THE INTERACTIVE CASEBOOK SERIES™

CONSTITUTIONAL LAW

A Contemporary Approach

SECOND EDITION

———————

By

Gregory E. Maggs

PROFESSOR OF LAW AND SENIOR ASSOCIATE DEAN OF ACADEMIC AFFAIRS
GEORGE WASHINGTON UNIVERSITY LAW SCHOOL

and

Peter J. Smith

PROFESSOR OF LAW
GEORGE WASHINGTON UNIVERSITY LAW SCHOOL

———————

WEST®

A Thomson Reuters business

Mat #41105530

Interactive Casebook Series is a trademark registered in the U.S. Patent and Trademark Office.

© 2009 Thomson Reuters
© 2011 Thomson Reuters
      610 Opperman Drive
      St. Paul, MN 55123
      1–800–313–9378

Printed in the United States of America

ISBN: 978–0–314–27355–0

Preface

American Constitutional Law is a sprawling subject. Some law schools cover the topic in one course, others in two or three; some cover it in the first year, others only in the second and third years, and still others teach some of it in the first year and then more in the final two years. The subject is so large that most law schools also teach pieces of it in classes principally focused on Administrative Law, Criminal Procedure, Civil Procedure, Property, and many other topics.

American legal publishers have produced scores of casebooks to fit this range of approaches. It was thus with some trepidation that we decided to add our book to the mix. In the end, we concluded that we had a contribution to make, even to this rich market. There is, of course, something like a "canon" in constitutional law, which means that a book is unlikely to be distinctive for the cases that it chooses to cover; a constitutional law casebook would not be particularly useful, for example, if it did not include *Marbury v. Madison*, 5 U.S. (1 Cranch) 137 (1803), *McCulloch v. Maryland*, 17 U.S. (4 Wheat.) 316 (1819), *Brown v. Board of Education of Topeka*, 347 U.S. 483, 489 (1954), or many others. Instead, we think our book is distinctive—and thus will be especially effective in teaching the subject—for four principal reasons.

First, the book comes with an electronic version that students can access on their computers. The electronic version contains live hyperlinks to cases, statutes, law review articles, and other materials available on Westlaw and other websites. Accordingly, students who wish to explore the material in greater depth have the tools at their fingertips to do so. In addition, students who use laptop computers in the classroom will be able to view the course materials on their computers in class.

Second, we have selected the principal cases very carefully, and we have tried to avoid the problem created by the aggressive editing in many books, which present excerpts so brief that the students in effect read only *about* what the Supreme Court has decided. But Supreme Court opinions should be presented as more than a series of conclusory assertions that have been stitched together by a space-sensitive editor. We have tried to edit the principal cases to ensure that they are short enough to read, but rich enough to give the students a clear sense of the Court's reasoning. We have also chosen not to create the illusion of breadth that characterizes many books in the field. Rather than provide summaries of dozens of decisions in each area that we take up, we focus on fuller excerpts of the principal cases, which are designed to be illustrative. Our book is self-consciously a casebook, and does not aspire to be a treatise.

Third, rather than follow the principal cases with pages and pages of notes and questions—an ineffective approach that students universally resent—we include multiple sidebars in the excerpts of each principal case to focus the students' attention on important questions at the very moment when they are reading the relevant portions of the opinion. Among other things, the sidebars focus attention on particularly salient passages of the opinions; draw connections between the discussion in the case and other topics that the students have explored (or will explore) in the book; supply food for thought; and direct the students to secondary materials to enrich their studies. After each case, we provide brief points for discussion, to focus the students' attention on the central themes in the case. Each Chapter also contains hypothetical problems—often drawn from real cases—to encourage the students to apply the doctrine that they have learned, and ends with an "executive summary" of the material, to identify the main themes and doctrines covered in the Chapter.

Fourth, throughout the book we include "Point-Counterpoints," in which we provide arguments for and against central questions raised by the materials in the book. To be sure, throughout the book—in the points for discussion and in short excerpts from scholarly articles by leading experts in the field—we present a diversity of views on every subject. But the Point-Counterpoint discussions are presented in our own voices and reflect our genuine points of disagreement on the many disputed questions raised in the book. We think that the students will find these discussions rich and stimulating.

The first edition of the book covered decisions through the Supreme Court's October 2007 term, which ended in June 2008. The second edition expands the excerpts of many of the cases and includes cases decided since 2008. The principal cases range from the old chestnuts to significant cases of much more recent vintage; from (to take just a few examples) *Barron v. Baltimore*, 32 U.S. (7 Pet.) 243 (1833), to *McDonald v. City of Chicago*, 130 S.Ct. 3020 (2010); from *Youngstown Sheet & Tube Co. v. Sawyer*, 343 U.S. 579 (1952), to *Hamdi v. Rumsfeld*, 542 U.S. 507 (2004); from *Dred Scott v. Sandford*, 60 U.S. 393 (1857), to *Parents Involved in Comm. Schools v. Seattle Sch. Dist. No. 1*, 127 S. Ct. 2738 (2007). In addition, Part I, which provides background and an overview, ends with *District of Columbia v. Heller*, 554 U.S. 570 (2008), the recent Second Amendment decision, as an illustrative case to foreshadow the themes that will recur in the rest of the book.

Although we have attempted to provide fuller excerpts of the principal cases than is perhaps common in casebooks in the field, we of course nevertheless have had to do substantial editing. We have used three asterisks to indicate that text has been omitted within a paragraph, although we have often omitted entire paragraphs without providing a similar indication. (Because the cases are hyperlinked, students can easily read the full opinions, if they so choose.) We have omitted most footnotes from the cases; when we have included them, we have used the original numbering from the cases. Footnotes that we have inserted in the cases, on the other hand, are indicated by an asterisk and conclude with the notation "—Eds." We have also omitted many of the citations, but we have attempted to preserve the most important ones, which are also hyperlinked for the convenience of the students.

We wish to acknowledge the many people who have helped us to produce this book. Many people helped us with the first edition. Our colleagues Tom Colby, Chip Lupu, and Robert Tuttle gave helpful suggestions, both for organization and content. Jonathan Affleck, Julia Carrano, Bob Chen, Courtney Enlow, and Brad Sauer went above and beyond as research assistants, editing cases and offering insightful commentary. Holly Saari did a terrific job making a dry manuscript come alive on the page. Louis Higgins graciously invited us to write the book and provided constant guidance and aid in seeing it through to completion. Dean Fred Lawrence and the George Washington University Law School also offered generous support.

We have had a similar embarrassment of riches with the second edition. Brad Clark, Tom Colby, Chip Lupu, Jeff Powell, and David Stras gave us invaluable feedback on the first edition (which they were kind enough to use in their classes). James Brower, Jamie Goldman, Elizabeth Gray, Ann Hodulik, Brittany Honeyman, Lindsay Lane, Richard Martinelli, Kyle Noonan, and Corrina Sowden provided outstanding research assistance. And Megan Anderson and Holly Saari again transformed our messy mass of edits into a clean and attractive book.

Gregory Maggs dedicates his contributions to the book to his patient family and to the many generations of law students at the George Washington University who have contributed to his understanding of constitutional law. Peter Smith dedicates his contributions to the book to Eileen and David Smith and Laurie Sparling, who have always provided unconditional love and support, and to Jonah and Sarah, whose already highly refined sense of justice has consistently challenged his own.

We hope that reading this book is as enjoyable for you as writing it was for us.

GREGORY E. MAGGS
PETER J. SMITH

March 2011
Washington, DC

Table of Contents

PREFACE iii

TABLE OF CONTENTS..vii

TABLE OF CASES xxi

PART I: *INTRODUCTION*...1

CHAPTER 1 *History and Overview* 1

   A. HISTORICAL SETTING OF THE CONSTITUTION..2

      1. COLONIAL GOVERNANCE AND EVENTS PRECEDING THE REVOLUTION 2

      2. THE FIRST AND SECOND CONTINENTAL CONGRESSES..3

      3. THE ARTICLES OF CONFEDERATION AND THE CALLING OF A CONSTITUTIONAL
          CONVENTION 4

      4. PROCEEDINGS OF THE CONSTITUTIONAL CONVENTION 5

      5. RATIFICATION OF THE CONSTITUTION 7

      6. THE FIRST CONGRESS...9

   B. ORGANIZATION OF THE CONSTITUTION..10

   C. METHODS OF INTERPRETING THE CONSTITUTION...13

      1. ORIGINALISM 16

          PERSPECTIVES AND ANALYSIS: JUSTICE ANTONIN SCALIA..18

      2. NON-ORIGINALISM 18

          PERSPECTIVES AND ANALYSIS: JUSTICE WILLIAM BRENNAN, JR. 21

   D. AN ILLUSTRATIVE CASE...22

      District of Columbia v. Heller 23

POINT-COUNTERPOINT
Does *Heller* represent originalism's triumph or its failure? 39

PART II: *THE FEDERAL COURTS* 43

CHAPTER 2 *Judicial Power* 45
  A. JUDICIAL REVIEW 45
    Marbury v. Madison 46
    Martin v. Hunter's Lessee 55
    Cooper v. Aaron 61
    PERSPECTIVE AND ANALYSIS: TOM PARKER 66
  B. OBSTACLES TO JUDICIAL REVIEW 67
    1. THE POLITICAL QUESTION DOCTRINE 67
      Baker v. Carr 68
      Nixon v. United States 72
    2. THE REQUIREMENT OF "CASE" OR "CONTROVERSY" 78
      Muskrat v. United States 78
    3. STANDING 82
      Allen v. Wright 83
      PERSPECTIVE AND ANALYSIS: FRANK EASTERBROOK 89
      Lujan v. Defenders of Wildlife 90
      HYPOTHETICAL 97
      PERSPECTIVE AND ANALYSIS: JONATHAN SIEGEL 97
    4. CONGRESSIONAL CONTROL OVER FEDERAL COURT JURISDICTION 98
      Ex Parte McCardle 98
      HYPOTHETICAL 102
  EXECUTIVE SUMMARY 102

POINT-COUNTERPOINT
What is the role of the federal courts in our constitutional scheme? 102

PART III: *FEDERALISM* 107

CHAPTER 3 *Federal Legislative Power* 109
  A. EXPRESS AND IMPLIED FEDERAL POWERS 109
    McCulloch v. Maryland 110
    United States v. Comstock 122

B. THE COMMERCE POWER 128
  1. THE EARLY VIEW 129
    Gibbons v. Ogden 130
  2. THE MIDDLE YEARS: UNCERTAINTY AND A RESTRICTIVE VIEW 134
    United States v. E.C. Knight Co. 134
    Shreveport Rate Case 136
    Champion v. Ames 139
    Hammer v. Dagenhart 142
    Carter v. Carter Coal Co. 146
  3. THE NEW DEAL AND BEYOND: AN EXPANSIVE VIEW 149
    NLRB v. Jones & Laughlin Steel Corp. 149
    United States v. Darby 152
    Wickard v. Filburn 155
    Heart of Atlanta Motel, Inc. v. United States 158
    Katzenbach v. McClung 159
  4. RECENT CASES: NEW LIMITS—OR OLD? 163
    United States v. Lopez 163
    HYPOTHETICAL 173
    United States v. Morrison 173
    Gonzales v. Raich 178
C. THE TAXING POWER 186
    Child Labor Tax Case 187
    United States v. Kahriger 189
    HYPOTHETICAL 192
D. THE SPENDING POWER 192
    United States v. Butler 193
    South Dakota v. Dole 197
E. THE WAR AND TREATY POWERS 201
    Woods v. Cloyd W. Miller Co. 201
    Missouri v. Holland 203
F. STATE IMMUNITY FROM FEDERAL REGULATION 206
    National League of Cities v. Usery 206
    Garcia v. San Antonio Metropolitan Transit Authority 209
    New York v. United States 213
    Printz v. United States 219
    HYPOTHETICAL 228
G. STATE SOVEREIGN IMMUNITY AS A LIMIT ON FEDERAL POWER 228
    Alden v. Maine 229
EXECUTIVE SUMMARY 238

POINT-COUNTERPOINT
Was the expansion of federal powers inevitable? Is it defensible?....................................241

CHAPTER 4 *Limitations on State Power* 245
INTRODUCTION 245
A. PREEMPTION OF STATE LAW BY FEDERAL LAW 245
   Silkwood v. Kerr-McGee Corp. 247
   HYPOTHETICAL 253
B. THE DORMANT COMMERCE CLAUSE DOCTRINE.............................253
   1. EARLY CASES 255
     Gibbons v. Ogden...255
   2. THE "UNIFORM NATIONAL STANDARD" TEST 258
     Cooley v. Board of Wardens 259
     Wabash, St. L. & P. Ry. Co. v. Illinois 262
   3. THE "DISCRIMINATION AGAINST INTERSTATE COMMERCE" TEST ...264
     Dean Milk Co. v. City of Madison, Wisc. 265
     Hughes v. Oklahoma 268
   4. THE "EXCESSIVE BURDEN ON INTERSTATE COMMERCE" TEST 271
     South Carolina State Highway Dept. v. Barnwell Bros. 272
     Southern Pacific Co. v. State of Arizona 275
     Kassel v. Consolidated Freightways Corp. of Delaware 279
   5. THE MEANING OF "INTERSTATE COMMERCE"...........................283
     City of Philadelphia v. New Jersey 284
     Camps Newfound/Owatonna, Inc. v. Town of Harrison 287
   6. THE MARKET-PARTICIPANT EXCEPTION 292
     South-Central Timber Development, Inc. v. Wunnicke...........292
     United Haulers Ass'n, Inc. v. Oneida-Herkimer Solid Waste Management Auth. ...297
   7. CONGRESSIONAL CONSENT 302
     Prudential Ins. Co. v. Benjamin..302
     Metropolitan Life Ins. Co. v. Ward 306
C. PRIVILEES AND IMMUNITIES CLAUSE 308
   Baldwin v. Fish and Game Commission of Montana 310
D. STATE POWER TO REGULATE THE HOUSE AND SENATE......................313
   U.S. Term Limits, Inc. v. Thornton 314
EXECUTIVE SUMMARY 322

PART IV: *SEPARATION OF POWERS*...325

CHAPTER 5 *Federal Executive Power*...327

    INTRODUCTION 327
    A. DOMESTIC AFFAIRS...327
        Youngstown Sheet & Tube Co. v. Sawyer 328
    B. FOREIGN AFFAIRS 339
        Dames & Moore v. Regan..339
        United States v. Curtiss-Wright Export Corporation 345
        Goldwater v. Carter 351
    C. THE PRESIDENT'S POWERS IN TIMES OF WAR................................354
        Hamdi v. Rumsfeld 358
    D. EXECUTIVE PRIVILEGE 371
        United States v. Nixon..372
    E. EXECUTIVE IMMUNITY 377
        Nixon v. Fitzgerald 378
        Clinton v. Jones..382
    EXECUTIVE SUMMARY 388

POINT-COUNTERPOINT

Has the Court struck the right balance between the President's power and Congress's
    power in the "war on terror"? 391

CHAPTER 6 *The Separation of Powers: The Legislative Process* 395

    INTRODUCTION 395
    A. DELEGATION OF LEGISLATIVE POWER..395
        PERSPECTIVE AND ANALYSIS: RICHARD PIERCE 396
        Whitman v. American Trucking Associations 398
    B. EXCLUDING THE PRESIDENT FROM THE LEGISLATIVE PROCESS 403
        Immigration and Naturalization Service v. Chadha................405
    C. IMPLICATIONS OF BICAMERALISM AND PRESENTMENT 414
        Clinton v. New York 414
    D. CONGRESSIONAL CONTROL OVER EXECUTIVE OFFICIALS 421
        Myers v. United States 423
        Humphrey's Executor v. United States.....................................427
        Bowsher v. Synar..430
        Morrison v. Olson 440
        Free Enterprise Fund v. Public Company Accounting Oversight Board 451
    E. BILLS OF ATTAINDER...458
        Nixon v. Administrator of General Services 459
    EXECUTIVE SUMMARY 462

PART V: *THE CONSTITUTION AND INDIVIDUAL RIGHTS*......................465

CHAPTER 7 *Introduction and Background*................................467
   A. EARLY HISTORY 467
      Barron v. Baltimore......................................472
   B. PRIVILEGES OR IMMUNITIES......................................475
      Slaughter-House Cases....................................475
   C. INCORPORATION 485
      Adamson v. California....................................487
      McDonald v. City of Chicago 494
   EXECUTIVE SUMMARY 505

POINT-COUNTERPOINT
Is it too late to question the incorporation doctrine?..................507

PART VI: *DUE PROCESS*...511

CHAPTER 8 *Substantive Due Process* 513
   A. SUBSTANTIVE DUE PROCESS AND ECONOMIC LIBERTY..................514
      Lochner v. New York 515
      Nebbia v. New York 521
      West Coast Hotel Co. v. Parrish..........................523
      Williamson v. Lee Optical Co. 527
      PERSPECTIVE AND ANALYSIS: RICHARD EPSTEIN 530
   B. SUBSTANTIVE DUE PROCESS AND FUNDAMENTAL RIGHTS...............530
     1. PRELUDE 531
      Pierce v. Society of the Sisters........................531
      Skinner v. Oklahoma.....................................533
     2. CONTRACEPTION AND ABORTION 537
      Griswold v. Connecticut.................................537
      Roe v. Wade 546
      Planned Parenthood of Southeastern Penn. v. Casey.......553
      Gonzales v. Carhart.....................................568
     3. MARRIAGE AND FAMILY....................................574
      Loving v. Virginia......................................575
     4. SEXUALITY 582
      Lawrence v. Texas.......................................583

PERSPECTIVE AND ANALYSIS: ROBERT DELAHUNTY & JOHN YOO 591

PERSPECTIVE AND ANALYSIS: VICKI JACKSON......................................592

5. LIFE..592

DeShaney v. Winnebago County Dept. of Social Services 592

6. DEATH 598

Cruzan v. Director, Missouri Dep't of Health 599

Washington v. Glucksberg 606

EXECUTIVE SUMMARY 612

POINT-COUNTERPOINT

Does the Constitution protect unenumerated rights?......................................615

CHAPTER 9 *Procedural Due Process*..619

Cleveland Board of Education v. Loudermill 620

EXECUTIVE SUMMARY 629

PART VII: *EQUAL PROTECTION* 631

CHAPTER 10 *Introduction and Framework* 633

A. DISTINCTIONS AND CLASSIFICATIONS..633

PERSPECTIVE AND ANALYSIS: JOHN HART ELY 635

B. TO WHOM DOES THE OBLIGATION OF EQUAL PROTECTION APPLY? 636

Bolling v. Sharpe...636

C. RATIONALITY REVIEW 639

Railway Express Agency v. People of State of New York 639

New York City Transit Authority v. Beazer 643

EXECUTIVE SUMMARY 647

POINT-COUNTERPOINT

Was *Bolling v. Sharpe, 347 U.S. 497 (1954)*, correctly decided? 649

CHAPTER 11 *Status-Based Classifications* 653

A. CLASSIFICATIONS BASED ON RACE AND NATIONAL ORIGIN 654

1. HISTORICAL PERSPECTIVE: PRE-RECONSTRUCTION 654

Dred Scott v. Sandford..654

2. FACIAL DISCRIMINATION AGAINST MINORITIES 658

Strauder v. West Virginia..658

Korematsu v. United States...661

   3. DISCRIMINATORY APPLICATION OF FACIALLY NEUTRAL LAWS......................668

     Yick Wo v. Hopkins..669

   4. DISCRIMINATORY EFFECT OR PURPOSE...671

     Washington v. Davis...672

     HYPOTHETICAL...678

   5. RACE-SPECIFIC BUT FACIALLY SYMMETRICAL LAWS..............................678

     Plessy v. Ferguson...679

     Brown v. Board of Education of Topeka.......................................682

     Perspective and Analysis: Robert Bork...686

     Loving v. Virginia...689

   6. AFFIRMATIVE ACTION...693

     City of Richmond v. J. A. Croson Co...695

     Grutter v. Bollinger...701

     Gratz v. Bollinger...707

     Parents Involved in Community Schools v. Seattle School Dist. No. 1...................712

   7. RACE AND REDISTRICTING..722

     Shaw v. Reno...723

B. GENDER CLASSIFICATIONS..727

   1. THE EARLY VIEW..728

   2. HEIGHTENED SCRUTINY...729

     Craig v. Boren..730

     United States v. Virginia...734

     HYPOTHETICAL...739

   3. DEFINING GENDER DISCRIMINATION..740

     Geduldig v. Aiello...740

   4. SEX DIFFERENCES AND STEREOTYPES..743

     Orr v. Orr...743

     Michael M. v. Superior Court of Sonoma County..........................746

   5. PURPOSE AND EFFECT...751

     Personnel Administrator of Massachusetts v. Feeney.......................751

C. OTHER CLASSIFICATIONS..755

   1. ALIENAGE...755

     Graham v. Richardson...755

   2. PARENTS' MARITAL STATUS..759

     Clark v. Jeter...759

   3. AGE...761

     Massachusetts Bd. of Retirement v. Murgia.................................761

   4. DISABILITY...764

Cleburne v. Cleburne Living Center 764
   5. Sexual Orientation 771
      Romer v. Evans 771
   Executive Summary 776

Chapter 12 *Equal Protection and Fundamental Rights* 779
   Introduction 779
   A. The Franchise 780
      1. The Right to Vote 780
         Harper v. Virginia State Bd. of Elections 781
         Bush v. Gore 786
      2. Apportionment and Gerrymandering 792
         Reynolds v. Sims 792
         Vieth v. Jubelirer 798
   B. Welfare and Education 804
      Dandridge v. Williams 804
      San Antonio Independent School Dist. v. Rodriguez 807
      Plyler v. Doe 812
   C. Access to the Courts 817
      M. L. B. v. S. L. J 817
   Executive Summary 820

Part VIII: *Legislative Protection of Individual Rights* 821

Chapter 13 *Congress's Power to Enforce the Reconstruction Amendments* 823
   A. The Thirteenth Amendment 823
      Jones v. Alfred H. Mayer Co. 824
   B. The Fourteenth and Fifteenth Amendments 827
      United States v. Guest 828
      South Carolina v. Katzenbach 832
      Katzenbach v. Morgan 838
      City of Boerne v. Flores 842
      Perspective and Analysis: Robert Post and Reva Siegel 846
      United States v. Morrison 846
   Executive Summary 851

POINT-COUNTERPOINT

Should the Reconstruction Amendments be read in light of the Tenth Amendment? 853

PART IX: *THE FIRST AMENDMENT*..857

CHAPTER 14 *Freedom of Speech*..859
INTRODUCTION 859
A. GENERAL PRINCIPLES AND RULES FOR REGULATING SPEECH.........................862
   1. CONTENT-BASED RESTRICTIONS..863
      Renton v. Playtime Theatres, Inc. 865
      Turner Broadcasting System, Inc. v. F.C.C. 869
      Republican Party of Minnesota v. White..873
      HYPOTHETICAL 878
   2. REASONABLE TIME, PLACE, AND MANNER RESTRICTIONS............................878
      Ward v. Rock Against Racism 879
      HYPOTHETICAL 883
   3. GENERALLY APPLICABLE REGULATIONS THAT INCIDENTALLY AFFECT EXPRESSION 883
      United States v. O'Brien 884
      Barnes v. Glen Theatre, Inc....888
   4. PRIOR RESTRAINTS 894
      New York Times Co. v. United States 895
      HYPOTHETICAL 902
   5. VAGUE OR OVERBROAD RESTRICTIONS...902
      NAACP v. Button..904
      Schad v. Borough of Mount Ephraim..909
   6. UNCONSTITUTIONAL CONDITIONS 913
      Rust v. Sullivan..914
B. CATEGORIES OF SPEECH..920
   1. INCITEMENT AND ADVOCACY OF CRIME..921
      Brandenburg v. Ohio..925
   2. DEFAMATION 927
      New York Times Co. v. Sullivan..929
   3. OBSCENITY 937
      Roth v. United States...938
      New York v. Ferber 943
   4. SYMBOLIC CONDUCT 948
      Texas v. Johnson 949
   5. PROVOCATIVE SPEECH..957
      Chaplinsky v. State of New Hampshire..957

Cohen v. California 960

Hypothetical 964

R.A.V. v. City of St. Paul, Minn. 964

6. Commercial Speech 973

44 Liquormart, Inc. v. Rhode Island 976

7. Campaign Contributions and Expenditures 983

Buckley v. Valeo 983

Citizens United v. Federal Election Commission 992

8. Speech of Public Employees 1001

Garcetti v. Ceballos 1002

Hypothetical 1006

9. Other Categories? 1006

United States v. Stevens 1007

Executive Summary 1010

Chapter 15 *Freedom of the Press* 1015

Introduction 1015

A. Applicability of General Laws to the Press 1016

Branzburg v. Hayes 1017

Zurcher v. Stanford Daily 1023

Cohen v. Cowles Media Co. 1028

B. Requiring the Press to Provide Media Access to Others 1031

Red Lion Broadcasting Co. v. F.C.C. 1032

Hypothetical 1037

Miami Herald Publishing Co. v. Tornillo 1038

C. Press Access to Government Proceedings 1042

Richmond Newspapers, Inc. v. Virginia 1042

Executive Summary 1049

Chapter 16 *Freedom of Association* 1051

Introduction 1051

A. Penalizing Individuals for Joining Groups 1053

NAACP v. Claiborne Hardware Co. 1054

Baird v. State Bar of Arizona 1057

B. Disclosure of Membership Lists 1061

NAACP v. State of Alabama ex rel. Patterson 1061

C. Freedom Not to Associate with Others 1066

Hurley v. Irish-American Gay, Lesbian and Bisexual Group of Boston 1067

Boy Scouts of America v. Dale 1072

Rumsfeld v. Forum for Academic and Institutional Rights, Inc. 1078
Executive Summary 1082

Chapter 17 *Freedom of Religion* 1085

A. The Establishment Clause 1085
  1. Government Aid to Religious Institutions 1091
    Everson v. Board of Education of Ewing Township 1092
    Lemon v. Kurtzman 1101
    Zelman v. Simmons-Harris 1110
    Hypothetical 1119
    A Note on Standing and Establishment Clause Challenges 1119
  2. Religion In Governmental Institutions 1120
    Engel v. Vitale 1123
    Wallace v. Jaffree 1128
    Lee v. Weisman 1135
    Edwards v. Aguillard 1148
    Marsh v. Chambers 1153
    Lynch v. Donnelly 1158
    Hypothetical 1168
    McCreary County, Kentucky v. American Civil Liberties Union of Kentucky 1169
    Van Orden v. Perry 1176
B. The Free Exercise Clause 1185
    Sherbert v. Verner 1188
    Wisconsin v. Yoder 1194
    Employment Div., Dept. of Human Resources of Oregon v. Smith 1200
    Church of the Lukumi Babalu Aye, Inc. v. City of Hialeah 1211
    Hypothetical 1218
    Locke v. Davey 1219
C. Government Involvement in Religious Disputes 1223
    *Presbyterian Church in U.S. v. Mary Elizabeth Blue Hull Memorial
      Presbyterian Church* 1224
Executive Summary 1229

Point-Counterpoint

Has the Court properly answered the question, "Whom should the First Amendment
  protect"? 1231

Part X: *Protection of Economic Liberty*

....1235

CHAPTER **18** *Protection of Economic Liberty*.........................1237

    A. IMPAIRMENT OF CONTRACTS BY STATE LAWS 1237

        Home Building & Loan Ass'n v. Blaisdell.........................1238

        Allied Structural Steel Company v. Spannaus 1241

    B. TAKINGS OF PRIVATE PROPERTY 1245

        1. INTRODUCTION.........................1246

        United States v. Causby 1246

        2. PHYSICAL TAKINGS.........................1249

        Yee v. City of Escondido 1250

        3. REGULATORY TAKINGS 1253

        Penn Central Transportation Co. v. City of New York 1253

        Andrus v. Allard 1257

        Lucas v. South Carolina Coastal Council 1259

        4. PUBLIC USE 1263

        Kelo v. City of New London 1263

    EXECUTIVE SUMMARY 1269

PART **XI**: *CONSTITUTIONAL LIMITATIONS ON NON-GOVERNMENTAL CONDUCT* 1271

CHAPTER **19** *The State Action Doctrine*.........................1273

    A. THE GENERAL REQUIREMENT OF STATE ACTION 1273

        The Civil Rights Cases.........................1274

    B. THE PUBLIC FUNCTION EXCEPTION.........................1280

        Marsh v. State of Alabama.........................1281

        Hudgens v. National Labor Relations Board.........................1285

    C. THE JUDICIAL ENFORCEMENT EXCEPTION 1288

        Shelley v. Kraemer.........................1288

    D. THE JOINT PARTICIPATION (OR ENTANGLEMENT) EXCEPTION.........................1292

        Burton v. Wilmington Parking Authority.........................1293

        Edmonson v. Leesville Concrete Co., Inc. 1297

        National Collegiate Athletic Association v. Tarkanian 1300

    EXECUTIVE SUMMARY 1306

APPENDIX *The Constitution of the United States of America*.........1307

INDEX.........................1325

Table of Cases

The principal cases are in bold type. Cases cited or discussed in the text are in roman type. References are to pages. Cases cited in principal cases and within other quoted materials are not included.

Abbott Laboratories v. Gardner, 387 U.S. 136, 87 S.Ct. 1507, 18 L.Ed.2d 681 (1967), 82

Abrams v. United States, 250 U.S. 616, 40 S.Ct. 17, 63 L.Ed. 1173 (1919), 862

Adair v. United States, 208 U.S. 161, 28 S.Ct. 277, 52 L.Ed. 436 (1908), 520

Adamson v. People of State of California, 332 U.S. 46, 67 S.Ct. 1672, 91 L.Ed. 1903 (1947), **487**

Adarand Constructors, Inc. v. Pena, 515 U.S. 200, 115 S.Ct. 2097, 132 L.Ed.2d 158 (1995), 639, 693, 700

Adkins v. Children's Hospital of the District of Columbia, 261 U.S. 525, 43 S.Ct. 394, 67 L.Ed. 785 (1923), 520

Aetna Life Ins. Co. of Hartford, Conn. v. Haworth, 300 U.S. 227, 57 S.Ct. 461, 81 L.Ed. 617 (1937), 81

A.L.A. Schechter Poultry Corporation v. United States, 295 U.S. 495, 55 S.Ct. 837, 79 L.Ed. 1570 (1935), 145, 398

Alden v. Maine, 527 U.S. 706, 119 S.Ct. 2240, 144 L.Ed.2d 636 (1999), **229**

Alexander v. United States, 509 U.S. 544, 113 S.Ct. 2766, 125 L.Ed.2d 441 (1993), 894

Allegheny, County of v. American Civil Liberties Union Greater Pittsburgh Chapter, 492 U.S. 573, 109 S.Ct. 3086, 106 L.Ed.2d 472 (1989), 1135, 1168

Allen v. Wright, 468 U.S. 737, 104 S.Ct. 3315, 82 L.Ed.2d 556 (1984), **83,** 1119

Allied Structural Steel Co. v. Spannaus, 438 U.S. 234, 98 S.Ct. 2716, 57 L.Ed.2d 727 (1978), **1241**

American Jewish Congress v. City of Chicago, 827 F.2d 120 (7th Cir.1987), 1168

Andrus v. Allard, 444 U.S. 51, 100 S.Ct. 318, 62 L.Ed.2d 210 (1979), **1257**

Arkansas Elec. Co-op. Corp. v. Arkansas Public Service Com'n, 461 U.S. 375, 103 S.Ct. 1905, 76 L.Ed.2d 1 (1983), 275

Arlington Heights, Village of v. Metropolitan Housing Development Corp., 429 U.S. 252, 97 S.Ct. 555, 50 L.Ed.2d 450 (1977), 675

Ashcroft v. Free Speech Coalition, 535 U.S. 234, 122 S.Ct. 1389, 152 L.Ed.2d 403 (2002), 902, 947

Avery v. Midland County, Tex., 390 U.S. 474, 88 S.Ct. 1114, 20 L.Ed.2d 45 (1968), 796

Baird v. State Bar of Ariz., 401 U.S. 1, 91 S.Ct. 702, 27 L.Ed.2d 639 (1971), **1057**

Baker v. Carr, 369 U.S. 186, 82 S.Ct. 691, 7 L.Ed.2d 663 (1962), **68,** 792

Baldwin v. Fish and Game Commission of Montana, 436 U.S. 371, 98 S.Ct. 1852, 56 L.Ed.2d 354 (1978), 309, **310**

Ballard, United States v., 322 U.S. 78, 64 S.Ct. 882, 88 L.Ed. 1148 (1944), 1186

Barnes v. Glen Theatre, Inc., 501 U.S. 560, 111 S.Ct. 2456, 115 L.Ed.2d 504 (1991), **888,** 913

Barron v. City of Baltimore, 32 U.S. 243, 8 L.Ed. 672 (1833), **472**

Batson v. Kentucky, 476 U.S. 79, 106 S.Ct. 1712, 90 L.Ed.2d 69 (1986), 660

Beauharnais v. People of State of Ill., 343 U.S. 250, 72 S.Ct. 725, 96 L.Ed. 919 (1952), 928, 1011

Benton v. Maryland, 395 U.S. 784, 89 S.Ct. 2056, 23 L.Ed.2d 707 (1969), 492

Best & Co. v. Maxwell, 311 U.S. 454, 61 S.Ct. 334, 85 L.Ed. 275 (1940), 264

Blatchford v. Native Village of Noatak and Circle Village, 501 U.S. 775, 111 S.Ct. 2578, 115 L.Ed.2d 686 (1991), 237

Board of County Com'rs, Wabaunsee County, Kan. v. Umbehr, 518 U.S. 668, 116 S.Ct. 2342, 135 L.Ed.2d 843 (1996), 913, 1001

Board of Ed. of Central School Dist. No. 1 v. Allen, 392 U.S. 236, 88 S.Ct. 1923, 20 L.Ed.2d 1060 (1968), 1091, 1105

Board of Educ. of Kiryas Joel Village School Dist. v. Grumet, 512 U.S. 687, 114 S.Ct. 2481, 129 L.Ed.2d 546 (1994), 1219

Board of Regents of State Colleges v. Roth, 408 U.S. 564, 92 S.Ct. 2701, 33 L.Ed.2d 548 (1972), 626

Board of Trustees of University of Alabama v. Garrett, 531 U.S. 356, 121 S.Ct. 955, 148 L.Ed.2d 866 (2001), 238, 770

Bob Jones University v. United States, 461 U.S. 574, 103 S.Ct. 2017, 76 L.Ed.2d 157 (1983), 88

Boerne, City of v. Flores, 521 U.S. 507, 117 S.Ct. 2157, 138 L.Ed.2d 624 (1997), **842,** 1211

Bollard v. California Province of the Society of Jesus, 196 F.3d 940 (9th Cir.1999), 1228

Bolling v. Sharpe, 347 U.S. 497, 74 S.Ct. 693, 98 L.Ed. 884 (1954), 631, **636,** 649

Boos v. Barry, 485 U.S. 312, 108 S.Ct. 1157, 99 L.Ed.2d 333 (1988), 863, 868

Boumediene v. Bush, 553 U.S. 723, 128 S.Ct. 2229, 171 L.Ed.2d 41 (2008), 101, 371

Bowers v. DeVito, 686 F.2d 616 (7th Cir.1982), 596

Bowers v. Hardwick, 478 U.S. 186, 106 S.Ct. 2841, 92 L.Ed.2d 140 (1986), 582

Bowsher v. Synar, 478 U.S. 714, 106 S.Ct. 3181, 92 L.Ed.2d 583 (1986), **430**

Boy Scouts of America v. Dale, 530 U.S. 640, 120 S.Ct. 2446, 147 L.Ed.2d 554 (2000), **1072,** 1083

Bradwell v. People of State of Illinois, 83 U.S. 130, 21 L.Ed. 442 (1872), 20, 728

Brandenburg v. Ohio, 395 U.S. 444, 89 S.Ct. 1827, 23 L.Ed.2d 430 (1969), **925,** 1011, 1060

Branzburg v. Hayes, 408 U.S. 665, 92 S.Ct. 2646, 33 L.Ed.2d 626 (1972), 1016, **1017,** 1049

Braunfeld v. Brown, 366 U.S. 599, 81 S.Ct. 1144, 6 L.Ed.2d 563 (1961), 1186, 1187

Breard v. City of Alexandria, La., 341 U.S. 622, 71 S.Ct. 920, 95 L.Ed. 1233 (1951), 973

Brown v. Board of Ed. of Topeka, Shawnee County, Kan., 347 U.S. 483, 74 S.Ct. 686, 98 L.Ed. 873 (1954), 20, **682,** 1273

Brown v. Board of Educ. of Topeka, Kan., 349 U.S. 294, 75 S.Ct. 753, 99 L.Ed. 1083 (1955), 688

Buck v. Bell, 274 U.S. 200, 47 S.Ct. 584, 71 L.Ed. 1000 (1927), 533, 633

Buckley v. Valeo, 424 U.S. 1, 96 S.Ct. 612, 46 L.Ed.2d 659 (1976), 14, 442, 638, 816, **983,** 1013, 1065, 1271

Burton v. Wilmington Parking Authority, 365 U.S. 715, 81 S.Ct. 856, 6 L.Ed.2d 45 (1961), **1293,** 1306

Bush v. Gore, 531 U.S. 98, 121 S.Ct. 525, 148 L.Ed.2d 388 (2000), **786**

Bush v. Vera, 517 U.S. 952, 116 S.Ct. 1941, 135 L.Ed.2d 248 (1996), 726

Butler, United States v., 297 U.S. 1, 56 S.Ct. 312, 80 L.Ed. 477 (1936), **193**

Calder v. Bull, 3 U.S. 386, 3 Dall. 386, 1 L.Ed. 648 (1798), 469

Califano v. Webster, 430 U.S. 313, 97 S.Ct. 1192, 51 L.Ed.2d 360 (1977), 745

California, United States v., 436 U.S. 32, 98 S.Ct. 1662, 56 L.Ed.2d 94 (1978), 328

Camps Newfound/Owatonna, Inc. v. Town of Harrison, Me., 520 U.S. 564, 117 S.Ct. 1590, 137 L.Ed.2d 852 (1997), **287**

Cantwell v. State of Connecticut, 310 U.S. 296, 60 S.Ct. 900, 84 L.Ed. 1213 (1940), 492, 1086, 1089, 1186, 1229

Capital Cities Cable, Inc. v. Crisp, 467 U.S. 691, 104 S.Ct. 2694, 81 L.Ed.2d 580 (1984), 247

Carmack, United States v., 329 U.S. 230, 67 S.Ct. 252, 91 L.Ed. 209 (1946), 1245

Carolene Products Co., United States v., 304 U.S. 144, 58 S.Ct. 778, 82 L.Ed. 1234 (1938), 526, 634, 811

Carter v. Carter Coal Co., 298 U.S. 238, 56 S.Ct. 855, 80 L.Ed. 1160 (1936), **146**

Castle Rock, Colo., Town of v. Gonzales, 545 U.S. 748, 125 S.Ct. 2796, 162 L.Ed.2d 658 (2005), 598, 627

Causby, United States v., 328 U.S. 256, 66 S.Ct. 1062, 90 L.Ed. 1206 (1946), **1246,** 1259

Central Hudson Gas & Elec. Corp. v. Public Service Commission of New York, 447 U.S. 557, 100 S.Ct. 2343, 65 L.Ed.2d 341 (1980), 974, 1012

Champion v. Ames, 188 U.S. 321, 23 S.Ct. 321, 47 L.Ed. 492 (1903), 139

Chaplinsky v. State of New Hampshire, 315 U.S. 568, 62 S.Ct. 766, 86 L.Ed. 1031 (1942), 920, **957,** 1012

Charles C. Steward Mach. Co. v. Davis, 301 U.S. 548, 57 S.Ct. 883, 81 L.Ed. 1279 (1937), 196

Chicago, B. & Q.R. Co. v. City of Chicago, 166 U.S. 226, 17 S.Ct. 581, 41 L.Ed. 979 (1897), 486, 493, 1245

Chicago, City of v. Morales, 527 U.S. 41, 119 S.Ct. 1849, 144 L.Ed.2d 67 (1999), 1053

Child Labor Tax Case, 259 U.S. 20, 42 S.Ct. 449, 66 L.Ed. 817 (1922), **187**

Chisholm v. Georgia, 2 U.S. 419, 2 Dall. 419, 1 L.Ed. 440 (1793), 65, 229

Church of American Knights of Ku Klux Klan v. City of Gary, Indiana, 334 F.3d 676 (7th Cir.2003), 959

Church of the Lukumi Babalu Aye, Inc. v. City of Hialeah, 508 U.S. 520, 113 S.Ct. 2217, 124 L.Ed.2d 472 (1993), 844, 1187, **1211,** 1230

Citizens Against Rent Control/Coalition for Fair Housing v. City of Berkeley, Cal., 454 U.S. 290, 102 S.Ct. 434, 70 L.Ed.2d 492 (1981), 1052

Citizens United v. Federal Election Commission, ___ U.S. ___, 130 S.Ct. 876, 175 L.Ed.2d 753 (2010), **992,** 1013, 1065

City of (see name of city)

Civil Rights Cases, 109 U.S. 3, 3 S.Ct. 18, 27 L.Ed. 835 (1883), 828, 1271, **1274,** 1306

Clark v. Community for Creative NonBViolence, 468 U.S. 288, 104 S.Ct. 3065, 82 L.Ed.2d 221 (1984), 888

Clark v. Jeter, 486 U.S. 456, 108 S.Ct. 1910, 100 L.Ed.2d 465 (1988), **759**

Cleburne, Tex., City of v. Cleburne Living Center, 473 U.S. 432, 105 S.Ct. 3249, 87 L.Ed.2d 313 (1985), 528, **764**

Cleveland Bd. of Educ. v. Loudermill, 470 U.S. 532, 105 S.Ct. 1487, 84 L.Ed.2d 494 (1985), **620**

Clinton v. City of New York, 524 U.S. 417, 118 S.Ct. 2091, 141 L.Ed.2d 393 (1998), **414**

Clinton v. Jones, 520 U.S. 681, 117 S.Ct. 1636, 137 L.Ed.2d 945 (1997), **382**

Cohen v. California, 403 U.S. 15, 91 S.Ct. 1780, 29 L.Ed.2d 284 (1971), **960**, 1012

Cohen v. Cowles Media Co., 501 U.S. 663, 111 S.Ct. 2513, 115 L.Ed.2d 586 (1991), 1016, **1028**, 1049

Cohens v. State of Virginia, 19 U.S. 264, 5 L.Ed. 257 (1821), 54, 59

Collins v. City of Harker Heights, Tex., 503 U.S. 115, 112 S.Ct. 1061, 117 L.Ed.2d 261 (1992), 1042

Colorado Republican Federal Campaign Committee v. Federal Election Com'n, 518 U.S. 604, 116 S.Ct. 2309, 135 L.Ed.2d 795 (1996), 992

Comstock, United States v., ___ U.S. ___, 130 S.Ct. 1949, 176 L.Ed.2d 878 (2010), **122**

Connick v. Myers, 461 U.S. 138, 103 S.Ct. 1684, 75 L.Ed.2d 708 (1983), 1001, 1013

Consolidated Edison Co. of New York, Inc. v. Public Service Commission of New York, 447 U.S. 530, 100 S.Ct. 2326, 65 L.Ed.2d 319 (1980), 864

Cooley v. Board of Wardens of Port of Philadelphia, to Use of Soc for Relief of Distressed Pilots, Their Widows and Children, 53 U.S. 299, 12 How. 299, 13 L.Ed. 996 (1851), 258, **259**

Cooper v. Aaron, 358 U.S. 1, 78 S.Ct. 1401, 3 L.Ed.2d 5, 3 L.Ed.2d 19 (1958), **61**

Coppage v. State of Kansas, 236 U.S. 1, 35 S.Ct. 240, 59 L.Ed. 441 (1915), 520

County of (see name of county)

Craig v. Boren, 429 U.S. 190, 97 S.Ct. 451, 50 L.Ed.2d 397 (1976), **730**

Crane v. New York, 239 U.S. 195, 36 S.Ct. 85, 60 L.Ed. 218 (1915), 756

Cruzan by Cruzan v. Director, Missouri Dept. of Health, 497 U.S. 261, 110 S.Ct. 2841, 111 L.Ed.2d 224 (1990), **599**

Cuellar, United States v., 478 F.3d 282 (5th Cir.2007), 397

CurtissBWright Export Corporation, United States v., 299 U.S. 304, 57 S.Ct. 216, 81 L.Ed. 255 (1936), **345**

Dames & Moore v. Regan, 453 U.S. 654, 101 S.Ct. 2972, 69 L.Ed.2d 918 (1981), **339**

Dandridge v. Williams, 397 U.S. 471, 90 S.Ct. 1153, 25 L.Ed.2d 491 (1970), **804**

Darby, United States v., 312 U.S. 100, 312 U.S. 657, 61 S.Ct. 451, 85 L.Ed. 609 (1941), **152**

Davis v. Bandemer, 478 U.S. 109, 106 S.Ct. 2797, 92 L.Ed.2d 85 (1986), 797

Davis, Helvering v., 301 U.S. 619, 301 U.S. 672, 57 S.Ct. 904, 81 L.Ed. 1307 (1937), 196

Dean Milk Co. v. City of Madison, Wis., 340 U.S. 349, 71 S.Ct. 295, 95 L.Ed. 329 (1951), **265**

Dennis v. Sparks, 449 U.S. 24, 101 S.Ct. 183, 66 L.Ed.2d 185 (1980), 1305

Dennis v. United States, 341 U.S. 494, 71 S.Ct. 857, 95 L.Ed. 1137 (1951), 921

Denver Area Educational Telecommunications Consortium, Inc. v. F.C.C., 518 U.S. 727, 116 S.Ct. 2374, 135 L.Ed.2d 888 (1996), 971

DeShaney v. Winnebago County Dept. of Social Services, 489 U.S. 189, 109 S.Ct. 998, 103 L.Ed.2d 249 (1989), **592**

Dickerson v. United States, 530 U.S. 428, 120 S.Ct. 2326, 147 L.Ed.2d 405 (2000), 64

District of Columbia v. Heller, 554 U.S. 570, 128 S.Ct. 2783, 171 L.Ed.2d 637 (2008), **23**, 493, 646

Doe v. Bolton, 410 U.S. 179, 93 S.Ct. 739, 35 L.Ed.2d 201 (1973), 309, 551

Dorsey, United States v., 418 F.3d 1038 (9th Cir.2005), 172

Douglas v. People of State of Cal., 372 U.S. 353, 83 S.Ct. 814, 9 L.Ed.2d 811 (1963), 807

Dred Scott v. Sandford, 60 U.S. 393, 19 How. 393, 15 L.Ed. 691 (1856), 64, 65, 514, **654**

Dun & Bradstreet, Inc. v. Greenmoss Builders, Inc., 472 U.S. 749, 105 S.Ct. 2939, 86 L.Ed.2d 593 (1985), 936

Dyer v. Blair, 390 F.Supp. 1291 (N.D.Ill.1975), 353

Easley v. Cromartie, 532 U.S. 234, 121 S.Ct. 1452, 149 L.Ed.2d 430 (2001), 726

E. C. Knight Co., United States v., 156 U.S. 1, 15 S.Ct. 249, 39 L.Ed. 325 (1895), **134**

Edmonson v. Leesville Concrete Co., Inc., 500 U.S. 614, 111 S.Ct. 2077, 114 L.Ed.2d 660 (1991), 661, **1297**

Edwards v. Aguillard, 482 U.S. 578, 107 S.Ct. 2573, 96 L.Ed.2d 510 (1987), **1148**, 1156

Eichman, United States v., 496 U.S. 310, 110 S.Ct. 2404, 110 L.Ed.2d 287 (1990), 956

Eisenstadt v. Baird, 405 U.S. 438, 92 S.Ct. 1029, 31 L.Ed.2d 349 (1972), 546

Elk Grove Unified School Dist. v. Newdow, 542 U.S. 1, 124 S.Ct. 2301, 159 L.Ed.2d 98 (2004), 1089, 1168

Employment Div., Dept. of Human Resources of Oregon v. Smith, 494 U.S. 872, 110 S.Ct. 1595, 108 L.Ed.2d 876 (1990), 894, 1186, **1200**, 1230

Engel v. Vitale, 370 U.S. 421, 82 S.Ct. 1261, 8 L.Ed.2d 601 (1962), 1085, **1123**, 1230

Epperson v. State of Ark., 393 U.S. 97, 89 S.Ct. 266, 21 L.Ed.2d 228 (1968), 1147, 1149

Everson v. Board of Ed. of Ewing Tp., 330 U.S. 1, 67 S.Ct. 504, 91 L.Ed. 711 (1947), 492, 1086, 1088, 1091, **1092**, 1219, 1229

Ex parte (see name of party)

Federal Election Com'n v. Akins, 524 U.S. 11, 118 S.Ct. 1777, 141 L.Ed.2d 10 (1998), 96

Felker v. Turpin, 518 U.S. 651, 116 S.Ct. 2333, 135 L.Ed.2d 827 (1996), 101

Ferguson v. Skrupa, 372 U.S. 726, 83 S.Ct. 1028, 10 L.Ed.2d 93 (1963), 529

Flast v. Cohen, 392 U.S. 83, 88 S.Ct. 1942, 20 L.Ed.2d 947 (1968), 1119

Flemming v. Nestor, 363 U.S. 603, 80 S.Ct. 1367, 4 L.Ed.2d 1435 (1960), 643

Fletcher v. Peck, 10 U.S. 87, 3 L.Ed. 162 (1810), 470

Florida Bar v. Went For It, Inc., 515 U.S. 618, 115 S.Ct. 2371, 132 L.Ed.2d 541 (1995), 909

Florida Lime & Avocado Growers, Inc. v. Paul, 373 U.S. 132, 83 S.Ct. 1210, 10 L.Ed.2d 248 (1963), 246

Foley v. Connelie, 435 U.S. 291, 98 S.Ct. 1067, 55 L.Ed.2d 287 (1978), 758

44 Liquormart, Inc. v. Rhode Island, 517 U.S. 484, 116 S.Ct. 1495, 134 L.Ed.2d 711 (1996), **976**

Free Enterprise Fund v. Public Co. Accounting Oversight Bd., ___ U.S. ___, 130 S.Ct. 3138, 177 L.Ed.2d 706 (2010), **451**

Frontiero v. Richardson, 411 U.S. 677, 93 S.Ct. 1764, 36 L.Ed.2d 583 (1973), 729

Frothingham v. Mellon, 262 U.S. 447, 43 S.Ct. 597, 67 L.Ed. 1078 (1923), 1119

Fullilove v. Klutznick, 448 U.S. 448, 100 S.Ct. 2758, 65 L.Ed.2d 902 (1980), 696

Garcetti v. Ceballos, 547 U.S. 410, 126 S.Ct. 1951, 164 L.Ed.2d 689 (2006), **1002**, 1013

Garcia v. San Antonio Metropolitan Transit Authority, 469 U.S. 528, 105 S.Ct. 1005, 83 L.Ed.2d 1016 (1985), **209**

Gayle v. Browder, 352 U.S. 903, 77 S.Ct. 145, 1 L.Ed.2d 114 (1956), 685

Geduldig v. Aiello, 417 U.S. 484, 94 S.Ct. 2485, 41 L.Ed.2d 256 (1974), **740**

Gentile v. State Bar of Nevada, 501 U.S. 1030, 111 S.Ct. 2720, 115 L.Ed.2d 888 (1991), 903

Georgia v. McCollum, 505 U.S. 42, 112 S.Ct. 2348, 120 L.Ed.2d 33 (1992), 661, 1300

Gertz v. Robert Welch, Inc., 418 U.S. 323, 94 S.Ct. 2997, 41 L.Ed.2d 789 (1974), 928, 935

Gibbons v. Ogden, 22 U.S. 1, 6 L.Ed. 23 (1824), **130, 255**

Gibson v. Mississippi, 162 U.S. 565, 16 S.Ct. 904, 40 L.Ed. 1075 (1896), 637

Gideon v. Wainwright, 372 U.S. 335, 83 S.Ct. 792, 9 L.Ed.2d 799 (1963), 493

Gitlow v. People of State of New York, 268 U.S. 652, 45 S.Ct. 625, 69 L.Ed. 1138 (1925), 492, 504, 1015, 1049

Goldberg v. Kelly, 397 U.S. 254, 90 S.Ct. 1011, 25 L.Ed.2d 287 (1970), 626

Goldman v. Weinberger, 475 U.S. 503, 106 S.Ct. 1310, 89 L.Ed.2d 478 (1986), 1193, 1209

Goldwater v. Carter, 444 U.S. 996, 100 S.Ct. 533, 62 L.Ed.2d 428 (1979), **351**

Gomillion v. Lightfoot, 364 U.S. 339, 81 S.Ct. 125, 5 L.Ed.2d 110 (1960), 671, 722, 727

Gonzales v. Carhart, 550 U.S. 124, 127 S.Ct. 1610, 167 L.Ed.2d 480 (2007), **568**

Gonzales v. O Centro Espirita Beneficente Uniao do Vegetal, 546 U.S. 418, 126 S.Ct. 1211, 163 L.Ed.2d 1017 (2006), 1211

Gonzales v. Oregon, 546 U.S. 243, 126 S.Ct. 904, 163 L.Ed.2d 748 (2006), 610

Gonzales v. Raich, 545 U.S. 1, 125 S.Ct. 2195, 162 L.Ed.2d 1 (2005), **178**

Good News Club v. Milford Central School, 533 U.S. 98, 121 S.Ct. 2093, 150 L.Ed.2d 151 (2001), 1147

Goodridge v. Department of Public Health, 440 Mass. 309, 798 N.E.2d 941 (Mass.2003), 590, 776

Goss v. Lopez, 419 U.S. 565, 95 S.Ct. 729, 42 L.Ed.2d 725 (1975), 627

Graham v. Richardson, 403 U.S. 365, 91 S.Ct. 1848, 29 L.Ed.2d 534 (1971), **755**

Gratz v. Bollinger, 539 U.S. 244, 123 S.Ct. 2411, 156 L.Ed.2d 257 (2003), **707**

Green v. County School Bd. of New Kent County, Va., 391 U.S. 430, 88 S.Ct. 1689, 20 L.Ed.2d 716 (1968), 688

Greenya v. George Washington University, 512 F.2d 556, 167 U.S.App.D.C. 379 (D.C.Cir.1975), 1288

Griffin v. California, 380 U.S. 609, 85 S.Ct. 1229, 14 L.Ed.2d 106 (1965), 493

Griffin v. Illinois, 351 U.S. 12, 76 S.Ct. 585, 100 L.Ed. 891 (1956), 818

Griggs v. Duke Power Co., 401 U.S. 424, 91 S.Ct. 849, 28 L.Ed.2d 158 (1971), 675

Griswold v. Connecticut, 381 U.S. 479, 85 S.Ct. 1678, 14 L.Ed.2d 510 (1965), **537**

Grosjean v. American Press Co., 297 U.S. 233, 56 S.Ct. 444, 80 L.Ed. 660 (1936), 860, 1010

Grutter v. Bollinger, 539 U.S. 306, 123 S.Ct. 2325, 156 L.Ed.2d 304 (2003), **701**

Guest, United States v., 383 U.S. 745, 86 S.Ct. 1170, 16 L.Ed.2d 239 (1966), **828**

Hall v. Beals, 396 U.S. 45, 90 S.Ct. 200, 24 L.Ed.2d 214 (1969), 82

Hamdan v. Rumsfeld, 548 U.S. 557, 126 S.Ct. 2749, 165 L.Ed.2d 723 (2006), 370

Hamdi v. Rumsfeld, 542 U.S. 507, 124 S.Ct. 2633, 159 L.Ed.2d 578 (2004), **358**

Hamdi v. Rumsfeld, 316 F.3d 450 (4th Cir.2003), 369

Hammer v. Dagenhart, 247 U.S. 251, 38 S.Ct. 529, 62 L.Ed. 1101 (1918), **142**

Hans v. Louisiana, 134 U.S. 1, 10 S.Ct. 504, 33 L.Ed. 842 (1890), 237

Harper v. Virginia State Bd. of Elections, 383 U.S. 663, 86 S.Ct. 1079, 16 L.Ed.2d 169 (1966), **781,** 818

Hatfill v. The New York Times Co., 532 F.3d 312 (4th Cir.2008), 929

Heart of Atlanta Motel, Inc. v. United States, 379 U.S. 241, 85 S.Ct. 348, 13 L.Ed.2d 258 (1964), 11, **158,** 841

Hein v. Freedom From Religion Foundation, Inc., 551 U.S. 587, 127 S.Ct. 2553, 168 L.Ed.2d 424 (2007), 1120

Helvering v. _____ (see opposing party)

Hicklin v. Orbeck, 437 U.S. 518, 98 S.Ct. 2482, 57 L.Ed.2d 397 (1978), 309

Hines v. Davidowitz, 312 U.S. 52, 61 S.Ct. 399, 85 L.Ed. 581 (1941), 246, 816

Hipolite Egg Co. v. United States, 220 U.S. 45, 31 S.Ct. 364, 55 L.Ed. 364 (1911), 141

Hirabayashi v. United States, 320 U.S. 81, 63 S.Ct. 1375, 87 L.Ed. 1774 (1943), 636, 662

Hoke v. United States, 227 U.S. 308, 33 S.Ct. 281, 57 L.Ed. 523 (1913), 141

Holmes v. City of Atlanta, 350 U.S. 879, 76 S.Ct. 141, 100 L.Ed. 776 (1955), 685

Home Bldg. & Loan Ass'n v. Blaisdell, 290 U.S. 398, 54 S.Ct. 231, 78 L.Ed. 413 (1934), 21, **1238**

Hudgens v. N. L. R. B., 424 U.S. 507, 96 S.Ct. 1029, 47 L.Ed.2d 196 (1976), **1285,** 1291, 1306

Hughes v. Oklahoma, 441 U.S. 322, 99 S.Ct. 1727, 60 L.Ed.2d 250 (1979), **268**

Humphrey's Ex'r v. United States, 295 U.S. 602, 55 S.Ct. 869, 79 L.Ed. 1611 (1935), 12, **427**

Hunter v. Underwood, 471 U.S. 222, 105 S.Ct. 1916, 85 L.Ed.2d 222 (1985), 675

Hurley v. Irish-American Gay, Lesbian and Bisexual Group of Boston, 515 U.S. 557, 115 S.Ct. 2338, 132 L.Ed.2d 487 (1995), **1067,** 1083

Hurtado v. People of State of California, 110 U.S. 516, 4 S.Ct. 292, 28 L.Ed. 232 (1884), 486, 493

Hustler Magazine v. Falwell, 485 U.S. 46, 108 S.Ct. 876, 99 L.Ed.2d 41 (1988), 936

Illinois ex rel. McCollum v. Board of Educ., 333 U.S. 203, 68 S.Ct. 461, 92 L.Ed. 649 (1948), 1121

Industrial Union Dept., AFLBCIO v. American Petroleum Institute, 448 U.S. 607, 100 S.Ct. 2844, 65 L.Ed.2d 1010 (1980), 397

Ingraham v. Wright, 430 U.S. 651, 97 S.Ct. 1401, 51 L.Ed.2d 711 (1977), 627

In re (see name of party)

I.N.S. v. Chadha, 462 U.S. 919, 103 S.Ct. 2764, 77 L.Ed.2d 317 (1983), 11, **405**

Irvin v. Dowd, 366 U.S. 717, 81 S.Ct. 1639, 6 L.Ed.2d 751 (1961), 493

Jackson v. Metropolitan Edison Co., 419 U.S. 345, 95 S.Ct. 449, 42 L.Ed.2d 477 (1974), 1281

Jacobellis v. State of Ohio, 378 U.S. 184, 84 S.Ct. 1676, 12 L.Ed.2d 793 (1964), 937

J.E.B. v. Alabama ex rel. T.B., 511 U.S. 127, 114 S.Ct. 1419, 128 L.Ed.2d 89 (1994), 661

Johnson v. California, 543 U.S. 499, 125 S.Ct. 1141, 160 L.Ed.2d 949 (2005), 692

Jones v. Alfred H. Mayer Co., 392 U.S. 409, 88 S.Ct. 2186, 20 L.Ed.2d 1189 (1968), **824,** 1277

Kahriger, United States v., 345 U.S. 22, 73 S.Ct. 510, 97 L.Ed. 754 (1953), **189**

Karcher v. Daggett, 462 U.S. 725, 103 S.Ct. 2653, 77 L.Ed.2d 133 (1983), 796

Kassel v. Consolidated Freightways Corp. of Delaware, 450 U.S. 662, 101 S.Ct. 1309, 67 L.Ed.2d 580 (1981), **279**

Katzenbach v. McClung, 379 U.S. 294, 85 S.Ct. 377, 13 L.Ed.2d 290 (1964), 11, **159**

Katzenbach v. Morgan, 384 U.S. 641, 86 S.Ct. 1717, 16 L.Ed.2d 828 (1966), **838,** 843, 848

Kelo v. City of New London, Conn., 545 U.S. 469, 125 S.Ct. 2655, 162 L.Ed.2d 439 (2005), **1263**

Kerrigan v. Commissioner of Public Health, 289 Conn. 135, 957 A.2d 407 (2008), 776

Kirby Forest Industries, Inc. v. United States, 467 U.S. 1, 104 S.Ct. 2187, 81 L.Ed.2d 1 (1984), 1246

Kitzmiller v. Dover Area School Dist., 400 F.Supp.2d 707 (M.D.Pa.2005), 1153

Knowlton v. Moore, 178 U.S. 41, 20 S.Ct. 747, 44 L.Ed. 969 (1900), 633

Kolender v. Lawson, 461 U.S. 352, 103 S.Ct. 1855, 75 L.Ed.2d 903 (1983), 903

Konigsberg v. State Bar of Cal., 366 U.S. 36, 81 S.Ct. 997, 6 L.Ed.2d 105 (1961), 860

Korematsu v. United States, 323 U.S. 214, 65 S.Ct. 193, 89 L.Ed. 194 (1944), 636, **661**

Kovacs v. Cooper, 336 U.S. 77, 69 S.Ct. 448, 93 L.Ed. 513 (1949), 878

Krueger v. Mitchell, 112 Wis.2d 88, 332 N.W.2d 733 (Wis.1983), 1249

La Belle Iron Works v. United States, 256 U.S. 377, 41 S.Ct. 528, 65 L.Ed. 998 (1921), 638

Lamb's Chapel v. Center Moriches Union Free School Dist., 508 U.S. 384, 113 S.Ct. 2141, 124 L.Ed.2d 352 (1993), 1107

Lawrence v. Texas, 539 U.S. 558, 123 S.Ct. 2472, 156 L.Ed.2d 508 (2003), **583**

Law Students Civil Rights Research Council, Inc. v. Wadmond, 401 U.S. 154, 91 S.Ct. 720, 27 L.Ed.2d 749 (1971), 903, 1060

Lee, United States v., 455 U.S. 252, 102 S.Ct. 1051, 71 L.Ed.2d 127 (1982), 1186

Lee v. Weisman, 505 U.S. 577, 112 S.Ct. 2649, 120 L.Ed.2d 467 (1992), 1086, 1107, **1135,** 1157, 1230

Lemon v. Kurtzman, 403 U.S. 602, 91 S.Ct. 2105, 29 L.Ed.2d 745 (1971), 1091, **1101,** 1224, 1229

Lewis v. Harris, 188 N.J. 415, 908 A.2d 196 (N.J.2006), 776

Lochner v. New York, 198 U.S. 45, 25 S.Ct. 539, 49 L.Ed. 937 (1905), **515,** 729

Locke v. Davey, 540 U.S. 712, 124 S.Ct. 1307, 158 L.Ed.2d 1 (2004), 1219

Lopez, United States v., 514 U.S. 549, 115 S.Ct. 1624, 131 L.Ed.2d 626 (1995), 11, 154, **163**

Loretto v. Teleprompter Manhattan CATV Corp., 458 U.S. 419, 102 S.Ct. 3164, 73 L.Ed.2d 868 (1982), 1250

Los Angeles, City of v. Alameda Books, Inc., 535 U.S. 425, 122 S.Ct. 1728, 152 L.Ed.2d 670 (2002), 868

Loving v. United States, 517 U.S. 748, 116 S.Ct. 1737, 135 L.Ed.2d 36 (1996), 397

Loving v. Virginia, 388 U.S. 1, 87 S.Ct. 1817, 18 L.Ed.2d 1010 (1967), **575, 689,** 1271

Lucas v. South Carolina Coastal Council, 505 U.S. 1003, 112 S.Ct. 2886, 120 L.Ed.2d 798 (1992), **1259**

Lugar v. Edmondson Oil Co., Inc., 457 U.S. 922, 102 S.Ct. 2744, 73 L.Ed.2d 482 (1982), 1272, 1292, 1296, 1306

Lujan v. Defenders of Wildlife, 504 U.S. 555, 112 S.Ct. 2130, 119 L.Ed.2d 351 (1992), **90**

Lynch v. Donnelly, 465 U.S. 668, 104 S.Ct. 1355, 79 L.Ed.2d 604 (1984), 1086, **1158,** 1230

Maine v. Taylor, 477 U.S. 131, 106 S.Ct. 2440, 91 L.Ed.2d 110 (1986), 271

Malloy v. Hogan, 378 U.S. 1, 84 S.Ct. 1489, 12 L.Ed.2d 653 (1964), 493

Marbury v. Madison, 5 U.S. 137, 2 L.Ed. 60 (1803), 12, **46,** 236

Marriage Cases, In re, 76 Cal.Rptr.3d 683, 183 P.3d 384 (Cal.2008), 591, 776

Marsh v. Chambers, 463 U.S. 783, 103 S.Ct. 3330, 77 L.Ed.2d 1019 (1983), 1138, **1153,** 1230

Marsh v. State of Ala., 326 U.S. 501, 66 S.Ct. 276, 90 L.Ed. 265 (1946), **1281,** 1306

Martin v. Hunter's Lessee, 14 U.S. 304, 4 L.Ed. 97 (1816), **55**

Massachusetts Bd. of Retirement v. Murgia, 427 U.S. 307, 96 S.Ct. 2562, 49 L.Ed.2d 520 (1976), **761**

Masson v. New Yorker Magazine, Inc., 501 U.S. 496, 111 S.Ct. 2419, 115 L.Ed.2d 447 (1991), 928

Mathews v. Eldridge, 424 U.S. 319, 96 S.Ct. 893, 47 L.Ed.2d 18 (1976), 628

McAuliffe v. City of New Bedford, 155 Mass. 216, 29 N.E. 517 (Mass.1892), 625, 1001

McCardle, Ex parte, 74 U.S. 506, 19 L.Ed. 264 (1868), **98**

McCleskey v. Kemp, 481 U.S. 279, 107 S.Ct. 1756, 95 L.Ed.2d 262 (1987), 678

McConnell v. Federal Election Commission, 540 U.S. 93, 124 S.Ct. 619, 157 L.Ed.2d 491 (2003), 992

McCreary County, Ky. v. American Civil Liberties Union of Ky., 545 U.S. 844, 125 S.Ct. 2722, 162 L.Ed.2d 729 (2005), 1099, 1158, **1169**

McDaniel v. Paty, 435 U.S. 618, 98 S.Ct. 1322, 55 L.Ed.2d 593 (1978), 1186

McDonald v. City of Chicago, ___ U.S. ___, 130 S.Ct. 3020, 177 L.Ed.2d 894 (2010), **494,** 580

McIntyre v. Ohio Elections Com'n, 514 U.S. 334, 115 S.Ct. 1511, 131 L.Ed.2d 426 (1995), 937

M'Culloch v. State, 17 U.S. 316, 4 L.Ed. 579 (1819), **110**

Medtronic, Inc. v. Lohr, 518 U.S. 470, 116 S.Ct. 2240, 135 L.Ed.2d 700 (1996), 252

Members of City Council of City of Los Angeles v. Taxpayers for Vincent, 466 U.S. 789, 104 S.Ct. 2118, 80 L.Ed.2d 772 (1984), 903

Metro Broadcasting, Inc. v. F.C.C., 497 U.S. 547, 110 S.Ct. 2997, 111 L.Ed.2d 445 (1990), 638

Metropolitan Life Ins. Co. v. Ward, 470 U.S. 869, 105 S.Ct. 1676, 84 L.Ed.2d 751 (1985), **306**

Meyer v. Nebraska, 262 U.S. 390, 43 S.Ct. 625, 67 L.Ed. 1042 (1923), 531

Miami Herald Pub. Co. v. Tornillo, 418 U.S. 241, 94 S.Ct. 2831, 41 L.Ed.2d 730 (1974), **1038,** 1049

Michael H. v. Gerald D., 491 U.S. 110, 109 S.Ct. 2333, 105 L.Ed.2d 91 (1989), 578

Michael M. v. Superior Court of Sonoma County, 450 U.S. 464, 101 S.Ct. 1200, 67 L.Ed.2d 437 (1981), **746**

Miller v. California, 413 U.S. 15, 93 S.Ct. 2607, 37 L.Ed.2d 419 (1973), 937, 941, 942, 1012

Miller v. Johnson, 515 U.S. 900, 115 S.Ct. 2475, 132 L.Ed.2d 762 (1995), 726

Miller, United States v., 307 U.S. 174, 59 S.Ct. 816, 83 L.Ed. 1206 (1939), 37

Milligan, Ex parte, 71 U.S. 2, 18 L.Ed. 281 (1866), 356

Milliken v. Bradley, 433 U.S. 267, 97 S.Ct. 2749, 53 L.Ed.2d 745 (1977), 689

Milliken v. Bradley, 418 U.S. 717, 94 S.Ct. 3112, 41 L.Ed.2d 1069 (1974), 689

Minneapolis & St. L.R. Co. v. Bombolis, 241 U.S. 211, 36 S.Ct. 595, 60 L.Ed. 961 (1916), 486, 493

Miranda v. Arizona, 384 U.S. 436, 86 S.Ct. 1602, 16 L.Ed.2d 694 (1966), 64

Mississippi University for Women v. Hogan, 458 U.S. 718, 102 S.Ct. 3331, 73 L.Ed.2d 1090 (1982), 745

Missouri v. Holland, 252 U.S. 416, 40 S.Ct. 382, 64 L.Ed. 641 (1920), **203**

Missouri v. Jenkins, 495 U.S. 33, 110 S.Ct. 1651, 109 L.Ed.2d 31 (1990), 689

Mistretta v. United States, 488 U.S. 361, 109 S.Ct. 647, 102 L.Ed.2d 714 (1989), 397

Mitchell v. Helms, 530 U.S. 793, 120 S.Ct. 2530, 147 L.Ed.2d 660 (2000), 1099

M.L.B. v. S.L.J., 519 U.S. 102, 117 S.Ct. 555, 136 L.Ed.2d 473 (1996), **817**

Moore v. City of East Cleveland, Ohio, 431 U.S. 494, 97 S.Ct. 1932, 52 L.Ed.2d 531 (1977), 577

Morrison v. Olson, 487 U.S. 654, 108 S.Ct. 2597, 101 L.Ed.2d 569 (1988), 12, **440**

Morrison, United States v., 529 U.S. 598, 120 S.Ct. 1740, 146 L.Ed.2d 658 (2000), **173, 846,** 1279

Mueller v. Allen, 463 U.S. 388, 103 S.Ct. 3062, 77 L.Ed.2d 721 (1983), 1091, 1107

Muller v. State of Oregon, 208 U.S. 412, 28 S.Ct. 324, 52 L.Ed. 551 (1908), 520, 729

Muskrat v. United States, 219 U.S. 346, 31 S.Ct. 250, 55 L.Ed. 246 (1911), **78**

Myers v. United States, 272 U.S. 52, 47 S.Ct. 21, 71 L.Ed. 160 (1926), **423**

N. A. A. C. P. v. Button, 371 U.S. 415, 83 S.Ct. 328, 9 L.Ed.2d 405 (1963), **904,** 1011

N. A. A. C. P. v. Claiborne Hardware Co., 458 U.S. 886, 102 S.Ct. 3409, 73 L.Ed.2d 1215 (1982), **1054,** 1083

N. A. A. C. P. v. State of Ala. ex rel. Patterson, 357 U.S. 449, 78 S.Ct. 1163, 2 L.Ed.2d 1488 (1958), **1061,** 1083

National Broadcasting Co. v. United States, 319 U.S. 190, 63 S.Ct. 997, 87 L.Ed. 1344 (1943), 398

National Collegiate Athletic Ass'n v. Tarkanian, 488 U.S. 179, 109 S.Ct. 454, 102 L.Ed.2d 469 (1988), **1300,** 1306

National League of Cities v. Usery, 426 U.S. 833, 96 S.Ct. 2465, 49 L.Ed.2d 245 (1976), **206**

Near v. State of Minnesota ex rel. Olson, 283 U.S. 697, 51 S.Ct. 625, 75 L.Ed. 1357 (1931), 895, 1015

Nebbia v. People of New York, 291 U.S. 502, 54 S.Ct. 505, 78 L.Ed. 940 (1934), **521**

Nebraska Press Ass'n v. Stuart, 427 U.S. 539, 96 S.Ct. 2791, 49 L.Ed.2d 683 (1976), 894

New Energy Co. of Indiana v. Limbach, 486 U.S. 269, 108 S.Ct. 1803, 100 L.Ed.2d 302 (1988), 264, 292

New Orleans, City of v. Dukes, 427 U.S. 297, 96 S.Ct. 2513, 49 L.Ed.2d 511 (1976), 633

New Orleans City Park Improvement Association v. Detiege, 358 U.S. 54, 79 S.Ct. 99, 3 L.Ed.2d 46 (1958), 685

New York v. Ferber, 458 U.S. 747, 102 S.Ct. 3348, 73 L.Ed.2d 1113 (1982), **943,** 971, 1012

New York v. United States, 505 U.S. 144, 112 S.Ct. 2408, 120 L.Ed.2d 120 (1992), **213,** 794

New York City Transit Authority v. Beazer, 440 U.S. 568, 99 S.Ct. 1355, 59 L.Ed.2d 587 (1979), **643**

New York Times Co. v. Sullivan, 376 U.S. 254, 84 S.Ct. 710, 11 L.Ed.2d 686 (1964), 928, **929,** 994, 1012

New York Times Co. v. United States, 403 U.S. 713, 91 S.Ct. 2140, 29 L.Ed.2d 822 (1971), **895,** 1011

Nguyen v. I.N.S., 533 U.S. 53, 121 S.Ct. 2053, 150 L.Ed.2d 115 (2001), 751

Nixon v. Administrator of General Services, 433 U.S. 425, 97 S.Ct. 2777, 53 L.Ed.2d 867 (1977), 458, **459**

Nixon v. Fitzgerald, 457 U.S. 731, 102 S.Ct. 2690, 73 L.Ed.2d 349 (1982), **378**

Nixon v. Shrink Missouri Government PAC, 528 U.S. 377, 120 S.Ct. 897, 145 L.Ed.2d 886 (2000), 991

Nixon v. United States, 506 U.S. 224, 113 S.Ct. 732, 122 L.Ed.2d 1 (1993), **72**

Nixon, United States v., 418 U.S. 683, 94 S.Ct. 3090, 41 L.Ed.2d 1039 (1974), **372**

N.L.R.B. v. Jones & Laughlin Steel Corp., 301 U.S. 1, 57 S.Ct. 615, 81 L.Ed. 893 (1937), **149**

North American Cold Storage Co. v. City of Chicago, 211 U.S. 306, 29 S.Ct. 101, 53 L.Ed. 195 (1908), 628

Northeastern Florida Chapter of Associated General Contractors of America v. City of Jacksonville, Fla., 508 U.S. 656, 113 S.Ct. 2297, 124 L.Ed.2d 586 (1993), 82, 89

North Texas Speciality Physicians v. F.T.C., 528 F.3d 346 (5th Cir.2008), 974

Northwest Austin Mun. Utility Dist. No. One v. Holder, ___ U.S. ___, 129 S.Ct. 2504, 174 L.Ed.2d 140 (2009), 836

Norwich Gaslight Co. v. Norwich City Gas Co., 25 Conn. 19 (1856), 482

Noto v. United States, 367 U.S. 290, 81 S.Ct. 1517, 6 L.Ed.2d 836 (1961), 1054

O'Brien, United States v., 391 U.S. 367, 88 S.Ct. 1673, 20 L.Ed.2d 672 (1968), 14, 864, **884,** 948, 981, 1011, 1012, 1080, 1193

O'Connor v. Donaldson, 422 U.S. 563, 95 S.Ct. 2486, 45 L.Ed.2d 396 (1975), 627

Ogden v. Saunders, 25 U.S. 213, 6 L.Ed. 606 (1827), 1237

Opinion of the Justices to the Governor, 363 Mass. 899, 298 N.E.2d 840 (Mass.1973), 81

Oregon v. Mitchell, 400 U.S. 112, 91 S.Ct. 260, 27 L.Ed.2d 272 (1970), 65

Orr v. Orr, 440 U.S. 268, 99 S.Ct. 1102, 59 L.Ed.2d 306 (1979), **743**

O'Shea v. Littleton, 414 U.S. 488, 94 S.Ct. 669, 38 L.Ed.2d 674 (1974), 81

Overton v. Bazzetta, 539 U.S. 126, 123 S.Ct. 2162, 156 L.Ed.2d 162 (2003), 1052

Palko v. Connecticut, 302 U.S. 319, 58 S.Ct. 149, 82 L.Ed. 288 (1937), 486

Palmer v. Thompson, 403 U.S. 217, 91 S.Ct. 1940, 29 L.Ed.2d 438 (1971), 677

Palmore v. Sidoti, 466 U.S. 429, 104 S.Ct. 1879, 80 L.Ed.2d 421 (1984), 692, 705

Parents Involved in Community Schools v. Seattle School Dist. No. 1, 551 U.S. 701, 127 S.Ct. 2738, 168 L.Ed.2d 508 (2007), **712**

Paris Adult Theatre I v. Slaton, 413 U.S. 49, 93 S.Ct. 2628, 37 L.Ed.2d 446 (1973), 942

Paul v. State of Virginia, 75 U.S. 168, 19 L.Ed. 357 (1868), 309

Pell v. Procunier, 417 U.S. 817, 94 S.Ct. 2800, 41 L.Ed.2d 495 (1974), 1048

Penn Cent. Transp. Co. v. City of New York, 438 U.S. 104, 98 S.Ct. 2646, 57 L.Ed.2d 631 (1978), **1253**

Pennell v. City of San Jose, 485 U.S. 1, 108 S.Ct. 849, 99 L.Ed.2d 1 (1988), 1252

Pennsylvania v. Union Gas Co., 491 U.S. 1, 109 S.Ct. 2273, 105 L.Ed.2d 1 (1989), 238

Pennsylvania Coal Co. v. Mahon, 260 U.S. 393, 43 S.Ct. 158, 67 L.Ed. 322 (1922), 1253, 1258, 1259

Pennzoil Co. v. Texaco, Inc., 481 U.S. 1, 107 S.Ct. 1519, 95 L.Ed.2d 1 (1987), 819

Perry v. Schwarzenegger, 704 F.Supp.2d 921 (N.D.Cal.2010), 776

Perry v. Sindermann, 408 U.S. 593, 92 S.Ct. 2694, 33 L.Ed.2d 570 (1972), 626, 913

Personnel Adm'r of Massachusetts v. Feeney, 442 U.S. 256, 99 S.Ct. 2282, 60 L.Ed.2d 870 (1979), **751**

Philadelphia, City of v. New Jersey, 437 U.S. 617, 98 S.Ct. 2531, 57 L.Ed.2d 475 (1978), **284**

Pickering v. Board of Ed. of Tp. High School Dist. 205, Will County, Illinois, 391 U.S. 563, 88 S.Ct. 1731, 20 L.Ed.2d 811 (1968), 1001

Pierce v. Society of the Sisters of the Holy Names of Jesus and Mary, 268 U.S. 510, 45 S.Ct. 571, 69 L.Ed. 1070 (1925), **531**

Pike v. Bruce Church, Inc., 397 U.S. 137, 90 S.Ct. 844, 25 L.Ed.2d 174 (1970), 271, 275

Planned Parenthood of Southeastern Pennsylvania v. Casey, 505 U.S. 833, 112 S.Ct. 2791, 120 L.Ed.2d 674 (1992), **553**

Pleasant Grove City, Utah v. Summum, ___ U.S. ___, 129 S.Ct. 1125, 172 L.Ed.2d 853 (2009), 919

Plessy v. Ferguson, 163 U.S. 537, 16 S.Ct. 1138, 41 L.Ed. 256 (1896), **679**, 680

Plyler v. Doe, 457 U.S. 202, 102 S.Ct. 2382, 72 L.Ed.2d 786 (1982), **812**

Poe v. Ullman, 367 U.S. 497, 81 S.Ct. 1752, 6 L.Ed.2d 989 (1961), 544, 608

Police Dept. of City of Chicago v. Mosley, 408 U.S. 92, 92 S.Ct. 2286, 33 L.Ed.2d 212 (1972), 755

Pollock v. Farmers' Loan & Trust Co., 158 U.S. 601, 15 S.Ct. 912, 39 L.Ed. 1108 (1895), 65

Posadas de Puerto Rico Associates v. Tourism Co. of Puerto Rico, 478 U.S. 328, 106 S.Ct. 2968, 92 L.Ed.2d 266 (1986), **975**, 1012

Powell v. McCormack, 395 U.S. 486, 89 S.Ct. 1944, 23 L.Ed.2d 491 (1969), 71

Presbyterian Church in United States v. Mary Elizabeth Blue Hull Memorial Presbyterian Church, 393 U.S. 440, 89 S.Ct. 601, 21 L.Ed.2d 658 (1969), **1224**, 1230

Principality of Monaco v. State of Mississippi, 292 U.S. 313, 54 S.Ct. 745, 78 L.Ed. 1282 (1934), 237

Printz v. United States, 521 U.S. 898, 117 S.Ct. 2365, 138 L.Ed.2d 914 (1997), **219**

Prudential Ins. Co. v. Benjamin, 328 U.S. 408, 66 S.Ct. 1142, 90 L.Ed. 1342 (1946), 154, **302**

Quirin, Ex parte, 317 U.S. 1, 63 S.Ct. 1, 87 L.Ed. 3 (1942), 357, 365

Railroad Retirement Board v. Alton R. Co., 295 U.S. 330, 55 S.Ct. 758, 79 L.Ed. 1468 (1935), 145

Railway Exp. Agency v. People of State of N.Y., 336 U.S. 106, 69 S.Ct. 463, 93 L.Ed. 533 (1949), **639**

R.A.V. v. City of St. Paul, Minn., 505 U.S. 377, 112 S.Ct. 2538, 120 L.Ed.2d 305 (1992), **964**, 1012

Raymond U v. Duke University, 91 N.C.App. 171, 371 S.E.2d 701 (N.C.App.1988), 927

Red Lion Broadcasting Co. v. F.C.C., 395 U.S. 367, 89 S.Ct. 1794, 23 L.Ed.2d 371 (1969), **1032**, 1049

Reed v. Reed, 404 U.S. 71, 92 S.Ct. 251, 30 L.Ed.2d 225 (1971), 729, 734

Regents of University of California v. Bakke, 438 U.S. 265, 98 S.Ct. 2733, 57 L.Ed.2d 750 (1978), 89, 693

Reno v. Condon, 528 U.S. 141, 120 S.Ct. 666, 145 L.Ed.2d 587 (2000), 227

Renton, City of v. Playtime Theatres, Inc., 475 U.S. 41, 106 S.Ct. 925, 89 L.Ed.2d 29 (1986), **865**, 1010

Republican Party of Minnesota v. White, 536 U.S. 765, 122 S.Ct. 2528, 153 L.Ed.2d 694 (2002), **873**, 1011

Reynolds v. Sims, 377 U.S. 533, 84 S.Ct. 1362, 12 L.Ed.2d 506 (1964), 71, **792**

Reynolds v. United States, 98 U.S. 145, 25 L.Ed. 244 (1878), 1086, 1186

Rice v. Santa Fe Elevator Corp., 331 U.S. 218, 67 S.Ct. 1146, 91 L.Ed. 1447 (1947), 247

Richmond, City of v. J.A. Croson Co., 488 U.S. 469, 109 S.Ct. 706, 102 L.Ed.2d 854 (1989), **695**

Richmond Newspapers, Inc. v. Virginia, 448 U.S. 555, 100 S.Ct. 2814, 65 L.Ed.2d 973 (1980), **1042,** 1049

Roberts v. United States Jaycees, 468 U.S. 609, 104 S.Ct. 3244, 82 L.Ed.2d 462 (1984), 1052, 1066, 1083

Robinson v. California, 370 U.S. 660, 82 S.Ct. 1417, 8 L.Ed.2d 758 (1962), 493

Roe v. Wade, 410 U.S. 113, 93 S.Ct. 705, 35 L.Ed.2d 147 (1973), **546**

Rogers v. Lodge, 458 U.S. 613, 102 S.Ct. 3272, 73 L.Ed.2d 1012 (1982), 722, 803

Romer v. Evans, 517 U.S. 620, 116 S.Ct. 1620, 134 L.Ed.2d 855 (1996), **771**

Rosenberger v. Rector and Visitors of University of Virginia, 515 U.S. 819, 115 S.Ct. 2510, 132 L.Ed.2d 700 (1995), 918, 919, 1108, 1147

Rosenblatt v. Baer, 383 U.S. 75, 86 S.Ct. 669, 15 L.Ed.2d 597 (1966), 928

Rosenstock v. Board of Governors of University of North Carolina, 423 F.Supp. 1321 (M.D.N.C.1976), 309

Rostker v. Goldberg, 453 U.S. 57, 101 S.Ct. 2646, 69 L.Ed.2d 478 (1981), 754

Roth v. United States, 354 U.S. 476, 77 S.Ct. 1304, 1 L.Ed.2d 1498 (1957), 937, **938,** 1012

Rubin v. Coors Brewing Co., 514 U.S. 476, 115 S.Ct. 1585, 131 L.Ed.2d 532 (1995), 976

Rumsfeld v. Forum for Academic and Institutional Rights, Inc., 547 U.S. 47, 126 S.Ct. 1297, 164 L.Ed.2d 156 (2006), **1078,** 1083

Rumsfeld v. Padilla, 542 U.S. 426, 124 S.Ct. 2711, 159 L.Ed.2d 513 (2004), 369

Rust v. Sullivan, 500 U.S. 173, 111 S.Ct. 1759, 114 L.Ed.2d 233 (1991), **914,** 1011

Saenz v. Roe, 526 U.S. 489, 119 S.Ct. 1518, 143 L.Ed.2d 689 (1999), 309, 484

Salvation Army v. Department of Community Affairs of State of N.J., 919 F.2d 183 (3rd Cir.1990), 1052

San Antonio Independent School Dist. v. Rodriguez, 411 U.S. 1, 93 S.Ct. 1278, 36 L.Ed.2d 16 (1973), **807**

San Diego, Cal., City of v. Roe, 543 U.S. 77, 125 S.Ct. 521, 160 L.Ed.2d 410 (2004), 928

Santa Fe Independent School Dist. v. Doe, 530 U.S. 290, 120 S.Ct. 2266, 147 L.Ed.2d 295 (2000), 1147

Santosky v. Kramer, 455 U.S. 745, 102 S.Ct. 1388, 71 L.Ed.2d 599 (1982), 627

Scales v. United States, 367 U.S. 203, 81 S.Ct. 1469, 6 L.Ed.2d 782 (1961), 1053, 1083

Schad v. Borough of Mount Ephraim, 452 U.S. 61, 101 S.Ct. 2176, 68 L.Ed.2d 671 (1981), **909**

School Dist. of Abington Tp., Pa. v. Schempp, 374 U.S. 203, 83 S.Ct. 1560, 10 L.Ed.2d 844 (1963), 1090, 1127

School Dist. of City of Grand Rapids v. Ball, 473 U.S. 373, 105 S.Ct. 3216, 87 L.Ed.2d 267 (1985), 1091

Schweiker v. Wilson, 450 U.S. 221, 101 S.Ct. 1074, 67 L.Ed.2d 186 (1981), 529

Scott v. Emerson, 15 Mo. 576 (Mo.1852), 657

Selective Service System v. Minnesota Public Interest Research Group, 468 U.S. 841, 104 S.Ct. 3348, 82 L.Ed.2d 632 (1984), 458

Seminole Tribe of Florida v. Florida, 517 U.S. 44, 116 S.Ct. 1114, 134 L.Ed.2d 252 (1996), 236, 238

Shapero v. Kentucky Bar Ass'n, 486 U.S. 466, 108 S.Ct. 1916, 100 L.Ed.2d 475 (1988), 909

Shaw v. Reno, 509 U.S. 630, 113 S.Ct. 2816, 125 L.Ed.2d 511 (1993), **723**

Sheldon v. Sill, 49 U.S. 441, 8 How. 441, 12 L.Ed. 1147 (1850), 101

Shelley v. Kraemer, 334 U.S. 1, 68 S.Ct. 836, 92 L.Ed. 1161 (1948), 1273, **1288,** 1306

Sherbert v. Verner, 374 U.S. 398, 83 S.Ct. 1790, 10 L.Ed.2d 965 (1963), 625, **1188**

Shreveport Rate Case, 234 U.S. 342, 34 S.Ct. 833, 58 L..Ed. 1341 (1914), **136**

Silkwood v. Kerr-McGee Corp., 464 U.S. 238, 104 S.Ct. 615, 78 L.Ed.2d 443 (1984), **247**

Skinner v. Oklahoma, 316 U.S. 535, 62 S.Ct. 1110, 86 L.Ed. 1655 (1942), **533**

Slaughter-House Cases, 83 U.S. 36, 21 L.Ed. 394 (1872), **475,** 827

Smith v. Goguen, 415 U.S. 566, 94 S.Ct. 1242, 39 L.Ed.2d 605 (1974), 903

South Carolina v. Baker, 485 U.S. 505, 108 S.Ct. 1355, 99 L.Ed.2d 592 (1988), 227

South Carolina v. Katzenbach, 383 U.S. 301, 86 S.Ct. 803, 15 L.Ed.2d 769 (1966), **832,** 843, 848

South Carolina State Highway Department v. Barnwell Bros., 303 U.S. 177, 58 S.Ct. 510, 82 L.Ed. 734 (1938), **272**

South Carolina, State of v. United States, 199 U.S. 437, 26 S.Ct. 110, 50 L.Ed. 261 (1905), 21

South-Central Timber Development, Inc. v. Wunnicke, 467 U.S. 82, 104 S.Ct. 2237, 81 L.Ed.2d 71 (1984), **292**

South Dakota v. Dole, 483 U.S. 203, 107 S.Ct. 2793, 97 L.Ed.2d 171 (1987), **197,** 913, 1082

Southeastern Promotions, Ltd. v. Conrad, 420 U.S. 546, 95 S.Ct. 1239, 43 L.Ed.2d 448 (1975), 895

Southern Pac. Co. v. State of Ariz. ex rel. Sullivan, 325 U.S. 761, 65 S.Ct. 1515, 89 L.Ed. 1915 (1945), **275**

Spence v. State of Wash., 418 U.S. 405, 94 S.Ct. 2727, 41 L.Ed.2d 842 (1974), 948, 1012

Stafford v. Wallace, 258 U.S. 495, 42 S.Ct. 397, 66 L.Ed. 735 (1922), 138

State Commercial Fisheries Entry Com'n v. Carlson, 65 P.3d 851 (Alaska 2003), 291

State of (see name of state)

Steffel v. Thompson, 415 U.S. 452, 94 S.Ct. 1209, 39 L.Ed.2d 505 (1974), 903

Stenberg v. Carhart, 530 U.S. 914, 120 S.Ct. 2597, 147 L.Ed.2d 743 (2000), 567

Stevens, United States v., ___ U.S. ___, 130 S.Ct. 1577, 176 L.Ed.2d 435 (2010), **1007**

Stone v. Graham, 449 U.S. 39, 101 S.Ct. 192, 66 L.Ed.2d 199 (1980), 1169

Stone v. State of Mississippi, 101 U.S. 814, 25 L.Ed. 1079 (1879), 1237

Strauder v. State of West Virginia, 100 U.S. 303, 25 L.Ed. 664 (1879), **658**

Sugarman v. Dougall, 413 U.S. 634, 93 S.Ct. 2842, 37 L.Ed.2d 853 (1973), 758

Supreme Court of New Hampshire v. Piper, 470 U.S. 274, 105 S.Ct. 1272, 84 L.Ed.2d 205 (1985), 309

Swann v. Charlotte-Mecklenburg Bd. of Ed., 402 U.S. 1, 91 S.Ct. 1267, 28 L.Ed.2d 554 (1971), 689

Swift & Co. v. United States, 196 U.S. 375, 25 S.Ct. 276, 49 L.Ed. 518 (1905), 138

Syracuse Peace Council v. F.C.C., 867 F.2d 654, 276 U.S.App.D.C. 38 (D.C.Cir.1989), 1037

Talley v. California, 362 U.S. 60, 80 S.Ct. 536, 4 L.Ed.2d 559 (1960), 859

Tennessee v. Lane, 541 U.S. 509, 124 S.Ct. 1978, 158 L.Ed.2d 820 (2004), 850

Texas v. Johnson, 491 U.S. 397, 109 S.Ct. 2533, 105 L.Ed.2d 342 (1989), **949,** 1012, 1080

Thomas v. Chicago Park Dist., 534 U.S. 316, 122 S.Ct. 775, 151 L.Ed.2d 783 (2002), 861

Thompson v. Western States Medical Center, 535 U.S. 357, 122 S.Ct. 1497, 152 L.Ed.2d 563 (2002), 982

Thornburgh v. American College of Obstetricians and Gynecologists, 476 U.S. 747, 106 S.Ct. 2169, 90 L.Ed.2d 779 (1986), 553

Tinker v. Des Moines Independent Community School Dist., 393 U.S. 503, 89 S.Ct. 733, 21 L.Ed.2d 731 (1969), 894, 948

Tomic v. Catholic Diocese of Peoria, 442 F.3d 1036 (7th Cir.2006), 1228

Torcaso v. Watkins, 367 U.S. 488, 81 S.Ct. 1680, 6 L.Ed.2d 982 (1961), 1186

Town of (see name of town)

Troxel v. Granville, 530 U.S. 57, 120 S.Ct. 2054, 147 L.Ed.2d 49 (2000), 577

Turner Broadcasting System, Inc. v. F.C.C., 512 U.S. 622, 114 S.Ct. 2445, 129 L.Ed.2d 497 (1994), **869**

Twining v. New Jersey, 211 U.S. 78, 29 S.Ct. 14, 53 L.Ed. 97 (1908), 486

United Haulers Ass'n, Inc. v. Oneida-Herkimer Solid Waste Management Authority, 550 U.S. 330, 127 S.Ct. 1786, 167 L.Ed.2d 655 (2007), **297**

United States v. _____ (see opposing party)

United States Dept. of Agriculture v. Moreno, 413 U.S. 528, 93 S.Ct. 2821, 37 L.Ed.2d 782 (1973), 770

United States Parole Commission v. Geraghty, 445 U.S. 388, 100 S.Ct. 1202, 63 L.Ed.2d 479 (1980), 82

United States R.R. Retirement Bd. v. Fritz, 449 U.S. 166, 101 S.Ct. 453, 66 L.Ed.2d 368 (1980), 529, 642

United States Term Limits, Inc. v. Thornton, 514 U.S. 779, 115 S.Ct. 1842, 131 L.Ed.2d 881 (1995), 11, 22, **314**

United States Trust Co. of New York v. New Jersey, 431 U.S. 1, 97 S.Ct. 1505, 52 L.Ed.2d 92 (1977), 1245

Valentine v. Chrestensen, 316 U.S. 52, 62 S.Ct. 920, 86 L.Ed. 1262 (1942), 973

Van Orden v. Perry, 545 U.S. 677, 125 S.Ct. 2854, 162 L.Ed.2d 607 (2005), 1091, 1099, **1176**

Varnum v. Brien, 763 N.W.2d 862 (Iowa 2009), 776

Vieth v. Jubelirer, 541 U.S. 267, 124 S.Ct. 1769, 158 L.Ed.2d 546 (2004), **798**

Village of (see name of village)

Virginia v. Black, 538 U.S. 343, 123 S.Ct. 1536, 155 L.Ed.2d 535 (2003), 860, 972, 1010

Virginia, United States v., 518 U.S. 515, 116 S.Ct. 2264, 135 L.Ed.2d 735 (1996), **734,** 746

Virginia State Bd. of Pharmacy v. Virginia Citizens Consumer Council, Inc., 425 U.S. 748, 96 S.Ct. 1817, 48 L.Ed.2d 346 (1976), 973

Wabash, St. L. & P. Ry. Co. v. State of Illinois, 118 U.S. 557, 7 S.Ct. 4, 30 L.Ed. 244 (1886), 259, **262**

Wallace v. Jaffree, 472 U.S. 38, 105 S.Ct. 2479, 86 L.Ed.2d 29 (1985), 1087, **1128,** 1167, 1230

Walz v. Tax Commission of City of New York, 397 U.S. 664, 90 S.Ct. 1409, 25 L.Ed.2d 697 (1970), 1106

Ward v. Rock Against Racism, 491 U.S. 781, 109 S.Ct. 2746, 105 L.Ed.2d 661 (1989), **879,** 981, 1011

Washington v. Davis, 426 U.S. 229, 96 S.Ct. 2040, 48 L.Ed.2d 597 (1976), **672**, 1193

Washington v. Glucksberg, 521 U.S. 702, 117 S.Ct. 2258, 138 L.Ed.2d 772 (1997), **606**

Watts v. United States, 394 U.S. 705, 89 S.Ct. 1399, 22 L.Ed.2d 664 (1969), 972

Webster v. Reproductive Health Services, 492 U.S. 490, 109 S.Ct. 3040, 106 L.Ed.2d 410 (1989), 553

Weinberger v. Wiesenfeld, 420 U.S. 636, 95 S.Ct. 1225, 43 L.Ed.2d 514 (1975), 745

Wesberry v. Sanders, 376 U.S. 1, 84 S.Ct. 526, 11 L.Ed.2d 481 (1964), 796

West Coast Hotel Co. v. Parrish, 300 U.S. 379, 57 S.Ct. 578, 81 L.Ed. 703 (1937), **523**

West Lynn Creamery, Inc. v. Healy, 512 U.S. 186, 114 S.Ct. 2205, 129 L.Ed.2d 157 (1994), 291

West Virginia State Board of Education v. Barnette, 319 U.S. 624, 63 S.Ct. 1178, 87 L.Ed. 1628 (1943), 1127, 1201

Whitman v. American Trucking Associations, 531 U.S. 457, 121 S.Ct. 903, 149 L.Ed.2d 1 (2001), **398**

Whitney v. California, 274 U.S. 357, 47 S.Ct. 641, 71 L.Ed. 1095 (1927), 862

Whitney v. Robertson, 124 U.S. 190, 8 S.Ct. 456, 31 L.Ed. 386 (1888), 350

Wickard v. Filburn, 317 U.S. 111, 63 S.Ct. 82, 87 L.Ed. 122 (1942), **155**

Williams, United States v., 553 U.S. 285, 128 S.Ct. 1830, 170 L.Ed.2d 650 (2008), 947

Williamson v. Lee Optical of Oklahoma, 348 U.S. 483, 75 S.Ct. 461, 99 L.Ed. 563 (1955), **527**, 642

Willson v. Black-Bird Creek Marsh Co., 27 U.S. 245, 7 L.Ed. 412 (1829), 258

Wisconsin v. Yoder, 406 U.S. 205, 92 S.Ct. 1526, 32 L.Ed.2d 15 (1972), 1186, **1194,**

Wolf v. People of the State of Colo., 338 U.S. 25, 69 S.Ct. 1359, 93 L.Ed. 1782 (1949), 492

Wolman v. Walter, 433 U.S. 229, 97 S.Ct. 2593, 53 L.Ed.2d 714 (1977), 1099

Wolston v. Reader's Digest Ass'n, Inc., 443 U.S. 157, 99 S.Ct. 2701, 61 L.Ed.2d 450 (1979), 928

Wong Kim Ark, United States v., 169 U.S. 649, 18 S.Ct. 456, 42 L.Ed. 890 (1898), 682

Woods v. Cloyd W. Miller Co., 333 U.S. 138, 68 S.Ct. 421, 92 L.Ed. 596 (1948), **201**

Yee v. City of Escondido, Cal., 503 U.S. 519, 112 S.Ct. 1522, 118 L.Ed.2d 153 (1992), **1250**

Yerger, Ex parte, 75 U.S. 85, 19 L.Ed. 332 (1868), 101

Yick Wo v. Hopkins, 118 U.S. 356, 6 S.Ct. 1064, 30 L.Ed. 220 (1886), **669**

Youngstown Sheet & Tube Co. v. Sawyer, 343 U.S. 579, 72 S.Ct. 863, 96 L.Ed. 1153 (1952), 11, **328**, 370, 1271

Zablocki v. Redhail, 434 U.S. 374, 98 S.Ct. 673, 54 L.Ed.2d 618 (1978), 577

Zauderer v. Office of Disciplinary Counsel of Supreme Court of Ohio, 471 U.S. 626, 105 S.Ct. 2265, 85 L.Ed.2d 652 (1985), 909

Zelman v. Simmons-Harris, 536 U.S. 639, 122 S.Ct. 2460, 153 L.Ed.2d 604 (2002), **1110**, 1230

Zobel v. Williams, 457 U.S. 55, 102 S.Ct. 2309, 72 L.Ed.2d 672 (1982), 309

Zorach v. Clauson, 343 U.S. 306, 72 S.Ct. 679, 96 L.Ed. 954 (1952), 1121

Zurcher v. Stanford Daily, 436 U.S. 547, 98 S.Ct. 1970, 56 L.Ed.2d 525 (1978), **1023**, 1049

PART I: INTRODUCTION

CHAPTER 1

History and Overview

This book concerns the constitutional law of the United States. As you will see in reading it, the book focuses mostly on how the Supreme Court has interpreted various provisions of the U.S. Constitution. This introductory chapter provides some background for understanding the Court's cases. The chapter starts by describing the historical setting in which the Constitution came into being. It then briefly outlines the structure and content of the Constitution. Finally, it presents conflicting theories about how courts should interpret the Constitution.

A. Historical Setting of the Constitution

In the mid-1700s, the United Kingdom of Great Britain[1] possessed a number of colonies in North America. Thirteen of these colonies later declared their independence and joined together to form the United States of America: Connecticut, Delaware, Georgia, Maryland, Massachusetts, New Hampshire, New Jersey, New York, North Carolina, Pennsylvania,

> **Go Online**
>
> Many law students feel that they would benefit from a quick refresher on American history. For a concise and easily accessible survey, visit the U.S. State Department's "Outline of U.S. History," available at http://infousa.state.gov/government/overview/docs/historytln.pdf. Chapters 3 and 4 of this outline, titled "The Road to Independence" and "The Formation of a National Government," are especially relevant.

---

[1] "Great Britain" is the name of the large island that England, Scotland, and Wales occupy. The Kingdom of England annexed Wales through Acts of Parliament passed in 1536 and 1543. In 1707, the Act of Union merged the Kingdom of England and the Kingdom of Scotland to form a new nation called the "United Kingdom of Great Britain." Historical discussions often shorten the lengthy name of this nation to the "United Kingdom" or "Great Britain" or just "Britain."

Rhode Island, South Carolina and Virginia.[2]

What led these colonies to seek independence? What did they hope to accomplish in forming a new nation? How did they organize their government? These are questions that anyone studying the Constitution must consider.

1. Colonial Governance and Events Preceding the Revolution

The thirteen colonies that later formed the United States exercised a fair degree of self-governance for many years. Each of the colonies had an elected assembly or legislature, which had authority to pass laws. In addition, these assemblies generally had the sole power to impose taxes and the sole authority to set the budget. The assemblies' enactments were subject to disapproval by a governor (who was appointed by the King of England in all of the colonies except Connecticut and Rhode Island) and by an appointed legislative council (except in Pennsylvania). But actual disapproval of legislation was very rare, and until the mid-1700s, few disputes arose between the colonies and the King or Parliament.

Serious challenges to the colonies' self-governance did not come about until the end of the French and Indian War. In this conflict, which lasted from 1754 until 1763, the United Kingdom fought against France and France's American Indian allies in North America. Although the United Kingdom ultimately prevailed, it incurred enormous expenses in the process. To help recover some of that money, Parliament passed several acts that sought to raise revenue from the colonies. These acts included the Stamp Act of 1765 and Townshend Act of 1767, both of which imposed taxes on various goods within the colonies.

Many colonists believed that these acts exceeded the power of Parliament. They asserted that any taxation imposed on the colonists must come from their own assemblies. Some of the colonists consequently protested the legislation with petitions and civil disobedience. In 1770, to alleviate tensions, Parliament repealed the taxes on almost all goods. But Parliament retained a tax on tea, largely to demonstrate that it did have power to tax the colonies if it so chose.

Colonists responded to the remaining tax by boycotting British tea and by smuggling tea into the country without paying taxes on it. (John Hancock, who later played a key role in the formation of the United States, was indicted on criminal charges for illegally purchasing and reselling tea from Holland.) Parliament in turn passed the Tea Act of 1773, which allowed the English East India Company to import and sell tea at lower prices than what the colonial merchants were charging, with the hope of inducing Americans to stop their boycott of British tea. To thwart this measure, on December 16, 1773, a group called the Sons of Liberty boarded ships in Boston Harbor that were carrying East India Company tea and threw the tea into the water.

---

[2] In North America, the United Kingdom also possessed the colonies of Quebec, Nova Scotia, Prince Edward Island, East Florida, and West Florida, but these colonies did not seek independence at the time of the American Revolution. Prior to the Revolution, the territory that later became Vermont was not recognized as a separate colony; instead, it was claimed by the colonies of both New York and New Hampshire. Vermont declared its independence from Great Britain and from New York and New Hampshire in 1777, but did not participate in the government formed by the Articles of Confederation. It joined the United States, after ratification of the Constitution, in 1791. Massachusetts assumed control over Maine in the mid-1600s and retained that control until 1820. Maine accordingly did not sign the Declaration of Independence.

In 1774, in response to this famous "Boston Tea Party," Parliament passed five laws that the colonists called the "Intolerable Acts" or the "Coercive Acts." These acts, among other things, severely limited the civil and political rights of colonists in Massachusetts. The goal was to force the colonists to make restitution for the tea and generally cease their defiance of Parliament. The founders of the United States remembered the loss of their liberty when they later drafted the Constitution and Bill of Rights.

2. The First and Second Continental Congresses

The Intolerable Acts and other factors led concerned colonists from all of the colonies except Georgia to send delegates to a meeting in Philadelphia. The meeting became known as the "First Continental Congress." The delegates met peacefully between September 5 and October 26, 1774. In total, fifty delegates attended. They included many famous figures of the era, such as John Adams, Samuel Adams, Patrick Henry, John Jay, Richard Henry Lee, Peyton Randolph, Roger Sherman, and George Washington.

FYI

The **Intolerable Acts** consisted of five individual acts. The Boston Port Act closed Boston to commercial shipping. The Quartering Act allowed a governor to order that British soldiers be quartered in private buildings if quarters were not provided for them within 24 hours following a request. The Massachusetts Government Act gave the royal government the exclusive power to appoint judges and prosecutors and prohibited town meetings without the permission of the royal governor. The Administration of Justice Act allowed the governor to order trials of persons arrested in Massachusetts to take place in other colonies, in order to prevent magistrates and juries from acquitting local residents who were hostile to the governor. The Quebec Act permitted the free exercise of the Roman Catholic Religion in Quebec, but it also provided no elected legislative assembly, creating—as the other colonists saw it—a tyranny that might spread to the other colonies.

The delegates to the First Continental Congress did not act as if they had the power to pass laws or take any other governmental actions. Instead, the delegates merely adopted resolutions and submitted letters and petitions of grievances to the King. Before adjourning, the First Continental Congress agreed to reconvene on May 10, 1775, in Philadelphia.

FYI

The records of the First and Second Continental Congress are collected and published in the Journals of the Continental Congress, 1774-1789 (Worthington C. Ford *et al.* eds. 1904-37), the full text of which is available at the Library of Congress's website: http://memory.loc.gov/ammem/amlaw/lwjc.html

Before the appointed date for the Second Continental Congress arrived, war broke out in Massachusetts. The fighting started with the battle of Lexington and Concord on April 19, 1775. In that battle, local militiamen defeated British troops who had come to seize their stores of weapons. Following the battle, colonists drove the British troops back to Boston and surrounded the city.

It was in these circumstances that the Second Continental Congress began to meet in Philadelphia on May 10, 1775. The Congress included delegates from each of the thirteen colonies. These delegates included many famous men of the founding era, such as John Hancock, John Adams, Benjamin Franklin, George Washington, and Thomas Jefferson. Like the First Continental Congress, the Second Continental Congress had no clear legislative authority. It could adopt resolutions, but could not pass laws or impose taxes.

Nevertheless, on June 15, 1775, the Second Continental Congress decided to assume authority over the American forces surrounding Boston, resolving that "a General be appointed to command all the continental forces, raised, or to be raised, for the defence of American liberty." It then unanimously selected George Washington for this position. The Second Continental Congress also appointed additional subordinate officers, and it agreed to finance the military (although obtaining the funds for this purpose proved difficult). Over the course of the next eleven months, fighting between American and British forces continued.

By the summer of 1776, the war had convinced the colonists that the colonies could no longer remain a part of the United Kingdom. Accordingly, on July 4, 1776, the Second Continental Congress adopted the Declaration of Independence. With this declaration, the fighting with Great Britain became a war for independence. The war for independence—known now as the "Revolution" or "Revolutionary War"—lasted seven years. The American forces lost most of the battles, but held together and eventually prevailed. In 1783, the United Kingdom acknowledged the independence of the United States in the Treaty of Paris, and the war ended.

3. The Articles of Confederation and the Calling of a Constitutional Convention

The Declaration of Independence proclaimed that the colonies had become "free and independent states." But these independent states needed to work together to prevail against the United Kingdom. In 1777, while the Revolutionary War was still being fought, the Continental Congress drafted a document called the Articles of Confederation. This document was finally approved by all of the states in 1781.

The Articles of Confederation was more like a multilateral treaty among allies than a formal constitution for a new national government. The document announced that its purpose was to create a "firm league of friendship" among the former colonies, which had now become something more akin to separate states. It emphasized that each "state retains its sovereignty, freedom, and independence."

Food for Thought

The newly independent states did not create a strong national government in the Articles of Confederation. Why might they have felt reluctant to do that even though the Revolutionary War clearly showed that the states needed to work together?

Under the Articles of Confederation, the states would continue to send delegates to a Congress just as they had done before. The Congress had limited power to pass laws, with each state having one vote. But the government was not effective. All measures required the unanimous assent of the states. The Congress had no way to enforce laws or collect taxes. There were no national courts. In addition, the unity of the states became strained over trade and other issues.

In 1787, the weaknesses in the Articles of Confederation led the Congress to call for a convention "for the sole and express purpose of revising the Articles of Confederation and reporting to Congress and the several legislatures such alterations and provisions therein as shall when agreed to in Congress and confirmed by the states render the federal constitution adequate to the exigencies of Government & the preservation of the Union." Notwithstanding the Congress's mandate, the convention quickly adopted as its task the drafting of a new Constitution. Accordingly, the convention became known as the "Constitutional Convention of 1787" (or sometimes the "Philadelphia Convention" or the "Federal Convention").

The states each could send as many "deputies" as they wanted to the Constitutional Convention. At the Convention, however, the delegates decided that each state would have only one vote. In total, fifty-five men attended the Convention. These men represented all of the states except Rhode Island, which chose not to participate. The deputies, whom we now call the "Framers" of the Constitution, included grand eminences such as George Washington and Benjamin Franklin; visionary political thinkers such as James Madison, Alexander Hamilton, James Wilson, and Roger Sherman; and masters of written expression such as Gouverneur Morris, who did most of the final stylistic editing of the Constitution. The deputies also included dissenters, such as George Mason of Virginia, who refused to vote for the document because it did not contain a bill of rights, and Robert Yates and John Lansing, Jr., who left the Convention early because they believed that their instructions from the New York legislature did not permit them to participate in creating a new constitution.

> **FYI**
>
> Although the Constitutional Convention met in secret and the members agreed not to discuss what took place, we now know a great deal about what transpired at the proceedings. The Convention appointed a secretary, who kept an official journal. In addition, at least eight of the fifty-five members took notes at the Convention. By great fortune, James Madison, who was the intellectual leader of the delegates, took the most extensive notes. The records and notes are collected in *The Records of the Federal Convention of 1787* (Max Farrand, ed., 1911), a source cited by more than 100 Supreme Court cases. The Library of Congress's website contains the full text of this work: http://memory.loc. gov/ammem/amlaw/lwfr.html.

4. Proceedings of the Constitutional Convention

As the cases in this book will show, in interpreting the Constitution, the Supreme Court often looks very carefully at what the deputies argued and decided at the Constitutional Convention.[3] To understand the Court's frequent references to the deputies' debates, readers of the Court's opinions should know what happened in Philadelphia. Basically, the Convention took place in nine chronological segments:

1. *Full Convention (May 14 - May 29).* The Convention began by unanimously selecting George Washington to serve as the Convention's president. It then adopted rules gov-

---

[3] As discussed in Part C of this Chapter, many writers disagree about whether it is possible to discern the original meaning of the Constitution from these debates and, in any event, whether the original meaning should govern modern interpretation of the Constitution.

erning the proceedings. These rules specified, among other things, that each state present and fully represented would have one vote and that the proceedings would be kept secret.

On May 29, 1787, Edmund Randolph offered 15 resolutions, each just one sentence in length. These resolutions—which became known as the "Virginia Plan" for government—reflected the ideas of James Madison. Under the plan, there would be a national legislature that would have two chambers, one directly elected and the other appointed by the state legislatures. The plan generally favored the states with large populations (Massachusetts, Pennsylvania, New York, and Virginia) because it called for proportional representation in both houses. After Randolph made this proposal, the Convention decided to deliberate as a committee of the whole (i.e., a gathering where all of the deputies could discuss the issues under informal rules of debate).

2. *Committee of the Whole (May 30 - June 13)*. On the first day when the deputies met as a committee of the whole, Gouverneur Morris urged Randolph to modify his resolutions to include the following proposal: "Resolved, that a national government ought to be established consisting of a supreme Legislature, Executive, and Judiciary." The committee of the whole voted to adopt this resolution. With this action, the committee of the whole implicitly endorsed creating a new Constitution as the goal of the Convention, rather than merely amending the Articles of Confederation.

3. *Full Convention (June 13 - June 15)*. The Convention formally debated the Virginia Plan from June 13 to June 15. The small states opposed the Virginia Plan because they believed that their votes would be diluted in a national legislature with proportional representation. On June 15, William Paterson of New Jersey proposed a set of nine alternative resolutions, which became known as the "New Jersey Plan." The New Jersey Plan favored small states. Most significantly, the plan called for a unicameral legislature with equal representation for each state. The Convention again decided to meet as a committee of the whole, this time to discuss the New Jersey Plan.

4. *Committee of the Whole (June 16 - June 19)*. The committee of the whole debated and ultimately rejected the New Jersey Plan. It also considered an alternative plan proposed by Alexander Hamilton. Hamilton's plan called for an executive elected for life and senators chosen for life. The plan would have reduced state sovereignty by allowing the national executive to appoint executives for each state government.

5. *Full Convention (June 19 - July 26)*. Important debates about representation in the legislative branch followed the rejection of the New Jersey Plan. The large and small states could not agree on the composition of the legislative branch. Ultimately, a modified version of the Virginia Plan became acceptable to the Convention after the delegates agreed to what has become known as the "Great Compromise" (or alternatively as the "Connecticut Compromise"). In this compromise, the states would have equal representation in the Senate and proportional representation in the House. This compromise balanced the interests of large and small states. The Convention also adopted the closely related three-fifths rule, under which only three-fifths of a state's slave population would be counted for determining representation in the House. This feature split the difference between Southern states, which wanted all slaves counted for this purpose, and Northern states, which opposed

counting any slaves in determining state entitlement to representation in the House.

In addition to the Great Compromise, the Convention also addressed a variety of other important topics. These included the term of the executive's service, the appointment of judges, and the process for ratifying the Constitution. On July 26th, with the general structure of the government settled, the Convention created a "Committee of Detail" to turn the plan into a draft. The Convention recessed while the Committee of Detail performed its work.

6. *Committee of Detail (July 27 - August 5)*. John Rutledge, Edmund Randolph, and James Wilson did most of the work of the Committee of Detail. In addition to describing the government and the selection of its members, the Committee of Detail added the list of congressional powers and the list of limitations on state powers now found in Article I. When the Committee of Detail finished, its draft was printed and distributed to all of the deputies.

7. *Full Convention (August 6 - September 6)*. The Full Convention then debated the Committee of Detail's draft and other important matters. They considered suffrage qualifications, immigration, slavery, and the veto power. During this time, the Convention referred some matters to separate committees, which met and reported back to the Convention. After reaching final conclusions on most items, the Convention appointed a "Committee of Style" (sometimes called the "Committee on Style and Arrangement"). The Committee of Style was charged with the task of putting the Constitution in a consistent form.

8. *Committee of Style (September 6 - September 12)*. The Committee of Style put all of the Convention's changes into the draft and polished the text. Gouverneur Morris did much of the work, although the Committee also included James Madison, William Johnson, Rufus King, and Alexander Hamilton. Their work is seen as very important because they formulated the precise expression of many of the Constitution's great clauses. The Committee of Style finished its assignment on September 12, and a printer made copies of its draft for all of the deputies.

9. *Full Convention (September 12 - September 17)*. The Convention then debated the Committee of Style's draft for several days. During this time, George Mason and Elbridge Gerry proposed the inclusion of a bill of rights. The Convention debated but rejected this proposal. Two days later, on September 17, 1787, the state delegations present at the Convention unanimously approved the Constitution. All of the individual delegates present except for Gerry, Mason, and Randolph signed the Constitution. The Convention then adjourned.

5. Ratification of the Constitution

The Constitution, by its own terms, could not go into effect until ratified. Article VII said: "The Ratification of the Conventions of nine States, shall be sufficient for the Establishment of this Constitution between the States so ratifying the Same." Under this provision, each state legislature was expected to form a ratifying convention to debate and vote on the Constitution. In the fall of 1787 and spring and early summer of 1788, the states held these ratifying conventions.

Whether the proposed Constitution would be ratified was an open question. The Constitution would make many substantial changes to the status quo. Although some people favored ratification, many others did not. Public debate spread throughout the states on the subject. Supporters of the Constitution became known as the "Federalists," while opponents became known as the "Anti-Federalists."

Three of the best known Federalists were Alexander Hamilton, James Madison, and John Jay. In the fall of 1787 and spring of 1788, they wrote a series of 85 essays explaining the Constitution and urging its ratification in the State of New York. Each of these essays was titled "The Federalist" followed by a number designating its order in the series. Historians typically refer to the 85 essays as the "Federalist Papers." These essays, all of which are available online, address nearly every aspect of the Constitution. Although the essays are advocacy documents and not dispassionate legal analyses, they have been remarkably influential. As you will see in reading the cases in this book, the Supreme Court regularly relies on these essays in attempting to discern the original meaning of the Constitution.

> **FYI**
>
> The Federalist Papers are clearly the most influential source of the original meaning of the Constitution other than the text of the Constitution itself. The Supreme Court has cited the Federalist Papers in more than 400 cases. The Library of Congress's website contains the full text of the Federalist Papers: http://thomas.loc. gov/home/histdox/fedpapers.html. For more information on the Federalist Papers, see *Gregory Maggs, A Concise Guide to the Records of the State Ratifying Conventions as a Source of the Original Meaning of the U.S. Constitution,* 2009 U. Ill. L. Rev. 457.

The Anti-Federalists opposed the Constitution for a number of reasons. Two of the most important concerned the protection of state sovereignty and individual rights. Opponents felt that the Constitution gave too much power to the federal government at the expense of the states. They also worried that the Constitution did not contain a bill of rights that would limit the powers of the government. In thinking about these opponents of the Constitution, modern readers should remember that their concerns stemmed from having lived through Parliament's oppression of the colonies.

> **FYI**
>
> Many records from the state ratifying conventions are collected in *The Debates in the Several State Conventions on the Adoption of the Federal Constitution, As Recommended by the General Convention at Philadelphia, in 1787* (Jonathan Elliot, ed. 1836-59). This work, often called *Elliot's Debates* for short, has been very influential; the Supreme Court has cited it in over 100 cases. The full text is available online at the Library of Congress's website: http://memory. loc.gov/ammem/amlaw/lwed.html.

By the summer of 1788, conventions in nine states had approved the Constitution, putting it into effect among the ratifying states. As the following table indicates, ratification was uncontroversial in Delaware, New Jersey, and Georgia. Each of these small states unanimously ratified the document.

But the Constitution was much more controversial in other states. Indeed, switching just a few votes in big states like New York or Virginia might have scuttled the entire project.

State	Date of Ratification	Vote
Delaware	Dec. 7, 1787	30-0
Pennsylvania	Dec. 12, 1787	46-23
New Jersey	Dec. 18, 1787	38-0
Georgia	Jan. 2, 1788	26-0
Connecticut	Jan. 9, 1788	128-40
Massachusetts	Feb. 6, 1788	187-168
Maryland	Apr. 28, 1788	63-11
South Carolina	May 23, 1788	149-73
New Hampshire	Jun. 21, 1788	57-47
Virginia	Jun. 25, 1788	89-79
New York	Jul. 26, 1788	30-27
North Carolina	Nov. 21, 1789	195-77
Rhode Island	May 29, 1790	34-32

6. The First Congress

Federal elections took place during the fall of 1788, and the new government under the Constitution began in 1789. George Washington, of course, became the first President. In the First Congress, which met from March 1789 to March 1791, a total of 29 persons served as senators and 66 served as representatives.

FYI

Because the First Congress laid so much of the foundation for the new nation, the Supreme Court often looks to its acts for guidance in determining the original meaning of the Constitution. The acts of the First Congress are published in volume 1 of *The Public Statutes at Large of the United States of America* (1845), the citation of which is abbreviated as "1 Stat." The Library of Congress has the full text at its website: http://memory.loc.gov/ammem/amlaw/lwsl.html.

Many of these senators and representatives justifiably could consider themselves experts on the Constitution. Ten of the senators and eleven of the representatives had served as deputies at the Constitutional Convention. Some of them, including James Madison, Oliver Ellsworth, and Roger Sherman, had played prominent roles in the Constitution's drafting. Other members of the First Congress, such as Richard Henry Lee, had participated at state ratifying conventions even though they had not attended the Constitutional Convention.

During its two-year term, the First Congress passed an astounding 96 acts. Among its many other accomplishments, the First Congress:

- imposed taxes on imported goods and on vessels entering United States ports, providing the first source of federal revenue;

- shaped the executive branch by establishing the Departments of Foreign Affairs, War, and Treasury;

- created the federal judicial system;

- passed laws on naturalization, patents, copyrights, and other subjects still governed by federal law;

- established a system of lighthouses, the post office, and the Bank of the United States;

- provided for the assumption of state revolutionary war debts and paying of the national debt; and

- located the seat of government in the District of Columbia and admitted Kentucky and Vermont into the Union.

- The First Congress also proposed twelve amendments to the Constitution, ten of which (now known as the Bill of Rights) received quick ratification by the states.

—————————

B. Organization of the Constitution

The Constitution contains a number of different parts. No one expects a new student of constitutional law to commit the document to memory or to master its provisions in one reading. But before going further, you should take some time to become familiar with its organization.

Preamble

The Constitution starts with an introduction, or "Preamble," which lists the six goals of the People in adopting the Constitution: "to form a more perfect Union, establish Justice, insure domestic Tranquility, provide for the common defence, promote the general Welfare, and secure the Blessings of Liberty to ourselves and our Posterity." Although lofty in tone, the courts mostly have concluded that the language of the Preamble is precatory. In other words, it does not create legal rights, duties, or powers. But the Preamble is still important. For example, it makes clear that the "People" rather than the states adopted the Constitution. We will consider this distinction in cases about the nature of the United States' sovereignty.

Article I

Following the Preamble, the Constitution contains seven articles. The first three articles reflect the Framers' vision that there are three branches of government: the legislative branch, the executive branch, and the judicial branch. Each has its own powers and has some ability to provide checks on the others. But as we will see in Chapter 6, sometimes questions arise about whether one branch is attempting to exercise powers belonging to another branch.

Article I contains ten sections that address the legislative branch. Section 1 establishes the fundamental point that "[a]ll legislative Powers herein granted shall be vested in a Congress of the United States, which shall consist of a Senate and House of Representatives." This means, among other things, that Congress has these powers, and that the President and the courts do not. You will read about this provision in famous cases like *Youngstown Sheet & Tube v. Sawyer*, 343 U.S. 579 (1952), in which the Court held that the President was unconstitutionally attempting to assert powers that were legislative in nature.

Sections 2 through 6 then tell how senators and representatives are selected, what their qualifications must be, how they are paid, and so forth. These provisions come up in the important case of *U.S. Term Limits v. Thornton*, 514 U.S. 779 (1995), a case invalidating an attempt to add what amounted to additional restrictions on who could run for the House or Senate.

Section 7 describes the procedure that Congress must follow in order to pass a law. As most high school civics classes teach, the House and Senate have to approve a bill, and the President must sign it. If the President vetoes a bill (i.e., rejects it), the House and Senate can override the veto with a two-thirds vote. But we will see in *INS v. Chadha*, 462 U.S. 919 (1983), that Congress has sometimes been tempted to look for ways to exercise power without involving the President.

Section 8 then lists the subjects upon which Congress may pass laws. It says that Congress may collect taxes, regulate commerce, establish a post office, and so forth. Chapter 3 of this book covers what Congress may and may not do under Article I, section 8. We will see in *Heart of Atlanta Motel v. United States*, 379 U.S. 241 (1964), and *Katzenbach v. McClung*, 379 U.S. 294 (1964), that Congress has the power to pass legislation protecting civil rights. On the other hand, we will see in *United States v. Lopez*, 514 U.S. 549 (1995), and *New York v. United States*, 505 U.S. 144 (1992), that the Supreme Court has struck down laws attempting to ban guns from schools or order the states to provide for the disposal of radioactive waste as being beyond the power of Congress to enact.

Sections 9 and 10 state various specific prohibitions. Section 9 says that Congress generally cannot suspend the writ of habeas corpus, pass ex post facto laws, tax exports from states, or give preference to one state's ports. Section 10 then tells us some of the things that the states may not do. They cannot enter treaties or coin money, impose duties on imports and exports, and so forth.

Article II

Article II concerns the executive branch. The Chief Executive, of course, is the President of the United States. Article II, section 1 says: "The executive Power shall be vested in a President of the United States of America." But the President does not act alone. The federal departments and agencies assist the President. The Constitution does not create these departments, but in various provisions it contemplates their existence. Congress has created many such departments, including the Department of Justice, the Department of Defense, the State Department, and so forth.

The President is the chief executive. In general, that makes everyone else in the executive branch subordinate to the President. The President generally exercises control by firing or threatening to fire those who will not carry out his lawful policies. But we will see in cases like *Humphrey's Executor v. United States*, 295 U.S. 602 (1935), and *Morrison v. Olson*, 487 U.S. 654 (1988), that Congress may place some limits on the ability of the President to control subordinates in this manner.

Section 2 puts the President in charge of the military, and allows him to grant pardons and appoint judges and other office holders. Section 3 requires the President to report to Congress, receive ambassadors, make sure that the laws are faithfully executed, and so forth.

Article III

Article III describes the power of the federal judiciary. The first sentence of Section 1 tells us that "[t]he judicial Power of the United States, shall be vested in one supreme Court, and in such inferior Courts as the Congress may from time to time ordain and establish." Section 2 then tells about the subject matter jurisdiction of federal courts. For example, it says that they can hear lawsuits between "Citizens of different States," which we know as diversity jurisdiction. We will see in the first case included in Chapter 2, *Marbury v. Madison*, 5 U.S. (1 Cranch) 137 (1803), that the Court struck down a federal statute that attempted to give the Court jurisdiction beyond the limits of Article III, section 2.

Articles IV - VII

Articles IV through VII contain a variety of different provisions. Article IV generally addresses relations among the states. As we will see in Chapter 4, the Privileges and Immunities Clause in Article IV limits discrimination by states against citizens of other states. Article V discusses the amendment process. The House and Senate can propose amendments by a two-thirds vote or two-thirds of the states can call a convention. (The latter route for amendment has never been used.) Proposals for amending the Constitution become effective when three-fourths of the states have ratified them in their legislatures or in conventions. Article VI tells us, among other things, that the "Constitution, and the Laws of the United States *** shall be the supreme Law of the Land." Article VII describes the ratification process that had to occur before the Constitution could take effect.

Amendments

The Constitution now contains 27 amendments. The first 10 amendments, commonly called the Bill of Rights, protect a large number of individual rights. Amendments 13 through 15 are known as the "Civil War Era Amendments" or the "Reconstruction Amendments" because they were passed at the end of the Civil War during the process of Reconstruction. They abolish slavery, bar states from denying equal protection of the laws or due process of the law to any person, and protect voting rights. We will be looking extensively at the First Amendment's protection of Free Speech, Free Press, and Religion, and at the Fourteenth Amendment's guarantees of Equal Protection and Due Process, in the second half of this book.

C. Methods of Interpreting the Constitution

One of the many things that distinguished the American Constitution at the time of its ratification was the simple fact that it was written down. (Although the United Kingdom—the nation from which the United States broke but from which it inherited its legal tradition—also had a "constitution," it was developed over time, in a common-law fashion, rather than codified.) At first blush, one might expect there to be little need for a thick casebook of judicial opinions for matters governed by a written document. But the study of American constitutional law has, from the very beginning, been as much a study of judicial interpretations of the Constitution as it has been of the document itself. We will see one of the reasons why this is so in Chapter 2 when we consider *Marbury v. Madison* and the topic of judicial review. But answering the question of who should get to interpret the Constitution—a question on which there is substantial continuing debate, as we will see in Chapter 2—does not tell us why a written Constitution should so frequently require interpretation in the first place. As it turns out, there has long been a need for interpretation of the Constitution because it is often not obvious, even after careful consultation of the text of the Constitution, what the Constitution tells us about important questions.

There are several reasons why this is so. First, the Framers of the Constitution (and those who ratified it) sought to preserve some degree of flexibility for subsequent generations to address pressing problems and, if necessary, to structure the government accordingly. Second, as described above, although the Framers were able to achieve consensus by compromising on some controversial questions, they masked their disagreement on other questions by writing general and vague provisions. Third, the Framers simply did not anticipate some of the questions that would arise in the future. Today's problems often look very different from the problems of 1789—or 1868, when the Fourteenth Amendment was ratified. Accordingly, the plain text of the Constitution often does not speak directly to questions that are likely to arise today.

One possible response to constitutional silence would be to conclude that if the Constitution does not expressly prohibit a particular action, it permits it. The Constitution, after all, is almost entirely about the limits on governmental, rather than private, action—the sole (and obviously incredibly important) exception being the Thirteenth Amendment, which prohibits slavery—and one could sensibly conclude that if the Constitution does not prohibit the government from taking a certain action, it implicitly permits it. There is great appeal to this approach; indeed, as we will see, among other things, it attempts to preserve democratic government by preventing judicial interference with the modern choices of democratically elected officials. But even if one is persuaded that it is the proper response to constitutional silence, it does not help us to determine *when* in fact the Constitution is silent on a particular question. This is because the Constitution's broad provisions arguably touch on a wide range of topics, even though they fail to provide specific guidance on most controversial questions that are likely to arise.

Indeed, the Constitution tends to speak at very high levels of generality. There is little doubt, for example, that the First Amendment protects the freedom of speech, but it does not define "freedom" or "speech." Is a contribution to a candidate for public office a form of "speech"? See *Buckley v. Valeo*, 424 U.S. 1 (1976), which we will consider in Chapter 14. What about publicly burning a draft card as a form of protest against an ongoing war? See *United States v. O'Brien*, 391 U.S. 367 (1968), which we will also consider in Chapter 14. And even if we can agree on what counts as speech, does a law imposing some limits on the ability to engage in a particular form of speech—but not prohibiting it entirely— "abridg[e]" the "freedom" protected by the Amendment? Similarly, the Fourteenth Amendment prohibits the States from denying to persons the "equal protection of the laws," but it does not give any more guidance about what those terms mean—whether, for example, the government is ever permitted to distinguish among citizens and, if so, whether some bases for classification are more problematic than others; and, if so, whether a State can justify a particular suspect classification—such as a requirement that drivers over 70 years old, but not younger drivers, get annual eye exams, or a ban on women serving in combat in the military—with sufficiently compelling reasons. Even determining whether the Constitution is "silent," therefore, requires interpretation of the document's broad terms.

Of course, the Constitution is not unusual among written texts in requiring interpretation to determine its meaning. Courts routinely are called upon, for example, to interpret statutes and contracts, written texts that only sometimes speak with great detail, and often speak in broad generalities—or, with respect to issues that are litigated, are entirely silent. Although interpretation of such documents is commonplace, there are a range of interpretive approaches that courts follow—and substantial debate over which are appropriate and defensible. In the context of statutory interpretation, for example, there are lively debates over whether judges should consider legislative history to determine statutory meaning, or whether courts should seek to discern congressional purposes in order to shed light on how Congress would have chosen to address particular circumstances about which the statute is silent. Similarly, there is a long-standing debate over whether, in interpreting a contract, courts should consider only the plain meaning of the contract's terms or instead may consider extrinsic evidence to determine a contract's meaning.

> **FYI**
>
> There is an extensive literature on the appropriate way for courts to interpret statutes. For a taste of the debate, compare John F. Manning, *Textualism as a Nondelegation Doctrine*, 97 Colum. L. Rev. 673 (1997), with Alexander Alienikoff, *Updating Statutory Interpretation*, 87 Mich. L. Rev. 20, 47-61 (1988).

But even assuming that there is a "correct" way to interpret statutes and contracts, matters are at least arguably more complex when the document at issue is the Constitution, because the Constitution is quite different from a statute or a contract in many important ways. First, as we will see when we consider <u>Marbury v. Madison</u> in Chapter 2, the Constitution is understood to be a form of "higher" law—that is, it cannot be superseded by an ordinary statute enacted by Congress, and (by its own express terms, in the Supremacy Clause of Article VI) it trumps state law that is inconsistent with its provisions. Second, by its own terms (in Article V), the Constitution can be amended only after obtaining a supermajority consensus—a two-thirds majority in both Houses of Congress and ratification by three-quarters of the States—that has rarely been achieved in over two hundred years. As noted above, there have been only 27 Amendments, and even that number tends to overstate the ease with which the Constitution may be amended: the ten Amendments in the Bill of Rights were adopted together two years after ratification of the original document, and one other (the Twenty-Seventh) was proposed along with the original Bill of Rights; three Amendments were adopted within only a few years after the Civil War; and two of the Amendments—the Eighteenth, enshrining Prohibition, and the Twenty-First, repealing it—effectively cancel each other out. Indeed, not only is it difficult to amend the Constitution, but Article V actually states that some of its provisions cannot be amended at all, even with the requisite support of two-thirds of both Houses of Congress and three-fourths of the states. Perhaps more strikingly, the provision that cannot be amended today is the one that gives each state an equal voice in the Senate, even though that provision arguably is the single most anti-democratic provision in the Constitution itself. Third, and particularly important in light of the first two distinctive features, the Constitution is over 200 years old.

Food for Thought

The provision in the Constitution providing the requirements for its ratification itself was inconsistent with the "constitution" that was in force at the time it was adopted. Although Article VII provided that the Constitution would become effective upon ratification by nine of the thirteen states, the Articles of Confederation expressly required *unanimous* consent of the states for any amendments to its terms. What does this suggest about the extent to which we should treat the *current* Constitution as binding?

Together, these features of the Constitution—its status as higher law, the difficulty of amending it, and its age—stand in uneasy tension with the notion of democracy. Indeed, the very notion of constitutionalism means that democratically elected majorities today cannot decide to govern themselves in the manner of their choosing if their choices would conflict with the Constitution. This tension is generally known as the "dead-hand problem": to embrace constitutionalism is to accept that the men who wrote and ratified the Constitution to govern *them* over 200 years ago should also be able to reach into the future, with their now-dead hands, and tell *us* how to live *our* lives.

One possible response to the dead-hand problem, of course, would be to deny the continuing binding force of the Constitution. It is, after all, merely a collection of words with no independent force beyond our willingness to follow it. But this response historically has held little appeal, because each successive generation has seen great value in binding itself to a charter for self-governance. First, it would be difficult for government to function without rules for the proper exercise of its power. Second, there is good reason to limit the power of democratic majorities. The Constitution is a form of self-imposed paternalism, to prevent us from letting the perceived exigencies of the moment lead us to decisions that, upon reflection and with the clarity of hindsight, we know are destructive of our most deeply held values.

And, as explained above, if we are to embrace the Constitution, then we must have some way to interpret it. The debate over how to interpret the Constitution is at least as old as the Constitution itself and tends to reflect the basic tension created by the very notion of constitutionalism. On the one hand, if we accept that the Constitution is a form of law (albeit higher law), then there is a strong argument that we should interpret it as we would any other law—to have a generally fixed content, determined by the will of those who enacted it, embodied either in their intentions, in the text itself, or in the understanding of that text at the time it was enacted. Indeed, one could forcefully argue that if the Constitution did not mean what its Framers thought it meant—or at least something closely approximating, at some level of generality, what they thought it meant—then the Constitution would not truly be a form of law in any conventional sense. This conception of the proper way to interpret the Constitution forms the theoretical basis of the approach to interpretation known as "originalism." Proponents of originalism argue that a provision of the Constitution must mean today what it meant, or perhaps was understood to mean, when it was ratified.

On the other hand, if we are concerned about the dead-hand problem and its seeming inconsistency with our democratic impulses today, then we might seek to interpret the Constitution in a way that reflects values that have enduring support, and not simply those that were important at the time of the Founding. According to this view, if the Constitution is binding principally because we agree to be bound by it, and we are eager to be bound by it only if we perceive it to be legitimate according to contemporary values, then we must update the Constitution in order to preserve it. This conception of the proper way to interpret the Constitution is often called "non-originalism," defined in contrast to what it is not. Most non-originalists rely to some degree on the original meaning of the Constitution, at least at a high level of generality, but also see room for constitutional meaning to evolve.

The debate over these competing views reflects the fundamental paradox of constitutionalism: if the Constitution is a form of law, then its meaning to the people who adopted it must be central to its meaning today. But do those people have a right to bind *us* to *their* choices? In the sections that follow, we consider the conventional arguments for and against originalism and non-originalism.

1. Originalism

Originalism is an approach to interpretation that accords dispositive weight to the original meaning of the Constitution. According to this approach, a provision of the Constitution must mean today what it meant when it was adopted. Under an originalist approach, for example, if the Constitution did not prohibit capital punishment in 1789— or in 1791, when the Bill of Rights was ratified, or in 1868, when the Fourteenth Amend-

Some originalists seek the original "intent" of the Framers, some seek the original "understanding" of the Constitution by the Framers or the ratifiers, and still others seek the original "objective meaning" of the Constitution. What are the differences among those three concepts? Should judges apply different inquiries depending upon whether they seek original intent, understanding, or objective meaning?

ment was ratified—then it does not prohibit it today. Conversely, under an originalist approach, if the Constitution in 1789—or, again, in 1791 or 1868—did not authorize Congress to rely on its authority under the Commerce Clause to regulate certain matters, then arguably Congress lacks that power today, as well. (We will consider in Chapter 3 whether changes in the nature of "commerce" inevitably should lead to the conclusion that Congress has greater power to regulate local matters today than it did at the time of the Framing.)

Proponents of originalism generally offer three principal arguments in support of their approach to interpreting the Constitution. First, they argue that originalism is the only approach to constitutional interpretation that properly recognizes the Constitution's status as law. Second, they argue that originalism is necessary to preserve democratic values. Third, they argue that originalism is uniquely promising for constraining the ability of judges to impose their own personal views under the guise of constitutional interpretation. We discuss these claims in turn.

First, originalists generally argue that because we have always treated written law as having a fixed meaning—this is true, for example, for statutes, whose meaning does not generally evolve over time—the Constitution, which is a form of law, must have a fixed meaning, as well. And, originalists argue, just as a statute's meaning is determined by reference to the understandings of the people who enacted it, the meaning of a provision of the Constitution must also be determined by reference to the people who were responsible for its enactment. Originalists do not necessarily deny the existence of the dead-hand problem, but they argue that if the Constitution is authoritative only to the extent that we agree with it today, then it is not really law at all but instead is simply a makeweight.

Second, proponents of originalism argue that only their approach is consistent with the proper judicial role in a democratic society. Any approach other than originalism, they argue, inevitably seeks constitutional meaning in evolving or current values. But a democratic system, they argue, does not need constitutional guarantees to ensure that its laws reflect current values. And it is fundamentally anti-democratic, they contend, to permit unelected judges to invalidate democratically enacted laws that are not inconsistent with the original meaning of the Constitution.

Third, originalists contend that because judicial review is by its very nature counter-majoritarian—a theme that we will explore in detail in Chapter 2—it is essential to ensure that judges employing it exercise, in Alexander Hamilton's words, "judgment" rather than "will," The Federalist No. 78—that is, that judges simply *interpret* the law rather than *make* the law. Because the original meaning of the Constitution is fixed, originalists argue, it can be objectively determined by a judge without reference to his own political preferences. In contrast, they argue, if the Constitution's meaning "evolves," but derives from something other than democratic enactments, then the judges seeking the Constitution's meaning will not be restrained in their ability to impose their own personal views under the guise of constitutional interpretation.

The basic approach of originalism, of course, is not a new approach to interpretation. But it has attracted renewed attention and support in the last few decades, in part as a response to the perceived non-originalism of the Supreme Court in the 1950s and 1960s, an era that saw a substantial judicial expansion of rights subject to constitutional protection.

Perspective and Analysis

Justice Antonin Scalia has arguably been the most well-known and influential originalist. Consider his defense of the approach:

> [O]riginalism seems to me more compatible with the nature and purpose of a Constitution in a democratic system. A democratic society does not, by and large, need constitutional guarantees to insure that its laws will reflect "current values." Elections take care of that quite well. The purpose of constitutional guarantees *** is precisely to prevent the law from reflecting certain changes in original values that the society adopting the Constitution thinks fundamentally undesirable.

He has also criticized the alternatives to originalism:

> [T]he central practical defect of nonoriginalism is fundamental and irreparable: the impossibility of achieving any consensus on what, precisely, is to replace original meaning, once that is abandoned. *** [In contrast, originalism] establishes a historical criterion that is conceptually quite separate from the preferences of the judge himself.

Antonin Scalia, *Originalism: The Lesser Evil*, 57 U. Cin. L. Rev. 849, 862-64 (1989).

---

2. Non-Originalism

In contrast, non-originalists generally believe that the Constitution's meaning today is not always the meaning that it had when it was ratified. Non-originalists accordingly look to a range of sources in interpreting the Constitution. This is not to say that all non-originalists believe that the original meaning is irrelevant to constitutional interpretation; to the contrary, virtually all theories of constitutional interpretation accord significant—and in some cases dispositive—weight to the original meaning. Non-originalists often conclude that the original meaning of a constitutional provision, expressed at a very high level of generality, provides guidance for ascertaining the relevant constitutional rule. Non-originalists, for example, might read the Equal Protection Clause of the Fourteenth Amendment to announce a general rule about equal treatment, which they might be willing to apply in a manner that the Framers of the Fourteenth Amendment did not contemplate, such as to discrimination on the basis of gender. But, for the reasons discussed below, non-originalists sometimes are willing to depart from the original meaning.

Non-originalists also often look to judicial precedent in seeking constitutional meaning. In this way, many non-originalists view constitutional interpretation as something akin to common-law decision-making, with constitutional principles evolving gradually over time. Non-originalists also often look to state practices to determine whether broad consensus has developed that a particular action or practice is acceptable or unacceptable.

Make the Connection

As we will see in Chapter 7, the Supreme Court has held that the Due Process Clause of the Fourteenth Amendment "incorporated" most of the provisions in the Bill of Rights, applying their limits to state, as well as federal, action.

For example, if public flogging is banned in all states but one—and has been illegal in all states but one for decades—then a non-originalist might conclude that public flogging today is a "cruel and unusual" punishment within the meaning of the Eighth Amendment, even though it likely was not thought to be cruel and unusual in 1791, when the Eighth Amendment was ratified, or in 1868, when the Fourteenth Amendment was ratified.

Non-originalists are willing to depart from the original meaning of the Constitution because of concerns about originalism itself. Non-originalists have generally disputed originalists' claims that originalism is likely to produce determinate constitutional meaning today. More fundamentally, non-originalists argue that departure from the original meaning often is necessary to ensure that the Constitution retains legitimacy, which is essential if the public is to continue to accept the Constitution's binding character. We discuss these claims in turn.

First, non-originalists contend that most difficult constitutional questions that arise today cannot be answered by simple reference to the original understanding. They observe that the historical record is silent on many important provisions of the Constitution; that when the Framers did discuss the meaning of a particular provision of the Constitution, they often disagreed about its meaning; and that, in any event, the Framers did not contemplate, let alone discuss, most of the difficult questions that arise today or how the Constitution would apply to those problems. Accordingly, non-originalists argue that resort to the original meaning is unlikely to produce determinate constitutional meaning today. Non-originalists also argue that this likely indeterminism undermines the claim that originalism is uniquely promising as a way to constrain judges from imposing their own views under the guise of constitutional interpretation; faced with an ambiguous or indeterminate historical record, non-originalists contend, judges have discretion to choose the evidence of original meaning that best reflects their own personal values.

Second, and more important, non-originalists argue that originalism fails to account for the dead-hand problem, and thus risks producing a Constitution that fails the test of legitimacy. Originalism, non-originalists note, by definition gives voice to the values of the framing generation, and thus risks producing results that the American public today might find problematic. An originalist approach to the Fourteenth Amendment, for example, arguably would have required the Court to conclude, contrary to the decision in *Brown v. Board of Education*, 347 U.S. 483 (1954), that racial segregation in public schools does not violate the Equal Protection Clause. Similarly, discrimination on the basis of gender was commonplace in 1868 when the Fourteenth Amendment was ratified; a faithfully originalist approach almost certainly would permit the states today to prohibit women from (among other things) serving as lawyers, as they did at the time that the Amendment was ratified. See *Bradwell v. Illinois*, 83 U.S. (16 Wall.) 130 (1873).

> **Food for Thought**
>
> There is a debate among scholars about whether <u>*Brown*</u> was correct as an originalist matter. Compare Robert H. Bork, The Tempting of America 76 (1990), and Michael W. McConnell, *Originalism and the Desegregation Decisions*, 81 Va. L. Rev. 947 (1995) (arguing that <u>*Brown*</u> was consistent with the original understanding of the Fourteenth Amendment), with Alexander Bickel, *The Original Understanding and the Segregation Decision*, 69 Harv. L. Rev. 1 (1955), and Michael Klarman, Brown, *Originalism, and Constitutional Theory*, 81 Va. L. Rev. 1881 (1995) (arguing that <u>*Brown*</u> was inconsistent with the original understanding of the Fourteenth Amendment). We will consider the decision in <u>*Brown*</u>, and discrimination on the basis of race and gender, in Chapter 11.

Non-originalists recognize that the Constitution (in Article V) makes explicit provision for the adoption of amendments, but they argue that the potential of the amendment process to incorporate modern values into the Constitution is illusory. In 1954, for example, when the Court decided <u>*Brown*</u>, Southern resistance would have prevented the ratification of an amendment prohibiting racial segregation. Similarly, as recently as the 1970s, a proposed amendment to prohibit discrimination on the basis of gender failed to achieve ratification in the required three-quarters of the States. These results, non-originalists contend, would substantially undermine respect for the Constitution, and thus the public's willingness to be bound by the Constitution.

Perspective and Analysis

Justice William Brennan was an influential critic of originalism and a proponent of what some call "Living Constitutionalism." Consider his view:

> A position that upholds constitutional claims only if they were within the specific contemplation of the Framers in effect establishes a presumption of resolving textual ambiguities against the claim of constitutional right. *** This is a choice no less political than any other; it expresses antipathy to claims of the minority to rights against the majority. ***

Justice Brennan did not reject the notion that the Constitution has enduring principles, defined by the Framers' choices. But he disagreed with a formulaic application of those principles:

> Current Justices read the Constitution in the only way that we can: as twentieth-century Americans. We look to the history of the time of the framing and to the intervening history of interpretation. But the ultimate question must be: What do the words of the text mean in our time? For the genius of the Constitution rests not in any static meaning it might have had in a world that is dead and gone, but in the adaptability of its great principles to cope with current problems and current needs.

William J. Brennan, Jr., *The Constitution of the United States: Contemporary Ratification*, 27 S. Tex. L. Rev. 433, 436 (1986).

All of this discussion leads to an important question: Which interpretive method does the Supreme Court use? As you will see, this question has no simple answer. As you read the Court's cases, you will find three categories of decisions.

In some cases, especially older ones, the Supreme Court has insisted emphatically that only the original meaning of the Constitution matters. The decision in *South Carolina v. United States*, 199 U.S. 437 (1905), made this point with unmistakable clarity. The Court said: "The Constitution is a written instrument. As such its meaning does not alter. That which it meant when adopted, it means now." *Id.* at 448.

In other cases, however, the Court has squarely rejected the idea that it must follow the original meaning of the Constitution. For example, in *Home Building & Loan Assn. v. Blaisdell*, 290 U.S. 398 (1934), which we will consider in Chapter 18, the Court allowed a state law to alter the obligation of a mortgage contract even though it recognized that this result likely conflicted with the original understanding of Contracts Clause in Article I, Section 10. The Court unapologetically rejected the idea that "the great clauses of the Constitution must be confined to the interpretation which the framers, with the conditions and outlook of their time, would have placed upon them." *Id.* at 443.

Most modern cases fall somewhere in between these two extremes. Usually, the Court considers evidence of the original meaning without making broad pronouncements about whether the original meaning must control. Sometimes the Court follows the original meaning, and sometimes it does not. Interestingly, even though the current Justices have very different views on constitutional interpretation, they all cite the Federalist Papers, the records of the Constitutional Convention, and the state ratifying debates from time to time because they all consider these sources to be influential. In many cases, the Court tries to follow the original meaning, but simply cannot agree on what it was. For example, as we will see in Chapter 4 in *U.S. Term Limits, Inc. v. Thornton,* 514 U.S. 779 (1995), both the majority and dissenting opinions claim to follow the original meaning.

In reading the cases in this book, consider not only the results that the Supreme Court reaches, but also what interpretive methodology the Court is using.

———————

This section has provided an overview of the competing approaches to constitutional interpretation. Although we directly address the arguments for originalism and non-originalism here, in many respects all of the material that follows in this book speaks, even if only indirectly, to the same question. Indeed, the judicial decisions in this book about what the Constitution means often are as much about the appropriate way to interpret the Constitution as they are about the meaning of the particular provisions at issue. As you read those materials, be sensitive to the relationship between arguments about the meaning of particular provisions of the Constitution and arguments about the appropriate way to interpret the Constitution more generally.

———————

D. An Illustrative Case

As we have discussed, constitutional interpretation often involves the need to ascribe concrete meaning to ambiguous text and the need to apply that text to concrete circumstances. What considerations are relevant in engaging in those inquiries?

In the case that follows, the Court considered the constitutionality under the Second Amendment of the District of Columbia's prohibition on the possession of handguns in the home. As you read the three opinions in the case—one for the Court and two in dissent—consider the roles that text, history, structure, and policy play in the interpretations that the Justices advanced.

———————

District of Columbia v. Heller

554 U.S. 570 (2008)

Justice SCALIA delivered the opinion of the Court.

The District of Columbia generally prohibits the possession of handguns. It is a crime to carry an unregistered firearm, and the registration of handguns is prohibited. See D.C.Code §§ 7-2501.01(12), 7-2502.01(a), 7-2502.02(a)(4) (2001). Wholly apart from that prohibition, no person may carry a handgun without a license, but the chief of police may issue licenses for 1-year periods. See §§ 22-4504(a), 22-4506. District of Columbia law also requires residents to keep their lawfully owned firearms, such as registered long guns, "unloaded and dissembled or bound by a trigger lock or similar device" unless they are located in a place of business or are being used for lawful recreational activities. See § 7-2507.02.

[Respondent Dick Heller, a D.C. special police officer authorized to carry a handgun while on duty at the Federal Judicial Center, wished to keep a handgun at home. He filed a lawsuit in District Court challenging these provisions under the Second Amendment. The District Court dismissed respondent's complaint, but the Court of Appeals directed the District Court to enter summary judgment for respondent.]

The Second Amendment provides: "A well regulated Militia, being necessary to the security of a free State, the right of the people to keep and bear Arms, shall not be infringed." *** The two sides in this case have set out very different interpretations of the Amendment. Petitioners and today's dissenting Justices believe that it protects only the right to possess and carry a firearm in connection with militia service. Respondent argues that it protects an individual right to possess a firearm unconnected with service in a militia, and to use that arm for traditionally lawful purposes, such as self-defense within the home.

The Second Amendment is naturally divided into two parts: its prefatory clause and its operative clause. *** Logic demands that there be a link between the stated purpose and the command. [That] requirement of logical connection may cause a prefatory clause to resolve an ambiguity in the operative clause ***. But apart from that clarifying function, a prefatory clause does not limit or expand the scope of the operative clause. Therefore, while we will begin our textual analysis with the operative clause, we will return to the prefatory clause to ensure that our reading of the operative clause is consistent with the announced purpose.

Operative Clause

"Right of the People." The first salient feature of the operative clause is that it codifies a "right of the people." The unamended Constitution and the Bill of Rights use the phrase "right of the people" two other times, in the First Amendment's Assembly-and-Petition Clause and in the Fourth Amendment's Search-and-Seizure Clause. The Ninth Amendment uses very similar terminology ***. All three of these instances unambiguously refer to individual rights, not "collective" rights, or rights that may be exercised only through participation in some corporate body. *** What is more, in all [other] provisions of the

Constitution that mention "the people," the term unambiguously refers to all members of the political community, not an unspecified subset. [This] contrasts markedly with the phrase "the militia" in the prefatory clause. As we will describe below, the "militia" in colonial America consisted of a subset of "the people"—those who were male, able bodied, and within a certain age range. Reading the Second Amendment as protecting only the right to "keep and bear Arms" in an organized militia therefore fits poorly with the operative clause's description of the holder of that right as "the people." We start therefore with a strong presumption that the Second Amendment right is exercised individually and belongs to all Americans.

   "Keep and bear Arms." We move now from the holder of the right—"the people"—to the substance of the right: "to keep and bear Arms." Before addressing the verbs "keep" and "bear," we interpret their object: "Arms." The 18th-century meaning is no different from the meaning today. The 1773 edition of Samuel Johnson's dictionary defined "arms" as "weapons of offence, or armour of defence." 1 Dictionary of the English Language 107 (4th ed.) (hereinafter Johnson). *** The term was applied, then as now, to weapons that were not specifically designed for military use and were not employed in a military capacity.

   We turn to the phrases "keep arms" and "bear arms." Johnson defined "keep" as, most relevantly, "[t]o retain; not to lose," and "[t]o have in custody." Johnson 1095. *** Thus, the most natural reading of "keep Arms" in the Second Amendment is to "have weapons."

   At the time of the founding, as now, to "bear" meant to "carry." When used with "arms," however, the term has a meaning that refers to carrying for a particular purpose—confrontation. *** Although the phrase implies that the carrying of the weapon is for the purpose of "offensive or defensive action," it in no way connotes participation in a structured military organization. From our review of founding-era sources, we conclude that this natural meaning was also the meaning that "bear arms" had in the 18th century. In numerous instances, "bear arms" was unambiguously used to refer to the carrying of weapons outside of an organized militia. The most prominent examples are those most relevant to the Second Amendment: Nine state constitutional provisions written in the 18th century or the first two decades of the 19th, which enshrined a right of citizens to "bear arms in defense of themselves and the state" or "bear arms in defense of himself and the state." It is clear from those formulations that "bear arms" did not refer only to carrying a weapon in an organized military unit.

> **Food for Thought**
>
> As the Court's discussion makes clear, some state constitutions explicitly extended the right to bear arms to self-defense. Does this fact support or undermine the Court's interpretation?

   Meaning of the Operative Clause. Putting all of these textual elements together, we find that they guarantee the individual right to possess and carry weapons in case of confrontation. This meaning is strongly confirmed by the historical background of the Second Amendment. *** Between the Restoration and the Glorious Revolution, the Stuart Kings Charles II and James II succeeded in using select militias loyal to them to suppress political dissidents, in part by disarming their opponents. These experiences caused Englishmen to be extremely wary of concentrated military forces run by the state and to be jealous of their arms. They accordingly obtained an assurance from William and Mary, in the Declaration of Right (which was codified as the English Bill of Rights), that Protestants would never be disarmed ***. This right has long been understood to be the predecessor to our Second Amendment.

By the time of the founding, the right to have arms had become fundamental for English subjects. Blackstone [cited] the arms provision of the Bill of Rights as one of the fundamental rights of Englishmen, [describing it as] "the natural right of resistance and self-preservation" ***. Thus, the right secured in 1689 as a result of the Stuarts' abuses was by the time of the founding understood to be an individual right protecting against both public and private violence. And, of course, what the Stuarts had tried to do to their political enemies, George III had tried to do to the colonists.

There seems to us no doubt, on the basis of both text and history, that the Second Amendment conferred an individual right to keep and bear arms. [We now determine] whether the prefatory clause of the Second Amendment comports with our interpretation of the operative clause. ***

Relationship between Prefatory Clause and Operative Clause

*** The debate with respect to the right to keep and bear arms, as with other guarantees in the Bill of Rights, was not over whether it was desirable (all agreed that it was) but over whether it needed to be codified in the Constitution. During the 1788 ratification debates, the fear that the federal government would disarm the people in order to impose rule through a standing army or select militia was pervasive in Antifederalist rhetoric. Federalists responded that because Congress was given no power to abridge the ancient right of individuals to keep and bear arms, such a force could never oppress the people. It was understood across the political spectrum that the right helped to secure the ideal of a citizen militia, which might be necessary to oppose an oppressive military force if the constitutional order broke down.

It is therefore entirely sensible that the Second Amendment's prefatory clause announces the purpose for which the right was codified: to prevent elimination of the militia. The prefatory clause does not suggest that preserving the militia was the only reason Americans valued the ancient right; most undoubtedly thought it even more important for self-defense and hunting. But the threat that the new Federal Government would destroy the citizens' militia by taking away their arms was the reason that right—unlike some other English rights—was codified in a written Constitution.

[P]etitioners' interpretation does not even achieve the narrower purpose that prompted codification of the right. If, as they believe, the Second Amendment right is no more than the right to keep and use weapons as a member of an organized militia, [then] it does not assure the existence of a "citizens' militia" as a safeguard against tyranny. For Congress retains plenary authority to organize the militia, which must include the authority to say who will belong to the organized force. *** Thus, if petitioners are correct, the Second Amendment protects citizens' right to use a gun in an organization from which Congress has plenary authority to exclude them. It guarantees a select militia of the sort the Stuart kings found useful, but not the people's militia that was the concern of the founding generation.

> **FYI**
>
> Article I, § 8, cl. 16 gives Congress the power "[t]o provide for organizing, arming, and disciplining, the Militia, and for governing such Part of them as may be employed in the Service of the United States, reserving to the States respectively, the Appointment of the Officers, and the Authority of training the Militia according to the discipline prescribed by Congress." Is it clear that this provision, especially when viewed in conjunction with cl. 15, authorizes Congress to determine the membership in the various state-controlled militias?

Our interpretation is confirmed by analogous arms-bearing rights in state constitutions that preceded and immediately followed adoption of the Second Amendment. Four States adopted analogues to the Federal Second Amendment in the period between independence and the ratification of the Bill of Rights. Two of them—Pennsylvania and Vermont—clearly adopted individual rights unconnected to militia service. Pennsylvania's Declaration of Rights of 1776 said: "That the people have a right to bear arms *for the defence of themselves,* and the state ***." In 1777, Vermont adopted the identical provision, except for inconsequential differences in punctuation and capitalization. *** North Carolina also codified a right to bear arms in 1776: "That the people have a right to bear arms, for the defence of the State ***." Declaration of Rights § XVII. This could plausibly be read to support only a right to bear arms in a militia—but that is a peculiar way to make the point in a constitution that elsewhere repeatedly mentions the militia explicitly. We [believe] that the most likely reading of [these] pre-Second Amendment state constitutional provisions is that they secured an individual right to bear arms for defensive purposes. [That] is strong evidence that that is how the founding generation conceived of the right.

Justice STEVENS places overwhelming reliance upon this Court's decision in *United States v. Miller,* 307 U.S. 174 (1939). [According to Justice STEVENS, <u>Miller</u> held that] the Second Amendment "protects the right to keep and bear arms for certain military purposes, but that it does not curtail the legislature's power to regulate the nonmilitary use and ownership of weapons." [But] *Miller* did not hold that and cannot possibly be read to have held that. The judgment in the case upheld against a Second Amendment challenge two men's federal convictions for transporting an unregistered short-barreled shotgun in interstate commerce, in violation of the National Firearms Act, 48 Stat. 1236. It is entirely clear that the Court's basis for saying that the Second Amendment did not apply was [that] the *type of weapon at issue* was not eligible for Second Amendment protection: "In the absence of any evidence tending to show that the possession or use of a [short-barreled shotgun] at this time has some reasonable relationship to the preservation or efficiency of a well regulated militia, we cannot say that the Second Amendment guarantees the right to keep and bear *such an instrument.*" 307 U.S. at 178 (emphasis added). "Certainly," the Court continued, "it is not within judicial notice that this weapon is any part of the ordinary military equipment or that its use could contribute to the common defense." *Ibid.* [H]ad the Court believed that the Second Amendment protects only those serving in the militia, it would have been odd to examine the character of the weapon rather than simply note that the two crooks were not militiamen. *** We therefore read *Miller* to say only that the Second Amendment does not protect those weapons not typically possessed by law-abiding citizens for lawful purposes, such as short-barreled shotguns.

Like most rights, the right secured by the Second Amendment is not unlimited. *** Although we do not undertake an exhaustive historical analysis today of the full scope of the Second Amendment, nothing in our opinion should be taken to cast doubt on longstanding prohibitions on the possession of firearms by felons and the mentally ill, or laws forbidding the carrying of firearms in sensitive places such as schools and government buildings, or laws imposing conditions and qualifications on the commercial sale of arms. *** We also recognize another important limitation on the right to keep and carry arms. *Miller* said, as we have explained, that the sorts of weapons protected were those "in common use at the time." 307 U.S. at 179. We think that limitation is fairly supported by the historical tradition of prohibiting the carrying of "dangerous and unusual weapons."

We turn finally to the law at issue here. [As we have demonstrated,] the inherent right of self-defense has been central to the Second Amendment right. The handgun ban amounts to a prohibition of an entire class of "arms" that is overwhelmingly chosen by American society for that lawful purpose. The prohibition extends, moreover, to the home, where the need for defense of self, family, and property is most acute. Under any of the standards of scrutiny that we have applied to enumerated constitutional rights, banning from the home "the most preferred firearm in the nation to 'keep' and use for protection of one's home and family," 478 F.3d, at 400, would fail constitutional muster. *** Whatever the reason, handguns are the most popular weapon chosen by Americans for self-defense in the home, and a complete prohibition of their use is invalid.

[T]he District's requirement (as applied to respondent's handgun) that firearms in the home be rendered and kept inoperable at all times [makes] it impossible for citizens to use them for the core lawful purpose of self-defense and is hence unconstitutional.

Before this Court petitioners have stated that "if the handgun ban is struck down and respondent registers a handgun, he could obtain a license, assuming he is not otherwise disqualified," by which they apparently mean if he is not a felon and is not insane. Respondent conceded at oral argument that he does not "have a problem [with] licensing" and that the District's law is permissible so long as it is "not enforced in an arbitrary and capricious manner." We therefore assume that petitioners' issuance of a license will satisfy respondent's prayer for relief and do not address the licensing requirement.

Justice BREYER [criticizes] us for declining to establish a level of scrutiny for evaluating Second Amendment restrictions. He proposes, explicitly at least, none of the traditionally expressed levels (strict scrutiny, intermediate scrutiny, rational basis), but rather a judge-empowering "interest-balancing inquiry" that "asks whether the statute burdens a protected interest in a way or to an extent that is out of proportion to the statute's salutary effects upon other important governmental interests." *** We know of no other enumerated constitutional right whose core protection has been subjected to a freestanding "interest-balancing" approach. The very enumeration of the right takes out of the hands of government—even the Third Branch of Government—the power to decide on a case-by-case basis whether the right is *really worth* insisting upon. *** Constitutional rights are enshrined with the scope they were understood to have when the people adopted them, whether or not future legislatures or (yes) even future judges think that scope too broad. [The Second Amendment] is the very *product* of an interest-balancing by the people—which Justice BREYER would now conduct for them anew. And whatever else it leaves to future evaluation, it surely elevates above all other interests the right of law-abiding, responsible citizens to use arms in defense of hearth and home.

We are aware of the problem of handgun violence in this country, and we take seriously the concerns raised by the many *amici* who believe that prohibition of handgun ownership is a solution. [But] the enshrinement of constitutional rights necessarily takes certain policy choices off the table. These include the absolute prohibition of handguns held and used for self-defense in the home. Undoubtedly some think that the Second Amendment is outmoded in a society where our standing army is the pride of our Nation, where well-trained police forces provide personal security, and where gun violence is a serious problem. That is perhaps debatable, but what is not debatable is that it is not the role of this Court to pronounce the Second Amendment extinct. [Affirmed.]

Justice STEVENS, with whom Justice SOUTER, Justice GINSBURG, and Justice BREYER join, dissenting.

The Second Amendment was adopted to protect the right of the people of each of the several States to maintain a well-regulated militia. It was a response to concerns raised during the ratification of the Constitution that the power of Congress to disarm the state militias and create a national standing army posed an intolerable threat to the sovereignty of the several States. Neither the text of the Amendment nor the arguments advanced by its proponents evidenced the slightest interest in limiting any legislature's authority to regulate private civilian uses of firearms. Specifically, there is no indication that the Framers of the Amendment intended to enshrine the common-law right of self-defense in the Constitution.

In 1934, Congress enacted the National Firearms Act, the first major federal firearms law. Upholding a conviction under that Act, this Court held that, "[i]n the absence of any evidence tending to show that possession or use of a 'shotgun having a barrel of less than eighteen inches in length' at this time has some reasonable relationship to the preservation or efficiency of a well regulated militia, we cannot say that the Second Amendment guarantees the right to keep and bear such an instrument." *Miller,* 307 U.S. at 178. The view of the Amendment we took in *Miller*—that it protects the right to keep and bear arms for certain military purposes, but that it does not curtail the Legislature's power to regulate the nonmilitary use and ownership of weapons—is both the most natural reading of the Amendment's text and the interpretation most faithful to the history of its adoption.

*** The preamble to the Second Amendment [is] comparable to provisions in several State Declarations of Rights that were adopted roughly contemporaneously with the Declaration of Independence.[5] Those state provisions highlight the importance members of the founding generation attached to the maintenance of state militias; they also underscore the profound fear shared by many in that era of the dangers posed by standing armies. While the need for state militias has not been a matter of significant public interest for almost two centuries, that fact should not obscure the contemporary concerns that animated the Framers.

The parallels between the Second Amendment and these state declarations, and the Second Amendment's omission of any statement of purpose related to the right to use firearms for hunting or personal self-defense, is especially striking in light of the fact that the Declarations of Rights of Pennsylvania and Vermont *did* expressly protect such civilian uses at the time. Article XIII of Pennsylvania's 1776 Declaration of Rights announced that "the people have a right to bear arms for the defence *of themselves* and the state"; § 43 of the Declaration assured that "the inhabitants of this state shall have the liberty to fowl and hunt in seasonable times on the lands they hold, and on all other lands therein not inclosed." And Article XV of the 1777 Vermont Declaration of Rights guaranteed "[t]hat the people have a right to bear arms for the defence *of themselves* and the State." The contrast between those two declarations and the Second Amendment reinforces the clear statement of purpose announced in the Amendment's preamble. It confirms that the Framers' single-minded focus in crafting the constitutional guarantee "to keep and bear arms" was on military uses of firearms, which they viewed in the context of service in state militias.

The preamble thus both sets forth the object of the Amendment and informs the meaning of the remainder of its text. *** The Court today tries to denigrate the importance of this clause of the Amendment by beginning its analysis with the Amendment's operative provision and returning to the preamble merely "to ensure that our reading of the operative clause is consistent with the announced purpose." That is not how this Court ordinarily reads such texts, and it is not how the preamble would have been viewed at the time the Amendment was adopted. *** Without identifying any language in the text that even mentions civilian uses of firearms, the Court proceeds to "find" its preferred reading in what is at best an ambiguous text, and then concludes that its reading is not foreclosed by the preamble. Perhaps the Court's approach to the text is acceptable advocacy, but it is surely an unusual approach for judges to follow.

[T]he words "the people" in the Second Amendment refer back to the object announced in the Amendment's preamble. They remind us that it is the collective action of individuals having a duty to serve in the militia that the text directly protects and, perhaps more importantly, that the ultimate purpose of the Amendment was to protect the States' share of the divided sovereignty created by the Constitution.

Although the Court's discussion of [the words "to keep and bear Arms"] treats them as two "phrases"—as if they read "to keep" and "to bear"—they describe a unitary right: to

---

[5] The Virginia Declaration of Rights ¶ 13 (1776), provided: "That a well-regulated militia, composed of the body of the people, trained to arms, is the proper, natural, and safe defence of a free State; that Standing Armies, in time of peace, should be avoided, as dangerous to liberty; and that, in all cases, the military should be under strict subordination to, and governed by, the civil power." [Maryland, Delaware, and New Hampshire had similar provisions.]

possess arms if needed for military purposes and to use them in conjunction with military activities. *** The term "bear arms" is a familiar idiom; when used unadorned by any additional words, its meaning is "to serve as a soldier, do military service, fight." 1 Oxford English Dictionary 634 (2d ed.1989). It is derived from the Latin *arma ferre,* which, translated literally, means "to bear [*ferre*] war equipment [*arma*]." *** Had the Framers wished to expand the meaning of the phrase "bear arms" to encompass civilian possession and use, they could have done so by the addition of phrases such as "for the defense of themselves," as was done in the Pennsylvania and Vermont Declarations of Rights. The *unmodified* use of "bear arms," by contrast, refers most naturally to a military purpose, as evidenced by its use in literally dozens of contemporary texts. *** When, as in this case, there is no [qualifier], the most natural meaning is the military one; and, in the absence of any qualifier, it is all the more appropriate to look to the preamble to confirm the natural meaning of the text.

The Amendment's use of the term "keep" in no way contradicts the military meaning conveyed by the phrase "bear arms" and the Amendment's preamble. To the contrary, a number of state militia laws in effect at the time of the Second Amendment's drafting used the term "keep" to describe the requirement that militia members store their arms at their homes, ready to be used for service when necessary. The Virginia military law, for example, ordered that "every one of the said officers, non-commissioned officers, and privates, shall constantly *keep* the aforesaid arms, accoutrements, and ammunition, ready to be produced whenever called for by his commanding officer." Act for Regulating and Disciplining the Militia, 1785 Va. Acts ch. 1, § 3, p. 2. "[K]eep and bear arms" thus perfectly describes the responsibilities of a framing-era militia member.

[T]he single right that [the clause describes] is both a duty and a right to have arms available and ready for military service, and to use them for military purposes when necessary. *** When each word in the text is given full effect, the Amendment is most naturally read to secure to the people a right to use and possess arms in conjunction with service in a well-regulated militia.

Two themes relevant to our current interpretive task ran through the debates on the original Constitution. "On the one hand, there was a widespread fear that a national standing Army posed an intolerable threat to individual liberty and to the sovereignty of the separate States." *Perpich v. Department of Defense,* 496 U.S. 334, 340 (1990). On the other hand, the Framers recognized the dangers inherent in relying on inadequately trained militia members "as the primary means of providing for the common defense," *Perpich,* 496 U.S. at 340. *** In order to respond to those twin concerns, a compromise was reached: Congress would be authorized to raise and support a national Army and Navy, and also to organize, arm, discipline, and provide for the calling forth of "the Militia." U.S. Const., Art. I, § 8, cls. 12-16. The President, at the same time, was empowered as the "Commander in Chief of the Army and Navy of the United States, and of the Militia of the several States, when called into the actual Service of the United States." Art. II, § 2. But, with respect to the militia, a significant reservation was made to the States: [the] States respectively would retain the right to appoint the officers and to train the militia in accordance with the discipline prescribed by Congress. Art. I, § 8, cl. 16.[20]

But the original Constitution's retention of the militia and its creation of divided authority over that body did not prove sufficient to allay fears about the dangers posed by a standing army [because] it did not prevent Congress from providing for the militia's *dis*armament. *** This sentiment was echoed at a number of state ratification conventions; indeed, it was one of the primary objections to the original Constitution voiced by its opponents.

[In response, upon ratifying the Constitution several states proposed amendments to the document.] The relevant proposals sent by the Virginia Ratifying Convention read as follows:

> "17th, That the people have a right to keep and bear arms; that a well regulated Militia composed of the body of the people trained to arms is the proper, natural and safe defence of a free State. That standing armies are dangerous to liberty, and therefore ought to be avoided, as far as the circumstances and protection of the Community will admit; and that in all cases the military should be under strict subordination to and be governed by the civil power."

> "19th. That any person religiously scrupulous of bearing arms ought to be exempted, upon payment of an equivalent to employ another to bear arms in his stead."

Take Note

Virginia's proposal—and Madison's original draft of the Second Amendment—included a provision to exempt conscientious objectors from service in the militias. What does this provision suggest about the contexts in which the Amendment protects the right to keep and bear arms?

North Carolina adopted Virginia's proposals and sent them to Congress as its own ***. New York produced a proposal with nearly identical language. Notably, each of these proposals used the phrase "keep and bear arms" [and] embedded the phrase within a group of principles that are distinctly military in meaning.

By contrast, New Hampshire's proposal [described] the protection involved in more clearly personal terms[:] "Congress shall never disarm any Citizen unless such as are or have been in Actual Rebellion."

[James] Madison, charged with the task of assembling the proposals for amendments sent by the ratifying States, was the principal draftsman of the Second Amendment. [His] decision to model the Second Amendment on the distinctly military Virginia proposal is therefore revealing, since it is clear that he considered and rejected formulations that would have unambiguously protected civilian uses of firearms. When [his draft proposal] was debated and modified, it is reasonable to assume that all participants in the drafting process

---

[20] The Court assumes—incorrectly, in my view—that even when a state militia was not called into service, Congress would have had the power to exclude individuals from enlistment in that state militia. That assumption is not supported by the text of the Militia Clauses of the original Constitution, which confer upon Congress the power to "organiz[e], ar[m], and disciplin[e], the Militia," Art. I, § 8, cl. 16, but not the power to say who will be members of a state militia. It is also flatly inconsistent with the Second Amendment. ***

were fully aware of the other formulations that would have protected civilian use and possession of weapons and that their choice to craft the Amendment as they did represented a rejection of those alternative formulations.

Until today, it has been understood that legislatures may regulate the civilian use and misuse of firearms so long as they do not interfere with the preservation of a well-regulated militia. The Court's announcement of a new constitutional right to own and use firearms for private purposes upsets that settled understanding ***.

Justice BREYER, with whom Justice STEVENS, Justice SOUTER, and Justice GINSBURG join, dissenting.

[T]he protection the [Second] Amendment provides is not absolute. The Amendment permits government to regulate the interests that it serves. Thus, irrespective of what those interests are—whether they do or do not include an independent interest in self-defense—the majority's view cannot be correct unless it can show that the District's regulation is unreasonable or inappropriate in Second Amendment terms. This the majority cannot do.

The majority is wrong when it says that the District's law is unconstitutional "[u]nder any of the standards of scrutiny that we have applied to enumerated constitutional rights." [It] certainly would not be unconstitutional under, for example, a "rational basis" standard, which requires a court to uphold regulation so long as it bears a "rational relationship" to a "legitimate governmental purpose." *Heller v. Doe,* 509 U.S. 312, 320 (1993). The law at issue here, which in part seeks to prevent gun-related accidents, at least bears a "rational relationship" to that "legitimate" life-saving objective.

Respondent proposes that the Court adopt a "strict scrutiny" test, which would require reviewing with care each gun law to determine whether it is "narrowly tailored to achieve a compelling governmental interest." *Abrams v. Johnson,* 521 U.S. 74, 82 (1997). But the majority implicitly, and appropriately, rejects that suggestion by broadly approving a set of laws [whose] constitutionality under a strict scrutiny standard would be far from clear. Indeed, [almost] every gun-control regulation will seek to advance (as the one here does) a "primary concern of every government—a concern for the safety and indeed the lives of its citizens." *United States v. Salerno,* 481 U.S. 739, 755 (1987). *** Thus, any attempt *in theory* to apply strict scrutiny to gun regulations will *in practice* turn into an interest-balancing inquiry, with the interests protected by the Second Amendment on one side and the governmental public-safety concerns on the other, the only question being whether the regulation at issue impermissibly burdens the former in the course of advancing the latter.

I would simply adopt such an interest-balancing inquiry explicitly. *** "[W]here a law significantly implicates competing constitutionally protected interests in complex ways," the Court generally asks whether the statute burdens a protected interest in a way or to an extent that is out of proportion to the statute's salutary effects upon other important governmental interests. See *Nixon v. Shrink Missouri Government PAC,* 528 U.S. 377, 402 (2000) (BREYER, J., concurring). Any answer would take account both of the statute's effects upon the competing interests and the existence of any clearly superior less restrictive alternative.

The only dispute regarding [the trigger-lock] provision appears to be whether the Constitution requires an exception that would allow someone to render a firearm operational when necessary for self-defense ***. The District concedes that such an exception exists. *** And because I see nothing in the District law that would *preclude* the existence of a background common-law self-defense exception, I would avoid the constitutional question by interpreting the statute to include it. See *Ashwander v. TVA*, 297 U.S. 288, 348 (1936) (Brandeis, J., concurring).

No one doubts the constitutional importance of [the] basic objective [of the District's ban on handgun possession], saving lives. But there is considerable debate about whether the [provision] helps to achieve that objective. *** Petitioners, and their *amici*, have presented us with [statistics about handgun violence.] *** From 1993 to 1997, there were 180,533 firearm-related deaths in the United States, an average of over 36,000 per year. *** In over one in every eight firearm-related deaths in 1997, the victim was someone under the age of 20. *** From 1993 to 1997, 81% of firearm-homicide victims were killed by handgun. *** Handguns also appear to be a very popular weapon among criminals. *** Statistics further suggest that urban areas, such as the District, have different experiences with gun-related death, injury, and crime, than do less densely populated rural areas. A disproportionate amount of violent and property crimes occur in urban areas, and urban criminals are more likely than other offenders to use a firearm during the commission of a violent crime.

Respondent and his many *amici* [disagree] strongly with the District's *predictive judgment* that a ban on handguns will help solve the crime and accident problems that those figures disclose. *** First, they point out that, since the ban took effect [in 1976], violent crime in the District has increased, not decreased. *** Second, respondent's *amici* point to a statistical analysis that [concludes] that strict gun laws are correlated with *more* murders, not fewer. *** Third, they point to evidence indicating that firearm ownership does have a beneficial self-defense effect. *** Fourth, respondent's *amici* argue that laws criminalizing gun possession are self-defeating, as evidence suggests that they will have the effect only of restricting law-abiding citizens, but not criminals, from acquiring guns.

[T]he District and its *amici* [respond] with studies of their own. *** The upshot is a set of studies and counterstudies that, at most, could leave a judge uncertain about the proper policy conclusion. [But] legislators, not judges, have primary responsibility for drawing policy conclusions from empirical fact. [D]eference to legislative judgment seems particularly appropriate here, where the judgment has been made by a local legislature, with particular knowledge of local problems and insight into appropriate local solutions. *** For these reasons, I conclude that the District's statute properly seeks to further the sort of life-preserving and public-safety interests that the Court has called "compelling."

The District's statute burdens the Amendment's first and primary objective hardly at all. [T]here is general agreement among the Members of the Court that the principal (if not the only) purpose of the Second Amendment is found in the Amendment's text: the preservation of a "well regulated Militia." *** To begin with, the present case has nothing to do with *actual* military service. [And] the District's law does not seriously affect military training interests. The law permits residents to engage in activities that will increase their familiarity with firearms. They may register (and thus possess in their homes) weapons other than handguns, such as rifles and shotguns. *** And while the District law prevents citizens from training with handguns *within the District,* [the] adjacent States do permit the use of handguns for target practice, and those States are only a brief subway ride away. [G]iven the costs already associated with gun ownership and firearms training, I cannot say that a subway ticket and a short subway ride (and storage costs) create more than a minimal burden.

The District's law does prevent a resident from keeping a loaded handgun in his home. And it consequently makes it more difficult for the householder to use the handgun for self-defense in the home against intruders, such as burglars. [But] there is no clearly superior, less restrictive alternative to the District's handgun ban [because] the ban's very objective is to reduce significantly the number of handguns in the District ***. [A]ny measure less restrictive in respect to the use of handguns for self-defense will, to that same extent, prove less effective in preventing the use of handguns for illicit purposes. If a resident has a handgun in the home that he can use for self-defense, then he has a handgun in the home that he can use to commit suicide or engage in acts of domestic violence. *** [T]he District law is tailored to the life-threatening problems it attempts to address. The law concerns one class of weapons, handguns, leaving residents free to possess shotguns and rifles, along with ammunition. The area that falls within its scope is totally urban. ***

The majority derides my approach as "judge-empowering." I take this criticism seriously, but I do not think it accurate. *** Application of such an approach, of course, requires judgment, but the very nature of the approach—requiring careful identification of the relevant interests and evaluating the law's effect upon them—limits the judge's choices; and the method's necessary transparency lays bare the judge's reasoning for all to see and to criticize.

The majority's methodology is, in my view, substantially less transparent than mine. *** "Putting all of [the Second Amendment's] textual elements together," the majority says, "we find that they guarantee the individual right to possess and carry weapons in case of confrontation." Then, three pages later, it says that "we do not read the Second Amendment to permit citizens to carry arms for *any sort* of confrontation." Yet, with one critical exception, it does not explain which confrontations count. It simply leaves that question unanswered.

Nor is it at all clear to me how the majority decides *which* loaded "arms" a homeowner may keep. The majority says that that Amendment protects those weapons "typically possessed by law-abiding citizens for lawful purposes." This definition conveniently excludes machineguns, but permits handguns, which the majority describes as "the most popular weapon chosen by Americans for self-defense in the home." But what sense does this approach make? According to the majority's reasoning, if Congress and the States lift restrictions on the possession and use of machineguns, and people buy machineguns to protect their homes, the Court will have to reverse course and find that the Second Amendment *does,* in fact, protect the individual self-defense-related right to possess a machinegun. On the majority's reasoning, if tomorrow someone invents a particularly useful, highly dangerous self-defense weapon, Congress and the States had better ban it immediately, for once it becomes popular Congress will no longer possess the constitutional authority to do so. *** There is no basis for believing that the Framers intended such circular reasoning.

I am similarly puzzled by the majority's list [of] provisions that in its view would survive Second Amendment scrutiny. *** Why these? Is it that similar restrictions existed in the late 18th century? The majority fails to cite any colonial analogues. ***

The argument about method, however, is by far the less important argument surrounding today's decision. Far more important are the unfortunate consequences that today's decision is likely to spawn. Not least of these [is] the fact that the decision threatens to throw into doubt the constitutionality of gun laws throughout the United States. I can find no sound legal basis for launching the courts on so formidable and potentially dangerous a mission. In my view, there simply is no untouchable constitutional right guaranteed by the Second Amendment to keep loaded handguns in the house in crime-ridden urban areas.

Points for Discussion

a. The Judicial Role and the Counter-Majoritarian Difficulty

In holding that the challenged regulations were unconstitutional, the Court noted that "the enshrinement of constitutional rights necessarily takes certain policy choices off the table." Notice that in making this statement, the Court is also asserting its authority both to determine the meaning of the Constitution and to invalidate democratically enacted laws. Is it problematic to permit the Court to act in such a counter-majoritarian, and arguably anti-democratic, fashion? Or is it essential that the Court do so? This question will be the subtext of all the material that follows, but it will be the particular focus of Chapter 2.

b. Structural and Institutional Arrangements or Individual Rights?

Justice Scalia concluded that the Second Amendment protects an individual right to keep and bear arms for purposes unrelated to participation in a state militia. Justice Stevens, by contrast, would have held that the Amendment is principally a structural protection to ensure that Congress cannot disarm the state militias. Which view do you find more convincing?

Notice that Justice Scalia did not deny the structural aims of the Second Amendment, and that Justice Stevens did deny that its structural aims advance the interest in liberty. The first several Parts of this book will focus on the principal structural and institutional arrangements that the Constitution creates, federalism and separation of powers. As we will see in detail, the Framers clearly viewed these arrangements as essential to preserving individual liberty. The remainder of the book will focus on the Constitution's explicit and direct protections for individual rights. Does it make sense to treat structural provisions and rights provisions as separate and discrete features of the constitutional scheme?

c. Interpretive Methodology: Originalism v. Non-Originalism

In interpreting the Second Amendment, Justice Scalia sought to determine its meaning at the time of the Framing. He relied on contemporaneous sources, such as eighteenth-century dictionaries and state constitutional provisions. Justice Breyer focused on the competing state and individual interests implicated by the challenged regulation. Was his approach non-originalist? Or did he simply seek to apply the original meaning of the Second Amendment to modern circumstances? Which approach did you find more sensible or convincing?

d. Interpretive Methodology: Originalism v. Originalism

Like Justice Scalia, Justice Stevens took an originalist approach to the Second Amendment, but he reached a very different conclusion about the Amendment's meaning. To the extent that the two Justices relied on similar materials, whose arguments did you find more convincing? What does the fact that they relied in part on *competing* sources say about the viability of originalism as an approach to interpreting the Constitution?

Did their inquiries have the same objective? Notice that Justice Scalia focused principally on what the language of the Second Amendment likely would have *meant* at the time of its ratification. Justice Stevens spent considerable time addressing the Amendment's drafting history. Does that mean that Justice Stevens was attempting to discern Madison's—and the other Framers'—*intent* in ratifying the Amendment? Is there a difference between the original "objective meaning" and the original "intent"? Is there a difference in the evidence that one might use to establish meaning and intent?

Notice also that Justice Scalia read the individual phrases in the Second Amendment atomistically, asking what each phrase means before assembling those individual meanings into one, broader meaning. Justice Stevens, by contrast, read the Amendment more holistically, with a particular emphasis on what the preamble suggests about the meaning of what Justice Scalia referred to as the "operative" clause. Given that many of the Constitution's most important provisions are written at a high level of generality and often are ambiguous in their application, what is the role of text in constitutional interpretation? Whose approach in <u>Heller</u> to the text did you find most convincing?

e. Level of Scrutiny

As the competing opinions suggested, the Court often assesses the constitutionality of government action by evaluating the governmental interests advanced by the action and the burden that the action imposes on the constitutional right at issue. For example, the Court has never interpreted the Equal Protection Clause of the Fourteenth Amendment absolutely to prohibit the government from treating different classes of citizens differently. Some classifications—such as a law providing that only persons over sixteen years of age are eligible to obtain driver's licenses—do not seem problematic, and accordingly are subjected only to "rational basis review," under which they are upheld as long as the classification is reasonably related to some legitimate governmental interest. Other classifications—such as laws that deny government benefits on the basis of race—are deeply suspect, and

Make the Connection

We discuss levels of scrutiny in Chapter 10, and in Chapters 8, 11, 12, and 14 we consider their application in detail.

accordingly are subjected to "strict scrutiny," under which they can be upheld only if they are narrowly tailored to achieve a compelling governmental interest. Still other classifications—such as those that distinguish on the basis of gender—are subjected to "intermediate scrutiny," which falls somewhere between rational basis review and strict scrutiny. The various levels of scrutiny generally reflect a judgment that few constitutional prohibitions are absolute, and that some government actions that burden protected rights nevertheless are defensible.

What level of scrutiny did the majority apply to the challenged regulations? Did the majority consider the government's interest in the challenged regulations? Or did the majority simply suggest that regulations that would have been prohibited in 1791 are prohibited today? Does the majority's suggestion that many regulations of the right to bear arms would be constitutional shed any light on this question? What level of scrutiny did Justice Stevens apply?

Justice Breyer explicitly proposed a test under which the challenged regulation's constitutionality turns on whether the statute "burdens a protected interest in a way or to an extent that is out of proportion to the statute's salutary effects upon other important governmental interests." Is this approach preferable to the majority's apparent approach of recognizing categories of absolutely forbidden regulations and of clearly permissible regulations?

f. Role of Precedent

Before *Heller*, the Court had decided very few cases that even circumspectly interpreted the Second Amendment. Perhaps the most important was *United States v. Miller,* 307 U.S. 174 (1939), a brief opinion whose reasoning, as the competing approaches in *Heller* show, was far from clear. What is the role of precedent in interpreting the Constitution? Suppose that the Court in *Miller* had clearly held that the Second Amendment protects the right to keep and bear arms only in conjunction with participation in a state militia. Would the Court in *Heller* have been bound by that holding if it concluded that the Court in *Miller* had failed properly to discern the original meaning of the Amendment? When is it appropriate for the Court to overrule prior decisions that interpreted the Constitution? In answering this question, consider what remedies exist when the Court "errs" in interpreting the Constitution.

g. The Constitution and Ambiguity

The issue in *Heller* was both of great importance and seemingly fundamental. Why do you think it took the Court over 200 years squarely to resolve that issue? In fact, as we will see throughout this book, a surprising number of important constitutional questions have never been addressed by the Court. As you read the materials that follow, consider why, and whether constitutional ambiguity is a good or bad thing.

h. Role of the Dissenting Opinions

Why did Justices Breyer and Stevens write such extensive dissenting opinions? Dissenting opinions do not carry any precedential value, as they represent the views of a minority of Justices. Are dissenting opinions simply an expression of disagreement for disagreement's sake? Are they templates for criticism of the Court's decision? If so, to what end? Are they in effect intended as the groundwork for a future change of course on the Court? In this book, we will regularly see dissenting opinions. If nothing else, does the Court's frequent inability to achieve unanimity suggest anything about the nature of constitutional interpretation?

————

POINT-COUNTERPOINT

Does *Heller* represent originalism's triumph or its failure?

POINT: GREGORY E. MAGGS

"Originalism" is a doctrine saying that judges should interpret the Constitution according to its original meaning. Proponents of originalism disagree on some points, such as whether judges should focus on the original intent of the Framers, the original understanding of the ratifiers, or the original objective meaning of the Constitution's text. But they all agree that none of these meanings change over time and that judges should not allow current policy considerations to affect their interpretation of the Constitution.

One common objection to originalism is that it does not produce certain results. The argument supporting this objection is that the text of the Constitution and the relevant historical materials are often too sparse or inconclusive to produce definitive answers to current constitutional issues. This deficiency may prevent judges from determining answers to important constitutional questions. Worse, it may allow judges to decide cases according to their own political preferences and then cover up what they are doing with make-weight arguments resting on vague historical documents.

At first glance, the Supreme Court's decision in *District of Columbia v. Heller*, 128 S. Ct. 2783 (2008), might appear to support this objection to originalism. Justice Scalia's opinion for the Court and Justice Stevens's dissenting opinion both claim to use originalist methodology, but they reach different conclusions. This result may suggest to some that originalism cannot answer the question of what the Second Amendment means. In addition, the Court's conservatives concluded that the gun control law at issue was unconstitutional, while the Court's liberals concluded that it was not. Because conservative politicians tend to oppose gun control, and liberal politicians tend to favor it, this division of the Justices might suggest that politics determined the Justices' positions.

But further reflection should reveal that *Heller* does not represent a failure of originalism. Any method of constitutional interpretation may produce differing conclusions. But originalism appears to be generally more determinate than other interpretative methods. Most of the cases in this book contain both majority and dissenting opinions, yet in very few of these cases did both sides attempt to use originalist methodology. *Heller* is an example, as is *U.S. Term Limits v. Thornton*, 514 U.S. 779 (1995), but not many others come to mind. Has any other method of constitutional interpretation produced comparable certainty?

As for policy preferences, a closer look casts doubt on suspicions that either the majority or the dissent in *Heller* was just voting for the outcome that it favored as a matter of policy. The District of Columbia statute was among the most extreme gun control laws in the nation. Even without knowing what the individual Justices actually think about gun control, it is difficult to believe that all of the members of the dissent, who generally favor personal rights, would want laws that effectively ban all handgun ownership. The majority meanwhile went out of its way to make clear, in dicta, that many kinds of gun regulations are still constitutional. Again, it is hard to imagine that all of the Justices in the majority would favor every possible regulation. Instead, _Heller_ appears to represent a good faith effort to determine what the Second Amendment originally meant, and is thus a triumph of originalism.

————————

COUNTERPOINT: PETER J. SMITH

Originalism's proponents contend that it is the only legitimate approach to constitutional interpretation because (they say) it is the only approach that accords to the Constitution an objectively identifiable fixed meaning and, in so doing, prevents the Justices from imposing their personal policy preferences under the guise of constitutional interpretation. Yet the dueling opinions in _Heller_ demonstrate why originalism fails to live up to its promise.

The 27 words of the Second Amendment provoked over 100 pages of interpretive analysis, and led two incredibly intelligent, historically well-versed, and widely respected Justices to diametrically different interpretations. And this should not be surprising. Most constitutional provisions are written at a very high level of generality—such as "Equal Protection" or "Due Process"—that give few hints about their "original" meaning as applied to concrete circumstances. And even those—such as the Second Amendment—that seem to speak at a higher level of specificity often are susceptible to multiple (and irreconcilable) interpretations. (The language of the Amendment, with its prefatory and operative clauses, is particularly obscure.) Add to these textual ambiguities the historical ambiguities that originalism invites—Would a "reasonable person" in 1791 have understood the first half of the Second Amendment to qualify the second half? Even assuming we can find enough evidence of such understanding, what if reasonable people in 1791 (like reasonable people today) disagreed about the meaning of the Amendment?—and originalism rarely produces meaning any more determinate than any other approach to constitutional interpretation.

If originalism is unlikely (at least in difficult cases, which, after all, are the only ones that end up seeing the light of day in a courtroom) to produce determinate meaning, then originalists' claims about how it constrains judges begin to fall apart. A judge seeking the original meaning of the Second Amendment can focus either on early militia provisions in state Declarations of Rights (as did Justice Stevens) or instead on the even-earlier English Bill of Rights or the writings of Blackstone (as did Justice Scalia); on contemporaneous dictionary definitions (as did Justice Scalia) or instead on contemporaneous state militia laws that used similar words (as did Justice Stevens). A judge can read early state constitutional provisions referring explicitly to the right to bear arms for self-defense either to confirm (as did Justice Scalia) or to refute (as did Justice Stevens) the view that the Second Amendment similarly protects such a right. And although there is no obvious reason to doubt the sincerity with which the Justices approached the question, one cannot ignore that the Justices widely viewed as the most conservative sided with the view preferred by political conservatives and that the more liberal Justices sided with the view preferred by political liberals. Originalism, it seems, is not nearly as constraining as its proponents claim.

Legal scholars have long debated the original meaning of the Second Amendment. But historians recognize that any such question is not susceptible to one authoritative answer; the Constitution, after all, was ratified by collective decision-making (in each state, no less), which reflected a dizzying array of (often dueling) intentions, expectations, hopes, and fears. One can debate whether the majority or the dissent had the better of the arguments. But it is time that we stopped pretending that this particular approach to constitutional interpretation is any better than others at establishing rules for judges to do what they must: to exercise judgment.

PART II: THE FEDERAL COURTS

Article III of the Constitution delineates the limits of the "judicial Power" and vests that power in the Supreme Court and "in such inferior Courts as the Congress may from time to time ordain and establish." It further provides that those courts will be staffed by judges who "hold their Offices during good Behaviour" and whose compensation "shall not be diminished during their Continuance in Office." In other words, federal judges enjoy life tenure and protection from certain forms of political retribution for their decisions. Indeed, the only method specified for removal of a federal judge is conviction after impeachment, which requires a super-majority vote of the Senate. See U.S. Const., art. II, § 4; art. I, § 3, cl. 6.

U.S. Constitution, <u>Article III, Section 1</u>

The judicial Power of the United States, shall be vested in one supreme Court, and in such inferior Courts as the Congress may from time to time ordain and establish. The Judges, both of the supreme and inferior Courts, shall hold their Offices during good Behaviour, and shall, at stated Times, receive for their Services, a Compensation, which shall not be diminished during their Continuance in Office.

FYI

Brutus is thought to be the pseudonym for Judge Robert Yates. Yates had been one of the delegates to the Constitutional Convention from New York, but he left the Convention before its conclusion because he believed (with some justification) that the delegates were exceeding their authority by proposing a new constitution instead of merely amending the Articles of Confederation. After the Convention, he devoted efforts to opposing ratification. Writing as Brutus, he sparred with Alexander Hamilton, his former colleague at the Convention, who argued for ratification.

Judicial independence was thought necessary to check overreaching by the political branches; after all, judges who are immune from majoritarian pressures perhaps can be expected to protect individual rights against majoritarian incursion. But Anti-Federalist opponents of the Constitution attacked the proposed allocation of judicial power to an independent judiciary as constituting a threat to the authority of the states and to democracy itself. "Brutus," an influential critic, charged that the "real effect" of the federal system of government would "be brought home to the feelings of the people, through the medium of the judicial power." Because federal judges would be "totally independent, both of the people and the legislature," judicial overreaching could not be "corrected by any power above them"—a situation that, he argued, was "altogether unprecedented in a free country."

Essays of Brutus No. 11, New York Journal (Jan. 31, 1788).

Alexander Hamilton responded to these criticisms by noting the important limits on the power of the judiciary. The federal judiciary, he argued, "from the nature of its functions, will always be the least dangerous to the political rights of the Constitution; because it will be least in a capacity to annoy or injure them." Unlike the Executive, who "holds the sword of the community," and Congress, which "commands the purse" and "prescribes the rules by which the duties and rights of every citizen are to be regulated," the judiciary "has no influence over either the sword or the purse; no direction either of the strength or of the wealth of the society; and can take no active resolution whatever. It may truly be said to have neither FORCE nor WILL, but merely judgment; and must ultimately depend upon the aid of the executive arm even for the efficacy of its judgments." The Federalist No. 78.

These competing positions continue to have resonance today. As we will see, judicial power often is an important antidote to overreaching by the political branches, particularly to actions that burden the rights of minorities. And it is important to note that the term "minorities" includes not just racial minorities, holders of unpopular views, criminal defendants, and adherents to non-mainstream religions, but also members of other groups that are not always protected by majoritarian politics, such as farmers, gun owners, and property owners. But when the courts exercise their power to invalidate decisions that are the product of democratic action, they arguably act anti-democratically. This "counter-majoritarian difficulty" has long plagued the exercise of judicial power in the United States. See Alexander Bickel, The Least Dangerous Branch (2d Ed. 1986). As we progress through the materials in this Part, these competing elements of judicial power will never be far from the surface.

————————

CHAPTER 2

Judicial Power

The most important—and controversial—power that the federal courts exercise is the power of judicial review. We take up that topic in Section A. We then turn in section B to obstacles to the exercise of this power. These obstacles include the political question doctrine, the requirement of a case or controversy before a federal court can exercise jurisdiction, the requirement that litigants have "standing" to present issues in court, and the power of Congress to control certain aspects of federal court jursidction.

A. Judicial Review

In November 1800, Thomas Jefferson received more votes in the presidential election than John Adams, the incumbent. Because no candidate received a majority of the electoral votes, however, the power to decide the election passed to the House of Representatives. In January 1801, President Adams nominated John Marshall, the Secretary of State, to serve as Chief Justice of the Supreme Court. He was confirmed by Congress and took the oath of office on February 4, 1801. He continued to serve simultaneously as Secretary of State. On February 17, the House of Representatives elected Thomas Jefferson, a Republican, as President. He would not be sworn in as President, however, until March 4, and in late February the Federalist Congress created many new judgeships in an attempt to maintain control of the federal judiciary.

Pursuant to an Act passed on February 27, President Adams on March 2 nominated 42 judges—including William Marbury, who was nominated to be a Justice of the Peace in the District of Columbia. The Senate confirmed

FYI

The election of 1800 revealed a defect in the Constitution's mechanism for selecting a President. Article II, § 1, cl. 3 provided that each elector would vote for two persons, and (if one candidate had the majority of electoral votes) the winner would become President and the candidate with the second-most electoral votes would become Vice President. Although Jefferson's Republican party had planned to have one elector withhold a vote for Aaron Burr (the candidate they hoped would become Vice President) in order to ensure that Jefferson would have the most votes, Jefferson and Burr ended up tied, and neither had a majority. The lame-duck, Federalist-controlled Congress came close to awarding the Presidency to Adams, but they eventually relented. The Twelfth Amendment, ratified in 1804, addressed the problem.

them on March 3, Adams's last day in office. Marshall, in his capacity as Secretary of State, signed and sealed the commissions of the judges but was unable to effect delivery of all of them by the end of the day. (John Marshall's brother James Marshall personally set out from the State Department on March 3 to deliver commissions to judges in the District of Columbia, but he could not cover the distance in time and returned the undelivered commissions to the State Department. See Jean E. Smith, John Marshall: Definer of a Nation 317-18 (1996).) On March 4, Marshall, as Chief Justice, administered the oath of office to President Jefferson, who did not deliver the remaining commissions and treated them as legally void. Jefferson subsequently appointed James Madison as Secretary of State.

Republicans responded swiftly to the Federalist attempts to entrench themselves in the judiciary. Republicans in Congress repealed a statute that the lame-duck Federalists had passed creating more federal judgeships that had not yet been filled; limited the Supreme Court, which was composed entirely of Federalist appointees, to one sitting per year; and impeached and removed John Pickering, a Federalist district judge in New Hampshire. They also hinted that the Justices on the Supreme Court would be next. (Indeed, in 1805, not long after the decision in *Marbury*, the House impeached Federalist Supreme Court Justice Samuel Chase, although the Senate did not convict him.) This was the context in which the Supreme Court decided *Marbury v. Madison*.

Marbury v. Madison

5 U.S. (1 Cranch) 137 (1803)

MARSHALL, C.J., announced the opinion of the Court:

At the last term on the affidavits then read and filed with the clerk, a rule was granted in this case, requiring the Secretary of State to show cause why a mandamus should not issue, directing him to deliver to William Marbury his commission as a justice of the peace for the county of Washington, in the District of Columbia. No cause has been shown, and the present motion is for a mandamus.

> **Definition**
>
> Mandamus is Latin for "We command." A writ of mandamus is an order to an executive, administrative, or judicial officer commanding the performance of a particular act required by law.

> **FYI**
>
> Chief Justice Marshall is speaking somewhat euphemistically here in saying that no cause was shown. Neither Secretary of State Madison nor anyone else from the Jefferson Administration had appeared to respond to the Court's order to show cause.

In the order in which the court has viewed this subject, the following questions have been considered and decided. 1st. Has the applicant a right to the commission he demands? 2d. If he has a right, and that right has been violated, do the laws of his country afford him a remedy? 3d. If they do afford him a remedy, is it a *man-*

damus issuing from this court?

The first object of inquiry is, 1st. Has the applicant a right to the commission he demands? His right originates in an Act of Congress passed in February 1801, concerning the District of Columbia. *** In order to determine whether he is entitled to this commission, it becomes necessary to enquire whether he has been appointed to the office. For if he has been appointed, the law continues him in office for five years, and he is entitled to the possession of those evidences of office, which, being completed, became his property.

[The constitutional power of appointment] has been exercised when the last act, required from the person possessing the power, has been performed. This last act is the signature [by the President] of the commission. *** The commission being signed, the subsequent duty of the Secretary of State is prescribed by law, and not to be guided by the will of the President. He is to affix the seal of the United States to the commission, and is to record it. *** The transmission of the commission, is a practice directed by convenience, but not by law. It cannot therefore be necessary to constitute the appointment which must precede it, and which is the mere act of the President.

It is therefore decidedly the opinion of the court, that when a commission has been signed by the President, the appointment is made; and that the commission is complete, when the seal of the United States has been affixed to it by the Secretary of State. *** Mr. Marbury, then, since his commission was signed by the President, and sealed by the Secretary of State, was appointed; and as the law creating the office, gave the officer a right to hold for five years, independent of the executive, the appointment was not revocable; but vested in the officer legal rights, which are protected by the laws of this country. To withhold his commission, therefore, is an act deemed by the court not warranted by law, but violative of a vested legal right.

This brings us to the second inquiry; which is: If he has a right, and that right has been violated, do the laws of this country afford him a remedy? The very essence of civil liberty certainly consists in the right of every individual to claim the protection of the laws, whenever he receives an injury. One of the first duties of government is to afford that protection. *** The government of the United States has been emphatically termed a government of laws, and not of men. It will certainly cease to deserve this high appellation, if the laws furnish no remedy for the violation of a vested legal right. If this obloquy is to be cast on the jurisprudence of our country, it must arise from the peculiar character of the case.

It behooves us then to enquire whether there be in its composition any ingredient which shall exempt it from legal investigation, or exclude the injured party from legal redress. Is it in the nature of the transaction? Is the act of delivering or withholding a commission to be considered as a mere political act, belonging to the executive department alone, for the performance of which, entire confidence is placed by our constitution in the supreme executive; and for any misconduct respecting which, the injured individual has no remedy. That there may be such cases is not to be questioned; but that every act of duty, to be performed in any of the great departments of government, constitutes such a case, is not to be admitted.

It follows then that the question, whether the legality of an act of the head of a department be examinable in a court of justice or not, must always depend on the nature of that act. *** [W]here the heads of departments are

Make the Connection

The Court here suggests that certain government actions are only "politically examinable." What sorts of actions fall into this category? We will consider this question, and the "political question doctrine," later in this Chapter.

the political or confidential agents of the executive, merely to execute the will of the President, or rather to act in cases in which the executive possesses a constitutional or legal discretion, nothing can be more perfectly clear than that their acts are only politically examinable. But where a specific duty is assigned by law, and individual rights depend upon the performance of that duty, it seems equally clear that the individual who considers himself injured, has a right to resort to the laws of his country for a remedy. [It] is then the opinion of the court, [that Marbury has a] right to the commission; a refusal to deliver which, is a plain violation of that right, for which the laws of his country afford him a remedy.

It remains to be inquired whether, [thirdly, he] is entitled to the remedy for which he applies. This depends on, 1st. The nature of the writ applied for; and 2d. The power of this court.

1st. The nature of the writ. *** This writ, if awarded, would be directed to an officer of government, and its mandate to him would be, to use the words of Blackstone, "to do a particular thing therein specified, which appertains to his office and duty and which the court has previously determined, or at least supposes, to be consonant to right and justice." Or, in the words of Lord Mansfield, the applicant, in this case, has a right to execute an office of public concern, and is kept out of possession of that right. These circumstances certainly concur in this case.

Still, to render the mandamus a proper remedy, the officer to whom it is to be directed, must be one to whom, on legal principles, such writ may be directed. *** The intimate political relation, subsisting between the President of the United States and the heads of departments, necessarily renders any legal investigation of the acts of one of those high officers peculiarly irksome, as well as delicate; and excites some hesitation with respect to the propriety of entering into such investigation.

Take Note

Chief Justice Marshall was fully aware that President Jefferson was likely to ignore, and to direct Madison to ignore, any judicial order commanding the delivery of Marbury's commission. How might this knowledge have affected Marshall's resolution of the case?

Impressions are often received without much reflection or examination, and it is not wonderful that in such a case as this, the assertion, by an individual, of his legal claims in a court of justice, to which claims it is the duty of that court to attend, should at first view be considered by some, as an attempt to intrude into the cabinet, and to intermeddle with the prerogatives of the executive.

It is scarcely necessary for the court to disclaim all pretensions to such a jurisdiction. An extravagance, so absurd and excessive, could not have been entertained for a moment. The province of the court is, solely, to decide on the rights of individuals, not to enquire how the executive, or executive officers, perform duties in which they have a discretion. Questions, in their nature political, or which are, by the constitution and laws, submitted to the executive, can never be made in this court.

But [when the head of a department] is directed by law to do a certain act affecting the absolute rights of individuals, in the performance of which he is not placed under the particular direction of the President, and the performance of which, the President cannot lawfully forbid, *** it is not perceived on what ground the courts of the country are further excused from the duty of giving judgment.

Take Note

Chief Justice Marshall addresses the question of the Court's own jurisdiction only after considering both whether Marbury has a right to his commission and whether the Jefferson Administration is obligated to deliver it. Typically, however, courts address jurisdictional questions before proceeding to the merits. Was it appropriate for Marshall to proceed in this fashion? Why do you suppose that he left the jurisdictional question for last?

This, then, is a plain case for a mandamus, either to deliver the commission, or a copy of it from the record; and it only remains to be inquired: Whether it can issue from this court. The act to establish the judicial courts of the United States authorizes the Supreme Court "to issue writs of mandamus, in cases warranted by the principles and usages of law, to any courts appointed, or persons holding office, under the authority of the United States."

The secretary of state, being a person holding an office under the authority of the United States, is precisely within the letter of the description; and if this court is not authorized to issue a writ of mandamus to such an officer, it must be because the law is unconstitutional, and therefore absolutely incapable of conferring the authority, and assigning the duties which its words purport to confer and assign.

The constitution [in Article III, § 1] vests the whole judicial power of the United States in one Supreme Court, and such inferior courts as congress shall, from time to time, ordain and establish. This power is expressly extended to all cases arising under the laws of the United States; and consequently, in some form, may be exercised over the present case; because the right claimed is given by a law of the United States.

In the distribution of this power it is declared [in Article III, § 2, cl. 2] that "the Supreme Court shall have original jurisdiction in all cases affecting ambassadors, other public ministers and consuls, and those in which a state shall be a party. In all other cases, the supreme court shall have appellate jurisdiction." [It] has been insisted, at the bar, that as the original grant of jurisdiction,

Definition

Note that the terms "ambassadors, other public ministers, and consuls" refer to different classes of diplomats from foreign countries. See *Black's Law Dictionary* (8th ed. 2004). These terms would not cover Madison in his role as the U.S. Secretary of State.

to the supreme and inferior courts, is general, and the clause, assigning original jurisdiction to the Supreme Court, contains no negative or restrictive words; the power remains to the legislature, to assign original jurisdiction to that court in other cases than those specified in the article which has been recited; provided those cases belong to the judicial power of the United States.

If it had been intended to leave it in the discretion of the legislature to apportion the judicial power between the supreme and inferior courts according to the will of that body, it would certainly have been useless to have proceeded further than to have defined the judicial power, and the tribunals in which it should be vested. The subsequent part of the section is mere surplusage, is entirely without meaning, if such is to be the construction. *** It cannot be presumed that any clause in the constitution is intended to be without effect; and therefore such a construction is inadmissible, unless the words require it.

When an instrument organizing fundamentally a judicial system, divides it into one supreme, and so many inferior courts as the legislature may ordain and establish; then enumerates its powers, and proceeds so far to distribute them, as to define the jurisdiction of the Supreme Court by declaring the cases in which it shall take original jurisdiction, and that in others it shall take appellate jurisdiction; the plain import of the words seems to be, that in one class of cases its jurisdiction is original, and not appellate; in the other it is appellate, and not original. If any other construction would render the clause inoperative, that is an additional reason for rejecting such other construction, and for adhering to their obvious meaning.

To enable this court then to issue a mandamus, it must be shown to be an exercise of appellate jurisdiction, or to be necessary to enable them to exercise appellate jurisdiction. It is the essential criterion of appellate jurisdiction, that it revises and corrects the proceedings in a cause already instituted, and does not create that cause. Although, therefore, a mandamus may be directed to courts, yet to issue such a writ to an officer for the delivery of a paper, is in effect the same as to sustain an original action for that paper, and therefore seems not to belong to appellate, but to original jurisdiction. Neither is it necessary in such a case as this, to enable the court to exercise its appellate jurisdiction.

The authority, therefore, given to the Supreme Court, by the act establishing the judicial courts of the United States, to issue writs of mandamus to public officers, appears not to be warranted by the Constitution; and it becomes necessary to enquire whether a jurisdiction, so conferred, can be exercised.

The question, whether an act, repugnant to the constitution, can become the law of the land, is a question deeply interesting to the United States; but, happily, not of an intricacy proportioned to its interest. It seems only necessary to recognize certain principles, supposed to have been long and well established, to decide it.

That the people have an original right to establish, for their future government, such principles as, in their opinion, shall most conduce to their own happiness, is the basis on which the whole American fabric has been erected. The exercise of this original right is a very great exertion; nor can it, nor ought it to be, frequently repeated. The principles, therefore, so established, are deemed fundamental. And as the authority, from which they proceed, is supreme, and can seldom act, they are designed to be permanent.

This original and supreme will organizes the government, and assigns, to different departments, their respective powers. It may either stop here; or establish certain limits not to be transcended by those departments. The government of the United States is of the latter description. The powers of the legislature are defined, and limited; and that those limits may not be mistaken, or forgotten, the constitution is written. To what purpose are powers limited, and to what purpose is that limitation committed to writing, if these limits may, at any time, be passed by those intended to be restrained? The distinction, between a government with limited and unlimited powers, is abolished, if those limits do not confine the persons on whom they are imposed, and if acts prohibited and acts allowed, are of equal obligation. It is a proposition too plain to be contested, that the Constitution controls any legislative act repugnant to it; or, that the legislature may alter the Constitution by an ordinary act.

Between these alternatives there is no middle ground. The constitution is either a superior, paramount law, unchangeable by ordinary means, or it is on a level with ordinary legislative acts, and like other acts, is alterable when the legislature shall please to alter it. If the former part of the alternative be true, then a legislative act contrary to the Constitution is not law: if the latter part be true, then written Constitutions are absurd attempts, on the part of the people, to limit a power in its own nature illimitable.

Certainly all those who have framed written constitutions contemplate them as forming the fundamental and paramount law of the nation, and consequently the theory of every such government must be, that an act of the legislature, repugnant to the constitution, is void. This theory is essentially attached to a written constitution, and is consequently to be considered, by this court, as one of the fundamental principles of our society.

If an act of the legislature, repugnant to the constitution, is void, does it, notwithstanding its invalidity, bind the courts, and oblige them to give it effect? Or, in other words, though it be not law, does it constitute a rule as operative as if it was a law? This would be to overthrow in fact what was established in theory; and would seem, at first view, an absurdity too gross to be insisted on. It shall, however, receive a more attentive consideration.

It is emphatically the province and duty of the judicial department to say what the law is. Those who apply the rule to particular cases, must of necessity expound and interpret that rule. If two laws conflict with each other, the courts must decide on the operation of each. *** This is of the very essence of judicial duty. If then the courts are to regard the Constitution; and the Constitution is superior to any ordinary act of the legislature; the Constitution, and not such ordinary act, must govern the case to which they both apply. Those then who controvert the principle that the Constitution is to be considered, in court, as a paramount law, are reduced to the necessity of maintaining that courts must close their eyes on the Constitution, and see only the law.

This doctrine would subvert the very foundation of all written constitutions. It would declare that an act, which, according to the principles and theory of our government, is entirely void; is yet, in practice, completely obligatory. It would declare, that if the legislature shall do what is expressly forbidden, such act, notwithstanding the express prohibition, is in reality effectual. It would be giving to the legislature a practical and real omnipotence, with the same breath which professes to restrict their powers within narrow limits. It is prescribing limits, and declaring that those limits may be passed at pleasure.

That it thus reduces to nothing what we have deemed the greatest improvement on political institutions—a written constitution—would of itself be sufficient, in America, where written constitutions have been viewed with so much reverence, for rejecting the construction. But the peculiar expressions of the Constitution of the United States furnish additional arguments in favour of its rejection.

The judicial power of the United States is extended to all cases arising under the Constitution. Could it be the intention of those who gave this power, to say that, in using it, the Constitution should not be looked into? That a case arising under the Constitution should be decided without examining the instrument under which it arises? This is too extravagant to be maintained. In some cases then, the Constitution must be looked into by the judges. And if they can open it at all, what part of it are they forbidden to read, or to obey?

There are many other parts of the Constitution which serve to illustrate this subject. It is declared that "no tax or duty shall be laid on articles exported from any state." Suppose a duty on the export of cotton, of tobacco, or of flour; and a suit instituted to recover it. Ought judgment to be rendered in such a case? Ought the judges to close their eyes on the constitution, and only see the law?

The Constitution declares that "no bill of attainder or *ex post facto* law shall be passed." If, however, such a bill should be passed and a person should be prosecuted under it; must the court condemn to death those victims whom the constitution endeavors to preserve?

"No person," says the Constitution, "shall be convicted of treason unless on the testimony of two witnesses to the same overt act, or on confession in open court." Here the language of the Constitution is addressed especially to the courts. It prescribes, directly for them, a rule of evidence not to be departed from. If the legislature should change that rule, and declare *one* witness, or a confession *out of* court, sufficient for conviction, must the constitutional principle yield to the legislative act?

From these, and many other selections which might be made, it is apparent, that the framers of the Constitution contemplated that instrument, as a rule for the government of *courts,* as well as of the legislature. [Why] otherwise does it direct the judges to take an oath to support it? This oath certainly applies, in an especial manner, to their conduct in their official character.

How immoral to impose it on them, if they were to be used as the instruments, and the knowing instruments, for violating what they swear to support! Why does a judge swear to discharge his duties agreeably to the Constitution of the United States, if that constitution forms no rule for his government? If it is closed upon him, and cannot be inspected

Take Note

Does the Constitution require any other government actors to take an oath to support the Constitution? If so, what does this suggest about Marshall's argument?

by him? If such be the real state of things, this is worse than solemn mockery. To prescribe, or to take this oath, becomes equally a crime.

It is also not entirely unworthy of observation, that in declaring what shall be the *supreme* law of the land, the *Constitution* itself is first mentioned; and not the laws of the United States generally, but those only which shall be made in *pursuance* of the constitution, have that rank.

Thus, the particular phraseology of the Constitution of the United States confirms and strengthens the principle, supposed to be essential to all written constitutions, that a law repugnant to the constitution is void; and that *courts,* as well as other departments, are bound by that instrument.

The rule must be discharged.

Points for Discussion

a. The Judiciary Act of 1789

Section 13 of the Judiciary Act of 1789—the provision at issue in *Marbury*—delineated the jurisdiction of the Supreme Court. After conferring original jurisdiction on the Court over cases involving states and ambassadors, the section stated: "The Supreme Court shall also have appellate jurisdiction from the circuit courts and courts of the several states, in the cases herein after specially provided for; and shall have power to issue writs of prohibition to the district courts, when proceeding as courts of admiralty and maritime jurisdiction, and writs of mandamus, in cases warranted by the principles and usages of law, to any courts appointed, or persons holding office, under the authority of the United States." 1 Stat. 73. In light of the clauses that immediately preceded the clause granting authority to the Court to issue writs of mandamus, do you find convincing the Court's conclusion that the Act authorized the Supreme Court to exercise *original* jurisdiction over suits seeking writs of mandamus against federal officers?

b. Article III

Article III, § 2, cl. 2 provides: "In all Cases involving Ambassadors, other public Ministers and Counsuls, and those in which a State shall be Party, the Supreme Court shall have original Jurisdiction. In all other Cases before mentioned [in clause 1], the supreme Court shall have appellate Jurisdiction ***." The Court concluded, in effect, that this provision creates mutually exclusive categories of original and appellate jurisdiction, such that Congress lacks power to confer original jurisdiction over cases that fall within the Supreme Court's appellate jurisdiction and vice versa. Is this the only plausible interpretation of the provision? In light of the language of the provision—that the Court "shall" have original jurisdiction over some cases and "shall" have appellate jurisdiction over others—is it the most compelling interpretation? What other meanings can the word "shall" connote? In answering these questions, consider that 20 years after the decision in <u>Marbury</u>, the Court—in an opinion by Chief Justice Marshall—held that Congress may authorize the Court to exercise appellate jurisdiction over a case involving a State, even though such cases plainly fall within the Court's original jurisdiction as defined in <u>Marbury</u>. *Cohens v. Virginia*, 19 U.S. (6 Wheat.) 264, 399-400 (1821).

c. Arguments For and Against Judicial Review of Federal Statutes

The Court concluded that it has authority to determine whether a federal statute is inconsistent with the Constitution and thus void. What specific reasons did it give for this conclusion? Are these reasons based on the text of the Constitution, on the original intent or understanding of the Constitution, or on policy or other considerations?

The Court's assertion that "all those who have framed written constitutions contemplate them as forming the fundamental and paramount law of the nation, and *** an act of the legislature, repugnant to the constitution, is void" is consistent with views expressed by Alexander Hamilton in the Federalist Papers. In The Federalist No. 78, Hamilton wrote:

> The complete independence of the courts of justice is peculiarly essential in a limited Constitution. By a limited Constitution, I understand one which contains certain specified exceptions to the legislative authority; such, for instance, as that it shall pass no bills of attainder, no ex-post-facto laws, and the like. Limitations of this kind can be preserved in practice no other way than through the medium of courts of justice, whose duty it must be to declare all acts contrary to the manifest tenor of the Constitution void. Without this, all the reservations of particular rights or privileges would amount to nothing.

Historians debate, however, whether this view of the Constitution was widely shared at the time of ratification.

In any event, it is worth noting that Chief Justice Marshall did not consider any possible counterarguments. Are there any arguments against judicial review of federal statutes? For example, is it relevant that there is no clause in the Constitution that says that courts may invalidate federal statutes, even though there is a provision—the Supremacy Clause in Article VI—that says that state judges may not enforce unconstitutional state laws? Is it worth noting that the Court's opinion cites no precedent to support its reasoning? Should it matter that Article I, § 7 says that a bill passed by the House and Senate and signed by the President is "a law" without qualification (i.e., without saying that it is "a law if the courts say it is constitutional")? With respect to this last point, consider that many of the Members of the Congress that enacted the Judiciary Act not only had taken an oath to support the Constitution, but also had served at the Constitutional Convention or in the state ratifying conventions. (Oliver Ellsworth, the principal drafter of the Judiciary Act, was a central figure at the former and an important figure at the Connecticut ratifying convention.) Do you suppose that they thought that section 13 of the Judiciary Act was constitutional? Why is the Court's interpretation of the Constitution superior to Congress's interpretation?

In light of this discussion, notice finally that Chief Justice Marshall stated that the central question in the case was "whether an act, repugnant to the constitution, can become the law of the land." He concluded, perhaps not surprisingly, that the answer must be "no." Was there really any debate about this proposition? Was the question that the Court answered really the central question in the case?

d. The Constitution and Ordinary Law

It is deeply ingrained in our social and political conscience—at least in part because of the conclusion in *Marbury v. Madison*—that statutes that conflict with the Constitution are void. But at least theoretically, statutes enacted today reflect the current democratic consensus. Why should we be deprived of the right to decide for ourselves, through democratic means, how to govern ourselves—and be so deprived, moreover, by un-elected judges enforcing a charter that represents the judgments of people who are long dead and gone? Even assuming that Chief Justice Marshall asked and answered the right question in *Marbury*, is it so clear that the Court should invalidate democratically enacted statutes on the ground that they are inconsistent with the Constitution? Why is the Constitution binding on us today?

e. Who Won in *Marbury*?

Who "won" in *Marbury*? Did Jefferson and Madison win? After all, the import of the holding—that the Court lacked jurisdiction to grant Marbury's petition—was that the Court could not order them to deliver Marbury's commission. In fact, Marbury never received his commission, even though according to the Court he had a right to it. But Jefferson and Madison's success came at a high price. They were also told by the Court that in one of their very first acts in office they had violated Marbury's vested legal rights. And the Federalists, who at the time controlled the federal courts, gained or solidified the power of judicial review. Was this a Pyrrhic victory?

Martin v. Hunter's Lessee

14 U.S. (1 Wheat.) 304 (1816)

[This case concerned a long-running dispute over a huge piece of land in Virginia that once was owned by Lord Fairfax, a British loyalist. The State of Virginia claimed that it had lawfully seized Fairfax's land prior to the Treaty of Paris in 1783, which ended the Revolutionary War. Virginia subsequently granted parcels of the land to some of its citizens, including Hunter. Martin claimed ownership of the same parcel of land, tracing his claim to a devise from Fairfax in 1781. Martin claimed that Fairfax's lands had been protected from seizure by the Treaty of Paris in 1783 and by the Jay Treaty of 1794.

Hunter filed a lawsuit in Virginia state court in 1791. The litigation itself was on hold for about 20 years, during which time John Marshall and his brother James contracted to purchase a large part of the Fairfax estate from Fairfax's heirs. The Virginia Court of

Appeals (the highest court in the state) first ruled in the case in 1810, upholding Virginia's earlier seizure of Fairfax's land and thus ruling in favor of Hunter. The United States Supreme Court reversed that judgment in *Fairfax's Devisee v. Hunter's Lessee*, 11 U.S. (7 Cranch) 603 (1813), and "instructed" and "commanded" the Virginia judges to enter judgment for Martin.

On remand, the Virginia Court of Appeals refused to enter judgment for Martin. It concluded that "the appellate power of the Supreme Court of the United States does not extend to this court," and that section 25 of the Judiciary Act of 1789, which authorized Supreme Court review of final decisions of the highest state courts rejecting claims, such as Martin's, based on federal law, thus was unconstitutional. The Virginia Court suggested that if Congress wanted to ensure United States Supreme Court review of all issues of federal law, it could create more inferior federal courts and confer on them jurisdiction—including by removal—over all issues arising under federal law. The Supreme Court reviewed that judgment in the opinion that follows.]

STORY, J., delivered the opinion of the court.

The third article of the constitution is that which must principally attract our attention. *** The language of the article throughout is manifestly designed to be mandatory upon the legislature. *** The judicial power of the United States *shall be vested* (not may be vested) in one supreme court, and in such inferior courts as congress may, from time to time, ordain and establish. Could congress have lawfully refused to create a supreme court, or to vest in it the constitutional jurisdiction?

The judicial power must [be] vested in some court, by congress; and to suppose that it was not an obligation binding on them, but might, at their pleasure, be omitted or declined, is to suppose that, under the sanction of the constitution, they might defeat the constitution itself; a construction which would lead to such a result cannot be sound.

If, then, it is a duty of congress to vest the judicial power of the United States, it is a duty to vest the *whole judicial power*. The language, if imperative as to one part, is imperative as to all. If it were otherwise, this anomaly would exist, that congress might successively refuse to vest the jurisdiction in any one class of cases enumerated in the constitution, and thereby defeat the jurisdiction as to all; for the constitution has not singled out any class on which congress are bound to act in preference to others.

> **FYI**
>
> *Martin* is the most significant case decided by the Marshall Court that Chief Justice Marshall did not write. He recused himself because of his claim to some of the Fairfax lands, which gave him an obvious stake in the outcome. Justice Joseph Story (1779-1845) was a great jurist in his own right. He became a Supreme Court Justice at age 32 and served on the Court for 34 years. Story was also a professor of law at Harvard and wrote a highly influential treatise, *Commentaries on the Constitution of the United States* (1833). This treatise, which the Supreme Court has cited in over 200 cases, is available online at http://www.constitution.org/js/js_000.htm.

This leads us to the consideration of the great question as to the nature and extent of the appellate jurisdiction of the United States. *** As [the] appellate jurisdiction is not limited as to the supreme court, and as to this court it may be exercised in all other cases than those of which it has original cognizance, what is there to restrain its exercise over state tribunals in the enumerated cases? The appellate power is not limited by the terms of the third article to any particular courts. The words are, "the judicial power (which includes appellate power) shall extend *to all cases*," &c., and "in all other cases before mentioned the supreme court shall have appellate jurisdiction." It is the *case*, then, and not *the court*, that gives the jurisdiction. If the judicial power extends to the case, it will be in vain to search in the letter of the constitution for any qualification as to the tribunal where it depends.

If the constitution meant to limit the appellate jurisdiction to cases pending in the courts of the United States, it would necessarily follow that the jurisdiction of these courts would, in all the cases enumerated in the constitution, be exclusive of state tribunals. How otherwise could the jurisdiction extend to *all* cases arising under the constitution, laws, and treaties of the United States, or *to all cases* of admiralty and maritime jurisdiction? If some of these cases might be entertained by state tribunals, and no appellate jurisdiction as to them should exist, then the appellate power would not extend to *all*, but to *some*, cases.

On the other hand, if [a] discretion be vested in congress to establish, or not to establish, inferior courts at their own pleasure, and congress should not establish such courts, the appellate jurisdiction of the supreme Court would have nothing to act upon, unless it could act upon cases pending in the state courts.

But it is plain that the framers of the constitution did contemplate that cases within the judicial cognizance of the United States not only might but would arise in the state courts, in the exercise of their ordinary jurisdiction. With this view the sixth article declares, that "this constitution, and the laws of the United States which shall be made in pursuance thereof, and all treaties made, or which shall be made, under the authority of the United States, shall be the supreme law of the land, and the judges in every state shall be bound thereby, any thing in the constitution or laws of any state to the contrary notwithstanding."

It must, therefore, be conceded that the constitution not only contemplated, but meant to provide for cases within the scope of the judicial power of the United States, which might yet depend before state tribunals. It was foreseen that in the exercise of their ordinary jurisdiction, state courts would incidentally take cognizance of cases arising under the constitution, the laws, and treaties of the United States. Yet to all these cases the judicial power, by the very terms of the constitution, is to extend. It cannot extend by original jurisdiction if that was already rightfully and exclusively attached in the state courts, which (as has been already shown) may occur; it must, therefore, extend by appellate jurisdiction, or not at all. It would seem to follow that the appellate power of the United States must, in such cases, extend to state tribunals; and if in such cases, there is no reason why it should not equally attach upon all others within the purview of the constitution.

It has been argued that such an appellate jurisdiction over state courts is inconsistent with the genius of our governments, and the spirit of the constitution. That the latter was never designed to act upon state sovereignties, but only upon the people, and that if the power exists, it will materially impair the sovereignty of the states, and the independence of their courts. We cannot yield to the force of this reasoning; it assumes principles which we cannot admit, and draws conclusions to which we do not yield our assent.

It is a mistake that the constitution was not designed to operate upon states, in their corporate capacities. It is crowded with provisions which restrain or annul the sovereignty of the states in some of the highest branches of their prerogatives. *** Nor can such a right be deemed to impair the independence of state judges. It is assuming the very ground in controversy to assert that they possess an absolute independence of the United States. In respect to the powers granted to the United States, they are not independent; they are expressly bound to obedience by the letter of the constitution; and if they should unintentionally transcend their authority, or misconstrue the constitution, there is no more reason for giving their judgments an absolute and irresistible force, than for giving it to the acts of the other co-ordinate departments of state sovereignty.

The argument urged from the possibility of the abuse of the revising power, is equally unsatisfactory. It is always a doubtful course, to argue against the use or existence of a power, from the possibility of its abuse. *** From the very nature of things, the absolute right of decision, in the last resort, must rest somewhere—wherever it may be vested it is susceptible of abuse.

It is further argued, that no great public mischief can result from a construction which shall limit the appellate power of the United States to cases in their own courts: first, because state judges are bound by an oath to support the constitution of the United States, and must be presumed to be men of learning and integrity; and, secondly, because congress must have an unquestionable right to remove all cases within the scope of the judicial power from the state courts to the courts of the United States, at any time before final judgment, though not after final judgment. [A]dmitting that the judges of the state courts are, and always will be, of as much learning, integrity, and wisdom, as those of the courts of the United States, (which we very cheerfully admit) [does] not aid the argument. It is manifest that the constitution has proceeded upon a theory of its own, [presuming] (whether rightly or wrongly we do not inquire) that state attachments, state prejudices, state jealousies, and state interests, might some times obstruct, or control, or be supposed to obstruct or control, the regular administration of justice.

> **Food for Thought**
>
> Can you think of any provisions of the Constitution that appear to presume that state judges might at times be biased in some way in the performance of their duties?

A motive of another kind, perfectly compatible with the most sincere respect for state tribunals, might induce the grant of appellate power over their decisions. That motive is the importance, and even necessity of *uniformity* of decisions throughout the whole United States, upon all subjects within the purview of the constitution. Judges of equal learning and integrity, in different states, might differently interpret a statute, or a treaty of the United States, or even the constitution itself: If there were no revising authority to control these jarring and discordant judgments, and harmonize them into uniformity, the laws, the treaties, and the constitution of the United States would be different in different states, and might, perhaps, never have precisely the same construction, obligation, or efficacy, in any two states. The public mischiefs that would attend such a state of things would be truly deplorable; and it cannot be believed that they could have escaped the enlightened convention which formed the constitution.

The remedy, too, of removal of suits would be utterly inadequate to the purposes of the constitution, if it could act only on the parties, and not upon the state courts. *** If state courts should deny the constitutionality of the authority to remove suits from their cognizance, in what manner could they be compelled to relinquish the jurisdiction?

On the whole, the court are of opinion, that the appellate power of the United States does extend to cases pending in the state courts; and that the 25th section of the judiciary act, which authorizes the exercise of this jurisdiction in the specified cases, by a writ of error, is supported by the letter and spirit of the constitution.

Points for Discussion

a. Text and History

Delegates at the Constitutional Convention were divided over whether to create lower federal courts. Some argued that the Constitution itself should create not only a Supreme Court but also inferior federal courts, to ensure a neutral forum for the assertion of federal rights. Others argued that the existing state courts would be adequate fora. The provision in Article III authorizing, but not requiring, Congress to create inferior federal courts was a compromise between the competing positions. What does the compromise reflect about the Framers' likely expectations about the Supreme Court's power to review state-court judgments? In addition, Article VI provides that "the Judges in every State shall be bound" by federal law, "any Thing in the Constitution or Laws of any State to the Contrary notwithstanding." Does this provision help Justice Story's reasoning?

b. State Court Hostility to Federal Law

Justice Story suggested that the Constitution presupposes the possibility of hostility by state court judges to federal law or claims arising under federal law. Is this a realistic fear? If so, why might we expect such hostility? And if it made sense to fear it in 1789 (or 1816), does it make sense to fear it today?

Chief Justice Marshall did not participate in the decision in *Martin*. But five years later, in *Cohens v. Virginia*, 19 U.S. (6 Wheat.) 264, 399-400 (1821), Marshall addressed the constitutionality of section 25 of the Judiciary Act in a case in which one of the parties was a state. Virginia argued (among other things) that the provision in Article III conferring original jurisdiction on the Supreme Court in cases "in which a State shall be a Party" precluded the Supreme Court from exercising appellate jurisdiction in the case. (Recall that the Court in *Marbury* had concluded that the categories of original and appellate jurisdiction in Article III were mutually exclusive.) The Court rejected Virginia's argument. Echoing Justice Story's opinion in _Martin_, the Court concluded that "the judicial power, as originally given, extends to all cases arising under the constitution or a law of the United States, whoever may be the parties." (Chief Justice Marshall concluded that the discussion in _Marbury_—which, of course, he had written—about the Court's appellate jurisdiction was unpersuasive dicta.) Marshall also agreed with Story that state courts might exhibit hostility to federal law: "It would be hazarding too much to assert, that the judicatures of the States will be exempt from the prejudices by which the legislatures and people are influenced, and will constitute perfectly impartial tribunals. In many States the judges are dependent for office and for salary on the will of the legislature. *** When we observe the importance which that constitution attaches to the independence of judges, we are the less inclined to suppose that it can have intended to leave these constitutional questions to tribunals where this independence may not exist ***. There is certainly nothing in the circumstances under which our constitution was formed; nothing in the history of the times, which would justify the opinion that the confidence reposed in the States was so implicit as to leave in them and their tribunals the power of resisting or defeating, in the form of law, the legitimate measures of the Union."

c. Uniformity

Justice Story also reasoned that Supreme Court review of state court judgments was necessary to ensure the uniformity of federal law. Why isn't removal to federal court of cases involving questions of federal law a sufficient response to the concern about uniformity?

———————————

Together, _Marbury_ and _Martin_ stand for the proposition that the Court has the power of judicial review, which it can exercise in cases arising in state and federal court and in cases involving the constitutionality of state or federal laws. These undoubtedly are profoundly important propositions in our system of government. But just how profound turns on the scope of the power of judicial review. Did the Court in _Marbury_ hold that judicial interpretations of the Constitution are binding on all actors subject to the provisions of the Constitution? Or did the Court in _Marbury_ simply hold that judicial review is the mere consequence of a court's obligation to decide cases that come before it in accordance with the governing law, including the Constitution? If this is the case, then judicial interpretations of the Constitution would be binding on the parties to the litigation that produced the interpretation, but perhaps on no one else.

Perhaps because of the delicacy of the Court's role in a democratic society—and because of the controversy that surrounds so many of the Court's important decisions— many prominent voices have long urged that only the latter, more narrow account of the power of judicial review is correct. Abraham Lincoln, for example, argued that "the candid citizen must confess that if the policy of the Government upon vital questions affecting the whole people is to be irrevocably fixed by decisions of the Supreme Court, the instant they are made in ordinary litigation between parties in personal actions, the people will have ceased to be their own rulers, having to that extent practically resigned their Government into the hands of that eminent tribunal." First Inaugural Address, March 4, 1861. The Court finally took the opportunity in the case that follows to address the question of the scope of *Marbury's* holding.

Cooper v. Aaron

358 U.S. 1 (1958)

Opinion of the Court by The CHIEF JUSTICE, Mr. Justice BLACK, Mr. Justice FRANK-FURTER, Mr. Justice DOUGLAS, Mr. Justice BURTON, Mr. Justice CLARK, Mr. Justice HARLAN, Mr. Justice BRENNAN, and Mr. Justice WHITTAKER.

As this case reaches us it raises questions of the highest importance to the maintenance of our federal system of government. It necessarily involves a claim by the Governor and Legislature of a State that there is no duty on state officials to obey federal court orders resting on this Court's considered interpretation of the United States Constitution. Specifically it involves actions by the Governor and Legislature of Arkansas upon the premise that they are not bound by our holding in *Brown v. Board of Education* [that] the Fourteenth Amendment forbids States to use their governmental powers to bar children on racial grounds from attending schools where there is state participation through any arrangement, management, funds or property. We are urged to uphold a suspension of the Little Rock School Board's plan to do away with segregated public schools in Little Rock until state laws and efforts to upset and nullify our holding in *Brown* have been further challenged and tested in the courts. We reject these contentions.

> **Take Note**
>
> The opinion of the Court was not announced either by one Justice or "per curiam," which means "by the Court." The Court took the highly unusual step of issuing a jointly signed opinion. Why would the Court do so in this case?

> **FYI**
>
> The Court issued two decisions in *Brown v. Board of Education*; the second, known as *Brown II*, ordered desegregation "with all deliberate speed." The litigation that followed directly involved lower federal courts around the country in overseeing desegregation plans. We will consider *Brown* and this line of cases in Chapter 11.

[Shortly after the decision in *Brown*, the Little Rock District School Board adopted a desegregation plan.] While the School Board was thus going forward with its preparation for desegregating the Little Rock school system, other state authorities, in contrast, were actively pursuing a program designed to perpetuate in Arkansas the system of racial segregation which this Court had held violated the Fourteenth Amendment. [The Arkansas state Constitution was amended to command the state legislature to oppose "in every Constitutional manner the unconstitutional desegregation decisions of the United States Supreme Court," and the legislature responded by enacting laws relieving school children from compulsory attendance at racially mixed schools. Although the Little Rock School Board continued with preparations to implement the first phase of a desegregation program, which entailed the enrollment of nine African-American children at Central High School, a school with more than two thousand students, the Governor of Arkansas dispatched units of the Arkansas National Guard to Central High School the day before the students arrived and placed the school "off limits" to the black students. Every school day for the next three weeks, members of the Guard, acting pursuant to the Governor's order, stood shoulder to shoulder at the school grounds and forcibly prevented the black students from entering.]

[After intervention of the Attorney General of the United States, the District Court overseeing the implementation of the desegregation plan enjoined] the Governor and the officers of the Guard from preventing the attendance of Negro children at Central High School, and from otherwise obstructing or interfering with the orders of the court in connection with the plan. The National Guard was then withdrawn from the school. [The next school day the children] entered the high school [under] the protection of the Little Rock Police Department and members of the Arkansas State Police[, but] the officers caused the children to be removed from the school during the morning because they had difficulty controlling a large and demonstrating crowd which had gathered at the high school. [Two days later], however, the President of the United States dispatched federal troops to Central High School and admission of the Negro students to the school was thereby effected. Regular army troops continued at the high school until November 27, 1957. They were then replaced by federalized National Guardsmen who remained throughout the balance of the school year. Eight of the Negro students remained in attendance at the school throughout the school year.

[On] February 20, 1958, the School Board and the Superintendent of Schools filed a petition in the District Court seeking a postponement of their program for desegregation. Their position in essence was that because of extreme public hostility, which they stated had been engendered largely by the official attitudes and actions of the Governor and the Legislature, the maintenance of a sound educational program at Central High School, with the Negro students in attendance, would be impossible. The Board therefore proposed that the Negro students already admitted to the school be withdrawn and sent to segregated schools, and that all further steps to carry out the Board's desegregation program be postponed for a period later suggested by the Board to be two and one-half years. After a hearing the District Court granted the relief requested by the Board [finding that] the past year at Central High School had been attended by conditions of "chaos, bedlam and turmoil" [and] that there were "repeated incidents of more or less serious violence directed against the Negro students and their property." [The court of appeals reversed.]

In affirming the judgment of the Court of Appeals which reversed the District Court we have accepted without reservation the position of the School Board, the Superintendent of Schools, and their counsel that they displayed entire good faith in the conduct of these proceedings and in dealing with the unfortunate and distressing sequence of events which has been outlined. We likewise have accepted the findings of the District Court as to the conditions at Central High School during the 1957-1958 school year, and also the findings that the educational progress of all the students, white and colored, of that school has suffered and will continue to suffer if the conditions which prevailed last year are permitted to continue.

The significance of these findings, however, is to be considered in light of the fact, indisputably revealed by the record before us, that the conditions they depict are directly traceable to the actions of legislators and executive officials of the State of Arkansas, taken in their official capacities, which reflect their own determination to resist this Court's decision in the _Brown_ case and which have brought about violent resistance to that decision in Arkansas. *** One may well sympathize with the position of the Board in the face of the frustrating conditions which have confronted it, but, regardless of the Board's good faith, the actions of the other state agencies responsible for those conditions compel us to reject the Board's legal position.

[T]he constitutional rights of children not to be discriminated against in school admission on grounds of race or color declared by this Court in the _Brown_ case can neither be nullified openly and directly by state legislators or state executive or judicial officers, nor nullified indirectly by them through evasive schemes for segregation whether attempted "ingeniously or ingenuously."

What has been said, in the light of the facts developed, is enough to dispose of the case. However, we should answer the premise of the actions of the Governor and Legislature that they are not bound by our holding in the _Brown_ case. *** Article VI of the Constitution makes the Constitution the "supreme Law of the Land." In 1803, Chief Justice Marshall, speaking for a unanimous Court, referring to the Constitution as "the fundamental and paramount law of the nation," declared in the notable case of _Marbury v. Madison_ that "It is emphatically the province and duty of the judicial department to say what the law is." This decision declared the basic principle that the federal judiciary is supreme in the exposition of the law of the Constitution, and that principle has ever since been respected by this Court and the Country as a permanent and indispensable feature of our constitutional system. It follows that the interpretation of the Fourteenth Amendment enunciated by this Court in the _Brown_ case is the supreme law of the land, and Art. VI of the Constitution makes it of binding effect on the States "any Thing in the Constitution or Laws of any State to the Contrary notwithstanding." Every state legislator and executive and judicial officer is solemnly committed by oath taken pursuant to Art. VI, cl. 3 "to support this Constitution."

No state legislator or executive or judicial officer can war against the Constitution without violating his undertaking to support it. *** A Governor who asserts a power to nullify a federal court order is similarly restrained. If he had such power, said Chief Justice Hughes, in 1932, also for a unanimous Court, "it is manifest that the fiat of a state Governor, and not the Constitution of the United States, would be the supreme law of the land; that the restrictions of the Federal Constitution upon the exercise of state power would be but impotent phrases."

The basic decision in _Brown_ was unanimously reached by this Court only after the case had been briefed and twice argued and the issues had been given the most serious consideration. Since the first <u>Brown</u> opinion three new Justices have come to the Court. They are at one with the Justices still on the Court who participated in that basic decision as to its correctness, and that decision is now unanimously reaffirmed. The principles announced in that decision and the obedience of the States to them, according to the command of the Constitution, are indispensable for the protection of the freedoms guaranteed by our fundamental charter for all of us. Our constitutional ideal of equal justice under law is thus made a living truth.

———————

Points for Discussion

a. Implications of Judicial Supremacy

The Court in <u>Cooper</u> emphatically rejected the view that government officials may ignore the Supreme Court's interpretation of the Constitution if they were not parties to the litigation that produced the interpretation. According to the decision in <u>Cooper</u>, it is not simply the "Constitution," but rather the Court's interpretation of the Constitution, that is the "supreme Law of the Land." In one sense, there is great appeal to this proposition. If political figures could ignore the Court and substitute their own interpretations of the Constitution, then the meaning of the Constitution would be left to the political process, and the courts' ability to protect individual rights against majoritarian incursion would be substantially diminished. The circumstances in <u>Cooper</u>—which led the Court firmly to insist that state-sanctioned racial segregation was intolerable—are perhaps the perfect example of the appeal of this view of judicial power.

But the principle of judicial supremacy might also lead, in at least some cases, to the entrenchment of deeply troubling views about constitutional meaning. President Lincoln offered his view of judicial supremacy, with which we introduced the decision in <u>Cooper</u>, in response to the Supreme Court's decision in *Dred Scott v. Sandford*, 60 U.S. (19 How.) 393 (1857), which held that persons of African descent could not become citizens of the United States, and that Congress lacked power to prohibit slavery in territories of the United States. Judicial supremacy is significantly less appealing when one considers that it applies to all judicial interpretations of the Constitution.

In light of this tension, was the Court's decision in <u>Cooper</u> correct?

b. Judicial Supremacy and Congress

<u>Cooper</u> was decided against the backdrop of state resistance to Supreme Court inter-pretations of the Constitution. Is the binding force of the Court's interpretations any dif-ferent when it is Congress, rather than a state or state official, that disagrees? In *Dickerson v. United States*, 530 U.S. 428 (2000), the Court considered the constitutionality of 18 U.S.C. § 3501, which purported to overrule the requirement announced in *Miranda v. Arizona*, 384 U.S. 436 (1966), that certain warnings must be given to a suspect subject to custodial interrogation in order to permit subsequent admission of the suspect's statements as evidence. The Court concluded that Congress "may not legislatively supersede our

decisions interpreting and applying the Constitution." Because the Court concluded that in <u>Miranda</u> it had announced a "constitutional rule" rather than "merely exercised its supervisory authority to regulate evidence in the absence of congressional direction," the Court invalidated the statute. Justice Scalia, joined by Justice Thomas, dissented, concluding that the Court in <u>Miranda</u> had not in fact announced a constitutional rule.

c. Historical Responses to Judicial Supremacy

Judicial supremacy is not absolute. On the contrary, history has shown that there are at least two possible, but limited, ways to undo constitutional decisions by the Supreme Court.

One method to negate the Court's decisions is to amend the Constitution, under the procedures in Article V, to say the opposite of what the Supreme Court previously interpreted the Constitution to mean. The Constitution has been amended to overturn at least four Supreme Court decisions in this manner: the Eleventh Amendment overruled *Chisholm v. Georgia*, 2 U.S. (2 Dall.) 419 (1793) (concerning federal court jurisdiction over state governments); the Thirteenth and Fourteenth Amendments overruled *Dred Scott v. Sandford*, 60 U.S. (19 How.) 393 (1856) (described above); the Sixteenth Amendment overruled *Pollock v. Farmers' Loan & Trust Co.*, 158 U.S. 601 (1895) (concerning income taxes); and the Twenty-Sixth Amendment overruled *Oregon v. Mitchell*, 400 U.S. 112 (1970) (concerning the voting age).

Consider, for example, the <u>Dred Scott</u> case. How does the first sentence of the 14th Amendment affect <u>Dred Scott</u>'s holding that persons of African ancestry cannot be citizens? How does the 13th Amendment affect <u>Dred Scott</u>'s holding that Congress cannot prohibit slavery in federal territories? Does the possibility of amending the Constitution eliminate all concerns about judicial supremacy?

The other way to undo constitutional decisions is to replace justices, when they retire, with justices who hold different views and who are willing to overturn precedents that they consider incorrect. We will see a famous example in Chapter 3 when we consider how changes in Court personnel during the 1930s led to the overturning of numerous cases that had limited federal power. But altering the membership of the Supreme Court to affect the outcome of cases is not easy for two reasons. First, replacing the personnel of the Supreme Court generally cannot happen quickly, because the justices have life tenure. Should the Constitution be amended to address this difficulty? See Steven G. Calabresi, *Term Limits for the Supreme Court: Life Tenure Reconsidered*, 29 Harv. J.L. & Pub. Pol'y 769 (2006) (arguing for term limits in part because of the difficulty of overturning Supreme Court decisions by amending the Constitution). Second, political obstacles may prevent the nomination and confirmation of justices who disagree with precedent. Consider, for example, the opposition to judicial nominees who would overturn the Supreme Court's decisions concerning abortion.

Notice in the last paragraph of the <u>Cooper v. Aaron</u> opinion that the Court mentions the change in its membership since the <u>Brown</u> decision. Why do you think that the Court raised this topic?

Modern Challenges to Judicial Supremacy

Notwithstanding the decisions in <u>Martin</u> and <u>Cooper</u>—and powerful arguments, based on text, history, and structure, that the Court has authority to review state court judgments and declare actions by the States unconstitutional—attacks on the Court's power of judicial review have been a constant refrain throughout American history. From the Virginia and Kentucky Resolutions of 1798—legislative resolutions drafted by James Madison and Thomas Jefferson that argued that the states are entitled to ignore federal laws or actions that they believe exceed the federal government's constitutional authority—to the Nullification Crisis of the 1830s—in which John C. Calhoun and South Carolina similarly asserted such a right—to the Civil Rights struggles of the 1950s and '60s, such attacks have been commonplace. For a modern example, consider the following.

Perspective and Analysis

In 2004, the Alabama Supreme Court, relying on the United States Supreme Court's decision in *Roper v. Simmons*, vacated the death sentence imposed on Renaldo Adams, who had been convicted of rape and murder. In <u>Roper</u>, the Supreme Court held that it violates the Eighth Amendment's prohibition on "cruel and unusual punishment" to execute a person who committed a crime while still a minor. Tom Parker, an Associate Justice on the Alabama Supreme Court who had recused himself from the case, responded with this editorial:

> [M]y fellow Alabama justices freed Adams from death row not because of any error of our courts but because they chose to passively accommodate—rather than actively resist—the unconstitutional opinion of five liberal justices on the U.S. Supreme Court. Those liberal justices *** based their ruling [in <u>Roper</u>] not on the original intent or actual language of the United States Constitution but on foreign law, including United Nations treaties. *** The proper response to such blatant judicial tyranny would have been for the Alabama Supreme Court to decline to follow <u>Roper</u> in the <u>Adams</u> case. *** State supreme courts may decline to follow bad U.S. Supreme Court precedents because those decisions bind only the parties to the particular case. Judges *** should not follow obviously wrong decisions simply because they are "precedents." After all, a judge takes an oath to support the constitution—not to automatically follow activist justices who believe their own devolving standards of decency trump the text of the constitution.

Tom Parker, Op-Ed: Alabama Justices Surrender to Judicial Activism, *Birmingham News*, **January 1, 2005, p. 4B.**

Points for Discussion

a. The Binding Force of Precedent

Is Justice Parker's discussion of the precedential effect of Supreme Court decisions interpreting the Constitution consistent with the view expressed in *Cooper*? If not, is his view nevertheless convincing? To what extent does this reasoning echo Chief Justice Marshall's reasoning in *Marbury*? To what extent does it conflict with it?

b. Reliance on "Foreign" Law in Interpreting the Constitution

As Justice Parker suggests in his article, the majority in the decision in *Roper* cited some foreign-law sources in reaching its conclusion about the meaning of the Eighth Amendment. We will explore the validity of this approach in Chapter 8, when we consider *Lawrence v. Texas*.

B. Obstacles to Judicial Review

Although the Supreme Court has held that courts generally have the power of judicial review, litigants face at least four important obstacles in attempting to persuade courts to strike down legislation or executive actions as unconstitutional. First, the Supreme Court has said that some issues are not "justiciable"—that is, capable of being resolved by the courts—because they present "political questions" that only the political branches (Congress and the President) may resolve. Second, long-standing practice holds that federal courts cannot give legal advice or make abstract decisions, but instead may decide only actual "cases and controversies." Third, federal courts will entertain claims only by persons who have "standing" to present them because they have something at stake in the litigation. Fourth, Congress can limit federal court jurisdiction by statute and thus constrain the ability of federal courts to engage in judicial review. In reading this material, consider not only what the legal rules are, but also where the rules come from, and how they affect constitutional litigation.

---

1. The Political Question Doctrine

In *Marbury*, the Court stated that "where the heads of departments are the political or confidential agents of the executive, merely to execute the will of the President, or rather to act in cases in which the executive possesses a constitutional or legal discretion, nothing can be more perfectly clear than that their acts are only politically examinable." The Court, of course, concluded that *Marbury* did not involve such actions. But the Court's statement gave rise to cases in which the Court declined to review challenged government actions, on the ground that the cases involved "political questions" that were outside of the province of the judicial power. The following case addresses how a court should decide whether a political question is presented in any given case.

———————

Baker v. Carr

369 U.S. 186 (1962)

Mr. Justice BRENNAN delivered the opinion of the Court.

[The plaintiffs were Tennessee voters who claimed that the apportionment of the state legislature violated their rights under the Equal Protection Clause. Although Tennessee law allocated legislative representation among its counties according to the total number of qualified voters who resided in each county, the state legislature had not reapportioned— that is, redrawn legislative district lines—in over 60 years. The plaintiffs, who lived in areas of the state that had experienced significant growth in population, claimed that the state's failure to reapportion had, in light of these substantial demographic changes, result- ed in the "debasement of their votes." They sought an injunction requiring either "reap- portionment by mathematical application of the Tennessee constitutional formulae to the most recent Federal Census figures" or elections conducted at large. The district court held that the suit presented a "political question" and was therefore nonjusticiable.]

We hold that this challenge to an apportionment presents no nonjusticiable "politi- cal question." Of course the mere fact that the suit seeks protection of a political right does not mean it presents a political question.
*** Rather, it is argued that apportionment cases *** can involve no federal constitutional right except one resting on the guaranty of a republican form of government[, Art. IV., § 4,] and that complaints based on that clause have been held to present political questions which are nonjusticiable. [B]ecause there appears to be some uncertainty as to why those cases did present political questions, and specifically as to whether this apportionment case is like those cases, we deem it necessary first to consider the contours of the "political question" doctrine.

> **FYI**
>
> Article IV, § 4 provides in relevant part: "The United States shall guar- antee to every State in this Union a Republican Form of Government ***." What is a "Republican" form of government? If it means govern- ment by representatives selected by the people, isn't this provision argu- ably violated by a representative sys- tem in which some voters' votes are worth substantially less than others'?

Our discussion *** requires review of a number of political question cases, in order to expose the attributes of the doctrine—attributes which, in various settings, diverge, combine, appear, and disappear in seeming disorderliness. *** That review reveals that *** it is the relationship between the judiciary and the coordinate branches of the Federal Government, and not the federal judiciary's relationship to the States, which gives rise to the "political question."

Deciding whether a matter has in any measure been committed by the Constitution to another branch of government, or whether the action of that branch exceeds whatever authority has been committed, is itself a delicate exercise in constitutional interpretation, and is a responsibility of this Court as ultimate interpreter of the Constitution. [It] is apparent [from our cases] that several formulations which vary slightly according to the settings in which the questions arise may describe a political question, although each has one or more elements which identify it as essentially a function of the separation of powers. Prominent on the surface of any case held to involve a political question is found a textually demonstrable constitutional commitment of the issue to a coordinate political department; or a lack of judicially discoverable and manageable standards for resolving it; or the impossibility of deciding without an initial policy determination of a kind clearly for nonjudicial discretion; or the impossibility of a court's undertaking independent resolution without expressing lack of the respect due coordinate branches of government; or an unusual need for unquestioning adherence to a political decision already made; or the potentiality of embarrassment from multifarious pronouncements by various departments on one question. *** The cases we have reviewed show the necessity for discriminating inquiry into the precise facts and posture of the particular case, and the impossibility of resolution by any semantic cataloguing.

But it is argued that this case shares the characteristics of *** cases concerning the Constitution's guaranty *** of a republican form of government. [Our review demonstrates] that Guaranty Clause claims involve those elements which define a "political question," and for that reason and no other, they are nonjusticiable. In particular, [the] nonjusticiability of such claims has nothing to do with their touching upon matters of state governmental organization. [Instead, the Court has found that] the Guaranty Clause is not a repository of judicially manageable standards *** for invalidating state action.

We come, finally, to the ultimate inquiry[:] whether our precedents as to what constitutes a nonjusticiable "political question" bring the case before us under the umbrella of that doctrine. A natural beginning is to note whether any of the common characteristics which we have been able to identify and label descriptively are present. We find none: The question here is the consistency of state action with the Federal Constitution. We have no question decided, or to be decided, by a political branch of government coequal with this Court. Nor do we risk embarrassment of our government abroad, or grave disturbance at home if we take issue with Tennessee as to the constitutionality of her action here challenged. Nor need the appellants, in order to succeed in this action, ask the Court to enter upon policy determinations for which judicially manageable standards are lacking. Judicial standards under the Equal Protection Clause are well developed and familiar, and it has been open to courts since the enactment of the Fourteenth Amendment to determine, if on the particular facts they must, that a discrimination reflects no policy, but simply arbitrary and capricious action. This case does, in one sense, involve the allocation of political power within a State, and the appellants might conceivably have added a claim under the Guaranty Clause. Of course, as we have seen, any reliance on that clause would be futile. But because any reliance on the Guaranty Clause could not have succeeded it does not follow that appellants may not be heard on the equal protection claim which in fact they tender.   True, it must be clear that the Fourteenth Amendment claim is not so enmeshed with those political question elements which render Guaranty Clause claims nonjusticiable as actually to present a political question itself.   But we have found that not to be the case here.   *** The right asserted is within the reach of judicial protection under the Fourteenth Amendment.

Mr. Justice FRANKFURTER, whom Mr. Justice HARLAN joins, dissenting.

[The] Court's authority—possessed of neither the purse nor the sword—ultimately rests on sustained public confidence in its moral sanction.   Such feeling must be nourished by the Court's complete detachment, in fact and in appearance, from political entanglements and by abstention from injecting itself into the clash of political forces in political settlements.   *** Even assuming the indispensable intellectual disinterestedness on the part of judges in such matters, they do not have accepted legal standards or criteria or even reliable analogies to draw upon for making judicial judgments.   To charge courts with the task of accommodating the incommensurable factors of policy that underlie these mathematical puzzles is to attribute, however flatteringly, omnicompetence to judges.

The present case involves all of the elements that have made the Guarantee Clause cases non-justiciable.   It is, in effect, a Guarantee Clause claim masquerading under a different label.   But it cannot make the case more fit for judicial action that appellants invoke the Fourteenth Amendment rather than Art. IV, § 4, where, in fact, the gist of their complaint is the same—unless it can be found that the Fourteenth Amendment speaks with greater particularity to their situation.

Appellants invoke the right to vote and to have their votes counted.   But ***[t]alk of "debasement" or "dilution" is circular talk.   One cannot speak of "debasement" or "dilution" of the value of a vote until there is first defined a standard of reference as to what a vote should be worth.   What is actually asked of the Court in this case is to choose among competing bases of representation—ultimately, really, among competing theories of political philosophy—in order to establish an appropriate frame of government for the State of Tennessee and thereby for all the States of the Union.

Apportionment, by its character, is a subject of extraordinary complexity, involving— even after the fundamental theoretical issues concerning what is to be represented in a representative legislature have been fought out or compromised—considerations of geography, demography, electoral convenience, economic and social cohesions or divergences among particular local groups, communications, the practical effects of political institutions like the lobby and the city machine, ancient traditions and ties of settled usage, respect for proven incumbents of long experience and senior status, mathematical mechanics, censuses compiling relevant data, and a host of others.   Legislative responses throughout the country to the reapportionment demands of the 1960 Census have glaringly confirmed that these are not factors that lend themselves to evaluations of a nature that are the staple of judicial determinations or for which judges are equipped to adjudicate by legal training or experience or native wit. And this is the more so true because in every strand of this complicated, intricate web of values meet the contending forces of partisan politics.   The practical significance of apportionment is that the next election results may differ because of it. Apportionment battles are overwhelmingly party or intra-party contests. It will add a virulent source of friction and tension in federal-state relations to embroil the federal judiciary in them.

Points for Discussion

a. Factors for Determining When a Question is a Political Question

The Court in *Baker* offered a list of factors to consider in deciding whether a case presents a political question. Which of these factors did Justice Frankfurter, in dissent, believe required the Court to decline to resolve the plaintiffs' claims?

b. Applying the Factors

The Court held that because judicial standards under the Equal Protection Clause of the Fourteenth Amendment were "well developed and familiar," there were judicially manageable standards to govern the resolution of plaintiffs' apportionment claims. What were those judicially manageable standards? If they were well developed and familiar, why didn't the Court identify them in its opinion?

> **Make the Connection**
>
> We will consider the right to vote, and standards for apportionment claims that the Court subsequently announced in *Reynolds v. Sims*, 377 U.S. 533 (1964), in Chapter 12.

Is it likely that the Court will encounter difficulty in applying the *Baker* factors? Consider *Powell v. McCormack*, 395 U.S. 486 (1969), which involved a claim by Congressman Adam Clayton Powell that the House of Representatives had improperly refused to seat him after he was elected. After a House committee determined that Powell had presented false travel vouchers in seeking reimbursement for official travel and that he had used government funds to make illegal payments to his wife, the full House refused to seat Powell. The defendants urged the Court to dismiss the suit under the political question doctrine, arguing that Article I, § 5, which provides that each House of Congress "shall be the Judge of the Qualifications of its Members," was a textual commitment to the House of the power to decide whether a Member was ethically qualified to sit in the House. The Court rejected the defendants' claims and found the question justiciable. The Court noted that Article I, § 2, cl. 1 lists the "qualifications"—age, citizenship, and residence—to which section 5 refers, and that Powell had plainly satisfied them. The Court concluded that Article I, § 5 was at most a "textually demonstrable commitment to Congress to judge only the qualifications expressly set forth" in Article I, §2, cl. 1.

If the defendants were correct that Article I, § 5 was a textual commitment to the House to decide on a Member's qualifications, would it have meant that the Court could not decide a claim that the House had refused to seat Powell, who was 59 years old at the time, on the ground that he did not meet the Constitution's age requirements for Members of the House? If the House had refused to seat him because of his race? Does Article I, § 5, cl. 2, which provides that "Each House may ***, with the Concurrence of two thirds, expel a Member," shed any light on defendants' position in *Powell*? (Although a majority of the House voted to refuse to seat Powell, the vote fell short of the two-thirds required for expulsion.)

Nixon v. United States

506 U.S. 224 (1993)

Chief Justice REHNQUIST delivered the opinion of the Court.

Petitioner Walter L. Nixon, Jr., asks this Court to decide whether Senate Rule XI, which allows a committee of Senators to hear evidence against an individual who has been impeached and to report that evidence to the full Senate, violates the Impeachment Trial Clause, Art. I, § 3, cl. 6. That Clause provides that the "Senate shall have the sole Power to try all Impeachments." But before we reach the merits of such a claim, we must decide whether it is "justiciable," that is, whether it is a claim that may be resolved by the courts. We conclude that it is not.

Nixon, a former Chief Judge of the United States District Court for the Southern District of Mississippi, was convicted by a jury of two counts of making false statements before a federal grand jury and sentenced to prison. The grand jury investigation stemmed from reports that Nixon had accepted a gratuity from a Mississippi businessman in exchange for asking a local district attorney to halt the prosecution of the businessman's son. Because Nixon refused to resign from his office as a United States District Judge, he continued to collect his judicial salary while serving out his prison sentence. On May 10, 1989, the House of Representatives adopted three articles of impeachment for high crimes and misdemeanors. The first two articles charged Nixon with giving false testimony before the grand jury and the third article charged him with bringing disrepute on the Federal Judiciary.

After the House presented the articles to the Senate, the Senate voted to invoke its own

> **Food for Thought**
>
> Judge Nixon was impeached in part for "bringing disrepute on the Federal Judiciary." Is this a valid ground for impeachment? Does the language of Article II, § 4—which provides that "The President, Vice President and all civil Officers of the United States, shall be removed from Office on Impeachment for, and Conviction of, Treason, Bribery, or other high Crimes and Misdemeanors"—shed any light on that question? Is the validity of a decision by the House to impeach itself a political question? Consider that in 1970, when Congressman Gerald Ford proposed the impeachment of Justice William Douglas for his liberal views, Ford argued that "an impeachable offense is whatever a majority of the House of Representatives considers [it] to be." 116 Cong. Rec. 11913 (1970). Can a judge be impeached for making decisions with which Members of Congress disagree?

Impeachment Rule XI, under which the presiding officer appoints a committee of Senators to "receive evidence and take testimony." The Senate committee held four days of hearings, during which 10 witnesses, including Nixon, testified. Pursuant to Rule XI, the committee presented the full Senate with a complete transcript of the proceeding and a Report stating the uncontested facts and summarizing the evidence on the contested facts. Nixon and the House impeachment managers submitted extensive final briefs to the full Senate and delivered arguments from the Senate floor during the three hours set aside for oral argument in front of that body. Nixon himself gave a personal appeal, and several Senators posed questions directly to both parties. The Senate voted by more than the constitutionally required two-thirds majority to convict Nixon on the first two articles. The presiding officer then entered judgment removing Nixon from his office as United States District Judge.

Nixon thereafter commenced the present suit, arguing that Senate Rule XI violates the constitutional grant of authority to the Senate to "try" all impeachments because it prohibits the whole Senate from taking part in the evidentiary hearings. Nixon sought a declaratory judgment that his impeachment conviction was void and that his judicial salary and privileges should be reinstated.

A controversy is nonjusticiable—*i.e.,* involves a political question—where there is "a textually demonstrable constitutional commitment of the issue to a coordinate political department; or a lack of judicially discoverable and manageable standards for resolving it." *Baker v. Carr*. But the courts must, in the first instance, interpret the text in question and determine whether and to what extent the issue is textually committed. [T]he concept of a textual commitment to a coordinate political department is not completely separate from the concept of a lack of judicially discoverable and manageable standards for resolving it; the lack of judicially manageable standards may strengthen the conclusion that there is a textually demonstrable commitment to a coordinate branch.

Petitioner argues that the word "try" in the first sentence [of Art. I, § 3, cl. 6] imposes by implication [a] requirement on the Senate in that the proceedings must be in the nature of a judicial trial. From there petitioner goes on to argue that this limitation precludes the Senate from delegating to a select committee the task of hearing the testimony of witnesses ***. Petitioner concludes from this that courts may review whether or not the Senate "tried" him before convicting him.

There are several difficulties with this position ***. The word "try," both in 1787 and later, has considerably broader meanings than those to which petitioner would limit it. *** Based on the variety of definitions, [we] cannot say that the Framers used the word "try" as an implied limitation on the method by which the Senate might proceed in trying impeachments. *** The conclusion that the use of the word "try" in the first sentence of the Impeachment Trial Clause lacks sufficient precision to afford any judicially manageable standard of review of the Senate's actions is fortified by the existence of the three very specific requirements that the Constitution does impose on the Senate when trying impeachments: The Members must be under oath, a two-thirds vote is required to convict, and the Chief Justice presides when the President is tried. These limitations are quite precise, and their nature suggests that the Framers did not intend to impose additional limitations on the form of the Senate proceedings by the use of the word "try" in the first sentence.

Petitioner devotes only two pages in his brief to negating the significance of the word "sole" in the first sentence of Clause 6. *** We think that the word "sole" is of considerable significance. Indeed, the word "sole" appears only one other time in the Constitution—with respect to the House of Representatives' "sole Power of Impeachment." Art. I, § 2, cl. 5 The commonsense meaning of the word "sole" is that the Senate alone shall have authority to determine whether an individual should be acquitted or convicted. *** Petitioner [argues] that even if significance be attributed to the word "sole" in the first sentence of the Clause, the authority granted is to the Senate, and this means that "the Senate—not the courts, not a lay jury, not a Senate Committee—shall try impeachments." It would be possible to read the first sentence of the Clause this way, but it is not a natural reading. Petitioner's interpretation would bring into judicial purview not merely the sort of claim made by petitioner, but other similar claims based on the conclusion that the word "Senate" has imposed by implication limitations on procedures which the Senate might adopt. Such limitations would be inconsistent with the construction of the Clause as a whole, which, as we have noted, sets out three express limitations in separate sentences.

The history and contemporary understanding of the impeachment provisions support our reading of the constitutional language. *** Despite [proposals to place the power of impeachment with the federal judiciary], the Convention ultimately decided that the Senate would have "the sole Power to try all Impeachments." The Supreme Court was not the proper body because the Framers [doubted whether the Court] "would possess the degree of credit and authority" to carry out its judgment if it conflicted with the accusation brought by the Legislature—the people's representative. [In addition,] judicial review would be inconsistent with the Framers' insistence that our system be one of checks and balances. In our constitutional system, impeachment was designed to be the *only* check on the Judicial Branch by the Legislature. *** Nixon's argument would place final reviewing authority with respect to impeachments in the hands of the same body that the impeachment process is meant to regulate.

Nevertheless, Nixon argues that judicial review is necessary in order to place a check on the Legislature. *** The Framers anticipated this objection and created two constitutional safeguards to keep the Senate in check. The first safeguard is that the whole of the impeachment power is divided between the two legislative bodies, with the House given the right to accuse and the Senate given the right to judge. *** The second safeguard is the two-thirds supermajority vote requirement.

In addition to the textual commitment argument, we are persuaded that the lack of finality and the difficulty of fashioning relief counsel against justiciability. *** This lack of finality would manifest itself most dramatically if the President were impeached. The legitimacy of any successor, and hence his effectiveness, would be impaired severely, not merely while the judicial process was running its course, but during any retrial that a differently constituted Senate might conduct if its first judgment of conviction were invalidated. Equally uncertain is the question of what relief a court may give other than simply setting aside the judgment of conviction. Could it order the reinstatement of a convicted federal judge, or order Congress to create an additional judgeship if the seat had been filled in the interim?

[W]e conclude *** that the word "try" in the Impeachment Trial Clause does not provide an identifiable textual limit on the authority which is committed to the Senate.

Justice STEVENS, concurring.

For me, the debate about the strength of the inferences to be drawn from the use of the words "sole" and "try" is far less significant than the central fact that the Framers decided to assign the impeachment power to the Legislative Branch. The disposition of the impeachment of Samuel Chase in 1805 demonstrated that the Senate is fully conscious of the profound importance of that assignment, and nothing in the subsequent history of the Senate's exercise of this extraordinary power suggests otherwise.

> **FYI**
>
> Justice Chase, a Federalist appointed to the Court by President Washington, was impeached by the House of Representatives for demonstrating political bias on the bench. Although the Senate was controlled by Jeffersonian Republicans, the Senate acquitted Chase of all charges, and he served on the Court until his death.

Respect for a coordinate branch of the Government forecloses any assumption that improbable hypotheticals like those mentioned by *** Justice SOUTER will ever occur. Accordingly, the wise policy of judicial restraint, coupled with the potential anomalies associated with a contrary view, provide a sufficient justification for my agreement with the [Court].

Justice WHITE, with whom Justice BLACKMUN joins, concurring in the judgment.

The Court is of the view that the Constitution forbids us even to consider [Nixon's] contention. I find no such prohibition and would therefore reach the merits of the claim. I concur in the judgment because the Senate fulfilled its constitutional obligation to "try" petitioner.

[The] issue in the political question doctrine is *not* whether the constitutional text commits exclusive responsibility for a particular governmental function to one of the political branches. There are numerous instances of this sort of textual commitment, *e.g.*, Art. I, § 8, and it is not thought that disputes implicating these provisions are nonjusticiable. Rather, the issue is whether the Constitution has given one of the political branches final responsibility for interpreting the scope and nature of such a power.

The significance of the Constitution's use of the term "sole" lies not in the infrequency with which the term appears, but in the fact that it appears exactly twice, in parallel provisions concerning impeachment. That the word "sole" is found only in the House and Senate Impeachment Clauses demonstrates that its purpose is to emphasize the distinct role of each in the impeachment process. *** While the majority is thus right to interpret the term "sole" to indicate that the Senate ought to "function independently and without assistance or interference," it wrongly identifies the Judiciary, rather than the House, as the source of potential interference with which the Framers were concerned when they employed the term "sole."

In essence, the majority suggests that the Framers conferred upon Congress a potential tool of legislative dominance yet at the same time rendered Congress' exercise of that power one of the very few areas of legislative authority immune from any judicial review. *** In a truly balanced system, impeachments tried by the Senate would serve as a means of controlling the largely unaccountable Judiciary, even as judicial review would ensure that the Senate adhered to a minimal set of procedural standards in conducting impeachment trials.

The majority also contends that the term "try" does not present a judicially manageable standard. [T]he term "try" is hardly so elusive as the majority would have it. Were the Senate, for example, to adopt the practice of automatically entering a judgment of conviction whenever articles of impeachment were delivered from the House, it is quite clear that the Senate will have failed to "try" impeachments. Indeed in this respect, "try" presents no greater, and perhaps fewer, interpretive difficulties than some other constitutional standards that have been found amenable to familiar techniques of judicial construction, including, for example, "Commerce [among] the several States" and "due process of law." The majority's conclusion that "try" is incapable of meaningful judicial construction is not without irony. One might think that if any class of concepts would fall within the definitional abilities of the Judiciary, it would be that class having to do with procedural justice.

[T]extual and historical evidence reveals that the Impeachment Trial Clause was not meant to bind the hands of the Senate beyond establishing a set of minimal procedures. Without identifying the exact contours of these procedures, it is sufficient to say that the Senate's use of a factfinding committee under Rule XI is entirely compatible with the Constitution's command that the Senate "try all impeachments." Petitioner's challenge to his conviction must therefore fail.

Justice SOUTER, concurring in the judgment.

I agree with the Court that this case presents a nonjusticiable political question. Because my analysis differs somewhat from the Court's, however, I concur in its judgment by this separate opinion. [T]he political question doctrine is "essentially a function of the separation of powers," existing to restrain courts "from inappropriate interference in the business of the other branches of Government," and deriving in large part from prudential concerns about the respect we owe the political departments. Not all interference is inappropriate or disrespectful, however, and application of the doctrine ultimately turns, as Learned Hand put it, on "how importunately the occasion demands an answer."

This occasion does not demand an answer. *** It seems fair to conclude that the [Impeachment Trial] Clause contemplates that the Senate may determine, within broad boundaries, such subsidiary issues as the procedures for receipt and consideration of evidence necessary to satisfy its duty to "try" impeachments. Other significant considerations confirm a conclusion that this case presents a nonjusticiable political question: the "unusual need for unquestioning adherence to a political decision already made," as well as "the potentiality of embarrassment from multifarious pronouncements by various departments on one question." *Baker*. As the Court observes, judicial review of an impeachment trial would under the best of circumstances entail significant disruption of government.

One can, nevertheless, envision different and unusual circumstances that might justify a more searching review of impeachment proceedings. If the Senate were to act in a manner seriously threatening the integrity of its results, convicting, say, upon a coin toss, or upon a summary determination that an officer of the United States was simply "a bad guy," judicial interference might well be appropriate. In such circumstances, the Senate's action might be so far beyond the scope of its constitutional authority, and the consequent impact on the Republic so great, as to merit a judicial response despite the prudential concerns that would ordinarily counsel silence.

Points for Discussion

a. Textual Commitment

What is the meaning of Article I, § 3, cl. 6's conferral on the Senate of the "sole Power to try all Impeachments"? If Congress had explicitly been granted the "sole Power" to regulate commerce among the states—a topic we will take up in Chapters 3 and 4—would a claim that Congress had exceeded its power to regulate interstate commerce be a nonjusticiable political question?

b. Judicially Manageable Standards

Should the Court have been able to develop judicially manageable standards to apply the constitutional requirement that the Senate "try" all impeachments? Does that term provide less guidance than other constitutional provisions that the Court has concluded are justiciable? Is "try" more ambiguous and amorphous than, say, "due process," "equal protection," "cruel and unusual," or "freedom of speech"?

c. The Political Question Factors

Dean Erwin Chemerinsky, a prominent constitutional scholar, argues that the factors listed in *Baker v. Carr* "seem useless" for determining whether an issue is a political question. He explains: "[T]here is no place in the Constitution where the text states that the legislature or executive should decide whether a particular action constitutes a constitutional violation. The Constitution does not mention judicial review, much less limit it by creating 'textually demonstrable commitments' to other branches of government. Similarly, most important constitutional provisions are written in broad, open-textured language and certainly do not include 'judicially discoverable and manageable standards.' *** As such, it hardly is surprising that the doctrine is described as confusing and unsatisfactory." Erwin Chemerinsky, Constitutional Law: Principles and Policies 131 (3d ed. 2006). Is this criticism valid? If so, how should the courts determine what is a political question? Or should the courts simply decide that no issues are political questions?

---

2. The Requirement of "Case" or "Controversy"

Article III, § 2 specifies the jurisdiction of the federal courts. In reading this provision, notice two things. First, the provision gives federal courts jurisdiction over various kinds of "cases" and "controversies." Second, the provision does not give federal courts jurisdiction over anything other than "cases" and "controversies."

U.S. Constitution, Article III, Section 2

Clause 1. The judicial Power shall extend to all Cases, in Law and Equity, arising under this Constitution, the Laws of the United States, and Treaties made, or which shall be made, under their Authority;—to all Cases affecting Ambassadors, other public Ministers and Consuls;—to all Cases of admiralty and maritime Jurisdiction;—to Controversies to which the United States shall be a Party;—to Controversies between two or more States;— between a State and Citizens of another State;—between Citizens of different States;—between Citizens of the same State claiming Lands under Grants of different States, and between a State, or the Citizens thereof, and foreign States, Citizens or Subjects.

Clause 2. In all Cases affecting Ambassadors, other public Ministers and Consuls, and those in which a State shall be Party, the supreme Court shall have original Jurisdiction. In all the other Cases before mentioned, the supreme Court shall have appellate Jurisdiction, both as to Law and Fact, with such Exceptions, and under such Regulations as the Congress shall make.

On the basis of these two points, as the following case will show, the Supreme Court has concluded that the federal courts may decide only cases and controversies. But those terms are not easily defined.

Muskrat v. United States

219 U.S. 346 (1911)

DAY, J. delivered the opinion of the court:

[In 1902, Congress enacted legislation that reserved specific property for some Cherokee Indians. In 1904 and 1906, Congress enacted legislation that increased the number of persons who had claims to the same property. The property interests of persons whose claims derived from the 1902 statute accordingly were diminished by the 1904 and 1906 legislation. In 1907, Congress enacted a statute that authorized a discrete class of persons who had interests in the land pursuant to the original 1902 law to "institute their suits in the court of claims to determine the validity of any acts of Congress passed since [the] act of [1902]." The Act conferred jurisdiction "upon the court of claims, with the right of appeal, by either party, to the Supreme Court of the United States, to hear, determine, and adjudicate each of said suits." The 1907 Act further provided that "[t]he suits brought hereunder shall be brought *** against the United States as a party defendant, and, for the speedy disposition of the questions involved, preference shall be given to the same by said courts, and by the Attorney General, who is hereby charged with the defense of said suits." The plaintiffs filed suit pursuant to the 1907 Act.]

The first question in these cases, as in others, involves the jurisdiction of the court to entertain the proceeding, and that depends upon whether the jurisdiction conferred is within the power of Congress, having in view the limitations of the judicial power, as established by [Article III of] the Constitution of the United States.

It will serve to elucidate the nature and extent of the judicial power thus conferred by the Constitution to note certain instances in which this court has had occasion to examine and define the same. *** In 1793, by direction of the President, Secretary of State Jefferson addressed to the justices of the Supreme Court a communication soliciting their views upon the question whether their advice to the Executive would be available in the solution of important questions of the construction of treaties, laws of nations and laws of the land, which the Secretary said were often presented under circumstances which "do not give a cognizance of them to the tribunals of the country." [Chief] Justice Jay and his associates answered to President Washington that, in consideration of the lines of separation drawn by the Constitution between the three departments of government, and being judges of a court of last resort, afforded strong arguments against the propriety of extrajudicially deciding the questions alluded to, and expressing the view that the power given by the Constitution to the President, of calling on heads of departments for opinions, "seems to have been purposely, as well as expressly, united to the executive departments."

> **Food for Thought**
>
> Should the Justices even have answered Jefferson's request? After all, in answering, didn't they essentially create law—about the propriety of advisory opinions—even though there was no justiciable case or controversy presented to them? Is it proper to cite the decision as precedent?

"Judicial power *** is the power of a court to decide and pronounce a judgment and carry it into effect between persons and parties who bring a case before it for decision." [By] the express terms of the Constitution, the exercise of the judicial power is limited to "cases" and "controversies." Beyond this it does not extend, and unless it is asserted in a case or controversy within the meaning of the Constitution, the power to exercise it is nowhere conferred. A "case" was defined by Mr. Chief Justice Marshall as early as the leading case of *Marbury v. Madison* to be a suit instituted according to the regular course of judicial procedure. *** "The term 'controversies,' if distinguishable at all from 'cases,' is so in that it is less comprehensive than the latter, and includes only suits of a civil nature." *** The term [case] implies the existence of present or possible adverse parties, whose contentions are submitted to the court for adjudication.

[T]he object and purpose of [this] suit is wholly comprised in the determination of the constitutional validity of certain acts of Congress ***. Is such a determination within the judicial power conferred by the Constitution, as the same has been interpreted and defined in the authoritative decisions to which we have referred? We think it is not. That judicial power *** is the right to determine actual controversies arising between adverse litigants, duly instituted in courts of proper jurisdiction. The right to declare a law unconstitutional arises because an act of Congress relied upon by one or the other of such parties in determining their rights is in conflict with the fundamental law. The exercise of this, the most important and delicate duty of this court, is not given to it as a body with revisory power over the action of Congress, but because the rights of the litigants in justiciable controversies require the court to choose between the fundamental law and a law purporting to be enacted within constitutional authority, but in fact beyond the power delegated to the legislative branch of the government.

This attempt to obtain a judicial declaration of the validity of the act of Congress is not presented in a "case" or "controversy," to which, under the Constitution of the United States, the judicial power alone extends. It is true the United States is made a defendant to this action, but it has no interest adverse to the claimants. The object is not to assert a property right as against the government, or to demand compensation for alleged wrongs because of action upon its part. The whole purpose of the law is to determine the constitutional validity of this class of legislation, in a suit not arising between parties concerning a property right necessarily involved in the decision in question, but in a proceeding against the government in its sovereign capacity, and concerning which the only judgment required is to settle the doubtful character of the legislation in question. [W]e think the Congress, in the act of March 1, 1907,

> **Take Note**
>
> What does the Court mean by an "adverse" interest? Doesn't the United States have an interest in defending the constitutionality of its laws? Indeed, doesn't the Executive Branch have a duty to defend Acts of Congress when they are challenged? See Article II, § 3 (stating that the President "shall take Care that the Laws be faithfully executed ***").

exceeded the limitations of legislative authority, so far as it required of this court action not judicial in its nature within the meaning of the Constitution.

The questions involved in this proceeding as to the validity of the legislation may arise in suits between individuals, and when they do and are properly brought before this court for consideration they, of course, must be determined in the exercise of its judicial functions.

———————

Points for Discussion

a. The Ban on Advisory Opinions

Since the Court's refusal in 1793 to answer Secretary of State Jefferson's legal query about the United States' legal obligations to Britain and France during the war between those two nations, the Court has declined to provide "advisory opinions"—that is, opinions about the proper resolution of abstract legal questions that are presented in a setting divorced from an actual dispute between adverse parties. What is the rationale for the ban on advisory opinions? Does this ban come at a cost?

Note that the "case or controversy" requirement of Article III does not apply to state courts. Some state courts, like the Massachusetts Supreme Judicial Court, do issue advisory opinions—even on questions of federal constitutional law. See, e.g., *Opinion of the Justices to the Governor,* 298 N.E.2d 840 (Mass. 1973) (advisory opinion that proposed legislation to restrict busing of children to desegregate schools would violate the Constitution).

b. The Claims in *Muskrat*

The plaintiffs in *Muskrat* asserted that their interests in Cherokee lands had been adversely affected by the statutes that they challenged. Even assuming a ban on advisory opinions, why weren't those claims justiciable? Is it because the United States, the defendant in their suits, had no interest adverse to the plaintiffs' interests? If suits against the United States were not proper, how could the plaintiffs have obtained a resolution of their claims about the validity of the enlargement of the class of persons entitled to the Cherokee lands?

c. Declaratory Judgment Actions

The Declaratory Judgment Act, 28 U.S.C. § 2201, authorizes federal courts to "declare the rights and other legal relations of any interested party seeking such declaration, whether or not further relief is or could be sought." Are declaratory judgment actions consistent with the case and controversy requirement as applied in *Muskrat*? The Court has upheld the Act, holding that federal courts may issue declaratory judgments as long as there is an actual dispute between adverse litigants. See *Aetna Life Insu. Co. v. Haworth,* 300 U.S. 227 (1937).

d. Ripeness and Mootness

An action filed in federal court not only must have the proper hallmarks of adversity, but also must be filed and litigated at a time that ensures that the case or controversy between the parties is sufficiently live. First, the federal courts will not consider cases that are not yet "ripe"—that is, that have not yet developed into actual controversies. If the head of a federal agency announces at a press conference that the agency is merely considering proposing a rule to establish fuel-efficiency standards for automobiles, for example, a suit filed that day by car manufacturers challenging the agency's action likely will be dismissed because the agency has not yet acted and thus the plaintiffs have not yet been harmed. When the injury asserted by the plaintiffs is wholly speculative, the claim likely will be dismissed under the ripeness doctrine. See, e.g., *O'Shea v. Littleton,* 414 U.S. 488 (1974).

Second, the federal courts generally will not consider claims that are "moot"—that is, claims in which the parties no longer have any meaningful and concrete stake. For example, a suit by a person detained by the government seeking to force the government to release him likely will be rendered moot upon his release. The plaintiff's desire to learn whether his prior detention was lawful is not alone sufficient to give the plaintiff a concrete stake in the outcome of the suit, because the relief that he seeks has already been granted. (If, on the other hand, the plaintiff seeks damages for the prior unlawful detention, his suit likely would not be moot.) See, e.g., *United States Parole Comm'n v. Geraghty*, 445 U.S. 388, 397 (1980) (explaining that the "requisite personal interest *** must continue throughout" the litigation's existence).

In other words, suits filed too early—and thus lacking the requisite ripeness—and suits resolved too late—and thus lacking the requisite concrete stake in the relief sought—are generally not justiciable in federal court. Ripeness and mootness doctrines are both intended to effectuate the case and controversy requirement. See *Abbott Laboratories v. Gardner*, 387 U.S. 136 (1967) (stating that the basic rationale of ripeness doctrine is "to prevent the courts, through avoidance of premature adjudication, from entangling themselves in abstract disagreements"); *Hall v. Beals*, 396 U.S. 45 (1969) (explaining that mootness doctrine effectuates the ban on advisory opinions).

For More Information

For a detailed discussion of the interests served by the case or controversy requirement, see Lea Brilmayer, *The Jurisprudence of Article III: Perspectives on the "Case or Controversy" Requirement*, 93 Harv. L. Rev. 297 (1979); Mark Tushnet, *The Sociology of Article III: A Response to Professor Brilmayer*, 93 Harv. L. Rev. 1698 (1980).

3. Standing

Ordinary principles of contract law dictate that broken promises are not enforceable by just anyone who wants to bring a lawsuit. On the contrary, usually only the party to whom the promise was made, an assignee of the benefit of the promise, or an intended third-party beneficiary may enforce it. Accordingly, some broken promises may go unenforced because no proper plaintiff brings a lawsuit.

The Supreme Court has said that something very similar is true in constitutional law: only litigants who have "standing" may enforce constitutional provisions. According to the Court, a plaintiff must satisfy three requirements:

> (1) [I]njury in fact, by which we mean an invasion of a legally protected interest that is (a) concrete and particularized, and (b) actual or imminent, not conjectural or hypothetical; (2) a causal relationship between the injury and the challenged conduct, by which we mean that the injury fairly can be traced to the challenged action of the defendant, and has not resulted from the independent action of some third party not before the court; and (3) a likelihood that the injury will be redressed by a favorable decision, by which we mean that the prospect of obtaining relief from the injury as a result of a favorable ruling is not too speculative. These elements are the irreducible minimum, required by the Constitution.

Northeastern Florida Chapter of Associated General Contractors v. City of Jacksonville, 508 U.S.

656, 663-664 (1993) (internal quotation marks and citations omitted).

In reading the following cases, consider whether these requirements are met, how insisting on these factors affects the availability of judicial review, and what justifications the Supreme Court might have for requiring standing.

Allen v. Wright

468 U.S. 737 (1984)

Justice O'CONNOR delivered the opinion of the Court.

Parents of black public school children allege in this nation-wide class action that the Internal Revenue Service (IRS) has not adopted sufficient standards and procedures to fulfill its obligation to deny tax-exempt status to racially discriminatory private schools. *** The issue before us is whether plaintiffs have standing to bring this suit. We hold that they do not.

The IRS denies tax-exempt [status] to racially discriminatory private schools. *** To carry out this policy, the IRS has established guidelines and procedures for determining whether a particular school is in fact racially nondiscriminatory. *** In 1976 respondents challenged these guidelines and procedures in a suit [in federal court]. The plaintiffs named in the complaint are parents of black children who, at the time the complaint was filed, were attending public schools in seven States in school districts undergoing desegregation.

> **FYI**
>
> There are two related benefits to tax-exempt status under the tax code. First, the tax-exempt institution does not have to pay taxes on income. Second, contributions to the tax-exempt institution are deductible by the persons making the contribution—which means that persons are more likely to make such contributions (because they are relatively cheaper) and thus that the tax-exempt organization is more likely to receive charitable contributions.

Respondents allege in their complaint that many racially segregated private schools *** receive tax exemptions, [and that] some of the tax-exempt racially segregated private schools created or expanded in desegregating districts in fact have racially discriminatory policies. Respondents allege that the IRS grant of tax exemptions to such racially discriminatory schools is unlawful.

Respondents do not allege that their children have been the victims of discriminatory exclusion from the schools whose tax exemptions they challenge as unlawful. Indeed, they have not alleged at any stage of this litigation that their children have ever applied or would ever apply to any private school. Rather, respondents claim a direct injury from the mere fact of the challenged Government conduct and *** injury to their children's opportunity to receive a desegregated education. *** Respondents *** ask for a declaratory judgment that the challenged IRS tax-exemption practices are unlawful [and] an injunction requiring the IRS to deny tax exemptions to a considerably broader class of private schools than the class of racially discriminatory private schools. *** In May 1977 the District Court permitted intervention as a defendant by petitioner Allen, the head of one of the private school systems identified in the complaint.

Take Note

The Court is reviewing the district court's grant of the defendant's motion to dismiss the plaintiffs' complaint. Because the district court resolved this case at the threshold, it did not consider the merits of the plaintiffs' claims. Is it problematic that claims that might have had substantial legal merit will not be resolved on the merits? Must a challenge to a plaintiff's standing be raised at the threshold of a suit?

Article III of the Constitution confines the federal courts to adjudicating actual "cases" and "controversies." *** The several doctrines that have grown up to elaborate that requirement are "founded in concern about the proper—and properly limited—role of the courts in a democratic society." *Warth v. Seldin*, 422 U.S. 490, 498 (1975). The Article III doctrine that requires a litigant to have "standing" to invoke the power of a federal court is perhaps the most important of these doctrines. "In essence the question of standing is whether the litigant is entitled to have the court decide the merits of the dispute or of particular issues." *Warth*. Standing doctrine embraces several judicially self-imposed limits on the exercise of federal jurisdiction, such as the general prohibition on a litigant's raising another person's legal rights, the rule barring adjudication of generalized grievances more appropriately addressed in the representative branches, and the requirement that a plaintiff's complaint fall within the zone of interests protected by the law invoked. The requirement of standing, however, has a core component derived directly from the Constitution. A plaintiff must allege personal injury fairly traceable to the defendant's allegedly unlawful conduct and likely to be redressed by the requested relief.

Like the prudential component, the constitutional component of standing doctrine incorporates concepts concededly not susceptible of precise definition. The injury alleged must be, for example, "distinct and palpable" and not "abstract" or "conjectural" or "hypothetical." The injury must be "fairly" traceable to the challenged action, and relief from the injury must be "likely" to follow from a favorable decision. These terms cannot be defined so as to make application of the constitutional standing requirement a mechanical exercise.

Typically, [the] standing inquiry requires careful judicial examination of a complaint's allegations to ascertain whether the particular plaintiff is entitled to an adjudication of the particular claims asserted. [The question of standing] must be answered by reference to the Art. III notion that federal courts may exercise power only "in the last resort, and as a necessity," and only when adjudication is "consistent with a system of separated powers and [the dispute is one] traditionally thought to be capable of resolution through the judicial process." *Flast v. Cohen*, 392 U.S. 83, 97 (1968).

Respondents allege two injuries in their complaint to support their standing to bring this lawsuit. First, they say that they are harmed directly by the mere fact of Government financial aid to discriminatory private schools. Second, they say that the federal tax exemptions to racially discriminatory private schools in their communities impair their ability to have their public schools desegregated. We conclude that neither suffices to support respondents' standing. The first fails under clear precedents of this Court because it does not constitute judicially cognizable injury. The second fails because the alleged injury is not fairly traceable to the assertedly unlawful conduct of the IRS.[19]

Respondents' first claim of injury can be interpreted in two ways. It might be a claim simply to have the Government avoid the violation of law alleged in respondents' complaint. Alternatively, it might be a claim of stigmatic injury, or denigration, suffered by all members of a racial group when the Government discriminates on the basis of race. Under neither interpretation is this claim of injury judicially cognizable.

This Court has repeatedly held that an asserted right to have the Government act in accordance with law is not sufficient, standing alone, to confer jurisdiction on a federal court. *** "[A]ssertion of a right to a particular kind of Government conduct, which the Government has violated by acting differently, cannot alone satisfy the requirements of Art. III without draining those requirements of meaning." *Valley Forge Christian College v. Americans United for Separation of Church and State, Inc.*, 454 U.S. 464, 483 (1982). Respondents here have no standing to complain simply that their Government is violating the law.

> ### Food for Thought
>
> The Court seems to be suggesting that disputes by persons who simply disagree with the government's choices should be resolved in the political, rather than the judicial, arena. But aren't the plaintiffs in this case contending that the very question that they raise—whether the IRS is properly following the law as mandated by Congress—has already been decided by Congress in the political arena?

Neither do they have standing to litigate their claims based on the stigmatizing injury often caused by racial discrimination. There can be no doubt that this sort of noneconomic injury is one of the most serious consequences of discriminatory government action and is sufficient in some circumstances to support standing. Our cases make clear, however, that such injury accords a basis for standing only to "those persons who are personally denied equal treatment" by the challenged discriminatory conduct.

The consequences of recognizing respondents' standing on the basis of their first claim of injury illustrate why our cases plainly hold that such injury is not judicially cognizable. If the abstract stigmatic injury were cognizable, standing would extend nationwide to all

---

[19] The "fairly traceable" and "redressability" components of the constitutional standing inquiry were initially articulated by this Court as two facets of a single causation requirement. To the extent there is a difference, it is that the former examines the causal connection between the assertedly unlawful conduct and the alleged injury, whereas the latter examines the causal connection between the alleged injury and the judicial relief requested. Cases such as this, in which the relief requested goes well beyond the violation of law alleged, illustrate why it is important to keep the inquiries separate if the "redressability" component is to focus on the requested relief. Even if the relief respondents request might have a substantial effect on the desegregation of public schools, whatever deficiencies exist in the opportunities for desegregated education for respondents' children might not be traceable to IRS violations of law—grants of tax exemptions to racially discriminatory schools in respondents' communities.

members of the particular racial groups against which the Government was alleged to be discriminating by its grant of a tax exemption to a racially discriminatory school, regardless of the location of that school. *** A black person in Hawaii could challenge the grant of a tax exemption to a racially discriminatory school in Maine. Recognition of standing in such circumstances would transform the federal courts into "no more than a vehicle for the vindication of the value interests of concerned bystanders." *United States v. SCRAP*, 412 U.S. 669, 687 (1973). Constitutional limits on the role of the federal courts preclude such a transformation.

It is in their complaint's second claim of injury that respondents allege harm to a concrete, personal interest that can support standing in some circumstances. The injury they identify—their children's diminished ability to receive an education in a racially integrated school—is, beyond any doubt, not only judicially cognizable but *** one of the most serious injuries recognized in our legal system. Despite the constitutional importance of curing the injury alleged by respondents, however, [it] cannot support standing because the injury alleged is not fairly traceable to the Government conduct respondents challenge as unlawful.

The illegal conduct challenged by respondents is the IRS's grant of tax exemptions to some racially discriminatory schools. The line of causation between that conduct and desegregation of respondents' schools is attenuated at best. *** It is, first, uncertain how many racially discriminatory private schools are in fact receiving tax exemptions. Moreover, it is entirely speculative, as respondents themselves conceded in the Court of Appeals, whether withdrawal of a tax exemption from any particular school would lead the school to change its policies. It is just as speculative whether any given parent of a child attending such a private school would decide to transfer the child to public school as a result of any changes in educational or financial policy made by the private school once it was threatened with loss of tax-exempt status. It is also pure speculation whether, in a particular community, a large enough number of the numerous relevant school officials and parents would reach decisions that collectively would have a significant impact on the racial composition of the public schools.

The links in the chain of causation between the challenged Government conduct and the asserted injury are far too weak for the chain as a whole to sustain respondents' standing. *** "Carried to its logical end, [respondents'] approach would have the federal courts as virtually continuing monitors of the wisdom and soundness of Executive action; such a role is appropriate for the Congress acting through its committees and the 'power of the purse'; it is not the role of the judiciary, absent actual present or immediately threatened injury resulting from unlawful governmental action." *Laird v. Tatum*, 408 U.S. 1, 15 (1972). When transported into the Art. III context, that principle, grounded as it is in the idea of separation of powers, counsels against recognizing standing in a case brought, not to enforce specific legal obligations whose violation works a direct harm, but to seek a restructuring of the apparatus established by the Executive Branch to fulfill its legal duties. The Constitution, after all, assigns to the Executive Branch, and not to the Judicial Branch, the duty to "take Care that the Laws be faithfully executed." U.S. Const., Art. II, § 3. We could not recognize respondents' standing in this case without running afoul of that structural principle.

Justice STEVENS, with whom Justice BLACKMUN joins, dissenting.

Respondents, the parents of black school-children, have alleged that their children are unable to attend fully desegregated schools because large numbers of white children in the areas in which respondents reside attend private schools which do not admit minority children. The Court [and I] agree that this is an adequate allegation of "injury in fact." *** This kind of injury may be actionable whether it is caused by the exclusion of black children from public schools or by an official policy of encouraging white children to attend nonpublic schools. A subsidy for the withdrawal of a white child can have the same effect as a penalty for admitting a black child. *** The critical question in these cases, therefore, is whether respondents have alleged that the Government has created that kind of subsidy.

"Both tax exemptions and tax deductibility are a form of subsidy ***. A tax exemption has much the same effect as a cash grant to the organization of the amount of tax it would have to pay on its income. Deductible contributions are similar to cash grants of the amount of a portion of the individual's contributions." *Regan v. Taxation With Representation of Washington*, 461 U.S. 540, 544 (1983). The purpose of this scheme, like the purpose of any subsidy, is to promote the activity subsidized ***. If the granting of preferential tax treatment would "encourage" private segregated schools to conduct their "charitable" activities, it must follow that the withdrawal of the treatment would "discourage" them ***.

This causation analysis is nothing more than a restatement of elementary economics: when something becomes more expensive, less of it will be purchased. [The tax-exemption provisions] are premised on that recognition. If racially discriminatory private schools lose the "cash grants" that flow from the operation of the statutes, the education they provide will become more expensive and hence less of their services will be purchased. Conversely, maintenance of these tax benefits makes an education in segregated private schools relatively more attractive, by decreasing its cost. Accordingly, without tax-exempt status, private schools will either not be competitive in terms of cost, or have to change their admissions policies, hence reducing their competitiveness for parents seeking "a racially segregated alternative" to public schools, which is what respondents have alleged many white parents in desegregating school districts seek. In either event the process of desegregation will be advanced ***. Thus, the laws of economics, not to mention the laws of Congress embodied in [the tax code], compel the conclusion that the injury respondents have alleged—the increased segregation of their children's schools because of the ready availability of private schools that admit whites only—will be redressed if these schools' operations are inhibited through the denial of preferential tax treatment.

The Court could mean one of three things by its invocation of the separation of powers. First, it could simply be expressing the idea that if the plaintiff lacks Art. III standing to bring a lawsuit, then there is no "case or controversy" within the meaning of Art. III and hence the matter is not within the area of responsibility assigned to the Judiciary by the Constitution. *** While there can be no quarrel with this proposition, in itself it provides no guidance for determining if the injury respondents have alleged is fairly traceable to the conduct they have challenged. Second, the Court could be saying that it will require a more direct causal connection when it is troubled by the separation of powers implications of the case before it. That approach confuses the standing doctrine with the justiciability of the issues that respondents seek to raise. The purpose of the standing inquiry is to measure the plaintiff's stake in the outcome, not whether a court has the authority to provide it with the outcome it seeks. Third, the Court could be saying that it will not treat as legally cognizable injuries that stem from an administrative decision concerning how enforcement resources will be allocated. *** However, as the Court also recognizes, this principle does not apply when suit is brought "to enforce specific legal obligations whose violation works a direct harm." *** Here, respondents contend that the IRS is violating a specific constitutional limitation on its enforcement discretion. There is a solid basis for that contention.

Deciding whether the Treasury has violated a specific legal limitation on its enforcement discretion does not intrude upon the prerogatives of the Executive, for in so deciding we are merely saying "what the law is." Surely the question whether the Constitution or the Code limits enforcement discretion is one within the Judiciary's competence ***.

————————

Points for Discussion

a. Why Standing?

What is the objective of enforcing a standing requirement? Is it to ensure that the plaintiff has a sufficient stake in the outcome so that there will be adversity between the parties and thus the issues and arguments will be fully developed in the litigation? If so, is there reason to think that the parents who filed the suit in *Allen* had a sufficient stake in the outcome? Is the objective to enforce separation-of-powers norms by ensuring that courts do not micromanage the decisions of the Executive Branch? If so, is it problematic that a different plaintiff—for example, the headmaster of a private school that does not discriminate on the basis of race but that must compete for students with tax-exempt schools that do—would have standing to assert the identical challenge to the federal regulation that the plaintiffs in *Allen* attempted unsuccessfully to assert? In reaching the merits in such a suit, wouldn't the Court be acting as the monitor of "the wisdom and soundness of Executive action"?

b. Which Plaintiffs?

If the IRS had been aggressive in *denying* tax-exempt status to private schools that discriminate on the basis of race, there is little doubt that the headmaster of such a school would have had standing to challenge, under the principles announced in *Allen*, the legality of the IRS's policy. Cf. *Bob Jones University v. United States*, 461 U.S. 574, 579 (1983). Doesn't this suggest that the Court is more willing to entertain suits challenging *over*-regulation than it is to entertain suits challenging *under*-regulation? If Congress has ordered more aggressive regulation, as the plaintiffs in *Allen* alleged it had done, then why shouldn't the Court enforce that legislative judgment as willingly as it would enforce a legislative decision for the government to do less?

c. Precedent

In *Regents of the University of California v. Bakke,* 438 U.S. 265 (1978), the plaintiff, a white man, challenged an affirmative action plan at the University of California at Davis's medical school. Under that plan, the school "reserved" sixteen places in the entering class of 100 for "disadvantaged minority students." Bakke's application for admission was rejected, even though he had stronger quantitative credentials than some of the students who had been admitted for the "reserved" places. The facts showed, however, that even if there had been no affirmative action plan Bakke would not have been admitted, because there were many more than sixteen other white applicants who had been denied but who had better credentials than did Bakke. The Court concluded that Bakke had standing because he had been denied the opportunity "to compete for all 100 places in the class."

> **Make the Connection**
>
> We will consider the Court's decision in *Bakke,* and the subject of affirmative action, in Chapter 11.

Was the Court's conclusion in *Allen* that the plaintiffs lacked standing consistent with the Court's decision in *Bakke* that the plaintiff had standing? After *Allen,* the Court has continued to follow the *Bakke* approach to standing for plaintiffs challenging government affirmative action programs. See *Northeastern Florida Chapter of Associated General Contractors v. City of Jacksonville,* 508 U.S. 656, 666 (1993).

Perspective and Analysis

The Court's standing doctrine has provoked a significant amount of scholarly attention. Consider the following reaction to the decision in *Allen* by a commentator (and federal judge) closely associated with the law and economics school of legal analysis:

> [I]t is hard to take seriously the claim that enforcement of legal rules does not affect bystanders. The rule against murder is designed to prevent other people from slaying me, as well as others, and I suffer an injury if the police announce that they will no longer enforce that rule in my neighborhood. *** Only a judge who secretly believes that the law does not influence behavior would find no injury in fact. *** The same reasoning establishes injury in fact when the government declines to enforce a law that was designed in part for my benefit.

Frank H. Easterbrook, *Foreword: The Court and the Economic System,* 98 Harv. L. Rev. 4, 40 (1984).

Lujan v. Defenders of Wildlife

504 U.S. 555 (1992)

Justice SCALIA delivered the opinion of the Court with respect to Parts I, II, III-A, and IV, and an opinion with respect to Part III-B, in which THE CHIEF JUSTICE, Justice WHITE, and Justice THOMAS join.

I.

The [Endangered Species Act of 1973 (ESA)] seeks to protect species of animals against threats to their continuing existence caused by man. The ESA instructs the Secretary of the Interior to promulgate by regulation a list of those species which are either endangered or threatened under enumerated criteria, and to define the critical habitat of these species. Section 7(a)(2) of the Act then provides, in pertinent part: "Each Federal agency shall, in consultation with and with the assistance of the Secretary [of the Interior], insure that any action authorized, funded, or carried out by such agency [is] not likely to jeopardize the continued existence of any endangered species or threatened species or result in the destruction or adverse modification of [critical] habitat[s] of such species ***." [In 1986, the Fish and Wildlife Service and the National Marine Fisheries Service, on behalf of the Secretary of the Interior and the Secretary of Commerce respectively, promulgated a joint regulation] interpreting § 7(a)(2) to require consultation only for actions taken in the United States or on the high seas ***. Shortly thereafter, respondents, organizations dedicated to wildlife conservation and other environmental causes, filed this action against the Secretary of the Interior, seeking a declaratory judgment that the [regulation] is in error as to the geographic scope of § 7(a)(2) and an injunction requiring the Secretary to promulgate a new regulation restoring the initial interpretation.

II.

Over the years, our cases have established that the irreducible constitutional minimum of standing contains three elements. First, the plaintiff must have suffered an "injury in fact"—an invasion of a legally protected interest which is (a) concrete and particularized, and (b) "actual or imminent, not 'conjectural' or 'hypothetical.'" Second, there must be a causal connection between the injury and the conduct complained of—the injury has to be "fairly [traceable] to the challenged action of the defendant, and not [the result of] the independent action of some third party not before the court." Third, it must be "likely," as opposed to merely "speculative," that the injury will be "redressed by a favorable decision."

When the suit is one challenging the legality of government action or inaction, the nature and extent of facts that must be averred (at the summary judgment stage) or proved (at the trial stage) in order to establish standing depends considerably upon whether the plaintiff is himself an object of the action (or forgone action) at issue. If he is, there is ordinarily little question that the action or inaction has caused him injury, and that a judgment preventing or requiring the action will redress it. When, however, as in this case, a plaintiff's asserted injury arises from the government's allegedly unlawful regulation (or lack of regulation) of *someone else,* much more is needed. In that circumstance, causation

Take Note

The Court is stating explicitly that persons directly regulated by the government are much more likely to be able to establish standing to challenge the regulation than are persons who are beneficiaries of the government's regulation of others. Doesn't this distinction presuppose some theory about what the government's proper regulatory role is—a theory that we might expect to find embodied in the very statutes on which plaintiffs such as those in *Lujan* rely? See Cass R. Sunstein, *Standing and the Privatization of Public Law*, 88 Colum. L. Rev. 1432 (1988).

and redressability ordinarily hinge on the response of the regulated (or regulable) third party to the government action or inaction—and perhaps on the response of others as well. *** Thus, when the plaintiff is not himself the object of the government action or inaction he challenges, standing is not precluded, but it is ordinarily "substantially more difficult" to establish. *Allen*.

III.

A.

Respondents' claim to injury is that the lack of consultation with respect to certain funded activities abroad "increas[es] the rate of extinction of endangered and threatened species." Of course, the desire to use or observe an animal species, even for purely esthetic purposes, is undeniably a cognizable interest for purpose of standing. See, e.g., *Sierra Club v. Morton*, 405 U.S. 727 (1972). "But the 'injury in fact' test requires more than an injury to a cognizable interest. It requires that the party seeking review be himself among the injured." *Id.* To survive the Secretary's summary judgment motion, respondents had to submit affidavits or other evidence showing, through specific facts, not only that listed species were in fact being threatened by funded activities abroad, but also that one or more of respondents' members would thereby be "directly" affected apart from their "'special interest' in [the] subject."

[The] Court of Appeals focused on the affidavits of two Defenders' members—Joyce Kelly and Amy Skilbred. Ms. Kelly stated that she traveled to Egypt in 1986 and "observed the traditional habitat of the endangered nile crocodile there and intend[s] to do so again, and hope[s] to observe the crocodile directly." *** Ms. Skilbred averred that she traveled to Sri Lanka in 1981 and "observed [the] habitat" of "endangered species such as the Asian elephant and the leopard" at what is now the site of [a] project funded by the Agency for International Development (AID), although she "was unable to see any of the endangered species." [She alleged that the project threatened endangered species, and that the threat] harmed her because she "intend[s] to return to Sri Lanka in the future and hope[s] to be more fortunate in spotting at least the endangered elephant and leopard." When Ms. Skilbred was asked at a subsequent deposition if and when she had any plans to return to Sri Lanka, she reiterated that "I intend to go back to Sri Lanka," but confessed that she had no current plans: "I don't know [when]. There is a civil war going on right now. *** Not next year, I will say. In the future."

We shall assume for the sake of argument that these affidavits contain facts showing that certain agency-funded projects threaten listed species—though that is questionable.

They plainly contain no facts, however, showing how damage to the species will produce "imminent" injury to Mses. Kelly and Skilbred. That the women "had visited" the areas of the projects before the projects commenced proves nothing. *** And the affiants' profession of an "inten[t]" to return to the places they had visited before—where they will presumably, this time, be deprived of the opportunity to observe animals of the endangered species— is simply not enough. Such "some day" intentions—without any description of concrete plans, or indeed even any specification of *when* the some day will be—do not support a finding of the "actual or imminent" injury that our cases require.

> **Food for Thought**
>
> Couldn't the plaintiffs in *Lujan* have established injury in fact merely by purchasing plane tickets to visit the areas affected by the government-funded projects? If so, what is the point of insisting that they do so?

Besides relying upon the Kelly and Skilbred affidavits, respondents propose a series of novel standing theories. The first, inelegantly styled "ecosystem nexus," proposes that any person who uses *any part* of a "contiguous ecosystem" adversely affected by a funded activity has standing even if the activity is located a great distance away. [But] a plaintiff claiming injury from environmental damage must use the area affected by the challenged activity and not an area roughly "in the vicinity" of it. *** To say that the Act protects ecosystems is not to say that the Act creates (if it were possible) rights of action in persons who have not been injured in fact, that is, persons who use portions of an ecosystem not perceptibly affected by the unlawful action in question.

Respondents' other theories are called, alas, the "animal nexus" approach, whereby anyone who has an interest in studying or seeing the endangered animals anywhere on the globe has standing; and the "vocational nexus" approach, under which anyone with a professional interest in such animals can sue. Under these theories, anyone who goes to see Asian elephants in the Bronx Zoo, and anyone who is a keeper of Asian elephants in the Bronx Zoo, has standing to sue because the Director of AID did not consult with the Secretary regarding the AID-funded project in Sri Lanka. This is beyond all reason. Standing is not "an ingenious academic exercise in the conceivable," but as we have said requires, at the summary judgment stage, a factual showing of perceptible harm. It is clear that the person who observes or works with a particular animal threatened by a federal decision is facing perceptible harm, since the very subject of his interest will no longer exist. It is even plausible—though it goes to the outermost limit of plausibility—to think that a person who observes or works with animals of a particular species in the very area of the world where that species is threatened by a federal decision is facing such harm, since some animals that might have been the subject of his interest will no longer exist. It goes beyond the limit, however, and into pure speculation and fantasy, to say that anyone who observes or works with an endangered species, anywhere in the world, is appreciably harmed by a single project affecting some portion of that species with which he has no more specific connection.

B.

Besides failing to show injury, respondents failed to demonstrate redressability. Instead of attacking the separate decisions to fund particular projects allegedly causing them harm, respondents chose to challenge a more generalized level of Government action (rules regarding consultation), the invalidation of which would affect all overseas projects. *** Since the agencies funding the projects were not parties to the case, the District Court could accord relief only against the Secretary: He could be ordered to revise his regulation to require consultation for foreign projects. But this would not remedy respondents' alleged injury unless the funding agencies were bound by the Secretary's regulation, which is very much an open question. *** The short of the matter is that redress of the only injury in fact respondents complain of requires action (termination of funding until consultation) by the individual funding agencies; and any relief the District Court could have provided in this suit against the Secretary was not likely to produce that action.

A further impediment to redressability is the fact that the agencies generally supply only a fraction of the funding for a foreign project. AID, for example, has provided less than 10% of the funding for the [Sri Lanka] project. Respondents have produced nothing to indicate that the projects they have named will either be suspended, or do less harm to listed species, if that fraction is eliminated. [I]t is entirely conjectural whether the nonagency activity that affects respondents will be altered or affected by the agency activity they seek to achieve.

IV.

The Court of Appeals found that respondents had standing for an additional reason: because they had suffered a "procedural injury." The so-called "citizen-suit" provision of the ESA provides, in pertinent part, that "any person may commence a civil suit on his own behalf [to] enjoin any person, including the United States and any other governmental instrumentality or agency [who] is alleged to be in violation of any provision of this chapter." *** This is not a case where plaintiffs are seeking to enforce a procedural requirement the disregard of which could impair a separate concrete interest of theirs (*e.g.*, the procedural requirement for a hearing prior to denial of their license application, or the procedural requirement for an environmental impact statement before a federal facility is constructed next door to them). Nor is it simply a case where concrete injury has been suffered by many persons, as in mass fraud or mass tort situations. Nor, finally, is it the unusual case in which Congress has created a concrete private interest in the outcome of a suit against a private party for the government's benefit, by providing a cash bounty for the victorious plaintiff. Rather, the court held that the injury-in-fact requirement had been satisfied by congressional conferral upon *all* persons of an abstract, self-contained, noninstrumental "right" to have the Executive observe the procedures required by law. We reject this view.

Whether the courts were to act on their own, or at the invitation of Congress, in ignoring the concrete injury requirement described in our cases, they would be discarding a principle fundamental to the separate and distinct constitutional role of the Third Branch—one of the essential elements that identifies those "Cases" and "Controversies" that are the business of the courts rather than of the political branches. "The province of the court," as Chief Justice Marshall said in *Marbury v. Madison* "is, solely, to decide on the rights of individuals." Vindicating the *public* interest (including the public interest in Government observance of the Constitution and laws) is the function of Congress and the Chief Executive. The question presented here is whether the public interest in proper administration of the laws (specifically, in agencies' observance of a particular, statutorily prescribed procedure) can be converted into an individual right by a statute that denominates it as such, and that permits all citizens (or, for that matter, a subclass of citizens who suffer no distinctive concrete harm) to sue. If the concrete injury requirement has the separation-of-powers significance we have always said, the answer must be obvious: To permit Congress to convert the undifferentiated public interest in executive officers' compliance with the law into an "individual right" vindicable in the courts is to permit Congress to transfer from the President to the courts the Chief Executive's most important constitutional duty, to "take Care that the Laws be faithfully executed." It would enable the courts, with the permission of Congress, "to assume a position of authority over the governmental acts of another and co-equal department," and to become "virtually continuing monitors of the wisdom and soundness of Executive action." *Allen.* We have always rejected that vision of our role. We hold that respondents lack standing to bring this action.

> ### Food for Thought
>
> There is a long history of Congress's authorizing "private attorneys general" to file suits on behalf of the United States, with a bounty of part of the government's recovery as incentive for the suit. The False Claims Act, 31 U.S.C. §§ 3729-3733, for example, authorizes individuals to file suits on behalf of the United States against defendants who have defrauded the government and authorizes an award of up to 25% of the recovery for the private plaintiff. Id. § 3730(d). Can such statutory devices survive the Court's reasoning in this section of the opinion?

> ### Make the Connection
>
> We will consider the meaning of the "take Care" clause of Article II in Chapter 5.

Justice KENNEDY, with whom Justice SOUTER joins, concurring in part and concurring in the judgment.

Although I agree with the essential parts of the Court's analysis, I write separately to make several observations. While it may seem trivial to require that Mses. Kelly and Skilbred acquire airline tickets to the project sites or announce a date certain upon which they will return, this is not a case where it is reasonable to assume that the affiants will be using the sites on a regular basis, nor do the affiants claim to have visited the sites since the projects commenced. With respect to the Court's discussion of respondents' "ecosystem nexus," "animal nexus," and "vocational nexus" theories, I agree that on this record respondents' showing is insufficient to establish standing on any of these bases. I am not willing to foreclose the possibility, however, that in different circumstances a nexus theory similar to those proffered here might support a claim to standing. *** In light of the conclusion that respondents have not demonstrated a concrete injury here sufficient to support standing under our precedents, I would not reach the issue of redressability that is discussed by the plurality in Part III-B.

I also join Part IV of the Court's opinion with the following observations. As Government programs and policies become more complex and farreaching, we must be sensitive to the articulation of new rights of action that do not have clear analogs in our common-law tradition. Modern litigation has progressed far from the paradigm of Marbury suing Madison to get his commission ***. In my view, Congress has the power to define injuries and articulate chains of causation that will give rise to a case or controversy where none existed before, and I do not read the Court's opinion to suggest a contrary view. In exercising this power, however, Congress must at the very least identify the injury it seeks to vindicate and relate the injury to the class of persons entitled to bring suit. The citizen-suit provision of the Endangered Species Act does not meet these minimal requirements, because while the statute purports to confer a right on "any person [to enjoin] the United States and any other governmental instrumentality or agency [who] is alleged to be in violation of any provision of this chapter," it does not of its own force establish that there is an injury in "any person" by virtue of any "violation."

While it does not matter how many persons have been injured by the challenged action, the party bringing suit must show that the action injures him in a concrete and personal way. This requirement is not just an empty formality. It preserves the vitality of the adversarial process by assuring both that the parties before the court have an actual, as opposed to professed, stake in the outcome, and that "the legal questions presented [will] be resolved, not in the rarified atmosphere of a debating society, but in a concrete factual context conducive to a realistic appreciation of the consequences of judicial action." In addition, the requirement of concrete injury confines the Judicial Branch to its proper, limited role in the constitutional framework of Government.

Justice BLACKMUN, with whom Justice O'CONNOR joins, dissenting.

I think a reasonable finder of fact could conclude from the information in the affidavits and deposition testimony that either Kelly or Skilbred will soon return to the project sites, thereby satisfying the "actual or imminent" injury standard. *** By requiring a "description of concrete plans" or "specification of *when* the some day [for a return visit] will be," the Court, in my view, demands what is likely an empty formality. No substantial barriers prevent Kelly or Skilbred from simply purchasing plane tickets to return to the Aswan and Mahaweli projects.

The Court [also] expresses concern that allowing judicial enforcement of "agencies' observance of a particular, statutorily prescribed procedure" would "transfer from the President to the courts the Chief Executive's most important constitutional duty, to 'take Care that the Laws be faithfully executed.'" In fact, the principal effect of foreclosing judicial enforcement of such procedures is to transfer power into the hands of the Executive at the expense—not of the courts—but of Congress, from which that power originates and emanates.

Under the Court's anachronistically formal view of the separation of powers, Congress legislates pure, substantive mandates and has no business structuring the procedural manner in which the Executive implements these mandates. *** In complex regulatory areas, however, Congress often legislates, as it were, in procedural shades of gray. That is, it sets forth substantive policy goals and provides for their attainment by requiring Executive Branch officials to follow certain procedures, for example, in the form of reporting, consultation, and certification requirements.

The consultation requirement of § 7 of the Endangered Species Act is [an] action-forcing statute. Consultation is designed as an integral check on federal agency action, ensuring that such action does not go forward without full consideration of its effects on listed species. *** Congress legislates in procedural shades of gray not to aggrandize its own power but to allow maximum Executive discretion in the attainment of Congress' legislative goals. *** The Court never has questioned Congress' authority to impose such procedural constraints on Executive power. Just as Congress does not violate separation of powers by structuring the procedural manner in which the Executive shall carry out the laws, surely the federal courts do not violate separation of powers when, at the very instruction and command of Congress, they enforce these procedures.

[I] cannot join the Court on what amounts to a slash-and-burn expedition through the law of environmental standing. In my view, "[t]he very essence of civil liberty certainly consists in the right of every individual to claim the protection of the laws, whenever he receives an injury." *Marbury v. Madison*. I dissent.

Points for Discussion

a. Injury in Fact

What criteria should the courts apply in deciding whether an alleged injury is a cognizable injury for purposes of Article III? If the point of the standing doctrine is to ensure that the plaintiff has the requisite stake in the outcome such that the suit is truly an adversarial contest between interested parties, are intangible, moral, or aesthetic injuries as cognizable as economic injuries?

b. Citizen-Suit Provisions

The Court held in *Lujan* that Congress cannot authorize a person to sue if that person has not suffered a cognizable injury, and thus that open-ended "citizen-suit provisions" are unconstitutional as applied to plaintiffs who have not actually suffered any cognizable injury. Justice Kennedy, however, stated in his concurring opinion that "Congress has the power to define injuries and articulate chains of causation that will give rise to a case or controversy where none existed before." Who gets to define "injury in fact"—Congress or the courts? In *Federal Election Commission v. Akins*, 524 U.S. 11 (1998), a divided Court held that voters who challenged a determination by the FEC that the American Israel Public Affairs Committee (AIPAC) was not a political committee subject to certain disclosure requirements under the Federal Election Campaign Act had standing. The Act authorizes "[a]ny person who believes a violation" of the Act has occurred to file a complaint with the FEC and to file a petition in federal court challenging the FEC's denial of such a complaint. 2 U.S.C. § 437g(a). The Court held that the plaintiffs' inability to obtain information about AIPAC's donors and campaign-related contributions and expenditures—information that "would help them (and others to whom they would communicate it) to evaluate candidates for public office, especially candidates who received assistance from AIPAC, and to evaluate the role that AIPAC's financial assistance might play in a specific election"—constituted a cognizable injury in fact. Is this decision consistent with *Lujan*?

Hypothetical

Congress enacts a statute that requires the Nuclear Regulatory Commission (NRC) to "provide adequate training to managers of nuclear plants" in order to lower the risk of nuclear catastrophes. Residents who live near a nuclear power plant file suit against the NRC claiming that the agency failed adequately to train the plant's managers. The NRC moves to dismiss the suit for lack of standing. How should the Court rule?

Perspective and Analysis

What purpose is served by the various justiciability doctrines? Consider the following:

> [T]he intricate set of constraints that the Supreme Court has found to be implicit in the terse language of Article III do not serve any apparent purpose. *** If we had no doctrines of justiciability whatsoever, the courts would still play only a proper, and properly limited, role in our democratic society, so long as they confined themselves to enforcing legal constraints on executive and congressional action. *** [C]ourts should always permit actions *if Congress authorizes them*. *** [D]emocracy requires courts to limit the substance of their rulings but does not imply a limit on the permitted modes of judicial proceeding.

Jonathan R. Siegel, *A Theory of Justiciability*, 86 Tex. L. Rev. 73 (2007). How might a supporter of justiciability requirements respond to Professor Siegel?

---

4. Congressional Control Over Federal Court Jurisdiction

The barriers to the exercise of judicial power that we have considered so far—the political question doctrine, the case and controversy requirement, and standing—are all judicially developed doctrines based on interpretations of the Constitution. But sometimes the courts are disabled from action because Congress divests them of the power to act. Look carefully at the language of Article III. Section 1 does not require Congress to create lower federal courts, and Congress traditionally has defined the jurisdiction of the lower courts that it has created. In addition, section 2, clause 2 says that the Supreme Court has appellate jurisdiction subject to "such Exceptions, and under such Regulations as the Congress shall make." Congress thus has the power to limit opportunities for judicial review by restricting the jurisdiction of both the lower federal courts and the Supreme Court. Are there limits on Congress's power to strip the federal courts of jurisdiction?

———

Ex Parte McCardle

74 U.S. 506 (1869)

[In the late 1860s, William McCardle published several editorials in the *Vicksburg Times* that sharply criticized federal military rule in the South during Reconstruction. (In one, for example, he called several military commanders "infamous, cowardly, and abandoned villains who, instead of wearing shoulder straps and ruling millions of people should have their heads shaved, their ears cropped, their foreheads branded, and their persons lodged in a penitentiary.") These editorials led to his arrest and detention by federal military officials, who convened a military commission to try him on charges that included impeding reconstruction and inciting insurrection. McCardle filed an action in federal court seeking a writ of habeas corpus, relying on a statute that Congress had enacted on February 5, 1867, called the Habeas Corpus Act, which gave the federal courts jurisdiction over habeas petitions challenging confinement by state or federal officials in violation of federal law. (The Judiciary Act of 1789, which the Habeas Corpus Act did not purport to repeal, had authorized jurisdiction over habeas petitions only by those held by federal officials.) McCardle claimed that the Military Reconstruction Act, which authorized military rule in the South, was unconstitutional because it permitted the trial of civilians by military tribunals rather than regularly constituted courts. He also argued that the prosecution violated his rights under the First, Fifth, and Sixth Amendments.

> **Definition**
>
> *Habeas Corpus* literally means "you have the body." The writ of habeas corpus is an ancient writ from a court ordering the release of a person unlawfully held by the government.

The Habeas Corpus Act also authorized habeas petitioners to appeal lower-court judgments to the Supreme Court, and after the federal circuit court denied the writ, McCardle appealed to the Supreme Court. After the Supreme Court denied the government's motion to dismiss and held oral arguments on the merits of McCardle's petition, members of Congress became concerned that the Court might invalidate the Military Reconstruction Act. Congress responded by passing a bill repealing the portion of the Habeas Corpus Act that conferred on the Supreme Court appellate jurisdiction over cases involving petitions for habeas corpus. President Johnson, who was facing an impeachment trial in the Senate for his alleged obstruction of Reconstruction efforts, vetoed the bill, but Congress immediately overrode the veto, and the provision, known as the Repealer Act, became law on March 27, 1868. One year later, after arguments on the effect of the Repealer Act on the Court's jurisdiction, the Court issued the following opinion.]

Chief Justice CHASE delivered the opinion of the court.

The first question necessarily is that of jurisdiction; for, if the act of March [27,] 1868, takes away the jurisdiction defined by the act of February [5], 1867, it is useless, if not improper, to enter into any discussion of other questions.

It is quite true, as was argued by the counsel for the petitioner, that the appellate jurisdiction of this court is not derived from acts of Congress. It is, strictly speaking, conferred by the Constitution. But it is conferred "with such exceptions and under such regulations as Congress shall make."

The exception to appellate jurisdiction in the case before us [is] not an inference from the affirmation of other appellate jurisdiction. It is made in terms. The provision of the act of 1867, affirming the appellate jurisdiction of this court in cases of habeas corpus is expressly repealed. It is hardly possible to imagine a plainer instance of positive exception. We are not at liberty to inquire into the motives of the legislature. We can only examine into its power under the Constitution; and the power to make exceptions to the appellate jurisdiction of this court is given by express words.

What, then, is the effect of the repealing act upon the case before us? We cannot doubt as to this. Without jurisdiction the court cannot proceed at all in any cause. Jurisdiction is power to declare the law, and when it ceases to exist, the only function remaining to the court is that of announcing the fact and dismissing the cause. And this is not less clear upon authority than upon principle.

> **FYI**
>
> The Congressman who introduced the Act of March 27, 1868 explained that the provision was intended to "sweep[] the [*McCardle*] case from the docket by taking away the jurisdiction of the court [to] prevent" the Court from determining "the invalidity and unconstitutionality of the reconstruction laws of Congress." Cong. Globe, 40th Cong., 2d Sess. 2062 (1868). Should this stated congressional motive matter?

It is quite clear, therefore, that this court cannot proceed to pronounce judgment in this case, for it has no longer jurisdiction of the appeal; and judicial duty is not less fitly performed by declining ungranted jurisdiction than in exercising firmly that which the Constitution and the laws confer.

Counsel seem to have supposed, if effect be given to the repealing act in question, that the whole appellate power of the court, in cases of habeas corpus, is denied. But this is an error. The act of 1868 does not except from that jurisdiction any cases but appeals from Circuit Courts under the act of 1867. It does not affect the jurisdiction which was previously exercised.

Take Note

What other source of jurisdiction is the Court referring to here? Had Congress actually stripped the Supreme Court of all jurisdiction to review habeas petitions?

The appeal of the petitioner in this case must be dismissed for want of jurisdiction.

Points for Discussion

a. The Exceptions Clause and the Supreme Court's Appellate Jurisdiction

Recall from our discussion of <u>Marbury v. Madison</u> that Article III confers on the Supreme Court appellate jurisdiction over most of the categories of cases within the judicial power. But the relevant provision states that in those cases the Supreme Court "shall have appellate jurisdiction, both as to Law and Fact, *with such Exceptions, and under such Regulations as the Congress shall make*" (emphasis added). What is the import of this language? The traditional view is that the Exceptions Clause confers on Congress plenary authority to deprive the Supreme Court of appellate jurisdiction—over either some class of cases or all cases otherwise within the federal judicial power. See, e.g., Herbert Wechsler, The Courts and the Constitution, 65 Colum. L. Rev. 1001 (1965). Subject to a very important caveat that we will discuss below, this appears to be the view that the Court in <u>McCardle</u> advanced.

Does this view mean that Congress could effectively achieve a *de facto* reversal of Supreme Court precedent with which it disagrees by stripping the Court of jurisdiction to hear cases of a certain type—for example, cases involving abortion, flag burning, or any other controversial practice? If so, is such a congressional power consistent with the broader notion of checks and balances that is central to the constitutional structure? Many commentators have concluded that Congress's power under the Exceptions Clause is in fact quite limited. Henry Hart, for example, famously suggested that Congress might lack power under the Exceptions Clause to "destroy the essential role of the Supreme Court in the constitutional plan." Henry M. Hart, Jr., *The Power of Congress to Limit the Jurisdiction of the Federal Courts: An Exercise in Dialectic*, 66 Harv. L. Rev. 1362, 1365 (1953).

b. The Holding in <u>McCardle</u>

Did the Court in <u>McCardle</u> in fact adopt the view that Congress's power under the Exceptions Clause is plenary? The Court concluded by noting that the Act of March 27, 1868 "did not except from [the Court's appellate] jurisdiction any cases but appeals from Circuit Courts under the act of 1867," and that it did "not affect the jurisdiction which was previously exercised." Indeed, one year after the decision in <u>McCardle</u>, the Court held in

Ex parte Yerger, 75 U.S. (8 Wall.) 85 (1869), that it had jurisdiction to entertain "original" habeas petitions pursuant to the Judiciary Act of 1789, which the Act of March 27, 1868 had not purported to disturb. In light of the existence of this alternative basis for Supreme Court jurisdiction, had Congress actually stripped the Court of jurisdiction? If not, what does that mean for the binding force of the Court's discussion of Congress's power to deprive the Court of appellate jurisdiction?

In 1996, the Court upheld restrictions on its power to review certain habeas decisions, reasoning that Congress had not purported to deprive the Court of its power under the Judiciary Act of 1789 to grant original habeas petitions. *Felker v. Turpin*, 518 U.S. 651 (1996). Should it matter that the Court has not granted such a petition since 1925?

William McCardle faced trial by military commission. In the Military Commissions Act of 2006, Congress authorized the use of military commissions to try "unlawful enemy combatants" suspected of war crimes arising out of the war on terror. One provision of this Act stated: "No court, justice, or judge shall have jurisdiction to hear or consider an application for a writ of habeas corpus filed by or on behalf of an alien detained by the United States who has been determined by the United States to have been properly detained as an enemy combatant or is awaiting such determination." 10 U.S.C. § 2241(e)(1). Is this provision constitutional? Might it matter that Congress has provided alternative means for detainees to challenge their confinement? In *Boumediene v. Bush*, 553 U.S. 723 (2008), the Court held that the provision effected an unconstitutional suspension of habeas corpus. We will explore this question in further detail in Chapter 5.

c. Congressional Control of the Jurisdiction of the Lower Federal Courts

Are there limits on Congress's power to control the jurisdiction of the lower federal courts? The conventional view is that there are no meaningful limits. After all, Article III does not even require Congress to create inferior courts; if Congress can refuse to create lower courts, then it should follow that Congress can create them but decline to confer the full range of Article III jurisdiction upon them. See *Sheldon v. Sill*, 49 U.S. (8 How.) 441 (1850). Indeed, that is what Congress effectively has done by imposing limits, for example, on the exercise of diversity jurisdiction. See 28 U.S.C. § 1332.

Over the years, however, many prominent commentators have taken issue with this view, arguing that Congress is required, at least under some circumstances, both to create lower federal courts and to confer upon them all, or at least some, of the judicial power. In *Martin v. Hunter's Lessee*, for example, Justice Story argued that because the Supreme Court can have original jurisdiction in only two classes of cases, it "would seem *** to follow that congress are bound to create some inferior courts, in which to vest all that jurisdiction which, under the constitution, is *exclusively* vested in the United States, and of which the supreme court cannot take original cognizance. They might establish one or more inferior courts; they might parcel out the jurisdiction among such courts, from time to time, at their own pleasure. But the whole judicial power of the United States should be, at all times, vested either in an original or appellate form, in some courts created under its authority." *Martin*, 14 U.S. (1 Wheat.) at 331; see also Akhil Reed Amar, *A Neo-Federalist View of Article*

III: Separating the Two Tiers of Federal Jurisdiction, 65 B.U. L. Rev. 205, 206, 229-30 (1985); Lawrence Gene Sager, *Foreword: Constitutional Limitations on Congress' Authority to Regulate the Jurisdiction of the Federal Courts*, 95 Harv. L. Rev. 17, 66 (1981).

———————

Taken together, these arguments suggest that Congress very well might have authority to deprive the Supreme Court of at least some of its appellate jurisdiction and to deprive the lower federal courts of at least some of their original jurisdiction. But what if Congress attempts to divest all federal courts of jurisdiction, original and appellate, over particular types of cases?

Hypothetical

In 2005, the House of Representatives passed the "Pledge Protection Act." The bill would have amended title 28 of the United States Code as follows, in relevant part:

Sec. 1632. Limitation on jurisdiction

(a) Except as provided in subsection (b), no court created by Act of Congress shall have any jurisdiction, and the Supreme Court shall have no appellate jurisdiction, to hear or decide any question pertaining to the interpretation of, or the validity under the Constitution of, the Pledge of Allegiance *** or its recitation.

(b) The limitation in subsection (a) does not apply to (1) any court established by Congress under its power to make needful rules and regulation respecting the territory of the United States; or (2) the Superior Court of the District of Columbia or the District of Columbia Court of Appeals.

If the bill had been enacted into law, would it have been constitutional?

———————

Executive Summary of This Chapter

The United States Supreme Court enjoys the power of **judicial review**—that is, the power to invalidate statutes that are unconstitutional. *Marbury v. Madison* (1803). This power includes the authority to review and invalidate state laws that are inconsistent with the Constitution. *Martin v. Hunter's Lessee* (1816).

Under the doctrine of **judicial supremacy**, decisions of the Court interpreting the Constitution are the "supreme Law of the Land" for purposes of Article VI of the Constitution, and therefore are binding on all state officers, *Cooper v. Aaron* (1958), and federal officers, *Dickerson v. United States* (2000).

Some constitutional questions are non-justiciable pursuant to the **political question doctrine**. Determining whether a political question exists in any given case requires consideration of several factors: (1) whether there is a textually demonstrable commitment in the Constitution of the issue to the President or Congress; (2) whether there are judicially discoverable and manageable standards for resolving the question; (3) whether resolution of the question calls for policy decisions inappropriate for judicial resolution; (4) whether resolution of the question will express a lack of due respect for other branches of government; (5) whether there is an unusual need for unquestioning adherence to a political decision that has already been made; and (6) whether there is the potential for embarrassment from inconsistent resolutions of the issue by the Court and one or more of the political branches. *Baker v. Carr* (1962).

Whether a state's legislative apportionment scheme violates the Equal Protection Clause is not a political question. *Baker v. Carr* (1962). Neither is a claim by a Member of Congress that he has been improperly excluded from his seat. *Powell v. McCormack* (1969). A claim that the Senate improperly delegated the task of "trying" an impeached federal judge, on the other hand, does present a political question. *Nixon v. United States* (1993).

The federal judicial power under Article III extends only to "Cases" and "Controversies." Accordingly, the Court lacks authority to issue **advisory opinions** about the proper resolution of abstract legal questions divorced from an actual dispute between adverse parties. In addition, the **case or controversy requirement** precludes Congress from conferring jurisdiction on the federal courts to decide abstract legal questions in suits that lack litigants with the requisite adversity of interests. *Muskrat v. United States* (1911).

The doctrines of **ripeness** and **mootness** also derive from the case or controversy requirement. A federal court will decline to resolve a controversy that is not **ripe**. A legal dispute is not ripe if it has not yet developed into an actual controversy, has not yet caused injury, or is otherwise asserted prematurely. *O'Shea v. Littleton* (1974). A federal court will also generally decline to resolve a controversy that is **moot**. A controversy is moot if the parties no longer have any meaningful and concrete stake in its resolution. *United States Parole Comm'n v. Geraghty* (1980).

A federal court lacks authority to assert jurisdiction over a case in which the plaintiff or plaintiffs lack **standing**. In order to satisfy the requirements of Article III standing doctrine, a plaintiff must properly allege: (1) that he has suffered an "**injury in fact**"; (2) that the injury is **fairly traceable** to the challenged conduct; and (3) that the injury is **redressable** by a favorable decision. *Allen v. Wright* (1984).

To constitute a cognizable injury in fact, the plaintiff must assert something more than simply a "generalized grievance"—that is, a grievance that is widely shared and undifferentiated. *Allen v. Wright* (1984). In addition, the injury must be concrete and particularized, and actual or imminent, rather than speculative or conjectural. *Lujan v. Defenders of Wildlife* (1992). To satisfy the causation prongs of the test, the link between the challenged conduct and the alleged injury must not be unduly attenuated or speculative. *Allen v. Wright* (1984). Congress lacks power to authorize suits by persons who do not satisfy the test for Article III standing. *Lujan v. Defenders of Wildlife* (1992).

Congress has authority to deprive the lower federal courts of jurisdiction. *Sheldon v. Sill* (1850). Congress also has some authority pursuant to the Exceptions Clause of Article III to deprive the Supreme Court of appellate jurisdiction, *Ex Parte McCardle* (1869), but the Supreme Court has never squarely decided whether Congress can completely deprive the Supreme Court of jurisdiction over a particular federal question. There might also be limits on Congress's power to strip all of the federal courts—lower courts and the Supreme Court—of jurisdiction over particular federal questions, but the question remains unresolved.

POINT-COUNTERPOINT

What is the role of the federal courts in our constitutional scheme?

POINT: PETER J. SMITH

The federal courts' essential functions are to protect individual rights from majoritarian incursion and to uphold the rule of law against government abuses of authority. When the government seeks to deprive an unpopular minority of the right to vote, for example, or seeks to suppress a citizen's ability to express an unpopular opinion, ordinary majoritarian politics by definition provide no means of redress. If we take seriously the notion that there are fundamental rights that are immune from governmental interference—a subject that we will take up in later Chapters—then the federal courts, which are in very important ways independent from the political process, must stand open to vindicate those rights when they are threatened. At bottom, this is the most compelling justification for conferring the power of judicial review on the federal courts.

Of course, not all claims asserted in federal court seek to vindicate fundamental rights. Some claims seek to enforce against the government rights that are important simply by virtue of the fact that Congress has conferred them—such as the right to have clean water or air. When faced with such claims, the federal courts have an obligation to ensure that the government is following the rules that it has previously established for itself. After all, insisting that government officials follow the law ensures that we live under the rule of law, rather than the rule of men (or women) subject only to their own caprice, which is the conventional definition of tyranny.

If the federal courts are to fulfill these functions, then they must be generally open to the assertion of bona fide claims. Accordingly, we must be wary of barriers erected to limit the authority of the courts to intervene to protect individual rights or to uphold the rule of law. The maze of rules that we have seen in this Part, however, has often frustrated the courts' ability to fulfill those functions. For example, it is difficult to resist the conclusion that the Court has deployed standing doctrine to keep from adjudication claims (or litigants) of which the Justices disapprove. (How else can we explain the fact that Allan Bakke, but not the plaintiffs in _Allen_, had standing to assert a race-based injury?) The political question doctrine, in theory a sensible idea, in practice lurks, because of its indeterminacy, as a tool for the Court to ratify problematic governmental decisions. And permitting Congress to divest the federal courts of jurisdiction over particular, disfavored issues—something that the Court has hinted, but fortunately never decided, that Congress could do—would strike at the core of the federal courts' essential function.

No one denies that the federal courts' role in our democratic society must be limited. But if we want to continue to have a Constitution that imposes meaningful limits on the authority of the political branches, then we must accept the power of judicial review and ensure that the courts can, in appropriate cases, exercise their authority to insist on the faithful and neutral application of the law.

———————

COUNTERPOINT: GREGORY E. MAGGS

"A circumstance which crowns the defects of the Confederation," Alexander Hamilton wrote in the *The Federalist Papers*, "[is] the want of a judiciary power." The Federalist No. 22. To remedy this deficiency of the Articles of Confederation, the Constitution prominently provided for "one supreme Court, and *** such inferior Courts as the Congress may from time to time ordain and establish." U.S. Const. art. III, § 1. But what role were the new federal courts to have? This question does not have a single answer. The Framers envisioned several important functions.

Hamilton, for example, argued that the Supreme Court could promote uniform interpretations of federal law, something numerous state courts could not accomplish. The Federalist No. 22. With its original jurisdiction, the Supreme Court also could quickly resolve sensitive cases involving ambassadors and states. The Federalist No. 81. Federal courts could serve as impartial tribunals in the "determination of controversies between different States and their citizens." The Federalist No. 80. And they would be a neutral forum for federal questions when "the prevalency of a local spirit may be found to disqualify the local [state] tribunals for the jurisdiction of national causes." The Federalist No. 81.

Hamilton advocated that federal courts should have the power of judicial review. The courts, he said, should exercise "a direct negative [on] State laws *** as might be in manifest contravention of the articles of Union." The Federalist No. 80. And after observing that the Constitution "contains certain specified exceptions to the [federal] legislative authority; such, for instance, as that it shall pass no bills of attainder, no ex-post-facto laws, and the like," Hamilton also famously wrote: "Limitations of this kind can be preserved in practice no other way than through the medium of courts of justice, whose duty it must be to declare all acts contrary to the manifest tenor of the Constitution void." The Federalist No. 78.

But a role no one supposed the federal courts would assume is that of the inventor of new constitutional rights and the final arbiter of social policy. Hamilton said: "To avoid an arbitrary discretion in the courts, it is indispensable that they should be bound down by strict rules and precedents, which serve to define and point out their duty in every particular case that comes before them ***." The Federalist No. 78. And yet, as we will see in subsequent Chapters, the federal courts have strayed from this vision. We now have the peculiar situation where courts, rather than Congress or the state legislatures, decide on a clean slate the most contentious issues of our times: what the nation's abortion policies should be, how we fight our wars, the precise circumstances in which capital punishment may be imposed, whether adults may choose to end their lives, how states must accommodate homosexuality, and so forth. Someone has to decide these matters, but it seems awfully undemocratic and thoroughly inconsistent with the original vision to leave the choices to elite federal judges.

PART III: FEDERALISM

One of the most important and divisive issues at the Constitutional Convention and subsequently in the ratification conventions was federalism: the relationship between the federal government and the states, and the relationship among the states. There was, to be sure, widespread agreement that the Articles of Confederation had created an unacceptably weak national government. Under the Articles, Congress lacked authority to impose taxes, and states often refused to contribute money when Congress requested it. Congress had no power to regulate commerce among the states, which enacted barriers to the importation of goods. And although the Articles conferred upon Congress power over foreign affairs, the power was ineffective because Congress was forced to rely on the states to implement its directives—there was, after all, no federal executive—and the states often refused to cooperate. Congress often had no choice but to sit idly by while the states fought among themselves, taxed and discriminated against goods produced in other states, and produced a deepening economic depression.

> **Make the Connection**
>
> We discussed the Articles of Confederation in Chapter 1.

Dissatisfaction with Congress's weakness under the Articles of Confederation was the impetus for the Constitutional Convention, but the proposed solution was not total consolidation of authority. On the one hand, the proposal that the Convention produced included some suggestions of very broad federal power. In addition to curing the most obvious defects of the Articles—such as conferring upon Congress the power to tax and the power to regulate interstate and foreign commerce—it authorized Congress to "make all Laws which shall be necessary and proper for carrying into Execution" not only the powers of Congress, but also "all other Powers vested by this Constitution in the Government of the United Sates, or in any Department or Officer thereof." Article I, § 8, cl. 18. It also provided that federal law "shall be the supreme Law of the Land ***, any Thing in the Constitution or Laws of any State to the Contrary notwithstanding." Article VI, cl. 2. But the proposed Constitution also contained provisions that suggested important limits on the power of the federal government. The Constitution presupposed the continuing existence of the states, see Article IV, § 4, and entitled the states to equal representation in the Senate, Article I, § 3, cl. 1; Article 5. More important, Congress's powers were enumerated, which suggested that Congress could not exercise powers not enumerated— a view confirmed upon the ratification of the Tenth Amendment, which provides, "The powers not delegated to the United States by the Constitution, nor prohibited by it to the States, are reserved to the States respectively, or to the people." Indeed, although the Constitution imposed some specific limits on the exercise of the states' power, see Article I, § 10, it did not purport to define the extent or scope of the power of the states.

Why Federalism?

The Constitution, in other words, obviously divides powers between the federal and state governments, but it doesn't give perfect guidance about where exactly the lines between competing sources of authority should be drawn. This ambiguity—particularly in the Constitution's application to modern problems—often leads to reliance, explicitly or implicitly, on arguments about the relative desirability of divided authority. What are the virtues of dividing authority between the states and the federal government in the first place? Conversely, what are the arguments in favor of consolidating power in one national government? Obviously, over the years many of the participants in these debates have had self-interested reasons to support one view or another. At the Convention, for example, the small states supported limits on federal authority to prevent dilution of their influence at the hands of the larger states. And individuals prosecuted for violating federal criminal statutes today have an obvious incentive to argue against the constitutional validity of the statutes under which they have been charged. Conversely, litigants relying on federal statutes that confer some benefit upon them can be expected to argue in favor of federal authority. But the arguments for and against the centralization of authority go beyond the mere self-interest of participants in the debates.

Proponents of de-centralization generally argue that such an approach better reflects the diversity of interests and preferences of individuals in different parts of the nation and encourages innovation in government, whereas centralization leads to one-size-fits-all decisions that stifle choice. See, e.g., Michael W. McConnell, *Federalism: Evaluating the Founders' Design*, 54 U. Chi. L. Rev. 1484 (1987). They also argue that dispersing government power is likely to protect individual liberty by limiting the power of any one government to act oppressively, see The Federalist No. 51, and that local officials are more likely than federal officials to be responsive to citizens, see The Federalist No. 45. Supporters of more robust centralized authority generally respond that centralization often is necessary to prevent individual states from imposing "externalities"—such as polluted air—on citizens of other states. See, e.g., David L. Shapiro, Federalism: A Dialogue (1995). James Madison argued, moreover, that the greatest threat to individual liberty comes from the tyranny of a majority faction, which is more likely to occur in a smaller, more homogenous political unit such as a state legislature. See The Federalist No. 10.

We would not presume to resolve a controversy as intractable as this one, but these arguments about the value of federalism are never far from the surface in the cases that follow. We begin our consideration of federalism with the powers of Congress. We will turn in Chapter 4 to the limits that the Constitution imposes on state power.

————

CHAPTER 3

Federal Legislative Power

A. Express and Implied Federal Powers

During the ratification debates, Anti-Federalist opponents of the Constitution argued that it would create an unduly powerful national government that would threaten both the separate existence of the states and the individual liberties over which the Revolution had been fought. Federalist supporters of the Constitution responded by arguing that such threats were illusory, because the national government would be authorized to exercise only those powers delegated "by positive grant expressed in the instrument of the union"—that is, only those powers enumerated in the Constitution. James Wilson, Speech at the Pennsylvania Statehouse, reprinted in 13 Merrill Jensen, John Kaminski, and Gaspare Saladino, The Documentary History of the Ratification of the Constitution 344 (1976); see also The Federalist No. 45 (James Madison) ("The powers delegated by the proposed Constitution to the federal government are few and defined. Those which are to remain in the State governments are numerous and indefinite."). The implications of this theory of enumeration, however, turned at least in part on how expansively or restrictively the powers actually enumerated would be construed.

To understand this debate, look carefully at Article I, section 8. This section enumerates the powers of Congress. The first 17 clauses grant Congress power to impose taxes, spend money, regulate commerce, set immigration standards, raise an Army and Navy, and so forth. All of these powers seem very important. But notice that these powers are stated in quite broad terms and do not specify many details. For example, clause 7 says that Congress may "establish Post Offices," but it does not say anything about procuring mail trucks, selling postage stamps, or hiring postal workers. Despite this omission, no one doubts that Congress may provide for these things. One reason for this conclusion is that clause 18 (the "Necessary and Proper Clause" or so-called "sweeping clause") grants Congress the power "[t]o make all Laws which shall be necessary and proper for carrying into Execution the foregoing Powers ***." Perhaps the reasonable implication of Congress's power to establish post offices is the related power to authorize the use of mail trucks, postage stamps, and postal workers; in any event, such incidents, simply put, are necessary and proper for carrying into execution the power to establish post offices.

A significant question is how broadly or how narrowly courts should read the Necessary and Proper Clause. A broad reading would enable Congress to exercise many implied powers that are not expressly stated. A narrow reading, by contrast, would confine Congress more closely to its express powers. The case that follows, one of the most famous in all of American constitutional law, takes up that question.

McCulloch v. Maryland

17 U.S. (4 Wheat.) 316 (1819)

[In 1791, a debate arose about whether Congress had the power to charter a bank. President Washington sought advice from Alexander Hamilton, his Secretary of the Treasury, and Thomas Jefferson, his Secretary of State. Hamilton argued that Congress had power, and Jefferson disagreed. Ultimately, Congress passed a bill chartering the Bank of the United States as a corporation, and President Washington signed the bill into law. The Bank was owned by private investors and largely dealt with commercial customers. Like other financial institutions, the Bank could make loans and it could take deposits (which it promised to repay by issuing promissory notes). But the Bank also had a special relationship with the federal government. The Treasury deposited funds in the Bank, and the Bank stood ready to make loans to the United States in times of need. Because of the Bank's large size, its policies on making and calling loans could have a substantial effect on the national economy. The charter of the Bank expired in 1811, but fiscal challenges led to pressure on Congress to create a new national bank. In 1816, Congress passed a bill creating the Second Bank of the United States, and President Madison, who years earlier had argued that Congress lacked power to create a national bank, signed the bill.

> **Definition**
>
> Businesses, banks, universities, hospitals, and many other entities are typically organized as corporations. This means that they have their own legal identities that are distinct from the people who own them or who work for them. For example, a corporation can enter into contracts, acquire and own property, and incur liability just like a real person. If investors want to start a corporation, they must obtain a corporate charter from the government, usually by paying a small fee and meeting various organizational requirements. Most corporate charters are issued at the state level. But the federal government also issues charters. Examples include Amtrak, the George Washington University, and Sallie Mae.

The Bank established branches in many states, including Maryland. In 1818, a nationwide financial panic led the Bank to call in loans, which exacerbated the economic depression that the country was already experiencing. Public anger mounted against the Bank, which was also accused of mismanagement and corruption. Maryland responded by imposing a tax on all banks operating in the state that were "not chartered by the Legislature." The law required uncharted banks either to issue bank notes only on stamped paper provided by the state for a fee for each issuance or to pay an annual lump sum of

$15,000. The law imposed on the officers of banks that failed to comply a penalty of $500 for each offense, and made the penalties enforceable in an "action of debt," which could be maintained by any person who discovered non-compliance with the law. (The law authorized the plaintiff in such an action to recover half of the penalty as a bounty for bringing the suit.)

John James filed this action of debt on behalf of Maryland against James McCulloch, the Cashier of the Baltimore branch of the Bank of the United States. (As Cashier, McCulloch effectively ran the branch. He had also been accused of complicity in financial improprieties at the Bank.) McCulloch conceded that the Bank was operating without a charter from the state of Maryland and that the Bank had issued notes without complying with the Maryland law. The Maryland Court of Appeals ruled in favor of the state.]

Chief Justice MARSHALL delivered the opinion of the Court.

In the case now to be determined, [Maryland], a sovereign state, denies the obligation of a law enacted by the legislature of the Union, and the [plaintiff in error] contests the validity of an act which has been passed by the legislature of that state. *** The first question made in the cause is—has congress power to incorporate a bank? [T]his can scarcely be considered as an open question, entirely unprejudiced by the former proceedings of the nation respecting it. The principle now contested was introduced at a very early period of our history, has been recognized by many successive legislatures, and has been acted upon by the judicial department, in cases of peculiar delicacy, as a law of undoubted obligation.

> **Food for Thought**
>
> In light of *Marbury v. Madison*, should the fact that Congress has asserted a particular power be treated as evidence that the Constitution in fact confers that power upon Congress?

It will not be denied, that a bold and daring usurpation might be resisted, after an acquiescence still longer and more complete than this. But *** [a]n exposition of the constitution, deliberately established by legislative acts, on the faith of which an immense property has been advanced, ought not to be lightly disregarded. The power now contested was exercised by the first congress elected under the present constitution. The bill for incorporating the Bank of the United States did not steal upon an unsuspecting legislature, and pass unobserved. Its principle was completely understood, and was opposed with equal zeal and ability. After being resisted, first, in the fair and open field of debate, and afterwards, in the executive cabinet, with as much persevering talent as any measure has ever experienced, and being supported by arguments which convinced

> **FYI**
>
> The Court was aware of the earlier debate over the constitutionality of the Bank, and that Madison had changed his view and signed a bill to charter the Bank. Madison stated at the time that the question of Congress's power to create the Bank was "precluded in my judgment by repeated recognitions under varied circumstances of the validity of such an institution in acts of the legislative, executive, and judicial branches of Government."

minds as pure and as intelligent as this country can boast, it became a law. The original act was permitted to expire; but a short experience of the embarrassments to which the refusal to revive it exposed the government, convinced those who were most prejudiced against the measure of its necessity, and induced the passage of the present law.

It would require no ordinary share of intrepidity, to assert that a measure adopted under these circumstances, was a bold and plain usurpation, to which the constitution gave no countenance. These observations belong to the cause; but they are not made under the impression, that, were the question entirely new, the law would be found irreconcilable with the constitution.

In discussing this question, the counsel for the state of Maryland [urge the Court to consider the Constitution] not as emanating from the people, but as the act of sovereign and independent states. The powers of the general government, it has been said, are delegated by the states, who alone are truly sovereign; and must be exercised in subordination to the states, who alone possess supreme dominion. It would be difficult to sustain this proposition. The convention which framed the constitution was indeed elected by the state legislatures. But the instrument *** was submitted to the *people*. They acted upon it in the only manner in which they can act safely, effectively and wisely, on such a subject, by assembling in convention. It is true, they assembled in their several states—and where else should they have assembled? No political dreamer was ever wild enough to think of breaking down the lines which separate the states, and of compounding the American people into one common mass. Of consequence, when they act, they act in their states. But the measures they adopt do not, on that account, cease to be the measures of the people themselves, or become the measures of the state governments.

From these conventions, the constitution derives its whole authority. The government proceeds directly from the people; is "ordained and established" in the name of the people. *** The assent of the states, in their sovereign capacity, is implied, in calling a convention, and thus submitting that instrument to the people. But the people were at perfect liberty to accept or reject it; and their act was final. It required not the affirmance, and could not be negatived, by the state governments. The constitution, when thus adopted, was of complete obligation, and bound the state sovereignties. The government of the Union, then (whatever may be the influence of this fact on the case), is, emphatically and truly, a government of the people. In form, and in substance, it emanates from them. Its powers are granted by them, and are to be exercised directly on them, and for their benefit.

> ### Food for Thought
>
> Referring to the Preamble, Patrick Henry, a prominent opponent of the proposed Constitution, asked at the Virginia ratifying convention, "who authorized them to speak the language of, We, the People, instead of We, the States? States are the characteristics, and the soul of a confederation. If the States be not the agents of this compact, it must be one great consolidated National Government of the people of all the States." For Henry, this was a reason to oppose ratification, but of course he did not ultimately prevail in his argument. Given this history of debate, do you find the Court's view of the nature of sovereignty under the Constitution convincing?

This government is acknowledged by all to be one of enumerated powers. *** If any one proposition could command the universal assent of mankind, we might expect it would be this—that the government of the Union, though limited in its powers, is supreme within its sphere of action.

Among the enumerated powers, we do not find that of establishing a bank or creating a corporation. But there is no phrase in the instrument which, like the articles of confederation, excludes incidental or implied powers; and which requires that everything granted shall be expressly and minutely described. Even the 10th amendment, which was framed for the purpose of quieting the excessive jealousies which had been excited, omits the word "expressly," and declares only that the powers "not delegated to the United States, nor prohibited to the states, are reserved to the states or to the people;" thus leaving the question, whether the particular power which may become the subject of contest has been delegated to the one government, or prohibited to the other, to depend on a fair construction of the whole instrument. The men who drew and adopted this amendment had experienced the embarrassments resulting from the insertion of this word in the articles of confederation, and probably omitted it, to avoid those embarrassments.

> **Take Note**
>
> The Articles of Confederation provided that each state "retains" every power "not expressly granted." The Court interprets the text of the Constitution in light of its contrast with the Articles of Confederation. Is this a sensible approach to interpretation?

A constitution, to contain an accurate detail of all the subdivisions of which its great powers will admit, and of all the means by which they may be carried into execution, would partake of the prolixity of a legal code, and could scarcely be embraced by the human mind. It would, probably, never be understood by the public. Its nature, therefore, requires that only its great outlines should be marked, its important objects designated, and the minor ingredients which compose those objects be deduced from the nature of the objects themselves. That this idea was entertained by the framers of the American constitution, is not only to be inferred from the nature of the instrument, but from the language. Why else were some of the limitations, found in the 9th section of the 1st article, introduced? It is also, in some degree, warranted by their having omitted to use any restrictive term which might prevent its receiving a fair and just interpretation. In considering this question, then, we must never forget that it is a *constitution* we are expounding.

> **FYI**
>
> Justice Frankfurter called this statement—"we must never forget, this is a constitution we are expounding"— the "single most important utterance in the literature of constitutional law." Felix Frankfurter, *John Marshall and the Judicial Function*, 69 Harv. L. Rev. 217, 218-19 (1955). What does the statement mean, and what does it suggest about the proper way to interpret the Constitution? In this opinion, is Chief Justice Marshall "expounding" the federal powers or "expanding" them?

Although, among the enumerated powers of government, we do not find the word "bank" or "incorporation," we find the great powers to lay and collect taxes; to borrow money; to regulate commerce; to declare and conduct a war; and to raise and support armies and navies. The sword and the purse, all the external relations, and no inconsiderable portion of the industry of the nation, are entrusted to its government. It can never be pretended that these vast powers draw after them others of inferior importance, merely because they are inferior. Such an idea can never be advanced. But it may with great reason be contended that a government, entrusted with such ample powers, on the due execution of which the happiness and prosperity of the nation so vitally depends, must also be entrusted with ample means for their execution. The power being given, it is the interest of the nation to facilitate its execution. It can never be their interest, and cannot be presumed to have been their intention, to clog and embarrass its execution, by withholding the most appropriate means. *** Can we adopt that construction (unless the words imperiously require it), which would impute to the framers of that instrument, when granting these powers for the public good, the intention of impeding their exercise, by withholding a choice of means? If, indeed, such be the mandate of the constitution, we have only to obey; but that instrument does not profess to enumerate the means by which the powers it confers may be executed; nor does it prohibit the creation of a corporation, if the existence of such a being be essential to the beneficial exercise of those powers. It is, then, the subject of fair inquiry, how far such means may be employed.

[Maryland argues that] the power of creating a corporation is one appertaining to sovereignty, and is not expressly conferred on congress. *** [But] the government which has a right to do an act, and has imposed on it the duty of performing that act, must, according to the dictates of reason, be allowed to select the means ***. The power of creating a corporation, though appertaining to sovereignty, is not like the power of making war, or levying taxes, or of regulating commerce, a great substantive and independent power, which cannot be implied as incidental to other powers, or used as a means of executing them. It is never the end for which other powers are exercised, but a means by which other objects are accomplished. *** No sufficient reason is, therefore, perceived, why it may not pass as incidental to those powers which are expressly given, if it be a direct mode of executing them.

But the constitution of the United States has not left the right of congress to employ the necessary means, for the execution of the powers conferred on the government, to general reasoning. To its enumeration of powers is added, that of making "all laws which shall be necessary and proper, for carrying into execution the foregoing powers, and all other powers vested by this constitution, in the government of the United States, or in any department thereof." The counsel for the state of Maryland have urged various arguments, to prove that this clause, though, in terms, a grant of power, is not so, in effect; but is really restrictive of the general right, which might otherwise be implied, of selecting means for executing the enumerated powers. *** Congress is not empowered by it to make all laws, which may have relation to the powers conferred on the government, but such only as may be "*necessary and proper*" for carrying them into execution. The word "*necessary*" is considered as controlling the whole sentence, and as limiting the right to pass laws for the execution of the granted powers, to such as are indispensable, and without which the power would be nugatory. That it excludes the choice of means, and leaves to congress, in each case, that only which is most direct and simple.

Is it true that this is the sense in which the word "necessary" is always used? Does it always import an absolute physical necessity, so strong that one thing to which another may be termed necessary, cannot exist without that other? We think it does not. [W]e find that it frequently imports no more than that one thing is convenient, or useful, or essential to another. To employ the means necessary to an end, is generally understood as employing any means calculated to produce the end, and not as being confined to those single means, without which the end would be entirely unattainable. *** It is essential to just construction that many words which import something excessive should be understood in a more mitigated sense—in that sense which common usage justifies. The word "necessary" *** admits of all degrees of comparison; and is often connected with other words, which increase or diminish the impression the mind receives of the urgency it imports. A thing may be necessary, very necessary, absolutely or indispensably necessary. To no mind would the same idea be conveyed by these several phrases. The comment on the word is well illustrated by *** the 10th section of the 1st article of the constitution. It is, we think, impossible to compare the sentence which prohibits a state from laying "imposts, or duties on imports or exports, except what may be *absolutely* necessary for executing its inspection laws," with that which authorizes congress "to make all laws which shall be necessary and proper for carrying into execution" the powers of the general government, without feeling a conviction that the convention understood itself to change materially the meaning of the word "necessary" by prefixing the word "absolutely." This word, then, like others, is used in various senses; and, in its construction, the subject, the context, the intention of the person using them, are all to be taken into view.

Let this be done in the case under consideration. The subject is the execution of those great powers on which the welfare of a nation essentially depends. It must have been the intention of those who gave these powers, to insure, so far as human prudence could insure, their beneficial execution. This could not be done by confiding the choice of means to such narrow limits as not to leave it in the power of congress to adopt any which might be appropriate, and which were conducive to the end. This provision is made in a constitution, intended to endure for ages to come, and consequently, to be adapted to the various *crises* of human affairs. To have prescribed the means by which government should, in all future time, execute its powers, would have been to change, entirely, the character of the instrument, and give it the properties of a legal code. It would have been an unwise attempt to provide, by immutable rules, for exigencies which, if foreseen at all, must have been seen dimly, and which can be best provided for as they occur. To have declared that the best means shall not be used, but those alone, without which the power given would be nugatory, would have been to deprive the legislature of the capacity to avail itself of experience, to exercise its reason, and to accommodate its legislation to circumstances.

If we apply this principle of construction to any of the powers of the government, we shall find it so pernicious in its operation that we shall be compelled to discard it. *** Take, for example, the power "to establish post-offices and post-roads." This power is executed by the single act of making the establishment. But, from this has been inferred the power and duty of carrying the mail along the post-road, from one post-office to another.

And from this implied power, has again been inferred the right to punish those who steal letters from the post-office, or rob the mail. It may be said, with some plausibility, that the right to carry the mail, and to punish those who rob it, is not indispensably necessary to the establishment of a post-office and post-road. This right is indeed essential to the beneficial exercise of the power, but not indispensably necessary to its existence. *** If the word "necessary" means "needful," "requisite," "essential," "conducive to," in order to let in the power of punishment for the infraction of law; why is it not equally comprehensive, when required to authorize the use of means which facilitate the execution of the powers of government, without the infliction of punishment?

In ascertaining the sense in which the word "necessary" is used in this clause of the constitution, we may derive some aid from that with which it is associated. Congress shall have power "to make all laws which shall be necessary *and proper* to carry into execution" the powers of the government. If the word "necessary" was used in that strict and rigorous sense for which the counsel for the state of Maryland contend, it would be an extraordinary departure from the usual course of the human mind, as exhibited in composition, to add a word, the only possible effect of which is, to qualify that strict and rigorous meaning; to present to the mind the idea of some choice of means of legislation, not strained and compressed within the narrow limits for which gentlemen contend.

But the argument which most conclusively demonstrates the error of the construction contended for by the counsel for the state of Maryland is founded on the intention of the convention, as manifested in the whole clause. *** 1st. The clause is placed among the powers of congress, not among the limitations on those powers. 2d. Its terms purport to enlarge, not to diminish the powers vested in the government. It purports to be an additional power, not a restriction on those already granted. No reason has been, or can be assigned, for thus concealing an intention to narrow the discretion of the national legislature, under words which purport to enlarge it.

The result of the most careful and attentive consideration bestowed upon this clause is, that if it does not enlarge, it cannot be construed to restrain the powers of congress, or to impair the right of the legislature to exercise its best judgment in the selection of measures to carry into execution the constitutional powers of the government. If no other motive for its insertion can be suggested, a sufficient one is found in the desire to remove all doubts respecting the right to legislate on that vast mass of incidental powers which must be involved in the constitution, if that instrument be not a splendid bauble.

> **Take Note**
>
> The last sentence of this paragraph is often quoted as the holding of *Mc-Culloch v. Maryland*. What exactly does it mean?

We admit, as all must admit, that the powers of the government are limited, and that its limits are not to be transcended. But we think the sound construction of the constitution must allow to the national legislature that discretion, with respect to the means by which the powers it confers are to be carried into execution, which will enable that body to perform the high duties assigned to it, in the manner most beneficial to the people. Let the end be legitimate, let it be within the scope of the constitution, and all means which are appropriate, which are plainly adapted to that end, which are not prohibited, but consist with the letter and spirit of the constitution, are constitutional.

If a corporation may be employed, indiscriminately with other means, to carry into execution the powers of the government, no particular reason can be assigned for excluding the use of a bank, if required for its fiscal operations. To use one, must be within the discretion of congress, if it be an appropriate mode of executing the powers of government. That it is a convenient, a useful, and essential instrument in the prosecution of its fiscal operations, is not now a subject of controversy. All those who have been concerned in the administration of our finances, have concurred in representing its importance and necessity; and so strongly have they been felt, that statesmen of the first class, whose previous opinions against it had been confirmed by every circumstance which can fix the human judgment, have yielded those opinions to the exigencies of the nation. *** The time has passed away, when it can be necessary to enter into any discussion, in order to prove the importance of this instrument, as a means to effect the legitimate objects of the government.

But were its necessity less apparent, none can deny its being an appropriate measure; and if it is, the decree of its necessity, as has been very justly observed, is to be discussed in another place. Should congress, in the execution of its powers, adopt measures which are prohibited by the constitution; or should congress, under the pretext of executing its powers, pass laws for the accomplishment of objects not entrusted to the government; it would become the painful duty of this tribunal, should a case requiring such a decision come before it, to say that such an act was not the law of the land. But where the law is not prohibited, and is really calculated to effect any of the objects entrusted to the government, to undertake here to inquire into the degree of its necessity would be to pass the line which circumscribes the judicial department, and to tread on legislative ground. This court disclaims all pretensions to such a power.

> **Take Note**
>
> How does a Court determine whether Congress has enacted a particular statute in an attempt to accomplish "objects not entrusted to the government"? Should the Court determine Congress's motive in enacting the statute? If so, how can a Court determine the motive of a body composed of hundreds of individuals, each with his or her own particular (and perhaps complex) motives?

It being the opinion of the court, that the act incorporating the bank is constitutional; and that the power of establishing a branch in the state of Maryland might be properly exercised by the bank itself, we proceed to inquire—

2. Whether the state of Maryland may, without violating the constitution, tax that branch? That the power of taxation is one of vital importance; that it is retained by the states; that it is not abridged by the grant of a similar power to the government of the Union; that it is to be concurrently exercised by the two governments—are truths which have never been denied. But such is the paramount character of the constitution, that its capacity to withdraw any subject from the action of even this power is admitted. The states are expressly forbidden to lay any duties on imports or exports, except what may be abso-

lutely necessary for executing their inspection laws. If the obligation of this prohibition must be conceded—if it may restrain a state from the exercise of its taxing power on imports and exports—the same paramount character would seem to restrain, as it certainly may restrain, a state from such other exercise of this power, as is in its nature incompatible with, and repugnant to, the constitutional laws of the Union. A law, absolutely repugnant to another, as entirely repeals that other as if express terms of repeal were used.

Food for Thought

Does the inclusion in Article I, section 10 of a specific limitation on some forms of state taxation help Marshall's argument, or undermine it? And is his argument here consistent with his argument in the prior section of the opinion about the import of express limitations in the text of the Constitution?

On this ground, the counsel for the bank place its claim to be exempted from the power of a state to tax its operations. There is no express provision for the case, but the claim has been sustained on a principle which so entirely pervades the constitution, is so intermixed with the materials which compose it, so interwoven with its web, so blended with its texture, as to be incapable of being separated from it, without rending it into shreds. This great principle is that the constitution and the laws made in pursuance thereof are supreme; that they control the constitution and laws of the respective states, and cannot be controlled by them. From this, which may be almost termed an axiom, other propositions are deduced as corollaries ***. These are, 1st. That a power to create implies a power to preserve; 2d. That a power to destroy, if wielded by a different hand, is hostile to, and incompatible with these powers to create and to preserve; 3d. That where this repugnancy exists, that authority which is supreme must control, not yield to that over which it is supreme.

It is admitted, that the power of taxing the people and their property, is essential to the very existence of government, and may be legitimately exercised on the objects to which it is applicable, to the utmost extent to which the government may choose to carry it. The only security against the abuse of this power is found in the structure of the government itself. In imposing a tax, the legislature acts upon its constituents. This is, in general, a sufficient security against erroneous and oppressive taxation.

The people of a state, therefore, give to their government a right of taxing themselves and their property, and as the exigencies of government cannot be limited, they prescribe no limits to the exercise of this right, resting confidently on the interest of the legislator, and on the influence of the constituent over their representative, to guard them against its abuse. But the means employed by the government of the Union have no such security, nor is the right of a state to tax them sustained by the same theory. Those means are not given by the people of a particular state, not given by the constituents of the legislature, which claim the right to tax them, but by the people of all the states. They are given by all, for the benefit of all—and upon theory, should be subjected to that government only which belongs to all.

We are not driven to the perplexing inquiry, so unfit for the judicial department, what degree of taxation is the legitimate use, and what degree may amount to the abuse of the power. The attempt to use it on the means employed by the government of the Union, in pursuance of the constitution, is itself an abuse, because it is the usurpation of a power which the people of a single state cannot give. We find, then, on just theory, a total failure of this original right to tax the means employed by the government of the Union, for the execution of its powers. The right never existed, and the question whether it has been surrendered, cannot arise.

But, waiving this theory for the present, let us resume the inquiry, whether this power can be exercised by the respective states, consistently with a fair construction of the constitution? That the power to tax involves the power to destroy; that the power to destroy may defeat and render useless the power to create; that there is a plain repugnance in conferring on one government a power to control the constitutional measures of another, which other, with respect to those very measures, is declared to be supreme over that which exerts the control, are propositions not to be denied. But all inconsistencies are to be reconciled by the magic of the word *confidence*. Taxation, it is said, does not necessarily and unavoidably destroy. To carry it to the excess of destruction, would be an abuse, to presume which, would banish that confidence which is essential to all government. But is this a case of confidence? Would the people of any one state trust those of another with a power to control the most insignificant operations of their state government? We know they would not. Why, then, should we suppose, that the people of any one state should be willing to trust those of another with a power to control the operations of a government to which they have confided their most important and most valuable interests? In the legislature of the Union alone, are all represented. The legislature of the Union alone, therefore, can be trusted by the people with the power of controlling measures which concern all, in the confidence that it will not be abused. This, then, is not a case of confidence, and we must consider it is as it really is.

> ### Make the Connection
>
> The Court reasons that when Congress acts, it necessarily represents the views of all of the people in all of the several States. Doesn't this argument suggest that there is no need for the Courts to police federal statutes for compliance with federalism norms?

If we apply the principle for which the state of Maryland contends, to the constitution, generally, we shall find it capable of changing totally the character of that instrument. *** If the states may tax one instrument, employed by the government in the execution of its powers, they may tax any and every other instrument. They may tax the mail; they may tax the mint; they may tax patent-rights; they may tax the papers of the custom-house; they may tax judicial process; they may tax all the means employed by the government, to an excess which would defeat all the ends of government. This was not intended by the American people. They did not design to make their government dependent on the states.

It has also been insisted, that, as the power of taxation in the general and state governments is acknowledged to be concurrent, every argument which would sustain the right of the general government to tax banks chartered by the states will equally sustain the right of the states to tax banks chartered by the general government. But the two cases are not on the same reason. The people of all the states have created the general government, and have conferred upon it the general power of taxation. The people of all the states, and the states themselves, are represented in congress, and, by their representatives, exercise this power. When they tax the chartered institutions of the states, they tax their constituents; and these taxes must be uniform. But when a state taxes the operations of the government of the United States, it acts upon institutions created, not by their own constituents, but by people over whom they claim no control. It acts upon the measures of a government created by others as well as themselves, for the benefit of others in common with themselves. The difference is that which always exists, and always must exist, between the action of the whole on a part, and the action of a part on the whole—between the laws of a government declared to be supreme, and those of a government which, when in opposition to those laws, is not supreme. But if the full application of this argument could be admitted, it might bring into question the right of congress to tax the state banks, and could not prove the rights of the states to tax the Bank of the United States.

[T]he states have no power, by taxation or otherwise, to retard, impede, burden, or in any manner control, the operations of the constitutional laws enacted by congress to carry into execution the powers vested in the general government. This is, we think, the unavoidable consequence of that supremacy which the constitution has declared. [T]his is a tax on the operations of the bank, and is, consequently, a tax on the operation of an instrument employed by the government of the Union to carry its powers into execution. Such a tax must be unconstitutional.

Points for Discussion

a. We the People v. We the States

There is little doubt that the Framers believed deeply in the concept of popular sovereignty. But did they conceive of a single, undifferentiated national polity, as perhaps is indicated by the opening phrase of the Preamble, "We the People of the United States"? Or did they instead view the states as the proper repositories of popular sovereignty, as indicated by the requirement that the Constitution—and any subsequent Amendments—be ratified by conventions in three-fourths of the states? What are the implications of preferring one view over the other?

b. Implied Powers

Before even referring to the Necessary and Proper Clause, Chief Justice Marshall reasoned that Congress's enumerated powers were properly interpreted to imply subsidiary powers. What are the implications of this reasoning on the theory that Congress is limited to the powers enumerated in the text? What would be the implications of accepting Maryland's arguments against the existence of implied congressional powers?

c. Implied From What?

From which enumerated power is the authority to create a bank implied? Does Marshall answer this seemingly essential question? If not, what does that mean for his arguments?

d. "The Sweeping Clause"

The question presented in *McCulloch* was not new. Anti-Federalist opponents of the Constitution had trained much of their fire on the Necessary and Proper Clause, which they called the "sweeping clause," arguing that it would authorize the federal government to do almost anything. The first important test of the Clause's meaning came in 1791, when, at the urging of Secretary of the Treasury Alexander Hamilton, Congress enacted a bill creating the First Bank of the United States. Washington sought the views of Hamilton and Thomas Jefferson, who was Secretary of State, about the bill's constitutionality. In a now-famous opinion, Jefferson argued that the bill was unconstitutional. He began by noting that the power to incorporate a bank did not fall within any of the "powers especially enumerated" in Article I. In his view, the power to "lay taxes for the purpose of paying the debts of the United States" did not authorize the bill because "no debt is paid by this bill, nor any tax laid;" the power to "borrow money" did not authorize it because the bill "neither borrows money nor ensures the borrowing it;" and the power to regulate commerce did not authorize it because to "make a thing which may be bought and sold, is not to prescribe regulations for buying and selling." Jefferson then turned to the Necessary and Proper Clause:

> The [general] phrase is, "to make all laws necessary and proper for carrying into execution the enumerated powers." But they can all be carried into execution without a bank. A bank therefore is not necessary, and consequently not authorized by this phrase. It has been urged that a bank will give great facility or convenience in the collection of taxes. Suppose this were true: yet the Constitution allows only the means which are "necessary," not those which are merely "convenient" for effecting the enumerated powers. If such a latitude of construction be allowed to this phrase as to give any non-enumerated power, it will go to everyone, for there is not one which ingenuity may not torture into a convenience in some instance or other, to some one of so long a list of enumerated powers. It would swallow up all the delegated powers, and reduce the whole to one power ***. Therefore it was that the Constitution restrained them to the necessary means, that is to say, to those means without which the grant of power would be nugatory. *** Perhaps, indeed, bank bills may be a more convenient vehicle ***. But a little difference in the degree of convenience cannot constitute the necessity which the Constitution makes the ground for assuming any non-enumerated power.

A few years later, shortly before he became President, Jefferson criticized the view of the Necessary and Proper Clause that Chief Justice Marshall would later advance. Responding to a federal bill to charter a mining company, Jefferson mocked: "Congress are authorized to defend the nation. Ships are necessary for defence; copper is necessary for ships; mines, necessary for copper; a company necessary to work the mines; and who can doubt this reasoning who has ever played at 'This is the House that Jack Built'? Under such a process of filiation of necessities the sweeping clause makes clean work." 10 The Writings of Thomas Jefferson 165 (Lipscomb & Bergh, eds. 1904). Jefferson clearly believed, at least at the time, that such arguments impermissibly expanded the powers of the federal government. Under Jefferson's view, what would the Necessary and Proper Clause mean? And how would the courts go about enforcing the limits that such a view would entail?

e. Types of Arguments About Constitutional Meaning

Chief Justice Marshall's opinion in *McCulloch* is a classic compendium of the various forms of constitutional arguments. Can you identify points that he makes based on constitutional text? Constitutional structure? History? Original Meaning? Political Theory? Pragmatic considerations? Are arguments of these sorts of equal value in interpreting the Constitution?

> **Make the Connection**
>
> We discussed theories of interpreting the Constitution in Chapter 1.

United States v. Comstock

130 S. Ct. 1949 (2010)

Justice BREYER delivered the opinion of the Court.

The federal statute before us allows a district court to order the civil commitment of an individual who is currently "in the custody of the [Federal] Bureau of Prisons," 18 U.S.C. § 4248, if that individual (1) has previously "engaged or attempted to engage in sexually violent conduct or child molestation," (2) currently "suffers from a serious mental illness, abnormality, or disorder," and (3) "as a result of" that mental illness, abnormality, or disorder is "sexually dangerous to others," in that "he would have serious difficulty in refraining from sexually violent conduct or child molestation if released." §§ 4247(a)(5)-(6).

Confinement in the federal facility will last until either (1) the person's mental condition improves to the point where he is no longer dangerous (with or without appropriate ongoing treatment), in which case he will be released; or (2) a State assumes responsibility for his custody, care, and treatment, in which case he will be transferred to the custody of that State. §§ 4248(d)(1)-(2). The statute establishes a system for ongoing psychiatric and judicial review of the individual's case, including judicial hearings at the request of the confined person at six-month intervals. §§ 4247(e)(1)(B), (h).

In November and December 2006, the Government instituted proceedings [under § 4248] in the Federal District Court for the Eastern District of North Carolina against the five respondents in this case. *** Each of the five respondents moved to dismiss the civil-commitment proceeding on constitutional grounds.

The question presented is whether the Necessary and Proper Clause, Art. I, § 8, cl. 18, grants Congress authority sufficient to enact the statute before us. In resolving that question, we assume, but we do not decide, that other provisions of the Constitution—such as the Due Process Clause—do not prohibit civil commitment in these circumstances. *Cf. Addington v. Texas*, 441 U.S. 418 (1979). In other words, we assume for argument's sake that the Federal Constitution would permit a State to enact this statute, and we ask solely whether the Federal Government, exercising its enumerated powers, may enact such a statute as well. On that assumption, we conclude that the Constitution grants Congress legislative power sufficient to enact § 4248. We base this conclusion on five considerations, taken together.

First, the Necessary and Proper Clause grants Congress broad authority to enact federal legislation. Nearly 200 years ago, this Court stated that the Federal "[G]overnment is acknowledged by all to be one of enumerated powers," *McCulloch v. Maryland*, 4 Wheat. 316, 405 (1819), which means that "[e]very law enacted by Congress must be based on one or more of" those powers, *United States v. Morrison*, 529 U.S. 598, 607 (2000). But, at the same time, "a government, entrusted with such" powers "must also be entrusted with ample means for their execution." *McCulloch*, 4 Wheat., at 408. Accordingly, the Necessary and Proper Clause makes clear that the Constitution's grants of specific federal legislative authority are accompanied by broad power to enact laws that are "convenient, or useful" or "conducive" to the authority's "beneficial exercise." Chief Justice Marshall emphasized that the word "necessary" does not mean "absolutely necessary." In language that has come to define the scope of the Necessary and Proper Clause, he wrote: "Let the end be legitimate, let it be within the scope of the constitution, and all means which are appropriate, which are plainly adapted to that end, which are not prohibited, but consist with the letter and spirit of the constitution, are constitutional." We have since made clear that, in determining whether the Necessary and Proper Clause grants Congress the legislative authority to enact a particular federal statute, we look to see whether the statute constitutes a means that is rationally related to the implementation of a constitutionally enumerated power. *Sabri v. United States*, 541 U.S. 600, 605 (2004).

Thus, the Constitution, which nowhere speaks explicitly about the creation of federal crimes beyond those related to "counterfeiting," "treason," or "Piracies and Felonies committed on the high Seas" or "against the Law of Nations," Art. I, § 8, cls. 6, 10; Art. III, § 3, nonetheless grants Congress broad authority to create such crimes. See *McCulloch, 4 Wheat.*, at 416 ("All admit that the government may, legitimately, punish any violation of its laws; and yet, this is not among the enumerated powers of Congress"). And Congress routinely exercises its authority to enact criminal laws in furtherance of, for example, its enumerated powers to regulate interstate and foreign commerce, to enforce civil rights, to spend funds for the general welfare, to establish federal courts, to establish post offices, to regulate bankruptcy, to regulate naturalization, and so forth.

Similarly, Congress, in order to help ensure the enforcement of federal criminal laws enacted in furtherance of its enumerated powers, "can cause a prison to be erected at any place within the jurisdiction of the United States, and direct that all persons sentenced to imprisonment under the laws of the United States shall be confined there." *Ex parte Karstendick*, 93 U.S. 396, 400 (1876). *** Neither Congress' power to criminalize conduct, nor its power to imprison individuals who engage in that conduct, nor its power to enact laws governing prisons and prisoners, is explicitly mentioned in the Constitution. But Congress nonetheless possesses broad authority to do each of those things in the course of "carrying into Execution" the enumerated powers "vested by" the "Constitution in the Government of the United States," Art. I, § 8, cl. 18—authority granted by the Necessary and Proper Clause.

Second, the civil-commitment statute before us constitutes a modest addition to a set of federal prison-related mental-health statutes that have existed for many decades. We recognize that even a longstanding history of related federal action does not demonstrate a statute's constitutionality. See, *e.g., Walz v. Tax Comm'n of City of New York*, 397 U.S. 664, 678 (1970). A history of involvement, however, can nonetheless be "helpful in reviewing the substance of a congressional statutory scheme," *Gonzales v. Raich*, 545 U.S. 1, 21 (2005), and, in particular, the reasonableness of the relation between the new statute and pre-existing federal interests.

Here, Congress has long been involved in the delivery of mental health care to federal prisoners, and has long provided for their civil commitment. In 1855 it established Saint Elizabeth's Hospital in the District of Columbia to provide treatment to "the insane of the army and navy . . . and of the District of Columbia." Act of Mar. 3, 1855, 10 Stat. 682; 39 Stat. 309. In 1857 it provided for confinement at Saint Elizabeth's of any person within the District of Columbia who had been "charged with [a] crime" and who was "insane" or later became "insane during the continuance of his or her sentence in the United States penitentiary." Act of Feb. 7, 1857, §§ 5-6, 11 Stat. 158. In 1874, expanding the geographic scope of its statutes, Congress provided for civil commitment in federal facilities (or in state facilities if a State so agreed) of "*all* persons who have been or shall be convicted of *any* offense in any court of the United States" and who are or "shall become" insane "during the term of their imprisonment." Act of June 23, 1874, ch. 465, 18 Stat. 251 (emphasis added). And in 1882 Congress provided for similar commitment of those "charged" with federal offenses who become "insane" while in the "custody" of the United States. Act of Aug. 7, 1882, 22 Stat. 330 (emphasis added). Thus, over the span of three decades, Congress created a national, federal civil-commitment program under which any person who was either charged with or convicted of any federal offense in any federal court could be confined in a federal mental institution. [In 1948 and 1949, Congress] provided for the civil commitment of individuals who are, or who become, mentally incompetent at any time after their arrest and before the expiration of their federal sentence, 18 U.S.C. §§ 4241, 4244, 4247-4248, [and in] 1984 Congress modified these basic statutes [before enacting the particular statute here at issue in 2006.]

Third, Congress reasonably extended its longstanding civil-commitment system to cover mentally ill and sexually dangerous persons who are already in federal custody, even if doing so detains them beyond the termination of their criminal sentence. For one thing, the Federal Government is the custodian of its prisoners. As federal custodian, it has the constitutional power to act in order to protect nearby (and other) communities from the danger federal prisoners may pose. Indeed, at common law, one "who takes charge of a third person" is "under a duty to exercise reasonable care to control" that person to prevent him from causing reasonably foreseeable "bodily harm to others." Restatement (Second) of Torts § 319, p. 129 (1963-1964). If a federal prisoner is infected with a communicable disease that threatens others, surely it would be "necessary and proper" for the Federal Government to take action, pursuant to its role as federal custodian, to refuse (at least until the threat diminishes) to release that individual among the general public, where he might infect others (even if not threatening an interstate epidemic, cf. Art. I, § 8, cl. 3). And if confinement of such an individual is a "necessary and proper" thing to do, then how could it not be similarly "necessary and proper" to confine an individual whose mental illness threatens others to the same degree?

Fourth, the statute properly accounts for state interests. Respondents and the dissent contend that § 4248 violates the Tenth Amendment because it "invades the province of state sovereignty" in an area typically left to state control. *New York v. United States*, 505 U.S. 144, 155 (1992). But the Tenth Amendment's text is clear: "The powers *not delegated to the United States* by the Constitution, nor prohibited by it to the States, are reserved to the States respectively, or to the people." (Emphasis added.) The powers "delegated to the United States by the Constitution" include those specifically enumerated powers listed in Article I along with the implementation authority granted by the Necessary and Proper Clause. Virtually by definition, these powers are not powers that the Constitution "reserved to the States."

Fifth, the links between § 4248 and an enumerated Article I power are not too attenuated. * * * [T]he same enumerated power that justifies the creation of a federal criminal statute, and that justifies the additional implied federal powers that the dissent considers legitimate, justifies civil commitment under § 4248 as well. Thus, we must reject respondents' argument that the Necessary and Proper Clause permits no more than a single step between an enumerated power and an Act of Congress.

Taken together, these [five] considerations lead us to conclude that the statute is a "necessary and proper" means of exercising the federal authority that permits Congress to create federal criminal laws, to punish their violation, to imprison violators, to provide appropriately for those imprisoned, and to maintain the security of those who are not imprisoned but who may be affected by the federal imprisonment of others. The Constitution consequently authorizes Congress to enact the statute.

Justice ALITO, concurring in the judgment.

I entirely agree with the dissent that "[t]he Necessary and Proper Clause empowers Congress to enact only those laws that 'carr[y] into Execution' one or more of the federal powers enumerated in the Constitution," but § 4248 satisfies that requirement because it is a neces-

> **Take Note**
>
> Why did the Court take these five considerations into account? Is this list of considerations based on the text of the Constitution or on precedent? Did the Court identify these considerations by looking at sources that might show the original meaning of the Constitution? Or did the Court simply select them in an effort to create a reasonable way of deciding Necessary and Proper Clause cases? Are they all relevant? Can you think of additional relevant considerations?

sary and proper means of carrying into execution the enumerated powers that support the federal criminal statutes under which the affected prisoners were convicted. The Necessary and Proper Clause provides the constitutional authority for most federal criminal statutes. In other words, most federal criminal statutes rest upon a congressional judgment that, in order to execute one or more of the powers conferred on Congress, it is necessary and proper to criminalize certain conduct, and in order to do that it is obviously necessary and proper to provide for the operation of a federal criminal justice system and a federal prison system.

The only additional question presented here is whether, in order to carry into execution the enumerated powers on which the federal criminal laws rest, it is also necessary and proper for Congress to protect the public from dangers created by the federal criminal justice and prison systems. In my view, the answer to that question is "yes." Just as it is necessary and proper for Congress to provide for the apprehension of escaped federal prisoners, it is necessary and proper for Congress to provide for the civil commitment of dangerous federal prisoners who would otherwise escape civil commitment as a result of federal imprisonment.

This is not a case in which it is merely possible for a court to think of a rational basis on which Congress might have perceived an attenuated link between the powers underlying the federal criminal statutes and the challenged civil commitment provision. Here, there is a substantial link to Congress' constitutional powers. For this reason, I concur in the judgment that Congress had the constitutional authority to enact 18 U.S.C. § 4248.

[Justice KENNEDY's opinion concurring in the judgment is omitted.]

Justice THOMAS, with whom Justice SCALIA joins ***, dissenting.

No enumerated power in Article I, § 8, expressly delegates to Congress the power to enact a civil-commitment regime for sexually dangerous persons, nor does any other provision in the Constitution vest Congress or the other branches of the Federal Government with such a power. Accordingly, § 4248 can be a valid exercise of congressional authority only if it is "necessary and proper for carrying into Execution" one or more of those federal powers actually enumerated in the Constitution.

Section 4248 does not fall within any of those powers. The Government identifies no specific enumerated power or powers as a constitutional predicate for § 4248, and none are readily discernable. Indeed, not even the Commerce Clause—the enumerated power this Court has interpreted most expansively, see, *e.g.*, *NLRB v. Jones & Laughlin Steel Corp.*, 301 U.S. 1, 37 (1937)—can justify federal civil detention of sex offenders. Under the Court's precedents, Congress may not regulate noneconomic activity (such as sexual violence) based solely on the effect such activity may have, in individual cases or in the aggregate, on interstate commerce. *United States v. Morrison*, 529 U.S. 598, 617-618 (2000); *United States v. Lopez*, 514 U.S. 549, 563-567 (1995). That limitation fore-

> **Make the Connection**
>
> We will consider Congress's power under the Commerce Clause, and the Court's decisions in *Morrison* and *Lopez*, later in this Chapter.

closes any claim that § 4248 carries into execution Congress' Commerce Clause power, and the Government has never argued otherwise.

To be sure, protecting society from violent sexual offenders is certainly an important end. Sexual abuse is a despicable act with untold consequences for the victim personally and society generally. But the Constitution does not vest in Congress the authority to protect society from every bad act that might befall it.

The Court observes that Congress has the undisputed authority to "criminalize conduct" that interferes with enumerated powers; to "imprison individuals who engage in that conduct"; to "enact laws governing [those] prisons"; and to serve as a "custodian of its prisoners." From this, the Court assumes that § 4248 must also be a valid exercise of congressional power because it is "reasonably adapted" to *those* exercises of Congress' incidental—and thus unenumerated—authorities. But that is not the question. The Necessary and Proper Clause does not provide Congress with authority to enact any law simply because it furthers *other laws* Congress has enacted in the exercise of its incidental authority; the Clause plainly requires a showing that every federal statute "carr[ies] into Execution" one or more of the Federal Government's *enumerated powers*.[1]

Federal laws that criminalize conduct that interferes with enumerated powers, establish prisons for those who engage in that conduct, and set rules for the care and treatment of prisoners awaiting trial or serving a criminal sentence satisfy this test because each helps to "carr[y] into Execution" the enumerated powers that justify a criminal defendant's arrest or conviction. *** Civil detention under § 4248, on the other hand, lacks any such connection to an enumerated power.

[T]he Court finally concludes that the civil detention of a "sexually dangerous person" under § 4248 carries into execution the enumerated power that justified that person's arrest or conviction in the first place. [But § 4248] does not require a federal court to find any connection between the reasons supporting civil commitment and the enumerated power with which that person's criminal conduct interfered. *** [Section] 4248 permits the term of federal civil commitment to continue beyond the date on which a convicted prisoner's sentence expires or the date on which the statute of limitations on an untried defendant's crime has run, [authorizing] federal custody over a person at a time when the Government would lack jurisdiction to detain him for violating a criminal law that executes an enumerated power. [And] the definition of a "sexually dangerous person" relevant to § 4248 does not require the court to find that the person is likely to violate a law executing an enumerated power in the future. In sum, the enumerated powers that justify a criminal defendant's arrest or conviction cannot justify his subsequent civil detention under § 4248.

---

[1] Justice Scalia did not join this paragraph or the one that follows. –*Eds.*

Points for Discussion

a. Necessary and Proper for What?

Article I, § 8, clause 18 grants Congress the power "[t]o make all Laws which shall be necessary and proper for carrying into Execution the foregoing Powers [i.e., the powers expressly enumerated in Art. I, § 8, clauses 1-17], and all other Powers vested by this Constitution." Which, if any, of Congress's granted constitutional powers is the statute at issue necessary and proper for carrying into execution? Is it the Commerce Power? If so, why? Why didn't the Court specify one such enumerated power? If Congress can use the Necessary and Proper Clause to enact a law merely because it is incidental to other federal laws, what would be an example of a law that falls beyond the scope of the Necessary and Proper Clause?

b. Weighing the Factors

The Court listed five considerations to take into account when applying the Necessary and Proper Clause. In this case, all of the considerations appeared to point in the same direction. How would the case have come out if some of the considerations weighed against federal power? For example, what would be the result if there were no long history of federal involvement in this arena or no attempt to accommodate state interests?

c. Drawing Lines

The dissent reasoned that some federal laws governing the treatment of prisoners properly carry into execution the enumerated power that justified the prisoners' conviction in the first place, but that the law at issue in *Comstock* did not. If the Court adopted the dissent's approach, how would it decide which laws are incidental to enumerated powers and which are merely incidental to laws that are themselves incidental to enumerated powers?

———————

B. The Commerce Power

McCulloch demonstrates that federal power can be either express or implied—and that the same is true of limits on state power, a subject that we will revisit in Chapter 4. The Constitution, after all, does not expressly confer upon Congress the power to create a Bank of the United States, but the Court in *McCulloch* concluded that such a power is fairly implied from other grants of power in Article I.

Even when the Constitution expressly confers power on Congress, questions arise about the scope and extent of that power. Although there are 17 clauses in Article I, section 8 conferring specific powers on Congress—in addition to the Necessary and Proper Clause, which was an important focus of the Court's decision in *McCulloch*—the one that historically has been the most important is the Commerce Clause.

> ### U.S. Constitution, <u>Article I, Section 8, Clause 3</u>
>
> The Congress shall have Power *** To regulate Commerce with foreign Nations, and among the several States, and with the Indian Tribes.

Under the Articles of Confederation, the states engaged in bitter trade wars, imposing tariffs on each other's goods. These trade battles worsened an already fragile economy, but Congress was largely powerless to act. There was widespread agreement that Congress ought to have the power to protect the national market, and the Framers responded by including the Commerce Clause in the new Constitution.

One consequence of this history is that, from the very earliest years of the Republic, there has been substantial support for the view that the states should be disabled from protectionist actions that resemble the trade wars under the Articles of Confederation. We will take up this topic in Chapter 4 when we consider the so-called Dormant Commerce Clause Doctrine. But first, we consider Congress's affirmative power to act pursuant to the Commerce Clause. As we will see, this clause has served as the basis for the vast majority of federal law enacted in the last 120 years. During that time—indeed, since the ratification of the Constitution—the nature of commerce has changed dramatically, and the nature of the national market that was a central concern of the Framers has changed and expanded as well.

Over the years, the Court has had many opportunities to consider the extent of the Commerce Power. Current law holds that Congress may regulate not only interstate commerce itself, but also the channels and instrumentalities of interstate commerce and intrastate economic activities that in the aggregate have a substantial effect on interstate commerce. How did this doctrine develop? We start at the beginning.

---

1. The Early View

The Marshall Court did not have many opportunities to consider the scope of Congress's power to regulate pursuant to the Commerce Clause. The case that follows provided Chief Justice Marshall with his first meaningful opportunity to opine on the scope of Congress's power to regulate interstate commerce.

Gibbons v. Ogden

22 U.S. (9 Wheat.) 1 (1824)

[The New York legislature in 1808 granted an exclusive right to Robert Livingston and Robert Fulton to operate steamboats in New York waters. Livingston and Fulton in turn licensed Ogden to operate a ferry between New York City and Elizabethtown, New Jersey. Gibbons, who originally had been Ogden's partner, began to operate a steamboat in competition with Ogden's service. Ogden sued Gibbons, relying on his monopoly under New York state law. Gibbons responded by demonstrating that he had been granted a license to operate ferries as "vessels to be employed in the coasting trade" pursuant to a 1793 federal statute. If the federal license meant that Gibbons was free to steam from state to state, it would have been impossible for a court to give effect both to Ogden's monopoly rights under the New York law and to Gibbons's rights under federal law. Gibbons argued that Ogden's exclusive right under New York law was preempted by the federal statute pursuant to the Supremacy Clause of Article VI. The New York courts sided with Ogden and enjoined Gibbons from operating his ferries in New York waters, and Gibbons appealed to the Supreme Court.]

> **Make the Connection**
>
> We will consider Congress's power to preempt state law—and the Court's role in determining when Congress has in fact preempted state law—in Chapter 4.

Mr. Chief Justice MARSHALL delivered the opinion of the Court:

The appellant contends that this decree is erroneous, because the laws which purport to give the exclusive privilege it sustains are repugnant to the constitution and laws of the United States. They are said to be repugnant [t]o that clause in the constitution which authorizes Congress to regulate commerce.

The words are, "Congress shall have power to regulate commerce with foreign nations, and among the several States, and with the Indian tribes." The subject to be regulated is commerce; and our constitution being *** one of enumeration, and not of definition, to

> **Food for Thought**
>
> The Court relies both on the original understanding of the word "commerce" and the original intent of those who drafted and ratified the Constitution. Does this suggest that the meaning of the word "commerce" is frozen at its meaning in 1789? What would that view mean for Congress's power to adapt to changes in the nature of commerce and the American economy?

ascertain the extent of the power, it becomes necessary to settle the meaning of the word. The counsel for the appellee would limit it to traffic, to buying and selling, or the interchange of commodities, and do not admit that it comprehends navigation. This would restrict a general term, applicable to many objects, to one of its significations. Commerce, undoubtedly, is traffic, but it is something more: it is intercourse. It describes the commercial intercourse between nations, and parts of nations, in all its branches, and is regulated by prescribing rules for carrying on that intercourse. *** All America understands, and has uniformly understood, the word "commerce," to comprehend navigation. It was so understood, and must have been so understood, when the constitution was framed. The power over commerce, including navigation, was one of the primary objects for which the people of America adopted their government, and must have been contemplated in forming it. The convention must have used the word in that sense, because all have understood it in that sense; and the attempt to restrict it comes too late.

[A]dditional confirmation is, we think, furnished by the words of the instrument itself. The 9th section of the 1st article declares that "no preference shall be given, by any regulation of commerce or revenue, to the ports of one State over those of another." [T]he most obvious preference which can be given to one port over another, in regulating commerce, relates to navigation. But the subsequent part of the sentence is still more explicit. It is, "nor shall vessels bound to or from one State, be obliged to enter, clear, or pay duties, in another." These words have a direct reference to navigation. *** The word used in the constitution, then, comprehends, and has been always understood to comprehend, navigation within its meaning; and a power to regulate navigation, is as expressly granted, as if that term had been added to the word "commerce."

The subject to which the power is *** applied, is to commerce "among the several States." The word "among" means intermingled with. A thing which is among others is intermingled with them. Commerce among the States cannot stop at the external boundary line of each State, but may be introduced into the interior.

It is not intended to say that these words comprehend that commerce, which is completely internal, which is carried on between man and man in a State, or between different parts of the same State, and which does not extend to or affect other States. Such a power would be inconvenient, and is certainly unnecessary.

Comprehensive as the word "among" is, it may very properly be restricted to that commerce which concerns more States than one. The phrase is not one which would probably have been selected to indicate the completely interior traffic of a State, because it is not an apt phrase for that purpose; and the enumeration of the particular classes of commerce, to which the power was to be extended, would not have been made, had the intention been to extend the power to every description. The enumeration presupposes something not enumerated; and that something, if we regard the language or the subject of the sentence, must be the exclusively internal commerce of a State. The genius and character of the whole government seem to be that its action is to be applied to all the external concerns of the nation, and to those internal concerns which affect the States generally; but not to those which are completely within a particular State, which do not affect other States, and with which it is not necessary to interfere, for the purpose of executing some of the general powers of the government. The completely internal commerce of a State, then, may be considered as reserved for the State itself.

We are now arrived at the inquiry—What is this power? It is the power to regulate; that is, to prescribe the rule by which commerce is to be governed. This power, like all others vested in Congress, is complete in itself, may be exercised to its utmost extent, and acknowledges no limitations, other than are prescribed in the constitution. *** [T]he sovereignty of Congress, though limited to specified objects, is plenary as to those objects ***. The wisdom and the discretion of Congress, their identity with the people, and the influence which their constituents possess at elections, are, in this, as in many other instances, as that, for example, of declaring war, the sole restraints on which they have relied, to secure them from its abuse. They are the restraints on which the people must often [rely] solely, in all representative governments.

> **Take Note**
>
> The Court declares that Congress's power to regulate is "plenary." "Plenary" means "completed" or "unqualified." This means that Congress can impose any kind of regulation that it chooses—prohibitions, taxes, quality standards, and so forth. As we see more cases in this Chapter, consider whether the Court has in fact treated this power as plenary.

The power of Congress, then, comprehends navigation, within the limits of every State in the Union; so far as that navigation may be, in any manner, connected with "commerce with foreign nations, or among the several States, or with the Indian tribes." It may, of consequence, pass the jurisdictional line of New York, and act upon the very waters to which the prohibition now under consideration applies.

[The Court's discussion of the argument that the Commerce Clause prevents states from acting, even in the absence of federal legislation, to regulate commerce is discussed in Chapter 4.]

[I]n exercising the power of regulating their own purely internal affairs, whether of trading or police, the States may sometimes enact laws, the validity of which depends on their interfering with, and being contrary to, an act of Congress passed in pursuance of the constitution. [Accordingly,] the Court will enter upon the inquiry, whether the laws of New York, as expounded by the highest tribunal of that State, have, in their application to this case, come into collision with an act of Congress, and deprived a citizen of a right to which that act entitles him. Should this collision exist, *** the acts of New York must yield to the law of Congress; and the decision sustaining the privilege they confer, against a right given by a law of the Union, must be erroneous.

[The federal statute pursuant to which Gibbons received his license] demonstrates the opinion of Congress that steam boats may be enrolled and licensed, in common with vessels using sails. They are, of course, entitled to the same privileges, and can no more be restrained from navigating waters, and entering ports which are free to such vessels, than if they were wafted on their voyage by the winds, instead of being propelled by the agency of fire. The one element may be as legitimately used as the other, for every commercial purpose authorized by the laws of the Union; and the act of a State inhibiting the use of either to any vessel having a license under the act of Congress, comes, we think, in direct collision with that act.

Mr. Justice JOHNSON[, concurring:]

For a century the States had submitted, with murmurs, to the commercial restrictions imposed by the parent State; and now, finding themselves in the unlimited possession of those powers over their own commerce, which they had so long been deprived of, and so

FYI

Justice Johnson was President Jefferson's first appointment to the Court. Yet his view of federal power arguably was even broader than that advanced by Marshall, a Federalist and a nationalist until the end.

earnestly coveted, that selfish principle which, well controlled, is so salutary, and which, unrestricted, is so unjust and tyrannical, guided by inexperience and jealousy, began to show itself in iniquitous laws and impolitic measures, from which grew up a conflict of commercial regulations, destructive to the harmony of the States, and fatal to their commercial interests abroad. This was the immediate cause that led to the forming of a convention.

The history of the times will, therefore, sustain the opinion, that the grant of power over commerce, if intended to be commensurate with the evils existing, and the purpose of remedying those evils, could be only commensurate with the power of the States over the subject. And this opinion is supported by a very remarkable evidence of the general understanding of the whole American people, when the grant was made. *** The power of a sovereign state over commerce *** amounts to nothing more than a power to limit and restrain it at pleasure.

Points for Discussion

a. Questions the Court Answers

The Court answers three questions about Article I, § 8, cl. 3: (1) What does "commerce" mean? Is it just buying and selling or is it something else? (2) What is commerce "among the several states"? Is it only shipping goods from one state to another or is it something more? (3) What is the power to "regulate"? Can Congress impose any kind of restriction or requirement on commerce among the states or is its power subject to limitations?

b. Political Safeguards of Federalism

Chief Justice Marshall stated that "[t]he wisdom and the discretion of Congress, their identity with the people, and the influence which their constituents possess at elections, are *** the sole restraints on which [the people] have relied, to secure them from its abuse." Taken to its logical extreme, doesn't this argument suggest that the Court should *never* invalidate an Act of Congress on the ground that it is inconsistent with federalism norms?

c. Express and Implied Limitations on State Power

In *Gibbons*, the Court was confronted with conflicting claims of right, one arising under federal law and the other arising under state law. The Court concluded that the federal statute preempted the state law. In light of the history on which Justice Johnson relied, should the states be disabled from regulating interstate commerce even in the absence of affirmative legislation from Congress? We will consider that question in Chapter 4.

---

2. The Middle Years: Uncertainty and a Restrictive View

In the first half of the nineteenth century, the Court had few occasions to construe the scope of Congress's power to regulate commerce, because Congress rarely exercised that power. And the cases during that time that did involve the Commerce Clause generally involved challenges to state, rather than federal, action, pursuant to the Dormant Commerce Clause Doctrine, which we will consider in Chapter 4. In the second half of the nineteenth century, however, the effects of industrialization led to several federal legislative responses. Congress regulated railroads, which were rapidly expanding across the continent, and attempted to regulate monopolies and unreasonable restraints of trade. Those efforts at regulation were challenged by parties on whom they imposed burdens, and the Court's responses were not entirely consistent. In some cases, such as the *E.C. Knight* case that follows, the Court offered a restrictive reading of Congress's power. In others—such as the *Shreveport Rate Case*, below—the Court construed Congress's power to regulate interstate commerce broadly.

United States v. E.C. Knight Co.

156 U.S. 1 (1895)

> **FYI**
>
> The Sherman Antitrust Act prohibits "[e]very contract, combination in the form of trust or otherwise, or conspiracy, in restraint of trade or commerce among the several States, or with foreign nations," 15 U.S.C. § 1, and prohibits attempts "to monopolize any part of the trade or commerce among the several States, or with foreign nations," 15 U.S.C. § 2.

Mr. Chief Justice FULLER *** delivered the opinion of the Court.

By the purchase of the stock of the four Philadelphia refineries with shares of its own stock the American Sugar Refining Company acquired nearly complete control of the manufacture of refined sugar within the United States. The bill charged that the contracts under which these purchases were made constituted combinations in restraint of trade *** contrary to the [federal Sherman Antitrust Act]. The fundamental question is whether, conceding that the existence of a monopoly in manufacture is established by the evidence, that monopoly can be directly suppressed under the act of congress in the mode attempted by this bill. *** That which belongs to commerce is within the jurisdiction of the United States, but that which does not belong to commerce is within the jurisdiction of the police power of the state.

The argument is that the power to control the manufacture of refined sugar is a monopoly over a necessary of life, to the enjoyment of which by a large part of the population of the United States interstate commerce is indispensable, and that, therefore, the general government, in the exercise of the power to regulate commerce, may repress such monopoly directly, and set aside the instruments which have created it. But this argument cannot be confined to necessaries of life merely, and must include all articles of general consumption. Doubtless the power to control the manufacture of a given thing involves, in a certain sense, the control of its disposition, but this is a secondary, and not the primary, sense; and, although the exercise of that power may result in bringing the operation of commerce into play, it does not control it, and affects it only incidentally and indirectly. Commerce succeeds to manufacture, and is not a part of it.

It will be perceived how far-reaching the proposition is that the power of dealing with a monopoly directly may be exercised by the general government whenever interstate or international commerce may be ultimately affected. *** [I]f the national power extends to all contracts and combinations in manufacture, agriculture, mining, and other productive industries, whose ultimate result may affect external commerce, comparatively little of business operations and affairs would be left for state control.

It was in the light of well-settled principles that the [Sherman Act] was framed. *** [W]hat the law struck at was combinations, contracts, and conspiracies to monopolize trade and commerce among the several states or with foreign nations; but the contracts and acts of the defendants related exclusively to the acquisition of the Philadelphia refineries and the business of sugar refining in Pennsylvania, and bore no direct relation to commerce between the states or with foreign nations. The object was manifestly private gain in the manufacture of the commodity, but not through the control of interstate or foreign commerce. *** There was nothing in the proofs to indicate any intention to put a restraint upon trade or commerce, and the fact, as we have seen, that trade or commerce might be indirectly affected, was not enough to entitle complainants to a decree.

> **Food for Thought**
>
> Why do you suppose the American Sugar Refining Company sought to acquire all other sugar refiners in the United States? Should it have been difficult to adduce proof of the defendant's "intention to put a restraint upon trade or commerce"? What effect should evidence of such an intention have on the Court's analysis?

The circuit court declined *** to grant the relief prayed, and dismissed the bill. [Affirmed.]

Mr. Justice HARLAN, dissenting.

Any combination *** that disturbs or unreasonably obstructs freedom in buying and selling articles manufactured to be sold to persons in other states, or to be carried to other states—a freedom that cannot exist if the right to buy and sell is fettered by unlawful restraints that crush out competition—affects, not incidentally, but directly, the people of all the states; and the remedy for such an evil is found only in the exercise of powers confided to a government which, this court has said, was the government of all, exercising powers delegated by all, representing all, acting for all.

[T]he act of 1890 *** does not strike at the manufacture simply of articles that are legitimate or recognized subjects of commerce, but at combinations that unduly restrain, because they monopolize, the buying and selling of articles which are to go into interstate commerce.

[The Court's] view of the scope of the act leaves the public, so far as national power is concerned, entirely at the mercy of combinations which arbitrarily control the prices of articles purchased to be transported from one state to another state. I cannot assent to that view. In my judgment, the general government is not placed by the constitution in such a condition of helplessness that it must fold its arms and remain inactive while capital combines, under the name of a corporation, to destroy competition, not in one state only, but throughout the entire country, in the buying and selling of articles—especially the necessaries of life—that go into commerce among the states. The doctrine of the autonomy of the states cannot properly be invoked to justify a denial of power in the national government to meet such an emergency, involving, as it does, that freedom of commercial intercourse among the states which the constitution sought to attain.

———————

Points for Discussion

a. The Constitution and Statutory Interpretation

Did the Court hold that the Sherman Antitrust Act was unconstitutional? Or did it hold that Congress did not purport to reach the type of conduct that gave rise to the United States' claims against the American Sugar Refining Company? If the latter, what role did the Court's interpretation of the Constitution play in interpreting the scope of the statute? Do you think that Congress meant to regulate the type of conduct in which the defendant was accused of engaging?

b. Precedent

Is it possible to reconcile the decision in *E.C. Knight* with Chief Justice Marshall's statement in *Gibbons* that Congress has power to regulate commerce that "concerns more States than one"?

———————

Shreveport Rate Case

234 U.S. 342 (1914)

Mr. Justice HUGHES delivered the opinion of the court:

[The Interstate Commerce Commission established rates for transporting goods by rail from Shreveport, Louisiana, to various stops in Texas. The Commission then ordered several railroads to cease charging rates for transporting goods within Texas that were disproportionately lower than the prevailing rates for the transportation of goods between points in Texas and Shreveport. (The railroads had been charging more for shorter trips from points in Texas to Shreveport than they had been charging for longer trips entirely in

Texas.) The ICC concluded that such rates "unjustly discriminated in favor of traffic within the state of Texas, and against similar traffic between Louisiana and Texas." Three railroads filed suit to set aside the Commission's order.]

[Congress's] authority, extending to these interstate carriers as instruments of interstate commerce, necessarily embraces the right to control their operations in all matters having such a close and substantial relation to interstate traffic that the control is essential or appropriate to the security of that traffic, to the efficiency of the interstate service, and to the maintenance of conditions under which interstate commerce may be conducted upon fair terms and without molestation or hindrance. As it is competent for Congress to legislate to these ends, unquestionably it may seek their attainment by requiring that the agencies of interstate commerce shall not be used in such manner as to cripple, retard, or destroy it. The fact that carriers are instruments of intrastate commerce, as well as of interstate commerce, does not derogate from the complete and paramount authority of Congress over the latter, or preclude the Federal power from being exerted to prevent the intrastate operations of such carriers from being made a means of injury to that which has been confided to Federal care. Wherever the interstate and intrastate transactions of carriers are so related that the government of the one involves the control of the other, it is Congress, and not the state, that is entitled to prescribe the final and dominant rule, for otherwise Congress would be denied the exercise of its constitutional authority, and the state, and not the nation, would be supreme within the national field.

> **Make the Connection**
>
> The ICC was exercising power that Congress delegated to it to regulate rates for shipping by rail. The suit thus involved the issue of whether the power that Congress delegated was within Congress's power under the Commerce Clause. We will consider Congress's power to delegate decision-making authority to agencies in Chapter 6. We will also consider state attempts to regulate interstate rail traffic, in the *Wabash* case, in Chapter 4.

Congress, in the exercise of its paramount power, may prevent the common instrumentalities of interstate and intrastate commercial intercourse from being used in their intrastate operations to the injury of interstate commerce. This is not to say that Congress possesses the authority to regulate the internal commerce of a state, as such, but that it does possess the power to foster and protect interstate commerce, and to take all measures necessary or appropriate to that end, although intrastate transactions of interstate carriers may thereby be controlled.

> **Food for Thought**
>
> In what way did the comparatively lower rates for intrastate shipping affect the *interstate* shipping market? In light of those effects, did it make sense to conclude that Congress was protecting the interstate market by regulating rates in the intrastate market?

This principle is applicable here. We find no reason to doubt that Congress is entitled to keep the highways of interstate communication open to interstate traffic upon fair and equal terms. *** It is immaterial, so far as the protecting power of Congress is concerned, that the discrimination arises from intrastate rates as compared with interstate rates. The use of the instrument of interstate commerce in a discriminatory manner so as to inflict injury upon that commerce, or some part thereof, furnishes abundant ground for Federal intervention.

———————————

Points for Discussion

a. Precedent

Is the holding in the *Shreveport Rate Case* reconcilable with the decision in *E.C. Knight*? If Congress has the "power to foster and protect interstate commerce," why doesn't it have the power to prevent monopolization that will affect the prices of goods sold interstate? Conversely, if Congress does not have authority to regulate manufacturing, on the theory that manufacturing is not "commerce" and affects commerce only indirectly, then why does it have authority to regulate intrastate shipping? Is the transportation of goods by railroad "commerce" in a way that manufacturing is not?

b. Textual Sources of Authority

Is the Court relying only on the Commerce Clause in reaching its conclusion in the *Shreveport Rate Case*? Or is it implicitly relying on the Necessary and Proper Clause, as well? Recall that the Court in *McCulloch* held that the Necessary and Proper Clause authorizes Congress to enact measures "plainly adapted" to the effectuation of ends legitimately sought pursuant to Congress's other affirmative powers. What is the relevance of the Necessary and Proper Clause in cases involving Congress's power to regulate interstate commerce?

———————————

The view of the Court in *E.C. Knight*—that Congress has power only to regulate commerce narrowly defined, and not the effects of local activity on interstate commerce—could not for long coexist peacefully with the view of the Court in the <u>Shreveport Rate Case</u>, under which Congress has authority to regulate intrastate matters that have such a "close and substantial relation to interstate traffic that the control is essential or appropriate to the security of that traffic, to the efficiency of interstate service, and to the maintenance of conditions under which interstate commerce may be conducted upon fair terms and without molestation or hindrance." But at least for a time, the Court unpredictably vacillated between *E.C. Knight*'s formal view of commerce and the <u>Shreveport Rate Case</u>'s more flexible effects test. The Court also sometimes upheld legislation on the ground that Congress may regulate local activities that are part of a larger "current of commerce among the States." *Swift & Co. v. United States*, 196 U.S. 375 (1905) (upholding an injunction under the Sherman Act against price fixing by local meat sellers); *Stafford v. Wallace*, 258 U.S. 495 (1922) (holding that the Packers and Stockyards Act of 1921 could constitutionally be applied to local dealers).

But the doctrine was even more confused than that. In the late nineteenth and early twentieth century, Congress enacted a series of statutes that regulated interstate shipments and transactions—that is, something like the "commerce" to which the Court in *E.C. Knight* had limited Congress's power—but that clearly appeared motivated as much by social and moral concerns as by economic concerns. The Court was often divided in its responses to such statutes. Consider the case that follows.

_____

Champion v. Ames

188 U.S. 321 (1903)

Mr. Justice HARLAN delivered the opinion of the court:

[The appellant was indicted for conspiring to violate an 1895 federal statute criminalizing the interstate transportation of lottery tickets, by arranging for the shipment of lottery tickets from Texas to California. He sought a writ of habeas corpus on the ground that the 1895 Act was unconstitutional.]

The appellant insists that the carrying of lottery tickets from one state to another state by an express company engaged in carrying freight and packages from state to state, although such tickets may be contained in a box or package, does not constitute, and cannot by any act of Congress be legally made to constitute, commerce among the states within the meaning of the [Commerce Clause]. *** We are of opinion that lottery tickets are subjects of traffic, and therefore are subjects of commerce, and the regulation of the carriage of such tickets from state to state, at least by independent carriers, is a regulation of commerce among the several states.

But it is said that the statute in question does not regulate the carrying of lottery tickets from state to state, but by punishing those who cause them to be so carried Congress in effect prohibits such carrying; that in respect of the carrying from one state to another of articles or things that are, in fact, or according to usage in business, the subjects of commerce, the authority given Congress was not to *prohibit*, but only to *regulate*. *** If lottery traffic, *carried on through interstate commerce*, is a matter of which Congress may take cognizance and over which its power may be exerted, can it be possible that it must tolerate the traffic, and simply regulate the manner in which it may be carried on? Or may not Congress, for the protection of the people of all the states, and under the power to regulate interstate commerce, devise such means, within the scope of the Constitution, and not prohibited by it, as will drive that traffic out of commerce among the states?

If a state, when considering legislation for the suppression of lotteries within its own limits, may properly take into view the evils that inhere in the raising of money, in that mode, why may not Congress, invested with the power to regulate commerce among the several states, provide that such commerce shall not be polluted by the carrying of lottery tickets from one state to another? In this connection it must not be forgotten that the power of Congress to regulate commerce among the states is plenary, is complete in itself, and is subject to no limitations except such as may be found in the Constitution. *** If it be said that [the Act] is inconsistent with the 10th Amendment, [the] answer is that the power to regulate commerce among the states has been expressly delegated to Congress.

Besides, Congress, by that act, does not assume to interfere with traffic or commerce in lottery tickets carried on exclusively within the limits of any state, but has in view only commerce of that kind among the several states. It has not assumed to interfere with the completely internal affairs of any state, and has only legislated in respect of a matter which concerns the people of the United States. As a state may, for the purpose of guarding the morals of its own people, forbid all sales of lottery tickets within its limits, so Congress, for the purpose of guarding the people of the United States against the "widespread pestilence of lotteries" and to protect the commerce which concerns all the states, may prohibit the carrying of lottery tickets from one state to another. In legislating upon the subject of the traffic in lottery tickets, as carried on through interstate commerce, Congress only supplemented the action of those states—perhaps all of them—which, for the protection of the public morals, prohibit the drawing of lotteries, as well as the sale or circulation of lottery tickets, within their respective limits. It said, in effect, that it would not permit the declared policy of the states, which sought to protect their people against the mischiefs of the lottery business, to be overthrown or disregarded by the agency of interstate commerce. We should hesitate long before adjudging that an evil of such appalling character, carried on through interstate commerce, cannot be met and crushed by the only power competent to that end. We say competent to that end, because Congress alone has the power to occupy, by legislation, the whole field of interstate commerce.

It is said, however, that if, in order to suppress lotteries carried on through interstate commerce, Congress may exclude lottery tickets from such commerce, that principle leads necessarily to the conclusion that Congress may arbitrarily exclude from commerce among the states any article, commodity, or thing, of whatever kind or nature, or however useful or valuable, which it may choose, no matter with what motive, to declare shall not be carried from one state to another. It will be time enough to consider the constitutionality of such legislation when we must do so. The present case does not require the court to declare the full extent of the power that Congress may exercise in the regulation of commerce among the states. *** It would not be difficult to imagine legislation that would be justly liable to such an objection as that stated, and be hostile to the objects for the accomplishment of which Congress was invested with the general power to regulate commerce among the several states. But, as often said, the possible abuse of a power is not an argument against its existence. [Affirmed.]

Mr. Chief Justice FULLER, with whom concur Mr. Justice BREWER, Mr. Justice SHIRAS, and Mr. Justice PECKHAM, dissenting:

That the purpose of Congress in this enactment was the suppression of lotteries cannot reasonably be denied. That purpose is avowed in the title of the act, and is its natural and reasonable effect, and by that its validity must be tested. It is urged [that] because Congress is empowered to regulate commerce between the several states, it, therefore, may suppress

> **FYI**
>
> The federal statute was entitled "An Act for the Suppression of Lottery Traffic through National and Interstate Commerce and the Postal Service, Subject to the Jurisdiction and Laws of the United States."

lotteries by prohibiting the carriage of lottery matter. Congress may, indeed, make all laws necessary and proper for carrying the powers granted to it into execution, and doubtless an act prohibiting the carriage of lottery matter would be necessary and proper to the execution of a power to suppress lotteries; but that power belongs to the states and not to Congress. To hold that Congress has general police power would be to hold that it may accomplish objects not [entrusted] to the general government, and to defeat the operation of the 10th Amendment.

Points for Discussion

a. Commerce "Among the States"

The federal statute at issue in *Champion* prohibited, among other things, the mere interstate transportation of lottery tickets by mail, even if the tickets were not sold across state lines. Is there an argument that such acts do not constitute commerce, even under the *E.C. Knight* Court's conception of the term? Or should it be enough that the regulated activity spanned state lines?

b. Federal Objectives

Recall that in *McCulloch* the Court declared, "should congress, under the pretext of executing its powers, pass laws for the accomplishment of objects not entrusted to the government; it would become the painful duty of this tribunal, should a case requiring such a decision come before it, to say that such an act was not the law of the land." Does this mean that when Congress invokes the commerce power in an attempt to regulate some local matter, the Court should invalidate the regulation? Should Congress's motives matter in deciding whether it has properly invoked its power under the Commerce Clause? The Court in *Champion* seemed to conclude that it was of no moment that Congress apparently enacted the statute to protect the people "against the widespread pestilence of lotteries," because the statute, in prohibiting an article from interstate commerce, regulated interstate transactions, a matter always within Congress's competence.

Champion v. Ames was one of a series of cases in which the Court upheld Congress's authority to regulate interstate transactions as a means of achieving social and moral objectives. Following this approach, for example, the Court upheld a statute that prohibited from interstate commerce food and drug items that contained a "deleterious" ingredient, *Hipolite Egg Co. v. United States*, 220 U.S. 45 (1911), and a statute prohibiting the transportation in interstate commerce of women for immoral purposes, *Hoke v. United States*, 227 U.S. 308 (1913). But the Court's decisions did not apply this principle uniformly, and the Court soon moved towards a more narrow and formal view of Congress's power under the Commerce Clause. Consider the cases that follow.

Hammer v. Dagenhart

247 U.S. 251 (1918)

Mr. Justice DAY delivered the opinion of the Court.

A bill was filed in the United States District Court for the Western District of North Carolina by a father in his own behalf and as next friend of his two minor sons, one under the age of fourteen years and the other between the ages of fourteen and sixteen years, employ[ees] in a cotton mill at Charlotte, North Carolina, to enjoin the enforcement of the act of Congress intended to prevent interstate commerce in the products of child labor. [The law prohibited the transportation in interstate commerce of goods produced in factories that employed (1) children under fourteen years old or (2) children between fourteen and sixteen years old (a) at night, (b) for more than eight hours per day, or (c) for more than six days per week.]

[I]t is insisted that adjudged cases in this court establish the doctrine that the power to regulate given to Congress incidentally includes the authority to prohibit the movement of ordinary commodities ***. The cases demonstrate the contrary. They rest upon the character of the particular subjects dealt with and the fact that the scope of governmental authority, state or national, possessed over them is such that the authority to prohibit is as to them but the exertion of the power to regulate. [In *Champion*, *Hipolite Egg*, and *Hoke*,] the use of interstate transportation was necessary to the accomplishment of harmful results. In other words, although the power over interstate transportation was to regulate, that could only be accomplished by prohibiting the use of the facilities of interstate commerce to effect the evil intended.

This element is wanting in the present case. The thing intended to be accomplished by this statute is the denial of the facilities of interstate commerce to those manufacturers in the states who employ children within the prohibited ages. The act in its effect does not regulate transportation among the states, but aims to standardize the ages at which children may be employed in mining and manufacturing within the states. The goods shipped are of themselves harmless. *** When offered for shipment, and before transportation begins, the labor of their production is over, and the mere fact that they were intended for interstate commerce transportation does not make their production subject to federal control under the commerce power.

The making of goods and the mining of coal are not commerce, nor does the fact that these things are to be afterwards shipped, or used in interstate commerce, make their production a part thereof. [T]he production of articles,

> **Take Note**
>
> Under the *E.C. Knight* conception of commerce, manufacturing and other "local" activities were not within Congress's power to regulate, even if they had significant "indirect" effects on commerce. But the statute at issue in *Hammer* regulated the interstate shipment of goods, which would appear to constitute interstate commerce even within the *E.C. Knight* view. Is the Court applying the *E.C. Knight* test—which, we have seen, was a relatively narrow view of Congress's power—or some other, even more restrictive, test?

intended for interstate commerce, is a matter of local regulation. *** If it were otherwise, all manufacture intended for interstate shipment would be brought under federal control to the practical exclusion of the authority of the states, a result certainly not contemplated by the framers of the Constitution when they vested in Congress the authority to regulate commerce among the States.

It is further contended that the authority of Congress may be exerted to control interstate commerce in the shipment of child-made goods because of the effect of the circulation of such goods in other states where the evil of this class of labor has been recognized by local legislation, and the right to thus employ child labor has been more rigorously restrained than in the state of production. In other words, that the unfair competition, thus engendered, may be controlled by closing the channels of interstate commerce to manufacturers in those states where the local laws do not meet what Congress deems to be the more just standard of other states.

There is no power vested in Congress to require the states to exercise their police power so as to prevent possible unfair competition. Many causes may co-operate to give one state, by reason of local laws or conditions, an economic advantage over others. The commerce clause was not intended to give to Congress a general authority to equalize such conditions. *** The grant of authority over a purely federal matter was not intended to destroy the local power always existing and carefully reserved to the states in the Tenth Amendment to the Constitution.

To sustain this statute would not be in our judgment a recognition of the lawful exertion of congressional authority over interstate commerce, but would sanction an invasion by the federal power of the control of a matter purely local in its character, and over which no authority has been delegated to Congress in conferring the power to regulate commerce among the states. *** Thus the act in a two-fold sense is repugnant to the Constitution. It not only transcends the authority delegated to Congress over commerce but also exerts a power as to a purely local matter to which the federal authority does not extend. The far reaching result of upholding the act cannot be more plainly indicated than by pointing out that if Congress can thus regulate matters entrusted to local authority by prohibition of the movement of commodities in interstate commerce, all freedom of commerce will be at an end, and the power of the states over local matters may be eliminated, and thus our system of government be practically destroyed. [For] these reasons we hold that this law exceeds the constitutional authority of Congress.

Mr. Justice HOLMES, [joined by Mr. Justice McKENNA, Mr. Justice BRANDEIS, and Mr. Justice CLARKE,] dissenting.

[I]f an act is within the powers specifically conferred upon Congress, it seems to me that it is not made any less constitutional because of the indirect effects that it may have, however obvious it may be that it will have those effects, and that we are not at liberty upon such grounds to hold it void. *** The statute confines itself to prohibiting the carriage of certain goods in interstate or foreign commerce. Congress is given power to regulate such commerce in unqualified terms. [A] law is not beyond the regulative power of Congress merely because it prohibits certain transportation out and out. *Champion v. Ames*.

The question then is narrowed to whether the exercise of its otherwise constitutional power by Congress can be pronounced unconstitutional because of its possible reaction upon the conduct of the States in a matter upon which I have admitted that they are free from direct control. [T]he power to regulate commerce and other constitutional powers could not be cut down or qualified by the fact that it might interfere with the carrying out of the domestic policy of any State.

The notion that prohibition is any less prohibition when applied to things now thought evil I do not understand. But if there is any matter upon which civilized countries have agreed[,] it is the evil of premature and excessive child labor. I should have thought that if we were to introduce our own moral conceptions where in my opinion they do not belong, this was preeminently a case for upholding the exercise of all its powers by the United States. But I had thought that the propriety of the exercise of a power admitted to exist in some cases was for the consideration of Congress alone and that this Court always had disavowed the right to intrude its judgment upon questions of policy or morals. It is not for this Court to pronounce when prohibition is necessary to regulation if it ever may be necessary—to say that it is permissible as against strong drink but not as against the product of ruined lives. *** The national welfare as understood by Congress may require a different attitude within its sphere from that of some self-seeking State. It seems to me entirely constitutional for Congress to enforce its understanding by all the means at its command.

————————

Points for Discussion

a. Precedent

The federal statute at issue in *Hammer* prohibited the interstate shipment of goods produced with child labor. In *Champion v. Ames*, the Court had sustained Congress's power to regulate the interstate shipment of goods even though Congress's apparent motive was to enforce its own social and moral views. Yet the Court in *Hammer* appears to have held that Congress cannot regulate even *inter*state commerce if the effect of that regulation is to control *intra*state activity. Why didn't the Court feel bound by *Champion* and related cases? Is the ground on which the Court distinguished those cases convincing?

b. "Two-Fold" Repugnancy

The Court stated that the act "in a two-fold sense is repugnant to the Constitution" because it both exceeds Congress's power under the Commerce Clause and regulates a matter "purely local in character." Are these different grounds for unconstitutionality? If the Tenth Amendment is the basis for the latter form of repugnancy, does the Court's view represent a sensible interpretation of the Tenth Amendment?

————————

Hammer reveals that the Court in the first third of the twentieth century was increasingly emboldened in enforcing or perhaps imposing limits on Congress's power to regulate the economy. But at the same time that the Court was settling on a restrictive test for federal power, large majorities of voters in the country were beginning to look to the federal government to address serious economic problems. In the 1930s, the nation was in the worst economic depression in its history; over 30 million Americans—25 percent of the population—had no source of income at all. Franklin D. Roosevelt was elected President after promising to solve the economic crisis with strong national regulation of the marketplace. Roosevelt proposed the "New Deal," which would use federal law to restrain what he viewed as abusive labor practices and other excesses of big businesses. He also promised to promote healthy competition, to protect consumer and employee health, safety, and morality, and to create a social safety net. A sympathetic Congress enacted dozens of federal statutes to regulate numerous aspects of the national economy.

The Court initially responded to these aggressive assertions of federal authority by invalidating the statutes that came before it. In *Railroad Retirement Board v. Alton Railroad Co.*, 295 U.S. 330 (1935), the Court held that the Commerce Clause did not permit Congress to create a compulsory retirement and pension plan for all carriers subject to the Interstate Commerce Act. In *A.L.A. Schechter Poultry Corp. v. United States*, 295 U.S. 495 (1935), the Court struck down the National Industrial Recovery Act of 1933 (NIRA), which authorized the President to issue "codes of fair competition for *** trade or industry." These codes, which were industry-specific and which the President typically issued after consultation with trade associations in the relevant industries, generally regulated employee wages and hours and identified and prohibited unfair trade practices. The Court concluded both that the Act unconstitutionally delegated legislative power and that the Act's authorization of regulation of employee wages and hours exceeded Congress's power under the Commerce Clause.

> **Make the Connection**
>
> We will consider Congress's power to delegate decision-making authority, and the non-delegation doctrine specifically, in Chapter 6.

President Roosevelt and Congress, however, were not chastened by these decisions. Roosevelt asked Congress to enact a regulatory scheme for the coal industry that was very similar in nature to the codes promulgated under the NIRA. Congress responded by enacting the Bituminous Coal Conservation Act of 1935, which was immediately challenged on the ground, among others, that it exceeded Congress's power under the Commerce Clause. The statute created a Commission in the Department of Interior that was authorized to create a code applicable to the coal industry that would regulate the maximum hours and minimum wages of workers in coal mines and establish minimum prices for the sale of coal. The statute also conferred collective bargaining rights on coal workers. To ensure compliance, the statute provided that any coal company that refused to comply with the code would have to pay a substantial tax. The following case was the culmination of a challenge to that statute. Unlike the statute at issue in *Hammer*, the statute at issue in *Carter Coal* did not purport to regulate the interstate shipment of a particular good or type of goods. Instead, the Bituminous Coal Conservation Act regulated labor practices in a particular industry. Was such a statute more vulnerable under the case-law as it existed in 1936, or less?

———————

Carter v. Carter Coal Co.

298 U.S. 238 (1936)

Mr. Justice SUTHERLAND delivered the opinion of the Court.

That commodities produced or manufactured within a state are intended to be sold or transported outside the state does not render their production or manufacture subject to federal regulation under the commerce clause. *** One who produces or manufactures a commodity, subsequently sold and shipped by him in interstate commerce, whether such sale and shipment were originally intended or not, has engaged in two distinct and separate activities. So far as he produces or manufactures a commodity, his business is purely local. So far as he sells and ships, or contracts to sell and ship, the commodity to customers in another state, he engages in interstate commerce. In respect of the former, he is subject only to regulation by the state; in respect of the latter, to regulation only by the federal government. Production is not commerce; but a step in preparation for commerce.

The employment of men, the fixing of their wages, hours of labor, and working conditions, the bargaining in respect of these things—whether carried on separately or collectively—each and all constitute intercourse for the purposes of production, not of trade. *** [T]he effect of the labor provisions of the act, including those in respect of minimum wages, wage agreements, collective bargaining, and the Labor Board and its powers, primarily falls upon production and not upon commerce; and confirms the further resulting conclusion that production is a purely local activity. It follows that none of these essential antecedents of production constitutes a transaction in or forms any part of interstate commerce.

That the production of every commodity intended for interstate sale and transportation has some effect upon interstate commerce may be, if it has not already been, freely granted; and we are brought to the final and decisive inquiry, whether here that effect is direct *** or indirect. The distinction is not formal, but substantial in the highest degree. Whether the effect of a given activity or condition is direct or indirect is not always easy to determine. The word "direct" implies that the activity or condition invoked or blamed shall operate proximately—not mediately, remotely, or collaterally—to produce the effect. It connotes the absence of an efficient intervening

> **Food for Thought**
>
> In other contexts—such as determining causation in tort suits—it is commonplace for courts to distinguish between causal connections that are direct (or proximate) and those that are indirect. Is there any reason why such judicial determinations are more problematic in this context?

agency or condition. And the extent of the effect bears no logical relation to its character. The distinction between a direct and an indirect effect turns, not upon the magnitude of either the cause or the effect, but entirely upon the manner in which the effect has been brought about. If the production by one man of a single ton of coal intended for interstate sale and shipment, and actually so sold and shipped, affects interstate commerce indirectly, the effect does not become direct by multiplying the tonnage, or increasing the number of men employed, or adding to the expense or complexities of the business, or by all combined.

The relation of employer and employee is a local relation. *** The wages are paid for the doing of local work. Working conditions are obviously local conditions. The employees are not engaged in or about commerce, but exclusively in producing a commodity. And the controversies and evils, which it is the object of the act to regulate and minimize, are local controversies and evils affecting local work undertaken to accomplish that local result. Such effect as they may have upon commerce, however extensive it may be, is secondary and indirect. An increase in the greatness of the effect adds to its importance. It does not alter its character.

Justice CARDOZO, joined by Justice BRANDEIS and Justice STONE, dissenting.

To regulate the price for [interstate] transactions is to regulate commerce itself, and not alone its antecedent conditions or its ultimate consequences. Regulation of prices being an exercise of the commerce power in respect of interstate transactions, the question remains whether it comes within that power as applied to intrastate sales where interstate prices are directly or intimately affected. Mining and agriculture and manufacture are not interstate commerce considered by themselves, yet their relation to that commerce may be such that for the protection of the one there is need to regulate the other. Sometimes it is said that the relation must be "direct" to bring that power into play. In many circumstances such a description will be sufficiently precise to meet the needs of the occasion. But a great principle of constitutional law is not susceptible of comprehensive statement in an adjective. The underlying thought is merely this, that "the law is not indifferent to considerations of degree." At times *** the waves of causation will have radiated so far that their undulatory motion, if discernible at all, will be too faint or obscure, too broken by cross-currents, to be heeded by the law. *** Perhaps, if one group of adjectives is to be chosen in preference to another, "intimate" and "remote" will be found to be as good as any. At all events, "direct" and "indirect," even if accepted as sufficient, must not be read too narrowly. A survey of the cases shows that the words have been interpreted with suppleness of adaptation and flexibility of meaning. The power is as broad as the need that evokes it. *** [T]he prices for intrastate sales of coal have so inescapable a relation to those for interstate sales that a system of regulation for transactions of the one class is necessary to give adequate protection to the system of regulation adopted for the other.

Points for Discussion

a. Direct and Indirect Effects

The Court holds that Congress has power to regulate only an intrastate activity's direct effects on interstate commerce. How should a Court decide whether effects are indirect? Does a statute guaranteeing the right of labor unions representing workers at large factories to strike regulate an activity with a direct effect or an indirect effect on interstate commerce?

b. Precedent

In *McCulloch*, the Court stated that where a law "is really calculated to effect any of the objects entrusted to the government, to undertake [to] inquire into the degree of its necessity would be to pass the line which circumscribes the judicial department, and to tread on legislative ground." Is the Court's approach in *Carter Coal* consistent with *McCulloch*? Was the statute challenged in *Carter Coal* "really calculated to effect" an object entrusted to the federal government? Was the Court's tolerance only for laws that regulate the "direct" effects of local activity on interstate commerce consistent with *McCulloch*'s deference to legislative judgments?

———————————

After the decision in *Carter Coal*, it seemed likely that the Court would strike down the central legislative measures of the New Deal—in particular, the National Labor Relations Act, which regulated the relationship between unions and management, and the Social Security Act—at the first opportunity. In response, shortly after his re-election in 1936, President Roosevelt announced his "Court-packing plan." Arguing that the Justices were too "aged and infirm," "laboring under a heavy burden," and generally out of touch with the complexities of the modern world, Roosevelt proposed adding a new seat on the Court for every Justice over age 70 who stayed on the bench, until the Court included fifteen members. Message to Congress (Feb. 5, 1937). At the time, six of the Justices—including the Justices who most consistently supported a restrictive view of federal power—were over 70 years old. Roosevelt argued to the nation that we must "save the Constitution from the Court and the Court from itself." Radio Address (March 9, 1937).

> **Make the Connection**
>
> We discussed ways in which Congress can control judicial decision-making in Chapter 2, when we considered Congress's power to control the jurisdiction of the federal courts. Is there any express or implicit constitutional prohibition on a plan to increase the size of the Supreme Court? What about a plan to decrease the size of the Supreme Court? Would it matter if Congress's motive were to respond to an increase in the federal courts' docket? Or if Congress's motive were to work a *de facto* reversal of unpopular Supreme Court precedent?

Although Congress was controlled by Democrats sympathetic to President Roosevelt, the Senate, after lively debate, rejected a bill based on Roosevelt's proposal. By that point, however, there were already signs that the Court was changing course—as illustrated by the decision in *NLRB v. Jones & Laughlin Steel Corp.*, below, and *West Coast Hotel Co. v. Par-*

For More Information

For More Information on the Court-Packing Plan and the "switch in time," see Michael Ariens, *A Thrice-Told Tale, or Felix the Cat*, 107 Harv. L. Rev. 620 (1994); Richard D. Friedman, *Switching Time and Other Thought Experiments: The Hughes Court and Constitutional Transformation*, 142 U. Pa. L. Rev. 1891 (1994).

rish, which we will take up in Chapter 8. In those cases, Justice Roberts, who previously had voted with the Court's conservative majority, voted to uphold government claims of power. There is debate over whether Roberts's change of heart—the famous "switch in time that saved the Nine"—was in response to Roosevelt's Court-packing plan or instead was because of a change of mind independent of political pressure.

But regardless of the cause, the Court began to chart a new approach that was highly deferential to the assertion of federal authority under the Commerce Clause.

3. The New Deal and Beyond: An Expansive View

NLRB v. Jones & Laughlin Steel Corp.

301 U.S. 1 (1937)

Mr. Chief Justice HUGHES delivered the opinion of the Court.

In a proceeding under the National Labor Relations Act of 1935 the National Labor Relations Board found that the respondent, Jones & Laughlin Steel Corporation, had violated the act by *** discriminating against members of the union with regard to hire and tenure of employment, and [by] coercing and intimidating its employees in order to interfere with their self-organization. The [NLRB] ordered the corporation to cease and desist from such discrimination and coercion [and] to offer reinstatement [to discharged employees].

[Jones & Laughlin manufactured iron and steel in plants in Pennsylvania and was the fourth largest producer of steel in the United States. With its nineteen subsidiaries, it owned and operated mines, lake and river transportation facilities, and terminal railroads located at its manufacturing plants. It owned or controlled mines in Michigan, Minnesota, Pennsylvania, and West Virginia, operated ships and railroads for the interstate transportation of raw materials, and maintained warehouses in Illinois, Michigan, Ohio, and Tennessee. It also operated steel fabricating shops in New York and Louisiana and owned or controlled stores and warehouses around the country and maintained sales offices in twenty United States cities.]

We think it clear that the [Act] may be construed so as to operate within the sphere of constitutional authority. The jurisdiction conferred upon the Board, and invoked in this instance, is found in section 10(a), which provides: "The Board is empowered *** to prevent any person from engaging in any unfair labor practice *** affecting commerce." *** It is a familiar principle that acts which directly burden or obstruct interstate or foreign commerce, or its free flow, are within the reach of the congressional power. Acts having that effect are not rendered immune because they grow out of labor disputes. It is the effect upon commerce, not the source of the injury, which is the criterion. Whether or not particular action does affect commerce in such a close and intimate fashion as to be subject to federal control, and hence to lie within the authority conferred upon the Board, is left by the statute to be determined as individual cases arise.

Respondent *** rests upon the proposition that manufacturing in itself is not commerce. *** Although activities may be intrastate in character when separately considered, if they have such a close and substantial relation to interstate commerce that their control is essential or appropriate to protect that commerce from burdens and obstructions, Congress cannot be denied the power to exercise that control. Undoubtedly the scope of this power must be considered in the light of our dual system of government and may not be extended so as to embrace effects upon interstate commerce so indirect and remote that to embrace them, in view of our complex society, would effectually obliterate the distinction between what is national and what is local and create a completely centralized government. The question is necessarily one of degree.

That intrastate activities, by reason of close and intimate relation to interstate commerce, may fall within federal control is demonstrated in the case of carriers who are engaged in both interstate and intrastate transportation. *Shreveport Rate Case.* The close and intimate effect which brings the subject within the reach of federal power may be due to activities in relation to productive industry although the industry when separately viewed is local.

[T]he fact that the employees here concerned were engaged in production is not determinative. The question remains as to the effect upon interstate commerce of the labor practice involved. In [*Schechter*] we found that the effect there was so remote as to be beyond the federal power. To find "immediacy or directness" there was to find it "almost everywhere," a result inconsistent with the maintenance of our federal system. In [*Carter Coal*], the Court was of the opinion that the provisions of the statute relating to production were invalid upon several grounds [including] improper delegation of legislative power [and a violation of] due process. These cases are not controlling here.

[The] stoppage of [respondent's] operations by industrial strife would have a most serious effect upon interstate commerce. In view of respondent's far-flung activities, it is idle to say that the effect would be indirect or

> **FYI**
>
> In sections of the opinion not included in this casebook, the Court in *Carter Coal* concluded that the Bituminous Coal Conservation Act violated the Due Process Clause of the Fifth Amendment and improperly delegated legislative authority, subjects that we will consider in Chapters 8 and 6, respectively. But in light of the section of the opinion in that case that is reproduced here, is it fair for the Court in *Jones & Laughlin* to suggest that the case's discussion of Congress's power under the Commerce Clause is not controlling?

remote. It is obvious that it would be immediate and might be catastrophic. *** When industries organize themselves on a national scale, making their relation to interstate commerce the dominant factor in their activities, how can it be maintained that their industrial labor relations constitute a forbidden field into which Congress may not enter when it is necessary to protect interstate commerce from the paralyzing consequences of industrial war? We have often said that interstate commerce itself is a practical conception. It is equally true that interferences with that commerce must be appraised by a judgment that does not ignore actual experience.

The steel industry is one of the great basic industries of the United States, with ramifying activities affecting interstate commerce at every point. [Respondent's enterprise] presents in a most striking way the close and intimate relation which a manufacturing industry may have to interstate commerce and we have no doubt that Congress had constitutional authority to safeguard the right of respondent's employees to self-organization and freedom in the choice of representatives for collective bargaining.

> **Practice Pointer**
>
> It is no coincidence that the first case under the NLRA to make it to the Court was an action against a giant steel conglomerate. The lawyers at the agency clearly concluded that there was a substantially better chance of prevailing on their constitutional defense of the statute if they sought to apply to it an employer whose activities so obviously affected interstate commerce.

Mr. Justice McREYNOLDS, joined by Justice VAN DEVANTER, Justice SUTHERLAND, and Justice BUTLER, dissenting.

Manifestly [the Court's] view of congressional power would extend it into almost every field of human industry. Any effect on interstate commerce by the discharge of employees shown here would be indirect and remote in the highest degree, as consideration of the facts will show. The immediate effect in the factory may be to create discontent among all those employed and a strike may follow, which, in turn, may result in reducing production, which ultimately may reduce the volume of goods moving in interstate commerce. By this chain of indirect and progressively remote events we finally reach the evil with which it is said the legislation under consideration undertakes to deal. A more remote and indirect interference with interstate commerce or a more definite invasion of the powers reserved to the states is difficult, if not impossible, to imagine. *** Almost anything—marriage, birth, death—may in some fashion affect commerce. *** It seems clear to us that Congress has transcended the powers granted.

United States v. Darby

312 U.S. 100 (1941)

Mr. Justice STONE delivered the opinion of the Court.

[Appellee was a lumber manufacturer in Georgia who was indicted for violating the Fair Labor Standards Act of 1938. The indictment charged that appellee shipped lumber in interstate commerce to customers outside the state, and that in the production of that lumber appellee employed workmen at less than the prescribed minimum wage or more than the prescribed maximum hours without payment to them of any wage for overtime. The indictment also charged that appellee employed workmen in the production of lumber for interstate commerce at wages below the minimum wage or for more than the maximum hours per week without payment to them of the prescribed overtime wage. The district court quashed the indictment.]

The prohibition of shipment of the proscribed goods in interstate commerce. Section 15(a)(1) [of the FLSA] prohibits *** the shipment in interstate commerce of goods produced for interstate commerce by employees whose wages and hours of employment do not conform to the requirements of the Act. *** While manufacture is not of itself interstate commerce[,] the shipment of manufactured goods interstate is such commerce and the prohibition of such shipment by Congress is indubitably a regulation of the commerce. The power to regulate commerce is the power "to prescribe the rule by which commerce is to be governed." *Gibbons.* It extends not only to those regulations which aid, foster and protect the commerce, but embraces those which prohibit it.

But it is said that *** while the prohibition is nominally a regulation of the commerce its motive or purpose is regulation of wages and hours of persons engaged in manufacture, the control of which has been reserved to the states and upon which Georgia and some of the states of destination have placed no restriction ***. The power of Congress over interstate commerce *** is not a forbidden invasion of state power merely because either its motive or its consequence is to restrict the use of articles of commerce within the states of destination ***. The motive and purpose of a regulation of interstate commerce are matters for the legislative judgment upon the exercise of which the Constitution places no restriction and over which the courts are given no control. *** [W]e conclude that the prohibition of the shipment interstate of goods produced under the forbidden substandard labor conditions is within the constitutional authority of Congress.

In the more than a century which has elapsed since the decision of *Gibbons v. Ogden*, these principles of constitutional interpretation have been so long and repeatedly recognized by this Court as applicable to the Commerce Clause, that there would be little occasion for repeating them now were it not for the decision of this Court twenty-two years ago in *Hammer v. Dagenhart*. *** The reasoning and conclusion of the Court's opinion there cannot be reconciled with the conclusion which we have reached, that the power of Congress under the Commerce Clause is plenary to exclude any article from interstate commerce subject only to the specific prohibitions of the Constitution. *** The distinction on which the decision was rested that Congressional power to prohibit interstate commerce is limited to articles which in themselves have some harmful or deleterious property—a distinction which was novel when made and unsupported by any provision of the Constitution—has long since been abandoned. The thesis of the opinion that the motive of the prohibition or its effect to control in some measure the use or production within the states of the article thus excluded from the commerce can operate to deprive the regulation of its constitutional authority has long since ceased to have force. *** The conclusion is inescapable that *Hammer v. Dagenhart* was a departure from the principles which have prevailed in the interpretation of the commerce clause both before and since the decision and that such vitality, as a precedent, as it then had has long since been exhausted. It should be and now is overruled.

> **Take Note**
>
> The decision in *Jones & Laughlin* arguably was in as much tension with the earlier decision in *Carter Coal* as the decision in *Darby* was with the earlier decision in *Hammer*. Why do you suppose the Court chose in this case to overrule *Hammer*, but chose in *Jones & Laughlin* only to distinguish *Carter Coal*?

Validity of the wage and hour requirements. Section 15(a)(2) *** require[s] employers to conform to the wage and hour provisions with respect to all employees engaged in the production of goods for interstate commerce. *** The power of Congress over interstate commerce is not confined to the regulation of commerce among the states. It extends to those activities intrastate which so affect interstate commerce or the exercise of the power of Congress over it as to make regulation of them appropriate means to the attainment of a legitimate end, the exercise of the granted power of Congress to regulate interstate commerce. *McCulloch.* *** Congress *** may choose the means reasonably adapted to the attainment of the permitted end, even though they involve control of intrastate activities. [The Court has sustained congressional] regulation of intrastate transactions which are so commingled with or related to interstate commerce that all must be regulated if the interstate commerce is to be effectively controlled. [*Shreveport Rate Case.*] *** The means adopted by § 15(a)(2) for the protection of interstate commerce by the suppression of the production of the condemned goods for interstate commerce is so related to the commerce and so affects it as to be within the reach of the commerce power. Congress *** recognized that in present day industry, competition by a small part may affect the whole and that the total effect of the competition of many small producers may be great.

So far as *Carter Coal* is inconsistent with this conclusion, its doctrine is limited in principle by the decisions [such as *Jones & Laughlin,*] which we follow.

Our conclusion is unaffected by the Tenth Amendment which provides: "The powers not delegated to the United States by the Constitution, nor prohibited by it to the States, are reserved to the States respectively, or to the people." The amendment states but a truism that all is retained which has not been surrendered. There is nothing in the history of its adoption to suggest that it was more than declaratory of the

> **Take Note**
>
> What does the Court mean when it says the Tenth Amendment merely states a "truism"? And of what part of the Constitution is the principle stated in the Tenth Amendment merely declaratory?

relationship between the national and state governments as it had been established by the Constitution before the amendment or that its purpose was other than to allay fears that the new national government might seek to exercise powers not granted, and that the states might not be able to exercise fully their reserved powers.

Reversed.

————————

Points for Discussion

a. More Switches in Time

The Court decided *Jones & Laughlin* in 1937 by a slim 5-4 majority. Yet *Darby*, which was decided only four years later, was unanimous. What do you suppose accounts for the sudden consensus on the Court?

b. "Constitutional Moments"

Article V provides the procedure for amending the Constitution, which requires ratification by the legislatures of (or conventions in) three-quarters of the states. Perhaps because the threshold for amendment is so high, the Constitution has been amended very few times in American history. Of the 27 amendments, ten were ratified together as the Bill of Rights (an eleventh, which was proposed with the original ten, was ratified years later as the Twenty-Seventh Amendment); three were ratified as part of the process of Reconstruction; and two—the Eighteenth and Twenty-First Amendments, relating to pro-hibition—cancel each other out.

Is it possible for the Constitution to be amended outside of the formal procedures identified in Article V? Bruce Ackerman has argued that the political consensus that pro-duced the New Deal—and the Court's ratification of Congress's authority to enact it—amounted to a "constitutional moment" that effectively inaugurated a new constitutional regime. See Bruce Ackerman, We the People: Foundations (1991). Even assuming that the Constitution can be changed in this manner, do the New Deal cases obviously depart from the principles that the Court had early on established to delimit Congress's power under the Commerce Clause?

c. The "Affectation Doctrine" or the "Effects Test"

The Court stated that Congress may regulate not only interstate commerce itself, but also "those activities intrastate which so affect interstate commerce or the exercise of the power of Congress over it as to make regulation of them appropriate means to a legiti-mate end." Subsequent cases have sometimes referred to the principle that Congress may regulate intrastate activities that affect interstate commerce as the "affectation doctrine," see, e.g., *Prudential Ins. Co. v. Benjamin*, 328 U.S. 408, 423 (1946), which we consider in Chapter 4, or the "effects test," see, e.g., *United States v. Lopez*, 514 U.S. 549 (1995), which we consider later in this Chapter.

————————

Wickard v. Filburn

317 U.S. 111 (1942)

Mr. Justice JACKSON delivered the opinion of the Court.

[Filburn sought to enjoin enforcement of a $117 penalty imposed under the Agricultural Adjustment Act of 1938 upon that part of his 1941 wheat crop that was in excess of the marketing quota established for his farm. Pursuant to the Act, the Secretary of Agriculture had established quotas for individual farms in order to "control the volume moving in interstate and foreign commerce in order to avoid surpluses and shortages and the consequent abnormally low or high wheat prices and obstructions to commerce." Filburn's allotment for 1941 was 223 bushels, but he exceeded that quota by 239 bushels. Filburn used the wheat that he grew on his farm to feed livestock, to seed his new crops, to make flour for consumption at home, and to sell on the market. Filburn argued that he intended to use some of the excess for personal consumption, and he challenged the Act as applied to wheat that he produced for personal consumption.]

The question would merit little consideration since our decision in *Darby*, sustaining the federal power to regulate production of goods for commerce[,] except for the fact that this Act extends federal regulation to production not intended in any part for commerce but wholly for consumption on the farm. *** Appellee says that this is a regulation of production and consumption of wheat [and that the effects of such activities] upon interstate commerce are at most "indirect." *** [But once] an economic measure of the reach of the power granted to Congress in the Commerce Clause is accepted, questions of federal power cannot be decided simply by finding the activity in question to be "production" nor can consideration of its economic effects be foreclosed by calling them "indirect." *** That an activity is of local character may help in a doubtful case to determine whether Congress intended to reach it. *** But even if appellee's activity be local and though it may not be regarded as commerce, it may still, whatever its nature, be reached by Congress if it exerts a substantial economic effect on interstate commerce and this irrespective of whether such effect is what might at some earlier time have been defined as "direct" or "indirect."

Commerce among the states in wheat is large and important. Although wheat is raised in every state but one, production in most states is not equal to consumption. [Some states produce more wheat than is needed in the state, and others produce less than is needed to satisfy in-state demand.] The decline in the export trade has left a large surplus in production which in connection with an abnormally large supply of wheat and other grains in recent years caused congestion in a number of markets; tied up railroad cars; and caused elevators in some instances to turn away grains, and railroads to institute embargoes to prevent further congestion. In the absence of regulation the price of wheat in the United States would be much affected by world conditions. During 1941 producers who cooperated with the Agricultural Adjustment program received an average price on the farm of about $1.16 a bushel as compared with the world market price of 40 cents a bushel.

The maintenance by government regulation of a price for wheat undoubtedly can be accomplished as effectively by sustaining or increasing the demand as by limiting the supply. The effect of the statute before us is to restrict the amount which may be produced for market and the extent as well to which one may forestall resort to the market by producing to meet his own needs. That appellee's own contribution to the demand for wheat may be trivial by itself is not enough to remove him from the scope of federal regulation where, as here, his contribution, taken together with that of many others similarly situated, is far from trivial.

It is well established by decisions of this Court that the power to regulate commerce includes the power to regulate the prices at which commodities in that commerce are dealt in and practices affecting such prices. One of the primary purposes of the Act in question was to increase the market price of wheat and to that end to limit the volume thereof that could affect the market. It can hardly be denied that a factor of such volume and variability as home-consumed wheat would have a substantial influence on price and market conditions. This may arise because being in marketable condition such wheat overhangs the market and if induced by rising prices tends to flow into the market and check price increases. But if we assume that it is never marketed, it supplies a need of the man who grew it which would otherwise be reflected by purchases in the open market. Home-grown wheat in this sense competes with wheat in commerce. *** This record leaves us in no doubt that Congress may properly have considered that wheat consumed on the farm where grown if wholly outside the scheme of regulation would have a substantial effect in defeating and obstructing its purpose to stimulate trade therein at increased prices.

> **Take Note**
>
> Filburn was simply growing wheat for personal consumption, rather than for selling it. In what way did such wheat "compete" with wheat grown by others and sold by them on the open market?

It is said, however, that this Act, forcing some farmers into the market to buy what they could provide for themselves, is an unfair promotion of the markets and prices of specializing wheat growers. It is of the essence of regulation that it lays a restraining hand on the self-interest of the regulated and that advantages from the regulation commonly fall to others. The conflicts of economic interest between the regulated and those who advantage by it are wisely left under our system to resolution by the Congress under its more flexible and responsible legislative process. Such conflicts rarely lend themselves to judicial determination. And with the wisdom, workability, or fairness, of the plan of regulation we have nothing to do.

Points for Discussion

a. The Aggregation Principle

Filburn's use of 239 bushels of home-grown wheat obviously did not have any discernable impact on the two-billion bushel interstate market for wheat. The Court, however, viewed Filburn's activity "taken together with that of many others similarly situated"—that is, the Court aggregated the effect on interstate commerce of all potential local use of home-grown wheat in excess of the statutory quota. If the Court instead had held that the Act could not be applied to Filburn's use of the wheat, on the ground that his use itself had no meaningful impact on interstate commerce, what would that have meant for the quota scheme as a whole?

b. The Rational-Basis Test

Wickard is emblematic of the "rational-basis" approach to reviewing exercises of the Commerce power, under which the Court asks whether Congress had a rational basis for concluding that the regulated conduct, when viewed in the aggregate, has a substantial effect on interstate commerce. Applying the aggregation principle and the rational-basis test, is there any local, intrastate conduct that is not within Congress's power to regulate?

Some law students react to *Wickard v. Filburn* with surprise and skepticism. They wonder how Congress can properly be called a government of limited powers if Congress can regulate how much wheat a person grows on his own property for his own consumption. As we will see shortly, some Justices have questioned whether the Supreme Court made a wrong turn by interpreting the Commerce power to allow Congress to regulate intrastate economic activities so long as in the aggregate those activities may affect interstate commerce. But before passing final judgment on the effects test and the aggregation principle, consider some of what Congress has accomplished with these broad powers.

In 1964, Congress enacted the Civil Rights Act, a sweeping law that sought to prohibit discrimination in several settings. Title II of the Act prohibited discrimination on the basis of "race, color, religion, or national origin" in places of "public accommodation." Title II specified that the facilities to which the prohibition applied included inns, hotels, motels, restaurants, cafeterias, lunch rooms, lunch counters, theaters, concert halls, and sports arenas. It further defined places of public accommodation as places whose "operations affect commerce," which included places that "offer[] to serve interstate travelers" or places where "a substantial portion of the food [served] has moved in commerce."

Make the Connection

We will consider the Fourteenth Amendment in Chapter 11, Congress's power to enforce the Fourteenth Amendment in Chapter 13, and the "state action" doctrine in Chapter 19.

The Act thus applied to many private—that is, non-state—actors. Because the Court has long interpreted the Fourteenth Amendment to apply only to state action, in enacting the Civil Rights Act Congress relied on its authority under the Commerce Clause. The Court upheld Title II of the Civil Rights Act in the two cases that follow.

Heart of Atlanta Motel, Inc. v. United States

379 U.S. 241 (1964)

Mr. Justice CLARK delivered the opinion of the Court.

Appellant owns and operates the Heart of Atlanta Motel which has 216 rooms available to transient guests [and which is] readily accessible to interstate highways ***. Appellant solicits patronage from outside the State of Georgia through various national advertising media, including magazines of national circulation; it maintains over 50 billboards and highway signs within the State, soliciting patronage for the motel; it accepts convention trade from outside Georgia and approximately 75% of its registered guests are from out of State. Prior to passage of the Act the motel had followed a practice of refusing to rent rooms to Negroes, and it alleged that it intended to continue to do so. In an effort to perpetuate that policy this suit was filed.

> **Food for Thought**
>
> The Court appears to rely heavily on evidence in the legislative record that Congress amassed in the course of enacting the statute. Given the standard that the Court applied in *Jones & Laughlin*, *Darby*, and *Wickard* for reviewing exercises of the commerce power, would it have mattered if Congress had not held any hearings or adduced any evidence before enacting the statutes?

While the Act as adopted carried no congressional findings the record of its passage through each house is replete with evidence of the burdens that discrimination by race or color places upon interstate commerce. [The] testimony included the fact that our people have become increasingly mobile with millions of people of all races traveling from State to State; that Negroes in particular have been the subject of discrimination in transient accommodations, having to travel great distances to secure the same; that often they have been unable to obtain accommodations and have had to call upon friends to put them up overnight; and that these conditions had become so acute as to require the listing of available lodging for Negroes in a special guidebook which was itself "dramatic testimony to the difficulties" Negroes encounter in travel. These exclusionary practices were found to be nationwide ***. This testimony indicated a qualitative as well as quantitative effect on interstate travel by Negroes. The former was the obvious impairment of the Negro traveler's pleasure and convenience that resulted when he continually was uncertain of finding lodging. As for the latter, there was evidence that this uncertainty stemming from racial discrimination had the effect of discouraging travel on the part of a substantial portion of the Negro community. [T]he voluminous testimony presents overwhelming evidence that discrimination by hotels and motels impedes interstate travel.

In framing Title II of this Act Congress was *** dealing with what it considered a moral problem. But that fact does not detract from the overwhelming evidence of the disruptive effect that racial discrimination has had on commercial intercourse. It was this burden which empowered Congress to enact appropriate legislation, and, given this basis for the exercise of its power, Congress was not restricted by the fact that the particular obstruction to interstate commerce with which it was dealing was also deemed a moral and social wrong.

It is said that the operation of the motel here is of a purely local character. But, assuming this to be true, *** the power of Congress to promote interstate commerce also includes the power to regulate the local incidents thereof, including local activities in both the States of origin and destination, which might have a substantial and harmful effect upon that commerce. One need only examine the evidence which we have discussed above to see that Congress may—as it has—prohibit racial discrimination by motels serving travelers, however "local" their operations may appear.

How obstructions in commerce may be removed—what means are to be employed— is within the sound and exclusive discretion of the Congress. It is subject only to one caveat—that the means chosen by it must be reasonably adapted to the end permitted by the Constitution. We cannot say that its choice here was not so adapted.

[The concurring opinions of Justices Black, Douglas, and Goldberg are reprinted below, after the Court's opinion in *Katzenbach v. McClung*.]

Katzenbach v. McClung

379 U.S. 294 (1964)

Mr. Justice CLARK delivered the opinion of the Court.

Ollie's Barbecue is a family-owned restaurant in Birmingham, Alabama, specializing in barbecued meats and homemade pies, with a seating capacity of 220 customers. It is located on a state highway 11 blocks from an interstate one and a somewhat greater distance from railroad and bus stations. The restaurant caters to a family and white-collar trade with a take-out service for Negroes. It employs 36 persons, two-thirds of whom are Negroes.

In the 12 months preceding the passage of the Act, the restaurant purchased locally approximately $150,000 worth of food, $69,683 or 46% of which was meat that it bought from a local supplier who had procured it from outside the State. The District Court expressly found that a substantial portion of the food served in the restaurant had moved in interstate commerce. The restaurant has refused to serve Negroes in its dining accommodations since its original opening in 1927, and since July 2, 1964, it has been operating in violation of the Act. The court below concluded that if it were required to serve Negroes it would lose a substantial amount of business.

[The relevant provisions of Title II] place any "restaurant *** principally engaged in selling food for consumption on the premises" under the Act [if] "a substantial portion of the food which it serves *** has moved in commerce." Ollie's Barbecue admits that it is covered by these provisions of the Act. *** There is no claim that interstate travelers frequented the restaurant. The sole question, therefore, narrows down to whether Title II, as applied to a restaurant annually receiving about $70,000 worth of food which has moved in commerce, is a valid exercise of the power of Congress.

The [legislative] record is replete with testimony of the burdens placed on interstate commerce by racial discrimination in restaurants. A comparison of per capita spending by Negroes in restaurants, theaters, and like establishments indicated less spending, after discounting income differences, in areas where discrimination is widely practiced. This condition, which was especially aggravated in the South, was attributed *** to racial segregation. This diminutive spending springing from a refusal to serve Negroes and their total loss as customers has, regardless of the absence of direct evidence, a close connection to interstate commerce. The fewer customers a restaurant enjoys the less food it sells and consequently the less it buys. *** In addition, there were many references to discriminatory situations causing wide unrest and having a depressant effect on general business conditions in the respective communities. Moreover there was an impressive array of testimony that discrimination in restaurants had a direct and highly restrictive effect upon interstate travel by Negroes[, for] one can hardly travel without eating. Likewise, it was said, that discrimination deterred professional, as well as skilled, people from moving into areas where such practices occurred and thereby caused industry to be reluctant to establish there.

> **Take Note**
>
> The Court in *McClung* considered an "as-applied" challenge to Title II of the Civil Rights Act—that is, a claim that the statute could not constitutionally be applied in this fashion, even if Congress generally had power to regulate others subject to the statute. If the Court had concluded that the statute was unconstitutional as applied to Ollie's Barbeque, then what would have been the implications for the constitutionality of the statute as applied in other contexts?

We believe that this testimony afforded ample basis for the conclusion that established restaurants in such areas sold less interstate goods because of the discrimination, that interstate travel was obstructed directly by it, that business in general suffered and that many new businesses refrained from establishing there as a result of it. It goes without saying that, viewed in isolation, the volume of food purchased by Ollie's Barbecue from sources supplied from out of state was insignificant when compared with the total foodstuffs moving in commerce. But, [as we held in] *Wickard*, "[that] contribution, taken together with that of many others similarly situated, is far from trivial."

Appellees *** object to the omission of a provision for a case-by-case determination—judicial or administrative—that racial discrimination in a particular restaurant affects commerce. But *** Congress has determined for itself that refusals of service to Negroes have imposed burdens both upon the interstate flow of food and upon the movement of products generally. Of course, the mere fact that Congress has said when particular activity shall be deemed to affect commerce does not preclude further examination by this Court. But where we find that the legislators, in light of the facts and testimony before them, have a rational basis for finding a chosen regulatory scheme necessary to the protection of commerce, our investigation is at an end. The only remaining question—one answered in the affirmative by the court below—is whether the particular restaurant either serves or offers to serve interstate travelers or serves food a substantial portion of which has moved in interstate commerce. The Civil Rights Act of 1964, as here applied, we find to be plainly appropriate in the resolution of what the Congress found to be a national commercial problem of the first magnitude.

[The following opinions apply as well to *Heart of Atlanta Motel*, above.]

Mr. Justice BLACK, concurring.

I recognize that every remote, possible, speculative effect on commerce should not be accepted as an adequate constitutional ground to uproot and throw into the discard all our traditional distinctions between what is purely local, and therefore controlled by state laws, and what affects the national interest and is therefore subject to control by federal laws. I recognize too that some isolated and remote lunchroom which sells only to local people and buys almost all its supplies in the locality may possibly be beyond the reach of the power of Congress to regulate commerce, just as such an establishment is not covered by the present Act.

> **Food for Thought**
>
> Applying the majority's approach, would, as Justice Black suggests, a restaurant that "sells only to local people and buys almost all its supplies in the locality" really be beyond Congress's power to regulate? Wouldn't the effects on spending by African-American customers and on interstate travel by African Americans be similar to those that the Court details with respect to restaurants that discriminate and that receive some percentage of their food from out of state?

But in deciding the constitutional power of Congress in cases like the two before us we do not consider the effect on interstate commerce of only one isolated, individual, local event, without regard to the fact that this single local event when added to many others of a similar nature may impose a burden on interstate commerce by reducing its volume or distorting its flow.

Mr. Justice DOUGLAS, concurring.

[T]he result reached by the Court is for me much more obvious as a protective measure under the Fourteenth Amendment than under the Commerce Clause. For the former deals with the constitutional status of the individual[,] not with the impact on commerce of local activities or vice versa. A decision based on the Fourteenth Amendment would have a more settling effect, making unnecessary litigation over whether a particular restaurant or inn is within the commerce definitions of the Act or whether a particular customer is an interstate traveler. Under my construction, the Act would apply to all customers in all the enumerated places of public accommodation. And that construction would put an end to all obstructionist strategies and finally close one door on a bitter chapter in American history.

Mr. Justice GOLDBERG, concurring.

The primary purpose of the Civil Rights Act of 1964 *** is the vindication of human dignity and not mere economics. [In my view,] § 1 of the Fourteenth Amendment guarantees to all Americans the constitutional right "to be treated as equal members of the community with respect to public accommodations," and *** "Congress has authority under § 5 of the Fourteenth Amendment, or under the Commerce Clause, to implement [those] rights ***."

———————

Points for Discussion

a. Food that has "Moved in Commerce"

On what theory of the Commerce Clause is Congress permitted to regulate a restaurant that serves food that itself has moved in interstate commerce? Can Congress criminalize the theft of a car on the theory that the car's muffler moved in interstate commerce before it was installed on the car? In light of today's economy, if Congress can regulate on this theory, is there anything that it can't regulate?

Or is the point that Congress can regulate local conduct on the theory that such conduct, when viewed in the aggregate, affects interstate commerce? If that is the theory on which the Court upheld Congress's assertion of power, then wouldn't the statute be constitutional even if there were no requirement that the restaurant serve food that has moved in interstate commerce?

b. Congressional Findings

What level of deference should the Court accord to "findings" that Congress makes in support of the enactment of a statute? On some accounts, because the courts are limited to the actual cases and controversies presented to them, Congress, which can hear wide-ranging testimony, is a better fact-finder than the courts. See, e.g., Lon Fuller, *The Forms and Limits of Adjudication*, 92 Harv. L. Rev. 353, 394-96 (1978). But can't Congress essentially "find" anything it wants? Can't Members of Congress simply stack the evidence presented in the fact-finding process to preordain the conclusion that they prefer?

c. An Odd Way of Looking at Things?

Under the effects test, Congress may regulate almost any subject, so long as Congress can link the activity somehow to commerce. But attempting to link all subjects of regulation to commerce causes Congress and the Supreme Court to look at social problems in an odd way—a way that perhaps only lawyers understand. Notice that in the last sentence of the majority opinion in *McClung*, the Court said that Congress may forbid racial discrimination in restaurants because this discrimination is a "national commercial problem of the first magnitude." Is that how you would have described the problem of racial discrimination before you started reading this Chapter of the casebook? ("Hey, Ollie, stop that! You might affect interstate commerce!") Would the Constitution be improved by adding a provision that would allow Congress to ban racial discrimination in a more straightforward way? Does it include such a provision?

d. The Civil Rights Struggle and the Constitution

Congress enacted the Civil Rights Act ten years after the Court's decision in *Brown v. Board of Education*, which declared racial segregation in public schools unconstitutional. (We will consider <u>Brown</u> in Chapter 11.) As we saw in *Cooper v. Aaron* in Chapter 2, <u>Brown</u> was met in the South with fierce resistance, and public and private discrimination on the basis of race continued. Notwithstanding the willingness of several Justices in <u>Heart of Atlanta Motel</u> and <u>McClung</u> to revisit the Court's precedents, the Court had long read the Fourteenth Amendment's Equal Protection Clause to prohibit only discrimination by state, rather than private, actors. Yet if Congress's power under the Commerce Clause extends to prohibiting local discrimination by private actors, then it is difficult to conceive of any limits on Congress's Commerce power. Would it have been feasible in the 1960s to amend the Constitution to authorize Congress to prohibit discrimination by private actors? If not, what does that suggest about the propriety of the Court's willingness to stretch the Commerce power to embrace the Civil Rights Act?

4. Recent Cases: New Limits—Or Old?

From 1937 to 1995, the Court did not invalidate any federal laws on the ground that they exceeded Congress's power under the Commerce Clause. During that time, as evidenced by the decisions in <u>Wickard</u>, <u>Heart of Atlanta Motel</u>, and <u>McClung</u>, the Court suggested that its role in enforcing federalism-based limits on federal power was sharply circumscribed. (During that time, even the occasional suggestions to the contrary—such as the Court's decision in <u>National League of Cities v. Usery</u>, which we will consider later in this Chapter—were quickly disavowed.) A generation of law students learned that there were virtually no—and perhaps actually no—limits on Congress's power to regulate pursuant to the Commerce Clause. In 1995, however, the Court invalidated a federal law on the ground that it exceeded Congress's power under the Commerce Clause.

United States v. Lopez

514 U.S. 549 (1995)

Chief Justice REHNQUIST delivered the opinion of the Court.

In the Gun-Free School Zones Act of 1990, [Pub. L. 101-647, sec. 1702, 104 Stat. 4789, 4844 (1990) (codified, as amended, at 18 U.S.C. § 922(q)),] Congress made it a federal offense "for any individual knowingly to possess a firearm at a place that the individual knows,

Take Note

Possession of a gun near a school was illegal under Texas law, as well. What does this suggest about the necessity of the federal statute at issue in this case? Should the content of state law be relevant to determining the scope of Congress's power under the Commerce Clause?

or has reasonable cause to believe, is a school zone." [The statute defined "school zone" as "in, or on the grounds of, a public, parochial or private school" or "within a distance of 1,000 feet from the grounds of a public, parochial or private school."] On March 10, 1992, respondent, who was then a 12th-grade student, arrived at Edison High School in San Antonio, Texas, carrying a concealed .38-caliber handgun and five bullets. He was arrested and charged under Texas law with firearm possession on school premises.

The next day, the state charges were dismissed after federal agents charged respondent by complaint with violating the Gun-Free School Zones Act of 1990. [Respondent moved to dismiss his federal indictment. The District Court denied the motion, and respondent was convicted and sentenced to six months' imprisonment and two years' supervised release.]

We start with first principles. The Constitution creates a Federal Government of enumerated powers. As James Madison wrote: "The powers delegated by the proposed Constitution to the federal government are few and defined. Those which are to remain in the State governments are numerous and indefinite." The Federalist No. 45 *** *Jones & Laughlin Steel*, *Darby*, and *Wickard* ushered in an era of Commerce Clause jurisprudence that greatly expanded the previously defined authority of Congress under that Clause. In part, this was a recognition of the great changes that had occurred in the way business was carried on in this country. Enterprises that had once been local or at most regional in nature had become national in scope. But the doctrinal change also reflected a view that earlier Commerce Clause cases artificially had constrained the authority of Congress to regulate interstate commerce. But even these modern-era precedents which have expanded congressional power under the Commerce Clause confirm that this power is subject to outer limits. [T]he Court has heeded [those warnings] and undertaken to decide whether a rational basis existed for concluding that a regulated activity sufficiently affected interstate commerce.

> **Practice Pointer**
>
> Some of the Commerce Clause challenges that we have seen so far were filed as declaratory judgment actions by parties who sought to avoid the requirements of federal law. The respondent in this case, in contrast, raised his constitutional challenge as a defense to prosecution for violation of the federal law. Do you think that the procedural posture in which the challenge was raised in this case was likely to make the Court more sympathetic to the respondent's claims, or less?

Consistent with this structure, we have identified three broad categories of activity that Congress may regulate under its commerce power. First, Congress may regulate the use of the channels of interstate commerce. [See *Darby*; *Heart of Atlanta Motel*] Second, Congress is empowered to regulate and protect the instrumentalities of interstate commerce, or persons or things in interstate commerce, even though the threat may come only from intrastate activities. [*Shreveport Rate Case*] Finally, Congress' commerce authority includes the power to regulate those activities having a substantial relation to interstate commerce, *i.e.*, those activities that substantially affect interstate commerce. [*Jones & Laughlin*]

We now turn to consider the power of Congress, in the light of this framework, to enact § 922(q). The first two categories of authority may be quickly disposed of: § 922(q) is not a regulation of the use of the channels of interstate commerce, nor is it an attempt to prohibit the interstate transportation of a commodity through the channels of commerce; nor can § 922(q) be justified as a regulation by which Congress has sought to protect an instrumentality of interstate commerce or a thing in interstate commerce. Thus, if § 922(q) is to be sustained, it must be under the third category as a regulation of an activity that substantially affects interstate commerce.

First, we have upheld a wide variety of congressional Acts regulating intrastate economic activity where we have concluded that the activity substantially affected interstate commerce. *** Where economic activity substantially affects interstate commerce, legislation regulating that activity will be sustained. Even *Wickard*, which is perhaps the most far reaching example of Commerce Clause authority over intrastate activity, involved economic activity in a way that the possession of a gun in a school zone does not. Section 922(q) is a criminal statute that by its terms has nothing to do with "commerce" or any sort of economic enterprise, however broadly one might define those terms. Section 922(q) is not an essential part of a larger regulation of economic activity, in which the regulatory scheme could be undercut unless the intrastate activity were regulated. It cannot, therefore, be sustained under our cases upholding regulations of activities that arise out of or are connected with a commercial transaction, which viewed in the aggregate, substantially affects interstate commerce.

Second, § 922(q) contains no jurisdictional element which would ensure, through case-by-case inquiry, that the firearm possession in question affects interstate commerce. ***

We agree with the Government that Congress normally is not required to make formal findings as to the substantial burdens that an activity has on interstate commerce. But to the extent that congressional findings would enable us to evaluate the legislative judgment that the activity in question substantially affected interstate commerce, even though no such substantial effect was visible to the naked eye, they are lacking here.

The Government's essential contention, *in fine,* is that we may determine here that § 922(q) is valid because possession of a firearm in a local school zone does indeed substantially affect interstate commerce. The Government argues that possession of a firearm in a school zone may result in violent crime and that violent crime can be expected to affect the functioning of the national economy in two ways. First, the costs of violent crime are substantial, and, through the mechanism of insurance, those costs are spread throughout the population. Second, violent crime reduces the willingness of individuals to travel to areas within the country that are perceived to be unsafe. The Government also argues that the presence of guns in schools poses a substantial threat to the educational process by threatening the learning environment. A handicapped educational process, in turn, will result in a less productive citizenry. That, in turn, would have an adverse effect on the Nation's economic well-being. As a result, the Government argues that Congress could rationally have concluded that § 922(q) substantially affects interstate commerce.

Take Note

Is the relationship of the regulated conduct to interstate commerce in this case any more attenuated than the relationship of the conduct at issue in *Heart of Atlanta Motel* and *Mc-Clung* to interstate commerce?

We pause to consider the implications of the Government's arguments. The Government admits, under its "costs of crime" reasoning, that Congress could regulate not only all violent crime, but all activities that might lead to violent crime, regardless of how tenuously they relate to interstate commerce. Similarly, under the Government's "national productivity" reasoning, Congress could regulate any activity that it found was related to the economic productivity of individual citizens: family law (including marriage, divorce, and child custody), for example. Under the theories that the Government presents in support of § 922(q), it is difficult to perceive any limitation on federal power, even in areas such as criminal law enforcement or education where States historically have been sovereign. Thus, if we were to accept the Government's arguments, we are hard pressed to posit any activity by an individual that Congress is without power to regulate.

Although Justice BREYER argues that acceptance of the Government's rationales would not authorize a general federal police power, he is unable to identify any activity that the States may regulate but Congress may not. *** Justice BREYER focuses, for the most part, on the threat that firearm possession in and near schools poses to the educational process and the potential economic consequences flowing from that threat. Specifically, the dissent reasons that (1) gun-related violence is a serious problem; (2) that problem, in turn, has an adverse effect on classroom learning; and (3) that adverse effect on classroom learning, in turn, represents a substantial threat to trade and commerce. This analysis would be equally applicable, if not more so, to subjects such as family law and direct regulation of education.

Justice BREYER rejects our reading of precedent and argues that "Congress could rationally conclude that schools fall on the commercial side of the line." [D]epending on the level of generality, any activity can be looked upon as commercial. Under the dissent's rationale, Congress could just as easily look at child rearing as "fall[ing] on the commercial side of the line" because it provides a "valuable service—namely, to equip [children] with the skills they need to survive in life and, more specifically, in the workplace." We do not doubt that Congress has authority under the Commerce Clause to regulate numerous commercial activities that substantially affect interstate commerce and also affect the educational process. That authority, though broad, does not include the authority to regulate each and every aspect of local schools.

The possession of a gun in a local school zone is in no sense an economic activity that might, through repetition elsewhere, substantially affect any sort of interstate commerce. To uphold the Government's contentions here, we would have to pile inference upon inference in a manner that would bid fair to convert congressional authority under the Commerce Clause to a general police power of the sort retained by the States. Admittedly, some of our prior cases have taken long steps down that road, giving great deference to congressional action. [W]e decline here to proceed any further. To do so would require us to conclude that the Constitution's enumeration of powers does not presuppose something not enumerated, and that there never will be a distinction between what is truly national and what is truly local. This we are unwilling to do.

Justice KENNEDY, with whom Justice O'CONNOR joins, concurring.

> **Take Note**
>
> Did the Court invalidate the Gun-Free School Zones Act as applied to the respondent? Or did it strike down the statute "on its face"—that is, as unconstitutional in all (or substantially all) of its applications, and thus categorically beyond Congress's power to enact in its present form?

The history of the judicial struggle to interpret the Commerce Clause during the transition from the economic system the Founders knew to the single, national market still emergent in our own era counsels great restraint before the Court determines that the Clause is insufficient to support an exercise of the national power. *** *Stare decisis* operates with great force in counseling us not to call in question the essential principles now in place respecting the congressional power to regulate transactions of a commercial nature. That fundamental restraint on our power forecloses us from reverting to an understanding of commerce that would serve only an 18th-century economy, dependent then upon production and trading practices that had changed but little over the preceding centuries; it also mandates against returning to the time when congressional authority to regulate undoubted commercial activities was limited by a judicial determination that those matters had an insufficient connection to an interstate system. Congress can regulate in the commercial sphere on the assumption that we have a single market and a unified purpose to build a stable national economy.

It does not follow, however, that in every instance the Court lacks the authority and responsibility to review congressional attempts to alter the federal balance. This case requires us to consider our place in the design of the Government and to appreciate the significance of federalism in the whole structure of the Constitution. Of the various structural elements in the Constitution, separation of powers, checks and balances, judicial review, and federalism, only concerning the last does there seem to be much uncertainty respecting the existence, and the content, of standards that allow the Judiciary to play a significant role in maintaining the design contemplated by the Framers. *** There is irony in this, because of the four structural elements in the Constitution just mentioned, federalism was the unique contribution of the Framers to political science and political theory. Though on the surface the idea may seem counterintuitive, it was the insight of the Framers that freedom was enhanced by the creation of two governments, not one.

The theory that two governments accord more liberty than one requires for its realization two distinct and discernable lines of political accountability: one between the citizens and the Federal Government; the second between the citizens and the States. *** Were the Federal Government to take over the regulation of entire areas of traditional state concern, areas having nothing to do with the regulation of commercial activities, the boundaries between the spheres of federal and state authority would blur and political responsibility would become illusory. The resultant inability to hold either branch of the government answerable to the citizens is more dangerous even than devolving too much authority to the remote central power.

Although it is the obligation of all officers of the Government to respect the constitutional design, the federal balance is too essential a part of our constitutional structure and plays too vital a role in securing freedom for us to admit inability to intervene when one or the other level of Government has tipped the scales too far.

Justice THOMAS, concurring.

[O]ur case law has drifted far from the original understanding of the Commerce Clause. In a future case, we ought to temper our Commerce Clause jurisprudence in a manner that both makes sense of our more recent case law and is more faithful to the original understanding of that Clause. *** In an appropriate case, I believe that we must further reconsider our "substantial effects" test with an eye toward constructing a standard that reflects the text and history of the Commerce Clause without totally rejecting our more recent Commerce Clause jurisprudence.

At the time the original Constitution was ratified, "commerce" consisted of selling, buying, and bartering, as well as transporting for these purposes. See 1 S. Johnson, A Dictionary of the English Language 361 (4th ed. 1773) (defining commerce as "Intercour[s]e; exchange of one thing for another; interchange of any thing; trade; traffick"); N. Bailey, An Universal Etymological English Dictionary (26th ed. 1789) ("trade or traffic"); T. Sheridan, A Complete Dictionary of the English Language (6th ed. 1796) ("Exchange of one thing for another; trade, traffick"). This understanding finds support in the etymology of the word, which literally means "with merchandise." See 3 Oxford English Dictionary 552 (2d ed. 1989) (com-

> **Take Note**
>
> Is Justice Thomas proposing the conceptual test for commerce that the Court followed in *E.C. Knight*, *Hammer*, and *Carter Coal*? Is his definition of commerce consistent with the test for commerce that the Court suggested in *Gibbons*? If not, does this undermine Justice Thomas's claims about the original understanding of the term "commerce"?

"with"; merci-"merchandise"). In fact, when Federalists and Anti-Federalists discussed the Commerce Clause during the ratification period, they often used trade (in its selling/bartering sense) and commerce interchangeably. See The Federalist No. 4 (J. Jay) (asserting that countries will cultivate our friendship when our "trade" is prudently regulated by Federal Government); id., No. 7 (A. Hamilton) (discussing "competitions of commerce" between States resulting from state "regulations of trade"); id., No. 40 (J. Madison) (asserting that it was an "acknowledged object of the Convention ... that the regulation of trade should be submitted to the general government"); Lee, Letters of a Federal Farmer No. 5, in Pamphlets on the Constitution of the United States 319 (P. Ford ed. 1888); Smith, An Address to the People of the State of New York, in id., at 107.

The Constitution not only uses the word "commerce" in a narrower sense than our case law might suggest, it also does not support the proposition that Congress has authority over all activities that "substantially affect" interstate commerce. [O]n this Court's understanding of congressional power, many of Congress' other enumerated powers under Art. I, § 8, are wholly superfluous. After all, if Congress may regulate all matters that substantially affect commerce, there is no need for the Constitution to specify that Congress may enact bankruptcy laws, or coin money and fix the standard of weights and measures, or punish counterfeiters of United States coin and securities. *** Put simply, much if not all of Art. I, § 8 (including portions of the Commerce Clause itself), would be surplusage if Congress had been given authority over matters that substantially affect interstate commerce. An interpretation of cl. 3 that makes the rest of § 8 superfluous simply cannot be correct.

My review of the case law indicates that the substantial effects test is but an innovation of the 20th century. *** If anything, the "wrong turn" was the Court's dramatic departure in the 1930's from a century and a half of precedent. Apart from its recent vintage and its corresponding lack of any grounding in the original understanding of the Constitution, the substantial effects test suffers from the further flaw that it appears to grant Congress a police power over the Nation. When asked at oral argument if there were *any* limits to the Commerce Clause, the Government was at a loss for words. Likewise, the principal dissent insists that there are limits, but it cannot muster even one example.

If we wish to be true to a Constitution that does not cede a police power to the Federal Government, our Commerce Clause's boundaries simply cannot be "defined" as being "commensurate with the national needs" or self-consciously intended to let the Federal Government "defend itself against economic forces that Congress decrees inimical or destructive of the national economy." See *post*, BREYER, J., dissenting. Such a formulation of federal power is no test at all: It is a blank check.

Justice STEVENS, dissenting.

Guns are both articles of commerce and articles that can be used to restrain commerce. Their possession is the consequence, either directly or indirectly, of commercial activity. In my judgment, Congress' power to regulate commerce in firearms includes the power to prohibit possession of guns at any location because of their potentially harmful use; it necessarily follows that Congress may also prohibit their possession in particular markets. The market for the possession of handguns by school-age children is, distressingly, substantial. Whether or not the national interest in eliminating that market would have justified federal legislation in 1789, it surely does today.

Justice SOUTER, dissenting.

In judicial review under the Commerce Clause, [the rational-basis test] reflects our respect for the institutional competence of the Congress on a subject expressly assigned to it by the Constitution and our appreciation of the legitimacy that comes from Congress's political accountability in dealing with matters open to a wide range of possible choices.

It was not ever thus, however, as even a brief overview of Commerce Clause history during the past century reminds us. The modern respect for the competence and primacy of Congress in matters affecting commerce developed only after one of this Court's most chastening experiences, when it perforce repudiated an earlier and untenably expansive conception of judicial review in derogation of congressional commerce power. [The] period from the turn of the century to 1937 is better noted for a series of cases applying highly formalistic notions of "commerce" to invalidate federal social and economic legislation. These restrictive views of commerce subject to congressional power complemented the Court's activism in limiting the enforceable scope of state economic regulation.

It is most familiar history that during this same period the Court routinely invalidated state social and economic legislation under an expansive conception of Fourteenth Amendment substantive due process. [U]nder each conception of judicial review the Court's character for the first third of the century showed itself in exacting judicial scrutiny of a legislature's choice of economic ends and of the legislative means selected to reach them.

> **Make the Connection**
>
> We will consider the cases to which Justice Souter alludes—in particular, the *Lochner* decision—and "substantive due process" in Chapter 8.

It was not merely coincidental, then, that sea changes in the Court's conceptions of its authority under the Due Process and Commerce Clauses occurred virtually together, in 1937. *** There is today, however, a backward glance at both the old pitfalls, as the Court treats deference under the rationality rule as subject to gradation according to the commercial or noncommercial nature of the immediate subject of the challenged regulation. The distinction between what is patently commercial and what is not looks much like the old distinction between what directly affects commerce and what touches it only indirectly. And the act of calibrating the level of deference by drawing a line between what is patently commercial and what is less purely so will probably resemble the process of deciding how much interference with contractual freedom was fatal. Thus, it seems fair to ask whether the step taken by the Court today does anything but portend a return to the untenable jurisprudence from which the Court extricated itself almost 60 years ago. The answer is not reassuring.

Justice BREYER, with whom Justice STEVENS, Justice SOUTER, and Justice GINSBURG join, dissenting.

[W]e must ask whether Congress could have had a *rational basis* for finding a significant (or substantial) connection between gun-related school violence and interstate commerce. *** Congress could reasonably have found the empirical connection that its law, implicitly or explicitly, asserts.

For one thing, reports, hearings, and other readily available literature make clear that the problem of guns in and around schools is widespread and extremely serious. *** Congress could therefore have found a substantial educational problem—teachers unable to teach, students unable to learn—and concluded that guns near schools contribute substantially to the size and scope of that problem. Having found that guns in schools significantly undermine the quality of education in our Nation's classrooms, Congress could also have found, given the effect of education upon interstate and foreign commerce, that gun-related violence in and around schools is a commercial, as well as a human, problem. Education, although far more than a matter of economics, has long been inextricably intertwined with the Nation's economy.

The economic links I have just sketched seem fairly obvious. Why then is it not equally obvious, in light of those links, that a widespread, serious, and substantial physical threat to teaching and learning *also* substantially threatens the commerce to which that teaching and learning is inextricably tied? *** At the very least, Congress could rationally have concluded that the links are "substantial."

[A] holding that the particular statute before us falls within the commerce power would not expand the scope of that Clause. Rather, it simply would apply preexisting law to changing economic circumstances. It would recognize that, in today's economic world, gun-related violence near the classroom makes a significant difference to our economic, as well as our social, well-being.

The majority's holding *** creates three serious legal problems. First, the majority's holding runs contrary to modern Supreme Court cases that have upheld congressional actions despite connections to interstate or foreign commerce that are less significant than the effect of school violence. *** The second legal problem the Court creates comes from its apparent belief that it can reconcile its holding with earlier cases by making a critical distinction between "commercial" and noncommercial "transaction[s]." The majority clearly cannot intend such a distinction to focus narrowly on an act of gun possession standing by itself, for such a reading could not be reconciled with [*McClung*, because in that case] the specific transaction (the race-based exclusion ***) was not itself "commercial." And, if the majority instead means to distinguish generally among broad categories of activities, differentiating what is educational from what is commercial, then, as a practical matter, the line becomes almost impossible to draw. Schools that teach reading, writing, mathematics, and related basic skills serve *both* social and commercial purposes, and one cannot easily separate the one from the other.

The third legal problem created by the Court's holding is that it threatens legal uncertainty in an area of law that, until this case, seemed reasonably well settled. Congress has enacted many statutes (more than 100 sections of the United States Code), including criminal statutes (at least 25 sections), that use the words "affecting commerce" to define their scope, and other statutes that contain no jurisdictional language at all. *** [T]he legal uncertainty now created will restrict Congress' ability to enact criminal laws aimed at criminal behavior that, considered problem by problem rather than instance by instance, seriously threatens the economic, as well as social, well-being of Americans.

Points for Discussion

a. Economic Activity

The Court in *Lopez* suggested that Congress has authority to regulate local activity on the theory that, in the aggregate, it substantially affects interstate commerce only if the activity is "economic" in nature. How should a Court determine whether an activity is economic? *Wickard* involved regulation of the cultivation and consumption of home-grown wheat. Were those economic activities? What about the discrimination at issue in *Heart of Atlanta Motel* and *McClung*?

b. Changes in the Nature of "Commerce"

The majority in *Lopez* acknowledged that the Court's view of permissible subjects for regulation under the Commerce Clause has changed as the nature of the interstate market has changed, but insisted that some semblance of the original understanding—that there are limits to Congress's power—must be preserved. Justice Thomas asserted that the meaning of the term "commerce" should be fixed according to the view of that term in 1789. And the dissenters asserted that as the world has changed, so must the scope of Congress's power to regulate commerce, defined in light of modern circumstances—even if this means, in practice, that Congress has virtually limitless power. Which of these views makes the most sense? Is it possible to be faithful to the "original meaning" of the Constitution and still conclude that Congress's power to regulate today is broader than it was in 1789?

c. Precedent and Original Meaning

In a footnote in his separate opinion, Justice Thomas said: "Although I might be willing to return to the original understanding, I recognize that many believe that it is too late in the day to undertake a fundamental reexamination of the past 60 years. Consideration of *stare decisis* and reliance interests may convince us that we cannot wipe the slate clean." Would it be appropriate, if more Justices were willing, to overrule 60 years worth of cases if they are inconsistent with the Constitution's original meaning? Not even self-professed originalists agree on this question. Compare Gary Lawson, *The Constitutional Case Against Precedent,* 17 Harv. J.L. & Publ. Pol'y 23 (1994)(arguing that it is unconstitutional for the Court to follow precedent that deviates from the Constitution's original, objective meaning), with Robert Bork, The Tempting of America: The Political Seduction of the Law 155-59 (1990) (arguing that some decisions are "so thoroughly embedded in our national life that [they] should not be overruled").

d. The Gun-Free School Zones Act Amended

To address the constitutional problem with the Gun-Free School Zones Act, Congress amended the statute to add a jurisdictional element. As amended, the statute now provides: "It shall be unlawful for any individual knowingly to possess a firearm that has moved in or that otherwise affects interstate or foreign commerce at a place that the individual knows, or has reasonable cause to believe, is a school zone." 18 U.S.C. § 922(q) Federal courts have upheld the statute as amended. See, e.g., *United States v. Dorsey,* 418 F.3d 1038, 1046 (9th Cir. 2005) Are these decisions consistent with *Lopez*? If so, how important was the *Lopez* decision in light of these subsequent developments?

Hypothetical

Congress enacts the "Dead-Beat Parent Act of 2007." It provides in relevant part: "The failure to pay child support in compliance with a state-court order shall be punishable by a fine of not more than $10,000 and imprisonment of not more than 2 years." Dennis Dilbert, a California resident, is indicted under the Act for failing to pay child support to his former spouse, who also lives, with the couple's children, in California. He has moved to quash the indictment on the ground that the Act exceeds Congress's power. How should the court rule? Could the statute be amended to remove doubts about its constitutionality without significantly changing its substance?

United States v. Morrison

529 U.S. 598 (2000)

Chief Justice REHNQUIST delivered the opinion of the Court.

In these cases we consider the constitutionality of 42 U.S.C. § 13981, which provides a federal civil remedy for the victims of gender-motivated violence. *** Petitioner Christy Brzonkala enrolled at [Virginia Tech, where she] met respondents Antonio Morrison and James Crawford, who were both students and members of its varsity football team. Brzonkala alleges that, within 30 minutes of meeting [them], they assaulted and repeatedly raped her. *** In early 1995, Brzonkala filed a complaint against respondents under Virginia Tech's Sexual Assault Policy. After the hearing, Virginia Tech's Judicial Committee found *** Morrison guilty of sexual assault and sentenced him to immediate suspension for two semesters. *** Morrison appealed his second conviction through the university's administrative system. On August 21, 1995, Virginia Tech's [provost] set aside Morrison's punishment[, concluding that it was "excessive." As a result, Brzonkala] dropped out of the university. In December 1995, Brzonkala sued Morrison, Crawford, and Virginia Tech [alleging] that Morrison's and Crawford's attack violated § 13981 ***. Morrison and Crawford moved to dismiss this complaint on the [ground] that § 13981's civil remedy is unconstitutional.

Section 13981 was part of the Violence Against Women Act of 1994. [Subsection (b)] states that "all persons within the United States shall have the right to be free from crimes of violence motivated by gender," [and subsection (c)] declares: "A person (including a person who acts under color of any statute, ordinance, regulation, custom, or usage of any State) who commits a crime of violence motivated by gender and thus deprives another of the right declared in subsection (b) of this section shall be liable to the party injured, in an action for the recovery of compensatory and punitive damages, injunctive and declaratory relief, and such other relief as a court may deem appropriate."

Petitioners *** seek to sustain § 13981 as a regulation of activity that substantially affects interstate commerce. Given § 13981's focus on gender-motivated violence wherever it occurs (rather than violence directed at the instrumentalities of interstate commerce, interstate markets, or things or persons in interstate commerce), we agree that this is the proper inquiry. *Lopez* *** provides the proper framework for conducting the required analysis of § 13981.

Gender-motivated crimes of violence are not, in any sense of the phrase, economic activity. While we need not adopt a categorical rule against aggregating the effects of any noneconomic activity in order to decide these cases, thus far in our Nation's history our cases have upheld Commerce Clause regulation of intrastate activity only where that activity is economic in nature.

Like the Gun-Free School Zones Act at issue in <u>Lopez</u>, § 13981 contains no jurisdictional element establishing that the federal cause of action is in pursuance of Congress' power to regulate interstate commerce. *** Congress elected to cast § 13981's remedy over a wider, and more purely intrastate, body of violent crime.

In contrast with the lack of congressional findings that we faced in <u>Lopez</u>, § 13981 is supported by numerous findings regarding the serious impact that gender-motivated violence has on victims and their families. But the existence of congressional findings is not sufficient, by itself, to sustain the constitutionality of Commerce Clause legislation. *** In these cases, Congress' findings are substantially weakened by the fact that they rely so heavily on a method of reasoning that we have already rejected as unworkable if we are to maintain the Constitution's enumeration of powers. Congress found that gender-motivated violence affects interstate commerce "by deterring potential victims from traveling interstate, from engaging in employment in interstate business, and from transacting with business, and in places involved in interstate commerce; by diminishing national productivity, increasing medical and other costs, and decreasing the supply of and the demand for interstate products."

Food for Thought

Is it realistic to fear that Congress will, if the prospect of judicial invalidation is substantially diminished, attempt comprehensively to regulate family law and violent crime? What might prevent Congress from doing so? What role should such considerations play in determining the consistency of federal law with federalism norms?

The reasoning that petitioners advance seeks to follow the but-for causal chain from the initial occurrence of violent crime (the suppression of which has always been the prime object of the States' police power) to every attenuated effect upon interstate commerce. If accepted, petitioners' reasoning would allow Congress to regulate any crime as long as the nationwide, aggregated impact of that crime has substantial effects on employment, production, transit, or consumption. Indeed, if Congress may regulate gender-motivated violence, it would be able to regulate murder or any other type of violence since gender-motivated violence, as a subset of all violent crime, is certain to have lesser economic impacts than the larger class of which it is a part. Petitioners' reasoning, moreover, will not limit Congress to regulating violence but may, as we suggested in *Lopez*, be applied equally as well to family law and other areas of traditional state regulation since the aggregate effect of marriage, divorce, and childrearing on the national economy is undoubtedly significant. Under our written Constitution, however, the limitation of congressional authority is not solely a matter of legislative grace.

We accordingly reject the argument that Congress may regulate noneconomic, violent criminal conduct based solely on that conduct's aggregate effect on interstate commerce. *** The regulation and punishment of intrastate violence that is not directed at the instrumentalities, channels, or goods involved in interstate commerce has always been the province of the States. Indeed, we can think of no better example of the police power, which the Founders denied the National Government and reposed in the States, than the suppression of violent crime and vindication of its victims.

If the allegations here are true, no civilized system of justice could fail to provide [Brzonkala] a remedy for the conduct of respondent Morrison. But under our federal system that remedy must be provided by the Commonwealth of Virginia, and not by the United States.

Justice THOMAS, concurring.

Make the Connection

The Court also held, in a portion of the opinion that we will consider in Chapter 13, that Congress's power to enforce the Fourteenth Amendment did not authorize it to enact the Violence Against Women Act.

[T]he very notion of a "substantial effects" test under the Commerce Clause is inconsistent with the original understanding of Congress' powers and with this Court's early Commerce Clause cases. *** Until this Court replaces its existing Commerce Clause jurisprudence with a standard more consistent with the original understanding, we will continue to see Congress appropriating state police powers under the guise of regulating commerce.

Justice SOUTER, with whom Justice STEVENS, Justice GINSBURG, and Justice BREYER join, dissenting.

Our cases, which remain at least nominally undisturbed, stand for the following propositions. Congress has the power to legislate with regard to activity that, in the aggregate, has a substantial effect on interstate commerce. The fact of such a substantial effect is not an issue for the courts in the first instance, but for the Congress, whose institutional capacity for gathering evidence and taking testimony far exceeds ours. By passing legislation, Congress indicates its conclusion, whether explicitly or not, that facts support its exercise of the commerce power. The business of the courts is to review the congressional assessment, not for soundness but simply for the rationality of concluding that a jurisdictional basis exists in fact. Any explicit findings that Congress chooses to make, though not dispositive of the question of rationality, may advance judicial review by identifying factual authority on which Congress relied. Applying those propositions in these cases can lead to only one conclusion.

One obvious difference from *Lopez* is the mountain of data assembled by Congress, here showing the effects of violence against women on interstate commerce. Passage of the Act in 1994 was preceded by four years of hearings, which included testimony from physicians and law professors; from survivors of rape and domestic violence; and from representatives of state law enforcement and private business. The record includes reports on gender bias from task forces in 21 States, and we have the benefit of specific factual findings in the eight separate Reports issued by Congress and its committees over the long course leading to enactment.

Congress thereby explicitly stated the predicate for the exercise of its Commerce Clause power. Is its conclusion irrational in view of the data amassed? [T]he sufficiency of the evidence before Congress to provide a rational basis for the finding cannot seriously be questioned. Indeed, the legislative record here is far more voluminous than the record compiled by Congress and found sufficient in two prior cases upholding Title II of the Civil Rights Act of 1964 against Commerce Clause challenges. *Heart of Atlanta Motel*; *McClung*.

The Act would have passed muster at any time between *Wickard* in 1942 and *Lopez* in 1995 ***. The fact that the Act does not pass muster before the Court today is therefore proof, to a degree that *Lopez* was not, that the Court's nominal adherence to the substantial effects test is merely that. Although a new jurisprudence has not emerged with any distinctness, it is clear that some congressional conclusions about obviously substantial, cumulative effects on commerce are being assigned lesser values than the once-stable doctrine would assign them. These devaluations are accomplished not by any express repudiation of the substantial effects test or its application through the aggregation of individual conduct, but by supplanting rational basis scrutiny with a new criterion of review.

The premise that the enumeration of powers implies that other powers are withheld is sound; the conclusion that some particular categories of subject matter are therefore presumptively beyond the reach of the commerce power is, however, a non sequitur. *** [H]istory has shown that categorical exclusions have proven as unworkable in practice as they are unsupportable in theory. [See, *e.g.*, *E.C. Knight*, *Hammer*, *Schechter Poultry*, *Carter Coal*.] Why is the majority tempted to reject the lesson so painfully learned in 1937? An answer emerges from contrasting *Wickard* with [*Carter Coal*.] *** The Court in *Carter Coal* was still trying to create a laissez-faire world out of the 20th-century economy, and formalistic commercial distinctions were thought to be useful instruments in achieving that object. The Court in *Wickard* knew it could not do any such thing and in the aftermath of the New Deal had long since stopped attempting the impossible.

If we now ask why the formalistic economic/noneconomic distinction might matter today, after its rejection in *Wickard*, the answer is not that the majority fails to see causal connections in an integrated economic world. The answer is that in the minds of the majority there is a new animating theory that makes categorical formalism seem useful again. Just as the old formalism had value in the service of an economic conception, the new one is useful in serving a conception of federalism. It is the instrument by which assertions of national power are to be limited in favor of preserving a supposedly discernible, proper sphere of state autonomy to legislate or refrain from legislating as the individual States see fit. [But as] with "conflicts of economic interest," so with supposed conflicts of sovereign political interests implicated by the Commerce Clause: the Constitution remits them to politics.

Today's majority *** finds no significance whatever in the state support for the Act based upon the States' acknowledged failure to deal adequately with gender-based violence in state courts, and the belief of their own law enforcement agencies that national action is essential. The National Association of Attorneys General supported the Act unanimously, and Attorneys General from 38 States urged Congress to enact the Civil Rights Remedy, representing that "the current system for dealing with violence against women is inadequate." *** Thirty-six [States] have filed an *amicus* brief in support of petitioners in these cases, and only one State has taken respondents' side. It is, then, not the least irony of these cases that the States will be forced to enjoy the new federalism whether they want it or not.

Justice BREYER, with whom Justice STEVENS joins, and with whom Justice SOUTER and Justice GINSBURG join as to Part I-A, dissenting.

The "economic/noneconomic" distinction is not easy to apply. Does the local street corner mugger engage in "economic" activity or "noneconomic" activity when he mugs for money? Would evidence that desire for economic domination underlies many brutal crimes against women save the present statute? *** [C]an Congress simply rewrite the present law and limit its application to restaurants, hotels, perhaps universities, and other places of public accommodation? Given the latter exception, can Congress save the present law by including it, or much of it, in a broader "Safe Transport" or "Workplace Safety" act?

More important, why should we give critical constitutional importance to the economic, or noneconomic, nature of an interstate-commerce-affecting *cause*? If chemical emanations through indirect environmental change cause identical, severe commercial harm outside a State, why should it matter whether local factories or home fireplaces release them? *** Nothing in the Constitution's language, or that of earlier cases prior to *Lopez*, explains why the Court should ignore one highly relevant characteristic of an interstate-commerce-affecting cause (how "local" it is), while placing critical constitutional weight upon a different, less obviously relevant, feature (how "economic" it is).

Most importantly, the Court's complex rules seem unlikely to help secure the very object that they seek, namely, the protection of "areas of traditional state regulation" from federal intrusion. *** [I]n a world where most everyday products or their component parts cross interstate boundaries, Congress will frequently find it possible to redraft a statute using language that ties the regulation to the interstate movement of some relevant object, thereby regulating local criminal activity or, for that matter, family affairs. Although this possibility does not give the Federal Government the power to regulate everything, it means that any substantive limitation will apply randomly in terms of the interests the majority seeks to protect. *** Complex Commerce Clause rules creating fine distinctions that achieve only random results do little to further the important federalist interests that called them into being. That is why modern (pre-*Lopez*) case law rejected them.

We live in a Nation knit together by two centuries of scientific, technological, commercial, and environmental change. Those changes, taken together, mean that virtually every kind of activity, no matter how local, genuinely can affect commerce, or its conditions, outside the State—at least when considered in the aggregate. And that fact makes it close to impossible for courts to develop meaningful subject-matter categories that would exclude some kinds of local activities from ordinary Commerce Clause "aggregation" rules without, at the same time, depriving Congress of the power to regulate activities that have a genuine and important effect upon interstate commerce. Since judges cannot change the world, the "defect" means that, within the bounds of the rational, Congress, not the courts, must remain primarily responsible for striking the appropriate state/federal balance. Congress is institutionally motivated to do so. Its Members represent state and local district interests. They consider the views of state and local officials when they legislate, and they have even developed formal procedures to ensure that such consideration takes place.

Points for Discussion

a. Institutional Roles

The majority in Morrison insisted on preserving a meaningful role for the Court in policing the boundaries between federal and state authority, whereas the dissenting Justices argued for substantial—and virtually complete—deference to Congress's judgment about the limits of its own power. What are the most compelling arguments for these contrasting views of the Court's and Congress's institutional roles?

b. State Support

Justice Souter argued that it is ironic for the Court to invalidate on federalism grounds a federal statute that officials from the states overwhelmingly supported and defended. Should state support be relevant to the Court's analysis of the constitutionality of a federal statute? Can the states "waive" a federalism challenge by supporting the enactment of a federal statute? What if officials from all 50 states, rather than simply a majority, had demonstrably supported the enactment (and constitutionality) of the Violence Against Women Act?

Gonzales v. Raich

545 U.S. 1 (2005)

Justice STEVENS delivered the opinion of the Court.

California is one of at least nine States that authorize the use of marijuana for medicinal purposes. The question presented in this case is whether the power vested in Congress by Article I, § 8, of the Constitution "[t]o make all Laws which shall be necessary and proper for carrying into Execution" its authority to "regulate Commerce with foreign Nations, and among the several States" includes the power to prohibit the local cultivation and use of marijuana in compliance with California law.

In 1996, California voters passed Proposition 215, now codified as the Compassionate Use Act of 1996. *** The Act creates an exemption from criminal prosecution for physicians, as well as for patients and primary caregivers, who possess or cultivate marijuana for medicinal purposes with the recommendation or approval of a physician. Respondents Angel Raich and Diane Monson are California residents who suffer from a variety of serious medical conditions and have sought to avail themselves of medical marijuana pursuant to the terms of the Compassionate Use Act. *** [They] thereafter brought this action *** seeking injunctive and declaratory relief prohibiting the enforcement of the federal Controlled Substances Act (CSA) to the extent it prevents them from possessing, obtaining, or manufacturing cannabis for their personal medical use. [Under the CSA, the manufacture, distribution, or possession of marijuana is a criminal offense.]

Respondents in this case do not dispute that passage of the CSA *** was well within Congress' commerce power. *** Rather, [they] argue that the CSA's categorical prohibition of the manufacture and possession of marijuana as applied to the intrastate manufacture and possession of marijuana for medical purposes pursuant to California law exceeds Congress' authority under the Commerce Clause.

Our case law firmly establishes Congress' power to regulate purely local activities that are part of an economic "class of activities" that have a substantial effect on interstate commerce. *** [*Wickard*] establishes that Congress can regulate purely intrastate activity that is not itself "commercial," in that it is not produced for sale, if it concludes that failure to regulate that class of activity would undercut the regulation of the interstate market in that commodity. The similarities between this case and *Wickard* are striking. Like the farmer in *Wickard*, respondents are cultivating, for home consumption, a fungible commodity for which there is an established, albeit illegal, interstate market. Just as the Agricultural Adjustment Act was designed "to control the volume [of wheat] moving in interstate and foreign commerce in order to avoid surpluses" and consequently control the market price, a primary purpose of the CSA is to control the supply and demand of controlled substances in both lawful and unlawful drug markets. In *Wickard*, we had no difficulty concluding that Congress had a rational basis for believing that, when viewed in the aggregate, leaving home-consumed wheat outside the regulatory scheme would have a substantial influence on price and market conditions. Here too, Congress had a rational basis for concluding that leaving home-consumed marijuana outside federal control would similarly affect price and market conditions.

More concretely, one concern prompting inclusion of wheat grown for home consumption in the 1938 Act was that rising market prices could draw such wheat into the interstate market, resulting in lower market prices. The parallel concern making it appropriate to include marijuana grown for home consumption in the CSA is the likelihood that the high demand in the interstate market will draw such marijuana into that market. While the diversion of homegrown wheat tended to frustrate the federal interest in stabilizing prices by regulating the volume of commercial transactions in the interstate market, the diversion of homegrown marijuana tends to frustrate the federal interest in eliminating commercial transactions in the interstate market in their entirety. In both cases, the regulation is squarely within Congress' commerce power because production of the commodity meant for home consumption, be it wheat or marijuana, has a substantial effect on supply and demand in the national market for that commodity.

Food for Thought

Would it make sense to require congressional findings about the relationship between interstate commerce and the particular conduct at issue? Is it reasonable to expect that Congress would make findings about any possible conduct that might be embraced by the prohibition in the statute? Or is the point that the likely failure of Congress to do so suggests something about the breadth of the statute in the first place?

Congress did not make a specific finding that the intrastate cultivation and possession of marijuana for medical purposes based on the recommendation of a physician would substantially affect the larger interstate marijuana market. [But] we have never required Congress to make particularized findings in order to legislate. While congressional findings are certainly helpful in reviewing the substance of a congressional statutory scheme, particularly when the connection to commerce is not self-evident, *** the absence of particularized findings does not call into question Congress' authority to legislate.

We need not determine whether respondents' activities, taken in the aggregate, substantially affect interstate commerce in fact, but only whether a "rational basis" exists for so concluding. Given the enforcement difficulties that attend distinguishing between marijuana cultivated locally and marijuana grown elsewhere, and concerns about diversion into illicit channels, we have no difficulty concluding that Congress had a rational basis for believing that failure to regulate the intrastate manufacture and possession of marijuana would leave a gaping hole in the CSA. *** That the regulation ensnares some purely intrastate activity is of no moment. As we have done many times before, we refuse to excise individual components of that larger scheme.

[R]espondents rely heavily on ****Lopez* and *Morrison*. As an initial matter, the statutory challenges at issue in those cases were markedly different from the challenge respondents pursue in the case at hand. Here, respondents ask us to excise individual applications of a concededly valid statutory scheme. In contrast, in both _Lopez_ and _Morrison_, the parties asserted that a particular statute or provision fell outside Congress' commerce power in its entirety. [W]e have often reiterated that "[w]here the class of activities is regulated and that class is within the reach of federal power, the courts have no power 'to excise, as trivial, individual instances' of the class."

At issue in _Lopez_ was the validity of *** a brief, single-subject statute making it a crime for an individual to possess a gun in a school zone. The Act did not regulate any economic activity and did not contain any requirement that the possession of a gun have any connection to past interstate activity or a predictable impact on future commercial activity. *** [The CSA is] a lengthy and detailed statute creating a comprehensive framework for regulating the production, distribution, and possession of five classes of "controlled substances." Our opinion in _Lopez_ casts no doubt on the validity of such a program.

Unlike those at issue in <u>Lopez</u> and <u>Morrison</u>, the activities regulated by the CSA are quintessentially economic. *** The CSA is a statute that regulates the production, distribution, and consumption of commodities for which there is an established, and lucrative, interstate market. Prohibiting the intrastate possession or manufacture of an article of commerce is a rational (and commonly utilized) means of regulating commerce in that product. Because the CSA is a statute that directly regulates economic, commercial activity, our opinion in <u>Morrison</u> casts no doubt on its constitutionality.

[I]f, as the principal dissent contends, the personal cultivation, possession, and use of marijuana for medicinal purposes is beyond the "outer limits of Congress' Commerce Clause authority," it must also be true that such personal use of marijuana (or any other homegrown drug) for *recreational* purposes is also beyond those "outer limits," whether or not a State elects to authorize or even regulate such use. *** One need not have a degree in economics to understand why a nationwide exemption for the vast quantity of marijuana (or other drugs) locally cultivated for personal use (which presumably would include use by friends, neighbors, and family members) may have a substantial impact on the interstate market for this extraordinarily popular substance. The congressional judgment that an exemption for such a significant segment of the total market would undermine the orderly enforcement of the entire regulatory scheme *** is not only rational, but "visible to the naked eye" under any commonsense appraisal of the probable consequences of such an open-ended exemption.

The exemption for cultivation by patients and caregivers can only increase the supply of marijuana in the California market. The likelihood that all such production will promptly terminate when patients recover or will precisely match the patients' medical needs during their convalescence seems remote; whereas the danger that excesses will satisfy some of the admittedly enormous demand for recreational use seems obvious. Moreover, that the national and international narcotics trade has thrived in the face of vigorous criminal enforcement efforts suggests that no small number of unscrupulous people will make use of the California exemptions to serve their commercial ends whenever it is feasible to do so. *** Congress could have rationally concluded that the aggregate impact on the national market of all the transactions exempted from federal supervision is unquestionably substantial.

Justice SCALIA, concurring in the judgment.

[U]nlike the channels, instrumentalities, and agents of interstate commerce, activities that substantially affect interstate commerce are not themselves part of interstate commerce, and thus the power to regulate them cannot come from the Commerce Clause alone. Rather, *** Congress's regulatory authority over intrastate activities that are not themselves part of interstate commerce (including activities that have a substantial effect on interstate commerce) derives from the Necessary and Proper Clause.

And the *** authority to enact laws necessary and proper for the regulation of interstate commerce is not limited to laws governing intrastate activities that substantially affect interstate commerce. Where necessary to make a regulation of interstate commerce effective, Congress may regulate even those intrastate activities that do not themselves substantially affect interstate commerce.　***　Moreover, *** Congress may regulate even noneconomic local activity if that regulation is a necessary part of a more general regulation of interstate commerce.　The relevant question is simply whether the means chosen are "reasonably adapted" to the attainment of a legitimate end under the commerce power.

Today's principal dissent objects that, by permitting Congress to regulate activities necessary to effective interstate regulation, the Court reduces *Lopez* and *Morrison* to "little more than a drafting guide." Unlike the power to regulate activities that have a substantial effect on interstate commerce, the power to enact laws enabling effective regulation of interstate commerce can only be exercised in conjunction with congressional regulation of an interstate market, and it extends only to those measures necessary to make the interstate regulation effective.　Neither [*Lopez* nor *Morrison*] involved the power of Congress to exert control over intrastate activities in connection with a more comprehensive scheme of regulation.

In the CSA, Congress has undertaken to extinguish the interstate market in Schedule I controlled substances, including marijuana.　The Commerce Clause unquestionably permits this.　***　To effectuate its objective, Congress has prohibited almost all intrastate activities related to [marijuana]—both economic activities (manufacture, distribution, possession with the intent to distribute) and noneconomic activities (simple possession).　That simple possession is a noneconomic activity is immaterial to whether it can be prohibited as a necessary part of a larger regulation.　Rather, Congress's authority to enact all of these prohibitions of intrastate controlled-substance activities depends only upon whether they are appropriate means of achieving the legitimate end of eradicating [those] substances from interstate commerce.

By this measure, I think the regulation must be sustained.　***　Drugs like marijuana are fungible commodities.　[M]arijuana that is grown at home and possessed for personal use is never more than an instant from the interstate market—and this is so whether or not the possession is for medicinal use or lawful use under the laws of a particular State.

Justice O'CONNOR, with whom THE CHIEF JUSTICE and Justice THOMAS join as to all but Part III, dissenting.

> **Take Note**
>
> Justice Scalia joined the majority in *Lopez* and *Morrison*, as did Justice Kennedy, who did not write separately in *Raich*.　The other Justices in the majority in *Lopez* and *Morrison* dissented in *Raich*, and the dissenters from *Lopez* and *Morrison* were in the majority in *Raich*.　Does Justice Scalia's opinion (which Justice Kennedy did not join) provide a convincing reason to treat the cases differently?

One of federalism's chief virtues [is] that it promotes innovation by allowing for the possibility that "a single courageous State may, if its citizens choose, serve as a laboratory; and try novel social and economic experiments without risk to the rest of the country." *New State Ice Co. v. Liebmann*, 285 U.S. 262, 311 (1932) (Brandeis, J., dissenting).　This case exemplifies the role of States as laboratories.　[California] has come to its own conclusion about the difficult and sensitive question of whether marijuana should be available to relieve severe pain and suffering.　Today the Court sanctions an application of the federal

Controlled Substances Act that extinguishes that experiment, without any proof that the personal cultivation, possession, and use of marijuana for medicinal purposes, if economic activity in the first place, has a substantial effect on interstate commerce and is therefore an appropriate subject of federal regulation. In so doing, the Court announces a rule that gives Congress a perverse incentive to legislate broadly pursuant to the Commerce Clause—nestling questionable assertions of its authority into comprehensive regulatory schemes—rather than with precision. That rule and the result it produces in this case are irreconcilable with our decisions in *Lopez* and *Morrison*.

I. Our decision [in *Lopez*] about whether gun possession in school zones substantially affected interstate commerce turned on four considerations. First, we observed that our "substantial effects" cases generally have upheld federal regulation of economic activity that affected interstate commerce, but that [the Gun-Free School Zones Act] was a criminal statute having "nothing to do with 'commerce' or any sort of economic enterprise." *** Second, we noted that the statute contained no express jurisdictional requirement establishing its connection to interstate commerce. Third, we found telling the absence of legislative findings about the regulated conduct's impact on interstate commerce. *** Finally, we rejected as too attenuated the Government's argument that firearm possession in school zones could result in violent crime which in turn could adversely affect the national economy. *** Later in *Morrison*, we relied on the same four considerations ***. In my view, the case before us is materially indistinguishable from *Lopez* and *Morrison* when the same considerations are taken into account.

II. [T]he Court appears to reason that the placement of local activity in a comprehensive scheme confirms that it is essential to that scheme. If the Court is right, then *Lopez* stands for nothing more than a drafting guide: Congress should have described the relevant crime as "transfer or possession of a firearm anywhere in the nation"—thus including commercial and noncommercial activity, and clearly encompassing some activity with assuredly substantial effect on interstate commerce. Had it done so, the majority hints, we would have sustained its authority to regulate possession of firearms in school zones. Furthermore, today's decision suggests we would readily sustain a congressional decision to attach the regulation of intrastate activity to a pre-existing comprehensive (or even not-so-comprehensive) scheme. If so, the Court invites increased federal regulation of local activity even if, as it suggests, Congress would not enact a *new* interstate scheme exclusively for the sake of reaching intrastate activity.

> **Food for Thought**
>
> Justice O'Connor asserts that the Court's conclusion will encourage Congress to enact broad, comprehensive regulatory schemes in order to reach more particularized and localized forms of activity. Is this a realistic threat? What might limit Congress's willingness or ability to do so?

The hard work for courts [is] to identify objective markers for confining the analysis in Commerce Clause cases. *** A number of objective markers are available to confine the scope of constitutional review here. [M]edical and nonmedical (*i.e.*, recreational) uses of drugs are realistically distinct and can be segregated.

Moreover, *** it is relevant that this case involves the interplay of federal and state regulation in areas of criminal law and social policy, where "States lay claim by right of history and expertise." To ascertain whether Congress' encroachment is constitutionally justified in this case, then, I would focus here on the personal cultivation, possession, and use of marijuana for medicinal purposes.

Take Note

Do you agree that defining the regulated conduct as the local possession of marijuana for medicinal purposes pursuant to a doctor's order in compliance with state law is an "objective" way to apply the *Lopez* and *Morrison* tests? Doesn't defining the regulated conduct that way effectively pre-ordain the conclusion that Congress lacks the power asserted? Conversely, doesn't the majority's approach—to define the regulated conduct as the unlawful sale of marijuana in an established market—virtually pre-ordain the opposite conclusion? How should the Court address this problem of level of generality?

Having thus defined the relevant conduct, we must determine whether, under our precedents, the conduct is economic and, in the aggregate, substantially affects interstate commerce. *** The Court's definition of economic activity is breathtaking. It defines as economic any activity involving the production, distribution, and consumption of commodities. [T]he Court's definition of economic activity for purposes of Commerce Clause jurisprudence threatens to sweep all of productive human activity into federal regulatory reach. *** It will not do to say that Congress may regulate noncommercial activity simply because it may have an effect on the demand for commercial goods, or because the noncommercial endeavor can, in some sense, substitute for commercial activity. Most commercial goods or services have some sort of privately producible analogue. Home care substitutes for daycare. Charades games substitute for movie tickets. *** To draw the line wherever private activity affects the demand for market goods is to draw no line at all, and to declare everything economic. We have already rejected the result that would follow—a federal police power.

The homegrown cultivation and personal possession and use of marijuana for medicinal purposes has no apparent commercial character. *** *Lopez* makes clear that possession is not itself commercial activity. And respondents have not come into possession by means of any commercial transaction; they have simply grown, in their own homes, marijuana for their own use, without acquiring, buying, selling, or bartering a thing of value. *** Even assuming that economic activity is at issue in this case, [t]here is simply no evidence that homegrown medicinal marijuana users constitute, in the aggregate, a sizable enough class to have a discernable, let alone substantial, impact on the national illicit drug market—or otherwise to threaten the CSA regime.

III. If I were a California citizen, I would not have voted for the medical marijuana ballot initiative; if I were a California legislator I would not have supported the Compassionate Use Act. But whatever the wisdom of California's experiment with medical marijuana, the federalism principles that have driven our Commerce Clause cases require that room for experiment be protected in this case. For these reasons I dissent.

Justice THOMAS, dissenting.

[N]o evidence from the founding suggests that "commerce" included the mere possession of a good or some purely personal activity that did not involve trade or exchange for value. In the early days of the Republic, it would have been unthinkable that Congress could prohibit the local cultivation, possession, and consumption of marijuana.

We normally presume that States enforce their own laws, and there is no reason to depart from that presumption here. *** But even assuming that States' controls allow some seepage of medical marijuana into the illicit drug market, there is a multibillion-dollar interstate market for marijuana. It is difficult to see how this vast market could be affected by diverted medical cannabis, let alone in a way that makes regulating intrastate medical marijuana obviously essential to controlling the interstate drug market. *** Congress' goal of curtailing the interstate drug trade would not plainly be thwarted if it could not apply the CSA to patients like Monson and Raich. That is, unless Congress' aim is really to exercise police power of the sort reserved to the States in order to eliminate even the intrastate possession and use of marijuana.

The majority's treatment of the substantial effects test is malleable, because the majority expands the relevant conduct. By defining the class at a high level of generality (as the intrastate manufacture and possession of marijuana), the majority overlooks that individuals authorized by state law to manufacture and possess medical marijuana exert no demonstrable effect on the interstate drug market. [T]he majority defines economic activity in the broadest possible terms ***. This carves out a vast swath of activities that are subject to federal regulation. If the majority is to be taken seriously, the Federal Government may now regulate quilting bees, clothes drives, and potluck suppers throughout the 50 States.

The majority's opinion only illustrates the steady drift away from the text of the Commerce Clause. There is an inexorable expansion from "commerce" to "commercial" and "economic" activity, and finally to all "production, distribution, and consumption" of goods or services for which there is an "established interstate market." Federal power expands, but never contracts, with each new locution. The majority is not interpreting the Commerce Clause, but rewriting it. *** One searches the Court's opinion in vain for any hint of what aspect of American life is reserved to the States. *** Our federalist system, properly understood, allows California and a growing number of other States to decide for themselves how to safeguard the health and welfare of their citizens.

——————

Points for Discussion

a. As-Applied v. Facial Challenges

The plaintiffs in *Raich* raised an "as-applied" challenge to the CSA—that is, they argued that it was unconstitutional as applied to their conduct—and the court rejected their challenge. In *Lopez*, in contrast, the Court struck down the statute there at issue "on its face"—

that is, it held that the statute was unconstitutional in its entirety, and should be declared unconstitutional in all applications. In other contexts, it is generally substantially more difficult to prevail on a facial challenge than it is to prevail on an as-applied challenge. (We will see examples when we turn to the First Amendment in Chapter 14.) The implication of the decisions in *Raich* and *Lopez*, however, is that it might be easier in Commerce Clause cases to prevail on a facial challenge—at least if Congress has not created a comprehensive scheme of regulation. Does this approach make sense?

b. Comprehensive Schemes

Central to the Court's conclusion in *Raich* was that the ban on local cultivation and possession was essential to the more comprehensive scheme of regulation under the CSA. Does this mean that federal statutes enacted pursuant to the commerce power are more likely to survive scrutiny if they sweep broadly—regulating a larger range of conduct, including more local conduct—rather than narrowly? If so, does this make sense from a federalism standpoint?

————————

C. The Taxing Power

Although the Commerce Clause has been the basis for a significant number of statutes over the last 70 years, it is not Congress's only meaningful power. Article I, § 8, which enumerates the powers of Congress, also confers on Congress the power to tax and spend, powers that Congress has used frequently to achieve its regulatory objectives. We address Congress's power to tax first, and then turn to Congress's spending power.

> ### U.S. Constitution, <u>Article I, Section 8, Clause 1</u>
>
> The Congress shall have Power To lay and collect Taxes, Duties, Imposts and Excises, to pay the Debts and provide for the common Defence and general Welfare of the United States; but all Duties, Imposts and Excises shall be uniform throughout the United States ***.

Taxes serve multiple functions. First, they raise revenue for the government. Second, by raising the cost of certain forms of behavior, they create disincentives to engage in that behavior—and incentives to engage in other, comparatively cheaper, behavior.

When a tax is particularly successful at the second function, it is little different in practice and effect from direct regulation of the behavior at issue. Assuming that there are limits on Congress's power to regulate certain forms of conduct pursuant to the Commerce Clause, can Congress circumvent those limits by reliance on its power to tax?

————————

Child Labor Tax Case

259 U.S. 20 (1922)

Mr. Chief Justice TAFT delivered the opinion of the Court.

This case presents the question of the constitutional validity of the Child Labor Tax Law. [Pursuant to that Act, the United States assessed Drexel Furniture Company $6,312.79—10 per cent of its net profits for 1919—for employing in its factory a boy under 14 years of age.] The company paid the tax under protest, and, after rejection of its claim for a refund, brought this suit.

The law is attacked on the ground that it is a regulation of the employment of child labor in the states—an exclusively state function under the federal Constitution and within the reservations of the Tenth Amendment. It is defended on the ground that it is a mere excise tax levied by the Congress of the United States under its broad power of taxation conferred by section 8, article 1, of the federal Constitution.

> **Make the Connection**
>
> The Court decided this case only four years after its decision in *Hammer v. Dagenhart*, which held that Congress lacks power pursuant to the Commerce Clause to regulate the practice of child labor.

We must construe the law and interpret the intent and meaning of Congress from the language of the act. *** Does this law impose a tax with only that incidental restraint and regulation which a tax must inevitably involve? Or does it regulate by the use of the so-called tax as a penalty? [The tax] provides a heavy exaction for a departure from a detailed and specified course of conduct in business. That course of business is that employers shall employ in mines and quarries, children of an age greater than 16 years; in mills and factories, children of an age greater than 14 years, and shall prevent children of less than 16 years in mills and factories from working more than 8 hours a day or 6 days in the week. If an employer departs from this prescribed course of business, he is to pay to the government one-tenth of his entire net income in the business for a full year. [I]t is only where he knowingly departs from the prescribed course that payment is to be exacted. Scienters are associated with penalties, not with taxes. The employer's factory is to be subject to inspection at any time not only by the taxing officers of the Treasury, the Department normally charged with the collection of taxes, but also by the Secretary of Labor and his subordinates, whose normal function is the advancement and protection of the welfare of the workers. In the light of these features of the act, a court must be blind not to see that the so-called tax is imposed to stop the employment of children within the age limits prescribed. Its prohibitory and regulatory effect and purpose are palpable. All others can see and understand this. How can we properly shut our minds to it?

> **Definition**
>
> An "excise tax" is a tax on the manufacture, sale, or use of goods, or on the carrying on of some specified activity.

Out of a proper respect for the acts of a co-ordinate branch of the government, this court has gone far to sustain taxing acts as such, even though there has been ground for suspecting, from the weight of the tax, it was intended to destroy its subject. But in the act before us the presumption of validity cannot prevail, because the proof of the contrary is found on the very face of its provisions. Grant the validity of this law, and all that Congress would need to do, hereafter, in seeking to take over to its control any one of the great number of subjects *** reserved to [the states] by the Tenth Amendment, would be to enact a detailed measure of complete regulation of the subject and enforce it by a so-called tax upon departures from it. To give such magic to the word "tax" would be to break down all constitutional limitation of the powers of Congress and completely wipe out the sovereignty of the states.

> **Food for Thought**
>
> It is notoriously difficult to determine the purpose or motive of a collective body such as a legislature, in which each member who voted for a proposal may have had individualized—and complex—reasons for doing so. See Frank H. Easterbrook, *Statutes' Domains*, 50 U. Chi. L. Rev. 533, 547-48 (1983). Should the Court consider Congress's purpose or motive here?

The difference between a tax and a penalty is sometimes difficult to define, and yet the consequences of the distinction in the required method of their collection often are important. Where the sovereign enacting the law has power to impose both tax and penalty, the difference between revenue production and mere regulation may be immaterial, but not so when one sovereign can impose a tax only, and the power of regulation rests in another. Taxes are occasionally imposed in the discretion of the Legislature on proper subjects with the primary motive of obtaining revenue from them and with the incidental motive of discouraging them by making their continuance onerous. They do not lose their character as taxes because of the incidental motive. But there comes a time in the extension of the penalizing features of the so-called tax when it loses its character as such and becomes a mere penalty, with the characteristics of regulation and punishment. Such is the case in the law before us. Although Congress does not invalidate the contract of employment or expressly declare that the employment within the mentioned ages is illegal, it does exhibit its intent practically to achieve the latter result by adopting the criteria of wrongdoing and imposing its principal consequence on those who transgress its standard.

The case before us cannot be distinguished from that of *Hammer v. Dagenhart.* *** The congressional power over interstate commerce is, within its proper scope, just as complete and unlimited as the congressional power to tax, and the legislative motive in its exercise is just as free from judicial suspicion and inquiry. Yet when Congress threatened to stop interstate commerce in ordinary and necessary commodities, unobjectionable as subjects of transportation, and to deny the same to the people of a state in order to coerce them into compliance with Congress' regulation of state concerns, the court said this was not in fact regulation of interstate commerce, but rather that of state concerns and was invalid. So here the so-called tax is a penalty to coerce people of a state to act as Congress wishes them to act in respect of a matter completely the business of the state government under the federal Constitution. This case requires as did [*Hammer*] the application of the principle announced [in *McCulloch*]: "Should Congress, *** under the pretext of executing its powers, pass laws for the accomplishment of objects not entrusted to the government; it would become the painful duty of this tribunal *** to say that such an act was not the law of the land."

For the reasons given, we must hold the Child Labor Tax Law invalid ***.

Points for Discussion

a. The Scope of the Taxing Power

If Congress has power pursuant to the Commerce Clause to regulate a particular activity, does it have power to impose a tax on that activity, even if the tax amounts to a "penalty"? Notice that the Court decided the *Child Labor Tax Case* only a few years after it decided *Hammer v. Dagenhart*, which considered the constitutionality of a federal law prohibiting the transportation in interstate commerce of goods produced in factories that used child labor. When the Court subsequently overruled *Hammer*, did it also overrule the *Child Labor Tax Case* sub silentio?

b. Taxes v. Penalties

What criteria should a court apply to determine whether a tax is a revenue-raising measure with an incidental motive to regulate or instead a penalty that constitutes impermissible regulation? Don't all taxes seek both to raise revenue and affect private choices?

There is currently a federal tax on the purchase of gasoline. Suppose that Congress today raised that tax $0.50 per gallon. Would the increase be a "penalty" or simply a "tax"? Would the answer be different if the tax before the increase took effect were already $2.00 per gallon? Given the scope of the Commerce Clause, does the answer to this question matter for the tax's constitutionality?

United States v. Kahriger

345 U.S. 22 (1953)

Mr. Justice REED delivered the opinion of the Court.

The issue raised by this appeal is the constitutionality of the occupational tax provisions of the Revenue Act of 1951, which levy a tax on persons engaged in the business of accepting wagers, and require such persons to register with the Collector of Internal Revenue. The unconstitutionality of the tax is asserted on two grounds. First, it is said that Congress, under the pretense of exercising its power to tax has attempted to penalize illegal intrastate gambling through the regulatory features of the Act, and has thus infringed the police power which is reserved to the states. Secondly, it is urged that the registration provisions of the tax violate the privilege against self-incrimination and are arbitrary and vague, contrary to the guarantees of the Fifth Amendment.

[Respondent Kahriger was charged with violating the Act on grounds that he was in the business of accepting wagers and that he willfully failed to register for and pay the occupational tax in question. Kahriger presumably did not register because his gambling activities were illegal under state law and he did not want to call attention to himself.]

The substance of respondent's position with respect to the Tenth Amendment is that Congress has chosen to tax a specified business which is not within its power to regulate. *** Appellee would have us say that because there is legislative history indicating a congressional motive to suppress wagering, this tax is not a proper exercise of such taxing power. *** [But we have upheld other taxes even though the] intent to curtail and hinder [was] manifest. [The] tax is [not] invalid [simply] because the revenue obtained is negligible. Appellee *** argues that the sole purpose of the statute is to penalize only illegal gambling in the states through the guise of a tax measure. [T]he instant tax has a regulatory effect. But regardless of its regulatory effect, the wagering tax produces revenue. As such it [is similar to other taxes that] we have found valid.

> **Take Note**
>
> Isn't it fair to assume that the tax invalidated in the *Child Labor Tax Case* also raised revenue for the government? (Indeed, the plaintiff in that case had been assessed several thousand dollars in taxes.) If so, can the *Child Labor Tax Case* be distinguished from this case? Does the Court even attempt to distinguish it?

Where federal legislation has rested on other congressional powers, such as the Necessary and Proper Clause or the Commerce Clause, this Court has generally sustained the statutes, despite their effect on matters ordinarily considered state concern. *** Where Congress has employed the taxing clause a greater variation in the decisions has resulted. *** It is hard to understand why the power to tax should raise more doubts because of indirect effects than other federal powers.

Penalty provisions in tax statutes added for breach of a regulation concerning activities in themselves subject only to state regulation have caused this Court to declare the enactments invalid. *Child Labor Tax Case.* Unless there are provisions, extraneous to any tax need, courts are without authority to limit the exercise of the taxing power. All the provisions of this excise are adapted to the collection of a valid tax.

[In an omitted portion of the opinion, the Court held that applying the registration provisions to Kahriger did not violate the privilege against self incrimination.]

Mr. Justice JACKSON, concurring.

I concur in the judgment and opinion of the Court, but with such doubt that if the minority agreed upon an opinion which did not impair legitimate use of the taxing power I probably would join it. But we deal here with important and contrasting values in our scheme of government, and it is important that neither be allowed to destroy the other. Of course, all taxation has a tendency proportioned to its burdensomeness to discourage the activity taxed. One cannot formulate a revenue-raising plan that would not have economic and social consequences. Congress may and should place the burden of taxes where it will least handicap desirable activities and bear most heavily on useless or harmful ones. If Congress may tax one citizen to the point of discouragement for making an honest living, it is hard to say that it may not do the same to another just because he makes a sinister living.

But here is a purported tax law which *** lays no tax except on specified gamblers whose calling in most states is illegal. It requires this group to step forward and identify themselves, not because they like others have income, but because of its source. This is difficult to regard as a rational or good-faith revenue measure, despite the deference that is due Congress. On the contrary, it seems to be a plan to tax out of existence the professional gambler whom it has been found impossible to prosecute out of existence.

> **Make the Connection**
>
> Recall that in the second half of the decision in *McCulloch v. Maryland*, the Court suggested that politics is the only protection for citizens subject to a tax imposed by a government whose representatives they get to choose. Is Justice Jackson, notwithstanding his concerns about the tax in this case, effectively adopting that view?

It will be a sad day for the revenues if the good will of the people toward their taxing system is frittered away in efforts to accomplish by taxation moral reforms that cannot be accomplished by direct legislation. But the evil that can come from this statute will probably soon make itself manifest to Congress. The evil of a judicial decision impairing the legitimate taxing power by extreme constitutional interpretations might not be transient.

Even though this statute approaches the fair limits of constitutionality, I join the decision of the Court.

Mr. Justice FRANKFURTER, dissenting.

Congress may make an oblique use of the taxing power in relation to activities with which Congress may deal directly, as for instance, commerce between the States. *** However, when oblique use is made of the taxing power as to matters which substantively are not within the powers delegated to Congress, the Court cannot shut its eyes to what is obviously, because designedly, an attempt to control conduct which the Constitution left to the responsibility of the States, merely because Congress wrapped the legislation in the verbal cellophane of a revenue measure. [T]he context of the circumstances which brought forth this enactment *** emphatically supports what was revealed on the floor of Congress, namely, that what was formally a means of raising revenue for the Federal Government was essentially an effort to check if not to stamp out professional gambling.

Points for Discussion

a. Precedent

Did the Court in *Kahriger* overrule the *Child Labor Tax Case*? It noted that "[p]enalty provisions in tax statutes added for breach of a regulation concerning activities in themselves subject only to state regulation have caused this Court to declare the enactments invalid," but it also suggested that such provisions are unconstitutional only if they are "extraneous to any tax need"—that is, only if they do not produce any revenue. Is it possible to conceive of a tax that is imposed for the "breach" of a federal regulation and that is entirely "extraneous to any tax need"?

b. Current Law

Since the decision in *Kahriger*, the Court has not invalidated a federal tax on the ground that it exceeds Congress's power to tax. Do you suppose that this is because of the test for the taxing power announced in *Kahriger*, the modern scope of Congress's power under the Commerce Clause, or both?

Hypothetical

Some experts believe that the best way to reform health care coverage in the United States is to require everyone who does not have government-provided health benefits to purchase private health insurance. Could Congress use its Commerce power to require someone to purchase private health insurance? Alternatively, could Congress impose a tax on any person who does not buy private health insurance in order to induce such purchases?

D. The Spending Power

Given that Congress has the power to tax, it is not surprising that it also has the power to spend the money that it raises through taxation. Article I, § 8, cl. 1 authorizes Congress "to pay the Debts and provide for the common Defence and general Welfare of the United States." Read literally, this appears to be an incredibly broad grant of authority. Can Congress use its spending power to achieve goals that it cannot achieve directly through the exercise of the commerce power? Does it matter whether Congress is granting money to private actors or instead to the state governments? The cases that follow grapple with those questions.

United States v. Butler

297 U.S. 1 (1936)

Mr. Justice ROBERTS delivered the opinion of the Court.

In this case we must determine whether certain provisions of the Agricultural Adjustment Act [of] 1933 conflict with the Federal Constitution. [In order to achieve the Act's stated purpose of stabilizing prices for agricultural commodities, the Act empowered the Secretary of Agriculture to pay farmers to reduce the number of acres dedicated to production for market. The Act further provided that the Secretary would obtain revenue for such payments by taxing processors of the particular agricultural commodity whose production the Secretary sought to limit. After the Secretary decided to stabilize cotton prices, the United States sought to impose a tax on the Hoosac Mills Corporation. The receivers of the company challenged the tax and the statutory scheme that authorized it.]

> **Take Note**
>
> Justice Roberts is the Justice who "switched" his vote on the scope of federal power in 1937, one year after the decision in *Butler* (and *Carter Coal*). As you read his opinion here, consider whether it gives any hints of the switch to come.

It is not contended that [Article I, § 8, cl. 1] grants power to regulate agricultural production upon the theory that such legislation would promote the general welfare. The government concedes that the phrase "to provide for the general welfare" qualifies the power "to lay and collect taxes." The view that the clause grants power to provide for the general welfare, independently of the taxing power, has never been authoritatively accepted. Mr. Justice Story points out that, if it were adopted, "it is obvious that under color of the generality of the words, to 'provide for the common defence and general welfare,' the government of the United States is, in reality, a government of general and unlimited powers, notwithstanding the subsequent enumeration of specific powers." The true construction undoubtedly is that the only thing granted is the power to tax for the purpose of providing funds for payment of the nation's debts and making provision for the general welfare.

Nevertheless, the government asserts that warrant is found in this clause for the adoption of the Agricultural Adjustment Act. *** Since the foundation of the nation, sharp differences of opinion have persisted as to the true interpretation of the phrase ["to provide for the general Welfare of the United States."] Madison asserted it amounted to no more than a reference to the other powers enumerated in the subsequent clauses of the same section; that, as the United States is a government of limited and enumerated powers, the grant of power to tax and spend for the general national welfare must be confined to the enumerated legislative fields committed to the Congress. In this view the phrase is mere tautology, for taxation and appropriation are or may be necessary incidents of the exercise of any of the enumerated legislative powers. Hamilton, on the other hand, maintained the clause confers a power separate and distinct from those later enumerated, is not restricted in meaning by the grant of them, and Congress consequently has a substantive power to tax and to appropriate, limited only by the requirement that it shall be exercised to provide for the general welfare of the United States. Each contention has had the support of those whose views are entitled to weight.

[We] conclude that the reading advocated by [Hamilton] is the correct one. While, therefore, the power to tax is not unlimited, its confines are set in the clause which confers it, and not in those of section 8 which bestow and define the legislative powers of the Congress. It results that the power of Congress to authorize expenditure of public moneys for public purposes is not limited by the direct grants of legislative power found in the Constitution.

We are not now required to ascertain the scope of the phrase "general welfare of the United States" or to determine whether an appropriation in aid of agriculture falls within it. Wholly apart from that question, another principle embedded in our Constitution prohibits the enforcement of the Agricultural Adjustment Act. The act invades the reserved rights of the states. It is a statutory plan to regulate and control agricultural production, a matter beyond the powers delegated to the federal government. The tax, the appropriation of the funds raised, and the direction for their disbursement are but parts of the plan. They are but means to an unconstitutional end.

From the accepted doctrine that the United States is a government of delegated powers, it follows that those not expressly granted, or reasonably to be implied from such as are conferred, are reserved to the states or to the people. To forestall any suggestion to the contrary, the Tenth Amendment was adopted. The same proposition, otherwise stated, is that powers not granted are prohibited. None to regulate agricultural production is given, and therefore legislation by Congress for that purpose is forbidden.

The government asserts that [the plan] is constitutionally sound because the end is accomplished by voluntary co-operation. [But the] regulation is not in fact voluntary. The farmer, of course, may refuse to comply, but the price of such refusal is the loss of benefits. *** This is coercion by economic pressure. The asserted power of choice is illusory. But if the plan were one for purely voluntary co-operation it would stand no better so far as federal power is concerned. At best, it is a scheme for purchasing with federal funds submission to federal regulation of a subject reserved to the states. *** [C]ontracts for the reduction of acreage and the control of production are outside the range of [federal] power. *** The Congress cannot invade state jurisdiction to compel individual action; no more can it purchase such action.

Mr. Justice STONE, [joined by Mr. Justice BRANDEIS and Mr. Justice CARDOZO,] dissenting.

The suggestion of coercion finds no support in the record or in any data showing the actual operation of the act. Threat of loss, not hope of gain, is the essence of economic coercion.

It is upon the contention that state power is infringed by purchased regulation of agricultural production that chief reliance is placed. *** The Constitution requires that public funds shall be spent for a defined purpose, the promotion of the general welfare. *** Expenditures would fail of their purpose and thus lose their constitutional sanction if the terms of payment were not such that by their influence on the action of the recipients the permitted end would be attained. *** Congress may not command that the science of agriculture be taught in state universities. But if it would aid the teaching of that science by grants to state institutions, it is appropriate, if not necessary, that the grant be on the condition that it be used for the intended purpose. *** It is a contradiction in terms to say that there is power to spend for the national welfare, while rejecting any power to impose conditions reasonably adapted to the attainment of the end which alone would justify the expenditure.

The limitation now sanctioned must lead to absurd consequences. The government may give seeds to farmers, but may not condition the gift upon their being planted in places where they are most needed or even planted at all. The government may give money to the unemployed, but may not ask that those who get it shall give labor in return, or even use it to support their families. *** If the expenditure is for a national public purpose, that purpose will not be thwarted because payment is on condition which will advance that purpose.

The power to tax and spend is not without constitutional restraints. One restriction is that the purpose must be truly national. Another is that it may not be used to coerce action left to state control. Another is the conscience and patriotism of Congress and the Executive. [But] interpretation of our great charter of government which proceeds on any assumption that the responsibility for the preservation of our institutions is the exclusive concern of any one of the three branches of government *** is far more likely, in the long run, "to obliterate the constituent members" of "an indestructible union of indestructible states" than the frank recognition that language, even of a constitution, may mean what it says: that the power to tax and spend includes the power to relieve a nationwide economic maladjustment by conditional gifts of money.

––––––––––––

Points for Discussion

a. Competing Views of the General Welfare Clause

As a textual matter, there are three potential interpretations of the General Welfare Clause. First, one could read the clause as a grant of authority that is separate from the preceding provision that confers the power to tax—in effect, to read, "Congress shall have Power To … provide for the common Defence and general Welfare of the United States." Under this reading, Congress would have the power to pass virtually any regulation, subject only to the requirement that the regulation be in the general welfare. If this reading were correct, then limits on Congress's other powers would be irrelevant.

Second, one could read the General Welfare Clause simply as a shorthand reference to the enumerated powers that follow in Article I, § 8. Under this view, which James Madison advanced, Congress would have power to tax or spend only when it is acting legitimately pursuant to one of its other enumerated powers. If this reading were correct, then Congress would have no authority to spend beyond that which it is already authorized to do pursuant to its other enumerated powers in conjunction with the Necessary and Proper Clause. On this view, the General Welfare Clause would simply confirm that one of the permissible means of effectuating the enumerated powers is the expenditure of money.

Third, one could read the General Welfare Clause to permit Congress to spend for the general welfare even if Congress could not achieve its desired objective pursuant to its other enumerated powers. This view, which Alexander Hamilton advanced, mediates between the broad implications of the first view and the constraining implications of the Madisonian view. On this view, Congress's power to spend would be broader than its power to regulate pursuant to its other enumerated powers.

The Court in *Butler* stated that the Hamiltonian view was the correct interpretation of the General Welfare Clause. Did the Court properly apply that view to the federal spending program challenged in the case?

b. The New Deal and Federal Spending Programs

Butler was one of several cases—many of which we have already seen—in which the Court invalidated federal enactments that were part of the New Deal. But just as the Court began in 1937 to recognize broader federal authority under the Commerce Clause and broader governmental power to regulate social and economic matters—a topic we will consider in Chapter 9—the Court began that year to uphold federal spending programs, as well. In *Charles C. Steward Machine Co. v. Davis*, 301 U.S. 548 (1937), the Court upheld, in a 5-4 decision, the unemployment compensation provisions of the Social Security Act, which had been a centerpiece of the New Deal legislative program. The challenged provision imposed a payroll tax on employers but provided a rebate to employers who contributed to a state unemployment compensation fund. The Court acknowledged that "every rebate from a tax when conditioned upon conduct is in some measure a temptation. But to hold that motive or temptation is equivalent to coercion is to plunge the law in endless difficulties." And in *Helvering v. Davis*, 301 U.S. 619 (1937), the Court upheld, in a 7-2 decision, the old-age benefits provisions of the Social Security Act, which imposed a tax on employees to fund payments to older citizens. The Court noted that the discretion to draw the line between matters of local and general welfare "belongs to Congress, unless the choice is clearly wrong, a display of arbitrary power."

The Court's view of Congress's spending power in the modern era has been similarly broad, as the following case demonstrates.

South Dakota v. Dole

483 U.S. 203 (1987)

Chief Justice REHNQUIST delivered the opinion of the Court.

Petitioner South Dakota permits persons 19 years of age or older to purchase beer containing up to 3.2% alcohol. In 1984 Congress enacted 23 U.S.C. § 158, which directs the Secretary of Transportation to withhold a percentage of federal highway funds otherwise allocable from States "in which the purchase or public possession [of] any alcoholic beverage by a person who is less than twenty-one years of age is lawful." The State sued *** seeking a declaratory judgment that § 158 violates the constitutional limitations on congressional exercise of the spending power and violates the Twenty-first Amendment to the United States Constitution.

> **FYI**
>
> The Twenty-First Amendment, which repealed Prohibition, provides in relevant part: "The transportation or importation into any State, Territory, or possession of the United States for delivery or use therein of intoxicating liquors, in violation of the laws thereof, is hereby prohibited." One reading of this language—though certainly not the only plausible one—is that the States' control over the lawfulness of the sale or possession of alcohol is plenary, notwithstanding Congress's affirmative powers. But see *Granholm v. Heald*, 544 U.S. 460 (2005).

In this Court, the parties direct most of their efforts to defining the proper scope of the Twenty-first Amendment[,] the bounds of which have escaped precise definition. Despite the extended treatment of the question by the parties, however, we need not decide in this case whether that Amendment would prohibit an attempt by Congress to legislate directly a national minimum drinking age. Here, Congress has acted indirectly under its spending power to encourage uniformity in the States' drinking ages. [W]e find this legislative effort within constitutional bounds even if Congress may not regulate drinking ages directly.

Incident to [the spending] power, Congress may attach conditions on the receipt of federal funds ***. The breadth of this power was made clear in *Butler*, where the Court [determined that] objectives not thought to be within Article I's "enumerated legislative fields" may nevertheless be attained through the use of the spending power and the conditional grant of federal funds.

The spending power is of course not unlimited, but is instead subject to several general restrictions articulated in our cases. The first of these limitations is derived from the language of the Constitution itself: the exercise of the spending power must be in pursuit of "the general welfare." In considering whether a particular expenditure is intended to serve general public purposes, courts should defer substantially to the judgment of Congress. Second, we have required that if Congress desires to condition the States' receipt of federal funds, it "must do so unambiguously, enabling the States to exercise their choice knowingly, cognizant of the consequences of their participation." Third, our cases have suggested (without significant elaboration) that conditions on federal grants might be illegitimate if they are unrelated "to the federal interest in particular national projects or programs." Finally, we have noted that other constitutional provisions may provide an independent bar to the conditional grant of federal funds.

We can readily conclude that the provision is designed to serve the general welfare ***. Congress found that the differing drinking ages in the States created particular incentives for young persons to combine their desire to drink with their ability to drive, and that this interstate problem required a national solution. *** The conditions upon which States receive the funds, moreover, could not be more clearly stated by Congress. And *** the condition imposed by Congress is directly related to one of the main purposes for which highway funds are expended—safe interstate travel. *** [T]he lack of uniformity in the States' drinking ages create[s] "an incentive to drink and drive" because "young persons commute to border States where the drinking age is lower." By enacting § 158, Congress conditioned the receipt of federal funds in a way reasonably calculated to address this particular impediment to a purpose for which the funds are expended.

> **Food for Thought**
>
> What is the point of the "germaneness" requirement? If the Hamiltonian view of the spending power is correct, then the consequence is that Congress may achieve pursuant to the spending power objectives that it could not achieve directly pursuant to the commerce power. If this is true, then why does it matter whether the condition imposed on the receipt of funds is related to the purpose for which the funds are granted?

The remaining question about the validity of § 158—and the basic point of disagreement between the parties—is whether the Twenty-first Amendment constitutes an "independent constitutional bar" to the conditional grant of federal funds. *** [T]he "independent constitutional bar" limitation on the spending power is not, as petitioner suggests, a prohibition on the indirect achievement of objectives which Congress is not empowered to achieve directly. Instead, we think that the language in our earlier opinions stands for the unexceptionable proposition that the power may not be used to induce the States to engage in activities that would themselves be unconstitutional. Thus, for example, a grant of federal funds conditioned on invidiously discriminatory state action or the infliction of cruel and unusual punishment would be an illegitimate exercise of the Congress' broad spending power. But no such claim can be or is made here. Were South Dakota to succumb to the blandishments offered by Congress and raise its drinking age to 21, the State's action in so doing would not violate the constitutional rights of anyone.

Our decisions have recognized that in some circumstances the financial inducement offered by Congress might be so coercive as to pass the point at which "pressure turns into compulsion." *Steward Machine*. Here, however, Congress has directed only that a State desiring to establish a minimum drinking age lower than 21 lose a relatively small percentage of certain federal highway funds. Petitioner contends that the coercive nature of this program is evident from the degree of success it has achieved. We cannot conclude, however, that a conditional grant of federal money of this sort is unconstitutional simply by reason of its success in achieving the congressional objective. When we consider *** that all South Dakota would lose if she adheres to her chosen course as to a suitable minimum drinking age is 5% of the funds otherwise obtainable under specified highway grant programs, the argument as to coercion is shown to be more rhetoric than fact.

Here Congress has offered relatively mild encouragement to the States to enact higher minimum drinking ages than they would otherwise choose. But the enactment of such laws remains the prerogative of the States not merely in theory but in fact. Even if Congress might lack the power to impose a national minimum drinking age directly, we conclude that encouragement to state action found in § 158 is a valid use of the spending power.

Justice BRENNAN, dissenting.

[R]egulation of the minimum age of purchasers of liquor falls squarely within the ambit of those powers reserved to the States by the Twenty-first Amendment. Since States possess this constitutional power, Congress cannot condition a federal grant in a manner that abridges this right. The Amendment, itself, strikes the proper balance between federal and state authority.

Justice O'CONNOR, dissenting.

My disagreement with the Court *** on the spending power issue *** is a disagreement about the application of a principle rather than a disagreement on the principle itself. *** In my view, establishment of a minimum drinking age of 21 is not sufficiently related to interstate highway construction to justify so conditioning funds appropriated for that purpose.

[I]f the purpose of § 158 is to deter drunken driving, it is far too over and under-inclusive. It is over-inclusive because it stops teenagers from drinking even when they are not about to drive on interstate highways. It is under-inclusive because teenagers pose only a small part of the drunken driving problem in this Nation. When Congress appropriates money to build a highway, it is entitled to insist that the highway be a safe one. But it is not entitled to insist as a condition of the use of highway funds that the State impose or change regulations in other areas of the State's social and economic life because of an attenuated or tangential relationship to highway use or safety. Indeed, if the rule were otherwise, the Congress could effectively regulate almost any area of a State's social, political, or economic life on the theory that use of the interstate transportation system is somehow enhanced.

"Congress has no power under the Spending Clause to impose requirements on a grant that go beyond specifying how the money should be spent. A requirement that is not such a specification is not a condition, but a regulation, which is valid only if it falls within one of Congress' delegated regulatory powers." [Br. for the National Conf. of State Legislatures as *Amicus Curiae*.] This approach harks back to *Butler*. *** The *Butler* Court saw the Agricultural Adjustment Act for what it was— an exercise of regulatory, not spending, power. The error in *Butler* was not the Court's conclusion that the Act was essentially regulatory, but rather its crabbed view of the extent of Congress' regulatory power under the Commerce Clause. The Agricultural Adjustment Act was regulatory but it was regulation that today would likely be considered within Congress' commerce power. *Wickard*.

> **Take Note**
>
> Justice O'Connor reasons that Congress should be permitted to impose conditions on a state's receipt of funds only if the condition dictates how the granted funds may be spent. In light of this position, would you say that her disagreement with the Court is over the "application of a principle rather than a disagreement on the principle itself"?

If the spending power is to be limited only by Congress' notion of the general welfare, the reality, given the vast financial resources of the Federal Government, is that the Spending Clause gives "power to the Congress to tear down the barriers, to invade the states' jurisdiction, and to become a parliament of the whole people, subject to no restrictions save such as are self-imposed." *Butler*.

————————————

Points for Discussion

a. Conditioned Spending

The statute in *Dole*, unlike the statute in *Butler*, involved a grant of funds to the states, rather than to private persons. When Congress grants funds to the states with conditions attached, Congress seeks to encourage—or perhaps force—the states to regulate pursuant to federal directives. Should such grants to the states be viewed as presumptively more constitutionally suspect than conditional grants to private persons?

b. The Limits on the Spending Power

The Court in *Dole* articulated five requirements for the exercise of the spending power: (1) Congress must act in pursuit of the general welfare; (2) any conditions on the states' receipt of federal funds must be imposed unambiguously; (3) the conditions imposed on the receipt of funds must be germane to the purposes for which Congress approved the grant; (4) the condition cannot require action that would violate some other constitutional provision; and (5) Congress cannot offer the states financial inducements that amount to coercion. Given the Court's application of these requirements, are there meaningful limits on Congress's power to achieve its regulatory objectives through the exercise of the spending power? Can you think of examples of laws that would violate each of these requirements? Why has the Court permitted Congress such broad leeway to act pursuant to the spending power while imposing more limits on Congress's power to act pursuant to the Commerce Clause?

————————————

E. The War and Treaty Powers

Article I, § 8 gives Congress the power to declare war, to raise and support armies, to provide and maintain a navy, and to make rules for the regulation of those forces. In addition, Article II, § 2 makes the President the Commander in Chief of the Armed Forces and gives the President the authority to make treaties, subject to the consent of two-thirds of the Senate. Do these powers, particularly when viewed in conjunction with the Necessary and Proper Clause, authorize Congress to legislate on any matter arguably related to war and foreign relations? Consider the two cases that follow.

Woods v. Cloyd W. Miller Co.

333 U.S. 138 (1948)

Mr. Justice DOUGLAS delivered the opinion of the Court.

The case is here on a direct appeal [from] a judgment of the District Court holding unconstitutional Title II of the Housing and Rent Act of 1947. [The Act made it unlawful "to offer, solicit, demand, accept, or receive any rent for the use or occupancy of any controlled housing accommodations in excess of the maximum rent" prescribed by an agency pursuant to authority under the Act and the Emergency Price Control Act of 1942.] The Act became effective on July 1, 1947, and the following day the appellee demanded of its tenants increases of 40% and 60% for rental accommodations in the Cleveland Defense-Rental Area, and admitted violation of the Act and regulations adopted pursuant thereto. Appellant thereupon instituted this proceeding to enjoin the violations.

The District Court was of the view that the authority of Congress to regulate rents by virtue of the war power ended with the Presidential Proclamation terminating hostilities on December 31, 1946, since that proclamation inaugurated "peace-in-fact" though it did not mark termination of the war. It also concluded that even if the war power continues, Congress did not act under it because it did not say so, and only if Congress says so, or enacts provisions so implying, can it be held that Congress intended to exercise such power.

We conclude, in the first place, that the war power sustains this legislation. The Court said in *Hamilton v. Kentucky Distilleries and Warehouse Co.*, 251 U.S. 146, 161 (1919), that the war power includes the power "to remedy the evils which have arisen from its rise and progress" and continues for the duration of that emergency.

> **FYI**
>
> Germany and Japan surrendered in 1945, and President Truman in December 1946 proclaimed the "end of hostilities." On December 31, 1946, however, President Truman declared that "a state of war still exists." 12 Fed.Reg. 1. In addition, on July 25, 1947, upon approving a joint resolution terminating various war statutes, President Truman issued a statement declaring that the "emergencies declared by the President on September 8, 1939, and May 27, 1941, and the state of war continue to exist."

Whatever may be the consequences when war is officially terminated, the war power does not necessarily end with the cessation of hostilities. *** In *Hamilton* and *Ruppert v. Caffey*, 251 U.S. 264 (1920), prohibition laws which were enacted after the Armistice in World War I were sustained as exercises of the war power because they conserved manpower and increased efficiency of production in the critical days during the period of demobilization, and helped to husband the supply of grains and cereals depleted by the war effort. Those cases followed the reasoning of *Stewart v. Kahn*, 11 Wall. 493 (1870), which held that Congress had the power to toll the statute of limitations of the States during the period when the process of their courts was not available to litigants due to the conditions obtaining in the Civil War.

The constitutional validity of the present legislation follows a fortiori from those cases. The legislative history of the present Act makes abundantly clear that there has not yet been eliminated the deficit in housing which in considerable measure was caused by the heavy demobilization of veterans and by the cessation or reduction in residential construction during the period of hostilities due to the allocation of building materials to military projects. Since the war effort contributed heavily to that deficit, Congress has the power even after the cessation of hostilities to act to control the forces that a short supply of the needed article created. If that were not true, the Necessary and Proper Clause would be drastically limited in its application to the several war powers. [Such a limit] would render Congress powerless to remedy conditions the creation of which necessarily followed from the mobilization of men and materials for successful prosecution of the war. So to read the Constitution would be to make it self-defeating.

We recognize the force of the argument that the effects of war under modern conditions may be felt in the economy for years and years, and that if the war power can be used in days of peace to treat all the wounds which war inflicts on our society, it may not only swallow up all other powers of Congress but largely obliterate the Ninth and the Tenth Amendments as well. There are no such implications in today's decision. We deal here with the consequences of a housing deficit greatly intensified during the period of hostilities by the war effort. Any power, of course, can be abused. But we cannot assume that Congress is not alert to its constitutional responsibilities.

The question of the constitutionality of action taken by Congress does not depend on recitals of the power which it undertakes to exercise. Here it is plain from the legislative history that Congress was invoking its war power to cope with a current condition of which the war was a direct and immediate cause. Its judgment on that score is entitled to the respect granted like legislation enacted pursuant to the police power.

Reversed.

Mr. Justice JACKSON, concurring.

I agree with the result in this case, but the arguments that have been addressed to us lead me to utter more explicit misgivings about war powers than the Court has done. The Government asserts no constitutional basis for this legislation other than this vague, undefined and undefinable "war power."

No one will question that this power is the most dangerous one to free government in the whole catalogue of powers. It usually is invoked in haste and excitement when calm legislative consideration of constitutional limitation is difficult. It is executed in a time of patriotic fervor that makes moderation unpopular. And, worst of all, it is interpreted by the Judges under the influence of the same passions and pressures. Always, as in this case, the Government urges hasty decision to forestall some emergency or serve some purpose and pleads that paralysis will result if its claims to power are denied or their confirmation delayed. Particularly when the war power is invoked to do things to the liberties of people, or to their property or economy that only indirectly affect conduct of the war and do not relate to the management of the war itself, the constitutional basis should be scrutinized with care.

I think we can hardly deny that the war power is as valid a ground for federal rent control now as it has been at any time. We still are technically in a state of war. I would not be willing to hold that war powers may be indefinitely prolonged merely by keeping legally alive a state of war that had in fact ended. I cannot accept the argument that war powers last as long as the effects and consequences of war for if so they are permanent—as permanent as the war debts. But I find no reason to conclude that we could find fairly that the present state of war is merely technical. We have armies abroad exercising our war power and have made no peace terms with our allies not to mention our principal enemies. I think the conclusion that the war power has been applicable during the lifetime of this legislation is unavoidable.

Missouri v. Holland

252 U.S. 416 (1920)

Mr. Justice HOLMES delivered the opinion of the Court.

This is a bill in equity brought by the State of Missouri to prevent a game warden of the United States from attempting to enforce the Migratory Bird Treaty Act of July 3, 1918 ***. The ground of the bill is that the statute is an unconstitutional interference with the rights reserved to the States by the Tenth Amendment ***.

On December 8, 1916, a treaty between the United States and Great Britain was proclaimed by the President. It recited that many species of birds in their annual migrations traversed many parts of the United States and of Canada, that they were of great value as a source of food and in destroying insects injurious to vegetation, but were in danger of extermination through lack of adequate protection. It therefore provided for specified closed seasons and protection in other forms, and agreed that the two powers would take or propose to their lawmaking bodies the necessary measures for carrying the treaty out. The [1918 Act], entitled an act to give effect to the convention, prohibited the killing, capturing or selling any of the migratory birds included in the terms of the treaty except as permitted by regulations compatible with those terms, to be made by the Secretary of Agriculture.

To answer this question it is not enough to refer to the Tenth Amendment, reserving the powers not delegated to the United States, because by Article II, Section 2, the power to make treaties is delegated expressly, and by Article VI treaties made under the authority of the United States, along with the Constitution and laws of the United States made in pursuance thereof, are declared the supreme law of the land. If the treaty is valid there can be no dispute about the validity of the statute under Article 1, Section 8, as a necessary and proper means to execute the powers of the Government. The language of the Constitution as to the supremacy of treaties being general, the question before us is narrowed to an inquiry into the ground upon which the present supposed exception is placed.

It is said that a treaty cannot be valid if it infringes the Constitution, that there are limits, therefore, to the treaty-making power, and that one such limit is that what an act of Congress could not do unaided, in derogation of the powers reserved to the States, a treaty cannot do. An earlier act of Congress that attempted by itself and not in pursuance of a treaty to regulate the killing of migratory birds within the States had been held bad in the District Court. *United States v. Shauver*, 214 Fed. 154; *United States v. McCullagh*, 221 Fed. 288.

Whether the two cases cited were decided rightly or not they cannot be accepted as a test of the treaty power. Acts of Congress are the supreme law of the land only when made in pursuance of the Constitution, while treaties are declared to be so when made under the authority of the United States. It is open to question whether the authority of the United States means more than the formal acts prescribed to make the convention.

We do not mean to imply that there are no qualifications to the treaty-making power; but they must be ascertained in a different way. It is obvious that there may be matters of the sharpest exigency for the national well being that an act of Congress could not deal with but that a treaty followed by such an act could, and it is not lightly to be assumed that, in matters requiring national action, "a power which must belong to and somewhere reside in every civilized government" is not to be found. *Andrews v. Andrews,* 188 U.S. 14, 33 (1903). *** [W]e may add that when we are dealing with words that also are a constituent act, like the Constitution of the United States, we must realize that they have called into life a being the development of which could not have been foreseen completely by the most gifted of its begetters. It was enough for them to realize or to hope that they had created an organism; it has taken a century and has cost their successors much sweat and blood to prove that they created a nation. The case before us must be considered in the light of our whole experience and not merely in that of what was said a hundred years ago. The treaty in question does not contravene any prohibitory words to be found in the Constitution. The only question is

> ### Food for Thought
>
> What are the "formal acts" that the Constitution prescribes for the creation of a binding treaty? Is it possible that there are no constraints on the treaty power other than compliance with those requirements? Would a treaty be valid if it were inconsistent with the First Amendment or some other protection for individual rights? If not, should federalism-based limits on the government's power be treated any differently?

whether it is forbidden by some invisible radiation from the general terms of the Tenth Amendment. We must consider what this country has become in deciding what that amendment has reserved.

The State as we have intimated founds its claim of exclusive authority upon an assertion of title to migratory birds, an assertion that is embodied in statute. No doubt it is true that as between a State and its inhabitants the State may regulate the killing and sale of such birds, but it does not follow that its authority is exclusive of paramount powers. *** Here a national interest of very nearly the first magnitude is involved. It can be protected only by national action in concert with that of another power. The subject matter is only transitorily within the State and has no permanent habitat therein. But for the treaty and the statute there soon might be no birds for any powers to deal with. We see nothing in the Constitution that compels the Government to sit by while a food supply is cut off and the protectors of our forests and our crops are destroyed. It is not sufficient to rely upon the States. The reliance is vain, and were it otherwise, the question is whether the United States is forbidden to act. We are of opinion that the treaty and statute must be upheld.

Mr. Justice VAN DEVANTER and Mr. Justice PITNEY dissent.

Points for Discussion

a. The War Power

Article I enumerates several powers related to matters of war. Do those grants of specific authority imply a more general "war power"? What limits might apply to the exercise of such a power? If Congress enjoys such a power after it formally declares war, at what point after the end of a war does the power cease to authorize broad action? Does the power authorize the same sorts of actions when the United States becomes involved in a military conflict without a formal declaration of war, as it has several times in the last half century?

b. The Treaty Power

Article VI provides that treaties made under the authority of the United States, along with the Constitution and statutes "made in pursuance thereof," are the "supreme Law of the Land." Can treaties validly regulate matters that Congress could not regulate pursuant to its other affirmative sources of authority, such as the Commerce Clause? Congress often passes legislation to implement treaties, acting pursuant to the Treaty Power and the Necessary and Proper Clause. Doesn't the Court's decision in *Missouri v. Holland* effectively permit Congress to use this approach to enact laws that would otherwise be inconsistent with federalism norms? Is there a realistic threat that Congress will do so?

F. State Immunity from Federal Regulation

The cases that we have considered thus far on the scope of Congress's power have mostly addressed Congress's power to regulate private—that is, non-state—conduct. Indeed, the central question for the exercise of Congress's affirmative powers under Article I has been whether Congress has authority to regulate localized conduct on the theory that the conduct has a sufficient relationship to matters expressly within Congress's competence. Should the question of the scope of Congress's power be answered differently when Congress seeks to regulate state, rather than private, action? (The decision in <u>South Dakota v. Dole</u> arguably was an introduction to this question.) We will put to one side for now Congress's power to force state action when acting pursuant to its authority to enforce the Reconstruction Amendments (i.e., the 13th-15th Amendments), which contain explicit limits on the power of the states.

We are concerned here with instances in which Congress seeks to exercise its Article I powers to regulate the states, either in the same fashion that it regulates private actors or in a fashion unique to state actors. Are the states immune from all forms of federal regulation? Are they immune from any forms of federal regulation? In the last few decades, the Court has struggled with this question, as the cases that follow will demonstrate.

> **Make the Connection**
>
> We will consider Congress's power to enforce the Reconstruction Amendments in Chapter 13.

National League of Cities v. Usery

426 U.S. 833 (1976)

Mr. Justice REHNQUIST delivered the opinion of the Court.

> **Make the Connection**
>
> Recall that the Court upheld the validity of the wage and hour provisions of the FLSA in <u>Darby</u>.

The original Fair Labor Standards Act[, which required employers covered by the Act to pay their employees a minimum hourly wage and time and a half for overtime,] specifically excluded the States and their political subdivisions from its coverage. In 1974, however, Congress *** extended the minimum wage and maximum hour provisions to almost all public employees employed by the States and by their various political subdivisions.

It is one thing to recognize the authority of Congress to enact laws regulating individual businesses necessarily subject to the dual sovereignty of the government of the Nation and of the State in which they reside. It is quite another to uphold a similar exercise of congressional authority directed, not to private citizens, but to the States as States. [T]here are attributes of sovereignty attaching to every state government which may not be impaired by Congress ***.

Quite apart from the substantial costs imposed [by the minimum-wage and overtime provisions] upon the States and their political subdivisions, the Act displaces state policies regarding the manner in which they will structure delivery of those governmental services which their citizens require. The Act *** directly supplants the considered policy choices of the States' elected officials and administrators as to how they wish to structure pay scales in state employment. The State might wish to employ persons with little or no training, or those who wish to work on a casual basis, or those who for some other reason do not possess minimum employment requirements, and pay them less than the federally prescribed minimum wage. *** But the Act would forbid such choices by the States. The only "discretion" left to them under the Act is either to attempt to increase their revenue to meet the additional financial burden imposed upon them by paying congressionally prescribed wages to their existing complement of employees, or to reduce that complement to a number which can be paid the federal minimum wage without increasing revenue.

> **Food for Thought**
>
> Doesn't every employer subject to the FLSA face the same dilemma that the Court says the states will face? Of course, private employers cannot raise taxes to pay for higher wages, but they can raise the price of the goods or services that they provide. Is there something about the public context that makes congressional imposition of such a choice on the states impermissible?

[The challenged] provisions will impermissibly interfere with the integral governmental functions of [States and their political subdivisions]. [T]heir application will *** significantly alter or displace the States' abilities to structure employer-employee relationships in such areas as fire prevention, police protection, sanitation, public health, and parks and recreation. These activities are typical of those performed by state and local governments in discharging their dual functions of administering the public law and furnishing public services. Indeed, it is functions such as these which governments are created to provide, services such as these which the States have traditionally afforded their citizens. If Congress may withdraw from the States the authority to make those fundamental employment decisions upon which their systems for performance of these functions must rest, we think there would be little left of the States' "separate and independent existence." *** We hold that insofar as the challenged amendments operate to directly displace the States' freedom to structure integral operations in areas of traditional governmental functions, they are not within the authority granted Congress by Art. I, § 8, cl. 3.

Mr. Justice BLACKMUN, concurring.

Although I am not untroubled by certain possible implications of the Court's opinion[,] I do not read the opinion so despairingly as does my Brother BRENNAN. *** I may misinterpret the Court's opinion, but it seems to me that it adopts a balancing approach, and does not outlaw federal power in areas such as environmental protection, where the federal interest is demonstrably greater and where state facility compliance with imposed federal standards would be essential. With this understanding on my part of the Court's opinion, I join it.

Mr. Justice BRENNAN, with whom Mr. Justice WHITE and Mr. Justice MARSHALL join, dissenting.

Take Note

Justice Blackmun provided the fifth vote for the Court's decision to invalidate the FLSA as it applied to these public employers, but his view of Congress's power to regulate the States appears different from the majority's. Under such circumstances, what is the precedential force of Chief Rehnquist's opinion? Of Justice Blackmun's?

The Court *** repudiate[s] principles governing judicial interpretation of our Constitution settled since the time of Mr. Chief Justice John Marshall, discarding his postulate that the Constitution contemplates that restraints upon exercise by Congress of its plenary commerce power lie in the political process and not in the judicial process.

My Brethren *** have today manufactured an abstraction without substance, founded neither in the words of the Constitution nor on precedent. An abstraction having such profoundly pernicious consequences is not made less so by characterizing the 1974 amendments as legislation directed against the "States Qua States." *** [M]y Brethren are also repudiating the long line of our precedents holding that a judicial finding that Congress has not unreasonably regulated a subject matter of "commerce" brings to an end the judicial role. [*McCulloch*.]

Today's repudiation of this unbroken line of precedents *** can only be regarded as a transparent cover for invalidating a congressional judgment with which they disagree. The only analysis even remotely resembling that adopted today is found in a line of opinions dealing with the Commerce Clause and the Tenth Amendment that ultimately provoked a constitutional crisis for the Court in the 1930's. E.g., *Carter Coal*; *Butler*; *Hammer*.

Mr. Justice STEVENS, dissenting.

[T]he Federal Government's power over the labor market is adequate to embrace these employees. Since I am unable to identify a limitation on that federal power that would not also invalidate federal regulation of state activities that I consider unquestionably permissible, I am persuaded that this statute is valid.

───────────

Garcia v. San Antonio Metropolitan Transit Authority

469 U.S. 528 (1985)

Justice BLACKMUN delivered the opinion of the Court.

[As explained in the previous case, *National League of Cities v. Usery* (1976), the Fair Labor Standards Act (FLSA) requires certain employers to pay their employees a minimum hourly rate and also an "overtime" wage for hours worked in excess of 40 hours a week. When the San Antonio Metropolitan Transit Authority refused to pay overtime wages to bus driver Joe G. Garcia and other employees, they sued the Transit Authority to enforce the Act. The Transit Authority argued that it was a state governmental entity engaged in a traditional governmental function (i.e., operating the city's mass transit system) and was thus constitutionally immune from the requirements of the Act.]

In the present cases, a Federal District Court concluded that municipal ownership and operation of a mass-transit system is a traditional governmental function and thus *** is exempt from the obligations imposed by the FLSA. *** [T]the attempt to draw the boundaries of state regulatory immunity in terms of "traditional governmental function" is not only unworkable but is also inconsistent with established principles of federalism and, indeed, with those very federalism principles on which *National League of Cities* purported to rest. That case, accordingly, is overruled.

Any rule of state immunity that looks to the "traditional," "integral," or "necessary" nature of governmental functions inevitably invites an unelected federal judiciary to make decisions about which state policies it favors and which ones it dislikes. We therefore now reject, as unsound in principle and unworkable in practice, a rule of state immunity from federal regulation that turns on a judicial appraisal of whether a particular governmental function is "integral" or "traditional." Any such rule leads to inconsistent results at the same time that it disserves principles of democratic self-governance, and it breeds inconsistency precisely because it is divorced from those principles. If there are to be limits on the Federal Government's power to interfere with state functions—as undoubtedly there are—we must look elsewhere to find them.

We doubt that courts ultimately can identify principled constitutional limitations on the scope of Congress' Commerce Clause powers over the States merely by relying on *a priori* definitions of state sovereignty. *** Apart from the limitation on federal authority inherent in the delegated nature of Congress' Article I powers, the principal means chosen by the Framers to ensure the role of the States in the federal system lies in the structure of the Federal Government itself. It is no novelty to observe that the composition of the Federal Government was designed in large part to protect the States from overreaching by Congress. The Framers thus gave the States a role in the selection both of the Executive and the Legislative Branches of the Federal Government. The States were vested with indirect influence over the House of Representatives and the Presidency by their control of electoral qualifications and their role in Presidential elections. U.S. Const., Art. I, § 2, and Art. II, § 1. They were given more direct influence in the Senate, where each State received equal representation and each Senator was to be selected by the legislature of his State.

Art. I, § 3. The significance attached to the States' equal representation in the Senate is underscored by the prohibition of any constitutional amendment divesting a State of equal representation without the State's consent. Art. V.

In short, the Framers chose to rely on a federal system in which special restraints on federal power over the States inhered principally in the workings of the National Government itself, rather than in discrete limitations on the objects of federal authority. State sovereign interests, then, are more properly protected by procedural safeguards inherent in the structure of the federal system than by judicially created limitations on federal power. *** We realize that changes in the structure of the Federal Government have taken place since 1789, not the least of which has been the substitution of popular election of Senators by the adoption of the Seventeenth Amendment in 1913, and that these changes may work to alter the influence of the States in the federal political process. Nonetheless, against this background, we are convinced that the fundamental limitation that the constitutional scheme imposes on the Commerce Clause to protect the "States as States" is one of process rather than one of result. Any substantive restraint on the exercise of Commerce Clause powers must find its justification in the procedural nature of this basic limitation, and it must be tailored to compensate for possible failings in the national political process rather than to dictate a "sacred province of state autonomy."

> **Food for Thought**
>
> Does the conclusion that the courts should decline to enforce state-autonomy-based limitations against congressional exercises of authority necessarily follow from the premise that the Framers sought to create a governmental structure to minimize the risk of federal overreaching? Isn't it possible that there are both structural protections against federal overreaching *and* judicially enforceable ones? See, e.g., Bradford R. Clark, *Putting the Safeguards Back Into the Political Safeguards of Federalism*, 80 Tex. L. Rev. 327 (2001).

Congress' action in affording SAMTA employees the protections of the wage and hour provisions of the FLSA contravened no affirmative limit on Congress' power under the Commerce Clause. *** [T]he principal and basic limit on the federal commerce power is that inherent in all congressional action—the built-in restraints that our system provides through state participation in federal governmental action.

We do not lightly overrule recent precedent. We have not hesitated, however, when it has become apparent that a prior decision has departed from a proper understanding of congressional power under the Commerce Clause. See *Darby*. Due respect for the reach of congressional power within the federal system mandates that we do so now. *National League of Cities v. Usery* is overruled.

Justice POWELL, with whom THE CHIEF JUSTICE, Justice REHNQUIST, and Justice O'CONNOR join, dissenting.

A unique feature of the United States is the *federal* system of government guaranteed by the Constitution and implicit in the very name of our country. Despite some genuflecting in the Court's opinion to the concept of federalism, today's decision effectively reduces the Tenth Amendment to meaningless rhetoric when Congress acts pursuant to the Commerce Clause.

[According to the Court,] the extent to which the States may exercise their authority, when Congress purports to act under the Commerce Clause, henceforth is to be determined from time to time by political decisions made by members of the Federal Government, decisions the Court says will not be subject to judicial review. I note that it does not seem to have occurred to the Court that *it*—an unelected majority of five Justices—today rejects almost 200 years of the understanding of the constitutional status of federalism.

Members of Congress are elected from the various States, but once in office they are Members of the Federal Government. Although the States participate in the Electoral College, this is hardly a reason to view the President as a representative of the States' interest against federal encroachment.[9] *** The fact that Congress generally does not transgress constitutional limits on its power to reach state activities does not make judicial review any less necessary to rectify the cases in which it does do so. The States' role in our system of government is a matter of constitutional law, not of legislative grace.

[The Court's holding] is inconsistent with the fundamental principles of our constitutional system. At least since *Marbury*, it has been the settled province of the federal judiciary "to say what the law is" with respect to the constitutionality of Acts of Congress. *** In our federal system, the States have a major role that cannot be pre-empted by the National Government. [T]he States' ratification of the Constitution was predicated on this understanding of federalism. Indeed, the Tenth Amendment was adopted specifically to ensure that the important role promised the States by the proponents of the Constitution was realized. *** [B]y usurping functions traditionally performed by the States, federal overreaching under the Commerce Clause undermines the constitutionally mandated balance of power between the States and the Federal Government, a balance designed to protect our fundamental liberties.

> **Take Note**
>
> Justice Powell appears to suggest that the Tenth Amendment sometimes deprives Congress of the power to regulate, even though Congress might otherwise have affirmative power under the Commerce Clause to regulate the matters in question. Is this view of the Tenth Amendment consistent with the view of the Tenth Amendment that the Court advanced in *Darby*?

---

[9] At one time in our history, the view that the structure of the Federal Government sufficed to protect the States might have had a somewhat more practical, although not a more logical, basis. Professor Wechsler, whose seminal article in 1954 proposed the view adopted by the Court today, predicated his argument on assumptions that simply do not accord with current reality. *** The adoption of the Seventeenth Amendment (providing for direct election of Senators), the weakening of political parties on the local level, and the rise of national media, among other things, have made Congress increasingly less representative of state and local interests, and more likely to be responsive to the demands of various national constituencies. ***

Justice REHNQUIST, dissenting.

I join both Justice POWELL's and Justice O'CONNOR's thoughtful dissents. [U]nder any one of [their] approaches the judgment in these cases should be affirmed, and I do not think it incumbent on those of us in dissent to spell out further the fine points of a principle that will, I am confident, in time again command the support of a majority of this Court.

Justice O'CONNOR, with whom Justice POWELL and Justice REHNQUIST join, dissenting.

Incidental to [the] expansion of the commerce power, Congress has been given an ability it lacked prior to the emergence of an integrated national economy. Because virtually every *state* activity, like virtually every activity of a private individual, arguably "affects" interstate commerce, Congress can now supplant the States from the significant sphere of activities envisioned for them by the Framers.

The last two decades have seen an unprecedented growth of federal regulatory activity. *** The political process has not protected against these encroachments on state activities, even though they directly impinge on a State's ability to make and enforce its laws. With the abandonment of *National League of Cities,* all that stands between the remaining essentials of state sovereignty and Congress is the latter's underdeveloped capacity for self-restraint.

The problems of federalism in an integrated national economy are capable of more responsible resolution than holding that the States as States retain no status apart from that which Congress chooses to let them retain. The proper resolution, I suggest, lies in weighing state autonomy as a factor in the balance when interpreting the means by which Congress can exercise its authority on the States as States.

It has been difficult for this Court to craft bright lines defining the scope of the state autonomy protected by *National League of Cities.* Such difficulty is to be expected whenever constitutional concerns as important as federalism and the effectiveness of the commerce power come into conflict. *** I would not shirk the duty ***.

Points for Discussion

a. The Political Safeguards of Federalism

The Court's conclusion in *Garcia* represents an embrace of the "political safeguards of federalism" as the principal—and perhaps the only—limit on Congress's ability to regulate the states. On this theory, the states' essential role in the selection of the President and the composition of Congress provide robust protection for the states' interests from federal interference. But state legislatures no longer select Senators, and although the Electoral College in theory provides an important role for the states in the election of the President, all states now award electoral votes based on the outcome of the popular vote in the state. Does this suggest that the political safeguards cannot be expected to function as well today as the Framers perhaps originally believed? Or can we expect national decisions about whether to regulate state institutions to reflect the proper operation of those safeguards? Should we be concerned that, in effect, citizens from states that supply a majority of both houses of Congress can force regulation of dissenting states, whose citizens oppose the federal choice? Or is that just a natural by-product of majoritarian rule?

b. Means Restrictions on the Exercise of Federal Power

Notice that there was no dispute in *Garcia* that Congress has power pursuant to the Commerce Clause to regulate the wages and hours of employees. See <u>Darby</u>. Should that be the end of the matter? Sometimes it is clear that it cannot be the end of the matter. For example, even though Congress has power to regulate wages, it is clear that it could not enact a statute providing that only registered Democrats are guaranteed a minimum wage; such a statute would violate the First Amendment, even though it would regulate a subject—employee wages—that otherwise is within the commerce power. If the Court recognizes that other provisions of the Constitution limit the manner in which Congress may exercise its power under the Commerce Clause, then why shouldn't it recognize the same for the Tenth Amendment? Are there any important differences for these purposes between the Tenth Amendment and the other rights-granting provisions in the Bill of Rights?

New York v. United States

505 U.S. 144 (1992)

Justice O'CONNOR delivered the opinion of the Court.

In these cases, we address the constitutionality of three provisions of the Low-Level Radioactive Waste Policy Amendments Act of 1985. *** We conclude that while Congress has substantial power under the Constitution to encourage the States to provide for the disposal of the radioactive waste generated within their borders, the Constitution does not confer upon Congress the ability simply to compel the States to do so.

We live in a world full of low level radioactive waste. Radioactive material is present in luminous watch dials, smoke alarms, measurement devices, medical fluids, research materials, and the protective gear and construction materials used by workers at nuclear power plants. *** The waste must be isolated from humans for long periods of time, often for hundreds of years. Millions of cubic feet of low level radioactive waste must be disposed of each year. *** [S]ince 1979 only three disposal sites—those in Nevada, Washington, and South Carolina—have been in operation. Waste generated in the rest of the country must be shipped to one of these three sites for disposal. *** In 1979, both the Washington and

Nevada sites were forced to shut down temporarily, leaving South Carolina to shoulder the responsibility of storing low level radioactive waste produced in every part of the country. The Governor of South Carolina, understandably perturbed, ordered a 50% reduction in the quantity of waste accepted at the Barnwell site. The Governors of Washington and Nevada announced plans to shut their sites permanently.

Faced with the possibility that the Nation would be left with no disposal sites for low level radioactive waste, Congress responded by enacting [the statute at issue here.] The Act provides three types of incentives to encourage the States to comply with their statutory obligation to provide for the disposal of waste generated within their borders. [The "monetary incentives" permitted states with disposal sites to levy a surcharge on the disposal of waste received from other states. The "access incentives" permitted states with disposal sites to increase the cost of access to their sites and then to deny access entirely to waste generated in states that failed to meet a federal deadline for the establishment of disposal sites of their own. And the "take title" provision required states that failed by a particular date to dispose of all waste generated within their borders to take title to the waste and, if the states failed to take possession of the waste, to face liability for all damages incurred by waste generators as a consequence of that failure.] New York *** has identified five potential sites [for disposal facilities, in two counties.] Residents of the two counties oppose the State's choice of location. [The] State of New York and the two counties *** filed this suit against the United States in 1990.

[Federalism] questions can be viewed in either of two ways. In some cases the Court has inquired whether an Act of Congress is authorized by one of the powers delegated to Congress in Article I of the Constitution. In other cases the Court has sought to determine whether an Act of Congress invades the province of state sovereignty reserved by the Tenth Amendment. In a case like [this], involving the division of authority between federal and state governments, the two inquiries are mirror images of each other. If a power is delegated to Congress in the Constitution, the Tenth Amendment expressly disclaims any reservation of that power to the States; if a power is an attribute of state sovereignty reserved by the Tenth Amendment, it is necessarily a power the Constitution has not conferred on Congress.

It is in this sense that the Tenth Amendment "states but a truism that all is retained which has not been surrendered." *Darby*. *** The Tenth Amendment thus directs us to determine, as in this case, whether an incident of state sovereignty is protected by a limitation on an Article I power. *** In the end, just as a cup may be half empty or half full, it makes no difference whether one views the question at issue in these cases as one of ascertaining the limits of the power delegated to the Federal Government under the affirmative provisions of the Constitution or one of discerning the core of sovereignty retained by the States under the Tenth Amendment. Either way, we must determine whether any of the three challenged provisions of the [Act] oversteps the boundary between federal and state authority.

Petitioners do not contend that Congress lacks the power to regulate the disposal of low level radioactive waste, [and they] do not dispute that under the Supremacy Clause

Congress could, if it wished, pre-empt state radioactive waste regulation. Petitioners contend only that the Tenth Amendment limits the power of Congress to regulate in the way it has chosen.

Most of our recent cases interpreting the Tenth Amendment have concerned the authority of Congress to subject state governments to generally applicable laws. *** [T]his is not a case in which Congress has subjected a State to the same legislation applicable to private parties. This litigation instead concerns the circumstances under which Congress may use the States as implements of regulation; that is, whether Congress may direct or otherwise motivate the States to regulate in a particular field or a particular way.

> **Make the Connection**
>
> The Court did not question Congress's power to regulate the disposal of radioactive waste. Yet such disposal is inherently a local activity, at least with respect to waste generated in-state. On what theory does Congress have power under the Commerce Clause to regulate the disposal of radioactive waste?

As an initial matter, Congress may not simply "commandee[r] the legislative processes of the States by directly compelling them to enact and enforce a federal regulatory program." *Hodel v. Virginia Surface Mining & Reclamation Assn.*, 452 U.S. 264, 288 (1981). *** While Congress has substantial powers to govern the Nation directly, including in areas of intimate concern to the States, the Constitution has never been understood to confer upon Congress the ability to require the States to govern according to Congress' instructions. Indeed, the question whether the Constitution should permit Congress to employ state governments as regulatory agencies was a topic of lively debate among the Framers. Under the Articles of Confederation, Congress lacked the authority in most respects to govern the people directly. *** The inadequacy of this governmental structure was responsible in part for the Constitutional Convention. Alexander Hamilton observed: "The great and radical vice in the construction of the existing Confederation is in the principle of LEGISLATION for STATES or GOVERNMENTS, in their CORPORATE or COLLECTIVE CAPACITIES, and as contra-distinguished from the INDIVIDUALS of whom they consist." The Federalist No. 15. As Hamilton saw it, "we must extend the authority of the Union to the persons of the citizens—the only proper objects of government."

The Convention generated a great number of proposals for the structure of the new Government, but two quickly took center stage. Under the Virginia Plan, as first introduced by Edmund Randolph, Congress would exercise legislative authority directly upon individuals, without employing the States as intermediaries. Under the New Jersey Plan, as first introduced by William Paterson, Congress would continue to require the approval of the States before legislating, as it had under the Articles of Confederation. *** In the end, the Convention opted for a Constitution in which Congress would exercise its legislative authority directly over individuals rather than over States. *** In providing for a stronger central government, therefore, the Framers explicitly chose a Constitution that confers upon Congress the power to regulate individuals, not States.

This is not to say that Congress lacks the ability to encourage a State to regulate in a particular way, or that Congress may not hold out incentives to the States as a method of influencing a State's policy choices. *** First, under Congress' spending power, "Congress may attach conditions on the receipt of federal funds." *South Dakota v. Dole*, 483 U.S. 203, 206 (1987). *** Second, where Congress has the authority to regulate private activity under the Commerce Clause, we have recognized Congress' power to offer States the choice of regulating that activity according to federal standards or having state law pre-empted by federal regulation. *Hodel v. Virginia Surface Mining & Reclamation Assn., Inc.* 452 U.S. 264, 288 (1981).

By either of these methods, *** the residents of the State retain the ultimate decision as to whether or not the State will comply. If a State's citizens view federal policy as sufficiently contrary to local interests, they may elect to decline a federal grant. If state residents would prefer their government to devote its attention and resources to problems other than those deemed important by Congress, they may choose to have the Federal Government rather than the State bear the expense of a federally mandated regulatory program, and they may continue to supplement that program to the extent state law is not pre-empted. Where Congress encourages state regulation rather than compelling it, state governments remain responsive to the local electorate's preferences; state officials remain accountable to the people.

By contrast, where the Federal Government compels States to regulate, the accountability of both state and federal officials is diminished. If the citizens of New York, for example, do not consider that making provision for the disposal of radioactive waste is in their best interest, they may elect state officials who share their view. That view can always be pre-empted under the Supremacy Clause if it is contrary to the national view, but in such a case it is the Federal Government that makes the decision in full view of the public, and it will be federal officials that suffer the consequences if the decision turns out to be detrimental or unpopular. But where the Federal Government directs the States to regulate, it may be state officials who will bear the brunt of public disapproval, while the federal officials who devised the regulatory program may remain insulated from the electoral ramifications of their decision. Accountability is thus diminished when, due to federal coercion, elected state officials cannot regulate in accordance with the views of the local electorate in matters not pre-empted by federal regulation.

[The monetary incentives are a permissible combination of] an unexceptionable exercise of Congress' power to authorize the States to burden interstate commerce[, a] federal tax on interstate commerce, [and a] conditional exercise of Congress' authority under the Spending Clause. [The access incentives are valid because they are within Congress's power] to authorize the States to discriminate against interstate commerce [and Congress's power to] offer States the choice of regulating that activity according to federal standards or having state

Make the Connection

Under the "Dormant Commerce Clause Doctrine," states generally do not have power to burden or discriminate against interstate commerce. If this is true, then how can Congress authorize them to discriminate without violating the Constitution? We will take up this question in Chapter 4.

law pre-empted by federal regulation.

The take title provision is of a different character. *** In this provision, Congress has crossed the line distinguishing encouragement from coercion. *** The take title provision offers state governments a "choice" of either accepting ownership of waste or regulating according to the instructions of Congress. *** [T]he Constitution would not permit Congress simply to transfer radioactive waste from generators to state governments. Such a forced transfer, standing alone, would in principle be no different than a congressionally compelled subsidy from state governments to radioactive waste producers. The same is true of the provision requiring the States to become liable for the generators' damages. *** Either type of federal action would "commandeer" state governments into the service of federal regulatory purposes, and would for this reason be inconsistent with the Constitution's division of authority between federal and state governments. [T]he second alternative held out to state governments—regulating pursuant to Congress' direction—would, standing alone, present a simple command to state governments to implement legislation enacted by Congress. As we have seen, the Constitution does not empower Congress to subject state governments to this type of instruction. Because [both options are beyond the authority of Congress to offer,] it follows that Congress lacks the power to offer the States a choice between the two.

Respondents note that the Act embodies a bargain among the sited and unsited States, a compromise to which New York was a willing participant and from which New York has reaped much benefit. [But the] Constitution does not protect the sovereignty of States for the benefit of the States or state governments as abstract political entities, or even for the benefit of the public officials governing the States. To the contrary, the Constitution divides authority between federal and state governments for the protection of individuals. Where Congress exceeds its authority relative to the States, therefore, the departure from the constitutional plan cannot be ratified by the "consent" of state officials.

States are not mere political subdivisions of the United States. State governments are neither regional offices nor administrative agencies of the Federal Government. The positions occupied by state officials appear nowhere on the Federal Government's most detailed organizational chart. *** The Federal Government may not compel the States to enact or administer a federal regulatory program.

Justice WHITE, with whom Justice BLACKMUN and Justice STEVENS join, concurring in part and dissenting in part.

Ultimately, I suppose, the entire structure of our federal constitutional government can be traced to an interest in establishing checks and balances to prevent the exercise of tyranny against individuals. But these fears seem extremely far distant to me in a situation such as this. We face a crisis of national proportions in the disposal of low-level radioactive waste, and Congress has acceded to the wishes of the States by permitting local decision-making rather than imposing a solution from Washington. New York itself participated and supported passage of this legislation at both the gubernatorial and federal representative levels, and then enacted state laws specifically to comply with the deadlines and time-tables agreed upon by the States in the 1985 Act. For me, the Court's civics lecture has a decidedly hollow ring at a time when action, rather than rhetoric, is needed to solve a national problem.

> **Take Note**
>
> Justice White reasons that the Court's holding will force Congress to regulate directly matters that it had attempted to leave, at least in part, to the discretion of state officials. Assuming Congress continues to believe that a national solution is needed to the problem of disposal of radioactive waste, what options are available to it after the decision in *New York*? Are those options more or less solicitous of state autonomy?

The ultimate irony of the decision today is that in its formalistically rigid obeisance to "federalism," the Court gives Congress fewer incentives to defer to the wishes of state officials in achieving local solutions to local problems. This legislation was a classic example of Congress acting as arbiter among the States in their attempts to accept responsibility for managing a problem of grave import. The States urged the National Legislature not to impose from Washington a solution to the country's low-level radioactive waste management problems. Instead, they sought a reasonable level of local and regional autonomy ***. By invalidating the measure designed to ensure compliance for recalcitrant States, such as New York, the Court upsets the delicate compromise achieved among the States and forces Congress to erect several additional formalistic hurdles to clear before achieving exactly the same objective.

Justice STEVENS, concurring in part and dissenting in part.

Under the Articles of Confederation, the Federal Government had the power to issue commands to the States. Because that indirect exercise of federal power proved ineffective, the Framers of the Constitution empowered the Federal Government to exercise legislative authority directly over individuals within the States, even though that direct authority constituted a greater intrusion on state sovereignty. Nothing in that history suggests that the Federal Government may not also impose its will upon the several States as it did under the Articles. The Constitution enhanced, rather than diminished, the power of the Federal Government.

Points for Discussion

a. The Tenth Amendment

The Court stated that "if a power is an attribute of state sovereignty reserved by the Tenth Amendment, it is necessarily a power the Constitution has not conferred on Congress." Is this consistent with the view of the Tenth Amendment advanced by the Court in *Darby*? In *Garcia*? If not, is it nevertheless a more sensible view?

b. Political Accountability

Do you agree that voters might be uncertain whom to blame if the federal government requires the state to open a radioactive waste dump? Wouldn't state officials be likely to proclaim—loudly and publicly—that the dump is there only because the federal government required it? Or is the problem that federal law didn't specify *where* in the state the dump should go, thus leaving the decision to state officials, who likely would be blamed for that decision? Would it help if Congress not only directed the state to create a dump, but also mandated where in the state the dump should go? Can you see why Congress would be unlikely to do that?

c. Means and Ends

The Court held that Congress could not require the state to take title to the waste, but it upheld Congress's power to attach conditions to the receipt of federal funds to encourage the state to provide for the disposal of radioactive waste. Given the wide scope of Congress's power pursuant to the General Welfare Clause, what is the point of the limitation announced in *New York v. United States*? If Congress can achieve all of its goals simply by offering money and attaching specific conditions, does the rule of *New York* provide any meaningful protection for state autonomy?

d. Basis for the Decision

How would you characterize the basis of the Court's decision? Is the Court relying on evidence of the original meaning, on precedent, or just on considerations of policy? For a textual argument that states have some immunity from federal regulation because the term "state" in the Constitution means "sovereign state," see Michael B. Rappaport, *Reconciling Textualism and Federalism: The Proper Textual Basis of the Supreme Court's Tenth and Eleventh Amendment Decisions*, 93 Nw. U. L. Rev. 819 (1999). Is that a satisfying basis for the decision?

Printz v. United States

521 U.S. 898 (1997)

Justice SCALIA delivered the opinion of the Court.

The [Brady Handgun Violence Prevention Act] requires the Attorney General to establish a national instant background-check system by November 30, 1998, and immediately puts in place certain interim provisions until that system becomes operative. Under the interim provisions, a firearms dealer who proposes to transfer a handgun must [obtain information from the transferee and provide that information to] the "chief law enforcement officer" (CLEO) of the transferee's residence. *** When a CLEO receives the required notice of a proposed transfer from the firearms dealer, the CLEO must "make a reasonable effort to ascertain within 5 business days whether receipt or possession would be in violation of the law, including research in whatever State and local recordkeeping systems are available and in a national system designated by the Attorney General." The Act does not require the CLEO to take any particular action if he determines that a pending transaction would be unlawful; he may notify the firearms dealer to that effect, but is not required to do so. If, however, the CLEO notifies a gun dealer that a prospective purchaser is ineligible to receive a handgun, he must, upon request, provide the would-be purchaser with a written statement of the reasons for that determination. Moreover, if the CLEO does not discover any basis for objecting to the sale, he must destroy any records in his possession relating to the transfer, including his copy of the Brady Form. [A]ny person who "knowingly violates [this provision] shall be [fined], imprisoned for not more than 1 year, or both." Petitioners Jay Printz and Richard Mack, the CLEOs for Ravalli County, Montana, and Graham County, Arizona, respectively, filed separate actions challenging the constitutionality of the Brady Act's interim provisions.

From the description set forth above, it is apparent that the Brady Act purports to direct state law enforcement officers to participate, albeit only temporarily, in the administration of a federally enacted regulatory scheme. *** Petitioners here object to being pressed into federal service, and contend that congressional action compelling state officers to execute federal laws is unconstitutional.

Because there is no constitutional text speaking to this precise question, the answer to the CLEOs' challenge must be sought in historical understanding and practice, in the structure of the Constitution, and in the jurisprudence of this Court.

Petitioners contend that compelled enlistment of state executive officers for the administration of federal programs is, until very recent years at least, unprecedented. The Government contends, to the contrary, that "the earliest Con-

> **Food for Thought**
>
> What is the relevance of the understanding of members of the early Congresses of their own powers? Is it evidence of the original meaning of the Constitution? Or is reliance on such evidence inconsistent with the principle of (and approach of the Court in) *Marbury v. Madison*?

gresses enacted statutes that required the participation of state officials in the implementation of federal laws." [E]arly congressional enactments "provide contemporaneous and weighty evidence of the Constitution's meaning." [Those statutes] required state courts to record applications for citizenship, to transmit abstracts of citizenship applications and other naturalization records to the Secretary of State, and to register aliens seeking naturalization and issue certificates of registry. *** These early laws establish, at most, that the Constitution was originally understood to permit imposition of an obligation on state *judges* to enforce federal prescriptions ***.

[W]e do not think the early statutes imposing obligations on state courts imply a power of Congress to impress the state executive into its service. Indeed, it can be argued that the numerousness of these statutes, contrasted with the utter lack of statutes imposing obligations on the States' executive (notwithstanding the attractiveness of that course to Congress), suggests an assumed *absence* of such power.

> **FYI**
>
> The Supremacy Clause of Article VI provides that state judges are "bound" by federal law. Does this suggest that Congress's power to require state judges to enforce federal law is different from its power to require state executive officials to implement federal law?

In addition to early legislation, the Government also appeals to other sources we have usually regarded as indicative of the original understanding of the Constitution. It points to portions of The Federalist [that suggest that Congress would rely on state officers to collect federal taxes.] But none of these statements necessarily implies—what is the critical point here—that Congress could impose these responsibilities *without the consent of the States.* They appear to rest on the natural assumption that the States would consent to allowing their officials to assist the Federal Government. The Federalist [No. 27 states that] "the legislatures, courts, and magistrates, of the [States] will be incorporated into the operations of the national government *as far as its just and constitutional authority extends;* and will be rendered auxiliary to the enforcement of its laws." [Justice Souter concludes that this demonstrates that the Constitution originally was understood to confer on the federal government the authority asserted in the Brady Act. But this reading] makes state *legislatures* subject to federal direction[, contrary to our holding in *New York v. United States*.] These problems are avoided, of course, if the calculatedly vague consequences the passage recites are taken to refer to nothing more (or less) than the duty owed to the National Government, on the part of *all* state officials, to enact, enforce, and interpret state law in such fashion as not to obstruct the operation of federal law.

The constitutional practice we have examined above tends to negate the existence of the congressional power asserted here, but is not conclusive. We turn next to consideration of the structure of the Constitution ***. It is incontestible that the Constitution established a system of "dual sovereignty." Although the States surrendered many of their powers to the new Federal Government, they retained "a residuary and inviolable sovereignty." The Federalist No. 39. This is reflected throughout the Constitution's text ***. The Framers' experience under the Articles of Confederation had persuaded them that using the States as the instruments of federal governance was both ineffectual and provocative of federal-state conflict. [They] rejected the concept of a central government that would act upon and through the States, and instead designed a system in which the State and Federal Governments would exercise concurrent authority over the people ***. The power of the Federal Government would be augmented immeasurably if it were able to impress into its service—and at no cost to itself—the police officers of the 50 States.

[F]ederal control of state officers *** would also have an effect upon *** the separation and equilibration of powers between the three branches of the Federal Government itself. The Constitution does not leave to speculation who is to administer the laws enacted by Congress; the President, it says, "shall take Care that the

> **Food for Thought**
>
> Can you identify provisions of the Constitution that confirm the structural principle on which Justice Scalia relies?

> **Make the Connection**
>
> Notwithstanding Justice Scalia's assertion, there is substantial debate about the degree to which the Constitution concentrates authority in the office of the President. We will discuss the President's powers—and the theory of the "unitary executive"—in Chapters 5 & 6.

Laws be faithfully executed," Art. II, § 3, personally and through officers whom he appoints ***. The Brady Act effectively transfers this responsibility to thousands of CLEOs in the 50 States, who are left to implement the program without meaningful Presidential control ***. The insistence of the Framers upon unity in the Federal Executive—to ensure both vigor and accountability—is well known. That unity would be shattered, and the power of the President would be subject to reduction, if Congress could act as effectively without the President as with him, by simply requiring state officers to execute its laws.

> **Make the Connection**
>
> This question of executive authority to exercise policy discretion arises as well when Congress delegates authority to Executive officials. We will discuss Congress's power to do so in Chapter 6.

Finally, and most conclusively in the present litigation, we turn to the prior jurisprudence of this Court. *** The Government contends that [u]nlike the "take title" provisions invalidated in [*New York v. United States*,] the background-check provision of the Brady Act does not require state legislative or executive officials to make policy, but instead issues a final directive to state CLEOs. *** Executive action that has utterly no policymaking component is rare, particularly at an executive level as high as a jurisdiction's chief law enforcement officer. Is it really true that there is no policymaking involved in deciding, for example, what "reasonable efforts" shall be expended to conduct a background check? *** It is quite impossible [to] draw the Government's proposed line at "no policymaking," and we would have to fall back upon a line of "not too much policymaking." How much is too much is not likely to be answered precisely; and an imprecise barrier against federal intrusion upon state authority is not likely to be an effective one.

Even assuming, moreover, that the Brady Act leaves no "policymaking" discretion with the States, we fail to see how that improves rather than worsens the intrusion upon state sovereignty. Preservation of the States as independent and autonomous political entities is arguably less undermined by requiring them to make policy in certain fields than *** by "reducing them to puppets of a ventriloquist Congress." It is an essential attribute of the States' retained sovereignty that they remain independent and autonomous within their proper sphere of authority.

The Government also maintains that requiring state officers to perform discrete, ministerial tasks specified by Congress does not violate the principle of *New York* because it does not diminish the accountability of state or federal officials. This argument fails even on its own terms. By forcing state governments to absorb the financial burden of implementing a federal regulatory program, Members of Congress can take credit for "solving" problems without having to ask their constituents to pay for the solutions with higher federal taxes. And even when the States are not forced to absorb the costs of implementing a federal program, they are still put in the position of taking the blame for its burdensomeness and for its defects. Under the present law, for example, it will be the CLEO and not some federal official who stands between the gun purchaser and immediate possession of his gun. And it will likely be the CLEO, not some federal official, who will be blamed for any error (even one in the designated federal database) that causes a purchaser to be mistakenly rejected.

Finally, the Government [argues that the Brady Act] places a minimal and only temporary burden upon state officers. There is considerable disagreement over the extent of the burden, but we need not pause over that detail. [The extent of the burden] might be relevant if we were evaluating whether the incidental application to the States of a federal law of general applicability excessively interfered with the functioning of state governments. But where, as here, it is the whole *object* of the law to direct the functioning of the state executive, and hence to compromise the structural framework of dual sovereignty, such a "balancing" analysis is inappropriate. It is the very *principle* of separate state sovereignty that such a law offends, and no comparative assessment of the various interests can overcome that fundamental defect.

We held in *New York* that Congress cannot compel the States to enact or enforce a federal regulatory program. Today we hold that Congress cannot circumvent that prohibition by conscripting the State's officers directly. The Federal Government may neither issue directives requiring the States to address particular problems, nor command the States' officers, or those of their political subdivisions, to administer or enforce a federal regulatory program. It matters not whether policymaking is involved, and no case-by-case weighing of the burdens or benefits is necessary; such commands are fundamentally incompatible with our constitutional system of dual sovereignty.

Justice O'CONNOR, concurring.

[T]he Court appropriately refrains from deciding whether other purely ministerial reporting requirements imposed by Congress on state and local authorities pursuant to its Commerce Clause powers are similarly invalid. The provisions invalidated here, however, which directly compel state officials to administer a federal regulatory program, utterly fail to adhere to the design and structure of our constitutional scheme.

Justice THOMAS, concurring.

[T]he Federal Government's authority under the Commerce Clause *** does not extend to the regulation of wholly *intra*state, point-of-sale transactions. Absent the underlying authority to regulate the intrastate transfer of firearms, Congress surely lacks the corollary power to impress state law enforcement officers into administering and enforcing such regulations. *** Even if we construe Congress' authority to regulate interstate commerce to encompass those intrastate transactions that "substantially affect" interstate commerce, I question whether Congress can regulate the particular transactions at issue here. *** The Second Amendment *** provides: "A well regulated Militia, being necessary to the security of a free State, the right of the people to keep and bear arms,

> **For More Information**
>
> The claim that the Second Amendment does not confer a "personal" right to bear arms is based on the argument that the opening clauses of the text—which provide, "A well regulated Militia, being necessary to the security of a free State"—modify the grant of the "right of the people to keep and bear Arms." After years of uncertainty, the Court held in 2008 that the Amendment does indeed protect an individual right to bear arms, unconnected to service in a state militia. See *District of Columbia v. Heller*, 128 S. Ct. 2783 (2008), which we considered in Chapter 1.

shall not be infringed."   [If] the Second Amendment is read to confer a *personal* right to "keep and bear arms," a colorable argument exists that the Federal Government's regulatory scheme, at least as it pertains to the purely intrastate sale or possession of firearms, runs afoul of that Amendment's protections. As the parties did not raise this argument, however, we need not consider it here.

Justice STEVENS, with whom Justice SOUTER, Justice GINSBURG, and Justice BREYER join, dissenting.

There is not a clause, sentence, or paragraph in the entire text of the Constitution of the United States that supports the proposition that a local police officer can ignore a command contained in a statute enacted by Congress pursuant to an express delegation of power enumerated in Article I.   Under the Articles of Confederation the National Government had the power to issue commands to the several sovereign States, but it had no authority to govern individuals directly. Thus, it raised an army and financed its operations by issuing requisitions to the constituent members of the Confederacy, rather than by creating federal agencies to draft soldiers or to impose taxes.

That method of governing proved to be unacceptable, not because it demeaned the sovereign character of the several States, but rather because it was cumbersome and inefficient.   *** The basic change in the character of the government that the Framers conceived was designed to enhance the power of the national government, not to provide some new, unmentioned immunity for state officers. *** Alexander Hamilton explained that "we must *extend* the authority of the Union to the persons of the citizens."   The Federalist No. 15. Indeed, the historical materials strongly suggest that the founders intended to enhance the capacity of the Federal Government by empowering it—as a part of the new authority to make demands directly on individual citizens—to act through local officials.   *** Opponents of the Constitution had repeatedly expressed fears that the new Federal Government's ability to impose taxes directly on the citizenry would result in an overbearing presence of federal tax collectors in the States. Federalists rejoined that this problem would not arise because, as Hamilton explained, "the United States will make use of the State officers and State regulations for collecting" certain taxes. [The Federalist] No. 36. Similarly, Madison made clear that the new central Government's power to raise taxes directly from the citizenry would "not be resorted to, except for supplemental purposes of revenue, and that the eventual collection, under the immediate authority of the Union, will generally be made by the officers appointed by the several States." The Federalist No. 45.

Bereft of support in the history of the founding, the Court rests its conclusion on the claim that there is little evidence the National Government actually exercised such a power in the early years of the Republic.   [But] we have never suggested that the failure of the early Congresses to address the scope of federal power in a particular area or to exercise a particular authority was an argument against its existence.   That position, if correct, would undermine most of our post-New Deal Commerce Clause jurisprudence. *** More importantly, the fact that Congress did elect to rely on state judges and the clerks of state courts to perform a variety of executive functions is surely evidence of a contemporary understanding that their status as state officials did not immunize them from federal service. *** The majority's insistence that this evidence of federal enlistment of state officials to serve executive functions is irrelevant simply because the assistance of "judges" was at issue rests on empty formalistic reasoning of the highest order.

Perversely, the majority's rule seems more likely to damage than to preserve the safeguards against tyranny provided by the existence of vital state governments. By limiting the ability of the Federal Government to enlist state officials in the implementation of its programs, the Court creates incentives for the National Government to aggrandize itself. In the name of State's rights, the majority would have the Federal Government create vast national bureaucracies to implement its policies. This is exactly the sort of thing that the early Federalists promised would not occur, in part as a result of the National Government's ability to rely on the magistracy of the States.

Justice SOUTER, dissenting.

In deciding these cases, which I have found closer than I had anticipated, it is The Federalist that finally determines my position. *** Hamilton in No. 27 first notes that because the new Constitution would authorize the National Government to bind individuals directly through national law, it could "employ the ordinary magistracy of each [State] in the execution of its laws." Were he to stop here, he would not necessarily be speaking of anything beyond the possibility of cooperative arrangements by agreement. But he then addresses the combined effect of the proposed Supremacy Clause, Art. VI, cl. 2, and state officers' oath requirement, Art. VI, cl. 3, and he states that "the Legislatures, Courts and Magistrates of the respective members will be incorporated into the operations of the national government, *as far as its just and constitutional authority extends;* and will be rendered auxiliary to the enforcement of its laws." The natural reading of this language is not merely that the officers of the various branches of state governments may be employed in the performance of national functions; Hamilton says that the state governmental machinery "will be incorporated" into the Nation's operation, and because the "auxiliary" status of the state officials will occur because they are "bound by the sanctity of an oath," I take him to mean that their auxiliary functions will be the products of their obligations thus undertaken to support federal law, not of their own, or the States', unfettered choices. Madison in No. 44 supports this reading [by arguing] that national officials "will have no agency in carrying the State Constitutions into effect. The members and officers of the State Governments, on the contrary, will have an essential agency in giving effect to the Federal Constitution." [This view is confirmed by The Federalist Nos. 36 and 45, which anticipated state collection of federal revenue.]

To be sure, it does not follow that any conceivable requirement may be imposed on any state official. I continue to agree, for example, that Congress may not require a state legislature to enact a regulatory scheme and that *New York v. United States* was rightly decided; after all, the essence of legislative power, within the limits of legislative jurisdiction, is a discretion not subject to command.[1] But insofar as national law would require nothing from a state officer inconsistent with the power proper to his branch of tripartite state government, *** I suppose that the reach of federal law as Hamilton described it would not be exceeded.

Justice BREYER, with whom Justice STEVENS joins, dissenting.

> **Food for Thought**
>
> What is the relevance of foreign law in determining the meaning of the United States Constitution? Does Justice Breyer treat the experience of other countries as an authoritative source of meaning for the United States Constitution? We will consider this question when we discuss *Lawrence v. Texas* in Chapter 8.

[T]he United States is not the only nation that seeks to reconcile the practical need for a central authority with the democratic virtues of more local control. At least some other countries, facing the same basic problem, have found that local control is better maintained through application of a principle that is the direct opposite of the principle the majority derives from the silence of our Constitution. The federal systems of Switzerland, Germany, and the European Union, for example, all provide that constituent states, not federal bureaucracies, will themselves implement many of the laws, rules, regulations, or decrees enacted by the central "federal" body. They do so in part because they believe that such a system interferes less, not more, with the independent authority of the "state," member nation, or other subsidiary government, and helps to safeguard individual liberty as well.

Of course, we are interpreting our own Constitution, not those of other nations, and there may be relevant political and structural differences between their systems and our own. But their experience may nonetheless cast an empirical light on the consequences of different solutions to a common legal problem—in this case the problem of reconciling central authority with the need to preserve the liberty-enhancing autonomy of a smaller constituent governmental entity. And that experience here offers empirical confirmation of the implied answer to a question Justice STEVENS asks: Why, or how, would what the majority sees as a constitutional alternative—the creation of a new federal gun-law bureaucracy, or the expansion of an existing federal bureaucracy—better promote either state sovereignty or individual liberty? As comparative experience suggests, there is no need to interpret the Constitution as containing an absolute principle forbidding the assignment of virtually any federal duty to any state official.

———————————   ———————————   ———————————

[1] The core power of an executive officer is to enforce a law in accordance with its terms; that is why a state executive "auxiliary" may be told what result to bring about. The core power of a legislator acting within the legislature's subject-matter jurisdiction is to make a discretionary decision on what the law should be; that is why a legislator may not be legally ordered to exercise discretion a particular way without damaging the legislative power as such.

Points for Discussion

a. The Dog that Didn't Bark

In reaching the conclusion that Congress lacks the power to direct state and local executive officials to enforce federal law, the Court relied on the absence of any early statutes imposing such obligations on such officials. Even assuming that actions by the early Congresses should be treated as evidence of constitutional meaning, should *inaction* by the early Congresses be treated as evidence of the original understanding of Congress's power? What else, aside from a congressional belief that it lacked the power in question, might explain Congress's failure to enact any such statutes in the early years of the Republic?

b. Implementation v. Compliance

The Court held in <u>Garcia</u> that Congress has power to require states to pay their employees a minimum wage according to federal standards. The Court held in <u>Printz</u> that Congress lacks power to require state executive officials to implement federal law. Is it possible to reconcile these two decisions? In order to comply with the federal minimum wage law, aren't state officials who oversee payroll matters for the state required to take actions—such as keeping track of overtime hours and preparing and issuing paychecks—to conform to federal requirements?

Is there a meaningful difference between complying with federal law—which is what Congress can force state officials to do—and implementing federal law—which Congress cannot force state officials to do? One way to distinguish between the two types of actions is by noting that when Congress directs state officials to implement federal law, it is in effect requiring state officials to enforce federal law against third parties. See *South Carolina v. Baker*, 485 U.S. 505 (1988) (holding that Congress had power to impose federal income tax on interest from bearer bonds issued by states, even though the tax in effect forced states to issue registered (and thus tax-exempt) bonds, because Congress did not "seek to control or influence the manner in which states regulate private parties"). In contrast, when Congress requires a state to pay its employees a federal minimum wage, it is regulating the states directly in the same manner that it regulates private parties—in this example, private employers. Does that mean that the crucial difference is whether Congress imposes requirements that it imposes on the states on similarly situated private parties, as well? See *Reno v. Condon*, 528 U.S. 141 (2000) (upholding the Driver's Privacy Protection Act, which restricted the states' ability to sell personal information that they collected on drivers, because the statute did "not require the States in their sovereign capacity to regulate their own citizens").

Hypothetical

Congress enacts legislation creating the "Federal Missing Children Database," which seeks to maintain information on children reported missing, in order to facilitate cooperative efforts to locate the children. In enacting the statute, Congress finds that abducted children often are transported across state lines, and that state law enforcement efforts to locate missing children often have been hampered by the lack of ready access to information about children missing in other states. The statute directs the Attorney General of the United States to maintain a database of information about children reported missing anywhere in the United States and to share the information in the database with state law enforcement officials. The statute also directs state law enforcement officials to report to the Attorney General (1) any report of a missing child, and (2) information about the missing child's physical appearance, birthday, and immediate family. A local sheriff objects to the reporting requirement. How should the court rule?

G. State Sovereign Immunity as a Limit on Federal Power

New York and *Printz* held that the states enjoy immunity from some forms of federal regulation. But they did not purport to overrule *Garcia*, which held that Congress can impose on the states substantive requirements similar to those that it imposes on private actors, such as the obligation to pay a minimum wage to employees. When Congress imposes such obligations, it often also provides for a private right of action to enforce the obligation. Accordingly, employees in private industry may sue their employers to recover wages unlawfully withheld. May Congress authorize similar remedies against the states for violation of statutory obligations that are otherwise validly imposed?

The Eleventh Amendment provides one possible answer.

U.S. Constitution, <u>Amend. XI</u>

The Judicial power of the United States shall not be construed to extend to any suit in law or equity, commenced or prosecuted against one of the United States by Citizens of another State, or by Citizens or Subjects of any Foreign State.

Recall that as originally written, Article III extended the judicial power to "Controversies *** between a State and Citizens of another State" and "between a State, or the Citizens thereof, and foreign States, Citizens or Subjects." By its terms, the Eleventh Amendment appears to remove these controversies from Article III's enumeration of the federal judicial power. How far does this language reach?

It is universally understood that the Eleventh Amendment was proposed and ratified in response to the Court's early decision in *Chisholm v. Georgia,* 2 U.S. (2. Dall.) 419 (1793), which read Article III literally to permit a state-law suit for damages by a citizen of South Carolina against the state of Georgia. But from there the disagreements begin. Consider the case that follows.

Alden v. Maine

527 U.S. 706 (1999)

Justice KENNEDY delivered the opinion of the Court.

[Petitioners, a group of probation officers, originally filed suit in federal court against their employer, the State of Maine, alleging that the State had violated the overtime provisions of the Fair Labor Standards Act of 1938 (FLSA), 29 U.S.C. § 201 et *seq.*, and seeking compensation and liquidated damages. The district court dismissed the suit, holding that Maine enjoyed sovereign immunity from such a suit in federal court.] Petitioners then filed the same action in state court. The state trial court dismissed the suit on the basis of sovereign immunity, and the Maine Supreme Judicial Court affirmed. *** We hold that the powers delegated to Congress under Article I of the United States Constitution do not include the power to subject nonconsenting States to private suits for damages in state courts.

The Eleventh Amendment makes explicit reference to the States' immunity from suits "commenced or prosecuted against one of the United States by Citizens of another State, or by Citizens or Subjects of any Foreign State." U.S. Const., Amdt. 11. We have, as a result, sometimes referred to the States' immunity from suit as "Eleventh Amendment immunity." The phrase is convenient shorthand but something of a misnomer, for the sovereign immunity of the States neither derives from, nor is limited by, the terms of the Eleventh Amendment. Rather, as the Constitution's structure, its history, and the authoritative interpretations by this Court make clear, the States' immunity from suit is a fundamental aspect of the sovereignty which the States enjoyed before the ratification of the Constitution, and which they retain today (either literally or by virtue of their admission into the Union upon an equal footing with the other States) except as altered by the plan of the Convention or certain constitutional Amendments.

The generation that designed and adopted our federal system considered immunity from private suits central to sovereign dignity. When the Constitution was ratified, it was well established in English law that the Crown could not be sued without consent in its own courts. *** Although the American people had rejected other aspects of English political theory, the doctrine that a sovereign could not be sued without its consent was universal in the States when the Constitution was drafted and ratified.

The ratification debates, furthermore, underscored the importance of the States' sovereign immunity to the American people. Grave concerns were raised by the provisions of Article III, which extended the federal judicial power to controversies between States and citizens of other States or foreign nations. *** The leading advocates of the Constitution assured the people in no uncertain terms that the Constitution would not strip the States of sovereign immunity. One assurance was contained in The Federalist No. 81, written by Alexander Hamilton: "It is inherent in the nature of sovereignty not to be amenable to the suit of an individual *without its consent.* This is the general sense and the general practice of mankind; and the exemption, as one of the attributes of sovereignty, is now enjoyed by the government of every State in the Union. Unless, therefore, there is a surrender of this immunity in the plan of the convention, it will remain with the States and the danger intimated must be merely ideal." At the Virginia ratifying convention, James Madison echoed this theme: "Its jurisdiction in controversies between a state and citizens of another state is much objected to, and perhaps without reason. It is not in the power of individuals to call any state into court. *** It appears to me that this [clause] can have no operation but this—to give a citizen a right to be heard in the federal courts; and if a state should condescend to be a party, this court may take cognizance of it." 3 Debates on the Federal Constitution 533 (J. Elliot 2d ed. 1854).

Although the state conventions which addressed the issue of sovereign immunity in their formal ratification documents sought to clarify the point by constitutional amendment, they made clear that they, like Hamilton [and] Madison, [understood] the Constitution as drafted to preserve the States' immunity from private suits. The Rhode Island Convention thus proclaimed that "[i]t is declared by the Convention, that the judicial power of the United States, in cases in which a state may be a party, does not extend to criminal prosecutions, or to authorize any suit by any person against a state." 1 *id.,* at 336. The convention sought, in addition, an express amendment "to remove all doubts or controversies respecting the same."

Despite the persuasive assurances of the Constitution's leading advocates and the expressed understanding of the only state conventions to address the issue in explicit terms, this Court held, just five years after the Constitution was adopted, that Article III authorized a private citizen of another State to sue the State of Georgia without its consent. *Chisholm v. Georgia,* 2 U.S. (2 Dall.) 419 (1793). Each of the four Justices who concurred in the judgment issued a separate opinion. The common theme of the opinions was that the case fell within the literal text of Article III, which by its terms granted jurisdiction over controversies "between a State and Citizens of another State," and "between a State, or the Citizens thereof, and foreign States, Citizens, or Subjects." U.S. Const., Art. III, § 2. *** Two Justices also argued that sovereign immunity was inconsistent with the principle of popular sovereignty established by the Constitution, 2 Dall., at 454-458 (Wilson, J.); *id.,* at 470-472 (Jay, C. J.).

The Court's decision "fell upon the country with a profound shock." *** The States, in particular, responded with outrage to the decision. *** An initial proposal to amend the Constitution was introduced in the House of Representatives the day after *Chisholm* was announced; the proposal adopted as the Eleventh Amendment was introduced in the Senate promptly following an intervening recess. Congress turned to the latter proposal with great dispatch; little more than two months after its introduction it had been endorsed by both Houses and forwarded to the States.

The text and history of the Eleventh Amendment [suggest] that Congress acted not to change but to restore the original constitutional design. By its terms, [the] Eleventh Amendment did not redefine the federal judicial power but instead overruled the Court. *** Congress chose not to enact language codifying the traditional understanding of sovereign immunity but rather to address the specific provisions of the Constitution that had raised concerns during the ratification debates and formed the basis of the *Chisholm* decision. *** The [most] natural inference is that the Constitution was understood, in light of its history and structure, to preserve the States' traditional immunity from private suits. As the Amendment clarified the only provisions of the Constitution that anyone had suggested might support a contrary understanding, there was no reason to draft with a broader brush.

As a consequence, we have looked to "history and experience, and the established order of things," rather than "[a]dhering to the mere letter" of the Eleventh Amendment, in determining the scope of the States' constitutional immunity from suit. Following this approach, the Court has upheld States' assertions of sovereign immunity in various contexts falling outside the literal text of the Eleventh Amendment. In *Hans v. Louisiana*, 134 U.S. 1 (1890), the Court held that sovereign immunity barred a citizen from suing his own State under the federal-question head of jurisdiction [notwithstanding] the petitioner's argument that the Eleventh Amendment, by its terms, applied only to suits brought by citizens of other States. *** Later decisions rejected similar requests to conform the principle of sovereign immunity to the strict language of the Eleventh Amendment in holding that nonconsenting States are immune from suits brought by federal corporations, *Smith v. Reeves*, 178 U.S. 436 (1900), foreign nations, *Principality of Monaco v. Mississippi*, 292 U.S. 313 (1934), or Indian tribes, *Blatchford v. Native Village of Noatak*, 501 U.S. 775 (1991), and in concluding that sovereign immunity is a defense to suits in admiralty, though the text of the Eleventh Amendment addresses only suits "in law or equity," *Ex parte New York*, 256 U.S. 490 (1921). These holdings reflect a settled doctrinal understanding [that the] Eleventh Amendment confirmed, rather than established, sovereign immunity as a constitutional principle; it follows that the scope of the States' immunity from suit is demarcated not by the text of the Amendment alone but by fundamental postulates implicit in the constitutional design.

In this case we must determine whether Congress has the power, under Article I, to subject nonconsenting States to private suits in their *own* courts. As the foregoing discussion makes clear, the fact that the Eleventh Amendment by its terms limits only "[t]he Judicial power of the United States" does not resolve the question. While the constitutional principle of sovereign immunity does pose a bar to federal jurisdiction over suits against nonconsenting States, this is not the only structural basis of sovereign immunity implicit in the constitutional design. Rather, "[t]here is also the postulate that States of the Union, still possessing attributes of sovereignty, shall be immune from suits, without their consent, save where there has been 'a surrender of this immunity in the plan of the convention.' " *Principality of Monaco*, 292 U.S., at 322-323 (quoting The Federalist No. 81). In exercising its Article I powers Congress may subject the States to private suits in their own courts only if there is "compelling evidence" that the States were required to surrender this power to Congress pursuant to the constitutional design.

The Constitution, by delegating to Congress the power to establish the supreme law of the land when acting within its enumerated powers, does not foreclose a State from asserting immunity to claims arising under federal law merely because that law derives not from the State itself but from the national power. *** We reject any contention that substantive federal law by its own force necessarily overrides the sovereign immunity of the States. When a State asserts its immunity to suit, the question is not the primacy of federal law but the implementation of the law in a manner consistent with the constitutional sovereignty of the States.

Nor can we conclude that the specific Article I powers delegated to Congress necessarily include, by virtue of the Necessary and Proper Clause or otherwise, the incidental authority to subject the States to private suits as a means of achieving objectives otherwise within the scope of the enumerated powers. *** Although the sovereign immunity of the States derives at least in part from the common-law tradition, the structure and history of the Constitution make clear that the immunity exists today by constitutional design.

Although the Constitution grants broad powers to Congress, our federalism requires that Congress treat the States in a manner consistent with their status as residuary sovereigns and joint participants in the governance of the Nation. The principle of sovereign immunity preserved by constitutional design "[accords] the States the respect owed them as members of the federation." *** Underlying constitutional form are considerations of great substance. Private suits against nonconsenting States—especially suits for money damages—may threaten the financial integrity of the States. [A]n unlimited congressional power to authorize suits in state court to levy upon the treasuries of the States for compensatory damages, attorney's fees, and even punitive damages could create staggering burdens, giving Congress a power and a leverage over the States that is not contemplated by our constitutional design.

The constitutional privilege of a State to assert its sovereign immunity in its own courts does not confer upon the State a concomitant right to disregard the Constitution or valid federal law. The States and their officers are bound by obligations imposed by the Constitution and by federal statutes that comport with the constitutional design. We are unwilling to assume the States will refuse to honor the Constitution or obey the binding laws of the United States.

Sovereign immunity, moreover, does not bar all judicial review of state compliance with the Constitution and valid federal law. [S]overeign immunity bars suits only in the absence of consent. Many States, on their own initiative, have enacted statutes consenting to a wide variety of suits. Nor, subject to constitutional limitations, does the Federal Government lack the authority or means to seek the States' voluntary consent to private suits. Cf. *South*

Make the Connection

We considered Congress's powers to grant funds to the states with strings attached earlier in this Chapter. We will consider Congress's power under Section 5 of the Fourteenth Amendment in Chapter 13.

Dakota v. Dole, 483 U.S. 203 (1987). [In addition, in] ratifying the Constitution, the States consented to suits brought by other States or by the Federal Government. *** [Moreover, we] have held also that in adopting the Fourteenth Amendment, the people required the States to surrender a portion of the sovereignty that had been preserved to them by the original Constitution, so that Congress may authorize private suits against nonconsenting States pursuant to its § 5 enforcement power. *Fitzpatrick v. Bitzer,* 427 U.S. 445 (1976). [T]he principle of sovereign immunity [bars] suits against States but not lesser entities [such as] municipal corporations. Nor does sovereign immunity bar [certain] actions against state officers for injunctive or declaratory relief. *Ex parte Young,* 209 U.S. 123 (1908). ***

When Congress legislates in matters affecting the States, it may not treat these sovereign entities as mere prefectures or corporations. Congress must accord States the esteem due to them as joint participants in a federal system, one beginning with the premise of sovereignty in both the central Government and the separate States. Congress has ample means to ensure compliance with valid federal laws, but it must respect the sovereignty of the States. [*Affirmed.*]

Justice SOUTER, with whom Justice STEVENS, Justice GINSBURG, and Justice BREYER join, dissenting.

The Court rests its decision principally on the claim that immunity from suit was "a fundamental aspect of the sovereignty which the States enjoyed before the ratification of the Constitution," an aspect which the Court understands to have survived the ratification of the Constitution in 1788 and to have been "confirm[ed]" and given constitutional status by the adoption of the Tenth Amendment in 1791. If the Court truly means by "sovereign immunity" what that term meant at common law, its argument would be insupportable. While sovereign immunity entered many new state legal systems as a part of the common law selectively received from England, it was not understood to be indefeasible or to have been given any such status by the new National Constitution, which did not mention it. Had the question been posed, state sovereign immunity could not have been thought to shield a State from suit under federal law on a subject committed to national jurisdiction by Article I of the Constitution. Congress exercising its conceded Article I power may unquestionably abrogate such immunity. [I]t is fair to read [the Court's] references to a "fundamental aspect" of state sovereignty as referring not to a prerogative inherited from the Crown, but to a conception necessarily implied by statehood itself. The conception is thus not one of common law so much as of natural law, a universally applicable proposition discoverable by reason.

The Court's principal rationale for today's result, then, turns on history: was the natural law conception of sovereign immunity as inherent in any notion of an independent State widely held in the United States in the period preceding the ratification of 1788 (or the adoption of the Tenth Amendment in 1791)? The answer is certainly no. There is almost no evidence that the generation of the Framers thought sovereign immunity was fundamental in the sense of being unalterable. Whether one looks at the period before the framing, to the ratification controversies, or to the early republican era, the evidence is the same. Some Framers thought sovereign immunity was an obsolete royal prerogative inapplicable in a republic; some thought sovereign immunity was a common law power defeasible, like other common law rights, by statute; and perhaps a few thought, in keeping with a natural law view distinct from the common law conception, that immunity was inherent in a sovereign because the body that made a law could not logically be bound by it. Natural law thinking on the part of a doubtful few will not, however, support the Court's position.

The only arguable support for the Court's absolutist view that I have found among the leading participants in the debate surrounding ratification was [Hamilton's statement in The Federalist No. 81,] where he described the sovereign immunity of the States in language suggesting principles associated with natural law. [T]he thrust of his argument was that sovereign immunity was "inherent in the nature of sovereignty." *** [Hamilton's statement] stands in contrast to formulations indicating no particular position on the natural-law-versus-common-law origin, to the more widespread view that sovereign immunity derived from common law, and to the more radical stance that the sovereignty of the people made sovereign immunity out of place in the United States.

In the Virginia ratifying convention, Madison was among those who debated sovereign immunity in terms of the result it produced, not its theoretical underpinnings. [But there] was no unanimity among the Virginians either on state- or federal-court immunity, however, for Edmund Randolph anticipated the position he would later espouse as plaintiff's counsel in *Chisholm v. Georgia*, 2 Dall. 419 (1793). He [argued that] the Constitution permitted suit against a State in federal court: "I think, whatever the law of nations may say, that any doubt respecting the construction that a state may be plaintiff, and not defendant, is taken away by the words *where a state shall be a party.*" 3 Elliot's Debates 573. Randolph clearly believed that the Constitution both could, and in fact by its language did, trump any inherent immunity enjoyed by the States.

At the furthest extreme from Hamilton, James Wilson made several comments in the Pennsylvania Convention that suggested his hostility to any idea of state sovereign immunity. [He argued that] "the government of each state ought to be subordinate to the government of

FYI

Edmund Randolph and James Wilson were both important figures at the Constitutional Convention and in the subsequent campaign to ratify the Constitution. Randolph proposed the "Virginia Plan," which was drafted by James Madison and which became the basis of the proposal ultimately adopted at the convention, but he refused to sign the final document, concerned that it lacked sufficient checks and balances. However, he supported ratification, and he later served as the first Attorney General of the United States. Wilson had signed the Declaration of Independence, during the ratification battles he gave an important speech laying out the theory of enumeration, and he subsequently served on the Supreme Court.

the United States." Wilson was also pointed in commenting on federal jurisdiction over cases between a State and citizens of another State: "When a citizen has a controversy with another state, there ought to be a tribunal where both parties may stand on a just and equal footing." Finally, Wilson laid out his view that sovereignty was in fact not located in the States at all: "Upon what principle is it contended that the sovereign power resides in the state governments? [M]y position is, that the sovereignty resides in the people; they have not parted with it; they have only dispensed such portions of the power as were conceived necessary for the public welfare." While this statement did not specifically address sovereign immunity, it expressed the major premise of what would later become Justice Wilson's position in *Chisholm*: that because the people, and not the States, are sovereign, sovereign immunity has no applicability to the States.

From a canvass of this spectrum of opinion expressed at the ratifying conventions, one thing is certain. No one was espousing an indefeasible, natural law view of sovereign immunity. The controversy over the enforceability of state debts subject to state law produced emphatic support for sovereign immunity from eminences as great as Madison and Marshall, but neither of them indicated adherence to any immunity conception outside the common law.

At the close of the ratification debates, the issue of the sovereign immunity of the States under Article III had not been definitively resolved, and in some instances the indeterminacy led the ratification conventions to respond in ways that point to the range of thinking about the doctrine. [T]he state ratifying conventions' felt need for clarification on the question of state suability demonstrates that uncertainty surrounded the matter even at the moment of ratification. This uncertainty set the stage for the divergent views expressed in *Chisholm*.

If the natural law conception of sovereign immunity as an inherent characteristic of sovereignty enjoyed by the States had been broadly accepted at the time of the founding, one would expect to find it reflected somewhere in the five opinions delivered by the Court in <u>Chisholm</u>. Yet that view did not appear in any of them. *** Not even Justice Iredell, who alone among the Justices thought that a State could not be sued in federal court, echoed Hamilton or hinted at a constitutionally immutable immunity doctrine. *** This dearth of support makes it very implausible for today's Court to argue that a substantial (let alone a dominant) body of thought at the time of the framing understood sovereign immunity to be an inherent right of statehood, adopted or confirmed by the Tenth Amendment.

The Court [also relies on] a structural basis in the Constitution's creation of a federal system. [But the] Court's argument that state-court sovereign immunity on federal questions is inherent in the very concept of federal structure is demonstrably mistaken. *** The State of Maine is not sovereign with respect to the national objectives of the FLSA. It is not the authority that promulgated the FLSA, on which the right of action in this case depends. That authority is the United States acting through the Congress, whose legislative power under Article I of the Constitution to extend FLSA coverage to state employees has already been decided, see *Garcia v. San Antonio Metropolitan Transit Authority*, and is not contested here.

It is symptomatic of the weakness of the structural notion proffered by the Court that it seeks to buttress the argument by relying on "the dignity and respect afforded a State, which the immunity is designed to protect." [T]he Court calls "immunity from private suits central to sovereign dignity" and assumes that this "dignity" is a quality easily translated from the person of the King to the participatory abstraction of a republican State. *** The thoroughly anomalous character of this appeal to dignity is obvious from a reading of Blackstone's description of royal dignity, which he sets out as a premise of his discussion of sovereignty: "Under every monarchical establishment, it is necessary to distinguish the prince from his subjects. [The] law therefore ascribes to the king [certain] attributes of a great and transcendent nature; by which the people are led to consider him in the light of a superior being, and to pay him that awful respect, which may enable him with greater ease to carry on the business of government." It would be hard to imagine anything more inimical to the republican conception, which rests on the understanding of its citizens precisely that the government is not above them, but of them, its actions being governed by law just like their own. Whatever justification there may be for an American government's immunity from private suit, it is not dignity.

[T]here is much irony in the Court's profession that it grounds its opinion on a deeply rooted historical tradition of sovereign immunity, when the Court abandons a principle nearly as inveterate, and much closer to the hearts of the Framers: that where there is a right, there must be a remedy. [*Marbury v. Madison*, 1 Cranch 137 (1803).] It will not do for the Court to respond that a remedy was never available where the right in question was against the sovereign. A State is not the sovereign when a federal claim is pressed against it ***. Before us, Maine has not claimed that petitioners are not covered by the FLSA, but only that it is protected from suit. *** Why the State of Maine has not rendered this case unnecessary by paying damages to petitioners under the FLSA of its own free will remains unclear to me.

———————

Points for Discussion

a. Constitutional Text and Structural Implications

The Court concluded in <u>Alden</u> that the states' immunity from suit derives not from the Eleventh Amendment, but instead from background constitutional postulates and structural implications of the federal system. On this view, what role does the Eleventh Amendment play? Does it add anything to the Constitution? We have already seen examples of the Court's relying on structural implications, but in most cases—such as in <u>McCulloch</u> and <u>Printz</u>—those implications have not run directly counter to constitutional text. Does the Eleventh Amendment's explicit focus on suits in *federal court* make the Court's analysis in <u>Alden</u> problematic?

Consider the disagreement between Chief Justice Rehnquist (for the Court) and Justice Souter (in dissent) in *Seminole Tribe of Fla. v. Florida*, 517 U.S. 44 (1996), which held that Congress lacks power under Article I to subject the states to private suits for damages in federal court. Chief Justice Rehnquist's opinion declined to rest on "a mere literal application of the words of § 2 of Article III," and instead focused on "postulates" "[b]ehind the words" of the Eleventh Amendment. Chief Justice Rehnquist thus criticized Justice Souter's dissenting opinion, which offered a "lengthy analysis of the text of the Eleventh Amendment," for being "directed at a straw man." Justice Souter responded by stating that "plain text is the Man of Steel in a confrontation with 'background principle[s]' and 'postulates which limit and control.'" Did the Court in *Alden* offer a different response to Justice Souter's criticism?

A conclusion that the Eleventh Amendment defines the full extent of constitutionally protected sovereign immunity would require the abandonment of a significant number of Supreme Court decisions. The suit that the Court permitted in <u>Chisholm</u> arose under state law; the plaintiff sought to recover a debt that he claimed the state owed him for goods that he had previously provided the state. One view of the Eleventh Amendment, accordingly, is that it simply deprived the federal courts of jurisdiction over suits by citizens of one state against another state arising under state law. (Indeed, many commentators have advanced this view. See, *e.g.*, William A. Fletcher, *A Historical Interpretation of the Eleventh Amendment: A Narrow Construction of an Affirmative Grant of Jurisdiction Rather Than a Prohibition Against Jurisdiction*, 35 Stan. L. Rev. 1033 (1983).) But at least since the late nineteenth century, the Court has advanced a much more robust view of the scope of state sovereign immunity.

In *Hans v. Louisiana*, 134 U.S. 1 (1890), the Court held that the Eleventh Amendment barred a federal-question suit by a citizen against his own state. And the Court has held that the Eleventh Amendment also bars suits against states in federal court by foreign nations, *Principality of Monaco v. Mississippi*, 292 U.S. 313 (1934), and Indian tribes, *Blatchford v. Native Village of Noatak*, 501 U.S. 775 (1991), notwithstanding the express language of the Amendment. The Court's view in <u>Alden</u>—which further extended the states' immunity to suits in state court—helped to free these decisions of the weight of the Eleventh Amendment. But in so doing, the Court effectively had to conclude that the Eleventh Amendment is constitutional surplusage. Do you find this approach convincing?

b. Sovereign Immunity and Political Theory

The doctrine of sovereign immunity derives from the notion that the "King can do no wrong," and thus cannot be subjected to suit for alleged wrongs. Given this historical pedigree, does the doctrine have any place in our constitutional system? Is it consistent with the foundational notion of popular sovereignty? Does it matter whether the doctrine is invoked to bar suits by the state's own citizens or instead citizens of other states (or countries)? If so, why?

c. State Immunity and Congressional Power

Even if the states presumptively enjoy sovereign immunity from private suits, is it clear that Congress lacks power to subject them to such suits as a remedy for state violation of requirements that Congress has otherwise validly imposed? As noted in <u>Alden</u>, the Court has held that Congress may authorize private suits for damages against the states pursuant to its authority to enforce the Fourteenth Amendment. That Amendment, after all, was designed to limit the power of the states, and thus effectively altered the federal-state balance, at least with respect to matters addressed by the substantive provisions of the Amendment. Can Congress also rely on its powers under Article I to subject the states to suit for violation of federal law enacted pursuant to those powers?

In *Pennsylvania v. Union Gas*, 491 U.S. 1 (1989), a plurality of the Court held that Congress can invoke its powers under Article I to "abrogate" the states' immunity from suit. Seven years later, however, the Court overruled *Union Gas* in *Seminole Tribe of Florida v. Florida*, 517 U.S. 44 (1996), which held (in a 5-4 decision) that Congress lacks power under Article I to subject the states to suit for violation of otherwise validly imposed federal requirements. Under current law, therefore, Congress may override the states' sovereign immunity (in federal and, presumably, state court) only when it acts properly to enforce the Fourteenth Amendment, a power that the Court has construed increasingly narrowly, see *Board of Trustees of Univ. of Alabama v. Garrett*, 531 U.S. 356 (2001) (holding that Congress did not have authority under Section 5 of the Fourteenth Amendment to subject the states to suit for violation of the Americans with Disabilities Act).

d. *National League of Cities* Redux?

Recall that the Court in *Garcia* overruled the prior decision in *National League of Cities*, which had held that Congress lacks authority pursuant to the Commerce Clause to regulate the states in the same fashion that it regulates private actors. The practical effect of the Court's decisions in *Seminole Tribe* and *Alden*, however, is that Congress cannot authorize a state employee to sue the state for damages when it fails to comply with the requirements of the Fair Labor Standards Act. Do those cases effectively overrule *Garcia*?

————

Executive Summary of this Chapter

Congress is limited to those powers enumerated in the Constitution. The enumerated powers, however, and the **Necessary and Proper Clause** imply the existence of subsidiary powers. Accordingly, Congress may seek to achieve any end that is legitimate under its express powers as long as its chosen means are reasonably adapted to achieving that end. *McCulloch v. Maryland* (1819). The Constitution also imposes some implied limits on the powers of the states, which lack power to tax instrumentalities of the federal government.

Under the **Commerce Clause**, Congress may regulate (1) interstate commerce, which is commerce that concerns more than one state; (2) the use of the "channels" of commerce, such as roads and navigable waters; (3) the "instrumentalities" of commerce, or persons or things in interstate commerce; and (4) intrastate "economic" activity that Congress might rationally believe **substantially affects** interstate commerce. *Gibbons v. Ogden* (1824); *United States v. Lopez* (1995).

Congress's power to regulate subjects within the scope of the Commerce Clause is plenary. *Gibbons v. Ogden* (1824). In reviewing legislation enacted under the Commerce

Clause, courts will not consider: (1) whether the actual purpose of the legislation is to regulate interstate commerce, *United States v. Darby* (1941); or (2) the wisdom, workability, or fairness of the legislation, *Wickard v. Filburn* (1942).

When determining whether the local activity that Congress seeks to regulate has the requisite connection to interstate commerce, the Court considers all of the regulated activity in the aggregate. *Wickard v. Filburn* (1942). Congress generally lacks authority to regulate local, non-economic conduct on the theory that, in the aggregate, the activity has a substantial effect on interstate commerce. *United States v. Morrison* (2000). In determining whether the local activity that Congress seeks to regulate is "economic" in nature, the Court sometimes considers other conduct for which the activity can serve as a substitute, *Gonzales v. Raich* (2005); *Wickard v. Filburn* (1942), and at other times appears to apply a more stringent test, *United States v. Morrison* (2000).

When Congress seeks to regulate local, non-economic conduct, the Court will consider congressional findings about the connection between the regulated conduct and interstate commerce, and whether the statute contains a "jurisdictional element," such as a provision limiting the statute to conduct "affecting commerce," *NLRB v. Jones & Laughlin Steel Corp.* (1937). It is not clear, however, whether findings and a jurisdictional element can save such a statute. By contrast, when Congress creates a comprehensive scheme that directly regulates economic, commercial activity, the Court will not, in an as-applied challenge, excise individual applications of the scheme even when it applies to local, non-economic conduct. *Gonzales v. Raich* (2005).

Congress has the **power to tax and spend for the general welfare**. Although Congress cannot rely on its power to tax when it seeks to regulate—by imposing a tax as a "penalty"—conduct not otherwise within the reach of Congress's affirmative powers, *Child Labor Tax Case* (1922), the Court will invalidate a tax on this ground only if it is "extraneous to any tax need"—that is, effectively, only if it does not produce any revenue, *United States v. Kahriger* (1953).

Pursuant to its power to spend for the general welfare, Congress may seek to accomplish objectives that it could not otherwise reach pursuant to its other enumerated powers. *United States v. Butler* (1936). Congress may also seek to accomplish its objectives by imposing conditions upon the receipt of federal funds by the states, as long as certain requirements are met: (1) the exercise of the spending power must be in pursuit of "the general welfare" (though the Court defers substantially to the judgment of Congress in this regard); (2) conditions imposed upon the states' receipt of federal funds must be unambiguous; (3) the conditions must be related to the federal interest in the spending program; (4) the conditions must not violate any independent constitutional bar; and (5) the financial inducement offered by Congress must not be so coercive as to pass the point at which "pressure turns into compulsion." *South Dakota v. Dole* (1987).

Congress's "**war power**" includes the authority to regulate "the evils which have arisen from [a war's] rise and progress," even if the war itself has already ended. *Woods v. Cloyd M. Miller Co.* (1948). The "**treaty power**," which derives from the authority of the President to make treaties subject to the consent of two-thirds of the Senate and from treaties' status under the Supremacy Clause, authorizes Congress to regulate matters that might otherwise be beyond the scope of federal power. *Missouri v. Holland* (1920).

When Congress acts pursuant to its powers under Article I, it may regulate the states in the same fashion that it regulates private actors. Accordingly, Congress has authority to require the states to pay their employees a minimum wage. *Garcia v. San Antonio Metropolitan Transit Authority* (1985). However, Congress cannot compel a state to enact or administer a federal regulatory program. *New York v. United States* (1992); *Printz v. United States* (1997).

Even though Congress has authority under Article I to regulate the states, it may not invoke those powers to subject the states to private suits for damages without their consent in federal court, *Seminole Tribe of Florida v. Florida* (1996), or state court, *Alden v. Maine* (1999), because of **state sovereign immunity**.

POINT-COUNTERPOINT

Was the expansion of federal powers inevitable? Is it defensible?

POINT: GREGORY E. MAGGS

Congress's powers have increased in three ways since 1789. First, several amendments to the Constitution have added federal powers. The Thirteenth, Fourteenth, and Fifteenth Amendments, for instance, now empower Congress to enforce their prohibitions on slavery, the denial of Due Process and Equal Protection, and voting discrimination. The Sixteenth Amendment now empowers Congress to impose income taxes. The Nineteenth, Twenty-Third, Twenty-Fourth, and Twenty-Sixth Amendments also grant new powers. Adding these powers might not have been inevitable; history could have turned out differently. But certainly the United States would be very different without them. In any event, the process by which these powers were added is clearly defensible. All were adopted according to the amendment procedures in Article V.

Second, changed circumstances have made some grants of power in the Constitution more significant. The Spending Power in Article I, § 8 provides one example. Over time the United States' revenue and credit have grown so much that the government now can spend $2.5 trillion per year, wildly more than it could have done in 1789. Congress's power to raise an Army and a Navy has become more significant now that the United States has the money, technology, and manpower to field the most powerful military forces in the world. Likewise, the power to regulate foreign commerce has taken on more importance now that the United States imports $2.3 trillion of goods and services annually. Similar conclusions hold true for many of Congress's other powers. The expansion of federal powers in this manner is also defensible. The Constitution's grants of power are written without qualification, and surely no one thought in 1789 that economic and other conditions would remain static. The original understanding and hope was that our nation would expand, prosper, and become more powerful.

Third, federal powers have expanded—at least in a practical sense—because the Supreme Court has allowed Congress to enact legislation that exceeds any powers granted in the Constitution. Most significantly, the Supreme Court has revised its interpretation of the Commerce Clause to allow Congress to regulate matters that are, quite simply, not "commerce *** among the several states": wages and hours, production of farm products, etc. Given overwhelming popular demand for federal regulation of these matters, it is perhaps understandable that Congress would attempt to push the bounds of its powers. But the manner of achieving this third type of expansion was neither inevitable nor defensible. If Congress and the people believed that the federal government needed more power, they could have amended the Constitution to grant it, as they have done many times in the past.

Perhaps the harm has not been so significant because Congress generally has enacted popular legislation. But by allowing Congress to skip the amendment process, the Supreme Court has undercut the doctrines of limited powers and judicial review. These doctrines are meant to prevent tyranny, and they should not be weakened when alternatives are so readily available.

———————

COUNTERPOINT: PETER J. SMITH

In 1789, most commerce in the United States was local. There were few reliable means of interstate transportation, and technology for the production of goods was rudimentary. Accordingly, the typical American used and consumed goods that were produced close to home—if not at home itself. Without nationwide (let alone global) economic integration, activity in one area of the country had little meaningful impact on activity elsewhere in the country. Congress thus rarely had occasion to exercise its power to regulate interstate commerce.

Then the world changed. Railroads facilitated the interstate transportation of goods, and new technology dramatically improved production and distribution. Formerly diffuse markets became linked. Wealth spread, but so did the problems that inevitably attend economic progress. And economic integration meant not only that the rising tide would lift many boats, but also that economic trouble could quickly spread far and wide. In this new world, which even the most forward-thinking of the Framers could not possibly have anticipated, activity in one part of the country had meaningful effects even in the most remote areas of the country. Patchwork regulation—if it occurred at all, in light of local pressures to attract jobs—was likely to produce as many negative systemic consequences as positive ones.

These changes alone were enough to lead many to conclude that federal regulation was necessary. And the Great Depression, which caused economic dislocation, unemployment, and general misery on a vast and unprecedented scale, convinced many of the remaining doubters. Economists, of course, continue to disagree about the wisdom of regulation of markets and industry, but that course tends to be popular whenever the market's failures stand in starkest relief—as they did in the 1930s. It thus was inevitable that Congress would assert the authority to regulate more expansively than it ever had before.

Judicial validation of Congress's expansive assertion of authority is fully justified, for at least three reasons. First, the original meaning of Congress's commerce power (not to mention its power under the Necessary and Proper Clause), when viewed at the appropriate level of generality, is entirely consistent with the modern understanding of the scope of Congress's authority. There is no more reason to think that the Framers sought to freeze into the word "commerce" the economic realities of 1789 than there is to think that they sought to freeze into the word "speech" in the First Amendment the limited modes of communication that existed in 1791. Just as no one would seriously contend that political films or webcasts do not count as protected "speech" simply because they did not exist two hundred years ago, we should not confine Congress's power to activity that would have been understood as "commerce," narrowly defined, two hundred years ago. As the world—and, with it, the nature of economic activity—has changed, so necessarily has Congress's power to regulate interstate commerce.

Second, a more restrictive reading of Congress's authority inevitably would require courts to make inherently policy-laden judgments about the propriety of economic regulation in particular circumstances. As we will see in Chapter 9, such an approach is fundamentally inconsistent with the judicial role.

Third, whereas there is considerable need for a judicial role to protect individual rights—because majoritarian political institutions by definition cannot always be trusted to protect minority rights—the need for judicial intervention to protect federalism values is small. Structural features of the Constitution—equal representation in the Senate, for example, and statewide, at-large elections for Senators—mean that there is a built-in check on excessive federal overreaching. And even if the "political safeguards of federalism" do not function perfectly due to changes to the original structural arrangement, they still appear to have some constraining effect. (Consider the presidential campaign of 1980 and the congressional campaign of 1994, both of which saw the election of candidates who pledged to devolve power to the states.)

The cost of judicial intervention, on the other hand, can be great: the invalidation of popular (and at least sometimes desirable) legislation, solely in the name of some amorphous concept of states' rights, a concept that (we must acknowledge) was also deployed cynically to defend slavery and to obstruct the civil rights movement of the twentieth century. The Court's interpretation of the Commerce Clause did not usurp the amendment process. It merely recognized that the Constitution was designed to adapt to change.

CHAPTER 4

Limitations on State Power

Introduction

This chapter covers four important constitutional limitations on state power that concern the role of the states in our federal system. The first limitation addresses the relationship of federal law to state law. As we will see, under the Supremacy Clause in Article VI, federal legislation may "preempt" or supersede state law. The second limitation relates to the power of states to regulate subjects that Congress also may regulate. Specifically, under the so-called "Dormant Commerce Clause Doctrine" (sometimes called the "Negative Commerce Clause Doctrine"), the Supreme Court has held that the grant of power to Congress to regulate interstate commerce implicitly restricts the power of the states to regulate commerce in several ways. The third limitation pertains to relations between states and citizens of other states. The Privileges and Immunities Clause in Article IV prevents states from engaging in certain types of discrimination against residents of other states. The fourth limitation concerns state attempts to regulate Congress by setting qualifications for members of the House and Senate.

These four limitations are by no means the only restrictions that the Constitution places on state law. On the contrary, Article I, § 10 bars the states from entering foreign treaties, coining money, and enacting bills of attainder, ex post facto laws, or laws impairing the obligation of contracts. The same provision says that states, without the consent of Congress, may not impose tariffs on imports or exports, keep troops and ships of war, or enter into compacts with other states. In addition, the Fourteenth Amendment prohibits states from denying any person equal protection or due process of law. The guarantee of due process of law is extremely important because the Supreme Court has held that it includes many of the limitations on governmental action found in the Bill of Rights. Other constitutional amendments impose further limitations on state law. We will consider many of these additional restrictions on state power in subsequent chapters.

A. Preemption of State Law by Federal Law

The **Supremacy Clause** in Article VI makes federal law "supreme" over state laws. As a result, federal law—including federal statutes, federal treaties, and the Constitution—

sometimes will supplant state law that otherwise would apply to a particular situation. The courts describe the displacement of state constitutions, statutes, regulations, and common law rules by federal law as "**federal preemption of state law**."

U.S. Constitution, Article VI, Clause 2

"This Constitution, and the Laws of the United States which shall be made in Pursuance thereof; and all Treaties made, or which shall be made, under the Authority of the United States, shall be the supreme Law of the Land."

This part of the chapter addresses preemption of state laws by federal legislation. Federal legislative preemption is clearly the most common constitutional ground upon which state laws are judicially invalidated. In 2006, for example, more than 2600 reported cases concerned federal preemption of state laws. As both Congress and the states enact new legislation, even more preemption cases may arise in the future.

Federal legislative preemption comes in two basic forms: "express preemption" and "implied preemption." **Express preemption** occurs when Congress expressly displaces state regulation of a particular subject. For example, a provision of the Federal Cigarette Labeling and Advertising Act provides that "[n]o requirement or prohibition based on smoking and health shall be imposed under State law with respect to the advertising or promotion of any cigarettes the packages of which are [lawfully] labeled." But Congress need not directly address the preemptive effect of its laws in order for a court to find preemption; a court can also find that Congress has impliedly preempted state law. **Implied preemption**, in turn, comes in two basic forms: "conflict preemption" and "field preemption." **Conflict preemption** occurs (1) when "compliance with both federal and state regulations is a physical impossibility," *Florida Lime & Avocado Growers, Inc. v. Paul*, 373 U.S. 132, 142-143 (1963), or (2) when state law "stands as an obstacle to the accomplishment and execution of the full purposes and objectives of Congress," *Hines v. Davidowitz*, 312 U.S. 52, 67 (1941). For example, for many years, federal law has required cigarette cartons to contain a label warning consumers of the dangers of tobacco. Even absent any express provision about the effect on state law, the federal law would preempt a state law that attempted to prohibit cigarette cartons from including a warning label, because a cigarette manufacturer could not comply with both the federal and state laws. In addition, the federal law would preempt a state law requiring cigarette cartons to have a label saying: "Don't believe the federal warning label. Smoking is good for you." Although a cigarette manufacturer could comply with the federal law and this hypothetical state law by including both the federal and state labels on each cigarette carton, a court surely would find that the state law undercuts the objective of the federal law (i.e., ensuring that smokers understand the risk of cigarettes). *Cf. Hines*, 312 U.S. at 52 (federal alien registration statute preempted a more burdensome Pennsylvania alien registration statute because the state law posed an obstacle to the federal goal of requiring registration while otherwise preserving aliens' civil liberties).

Field preemption happens when Congress chooses to regulate a subject exclusively by federal law. As the Supreme Court has said, in some instances a "scheme of federal regulation may be so pervasive as to make reasonable the inference that Congress left no room for the States to supplement it." *Rice v. Santa Fe Elevator Corp.*, 331 U.S. 218, 230 (1947). When field preemption occurs, no state laws may apply to the subject, even if the state laws do not directly conflict with the specific requirements of federal law. For example, Congress at one time preempted all state regulation of any type of signal carried by cable television systems. *See Capital Cities Cable, Inc. v. Crisp*, 467 U.S. 691, 698-99 (1984). Field preemption is rarer than conflict preemption. Usually, Congress attempts to regulate only certain aspects of a subject, while leaving additional, non-conflicting regulation to the states.

Silkwood v. Kerr-McGee Corp.

464 U.S. 238 (1984)

Justice WHITE delivered the opinion of the Court.

This case requires us to determine whether a state-authorized award of punitive damages arising out of the escape of plutonium from a federally-licensed nuclear facility is preempted either because it falls within that forbidden field or because it conflicts with some other aspect of the Atomic Energy Act.

Karen Silkwood was a laboratory analyst for Kerr-McGee at its Cimmaron plant near Crescent, Oklahoma. The plant fabricated plutonium fuel pins for use as reactor fuel in nuclear power plants. Accordingly, the plant was subject to licensing and regulation by the Nuclear Regulatory Commission (NRC) pursuant to the Atomic Energy Act, 42 U.S.C. §§ 2011-2284 (1976 ed. and Supp. V).

During a three-day period of November 1974, Silkwood was contaminated by plutonium from the Cimmaron plant. On November 5, Silkwood was grinding and polishing plutonium samples, utilizing glove boxes designed for that purpose. In accordance with established procedures, she checked her hands for contamination when she withdrew them from the glove box. *** A monitoring device revealed contamination on Silkwood's left hand, right wrist, upper arm, neck, hair, and nostrils. She was immediately decontaminated, and at the end of her shift, the monitors detected no contamination. *** The next day, Silkwood arrived at the plant and began doing paperwork in the laboratory. Upon leaving the laboratory, Silkwood monitored herself and again discovered surface contamination. Once again, she was decontaminated.

On the third day, November 7, Silkwood was monitored upon her arrival at the plant. High levels of contamination were detected. Four urine samples and one fecal sample submitted that morning were also highly contaminated. Suspecting that the contamination had spread to areas outside the plant, the company directed a decontamination squad to accompany Silkwood to her apartment. Silkwood's roommate, who was also an employee at the plant, was *** also contaminated, although to a lesser degree than Silkwood. The squad then monitored the apartment, finding contamination in several rooms, with especially high levels in the bathroom, the kitchen, and Silkwood's bedroom.

FYI

In 1983, Hollywood made a movie about Karen Silkwood's experience called *Silkwood*. Starring Meryl Streep, Kurt Russell, and Cher, the film was nominated for 5 Oscars. Generations of law students have rented this film while studying constitutional law.

The contamination level in Silkwood's apartment was such that many of her personal belongings had to be destroyed. Silkwood herself was sent to the Los Alamos Scientific Laboratory to determine the extent of contamination in her vital body organs. She returned to work on November 13. That night, she was killed in an unrelated automobile accident.

Bill Silkwood, Karen's father, brought the present diversity action in his capacity as administrator of her estate. The action was based on common law tort principles under Oklahoma law and was designed to recover for the contamination injuries to Karen's person and property. ***

The jury returned a verdict in favor of Silkwood, finding actual damages of $505,000 ($500,000 for personal injuries and $5,000 for property damage) and punitive damages of $10,000,000. [The Court of Appeals reversed the $500,000 award for personal injuries because the Oklahoma workers' compensation law did not permit this recovery. The Court of Appeals further held that federal laws regulating the Kerr-McGee facility preempted state tort law, barring recovery of punitive damages.]

As we recently observed in *Pacific Gas & Electric Co. v. State Energy Resources Conservation & Development Comm'n*, 461 U.S. 190 (1983), state law can be preempted in either of two general ways. If Congress evidences an intent to occupy a given field, any state law falling within that field is preempted. If Congress has not entirely displaced state regulation over the matter in question, state law is still preempted to the extent it actually conflicts with federal law, that is, when it is impossible to comply with both state and federal law, or where the state law stands as an obstacle to the accomplishment of the full purposes and objectives of Congress. Kerr-McGee contends that the award in this case is invalid under either analysis. We consider each of these contentions in turn.

Take Note

In this paragraph, the Court summarizes the different ways that federal law may impliedly preempt state law. The Supreme Court consistently uses this framework in federal preemption cases. Are the different types of preemption truly distinct, or is there often overlap between the two?

In *Pacific Gas & Electric*, an examination of the statutory scheme and legislative history of the Atomic Energy Act convinced us that "Congress . . . intended that the federal government regulate the radiological safety aspects involved . . . in the construction and operation of a nuclear plant." 461 U.S. at 205. Thus, we concluded that "the federal government has occupied the entire field of nuclear safety concerns, except the limited powers expressly ceded to the states." <u>Id. at 211</u>.

Kerr-McGee argues that our ruling in <u>Pacific Gas & Electric</u> is dispositive of the issue in this case. Noting that "regulation can be as effectively asserted through an award of damages as through some form of preventive relief," *San Diego Building Trades Council v. Garmon,* 359 U.S. 236, 247 (1959), Kerr-McGee submits that because the state-authorized award of punitive damages in this case punishes and deters conduct related to radiation hazards, it falls within the prohibited field. However, a review of the same legislative history which prompted our holding in <u>Pacific Gas & Electric,</u> coupled with an examination of Congress' actions with respect to other portions of the Atomic Energy Act, convinces us that the preempted field does not extend as far as Kerr-McGee would have it.

As we recounted in <u>Pacific Gas & Electric</u>, "[u]ntil 1954 [the] use, control and ownership of nuclear technology remained a federal monopoly." <u>461 U.S. at 206</u>. In that year, Congress enacted legislation which provided for private involvement in the development of atomic energy. However, the federal government retained extensive control over the manner in which this development occurred. In particular, the Atomic Energy Commission (the predecessor of the NRC) was given "exclusive jurisdiction to license the transfer, delivery, receipt, acquisition, possession and use of nuclear materials." *Id.* at 207.

In 1959 Congress amended the Atomic Energy Act in order to "clarify the respective responsibilities of the States and the Commission with respect to the regulation of byproduct, source, and special nuclear materials." 42 U.S.C. § 2021(a)(1). The Commission was authorized to turn some of its regulatory authority over to any state which would adopt a suitable regulatory program. However, the Commission was to retain exclusive regulatory authority over "the disposal of such . . . byproduct, source, or special nuclear material as the Commission determines . . . should, because of the hazards or potential hazards thereof, not be disposed of without a license from the Commission." 42 U.S.C. § 2021(c)(4). The states were therefore still precluded from regulating the safety aspects of these hazardous materials.

Congress' decision to prohibit the states from regulating the safety aspects of nuclear development was premised on its belief that the Commission was more qualified to determine what type of safety standards should be enacted in this complex area. As Congress was informed by the AEC, the 1959 legislation provided for continued federal control over the more hazardous materials because "the technical safety considerations are of such complexity that it is not likely that any State would be prepared to deal with them during the foreseeable future." H.R.Rep. No. 1125, 86th Cong., 1st Sess. 3 (1959). If there were nothing more, this concern over the states' inability to formulate effective standards and the foreclosure of the states from conditioning the operation of nuclear plants on compliance with state-imposed safety standards arguably would disallow resort to state-law remedies by those suffering injuries from radiation in a nuclear plant. There is, however, ample evidence that Congress had no intention of forbidding the states from providing such remedies.

Indeed, there is no indication that Congress even seriously considered precluding the use of such remedies either when it enacted the Atomic Energy Act in 1954 or when it amended it in 1959. This silence takes on added significance in light of Congress' failure to provide any federal remedy for persons injured by such conduct. It is difficult to believe that Congress would, without comment, remove all means of judicial recourse for those injured by illegal conduct.

More importantly, the only congressional discussion concerning the relationship between the Atomic Energy Act and state tort remedies indicates that Congress assumed that such remedies would be available. After the 1954 law was enacted, private companies contemplating entry into the nuclear industry expressed concern over potentially bankrupting state-law suits arising out of a nuclear incident. As a result, in 1957 Congress passed the Price-Anderson Act, an amendment to the Atomic Energy Act. Pub.L. 85-256, 71 Stat. 576 (1957). That Act established an indemnification scheme under which operators of licensed nuclear facilities could be required to obtain up to $60 million in private financial protection against such suits. The government would then provide indemnification for the next $500 million of liability, and the resulting $560 million would be the limit of liability for any one nuclear incident.

Although the Price-Anderson Act does not apply to the present situation, the discussion preceding its enactment and subsequent amendment indicates that Congress assumed that persons injured by nuclear accidents were free to utilize existing state tort law remedies. The Joint Committee Report on the original version of the Price-Anderson Act explained the relationship between the Act and existing state tort law as follows:

> "Since the rights of third parties who are injured are established by State law, there is no interference with the State law until there is a likelihood that the damages exceed the amount of financial responsibility required together with the amount of the indemnity. At that point the Federal interference is limited to the prohibition of making payments through the state courts and to prorating the proceeds available."

S.Rep. No. 296, 85th Cong., 1st Sess. 9 (1957), U.S. Code Cong. & Admin. News 1957, pp. 1803, 1810.

Kerr-McGee focuses on the differences between compensatory and punitive damages awards and asserts that, at most, Congress intended to allow the former. This argument, however, is misdirected because our inquiry is not whether Congress expressly allowed punitive damages awards. Punitive damages have long been a part of traditional state tort law. As we noted above, Congress assumed that traditional principles of state tort law would apply with full force unless they were expressly supplanted. Thus, it is Kerr-McGee's burden to show that Congress intended to preclude such awards. Yet, the company is unable to point to anything in the legislative history or in the regulations that indicates that punitive damages were not to be allowed. To the contrary, the regulations issued implementing the insurance provisions of the Price-Anderson Act themselves contemplate that punitive damages might be awarded under state law.

In sum, it is clear that in enacting and amending the Price-Anderson Act, Congress assumed that state-law remedies, in whatever form they might take, were available to those injured by nuclear incidents. This was so even though it was well aware of the NRC's exclusive authority to regulate safety matters. No doubt there is tension between the conclusion that safety regulation is the exclusive concern of the federal law and the conclusion that a state may nevertheless award damages based on its own law of liability. But as we understand what was done over the years in the legislation concerning nuclear energy, Congress intended to stand by both concepts and to tolerate whatever tension there was between them. We can do no less. It may be that the award of damages based on the state law of negligence or strict liability is regulatory in the sense that a nuclear plant will be threatened with damages liability if it does not conform to state standards, but that regulatory consequence was something that Congress was quite willing to accept.

Definition
The phrase *amicus curiae* means "friend of the court." The term refers to someone who is not a party to a lawsuit but whom a court allows to file a brief. The Supreme Court often invites the Solicitor General of the United States to file briefs as *amicus curiae* in cases concerning federal legislation when the United States is not a party.

The United States, as amicus curiae, contends that the award of punitive damages in this case is preempted because it conflicts with the federal remedial scheme, noting that the NRC is authorized to impose civil penalties on licensees when federal standards have been violated. However, the award of punitive damages in the present case does not conflict with that scheme. Paying both federal fines and state-imposed punitive damages for the same incident would not appear to be physically impossible. Nor does exposure to punitive damages frustrate any purpose of the federal remedial scheme.

Justice BLACKMUN, with whom Justice MARSHALL joins, dissenting.

The principles set forth in <u>Pacific Gas</u> compel the conclusion that the punitive damages awarded in this case, and now upheld, are pre-empted. The prospect of paying a large fine—in this case a potential $10 million—for failure to operate a nuclear facility in a particular manner has an obvious effect on the safety precautions that nuclear licensees will follow. The Court does not dispute, moreover, that punitive damages are expressly designed for this purpose. Punitive damages are "private fines levied by civil juries." *Gertz v. Robert Welch, Inc.*, 418 U.S. 323, 350 (1974). ***

Points for Discussion

a. Field Preemption and Conflict Preemption

What kind of preemption did Kerr-McGee ask the Court to find in this case? What kind of preemption did the United States as *amicus curiae* ask the court to find? What kind of preemption did the dissent think existed? Why did the Court find neither kind of preemption?

b. Reason for Federal Preemption of State Law

What policy consideration may have justified inclusion of the Supremacy Clause in the Constitution? Some history may help in answering this question. When the states were deciding whether to ratify the Constitution, federal preemption was a major issue. Opponents of the Constitution argued that the Supremacy Clause made the federal government too powerful. But Alexander Hamilton argued in response that federal laws had to be supreme if they were to have any force. He wrote in Federalist No. 33: "[W]hat would they amount to, if they were not to be supreme? It is evident they would amount to nothing. A LAW by the very meaning of the term includes supremacy. It is a rule which those to whom it is prescribed are bound to observe." Can you explain Hamilton's argument? Why would a federal law "amount to nothing" if it were not supreme over state law?

c. Basic Policy Question Regarding Preemption

A leading commentator on Constitutional Law has concisely summarized the basic policy question regarding preemption as follows: "Ultimately, preemption doctrines are about allocating governing authority between federal and state governments. A broad view of preemption leaves less room for governance by state and local governments." Erwin Chemerinsky, Constitutional Law: Principles and Policies 287 (1997). In considering this policy question, note that the Supreme Court has announced the following principle: "In all pre-emption cases, and particularly in those [where] Congress has legislated *** in a field which the States have traditionally occupied, we start with the assumption that the historic police powers of the States were not to be superseded by the Federal Act unless that was the clear and manifest purpose of Congress." *Medtronic, Inc. v. Lohr,* 518 U.S. 470, 485 (1996). What does this presumption regarding preemption say about the Court's position on the basic policy question?

——————————

Hypothetical

Federal law authorizes the Secretary of Agriculture to "establish and maintain minimum standards of quality and maturity" for agricultural commodities. Each year, the Secretary has promulgated a regulation that forbids the picking and shipping of avocados before a certain date, to ensure quality and maturity. California law prohibits the sale of avocados that contain less than 8 percent oil. A trade group representing Florida avocado growers filed suit to enjoin enforcement of the California law against Florida avocados certified as mature under the federal regulations. How should the Court rule?

B.   The Dormant Commerce Clause Doctrine

As we saw in Chapter 3, Article I, § 8 of the Constitution grants a number of important powers to Congress. Congress can impose taxes, spend money, regulate commerce, create post offices, raise an army and navy, and so forth. We have already considered what Congress may do with these powers. A separate issue, examined here, is whether the mere grant of these powers to Congress divests the state governments of any powers. This question does not have a simple answer.

Some of the powers listed in Article I, § 8 belong exclusively to Congress. For example, Article I, § 8, clause 5 gives Congress the right to coin money, and Article I, §10, clause 1 then says that the states may not coin money. Therefore, Congress may coin money but the states may not. But Congress and the states share other powers. For example, although Article I, § 8, clause 1 gives Congress the power to impose taxes and spend money, no one has ever thought that the states lost this power by ratifying the Constitution. On the contrary, although Congress raises revenue and spends money, the states have their own taxes, their own treasuries, and their own expenditures.

> **Make the Connection**
>
> Recall that the Court in *McCulloch* acknowledged that the states have concurrent power to tax, even though there may be some federalism-based limits on their ability to exercise that power.

Still other powers fall somewhere in between; they are neither exclusively federal nor equally shared between the federal and state governments. For example, Article I, § 8, clause 12 gives Congress the power to raise an Army. Article I, § 10, clause 3 then says that the states cannot keep troops "without the consent of Congress." In other words, states can have an armed force, but only if Congress allows it.

Into which of these different categories does the very important power of regulating commerce fall? It might seem that the power is concurrently enjoyed by the federal and state governments. We know from Chapter 3 that Congress has the power to regulate not only commerce itself, but also the instrumentalities and channels of commerce, and even intrastate economic activities that substantially affect interstate commerce. At the same time, no one doubts that the states also may regulate commerce. For example, as you will learn in your other law school classes, most contract law and commercial law is state law.

But the answer is not so simple. Over time, the Supreme Court has said that the grant of power to Congress in Article I, § 8, clause 3 to regulate interstate commerce imposes several implicit restrictions on state regulations of commerce, all of which we will see in the cases below. The Court has struggled to define the precise contours of these limitations. At one time, the Court insisted that states cannot regulate subjects for which national uniformity is necessary; at another time, the Court held that although the states can enact laws that have only an "indirect" effect on interstate commerce, they lack power to enact laws that "directly" interfere with interstate commerce. As we saw in our unit on Congress's power under the Commerce Clause, the Court has abandoned the direct-effects test for allocating power between the states and the federal government, but the Court has never formally abandoned the "uniform national standards" test.

Under current doctrine, which we explore in detail below, a state cannot treat interstate commerce differently from intrastate commerce when there is a reasonable, nondiscriminatory, alternative way of furthering the state's legitimate interests. Legitimate local interests include protecting health and safety, conserving natural resources, and similar things, but do not include protecting local businesses from competition. In addition, a state cannot impose a burden on interstate commerce that is excessive in relation to legitimate local interests.

These limitations make up the so-called "**Dormant Commerce Clause Doctrine**" (also known as the "**Negative Commerce Clause Doctrine**"). The name of this doctrine has a simple explanation. A power of Congress is "dormant" if the power exists but is not being exercised. Under the Dormant Commerce Clause Doctrine, even if Congress has not attempted to regulate a particular aspect of commerce that Congress could regulate, Congress's dormant power has a "negative" implication: namely, that the states are subject to the implied limitations discussed above.

The traditional justification given for the Dormant Commerce Clause Doctrine is that the United States adopted the Constitution to address problems that had arisen under the Articles of Confederation. One of the major issues facing the Union in the 1780s was that individual states were enacting tariffs and regulations that inhibited interstate commerce. In Federalist No. 22, Alexander Hamilton explained that these burdensome state-law restrictions on trade were causing discord among the states and that the impediments to trade were likely to get worse unless something were done about them on the national level. Hamilton wrote: "The interfering and unneighbourly regulations of some states contrary to the true spirit of the Union, have in different instances given just cause of umbrage and complaint to others; and it is to be feared that examples of this nature, if not restrained by a national controul, would be multiplied and extended till they became *** injurious impediments to the intercourse between the different parts of the confederacy."

Hamilton and other supporters of the Constitution clearly believed that including the Commerce Clause in Article I, § 8 would address this problem. The Supreme Court, accordingly, has concluded that the mere presence of the Commerce Clause in the Constitution may bar burdensome or discriminatory state commerce regulations. But critics of the Dormant Commerce Clause Doctrine have a different view. They believe that the Commerce Clause gives Congress the power to regulate interstate commerce, including the power to preempt state laws concerning commerce, but that Congress must exercise that power by enacting legislation before any preemption can occur. In their view, the Commerce Clause in its dormant state has no effect on state regulations. You will see this disagreement between the Court and the dissenting Justices in some of the cases included in this Chapter.

1. Early Cases

Early suggestions that the grant of power to Congress to regulate commerce might limit state power to regulate commerce appeared first in *Gibbons v. Ogden*, the landmark case on the Commerce Clause included at the start of Chapter 3.

Gibbons v. Ogden

22 U.S. (9 Wheat.) 1, 190 (1824)

[Recall that Gibbons, the appellant, challenged the constitutionality of a New York law that would restrain him from offering steamboat service from New Jersey to New York. One of Gibbons's arguments was that the New York law was unconstitutional because the Constitution grants Congress the exclusive power to regulate interstate commerce. The Supreme Court found it unnecessary to decide this question because the Court concluded that a federal statute, the Federal Licensing Act, preempted the New York law. But the Court addressed the argument briefly as follows.]

FYI

Gibbons was represented by one of the greatest lawyers in American history, Daniel Webster (1782-1852). Webster served in Congress as a member of the House of Representatives from New Hampshire and later as a Senator from Massachusetts. He also was a Secretary of State. Webster argued several important Supreme Court cases, including *McCulloch v. Maryland* and *Gibbons v. Ogden*.

The appellant *** contends that full power to regulate a particular subject implies the whole power, and leaves no residuum; that a grant of the whole is incompatible with the existence of a right in another to any part of it.

The grant of the power to lay and collect taxes is, like the power to regulate commerce, made in general terms, and has never been understood to interfere with the exercise of the same power by the State; and hence has been drawn an argument which has been applied to the question under consideration. But the two grants are not, it is conceived, similar in their terms or their nature. Although many of the powers formerly exercised by the States are transferred to the government of the Union, yet the State governments remain, and constitute a most important part of our system. The power of taxation is indispensable to their existence, and is a power which, in its own nature, is capable of residing in, and being exercised by, different authorities at the same time. *** When *** each government exercises the power of taxation, neither is exercising the power of the other. But, when a State proceeds to regulate commerce with foreign nations, or among the several States, it is exercising the very power that is granted to Congress, and is doing the very thing which Congress is authorized to do. There is no analogy, then, between the power of taxation and the power of regulating commerce.

In discussing the question, whether this power is still in the States, in the case under consideration, we may dismiss from it the inquiry, whether it is surrendered by the mere grant to Congress, or is retained until Congress shall exercise the power. We may dismiss that inquiry, because it has been exercised, and the regulations which Congress deemed it proper to make, are now in full operation. The sole question is, can a State regulate commerce with foreign nations and among the States, while Congress is regulating it?

It is obvious, that the government of the Union, in the exercise of its express powers, that, for example, of regulating commerce with foreign nations and among the States, may use means that may also be employed by a State, in the exercise of its acknowledged powers; that, for example, of regulating commerce within the State. If Congress license vessels to sail from one port to another, in the same State, the act is supposed to be, necessarily, incidental to the power expressly granted to Congress, and implies no claim of a direct power to regulate the purely internal commerce of a State, or to act directly on its system of police. So, if a State, in passing laws on subjects acknowledged to be within its control, and with a view to those subjects, shall adopt a measure of the same character with one which Congress may adopt, it does not derive its authority from the particular power which has been granted, but from some other, which remains with the State, and may be executed by the same means. All experience shows, that the same measures, or measures scarcely distinguishable from each other, may flow from distinct powers; but this does not prove that the powers themselves are identical. Although the means used in their execution may sometimes approach each other so nearly as to be confounded, there are other situations in which they are sufficiently distinct to establish their individuality.

In our complex system, presenting the rare and difficult scheme of one general government, whose action extends over the whole, but which possesses only certain enumerated powers; and of numerous State governments, which retain and exercise all powers not delegated to the Union, contests respecting power must arise. Were it even otherwise, the measures taken by the respective governments to execute their acknowledged powers, would often be of the same description, and might, sometimes, interfere. This, however, does not prove that the one is exercising, or has a right to exercise, the powers of the other.

It has been contended by the counsel for the appellant, that, as the word "to regulate" implies in its nature, full power over the thing to be regulated, it excludes, necessarily, the action of all others that would perform the same operation on the same thing. That regulation is designed for the entire result, applying to those parts which remain as they were, as well as to those which are altered. It produces a uniform whole, which is as much disturbed and deranged by changing what the regulating power designs to leave untouched, as that on which it has operated.

> **Take Note**
>
> The Supreme Court summarizes here what Gibbons argued about the effect of the Commerce Clause. What does the initial sentence of the paragraph mean? Does the Court agree or disagree with the argument?

There is great force in this argument, and the Court is not satisfied that it has been refuted.

Mr. Justice JOHNSON.

The judgment entered by the Court in this cause, has my entire approbation; but having adopted my conclusions on views of the subject materially different from those of my brethren, I feel it incumbent on me to exhibit those views. I have, also, another inducement: in questions of great importance and great delicacy, I feel my duty to the public best discharged, by an effort to maintain my opinions in my own way.

In attempts to construe the constitution, I have never found much benefit resulting from the inquiry, whether the whole, or any part of it, is to be construed strictly, or literally. The simple, classical, precise, yet comprehensive language, in which it is couched, leaves, at most, but very little latitude for construction; and when its intent and meaning is discovered, nothing remains but to execute the will of those who made it, in the best manner to effect the purposes intended. The great and paramount purpose, was to unite this mass of wealth and power, for the protection of the humblest individual; his rights, civil and political, his interests and prosperity, are the sole end; the rest are nothing but the means. But the principal of those means, one so essential as to approach nearer the characteristics of an end, was the independence and harmony of the States, that they may the better subserve the purposes of cherishing and protecting the respective families of this great republic.

If there was any one object riding over every other in the adoption of the constitution, it was to keep the commercial intercourse among the States free from all invidious and partial restraints. And I cannot overcome the conviction, that if the licensing act was repealed to-morrow, the rights of the appellant to a reversal of the decision complained of, would be as strong as it is under this license.

Points for Discussion

a. Relationship of Preemption to the Dormant Commerce Clause Doctrine

The majority opinion exhibits the standard understanding of the relationship of statutory preemption to the Dormant Commerce Clause Doctrine. If Congress has enacted legislation that governs a particular issue, then the federal statute preempts any state laws, and there is no need to apply the Dormant Commerce Clause Doctrine.

b. Meaning of the Concurring Opinion

Although the majority of the Court in *Gibbons* found it unnecessary to decide whether the state law would have violated the Commerce Clause in the absence of federal legislation, Justice Johnson reached this issue in his concurrence. How did he justify his conclusion? What was his method of interpreting the Constitution?

c. The Police Power of the States

In *Willson v. Black–Bird Creek Co.*, 27 U.S. (2 Pet.) 245 (1829), Delaware enacted legislation authorizing the Black Bird Creek Company to construct a dam over a small river. After the dam was built, the owners of a sloop broke up the dam so that their vessel could navigate the river. When the Black Bird Creek Company sued the owners of the sloop for damages, the owners argued in defense that they were not liable because they had a federal right to use the river and Delaware could not abridge this right by authorizing the construction of the dam. Chief Justice John Marshall, writing for the court, rejected this argument. He said: "We do not think that the act [of Delaware] empowering the Black Bird Creek Marsh Company to place a dam across the creek, can, under all the circumstances of the case, be considered as repugnant to the power [of Congress] to regulate commerce in its dormant state, or as being in conflict with any law passed on the subject." The Dormant Commerce Clause Doctrine acquired its name from this statement; the word "dormant" means "asleep." Why would the federal power to regulate commerce be considered dormant in this case?

For some years after the *Willson* decision, the Supreme Court suggested that the states might have a "police power"—meaning a power to regulate for the protection of local health and safety—unaffected by the Commerce Clause. But this theory that the states had a separate sphere of legislative authority ultimately "did not prove to be a useful tool" for deciding cases. John E. Nowak & Ronald D. Rotunda, Constitutional Law 284 (5th ed. 1995). The Supreme Court instead adopted different limitations, discussed below, as it searched for the limitations that now make up the Dormant Commerce Clause Doctrine.

—————

2. The "Uniform National Standard" Test

Two decades after the Supreme Court decided *Gibbons v. Ogden* and *Willson v. Black-Bird Creek*, the Court became more specific about the negative implications of the Commerce Clause. In *Cooley v. Board of Wardens*, 53 U.S. (12 How.) 299 (1851), reprinted below, the Court announced a situation in which the grant of power to Congress to regulate commerce would limit state laws: namely, when the states attempt to regulate a subject for which a **uniform national standard** is necessary. In *Cooley*, the Supreme Court ultimately concluded that a uniform national standard was not needed and therefore did not invalidate the state law at issue. But as you will see, the Court reached the opposite conclusion in the case that follows, *Wabash, St. L. & P. Ry. Co. v. Illinois*, 118 U.S. 557 (1886). Consider how the "uniform national standard" test came into being, and why the Court reached different conclusions about its application in the two cases.

Cooley v. Board of Wardens

53 U.S. (12 How.) 299 (1851)

Mr. Justice CURTIS delivered the opinion of the Court.

These cases are brought here by writs of error to the Supreme Court of the Commonwealth of Pennsylvania. They are actions to recover half pilotage fees under the 29th section of the act of the Legislature of Pennsylvania, passed on the second day of March, 1803. The plaintiff in error alleges that the highest court of the state has decided against a right *** to be exempted from the payment of the sums of money demanded, pursuant to the State law above referred to, because that law contravenes several provisions of the Constitution of the United States.

The particular section of the state law drawn in question is as follows:

> "That every ship or vessel arriving from or bound to any foreign port or place, and every ship or vessel of the burden of seventy-five tons or more, sailing from or bound to any port not within the river Delaware, shall be obliged to receive a pilot. *** And if the master of any such ship or vessel shall refuse or neglect to take a pilot, the master, owner or consignee of such vessel shall forfeit and pay *** a sum equal to the half-pilotage of such ship or vessel ***."

We think this particular regulation concerning half-pilotage fees, is an appropriate part of a general system of regulations of this subject. Testing it by the practice of commercial states and countries legislating on this subject, we find it has usually been deemed necessary to make similar provisions. Numerous laws of this kind are cited in the learned argument of the counsel for the defendant in error; and their fitness, as a part of the system of pilotage, in many places, may be inferred from their existence in so many different states and countries. Like other laws they are framed to meet the most usual cases ***; they rest upon the propriety of securing lives and property exposed to the perils of a dangerous navigation, by taking on board a person peculiarly skilled to encounter or avoid them; upon the policy of discouraging the commanders of vessels from refusing to receive such persons on board at the proper times and places; and upon the expediency, and even intrinsic justice, of not suffering those who have incurred labor, and expense, and danger, to place themselves in a position to render important service generally necessary, to go unrewarded, because the master of a particular vessel either rashly refuses their proffered assistance, or, contrary to the general experience, does not need it. ***

It remains to consider the objection, that it is repugnant to the third clause of the eighth section of the first article [of the Constitution]. *** That the power to regulate commerce includes the regulation of navigation, we consider settled. And when we look to the nature of the service performed by pilots, to the relations which that service and its compensations bear to navigation between the several states, and between the ports of the United States and foreign countries, we are brought to the conclusion, that the regulation of the qualifications of pilots, of the modes and times of offering and rendering their services, of the responsibilities which shall rest upon them, of the powers they shall possess, of the compensation they may demand, and of the penalties by which their rights and duties may be enforced, do constitute regulations of navigation, and consequently of commerce, within the just meaning of this clause of the Constitution.

> **Make the Connection**
>
> Recall that the Court held in *Gibbons* that "commerce" includes navigation.

*** [W]e are brought directly and unavoidably to the consideration of the question, whether the grant of the commercial power to Congress, did *per se* deprive the states of all power to regulate pilots. This question has never been decided by this court, nor, in our judgment, has any case depending upon all the considerations which must govern this one, come before this court. The grant of commercial power to Congress does not contain any terms which expressly exclude the states from exercising an authority over its subject-matter. If they are excluded it must be because the nature of the power, thus granted to Congress, requires that a similar authority should not exist in the states. If it were conceded on the one side, that the nature of this power, like that to legislate for the District of Columbia, is absolutely and totally repugnant to the existence of similar power in the states, probably no one would deny that the grant of the power to Congress, as effectually and perfectly excludes the states from all future legislation on the subject, as if express words had been used to exclude them. And on the other hand, if it were admitted that the existence of this power in Congress, like the power of taxation, is compatible with the existence of a similar power in the states, then it would be in conformity with the contemporary exposition of the Constitution (The Federalist, No. 32), and with the judicial construction, given from time to time by this court, after the most deliberate consideration, to hold that the mere grant of such a power to Congress, did not imply a prohibition on the states to exercise the same power; that it is not the mere existence of such a power, but its exercise by Congress, which may be incompatible with the exercise of the same power by the states, and that the states may legislate in the absence of congressional regulations.

Either absolutely to affirm, or deny that the nature of this power requires exclusive legislation by Congress, is to lose sight of the nature of the subjects of this power, and to assert concerning all of them, what is really applicable but to a part. Whatever subjects of this power are in their nature national, or admit only of one uniform system, or plan of regulation, may justly be said to be of such a nature as to require exclusive legislation by Congress. That this cannot be affirmed of laws for the regulation of pilots and pilotage is plain. The act of 1789[*] contains a clear and authoritative declaration by the first Congress, that the nature of this subject is such, that until Congress should find it necessary to exert its power, it should be left to the legislation of the states; that it is local and not national; that it is likely to be the best provided for, not by one system, or plan of regulations, but by as many as the legislative discretion of the several states should deem applicable to the local peculiarities of the ports within their limits.

Take Note

Here is where the Court establishes the rule that the Commerce Clause prevents the states from regulating subjects that require a uniform national standard. What logic leads the Court to create this rule?

Viewed in this light, so much of this act of 1789 as declares that pilots shall continue to be regulated "by such laws as the states may respectively hereafter enact for that purpose," instead of being held to be inoperative, as an attempt to confer on the states a power to legislate, of which the Constitution had deprived them, is allowed an appropriate and important signification. It manifests the understanding of Congress, at the outset of the government, that the nature of this subject is not such as to require its exclusive legislation. The practice of the states, and of the national government, has been in conformity with this declaration, from the origin of the national government to this time; and the nature of the subject when examined, is such as to leave no doubt of the superior fitness and propriety, not to say the absolute necessity, of different systems of regulation, drawn from local knowledge and experience, and conformed to local wants.

Food for Thought

If the states cannot regulate matters that require a uniform national standard, but the Court defers to Congress's judgment about what matters require such a standard, then why is there a need for a judicially enforced Dormant Commerce Clause Doctrine in the first place?

It is the opinion of a majority of the court that the mere grant to Congress of the power to regulate commerce, did not deprive the states of power to regulate pilots, and that although Congress has legislated on this subject, its legislation manifests an intention, with a single exception, not to regulate this subject, but to leave its regulation to the several states.

---

[*] In 1789, Congress enacted a law saying "all pilots in the bays, inlets, rivers, harbors, and ports of the United States shall continue to be regulated in conformity with the existing laws of the states, respectively, wherein such pilots may be, or with such laws as the states may respectively hereafter enact for the purpose, until further legislative provision shall be made by Congress." This law did not apply to the present case because the Pennsylvania law was enacted after 1789. But the federal law did indicate that Congress was content to allow some state regulations to govern pilotage.—Eds.

Wabash, St. L. & P. Ry. Co. v. Illinois

118 U.S. 557 (1886)

MILLER, J.

This is a writ of error to the supreme court of Illinois. *** The first count [charged] that the Wabash, St. Louis & Pacific Railway Company had, in violation of a statute of the state of Illinois, been guilty of an unjust discrimination in its rates or charges of toll and compensation for the transportation of freight. The specific allegation is that the railroad company charged Elder & McKinney for transporting 26,000 pounds of goods and chattels from Peoria, in the state of Illinois, to New York city, the sum of $39, being at the rate of 15 cents per hundred pounds for said car-load; and that on the same day they agreed to carry and transport for Isaac Bailey and F. O. Swannell another car-load of goods and chattels from Gilman, in the state of Illinois, to said city of New York, for which they charged the sum of $65, being at the rate of 25 cents per hundred pounds. *** This freight being of the same class in both instances, and carried over the same road, except as to the difference in the distance, it is obvious that a discrimination against Bailey & Swannell was made in the charges against them, as compared with those against Elder & McKinney; and this is true whether we regard the charge for the whole distance from the terminal points in Illinois to New York city, or the proportionate charge for the haul within the state of Illinois.

The language of the statute which is supposed to be violated by this transaction is *** that if any railroad corporation shall charge, collect, or receive, for the transportation of any passenger or freight of any description upon its railroad, for any distance within the state, the same or a greater amount of toll or compensation than is at the same time charged, collected, or received for the transportation in the same direction of any passenger or like quantity of freight of the same class over a greater distance of the same road, all such discriminating rates, charges, collections, or receipts, whether made directly or by means of rebate, drawback, or other shift or evasion, shall be deemed and taken against any such railroad corporation as *prima facie* evidence of unjust discrimination prohibited by the provisions of this act. ***

If the Illinois statute could be construed to apply exclusively to contracts for a carriage which begins and ends within the state, disconnected from a continuous transportation through or into other states, there does not seem to be any difficulty in holding it to be valid. For instance, a contract might be made to carry goods for a certain price from Cairo to Chicago, or from Chicago to Alton. The charges for these might be within the competency of the Illinois legislature to regulate. The reason for this is that both the charge and the actual transportation in such cases are exclusively confined to the limits of the territory of the state, and is not commerce among the states, or interstate commerce, but is exclusively commerce within the state. So far, therefore, as this class of trans-

Food for Thought

Alton, Cairo, and Chicago are cities in the state of Illinois. Given the Court's modern interpretation of the scope of the Commerce Clause, is it clear that such intrastate rates would not be within Congress's power to regulate? Recall the *Shreveport Rate Case*, which we considered in Chapter 3.

portation, as an element of commerce, is affected by the statute under consideration, it is not subject to the constitutional provision concerning commerce among the states. ***

The supreme court of Illinois does not place its judgment in the present case on the ground that the transportation and the charge are exclusively state commerce, but, conceding that it may be a case of commerce among the states, or interstate commerce, which congress would have the right to regulate if it had attempted to do so, argues that this statute of Illinois belongs to that class of commercial regulations which may be established by the laws of a state until congress shall have exercised its power on that subject ***.

[There is a] class of regulations of commerce which, like pilotage, bridging navigable rivers, and many others, could be acted upon by the states, in the absence of any legislation by congress on the same subject. By the slightest attention to the matter, it will be readily seen that the circumstances under which a bridge may be authorized across a navigable stream within the limits of a state for the use of a public highway, and the local rules which shall govern the conduct of the pilots of each of the varying harbors of the coasts of the United States, depend upon principles far more limited in their application and importance than those which should regulate the transportation of persons and property across the half or the whole of the continent, over the territories of half a dozen states, through which they are carried without change of car or breaking bulk.

Of the justice or propriety of the principle which lies at the foundation of the Illinois statute it is not the province of this court to speak. As restricted to a transportation which begins and ends within the limits of the state, it may be very just and equitable, and it certainly is the province of the state legislature to determine that question; but when it is attempted to apply to transportation through an entire series of states a principle of this kind, and each one of the states shall attempt to establish its own rates of transportation, its own methods to prevent discrimination in rates, or to permit it, the deleterious influence upon the freedom of commerce among the states, and upon the transit of goods through those states, cannot be overestimated. That this species of regulation is one which must be, if established at all, of a general and national character, and cannot be safely and wisely remitted to local rules and local regulations, we think is clear from

> **Take Note**
>
> The Court concludes here that, if rates for interstate transportation of goods are to be regulated, they must be regulated by a uniform national standard. Why does the Court reach this conclusion?

what has already been said. And if it be a regulation of commerce, as we think we have demonstrated it is, and as the Illinois court concedes it to be, it must be of that national character; and the regulation can only appropriately exist by general rules and principles, which demand that it should be done by the congress of the United States under the commerce clause of the constitution.

The judgment of the supreme court of Illinois is therefore reversed, and the case remanded to that court for further proceedings in conformity with this opinion.

Points for Discussion

a. Justifying the Court's Conclusion

Suppose a railroad wants to carry goods from New Jersey to Massachusetts. Suppose further that New Jersey law says that the railroad must charge a rate of 15¢ per hundred pounds for this interstate journey, but Massachusetts law says that the railroad may not charge a rate of more than 10¢ per hundred pounds for the journey. Does this hypothetical illustrate why, as the Court says in this case, state regulation of interstate transportation rates is "inappropriate" and that any regulation must be of "a general national character"?

b. Comparison

How does the regulation of railroad rates in this case differ from the regulation of ship pilotage in local harbors in *Cooley v. Board of Wardens*? Why did the Supreme Court think that a uniform national rule concerning piloting ships into harbors was not necessary, but that one for railroad rates was necessary?

c. Wisdom of the State Law

Notice how the Court refuses to consider the "justice or propriety" of the Illinois law, but instead focuses only on whether the law concerns a matter for which uniform national regulation is required. Why is the wisdom of the state law not at issue? Is it possible to apply the uniform national standard test without any consideration of the wisdom of the state regulation at issue?

---

3. The "Discrimination Against Interstate Commerce" Test

In *Cooley v. Board of Wardens*, the Supreme Court developed the rule that states cannot regulate subjects for which a uniform national standard is necessary. The Court has never abandoned this rule, and it continues to cite *Cooley* in Dormant Commerce Clause cases. In the second half of the Twentieth Century, however, the Court began to articulate other limitations imposed by the Dormant Commerce Clause Doctrine.

The first of these limitations is that a state may not engage in **discrimination against interstate commerce** unless necessary to further a legitimate state interest. The prohibition against discrimination applies to statutes that discriminate on their face or that have a discriminatory purpose or effect. The Supreme Court has said: "The commerce clause forbids discrimination, whether forthright or ingenious. In each case it is our duty to determine whether the statute under attack, whatever its name may be, will in its practical operation work discrimination against interstate commerce." *Best & Co. v. Maxwell*, 311 U.S. 454, 455-456 (1940). The prohibition against discrimination is strict, but not absolute. The Supreme Court has declared that "a State may validate a statute that discriminates against interstate commerce by showing that it advances a legitimate local purpose that cannot be adequately served by reasonable nondiscriminatory alternatives." *New Energy Co. v. Limbach*, 486 U.S. 269, 278 (1988).

As the following cases show, states have attempted to discriminate against interstate commerce in different ways. They may try, for example, to restrict imports and thus protect local producers from external competition. Or they may try to limit exports, preserving goods for local consumers. Either way, interstate commerce is treated differently from commerce wholly within the state. Once a court finds discrimination, it must consider the reason for discrimination and whether the state could have found nondiscriminatory ways to protect its interests.

Dean Milk Co. v. City of Madison, Wisc.

340 U.S. 349 (1951)

Mr. Justice CLARK delivered the opinion of the Court.

This appeal challenges the constitutional validity of two sections of an ordinance of the City of Madison, Wisconsin, regulating the sale of milk and milk products within the municipality's jurisdiction. One section in issue makes it unlawful to sell any milk as pasteurized unless it has been processed and bottled at an approved pasteurization plant within a radius of five miles from the central square of Madison. Another section, which prohibits the sale of milk, or the importation, receipt or storage of milk for sale, in Madison unless from a source of supply possessing a permit issued after inspection by Madison officials, is attacked insofar as it expressly relieves municipal authorities from any duty to inspect farms located beyond twenty-five miles from the center of the city.

The area defined by the ordinance with respect to milk sources encompasses practically all of Dane County and includes some 500 farms which supply milk for Madison. Within the five-mile area for pasteurization are plants of five processors, only three of which are engaged in the general wholesale and retail trade in Madison. Inspection of these farms and plants is scheduled once every thirty days and is performed by two municipal inspectors, one of whom is full-time. The courts below found that the ordinance in question promotes convenient, economical and efficient plant inspection.

Appellant purchases and gathers milk from approximately 950 farms in northern Illinois and southern Wisconsin, none being within twenty-five miles of Madison. Its pasteurization plants are located at Chemung and Huntley, Illinois, about 65 and 85 miles respectively from Madison. Appellant was denied a license to sell its products within Madison solely because its pasteurization plants were more than five miles away.

It is conceded that the milk which appellant seeks to sell in Madison is supplied from farms and processed in plants licensed and inspected by public health authorities of Chicago, and is labeled "Grade A" under the Chicago ordinance which adopts the rating standards recommended by the United States Public Health Service. Both the Chicago and Madison ordinances, though not the sections of the latter here in issue, are largely patterned after the Model Milk Ordinance of the Public Health Service. However, Madison contends and we assume that in some particulars its ordinance is more rigorous than that of Chicago.

Upon these facts we find it necessary to determine only the issue raised under the Commerce Clause, for we agree with appellant that the ordinance imposes an undue burden on interstate commerce. [This] is not an instance in which an enactment falls because of federal legislation which, as a proper exercise of paramount national power over commerce, excludes measures which might otherwise be within the police power of the states. ***

Nor can there be objection to the avowed purpose of this enactment. We assume that difficulties in sanitary regulation of milk and milk products originating in remote areas may present a situation in which "upon a consideration of all the relevant facts and circumstances it appears that the matter is one which may appropriately be regulated in the interest of the safety, health and well-being of local communities ***." *Parker v. Brown*, 317 U.S. 341, 362-363 (1943).

> **Make the Connection**
>
> Just as promoting safety is considered a legitimate interest in judging the constitutionality of discrimination against interstate commerce, so too is it seen as a legitimate state interest in evaluating burdens placed on interstate commerce, as we will see later in this Chapter.

But this regulation, like the provision invalidated in *Baldwin v. G.A.F. Seelig, Inc.*, 294 U.S. 511 (1935), in practical effect excludes from distribution in Madison wholesome milk produced and pasteurized in Illinois. "The importer [may] keep his milk or drink it, but sell it he may not." *Id.* at 521. In thus erecting an economic barrier protecting a major local industry against competition from without the State, Madison plainly discriminates against interstate commerce.[4] This it cannot do, even in the exercise of its unquestioned power to protect the health and safety of its people, if reasonable nondiscriminatory alternatives, adequate to conserve legitimate local interests, are available. A different view, that the ordinance is valid simply because it professes to be a health measure, would mean that the Commerce Clause of itself imposes no limitations on state action other than those laid down by the Due Process Clause, save for the rare instance where a state artlessly discloses an avowed purpose to discriminate against interstate goods. Our issue then is whether the discrimination inherent in the Madison ordinance can be justified in view of the character of the local interests and the available methods of protecting them.

> **Take Note**
>
> In this passage, the Court expresses the rule for when a state law violates the Dormant Commerce Clause Doctrine because of discrimination against interstate commerce. Can you articulate what constitutes "discrimination" within the meaning of the rule?

It appears that reasonable and adequate alternatives are available. If the City of Madi-

---

[4] It is immaterial that Wisconsin milk from outside the Madison area is subjected to the same proscription as that moving in interstate commerce.

son prefers to rely upon its own officials for inspection of distant milk sources, such inspection is readily open to it without hardship for it could charge the actual and reasonable cost of such inspection to the importing producers and processors. Moreover, appellee Health Commissioner of Madison testified that as proponent of the local milk ordinance he had submitted the provisions here in controversy and an alternative proposal based on § 11 of the Model Milk Ordinance recommended by the United States Public Health Service. The model provision imposes no geographical limitation on location of milk sources and processing plants but excludes from the municipality milk not produced and pasteurized conformably to standards as high as those enforced by the receiving city. In implementing such an ordinance, the importing city obtains milk ratings based on uniform standards and established by health authorities in the jurisdiction where production and processing occur. The receiving city may determine the extent of enforcement of sanitary standards in the exporting area by verifying the accuracy of safety ratings of specific plants or of the milkshed in the distant jurisdiction through the United States Public Health Service, which routinely and on request spot checks the local ratings. The Commissioner testified that Madison consumers "would be safeguarded adequately" under either proposal and that he had expressed no preference. The milk sanitarian of the Wisconsin State Board of Health testified that the State Health Department recommends the adoption of a provision based on the Model Ordinance. Both officials agreed that a local health officer would be justified in relying upon the evaluation by the Public Health Service of enforcement conditions in remote producing areas.

To permit Madison to adopt a regulation not essential for the protection of local health interests and placing a discriminatory burden on interstate commerce would invite a multiplication of preferential trade areas destructive of the very purpose of the Commerce Clause. Under the circumstances here presented, the regulation must yield to the principle that "one state in its dealings with another may not place itself in a position of economic isolation." *Baldwin v. G.A.F. Seeling, Inc.*, 294 U.S. at 527. *** [W]e conclude that the judgment below sustaining the five-mile provision as to pasteurization must be reversed.

The Supreme Court of Wisconsin thought it unnecessary to pass upon the validity of the twenty-five-mile limitation, apparently in part for the reason that this issue was made academic by its decision upholding the five-mile section. In view of our conclusion as to the latter provision, a determination of appellant's contention as to the other section is now necessary. As to this issue, therefore, we vacate the judgment below and remand for further proceedings not inconsistent with the principles announced in this opinion. It is so ordered.

Points for Discussion

a. Discrimination against Interstate Commerce

The Madison ordinance does not say anything about excluding products from other states. But the Court says the law "in practical effect excludes from distribution in Madison wholesome milk produced and pasteurized in Illinois." Why doesn't it make a difference that the discrimination is implicit and not explicit? Also, why doesn't it matter, as the Court says in footnote 4, that the law also excludes milk from other parts of Wisconsin?

b. Legitimate State Interest

What was the city's interest in having the law? Did the Court think that the interest was legitimate? Is it possible to conceive of the city's interest as being illegitimate, given the purposes of the Dormant Commerce Clause Doctrine?

c. Less Discriminatory Alternatives

How could the city have accomplished its goal without discriminating against interstate commerce? Is the Court the most competent actor to decide whether less discriminatory alternatives are viable alternatives?

d. Purpose of Prohibiting Discrimination

The Court says that permitting Madison to place "a discriminatory burden on interstate commerce would invite a multiplication of preferential trade areas destructive of the very purpose of the Commerce Clause." Why would upholding the Madison law invite other obstacles to trade?

e. Historical Basis for the Dormant Commerce Clause Doctrine

Recall that one of the principal defects of the Articles of Confederation was that it effectively permitted the states to engage in economically disastrous protectionism (i.e. protection of local businesses from non-local competition), and that the inclusion of the Commerce Clause in the new Constitution was a response to this problem. Does this history justify judicial enforcement, even absent legislation from Congress, of a ban on state regulation that discriminates against interstate commerce?

————————

Hughes v. Oklahoma

441 U.S. 322 (1979)

Mr. Justice BRENNAN delivered the opinion of the Court.

FYI

A minnow is a small fish often used as bait for catching other fish. A seine is a kind of net placed vertically in the water to trap fish.

The question presented for decision is whether Okl. Stat., Tit. 29, § 4-115(B) (Supp. 1978), violates the Commerce Clause, Art. I, § 8, cl. 3, of the United States Constitution, insofar as it provides that "[n]o person may transport or ship minnows for sale outside the state which were seined or procured within the waters of this state . . . ." The prohibition against transportation out of State for sale thus does not apply to hatchery-bred minnows, but only to "natural" minnows seined or procured from waters within the State.

Section 4-115(B) is part of the Oklahoma Wildlife Conservation Code. Another provision of that Code requires that persons have a minnow dealer's license before they can lawfully seine or trap minnows within the State—except for their own use as bait—§ 4-116 (Supp. 1978), but no limit is imposed on the number of minnows a licensed dealer may take from state waters. Nor is there any regulation except § 4-115(B) concerning the disposition of lawfully acquired minnows; they may be sold within Oklahoma to any person and for any purpose, and may be taken out of the State for any purpose except sale.

Appellant William Hughes holds a Texas license to operate a commercial minnow business near Wichita Falls, Tex. An Oklahoma game ranger arrested him on a charge of violating § 4-115(B) by transporting from Oklahoma to Wichita Falls a load of natural minnows purchased from a minnow dealer licensed to do business in Oklahoma. Hughes' defense that § 4-115(B) was unconstitutional because it was repugnant to the Commerce Clause was rejected, and he was convicted and fined. ***

Section 4-115(B) on its face discriminates against interstate commerce. It forbids the transportation of natural minnows out of the State for purposes of sale, and thus "overtly blocks the flow of interstate commerce at [the] State's borders." *Philadelphia v. New Jersey*, 437 U.S. 617 (1978). Such facial discrimination by itself may be a fatal defect, regardless of the State's purpose, because "the evil of protectionism can reside in legislative means as well as legislative ends." *Id.* at 626. At a minimum such facial discrimination invokes the strictest scrutiny of any purported legitimate local purpose and of the absence of nondiscriminatory alternatives.

> **FYI**
>
> *Facial discrimination* means discrimination that is apparent from the language of the statute. Some statutes discriminate on their face, while others are written in nondiscriminatory terms but are discriminatory in their effects.

Oklahoma argues that § 4-115(B) serves a legitimate local purpose in that it is "readily apparent as a conservation measure." The State's interest in maintaining the ecological balance in state waters by avoiding the removal of inordinate numbers of minnows may well qualify as a legitimate local purpose. We consider the States' interests in conservation and protection of wild animals as legitimate local purposes similar to the States' interests in protecting the health and safety of their citizens.

[But far] from choosing the least discriminatory alternative, Oklahoma has chosen to "conserve" its minnows in the way that most overtly discriminates against interstate commerce. The State places no limits on the numbers of minnows that can be taken by licensed minnow dealers; nor does it limit in any way how these minnows may be disposed of within the State. Yet it forbids the transportation of any commercially significant number of natural minnows out of the State for sale. Section 4-115(B) is certainly not a "last ditch" attempt at conservation after nondiscriminatory alternatives have proved unfeasible. It is rather a choice of the most discriminatory means even though nondiscriminatory alternatives would seem likely to fulfill the State's purported legitimate local purpose more effectively. We therefore hold that § 4-115(B) is repugnant to the Commerce Clause.

[Our decision] does not leave the States powerless to protect and conserve wild animal life within their borders. Today's decision makes clear, however, that States may promote this legitimate purpose only in ways consistent with the basic principle that "our economic unit is the Nation," *H.P. Hood & Sons, Inc. v. Du Mond*, 336 U.S. 525, 537 (1949), and that when a wild animal "becomes an article of commerce . . . its use cannot be limited to the citizens of one State to the exclusion of citizens of another State." *Geer v. Connecticut*, 161 U.S. 519, 538 (1896) (Field, J., dissenting). *Reversed.*

Mr. Justice REHNQUIST, with whom THE CHIEF JUSTICE joins, dissenting.

Contrary to the view of the Court, I do not think that Oklahoma's regulation of the commercial exploitation of natural minnows either discriminates against out-of-state enterprises in favor of local businesses or that it burdens the interstate commerce in minnows. At least, no such showing has been made on the record before us. This is not a case where a State's regulation permits residents to export naturally seined minnows but prohibits nonresidents from so doing. No person is allowed to export natural minnows for sale outside of Oklahoma; the statute is evenhanded in its application. The State has not used its power to protect its own citizens from outside competition. Nor is this a case where a State requires a nonresident business, as a condition to exporting minnows, to move a significant portion of its operations to the State or to use certain state resources in pursuit of its business for the benefit of the local economy. And, notwithstanding the Court's protestations to the contrary, Oklahoma has not blocked the flow of interstate commerce in minnows at the State's borders. Appellant, or anyone else, may freely export as many minnows as he wishes, so long as the minnows so transported are hatchery minnows and not naturally seined minnows. On this record, I simply fail to see how interstate commerce in minnows, the commodity at issue here, is impeded in the least by Oklahoma's regulatory scheme.

———

Point for Discussion

a. Discrimination

Why did the Court think that the law discriminated against interstate commerce? Why did the dissent think that the law did not? If the law was discriminatory, against whom or what did it discriminate?

b. Less Discriminatory Alternatives in Environmental Protection

Does this case limit how states may attempt to protect the environment? Or does it just invalidate the specific means chosen by Oklahoma? How, if at all, could the state have accomplished its goal of protecting minnows in a less discriminatory manner?

c. Importation of Minnows

In *Maine v. Taylor*, 477 U.S. 131 (1986), the Supreme Court upheld the conviction of a man who had violated a Maine statute prohibiting the importation of baitfish into Maine. The Court held that the state statute did not violate the Dormant Commerce Clause Doctrine. Even though the statute discriminated against interstate commerce, the state had a strong interest in protecting native fisheries from harms caused by non-native species. In addition, the Court concluded that the state could not further this interest through alternative non-discriminatory means. Why is this case different from *Hughes v. Oklahoma*? Why weren't non-discriminatory options available to Maine?

---

4. The "Excessive Burden on Interstate Commerce" Test

We have seen that the states may not discriminate against interstate commerce. But given the nature of commerce today, even state regulation that does not treat out-of-state interests differently from in-state interests has the potential to create effects on commerce outside the borders of the state imposing the regulation. Another limitation that the Court has developed, in a series of cases, is that states may not impose **a burden on interstate commerce that is excessive** in relation to legitimate local interests. In a frequently-quoted portion of *Pike v. Bruce Church*, 397 U.S. 137, 142 (1970), the Supreme Court more formally stated the modern rule as follows:

> "Where [a state law] regulates evenhandedly to effectuate a legitimate local public interest, and its effects on interstate commerce are only incidental, it will be upheld unless the burden imposed on such commerce is clearly excessive in relation to the putative local benefits. If a legitimate local purpose is found, then the question becomes one of degree. And the extent of the burden that will be tolerated will of course depend on the nature of the local interest involved, and on whether it could be promoted as well with a lesser impact on interstate activities."

Under this rule, legitimate local interests include protecting health and safety and conserving natural resources, but they do not include protecting local businesses from competition. This "excessive burden" rule did not reach its final form in a single case; rather, it took several decades for the rule to develop. In reading the following decisions, notice how the rule evolved and became more specific as the Supreme Court considered additional cases. Consider whether this rule is different from the "uniform national standards" test that we considered earlier in this Chapter. Also consider why some members of the Supreme Court have felt uncomfortable in weighing the importance of state interests when applying the test.

South Carolina State Highway Dept. v. Barnwell Bros.

303 U.S. 177 (1938)

Mr. Justice STONE delivered the opinion of the Court.

Act No. 259 of the General Assembly of South Carolina, of April 28, 1933, prohibits use on the state highways of motor trucks and "semi-trailer motor trucks" whose width exceeds 90 inches, and whose weight including load exceeds 20,000 pounds. For purposes of the weight limitation, section 2 of the statute provides that a semitrailer motortruck, which is a motor propelled truck with a trailer whose front end is designed to be attached to and supported by the truck, shall be considered a single unit. The principal question for decision is whether these prohibitions impose an unconstitutional burden upon interstate commerce.

The District Court of three judges, after hearing evidence, ruled that the challenged provisions of the statute have not been superseded by the Federal Motor Carrier Act, and *** that the challenged provisions, being an exercise of the state's power to regulate the use of its highways so as to protect them from injury and to insure their safe and economical use, do not violate the Fourteenth Amendment. But it held that the weight and width prohibitions place an unlawful burden on interstate motor traffic passing over specified highways of the state, which for the most part are of concrete or a concrete base surfaced with asphalt. It accordingly enjoined the enforcement of the weight provision against interstate motor carriers on the specified highway, and also the width limitation of 90 inches, except in the case of vehicles exceeding 96 inches in width. ***

The trial court rested its decision that the statute unreasonably burdens interstate commerce, upon findings, not assailed here, that there is a large amount of motortruck traffic passing interstate in the southeastern part of the United States, which would normally pass over the highways of South Carolina, but which will be barred from the state by the challenged restrictions if enforced, and upon its conclusion that, when viewed in the light of their effect upon interstate commerce, these restrictions are unreasonable.

To reach this conclusion the court weighed conflicting evidence and made its own determinations as to the weight and width of motortrucks commonly used in interstate traffic and the capacity of the specified highways of the state to accommodate such traffic without injury to them or danger to their users. It found that interstate carriage by motortrucks has become a national industry; that from 85 to 90 per cent of the motor trucks used in interstate transportation are 96 inches wide and of a gross weight, when loaded, of more than 10 tons; that only four other states prescribe a gross load weight as low as 20,000 pounds; and that the American Association of State Highway Officials and the National Conference on Street and Highway Safety in the Department of Commerce have recommended for adoption weight and width limitations in which weight is limited to axle loads of 16,000 to 18,000 pounds and width is limited to 96 inches.

While the constitutional grant to Congress of power to regulate interstate commerce has been held to operate of its own force to curtail state power in some measure,[2] it did not forestall all state action affecting interstate commerce.

Ever since *Willson v. Black-bird Creek Marsh Co.*, 27 U.S. (2 Pet.) 245 (1829), and *Cooley v. Board of Port Wardens*, 53 U.S. (12 How.) 299 (1851), it has been recognized that there are matters of local concern, the regulation of which unavoidably involves some regulation of interstate commerce but which, because of their local character and their number and diversity, may never be fully dealt with by Congress. Notwithstanding the commerce clause, such regulation in the absence of congressional action has for the most part been left to the states by the decisions of this Court, subject to the other applicable constitutional restraints.

> **Food for Thought**
>
> Footnote 2 contains a famous and often-cited political theory for why the Dormant Commerce Clause Doctrine should allow some state regulation of commerce but not all regulation. What does the last sentence of the footnote mean?

[T]he present case affords no occasion for saying that the bare possession of power by Congress to regulate the interstate traffic forces the states to conform to standards which Congress might, but has not adopted, or curtails their power to take measures to insure the safety and conservation of their highways which may be applied to like traffic moving intrastate. Few subjects of state regulation are so peculiarly of local concern as is the use of state highways. There are few, local regulation of which is so inseparable from a substantial effect on interstate commerce. Unlike the railroads, local highways are built, owned, and maintained by the state or its municipal subdivisions. The state has a primary and immediate concern in their safe and economical administration. The present regulations, or any others of like purpose, if they are to accomplish their end, must be applied alike to interstate and intrastate traffic both moving in large volume over the highways. The fact that they affect alike shippers in interstate and intrastate commerce in large number within as well as without the state is a safeguard against their abuse.

Congress, in the exercise of its plenary power to regulate interstate commerce, may determine whether the burdens imposed on it by state regulation, otherwise permissible, are too great, and may, by legislation designed to secure uniformity or in other respects to protect the national interest in the commerce, curtail to some extent the state's regulatory power. But that is a legislative, not a judicial, function, to be performed in the light of the congressional judgment of what is appropriate regulation of interstate commerce, and the

[handwritten margin note: Congress should determine if restriction are too much]

---

[2] State regulations affecting interstate commerce, whose purpose or effect is to gain for those within the state an advantage at the expense of those without, or to burden those out of the state without any corresponding advantage to those within, have been thought to impinge upon the constitutional prohibition even though Congress has not acted. Underlying the stated rule has been the thought, often expressed in judicial opinion, that when the regulation is of such a character that its burden falls principally upon those without the state, legislative action is not likely to be subjected to those political restraints which are normally exerted on legislation where it affects adversely some interests within the state.

extent to which, in that field, state power and local interests should be required to yield to the national authority and interest. In the absence of such legislation the judicial function, under the commerce clause, Const. art. 1, § 8, cl. 3, as well as the Fourteenth Amendment, stops with the inquiry whether the state Legislature in adopting regulations such as the present has acted within its province, and whether the means of regulation chosen are reasonably adapted to the end sought.

[In considering the challenged weight limitation, the district court relied on evidence that was] based on theoretical strength of concrete highways laid under ideal conditions, and none of it was based on an actual study of the highways of South Carolina or of the subgrade and other road building conditions which prevail there and which have a material bearing on the strength and durability of such highways. There is uncontradicted testimony that approximately 60 per cent. of the South Carolina standard paved highways in question were built without a longitudinal center joint which has since become standard practice, the portion of the concrete surface adjacent to the joint being strengthened by reinforcement or by increasing its thickness; and that owing to the distribution of the stresses on concrete roads when in use, those without a center joint have a tendency to develop irregular longitudinal cracks. As the concrete in the center of such roads is thinner than that at the edges, the result is that the highway is split into two irregular segments, each with a weak inner edge which, according to the expert testimony, is not capable of supporting indefinitely wheel loads in excess of 4,200 pounds.

> **Take Note**
>
> The Court says here that a state legislature may impose burdens on interstate commerce so long as it has "acted within its province" and the "means chosen" are reasonable. Modern cases do not follow this formulation of the rule. Instead, as explained above, they ask whether the burden on interstate commerce is excessive in comparison to legitimate local interests. Notice, however, the Court's analysis here in fact is similar to the modern approach.

These considerations, with the presumption of constitutionality, afford adequate support for the weight limitation without reference to other items of the testimony tending to support it. *** The fact that many states have adopted a different standard is not persuasive. The conditions under which highways must be built in the several states, their construction, and the demands made upon them, are not uniform. The road building art, as the record shows, is far from having attained a scientific certainty and precision, and scientific precision is not the criterion for the exercise of the constitutional regulatory power of the states. The Legislature, being free to exercise its own judgment, is not bound by that of other Legislatures. It would hardly be contended that if all the states had adopted a single standard none, in the light of its own experience and in the exercise of its judgment upon all the complex elements which enter into the problem, could change it.

Only a word need be said as to the width limitation. While a large part of the highways in question are from 18 to 20 feet in width, approximately 100 miles are only 16 feet wide. On all the use of a 96-inch truck leaves but a narrow margin for passing. On the road 16 feet wide it leaves none. The 90-inch limitation has been in force in South Carolina since 1920, and the concrete highways which it has built appear to be adopted to vehicles of that width. The record shows without contradiction that the use of heavy loaded trucks on the highways tends to force other traffic off the concrete surface onto the shoulders of the road adjoining its edges, and to increase repair costs materially. It appears also that as the width of trucks is increased it obstructs the view of the highway, causing much inconvenience and increased hazard in its use. It plainly cannot be said that the width of trucks used on the highways in South Carolina is unrelated to their safety and cost of maintenance, or that a 90-inch width limitation, adopted to safeguard the highways of the state, is not within the range of the permissible legislative choice.

The regulatory measures taken by South Carolina are within its legislative power. *** Reversed.

Points for Discussion

a. The *Pike v. Bruce Church* Test

The Supreme Court decided this case before it established the modern formulation of the rule regarding excessive burdens, quoted above, from *Pike v. Bruce Church*, 397 U.S. 137 (1970). But the Court has said that even though *Barnwell Bros.* used a "less formalistic approach," the decision is a "classic case" consistent with the modern understanding of the Dormant Commerce Clause. *Arkansas Elec. Co-op. Corp. v. Arkansas Public Service Comm'n*, 461 U.S. 375, 393 (1983).

b. Legitimate Interests

Why did the Court think that South Carolina had a legitimate interest in regulating the weight and width of trucks using its highways? Even if South Carolina has a legitimate interest in regulating the weight and width of trucks, does that mean that the state may enact any regulation that it desires? Do you agree that state highways are "peculiarly of local concern" today?

Southern Pacific Co. v. State of Arizona

325 U.S. 761 (1945)

Mr. Chief Justice STONE delivered the opinion of the Court.

The Arizona Train Limit Law of May 16, 1912, Arizona Code Ann., 1939, § 69-119, makes it unlawful for any person or corporation to operate within the state a railroad train of more than fourteen passenger or seventy freight cars, and authorizes the state to recover a money penalty for each violation of the Act. The questions for decision are whether Congress has, by legislative enactment, restricted the power of the states to regulate the length of interstate trains as a safety measure and, if not, whether the statute contravenes the commerce clause of the federal Constitution.

Congress, although asked to do so, has declined to pass legislation specifically limiting trains to seventy cars. We are therefore brought to appellant's principal contention, that the state statute contravenes the commerce clause of the Federal Constitution.

The findings show that the operation of long trains, that is trains of more than fourteen passenger and more than seventy freight cars, is standard practice over the main lines of the railroads of the United States, and that, if the length of trains is to be regulated at all, national uniformity in the regulation adopted, such as only Congress can prescribe, is practically indispensable to the operation of an efficient and economical national railway system. On many railroads passenger trains of more than fourteen cars and freight trains of more than seventy cars are operated, and on some systems freight trains are run ranging from one hundred and twenty-five to one hundred and sixty cars in length. Outside of Arizona, where the length of trains is not restricted, appellant runs a substantial proportion of long trains. In 1939 on its comparable route for through traffic through Utah and Nevada from 66 to 85% of its freight trains were over 70 cars in length and over 43% of its passenger trains included more than fourteen passenger cars.

In Arizona, approximately 93% of the freight traffic and 95% of the passenger traffic is interstate. Because of the Train Limit Law appellant is required to haul over 30% more trains in Arizona than would otherwise have been necessary. The record shows a definite relationship between operating costs and the length of trains, the increase in length resulting in a reduction of operating costs per car. The additional cost of operation of trains complying with the Train Limit Law in Arizona amounts for the two railroads traversing that state to about $1,000,000 a year. The reduction in train lengths also impedes efficient operation. More locomotives and more manpower are required; the necessary conversion and reconversion of train lengths at terminals and the delay caused by breaking up and remaking long trains upon entering and leaving the state in order to comply with the law, delays the traffic and diminishes its volume moved in a given time, especially when traffic is heavy.

At present the seventy freight car laws are enforced only in Arizona and Oklahoma, with a fourteen car passenger car limit in Arizona. The record here shows that the enforcement of the Arizona statute results in freight trains being broken up and reformed at the California border and in New Mexico, some distance from the Arizona line. Frequently it is not feasible to operate a newly assembled train from the New Mexico yard nearest to Arizona, with the result that the Arizona limitation governs the flow of traffic as far east as El Paso, Texas. For similar reasons the Arizona law often controls the length of passenger trains all the way from Los Angeles to El Paso.

If one state may regulate train lengths, so may all the others, and they need not prescribe the same maximum limitation. The practical effect of such regulation is to control train operations beyond the boundaries of the state exacting it because of the necessity of breaking up and reassembling long trains at the nearest terminal points before entering and after leaving the regulating state. The serious impediment to the free flow of commerce by the local regulation of train lengths and the practical necessity that such regulation, if any, must be prescribed by a single body having a nation-wide authority are apparent.

The trial court found that the Arizona law had no reasonable relation to safety, and made train operation more dangerous. Examination of the evidence and the detailed findings makes it clear that this conclusion was rested on facts found which indicate that such increased danger of accident and personal injury as may result from the greater length of trains is more than offset by the increase in the number of accidents resulting from the larger number of trains when train lengths are reduced. In considering the effect of the statute as a safety measure, therefore, the factor of controlling significance for present purposes is not whether there is basis for the conclusion of the Arizona Supreme Court that the increase in length of trains beyond the statutory maximum has an adverse effect upon safety of operation. The decisive question is whether in the circumstances the total effect of the law as a safety measure in reducing accidents and casualties is so slight or problematical as not to outweigh the national interest in keeping interstate commerce free from interferences which seriously impede it and subject it to local regulation which does not have a uniform effect on the interstate train journey which it interrupts.

> **Take Note**
>
> The Court announces that it will weigh the state's legitimate interests in enacting a law against the burden that the law places on interstate commerce. State laws that impose an excessive burden are unconstitutional. How exactly should a court go about balancing a state's interests in regulation against the burdens it imposes on commerce?

The principal source of danger of accident from increased length of trains is the resulting increase of "slack action" of the train. Slack action is the amount of free movement of one car before it transmits its motion to an adjoining coupled car. This free movement results from the fact that in railroad practice cars are loosely coupled, and the coupling is often combined with a stock-absorbing device, a "draft gear," which, under stress, substantially increases the free movement as the train is started or stopped. Loose coupling is necessary to enable the train to proceed freely around curves and is an aid in starting heavy trains, since the application of the locomotive power to the train operates on each car in the train successively, and the power is thus utilized to start only one car at a time.

As the trial court found, reduction of the length of trains also tends to increase the number of accidents because of the increase in the number of trains. The application of the Arizona law compelled appellant to operate 30.08%, or 4,304, more freight trains in 1938 than would otherwise have been necessary. And the record amply supports the trial court's conclusion that the frequency of accidents is closely related to the number of trains run. The number of accidents due to grade crossing collisions between trains and motor vehicles and pedestrians, and to collisions between trains, which are usually far more serious than those due to slack action, and accidents due to locomotive failures, in general vary with the number of trains. Increase in the number of trains results in more starts and stops, more "meets" and "passes," and more switching movements, all tending to increase the number of accidents not only to train operatives and other railroad employees, but to passengers and members of the public exposed to danger by train operations.

Here we conclude that the state does go too far. Its regulation of train lengths, admittedly obstructive to interstate train operation, and having a seriously adverse effect on transportation efficiency and economy, passes beyond what is plainly essential for safety since it does not appear that it will lessen rather than increase the danger of accident. Its attempted regulation of the operation of interstate trains cannot establish nation-wide control such as is essential to the maintenance of an efficient transportation system, which Congress alone can prescribe. The state interest cannot be preserved at the expense of the national interest by an enactment which regulates interstate train lengths without securing such control, which is a matter of national concern. To this the interest of the state here asserted is subordinate. Reversed.

Mr. Justice BLACK, dissenting.

[W]hether it is in the interest of society for the length of trains to be governmentally regulated is a matter of public policy. Someone must fix that policy—either the Congress, or the state, or the courts. A century and a half of constitutional history and government admonishes this Court to leave that choice to the elected legislative representatives of the people themselves, where it properly belongs both on democratic principles and the requirements of efficient government.

> **Food for Thought**
>
> Justice Hugo Black was an extremely influential member of the Court. Appointed in 1937, he supported a broad reading of Congress's commerce power. At the same time, Justice Black urged a narrow interpretation of the Dormant Commerce Clause Doctrine. See Earl M. Maltz, *The Impact of The Constitutional Revolution of 1937 on The Dormant Commerce Clause*, 19 Harv. J.L. & Pub. Pol'y 121, 129 (1995). Are these views consistent?

Points for Discussion

a. Understanding the Court's Reasoning

Why does the majority think that the state legislation goes too far? Is the majority saying that safety is not a legitimate state interest?

b. Political Theory

Recall what the Court said in footnote 2 of the *Barnwell Bros.* case: "when the regulation is of such a character that its burden falls principally upon those without the state, legislative action is not likely to be subjected to those political restraints which are normally exerted on legislation where it affects adversely some interests within the state." Does this case involve an example of such regulation?

c. Disagreement between the Majority and the Dissent

Does Justice Black disagree with how the majority weighs the state's interest in safety or is he making a different point in his dissent? Is the reasoning of the majority or the dissent closer to the earlier Dormant Commerce Clause Doctrine cases in which the Court disclaimed any pretension to consider the wisdom of state laws?

d. Origin of the Balancing Test

In an omitted portion of the opinion, the Court cited Columbia University Professor Noel Dowling's influential article, *Interstate Commerce and State Power*, 27 Va. L. Rev. 1 (1940). In this article, Dowling argued against trying to decide whether a state law violates the Commerce Clause based on whether the state law has more than an "incidental" effect on interstate commerce. Instead, Dowling recommended weighing the state's interest in the law against the burden that it imposes on interstate commerce. *See id.* at 21-22. What might be a problem with a test that focuses only on whether a state law imposes more than an "incidental burden"? Is there anything problematic about weighing state interests?

e. The Scope of the Commerce Power

We saw in Chapter 3 that the Court has concluded that Congress has extensive power to regulate local activity on the theory that such activity, when viewed in the aggregate, has a substantial effect on interstate commerce. Given the scope of Congress's power under the Commerce Clause and the Necessary and Proper Clause, is it possible to conceive of a state regulation that does not impose at least some burden on interstate commerce? How does a Court decide whether such a burden is "excessive"?

As the preceding cases have shown, a court must determine whether a state law that burdens interstate commerce furthers a legitimate state interest, such as promoting safety. In making this determination, a question arises whether a court must consider any possible justification for the law or whether the court must look at the actual motivation of the state legislature in creating the law. This issue divided the Supreme Court in the following case.

Kassel v. Consolidated Freightways Corp. of Delaware

450 U.S. 662 (1981)

Take Note

Justice Powell's opinion received the support of only four Justices. It thus represents the views of only a plurality, not a majority, of the Court. The plurality and the concurrence reach the same conclusion, but they use different reasoning. What is the difference?

Justice POWELL announced the judgment of the Court and delivered an opinion, in which Justice WHITE, Justice BLACKMUN, and Justice STEVENS joined.

The State of Iowa *** by statute restricts the length of vehicles that may use its highways. Unlike all other States in the West and Midwest, Iowa generally prohibits the use of 65-foot doubles within its borders. Instead, most truck combinations are restricted to 55 feet in length. Doubles, mobile homes, trucks carrying vehicles such as tractors and other farm equipment, and singles hauling livestock, are permitted to be as long as 60 feet. *** Notwithstanding these restrictions, Iowa's statute permits cities abutting the state line by local ordinance to adopt the length limitations of the adjoining State. Where a city has exercised this option, otherwise oversized trucks are permitted within the city limits and in nearby commercial zones.[6]

Because of Iowa's statutory scheme, Consolidated cannot use its 65-foot doubles to move commodities through the State. *** Consolidated filed this suit in the District Court averring that Iowa's statutory scheme unconstitutionally burdens interstate commerce. ***

[R]egulations that touch upon safety—especially highway safety—are those that "the Court has been most reluctant to invalidate." But the incantation of a purpose to promote the public health or safety does not insulate a state law from Commerce Clause attack. Regulations designed for that salutary purpose nevertheless may further the purpose so marginally, and interfere with commerce so substantially, as to be invalid under the Commerce Clause.

The evidence [at trial] showed, and the District Court found, that the 65-foot double was at least the equal of the 55-foot single in the ability to brake, turn, and maneuver. *** Consolidated, meanwhile, demonstrated that Iowa's law substantially burdens interstate commerce. Trucking companies that wish to continue to use 65-foot doubles must route them around Iowa or detach the trailers of the doubles and ship them through separately. Alternatively, trucking companies must use the smaller 55-foot singles or 60-foot doubles permitted under Iowa law. Each of these options engenders inefficiency and added expense.

In addition to increasing the costs of the trucking companies (and, indirectly, of the service to consumers), Iowa's law may aggravate, rather than ameliorate, the problem of highway accidents. Fifty-five foot singles carry less freight than 65-foot doubles. Either more small trucks must be used to carry the same quantity of goods through Iowa, or the same number of larger trucks must drive longer distances to bypass Iowa. In either case, [the] restriction requires more highway miles to be driven to transport the same quantity of goods. Other things being equal, accidents are proportional to distance traveled. Thus, if 65-foot doubles are as safe as 55-foot singles, Iowa's law tends to increase the number of accidents, and to shift the incidence of them from Iowa to other States.

Perhaps recognizing the weakness of the evidence supporting its safety argument, and the substantial burden on commerce that its regulations create, Iowa urges the Court simply to "defer" to the safety judgment of the State. It argues that the length of trucks is generally, although perhaps imprecisely, related to safety. The task of drawing a line is one that Iowa contends should be left to its legislature.

The Court normally does accord "special deference" to state highway safety regulations. This traditional deference "derives in part from the assumption that where such

---

[6] The Iowa Legislature in 1974 passed House Bill 671, which would have permitted 65-foot doubles. But Iowa Governor Ray vetoed the bill, noting that it "would benefit only a few Iowa-based companies while providing a great advantage for out-of-state trucking firms and competitors at the expense of our Iowa citizens." Governor's Veto Message of March 2, 1974, reprinted in App. 626. The "border-cities exemption" was passed by the General Assembly and signed by the Governor shortly thereafter. ***

regulations do not discriminate on their face against interstate commerce, their burden usually falls on local economic interests as well as other States' economic interests, thus insuring that a State's own political processes will serve as a check against unduly burdensome regulations." Less deference to the legislative judgment is due, however, where the local regulation bears disproportionately on out-of-state residents and businesses. Such a disproportionate burden is apparent here. Iowa's scheme, although generally banning large doubles from the State, nevertheless has several exemptions that secure to Iowans many of the benefits of large trucks while shunting to neighboring States many of the costs associated with their use.

At the time of trial there were two particularly significant exemptions. First, singles hauling livestock or farm vehicles were permitted to be as long as 60 feet. As the Court of Appeals noted, this provision undoubtedly was helpful to local interests. Second, cities abutting other States were permitted to enact local ordinances adopting the larger length limitation of the neighboring State. This exemption offered the benefits of longer trucks to individuals and businesses in important border cities without burdening Iowa's highways with interstate through traffic.

It is thus far from clear that Iowa was motivated primarily by a judgment that 65-foot doubles are less safe than 55-foot singles. Rather, Iowa seems to have hoped to limit the use of its highways by deflecting some through traffic. [T]he statutory exemptions, their history, and the arguments Iowa has advanced in support of its law in this litigation, all suggest that the deference traditionally accorded a State's safety judgment is not warranted. The controlling factors thus are the findings of the District Court [with] respect to the relative safety of the types of trucks at issue, and the substantiality of the burden on interstate commerce. Because Iowa has imposed this burden without any significant countervailing safety interest, its statute violates the Commerce Clause.

Justice BRENNAN, with whom Justice MARSHALL joins, concurring in the judgment.

My Brothers POWELL and REHNQUIST make the mistake of disregarding the intention of Iowa's lawmakers and assuming that resolution of the case must hinge upon the argument offered by Iowa's attorneys: that 65-foot doubles are more dangerous than shorter trucks. They then canvass the factual record and findings of the courts below and reach opposite conclusions as to whether the evidence adequately supports that empirical judgment. I repeat: my Brothers POWELL and REHNQUIST have asked and answered the wrong question. For although Iowa's lawyers in this litigation have defended the truck-length regulation on the basis of the safety advantages of 55-foot singles and 60-foot doubles over 65-foot doubles, Iowa's actual rationale for maintaining the regulation had nothing to do with these purported differences. Rather, Iowa sought to discourage interstate truck traffic on Iowa's highways. Thus, the safety advantages and disadvantages of the types and lengths of trucks involved in this case are irrelevant to the decision.

The Iowa Legislature has consistently taken the position that size, weight, and speed restrictions on interstate traffic should be set in accordance with uniform national standards. *** In 1974, the Iowa Legislature [voted] to increase the permissible length of trucks to conform to uniform standards then in effect in most other States. *** But Governor Ray broke from prior state policy, and vetoed the legislation. [Governor Ray's] principal concern was that to allow 65-foot doubles would "basically ope[n] our state to literally thousands and thousands more trucks per year." This increase in interstate truck traffic would, in the Governor's estimation, greatly increase highway maintenance costs, which are borne by the citizens of the State, and increase the number of accidents and fatalities within the State. The legislative response was not to override the veto, but to accede to the Governor's action, and in accord with his basic premise, to enact a "border cities exemption." This permitted cities within border areas to allow 65-foot doubles while otherwise maintaining the 60-foot limit throughout the State to discourage interstate truck traffic. *** The Governor admitted that he blocked legislative efforts to raise the length of trucks because the change "would benefit only a few Iowa-based companies while providing a great advantage for out-of-state trucking firms and competitors at the expense of our Iowa citizens."

> **Take Note**
>
> Did Justice Brennan conclude that the burdens imposed on interstate commerce by the challenged regulation outweigh the state's interests in enacting it? Or did he conclude that the regulation is defective for a different reason?

Iowa may not shunt off its fair share of the burden of maintaining interstate truck routes, nor may it create increased hazards on the highways of neighboring States in order to decrease the hazards on Iowa highways. Such an attempt has all the hallmarks of the "simple ... protectionism" this Court has condemned in the economic area. *Philadelphia v. New Jersey*, 437 U.S. 617 (1978). Just as a State's attempt to avoid interstate competition in economic goods may damage the prosperity of the Nation as a whole, so Iowa's attempt to deflect interstate truck traffic has been found to make the Nation's highways as a whole more hazardous. That attempt should therefore be subject to "a virtually *per se* rule of invalidity."

Justice REHNQUIST, with whom THE CHIEF JUSTICE and Justice STEWART join, dissenting.

It is emphatically not our task to balance any incremental safety benefits from prohibiting 65-foot doubles as opposed to 60-foot doubles against the burden on interstate commerce. Lines drawn for safety purposes will rarely pass muster if the question is whether a slight increment can be permitted without sacrificing safety.

My Brother BRENNAN argues that the Court should consider only *the* purpose the Iowa legislators *actually* sought to achieve by the length limit, and not the purposes advanced by Iowa's lawyers in defense of the statute. This argument calls to mind what was said of the Roman Legions: that they may have lost battles, but they never lost a war, since they never let a war end until they had won it. The argument has been consistently rejected by the Court in other contexts, and Justice BRENNAN can cite no authority for the proposition that possible legislative purposes suggested by a State's lawyers should not be considered in

Commerce Clause cases. The problems with a view such as that advanced in the opinion concurring in the judgment are apparent. To name just a few, it assumes that individual legislators are motivated by one discernible "actual" purpose, and ignores the fact that different legislators may vote for a single piece of legislation for widely different reasons. How, for example, would a court adhering to the views expressed in the opinion concurring in the judgment approach a statute, the legislative history of which indicated that 10 votes were based on safety considerations, 10 votes were based on protectionism, and the statute passed by a vote of 40-20? What would the *actual* purpose of the *legislature* have been in that case? This Court has wisely "never insisted that a legislative body articulate its reasons for enacting a statute." *United States R.R. Retirement Bd v. Fritz*, 449 U.S. 166, 179 (1980).

Points for Discussion

a. Plurality, Concurrence in Judgment, and Dissent

Why did the plurality think the law was unconstitutional? Why did the concurring Justices reach the same conclusion? Why did the dissent think that both the majority and the concurring Justices were wrong?

b. Actual Motivation v. Putative Benefits

The members of the Court disagreed about whether they should consider only a state's actual interest in enacting a law or instead any putative possible benefits of the law. This case did not finally resolve that question, because there was no majority opinion, and only an opinion joined by five members of the Supreme Court can establish precedent of the Court. (Anyone citing Justice Powell's opinion should identify it as a plurality opinion; a plurality opinion carries less weight than a majority opinion, but perhaps more weight than a concurrence in the judgment that is not a plurality opinion.)

---

5. The Meaning of "Interstate Commerce"

We have seen that, under the Dormant Commerce Clause Doctrine, a state cannot generally discriminate against interstate commerce or impose an excessive burden on interstate commerce. Under these two limitations, questions sometimes arise about just what constitutes "interstate commerce." The question has taken on particular salience as the Court has expansively construed Congress's power to regulate interstate commerce. Does the term include the transportation of garbage? Does it embrace the operation of property for charitable purposes? For answers to these illustrative questions, consider the following cases.

City of Philadelphia v. New Jersey

437 U.S. 617 (1978)

Mr. Justice STEWART delivered the opinion of the Court.

A New Jersey law prohibits the importation of most "solid or liquid waste which originated or was collected outside the territorial limits of the State . . . ." In this case we are required to decide whether this statutory prohibition violates the Commerce Clause of the United States Constitution.

The statutory provision in question is ch. 363 of 1973 N.J. Laws, which took effect in early 1974. In pertinent part it provides:

> "No person shall bring into this State any solid or liquid waste which originated or was collected outside the territorial limits of the State, except garbage to be fed to swine in the State of New Jersey, until the commissioner [of the State Department of Environmental Protection] shall determine that such action can be permitted without endangering the public health, safety and welfare and has promulgated regulations permitting and regulating the treatment and disposal of such waste in this State."

As authorized by ch. 363, the Commissioner promulgated regulations permitting four categories of waste to enter the State. Apart from these narrow exceptions, however, New Jersey closed its borders to all waste from other States. *** Immediately affected by these developments were the operators of private landfills in New Jersey, and several cities in other States that had agreements with these operators for waste disposal. They brought suit against New Jersey and its Department of Environmental Protection in state court, attacking the statute and regulations [under the Dormant Commerce Clause Doctrine].

Before it addressed the merits of the appellants' claim, the New Jersey Supreme Court questioned whether the interstate movement of those wastes banned by ch. 363 is "commerce" at all within the meaning of the Commerce Clause. Any doubts on that score should be laid to rest at the outset.

The state court expressed the view that there may be two definitions of "commerce" for constitutional purposes. When relied on "to support some exertion of federal control or regulation," the Commerce Clause permits "a very sweeping concept" of commerce. But when relied on "to strike down or restrict state legislation," that Clause and the term "commerce" have a "much more confined . . . reach."

The state court reached this conclusion in an attempt to reconcile modern Commerce Clause concepts with several old cases of this Court holding that States can prohibit the importation of some objects because they "are not legitimate subjects of trade and commerce." *Bowman v. Chicago & Northwestern R. Co.,* 125 U.S. 465, 489 (1888). These articles include items "which, on account of their existing condition, would bring in and spread disease, pestilence, and death, such as rags or other substances infected with the germs of yellow fever or the virus of small-pox, or cattle or meat or other provisions that are diseased or decayed, or otherwise, from their condition and quality, unfit for human use or consumption." *Ibid.* See also *Baldwin v. G. A. F. Seelig, Inc.,* 294 U.S. 511, 525 (1935), and cases cited therein. The state court found that ch. 363, as narrowed by the state regulations, banned only "those wastes which can[not] be put to effective use," and therefore those wastes were not commerce at all, unless "the mere transportation and disposal of valueless waste between states constitutes interstate commerce within the meaning of the constitutional provision."

We think the state court misread our cases, and thus erred in assuming that they require a two-tiered definition of commerce. In saying that innately harmful articles "are not legitimate subjects of trade and commerce," the *Bowman* Court was stating its conclusion, not the starting point of its reasoning. All objects of interstate trade merit Commerce Clause protection; none is excluded by definition at the outset. In *Bowman* and similar cases, the Court held simply that because the articles' worth in interstate commerce was far outweighed by the dangers inhering in their very movement, States could prohibit their transportation across state lines. Hence, we reject the state court's suggestion that the banning of "valueless" out-of-state wastes by ch. 363 implicates no constitutional protection. Just as Congress has power to regulate the interstate movement of these wastes, States are not free from constitutional scrutiny when they restrict that movement.

> **Take Note**
>
> The Court explains here what "interstate commerce" is for the purpose of the Dormant Commerce Clause Doctrine. Is the Court's definition of interstate commerce identical to the phrase's definition for purposes of determining Congress's power to regulate under the Commerce Clause?

The crucial inquiry, therefore, must be directed to determining whether ch. 363 is basically a protectionist measure, or whether it can fairly be viewed as a law directed to legitimate local concerns, with effects upon interstate commerce that are only incidental.

The purpose of ch. 363 is set out in the statute itself as follows:

"The Legislature finds and determines that . . . the volume of solid and liquid waste continues to rapidly increase, that the treatment and disposal of these wastes continues to pose an even greater threat to the quality of the environment of New Jersey, that the available and appropriate land fill sites within the State are being diminished, that the environment continues to be threatened by the treatment and disposal of waste which originated or was collected outside the State, and that the public health, safety and welfare require that the treatment and disposal within this State of all wastes generated outside of the State be prohibited."

> **Food for Thought**
>
> Garbage is different from the goods that the states sought to protect in other cases that we have seen in this Chapter, in that, generally speaking, no one wants it. So what is the good—the "scarce natural resource"—that New Jersey sought to protect and that is at issue in this case?

The New Jersey law at issue in this case falls squarely within the area that the Commerce Clause puts off limits to state regulation. On its face, it imposes on out-of-state commercial interests the full burden of conserving the State's remaining landfill space. It is true that in our previous cases the scarce natural resource was itself the article of commerce, whereas here the scarce resource and the article of commerce are distinct. But that difference is without consequence. In both instances, the State has overtly moved to slow or freeze the flow of commerce for protectionist reasons. It does not matter that the State has shut the article of commerce inside the State in one case and outside the State in the other. What is crucial is the attempt by one State to isolate itself from a problem common to many by erecting a barrier against the movement of interstate trade.

Today, cities in Pennsylvania and New York find it expedient or necessary to send their waste into New Jersey for disposal, and New Jersey claims the right to close its borders to such traffic. Tomorrow, cities in New Jersey may find it expedient or necessary to send their waste into Pennsylvania or New York for disposal, and those States might then claim the right to close their borders. The Commerce Clause will protect New Jersey in the future, just as it protects her neighbors now, from efforts by one State to isolate itself in the stream of interstate commerce from a problem shared by all. *** *Reversed.*

Mr. Justice REHNQUIST, with whom THE CHIEF JUSTICE joins, dissenting.

The Supreme Court of New Jersey expressly found that ch. 363 was passed "to preserve the health of New Jersey residents by keeping their exposure to solid waste and landfill areas to a minimum." The Court points to absolutely no evidence that would contradict this finding by the New Jersey Supreme Court. Because I find no basis for distinguishing the laws under challenge here from our past cases upholding state laws that prohibit the importation of items that could endanger the population of the State, I dissent.

Points for Discussion

a. Meaning of Interstate Commerce

Why does the Court think that this case involves interstate commerce even if no one (by virtue of the New Jersey regulation) is buying or selling the trash? Does a broad reading of the term commerce transform the Dormant Commerce Clause Doctrine into a general anti-discrimination prohibition? Or is trash in fact considerably more "valuable" than New Jersey claimed?

b. Environmental Justice

One commentator criticizes this decision in terms of both constitutional law and environmental justice: "The constitutional critique of the Court's interstate waste decisions [is that there is] a political imbalance in the system: by pursuing a national, unfettered market above all else, the Court inappropriately diminishes state and local autonomy in confronting serious health and environmental concerns. The evolving theory of environmental justice urges us to recognize a social imbalance as well: this same commitment to an unfettered market in waste undercuts the ability of local residents to affect more equitable distribution patterns of migrating waste." Robert R.M. Verchick, *The Commerce*

Clause, Environmental Justice, And The Interstate Garbage Wars, 70 S. Cal. L. Rev. 1239, 1289 (1997). How might the Court respond to this criticism?

The following case also concerns the definition of interstate commerce. Beyond this specific issue, however, the decision has become well known because the two dissenting opinions show that great disagreement has arisen in recent years about the scope and legitimacy of the Dormant Commerce Clause Doctrine.

Camps Newfound/Owatonna, Inc. v. Town of Harrison

520 U.S. 564 (1997)

Justice STEVENS delivered the opinion of the Court.

The question presented is whether an otherwise generally applicable state property tax violates the Commerce Clause of the United States Constitution, Art. I, § 8, cl. 3, because its exemption for property owned by charitable institutions excludes organizations operated principally for the benefit of nonresidents.

Petitioner is a Maine nonprofit corporation that operates a summer camp for the benefit of children of the Christian Science faith. The regimen at the camp includes supervised prayer, meditation, and church services designed to help the children grow spiritually and physically in accordance with the tenets of their religion. About 95 percent of the campers are not residents of Maine.

The camp is located in the town of Harrison (Town); it occupies 180 acres on the shores of a lake about 40 miles northwest of Portland. Petitioner's revenues include camper tuition averaging about $400 per week for each student, contributions from private donors, and income from a "modest endowment." In recent years, the camp has had an annual operating deficit of approximately $175,000. From 1989 to 1991, it paid over $20,000 in real estate and personal property taxes each year.

The Maine statute at issue provides a general exemption from real estate and personal property taxes for "benevolent and charitable institutions incorporated" in the State. With respect to institutions that are "in fact conducted or operated principally for the benefit of persons who are not residents of Maine," however, a charity may only qualify for a more limited tax benefit, and then only if the weekly charge for services provided does not exceed $30 per person. *** Because most of the campers come from out of State, petitioner could not qualify for a complete exemption. And, since the weekly tuition was roughly $400, petitioner was ineligible for any charitable tax exemption at all.

This case involves an issue that we have not previously addressed—the disparate real estate tax treatment of a nonprofit service provider based on the residence of the consumers that it serves. The Town argues that our dormant Commerce Clause jurisprudence is wholly inapplicable to this case, because interstate commerce is not implicated here and Congress has no power to enact a tax on real estate. ***

We are unpersuaded by the Town's argument that the dormant Commerce Clause is inapplicable here, either because campers are not "articles of commerce," or, more generally, because the camp's "product is delivered and 'consumed' entirely within Maine." Even though petitioner's camp does not make a profit, it is unquestionably engaged in commerce, not only as a purchaser, see *Katzenbach v. McClung,* 379 U.S. 294, 300-301 (1964); *United States v. Lopez,* 514 U.S. 549, 558 (1995), but also as a provider of goods and services. It markets those services, together with an opportunity to enjoy the natural beauty of an inland lake in Maine, to campers who are attracted to its facility from all parts of the Nation. The record reflects that petitioner "advertises for campers in [out-of-state] periodicals . . . and sends its Executive Director annually on camper recruiting trips across the country." Petitioner's efforts are quite successful; 95 percent of its campers come from out of State. The attendance of these campers necessarily generates the transportation of persons across state lines that has long been recognized as a form of "commerce."

Summer camps are comparable to hotels that offer their guests goods and services that are consumed locally. In *Heart of Atlanta Motel, Inc. v. United States,* 379 U.S. 241 (1964), we recognized that interstate commerce is substantially affected by the activities of a hotel that "solicits patronage from outside the State of Georgia through various national advertising media, including magazines of national circulation." *Id.* at 243. In that case, we held that commerce was substantially affected by private race discrimination that limited access to the hotel and thereby impeded interstate commerce in the form of travel. *Id.* Official discrimination that limits the access of nonresidents to summer camps creates a similar impediment. Even when business activities are purely local, if "it is interstate commerce that feels the pinch, it does not matter how local the operation which applies the squeeze." *Heart of Atlanta* (quoting *United States v. Women's Sportswear Mfrs. Assn.,* 336 U.S. 460, 464 (1949)).

> **Take Note**
>
> In this passage, the Court explains why this case involves interstate commerce. Must Congress have had power to enact a regulation similar to the challenged state regulation in order for the state regulation to be vulnerable under the Dormant Commerce Clause Doctrine? If not, why is the state regulation problematic?

Although *Heart of Atlanta* involved Congress' affirmative Commerce Clause powers, its reasoning is applicable here. As we stated in *Hughes v. Oklahoma,* 441 U.S. 322 (1979): "The definition of 'commerce' is the same when relied on to strike down or restrict state legislation as when relied on to support some exertion of federal control or regulation." *Id., at 326, n. 2.* ***

There is no question that were this statute targeted at profit-making entities, it would violate the dormant Commerce Clause. "State laws discriminating against interstate commerce on their face are 'virtually *per se* invalid.' " *Fulton Corp. v. Faulkner,* 516 U.S. 325, 331 (1996) (quoting *Oregon Waste Systems, Inc. v. Department of Environmental Quality of Ore.,* 511 U.S. 93 (1994)). It is not necessary to look beyond the text of this statute to determine that it discriminates against interstate commerce. The Maine law expressly distinguishes between entities that serve a principally interstate clientele and those that primarily serve an intrastate market, singling out camps that serve mostly in-staters for beneficial tax treatment, and penalizing those camps that do a principally interstate business. As a practical matter, the statute encourages affected entities to limit their out-of-state clientele, and penalizes the principally nonresident customers of businesses catering to a primarily interstate market.

> **Food for Thought**
>
> In what way does the challenged tax provision, which applies only to in-state businesses, penalize the non-resident customers of the camp and other similar businesses?

We see no reason why the nonprofit character of an enterprise should exclude it from the coverage of either the affirmative or the negative aspect of the Commerce Clause. There are a number of lines of commerce in which both for-profit and nonprofit entities participate. Some educational institutions, some hospitals, some child care facilities, some research organizations, and some museums generate significant earnings; and some are operated by not-for-profit corporations.

For purposes of Commerce Clause analysis, any categorical distinction between the activities of profit-making enterprises and not-for-profit entities is therefore wholly illusory. Entities in both categories are major participants in interstate markets. And, although the summer camp involved in this case may have a relatively insignificant impact on the commerce of the entire Nation, the interstate commercial activities of nonprofit entities as a class are unquestionably significant. See *Wickard v. Filburn,* 317 U.S. 111, 127-128 (1942); *Lopez,* 514 U.S. at 556, 559-560.

Justice SCALIA, with whom THE CHIEF JUSTICE, Justice THOMAS, and Justice GINSBURG join, dissenting.

Facially discriminatory or not, the exemption is no more an artifice of economic protectionism than any state law which dispenses public assistance only to the State's residents. Our cases have always recognized the legitimacy of limiting state-provided welfare benefits to bona fide residents. *** If [a] State that provides social services directly may limit its largesse to its own residents, I see no reason why a State that chooses to provide some of its social services indirectly—by compensating or subsidizing private charitable providers—cannot be similarly restrictive.

Justice THOMAS, with whom Justice SCALIA joins, and with whom THE CHIEF JUSTICE joins [in relevant part], dissenting.

The negative Commerce Clause has no basis in the text of the Constitution, makes little sense, and has proved virtually unworkable in application. In one fashion or another, every Member of the current Court and a goodly number of our predecessors have at least recognized these problems, if not been troubled by them. Because the expansion effected by today's holding further undermines the delicate balance in what we have termed "Our Federalism," *Younger v. Harris,* 401 U.S. 37, 44 (1971), I think it worth revisiting the underlying justifications for our involvement in the negative aspects of the Commerce Clause, and the compelling arguments demonstrating why those justifications are illusory.

To cover its exercise of judicial power in an area for which there is no textual basis, the Court has historically offered two different theories in support of its negative Commerce Clause jurisprudence. The first theory posited was that the Commerce Clause itself constituted an *exclusive* grant of power to Congress. The "exclusivity" rationale was likely wrong from the outset, however. See, *e.g., The Federalist No. 32 *** (A. Hamilton)* ("[N]otwithstanding the affirmative grants of general authorities, there has been the most pointed care in those cases where it was deemed improper that the like authorities should reside in the states, to insert negative clauses prohibiting the exercise of them by the states"). It was seriously questioned even in early cases. See, *e.g., Southern Pacific Co. v. Arizona ex rel. Sullivan,* 325 U.S. 761, 766-767 (1945) ("Ever since *Willson v. Black-Bird Creek Marsh Co.,* 27 U.S. (2 Pet.) 245 (1829), and *Cooley v. Board of Wardens,* 53 U.S. (12 How.) 299 (1851), it has been recognized that, in the absence of conflicting legislation by Congress, there is a residuum of power in the state to make laws governing matters of local concern which nevertheless in some measure affect interstate commerce or even, to some extent, regulate it").

The second theory offered to justify creation of a negative Commerce Clause is that Congress, by its silence, pre-empts state legislation. In other words, we presumed that congressional "inaction" was "equivalent to a declaration that inter-State commerce shall be free and untrammelled." *Welton v. Missouri,* 91 U.S. 275, 282 (1876). To the extent that the "pre-emption-by-silence" rationale ever made sense, it, too, has long since been rejected by this Court in virtually every analogous area of the law.

For example, ever since the watershed case of *Erie R. Co. v. Tompkins,* 304 U.S. 64, (1938), this Court has rejected the notion that it can create a federal common law to fill in great silences left by Congress, and thereby pre-empt state law. We have recognized that "a federal court could not generally apply a federal rule of decision, despite the existence of jurisdiction, in the absence of an applicable Act of Congress." *Milwaukee v. Illinois,* 451 U.S. 304, 313 (1981).

Moreover, our negative Commerce Clause jurisprudence has taken us well beyond the invalidation of obviously discriminatory taxes on interstate commerce. We have used the Clause to make policy-laden judgments that we are ill equipped and arguably unauthorized to make. ***

Any test that requires us to assess (1) whether a particular statute serves a "legitimate" local public interest; (2) whether the effects of the statute on interstate commerce are merely "incidental" or "clearly excessive in relation to the putative benefits"; (3) the "nature" of the local interest; and (4) whether there are alternative means of furthering the local interest that

Make the Connection

The Court often considers governmental interests and the availability of other regulatory choices when it addresses challenges under the Due Process Clause, the Equal Protection Clause, and the First Amendment, topics that we will consider in Chapters 8, 10-12, and 14-16. Is it more problematic for judges to apply such scrutiny when the Dormant Commerce Clause Doctrine is at issue?

have a "lesser impact" on interstate commerce, and even then makes the question "one of degree," surely invites us, if not compels us, to function more as legislators than as judges.

In my view, none of this policy-laden decision making is proper. Rather, the Court should confine itself to interpreting the text of the Constitution ***.

Points for Discussion

a. Subsidies

Does this case mean that state governments cannot give any benefits or subsidies to state residents (while withholding them from out-of-state residents) if the subsidy might affect interstate commerce? In *West Lynn Creamery, Inc. v. Healy*, 512 U.S. 186 (1994), the Court invalidated a Massachusetts law that imposed a tax on all sales of milk to Massachusetts retailers but then rebated the proceeds of the tax to Massachusetts dairy farmers, even though two-thirds of milk sold in Massachusetts came from outside the state. The Court acknowledged that a "pure subsidy funded out of general revenue ordinarily imposes no burden on interstate commerce, but merely assists local business," but it invalidated the Massachusetts law because "a State may not benefit in-state economic interests by burdening out-of-state competitors." Don't all subsidies limited to in-state businesses effectively burden out-of-state competitors by lowering the cost of goods or services for in-state businesses?

In contrast, consider *State Commercial Fisheries Entry Com'n v. Carlson*, 65 P.3d 851 (Alaska 2003), which involved a challenge by out-of-state commercial fisherman to an Alaska law that charged them three times as much for commercial fishing licenses as it did in-state residents. The Alaska Supreme Court upheld the Alaska law, distinguishing *Camps NewFound* as follows:

> In *Camps Newfound*, the United States Supreme Court struck down a local Maine property tax exemption for a charitable camp that primarily served state residents. A Maine town had attempted to argue that the business of the camp did not involve articles of commerce because the services of the camp were "delivered and 'consumed' entirely within Maine." The Court noted that "[t]he attendance of these campers necessarily generates the transportation of persons across state lines that has long been recognized as a form of 'commerce.'" We find there to be no direct analogy between the campers in *Camps Newfound* and the movement of commercial fishers into Alaska. The Court in *Camps Newfound* drew a comparison of the summer camps to hotels. This comparison indicates a sufficient distinction from commercial fishing licenses and permits to allay concerns about the constitutionality of the fee differential.

Id. at 862 (footnotes omitted). Is this distinction convincing? Can you think of any other ground that might justify a state's charging out-of-state commercial fisherman more money for their licenses?

b. Policy Judgments

Is Justice Thomas correct in saying that the Dormant Commerce Clause Doctrine requires the courts to make policy-laden judgments? What would happen if the Supreme Court abandoned the Dormant Commerce Clause Doctrine?

c. Text, History, and Structure

Justice Thomas asserts that the Dormant Commerce Clause Doctrine is illegitimate because (1) it is not based on constitutional text and (2) no theory justifies the doctrine absent a textual basis. Does Justice Thomas apply the same approach to interpreting the Constitution here as he does in cases involving limits on Congress's power? Should historical understandings of the nature of the commerce power be relevant to determining whether it disables the states from acting, even if those understandings are not explicit in the text? And does Justice Thomas acknowledge the political process argument, which we saw advanced in footnote 2 in the *Barnwell Bros.* opinion, for the Dormant Commerce Clause Doctrine?

———————

6. The Market-Participant Exception

The Supreme Court has recognized a "market-participant" exception to the Dormant Commerce Clause Doctrine. The exception applies when a state government acts like a private business, buying or selling goods or services in the market. Just as the courts would not scrutinize a business's decisions about whom to buy from or sell to, the Supreme Court has said that courts should not limit a state government's market activities, even if the state government favors in-state buyers or sellers. The market participation exception, as the Court has said, "differentiates between a State's acting in its distinctive governmental capacity, and a State's acting in the more general capacity of a market participant; only the former is subject to the limitations of the negative Commerce Clause." *New Energy Co. of Indiana v. Limbach*, 486 U.S. 269, 277 (1988).

———————

South-Central Timber Development, Inc. v. Wunnicke

467 U.S. 82 (1984)

Justice WHITE announced the judgment of the Court and delivered the opinion of the Court with respect to Parts I and II, and an opinion with respect to Parts III and IV, in which Justice BRENNAN, Justice BLACKMUN, and Justice STEVENS joined.

We granted certiorari in this case to review a decision of the Court of Appeals for the Ninth Circuit that held that Alaska's requirement that timber taken from state lands be processed within the State prior to export was "implicitly authorized" by Congress and therefore does not violate the Commerce Clause. We hold that it was not authorized and reverse the judgment of the Court of Appeals.

I

In September 1980, the Alaska Department of Natural Resources published a notice that it would sell approximately 49 million board-feet of timber in the area of Icy Cape, Alaska, on October 23, 1980. The notice of sale, the prospectus, and the proposed contract for the sale all provided, pursuant to 11 Alaska Admin.Code § 76.130 (1974), that "[p]rimary manufacture within the State of Alaska will be required as a special provision of the contract." Under the primary-manufacture requirement, the successful bidder must partially process the timber prior to shipping it outside of the State. The requirement is imposed by contract and does not limit the export of unprocessed timber not owned by the State. The stated purpose of the requirement is to "protect existing industries, provide for the establishment of new industries, derive revenue from all timber resources, and manage the State's forests on a sustained yield basis." When it imposes the requirement, the State charges a significantly lower price for the timber than it otherwise would.

The major method of complying with the primary-manufacture requirement is to convert the logs into cants, which are logs slabbed on at least one side. In order to satisfy the Alaska requirement, cants must be either sawed to a maximum thickness of 12 inches or squared on four sides along their entire length.

> **FYI**
>
> Logs are *slabbed* by sawing one side lengthwise to form a square edge.

Petitioner, South-Central Timber Development, Inc., is an Alaska corporation engaged in the business of purchasing standing timber, logging the timber, and shipping the logs into foreign commerce, almost exclusively to Japan. It does not operate a mill in Alaska and customarily sells unprocessed logs. When it learned that the primary-manufacture requirement was to be imposed on the Icy Cape sale, it brought an action in Federal District Court seeking an injunction, arguing that the requirement violated the negative implications of the Commerce Clause.

> **Make the Connection**
>
> The possibility that Congress may consent to state discrimination against interstate commerce is addressed in the next section of this Chapter.

II

[The Court held that Congress had not authorized the state regulation.]

III

We now turn to the issues left unresolved by the Court of Appeals. The first of these issues is whether Alaska's restrictions on export of unprocessed timber from state-owned lands are exempt from Commerce Clause scrutiny under the "market-participant doctrine."

Our cases make clear that if a State is acting as a market participant, rather than as a market regulator, the dormant Commerce Clause places no limitation on its activities. The precise contours of the market-participant doctrine have yet to be established, however, the doctrine having been applied in only three cases of this Court to date.

The first of the cases, *Hughes v. Alexandria Scrap Corp.*, 426 U.S. 794 (1976), involved a Maryland program designed to reduce the number of junked automobiles in the State. A "bounty" was established on Maryland-licensed junk cars, and the State imposed more stringent documentation requirements on out-of-state scrap processors than on in-state ones. The Court rejected a Commerce Clause attack on the program, although it noted that under traditional Commerce Clause analysis the program might well be invalid because it had the effect of reducing the flow of goods in interstate commerce. The Court concluded that Maryland's action was not "the kind of action with which the Commerce Clause is concerned," because "[n]othing in the purposes animating the Commerce Clause prohibits a State, in the absence of congressional action, from participating in the market and exercising the right to favor its own citizens over others."

In *Reeves, Inc. v. Stake*, 447 U.S. 429 (1980), the Court upheld a South Dakota policy of restricting the sale of cement from a state-owned plant to state residents, declaring that "[t]he basic distinction drawn in *Alexandria Scrap* between States as market participants and States as market regulators makes good sense and sound law." The Court relied upon " 'the long recognized right of trader or manufacturer, engaged in an entirely private business, freely to exercise his own independent discretion as to parties with whom he will deal.' " *Id., at 438-439* (quoting *United States v. Colgate & Co.*, 250 U.S. 300, 307 (1919)). In essence, the Court recognized the principle that the Commerce Clause places no limitations on a State's refusal to deal with particular parties when it is participating in the interstate market in goods.

The most recent of this Court's cases developing the market-participant doctrine is *White v. Massachusetts Council of Construction Employers, Inc.*, 460 U.S. 204 (1983), in which the Court sustained against a Commerce Clause challenge an executive order of the Mayor of Boston that required all construction projects funded in whole or in part by city funds or city-administered funds to be performed by a work force of at least 50% city residents. The Court rejected the argument that the city was not entitled to the protection of the doctrine because the order had the effect of regulating employment contracts between public contractors and their employees. Recognizing that "there are some limits on a state or local government's ability to impose restrictions that reach beyond the immediate parties with which the government transacts business," the Court found it unnecessary to define those limits because "[e]veryone affected by the order [was], in a substantial if informal sense, 'working for the city.' " The fact that the employees were "working for the city" was "crucial" to the market-participant analysis in *White*.

The State of Alaska contends that its primary-manufacture requirement fits squarely within the market-participant doctrine, arguing that "Alaska's entry into the market may be viewed as precisely the same type of subsidy to local interests that the Court found unobjectionable in *Alexandria Scrap*." However, when Maryland became involved in the scrap market it was as a purchaser of scrap; Alaska, on the other hand, participates in the timber market, but imposes conditions downstream in the timber-processing market. Alaska is not merely subsidizing local timber processing in an amount "roughly equal to the difference between the price the timber would fetch in the absence of such a requirement and the amount the state actually receives." If the State directly subsidized the timber-processing industry by such an amount, the purchaser would retain the option of taking advantage of the subsidy by processing timber in the State or forgoing the benefits of the subsidy and exporting unprocessed timber. Under the Alaska requirement, however, the choice is made for him: if he buys timber from the State he is not free to take the timber out of state prior to processing.

The State also would have us find *Reeves* controlling. *** Although the Court in *Reeves* did strongly endorse the right of a State to deal with whomever it chooses when it participates in the market, it did not—and did not purport to—sanction the imposition of any terms that the State might desire. For example, the Court expressly noted in *Reeves* that "Commerce Clause scrutiny may well be more rigorous when a restraint on foreign commerce is alleged," that a natural resource "like coal, timber, wild game, or minerals" was not involved, but instead the cement was "the end product of a complex process whereby a costly physical plant and human labor act on raw materials," and that South Dakota did not bar resale of South Dakota cement to out-of-state purchasers. In this case, all three of the elements that were not present in *Reeves*—foreign commerce, a natural resource, and restrictions on resale—are present.

Finally, Alaska argues that since the Court in *White* upheld a requirement that reached beyond "the boundary of formal privity of contract," then, a fortiori, the primary-manu-facture requirement is permissible, because the State is not regulating contracts for resale of timber or regulating the buying and selling of timber, but is instead "a seller of timber, pure and simple." Yet it is clear that the State is more than merely a seller of timber. In the commercial context, the seller usually has no say over, and no interest in, how the product is to be used after sale; in this case, however, payment for the timber does not end the obligations of the purchaser, for, despite the fact that the purchaser has taken delivery of the timber and has paid for it, he cannot do with it as he pleases. Instead, he is obligated to deal with a stranger to the contract after completion of the sale.

That privity of contract is not always the outer boundary of permissible state activity does not necessarily mean that the Commerce Clause has no application within the boundary of formal privity. The market-participant doctrine permits a State to influence "a discrete, identifiable class of economic activity in which [it] is a major participant." *White*, 460 U.S., at 211, n. 7. Contrary to the State's contention, the doctrine is not carte blanche to impose any conditions that the State has the economic power to dictate, and does not validate any requirement merely because the State imposes it upon someone with whom it is in contractual privity.

The limit of the market-participant doctrine must be that it allows a State to impose burdens on commerce within the market in which it is a participant, but allows it to go no further. The State may not impose conditions, whether by statute, regulation, or contract, that have a substantial regulatory effect outside of that particular market. Unless the "market" is relatively narrowly defined, the doctrine has the potential of swallowing up the rule that States may not impose substantial burdens on interstate commerce even if they act with the permissible state purpose of fostering local industry.

IV

Finally, the State argues that even if we find that Congress did not authorize the processing restriction, and even if we conclude that its actions do not qualify for the market-participant exception, the restriction does not substantially burden interstate or foreign commerce under ordinary Commerce Clause principles. We need not labor long over that contention.

Take Note

Part IV is also a plurality opinion. Why did the other members of the Court consider it unnecessary to reach the question whether the Alaska law violated the Dormant Commerce Clause Doctrine?

Viewed as a naked restraint on export of unprocessed logs, there is little question that the processing requirement cannot survive scrutiny under the precedents of the Court. *** Because of the protectionist nature of Alaska's local-processing requirement and the burden on commerce resulting therefrom, we conclude that it falls within the rule of virtual per se invalidity of laws that "bloc[k] the flow of interstate commerce at a State's borders." *City of Philadelphia v. New Jersey*, 437 U.S. 617, 624 (1978).

Justice POWELL, with whom THE CHIEF JUSTICE joins, concurring in part and concurring in the judgment.

I join Parts I and II of Justice WHITE's opinion. I would remand the case to the Court of Appeals to allow that court to consider whether Alaska was acting as a "market participant" and whether Alaska's primary-manufacture requirement substantially burdened interstate commerce ***.

Justice REHNQUIST, with whom Justice O'CONNOR joins, dissenting.

In my view, the line of distinction drawn in the plurality opinion between the State as market participant and the State as market regulator is both artificial and unconvincing. *** The contractual term at issue here no more transforms Alaska's sale of timber into "regulation" of the processing industry than the resident-hiring preference imposed by the city of Boston in <u>White</u> constituted regulation of the construction industry. Alaska is merely paying the buyer of the timber indirectly, by means of a reduced price, to hire Alaska residents to process the timber. Under existing precedent, the State could accomplish that same result in any number of ways. For example, the State could choose to sell its timber only to those companies that maintain active primary-processing plants in Alaska. *Reeves, Inc. v. Stake*, 447 U.S. 429 (1980). Or the State could directly subsidize the primary-processing industry within the State. *Hughes v. Alexandria Scrap Corp.*, 426 U.S. 794 (1976). The State could even pay to have the logs processed and then enter the market only to sell processed logs. It seems to me unduly formalistic to conclude that the one path chosen by the State as best suited to promote its concerns is the path forbidden it by the Commerce Clause.

Points for Discussion

a. Distinctions

How did the plurality opinion distinguish the *White*, *Reeves*, and *Hughes* cases? Why did the dissent find these distinctions unconvincing?

b. Dangers of the Market-Participant Exception

The plurality says: "Unless the 'market' is relatively narrowly defined, the [market-participant exception] has the potential of swallowing up the rule that States may not impose substantial burdens on interstate commerce even if they act with the permissible state purpose of fostering local industry." Can you think of examples that would illustrate this concern?

c. Alternatives

Is Justice Rehnquist correct that the state could accomplish its goal of supporting the Alaska timber-processing industry in several other permissible ways? If so, what does that suggest about the market-participant exception? About the Dormant Commerce Clause Doctrine more generally?

———————————

In some instances, state and local governments enact laws that favor themselves at the expense of all others. For example, laws may give a governmental unit a monopoly over certain kinds of goods or services, like trash collection or mass transit. Because these laws exclude all businesses from competition, they necessarily exclude out-of-state businesses. As a result, the question arises whether these laws should be viewed as discriminating against interstate commerce. The market-participant exception does not apply in these cases because the government is not simply competing in the marketplace with other businesses, but instead has enacted laws that give it advantages. But as the following decision concludes, this does not necessarily mean that the states that enact such laws are violating the Dormant Commerce Clause Doctrine.

———————————

United Haulers Ass'n, Inc. v. Oneida-Herkimer Solid Waste Management Auth.

550 U.S. 330 (2007)

Chief Justice ROBERTS delivered the opinion of the Court, except as to Part II-D.

"Flow control" ordinances require trash haulers to deliver solid waste to a particular waste processing facility. In *C & A Carbone, Inc. v. Clarkstown,* 511 U.S. 383 (1994), this Court struck down under the Commerce Clause a flow control ordinance that forced haulers to deliver waste to a particular *private* processing facility. In this case, we face flow control ordinances quite similar to the one invalidated in *Carbone*. The only salient difference is that the laws at issue here require haulers to bring waste to facilities owned and operated by a state-created public benefit corporation. We find this difference constitutionally significant. Disposing of trash has been a traditional government activity for years, and laws that favor the government in such areas—but treat every private business, whether in-state or out-of-state, exactly the same—do not discriminate against interstate commerce for purposes of the Commerce Clause. Applying the Commerce Clause test reserved for regulations that do not discriminate against interstate commerce, we uphold these ordinances because any incidental burden they may have on interstate commerce does not outweigh the benefits they confer on the citizens of Oneida and Herkimer Counties.

I

[The New York legislature created the Oneida-Herkimer Solid Waste Management Authority and empowered it to dispose of solid waste generated in Oneida and Herkimer counties. The Authority established waste disposal sites in these counties.] In 1989, the Authority and the Counties entered into a Solid Waste Management Agreement, under which the Authority agreed to manage all solid waste within the Counties. Private haulers would remain free to pick up citizens' trash from the curb, but the Authority would take over the job of processing the trash, sorting it, and sending it off for disposal. To fulfill its part of the bargain, the Authority agreed to purchase and develop facilities for the processing and disposal of solid waste and recyclables generated in the Counties.

The Authority collected "tipping fees" to cover its operating and maintenance costs for these facilities.[1] The tipping fees significantly exceeded those charged for waste removal on the open market, but they allowed the Authority to do more than the average private waste disposer. In addition to landfill transportation and solid waste disposal, the fees enabled the Authority to provide recycling of 33 kinds of materials, as well as composting, household hazardous waste disposal, and a number of other services. If the Authority's operating costs and debt service were not recouped through tipping fees and other charges, the agreement provided that the Counties would make up the difference.

As described, the agreement had a flaw: Citizens might opt to have their waste hauled to facilities with lower tipping fees. To avoid being stuck with the bill for facilities that citizens voted for but then chose not to use, the Counties enacted "flow control" ordinances requiring that all solid waste generated within the Counties be delivered to the Authority's processing sites. Private haulers must obtain a permit from the Authority to collect waste in the Counties. Penalties for noncompliance with the ordinances include permit revocation, fines, and imprisonment.

Petitioners are United Haulers Association, Inc., a trade association made up of solid waste management companies, and six haulers that operated in Oneida and Herkimer Counties when this action was filed. In 1995, they sued the Counties and the Authority, alleging that the flow control laws violate the Commerce Clause by discriminating against

---

[1] Tipping fees are disposal charges levied against collectors who drop off waste at a processing facility. They are called "tipping" fees because garbage trucks literally tip their back end to dump out the carried waste. As of 1995, haulers in the Counties had to pay tipping fees of at least $86 per ton, a price that ballooned to as much as $172 per ton if a particular load contained more than 25% recyclables.

interstate commerce. They submitted evidence that without the flow control laws and the associated $86-per-ton tipping fees, they could dispose of solid waste at out-of-state facilities for between $37 and $55 per ton, including transportation.

[II-C]

The flow control ordinances in this case benefit a clearly public facility, while treating all private companies exactly the same. Because the question is now squarely presented on the facts of the case before us, we decide that such flow control ordinances do not discriminate against interstate commerce for purposes of the dormant Commerce Clause.

Compelling reasons justify treating these laws differently from laws favoring particular private businesses over their competitors. "Conceptually, of course, any notion of discrimination assumes a comparison of substantially similar entities." *General Motors Corp. v. Tracy*, 519 U.S. 278, 298 (1997). But States and municipalities are not private businesses—far from it. Unlike private enterprise, government is vested with the responsibility of protecting the health, safety, and welfare of its citizens. These important responsibilities set state and local government apart from a typical private business.

Given these differences, it does not make sense to regard laws favoring local government and laws favoring private industry with equal skepticism. As our local processing cases demonstrate, when a law favors in-state business over out-of-state competition, rigorous scrutiny is appropriate because the law is often the product of "simple economic protectionism." *Wyoming v. Oklahoma*, 502 U.S. 437, 454 (1992). Laws favoring local government, by contrast, may be directed toward any number of legitimate goals unrelated to protectionism. Here the flow control ordinances enable the Counties to pursue particular policies with respect to the handling and treatment of waste generated in the Counties, while allocating the costs of those policies on citizens and businesses according to the volume of waste they generate.

> **Take Note**
>
> In this paragraph and those that follow, the Court explains why laws favoring the government should not be viewed as laws discriminating against interstate commerce. What exactly is the Court's theory?

The contrary approach of treating public and private entities the same under the dormant Commerce Clause would lead to unprecedented and unbounded interference by the courts with state and local government. The dormant Commerce Clause is not a roving license for federal courts to decide what activities are appropriate for state and local government to undertake, and what activities must be the province of private market competition. In this case, the citizens of Oneida and Herkimer Counties have chosen the government to provide waste management services, with a limited role for the private sector in arranging for transport of waste from the curb to the public facilities. The citizens could have left the entire matter for the private sector, in which case any regulation they undertook could not discriminate against interstate commerce. But it was also open to them to vest responsibility for the matter with their government, and to adopt flow control ordinances to support the government effort. It is not the office of the Commerce Clause to control the decision of the voters on whether government or the private sector should provide waste management services. *** "The Commerce Clause significantly limits the ability of States and localities to regulate or otherwise burden the flow of interstate commerce, but it does not elevate free trade above all other values." *Maine v. Taylor*, 477 U.S., at 151.

Finally, it bears mentioning that the most palpable harm imposed by the ordinances—more expensive trash removal—is likely to fall upon the very people who voted for the laws. Our dormant Commerce Clause cases often find discrimination when a State shifts the costs of regulation to other States, because when "the burden of state regulation falls on interests outside the state, it is unlikely to be alleviated by the operation of those political restraints normally exerted when interests within the state are affected." *Southern Pacific Co. v. Arizona ex rel. Sullivan*, 325 U.S. 761, 767-768, n. 2 (1945). Here, the citizens and businesses of the Counties bear the costs of the ordinances. There is no reason to step in and hand local businesses a victory they could not obtain through the political process.

We hold that the Counties' flow control ordinances, which treat in-state private business interests exactly the same as out-of-state ones, do not "discriminate against interstate commerce" for purposes of the dormant Commerce Clause.

[II-D]

The Counties' flow control ordinances are properly analyzed under the test set forth in *Pike v. Bruce Church, Inc.*, 397 U.S. 137 (1970), which is reserved for laws "directed to legitimate local concerns, with effects upon interstate commerce that are only incidental." *Philadelphia v. New Jersey*, 437 U.S. 617, 624 (1978). Under the *Pike* test, we will uphold a nondiscriminatory statute like this one "unless the burden imposed on [interstate] commerce is clearly excessive in relation to the putative local benefits." 397 U.S. at 142.

> **Take Note**
>
> Part II-D is a plurality opinion because it received the votes of only four justices. Why do you think the other five Justices decided not to join this part?

After years of discovery, both the Magistrate Judge and the District Court could not detect *any* disparate impact on out-of-state as opposed to in-state businesses. The Second Circuit alluded to, but did not endorse, a "rather abstract harm" that may exist because "the Counties' flow control ordinances have removed the waste generated in Oneida and Herkimer Counties from the national marketplace for waste processing services." We find it unnecessary to decide whether the ordinances impose any incidental burden on interstate commerce because any arguable burden does not exceed the public benefits of the ordinances.

Justice SCALIA concurring in part.

I have been willing to enforce on *stare decisis* grounds a "negative" self-executing Commerce Clause in two situations: "(1) against a state law that facially discriminates against interstate commerce, and (2) against a state law that is indistinguishable from a type of law previously held unconstitutional by the Court." *West Lynn Creamery, Inc. v. Healy,* 512 U.S.

186, 210 (1994) (SCALIA, J., concurring in judgment). As today's opinion makes clear, the flow-control law at issue in this case meets neither condition. It benefits a *public entity* performing a traditional local-government function and treats *all private entities* precisely the same way. "Disparate treatment constitutes discrimination only if the objects of the disparate treatment are, for the relevant purposes, similarly situated." *Camps Newfound/ Owatonna, Inc. v. Town of Harrison,* 520 U.S. 564, 601 (1997) (SCALIA, J., dissenting). None of this Court's cases concludes that public entities and private entities are similarly situated for Commerce Clause purposes. To hold that they are "would broaden the negative Commerce Clause beyond its existing scope, and intrude on a regulatory sphere traditionally occupied by . . . the States." *General Motors Corp. v. Tracy,* 519 U.S. 278, 313 (1997) (SCALIA, J., concurring).

I am unable to join Part II-D of the principal opinion, in which the plurality performs so-called "*Pike* balancing." Generally speaking, the balancing of various values is left to Congress—which is precisely what the Commerce Clause (the *real* Commerce Clause) envisions.

Justice THOMAS concurring in the judgment.

I concur in the judgment. Although I joined *C & A Carbone, Inc. v. Clarkstown,* 511 U.S. 383 (1994), I no longer believe it was correctly decided. The negative Commerce Clause has no basis in the Constitution and has proved unworkable in practice. See *Camps Newfound/Owatonna, Inc. v. Town of Harrison,* 520 U.S. 564, 610-620 (1997) (THOMAS, J., dissenting). As the debate between the majority and dissent shows, application of the negative Commerce Clause turns solely on policy considerations, not on the Constitution. Because this Court has no policy role in regulating interstate commerce, I would discard the Court's negative Commerce Clause jurisprudence.

> ### Make the Connection
>
> The *Camps Newfound/Owatonna Inc.* case appears above. Justice Thomas explained in more depth in his dissent in that case why he objects to the Dormant Commerce Clause Doctrine.

Justice ALITO, with whom Justice STEVENS and Justice KENNEDY join, dissenting.

In *C & A Carbone, Inc. v. Clarkstown,* 511 U.S. 383 (1994), we held that "a so-called flow control ordinance, which require[d] all solid waste to be processed at a designated transfer station before leaving the municipality," discriminated against interstate commerce and was invalid under the Commerce Clause because it "depriv[ed] competitors, including out-of-state firms, of access to a local market." *Id.* at 386. Because the provisions challenged in this case are essentially identical to the ordinance invalidated in *Carbone* I respectfully dissent.

———————————

Points for Discussion

a. Market-Participant Exception

Why didn't the market-participant exception apply in this case? Isn't the state acting in the way that private competitors would act if given the opportunity?

b. Future of the Dormant Commerce Clause Doctrine

For many decades, the Supreme Court expanded the Dormant Commerce Clause Doctrine. As we have seen, in a series of cases, the Court progressively added new restrictions on state laws pertaining to commerce, including the uniform-national-standard, excessive-burden, and discrimination limitations. More recently, though, the Court seems to be moving in the other direction. The Supreme Court has created the market-participant exception, and it has limited the definition of discrimination against interstate commerce. Some members of the Court have called for even further limitation. What does this trend suggest for the future of the Dormant Commerce Clause Doctrine?

---

7. Congressional Consent

We now have seen several limitations that the Dormant Commerce Clause Doctrine imposes on the power of the states to regulate. The following decisions consider whether Congress may remove these limitations by legislation. In other words, may Congress authorize the states to pass legislation that otherwise would violate the Dormant Commerce Clause Doctrine? As you will see, the answer is yes, even though ordinarily Congress cannot authorize conduct that otherwise violates the Constitution. In reading the cases, consider why Congress has this power in the context of the Dormant Commerce Clause Doctrine.

Prudential Ins. Co. v. Benjamin

328 U.S. 408 (1946)

Mr. Justice RUTLEDGE delivered the opinion of the Court.

[In *Paul v. Virginia*, 75 U.S. (8 Wall.) 168, 183 (1869), the Supreme Court held that a Virginia statute that discriminated against out-of-state insurance companies did not violate the Dormant Commerce Clause Doctrine because "issuing a policy of insurance is not a transaction of commerce." But 75 years later, in *United States v. South-Eastern Underwriters Ass'n*, 322 U.S. 533 (1944), the Supreme Court held that Congress could regulate the business of insurance through the federal antitrust laws because insurance is a commercial enterprise and "[n]o commercial enterprise of any kind which conducts its activities across state lines [is] wholly beyond the regulatory power of Congress under the Commerce

Clause." *Id.* at 553. The <u>*South-Eastern Underwriters*</u> decision created uncertainty about whether the reasoning in <u>*Paul v. Virginia*</u>—that issuing an insurance policy was not commerce—was still valid, and consequently doubt about whether the Dormant Commerce Clause Doctrine would apply to discriminatory state insurance laws. Congress partially responded to this concern by passing the McCarran Act, 59 Stat. 33, 34 (1945), which says that federal law generally will regulate insurance only "to the extent that such business is not regulated by State law." In this case, Prudential Insurance Co., a business incorporated in New Jersey, challenged a South Carolina tax on "foreign" (i.e., out-of-state) insurance companies doing business in South Carolina. The case raised the question whether the McCarran Act was sufficient to make the South Carolina tax constitutional.]

The tax is laid on foreign insurance companies and must be paid annually as a condition of receiving a certificate of authority to carry on the business of insurance within the state. The exaction amounts to three per cent of the aggregate of premiums received from business done in South Carolina, without reference to its interstate or local character. No similar tax is required of South Carolina corporations.

Prudential insists that the tax discriminates against interstate commerce and in favor of local business, since it is laid only on foreign corporations and is measured by their gross receipts from premiums derived from business done in the state, regardless of its interstate or local character. Accordingly it says the tax cannot stand consistently with many decisions of this Court outlawing state taxes which discriminate against interstate commerce. South Carolina denies that the tax is discriminatory or has been affected by the *South-Eastern Underwriters* decision. But in any event it maintains that the tax is valid, more particularly in view of the McCarran Act, by which it is claimed Congress has consented to continuance of this form of taxation and thus has removed any possible constitutional objection which otherwise might exist. This Prudential asserts Congress has not done and could not do.

We are not required however to consider whether *** the authorities on which Prudential chiefly relies would require invalidation of South Carolina's tax. For they are not on point. *** [T]hey are the cases which from *Welton v. Missouri*, 91 U.S. 91 U.S. (1 Otto) 275 (1875), until now have outlawed state taxes found to discriminate against interstate commerce. No one of them involved a situation like that now here. In each the question of validity of the state taxing statute arose when Congress' power lay dormant. In none had Congress acted or purported to act, either by way of consenting to the state's tax or otherwise. Those cases therefore presented no question of the validity of such a tax where Congress had taken affirmative action consenting to it or purporting to give it validity. Nor, consequently, could they stand as controlling precedents for such a case.

This would seem so obvious as hardly to require further comment, except for the fact that Prudential has argued so earnestly to the contrary. Its position puts the McCarran Act to one side, either as not intended to have effect toward validating this sort of tax or, if construed otherwise, as constitutionally ineffective to do so. Those questions present the controlling issues in this case. But before we turn to them it will be helpful to note the exact effects of Prudential's argument.

Fundamentally it maintains that the commerce clause "of its own force" and without reference to any action by Congress, whether through its silence or otherwise, forbids discriminatory state taxation of interstate commerce. This is to say, in effect, that neither Congress acting affirmatively nor Congress and the states thus acting coordinately can validly impose any regulation which the Court has found or would find to be forbidden by the commerce clause, if laid only by state action taken while Congress' power lies dormant. In this view the limits of state power to regulate commerce in the absence of affirmative action by Congress are also the limits of Congress' permissible action in this respect, whether taken alone or in coordination with state legislation.

Merely to state the position in this way compels its rejection. So conceived, Congress' power over commerce would be nullified to a very large extent. For in all the variations of commerce clause theory it has never been the law that what the states may do in the regulation of commerce, Congress being silent, is the full measure of its power. Much less has this boundary been thought to confine what Congress and the states acting together may accomplish. So to regard the matter would invert the constitutional grant into a limitation upon the very power it confers.

The commerce clause is in no sense a limitation upon the power of Congress over interstate and foreign commerce. On the contrary, it is, as Marshall declared in *Gibbons v. Ogden*, a grant to Congress of plenary and supreme authority over those subjects. The only limitation it places upon Congress' power is in respect to what constitutes commerce, including whatever rightly may be found to affect it sufficiently to make Congressional regulation necessary or appropriate. This limitation, of course, is entirely distinct from the implied prohibition of the commerce clause. The one is concerned with defining commerce, with fixing the outer boundary of the field over which the authority granted shall govern. The other relates only to matters within the field of commerce, once this is defined, including whatever may fall within the "affectation" doctrine. The one limitation bounds the power of Congress. The other confines only the powers of the states. And the two areas are not coextensive. The distinction is not always clearly observed, for both questions may and indeed at times do arise in the same case and in close relationship. But, to blur them, and thereby equate the implied prohibition with the affirmative endowment is altogether fallacious. There is no such equivalence.

It is not necessary to spend much time with interpreting the McCarran Act. Pertinently it is as follows:

"Sec. 1. The Congress hereby declares that the continued regulation and taxation by the several States of the business of insurance is in the public interest, and that silence on the part of the Congress shall not be construed to impose any barrier to the regulation or taxation of such business by the several States.

"Sec. 2. (a) The business of insurance, and every person engaged therein, shall be subject to the laws of the several States which relate to the regulation or taxation of such business.

"(b) No Act of Congress shall be construed to invalidate, impair, or supersede any law enacted by any State for the purpose of regulating the business of insurance, or which imposes a fee or tax upon such business, unless such Act specifically relates to the business of insurance. ***" 59 Stat. 34.

Two conclusions, corollary in character and important for this case, must be drawn from Congress' action and the circumstances in which it was taken. *** Congress intended to declare, and in effect declared, that uniformity of regulation, and of state taxation, are not required in reference to the business of insurance, by the national public interest, except in the specific respects otherwise expressly provided for. This necessarily was a determination by Congress that state taxes, which in its silence might be held invalid as discriminatory, do not place on interstate insurance business a burden which it is unable generally to bear or should not bear in the competition with local business. Such taxes were not uncommon, among the states, and the statute clearly included South Carolina's tax now in issue.

In view of all these considerations, we would be going very far to rule that South Carolina no longer may collect her tax. To do so would flout the expressly declared policies of both Congress and the state. Moreover it would establish a ruling never heretofore made and in doing this would depart from the whole trend of decision in a great variety of situations most analogous to the one now presented. For, as we have already emphasized, the authorities most closely in point upon the problem are not, as appellant insists, those relating to discriminatory state taxes laid in the dormancy of Congress' power. They are rather the decisions which, in every instance thus far not later overturned, have sustained coordinated action taken by Congress and the states in the regulation of commerce.

Points for Discussion

a. Can Congress Overrule the Supreme Court?

In discussing how Congress may authorize states to enact laws that otherwise would violate the Dormant Commerce Clause Doctrine, a leading commentator writes: "[T]his is one of the few areas where Congress has clear authority to overrule a Supreme Court decision interpreting the Constitution. If the Court deems a matter to violate the dormant commerce clause, Congress can respond by enacting a law approving the action, thereby effectively overruling the Supreme Court." Erwin Chemerinsky, Constitutional Law: Principles and Policies 449 (3d ed. 2006). Why can Congress overrule the Supreme Court in this area? Is this consistent with *Marbury v. Madison*?

b. Policy Considerations

Under what circumstances should Congress authorize states to discriminate against interstate commerce? Don't all discriminatory measures cause problems of the kind the Commerce Clause was designed to prevent?

c. Extent of Congress's Power

The Court cites the familiar rule that Congress has plenary power to regulate interstate commerce, meaning that Congress can regulate it in any otherwise constitutional way that it chooses. Congress therefore can authorize all of the states to discriminate in the insurance context. But under this theory, may Congress authorize some states to discriminate against interstate commerce but not others? For example, may Congress validly enact legislation saying that South Carolina may impose discriminatory taxes on out-of-state insurance companies but that North Carolina may not? See Thomas B. Colby, *Revitalizing the Forgotten Uniformity Constraint on the Commerce Power*, 91 Va. L. Rev. 249, 262 (2005) (recognizing that modern decisions permit Congress to discriminate among the states, but arguing that these decisions are "directly contrary both to the original intent of the Framers and to the once-settled general understanding of the scope of the commerce power").

———

Even if Congress has consented to the enactment of state legislation that would otherwise violate the Dormant Commerce Clause, it does not follow that the state legislation is automatically constitutional. As the following case shows, the Dormant Commerce Clause is not the only provision in the Constitution that prohibits discrimination. On the contrary, the Equal Protection Clause of the Fourteenth Amendment also bars certain types of discriminatory legislation.

U.S. Constitution, <u>Amend. XIV</u>

Section 1. "No State shall make or enforce any law which shall *** deny to any person within its jurisdiction the equal protection of the laws."

Metropolitan Life Ins. Co. v. Ward

470 U.S. 869 (1985)

Justice POWELL delivered the opinion of the Court.

Since 1955, the State of Alabama has granted a preference to its domestic insurance companies by imposing a substantially lower gross premiums tax rate on them than on out-of-state (foreign) companies. Under the current statutory provisions, foreign life insurance companies pay a tax on their gross premiums received from business conducted in Alabama at a rate of three percent, and foreign companies selling other types of insurance pay at a rate of four percent. All domestic insurance companies, in contrast, pay at a rate of only one percent on all types of insurance premiums. As a result, a foreign insurance company doing the same type and volume of business in Alabama as a domestic company generally will pay three to four times as much in gross premiums taxes as its domestic competitor.

Appellants, a group of insurance companies incorporated outside of the State of Alabama, filed claims with the Alabama Department of Insurance in 1981, contending that the domestic preference tax statute, as applied to them, violated the Equal Protection Clause. They sought refunds of taxes paid for the tax years 1977 through 1980. The Commissioner of Insurance denied all of their claims on July 8, 1981.

The State argues *** that it is impermissible to view a discriminatory tax such as the one at issue here as violative of the Equal Protection Clause. This approach, it contends, amounts to no more than "Commerce Clause rhetoric in equal protection clothing." The State maintains that because Congress, in enacting the McCarran-Ferguson Act, intended to authorize States to impose taxes that burden interstate commerce in the insurance field, the tax at issue here must stand. Our concerns are much more fundamental than as characterized by the State. Although the McCarran-Ferguson Act exempts the insurance industry from Commerce Clause restrictions, it does not purport to limit in any way the applicability of the Equal Protection Clause.

Moreover, the State's view ignores the differences between Commerce Clause and equal protection analysis and the consequent different purposes those two constitutional provisions serve. Under Commerce Clause analysis, the State's interest, if legitimate, is weighed against the burden the state law would impose on interstate commerce. In the equal protection context, however, if the State's purpose is found to be legitimate, the state law stands as long as the burden it imposes is found to be rationally related to that purpose, a relationship that is not difficult to establish.

> **Take Note**
>
> The Court explains here the differences in the prohibitions against discrimination under the Equal Protection Clause and under the Dormant Commerce Clause Doctrine. Can you think of examples where the differences would matter?

The two constitutional provisions perform different functions in the analysis of the permissible scope of a State's power—one protects interstate commerce, and the other protects persons[9] from unconstitutional discrimination by the States. The effect of the statute at issue here is to place a discriminatory tax burden on foreign insurers who desire to do business within the State, thereby also incidentally placing a burden on interstate commerce. Equal protection restraints are applicable even though the *effect* of the discrimination in this case is similar to the type of burden with which the Commerce Clause also would be concerned.

We hold that under the circumstances of this case, promotion of domestic business by discriminating against nonresident competitors is not a legitimate state purpose.

Justice O'CONNOR, with whom Justice BRENNAN, Justice MARSHALL, and Justice REHNQUIST join, dissenting.

[T]he Court has held in the dormant Commerce Clause context that a State may provide subsidies or rebates to domestic but not to foreign enterprises if it rationally believes that the former contribute to the State's welfare in ways that the latter do not. *Hughes v. Alexandria Scrap Corp.*, 426 U.S. 794 (1976). *** See also *Western & Southern Life Ins. Co. v. State Board of Equalization of California*, 451 U.S. 648, 669 (1981) (with congressional approval, States may promote domestic insurers by seeking to deter other States from

---

[9] It is well established that a corporation is a "person" within the meaning of the Fourteenth Amendment.

enacting discriminatory or excessive taxes).

[T]he majority suggests that a state purpose might be legitimate for purposes of the Commerce Clause but somehow illegitimate for purposes of the Equal Protection Clause. No basis is advanced for this theory because no basis exists. The test of a legitimate state purpose must be whether it addresses valid state concerns. To suggest that the purpose's legitimacy, chameleon-like, changes according to the constitutional clause cited in the complaint is merely another pretext to escape the clear message of this Court's precedents.

————

Points for Discussion

a. Effect of the McCarran-Ferguson Act

The Court says that while the "McCarran-Ferguson Act exempts the insurance industry from Commerce Clause restrictions, it does not purport to limit in any way the applicability of the Equal Protection Clause." If the statute as applied in this case is unconstitutional, what did the McCarran-Ferguson Act accomplish?

b. The Equal Protection Clause and the Dormant Commerce Clause

If the state regulation at issue in *Metropolitan Life* violates the Equal Protection Clause because it seeks to protect in-state business by discriminating against out-of-state businesses, then is there any need for the "discrimination" limitation under the Dormant Commerce Clause? Is the Equal Protection Clause a more sensible textual basis for the Court's anti-discrimination rule than the Commerce Clause?

c. Other Constitutional Provisions

What other constitutional provisions might a discriminatory state commerce regulation violate? One additional possibility, discussed below, is the Privileges and Immunities Clause found in Article IV.

————

C. Privileges and Immunities Clause

This chapter already has considered two limitations on state power: the Supremacy Clause and the Dormant Commerce Clause Doctrine. In this section, we consider a third limitation, the Privileges and Immunities Clause found in article IV, section 2, clause 1 of the Constitution.

U.S. Constitution, Article IV, Section 2, Clause 1

"The Citizens of each State shall be entitled to all Privileges and Immunities of Citizens in the several States."

The Supreme Court's cases have established four important principles with respect to the Privileges and Immunities Clause. First, the clause is an anti-discrimination measure that limits the ability of states to treat citizens of other states differently from the state's own citizens. As the Supreme Court has said, the Privileges and Immunities Clause protects the citizens of each state because it "inhibits discriminating legislation against them by other States." *Paul v. Virginia*, 75 U.S. (8 Wall.) 168, 180 (1869).

Second, the Privileges and Immunities Clause limits discrimination only with respect to rights that are "fundamental to the promotion of interstate harmony." *Supreme Court of New Hampshire v. Piper*, 470 U.S. 274, 279 (U.S. 1985). These rights include important things, such as obtaining employment, *Hicklin v. Orbeck*, 437 U.S. 518 (1978), or obtaining medical services, *Doe v. Bolton*, 410 U.S. 179, 200 (1973). But the anti-discrimination privilege does not extend to less essential matters. States, for example, may discriminate against out-of-state residents in issuing recreational hunting licenses, *Baldwin v. Fish and Game Commission of Montana*, 436 U.S. 371 (1978), or even offering admissions to a state university, *Rosenstock v. Board of Governors of University of North Carolina*, 423 F. Supp. 1321 (D.C.N.C. 1976). The courts continue to develop the distinction between rights fundamental to the promotion of interstate harmony and other rights as they consider additional cases.

Third, the Privileges and Immunities Clause may allow a state to discriminate against non-residents, even with respect to certain very important rights, if the state has a "substantial reason" for the discrimination. *Saenz v. Roe*, 526 U.S. 489, 502 (1999). For example, as the Court has said, "no one would suggest that the Privileges and Immunities Clause requires a State to open its polls to a person who declines to assert that the State is the only one where he claims a right to vote." *Baldwin*, 436 U.S. at 383.

Fourth, the term "citizen" has a specific meaning. The term refers to United States citizens, a group that does not include aliens or corporations. *See Zobel v. Williams*, 457 U.S. 55, 74 (1982) (O'Connor, J., concurring). And in determining whether a person is a "citizen" of a particular state, "it is now established that the terms 'citizen' and 'resident' are essentially interchangeable, for purposes of analysis of most cases under the Privileges and Immunities Clause." *Hicklin*, 437 U.S. at 524.

Finally, note that there is another clause in the Constitution that addresses privileges and immunities. Section 1 of the Fourteenth Amendment provides: "No state shall make or enforce any law which shall abridge the privileges or immunities of citizens of the United States." Unlike the Privileges and Immunities Clause in Article IV, the Fourteenth Amendment speaks of the "privileges *or* immunities" of "citizens of the United States." We will consider this provision in Chapter 7.

In reading the following case, consider whether a state is discriminating against out-of-state residents, whether the discrimination is likely to jeopardize interstate harmony, and whether any state interest might justify the discrimination.

Baldwin v. Fish and Game Commission of Montana

436 U.S. 371 (1978)

Mr. Justice BLACKMUN delivered the opinion of the Court.

Appellant Lester Baldwin is a Montana resident. He also is an outfitter holding a state license as a hunting guide. The majority of his customers are nonresidents who come to Montana to hunt elk and other big game. Appellants Carlson, Huseby, Lee and Moris are residents of Minnesota. They have hunted big game, particularly elk, in Montana in past years and wish to continue to do so.

In 1975, the five appellants, disturbed by the difference in the kinds of Montana elk-hunting licenses available to nonresidents, as contrasted with those available to residents of the State, and by the difference in the fees the nonresident and the resident must pay for their respective licenses, instituted the present federal suit for declaratory and injunctive relief and for reimbursement, in part, of fees already paid. ***

The relevant facts are not in any real controversy and many of them are agreed. *** For the 1975 hunting season, a Montana resident could purchase a license solely for elk for $4. The nonresident, however, in order to hunt elk, was required to purchase a combination license at a cost of $151; this entitled him to take one elk and two deer. For the 1976 season, the Montana resident could purchase a license solely for elk for $9. The nonresident, in order to hunt elk, was required to purchase a combination license at a cost of $225; this entitled him to take one elk, one deer, one black bear, and game birds, and to fish with hook and line. A resident was not required to buy any combination of licenses, but if he did, the cost to him of all the privileges granted by the nonresident combination license was $30. The nonresident thus paid 7 1/2 times as much as the resident, and if the nonresident wished to hunt only elk, he paid 25 times as much as the resident.

Appellants strongly urge here that the Montana licensing scheme for the hunting of elk violates the Privileges and Immunities Clause of Art. IV, § 2, of our Constitution. That Clause is not one the contours of which have been precisely shaped by the process and wear of constant litigation and judicial interpretation over the years since 1789. ***

Perhaps because of the imposition of the Fourteenth Amendment upon our constitutional consciousness and the extraordinary emphasis that the Amendment received, it is not surprising that the contours of Art. IV, § 2, cl. 1, are not well developed, and that the relationship, if any, between the Privileges and Immunities Clause and the "privileges or immunities" language of the Fourteenth Amendment is less than clear. We are, nevertheless, not without some pronouncements by this Court as to the Clause's significance and reach. There are at least three general comments that deserve mention:

The first is that of Mr. Justice Field, writing for a unanimous Court in *Paul v. Virginia*, 75 U.S. (8 Wall.) 168, 180 (1869). He emphasized nationalism, the proscription of discrimination, and the assurance of equality of all citizens within any State:

> "It was undoubtedly the object of the clause in question to place the citizens of each State upon the same footing with citizens of other States, so far as the advantages resulting from citizenship

in those States are concerned. It relieves them from the disabilities of alienage in other States; it inhibits discriminating legislation against them by other States; it gives them the right of free ingress into other States, and egress from them; it insures to them in other States the same freedom possessed by the citizens of those States in the acquisition and enjoyment of property and in the pursuit of happiness; and it secures to them in other States the equal protection of their laws. It has been justly said that no provision in the Constitution has tended so strongly to constitute the citizens of the United States one people as this."

The second came 70 years later when Mr. Justice Roberts, writing for himself and Mr. Justice Black in *Hague v. CIO*, 307 U.S. 496, 511 (1939), summed up the history of the Clause and pointed out what he felt to be the difference in analysis in the earlier cases from the analysis in later ones:

"[P]rior to the adoption of the Fourteenth Amendment, there had been no constitutional definition of citizenship of the United States, or of the rights, privileges, and immunities secured thereby or springing therefrom. At one time it was thought that this section recognized a group of rights which, according to the jurisprudence of the day, were classed as 'natural rights'; and that the purpose of the section was to create rights of citizens of the United States by guaranteeing the citizens of every State the recognition of this group of rights by every other State. *** While this description of the civil rights of the citizens of the States has been quoted with approval, it has come to be the settled view that Article IV, § 2, does not import that a citizen of one State carries with him into another fundamental privileges and immunities which come to him necessarily by the mere fact of his citizenship in the State first mentioned, but, on the contrary, that in any State every citizen of any other State is to have the same privileges and immunities which the citizens of that State enjoy. The section, in effect, prevents a State from discriminating against citizens of other States in favor of its own."

The third and most recent general pronouncement is that authored by Mr. Justice Marshall for a nearly unanimous Court in *Austin v. New Hampshire*, 420 U.S. 656, 660-661 (1975), stressing the Clause's "norm of comity" and the Framers' concerns:

"The Clause thus establishes a norm of comity without specifying the particular subjects as to which citizens of one State coming within the jurisdiction of another are guaranteed equality of treatment. The origins of the Clause do reveal, however, the concerns of central import to the Framers. During the preconstitutional period, the practice of some States denying to outlanders the treatment that its citizens demanded for themselves was widespread. The fourth of the Articles of Confederation was intended to arrest this centrifugal tendency with some particularity. . . . The discriminations at which this Clause was aimed were by no means eradicated during the short life of the Confederation, and the provision was carried over into the comity article of the Constitution in briefer form but with no change of substance or intent, unless it was to strengthen the force of the Clause in fashioning a single nation."

When the Privileges and Immunities Clause has been applied to specific cases, it has been interpreted to prevent a State from imposing unreasonable burdens on citizens of other States in their pursuit of common callings within the State, *Ward v. Maryland*, 12 Wall. 418 (1871); in the ownership and disposition of privately held

Take Note

The Court gives examples of the kinds of discrimination that do, and that do not, jeopardize interstate harmony. Is it possible to discern a broader principle from these examples?

property within the State, *Blake v. McClung,* 172 U.S. 239 (1898); and in access to the courts of the State, *Canadian Northern R. Co. v. Eggen,* 252 U.S. 553 (1920).

It has not been suggested, however, that state citizenship or residency may never be used by a State to distinguish among persons. Suffrage, for example, always has been understood to be tied to an individual's identification with a particular State. No one would suggest that the Privileges and Immunities Clause requires a State to open its polls to a person who declines to assert that the State is the only one where he claims a right to vote. The same is true as to qualification for an elective office of the State. Nor must a State always apply all its laws or all its services equally to anyone, resident or nonresident, who may request it so to do. Some distinctions between residents and nonresidents merely reflect the fact that this is a Nation composed of individual States, and are permitted; other distinctions are prohibited because they hinder the formation, the purpose, or the development of a single Union of those States. Only with respect to those "privileges" and "immunities" bearing upon the vitality of the Nation as a single entity must the State treat all citizens, resident and nonresident, equally. Here we must decide into which category falls a distinction with respect to access to recreational big-game hunting.

Does the distinction made by Montana between residents and nonresidents in establishing access to elk hunting threaten a basic right in a way that offends the Privileges and Immunities Clause? Merely to ask the question seems to provide the answer. We repeat much of what already has been said above: Elk hunting by nonresidents in Montana is a recreation and a sport. In itself—wholly apart from license fees—it is costly and obviously available only to the wealthy nonresident or to the one so taken with the sport that he sacrifices other values in order to indulge in it and to enjoy what it offers. It is not a means to the nonresident's livelihood. The mastery of the animal and the trophy are the ends that are sought; appellants are not totally excluded from these. The elk supply, which has been entrusted to the care of the State by the people of Montana, is finite and must be carefully tended in order to be preserved.

Appellants' interest in sharing this limited resource on more equal terms with Montana residents simply does not fall within the purview of the Privileges and Immunities Clause. Equality in access to Montana elk is not basic to the maintenance or well-being of the Union. Appellants do not—and cannot—contend that they are deprived of a means of a livelihood by the system or of access to any part of the State to which they may seek to travel. We do not decide the full range of activities that are sufficiently basic to the livelihood of the Nation that the States may not interfere with a nonresident's participation therein without similarly interfering with a resident's participation. Whatever rights or activities may be "fundamental" under the Privileges and Immunities Clause, we are persuaded, and hold, that elk hunting by nonresidents in Montana is not one of them.

———————

Points for Discussion

a. Elements of the Rule

How did the Montana law discriminate against out-of-state residents? Was the discrimination likely to jeopardize interstate harmony? Did Montana have to show that the discrimination was necessary to further an important state interest? Should it have been required to make such a showing?

b. The Dormant Commerce Clause Doctrine and Equal Protection

How would you analyze the Montana law under the Dormant Commerce Clause Doctrine or under the Equal Protection Clause? Why didn't the Court analyze it under those provisions?

D. State Power to Regulate the House and Senate

Chapter 3, which addressed federal powers, began with the landmark case of *McCulloch v. Maryland*. That case presented two issues. Recall that the first issue was whether Congress has the power to create a national bank. The Supreme Court, relying in part on the Necessary and Proper Clause, concluded that Congress has this power. The second issue was whether the states could impose a tax on the notes issued by the national bank. The Court held that the state could not. Indeed, since *McCulloch*, the Court has announced that, as a general rule, instrumentalities of the federal government are immune from state taxes and regulations. California cannot tax the U.S. Postal Service, New York cannot tell the U.S. Navy how to operate its ships, and so forth. This principle serves as a general limitation on the power of the states, derived from the structure of the Constitution and the relationship between the states and the federal government.

But the scope of this limitation on state authority is somewhat uncertain. A major test of federal immunity from state regulation occurred in the early 1990s. A grass-roots movement arose throughout the country to impose term limits on members of Congress. The movement stemmed from a belief that members of Congress had become interested primarily in seeking reelection and therefore had become ineffective in running the country. Limiting the terms that a member of Congress could serve was thought to provide a solution to this problem. Legislatures in 23 states passed measures to restrict the ability of senior members of the House of Representatives and the Senate to seek reelection. If these restrictions were constitutional, at least 72 members of Congress would have been barred from standing for reelection in 1996. Many more would have faced term limits in the future. So when the Supreme Court agreed to consider the issue in the following case, quite a few politicians anxiously awaited its decision. *See* Deborah Kalb & Doug Obey, *Members Applaud, Decry Decision on Term Limits*, The Hill (May 24, 1995).

The Constitution includes provisions that speak directly to the question of the qualifications for Members of Congress. These provisions were predictably quite important in the challenge to the state term-limit provisions.

U.S. Constitution, <u>Article I, Section 3</u>

Clause 2. "No Person shall be a Representative who shall not have attained to the Age of twenty five Years, and been seven Years a Citizen of the United States, and who shall not, when elected, be an Inhabitant of that State in which he shall be chosen."

Clause 3. "No Person shall be a Senator who shall not have attained to the Age of thirty Years, and been nine Years a Citizen of the United States, and who shall not, when elected, be an Inhabitant of that State for which he shall be chosen."

U.S. Term Limits, Inc. v. Thornton

514 U.S. 779 (1995)

Justice STEVENS delivered the opinion of the Court.

At the general election on November 3, 1992, the voters of Arkansas adopted Amendment 73, [which had been proposed as a "Term Limitation Amendment,"] to their State Constitution. *** Section 3 [of the Amendment], the provision at issue in these cases, applies to the Arkansas Congressional Delegation. It provides:

"(a) Any person having been elected to three or more terms as a member of the United States House of Representatives from Arkansas shall not be certified as a candidate and shall not be eligible to have his/her name placed on the ballot for election to the United States House of Representatives from Arkansas.

"(b) Any person having been elected to two or more terms as a member of the United States Senate from Arkansas shall not be certified as a candidate and shall not be eligible to have his/her name placed on the ballot for election to the United States Senate from Arkansas."

Amendment 73 states that it is self-executing and shall apply to all persons seeking election after January 1, 1993.

On November 13, 1992, respondent Bobbie Hill, on behalf of herself, similarly situated Arkansas "citizens, residents, taxpayers and registered voters," and the League of Women Voters of Arkansas, filed a complaint in the Circuit Court for Pulaski County, Arkansas, seeking a declaratory judgment that § 3 of Amendment 73 is "unconstitutional and void." ***

Twenty-six years ago, in *Powell v. McCormack,* 395 U.S. 486 (1969), we reviewed the history and text of the Qualifications Clauses in a case involving an attempted exclusion of a duly elected Member of Congress. The principal issue was whether the power granted to each House in Art. I, § 5, cl. 1, to judge the "Qualifications of its own Members" includes

Make the Connection

We considered the Court's decision in *Powell* in Chapter 2, when we discussed the political question doctrine.

the power to impose qualifications other than those set forth in the text of the Constitution. In an opinion by Chief Justice Warren for eight Members of the Court, we held that it does not. * * *

[In *Powell*,] we viewed the Convention debates as manifesting the Framers' intent that the qualifications in the Constitution be fixed and exclusive. We found particularly revealing the debate concerning a proposal made by the Committee of Detail that would have given Congress the power to add property qualifications. James Madison argued that such a power would vest "an improper & dangerous power in the Legislature," by which the Legislature "can by degrees subvert the Constitution." 395 U.S. at 533-534, quoting 2 Records of the Federal Convention of 1787, pp. 249-250 (M. Farrand ed. 1911). Madison continued: "A Republic may be converted into an aristocracy or oligarchy as well by limiting the number capable of being elected, as the number authorised to elect." 395 U.S. at 534, quoting 2 Farrand 250.

The Framers further revealed their concerns about congressional abuse of power when Gouverneur Morris suggested modifying the proposal of the Committee of Detail to grant Congress unfettered power to add qualifications. We noted that Hugh Williamson "expressed concern that if a majority of the legislature should happen to be 'composed of any particular description of men, of lawyers for example, . . . the future elections might be secured to their own body.' " Id. at 535, quoting 2 Farrand 250. We noted, too, that Madison emphasized the British Parliament's attempts to regulate qualifications, and that he observed: "[T]he abuse they had made of it was a lesson worthy of our attention." 395 U.S. at 535, quoting 2 Farrand 250. We found significant that the Convention rejected both Morris' modification and the Committee's proposal.

We also recognized in *Powell* that the post Convention ratification debates confirmed that the Framers understood the qualifications in the Constitution to be fixed and unalterable by Congress. For example, we noted that in response to the antifederalist charge that the new Constitution favored the wealthy and well born, Alexander Hamilton wrote:

"The truth is that there is no method of securing to the rich the preference apprehended but by prescribing qualifications of property either for those who may elect or be elected. But this forms no part of the power to be conferred upon the national government. . . . *The qualifications of the persons who may choose or be chosen, as has been remarked upon other occasions, are defined and fixed in the Constitution, and are unalterable by the legislature.*" 395 U.S., at 539, quoting The Federalist No. 60, p. 371 (C. Rossiter ed. 1961) (emphasis added) (hereinafter The Federalist).

The exercise by Congress of its power to judge the qualifications of its Members further confirmed this understanding. We concluded that, during the first 100 years of its existence, "Congress strictly limited its power to judge the qualifications of its members to those enumerated in the Constitution." 395 U.S. at 542.

As this elaborate summary reveals, our historical analysis in *Powell* was both detailed and persuasive. We thus conclude now, as we did in *Powell*, that history shows that, with respect to Congress, the Framers intended the Constitution to establish fixed qualifications.

Our reaffirmation of *Powell* does not necessarily resolve the specific questions presented in these cases. For petitioners argue that whatever the constitutionality of additional qualifications for membership imposed by Congress, the historical and textual materials discussed in *Powell* do not support the conclusion that the Constitution prohibits additional qualifications imposed by States. In the absence of such a

constitutional prohibition, petitioners argue, the Tenth Amendment and the principle of reserved powers require that States be allowed to add such qualifications.

Contrary to petitioners' assertions, the power to add qualifications is not part of the original powers of sovereignty that the Tenth Amendment reserved to the States. Petitioners' Tenth Amendment argument misconceives the nature of the right at issue because that Amendment could only "reserve" that which existed before. As Justice Story recognized, "the states can exercise no powers whatsoever, which exclusively spring out of the existence of the national government, which the constitution does not delegate to them. . . . No state can say, that it has reserved, what it never possessed." 1 Story § 627.

Justice Story's position thus echoes that of Chief Justice Marshall in *McCulloch v. Maryland*, 4 Wheat. 316 (1819). In *McCulloch*, the Court rejected the argument that the Constitution's silence on the subject of state power to tax corporations chartered by Congress implies that the States have "reserved" power to tax such federal instrumentalities. As Chief Justice Marshall pointed out, an "original right to tax" such federal entities "never existed, and the question whether it has been surrendered, cannot arise." *Id.*, at 430.

With respect to setting qualifications for service in Congress, no such right existed before the Constitution was ratified. [Under the Articles of Confederation,] "the States retained most of their sovereignty, like independent nations bound together only by treaties." *Wesberry v. Sanders*, 376 U.S. 1, 9 (1964). *** In adopting [the Constitution], the Framers envisioned a uniform national system, rejecting the notion that the Nation was a collection of States, and instead creating a direct link between the National Government and the people of the United States. In that National Government, representatives owe primary allegiance not to the people of a State, but to the people of the Nation.

In short, as the Framers recognized, electing representatives to the National Legislature was a new right, arising from the Constitution itself. The Tenth Amendment thus provides no basis for concluding that the States possess reserved power to add qualifications to those that are fixed in the Constitution. Instead, any state power to set the qualifications for membership in Congress must derive not from the reserved powers of state sovereignty, but rather from the delegated powers of national sovereignty. In the absence of any constitutional delegation to the States of power to add qualifications to those enumerated in the Constitution, such a power does not exist.

The available affirmative evidence indicates the Framers' intent that States have no role in the setting of qualifications. In The Federalist No. 52, dealing with the House of Representatives, Madison addressed the "qualifications of the electors and the elected." Madison first noted the difficulty in achieving uniformity in the qualifications for electors, which resulted in the Framers' decision to require only that the qualifications for federal electors be the same as those for state electors. Madison argued that such a decision "must be satisfactory to every State, because it is comfortable to the standard already established, or which may be established, by the State itself." Madison then explicitly contrasted the state control over the qualifications of electors with the lack of state control over the qualifications of the elected:

> "The qualifications of the elected, being less carefully and properly defined by the State constitutions, and being at the same time more susceptible of uniformity, have been very properly considered and regulated by the convention. A representative of the United States must be of the age of twenty-five years; must have been seven years a citizen of the United States; must, at the time of his election be an inhabitant of the State he is to represent; and, during the time of his service must be in no office under the United States. Under these reasonable limitations, the door of this part of the federal government is open to merit of every description, whether native or adoptive, whether young or old, and without regard to poverty or wealth, or to any particular profession of religious faith."

We also find compelling the complete absence in the ratification debates of any assertion that States had the power to add qualifications. In those debates, the question whether to require term limits, or "rotation," was a major source of controversy. The draft of the Constitution that was submitted for ratification contained no provision for rotation. In arguments that echo in the preamble to Arkansas' Amendment 73, opponents of ratification condemned the absence of a rotation requirement, noting that "there is no doubt that senators will hold their office perpetually; and in this situation, they must of necessity lose their dependence, and their attachments to the people."

Regardless of which side has the better of the debate over rotation, it is most striking that nowhere in the extensive ratification debates have we found any statement by either a proponent or an opponent of rotation that the draft constitution would permit States to require rotation for the representatives of their own citizens. If the participants in the debate had believed that the States retained the authority to impose term limits, it is inconceivable that the Federalists would not have made this obvious response to the arguments of the pro-rotation forces. The absence in an otherwise freewheeling debate of any suggestion that States had the power to impose additional qualifications unquestionably reflects the Framers' common understanding that States lacked that power.

Our conclusion that States lack the power to impose qualifications vindicates the same "fundamental principle of our representative democracy" that we recognized in *Powell*, namely, that "the people should choose whom they please to govern them." *Id.*

Petitioners argue that, even if States may not add qualifications, Amendment 73 is constitutional because it is not such a qualification, and because Amendment 73 is a permissible exercise of state power to regulate the "Times, Places and Manner of holding

Elections." We reject these contentions. In our view, Amendment 73 is an indirect attempt to accomplish what the Constitution prohibits Arkansas from accomplishing directly. * * *

Justice THOMAS, with whom THE CHIEF JUSTICE, Justice O'CONNOR, and Justice SCALIA join, dissenting.

The Court holds [that] neither the elected legislature of [a] State nor the people themselves (acting by ballot initiative) may prescribe any qualifications for [federal] representatives. The majority therefore defends the right of the people of Arkansas to "choose whom they please to govern them" by invalidating a provision that won nearly 60% of the votes cast in a direct election and that carried every congressional district in the State.

When they adopted the Federal Constitution, of course, the people of each State surrendered some of their authority to the United States (and hence to entities accountable to the people of other States as well as to themselves). They affirmatively deprived their States of certain powers, see, *e.g.,* Art. I, § 10, and they affirmatively conferred certain powers upon the Federal Government, see, *e.g.,* Art. I, § 8. Because the people of the several States are the only true source of power, however, the Federal Government enjoys no authority beyond what the Constitution confers: The Federal Government's powers are limited and enumerated. In the words of Justice Black: "The United States is entirely a creature of the Constitution. Its power and authority have no other source." *Reid v. Covert,* 354 U.S. 1, 5-6 (1957) (plurality opinion).

In each State, the remainder of the people's powers—"[t]he powers not delegated to the United States by the Constitution, nor prohibited by it to the States," Amdt. 10—are either delegated to the state government or retained by the people. The Federal Constitution does not specify which of these two possibilities obtains; it is up to the various state constitutions to declare which powers the people of each State have delegated to their state government. As far as the Federal Constitution is concerned, then, the States can exercise all powers that the Constitution does not withhold from them. The Federal Government and the States thus face different default rules: Where the Constitution is silent about the exercise of a particular power—that is, where the Constitution does not speak either expressly or by necessary implication—the Federal Government lacks that power and the States enjoy it.

The majority's essential logic is that the state governments could not "reserve" any powers that they did not control at the time the Constitution was drafted. But it was not the state governments that were doing the reserving. The Constitution derives its authority instead from the consent of *the people* of the States. Given the fundamental principle that all governmental powers stem from the people of the States, it would simply be incoherent to assert that the people of the States could not reserve any powers that they had not previously controlled.

The majority also seeks support for its view of the Tenth Amendment in *McCulloch v. Maryland,* 4 Wheat. 316 (1819). But this effort is misplaced. * * * [The Court] held that the Constitution affirmatively prohibited Maryland's tax on the bank created by [a federal] statute. The Court relied principally on concepts that it deemed inherent in the Supremacy

Clause of Article VI, [concluding] that the very nature of state taxation on the bank's operations was "incompatible with, and repugnant to," the federal statute creating the bank. ***
For the majority, however, *McCulloch* apparently turned on the fact that before the Constitution was adopted, the States had possessed no power to tax the instrumentalities of the governmental institutions that the Constitution created. This understanding of *McCulloch* makes most of Chief Justice Marshall's opinion irrelevant; according to the majority, there was no need to inquire into whether federal law deprived Maryland of the power in question, because the power could not fall into the category of "reserved" powers anyway.

I take it to be established, then, that the people of Arkansas do enjoy "reserved" powers over the selection of their representatives in Congress. Purporting to exercise those reserved powers, they have agreed among themselves that the candidates covered by § 3 of Amendment 73—those whom they have already elected to three or more terms in the House of Representatives or to two or more terms in the Senate—should not be eligible to appear on the ballot for reelection, but should nonetheless be returned to Congress if enough voters are sufficiently enthusiastic about their candidacy to write in their names. Whatever one might think of the wisdom of this arrangement, we may not override the decision of the people of Arkansas unless something in the Federal Constitution deprives them of the power to enact such measures.

At least on their face, *** the Qualifications Clauses do nothing to prohibit the people of a State from establishing additional eligibility requirements for their own representatives. Joseph Story thought that such a prohibition was nonetheless implicit in the constitutional list of qualifications, because "[f]rom the very nature of such a provision, the affirmation of these qualifications would seem to imply a negative of all others." 1 Commentaries on the Constitution of the United States § 624 (1833). This argument rests on the maxim *expressio unius est exclusio alterius.* When the Framers decided which qualifications to include in the Constitution, they also decided not to include any other qualifications in the Constitution. In Story's view, it would conflict with this latter decision for the people of the individual States to decide, as a matter of state law, that they would like their own representatives in Congress to meet additional eligibility requirements.

> **Definition**
>
> *Expressio unius est exclusio alterius* means "to say one thing is to exclude the other." The *expressio unius* maxim says that an express inclusion of some things in a law implies the exclusion of others. What would this maxim mean with respect to the requirements included in Article I for members of the House and Senate?

To spell out the logic underlying this argument is to expose its weakness. Even if one were willing to ignore the distinction between requirements enshrined in the Constitution and other requirements that the Framers were content to leave within the reach of ordinary law, Story's application of the *expressio unius* maxim takes no account of federalism. At most, the specification of certain nationwide disqualifications in the Constitution implies the negation of other *nationwide* disqualifications; it does not imply that individual States or their people are barred from adopting their own disqualifications on a state-by-state basis. Thus, the one delegate to the Philadelphia Convention who voiced anything approaching

Story's argument said only that a recital of qualifications in the Constitution would imply that *Congress* lacked any qualification-setting power. See 2 Farrand 123 (remarks of John Dickinson).

The Qualifications Clauses do prevent the individual States from abolishing all eligibility requirements for Congress. This restriction on state power reflects the fact that when the people of one State send immature, disloyal, or unknowledgeable representatives to Congress, they jeopardize not only their own interests but also the interests of the people of other States. Because Congress wields power over all the States, the people of each State need some guarantee that the legislators elected by the people of other States will meet minimum standards of competence. The Qualifications Clauses provide that guarantee: They list the requirements that the Framers considered essential to protect the competence of the National Legislature.

If the people of a State decide that they would like their representatives to possess additional qualifications, however, they have done nothing to frustrate the policy behind the Qualifications Clauses. Anyone who possesses all of the constitutional qualifications, plus some qualifications required by state law, still has all of the federal qualifications. Accordingly, the fact that the Constitution specifies certain qualifications that the Framers deemed necessary to protect the competence of the National Legislature does not imply that it strips the people of the individual States of the power to protect their own interests by adding other requirements for their own representatives.

> **Take Note**
>
> The dissent concludes that the Qualifications Clause imposes a floor, not a ceiling. The majority, in contrast, concluded that the same text imposes not only a floor but also a ceiling. Which view do you find more persuasive?

The people of other States could legitimately complain if the people of Arkansas decide, in a particular election, to send a 6-year-old to Congress. But the Constitution gives the people of other States no basis to complain if the people of Arkansas elect a freshman representative in preference to a long-term incumbent. That being the case, it is hard to see why the rights of the people of other States have been violated when the people of Arkansas decide to enact a more general disqualification of long-term incumbents. Such a disqualification certainly is subject to scrutiny under other constitutional provisions, such as the First and Fourteenth Amendments. But as long as the candidate whom they send to Congress meets the constitutional age, citizenship, and inhabitancy requirements, the people of Arkansas have not violated the Qualifications Clauses.

In seeking ratification of the Constitution, James Madison did assert that "[u]nder these reasonable limitations [set out in the House Qualifications Clause], the door of this part of the federal government is open to merit of every description. . . ." The Federalist No. 52. The majority stresses this assertion, and others to the same effect, in support of its "egalitarian concept." But there is no reason to interpret these statements as anything more than claims that the Constitution itself imposes relatively few disqualifications for congressional office. One should not lightly assume that Madison and his colleagues, who were attempting to win support at the state level for the new Constitution, were proclaiming the inability of the people of the States or their state legislatures to prescribe any eligibility requirements for their own Representatives or Senators. Instead, they were merely responding to the charge that the Constitution was undemocratic and would lead to aristocracies in office. The statement that the qualifications imposed in the Constitution are not unduly restrictive hardly implies that the Constitution withdrew the power of the people of each State to prescribe additional eligibility requirements for their own Representatives if they so desired.

[S]tate practice immediately after the ratification of the Constitution refutes the majority's suggestion that the Qualifications Clauses were commonly understood as being exclusive. Five States supplemented the constitutional disqualifications in their very first election laws, and the surviving records suggest that the legislatures of these States considered and rejected the interpretation of the Constitution that the majority adopts today. [T]he first Virginia election law erected a property qualification for Virginia's contingent in the Federal House of Representatives. See Virginia Election Law (Nov. 20, 1788), in 2 Documentary History of the First Federal Elections, 1788-1790, pp. 293, 294 (G. DenBoer ed. 1984) (hereinafter First Federal Elections) (restricting possible candidates to "freeholder[s]"). What is more, while the Constitution merely requires representatives to be inhabitants of their State, the legislatures of five of the seven States that divided themselves into districts for House elections added that representatives also had to be inhabitants of the district that elected them. Three of these States adopted durational residency requirements too, insisting that representatives have resided within their districts for at least a year (or, in one case, three years) before being elected.[11]

It is radical enough for the majority to hold that the Constitution implicitly precludes the people of the States from prescribing any eligibility requirements for the congressional candidates who seek their votes. This holding, after all, does not stop with negating the term limits that many States have seen fit to impose on their Senators and Representatives. Today's decision also means that no State may disqualify congressional candidates whom a court has found to be mentally incompetent, see, e.g., Fla. Stat. §§ 97.041(2), 99.021(1) (a) (1991), who are currently in prison, see, e.g., Ill. Comp. Stat. Ann., ch. 10, §§ 5/3-5, 5/7-10, 5/10-5 (1993 and West Supp.1995), or who have past vote-fraud convictions, see, e.g., Ga. Code Ann. §§ 21-2-2(25), 21-2-8 (1993 and Supp.1994). Likewise, after today's decision, the people of each State must leave open the possibility that they

---

[11] See Georgia Election Law (Jan. 23, 1789) (restricting representatives from each district to "resident[s] of three years standing in the district"), in 2 First Federal Elections 456, 457; Maryland Election Law (Dec. 22, 1788) (simple district residency requirement), in 2 First Federal Elections 136, 138; Massachusetts Election Resolutions (Nov. 20, 1788) (same), in 1 First Federal Elections 508, 509 (M. Jensen & R. Becker eds. 1976); North Carolina Election Law (Dec. 16, 1789) (requiring the person elected from each district to have been "a Resident or Inhabitant of that Division for which he is elected, during the Space or Term of one Year before, and at the Time of Election"), in 4 First Federal Elections 347; Virginia Election Law (Nov. 20, 1788) (requiring each candidate to have been "a bona fide resident for twelve months within such District"), in 2 First Federal Elections 293, 294. Upon being admitted to the Union in 1796, Tennessee also required its Members in the Federal House of Representatives to have been Tennessee residents for three years and district residents for one year before their election. Act of Apr. 20, 1796, ch. 10, in Laws of the State of Tennessee 81 (1803).

will trust someone with their vote in Congress even though they do not trust him with a vote in the election for Congress. See, e.g., R.I. Gen. Laws § 17-14-1.2 (1988) (restricting candidacy to people "qualified to vote").

————

Points for Discussion

a. Method of Constitutional Interpretation

Do the majority and dissent disagree about whether the issue in this case should be determined by discerning the original meaning of the Constitution or do they just disagree about what the original meaning of the Constitution is?

b. Qualifications Other Than Term Limits

The dissent lists various statutes that impose qualifications on members of Congress other than term limits. Are all of these statutes unconstitutional? What might be the practical consequences of invalidating all of these statutes?

c. *U.S. Term Limits* and *McCulloch*

Recall that the decision in *McCulloch* addressed both (1) whether the states had "reserved" powers to regulate the national government and (2) whether under the Constitution sovereignty remained solely in the constituent political communities in the states or rather also lay in a national political community. Was the Court's approach in *U.S. Term Limits* consistent with the Court's approach in *McCulloch*? What about the approach of the dissent in *U.S. Term Limits*?

————

Executive Summary of this Chapter

This chapter covers several important constitutional limitations on state power. These limitations concern the role of the states in the federal system. The limitations address the relationship of state law to federal law, the power of the states to regulate what the federal government also may regulate, the relations between states and citizens of other states, and state power to restrict the membership of Congress.

Under the **Supremacy Clause**, federal law can preempt (i.e., supplant) state law expressly or impliedly. Congress impliedly preempts state law in two ways:

> (1) **Field Preemption**: "If Congress evidences an intent to occupy a given field, any state law falling within that field is preempted."

> (2) **Conflict Preemption**: "If Congress has not entirely displaced state regulation over the matter in question, state law is still preempted to the extent it actually conflicts with federal law . . . ." *Silkwood v. Kerr-McKee* (1984).

The **Dormant Commerce Clause Doctrine** says that a state law affecting interstate commerce is invalid in the following situations:

(1) The state law concerns a subject for which **national uniformity** is necessary. *Cooley v. Board of Wardens* (1851); *Wabash, St. Louis & Pacific Ry. Co. v. Illinois* (1886).

(2) The state law **discriminates against interstate commerce** either on its face or in its effects, unless the discrimination is necessary to further a legitimate state interest. *Dean Milk v. City of Madison* (1951), *Hughes v. Oklahoma* (1979).

(3) The state law imposes a **burden on interstate commerce** that is excessive in relation to legitimate local interests. *South Carolina Department of Transportation v. Barnwell Brothers* (1938), *Southern Pacific v. Arizona* (1945), *Kassel v. Consolidated Freightways Corp.* (1981).

In applying these limitations under the Dormant Commerce Clause Doctrine, the Court has followed the following principles:

(1) **Legitimate state interests** include protecting health and safety and conserving natural resources, but they do not include protecting local businesses from competition, *Dean Milk v. City of Madison* (1951), or isolating the state from a problem common to many states (like disposing of trash or avoiding traffic on state highways), *Kassel v. Consolidated Freightways Corp.* (1981); *City of Philadelphia v. New Jersey* (1978).

(2) The term "**interstate commerce**" has the same meaning for determining limitations on states under the Dormant Commerce Clause Doctrine as it does for determining the power of Congress under the Commerce Clause. *City of Philadelphia v. New Jersey* (1978); *Camps Newfound/Owatonna, Inc. v. Town of Harrison, Maine* (1996).

(3) Under the **Market-Participant Exception** to the Dormant Commerce Clause Doctrine, a state may discriminate against interstate commerce when buying or selling goods or services in the market (as opposed to regulating the market). *South-Central Timber Development, Inc. v. Wunnicke* (1982).

(4) A state does not discriminate against interstate commerce by enacting **laws that favor local government** as opposed to local citizens or businesses. *United Haulers Ass'n, Inc. v. Oneida-Herkimer Solid Waste Management Authority* (2007).

(5) In legislation enacted under its power to regulate interstate commerce, **Congress may consent to state laws** that would otherwise violate the Dormant Commerce Clause Doctrine. *Prudential Life Insurance Co. v. Benjamin* (1946). But even if discriminatory state laws do not violate the Dormant Commerce Clause Doctrine, they may violate the **Equal Protection Clause**. *Metropolitan Life Ins. Co. v. Ward* (1985).

The **Privileges and Immunities Clause** prohibits discrimination against out-of-state residents or citizens (but not corporations or aliens) if the discrimination might jeopardize interstate harmony, unless the discrimination is necessary to promote a substantial state interest. *Baldwin v. Fish & Game Commission* (1978).

States generally cannot **regulate the House and Senate** by restricting their membership. Article I sets forth the only qualifications for members of Congress, and the states may not attempt to impose additional qualifications by limiting the ability of candidates to have their names appear on general ballots. *U.S. Term Limits, Inc. v. Thornton* (1995).

Part IV: Separation of Powers

Our consideration of federalism was, in a very important sense, a consideration of the separation of powers—specifically, a consideration of the separation of powers between the federal government and the states, and among the states themselves. In addition, our consideration in Chapter 2 of the judicial power, which focused on the courts' relationship to the states and (more important for present purposes) to the other branches of the federal government, was a subset of the more general topic of the separation of powers.

We turn now directly to a consideration of the separation of powers among the branches of the federal government. In Chapter 5, we take up the scope of federal executive power. In Chapter 6, we will address the scope of the federal legislative power. Although we cover these topics in separate Chapters, they are closely related. Indeed, when we consider the scope of the President's power, it is often in relation to a (potential) competing claim of power by Congress. And when we discuss the legislative power, the President's role in that process—and Congress's authority to place limits on that role—will often be front and center. As we consider these questions, pay close attention to the broad themes that are common to them.

FYI

On May 30, 1787, at the Constitutional Convention in Philadelphia, Gouverneur Morris proposed that "a national government ought to be established consisting of a supreme Legislature, Executive, and Judiciary." 1 Records of the Federal Convention of 1787 38-39 (Max Farrand ed. 1937). The Convention adopted this proposal to separate the federal government into three branches. The Constitution embodies the separation of powers in the first sections of Article I, Article II, and Article III.

Gouverneur Morris was a delegate from Pennsylvania. At the Constitutional Convention, he spoke more than any other delegate, even more than James Madison, who was the next most loquacious. Morris was principally responsible for drafting the grand preamble of the Constitution and for putting much of the Constitution in its final, elegant form. Note that "Gouverneur" was his first name; it is not a title. (Gouverneur Morris was named after his mother, Sarah Gouverneur.)

U.S. Constitution

Article I, § 1: "All legislative Powers herein granted shall be vested in a Congress of the United States, which shall consist of a Senate and House of Representatives."

Article II, § 1: "The executive Power shall be vested in a President of the United States of America."

Article III, § 1: "The judicial Power of the United States shall be vested in one supreme Court, and in such inferior Courts as the Congress may from time to time ordain and establish."

The Framers of the Constitution believed that separating the basic powers of government and distributing them among different branches would protect the people. If the powers were not separated, then there might be no check on abuses by the government. As James Madison wrote in The Federalist No. 47: "The accumulation of all powers legislative, executive and judiciary in the same hands, whether of one, a few or many, and whether hereditary, self appointed, or elective, may justly be pronounced the very definition of tyranny."

This view continues to have influence. In modern times, no one disputes the basic idea that our system has and should have separated powers. But if the theory of the separation of powers is easy to state, its application in practice has often proved elusive. How should we read the grants of authority to the President and to Congress, which often are phrased in vague and general language? Does the actual structure of government created by the Constitution obviate the need for judicial intervention in inter-branch disputes? These are questions on which we will focus in the next two Chapters.

But the Constitution also mixes the powers of the branches in several important respects. Congress has the legislative power, but the President has the power of the veto. The President has the power of appointment, but the Senate has the power of "advice and consent." This mixing in many cases blurs the inquiry over the proper allocation of government power.

As we will see, sometimes a branch of government attempts to aggrandize its own power by exercising powers reserved to another branch. At other times, a branch will attempt to encroach on the power of another branch, by limiting that branch's power without attempting to exercise it itself. Still other times, one branch will attempt to yield its powers to another branch. The Supreme Court has decided several very important cases determining what the Constitution permits and what it does not. Pay close attention to the contexts in which these conflicts arise, and the particular way in which the separation of powers is alleged to have been violated.

Chapter 5

Federal Executive Power

Introduction

As noted above, Article II of the Constitution begins by declaring: "The executive Power shall be vested in a President of the United States of America." Executive power in general is the power to carry out and enforce federal laws, to represent the United States in its foreign relations, and to run the government. Sections 2 and 3 of Article II provide some details about the President and the President's executive power: The President is the Commander in Chief of the Armed Forces. The President may grant pardons. With the advice and consent of the Senate, the President may make treaties with foreign nations. Also with the advice and consent of the Senate, the President may appoint judges, ambassadors, and all other officers of the United States. In addition, the President may establish diplomatic relations with foreign nations by receiving their ambassadors. And the President must "take Care that the Laws be faithfully executed."

This chapter does not proceed with a clause-by-clause examination of the President's powers and duties. Instead, it focuses on difficult issues that have arisen when the President has pressed presidential authority to its limits. In reading the cases that follow, consider not only the rules announced by the Supreme Court, but also why the President may have felt a need to assert the disputed powers. Consider as well what the cases reveal about whether the Court should aggressively police the boundaries of presidential authority, and what checks might exist absent judicial intervention.

A. Domestic Affairs

When acting with respect to domestic affairs (i.e., non-international subjects), the President clearly can exercise any powers given to him by the Constitution or by (otherwise constitutional) federal legislation. For an example of a constitutional power, consider Article II, § 2, cl. 2, which says that the President may grant pardons. A pardon is an official act that eliminates consequences that the recipient of the pardon otherwise would suffer for having committed a crime. Even when a pardon is politically controversial—such as the pardon President Gerald Ford gave to former President Richard Nixon—no one doubts that the President has the power to grant the pardon. For an example of a statutory power, consider the Antiquities Act, 16 U.S.C. § 431, which authorizes the President to protect historic landmarks on federally owned land by designating them as national monuments. Pursuant to this Act, the President clearly has the power to establish national monuments. *See, e.g., United States v. California*, 436 U.S. 32 (1978). (We will consider Congress's power to delegate decision-making authority of this sort when we discuss the Federal Legislative Power in Chapter 6.)

A more difficult question is whether the President may take actions with respect to domestic affairs that both go beyond any statutory authorization and find no obvious sanction in expressly enumerated constitutional provisions. Unlike Article I, which purports to vest only the legislative powers "herein granted" in Congress, Article II simply vests the "executive Power" in the President. As noted above, some specific powers are listed in Article II. But is there reason to read Article II to permit the President to rely on unenumerated, inherent authority that he enjoys simply by virtue of the importance of the office?

The following case says that the answer is no. "The President's power, if any," according to the Court, "must stem either from an act of Congress or from the Constitution itself." As you read the case, consider why the President believed that he needed an additional power, the exercise of which gave rise to the challenge in the case.

Youngstown Sheet & Tube Co. v. Sawyer

343 U.S. 579 (1952)

Mr. Justice BLACK delivered the opinion of the Court.

We are asked to decide whether the President was acting within his constitutional power when he issued an order directing the Secretary of Commerce to take possession of and operate most of the Nation's steel mills. The mill owners argue that the President's order amounts to lawmaking, a legislative function which the Constitution has expressly confided to the Congress and not to the President. The Government's position is that the order was made on findings of the President that his action was necessary to avert a national catastrophe which would inevitably result from a stoppage of steel production, and that in meeting this grave emergency the President was acting within the aggregate of his constitutional powers as the Nation's Chief Executive and the Commander in Chief of the Armed Forces of the United States. The issue emerges here from the following series of events:

In the latter part of 1951 [during the Korean War], a dispute arose between the steel companies and their employees over terms and conditions that should be included in new collective bargaining agreements. Long-continued conferences failed to resolve the dispute. On December 18, 1951, the employees' representative, United Steelworkers of America, C.I.O., gave notice of an intention to strike when the existing bargaining agreements expired on December 31. The Federal Mediation and Conciliation Service then intervened in an effort to get labor and management to agree. This failing, the President on December 22, 1951, referred the dispute to the Federal Wage Stabilization Board to investigate and make recommendations for fair and equitable terms of settlement. This Board's report resulted in no settlement. On April 4, 1952, the Union gave notice of a nation-wide strike called to begin at 12:01 a.m. April 9. The indispensability of steel as a component of substantially all weapons and other war materials led the President to believe that the proposed work stoppage would immediately jeopardize our national defense and that governmental seizure of the steel mills was necessary in order to assure the continued availability of steel. Reciting these considerations for his action, the President, a few hours before the strike was to begin, issued Executive Order 10340, [which] directed the Secretary of Commerce to take possession of most of the steel mills and keep them running. The Secretary immediately issued his own possessory orders, calling upon the presidents of the various seized companies to serve as operating managers for the United States. They were directed to carry on their activities in accordance with regulations and directions of the Secretary. The next morning the President sent a message to Congress reporting his action. Twelve days later he sent a second message. Congress has taken no action.

Obeying the Secretary's orders under protest, the companies brought proceedings against him in the District Court. Their complaints charged that the seizure was not authorized by an act of Congress or by any constitutional provisions. The District Court was asked to declare the orders of the President and the Secretary invalid and to issue preliminary and permanent injunctions restraining their enforcement. *** [The] District Court on April 30 issued a preliminary injunction restraining the Secretary from "continuing the seizure and possession of the plant * * * and from acting under the purported authority of Executive Order No. 10340." On the same day the Court of Appeals stayed the District Court's injunction. Deeming it best that the issues raised be promptly decided by this Court, we granted certiorari on May 3 and set the cause for argument on May 12.

The President's power, if any, to issue the order must stem either from an act of Congress or from the Constitution itself. There is no statute that expressly authorizes the President to take possession of property as he did here. Nor is there any act of Congress to which our attention has been directed from which such a power can fairly be implied.

> ### Food for Thought
>
> Why are the two statutes cited in these paragraphs relevant to the Court's analysis? Does the Court hold that the President violated these two statutes? Or is the Court suggesting something else?

Indeed, we do not understand the Government to rely on statutory authorization for this seizure. There are two statutes [the Selective Service Act and the Defense Production Act of 1950] which do authorize the President to take both personal and real property under certain conditions.

However, the Government admits that these conditions were not met and that the President's order was not rooted in either of the statutes. The Government refers to the seizure provisions of [the Defense Production Act] as "much too cumbersome, involved, and time-consuming for the crisis which was at hand."

Moreover, the use of the seizure technique to solve labor disputes in order to prevent work stoppages was not only unauthorized by any congressional enactment; prior to this controversy, Congress had refused to adopt that method of settling labor disputes. When the Taft-Hartley Act was under consideration in 1947, Congress rejected an amendment which would have authorized such governmental seizures in cases of emergency. Apparently it was thought that the technique of seizure, like that of compulsory arbitration, would interfere with the process of collective bargaining. Consequently, the plan Congress adopted in that Act did not provide for seizure under any circumstances. Instead, the plan sought to bring about settlements by use of the customary devices of mediation, conciliation, investigation by boards of inquiry, and public reports.

It is clear that if the President had authority to issue the order he did, it must be found in some provisions of the Constitution. And it is not claimed that express constitutional language grants this power to the President. The contention is that presidential power should be implied from the aggregate of his powers under the Constitution. Particular reliance is placed on provisions in Article II which say that "the executive Power shall be vested in a President ***"; that "he shall take Care that the Laws be faithfully executed"; and that he "shall be Commander in Chief of the Army and Navy of the United States."

The order cannot properly be sustained as an exercise of the President's military power as Commander in Chief of the Armed Forces. The Government attempts to do so by citing a number of cases upholding broad powers in military commanders engaged in day-to-day fighting in a theater of war. Such cases need not concern us here. Even though "theater of war" be an expanding concept, we cannot with faithfulness to our constitutional system hold that the Commander in Chief of the Armed Forces has the ultimate power as such to take possession of private property in order to keep labor disputes from stopping production. This is a job for the Nation's lawmakers, not for its military authorities.

> **Make the Connection**
>
> In *McCulloch v. Maryland*, which we considered in Chapter 3, the Court held that Congress enjoys implied powers. Is the Court saying here that the same isn't true for the President?

Nor can the seizure order be sustained because of the several constitutional provisions that grant executive power to the President. In the framework of our Constitution, the President's power to see that the laws are faithfully executed refutes the idea that he is to be a lawmaker. The Constitution limits his functions in the lawmaking process to the recommending of laws he thinks wise and the vetoing of laws he thinks bad. And the Constitution is neither silent nor equivocal about who shall make laws which the President is to execute. The first section of the first article says that "All legislative Powers herein granted shall be vested in a Congress of the United States ***." After granting many powers to the Congress, Article I goes on to provide that Congress may "make all Laws which shall be necessary and proper for carrying into Execution the foregoing Powers and all other Powers vested by this Constitution in the Government of the United States, or in any Department or Officer thereof."

The President's order does not direct that a congressional policy be executed in a manner prescribed by Congress—it directs that a presidential policy be executed in a manner prescribed by the President. The preamble of the order itself, like that of many statutes, sets out reasons why the President believes certain policies should be adopted, proclaims these policies as rules of conduct to be followed, and again, like a statute, authorizes a government official to promulgate additional rules and regulations consistent with the policy proclaimed and needed to carry that policy into execution. The power of Congress to adopt such public policies as those proclaimed by the order is beyond question. It can authorize the taking of private property for public use. It can makes laws regulating the relationships between employers and employees, prescribing rules designed to settle labor disputes, and fixing wages and working conditions in certain fields of our economy. The Constitution did not subject this law-making power of Congress to presidential or military supervision or control.

> **Make the Connection**
>
> The Court states here that Congress had power to authorize the seizure of the steel plants. What would have been the source of Congress's authority to do so? Would such an action have been consistent with the Fifth Amendment?

It is said that other Presidents without congressional authority have taken possession of private business enterprises in order to settle labor disputes. But even if this be true, Congress has not thereby lost its exclusive constitutional authority to make laws necessary and proper to carry out the powers vested by the Constitution "in the Government of the United States, or in any Department or Officer thereof."

The Founders of this Nation entrusted the law making power to the Congress alone in both good and bad times. It would do no good to recall the historical events, the fears of power and the hopes for freedom that lay behind their choice. Such a review would but confirm our holding that this seizure order cannot stand.

Mr. Justice FRANKFURTER, concurring.

[For the Founders of this Nation,] the doctrine of separation of powers was not mere theory; it was a felt necessity. Not so long ago it was fashionable to find our system of checks and balances obstructive to effective government. It was easy to ridicule that system as outmoded—too easy. The experience through which the world has passed in our own day has made vivid the realization that the Framers of our Constitution were not inexperienced doctrinaires. These long-headed statesmen had no illusion that our people enjoyed biological or psychological or sociological immunities from the hazards of concentrated power.

The question before the Court comes in this setting. Congress has frequently—at least 16 times since 1916—specifically provided for executive seizure of production, transportation, communications, or storage facilities. In every case it has qualified this grant of power with limitations and safeguards. *** It cannot be contended that the President would have had power to issue this order had Congress explicitly negated such authority in formal legislation. Congress has expressed its will to withhold this power from the President as though it had said so in so many words. *** It is one thing to draw an intention of Congress from general language and to say that Congress would have explicitly written what is inferred, where Congress has not addressed itself to a specific situation. It is quite impossible, however, when Congress did specifically address itself to a problem, as Congress did to that of seizure, to find secreted in the interstices of legislation the very grant of power which Congress consciously withheld. To find authority so explicitly withheld is not merely to disregard in a particular instance the clear will of Congress. It is to disrespect the whole legislative process and the constitutional division of authority between President and Congress.

The Constitution is a framework for government. Therefore the way the framework has consistently operated fairly establishes that it has operated according to its true nature. Deeply embedded traditional ways of conducting government cannot supplant the Constitution or legislation, but they give meaning to the words of a text or supply them. It is an inadmissibly narrow conception of American constitutional law to confine it to the words of the Constitution and to disregard the gloss which life has written upon them. In short, a systematic, unbroken, executive practice, long pursued to the knowledge of the Congress and never before questioned, engaged in by Presidents who have also sworn to uphold the Constitution, making as it were such exercise of power part of the structure of our government, may be treated as a gloss on "executive Power" vested in the President by § 1 of Art. II. ***

Down to the World War II period, [the] record is barren of instances comparable to the one before us. Of twelve seizures by President Roosevelt prior to the enactment of the War Labor Disputes Act in June, 1943, three were sanctioned by existing law, and six others were effected after Congress, on December 8, 1941, had declared the existence of a state of war. In this case, reliance on the powers that flow from declared war has been commendably disclaimed by the Solicitor General. Thus the list of executive assertions of the power of seizure in circumstances comparable to the present reduces to three in the six-month period from June to December of 1941. We need not split hairs in comparing those actions to the one before us, though much might be said by way of differentiation. Without passing on their validity, as we are not called upon to do, it suffices to say that these three isolated instances do not add up, either in number, scope, duration or contemporaneous legal justification, to the kind of executive construction of the Constitution [that would justify the action at issue]. Nor do they come to us sanctioned by long-continued acquiescence of Congress giving decisive weight to a construction by the Executive of its powers.

Mr. Justice JACKSON, concurring in the judgment and opinion of the court.

A judge, like an executive adviser, may be surprised at the poverty of really useful and unambiguous authority applicable to concrete problems of executive power as they actually present themselves. Just what our forefathers did envision, or would have envisioned had they foreseen modern conditions, must be divined from materials almost as enigmatic as the dreams Joseph was called upon to interpret for Pharaoh. A century and a half of partisan debate and scholarly speculation yields no net result but only supplies more or less apt quotations from respected sources on each side of any question. They largely cancel each other. And court decisions are indecisive because of the judicial practice of dealing with the largest questions in the most narrow way.

The actual art of governing under our Constitution does not and cannot conform to judicial definitions of the power of any of its branches based on isolated clauses or even single Articles torn from context. While the Constitution diffuses power the better to secure liberty, it also contemplates that practice will integrate the dispersed powers into a workable government. It enjoins upon its branches separateness but interdependence, autonomy but reciprocity. Presidential powers are not fixed but fluctuate, depending upon their disjunction or conjunction with those of Congress. We may well begin by a somewhat over-simplified grouping of practical situations in which a President may doubt, or others may challenge, his powers, and by distinguishing roughly the legal consequences of this factor of relativity.

> **Take Note**
>
> Although only a concurrence, Justice Jackson's description of the three categories of executive action quickly captured judicial imaginations. Scores of subsequent opinions, including several in this Chapter, have cited it. Can you think of examples for each category?

1. When the President acts pursuant to an express or implied authorization of Congress, his authority is at its maximum, for it includes all that he possesses in his own right plus all that Congress can delegate. In these circumstances, and in these only, may he be said (for what it may be worth), to personify the federal sovereignty. If his act is held unconstitutional under these circumstances, it usually means that the Federal Government as an undivided whole lacks power. A seizure executed by the President pursuant to an Act of Congress would be supported by the strongest of presumptions and the widest latitude of judicial interpretation, and the burden of persuasion would rest heavily upon any who might attack it.

2. When the President acts in absence of either a congressional grant or denial of authority, he can only rely upon his own independent powers, but there is a zone of twilight in which he and Congress may have concurrent authority, or in which its distribution is uncertain. Therefore, congressional inertia, indifference or quiescence may sometimes, at least as a practical matter, enable, if not invite, measures on independent presidential responsibility. In this area, any actual test of power is likely to depend on the imperatives of events and contemporary imponderables rather than on abstract theories of law.

3. When the President takes measures incompatible with the expressed or implied will of Congress, his power is at its lowest ebb, for then he can rely only upon his own constitutional powers minus any constitutional powers of Congress over the matter. Courts can sustain exclusive Presidential control in such a case only be disabling the Congress from acting upon the subject. Presidential claim to a power at once so conclusive and preclusive must be scrutinized with caution, for what is at stake is the equilibrium established by our constitutional system.

Into which of these classifications does this executive seizure of the steel industry fit? It is eliminated from the first by admission, for it is conceded that no congressional authorization exists for this seizure. That takes away also the support of the many precedents and declarations which were made in relation, and must be confined, to this category.

Can it then be defended under flexible tests available to the second category? It seems clearly eliminated from that class because Congress has not left seizure of private property an open field but has covered it by three statutory policies inconsistent with this seizure. ***

This leaves the current seizure to be justified only by the severe tests under the third grouping, where it can be supported only by any remainder of executive power after subtraction of such powers as Congress may have over the subject. In short, we can sustain the President only by holding that seizure of such strike-bound industries is within his domain and beyond control by Congress.

Take Note

Why didn't the President's action fall into Justice Jackson's second category, which involves congressional silence on the action in question? In Justice Jackson's view, has Congress been silent on the issue? How can one tell the difference among implied congressional authorization (category 1), implied congressional prohibition (category 3), and congressional silence (category 2)?

The Solicitor General seeks the power of seizure in three clauses of the Executive Article, the first reading, "The executive Power shall be vested in a President of the United States of America." Lest I be thought to exaggerate, I quote the interpretation which his brief puts upon it: "In our view, this clause constitutes a grant of all the executive powers of which the Government is capable." If that be true, it is difficult to see why the forefathers bothered to add several specific items, including some trifling ones.

The example of such unlimited executive power that must have most impressed the forefathers was the prerogative exercised by George III, and the description of its evils in the Declaration of Independence leads me to doubt that they were creating their new Executive in his image. Continental European examples were no more appealing. And if we seek instruction from our own times, we can match it only from the executive powers in those governments we disparagingly describe as totalitarian. I cannot accept the view that this clause is a grant in bulk of all conceivable executive power but regard it as an allocation to the presidential office of the generic powers thereafter stated.

The clause on which the Government next relies is that "The President shall be Commander in Chief of the Army and Navy of the United States ***." These cryptic words have given rise to some of the most persistent controversies in our constitutional history. Of course, they imply something more than an empty title. But just what authority goes with the name has plagued Presidential advisers who would not waive or narrow it by nonassertion yet cannot say where it begins or ends. It undoubtedly puts the Nation's armed forces under Presidential command. Hence, this loose appellation is sometimes advanced as support for any Presidential action, internal or external, involving use of force, the idea being that it vests power to do anything, anywhere, that can be done with an army or navy.

That seems to be the logic of an argument tendered at our bar—that the President having, on his own responsibility, sent American troops abroad derives from that act "affirmative power" to seize the means of producing a supply of steel for them. To quote, "Perhaps the most forceful illustrations of the scope of Presidential power in this connection is the fact that American troops in Korea, whose safety and effectiveness are so directly involved here, were sent to the field by an exercise of the President's constitutional powers." Thus, it is said he has invested himself with "war powers."

I cannot foresee all that it might entail if the Court should indorse this argument. Nothing in our Constitution is plainer than that declaration of a war is entrusted only to Congress. Of course, a state of war may in fact exist without a formal declaration. But no doctrine that the Court could promulgate would seem to me more sinister and alarming than that a President whose conduct of foreign affairs is so largely uncontrolled, and often even is unknown, can vastly enlarge his mastery over the internal affairs of the country by his own commitment of the Nation's armed forces to some foreign venture. I do not, however, find it necessary or appropriate to consider the legal status of the Korean enterprise to discountenance argument based on it. ***

> **FYI**
>
> Congress did not declare war in the Korean conflict. The United States contributed troops after the United Nations condemned North Korea's invasion of South Korea. President Truman characterized the United States' participation in the conflict as a "police action."

There are indications that the Constitution did not contemplate that the title Commander-in-Chief of the Army and Navy will constitute him also Commander-in-Chief of the country, its industries and its inhabitants. He has no monopoly of "war powers," whatever they are. While Congress cannot deprive the President of the command of the army and navy, only Congress can provide him an army or navy to command. It is also empowered to make rules for the "Government and Regulation of land and naval forces," by which it may to some unknown extent impinge upon even command functions. That military powers of the Commander-in-Chief were not to supersede representative government of internal affairs seems obvious from the Constitution and from elementary American history. *** The purpose of lodging dual titles in one man was to insure that the civilian would control the military, not to enable the military to subordinate the presidential office. ***

We should not use this occasion to circumscribe, much less to contract, the lawful role of the President as Commander-in-Chief. I should indulge the widest latitude of interpretation to sustain his exclusive function to command the instruments of national force, at least when turned against the outside world for the security of our society. But, when it is turned inward, not because of rebellion but because of a lawful economic struggle between industry and labor, it should have no such indulgence. His command power is not such an absolute as might be implied from that office in a militaristic system but is subject to limitations consistent with a constitutional Republic whose law and policy-making branch is a representative Congress. The purpose of lodging dual titles in one man was to insure that the civilian would control the military, not to enable the military to subordinate the presidential office. *** What the power of command may include I do not try to envision, but I think it is not a military prerogative, without support of law, to seize persons or property because they are important or even essential for the military and naval establishment.

The third clause in which the Solicitor General finds seizure powers is that "he shall take Care that the Laws be faithfully executed ***." That authority must be matched against words of the Fifth Amendment that "No person shall be *** deprived of life, liberty, or property, without due process of law ***." One gives a governmental authority that reaches so far as there is law, the other gives a private right that authority shall go no farther. These signify about all there is of the principle that ours is a government of laws, not of men, and that we submit ourselves to rulers only if under rules.

The Solicitor General lastly grounds support of the seizure upon nebulous, inherent powers never expressly granted but said to have accrued to the office from the customs and claims of preceding administrations. The plea is for a resulting power to deal with a crisis or an emergency according to the necessities of the case, the unarticulated assumption being that necessity knows no law.

The appeal, however, that we declare the existence of inherent powers *ex necessitate* to meet an emergency asks us to do what many think would be wise, although it is something the forefathers omitted. They knew what emergencies were, knew the pressures they engender for authoritative action, knew, too, how they afford a ready pretext for usurpation. We may also suspect that they suspected that emergency powers would tend to kindle emergencies. Aside from suspension of the privilege of the writ of habeas corpus in time of rebellion or invasion, when the public safety may require it, they made no express provision for exercise of extraordinary authority because of a crisis. I do not think we rightfully may so amend their work, and, if we could, I am not convinced it would be wise to do so, although many modern nations have forthrightly recognized that war and economic crises may upset the normal balance between liberty and authority. ***

With all its defects, delays and inconveniences, men have discovered no technique for long preserving free government except that the Executive be under the law, and that the law be made by parliamentary deliberations. Such institutions may be destined to pass away. But it is the duty of the Court to be last, not first, to give them up.

[Justice DOUGLAS's concurring opinion and Justice BURTON's and Justice CLARK's opinions concurring in the judgment are omitted.]

Mr. Chief Justice VINSON, with whom Mr. Justice REED and Mr. Justice MINTON join, dissenting.

In passing upon the question of Presidential powers in this case, we must first consider the context in which those powers were exercised. Those who suggest that this is a case involving extraordinary powers should be mindful that these are extraordinary times. A world not yet recovered from the devastation of World War II has been forced to face the threat of another and more terrifying global conflict.

The President has the duty to execute the [legislative programs that Congress created to support the Korean War effort]. Their successful execution depends upon continued production of steel and stabilized prices for steel. [T[he President acted to avert a complete shutdown of steel production. *** One is not here called upon even to consider the possibility of executive seizure of a farm, a corner grocery store or even a single industrial plant. Such considerations arise only when one ignores the central fact of this case—that the Nation's entire basic steel production would have shut down completely if there had been no Government seizure. *** Accordingly, if the President has any power under the Constitution to meet a critical situation in the absence of express statutory authorization, there is no basis whatever for criticizing the exercise of such power in this case.

The whole of the "executive Power" is vested in the President. *** This comprehensive grant of the executive power to a single person was bestowed soon after the country had thrown the yoke of monarchy. Only by instilling initiative and vigor in all of the three departments of Government, declared Madison, could tyranny in any from be avoided. *** It is thus apparent that the Presidency was deliberately fashioned as an office of power and independence. [The Framers did not] create an automaton impotent to exercise the powers of Government at a time when the survival of the Republic itself may be at stake.

A review of executive action demonstrates that our Presidents have on many occasions exhibited the leadership contemplated by the Framers when they made the President Commander in Chief, and imposed upon him the trust to "take Care that the Laws be faithfully executed." With or without explicit statutory authorization, Presidents have at such times dealt with national emergencies by acting promptly and resolutely to enforce legislative programs, at least to save those programs until Congress could act. Congress and the courts have responded to such executive initiative with consistent approval. ***

The fact that temporary executive seizures of industrial plants to meet an emergency have not been directly tested in this Court furnishes not the slightest suggestion that such actions have been illegal. Rather, the fact that Congress and the courts have consistently recognized and given their support to such executive action indicates that such a power of seizure has been accepted throughout our history. ***

Much of the argument in this case has been directed at straw men. We do not now have before us the case of a President acting solely on the basis of his own notions of the public welfare. Nor is there any question of unlimited executive power in this case. The President himself closed the door to any such claim when he sent his Message to Congress stating his purpose to abide by any action of Congress, whether approving or disapproving his seizure action. Here, the President immediately made sure that Congress was fully informed of the temporary action he had taken only to preserve the legislative programs from destruction until Congress could act. ***

Seizure of plaintiffs' property is not a pleasant undertaking. Similarly unpleasant to a free country are the draft which disrupts the home and military procurement which causes economic dislocation and compels adoption of price controls, wage stabilization and allocation of materials. The President informed Congress that even a temporary Government operation of plaintiffs' properties was "thoroughly distasteful" to him, but was necessary to prevent immediate paralysis of the mobilization program. Presidents have been in the past, and any man worthy of the Office should be in the future, free to take at least interim action necessary to execute legislative programs essential to survival of the Nation. A sturdy judiciary should not be swayed by the unpleasantness or unpopularity of necessary executive action, but must independently determine for itself whether the President was acting, as required by the Constitution, to "take Care that the Laws be faithfully executed."

—————

Points for Discussion

a. What Did the President Do Wrong?

Did the Court conclude that the President had acted in violation of a specific constitutional or statutory provision, or instead just that the President did not have authority to act? If the President lacked authority for his order, what effect if any could it have?

b. The Government's Argument

In defending the President's seizure of the steel mills in the district court, Assistant Attorney General Holmes Baldridge told the court: "It is our position that the President is accountable only to the country, and that the President's decisions are conclusive." District Judge David A. Pine asked in response: "Then the Constitution limits the Judiciary, but does not limit the Executive?" The Assistant Attorney General responded: "That is the way we read the constitution." *See* William H. Rehnquist, *The Supreme Court* 160 (2002) (recounting the proceedings in the District Court). What language in Article II might support the government's position? In what sense is the President accountable "to the country"? What consequences might flow from the government's position if the courts had accepted it? Can you think of a better argument for the government?

c. President Lincoln

During the Civil War, President Abraham Lincoln took a number of controversial executive actions, such as suspending the writ of habeas corpus (i.e., the power of courts to order the government to release persons who have been detained without a valid legal basis). When confronted with objections that he was violating the Constitution, Lincoln asked in response whether it is "possible to lose the nation and yet preserve the Constitution?" What was President Lincoln implying? What precedential value should Lincoln's actions have?

d. Inherent Powers

The Court concluded that the President does not enjoy inherent power to act, but instead is limited to those powers granted in the Constitution and by statute. (Justice Jackson's framework, in contrast, appeared to leave at least some room for the President to act absent authorization from Congress.) If an attack by a hostile power rendered Congress unable to act, would the President have power to take all necessary responsive actions? If so, doesn't that mean that the President has powers beyond those clearly enumerated in the Constitution, and that sometimes the President can act even without express constitutional or statutory authorization? And if not, is our constitutional structure sensible?

e. Emergency Powers

Several provisions of the Constitution refer to exigent circumstances that might arise because of war or other national emergencies. See, e.g., Art. I, § 9, cl. 2 ("The Privilege of the Writ of Habeas Corpus shall not be suspended, unless when in Cases of Rebellion or Invasion the public Safety may require it."); Art. I, § 8, cl. 15 ("The Congress shall have the Power *** To provide for calling forth the Militia to execute the Laws of the Union, suppress Insurrections and repel Invasions."); Amend. III ("No Soldier shall, in time of peace be quartered in any house, without the consent of the Owner, nor in time of war, but in a manner to be prescribed by law."); Amend. V ("No person shall be held to answer for a capital, or otherwise infamous crime, unless on a presentment or indictment of a Grand Jury, except in cases arising in the land or naval forces, or in the Militia, when in actual service in time of War or public danger."). Yet there is no provision in the Constitution expressly conferring upon either the President or Congress broad powers to act in the face of an emergency. Should the Court find such a power to be implied? If so, was *Youngstown* the case in which to do it?

B. Foreign Affairs

In *Youngstown Sheet & Tube Co. v. Sawyer*, the Supreme Court said that when acting with respect to domestic affairs the President has only the powers expressly or by implication conferred by the Constitution or by statute. Might the President have additional powers—powers not explicitly conferred by the Constitution or statute—when acting with respect to foreign affairs?

Dames & Moore v. Regan

453 U.S. 654 (1981)

Justice REHNQUIST delivered the opinion of the Court.

On November 4, 1979, the American Embassy in Tehran was seized and our diplomatic personnel were captured and held hostage. In response to that crisis, President Carter, acting pursuant to the International Emergency Economic Powers Act, 91 Stat. 1626 (hereinafter IEEPA), declared a national emergency on November 14, 1979, and blocked the removal or transfer of "all property and interests in property of the Government of Iran, its instrumentalities and controlled entities and the Central Bank of Iran which are or become subject to the jurisdiction of the United States. . . ."

On January 20, 1981, the Americans held hostage were released by Iran pursuant to an Agreement entered into the day before and embodied in two Declarations of the

Democratic and Popular Republic of Algeria. The Agreement stated that "[i]t is the purpose of [the United States and Iran] . . . to terminate all litigation as between the Government of each party and the nationals of the other, and to bring about the settlement and termination of all such claims through binding arbitration." In furtherance of this goal, the Agreement called for the establishment of an Iran-United States Claims Tribunal which would arbitrate any claims not settled within six months. Awards of the Claims Tribunal are to be "final and binding" and "enforceable . . . in the courts of any nation in accordance with its laws." ***

[To implement the Agreement, the President issued executive orders and the Treasury Department issued regulations. These executive orders and regulations sought to move pending cases from domestic courts to the Claims Tribunal. Among other things, they required courts to suspend pending litigation against Iran and they nullified liens and attachments against Iranian property in the United States. These executive orders affected petitioner *Dames & Moore*, which had sued the Government of Iran, the Atomic Energy Organization of Iran, and a number of Iranian banks in federal court, claiming that it was owed more than $3 million for breach of contract.]

On April 28, 1981, petitioner filed this action in the District Court for declaratory and injunctive relief against the United States and the Secretary of the Treasury, seeking to prevent enforcement of the Executive Orders and Treasury Department regulations implementing the Agreement with Iran. In its complaint, petitioner alleged that the actions of the President and the Secretary of the Treasury implementing the Agreement with Iran were beyond their statutory and constitutional powers and, in any event, were unconstitutional to the extent they adversely affect petitioner's final judgment against the Government of Iran and the Atomic Energy Organization, its execution of that judgment in the State of Washington, its prejudgment attachments, and its ability to continue to litigate against the Iranian banks. ***

The parties and the lower courts, confronted with the instant questions, have all agreed that much relevant analysis is contained in *Youngstown Sheet & Tube Co. v. Sawyer*, 343 U.S. 579 (1952). *** Although we have in the past found and do today find Justice Jackson's classification of executive actions into three general categories analytically useful, *** Jackson himself recognized that his three categories represented "a somewhat over-simplified grouping," 343 U.S. at 635, and it is doubtless the case that executive action in any particular instance falls, not neatly in one of three pigeonholes, but rather at some point along a spectrum running from explicit congressional authorization to explicit congressional prohibition. This is particularly true as respects cases such as the one before us, involving responses to international crises the nature of which Congress can hardly have been expected to anticipate in any detail.

Take Note

The Court here treats Justice Jackson's opinion in *Youngstown* as containing the proper framework for analyzing claims of presidential power, even though that opinion was merely a concurrence. Indeed, Jackson's opinion has been the most enduring of the several opinions in *Youngstown*. It might also interest you to learn that Chief Justice Rehnquist clerked for Justice Jackson after graduating from law school.

[The Court concluded that the IEEPA provided specific congressional authorization to the President to nullify the attachments and order the transfer of Iranian assets, but that neither the IEEPA nor the Hostage Act, 22 U.S.C. § 1732, authorized the suspension of the claims of American citizens against Iran.]

Although we have declined to conclude that the IEEPA or the Hostage Act directly authorizes the President's suspension of claims for the reasons noted, we cannot ignore the general tenor of Congress' legislation in this area in trying to determine whether the President is acting alone or at least with the acceptance of Congress. As we have noted, Congress cannot anticipate and legislate with regard to every possible action the President may find it necessary to take or every possible situation in which he might act. Such failure of Congress specifically to delegate authority does not, "especially . . . in the areas of foreign policy and national security," imply "congressional disapproval" of action taken by the Executive. *Haig v. Agee*, 453 U.S. 280, 291 (1981). On the contrary, the enactment of legislation closely related to the question of the President's authority in a particular case which evinces legislative intent to accord the President broad discretion may be considered to "invite" "measures on independent presidential responsibility," *Youngstown*, 343 U.S., at 637 (Jackson, J., concurring). At least this is so where there is no contrary indication of legislative intent and when, as here, there is a history of congressional acquiescence in conduct of the sort engaged in by the President. It is to that history which we now turn.

> **Take Note**
>
> How does the Court's statement here of the test for Presidential authority differ from Justice Jackson's statement in *Youngstown*?

Not infrequently in affairs between nations, outstanding claims by nationals of one country against the government of another country are "sources of friction" between the two sovereigns. *United States v. Pink*, 315 U.S. 203, 225 (1942). To resolve these difficulties, nations have often entered into agreements settling the claims of their respective nationals. As one treatise writer puts it, international agreements settling claims by nationals of one state against the government of another "are established international practice reflecting traditional international theory." L. Henkin, Foreign Affairs and the Constitution 262 (1972). Consistent with that principle, the United States has repeatedly exercised its sovereign authority to settle the claims of its nationals against foreign countries. Though those settlements have sometimes been made by treaty, there has also been a longstanding practice of settling such claims by executive agreement without the advice and consent of the Senate. Under such agreements, the President has agreed to renounce or extinguish claims of United States nationals against foreign governments in return for lump-sum payments or the establishment of arbitration procedures. To be sure, many of these settlements were encouraged by the United States claimants themselves, since a claimant's only hope of obtaining any payment at all might lie in having his Government negotiate a diplomatic settlement on his behalf. But it is also undisputed that the "United States has sometimes disposed of the claims of its citizens without their consent, or even without consultation with them, usually without exclusive regard for their interests, as distinguished from those of the nation as a whole." Henkin, *supra*, at 262-263. It is clear that the practice of settling claims continues today. Since 1952, the President has entered into at least 10 binding settlements with foreign nations, including an $80 million settlement with the People's Republic of China.

Crucial to our decision today is the conclusion that Congress has implicitly approved the practice of claim settlement by executive agreement. This is best demonstrated by Congress' enactment of the International Claims Settlement Act of 1949, 64 Stat. 13, as amended, 22 U.S.C. § 1621 *et seq.* (1976 ed. and Supp. IV). The Act had two purposes: (1) to allocate to United States nationals funds received in the course of an executive claims settlement with Yugoslavia, and (2) to provide a procedure whereby funds resulting from future settlements could be distributed. To achieve these ends Congress created the International Claims Commission, now the Foreign Claims Settlement Commission, and gave it jurisdiction to make final and binding decisions with respect to claims by United States nationals against settlement funds. By creating a procedure to implement future settlement agreements, Congress placed its stamp of approval on such agreements. Indeed, the legislative history of the Act observed that the United States was seeking settlements with countries other than Yugoslavia and that the bill contemplated settlements of a similar nature in the future.

Over the years Congress has frequently amended the International Claims Settlement Act to provide for particular problems arising out of settlement agreements, thus demonstrating Congress' continuing acceptance of the President's claim settlement authority. With respect to the Executive Agreement with the People's Republic of China, for example, Congress established an allocation formula for distribution of the funds received pursuant to the Agreement. As with legislation involving other executive agreements, Congress did not question the fact of the settlement or the power of the President to have concluded it. In 1976, Congress authorized the Foreign Claims Settlement Commission to adjudicate the merits of claims by United States nationals against East Germany, prior to any settlement with East Germany, so that the Executive would "be in a better position to negotiate an adequate settlement . . . of these claims." S. Rep. No. 94-1188, p. 2 (1976). Similarly, Congress recently amended the International Claims Settlement Act to facilitate the settlement of claims against Vietnam. ***

In addition to congressional acquiescence in the President's power to settle claims, prior cases of this Court have also recognized that the President does have some measure of power to enter into executive agreements without obtaining the advice and consent of the Senate. In *United States v. Pink*, 315 U.S. 203 (1942), for example, the Court upheld the validity of the Litvinov Assignment, which was part of an Executive Agreement whereby the Soviet Union assigned to the United States amounts owed to it by American nationals so that outstanding claims of other American nationals could be paid. The Court explained that the resolution of such claims was integrally connected with normalizing United States' relations with a foreign state:

> "Power to remove such obstacles to full recognition as settlement of claims of our nationals . . . certainly is a modest implied power of the President. . . . No such obstacle can be placed in the way of rehabilitation of relations between this country and another nation, unless the historic conception of the powers and responsibilities . . . is to be drastically revised." *Id.*, at 229-230.

In light of all of the foregoing—the inferences to be drawn from the character of the legislation Congress has enacted in the area, such as the IEEPA and the Hostage Act, and from the history of acquiescence in executive claims settlement—we conclude that the President was authorized to suspend pending claims pursuant to Executive Order No. 12294. As Justice Frankfurter pointed out in *Youngstown,* 343 U.S., at 610-611, "a systematic, unbroken, executive practice, long pursued to the knowledge of the Congress and never before questioned . . . may be treated as a gloss on 'Executive Power' vested in the President by § 1 of Art. II." Past practice does not, by itself, create power, but "long-continued practice, known to and acquiesced in by Congress, would raise a presumption that the [action] had been [taken] in pursuance of its consent. . . ." *United States v. Midwest Oil Co.*, 236 U.S. 459, 474 (1915). Such practice is present here and such a presumption is also appropriate. In light of the fact that Congress may be considered to have consented to the President's action in suspending claims, we cannot say that action exceeded the President's powers.

> **Food for Thought**
>
> The Court places emphasis on the historic practice of Presidents in settling claims and of Congress in acquiescing in this practice. Why should what the President and Congress have done in the past be relevant to the question whether the President has a particular power? Can Congress and the President create precedents comparable to those established in judicial decisions?

Just as importantly, Congress has not disapproved of the action taken here. Though Congress has held hearings on the Iranian Agreement itself, Congress has not enacted legislation, or even passed a resolution, indicating its displeasure with the Agreement. Quite the contrary, the relevant Senate Committee has stated that the establishment of the Tribunal is "of vital importance to the United States." S. Rep. No. 97-71, p. 5 (1981). We are thus clearly not confronted with a situation in which Congress has in some way resisted the exercise of Presidential authority.

Finally, we re-emphasize the narrowness of our decision. We do not decide that the President possesses plenary power to settle claims, even as against foreign governmental entities. *** But where, as here, the settlement of claims has been determined to be a necessary incident to the resolution of a major foreign policy dispute between our country and another, and where, as here, we can conclude that Congress acquiesced in the President's action, we are not prepared to say that the President lacks the power to settle such claims.

Points for Discussion

a. Domestic Affairs v. Foreign Affairs

Recall that the Court held in the *Youngstown* case that the President does not enjoy inherent authority to act; instead, the President has power to act only if the Constitution or a congressional statute confers such authority. Although the case involved President

Truman's actions during the Korean War, the Court viewed his act nationalizing the steel industry as one pertaining to matters of domestic affairs. After the decision in *Dames & Moore*, does the same approach apply when the President acts in the arena of foreign affairs? If not, in what way is the approach different? Does the Court adequately explain why the two contexts are different? And how can the Court identify when a President's actions concern domestic affairs and when they concern foreign affairs?

b. Nature of the President's Action

Does the Court hold that the President's executive order is federal law that is supreme over state law? If not, how can the President's order supersede private claims and liens under state law? Is this result consistent with the Supremacy Clause?

c. Executive Agreements

Article II, § 2 of the Constitution provides that the President "shall have Power, by and with the Advice and Consent of the Senate, to make Treaties, provided two thirds of the Senators present concur." An executive agreement, in contrast, is an agreement negotiated with a foreign nation by the President without subsequent ratification by the Senate. Are executive agreements constitutional? Some commentators have argued that they are not. See Bradford Clark, *Domesticating Sole Executive Agreements*, 93 Va. L. Rev. 1573, 1611-1612 (2007). Does the Constitution's treatment of the *states'* authority to enter agreements with foreign nations shed any light on the issue? Article I, § 10, cl. 1 provides that "[n]o State shall enter into any Treaty, Alliance, or Confederation," but clause 3 states that "[n]o State shall, without the Consent of Congress, *** enter into any Agreement or Compact with another State, or with a foreign Power." Does this suggest that there is a difference under the Constitution between "treaties" and "agreements"? If so, what is it?

The Court's opinion in *Dames & Moore* suggested that the President has greater leeway to act in matters of foreign affairs, but the Court still largely adhered to the *Youngstown* case's account of the scope of the President's powers. Does the Court's embrace of *Youngstown* suggest that the President does not enjoy any extra-constitutional powers when dealing with matters of international affairs? Consider the two cases that follow.

The issue in the following case requires some background to understand. In ordinary circumstances, Congress establishes federal criminal offenses by enacting statutes that specify conduct that is unlawful. The President then (through other officers) enforces the legislation by prosecuting offenders. For example, one provision of the Federal Criminal Code, 18 U.S.C. § 1002, makes it a federal crime to possess forged or counterfeit documents for the purpose of defrauding the government. The President, through the Justice Department, enforces the statute by bringing charges against and prosecuting suspected criminals. But suppose that Congress wanted to alter this usual model to give the President more authority and discretion. For example, suppose that Congress amended § 1002 to say that it shall be unlawful to possess forged or counterfeit documents for the purpose of defrauding the government "if and when the President by proclamation declares that this conduct shall be a crime." Would this statute be constitutional? At the time of the *Curtiss-Wright* decision, there was a serious argument that the answer was no because the hypothetical statute would impermissibly delegate legislative power (i.e., the power to decide what is a crime and what is not) to the President. In *Curtiss-Wright* the Court considered whether Congress could give the President greater discretion in the context of foreign affairs.

> **Make the Connection**
>
> We will discuss Congress's power to delegate decision-making authority to the President and to other officers in the course of our discussion of the federal legislative power, in Chapter 6.

United States v. Curtiss-Wright Export Corporation

299 U.S. 304 (1936)

Mr. Justice SUTHERLAND delivered the opinion of the Court.

> **FYI**
>
> In the 1930s, Bolivia and Paraguay fought a war in the Chaco, a plain that covers parts of Argentina, Bolivia, and Paraguay. American arms manufacturers were selling weapons to both sides in the conflict, complicating diplomatic relations.

On January 27, 1936, an indictment was returned in the court below, the first count of which charges that appellees, beginning with the 29th day of May, 1934, conspired to sell in the United States certain arms of war, namely, fifteen machine guns, to Bolivia, a country then engaged in armed conflict in the Chaco, in violation of the Joint Resolution of Congress approved May 28, 1934, and the provisions of a proclamation issued on the same day by the President of the United States pursuant to authority conferred by section 1 of the resolution. In pursuance of the conspiracy, the commission of certain overt acts was alleged, details of which need not be stated. The Joint Resolution (chapter 365, 48 Stat. 811) follows:

Resolved by the Senate and House of Representatives of the United States of America in Congress assembled, That if the President finds that the prohibition of the sale of arms and munitions of war in the United States to those countries now engaged in armed conflict in the Chaco may contribute to the reestablishment of peace between those countries, and if after consultation with the governments of other American Republics and with their cooperation, as well as that of such other governments as he may deem necessary, he makes proclamation to that effect, it shall be unlawful to sell, except under such limitations and exceptions as the President

> **FYI**
>
> A joint resolution is a resolution passed by both houses of Congress and presented to the President for his signature or veto. It has the force of law. (In contrast, a concurrent resolution is passed by both Houses of Congress but does not have the force of law because it is not presented to the President.)

prescribes, any arms or munitions of war in any place in the United States to the countries now engaged in that armed conflict, or to any person, company, or association acting in the interest of either country, until otherwise ordered by the President or by Congress.

Sec. 2. Whoever sells any arms or munitions of war in violation of section 1 shall, on conviction, be punished by a fine not exceeding $10,000 or by imprisonment not exceeding two years, or both.

The President's proclamation (48 Stat. 1744, No. 2087), after reciting the terms of the Joint Resolution, declares:

Now, Therefore, I, Franklin D. Roosevelt, President of the United States of America, acting under and by virtue of the authority conferred in me by the said joint resolution of Congress, do hereby declare and proclaim that I have found that the prohibition of the sale of arms and munitions of war in the United States to those countries now engaged in armed conflict in the Chaco may contribute to the reestablishment of peace between those countries, and that I have consulted with the governments of other American Republics and have been assured of the cooperation of such governments as I have deemed necessary as contemplated by the said joint resolution; and I do hereby admonish all citizens of the United States and every person to abstain from every violation of the provisions of the joint resolution above set forth, hereby made applicable to Bolivia and Paraguay, and I do hereby warn them that all violations of such provisions will be rigorously prosecuted.

Appellees severally demurred to [the indictment] on the [ground] that the Joint Resolution effects an invalid delegation of legislative power to the executive ***.

Whether, if the Joint Resolution had related solely to internal affairs, it would be open to the challenge that it constituted an unlawful delegation of legislative power to the Executive, we find it unnecessary to determine. The whole aim of the resolution is to affect a situation entirely external to the United States, and falling within the category of foreign affairs. The determination which we are called to make, therefore, is whether the Joint Resolution, as applied to that situation, is vulnerable to attack under the rule that forbids a delegation of the lawmaking power. In other words, assuming (but not deciding) that the challenged delegation, if it were confined to internal affairs, would be invalid, may it nevertheless be sustained on the ground that its exclusive aim is to afford a remedy for a hurtful condition within foreign territory?

> **Take Note**
>
> The Court acknowledges here that it might have concluded that the joint resolution might have been an unconstitutional delegation of power if it concerned internal affairs. But the Court makes clear that a different standard applies in matters of foreign affairs.

It will contribute to the elucidation of the question if we first consider the differences between the powers of the federal government in respect of foreign or external affairs and those in respect of domestic or internal affairs. That there are differences between them, and that these differences are fundamental, may not be doubted.

The two classes of powers are different, both in respect of their origin and their nature. The broad statement that the federal government can exercise no powers except those specifically enumerated in the Constitution, and such implied powers as are necessary and proper to carry into effect the enumerated powers, is categorically true only in respect of our internal affairs. In that field, the primary purpose of the Constitution was to carve from the general mass of legislative powers then possessed by the states such portions as it was thought desirable to vest in the federal government, leaving those not included in the enumeration still in the states. That this doctrine applies only to powers which the states had is self-evident. And since the states severally never possessed international powers, such powers could not have been carved from the mass of state powers but obviously were transmitted to the United States from some other source. During the Colonial period, those powers were possessed exclusively by and were entirely under the control of the Crown. By the Declaration of Independence, "the Representatives of the United States of America" declared the United (not the several) Colonies to be free and independent states, and as such to have "full Power to levy War, conclude Peace, contract Alliances, establish Commerce and to do all other Acts and Things which Independent States may of right do."

As a result of the separation from Great Britain by the colonies, acting as a unit, the powers of external sovereignty passed from the Crown not to the colonies severally, but to the colonies in their collective and corporate capacity as the United States of America. Even before the Declaration, the colonies were a unit in foreign affairs, acting through a common agency—namely, the Continental Congress, composed of delegates from the thirteen colonies. That agency exercised the powers of war and peace, raised an army, created a navy, and finally adopted the Declaration of Independence. Rulers come and go; governments end and forms of government change; but sovereignty survives. A political society cannot endure without a supreme will somewhere. Sovereignty is never held in suspense. When, therefore, the external sovereignty of Great Britain in respect of the colonies ceased, it immediately passed to the Union. That fact was given practical application almost at once. The treaty of peace, made on September 3, 1783, was concluded between his Brittanic Majesty and the "United States of America." 8 Stat., European Treaties, 80.

The Union existed before the Constitution, which was ordained and established among other things to form "a more perfect Union." Prior to that event, it is clear that the Union, declared by the Articles of Confederation to be "perpetual," was the sole possessor of external sovereignty, and in the Union it remained without change save in so far as the Constitution in express terms qualified its exercise. The Framers' Convention was called and exerted its powers upon the irrefutable postulate that though the states were several their people in respect of foreign affairs were one.

Take Note

In this passage, the Court concludes that the federal government has extra-constitutional powers, which are powers that do not "depend upon the affirmative grants of the Constitution." Where did these powers come from? What (and who) defines them?

It results that the investment of the federal government with the powers of external sovereignty did not depend upon the affirmative grants of the Constitution. The powers to declare and wage war, to conclude peace, to make treaties, to maintain diplomatic relations with other sovereignties, if they had never been mentioned in the Constitution, would have vested in the federal government as necessary concomitants of nationality. Neither the Constitution nor the laws passed in pursuance of it have any force in foreign territory unless in respect of our own citizens; and operations of the nation in such territory must be governed by treaties, international understandings and compacts, and the principles of international law. As a member of the family of nations, the right and power of the United States in that field are equal to the right and power of the other members of the international family. Otherwise, the United States is not completely sovereign. The power to acquire territory by discovery and occupation, the power to expel undesirable aliens, the power to make such international agreements as do not constitute treaties in the constitutional sense, none of which is expressly affirmed by the Constitution, nevertheless exist as inherently inseparable from the conception of nationality. This the court recognized, and in each of the cases cited found the warrant for its conclusions not in the provisions of the Constitution, but in the law of nations.

Not only, as we have shown, is the federal power over external affairs in origin and essential character different from that over internal affairs, but participation in the exercise of the power is significantly limited. In this vast external realm, with its important, complicated, delicate and manifold problems, the President alone has the power to speak or listen as a representative of the nation. He makes treaties with the advice and consent of the Senate; but he alone negotiates. Into the field of negotiation the Senate cannot intrude; and Congress itself is powerless to invade it. As Marshall said in his great argument of March 7, 1800, in the House of Representatives, "The President is the sole organ of the nation in its external relations, and its sole representative with foreign nations." Annals, 6th Cong., col. 613. *** It is important to bear in mind that we are here dealing not alone with an authority vested in the President by an exertion of legislative power, but with such an authority plus the very delicate, plenary and exclusive power of the President as the sole organ of the federal government in the field of international relations—a power which does not require as a basis for its exercise an act of Congress, but which, of course, like every other governmental power, must be exercised in subordination to the applicable provisions of the Constitution. It is quite apparent that if, in the maintenance of our international relations, embarrassment—perhaps serious embarrassment—is to be avoided and success for our aims achieved, congressional legislation which is to be made effective through negotiation and inquiry within the international field must often accord to the President a degree of discretion and freedom from statutory restriction which would not be admissible were domestic affairs alone involved.

> **Take Note**
>
> The Court explains here why Congress might need to give the President more discretion "within the international field" than with respect to "domestic affairs." What is the Court's reasoning? What kind of "serious embarrassment" might result if the President could not have discretion?

Moreover, he, not Congress, has the better opportunity of knowing the conditions which prevail in foreign countries, and especially is this true in time of war. He has his confidential sources of information. He has his agents in the form of diplomatic, consular and other officials. Secrecy in respect of information gathered by them may be highly necessary, and the premature disclosure of it productive of harmful results. Indeed, so clearly is this true that the first President refused to accede to a request to lay before the House of Representatives the instructions, correspondence and documents relating to the negotiation of the Jay Treaty—a refusal the wisdom of which was recognized by the House itself and has never since been doubted. In his reply to the request, President Washington said:

> "The nature of foreign negotiations requires caution, and their success must often depend on secrecy; and even when brought to a conclusion a full disclosure of all the measures, demands, or eventual concessions which may have been proposed or contemplated would be extremely impolitic; for this might have a pernicious influence on future negotiations, or produce immediate inconveniences, perhaps danger and mischief, in relation to other powers. The necessity of such caution and secrecy was one cogent reason for vesting the power of making treaties in the President, with the advice and consent of the Senate, the principle on which that body was formed confining it to a small number of members. To admit, then, a right in the House of Representatives to demand and to have as a matter of course all the papers respecting a negotiation with a foreign power would be to establish a dangerous precedent." 1 Messages and Papers of the Presidents, p. 194.

In the light of the foregoing observations, it is evident that this court should not be in haste to apply a general rule which will have the effect of condemning legislation like that under review as constituting an unlawful delegation of legislative power. The principles which justify such legislation find overwhelming support in the unbroken legislative practice which has prevailed almost from the inception of the national government to the present day.

Practically every volume of the United States Statutes contains one or more acts or joint resolutions of Congress authorizing action by the President in respect of subjects affecting foreign relations, which either leave the exercise of the power to his unrestricted judgment, or provide a standard far more general than that which has always been considered requisite with regard to domestic affairs.

> ### Food for Thought
>
> According to the Court's reasoning, are statutes delegating authority to the President a necessary predicate for the President's exercise of authority in the arena of foreign affairs?

The uniform, long-continued and undisputed legislative practice just disclosed rests upon an admissible view of the Constitution which, even if the practice found far less support in principle than we think it does, we should not feel at liberty at this late day to disturb.

[W]e conclude there is sufficient warrant for the broad discretion vested in the President to determine whether the enforcement of the statute will have a beneficial effect upon the re-establishment of peace in the affected countries; whether he shall make proclamation to bring the resolution into operation; whether and when the resolution shall cease to operate and to make proclamation accordingly; and to prescribe limitations and exceptions to which the enforcement of the resolution shall be subject.

Points for Discussion

a. "*Curtiss-Wright*, So I'm Right."

Presidents often justify controversial actions that they have taken in the field of foreign affairs by citing the *Curtiss-Wright* decision. (A longstanding inside joke among Justice Department lawyers is that the President's argument in the Supreme Court often boils down to "*Curtiss-Wright*, so I'm right.") Yet if the President has extra-constitutional powers over foreign affairs, how far do these powers extend? What limitations does the Court suggest might exist? And is the approach of the Court in *Youngstown* reconcilable with the approach of the Court in *Curtiss-Wright*?

b. Sovereignty and History

Not everyone agrees with the Court's understanding of the Revolutionary period. One prominent scholar has described the historical account of sovereignty as "shockingly inaccurate," contending that the various state governments actually exercised many foreign affairs powers following independence. *See* Charles A. Lofgren, United States v. Curtiss-Wright Export Corporation: *An Historical Reassessment*, 83 Yale L.J. 1, 30-32 (1973). Others believe that the Court's account (at least with respect to this question) was largely correct. See, e.g., Jack N. Rakove, *The Origins of Judicial Review: A Plea for New Contexts*, 49 Stan. L. Rev. 1031, 1043 (1997). How important is a correct assessment of history to the Court's conclusion?

c. Congressional Power Over Foreign Affairs

What is Congress's role in foreign affairs? Under Article I, Congress has authority to regulate commerce with foreign nations; to lay and collect duties (which presumably permits Congress to impose retaliatory sanctions on other nations' goods); to raise, support, and regulate the armed forces; and to declare war. This suggests at least some role for Congress in foreign affairs. Did the Court's analysis in *Curtiss-Wright* properly take account of that role?

———————

The Constitution specifies the manner in which the United States can enter into treaties with foreign countries. Article II, section 2, clause 2 says that the President "shall have Power, by and with the Advice and Consent of the Senate, to make Treaties, provided two thirds of the Senators present concur." Oddly, though, the Constitution does not specify a procedure for the United States to withdraw from treaties.

The Supreme Court ruled in *Whitney v. Robertson*, 124 U.S. 190 (1888), that Congress and the President, acting together, can abrogate a treaty by passing a statute that overrides the treaty. In that case, the United States made a treaty with the Dominican Republic saying that the United States would not impose a higher duty on articles imported from the Dominican Republic than from other countries. Congress subsequently passed a statute that contradicted this treaty by exempting Hawaii (then an independent nation), but not the Dominican Republic, from duties on centrifugal and molasses sugars. The Court rejected an argument by importers from the Dominican Republic that, under the treaty, they should not have to pay a duty. The Court reasoned:

By the constitution, a treaty is placed on the same footing, and made of like obligation, with an act of legislation. Both are declared by that instrument to be the supreme law of the land, and no superior efficacy is given to either over the other. When the two relate to the same subject, the courts will always endeavor to construe them so as to give effect to both, if that can be done without violating the language of either; but, if the two are inconsistent, the one last in date will control the other: provided, always, the stipulation of the treaty on the subject is self-executing.

Id. at 194.

The following case concerns the question whether it is possible for the President unilaterally, i.e., without the concurrence of Congress (or the Senate alone), to cause the United States to withdraw from a treaty. A little history is necessary for understanding what happened in the case. After World War II, two rival Chinese forces fought for control of China, and they formed two rival governments. The communist forces, led by Mao Zedong, established the People's Republic of China (PRC) with its capital in Peking. The nationalist forces, led by Chiang Kai-shek, established the Republic of China (ROC), with its capital on the island of Taiwan. Each government claimed to rule all of China. But in reality the PRC controlled the mainland, while the ROC controlled only Taiwan. In 1949, the United States entered into diplomatic relations and a mutual defense treaty with the ROC. But in 1978, President Carter announced that the United States would recognize the PRC as the sole government of China, effective January 1, 1979, and would simultaneously withdraw recognition from the ROC and terminate the mutual defense treaty. When Senator Barry Goldwater and others sued to enjoin this action, arguing that President Carter's action would violate the treaty, the Court of Appeals for the D.C. Circuit held that the President had not exceeded his authority. The case then went to the Supreme Court. Resolution of the issue divided the Court so much that a majority of justices could not agree on the proper analysis. But when all was said and done, the President did succeed in withdrawing the United States from the mutual defense treaty because neither the Supreme Court nor anyone else effectively intervened.

Goldwater v. Carter

444 U.S. 996 (1979)

ORDER

The petition for a writ of certiorari is granted. The judgment of the Court of Appeals is vacated and the case is remanded to the District Court with directions to dismiss the complaint.

Mr. Justice MARSHALL concurs in the result.

Mr. Justice POWELL, concurring.

Although I agree with the result reached by

Take Note

A majority of the Supreme Court agreed that the judgment of the Court of Appeals should be vacated and the case should be dismissed. But no group of five Justices could agree on the rationale for this result. So the Court simply issued this one-sentence order. Various Justices then wrote opinions explaining their views.

the Court, I would dismiss the complaint as not ripe for judicial review. This Court has recognized that an issue should not be decided if it is not ripe for judicial review. *Buckley v. Valeo*, 424 U.S. 1, 113-114 (1976) (*per curiam*). Prudential considerations persuade me that a dispute between Congress and the President is not ready for judicial review unless and until each branch has taken action asserting its constitutional authority. Differences between the President and the Congress are commonplace under our system. The differences should, and almost invariably do, turn on political rather than legal considerations. The Judicial Branch should not decide issues affecting the allocation of power between the President and Congress until the political branches reach a constitutional impasse. Otherwise, we would encourage small groups or even individual Members of Congress to seek judicial resolution of issues before the normal political process has the opportunity to resolve the conflict.

In this case, a few Members of Congress claim that the President's action in terminating the treaty with Taiwan has deprived them of their constitutional role with respect to a change in the supreme law of the land. Congress has taken no official action. In the present posture of this case, we do not know whether there ever will be an actual confrontation between the Legislative and Executive Branches. Although the Senate has considered a resolution declaring that Senate approval is necessary for the termination of any mutual defense treaty, see 125 Cong.Rec. S7015, S7038-S7039 (June 6, 1979), no final vote has been taken on the resolution. See *id.*, at S16683-S16692 (Nov. 15, 1979). Moreover, it is unclear whether the resolution would have retroactive effect. See *id.*, at S7054-S7064 (June 6, 1979); *id.*, at S7862 (June 18, 1979). It cannot be said that either the Senate or the House has rejected the President's claim. If the Congress chooses not to confront the President, it is not our task to do so. I therefore concur in the dismissal of this case.

Take Note

Justice Rehnquist's opinion was supported by four justices. It is the "plurality opinion" because it received more votes than any other opinion. But it is still only a concurrence in the judgment, rather than a majority opinion.

Mr. Justice REHNQUIST, with whom THE CHIEF JUSTICE, Mr. Justice STEWART, and Mr. Justice STEVENS join, concurring in the judgment.

I am of the view that the basic question presented by the petitioners in this case is "political" and therefore nonjusticiable because it involves the authority of the President in the conduct of our country's foreign relations and the extent to which the Senate or the Congress is authorized to negate the action of the President. *** Here, while the Constitution is express as to the manner in which the Senate shall participate in the ratification of a treaty, it is silent as to that body's participation in the abrogation of a treaty. In this respect the case is directly analogous to *Coleman v. Miller*, 307 U.S. 433 (1939) [in which a plurality decided that the question whether a state ratified or rejected a constitutional amendment is a non-justiciable political question].

In light of the absence of any constitutional provision governing the termination of a treaty, and the fact that different termination procedures may be appropriate for different treaties, the instant case in my view also "must surely be controlled by political standards [rather than standards easily characterized as judicially manageable]." [*Dyer v. Blair,* 390 F. Supp. 1291, 1302 (N.D.Ill.1975) (three-judge court).] I think that the justifications for concluding that the question here is political in nature are even more compelling *** because it involves foreign relations—specifically a treaty commitment to use military force in the defense of a foreign government if attacked.

> **Make the Connection**
>
> We discussed the political question doctrine in Chapter 2, in our consideration of the judicial power.

The present case differs in several important respects from *Youngstown Sheet & Tube Co. v. Sawyer,* 343 U.S. 579 (1952), cited by petitioners as authority both for reaching the merits of this dispute and for reversing the Court of Appeals. In *Youngstown,* private litigants brought a suit contesting the President's authority under his war powers to seize the Nation's steel industry, an action of profound and demonstrable domestic impact. Here, by contrast, we are asked to settle a dispute between coequal branches of our Government, each of which has resources available to protect and assert its interests, resources not available to private litigants outside the judicial forum. Moreover, as in *Curtiss-Wright,* the effect of this action, as far as we can tell, is "entirely external to the United States, and [falls] within the category of foreign affairs." Finally, as already noted, the situation presented here is closely akin to that presented in *Coleman,* where the Constitution spoke only to the procedure for ratification of an amendment, not to its rejection.

Mr. Justice BLACKMUN, with whom Mr. Justice WHITE joins, dissenting in part.

In my view, the time factor and its importance are illusory; if the President does not have the power to terminate the treaty (a substantial issue that we should address only after briefing and oral argument), the notice of intention to terminate surely has no legal effect. It is also indefensible, without further study, to pass on the issue of justiciability or on the issues of standing or ripeness. While I therefore join in the grant of the petition for certiorari, I would set the case for oral argument and give it the plenary consideration it so obviously deserves.

Mr. Justice BRENNAN, dissenting.

In stating that this case presents a nonjusticiable "political question," Mr. Justice Rehnquist, in my view, profoundly misapprehends the political-question principle as it applies to matters of foreign relations. Properly understood, the political-question doctrine restrains courts from reviewing an exercise of foreign policy judgment by the coordinate political branch to which authority to make that judgment has been "constitutional[ly] commit[ted]." *Baker v. Carr,* 369 U.S. 186, 211-213, 217 (1962). But the doctrine does not pertain when a court is faced with the *antecedent* question whether a particular branch has been constitutionally designated as the repository of political decisionmaking power. Cf. *Powell v. McCormack,* 395 U.S. 486, 519-521 (1969). The issue of decisionmaking authority must be resolved as a matter of constitutional law, not political discretion; accordingly, it falls within the competence of the courts.

The constitutional question raised here is prudently answered in narrow terms. Abrogation of the defense treaty with Taiwan was a necessary incident to Executive recognition of the Peking Government, because the defense treaty was predicated upon the now-abandoned view that the Taiwan Government was the only legitimate political authority in China. Our cases firmly establish that the Constitution commits to the President alone the power to recognize, and withdraw recognition from, foreign regimes. That mandate being clear, our judicial inquiry into the treaty rupture can go no further.

Points for Discussion

a. Counting the Votes

How many Justices thought that the President had the authority to terminate the treaty? How many Justices thought that he did not? How many Justices thought that the Supreme Court could not decide the issue because it was not ripe? How many Justices thought that the Supreme Court could not decide the issue because it was a non-justiciable political question?

b. Advising the President

Suppose that the President wants to withdraw from a treaty with another country. Because the President is concerned that Congress will not support this move by passing legislation abrogating the treaty, the President is contemplating acting alone. The President asks you, "Can I pull the United States out of the treaty all by myself?" What legal and practical advice would you give the President?

c. Role for Congress

Justice Powell concluded that the case was not yet ripe for review. Did he think that it might have become ripe for review in the future? What steps could Congress have taken in opposing the President's actions other than having individual members of Congress bring a lawsuit?

C. The President's Powers in Times of War

The Court in *Goldwater* declined to resolve an interbranch controversy over the respective powers of the President and Congress in a matter of foreign affairs. That controversy existed at least in part because the Constitution divides responsibility over matters of foreign affairs—and on the subject of treaties in particular—between the President and Congress.

Controversies have also long existed over the scope of the President's powers in times of war, in large part because the Constitution similarly divides responsibility between the

President and Congress over matters related to war. For example, the President is the Commander in Chief of the Armed Forces. But the Constitution also vests Congress with substantial authority over matters of war, including the power to "declare War" and to "make Rules concerning Captures on Land and Water," Art. I, § 8, cl. 11, to "raise and support Armies" and "provide and maintain a Navy," Art. I, § 8, cl. 12 & 13, and to "make Rules for the *** Regulation of the land and naval Forces," Art. I, § 8, cl. 14. Not surprisingly given this arrangement, questions have often arisen about the respective roles of the President and Congress in matters of war. And, as in the *Goldwater* case, some of those questions have never been resolved.

Consider the case of the War Powers Resolution of 1973. After the United States had been involved in the Vietnam War for many years without a formal congressional declaration of war, Congress adopted a joint resolution to govern and limit the President's authority to involve the armed forces in hostilities. The stated purpose of the resolution was to "fulfill the intent of the framers of the Constitution of the United States and insure that the collective judgment of both the Congress and the President will apply to the introduction of United States Armed Forces into hostilities, or into situations where imminent involvement in hostilities is clearly indicated by the circumstances, and to the continued use of such forces in hostilities or in such situations." Although President Nixon vetoed the resolution, stating that it "would attempt to take away, by a mere legislative act, authorities which the President has properly exercised under the Constitution for almost 200 years," Congress overrode the veto with a super-majority vote in both houses.

The Resolution provides in relevant part:

§ 2(c). The constitutional powers of the President as Commander-in-Chief to introduce United States Armed Forces into hostilities, or into situations where imminent involvement in hostilities is clearly indicated by the circumstances, are exercised only pursuant to (1) a declaration of war, (2) specific statutory authorization, or (3) a national emergency created by attack upon the United States, its territories or possessions, or its armed forces.

[§ 3 requires the President "in every possible instance" to "consult" with Congress before introducing the armed forces into hostilities and then regularly for the duration of the hostilities.]

§ 4(a). In the absence of a declaration of war, in any case in which United States Armed Forces are introduced [into hostilities,] the President shall submit within 48 hours to the Speaker of the House of Representatives and to the President pro tempore of the Senate a report, in writing, setting forth—(A) the circumstances necessitating the introduction of United States Armed Forces; (B) the constitutional and legislative authority under which such introduction took place; and (C) the estimated scope and duration of the hostilities or involvement.

[§ 4(b) requires the President to provide "such other information as the Congress may request."]

§ 5(b). Within sixty calendar days after a report is submitted or is required to be submitted pursuant to section 4(a)(1), whichever is earlier, the President shall terminate any use of United States Armed Forces with respect to which such report was submitted (or required to be submitted), unless the Congress (1) has declared war or has enacted a specific authorization for such use of United States Armed Forces, (2) has extended by law such sixty-day period, or (3) is physically unable to meet as a result of an armed attack upon the United States. Such sixty-day period shall be extended for not more than an additional thirty days if the President determines and certifies to the Congress in writing that unavoidable military necessity respecting the safety of United States Armed Forces requires the continued use of such armed forces in the course of bringing about a prompt removal of such forces.

§ 5(c). Notwithstanding subsection (b), at any time that United States Armed Forces are engaged in hostilities outside the territory of the United States, its possessions and territories without a declaration of war or specific statutory authorization, such forces shall be removed by the President if the Congress so directs by concurrent resolution.

Is the War Powers Resolution constitutional? Is it merely an implementation of Congress's authority to declare war—and effectively Congress's attempt to define what counts as war? Or is it an impermissible interference with the President's role as Commander-in-Chief? Does Congress possess any other authority, short of declaring war, effectively to control the President's commitment of the armed forces to hostilities?

Presidents of both parties have taken the position that the War Powers Resolution is unconstitutional. They have also read it narrowly. For example, Presidents of both parties have taken the view that the Resolution "recognizes and presupposes the existence of unilateral Presidential authority" to "introduce troops into hostilities or potential hostilities without prior authorization by the Congress." Opinion of the Office of Legal Counsel on the Deployment of United States Armed Forces Into Haiti (Sept. 27, 1994). (Do you agree with this interpretation?) Since 1973, Presidents have sometimes complied with the Resolution's reporting requirements; other times they have not.

The Court has never addressed the constitutionality of the War Powers Resolution. Is the absence of judicial resolution of this question problematic? Or does it leave the question of authority over matters of war in the proper forum?

————————————

When the Nation goes to war, the President not only must make decisions about how to use military force, but also must make decisions about how to deal with persons captured in the course of armed conflicts. We focus here on a question that has taken on particular urgency in recent years, in the wake of the terrorist attacks of September 11, 2001: the President's power to detain and create rules for trying persons accused of acting as enemy combatants.

The following very heavily edited case arose out of America's use of military force following the terrorist attack of September 11, 2001. We include it, rather than earlier decisions, because of its obvious contemporary significance and because it contains the latest words on the President's war powers. But a small amount of background about two significant earlier cases might be useful. In *Ex Parte Milligan*, 71 U.S. 2 (1866), the Court granted a writ of habeas corpus to Milligan, a citizen of Indiana who had not served in the armed forces during the Civil War. Milligan had been detained in 1864 by the United States military and accused of plotting against military authorities. He was tried, before the war ended, by a military commission and sentenced to death. Although a civilian grand jury convened after the end of the Civil War failed to indict Milligan, the government announced its intention to proceed with Milligan's execution. Milligan challenged that decision in federal court. Justice Davis, who had been Lincoln's friend and campaign manager, wrote the opinion shortly after the former President's assassination. The Court held that Milligan could not be tried by a military commission. The Court explained: "Civil liberty and this kind of martial law cannot endure together *** [and] can never exist where the courts are open, and in the proper and unobstructed exercise of their jurisdiction."

Ex Parte Quirin, 317 U.S. 1 (1942), concerned eight Nazi saboteurs who used a German submarine to sneak into the United States during World War II with orders to commit a series of attacks in the United States. After the saboteurs were captured, President Roosevelt ordered the men tried by a military commission. The government charged the saboteurs with violating the laws of war by, among other things, crossing military lines out of uniform. The men, at least one of whom was an American citizen, unsuccessfully challenged the legality of the tribunal. The Court distinguished <u>Ex Parte Milligan</u> on the ground that the petitioners had been charged with violating the laws of war rather than domestic law. <u>Ex Parte Quirin</u> is a famous but controversial case. It appears that two of the saboteurs never intended to carry out the plan, and that after landing they informed the FBI about the plot. They nevertheless were tried before the military commission and (at least initially) sentenced to death. In addition, the historical record reveals that President Roosevelt's Attorney General personally lobbied the Justices of the Supreme Court to uphold the military tribunal commissioned to try the eight men. The Court issued its opinion in the case only after six of the men (those who had not informed law enforcement authorities of the plot) had already been executed. See Jonathan Turley, *Art and the Constitution: The Supreme Court and the Rise of the Impressionist School of Constitutional Interpretation*, 2004 Cato Sup. Ct. Rev. 69.

Finally, in 1948, Congress enacted the Non-Detention Act, 18 U.S.C. § 4001(a), which provides: "No citizen shall be imprisoned or otherwise detained by the United States except pursuant to an Act of Congress." It was against this background that the Court decided the most recent cases on the scope of the President's authority to detain enemy combatants. In reading the case that follows, you will see that although the Court concluded that Congress gave the President authority to use military force, substantial questions still arose about the scope of that authority. Pay particularly close attention to two points: (1) the division of opinions among the Justices on basic issues regarding the President's war powers; and (2) the Justices' treatment of precedents from the World War II era.

Hamdi v. Rumsfeld

542 U.S. 507 (2004)

Justice O'CONNOR announced the judgment of the Court and delivered an opinion, in which THE CHIEF JUSTICE, Justice KENNEDY, and Justice BREYER join.

> **Take Note**
>
> Justice O'Connor's opinion was supported by four justices. It is the "plurality opinion" because it received more votes than any other.

At this difficult time in our Nation's history, we are called upon to consider the legality of the Government's detention of a United States citizen on United States soil as an "enemy combatant" and to address the process that is constitutionally owed to one who seeks to challenge his classification as such. The United States Court of Appeals for the Fourth Circuit held that petitioner's detention was legally authorized and that he was entitled to no further opportunity to challenge his enemy-combatant label. We now vacate and remand. We hold that although Congress authorized the detention of combatants in the narrow circumstances alleged here, due process demands that a citizen held in the United States as an enemy combatant be given a meaningful opportunity to contest the factual basis for that detention before a neutral decisionmaker.

On September 11, 2001, the al Qaeda terrorist network used hijacked commercial airliners to attack prominent targets in the United States. Approximately 3,000 people were killed in those attacks. One week later, in response to these "acts of treacherous violence," Congress passed a resolution authorizing the President to "use all necessary and appropriate force against those nations, organizations, or persons he determines planned, authorized, committed, or aided the terrorist attacks" or "harbored such organizations or persons, in order to prevent any future acts of international terrorism against the United States by such nations, organizations or persons." Authorization for Use of Military Force ("the AUMF"), 115 Stat. 224. Soon thereafter, the President ordered

> **Take Note**
>
> The joint resolution authorizes the President to use military force, but does not define the scope of this authority. In particular, it does not specify whether the authority extends to detaining enemy combatants. How should the Court determine the scope of that authority? How does the Court determine it?

United States Armed Forces to Afghanistan, with a mission to subdue al Qaeda and quell the Taliban regime that was known to support it.

This case arises out of the detention of a man whom the Government alleges took up arms with the Taliban during this conflict. His name is Yaser Esam Hamdi. Born an American citizen in Louisiana in 1980, Hamdi moved with his family to Saudi Arabia as a child. By 2001, the parties agree, he resided in Afghanistan. At some point that year, he was seized by members of the Northern Alliance, a coalition of military groups opposed to the Taliban government, and eventually was turned over to the United States military.

The Government asserts that it initially detained and interrogated Hamdi in Afghanistan before transferring him to the United States Naval Base in Guantanamo Bay in January 2002. In April 2002, upon learning that Hamdi is an American citizen, authorities transferred him to a naval brig in Norfolk, Virginia, where he remained until a recent transfer to a brig in Charleston, South Carolina. The Government contends that Hamdi is an "enemy combatant," and that this status justifies holding him in the United States indefinitely—without formal charges or proceedings—unless and until it makes the determination that access to counsel or further process is warranted.

The threshold question before us is whether the Executive has the authority to detain citizens who qualify as "enemy combatants." There is some debate as to the proper scope of this term, and the Government has never provided any court with the full criteria that it uses in classifying individuals as such. It has made clear, however, that, for purposes of this case, the "enemy combatant" that it is seeking to detain is an individual who, it alleges, was "part of or supporting forces hostile to the United States or coalition partners" in Afghanistan and who "engaged in an armed conflict against the United States" there. Brief for Respondents 3. We therefore answer only the narrow question before us: whether the detention of citizens falling within that definition is authorized.

The Government maintains that no explicit congressional authorization is required, because the Executive possesses plenary authority to detain pursuant to Article II of the Constitution. We do not reach the question whether Article II provides such authority, however, because we agree with the Government's alternative position, that Congress has in fact authorized Hamdi's detention, through the AUMF.

The AUMF authorizes the President to use "all necessary and appropriate force" against "nations, organizations, or persons" associated with the September 11, 2001, terrorist attacks. 115 Stat. 224. There can be no doubt that individuals who fought against the United States in Afghanistan as part of the Taliban, an organization known to have supported the al Qaeda terrorist network responsible for those attacks, are individuals Congress sought to target in passing the AUMF. We conclude that detention of individuals falling into the limited category we are considering, for the duration of the particular conflict in which they were captured, is so fundamental and accepted an incident to war as to be an exercise of the "necessary and appropriate force" Congress has authorized the President to use.

The capture and detention of lawful combatants and the capture, detention, and trial of unlawful combatants, by "universal agreement and practice," are "important incident[s] of war." *Ex parte Quirin,* 317 U.S. 1 (1942). The purpose of detention is to prevent captured individuals from returning to the field of battle and taking up arms once again.

There is no bar to this Nation's holding one of its own citizens as an enemy combatant. In <u>Quirin</u>, one of the detainees, Haupt, alleged that he was a naturalized United States citizen. <u>317 U.S., at 20</u>. We held that "[c]itizens who associate themselves with the military arm of the enemy government, and with its aid, guidance and direction enter this country bent on hostile acts, are enemy belligerents within the meaning of . . . the law of war." <u>Id., at 37-38</u>. While Haupt was tried for violations of the law of war, nothing in <u>Quirin</u> suggests that his citizenship would have precluded his mere detention for the duration of the relevant hostilities. See <u>id., at 30-31</u>. Nor can we see any reason for drawing such a line here. A citizen, no less than an alien, can be "part of or supporting forces hostile to the United States or coalition partners" and "engaged in an armed conflict against the United States," Brief for Respondents 3; such a citizen, if released, would pose the same threat of returning to the front during the ongoing conflict.

In light of these principles, it is of no moment that the AUMF does not use specific language of detention. Because detention to prevent a combatant's return to the battlefield is a fundamental incident of waging war, in permitting the use of "necessary and appropriate force," Congress has clearly and unmistakably authorized detention in the narrow circumstances considered here.

Take Note

Do you agree that Congress has "clearly and unmistakably" authorized detention in the particular circumstances at issue in this case? Would it matter if Congress had done so merely by implication?

Hamdi objects, nevertheless, that Congress has not authorized the *indefinite* detention to which he is now subject. The Government responds that "the detention of enemy combatants during World War II was just as 'indefinite' while that war was being fought." We take Hamdi's objection to be not to the lack of certainty regarding the date on which the conflict will end, but to the substantial prospect of perpetual detention. We recognize that the national security underpinnings of the "war on terror," although crucially important, are broad and malleable. As the Government concedes, "given its unconventional nature, the current conflict is unlikely to end with a formal cease-fire agreement." The prospect Hamdi raises is therefore not far-fetched. If the Government does not consider this unconventional war won for two generations, and if it maintains during that time that Hamdi might, if released, rejoin forces fighting against the United States, then the position it has taken throughout the litigation of this case suggests that Hamdi's detention could last for the rest of his life. It is a clearly established principle of the law of war that detention may last no longer than active hostilities. See Article 118 of the Geneva Convention (III) Relative to the Treatment of Prisoners of War, Aug. 12, 1949, [1955] 6 U.S.T. 3316, 3406, T.I.A.S. No. 3364 ("Prisoners of war shall be released and repatriated without delay after the cessation of active hostilities").

Hamdi contends that the AUMF does not authorize indefinite or perpetual detention. Certainly, we agree that indefinite detention for the purpose of interrogation is not authorized. Further, we understand Congress' grant of authority for the use of "necessary and appropriate force" to include the authority to detain for the duration of the relevant conflict, and our understanding is based on longstanding law-of-war principles. If the practical circumstances of a given conflict are entirely unlike those of the conflicts that informed the development of the law of war, that understanding may unravel. But that is not the situation we face as of this date. Active combat operations against Taliban fighters apparently are ongoing in Afghanistan. The United States may detain, for the duration of these hostilities, individuals legitimately determined to be Taliban combatants who "engaged in an armed conflict against the United States." If the record establishes that United States troops are still involved in active combat in Afghanistan, those detentions are part of the exercise of "necessary and appropriate force," and therefore are authorized by the AUMF.

[Although the plurality concluded that the AUMF authorized the President to detain enemy combatants, it concluded that the Due Process Clause requires that "a citizen-detainee seeking to challenge his classification as an enemy combatant *** receive notice of the factual basis for his classification, and a fair opportunity to rebut the Government's factual assertions before a neutral decisionmaker."]

In so holding, we necessarily reject the Government's assertion that separation of powers principles mandate a heavily circumscribed role for the courts in such circumstances. Indeed, the position that the courts must forgo any examination of the individual case and focus exclusively on the legality of the broader detention scheme cannot be mandated by any reasonable view of separation of powers, as this approach serves only to condense power into a single branch of government. We have long since made clear that a state of war is not a blank check for the President when it comes to the rights of the Nation's citizens. *Youngstown Sheet & Tube v. Sawyer*, 343 U.S. 579, 587 (1952). Whatever power the United States Constitution envisions for the Executive in its exchanges with other nations or with enemy organizations in times of conflict, it most assuredly envisions a role for all three branches when individual liberties are at stake. *** Thus, while we do not question that our due process assessment must pay keen attention to the particular burdens faced by the Executive in the context of military action, it would turn our system of checks and balances on its head to suggest that a citizen could not make his way to court with a challenge to the factual basis for his detention by his Government, simply because the Executive opposes making available such a challenge.

[The Court remanded the case to allow for a determination whether Hamdi actually was an enemy combatant.]

Justice SOUTER, with whom Justice GINSBURG joins, concurring in part, dissenting in part, and concurring in the judgment.

The threshold issue is how broadly or narrowly to read the Non-Detention Act, the tone of which is severe: "No citizen shall be imprisoned or otherwise detained by the United States except pursuant to an Act of Congress." 18 U.S.C. § 4001(a). Should the severity of the Act be relieved when the Government's stated factual justification for incommunicado detention is a war on terrorism, so that the Government may be said to act "pursuant" to congressional terms that fall short of explicit authority to imprison individuals? With one possible though important qualification, the answer has to be no.

The fact that Congress intended to guard against a repetition of the World War II internments when it *** gave us § 4001(a) provides a powerful reason to think that § 4001(a) was meant to require clear congressional authorization before any citizen can be placed in a cell. It is not merely that the legislative history shows that § 4001(a) was thought necessary in anticipation of times just like the present, in which the safety of the country is threatened. To appreciate what is most significant, one must only recall that the internments of the 1940s were accomplished by Executive action.

> **Make the Connection**
>
> We will consider the government's internment of Japanese-American citizens during World War II, and the Court's decision in *Korematsu v. United States*, in Chapter 11.

[E]ven if history had spared us the cautionary example of the internments in World War II, *** there would be a compelling reason to read § 4001(a) to demand manifest authority to detain before detention is authorized. The defining character of American constitutional government is its constant tension between security and liberty, serving both by partial helpings of each. In a government of separated powers, deciding finally on what is a reasonable degree of guaranteed liberty whether in peace or war (or some condition in between) is not well entrusted to the Executive Branch of Government, whose particular responsibility is to maintain security. For reasons of inescapable human nature, the branch of the Government asked to counter a serious threat is not the branch on which to rest the Nation's entire reliance in striking the balance between the will to win and the cost in liberty on the way to victory; the responsibility for security will naturally amplify the claim that security legitimately raises. A reasonable balance is more likely to be reached on the judgment of a different branch ***. Hence the need for an assessment by Congress before citizens are subject to lockup, and likewise the need for a clearly expressed congressional resolution of the competing claims.

Under this principle of reading § 4001(a) robustly to require a clear statement of authorization to detain, none of the Government's arguments suffices to justify Hamdi's detention. *** Since the Force Resolution was adopted one week after the attacks of September 11, 2001, it naturally speaks with some generality, but its focus is clear, and that is on the use of military power. It is fairly read to authorize the use of armies and weapons, whether against other armies or individual terrorists. But *** it never so much as uses the word detention, and there is no reason to think Congress might have perceived any need to augment Executive power to deal with dangerous citizens within the United States, given the well-stocked statutory arsenal of defined criminal offenses covering the gamut of actions that a citizen sympathetic to terrorists might commit. See, *e.g.,* 18 U.S.C. § 2339A (material support for various terrorist acts); § 2339B (material support to a foreign terrorist organization); § 2332a (use of a weapon of mass destruction, including conspiracy and attempt); § 2332b(a)(1) (acts of terrorism "transcending national boundaries," including threats, conspiracy, and attempt); 18 U.S.C. § 2339C (financing of certain terrorist acts); see also 18 U.S.C. § 3142(e) (pretrial detention).

Since the Government has given no reason either to deflect the application of § 4001(a) or to hold it to be satisfied, I need to go no further; the Government hints of a constitutional challenge to the statute, but it presents none here. I will, however, stray across the line between statutory and constitutional territory just far enough to note the weakness of the Government's mixed claim of inherent, extrastatutory authority under a combination of Article II of the Constitution and the usages of war. It is in fact in this connection that the Government developed its argument that the exercise of war powers justifies the detention, and what I have just said about its inadequacy applies here as well. Beyond that, it is instructive to recall Justice Jackson's observation that the President is not Commander in Chief of the country, only of the military. *Youngstown Sheet & Tube Co. v. Sawyer*, 343 U.S. 579, 643-644 (1952) (concurring opinion); *see also* id., at 637-638 (Presidential authority is "at its lowest ebb" where the President acts contrary to congressional will).

There may be room for one qualification to Justice Jackson's statement, however: in a moment of genuine emergency, when the Government must act with no time for deliberation, the Executive may be able to detain a citizen if there is reason to fear he is an imminent threat to the safety of the Nation and its people. This case, however, does not present that question, because an emergency power of necessity must at least be limited by the emergency; Hamdi has been locked up for over two years. Cf. *Ex parte Milligan*, 4 Wall. 2, 127 (1866) (martial law justified only by "actual and present" necessity as in a genuine invasion that closes civilian courts). *** Whether insisting on the careful scrutiny of emergency claims or on a vigorous reading of § 4001(a), we are heirs to a tradition given voice 800 years ago by Magna Carta, which, on the barons' insistence, confined executive power by "the law of the land."

Because I find Hamdi's detention forbidden by § 4001(a) and unauthorized by the Force Resolution, I would not reach any questions of what process he may be due in litigating disputed issues in a proceeding under the habeas statute or prior to the habeas enquiry itself. *** Since this disposition does not command a majority of the Court, however, the need to give practical effect to the conclusions of eight Members of the Court rejecting the Government's position calls for me to join with the plurality in ordering remand on terms closest to those I would impose.

> **Take Note**
>
> Why did Justice Souter decide that the President does not have authority to detain Hamdi? If Hamdi had been killed by American forces in armed combat on a battlefield in Afghanistan, would that action have been authorized? If so, why can't the government take the lesser step of detaining him in the United States indefinitely?

Justice SCALIA, with whom Justice STEVENS joins, dissenting.

Where the Government accuses a citizen of waging war against it, our constitutional tradition has been to prosecute him in federal court for treason or some other crime. Where the exigencies of war prevent that, the Constitution's Suspension Clause, Art. I, § 9, cl. 2, allows Congress to relax the usual protections temporarily. Absent suspension, however, the Executive's assertion of military exigency has not been thought sufficient to permit detention without charge. No one contends that the congressional Authorization for Use of Military Force, on which the Government relies to justify its actions here, is an implementation of the Suspension Clause. Accordingly, I would reverse the decision below.

The very core of liberty secured by our Anglo-Saxon system of separated powers has been freedom from indefinite imprisonment at the will of the Executive. *** The gist of the Due Process Clause, as understood at the founding and since, was to force the Government to follow those common-law procedures traditionally deemed necessary before depriving a person of life, liberty, or property. *** These due process rights have historically been vindicated by the writ of habeas corpus. In England before the founding, the writ developed into a tool for challenging executive confinement. *** The writ of habeas corpus was preserved in the Constitution—the only common-law writ to be explicitly mentioned. See Art. I, § 9, cl. 2.

The allegations here, of course, are no ordinary accusations of criminal activity. [Hamdi] has been imprisoned because the Government believes he participated in the waging of war against the United States. The relevant question, then, is whether there is a different, special procedure for imprisonment of a citizen accused of wrongdoing by aiding the enemy in wartime. [The plurality] asserts that captured enemy combatants (other than those suspected of war crimes) have traditionally been detained until the cessation of hostilities and then released. That is probably an accurate description of wartime practice with respect to enemy aliens. The tradition with respect to American citizens, however, has been quite different. Citizens aiding the enemy have been treated as traitors subject to the criminal process.

There are times when military exigency renders resort to the traditional criminal process impracticable. English law accommodated such exigencies by allowing legislative suspension of the writ of habeas corpus for brief periods. *** Our Federal Constitution contains a provision explicitly permitting suspension, but limiting the situations in which it may be invoked: "The privilege of the Writ of Habeas Corpus shall not be suspended, unless when in Cases of Rebellion or Invasion the public Safety may require it." Art. I, § 9, cl. 2. Although this provision does not state that suspension must be effected by, or authorized by, a legislative act, it has been so understood, consistent with English practice and the Clause's placement in Article I. See *Ex parte Merryman*, 17 F. Cas. 144, 151-152 (Cir. Ct. D Md. 1861) (Taney, C. J., rejecting Lincoln's unauthorized suspension); 3 Story § 1336, at 208-209.

The Suspension Clause was by design a safety valve, the Constitution's only "express provision for exercise of extraordinary authority because of a crisis," *Youngstown Sheet & Tube Co. v. Sawyer*, 343 U.S. 579, 650 (1952) (Jackson, J., concurring). Very early in the Nation's history, President Jefferson unsuccessfully sought a suspension of habeas corpus to deal with Aaron Burr's conspiracy to overthrow the Government. See 16 Annals of Congress 402-425 (1807). During the Civil War, Congress passed its first Act authorizing

Executive suspension of the writ of habeas corpus, see Act of Mar. 3, 1863, 12 Stat. 755, to the relief of those many who thought President Lincoln's unauthorized proclamations of suspension (*e.g.,* Proclamation No. 1, 13 Stat. 730 (1862)) unconstitutional. Later Presidential proclamations of suspension relied upon the congressional authorization, *e.g.,* Proclamation No. 7, 13 Stat. 734 (1863). During Reconstruction, Congress passed the Ku Klux Klan Act, which included a provision authorizing suspension of the writ, invoked by President Grant in quelling a rebellion in nine South Carolina counties.

[T]he reasoning and conclusion of *Milligan* logically cover the present case. The Government justifies imprisonment of Hamdi on principles of the law of war and admits that, absent the war, it would have no such authority. But if the law of war cannot be applied to citizens where courts are open, then Hamdi's imprisonment without criminal trial is no less unlawful than Milligan's trial by military tribunal.

The proposition that the Executive lacks indefinite wartime detention authority over citizens is consistent with the Founders' general mistrust of military power permanently at the Executive's disposal. In the Founders' view, the "blessings of liberty" were threatened by "those military establishments which must gradually poison its very fountain." The Federalist No. 45, p. 238 (J. Madison). *** Except for the actual command of military forces, all authorization for their maintenance and all explicit authorization for their use is placed in the control of Congress under Article I, rather than the President under Article II. As Hamilton explained, the President's military authority would be "much inferior" to that of the British King. [The Federalist No. 69, p. 357.] A view of the Constitution that gives the Executive authority to use military force rather than the force of law against citizens on American soil flies in the face of the mistrust that engendered these provisions.

The Government argues that our more recent jurisprudence ratifies its indefinite imprisonment of a citizen within the territorial jurisdiction of federal courts. *** In [*Ex parte Quirin*, 317 U.S. 1 (1942),] it was uncontested that the petitioners were members of enemy forces. *** But where those jurisdictional facts are not conceded—where the petitioner insists that he is not a belligerent—*Quirin* left the pre-existing law in place: Absent suspension of the writ, a citizen held where the courts are open is entitled either to criminal trial or to a judicial decree requiring his release.

It follows from what I have said that Hamdi is entitled to a habeas decree requiring his release unless (1) criminal proceedings are promptly brought, or (2) Congress has suspended the writ of habeas corpus. A suspension of the writ could, of course, lay down conditions for continued detention, similar to those that today's opinion prescribes under the Due Process Clause. But there is a world of difference between the people's representatives' determining the need for that suspension (and prescribing the conditions for it), and this Court's doing so.

Take Note

In what ways is Justice Scalia's view different from Justice Souter's? From the plurality's?

The plurality finds justification for Hamdi's imprisonment in the Authorization for Use of Military Force. *** This is not remotely a congressional suspension of the writ, and no one claims that it is. Contrary to the plurality's view,

I do not think this statute even authorizes detention of a citizen with the clarity necessary *** to overcome [18 U.S.C. § 4001(a).] But even if it did, I would not permit it to overcome Hamdi's entitlement to habeas corpus relief. The Suspension Clause of the Constitution, which carefully circumscribes the conditions under which the writ can be withheld, would be a sham if it could be evaded by congressional prescription of requirements other than the common-law requirement of committal for criminal prosecution that render the writ, though available, unavailing. If the Suspension Clause does not guarantee the citizen that he will either be tried or released, unless the conditions for suspending the writ exist and the grave action of suspending the writ has been taken; if it merely guarantees the citizen that he will not be detained unless Congress by ordinary legislation says he can be detained; it guarantees him very little indeed.

Several limitations give my views in this matter a relatively narrow compass. They apply only to citizens, accused of being enemy combatants, who are detained within the territorial jurisdiction of a federal court. *** Where the citizen is captured outside and held outside the United States, the constitutional requirements may be different. Moreover, even within the United States, the accused citizen-enemy combatant may lawfully be detained once prosecution is in progress or in contemplation.

I frankly do not know whether these tools are sufficient to meet the Government's security needs, including the need to obtain intelligence through interrogation. It is far beyond my competence, or the Court's competence, to determine that. But it is not beyond Congress's. If the situation demands it, the Executive can ask Congress to authorize suspension of the writ—which can be made subject to whatever conditions Congress deems appropriate, including even the procedural novelties invented by the plurality today. To be sure, suspension is limited by the Constitution to cases of rebellion or invasion. But whether the attacks of September 11, 2001, constitute an "invasion," and whether those attacks still justify suspension several years later, are questions for Congress rather than this Court. If civil rights are to be curtailed during wartime, it must be done openly and democratically, as the Constitution requires, rather than by silent erosion through an opinion of this Court.

> **Take Note**
>
> Justice Scalia suggests that the question whether the circumstances justifying suspension exist is a non-justiciable political question. If Congress can simply declare an emergency and suspend the writ indefinitely, without judicial oversight, is there sufficient protection for the liberty interests that Justice Scalia said are protected by the writ in the first place? See Amanda L. Tyler, *Is Suspension a Political Question?* 59 Stan. L. Rev. 333 (2006).

The Founders well understood the difficult tradeoff between safety and freedom. [They] warned us about the risk, and equipped us with a Constitution designed to deal with it. Many think it not only inevitable but entirely proper that liberty give way to security in times of national crisis ***. Whatever the general merits of the view that war silences law or modulates its voice, that view has no place in the interpretation and application of a Constitution designed precisely to confront war and, in a manner that accords with democratic principles, to accommodate it. Because the Court has proceeded to meet the current emergency in a manner the Constitution does not envision, I respectfully dissent.

Justice THOMAS, dissenting.

The Executive Branch, acting pursuant to the powers vested in the President by the Constitution and with explicit congressional approval, has determined that Hamdi is an enemy combatant and should be detained. This detention falls squarely within the Federal Government's war powers, and we lack the expertise and capacity to second-guess that decision.

[B]ecause the Founders understood that they could not foresee the myriad potential threats to national security that might later arise, they chose to create a Federal Government that necessarily possesses sufficient power to handle any threat to the security of the Nation. *** The Founders intended that the President have primary responsibility—along with the necessary power—to protect the national security and to conduct the Nation's foreign relations. They did so principally because the structural advantages of a unitary Executive are essential in these domains.

These structural advantages are most important in the national-security and foreign-affairs contexts. *** To this end, the Constitution vests in the President "[t]he executive Power," Art. II, § 1, provides that he "shall be Commander in Chief of the" Armed Forces, § 2, and places in him the power to recognize foreign governments, § 3. This Court has long recognized these features and has accordingly held that the President has constitutional authority to protect the national security and that this authority carries with it broad discretion. *** Congress, to be sure, has a substantial and essential role in both foreign affairs and national security. But it is crucial to recognize that judicial interference in these domains destroys the purpose of vesting primary responsibility in a unitary Executive.

For these institutional reasons and because "Congress cannot anticipate and legislate with regard to every possible action the President may find it necessary to take or every possible situation in which he might act," it should come as no surprise that "[s]uch failure of Congress does not, especially in the areas of foreign policy and national security, imply congressional disapproval of action taken by the Executive." *Dames & Moore v. Regan*, 453 U.S. 654, 678 (1981). Rather, in these domains, the fact that Congress has provided the President with broad authorities does not imply—and the Judicial Branch should not infer—that Congress intended to deprive him of particular powers not specifically enumerated. See *Dames & Moore, 453 U.S. at 678*.

I acknowledge that the question whether Hamdi's executive detention is lawful is a question properly resolved by the Judicial Branch, though the question comes to the Court with the strongest presumptions in favor of the Government. The plurality agrees that Hamdi's detention is lawful if he is an enemy combatant. But the question whether Hamdi is actually an enemy combatant is "of a kind for which the Judiciary has neither aptitude, facilities nor responsibility and which has long been held to belong in the domain of political power not subject to judicial intrusion or inquiry." *Chicago & Southern Air Lines, Inc. v. Waterman S.S. Corp.*, 333 U.S. 103, 111 (1948). That is, although it is appropriate for the Court to determine the judicial question whether the President has the asserted authority, we lack the information and expertise to question whether Hamdi is actually an enemy combatant, a question the resolution of which is committed to other branches.

Although the President very well may have inherent authority to detain those arrayed against our troops, I agree with the plurality that we need not decide that question because Congress [in the AUMF] has authorized the President to do so. *** But I do not think that the plurality has adequately explained the breadth of the President's authority to detain enemy combatants, an authority that includes making virtually conclusive factual findings. In my view, the structural considerations discussed above, as recognized in our precedent, demonstrate that we lack the capacity and responsibility to second-guess this determination. In a case strikingly similar to this one, the Court addressed a Governor's authority to detain for an extended period a person the executive believed to be responsible, in part, for a local insurrection. Justice Holmes wrote for a unanimous Court:

> "When it comes to a decision by the head of the State upon a matter involving its life, the ordinary rights of individuals must yield to what *he deems* the necessities of the moment. Public danger warrants the substitution of executive process for judicial process. This was admitted with regard to killing men in the actual clash of arms, and we think it obvious, although it was disputed, that the same is true of temporary detention to prevent apprehended harm." *Moyer v. Peabody*, 212 U.S. 78 (1909).

The Court answered Moyer's claim that he had been denied due process by emphasizing that

> "it is familiar that what is due process of law depends on circumstances. It varies with the subject-matter and the necessities of the situation. Thus summary proceedings suffice for taxes, and executive decisions for exclusion from the country . . . . Such arrests are not necessarily for punishment, but are by way of precaution to prevent the exercise of hostile power." *Id.*, at 84-85 (citations omitted).

In this context, due process requires nothing more than a good-faith executive determination. To be clear: The Court has held that an executive, acting pursuant to statutory and constitutional authority may, consistent with the Due Process Clause, unilaterally decide to detain an individual if the executive deems this necessary for the public safety *even if he is mistaken.*

—————

Points for Discussion

a. Comparing the Opinions

How is Justice Scalia's opinion different from Justice Souter's opinion?   How would each of them rule on a case involving the detention of a *non*-citizen? How is Justice O'Connor's opinion different from Justice Thomas's opinion? What are the various Justices' views about the President's statutory authority to detain a citizen? The President's constitutional authority?

b. Deference to the Executive

Justice Thomas agreed with the plurality opinion by Justice O'Connor that the Authorization to Use Military Force allowed the President to order the detention of enemy combatants. But he disagreed with the plurality's conclusion that the President's determination of who was an enemy combatant was subject to judicial interference. (Although Justice Thomas's position on this issue received only one vote at the Supreme Court, it was the view of the court of appeals. See *Hamdi v. Rumsfeld*, 316 F.3d 450 (4th Cir. 2003).) If the President or his military subordinate orders an airstrike against suspected enemy combatants, may a court assert jurisdiction to determine whether the intended targets actually are enemy combatants? If not, why is this case different?

c. Aftermath of the Decision

Following this decision, the Department of Defense created Combatant Status Review Tribunals (i.e., hearing bodies composed of military officers) to determine whether individual detainees in fact were combatants. Much litigation has followed over the adequacy of the procedures followed by these tribunals. The United States returned Yaser Hamdi to Saudi Arabia on October 11, 2004, pursuant to an agreement in which Hamdi renounced his American citizenship and promised not to leave Saudi Arabia for five years. Saudi Arabia took no action against him. *See* Joel Brinkley, *From Afghanistan to Saudi Arabia, via Guantanamo*, N.Y. Times, Oct. 16, 2004, at A4.

d. Detaining Citizens Captured in the United States

Hamdi concerned the President's power to detain a citizen captured on a battlefield abroad and alleged to be an enemy combatant. What are the limits on the President's power to detain a citizen captured *in the United States*? The Court was presented with this question in *Rumsfeld v. Padilla*, 542 U.S. 426 (2004), but a five-Justice majority declined to decide the issue, concluding that the respondent had filed his petition for a writ of habeas corpus in the wrong district court and against the wrong defendant. Justice Stevens, joined by Justices Souter, Ginsburg, and Breyer, dissented, concluding that Congress had not, in the AUMF, authorized the detention of an American citizen arrested in the United States. (Justice Breyer had reached the opposite conclusion in <u>Hamdi</u> with respect to citizens captured abroad.) Justice Stevens asserted:

> "At stake in this case is nothing less than the essence of a free society. Even more important than the method of selecting the people's rulers and their successors is the character of the constraints imposed on the Executive by the rule of law. Unconstrained executive detention for the purpose of investigating and preventing subversive activity is the hallmark of the Star Chamber. Access to counsel for the purpose of protecting the citizen from official mistakes and mistreatment is the hallmark of due process. Executive detention of subversive citizens, like detention of enemy soldiers to keep them off the battlefield, may sometimes be justified to prevent persons from launching or becoming missiles of destruction. It may not, however, be justified by the naked interest in using unlawful procedures to extract information. Incommunicado detention for months on end is such a procedure. Whether the information so procured is more or less reliable than that acquired by more extreme forms of torture is of no consequence. For if this Nation is to remain true to the ideals symbolized by its flag, it must not wield the tools of tyrants even to resist an assault by the forces of tyranny."

Justice Scalia's opinion in <u>Hamdi</u> makes clear that he would have agreed, in a properly filed case, that the President lacks authority (absent a suspension of the writ of habeas corpus) to detain without charges or access to a lawyer a citizen captured in the United States. Accordingly, five members of the Court (at least in 2004) appear to have believed that the President lacked such authority.

Do the Executive's reasons for detaining a citizen matter in resolving the question whether the Constitution permits detention without access to lawyers or judicial process? Should they?

───────────

In *Hamdi*, the Supreme Court considered whether the President had authority to order the military to detain, without trial or access to lawyers, American citizens alleged to be enemy combatants. Does the President have power to order the use of military tribunals to try *non*-citizen enemy combatants for war crimes? In 2001, President Bush issued an order to govern the "Detention, Treatment, and Trial of Certain Non-Citizens in the War Against Terrorism." 66 Fed. Reg. 57833. The order authorized trials by "military commissions" for non-citizens for whom the President determines "there is reason to believe" that he or she (1) "is or was" a member of al Qaeda or (2) has engaged or participated in terrorist activities aimed at or harmful to the United States. A Yemeni national charged with conspiring with Osama bin Laden and others to engage in acts of terrorism and deemed eligible for trial by military commission sought writs of habeas corpus and mandamus to challenge the Executive Branch's proposed means of prosecuting him on the charges.

In *Hamdan v. Rumsfeld*, 548 U.S. 557 (2006), the Court held that the President's order was inconsistent with a statutory requirement imposed by the Uniform Code of Military Justice (UCMJ) and also violated the laws of war as embodied in the Third Geneva Convention of 1949 on the Treatment of Prisoners of War. Citing *Youngstown Sheet & Tube Co. v. Sawyer*, 343 U.S. 579, 637 (1952), the Court declared, "Whether or not the President has independent power, absent congressional authorization, to convene military commissions, he may not disregard limitations that Congress has, in proper exercise of its own war powers, placed on his powers." The Court also concluded that neither the Authorization for Use of Military Force nor the Detainee Treatment Act (DTA), Pub. L. 109-163, 119 Stat 3136, 3474 (Jan. 6, 2006), which Congress had enacted after Hamdan's commission had been convened, provided "specific, overriding authorization" for the military commission that had been convened to try Hamdan.

Justice Thomas, joined in part by two other Justices, dissented. In his view, in the domains of foreign policy and national security, "the fact that Congress has provided the President with broad authorities does not imply—and the Judicial Branch should not infer—that Congress intended to deprive him of particular powers not specifically enumerated." Instead, he asserted that the President's decision was "entitled to a heavy measure of deference." He would have concluded that the AUMF authorized the President's order. In addition, he would have concluded that the proposed procedures for the military commissions were consistent with the UCMJ and the laws of war.

Congress responded to the Court's decision in *Hamdan* by enacting the Military Commissions Act of 2006. Among other things, this Act authorized the President to use military commissions to try suspected terrorists and allowed the commissions' procedures to differ from those of courts-martial. Congress specifically amended the UCMJ to overrule the Court's interpretation, rejecting Justice Stevens's view and adopting Justice Thomas's. See 10 U.S.C. § 836(1). In *Boumediene v. Bush*, 553 U.S. 723 (2008), however, the Court held that persons detained at Guantanamo Bay enjoy the privilege of habeas corpus because Guantanamo Bay is under the de facto control of the United States military, and that the procedures that Congress provided in the Detainee Treatment Act of 2005 and the Military Commissions Act of 2006 for those detainees were not an "adequate and effective substitute for habeas corpus." Because Congress had not formally suspended the writ of habeas corpus, the Court concluded that these procedures operated as "an unconstitutional suspension of the writ." The Court did not reach the question whether the President had authority to detain the petitioners, leaving that question "to be resolved in the first instance by the District Court."

Did the Court's decisions in *Hamdan* and *Boumediene* meaningfully constrain the President's authority to detain and try persons whom he considers threats to the United States? Did they constrain Congress's power to authorize the President to do so? If so, are those constraints justified?

D. Executive Privilege

A privilege is an exception to a general duty. For example, a witness who is properly called before a grand jury may have a general duty to testify. But the witness may assert certain privileges that limit this duty. For example, the Fifth Amendment privilege against self-incrimination may give the witness the right not to make statements exposing the witness to criminal liability. The attorney-client privilege similarly may allow the witness to refuse to disclose the content of prior communications with the witness's lawyer.

Presidents since Washington have claimed that the Constitution creates an "executive privilege" that allows them to keep secret their communications with close advisors. Presidents often assert this privilege when Congress is investigating executive actions and demands that the White House provide information. But the privilege also can arise in judicial proceedings, as the following case shows. In reading the decision, consider the arguments for concluding that an executive privilege exists and the nature of the restrictions that the Supreme Court places on the privilege that it recognizes.

Prior to the 1972 Presidential election, supporters of President Nixon were caught trying to break into the Democratic Party headquarters in the Watergate complex in Washington, D.C. There is no evidence that President Nixon knew about the crime in advance.

But President Nixon and his advisors plotted to cover up the incident because they correctly predicted that the attempted burglary would have negative political consequences. At the request of a special prosecutor appointed by the Attorney General, a grand jury subsequently investigated whether President Nixon and others had conspired to obstruct justice. The grand jury wanted access to tape recordings that President Nixon had made of his conversations with advisors in the White House concerning the cover-up. President Nixon's refusal to disclose them led to the decision that follows.

————————

United States v. Nixon

418 U.S. 683 (1974)

Mr. Chief Justice BURGER delivered the opinion of the Court.

On March 1, 1974, a grand jury of the United States District Court for the District of Columbia returned an indictment charging seven named individuals with various offenses, including conspiracy to defraud the United States and to obstruct justice. Although he was not designated as such in the indictment, the grand jury named the President, among others, as an unindicted coconspirator. On April 18, 1974, upon motion of the Special Prosecutor, a *subpoena duces tecum* was issued pursuant to Rule 17(c) to the President by the United States District Court and made returnable on May 2, 1974. This subpoena required the production, in advance of the September 9 trial date, of certain tapes, memoranda, papers, transcripts or other writings relating to certain precisely identified meetings between the President and others. The Special Prosecutor was able to fix the time, place, and persons present at these discussions because the White House daily logs and appointment records had been delivered to him. On April 30, the President publicly released edited transcripts of 43 conversations; portions of 20 conversations subject to subpoena in the present case were included. On May 1, 1974, the President's counsel filed a "special appearance" and a motion to quash the subpoena under Rule 17(c). This motion was accompanied by a formal claim of privilege.

> **Definition**
>
> A *subpoena duces tecum* is an order directing a witness to appear and bring documents or other items. *Black's Law Dictionary* (8th ed. 2004).

JUSTICIABILITY

In the District Court, the President's counsel argued that the court lacked jurisdiction to issue the subpoena because the matter was an intra-branch dispute between a subordinate and superior officer of the Executive Branch and hence not subject to judicial resolution. That argument has been renewed in this Court with emphasis on the contention that the dispute

> **FYI**
>
> The Supreme Court granted certiorari before the Court of Appeals decided the case. This is very rare, but the Court did so "because of the public importance of the issues presented and the need for their prompt resolution."

does not present a "case" or "controversy" which can be adjudicated in the federal courts.

Early in the controversy over the Watergate break-in, Attorney General Elliot Richardson appointed Archibald Cox, a law professor, as a special prosecutor to investigate the affair. After Cox subpoenaed recordings that the President had secretly made of conversations in the Oval Office, President Nixon ordered Richardson to fire Cox. Nixon fired Richardson and his deputy, William Ruckelshaus, when they refused to fire Cox. (These firings became known as the "Saturday Night Massacre.") Solicitor General Robert Bork then fired Cox. After more damaging disclosures of the President's role in a cover-up of the Watergate affair, the Nixon administration appointed a new special prosecutor, Leon Jaworski, who sought the evidence at issue here.

The President's counsel [views] the present dispute as essentially a "jurisdictional" dispute within the Executive Branch which he analogizes to a dispute between two congressional committees. Since the Executive Branch has exclusive authority and absolute discretion to decide whether to prosecute a case, it is contended that a President's decision is final in determining what evidence is to be used in a given criminal case. *** The Special Prosecutor's demand for the items therefore presents, in the view of the President's counsel, a political question under *Baker v. Carr*, 369 U.S. 186 (1962), since it involves a "textually demonstrable" grant of power under Art. II.

Our starting point is the nature of the proceeding for which the evidence is sought—here a pending criminal prosecution. It is a judicial proceeding in a federal court alleging violation of federal laws and is brought in the name of the United States as sovereign. Under the authority of Art. II, § 2, Congress has vested in the Attorney General the power to conduct the criminal litigation of the United States Government. It has also vested in him the power to appoint subordinate officers to assist him in the discharge of his duties. Acting pursuant to those statutes, the Attorney General has delegated the authority to represent the United States in these particular matters to a Special Prosecutor with unique authority and tenure.[8] The

---

[8] The regulation issued by the Attorney General pursuant to his statutory authority vests in the Special Prosecutor plenary authority to control the course of investigations and litigation related to "all offenses arising out of the 1972 Presidential Election for which the Special Prosecutor deems it necessary and appropriate to assume responsibility, allegations involving the President, members of the White House staff, or Presidential appointees, and any other matters which he consents to have assigned to him by the Attorney General." 38 Fed.Reg. 30739, as amended by 38 Fed.Reg. 32805. In particular, the Special Prosecutor was given full authority, inter alia, "to contest the assertion of 'Executive Privilege' . . . and handl(e) all aspects of any cases within his jurisdiction." Id., at 30739. The regulations then go on the provide:

"In exercising this authority, the Special Prosecutor will have the greatest degree of independence that is consistent with the Attorney General's statutory accountability for all matters falling within the jurisdiction of the Department of Justice. The Attorney General will not countermand or interfere with the Special Prosecutor's decisions or actions. The Special Prosecutor will determine whether and to what extent he will inform or consult with the Attorney General about the conduct of his duties and responsibilities. In accordance with assurances given by the President to the Attorney General that the President will not exercise his Constitutional powers to effect the discharge of the Special Prosecutor or to limit the independence that he is hereby given, the Special Prosecutor will not be removed from his duties except for extraordinary improprieties on his part and without the President's first consulting the Majority and the Minority Leaders and Chairmen and ranking Minority Members of the Judiciary Committees of the Senate and House of Representatives and ascertaining that their consensus is in accord with his proposed action."

regulation gives the Special Prosecutor explicit power to contest the invocation of executive privilege in the process of seeking evidence deemed relevant to the performance of these specially delegated duties.

[I]t is theoretically possible for the Attorney General to amend or revoke the regulation defining the Special Prosecutor's authority. But he has not done so. So long as this regulation remains in force the Executive Branch is bound by it, and indeed the United States as the sovereign composed of the three branches is bound to respect and to enforce it. Moreover, the delegation of authority to the Special Prosecutor in this case is not an ordinary delegation by the Attorney General to a subordinate officer: with the authorization of the President, the Acting Attorney General provided in the regulation that the Special Prosecutor was not to be removed without the "consensus" of eight designated leaders of Congress.

The demands of and the resistance to the subpoena present an obvious controversy in the ordinary sense, but that alone is not sufficient to meet constitutional standards. In the constitutional sense, controversy means more than disagreement and conflict; rather it means the kind of controversy courts traditionally resolve. Here at issue is the production or nonproduction of specified evidence deemed by the Special Prosecutor to be relevant and admissible in a pending criminal case. It is sought by one official of the Executive Branch within the scope of his express authority; it is resisted by the Chief Executive on the ground of his duty to preserve the confidentiality of the communications of the President. Whatever the correct answer on the merits, these issues are "of a type which are traditionally justiciable." The independent Special Prosecutor with his asserted need for the subpoenaed material in the underlying criminal prosecution is opposed by the President with his steadfast assertion of privilege against disclosure of the material. This setting assures there is "that concrete adverseness which sharpens the presentation of issues upon which the court so largely depends for illumination of difficult constitutional questions." *Baker v. Carr*, 369 U.S., at 204. Moreover, since the matter is one arising in the regular course of a federal criminal prosecution, it is within the traditional scope of Art. III power.

THE CLAIM OF PRIVILEGE

The first contention is a broad claim that the separation of powers doctrine precludes judicial review of a President's claim of privilege. The second contention is that if he does not prevail on the claim of absolute privilege, the court should hold as a matter of constitutional law that the privilege prevails over the subpoena. In the performance of assigned constitutional duties each branch of the Government must initially interpret the Constitution, and the interpretation of its powers by any branch is due great respect from the others. *** Many decisions of this Court, however, have unequivocally reaffirmed the holding of <u>Marbury v. Madison</u> that "[i]t is emphatically the province and duty of the judicial department to say what the law is." **** Since this Court has consistently exercised the power to construe and delineate claims arising under express powers, it must follow that the Court has authority to interpret claims with respect to powers alleged to derive from enumerated powers.

In support of his claim of absolute privilege, the President's counsel urges two grounds, one of which is common to all governments and one of which is peculiar to our system of separation of powers. The first ground is the valid need for protection of communications between high Government officials and those who advise and assist them in the performance of their manifold duties; the importance of this confidentiality is too plain to require further discussion. Human experience teaches that those who expect public dissemination of their remarks may well temper candor with a concern for appearances and for their own interests to the detriment of the decisionmaking process.

Take Note

Does the claimed executive privilege find support in the text of the Constitution? If not, where did President Nixon argue that it comes from?

Whatever the nature of the privilege of confidentiality of Presidential communications in the exercise of Art. II powers, the privilege can be said to derive from the supremacy of each branch within its own assigned area of constitutional duties. Certain powers and privileges flow from the nature of enumerated powers; the protection of the confidentiality of Presidential communications has similar constitutional underpinnings.

The second ground asserted by the President's counsel in support of the claim of absolute privilege rests on the doctrine of separation of powers. Here it is argued that the independence of the Executive Branch within its own sphere insulates a President from a judicial subpoena in an ongoing criminal prosecution, and thereby protects confidential Presidential communications.

However, neither the doctrine of separation of powers, nor the need for confidentiality of high-level communications, without more, can sustain an absolute, unqualified Presidential privilege of immunity from judicial process under all circumstances. The President's need for complete candor and objectivity from advisers calls for great deference from the courts. However, when the privilege depends solely on the broad, undifferentiated claim of public interest in the confidentiality of such conversations, a confrontation with other values arises. Absent a claim of need to protect military, diplomatic, or sensitive national

Definition

In camera means "in the judge's private chambers." Black's Law Dictionary (8th ed. 2004).

security secrets, we find it difficult to accept the argument that even the very important interest in confidentiality of Presidential communications is significantly diminished by production of such material for *in camera* inspection with all the protection that a district court will be obliged to provide.

The impediment that an absolute, unqualified privilege would place in the way of the primary constitutional duty of the Judicial Branch to do justice in criminal prosecutions would plainly conflict with the function of the courts under Art. III. In designing the structure of our Government and dividing and allocating the sovereign power among three co-equal branches, the Framers of the Constitution sought to provide a comprehensive system, but the separate powers were not intended to operate with absolute independence. To read the Art. II powers of the President as providing an absolute privilege as against a subpoena essential to enforcement of criminal statutes on no more than a generalized claim of the public interest in confidentiality of nonmilitary and nondiplomatic discussions would upset the constitutional balance of "a workable government" and gravely impair the role of the courts under Art. III.

Since we conclude that the legitimate needs of the judicial process may outweigh Presidential privilege, it is necessary to resolve those competing interests in a manner that preserves the essential functions of each branch. The right and indeed the duty to resolve that question does not free the Judiciary from according high respect to the representations made on behalf of the President.

The expectation of a President to the confidentiality of his conversations and correspondence, like the claim of confidentiality of judicial deliberations, for example, has all the values to which we accord deference for the privacy of all citizens and, added to those values, is the necessity for protection of the public interest in candid, objective, and even blunt or harsh opinions in Presidential decisionmaking. A President and those who assist him must be free to explore alternatives in the process of shaping policies and making decisions and to do so in a way many would be unwilling to express except privately. These are the considerations justifying a presumptive privilege for Presidential communications. The privilege is fundamental to the operation of Government and inextricably rooted in the separation of powers under the Constitution. ***

But this presumptive privilege must be considered in light of our historic commitment to the rule of law. This is nowhere more profoundly manifest than in our view that "the twofold aim (of criminal justice) is that guilt shall not escape or innocence suffer." *Berger v. United States*, 295 U.S. 78, 88 (1935). We have elected to employ an adversary system of criminal justice in which the parties contest all issues before a court of law. The need to develop all relevant facts in the adversary system is both fundamental and comprehensive. The ends of criminal justice would be defeated if judgments were to be founded on a partial or speculative presentation of the facts. The very integrity of the judicial system and public confidence in the system depend on full disclosure of all the facts, within the framework of the rules of evidence. To ensure that justice is done, it is imperative to the function of courts that compulsory process be available for the production of evidence needed either by the prosecution or by the defense.

In this case we must weigh the importance of the general privilege of confidentiality of Presidential communications in performance of the President's responsibilities against the inroads of such a privilege on the fair administration of criminal justice. The interest in preserving confidentiality is weighty indeed and entitled to great respect. However, we cannot conclude that advisers will be moved to temper the candor of their remarks by the infrequent occasions of disclosure because of the possibility that such conversations will be called for in the context of a criminal prosecution.

On the other hand, the allowance of the privilege to withhold evidence that is demonstrably relevant in a criminal trial would cut deeply into the guarantee of due process of law and gravely impair the basic function of the courts. A President's acknowledged need for confidentiality in the communications of his office is general in nature, whereas the constitutional need for production of relevant evidence in a criminal proceeding is specific and central to the fair adjudication of a particular criminal case in the administration of justice. Without access to specific facts a criminal prosecution may be totally frustrated. The President's broad interest in confidentiality of communications will not be vitiated by disclosure of a limited number of conversations preliminarily shown to have some bearing on the pending criminal cases.

We conclude that when the ground for asserting privilege as to subpoenaed materials sought for use in a criminal trial is based only on the generalized interest in confidentiality, it cannot prevail over the fundamental demands of due process of law in the fair administration of criminal justice. The generalized assertion of privilege must yield to the demonstrated, specific need for evidence in a pending criminal trial.

[The Court concluded by describing how a judge, when confronted with a claim of privilege, should inspect the evidence *in camera* before making a ruling.]

Affirmed.

Points for Discussion

a. Legal Question or Policy Question?

Is the question whether the President should have an executive privilege a legal question or a policy question? What legal sources does the Court cite in support of the privilege? What legal sources does the Court cite for limiting it? What policy considerations does the Court take into account?

b. Disputes with Congress

Suppose that Congress demands that the President turn over sensitive documents, and the President refuses to turn them over on grounds of executive privilege. How can Congress and the President settle the dispute over production of the documents? Is the Court's role in such a controversy different from the Court's role in *Nixon*?

E. Executive Immunity

The following two cases consider important and related questions. The first is whether Presidents face civil liability for actions that they take in their official capacity. This question is significant. If Presidents face no liability, then they might not take care to avoid violating the rights of individuals. On the other hand, if Presidents may incur civil liability for their official actions, then they may hesitate to carry out their duties for fear of being sued. The second question is whether courts may entertain a civil lawsuit against a President during the President's term of office for unofficial actions taken before the President's term in office. Allowing these lawsuits may burden the President because litigation can be time-consuming and distracting. But barring them may deny justice to plaintiffs who have valid claims.

————————

Nixon v. Fitzgerald

457 U.S. 731 (1982)

Justice POWELL delivered the opinion of the Court.

In January 1970 the respondent A. Ernest Fitzgerald lost his job as a management analyst with the Department of the Air Force. Fitzgerald's dismissal occurred in the context of a departmental reorganization and reduction in force, in which his job was eliminated. In announcing the reorganization, the Air Force characterized the action as taken to promote economy and efficiency in the Armed Forces.

Respondent's discharge attracted unusual attention in Congress and in the press. Fitzgerald had attained national prominence approximately one year earlier, during the waning months of the Presidency of Lyndon B. Johnson. On November 13, 1968, Fitzgerald appeared before the Subcommittee on Economy in Government of the Joint Economic Committee of the United States Congress. To the evident embarrassment of his superiors in the Department of Defense, Fitzgerald testified that cost-overruns on the C-5A transport plane could approximate $2 billion. He also revealed that unexpected technical difficulties had arisen during the development of the aircraft.

[Claiming that he had suffered retaliation for his congressional testimony, Fizgerald sued former President Richard Nixon and others for damages. President Nixon claimed that he had absolute immunity from liability for any action that he may have taken against Fitzgerald while he was President.]

This Court consistently has recognized that government officials are entitled to some form of immunity from suits for civil damages. In *Spalding v. Vilas*, 161 U.S. 483 (1896), the Court considered the immunity available to the Postmaster General in a suit for damages based upon his official acts. Drawing upon principles of immunity developed in English cases at common law, the Court concluded that "[t]he interests of the people" required a grant of absolute immunity to public officers. *Id., at 498.* In the absence of immunity, the Court reasoned, executive officials would hesitate to exercise their discretion in a way "injuriously affect[ing] the claims of particular individuals," *id., at 499*, even when the public interest required bold and unhesitating action. Considerations of "public policy and convenience" therefore compelled a judicial recognition of immunity from suits arising from official acts.

In *Scheuer v. Rhodes*, 416 U.S. 232 (1974), the Court considered the immunity available to state executive officials in a 42 U.S.C § 1983 suit alleging the violation of constitutional rights. *** As construed by subsequent cases, *Scheuer* established a two-tiered division of immunity defenses in § 1983 suits. To most [state] executive officers *Scheuer* accorded qualified immunity. For them the scope of the defense varied in proportion to the nature of their official functions and the range of decisions that conceivably might be taken in "good faith." This "functional" approach also defined a second tier, however, at which the especially sensitive duties of certain officials—notably judges and prosecutors—required the continued recognition of absolute immunity. See, e.g., *Imbler v. Pachtman*, 424 U.S. 409 (1976) (state prosecutors possess absolute immunity with respect to the initiation and pursuit of prosecutions); *Stump v. Sparkman*, 435 U.S. 349 (1978) (state judge possesses absolute immunity for all judicial acts).

This approach was reviewed in detail in *Butz v. Economou*, 438 U.S. 478 (1978), when we considered for the first time the kind of immunity possessed by *federal* executive officials who are sued for constitutional violations. In <u>Butz</u> the Court rejected an argument, based on decisions involving federal officials charged with common-law torts, that all high federal officials have a right to absolute immunity from constitutional damages actions. Concluding that a blanket recognition of absolute immunity would be anomalous in light of the qualified immunity standard applied to state executive officials, <u>id. at 504</u>, we held that federal officials generally have the same qualified immunity possessed by state officials in cases under § 1983. In so doing we reaffirmed our holdings that some officials, notably judges and prosecutors, "because of the special nature of their responsibilities," <u>id., at 511</u>," require a full exemption from liability." <u>Id. at 508</u>. In <u>Butz</u> [we] left open the question whether other federal officials could show that "public policy requires an exemption of that scope." <u>Id., at 506</u>.

Here a former President asserts his immunity from civil damages claims of two kinds. He stands named as a defendant in a direct action under the Constitution and in two statutory actions under federal laws of general applicability. In neither case has Congress taken express legislative action to subject the President to civil liability for his official acts.

Applying the principles of our cases to claims of this kind, we hold that petitioner, as a former President of the United States, is entitled to absolute immunity from damages liability predicated on his official acts. We consider this immunity a functionally mandated incident of the President's unique office, rooted in the constitutional tradition of the separation of powers and supported by our history. Justice Story's analysis remains persuasive:

> "There are . . . incidental powers, belonging to the executive department, which are necessarily implied from the nature of the functions, which are confided to it. Among these, must necessarily be included the power to perform them . . . . The president cannot, therefore, be liable to arrest, imprisonment, or detention, while he is in the discharge of the duties of his office; and for this purpose his person must be deemed, in civil cases at least, to possess an official inviolability." 3 J. Story, Commentaries on the Constitution of the United States § 1563, pp. 418-419 (1st ed. 1833).

The President occupies a unique position in the constitutional scheme. Article II, § 1, of the Constitution provides that "[t]he executive Power shall be vested in a President of the United States." This grant of authority establishes the President as the chief constitutional officer of the Executive Branch, entrusted with supervisory and policy responsibilities of utmost discretion and sensitivity. These include the enforcement of federal law—it is the President who is charged constitutionally to "take Care that the Laws be faithfully executed"; the conduct of foreign affairs—a realm in which the Court has recognized that "[i]t would be intolerable that courts, without the relevant information, should review and perhaps nullify actions of the Executive taken on information properly held secret"; and management of the Executive Branch—a task for which "imperative reasons requir[e] an unrestricted power [in the President] to remove the most important of his subordinates in their most important duties."

In arguing that the President is entitled only to qualified immunity, the respondent relies on cases in which we have recognized immunity of this scope for governors and cabinet officers. *E.g.*, *Butz v. Economou*, 438 U.S. 478 (1978); *Scheuer v. Rhodes*, 416 U.S. 232 (1974). We find these cases to be inapposite. The President's unique status under the Constitution distinguishes him from other executive officials.[31]

Because of the singular importance of the President's duties, diversion of his energies by concern with private lawsuits would raise unique risks to the effective functioning of

---

[31] Noting that the Speech and Debate Clause provides a textual basis for congressional immunity, respondent argues that the Framers must be assumed to have rejected any similar grant of executive immunity. This argument is unpersuasive. First, a specific textual basis has not been considered a prerequisite to the recognition of immunity. No provision expressly confers judicial immunity. Yet the immunity of judges is well settled. Second, this Court already has established that absolute immunity may be extended to certain officials of the Executive Branch. Third, there is historical evidence from which it may be inferred that the Framers assumed the President's immunity from damages liability. At the Constitutional Convention several delegates expressed concern that subjecting the President even to impeachment would impair his capacity to perform his duties of office. See 2 M. Farrand, Records of the Federal Convention of 1787, p. 64 (1911) (remarks of Gouverneur Morris); id., at 66 (remarks of Charles Pinckney). The delegates of course did agree to an Impeachment Clause. But nothing in their debates suggests an expectation that the President would be subjected to the distraction of suits by disappointed private citizens. ***

government. As is the case with prosecutors and judges—for whom absolute immunity now is established—a President must concern himself with matters likely to "arouse the most intense feelings." *Pierson v. Ray*, 386 U.S. 547, 554 (1967). Yet, as our decisions have recognized, it is in precisely such cases that there exists the greatest public interest in providing an official "the maximum ability to deal fearlessly and impartially with" the duties of his office. *Ferri v. Ackerman*, 444 U.S. 193, 203 (1979). This concern is compelling where the officeholder must make the most sensitive and far-reaching decisions entrusted to any official under our constitutional system.[32] Nor can the sheer prominence of the President's office be ignored. In view of the visibility of his office and the effect of his actions on countless people, the President would be an easily identifiable target for suits for civil damages. Cognizance of this personal vulnerability frequently could distract a President from his public duties, to the detriment of not only the President and his office but also the Nation that the Presidency was designed to serve.

Justice WHITE, with whom Justice BRENNAN, Justice MARSHALL, and Justice BLACKMUN join, dissenting.

[According to the Court, the] President, acting within the outer boundaries of what Presidents normally do, may, without liability, deliberately cause serious injury to any number of citizens even though he knows his conduct violates a statute or tramples on the constitutional rights of those who are injured. Even if the President in this case ordered Fitzgerald fired by means of a trumped-up reduction in force, knowing that such a discharge was contrary to the civil service laws, he would be absolutely immune from suit. By the same token, if a President, without following the statutory procedures which he knows apply to himself as well as to other federal officials, orders his subordinates to wiretap or break into a home for the purpose of installing a listening device, and the officers comply with his request, the President would be absolutely immune from suit. He would be immune regardless of the damage he inflicts, regardless of how violative of the statute and of the Constitution he knew his conduct to be, and regardless of his purpose.

Points for Discussion

a. Another Legal Question or Policy Question?

We previously have considered whether the executive privilege is rooted in law or policy. What about the question whether the President should have absolute immunity? Is that a legal question or a question of policy? Do the majority and dissenting opinions disagree on this question? Is it possible to find a justification in the Constitution's structure even if not in any express provision?

---

[32] Among the most persuasive reasons supporting official immunity is the prospect that damages liability may render an official unduly cautious in the discharge of his official duties. As Judge Learned Hand wrote in *Gregoire v. Biddle*, 177 F.2d 579, 581 (CA2 1949), *cert. denied*, 339 U.S. 949 (1950), "[t]he justification for [denying recovery] is that it is impossible to know whether the claim is well founded until the case has been tried, and to submit all officials, the innocent as well as the guilty, to the burden of a trial and to the inevitable danger of its outcome, would dampen the ardor of all but the most resolute . . . ."

b. Political Checks

Is there an adequate political check on presidential over-reaching such that judicial intervention is unnecessary? If not, is the conclusion in *Fitzgerald* nevertheless defensible?

c. Status of Presidential Immunity

The Court notes that Congress had not purported to authorize suits against the President. Could Congress enact a statute over-riding the President's immunity in some class of cases? In all cases?

d. The President's Subordinates

Suppose the President orders a subordinate to torture a suspected terrorist, in violation of the law. Would the President be liable for damages? Would the subordinate?

————————

Clinton v. Jones

520 U.S. 681 (1997)

Justice STEVENS delivered the opinion of the Court.

Petitioner, William Jefferson Clinton, was elected to the Presidency in 1992, and re-elected in 1996. His term of office expires on January 20, 2001. In 1991 he was the Governor of the State of Arkansas. Respondent, Paula Corbin Jones, is a resident of California. In 1991 she lived in Arkansas, and was an employee of the Arkansas Industrial Development Commission.

On May 6, 1994, she commenced this action in the United States District Court for the Eastern District of Arkansas by filing a complaint naming petitioner and Danny Ferguson, a former Arkansas State Police officer, as defendants. The complaint alleges two federal claims, and two state-law claims over which the federal court has jurisdiction because of the diverse citizenship of the parties. As the case comes to us, we are required to assume the truth of the detailed—but as yet untested—factual allegations in the complaint.

Those allegations principally describe events that are said to have occurred on the afternoon of May 8, 1991, during an official conference held at the Excelsior Hotel in Little Rock, Arkansas. The Governor delivered a speech at the conference; respondent—working as a state employee—staffed the registration desk. She alleges that Ferguson persuaded her to leave her desk and to visit the Governor in a business suite at the hotel, where he made "abhorrent" sexual advances that she vehemently rejected. She further claims that her superiors at work subsequently dealt with her in a hostile and rude manner, and changed her duties to punish her for rejecting those advances. Finally, she alleges that after petitioner was elected President, Ferguson defamed her by making a statement to a reporter that implied she had accepted petitioner's alleged overtures, and that various persons authorized to speak for the President publicly branded her a liar by denying that the incident had occurred. *** [I]t is perfectly clear that the alleged misconduct of petitioner was unrelated to any of his official duties as President of the United States and, indeed, occurred before he was elected to that office.

In response to the complaint, petitioner promptly advised the District Court that he intended to file a motion to dismiss on grounds of Presidential immunity, and requested the court to defer all other pleadings and motions until after the immunity issue was resolved. *** The District Judge denied the motion to dismiss on immunity grounds and ruled that discovery in the case could go forward, but ordered any trial stayed until the end of petitioner's Presidency. Although she recognized that a "thin majority" in *Nixon v. Fitzgerald,* 457 U.S. 731 (1982), had held that "the President has absolute immunity from civil damage actions arising out of the execution of official duties of office," she was not convinced that "a President has absolute immunity from civil causes of action arising prior to assuming the office." She was, however, persuaded by some of the reasoning in our opinion in *Fitzgerald* that deferring the trial if one were required would be appropriate. Relying in part on the fact that respondent had failed to bring her complaint until two days before the 3-year period of limitations expired, she concluded that the public interest in avoiding litigation that might hamper the President in conducting the duties of his office outweighed any demonstrated need for an immediate trial.

Petitioner's principal submission—that "in all but the most exceptional cases," the Constitution affords the President temporary immunity from civil damages litigation arising out of events that occurred before he took office—cannot be sustained on the basis of precedent.

Only three sitting Presidents have been defendants in civil litigation involving their actions prior to taking office. Complaints against Theodore Roosevelt and Harry Truman had been dismissed before they took office; the dismissals were affirmed after their respective inaugurations. Two companion cases arising out of an automobile accident were filed against John F. Kennedy in 1960 during the Presidential campaign. After taking office, he unsuccessfully argued that his status as Commander in Chief gave him a right to a stay under the Soldiers' and Sailors' Civil Relief Act of 1940. The motion for a stay was denied by the District Court, and the matter was settled out of court. Thus, none of those cases sheds any light on the constitutional issue before us.

The principal rationale for affording certain public servants immunity from suits for money damages arising out of their official acts is inapplicable to unofficial conduct. In cases involving prosecutors, legislators, and judges we have repeatedly explained that the immunity serves the public interest in enabling such officials to perform their designated functions effectively without fear that a particular decision may give rise to personal liability. *** That rationale provided the principal basis for our holding that a former President of the United States was "entitled to absolute immunity from damages liability predicated on his official acts," *Fitzgerald,* 457 U.S. at 749. Our central concern was to avoid rendering the President "unduly cautious in the discharge of his official duties." 457 U.S., at 752, n. 32.

This reasoning provides no support for an immunity for *unofficial* conduct. As we explained in *Fitzgerald,* "the sphere of protected action must be related closely to the immunity's justifying purposes." *Id.,* at 755. Because of the President's broad responsibilities, we recognized in that case an immunity from damages claims arising out of official acts extending to the "outer perimeter of his authority." *Id.,* at 757. But we have never suggested that the President, or any other official, has an immunity that extends beyond the scope of any action taken in an official capacity.

Moreover, when defining the scope of an immunity for acts clearly taken *within* an official capacity, we have applied a functional approach. "Frequently our decisions have held that an official's absolute immunity should extend only to acts in performance of particular functions of his office." *Id.,* at 755. Hence, for example, a judge's absolute immunity does not extend to actions performed in a purely administrative capacity. See *Forrester v. White,* 484 U.S. 219, 229-230 (1988). As our opinions have made clear, immunities are grounded in "the nature of the function performed, not the identity of the actor who performed it." *Id.,* at 229. Petitioner's effort to construct an immunity from suit for unofficial acts grounded purely in the identity of his office is unsupported by precedent.

We are also unpersuaded by the evidence from the historical record to which petitioner has called our attention. He points to a comment by Thomas Jefferson protesting the subpoena *duces tecum* Chief Justice Marshall directed to him in the Burr trial, a statement in the diaries kept by Senator William Maclay of the first Senate debates, in which then-Vice President John Adams and Senator Oliver Ellsworth are recorded as having said that "the President personally [is] not . . . subject to any process whatever," lest it be "put . . . in the power of a common Justice to exercise any Authority over him and Stop the Whole Machine of Government," and to a quotation from Justice Story's Commentaries on the Constitution. None of these sources sheds much light on the question at hand.

Respondent, in turn, has called our attention to conflicting historical evidence. Speaking in favor of the Constitution's adoption at the Pennsylvania Convention, James Wilson—who had participated in the Philadelphia Convention at which the document was drafted—explained that, although the President "is placed [on] high," "not a single privilege is annexed to his character; far from being above the laws, he is amenable to them in his private character as a citizen, and in his public character by impeachment." 2 J. Elliot, Debates on the Federal Constitution 480 (2d ed. 1863). This description is consistent with both the doctrine of Presidential immunity as set forth in *Fitzgerald* and rejection of the immunity claim in this case. With respect to acts taken in his "public character"—that is, official acts—the President may be disciplined principally by impeachment, not by private lawsuits for damages. But he is otherwise subject to the laws for his purely private acts.

Petitioner's strongest argument supporting his immunity claim is based on the text and structure of the Constitution. He does not contend that the occupant of the Office of the President is "above the law," in the sense that his conduct is entirely immune from judicial scrutiny. The President argues merely for a postponement of the judicial proceedings that

> **Take Note**
>
> Was the President seeking absolute immunity from suit? Or simply immunity while in office? If the latter, wasn't the President's claim substantially less sweeping than the claim upheld in *Fitzgerald*?

will determine whether he violated any law. His argument is grounded in the character of the office that was created by Article II of the Constitution, and relies on separation-of-powers principles that have structured our constitutional arrangement since the founding.

As a starting premise, petitioner contends that he occupies a unique office with powers and responsibilities so vast and important that the public interest demands that he devote his undivided time and attention to his public duties. He submits that—given the nature of the office—the doctrine of separation of powers places limits on the authority of the Federal Judiciary to interfere with the Executive Branch that would be transgressed by allowing this action to proceed.

We have no dispute with the initial premise of the argument. *** It does not follow, however, that separation-of-powers principles would be violated by allowing this action to proceed. The doctrine of separation of powers is concerned with the allocation of official power among the three coequal branches of our Government. ***

Of course the lines between the powers of the three branches are not always neatly defined. But in this case there is no suggestion that the Federal Judiciary is being asked to perform any function that might in some way be described as "executive." Respondent is merely asking the courts to exercise their core Article III jurisdiction to decide cases and controversies. Whatever the outcome of this case, there is no possibility that the decision will curtail the scope of the official powers of the Executive Branch. The litigation of questions that relate entirely to the unofficial conduct of the individual who happens to be the President poses no perceptible risk of misallocation of either judicial power or executive power.

Rather than arguing that the decision of the case will produce either an aggrandizement of judicial power or a narrowing of executive power, petitioner contends that—as a byproduct of an otherwise traditional exercise of judicial power—burdens will be placed on the President that will hamper the performance of his official duties. We have recognized that "[e]ven when a branch does not arrogate power to itself ... the separation-of-powers doctrine requires that a branch not impair another in the performance of its constitutional duties." *Loving v. United States,* 517 U.S. 748, 757 (1996). As a factual matter, petitioner contends that this particular case—as well as the potential additional litigation that an affirmance of the Court of Appeals' judgment might spawn—may impose an unacceptable burden on the President's time and energy, and thereby impair the effective performance of his office.

> **Food for Thought**
>
> Are courts well suited to making predictions of this sort? Was the Court's prediction here a good one?

Petitioner's predictive judgment finds little support in either history or the relatively narrow compass of the issues raised in this particular case. As we have already noted, in the more than 200-year history of the Republic, only three sitting Presidents have been subjected to suits for their private actions. If the past is any indicator, it seems unlikely that a deluge of such litigation will ever engulf the Presidency. As for the case at hand, if properly managed by the District Court, it appears to us highly unlikely to occupy any substantial amount of petitioner's time.

The District Court has broad discretion to stay proceedings as an incident to its power to control its own docket. See, *e.g., Landis v. North American Co.,* 299 U.S. 248, 254 (1936). As we have explained, "[e]specially in cases of extraordinary public moment, [a plaintiff] may be required to submit to delay not immoderate in extent and not oppressive in its consequences if the public welfare or convenience will thereby be promoted." *Id.,* at 256. Although we have rejected the argument that the potential burdens on the President violate separation-of-powers principles, those burdens are appropriate matters for the District Court to evaluate in its management of the case. The high respect that is owed to the office of the Chief Executive, though not justifying a rule of categorical immunity, is a matter that should inform the conduct of the entire proceeding, including the timing and scope of discovery.

Nevertheless, we are persuaded that it was an abuse of discretion for the District Court to defer the trial until after the President leaves office. Such a lengthy and categorical stay takes no account whatever of the respondent's interest in bringing the case to trial. The complaint was filed within the statutory limitations period—albeit near the end of that period—and delaying trial would increase the danger of prejudice resulting from the loss of evidence, including the inability of witnesses to recall specific facts, or the possible death of a party.

The decision to postpone the trial was, furthermore, premature. The proponent of a stay bears the burden of establishing its need. In this case, at the stage at which the District Court made its ruling, there was no way to assess whether a stay of trial after the completion of discovery would be warranted. Other than the fact that a trial may consume some of the President's time and attention, there is nothing in the record to enable a judge to assess the potential harm that may ensue from scheduling the trial promptly after discovery is concluded. We think the District Court may have given undue weight to the concern that a trial might generate unrelated civil actions that could conceivably hamper the President in conducting the duties of his office. If and when that should occur, the court's discretion would permit it to manage those actions in such fashion (including deferral of trial) that interference with the President's duties would not occur. But no such impingement upon the President's conduct of his office was shown here.

If Congress deems it appropriate to afford the President stronger protection, it may respond with appropriate legislation. As petitioner notes in his brief, Congress has enacted more than one statute providing for the deferral of civil litigation to accommodate important public interests. See, *e.g.,* 11 U.S.C. § 362 (litigation against debtor stayed upon filing of bankruptcy petition); Soldiers' and Sailors' Civil Relief Act of 1940, 50 U.S.C. App. §§ 501-525 (provisions

Food for Thought

In 1997, both Houses of Congress were controlled by the Republican party. President Clinton was a Democrat. Is the possibility of legislation conferring immunity, in such circumstances or more generally, a realistic form of protection for the President?

governing, *inter alia,* tolling or stay of civil claims by or against military personnel during course of active duty). ***

Justice BREYER, concurring in the judgment.

I agree with the majority that the Constitution does not automatically grant the President an immunity from civil lawsuits based upon his private conduct. Nor does the "doctrine of separation of powers require federal courts to stay" virtually "all private actions against the President until he leaves office." *** To obtain a postponement the President must "bear the burden of establishing its need."

In my view, however, once the President sets forth and explains a conflict between judicial proceeding and public duties, the matter changes. At that point, the Constitution permits a judge to schedule a trial in an ordinary civil damages action (where postponement normally is possible without overwhelming damage to a plaintiff) only within the constraints of a constitutional principle—a principle that forbids a federal judge in such a case to interfere with the President's discharge of his public duties. I have no doubt that the Constitution contains such a principle applicable to civil suits, based upon Article II's vesting of the entire "executive Power" in a single individual, implemented through the Constitution's structural separation of powers, and revealed both by history and case precedent. I recognize that this case does not require us now to apply the principle specifically, thereby delineating its contours; nor need we now decide whether lower courts are to apply it directly or categorically through the use of presumptions or rules of administration. Yet I fear that to disregard it now may appear to deny it.

The Constitution states that the "executive Power shall be vested in a President." Art. II, § 1. This constitutional delegation means that a sitting President is unusually busy, that his activities have an unusually important impact upon the lives of others, and that his conduct embodies an authority bestowed by the entire American electorate. He (along with his constitutionally subordinate Vice President) is the only official for whom the entire Nation votes, and is the only elected officer to represent the entire Nation both domestically and abroad. *** [T]his constitutional structure means that the President is not like Congress, for Congress can function as if it were whole, even when up to half of its members are absent, *see* U.S. Const., Art. I, § 5, cl. 1. It means that the President is not like the Judiciary, for judges often can designate other judges, e.g., from other judicial circuits, to sit even should an entire court be detained by personal litigation. It means that, unlike Congress, which is regularly out of session, U.S. Const., Art. I, §§ 4, 5, 7, the President never adjourns.

Nixon v. Fitzgerald strongly supports the principle that judges hearing a private civil damages action against a sitting President may not issue orders that could significantly distract a President from his official duties. *** The majority [overlooks] the fact that *Fitzgerald* set forth a single immunity (an absolute immunity) applicable both to sitting and former Presidents. Its reasoning focused upon both. Its key paragraph, explaining why the President enjoys an absolute immunity rather than a qualified immunity, contains seven sentences, four of which focus primarily upon time and energy *distraction* and three of which focus primarily upon official decision *distortion.*

This case is a private action for civil damages in which, as the District Court here found, it is possible to preserve evidence and in which later payment of interest can compensate for delay. The District Court in this case determined that the Constitution required the postponement of trial during the sitting President's term. It may well be that the trial of this case cannot take place without significantly interfering with the President's ability to carry out his official duties. Yet, I agree with the majority that there is no automatic temporary immunity and that the President should have to provide the District Court with a reasoned explanation of why the immunity is needed; and I also agree that, in the absence of that explanation, the court's postponement of the trial date was premature. For those reasons, I concur in the result.

Points for Discussion

a. Subsequent History

When Paula Jones's sexual harassment lawsuit went forward, Jones's attorneys deposed President Clinton. During the deposition, President Clinton misleadingly answered questions about his sexual activities with another subordinate, Monica Lewinsky, an intern at the White House. This testimony led President Clinton to be suspended from the bar, fined by the district court, and impeached by the House of Representatives (although not convicted of an offense by the Senate). Needless to say, the entire event caused a major disruption in the work of the President. Should the Court have anticipated this possible consequence of allowing a civil lawsuit to proceed? Judge Richard Posner has written: "In retrospect *** allowing Paula Jones's suit against the President to go forward before he left office [appears to be one of the Supreme Court's] naive, unintended, unpragmatic, and gratuitous body blows to the Presidency." Richard A. Posner, An Affair of State: The Investigation, Impeachment, and Trial of President Clinton 13 (1999).

b. Congressional Action

Could Congress grant the President protection from lawsuits while he is in office? If so, how would you draft a statute for this purpose? Would protection from all civil lawsuits while in office be a good idea?

Executive Summary of this Chapter

The Constitution establishes the **separation of powers** in the first sections of Articles I, II, and III by assigning legislative authority to Congress, executive authority to the President, and judicial authority to the Supreme Court (and inferior federal courts). Violations of the separation of powers may occur when one branch of government tries to exercise power that belongs to another branch, or when one branch tries to surrender its power to other branches.

With respect to **domestic affairs**, the Supreme Court has held that the President may exercise only those powers granted expressly or implicitly by a statute or by the Constitution. *Youngstown Sheet & Tube v. Sawyer* (1952). Accordingly, the President did not have the power to seize private property outside the theater of war except pursuant to a statute.

The President may enter into **international agreements** settling claims by United States citizens against a foreign government even in the absence of express statutory or constitutional authority and even if the agreements abrogate state-law rights. *Dames & Moore v. Regan* (1981).

With respect to **international affairs**, the theory of the "**extra-constitutional origin of the foreign affairs power**" says that the United States may exercise not only the powers that the Constitution expressly grants, but also other foreign affairs powers enjoyed by all sovereigns. *United States v. Curtiss-Wright Export* (1936).

As a practical matter, the President can exercise some foreign affairs powers not expressly granted in the Constitution, because the federal courts will decline to review the President's actions under the political question doctrine or other doctrines. For example, the Supreme Court declined in *Goldwater v. Carter* (1979) to decide whether the President had **the power to rescind treaty obligations**, effectively allowing the President to rescind the treaty.

If federal legislation grants the President **authority to use military force**, but does not specify the details, the President has only the powers granted by the Constitution, by other statutes, and by the laws of war. Exercising these powers, the President may detain enemy combatants, if they are accorded certain requirements imposed by the Due Process Clause. *Hamdi v. United States* (2004). But the President may not try them by military commissions if the procedures of those military commissions would violate other federal statutes or the laws of war. *Hamdan v. Rumsfeld* (2006).

The **Executive Privilege** doctrine, which is constitutionally implied by the need for the effective discharge of executive power, says that the President has a qualified privilege to keep confidential any communications with executive advisors. Although the privilege is not absolute, it generally will protect any communications with executive advisors regarding "military, diplomatic, or sensitive national security secrets." Conversely, "the demonstrated, specific need for evidence in a pending criminal trial" can overcome the assertion of executive privilege. *United States v. Nixon* (1974).

The President has **absolute immunity from civil liability** for official acts taken while President. *Nixon v. Fitzgerald* (1982). But the President does not have immunity from, and does not have a right to delay lawsuits for, **private acts**, even while still serving as President. *Clinton v. Jones* (1997).

Point-Counterpoint

Has the Court struck the right balance between the President's power and Congress's power in the "war on terror"?

POINT: PETER J. SMITH

In *Hamdi v. Rumsfeld*, 542 U.S. 507 (2004), and the other recent cases on the President's power in the "war on terror," the Court properly imposed limits on the President's authority to act in the face of congressional prohibition. The power that the President asserted in those cases was truly breathtaking, and fundamentally inconsistent with our constitutional design.

In our constitutional scheme, the President, like any other person, is subject to the rule of law. And generally speaking, it is Congress that creates the law, not the President. To be sure, it oversimplifies matters to suggest, as did Justice Black in *Youngstown Sheet & Tube Co. v. Sawyer*, 343 U.S. 579 (1952), that one can answer the question of the scope of the President's power by noting that the President is not a "lawmaker." After all, the Court has long recognized that Congress may delegate broad policy-making authority to the President. But when Congress affirmatively prohibits the President from acting, or when the President seeks without congressional authorization to take actions that touch on individual rights in matters that the Constitution commits in large part to congressional control, claims of presidential authority must be viewed with a skeptical eye.

The cases arising from the war on terror involved assertions of presidential power in just such circumstances. Article I specifically empowers Congress, and not the President, to "declare War," to "make Rules for *** the Regulation of the land and naval Forces," and to "make Rules concerning Captures on Land and Water," powers that, together, appear to embrace rules about how to detain and interrogate persons accused of taking up arms against the United States. And Congress has exercised those powers to impose limits on the detention, treatment, and trial of such persons. To be sure, the Constitution also makes the President the Commander in Chief of the armed forces. But that clause was designed largely to make clear that the military would be subject to civilian control—and thus to the rule of law. See The Federalist No. 69.

It is in light of this background that one must evaluate the President's claims of authority in the war on terror. Of course, the Constitution should not be read so inflexibly as to prevent the President from acting in an emergency, without congressional authorization, to protect the nation. For example, few doubt that the President would have authority, even before Congress has had the opportunity to act, to repel an imminent invasion. But the authority that the President claimed in the recent war on terror cases went far beyond this modest and unobjectionable power.

In *Hamdi*, the President essentially asserted the power to round up American citizens, declare them enemies of the state, and then, on the basis of nothing more than his personal, unsubstantiated declaration, detain them indefinitely—with no right to a lawyer or a hearing, and no opportunity for the courts or the Congress ever to intervene. The Court properly declined to find such a power in the broadly worded Authorization to Use Military Force. Indeed, such a power—even if exercised in good faith and with the best intentions—is fundamentally inconsistent with the rule of law and long-held constitutional values.

Resolving the proper relationship between Congress and the President is, of course, only one part of the task that confronts the courts in cases arising from the war on terror. Wholly aside from separation-of-powers concerns, constitutional protections for individual rights might preclude the President from taking these actions even *with* express congressional authorization, and *Hamdi* may well be vulnerable to criticism for failing fully to recognize those protections. But if nothing else, the Court has made clear in its recent cases that the President is subject to the rule of law. This is an essential step in the process of determining the proper balance of power between the President and Congress, even in matters of war and national security.

COUNTERPOINT: GREGORY E. MAGGS

The Supreme Court's first four war on terror cases together raise a serious separation of powers problem, but the problem does not concern the separation between the President and Congress. In each case, the President in fact acted with statutory authority from Congress. Instead, the problem concerns the actions of the Supreme Court. Although the Court began with restraint, it increasingly usurped the role of the political branches.

In *Hamdi v. Rumsfeld*, 542 U.S. 507 (2004), the President claimed that Congress by legislation had authorized him to use military force and that under this authority he could detain enemy combatants, including U.S. citizens. Five members of the Court correctly agreed, provided that the President properly determined that the persons detained actually were enemy combatants. This case is largely unremarkable from a separation of powers point of view.

In *Rasul v. Bush*, 542 U.S. 466 (2004), the President claimed that the habeas corpus statute enacted by Congress did not give the Court jurisdiction over a detainee held at Guantanamo Bay, Cuba. A majority of the Court, however, overruled prior precedent and misread the habeas corpus statute so that the Court could assert jurisdiction. The Court thus insinuated itself into policy matters that belonged to Congress and the President. In a bipartisan move, Congress promptly rebuked the Court for this usurpation by enacting the Detainee Treatment Act of 2005, which re-stripped the Court of habeas corpus jurisdiction.

In *Hamdan v. Rumsfeld*, 548 U.S. 557 (2006), the Supreme Court also abused its power by again misinterpreting congressional legislation. The Court wrongly held that the Detainee Treatment Act of 2005 did not apply to pending cases, contrary to its usual construction of jurisdictional statutes. It also incorrectly held that the Uniform Code of

Military Justice (UCMJ) prohibited the President from trying war criminals by military commission when the military commission procedures differed from those used by courts-martial. This decision was wrong because, although UCMJ imposed a uniformity requirement, the requirement meant only that Army military commissions had to be the same as Navy and Air Force military commissions. It did not mean that military commissions had to be uniform with courts-martial. In the Military Commissions Act of 2006, a bipartisan Congress again rebuked the Court by overruling both statutory interpretations in <u>*Hamdan*</u> and again granting authority to the President.

Finally, in *Boumediene v. Bush,* 553 U.S. 723 (2008), the Court apparently realized that it could no longer play games with the President and Congress by misconstruing legislation. Instead, it held that the Military Commissions Act of 2006 was unconstitutional. Again disregarding precedent, the Court ruled that enemy combatants detained outside the United States may have a constitutional right to habeas corpus. This incorrect decision represents the most serious separation of powers problem to date. Because the Court couched its usurpation in constitutional terms, Congress and the President have no means to respond. As a result, the Supreme Court is now in charge of an important part of military policy.

CHAPTER 6

The Separation of Powers: The Legislative Process

Introduction

In Chapter 5, we considered the Federal Executive Power. The discussion necessarily touched not only on the President's constitutional powers, but also the powers of Congress; after all, challenges to the President's assertion of power often are based on an assertion that the President has encroached on the powers of Congress, or at least acted in conflict with Congress's assertion of its own powers.

In this Chapter, we consider the federal legislative power more directly. But in so doing, we of course cannot treat Congress's power in isolation. Indeed, most of the cases that we consider in this Chapter involve either a conflict between Congress's power and the President's power or a claim that Congress has impermissibly given away its power to another branch. The issues that we raised in Chapter 5, therefore, remain highly relevant here. In the sections that follow, we consider Congress's authority to delegate power to other governmental actors, including the President and officials at administrative agencies; congressional attempts to exclude the President from the legislative process; the implications of the requirements of "bicameralism and presentment"; Congress's power to control Executive officials; and the limits imposed on Congress's power by the constitutional prohibition on Bills of Attainder.

A. Delegation of Legislative Power

In the traditional account of the law-making process, Congress passes specific laws, which the executive branch then carries out or enforces. The federal criminal law is the classic example of this process. Congress has passed statutes making it a criminal offense to rob a federally insured bank, to counterfeit money, to launder money, or to assassinate government officials. These statutes specify all of the elements of these offenses because Congress has made all of the legislative choices about what they should be. The role of the executive branch is simply to enforce them by obtaining indictments against suspected offenders and then prosecuting them.

On this account, Congress makes the important policy decisions in enacting the law— to take one of the examples above, Congress has decided that robbing a federally insured bank is an offense worthy of punishment, and has identified the specific elements of the offense, see 18 U.S.C. § 2113—and prosecutors in the executive branch merely enforce those decisions, by seeking indictments and prosecuting persons accused of violating the law.

Not every federal statute, however, contemplates this allocation of authority between Congress and the executive branch. Particularly since the emergence of the modern administrative state, Congress has passed general laws that give administrative agencies or other executive officers discretion to make and then enforce rules, regulations, and decisions for achieving the goals and objectives of the general laws. Indeed, this approach to law making is perhaps now more common. As the federal government has become enormous, the kinds of problems that it seeks to solve have become more complex. Congress, for example, wants to regulate the environment, the energy industry, the manufacture of food and drugs, and so forth. But Congress recognizes that its members do not have the knowledge or the time to figure out all of the details, or to respond to rapidly changing facts on the ground. As a result, Congress does not try to specify all of the regulatory details in the statutes that it passes. Instead, Congress passes laws that give administrative agencies discretion to formulate the necessary regulations for achieving various goals.

For example, Congress might pass statutes giving the Environmental Protection Agency (EPA) discretion to issue regulations to protect the air or water. Or Congress might pass laws giving the Food and Drug Administration (FDA) discretion to regulate drug safety. Any regulations promulgated by the EPA or FDA under these statutes have the force of law, and the executive branch will enforce them.

Perspective and Analysis

Consider the following account of how Congress relies on administrative agencies:

> Congress typically assigns to an agency responsibility for constructing a regulatory or benefit program that is consistent with a long, complicated statute. When that statute emerges from the sausage factory that is the legislative process, it invariably includes scores of gaps, ambiguities, and internally inconsistent provisions. *** An agency's task in this typical situation is to construct a coherent regulatory program within the boundaries created by the statutes that limit the agency's discretion.

Richard Pierce, *Reconciling Chevron and Stare Decisis*, 85 Geo. L.J. 2225, 2235 (1997). The course in Administrative Law considers this process—and the constitutional questions that it raises—in detail.

Such statutes, which delegate a substantial amount of policy-making authority to actors outside Congress, raise some constitutional questions. After all, Article I, § 1 gives the "legislative power" of the federal government to Congress; if only Congress is permitted to exercise that authority, then at some point a delegation of policy-making authority will be tantamount to a delegation of the legislative power itself. But the issue is substantially more complicated than it might seem at first blush.

First, the constitutional text does not expressly forbid Congress from delegating the legislative power to other government actors. Indeed, the comparable language in Article II—which vests the "executive Power" in the President—has never been thought to prevent the President from delegating to other officers the authority to enforce federal law. (As a result, the President may permit, for example, the Attorney General to make decisions about whom to indict, even though such a decision is a quintessentially executive function.) Some scholars have argued that the grant of the legislative power in Article I should be read the same way, to permit Congress to delegate its authority to other government actors. See Thomas W. Merrill, *Rethinking Article I, Section 1: From Nondelegation to Exclusive Delegation*, 104 Colum. L. Rev. 2097 (2004).

The Court, however, has always treated the grant of legislative power in Article I differently, concluding that Congress may not delegate its legislative power. The Court has ruled that "Congress may not delegate the power to make laws and so may delegate no more than the authority to make policies and rules that implement its statutes." *Loving v. United States*, 517 U.S. 748, 771 (1996). The Court has sometimes noted that this view derives from the writings of John Locke, a British political philosopher whose work was highly influential with the Framers. See, *e.g.*, *Industrial Union Dept., AFL-CIO v. American Petroleum Inst.*, 448 U.S. 607, 672-73 (1980) (Rehnquist, J., concurring in the judgment) ("Locke wrote that '[t]he power of the legislative [branch], being derived from the people by a positive voluntary grant and institution, can be no other than what that positive grant conveyed, which being only to make laws, and not to make legislators, the legislative [branch] can have no power to transfer their authority of making laws and place it in other hands.'" (quoting J. Locke, Second Treatise of Civil Government, in the Tradition of Freedom,¶ 141, p. 244 (M. Mayer ed. 1957)).

Second, even once one concludes that the Constitution prohibits delegation of the legislative power, difficult questions of definition arise. Article I, after all, does not define the term "legislative power." Must Congress make every policy choice, leaving to the executive branch only the ministerial task of enforcement? This, as it turns out, would be virtually impossible. Even specific statutes, such as the criminal laws mentioned above, inevitably delegate some policy-making authority to the individuals who will enforce them. To take just one example, should the money-laundering statute be applied to a person who conceals money under the floorboards of his car as a way of obscuring its illegal origins? See *United States v. Cuellar*, 478 F.3d 282 (5th Cir. 2007). As Justice Scalia has explained, "Once it is conceded, as it must be, that no statute can be entirely precise, and that some judgments, even some judgments involving policy considerations, must be left to the officers executing the law and to the judges applying it, the debate over unconstitutional delegation becomes a debate not over a point of principle but over a question of degree." *Mistretta v. United States*, 488 U.S. 361, 415 (1989) (Scalia, J., dissenting).

The Supreme Court has addressed this issue in numerous cases. The Court has concluded that Congress impermissibly delegates legislative power only when it fails to provide an "intelligible principle" to guide the agency's or the executive official's exercise of discretion. *Id.* This is known as the "**non-delegation doctrine**."

In actual practice, the Supreme Court has rejected almost all challenges claiming that federal legislation impermissibly delegates legislative authority. For example, in *National Broadcasting Co. v. United States*, 319 U.S. 190, 216-217 (1943), the Supreme Court upheld a statute so broad that it granted the Federal Communications Commission authority to regulate radio broadcasting according to "public interest, convenience, or necessity." Indeed, the Supreme Court has found delegations unconstitutional in only a few cases. Most recently, in *A.L.A. Schechter Poultry Corp. v. United States*, 295 U.S. 495 (1935), and *Panama Refining Co. v. Ryan*, 293 U.S. 388 (1935), the Supreme Court held that Congress had gone too far in the National Industrial Recovery Act when it authorized the President to prescribe "codes of fair competition" in business without giving the President further guidance. The Court decided these cases at a time when it was regularly invalidating New Deal legislation as beyond Congress's power to regulate under the Commerce Clause.

> **Make the Connection**
>
> We saw a hint of these cases in Chapter 3 when we considered the Court's decision in *Carter v. Carter Coal*.

The following case involves the non-delegation doctrine. In reading the case, consider why Congress might have wanted to give broad discretion to the EPA and why the Supreme Court chose not to interfere.

———————

Whitman v. American Trucking Associations

531 U.S. 457 (2001)

Justice SCALIA delivered the opinion of the Court.

Section 109(a) of the [Clean Air Act (CAA)] requires the Administrator of the EPA to promulgate [national ambient air quality standards (NAAQS)] for each air pollutant for which "air quality criteria" have been issued under § 108. Once a NAAQS has been promulgated, the Administrator must review the standard (and the criteria on which it is based) "at five-year intervals" and make "such revisions . . . as may be appropriate." CAA § 109(d)(1). These cases arose when, on July 18, 1997, the Administrator revised the NAAQS for particulate matter and ozone. American Trucking Associations, Inc., and its co-respondents—which include, in addition to other private companies, the States of Michigan, Ohio, and West Virginia—challenged the new standards in the Court of Appeals for the District of Columbia Circuit ***.

> **Take Note**
>
> Three states challenged the regulations at issue in this case. Does the case raise a federalism issue? If not, why did these states file a challenge?

The District of Columbia Circuit accepted some of the challenges and rejected others. It agreed *** that § 109(b)(1) delegated legislative power to the Administrator in contravention of the United States Constitution, Art. I, § 1, because it found that the EPA had interpreted the statute to provide no "intelligible principle" to guide the agency's exercise of authority. ***

[S]ince the first step in assessing whether a statute delegates legislative power is to determine what authority the statute confers, we address that issue of interpretation first and reach respondents' constitutional arguments [afterward]. Section 109(b)(1) instructs the EPA to set primary ambient air quality standards "the attainment and maintenance of which . . . are requisite to protect the public health" with "an adequate margin of safety." Were it not for the hundreds of pages of briefing respondents have submitted on the issue, one would have thought it fairly clear that this text does not permit the EPA to consider costs in setting the standards. The language, as one scholar has noted, "is absolute." D. Currie, Air Pollution: Federal Law and Analysis 4-15 (1981). The EPA, "based on" the information about health effects contained in the technical "criteria" documents compiled under § 108(a)(2), is to identify the maximum airborne concentration of a pollutant that the public health can tolerate, decrease the concentration to provide an "adequate" margin of safety, and set the standard at that level. Nowhere are the costs of achieving such a standard made part of that initial calculation.

Section 109(b)(1) of the CAA instructs the EPA to set "ambient air quality standards the attainment and maintenance of which in the judgment of the Administrator, based on [the] criteria [documents of § 108] and allowing an adequate margin of safety, are requisite to protect the public health." The Court of Appeals held that this section as interpreted by the Administrator did not provide an "intelligible principle" to guide the EPA's exercise of authority in setting NAAQS. "[The] EPA," it said, "lack[ed] any determinate criteria for drawing lines. It has failed to state intelligibly how much is too much." The court hence found that the EPA's interpretation (but not the statute itself) violated the nondelegation doctrine. We disagree.

In a delegation challenge, the constitutional question is whether the statute has delegated legislative power to the agency. Article I, § 1, of the Constitution vests "[a]ll legislative Powers herein granted . . . in a Congress of the United States." This text permits no delegation of those powers, *Loving v. United States,* 517 U.S. 748, 771 (1996), and so we repeatedly have said that when Congress confers decisionmaking authority upon agencies *Congress* must "lay down by legislative act an intelligible principle to which the person or body authorized to [act] is directed to conform." *J.W. Hampton, Jr., & Co. v. United States,* 276 U.S. 394, 409 (1928).

We agree with the Solicitor General that the text of § 109(b)(1) of the CAA at a minimum requires that "[f]or a discrete set of pollutants and based on published air quality criteria that reflect the latest scientific knowledge, [the] EPA must establish uniform national standards at a level that is requisite to protect public health from the adverse effects of the pollutant in the ambient air." Tr. of Oral Arg., p. 5. Requisite, in turn, "mean[s] sufficient, but not more than necessary." *Id.,* at 7. These limits on the EPA's discretion are strikingly similar to the ones we approved in *Touby v. United States,* 500 U.S. 160 (1991), which permitted the Attorney General to designate a drug as a controlled substance for purposes of criminal drug enforcement if doing so was "necessary to avoid an imminent hazard to the public safety." They also resemble the Occupational Safety and Health Act of 1970 provision requiring the agency to "set the standard which most adequately assures, to the extent feasible, on the basis of the best available evidence, that no employee will suffer any impairment of health"—which the Court upheld in *Industrial Union Dept., AFL-CIO v. American Petroleum Institute,* 448 U.S. 607, 646 (1980), and which even then-Justice REHNQUIST, who alone in that case thought the statute violated the nondelegation doctrine, see *id.* (opinion concurring in judgment), would have upheld if, like the statute here, it did not permit economic costs to be considered. See *American Textile Mfrs. Institute, Inc. v. Donovan,* 452 U.S. 490, 545 (1981) (REHNQUIST, J., dissenting).

> **Take Note**
>
> In this paragraph, the Court describes an "identifiable principle" that serves to channel the EPA's discretion. What is the principle? Can you think of regulations that might violate this principle?

The scope of discretion § 109(b)(1) allows is in fact well within the outer limits of our nondelegation precedents. In the history of the Court we have found the requisite "intelligible principle" lacking in only two statutes, one of which provided literally no guidance for the exercise of discretion, and the other of which conferred authority to regulate the entire economy on the basis of no more precise a standard than stimulating the economy by assuring "fair competition." See *Panama Refining Co. v. Ryan,* 293 U.S. 388 (1935); *A.L.A. Schechter Poultry Corp. v. United States,* 295 U.S. 495 (1935). We have, on the other hand, upheld the validity of § 11(b)(2) of the Public Utility Holding Company Act of 1935, 49 Stat. 821, which gave the Securities and Exchange Commission authority to modify the structure of holding company systems so as to ensure that they are not "unduly or unnecessarily complicate[d]" and do not "unfairly or inequitably distribute voting power among security holders." *American Power & Light Co. v. SEC,* 329 U.S. 90, 104 (1946). We have approved the wartime conferral of agency power to fix the prices of commodities at a level that "will be generally fair and equitable and will effectuate the [in some respects conflicting] purposes of th[e] Act." *Yakus v. United States,* 321 U.S. 414, 420 (1944). And we have found an "intelligible principle" in various statutes authorizing regulation in the "public interest." See, *e.g., National Broadcasting Co. v. United States,* 319 U.S. 190, 225-226 (1943) (Federal Communications Commission's power to regulate airwaves); *New York Central Securities Corp. v. United States,* 287 U.S. 12, 24-25 (1932) (Interstate Commerce Commission's power to approve railroad consolidations). In short, we have "almost never felt qualified to second-guess Congress regarding the permissible degree of policy judgment that can be left to those executing or applying the law." *Mistretta v. United States,* 488 U.S. 361, 416 (1989) (SCALIA, J., dissenting); see id., at 373 (majority opinion).

It is true enough that the degree of agency discretion that is acceptable varies according to the scope of the power congressionally conferred. While Congress need not provide any direction to the EPA regarding the manner in which it is to define "country elevators," which are to be exempt from new-stationary-source regulations governing grain elevators, it must provide substantial guidance on setting air standards that affect the entire national economy. But even in sweeping regulatory schemes we have never demanded, as the Court of Appeals did here, that statutes provide a "determinate criterion" for saying "how much [of the regulated harm] is too much." In *Touby* for example, we did not require the statute to decree how "imminent" was too imminent, or how "necessary" was necessary enough, or even—most relevant here—how "hazardous" was too hazardous. 500 U.S., at 165-167. Similarly, the statute at issue in *Lichter v. United States,* 334 U.S. 742, 783 (1948), authorized agencies to recoup "excess profits" paid under wartime Government contracts, yet we did not insist that Congress specify how much profit was too much. It is therefore not conclusive for delegation purposes that, as respondents argue, ozone and particulate matter are "nonthreshold" pollutants that inflict a continuum of adverse health effects at any airborne concentration greater than zero, and hence require the EPA to make judgments of degree. "[A] certain degree of discretion, and thus of lawmaking, inheres in most executive or judicial action." *Mistretta v. United States*, *supra*, at 417 (SCALIA, J., dissenting) (emphasis deleted). Section 109(b)(1) of the CAA, which to repeat we interpret as requiring the EPA to set air quality standards at the level that is "requisite"—that is, not lower or higher than is necessary—to protect the public health with an adequate margin of safety, fits comfortably within the scope of discretion permitted by our precedent.

> **Food for Thought**
>
> Is it possible to imagine a statute that leaves no discretion at all for the actor administering the statute? Suppose that the statute required the EPA to set a standard for particulate matter at the level that, "regardless of cost, ensured that no person would suffer any material health impairment." Would that statute leave policy-making discretion to the person administering it?

Justice THOMAS, concurring.

The parties to these cases who briefed the constitutional issue wrangled over constitutional doctrine with barely a nod to the text of the Constitution. Although this Court since 1928 has treated the "intelligible principle" requirement as the only constitutional limit on congressional grants of power to administrative agencies, see *J.W. Hampton, Jr., & Co. v. United States,* 276 U.S. 394, 409 (1928), the Constitution does not speak of "intelligible principles." Rather, it speaks in much simpler terms: "*All* legislative Powers herein granted shall be vested in a Congress." U.S. Const., Art. 1, § 1 (emphasis added). I am not convinced that the intelligible principle doctrine serves to prevent all cessions of legislative power. I believe that there are cases in which the principle is intelligible and yet the significance of the delegated decision is simply too great for the decision to be called anything other than "legislative."

> **Food for Thought**
>
> Justice Thomas laments that the parties did not explain how the text of the Constitution addresses the question in this case. What, if anything, does the text of the Constitution require? Does that text answer the question in this case?

As it is, none of the parties to these cases has examined the text of the Constitution or asked us to reconsider our precedents on cessions of legislative power. On a future day, however, I would be willing to address the question whether our delegation jurisprudence has strayed too far from our Founders' understanding of separation of powers.

Justice STEVENS, with whom Justice SOUTER joins, concurring in part and concurring in the judgment.

The Court has two choices. We could choose to articulate our ultimate disposition of this issue by frankly acknowledging that the power delegated to the EPA is "legislative" but nevertheless conclude that the delegation is constitutional because adequately limited by the terms of the authorizing statute. Alternatively, we could pretend, as the Court does, that the authority delegated to the EPA is somehow not "legislative power." *** I am persuaded that it would be both wiser and more faithful to what we have actually done in delegation cases to admit that agency rulemaking authority is "legislative power."

The proper characterization of governmental power should generally depend on the nature of the power, not on the identity of the person exercising it. If the NAAQS that the EPA promulgated had been prescribed by Congress, everyone would agree that those rules would be the product of an exercise of "legislative power." The same characterization is appropriate when an agency exercises rulemaking authority pursuant to a permissible delegation from Congress.

My view is not only more faithful to normal English usage, but is also fully consistent with the text of the Constitution. In Article I, the Framers vested "All legislative Powers" in the Congress, Art. I, § 1, just as in Article II they vested the "executive Power" in the President, Art. II, § 1. Those provisions do not purport to limit the authority of either recipient of power to delegate authority to others. ***

It seems clear that an executive agency's exercise of rulemaking authority pursuant to a valid delegation from Congress is "legislative." As long as the delegation provides a sufficiently intelligible principle, there is nothing inherently unconstitutional about it.

[Justice BREYER's opinion concurring in part and concurring in the judgment is omitted.]

———————————

Points for Discussion

a. The Need for Broad Discretion

Why might Congress have thought that it needed to give the EPA broad discretion to set "ambient air quality standards"? Could Congress have set those standards itself?

b. Justification for the Intelligible Principle Requirement

Why must legislation that gives an administrative agency authority to pass rules and regulations contain an "intelligible principle" to guide the agency's discretion? Is the administrative agency in effect legislating if it does not act under the constraint of some intelligible principle? Is it accurate to say that the administrative agency is not legislating if Congress does give the agency an intelligible principle to follow? If so, is it still true if the "intelligible principle" is phrased in very general terms?

c. Constitutional Text

Justice Thomas urged the Court to focus more on the constitutional text, presumably Article I, § 1. Yet other constitutional provisions appear to contemplate the existence of something like an administrative state. The Necessary and Proper Clause, for example, speaks of powers vested "in the Government of the United States, or in any Department or Officer thereof," Art. I, § 8, cl. 18, even though the Constitution doesn't specifically vest power in anyone other than Congress, the President, and the federal courts. The Opinion Clause, Art. II, § 2, cl. 1, similarly contemplates "executive Departments" with "principal Officer[s]" who will have legal "Duties." The Appointments Clause, Art. II, § 2, cl. 2, likewise contemplates "Officers" and "Departments." Do these provisions cast any light on the permissibility of delegation of decision-making authority?

d. History

Some scholars have criticized the modern non-delegation doctrine as being inconsistent with the original understanding. See, e.g., Gary Lawson, *Delegation and Original Meaning*, 88 Va. L. Rev. 327 (2002). But others have argued that early practice—under which Congress gave administrators broad statutory authority to regulate—suggests that modern cases are perhaps much closer to the original understanding of Congress's power to delegate authority than critics have suggested. See Jerry L. Mashaw, *Recovering American Administrative Law: Federalist Foundations, 1787-1801*, 115 Yale L.J. 1256 (2006).

e. Judicial Deference

As the <u>American Trucking</u> case makes clear, the Court affords Congress a good deal of leeway in reviewing cases challenging delegations of authority. Why has the Court been so deferential? Is the Court better suited than Congress to decide which policy choices Congress alone ought to make?

B. Excluding the President from the Legislative Process

The consequence of the Court's approach to delegation is that officials in the executive branch often have considerable power to make policy decisions. As we have seen, often Congress passes general rules, and administrative agencies then fill in many of the details. Congress recognizes that it cannot possibly make all of the policies necessary for running the government. But that does not mean that Congress wants to cede total control over all important policy making. Over the past several decades, Congress has looked for ways to oversee or check some of the policy-making by administrative agencies.

Congress's most common method of oversight involves calling executive branch officials to testify before congressional committees. For example, suppose that the Food and Drug Administration (FDA) refuses to approve as safe and effective a drug that many people think deserves approval. Someone might complain to the House or Senate committee charged with oversight of the FDA. The committee then might call FDA officials to participate in a hearing on the subject on Capital Hill. The committee might ask the FDA officials about the decision. If the committee disagrees with the FDA's position, members of the committee might berate the officials publicly and ask for a change of policy. Members of Congress might even threaten the agency with the loss of funds for essential operations.

In many instances, oversight hearings persuade officials from administrative agencies to back down and change their policies. These officials may wish to appease Congress, even though the officials are part of the executive branch. They know that Congress ultimately has the power to pass legislation overruling their decisions or to retaliate against the agency by limiting its future funding.

But sometimes, fundamental policy disputes occur, and mere oversight by Congress does not suffice to cause executive branch officials to change an agency's position. Congress, in these instances, sometimes carries through with its threats to pass legislation overruling the agency. But Congress faces several practical difficulties in attempting to control administrative agencies by enacting new statutes. Passing legislation is a long and difficult process. Even if Congress successfully acts, it may not be able to undo a particular unpopular decision because of limits on Congress's power to legislate retroactively. And even if Congress can enact a bill, the President has a veto, and may use it to support the agency's position over that of Congress.

The shortcomings in these methods of exercising control over administrative agencies led Congress in the 20th century to invent a controversial alternative tactic. The invention was the inclusion of "**legislative veto**" provisions in statutes delegating authority to administrative agencies. Legislative veto provisions typically said that Congress—or the House or the Senate acting alone—could rescind certain actions taken by agencies simply by passing a resolution. Legislative veto provisions thus made agency actions conditional. The agency could act, but the action would become invalid if one or both Houses of Congress disapproved.

In the following landmark case, the Supreme Court determined that legislative veto provisions are unconstitutional. In reading the case, consider why Congress desired the legislative veto and why the Supreme Court concluded that Congress could not give itself this tool.

Immigration and Naturalization Service v. Chadha

462 U.S. 919 (1983)

Chief Justice BURGER delivered the opinion of the Court.

Chadha is an East Indian who was born in Kenya and holds a British passport. He was lawfully admitted to the United States in 1966 on a nonimmigrant student visa. His visa expired on June 30, 1972. On October 11, 1973, the District Director of the Immigration and Naturalization Service ordered Chadha to show cause why he should not be deported for having "remained in the United States for a longer time than permitted." Pursuant to § 242(b) of the Immigration and Nationality Act, a deportation hearing was held before an immigration judge on January 11, 1974. Chadha conceded that he was deportable for overstaying his visa and the hearing was adjourned to enable him to file an application for suspension of deportation under § 244(a)(1) of the Act. Section 244(a)(1) provides [for suspension of deportation for persons of "good moral character" in certain cases of "extreme hardship."]

The immigration judge found that Chadha met the requirements of § 244(a)(1): he had resided continuously in the United States for over seven years, was of good moral character, and would suffer "extreme hardship" if deported. Pursuant to § 244(c)(1) of the Act, the immigration judge suspended Chadha's deportation ***. [This suspension became the Attorney General's recommendation.] Once the Attorney General's recommendation for suspension of Chadha's deportation was conveyed to Congress, Congress had the power under § 244(c)(2) of the Act, to veto[2] the Attorney General's determination that Chadha should not be deported. Section 244(c)(2) provides:

FYI

At the time of the decision in this case, the Immigration and Naturalization Service was a component of the Department of Justice. Chadha's deportation hearing was held before an "administrative law judge," an agency official with a good deal of independence from political decision-makers. But under the statute, the Attorney General was the final decision-maker for the agency. Does this structure itself raise concerns about the separation of powers?

"(2) In the case of an alien specified in paragraph (1) of subsection (a) of this subsection—if during the session of the Congress at which a case is reported, or prior to the close of the session of the Congress next following the session at which a case is reported, either the Senate or the House of Representatives passes a resolution stating in substance that it does not favor the suspension of such deportation, the Attorney General shall thereupon deport such alien or authorize the alien's voluntary departure at his own expense under the order of deportation in the manner provided by law. If, within the time above specified, neither the Senate nor the House of Representatives shall pass such a resolution, the Attorney General shall cancel deportation proceedings."

---

[2] In constitutional terms, "veto" is used to describe the President's power under Art. I, § 7 of the Constitution. It appears, however, that Congressional devices of the type authorized by § 244(c)(2) have come to be commonly referred to as a "veto." We refer to the Congressional "resolution" authorized by § 244(c)(2) as a "one-House veto" of the Attorney General's decision to allow a particular deportable alien to remain in the United States.

On December 12, 1975, Representative Eilberg, Chairman of the Judiciary Subcommittee on Immigration, Citizenship, and International Law, introduced a resolution opposing "the granting of permanent residence in the United States to [six] aliens," including Chadha. The resolution was referred to the House Committee on the Judiciary. On December 16, 1975, the resolution was discharged from further consideration by the House Committee on the Judiciary and submitted to the House of Representatives for a vote. The resolution had not been printed and was not made available to other Members of the House prior to or at the time it was voted on. So far as the record before us shows, the House consideration of the resolution was based on Representative Eilberg's statement from the floor that

> **FYI**
>
> Before Congress enacted § 244, suspension of deportation was done by "private bills," which are bills passed by both Houses of Congress and presented to the President and that relate only to one or a small number of persons or entities. Why do you suppose Congress changed that system?

"[i]t was the feeling of the committee, after reviewing 340 cases, that the aliens contained in the resolution [Chadha and five others] did not meet these statutory requirements, particularly as it relates to hardship; and it is the opinion of the committee that their deportation should not be suspended." *Ibid.*

The resolution was passed without debate or recorded vote. Since the House action was pursuant to § 244(c)(2), the resolution was not treated as an Article I legislative act; it was not submitted to the Senate or presented to the President for his action.

After the House veto of the Attorney General's decision to allow Chadha to remain in the United States, the immigration judge reopened the deportation proceedings to implement the House order deporting Chadha. Chadha moved to terminate the proceedings on the ground that § 244(c)(2) is unconstitutional.

> **Take Note**
>
> Chadha raised his separation of powers argument as a defense to a deportation proceeding. Is the Court's role in addressing such a challenge different from the Court's role when the dispute is directly between Congress and an Executive official—or the President himself?

The Presentment Clauses

The records of the Constitutional Convention reveal that the requirement that all legislation be presented to the President before becoming law was uniformly accepted by the Framers. Presentment to the President and the Presidential veto were considered so imperative that the draftsmen took special pains to assure that these requirements could not be circumvented. During the final debate on Art. I, § 7, cl. 2, James Madison expressed concern that it might easily be evaded by the simple expedient of calling a proposed law a "resolution" or "vote" rather than a "bill." 2 M. Farrand, The Records of the Federal Convention of 1787 301-302. As a consequence, Art. I, § 7, cl. 3, was added. *Id.,* at 304-305.

The decision to provide the President with a limited and qualified power to nullify proposed legislation by veto was based on the profound conviction of the Framers that the powers conferred on Congress were the powers to be most carefully circumscribed. It is beyond doubt that lawmaking was a power to be shared by both Houses and the President. In The Federalist No. 73, Hamilton focused on the President's role in making laws:

> "If even no propensity had ever discovered itself in the legislative body to invade the rights of the Executive, the rules of just reasoning and theoretic propriety would of themselves teach us that the one ought not to be left to the mercy of the other, but ought to possess a constitutional and effectual power of self-defense."

The President's role in the lawmaking process also reflects the Framers' careful efforts to check whatever propensity a particular Congress might have to enact oppressive, improvident, or ill-considered measures. [See The Federalist No. 73.] *** The Court also has observed that the Presentment Clauses serve the important purpose of assuring that a "national" perspective is grafted on the legislative process ***. *Myers v. United States,* 272 U.S. 52, 123 (1926).

Bicameralism

The bicameral requirement of Art. I, §§ 1, 7 was of scarcely less concern to the Framers than was the Presidential veto and indeed the two concepts are interdependent. By providing that no law could take effect without the concurrence of the prescribed majority of the Members of both Houses, the Framers reemphasized their belief, already remarked upon in connection with the Presentment Clauses, that legislation should not be enacted unless it has been carefully and fully considered by the Nation's elected officials. In the Constitutional Convention debates on the need for a bicameral legislature, James Wilson, later to become a Justice of this Court, commented:

> "Despotism comes on mankind in different shapes. Sometimes in an Executive, sometimes in a military, one. Is there danger of a Legislative despotism? Theory & practice both proclaim it. If the Legislative authority be not restrained, there can be neither liberty nor stability; and it can only be restrained by dividing it within itself, into distinct and independent branches. In a single house there is no check, but the inadequate one, of the virtue & good sense of those who compose it." 1 M. Farrand, *supra,* at 254.

Hamilton argued that [were] the Nation to adopt a Constitution providing for only one legislative organ, "we shall finally accumulate, in a single body, all the most important prerogatives of sovereignty, and thus *** create in reality that very tyranny which the adversaries of the new Constitution either are, or affect to be, solicitous to avert." The Federalist No. 22, *supra,* at 135. These observations are consistent with what many of the Framers expressed, none more cogently than Hamilton in pointing up the need to divide and disperse power in order to protect liberty: "In republican government, the legislative authority necessarily predominates. The remedy for this inconveniency is to divide the legislature into different branches; and to render them, by different modes of election and different principles of action, as little connected with each other as the nature of their common functions and their common dependence on the society will admit." The Federalist No. 51, *supra,* at 324.

We see therefore that the Framers were acutely conscious that the bicameral requirement and the Presentment Clauses would serve essential constitutional functions. The President's participation in the legislative process was to protect the Executive Branch from Congress and to protect the whole people from improvident laws. The division of the Congress into two distinctive bodies assures that the legislative power would be exercised only after opportunity for full study and debate in separate settings. The President's unilateral veto power, in turn, was limited by the power of two thirds of both Houses of Congress to overrule a veto thereby precluding final arbitrary action of one person. It emerges clearly that the prescription for legislative action in Art. I, §§ 1, 7 represents the Framers' decision that the legislative power of the Federal government be exercised in accord with a single, finely wrought and exhaustively considered, procedure.

Not every action taken by either House is subject to the bicameralism and presentment requirements of Art. I. Whether actions taken by either House are, in law and fact, an exercise of legislative power depends not on their form but upon "whether they contain matter which is properly to be regarded as legislative in its character and effect." S. Rep. No. 1335, 54th Cong., 2d Sess., 8 (1897).

Examination of the action taken here by one House pursuant to § 244(c)(2) reveals that it was essentially legislative in purpose and effect. In purporting to exercise power defined in Art. I, § 8, cl. 4 to "establish an uniform Rule of Naturalization," the House took action that had the purpose and effect of altering the legal rights, duties and relations of persons, including the Attorney General, Executive Branch officials and Chadha, all outside the legislative branch. Section 244(c)(2) purports to authorize one House of Congress to require the Attorney General to deport an individual alien whose deportation otherwise would be cancelled under § 244. The one-House veto operated in this case to overrule the Attorney General and mandate Chadha's deportation; absent the House action, Chadha would remain in the United States. Congress has *acted* and its action has altered Chadha's status.

> **Take Note**
>
> The Court says that the requirements of bicameralism and presentment apply only to "legislative" action. In reading the rest of the opinion, observe how the Court decides whether what the House did here is a form of legislative action. What actions by Congress do not count as "legislative" action? What is the test for what counts?

The legislative character of the one-House veto in this case is confirmed by the character of the Congressional action it supplants. Neither the House of Representatives nor the Senate contends that, absent the veto provision in § 244(c)(2), either of them, or both of them acting together, could effectively require the Attorney General to deport an alien once the Attorney General, in the exercise of legislatively delegated authority,[16] had determined the alien should remain in the United States. Without the challenged provision in § 244(c)(2), this could have been achieved, if at all, only by legislation requiring deportation. Similarly, a veto by one House of Congress under § 244(c)(2) cannot be justified as an attempt at amending the standards set out in § 244(a)(1), or as a repeal of § 244 as applied to Chadha. Amendment and repeal of statutes, no less than enactment, must conform with Art. I.

Finally, we see that when the Framers intended to authorize either House of Congress to act alone and outside of its prescribed bicameral legislative role, they narrowly and precisely defined the procedure for such action. There are but four provisions in the Constitution, explicit and unambiguous, by which one House may act alone with the unreviewable force of law, not subject to the President's veto: (a) The House of Representatives alone was given the power to initiate impeachments. Art. I, § 2, cl. 6; (b) The Senate alone was given the power to conduct trials following impeachment on charges initiated by the House and to convict following trial. Art. I, § 3, cl. 5; (c) The Senate alone was given final unreviewable power to approve or to disapprove presidential appointments. Art. II, § 2, cl. 2; (d) The Senate alone was given unreviewable power to ratify treaties negotiated by the President. Art. II, § 2, cl. 2. *** Clearly, when the Draftsmen sought to confer special powers on one House, independent of the other House, or of the President, they did so in explicit, unambiguous terms.

Since it is clear that the action by the House under § 244(c)(2) was not within any of the express constitutional exceptions authorizing one House to act alone, and equally clear that it was an exercise of legislative power, that action was subject to the standards prescribed in Article I.

The veto authorized by § 244(c)(2) doubtless has been in many respects a convenient shortcut; the "sharing" with the Executive by Congress of its authority over aliens in this manner is, on its face, an appealing compromise. In purely practical terms, it is obviously easier for action to be taken by one House without submission to the President; but it is crystal clear from the records of the Convention, contemporaneous writings and debates, that the Framers ranked other values higher than efficiency. The records of the Convention and debates in the States preceding ratification underscore the common desire to

---

[16] Congress protests that affirming the Court of Appeals in this case will sanction "lawmaking by the Attorney General." To be sure, some administrative agency action—rule making, for example—may resemble "lawmaking." [But when] the Attorney General performs his duties pursuant to § 244, he does not exercise "legislative" power. The bicameral process is not necessary as a check on the Executive's administration of the laws because his administrative activity cannot reach beyond the limits of the statute that created it—a statute duly enacted pursuant to Art. I, §§ 1, 7. The constitutionality of the Attorney General's execution of the authority delegated to him by § 244 involves only a question of delegation doctrine. *** Executive action under legislatively delegated authority that might resemble "legislative" action in some respects is not subject to the approval of both Houses of Congress and the President for the reason that the Constitution does not so require. That kind of Executive action is always subject to check by the terms of the legislation that authorized it; and if that authority is exceeded it is open to judicial review as well as the power of Congress to modify or revoke the authority entirely. A one-House veto is clearly legislative in both character and effect and is not so checked; the need for the check provided by Art. I, §§ 1, 7 is therefore clear. Congress' authority to delegate portions of its power to administrative agencies provides no support for the argument that Congress can constitutionally control administration of the laws by way of a Congressional veto.

define and limit the exercise of the newly created federal powers affecting the states and the people. There is unmistakable expression of a determination that legislation by the national Congress be a step-by-step, deliberate and deliberative process. We hold that the Congressional veto provision in § 244(c)(2) is severable from the Act and that it is unconstitutional.

Justice POWELL, concurring in the judgment.

The Court's decision, based on the Presentment Clauses, apparently will invalidate every use of the legislative veto. *** One reasonably may disagree with Congress' assessment of the veto's utility, but the respect due its judgment as a coordinate branch of Government cautions that our holding should be no more extensive than necessary to decide this case. In my view, the case may be decided on a narrower ground. When Congress finds that a particular person does not satisfy the statutory criteria for permanent residence in this country it has assumed a judicial function in violation of the principle of separation of powers.

[The Framers were concerned] that trial by a legislature lacks the safeguards necessary to prevent the abuse of power. *** On its face, the House's action appears clearly adjudicatory. The House did not enact a general rule; rather it made its own determination that six specific persons did not comply with certain statutory criteria. It thus undertook the type of decision that traditionally has been left to other branches.

> **Make the Connection**
>
> This concern led the Framers explicitly to prohibit Congress from enacting "Bills of Attainder," legislative acts that impose punishment. We will consider that prohibition later in this Chapter.

The impropriety of the House's assumption of this function is confirmed by the fact that its action raises the very danger the Framers sought to avoid—the exercise of unchecked power. In deciding whether Chadha deserves to be deported, Congress is not subject to any internal constraints that prevent it from arbitrarily depriving him of the right to remain in this country. Unlike the judiciary or an administrative agency, Congress is not bound by established substantive rules. Nor is it subject to the procedural safeguards, such as the right to counsel and a hearing before an impartial tribunal, that are present when a court or an agency adjudicates individual rights. The only effective constraint on Congress' power is political, but Congress is most accountable politically when it prescribes rules of general applicability. When it decides rights of specific persons, those rights are subject to "the tyranny of a shifting majority."

Justice WHITE, dissenting.

Today the Court not only invalidates § 244(c)(2) of the Immigration and Nationality Act, but also sounds the death knell for nearly 200 other statutory provisions in which Congress has reserved a "legislative veto." For this reason, the Court's decision is of surpassing importance. And it is for this reason that the Court would have been well-advised to decide the case, if possible, on the narrower grounds of separation of powers, leaving for full consideration the constitutionality of other congressional review statutes operating on such varied matters as war powers and agency rulemaking, some of which concern the independent regulatory agencies.

The prominence of the legislative veto mechanism in our contemporary political system and its importance to Congress can hardly be overstated. It has become a central means by which Congress secures the accountability of executive and independent agencies. Without the legislative veto, Congress is faced with a Hobson's choice: either to refrain from delegating the necessary authority, leaving itself with a hopeless task of writing laws with the requisite specificity to cover endless special circumstances across the entire policy landscape, or in the alternative, to abdicate its law-making function to the executive branch and independent agencies. To choose the former leaves major national problems unresolved; to opt for the latter risks unaccountable policymaking by those not elected to fill that role. Accordingly, over the past five decades, the legislative veto has been placed in nearly 200 statutes. The device is known in every field of governmental concern: reorganization, budgets, foreign affairs, war powers, and regulation of trade, safety, energy, the environment and the economy.

> **Take Note**
>
> Why does Justice White think that Congress needs the legislative veto? Does he make a constitutional argument or a policy argument for upholding the legislative veto?

The history of the legislative veto also makes clear that it has not been a sword with which Congress has struck out to aggrandize itself at the expense of the other branches—the concerns of Madison and Hamilton. Rather, the veto has been a means of defense, a reservation of ultimate authority necessary if Congress is to fulfill its designated role under Article I as the nation's lawmaker. While the President has often objected to particular legislative vetoes, generally those left in the hands of congressional committees, the Executive has more often agreed to legislative review as the price for a broad delegation of authority. To be sure, the President may have preferred unrestricted power, but that could be precisely why Congress thought it essential to retain a check on the exercise of delegated authority.

If the legislative veto were as plainly unconstitutional as the Court strives to suggest, its broad ruling today would be more comprehensible. But, the constitutionality of the legislative veto is anything but clearcut. *** The reality of the situation is that the constitutional question posed today is one of immense difficulty over which the executive and legislative branches—as well as scholars and judges—have understandably disagreed. That disagreement stems from the silence of the Constitution on the precise question: The Constitution does not directly authorize or prohibit the legislative veto. Thus, our task should be to determine whether the legislative veto is consistent with the purposes of Art. I and the principles of Separation of Powers which are reflected in that Article and throughout the Constitution. We should not find the lack of a specific constitutional authorization for the legislative veto surprising, and I would not infer disapproval of the mechanism from its absence. *** [O]ur Federal Government was intentionally chartered with the flexibility to respond to contemporary needs without losing sight of fundamental democratic principles.

The power to exercise a legislative veto is not the power to write new law without bicameral approval or presidential consideration. The veto must be authorized by statute and may only negative what an Executive department or independent agency has proposed. On its face, the legislative veto no more allows one House of Congress to make law than does the presidential veto confer such power upon the President.

If Congress may delegate lawmaking power to independent and executive agencies, it is most difficult to understand Article I as forbidding Congress from also reserving a check on legislative power for itself. Absent the veto, the agencies receiving delegations of legislative or quasi-legislative power may issue regulations having the force of law without bicameral approval and without the President's signature. It is thus not apparent why the reservation of a veto over the exercise of that legislative power must be subject to a more exacting test. In both cases, it is enough that the initial statutory authorizations comply with the Article I requirements. *** Under the Court's analysis, the Executive Branch and the independent agencies may make rules with the effect of law while Congress, in whom the Framers confided the legislative power, may not exercise a veto which precludes such rules from having operative force.

The central concern of the presentation and bicameralism requirements of Article I is that when a departure from the legal status quo is undertaken, it is done with the approval of the President and both Houses of Congress—or, in the event of a presidential veto, a two-thirds majority in both Houses. This interest is fully satisfied by the operation of § 244(c)(2). The President's approval is found in the Attorney General's action in recommending to Congress that the deportation order for a given alien be suspended. The House and the Senate indicate their approval of the Executive's action by not passing a resolution of disapproval within the statutory period. Thus, a change in the legal status quo—the deportability of the alien—is consummated only with the approval of each of the three relevant actors. The disagreement of any one of the three maintains the alien's pre-existing status: the Executive may choose not to recommend suspension; the House and Senate may each veto the recommendation. The effect on the rights and obligations of the affected individuals and upon the legislative system is precisely the same as if a private bill were introduced but failed to receive the necessary approval.

[T]he history of the separation of powers doctrine is [a] history of accommodation and practicality. Apprehensions of an overly powerful branch have not led to undue prophylactic measures that handicap the effective working of the national government as a whole. The Constitution does not contemplate total separation of the three branches of Government.

The legislative veto provision does not "prevent the Executive Branch from accomplishing its constitutionally assigned functions." *** § 244 grants the executive only a qualified suspension authority and it is only that authority which the President is constitutionally authorized to execute. Moreover, the Court believes that the legislative veto we consider today is best characterized as an exercise of legislative or quasi-legislative authority. Under this characterization, the practice does not, even on the surface, constitute an infringement of executive or judicial prerogative. *** Nor does § 244 infringe on the judicial power, as Justice POWELL would hold. *** Congressional action does not substitute for judicial review of the Attorney General's decisions.

[The Court's holding] reflects a profoundly different conception of the Constitution than that held by the Courts which sanctioned the modern administrative state. Today's decision strikes down in one fell swoop provisions in more laws enacted by Congress than the Court has cumulatively invalidated in its history. *** I must dissent.

Points for Discussion

a. The Reach of *Chadha*

Justice White observes that nearly 200 federal statutes contained legislative veto provisions. In light of the Court's decision, all of these federal statutes were (at least in part) unconstitutional. For this reason, *INS v. Chadha* could be said to have invalidated more federal statutes than any other case in the history of the United States. Was the number of statutes containing legislative veto provisions a reason for pause, or was it instead a reason for the Court to act as it did?

b. Aggrandizement v. Delegation

In the first part of this Chapter, we saw that the Court is not overly concerned about the possibility that Congress might delegate some of its power to administrative agencies. But here we see the Court is concerned when Congress reserves to itself a new method to check the exercise of those delegated powers. Why might the Court have seen this reservation as a more troubling separation of powers problem than delegation?

c. Formalism vs. Functionalism

Chief Justice Burger and Justice White both were concerned about preserving the separation of powers, but they clearly viewed the substantive content of that concept—and the Court's role in enforcing it—differently. Chief Justice Burger insisted that the Constitution creates a set form for the law-making process, and that any deviation from that form must therefore be unconstitutional. He reasoned, in other words, that the contours of the separation of powers are determined by constitutional form. Justice White, in contrast, argued that the Court's task was to determine whether the legislative veto presented an actual, functional threat to the notion of the separation of powers. If the legislative veto did not substantially or meaningfully shift the balance of power to one branch, he suggested, then the Court should not intervene.

What are the virtues of these two approaches—formalism and functionalism—to separation of powers issues? As you read the rest of the cases in this Chapter, be sensitive to the types of arguments on which the Court relies, and consider whether the Court is better suited for applying one or the other approach.

C. Implications of Bicameralism and Presentment

Congress often passes bills that include thousands of pages of new tax, spending, and regulatory provisions. The President traditionally has had a binary choice in dealing with these bills: the President either can sign such bills or veto them. If the President signs a bill, the President approves the bill in total, and all of the bill's provisions become law. If the President vetoes the bill, the President disapproves it, and none of the provisions becomes law. The President does not have the option to approve some of the bill but not the rest.

In many states, the system is different; state constitutions may allow governors to sign bills but selectively disapprove of some of their provisions. This power is typically called a **"line-item veto."** The bill becomes law, except for the items in the bill that the governor has disapproved. The following case concerns the question whether Congress may give the President similar authority.

————————————

Clinton v. New York

524 U.S. 417 (1998)

Justice STEVENS delivered the opinion of the Court.

The Line Item Veto Act gives the President the power to "cancel in whole" three types of provisions that have been signed into law: "(1) any dollar amount of discretionary budget authority; (2) any item of new direct spending; or (3) any limited tax benefit." 2 U.S.C. § 691(a) [110 Stat. 1200].

The Act requires the President to adhere to precise procedures whenever he exercises his cancellation authority. In identifying items for cancellation he must consider the legislative history, the purposes, and other relevant information about the items. See § 691(b). He must determine, with respect to each cancellation, that it will "(i) reduce the Federal budget deficit; (ii) not impair any essential Government functions; and (iii) not harm the national interest." § 691(a)(3)(A). Moreover, he must transmit a special message to Congress notifying it of each cancellation within five calendar days (excluding Sundays) after the enactment of the canceled provision. See § 691(a)(3)(B).

> **Food for Thought**
>
> Putting aside the particular separation of powers issue that the Court addresses in this case, does the Act contain an intelligible principle to guide the President's exercise of authority under the Act? Do the requirements in § 691 limit the President's policy-making discretion in any meaningful way?

A cancellation takes effect upon receipt by Congress of the special message from the President. See § 691b(a). If, however, a "disapproval bill" pertaining to a special message is enacted into law, the cancellations set forth in that message become "null and void." *Ibid.* The Act sets forth a detailed expedited procedure for the consideration of a "disapproval bill," see § 691d, but no such bill was passed for either of the cancellations involved in these cases. A majority vote of both Houses is sufficient to enact a disapproval bill. The Act does not grant the President the authority to cancel a disapproval bill, see § 691(c), but he does, of course, retain his constitutional authority to veto such a bill.

[Following these procedures, the President exercised his authority to cancel one provision in the Balanced Budget Act of 1997, 111 Stat. 251, 515, and two provisions in the Taxpayer Relief Act of 1997, 111 Stat. 788, 895-896, 990-993. The cancelled provision in the Balanced Budget Act would have, in effect, increased federal subsidies for medical care in the state of New York. The cancelled provisions in the Tax Payer Relief Act would have, in effect, reduced the taxes imposed on the sale of certain food refineries to farmers' cooperatives.]

Food for Thought

Why do you suppose Congress enacted the Line Item Veto Act? If it is to prevent wasteful spending, why can't Congress simply stop including wasteful provisions in its bills?

The effect of a cancellation is plainly stated in § 691e, which defines the principal terms used in the Act. With respect to both an item of new direct spending and a limited tax benefit, the cancellation prevents the item "from having legal force or effect." §§ 691e(4)(B)-(C). Thus, under the plain text of the statute, the two actions of the President that are challenged in these cases prevented one section of the Balanced Budget Act of 1997 and one section of the Taxpayer Relief Act of 1997 "from having legal force or effect." The remaining provisions of those statutes *** continue to have the same force and effect as they had when signed into law.

In both legal and practical effect, the President has amended two Acts of Congress by repealing a portion of each. "[R]epeal of statutes, no less than enactment, must conform with Art. I." *INS v. Chadha*, 462 U.S. 919, 954 (1983). There is no provision in the Constitution that authorizes the President to enact, to amend, or to repeal statutes. Both Article I and Article II assign responsibilities to the President that directly relate to the lawmaking process, but neither addresses the issue presented by these cases. *** [A]fter a bill has passed both Houses of Congress, but "before it become[s] a Law," it must be presented to the President. If he approves it, "he shall sign it, but if not he shall return it, with his Objections to that House in which it shall have originated, who shall enter the Objections at large on their Journal, and proceed to reconsider it." Art. I, § 7, cl. 2. His "return" of a bill, which is usually described as a "veto," is subject to being overridden by a two-thirds vote in each House.

There are important differences between the President's "return" of a bill pursuant to Article I, § 7, and the exercise of the President's cancellation authority pursuant to the Line Item Veto Act. The constitutional return takes place *before* the bill becomes law; the statutory cancellation occurs *after* the bill becomes law. The constitutional return is of the entire bill; the statutory cancellation is of only a part. Although the Constitution expressly authorizes the President to play a role in the process of enacting statutes, it is silent on the subject of unilateral Presidential action that either repeals or amends parts of duly enacted statutes.

There are powerful reasons for construing constitutional silence on this profoundly important issue as equivalent to an express prohibition. The procedures governing the enactment of statutes set forth in the text of Article I were the product of the great debates and compromises that produced the Constitution itself. Familiar historical materials provide abundant support for the conclusion that the power to enact statutes may only "be exercised in accord with a single, finely wrought and exhaustively considered, procedure." *Chadha,* 462 U.S., at 951. Our first President understood the text of the Presentment Clause as requiring that he either "approve all the parts of a Bill, or reject it in toto."[30] What has emerged in these cases from the President's exercise of his statutory cancellation powers, however, are truncated versions of two bills that passed both Houses of Congress. They are not the product of the "finely wrought" procedure that the Framers designed.

> **Take Note**
>
> The Court explains here why the Constitution does not permit the President to approve or disapprove parts of bills. What kinds of reasoning does the Court use? Is it functionalist or formalist?

The Government advances two related arguments to support its position that despite the unambiguous provisions of the Act, cancellations do not amend or repeal properly enacted statutes in violation of the Presentment Clause. First, relying primarily on *Field v. Clark,* 143 U.S. 649 (1892), the Government contends that the cancellations were merely exercises of discretionary authority granted to the President by the Balanced Budget Act and the Taxpayer Relief Act read in light of the previously enacted Line Item Veto Act. Second, the Government submits that the substance of the authority to cancel tax and spending items "is, in practical effect, no more and no less than the power to 'decline to spend' specified sums of money, or to 'decline to implement' specified tax measures." Neither argument is persuasive.

In *Field v. Clark,* the Court upheld the constitutionality of the Tariff Act of 1890. Act of Oct. 1, 1890, 26 Stat. 567. That statute contained a "free list" of almost 300 specific articles that were exempted from import duties "unless otherwise specially provided for in this act." *Id.,* at 602. Section 3 was a special provision that directed the President to suspend that exemption for sugar, molasses, coffee, tea, and hides "whenever, and so often" as he should be satisfied that any country producing and exporting those products imposed duties on the agricultural products of the United States that he deemed to be "reciprocally unequal and unreasonable." *Id.,*at 612. The section then specified the duties to be imposed on those products during any such suspension. The Court provided this explanation for its conclusion that § 3 had not delegated legislative power to the President:

> "[W]hen [the President] ascertained the fact [made relevant by the statute,] it became his duty to issue a proclamation declaring the suspension, as to that country, which Congress had determined should occur. He had no discretion in the premises except in respect to the duration of

---

[30] 33 Writings of George Washington 96 (J. Fitzpatrick ed., 1940); see also W. Taft, The Presidency: Its Duties, Its Powers, Its Opportunities and Its Limitations 11 (1916) (stating that the President "has no power to veto part of a bill and let the rest become a law").

the suspension so ordered. But that related only to the enforcement of the policy established by Congress. As the suspension was absolutely required when the President ascertained the existence of a particular fact, it cannot be said that in ascertaining that fact and in issuing his proclamation, in obedience to the legislative will, he exercised the function of making laws . . . . It was a part of the law itself as it left the hands of Congress that the provisions, full and complete in themselves, permitting the free introduction of sugars, molasses, coffee, tea and hides, from particular countries, should be suspended, in a given contingency, and that in case of such suspensions certain duties should be imposed." *Id.,* at 693.

This passage identifies three critical differences between the power to suspend the exemption from import duties and the power to cancel portions of a duly enacted statute. First, the exercise of the suspension power was contingent upon a condition that did not exist when the Tariff Act was passed: the imposition of "reciprocally unequal and unreasonable" import duties by other countries. In contrast, the exercise of the cancellation power within five days after the enactment of the Balanced Budget and Tax Reform Acts necessarily was based on the same conditions that Congress evaluated when it passed those statutes. Second, under the Tariff Act, when the President determined that the contingency had arisen, he had a duty to suspend; in contrast, while it is true that the President was required by the Act to make three determinations before he canceled a provision, those determinations did not qualify his discretion to cancel or not to cancel. Finally, whenever the President suspended an exemption under the Tariff Act, he was executing the policy that Congress had embodied in the statute. In contrast, whenever the President cancels an item of new direct spending or a limited tax benefit he is rejecting the policy judgment made by Congress and relying on his own policy judgment. Thus, the conclusion in *Field v. Clark* that the suspensions mandated by the Tariff Act were not exercises of legislative power does not undermine our opinion that cancellations pursuant to the Line Item Veto Act are the functional equivalent of partial repeals of Acts of Congress that fail to satisfy Article I, § 7. *** The Line Item Veto Act authorizes the President himself to effect the repeal of laws, for his own policy reasons, without observing the procedures set out in Article I, § 7. The fact that Congress intended such a result is of no moment. Although Congress presumably anticipated that the President might cancel some of the items in the Balanced Budget Act and in the Taxpayer Relief Act, Congress cannot alter the procedures set out in Article I, § 7, without amending the Constitution.

Neither are we persuaded by the Government's contention that the President's authority to cancel new direct spending and tax benefit items is no greater than his traditional authority to decline to spend appropriated funds. The Government has reviewed in some detail the series of statutes in which Congress has given the Executive broad discretion over the expenditure of appropriated funds. For example, the First Congress appropriated "sum[s] not exceeding" specified amounts to be spent on various Government operations. See, *e.g.,* Act of Sept. 29, 1789, ch. 23, § 1, 1 Stat. 95; Act of Mar. 26, 1790, ch. 4, 1 Stat. 104; Act of Feb. 11, 1791, ch. 6, 1 Stat. 190. In those statutes, as in later years, the President was given wide discretion with respect to both the amounts to be spent and how the money would be allocated among different functions. It is argued that the Line Item Veto Act merely confers comparable discretionary authority over the expenditure of appropriated funds. The critical difference between this statute and all of its predecessors, however, is that unlike any of them, this Act gives the President the unilateral power to change the text of duly enacted statutes. None of the Act's predecessors could even arguably have been construed to authorize such a change.

Justice KENNEDY, concurring.

A Nation cannot plunder its own treasury without putting its Constitution and its survival in peril. The statute before us, then, is of first importance, for it seems undeniable the Act will tend to restrain persistent excessive spending. Nevertheless, for the reasons given by Justice STEVENS in the opinion for the Court, the statute must be found invalid. Failure of political will does not justify unconstitutional remedies.

Justice SCALIA, with whom Justice O'CONNOR joins, and with whom Justice BREYER joins as to Part III, concurring in part and dissenting in part.

[Art. I, § 7] no more categorically prohibits the Executive reduction of congressional dispositions in the course of implementing statutes that authorize such reduction, than it categorically prohibits the Executive augmentation of congressional dispositions in the course of implementing statutes that authorize such augmentation—generally known as substantive rulemaking. There are, to be sure, limits upon the former just as there are limits upon the latter ***. Those limits are established, however, not by some categorical prohibition of Art. I, § 7, [but] by what has come to be known as the doctrine of unconstitutional delegation of legislative authority: When authorized Executive reduction or augmentation is allowed to go too far, it usurps the nondelegable function of Congress and violates the separation of powers. It is this doctrine, and not the Presentment Clause, that was discussed in the *Field* opinion, and it is this doctrine, and not the Presentment Clause, that is the issue presented by the statute before us here. Insofar as the degree of political, "lawmaking" power conferred upon the Executive is concerned, there is not a dime's worth of difference between Congress's authorizing the President to cancel a spending item, and Congress's authorizing money to be spent on a particular item at the President's discretion. And the latter has been done since the founding of the Nation.

The short of the matter is this: Had the Line Item Veto Act authorized the President to "decline to spend" any item of spending contained in the Balanced Budget Act of 1997, there is not the slightest doubt that authorization would have been constitutional. What the Line Item Veto Act does instead—authorizing the President to "cancel" an item of spending—is technically different. But the technical difference does *not* relate to the technicalities of the Presentment Clause, which have been fully complied with; and the doctrine of unconstitutional delegation, which *is* at issue here, is preeminently *not* a doctrine of technicalities. The title of the Line Item Veto Act, which was perhaps designed to simplify for public comprehension, or perhaps merely to comply with the terms of a campaign pledge, has succeeded in faking out the Supreme Court. The President's action it authorizes in fact is not a line-item veto and thus does not offend Art. I, § 7; and insofar as the substance of

> **Food for Thought**
>
> Why does Justice Scalia think that this case does not involve a genuine line-item veto?

that action is concerned, it is no different from what Congress has permitted the President to do since the formation of the Union.

Justice BREYER, with whom Justice O'CONNOR and Justice SCALIA join as to Part III, dissenting.

When our Nation was founded, Congress could easily have provided the President with [the kind of power at issue here]. In that time period, our population was less than 4 million, federal employees numbered fewer than 5,000, [and] annual federal budget outlays totaled approximately $4 million. At that time, a Congress, wishing to give a President the power to select among appropriations, could simply have embodied each appropriation in a separate bill, each bill subject to a separate Presidential veto. Today, however, our population is about 250 million, the Federal Government employs more than 4 million people, the annual federal budget is $1.5 trillion, and a typical budget appropriations bill may have a dozen titles, hundreds of sections, and spread across more than 500 pages of the Statutes at Large. Congress cannot divide such a bill into thousands, or tens of thousands, of separate appropriations bills, each one of which the President would have to sign, or to veto, separately. Thus, the question is whether the Constitution permits Congress to choose a particular novel means to achieve this same, constitutionally legitimate, end.

[We should] interpret nonliteral separation-of-powers principles in light of the need for "workable government." *Youngstown Sheet & Tube Co. v. Sawyer,* 343 U.S. 579, 635 (1952), J., concurring). If we apply those principles in light of that objective, as this Court has applied them in the past, the Act is constitutional.

The Court believes that the Act violates the literal text of the Constitution. A simple syllogism captures its basic reasoning: <u>Major Premise</u>: The Constitution sets forth an exclusive method for enacting, repealing, or amending laws. <u>Minor Premise</u>: The Act authorizes the President to "repea[l] or amen[d]" laws in a different way, namely by announcing a cancellation of a portion of a previously enacted law. <u>Conclusion</u>: The Act is inconsistent with the Constitution. I find this syllogism unconvincing, however, because its Minor Premise is faulty. When the President "canceled" the two appropriation measures now before us, he did not *repeal* any law nor did he *amend* any law. He simply *followed* the law, leaving the statutes, as they are literally written, intact.

To understand why one cannot say, *literally speaking,* that the President has repealed or amended any law, imagine [that] the canceled New York health care tax provision at issue here [had instead specifically said that] *"the President may prevent the just-mentioned provision from having legal force or effect if he determines x, y, and z."* (Assume x, y and z to be the same determinations required by the Line Item Veto Act). Whatever a person might say, or think, about the constitutionality of this imaginary law, [the] English language would prevent one from saying [that] a President who [prevents the tax from having legal force or effect] has either *repealed* or *amended* this particular hypothetical statute. Rather, the President has *followed* that law to the letter. He has exercised the power it explicitly delegates to him. He has executed the law, not repealed it.

It could make no significant difference to this linguistic point were the italicized proviso to appear, not as part of what I have called Section One, but, instead, at the bottom of the statute page, say, referenced by an asterisk, with a statement that it applies to every spending provision in the Act next to which a similar asterisk appears. And that being so, it could make no difference if that proviso appeared, instead, in a different, earlier enacted law, along with legal language that makes it applicable to every future spending provision picked out according to a specified formula. *** But, of course, this last mentioned possibility is this very case.

Because I disagree with the Court's holding of literal violation, I must consider whether the Act nonetheless violates separation-of-powers principles. *** Viewed conceptually, the power the Act conveys [is] "executive." As explained above, an exercise of that power "executes" the Act. *** The fact that one could also characterize this kind of power as "legislative," say, if Congress itself (by amending the appropriations bill) prevented a provision from taking effect, is beside the point. This Court has frequently found that the exercise of a particular power [can] fall within the constitutional purview of more than one branch of Government.

[O]ne cannot say that the Act "encroaches" upon Congress' power, when Congress retained the power to insert, by simple majority, into any future appropriations bill, into any section of any such bill, or into any phrase of any section, a provision that says the Act will not apply. See 2 U.S.C. § 691f(c)(1) (1994 ed., Supp. II). Congress also retained the power to "disapprov[e]," and thereby reinstate, any of the President's cancellations. See 2 U.S.C. § 691b(a). And it is Congress that drafts and enacts the appropriations statutes that are subject to the Act in the first place—and thereby defines the outer limits of the President's cancellation authority. *** Nor can one say the Act's grant of power "aggrandizes" the Presidential office. The grant is limited [to] the power to spend, or not to spend, particular appropriated items, and the power to permit, or not to permit, specific limited exemptions from generally applicable tax law from taking effect. These powers [resemble] those the President has exercised in the past on other occasions.

The "nondelegation" doctrine [raises] a more serious constitutional obstacle here. [The standards in the Act] are broad. But this Court has upheld standards that are equally broad, or broader. [In addition, the] President, unlike most agency decisionmakers, is an elected official. He is responsible to the voters, who, in principle, will judge the manner in which he exercises his delegated authority. Whether the President's expenditure decisions, for example, are arbitrary is a matter that in the past has been left primarily to those voters to consider.

[I] recognize that the Act before us is novel. In a sense, it skirts a constitutional edge. But that edge has to do with means, not ends. The means chosen do not amount literally to the enactment, repeal, or amendment of a law. *** Those means do not violate any basic separation-of-powers principle. They do not improperly shift the constitutionally foreseen balance of power from Congress to the President. Nor, since they comply with separation-of-powers principles, do they threaten the liberties of individual citizens. They represent an experiment that may, or may not, help representative government work better.

The Constitution, in my view, authorizes Congress and the President to try novel methods in this way. Consequently, with respect, I dissent.

Points for Discussion

a. Aggrandizement?

Does this case involve an attempt by Congress to aggrandize its own powers? If not, why should the Court care whether Congress has given the President additional powers? If Congress becomes concerned about the President's abuse of authority conferred by the statute, can't Congress simply repeal the Act?

b. Political Logrolling

The term "logrolling" in politics refers to a common way of accommodating differences of opinion when passing legislation. Politicians may support opponents' proposals, to induce these opponents to support their own objectives. For example, suppose that in setting the federal budget, Republicans want to increase defense spending, while Democrats desire to raise education spending. Rather than blocking each other's proposals, the two parties might agree to pass a single spending bill that increases both defense spending and education spending. How would giving the President a line-item veto affect logrolling compromises of this kind? What benefits and drawbacks might result? *Compare* J. Gregory Sidak, *The Line-Item Veto Amendment*, 80 Cornell L. Rev. 1498, 1498 (1995) ("The absence of a presidential line-item veto may have contributed to the seemingly irreversible growth of the federal government."), *with* Adrian Vermeule, *The Constitutional Law of Congressional Procedure*, 71 U. Chi. L. Rev. 361, 413 n. 169 (2004) ("Logrolling may permit, of course, either socially beneficial trades or the infliction of socially harmful externalities ***. Much depends on the details of the situation.").

c. Constitutional Alternatives?

After the decision in *Clinton*, is it possible to craft a constitutional statute that gives the President the authority to trim wasteful spending from the budget?

D. Congressional Control over Executive Officials

As we have seen, Article II vests the executive power of the United States in the President. But of course the President cannot administer the entire federal government alone. Instead, the President must act through subordinates, like the Secretary of State, the Attorney General, the Secretary of Defense, and so forth. The Constitution specifically requires the President to "take Care that the Laws be faithfully executed," Art. II, § 3, and it provides that the President "may require the Opinion, in writing, of the principal Officer in each of the executive Departments, upon any Subject relating to the Duties of their respective

Offices," Art. II, § 2.

But a question not fully addressed by the text of the Constitution is how or to what extent the President may control the actions of subordinates. The conventional way that a President, like any other supervisor, exercises control over subordinates is through the power to hire and to fire. The Constitution's assignment of responsibility for hiring and firing, therefore, is of the utmost importance in determining the extent of the President's authority to control the actions of subordinates.

The Constitution makes clear, in the Appointments Clause, Art. II, § 2, cl. 2, that the President has authority (subject to the "the Advice and Consent of the Senate") to appoint "Officers" of the United States, and that Congress may (but need not) vest in the President the power to appoint "inferior Officers," as well.

U.S. Constitution, Article II, <u>Section 2, Cl. 2</u>

[The President] shall nominate, and by and with the Advice and Consent of the Senate, shall appoint Ambassadors, other public Ministers and Consuls, Judges of the supreme Court, and all other Officers of the United States, whose Appointments are not herein otherwise provided for, and which shall be established by Law: but the Congress may by Law vest the Appointment of such inferior Officers, as they think proper, in the President alone, in the Courts of Law, or in the Heads of Departments.

The Court has held that Congress may not assign *to itself* the power to appoint executive officers. See *Buckley v. Valeo*, 424 U.S. 1 (1976) (holding that Congress could not constitutionally authorize Members of Congress to appoint members of the Federal Election Commission). But a Congress that seeks to limit the President's authority to control his subordinates might be able to achieve its goal by vesting the power to appoint in someone other than the President. As the language of the Appointments Clause makes clear, whether Congress can do so turns on whether the official whose appointment is at issue is an "Officer" or instead an "inferior Officer." We will defer until later in this Chapter—specifically in the discussion of the Court's decision in *Morrison v. Olson*—how the Court distinguishes between these two classes of officials.

But even officers whom the President has appointed might sometimes seek to make decisions with which the President disagrees. Suppose, for example, the President disagrees with the Secretary of the Treasury on a matter of policy or the President views the Secretary of Treasury's performance as unsatisfactory. What can the President do? Traditionally, the President has exercised control in these kinds of situations either by firing, or threatening to fire, subordinates who do not conform to the President's requirements. Indeed, the President might be able to control the decision-making even of officers whom he has *not* appointed if he has the power to remove them from office.

The next two cases consider the question whether Congress by statute can limit the

President's ability to discharge subordinates and thus restrict the ability of the President to control the executive branch. The two decisions, however, are not easy to reconcile. As a noted commentator has written, *Myers v. United States* "stands for the broad proposition that any congressional limits on the [the President's] removal power are unconstitutional," Erwin Chemerinsky, *Constitutional Law: Principles and Policies* 350 (3d ed. 2006), at least with respect to "Officers" of the United States. But *Humphrey's Executor v. United States* holds that, at least with respect to the heads of some administrative agencies, Congress "may limit removal to situations where there is just cause for firing." *Id.* at 351. In reading the cases, consider how the Court reconciles the difference.

Myers v. United States

272 U.S. 52 (1926)

Mr. Chief Justice TAFT delivered the opinion of the Court.

This case presents the question whether under the Constitution the President has the exclusive power of removing executive officers of the United States whom he has appointed by and with the advice and consent of the Senate.

> **FYI**
>
> William Howard Taft was the President of the United States from 1909-1913. In his tremendous legal and political career, he also served as Chief Justice of the United States, a federal circuit judge, the solicitor general of the United States, the civil governor of the Philippines, and a professor at Yale Law School.

Myers, appellant's intestate, was on July 21, 1917, appointed by the President, by and with the advice and consent of the Senate, to be a postmaster of the first class at Portland, Or., for a term of four years. On January 20, 1920, Myers' resignation was demanded. He refused the demand. On February 2, 1920, he was removed from office by order of the Postmaster General, acting by direction of the President. *** On April 21, 1921, he brought this suit in the Court of Claims for his salary from the date of his removal, which *** amounted to $8,838.71. In August, 1920, the President made a recess appointment of one Jones, who took office September 19, 1920.

By the sixth section of the Act of Congress of July 12, 1876, 19 Stat. 80, under which Myers was appointed with the advice and consent of the Senate as a first-class postmaster, it is provided that:

> "Postmasters of the first, second, and third classes shall be appointed and may be removed by the President by and with the advice and consent of the Senate, and shall hold their offices for four years unless sooner removed or suspended according to law."

The Senate did not consent to the President's removal of Myers during his term. If this statute in its requirement that his term should be four years unless sooner removed by the President by and with the consent of the Senate is valid, the appellant, Myers' administratrix, is entitled to recover his unpaid salary for his full term and the judgment of the Court of Claims must be reversed. The government maintains that the requirement is invalid, for the reason that under article 2 of the Constitution the President's power of removal of executive officers appointed by him with the advice and consent of the Senate is full and complete without consent of the Senate. If this view is sound, the removal of Myers by the President without the Senate's consent was legal, and the judgment of the Court of Claims against the appellant was correct, and must be affirmed ***. We are therefore confronted by the constitutional question and cannot avoid it.

In the House of Representatives of the First Congress, on Tuesday, May 18, 1789, Mr. Madison moved in the committee of the whole that there should be established three executive departments, one of Foreign Affairs, another of the Treasury, and a third of War, at the head of each of which there should be a Secretary, to be appointed by the President by and with the advice and consent of the Senate, and to be removable by the President. The committee agreed to the establishment of a Department of Foreign Affairs, but a discussion ensued as to making the Secretary removable by the President. 1 Annals of Congress, 370, 371. "The question was now taken and carried, by a considerable majority, in favor of declaring the power of removal to be in the President." 1 Annals of Congress, 383.

It is convenient in the course of our discussion of this case to review the reasons advanced by Mr. Madison and his associates for their conclusion, supplementing them, so far as may be, by additional considerations which lead this court to concur therein.

The debates in the Constitutional Convention indicated an intention to create a strong executive, and after a controversial discussion the executive power of the government was vested in one person and many of his important functions were specified so as to avoid the humiliating weakness of the Congress during the Revolution and under the Articles of Confederation.

Mr. Madison and his associates in the discussion in the House dwelt at length upon the necessity there was for construing article 2 to give the President the sole power of removal in his responsibility for the conduct of the executive branch, and enforced this by emphasizing his duty expressly declared in the third section of the article to "take care that the laws be faithfully executed." Madison, 1 Annals of Congress, 496, 497.

> **FYI**
>
> During the debate on Madison's proposal, a discussion of removal of officers arose. A small number of Representatives believed that impeachment was the only way to remove an officer, and the rest of the Members were divided roughly evenly among the following three views: (1) removal is the President's prerogative alone; (2) removal, like appointment, is vested jointly in the President and the Senate; and (3) because the Constitution is silent, Congress can settle the question of removal pursuant to its power under the Necessary and Proper Clause. See Edward S. Corwin, *Tenure of Office and the Removal Power Under the Constitution*, 27 Colum. L. Rev. 353 (1927). Proponents of the first view and the third view ultimately joined to confer the power on the President. Is it a fair inference from this record that the original understanding was that the removal power resided solely in the President?

The vesting of the executive power in the President was essentially a grant of the power to execute the laws. But the President alone and unaided could not execute the laws. He must execute them by the assistance of subordinates. This view has since been repeatedly affirmed by this court. As he is charged specifically to take care that they be faithfully executed, the reasonable implication, even in the absence of express words, was that as part of his executive power he should select those who were to act for him under his direction in the execution of the laws. The further implication must be, in the absence of any express limitation respecting removals, that as his selection of administrative officers is essential to the execution of the laws by him, so must be his power of removing those for whom he cannot continue to be responsible. Fisher Ames, 1 Annals of Congress, 474.

> **Take Note**
>
> The Court explains in this paragraph why the President must have the power to remove subordinates and explains in the next paragraph why Congress should not play a role in the removal decisions. What is the Court's reasoning? Does the Court offer legal or policy arguments?

The power to prevent the removal of an officer who has served under the President is different from the authority to consent to or reject his appointment. When a nomination is made, it may be presumed that the Senate is, or may become, as well advised as to the fitness of the nominee as the President, but in the nature of things the defects in ability or intelligence or loyalty in the administration of the laws of one who has served as an officer under the President are facts as to which the President, or his trusted subordinates, must be better informed than the Senate, and the power to remove him may therefore be regarded as confined for very sound and practical reasons, to the governmental authority which has administrative control. The power of removal is incident to the power of appointment, not to the power of advising and consenting to appointment, and when the grant of the executive power is enforced by the express mandate to take care that the laws be faithfully executed, it emphasizes the necessity for including within the executive power as conferred the exclusive power of removal.

We come now to consider an argument, advanced and strongly pressed on behalf of the complainant, that this case concerns only the removal of a postmaster, that a postmaster is an inferior officer, and that such an office was not included within the legislative decision of 1789, which related only to superior officers to be appointed by the President by and with the advice and consent of the Senate.***

Section 2 of article 2, after providing that the President shall nominate and with the consent of the Senate appoint ambassadors, other public ministers, consuls, judges of the Supreme Court and all other officers of the United States whose appointments are not herein otherwise provided for, and which shall be established by law, contains the proviso:

> "But the Congress may be law vest the appointment of such inferior officers, as they think proper, in the President alone, in the courts of law or in the heads of departments."

The power to remove inferior executive officers, like that to remove superior executive officers, is an incident of the power to appoint them, and is in its nature an executive power. The authority of Congress given by the excepting clause to vest the appointment of such inferior officers in the heads of departments carries with it authority incidentally to invest the heads of departments with power to remove. It has been the practice of Congress to do so and this court has recognized that power. *** But the court never has held, nor reasonably could hold, although it is argued to the contrary on behalf of the appellant, that the excepting clause enables Congress to draw to itself, or to either branch of it, the power to remove or the right to participate in the exercise of that power. To do this would be to go beyond the words and implications of that clause, and to infringe the constitutional principle of the separation of governmental powers.

For the reasons given, we must therefore hold that the provision of the law of 1876 by which the unrestricted power of removal of first-class postmasters is denied to the President is in violation of the Constitution and invalid.

> **Food for Thought**
>
> If Congress can vest the authority to appoint an "inferior" officer in someone other than the President, then why can't it limit the President's authority to fire such an officer, as well? Is the defect here not that Congress limited the *President's* right to remove, but instead that Congress reserved the power to *itself*?

Points for Discussion

a. Original Understanding

To what extent does the Court rely on the original understanding of the Constitution to support its conclusion? Is the evidence of the original understanding cited by the Court persuasive? What inference should we draw from the fact that the Constitution specifies the President's and the Senate's role in appointments, but is silent with respect to the President's power of removal? What weight should we put on the fact that Congress has the power to impeach and remove Officers of the United States? See Article II, § 4; Article I, § 2, cl. 5; Article I, § 3, cl. 6.

b. President Andrew Johnson's Firing of the Secretary of War

Vice President Andrew Johnson became President when Abraham Lincoln was assassinated in 1865. President Johnson soon disagreed with Secretary of War Edwin Stanton about the treatment of the defeated Southern states. Congress, which generally sided with Stanton, passed the Tenure of Office Act of 1867, 14 Stat 430 (over Johnson's veto), to prevent Johnson from firing Stanton and other officials. When Johnson removed Stanton in violation of this Act, the House of Representatives impeached him. But the Senate did not remove Johnson from office, acquitting him by a single vote. Does this historical incident support or undermine the Court's conclusion in <u>Myers</u>? To read more about this history, see Steven G. Calabresi & Christopher S. Yoo, *The Unitary Executive During the Second Half-Century*, 26 Harv. J. L & Pub. Pol'y 667, 737-759 (2003).

Humphrey's Executor v. United States

295 U.S. 602 (1935)

Mr. Justice SUTHERLAND delivered the opinion of the Court.

Plaintiff brought suit in the Court of Claims against the United States to recover a sum of money alleged to be due the deceased for salary as a Federal Trade Commissioner from October 8, 1933, when the President undertook to remove him from office, to the time of his death on February 14, 1934. The court below has certified to this court two questions in respect of the power of the President to make the removal. The material facts which give rise to the questions are as follows:

William E. Humphrey, the decedent, on December 10, 1931, was nominated by President Hoover to succeed himself as a member of the Federal Trade Commission, and was confirmed by the United States Senate. He was duly commissioned for a term of seven years, expiring September 25, 1938; and, after taking the required oath of office, entered upon his duties. On July 25, 1933, President Roosevelt addressed a letter to the commissioner asking for his resignation, on the ground "that the aims and purposes of the Administration with respect to the work of the Commission can be carried out most effectively with personnel of my own selection," but disclaiming any reflection upon the commissioner personally or upon his services. The commissioner replied, asking time to consult his friends. After some further correspondence upon the subject, the President on August 31, 1933, wrote the commissioner expressing the hope that the resignation would be forthcoming, and saying: "You will, I know, realize that I do not feel that your mind and my mind go along together on either the policies or the administering of the Federal Trade Commission, and, frankly, I think it is best for the people of this country that I should have a full confidence."

The commissioner declined to resign; and on October 7, 1933, the President wrote him: "Effective as of this date you are hereby removed from the office of Commissioner of the Federal Trade Commission."

Humphrey never acquiesced in this action, but continued thereafter to insist that he was still a member of the commission, entitled to perform its duties and receive the compensation provided by law at the rate of $10,000 per annum. Upon these and other facts set forth in the certificate, which we deem it unnecessary to recite, the following questions are certified:

1. Do the provisions of section 1 of the Federal Trade Commission Act, stating that "any commissioner may be removed by the President for inefficiency, neglect of duty, or malfeasance in office," restrict or limit the power of the President to remove a commissioner except upon one or more of the causes named?

If the foregoing question is answered in the affirmative, then—

2. If the power of the President to remove a commissioner is restricted or limited as shown by the foregoing interrogatory and the answer made thereto, is such a

restriction or limitation valid under the Constitution of the United States?

[The Court answered the first question in the affirmative.]

Second. To support its contention that the removal provision of section 1, as we have just construed it, is an unconstitutional interference with the executive power of the President, the government's chief reliance is *Myers v. United States*, 272 U.S. 52 (1926). ***

The office of a postmaster is so essentially unlike the office now involved that the decision in the *Myers* Case cannot be accepted as controlling our decision here. A postmaster is an executive officer restricted to the performance of executive functions. He is charged with no duty at all related to either the legislative or judicial power. The actual decision in the *Myers* Case finds support in the theory that such an officer is merely one of the units in the executive department and, hence, inherently subject to the exclusive and illimitable power of removal by the Chief Executive, whose subordinate and aid he is. Putting aside dicta, which may be followed if sufficiently persuasive but which are not controlling, the necessary reach of the decision goes far enough to include all purely executive officers. It goes no farther; much less does it include an officer who occupies no place in the executive department and who exercises no part of the executive power vested by the Constitution in the President.

> **Take Note**
>
> How does the Court distinguish *Myers v. United States*? Do you find the distinction convincing? Is there any other way to distinguish *Myers*?

The Federal Trade Commission is an administrative body created by Congress to carry into effect legislative policies embodied in the statute in accordance with the legislative standard therein prescribed, and to perform other specified duties as a legislative or as a judicial aid. Such a body cannot in any proper sense be characterized as an arm or an eye of the executive. Its duties are performed without executive leave and, in the contemplation of the statute, must be free from executive control. In administering the provisions of the statute in respect of "unfair methods of competition," that is to say, in filling in and administering the details embodied by that general standard, the commission acts in part quasi legislatively and in part quasi judicially. In making investigations and reports thereon for the information of Congress under section 6, in aid of the legislative power, it acts as a legislative agency. Under section 7, which authorizes the commission to act as a master in chancery under rules prescribed by the court, it acts as an agency of the judiciary. To the extent that it exercises any executive function, as distinguished from executive power in the constitutional sense, it does so in the discharge and effectuation of its quasi legislative or quasi judicial powers, or as an agency of the legislative or judicial departments of the government.

We think it plain under the Constitution that illimitable power of removal is not possessed by the President in respect of officers of the character of those just named. The authority of Congress, in creating quasi legislative or quasi judicial agencies, to require them to act in discharge of their duties independently of executive control cannot well be doubted; and that authority includes, as an appropriate incident, power to fix the period during which they shall continue, and to forbid their removal except for cause in the meantime. For it is quite evident that one who holds his office only during the pleasure of another cannot be depended upon to maintain an attitude of independence against the latter's will.

The fundamental necessity of maintaining each of the three general departments of government entirely free from the control or coercive influence, direct or indirect, of either of the others, has often been stressed and is hardly open to serious question. So much is implied in the very fact of the separation of the powers of these departments by the Constitution; and in the rule which recognizes their essential coequality. The sound application of a principle that makes one master in his own house precludes him from imposing his control in the house of another who is master there. ***

> **Take Note**
>
> The Court concludes here that Congress may restrict the President's power to remove officers at agencies exercising quasi-judicial or quasi-legislative power. How can Congress, consistent with the separation of powers, create an agency that exercises "quasi-judicial" or "quasi-legislative" power?

The power of removal here claimed for the President falls within this principle, since its coercive influence threatens the independence of a commission, which is not only wholly disconnected from the executive department, but which, as already fully appears, was created by Congress as a means of carrying into operation legislative and judicial powers, and as an agency of the legislative and judicial departments.

The result of what we now have said is this: Whether the power of the President to remove an officer shall prevail over the authority of Congress to condition the power by fixing a definite term and precluding a removal except for cause will depend upon the character of the office; the *Myers* decision, affirming the power of the President alone to make the removal, is confined to purely executive officers; and as to officers of the kind here under consideration, we hold that no removal can be made during the prescribed term for which the officer is appointed, except for one or more of the causes named in the applicable statute.

Points for Discussion

a. The "Unitary Executive"

Proponents of the theory of the "unitary executive" generally oppose efforts to vest executive power in persons whom the President cannot control. Does *Humphrey's Executor* suggest that our government now has two executive branches, one that is under the complete control of the President and another that operates largely independent of the President? Is a non-unitary executive branch consistent with the text of Article II, section 1? Or do other provisions in the Constitution contemplate officers beyond the complete control of the President?

b. Independent Administrative Agencies

Federal administrative agencies that are led by an official whom the President can fire only for good cause are now called "Independent Administrative Agencies." These agencies include the Central Intelligence Agency, the Environmental Protection Agency, the Federal Communications Commission, the Board of Governors of the Federal Reserve System, and the Federal Trade Commission. What do these agencies have in common? Do they all perform quasi-legislative or quasi-judicial functions? Should the President really have limited control over the important functions carried out by these governmental bodies? Conversely, why might independence be desirable for some or all of those agencies?

———————

As we will see shortly, the tension between *Myers* and *Humphrey's Executor* created an unstable place for the law to rest. But even assuming that the Court's focus, in deciding whether Congress can limit the President's power to remove an officer, on the "character of the office" is sensible, we must have some way to determine when in fact an officer exercises "executive," rather than "quasi-judicial" or "quasi-legislative," power. This can be a surprisingly difficult inquiry, particularly in certain contexts. Consider the case that follows.

The legislative branch of government includes more than the 100 senators in the Senate and the 435 representatives in the House. These politicians all have staffs that help them in their work. In addition, Congress employs important officials, such as the Sergeant at Arms, the Librarian of the Library of Congress, and the Architect of the Capitol, who all help carry out the functions of the legislative branch. No one doubts that Congress may employ these officials and restrict the President's ability to interfere with them. A separate question, however, is whether Congress can assign executive powers to them. The following case says that the answer is no. But determining whether an officer is in fact in the legislative branch of government and whether the official actually exercises executive power are not always easy tasks. Consider how the Court answers these questions in this case.

———————

Bowsher v. Synar

478 U.S. 714 (1986)

Chief Justice BURGER delivered the opinion of the Court.

On December 12, 1985, the President signed into law the Balanced Budget and Emergency Deficit Control Act of 1985, Pub.L. 99-177, 99 Stat. 1038, popularly known as the "Gramm-Rudman-Hollings Act." The purpose of the Act is to eliminate the federal budget deficit. To that end, the Act sets a "maximum deficit amount" for federal spending for each of fiscal years 1986 through 1991. The size of that maximum deficit amount progressively reduces to zero in fiscal year 1991. If in any fiscal year the federal budget deficit exceeds the maximum deficit amount by more than a specified sum, the Act requires across-the-board cuts in federal spending to reach the targeted deficit level, with half of the cuts made to defense programs and the other half made to nondefense programs. The Act exempts certain priority programs from these cuts.

These "automatic" reductions are accomplished through a rather complicated procedure, spelled out in § 251, the so-called "reporting provisions" of the Act. Each year, the Directors of the Office of Management and Budget (OMB) and the Congressional Budget Office (CBO) independently estimate the amount of the federal budget deficit for the upcoming fiscal year. If that deficit exceeds the maximum targeted deficit amount for that fiscal year by more than a specified amount, the Directors of OMB and CBO independently calculate, on a program-by-program basis, the budget reductions necessary to ensure that the deficit does not exceed the maximum deficit amount. The Act then requires the Directors to report jointly their deficit estimates and budget reduction calculations to the Comptroller General.

> **FYI**
>
> OMB is an entity within the Executive Office of the President. The Director of OMB is removable at will by the President.

The Comptroller General, after reviewing the Directors' reports, then reports his conclusions to the President. The President in turn must issue a "sequestration" order mandating the spending reductions specified by the Comptroller General. There follows a period during which Congress may by legislation reduce spending to obviate, in whole or in part, the need for the sequestration order. If such reductions are not enacted, the sequestration order becomes effective and the spending reductions included in that order are made.

Within hours of the President's signing of the Act, Congressman Synar, who had voted against the Act, filed a complaint seeking declaratory relief that the Act was unconstitutional. Eleven other Members later joined Congressman Synar's suit. A virtually identical lawsuit was also filed by the National Treasury Employees Union. The Union alleged that its members had been injured as a result of the Act's automatic spending reduction provisions, which have suspended certain cost-of-living benefit increases to the Union's members.

We noted recently that "[t]he Constitution sought to divide the delegated powers of the new Federal Government into three defined categories, Legislative, Executive, and Judicial." *INS v. Chadha,* 462 U.S. 919, 951 (1983). The declared purpose of separating and dividing the powers of government, of course, was to "diffus[e] power the better to secure liberty." *Youngstown Sheet & Tube Co. v. Sawyer,* 343 U.S. 579, 635 (1952) (Jackson, J., concurring). Justice Jackson's words echo the famous warning of Montesquieu, quoted by James Madison in The Federalist No. 47, that "there can be no liberty where the legislative and executive powers are united in the same person, or body of magistrates."

Even a cursory examination of the Constitution reveals the influence of Montesquieu's thesis that checks and balances were the foundation of a structure of government that would protect liberty. The Framers provided a vigorous Legislative Branch and a separate and wholly independent Executive Branch, with each branch responsible ultimately to the people. The Framers also provided for a Judicial Branch equally independent with "[t]he judicial Power . . . extend[ing] to all Cases, in Law and Equity, arising under this Constitution, and the Laws of the United States." Art. III, § 2.

Other, more subtle, examples of separated powers are evident as well. Unlike parliamentary systems such as that of Great Britain, no person who is an officer of the United States may serve as a Member of the Congress. Art. I, § 6. Moreover, unlike parliamentary systems, the President, under Article II, is responsible not to the Congress but to the people, subject only to impeachment proceedings which are exercised by the two Houses as representatives of the people. Art. II, § 4. And even in the impeachment of a President the presiding officer of the ultimate tribunal is not a member of the Legislative Branch, but the Chief Justice of the United States. Art. I, § 3.

The Constitution does not contemplate an active role for Congress in the supervision of officers charged with the execution of the laws it enacts. The President appoints "Officers of the United States" with the "Advice and Consent of the Senate. . . ." Art. II, § 2. Once the appointment has been made and confirmed, however, the Constitution explicitly provides for removal of Officers of the United States by Congress only upon impeachment by the House of Representatives and conviction by the Senate. An impeachment by the House and trial by the Senate can rest only on "Treason, Bribery or other high Crimes and Misdemeanors." Article II, § 4. A direct congressional role in the removal of officers charged with the execution of the laws beyond this limited one is inconsistent with separation of powers.

This Court first directly addressed this issue in *Myers v. United States,* 272 U.S. 52 (1925). At issue in *Myers* was a statute providing that certain postmasters could be removed only "by and with the advice and consent of the Senate." *** Chief Justice Taft, writing for the Court, declared the statute unconstitutional on the ground that for Congress to "draw to itself, or to either branch of it, the power to remove or the right to participate in the exercise of that power . . . would be . . . to infringe the constitutional principle of the separation of governmental powers." *Id.,* at 161.

A decade later, in *Humphrey's Executor v. United States,* 295 U.S. 602 (1935), relied upon heavily by appellants, a Federal Trade Commissioner who had been removed by the President sought backpay. *Humphrey's Executor* involved an issue not presented either in the *Myers* case or in this case—*i.e.,* the power of Congress to limit the President's powers of removal of a Federal Trade Commissioner. The relevant statute permitted removal "by the President," but only "for inefficiency, neglect of duty, or malfeasance in office." *** The Court distinguished *Myers,* reaffirming its holding that congressional participation in the removal of executive officers is unconstitutional. ***

In light of these precedents, we conclude that Congress cannot reserve for itself the power of removal of an officer charged with the execution of the laws except by impeachment. To permit the execution of the laws to be vested in an officer answerable only to Congress would, in practical terms, reserve in Congress control over the execution of the laws. *** The structure of the Constitution does not permit Congress to execute the laws; it follows that Congress cannot grant to an officer under its control what it does not possess. *** With these principles in mind, we turn to consideration of whether the Comptroller General is controlled by Congress.

The critical factor lies in the provisions of the statute defining the Comptroller General's office relating to removability. Although the Comptroller General is nominated by the President from a list of three individuals recommended by the Speaker of the House of Representatives and the President *pro tempore* of the Senate, see 31 U.S.C. § 703(a)(2), and confirmed by the Senate, he is removable only at the initiative of Congress. He may be removed not only by impeachment but also by joint resolution of Congress "at any time" resting on any one of the following bases: "(i) permanent disability"; "(ii) inefficiency"; "(iii) neglect of duty"; "(iv) malfeasance"; or "(v) a felony or conduct involving moral turpitude." 31 U.S.C. § 703(e)(1)(B).[7]

This provision was included, as one Congressman explained in urging passage of the Act, because Congress "felt that [the Comptroller General] should be brought under the sole control of Congress, so that Congress at any moment when it found he was inefficient and was not carrying on the duties of his office as he should and as the Congress expected, could remove him without the long, tedious process of a trial by impeachment." 61 Cong. Rec. 1081 (1921).

The removal provision was an important part of the legislative scheme, as a number of Congressmen recognized. Representative Hawley commented: "[H]e is our officer, in a measure, getting information for us.... If he does not do his work properly, we, as practically his employers, ought to be able to discharge him from his office." 58 Cong. Rec. 7136 (1919). Representative Sisson observed that the removal provisions would give "[t]he Congress of the United States ... absolute control of the man's destiny in office." 61 Cong. Rec. 987 (1921). The ultimate design was to "give the legislative branch of the Government control of the audit, not through the power of appointment, but through the power of removal." 58 Cong. Rec. 7211 (1919) (Rep. Temple).

> **Take Note**
>
> The Court recognizes that the Comptroller General traditionally has been viewed as an official within the legislative branch. Does this fact determine the outcome of the case, or are other facts more significant?

Over the years, the Comptrollers General have also viewed themselves as part of the Legislative Branch. In one of the early Annual Reports of Comptroller General, the official seal of his office was described as reflecting

"the independence of judgment to be exercised by the General Accounting Office, subject to the control of the legislative branch. . . . The combination represents an agency of the Congress independent of other authority auditing and checking the expenditures of the Government as required by law and subjecting any questions arising in that connection to quasi-judicial determination." GAO Ann. Rep. 5-6 (1924).

---

[7] Although the President could veto such a joint resolution, the veto could be overridden by a two-thirds vote of both Houses of Congress. Thus, the Comptroller General could be removed in the face of Presidential opposition. Like the District Court, 626 F.Supp., at 1393, n. 21, we therefore read the removal provision as authorizing removal by Congress alone.

Against this background, we see no escape from the conclusion that, because Congress has retained removal authority over the Comptroller General, he may not be entrusted with executive powers. The remaining question is whether the Comptroller General has been assigned such powers in the Balanced Budget and Emergency Deficit Control Act of 1985.

The primary responsibility of the Comptroller General under the instant Act is the preparation of a "report." This report must contain detailed estimates of projected federal revenues and expenditures. The report must also specify the reductions, if any, necessary to reduce the deficit to the target for the appropriate fiscal year. The reductions must be set forth on a program-by-program basis.

In preparing the report, the Comptroller General is to have "due regard" for the estimates and reductions set forth in a joint report submitted to him by the Director of CBO and the Director of OMB, the President's fiscal and budgetary adviser. However, the Act plainly contemplates that the Comptroller General will exercise his independent judgment and evaluation with respect to those estimates. The Act also provides that the Comptroller General's report "shall explain fully any differences between the contents of such report and the report of the Directors." § 251(b)(2).

Appellants suggest that the duties assigned to the Comptroller General in the Act are essentially ministerial and mechanical so that their performance does not constitute "execution of the law" in a meaningful sense. On the contrary, we view these functions as plainly entailing execution of the law in constitutional terms. Interpreting a law enacted by Congress to implement the legislative mandate is the very essence of "execution" of the law. Under § 251, the Comptroller General must exercise judgment concerning facts that affect the application of the Act. He must also interpret the provisions of the Act to determine precisely what budgetary calculations are required. Decisions of that kind are typically made by officers charged with executing a statute.

> **Food for Thought**
>
> Do you agree that "interpreting a law enacted by Congress" is the "very essence" of the executive function? Who else might be called upon to perform that function? And is "interpretation" really what the Comptroller General is required to do under the scheme at issue here?

> **Food for Thought**
>
> If the President must "carry out" the Comptroller General's directive, then isn't the Comptroller General's power more "legislative" in nature? Who ordinarily is responsible for deciding how much money the government will appropriate for its programs?

The executive nature of the Comptroller General's functions under the Act is revealed in § 252(a)(3) which gives the Comptroller General the ultimate authority to determine the budget cuts to be made. Indeed, the Comptroller General commands the President himself to carry out, without the slightest variation (with exceptions not relevant to the constitutional issues presented), the directive of the Comptroller General as to the budget reductions:

"The [Presidential] order *must provide* for reductions in the manner specified in section 251(a)

(3), *must incorporate* the provisions of the [Comptroller General's] report submitted under section 251(b), and *must be consistent with such report in all respects.* The President *may not modify or recalculate any of the estimates, determinations, specifications, bases, amounts, or percentages* set forth in the report submitted under section 251(b) in determining the reductions to be specified in the order with respect to programs, projects, and activities, or with respect to budget activities, within an account. . . ." § 252(a)(3) (emphasis added).

Congress of course initially determined the content of the Balanced Budget and Emergency Deficit Control Act; and undoubtedly the content of the Act determines the nature of the executive duty. However, as *Chadha* makes clear, once Congress makes its choice in enacting legislation, its participation ends. Congress can thereafter control the execution of its enactment only indirectly—by passing new legislation. *Chadha*, 462 U.S., at 958. By placing the responsibility for execution of the Balanced Budget and Emergency Deficit Control Act in the hands of an officer who is subject to removal only by itself, Congress in effect has retained control over the execution of the Act and has intruded into the executive function. The Constitution does not permit such intrusion.

Justice STEVENS, with whom Justice MARSHALL joins, concurring in the judgment.

I agree with the Court that the "Gramm-Rudman-Hollings" Act contains a constitutional infirmity so severe that the flawed provision may not stand. I disagree with the Court, however, on the reasons why the Constitution prohibits the Comptroller General from exercising the powers assigned to him by § 251(b) and § 251(c)(2) of the Act. It is not the dormant, carefully circumscribed congressional removal power that represents the primary constitutional evil. Nor do I agree with the conclusion of both the majority and the dissent that the analysis depends on a labeling of the functions assigned to the Comptroller General as "executive powers." Rather, I am convinced that the Comptroller General must be characterized as an agent of Congress because of his longstanding statutory responsibilities; that the powers assigned to him under the Gramm-Rudman-Hollings Act require him to make policy that will bind the Nation; and that, when Congress, or a component or an agent of Congress, seeks to make policy that will bind the Nation, it must follow the procedures mandated by Article I of the Constitution—through passage by both Houses and presentment to the President. In short, Congress may not exercise its fundamental power to formulate national policy by delegating that power to one of its two Houses, to a legislative committee, or to an individual agent of the Congress such as the Speaker of the House of Representatives, the Sergeant at Arms of the Senate, or the Director of the Congressional Budget Office. *INS v. Chadha*, 462 U.S. 919 (1983). That principle, I believe, is applicable to the Comptroller General.

> **Take Note**
>
> According to Justice Stevens, what is the nature of the power exercised by the Comptroller General? If he disagrees with the Court on this question, then why does he agree that the Act is unconstitutional?

Justice WHITE, dissenting.

The Court, acting in the name of separation of powers, takes upon itself to strike down the Gramm-Rudman-Hollings Act, one of the most novel and far-reaching legislative responses to a national crisis since the New Deal. *** I will not purport to speak to the wisdom of the policies incorporated in the legislation the Court invalidates ***. I will, however, address the wisdom of the Court's willingness to interpose its distressingly formalistic view of separation of powers as a bar to the attainment of governmental objectives through the means chosen by the Congress and the President in the legislative process established by the Constitution. *** [T]he Court's decision rests on a feature of the legislative scheme that is of minimal practical significance and that presents no substantial threat to the basic scheme of separation of powers.

It is evident (and nothing in the Court's opinion is to the contrary) that the powers exercised by the Comptroller General under the Gramm-Rudman-Hollings Act are not such that vesting them in an officer not subject to removal at will by the President would in itself improperly interfere with Presidential powers. Determining the level of spending by the Federal Government is not by nature a function central either to the exercise of the President's enumerated powers or to his general duty to ensure execution of the laws; rather, appropriating funds is a peculiarly legislative function, and one expressly committed to Congress by Art. I, § 9, which provides that "No Money shall be drawn from the Treasury, but in Consequence of Appropriations made by Law." In enacting Gramm-Rudman-Hollings, Congress has chosen to exercise this legislative power to establish the level of federal spending by providing a detailed set of criteria for reducing expenditures below the level of appropriations in the event that certain conditions are met. Delegating the execution of this legislation—that is, the power to apply the Act's criteria and make the required calculations—to an officer independent of the President's will does not deprive the President of any power that he would otherwise have or that is essential to the performance of the duties of his office. Rather, the result of such a delegation, from the standpoint of the President, is no different from the result of more traditional forms of appropriation: under either system, the level of funds available to the Executive Branch to carry out its duties is not within the President's discretionary control.

I have no quarrel with the proposition that the powers exercised by the Comptroller under the Act may be characterized as "executive" in that they involve the interpretation and carrying out of the Act's mandate. I can also accept the general proposition that although Congress has considerable authority in designating the officers who are to execute legislation, the constitutional scheme of separated powers does prevent Congress from reserving an executive role for itself or for its "agents." I cannot accept, however, that the exercise of authority by an officer removable for cause by a joint resolution of Congress is analogous to the impermissible execution of the law by Congress itself, nor would I hold that the congressional role in the removal process renders the Comptroller an "agent" of the Congress, incapable of receiving "executive" power.

The question to be answered is whether the threat of removal of the Comptroller General for cause through joint resolution as authorized by the Budget and Accounting Act renders the Comptroller sufficiently subservient to Congress that investing him with "executive" power can be realistically equated with the unlawful retention of such power by Congress itself; more generally, the question is whether there is a genuine threat of "encroachment or aggrandizement of one branch at the expense of the other," *Buckley v. Valeo*, 424 U.S., at 122. Common sense indicates that the existence of the removal provision poses no such threat to the principle of separation of powers.

The statute does not permit anyone to remove the Comptroller at will; removal is permitted only for specified cause, with the existence of cause to be determined by Congress following a hearing. *** These [limitations] on the removal power militate strongly against the characterization of the Comptroller as a mere agent of Congress by virtue of the removal authority.

More importantly, the substantial role played by the President in the process of removal through joint resolution reduces to utter insignificance the possibility that the threat of removal will induce subservience to the Congress. *** [A] joint resolution must be presented to the President and is ineffective if it is vetoed by him, unless the veto is overridden by the constitutionally prescribed two-thirds majority of both Houses of Congress. The requirement of Presidential approval obviates the possibility that the Comptroller will perceive himself as so completely at the mercy of Congress that he will function as its tool. If the Comptroller's conduct in office is not so unsatisfactory to the President as to convince the latter that removal is required under the statutory standard, Congress will have no independent power to coerce the Comptroller unless it can muster a two-thirds majority in both Houses—a feat of bipartisanship more difficult than that required to impeach and convict. The incremental *in terrorem* effect of the possibility of congressional removal in the face of a Presidential veto is therefore exceedingly unlikely to have any discernible impact on the extent of congressional influence over the Comptroller.

The practical result of the removal provision is not to render the Comptroller unduly dependent upon or subservient to Congress, but to render him one of the most independent officers in the entire federal establishment. Those who have studied the office agree that the procedural and substantive limits on the power of Congress and the President to remove the Comptroller make dislodging him against his will practically impossible. *** Realistic consideration of the nature of the Comptroller General's relation to Congress thus reveals that the threat to separation of powers conjured up by the majority is wholly chimerical.

The wisdom of vesting "executive" powers in an officer removable by joint resolution may indeed be debatable—as may be the wisdom of the entire scheme of permitting an unelected official to revise the budget enacted by Congress—but such matters are for the most part to be worked out between the Congress and the President through the legislative process, which affords each branch ample opportunity to defend its interests. Under such circumstances, the role of this Court should be limited to determining whether the Act so alters the balance of authority among the branches of government as to pose a genuine threat to the basic division between the lawmaking power and the power to execute the law. Because I see no such threat, I cannot join the Court in striking down the Act.

Justice BLACKMUN, dissenting.

The only relief sought in this case is nullification of the automatic budget-reduction provisions of the Deficit Control Act, and that relief should not be awarded even if the Court is correct that those provisions are constitutionally incompatible with Congress' authority to remove the Comptroller General by joint resolution. Any incompatibility, I feel, should be cured by refusing to allow congressional removal—if it ever is attempted— and not by striking down the central provisions of the Deficit Control Act. However wise or foolish it may be, that statute unquestionably ranks among the most important federal enactments of the past several decades. I cannot see the sense of invalidating legislation of this magnitude in order to preserve a cumbersome, 65-year-old removal power that has never been exercised and appears to have been all but forgotten until this litigation.

In the absence of express statutory direction, I think it is plain that, as both Houses urge, invalidating the Comptroller General's functions under the Deficit Control Act would frustrate congressional objectives far more seriously than would refusing to allow Congress to exercise its removal authority under the 1921 law. The majority suggests that the removal authority plays an important role in furthering Congress' desire to keep the Comptroller General under its control. But as Justice WHITE demonstrates, the removal provision serves feebly for such purposes, especially in comparison to other, more effective means of supervision at Congress' disposal. Unless Congress institutes impeachment proceedings—a course all agree the Constitution would permit—the 1921 law authorizes Congress to remove the Comptroller General only for specified cause, only after a hearing, and only by passing the procedural equivalent of a new public law. Congress has never attempted to use this cumbersome procedure, and the Comptroller General has shown few signs of subservience. If Congress in 1921 wished to make the Comptroller General its lackey, it did a remarkably poor job.

I do not claim that the 1921 removal provision is a piece of statutory deadwood utterly without contemporary significance. But it comes close. Rarely if ever invoked even for symbolic purposes, the removal provision certainly pales in importance beside the legislative scheme the Court strikes down today—an extraordinarily far-reaching response to a deficit problem of unprecedented proportions. Because I believe that the constitutional defect found by the Court cannot justify the remedy it has imposed, I respectfully dissent.

———————

Points for Discussion

a. An Alternative Remedy?

The Court announced that Congress cannot give the Comptroller General the executive powers that he would have under the Balanced Budget Act and at the same time reserve the power to remove him. Justice Blackmun reasoned in dissent that striking down the part of the Balanced Budget Act that gives the Comptroller General executive power is not the best solution to this problem. What would be another solution?

b. What is Executive Power?

Justice White questioned whether the Comptroller General really was exercising executive power under the Act. Why did the Court disagree? Whose view is more convincing? Is the line between executive and legislative authority obvious, particularly in this context? What was Justice Stevens's reasoning in agreeing with the Court's resolution of the case?

c. Who Controls the Comptroller General?

The Court reasoned that because Congress could override a presidential veto of a resolution approving the Comptroller General's removal, the removal provision in effect authorized "removal by Congress alone." Such an override vote would require a two-thirds majority in each House of Congress. See Article I, § 7, cl. 2. Yet Congress has authority to remove an executive official by impeachment, see Article II, § 4, and it can do so by a mere majority vote in the House and then a two-thirds vote in the Senate. See Article I, § 2, cl. 5; Article I, § 3, cl. 6. More important, the President has no authority to veto such a decision. In light of this scheme, is the Court's assertion about Congress's control over the Comptroller General convincing?

d. The *Myers* Principle

The members of the Court disagreed about the nature of the Comptroller General's authority and the extent of Congress's control over him. But notice that once one concludes (1) that he exercises executive power and (2) that he is subject to congressional control, the narrower principle of the *Myers* case—that Congress cannot *reserve to itself* the power to remove an executive official—controlled the outcome of the case.

Bowsher stands at least for the proposition that Congress cannot reserve to itself the power to remove an officer exercising executive authority. But can Congress limit the *President's* authority to remove such officers if it does not preserve a role for itself in the removal decision? Viewed together, *Myers* and *Humphrey's Executor* gave a somewhat unsatisfying answer to the question.

The case that follows addresses the question squarely. It concerns a very important conflict of ideas. In general, no one doubts that prosecuting criminal suspects is an executive branch function. But leaving prosecutorial decisions solely to the executive branch might be problematic if the criminal suspects are themselves government officials within the executive branch. After the Watergate scandal, Congress addressed this issue with the Ethics in Government Act of 1978, which allowed a panel of federal judges to appoint an independent counsel to investigate and, if necessary, to prosecute executive branch officials.

Morrison v. Olson

487 U.S. 654 (1988)

Chief Justice REHNQUIST delivered the opinion of the Court.

This case presents us with a challenge to the independent counsel provisions of the Ethics in Government Act of 1978. We hold today that these provisions of the Act do not violate the Appointments Clause of the Constitution, Art. II, § 2, cl. 2, or the limitations of Article III, nor do they impermissibly interfere with the President's authority under Article II in violation of the constitutional principle of separation of powers.

Title VI of the Ethics in Government Act allows for the appointment of an "independent counsel" to investigate and, if appropriate, prosecute certain high-ranking Government officials for violations of federal criminal laws. The Act requires the Attorney General, upon receipt of information that he determines is "sufficient to constitute grounds to investigate whether any person [covered by the Act] may have violated any Federal criminal law," to conduct a preliminary investigation of the matter. When the Attorney General has completed this investigation, or 90 days has elapsed, he is required to report to a special court (the Special Division) created by the Act "for the purpose of appointing independent counsels."[3] If the Attorney General determines that "there are no reasonable grounds to believe that further investigation is warranted," then he must notify the Special Division of this result. In such a case, "the division of the court shall have no power to appoint an independent counsel." If, however, the Attorney General has determined that there are "reasonable grounds to believe that further investigation or prosecution is warranted," then he "shall apply to the division of the court for the appointment of an independent counsel." The Attorney General's application to the court "shall contain sufficient information to assist the [court] in selecting an independent counsel and in defining that independent counsel's prosecutorial jurisdiction." Upon receiving this application, the Special Division "shall appoint an appropriate independent counsel and shall define that independent counsel's prosecutorial jurisdiction."

With respect to all matters within the independent counsel's jurisdiction, the Act grants the counsel "full power and independent authority to exercise all investigative and prosecutorial functions and powers of the Department of Justice, the Attorney General, and any other officer or employee of the Department of Justice." *** [The] procedure for removing an independent counsel [is governed by section 596(a)(1), which] provides:

> "An independent counsel appointed under this chapter may be removed from office, other than by impeachment and conviction, only by the personal action of the Attorney General and only for good cause, physical disability, mental incapacity, or any other condition that substantially impairs the performance of such independent counsel's duties."

---

[3] The Special Division is a division of the United States Court of Appeals for the District of Columbia Circuit. The court consists of three circuit court judges or justices appointed by the Chief Justice of the United States. One of the judges must be a judge of the United States Court of Appeals for the District of Columbia Circuit, and no two of the judges may be named to the Special Division from a particular court. The judges are appointed for 2-year terms, with any vacancy being filled only for the remainder of the 2-year period.

[In 1983, the White House refused to turn over certain documents regarding environmental policies to Congress on grounds of executive privilege. Congress called appellee, Theodore Olson, who was then the Assistant Attorney General for the Office of Legal Counsel (OLC), to testify about the Justice Department's role in this matter. Questions subsequently arose about whether Olson had testified truthfully. The Special Division eventually appointed Alexia Morrison (appellant) as an independent counsel to investigate the charges. In May and June 1987, appellant caused a grand jury to issue and serve subpoenas *ad testificandum* and *duces tecum* on Olson and two other government officials (appellees). All three appellees moved to quash the subpoenas on ground that the Ethics in Government Act was unconstitutional.]

> **FYI**
>
> After this case was decided, the Independent Counsel ultimately decided that no charges against Olson were warranted. Olson later represented President George W. Bush in litigation over the 2000 presidential election, and he subsequently became the Solicitor General of the United States.

[Appellees first claim that the Act violates the Appointments Clause, Article II, § 2, cl. 2.] The parties do not dispute that "[t]he Constitution for purposes of appointment . . . divides all its officers into two classes." *United States v. Germaine,* 99 U.S. (9 Otto) 508, 509 (1879). As we stated in *Buckley v. Valeo,* 424 U.S. 1, 132 (1976): "[P]rincipal officers are selected by the President with the advice and consent of the Senate. Inferior officers Congress may allow to be appointed by the President alone, by the heads of departments, or by the Judiciary." The initial question is, accordingly, whether appellant is an "inferior" or a "principal" officer. If she is the latter, as the Court of Appeals concluded, then the Act is in violation of the Appointments Clause.

> **Take Note**
>
> The Court in this part of the opinion reaches two conclusions. First, the independent counsel is an "inferior officer" of the United States. Second, Congress can vest in the courts of law the power to appoint inferior officers who exercise (at least some types of) executive authority. What leads the Court to these conclusions? Could Congress vest in the courts the power to appoint all inferior officers of the United States?

The line between "inferior" and "principal" officers is one that is far from clear, and the Framers provided little guidance into where it should be drawn. We need not attempt here to decide exactly where the line falls between the two types of officers, because in our view appellant clearly falls on the "inferior officer" side of that line. Several factors lead to this conclusion.

First, appellant is subject to removal by a higher Executive Branch official. Although appellant may not be "subordinate" to the Attorney General (and the President) insofar as she possesses a degree of independent discretion to exercise the powers delegated to her under the Act, the fact that she can be removed by the Attorney General indicates that she is to some degree "inferior" in rank and authority. Second, appellant is empowered by the Act to perform only certain, limited duties. An independent counsel's role is restricted primarily to investigation and, if appropriate, prosecution for certain federal crimes. Admittedly, the Act delegates to appellant "full power and independent authority to exercise all investigative and prosecutorial functions and powers of the Department of Justice," but this grant of authority does not include any authority to formulate policy for the Government or the Executive Branch, nor does it give appellant any administrative duties outside of those necessary to operate her office. The Act specifically provides that in policy matters appellant is to comply to the extent possible with the policies of the Department.

Third, appellant's office is limited in jurisdiction. Not only is the Act itself restricted in applicability to certain federal officials suspected of certain serious federal crimes, but an independent counsel can only act within the scope of the jurisdiction that has been granted by the Special Division pursuant to a request by the Attorney General. Finally, appellant's office is limited in tenure. There is concededly no time limit on the appointment of a particular counsel. Nonetheless, the office of independent counsel is "temporary" in the sense that an independent counsel is appointed essentially to accomplish a single task, and when that task is over the office is terminated, either by the counsel herself or by action of the Special Division. Unlike other prosecutors, appellant has no ongoing responsibilities that extend beyond the accomplishment of the mission that she was appointed for and authorized by the Special Division to undertake. In our view, these factors relating to the "ideas of tenure, duration ... and duties" of the independent counsel, _Germaine, supra, 9 Otto, at 511_, are sufficient to establish that appellant is an "inferior" officer in the constitutional sense.

This does not, however, end our inquiry under the Appointments Clause. Appellees argue that even if appellant is an "inferior" officer, the Clause does not empower Congress to place the power to appoint such an officer outside the Executive Branch. They contend that the Clause does not contemplate congressional authorization of "interbranch appointments," in which an officer of one branch is appointed by officers of another branch. *** On its face, [the Appointments Clause] admits of no limitation on interbranch appointments. Indeed, the inclusion of "as they think proper" seems clearly to give Congress significant discretion to determine whether it is "proper" to vest the appointment of, for example, executive officials in the "courts of Law." ***

> ### Food for Thought
>
> Could Congress vest the head of the FTC with the power to appoint the clerk of a United States District Court? The Chief Justice with the power to appoint the Deputy Secretary of Defense? If not, why is this case different? Does it make sense to read the absence of a specific limitation on interbranch appointments implicitly to permit them?

We also note that the history of the Clause provides no support for appellees' position. Throughout most of the process of drafting the Constitution, the Convention concentrated on the problem of who should have the authority to appoint judges. *** [T]here was little or no debate on the question whether the Clause empowers Congress to provide for interbranch appointments, and there is nothing to suggest that the Framers intended to prevent Congress from having that power.

We do not mean to say that Congress' power to provide for interbranch appointments of "inferior officers" is unlimited. [Congress'] decision to vest the appointment power in the courts would be improper if there was some "incongruity" between the functions normally performed by the courts and the performance of their duty to appoint. In this case, however, we do not think it impermissible for Congress to vest the power to appoint independent counsel in a specially created federal court. We thus disagree with the Court of Appeals' conclusion that there is an inherent incongruity about a court having the power to appoint prosecutorial officers. We have recognized that courts may appoint private attorneys to act as prosecutor for judicial contempt judgments.

Appellees next contend that the powers vested in the Special Division by the Act conflict with Article III of the Constitution. *** As a general rule, we have broadly stated that "executive or administrative duties of a nonjudicial nature may not be imposed on judges holding office under Art. III of the Constitution." *Buckley*, 424 U.S., at 123. The purpose of this limitation is to help ensure the independence of the Judicial Branch and to prevent the Judiciary from encroaching into areas reserved for the other branches.

In our view, Congress' power under the Clause to vest the "Appointment" of inferior officers in the courts may, in certain circumstances, allow Congress to give the courts some discretion in defining the nature and scope of the appointed official's authority. Particularly when, as here, Congress creates a temporary "office" the nature and duties of which will by necessity vary with the factual circumstances giving rise to the need for an appointment in the first place, it may vest the power to define the scope of the office in the court as an incident to the appointment of the officer pursuant to the Appointments Clause. ***

> ### Take Note
>
> The Court concludes here that Congress can give federal judges powers as "incident[s]" to the power of appointing inferior officers. Does the Court identify a clear test for what these powers include?

[W]e do not think that Article III absolutely prevents Congress from vesting [other] miscellaneous powers in the Special Division pursuant to the Act. *** [T]he miscellaneous powers [to grant extensions and refer matters to the counsel] do not impermissibly trespass upon the authority of the Executive Branch. *** [These functions] are not inherently "Executive"; indeed, they are directly analogous to functions that federal judges perform in other contexts, such as deciding whether to allow disclosure of matters occurring before a grand jury, deciding to extend a grand jury investigation, or awarding attorney's fees. [Although] the Special Division's power to terminate the office of the independent counsel pursuant to § 596(b)(2) *** is not a power that could be considered typically "judicial," *** we do not, as did the Court of Appeals, view this provision as a significant judicial encroachment upon executive power or upon the prosecutorial discretion of the independent counsel. *** The termination provisions of the Act do not give the Special Division anything approaching the power to *remove* the counsel while an investigation or court proceeding is still underway—this power is vested solely in the Attorney General. As we see it, "termination" may occur only when the duties of the counsel are truly "completed" or "so substantially completed" that there remains no need for any continuing action by the independent counsel. It is basically a device for removing from the public payroll an independent counsel who has served his or her purpose, but is unwilling to acknowledge the fact. So construed, the Special Division's power to terminate does not pose a sufficient threat of judicial intrusion into matters that are more properly within the Executive's authority to require that the Act be invalidated as inconsistent with Article III.

We now turn to consider whether the Act is invalid under the constitutional principle of separation of powers. Two related issues must be addressed: The first is whether the provision of the Act restricting the Attorney General's power to remove the independent counsel to only those instances in which he can show "good cause," taken by itself, impermissibly interferes with the President's exercise of his constitutionally appointed functions. The second is whether, taken as a whole, the Act violates the separation of powers by reducing the President's ability to control the prosecutorial powers wielded by the independent counsel.

Unlike both *Bowsher v. Synar,* 478 U.S. 714 (1986), and *Myers v. United States,* 272 U.S. 52 (1926), this case does not involve an attempt by Congress itself to gain a role in the removal of executive officials other than its established powers of impeachment and conviction.

The Act instead puts the removal power squarely in the hands of the Executive Branch; an independent counsel may be removed from office, "only by the personal action of the Attorney General, and only for good cause." There is no requirement of congressional approval of the Attorney General's removal decision, though the decision is subject to judicial review. In our view, the removal provisions of the Act make this case more analogous to *Humphrey's Executor v. United States,* 295 U.S. 602 (1935), than to <u>*Myers*</u> or <u>*Bowsher.*</u>

Appellees [argue] that our decision in <u>*Humphrey's Executor*</u> rests on a distinction between "purely executive" officials and officials who exercise "quasi-legislative" and "quasi-judicial" powers. In their view, when a "purely executive" official is involved, the governing precedent is <u>*Myers*</u>, not <u>*Humphrey's Executor*</u>. And, under <u>*Myers*</u>, the President must have absolute discretion to discharge "purely" executive officials at will.

We undoubtedly did rely on the terms "quasi-legislative" and "quasi-judicial" to distinguish the officials involved in <u>*Humphrey's Executor*</u> [from] those in <u>*Myers*</u>, but our present considered view is that the determination of whether the Constitution allows Congress to impose a "good cause"-type restriction on the President's power to remove an official cannot be made to turn on whether or not that official is classified as "purely executive." The analysis contained in our removal cases is designed not to define rigid categories of those officials who may or may not be removed at will by the President, but to ensure that Congress does not interfere with the President's exercise of the "executive power" and his constitutionally appointed duty to "take care that the laws be faithfully executed" under Article II. <u>*Myers*</u> was undoubtedly correct in its holding, and in its broader suggestion that there are some "purely executive" officials who must be removable by the President at will if he is to be able to accomplish his constitutional role. *** At the other end of the spectrum[,] the characterization of the [agency] in <u>*Humphrey's Executor*</u> [as] "quasi-legislative" or "quasi-judicial" in large part reflected our judgment that it was not essential to the

President's proper execution of his Article II powers that these agencies be headed up by individuals who were removable at will. We do not mean to suggest that an analysis of the functions served by the officials at issue is irrelevant. But the real question is whether the removal restrictions are of such a nature that they impede the President's ability to perform his constitutional duty, and the functions of the officials in question must be analyzed in that light.

Considering for the moment the "good cause" removal provision in isolation from the other parts of the Act at issue in this case, we cannot say that the imposition of a "good cause" standard for removal by itself unduly trammels on executive authority. There is no real dispute that the functions performed by the independent counsel are "executive" in the sense that they are law enforcement functions that typically have been undertaken by officials within the Executive Branch. As we noted above, however, the independent counsel is an inferior officer under the Appointments Clause, with limited jurisdiction and tenure and lacking policymaking or significant administrative authority. Although the counsel exercises no small amount of discretion and judgment in deciding how to carry out his or her duties under the Act, we simply do not see how the President's need to control the exercise of that discretion is so central to the functioning of the Executive Branch as to require as a matter of constitutional law that the counsel be terminable at will by the President.

The final question to be addressed is whether the Act, taken as a whole, violates the principle of separation of powers by unduly interfering with the role of the Executive Branch. *** We observe first that this case does not involve an attempt by Congress to increase its own powers at the expense of the Executive Branch. Unlike some of our previous cases, most recently *Bowsher v. Synar*, this case simply does not pose a "dange[r] of congressional usurpation of Executive Branch functions." 478 U.S., at 727; see also *INS v. Chadha,* 462 U.S. 919, 958 (1983). Indeed, with the exception of the power of impeachment—which applies to all officers of the United States—Congress retained for itself no powers of control or supervision over an independent counsel. The Act does empower certain Members of Congress to request the Attorney General to apply for the appointment of an independent counsel, but the Attorney General has no duty to comply with the request, although he must respond within a certain time limit. Other than that, Congress' role under the Act is limited to receiving reports or other information and oversight of the independent counsel's activities, functions that we have recognized generally as being incidental to the legislative function of Congress. See *McGrain v. Daugherty,* 273 U.S. 135, 174 (1927).

> **Food for Thought**
>
> The Court says here that the Act does not "unduly" interfere with executive authority. Does the Court indicate what kind of measures would constitute an undue interference? If not, are there manageable standards that a court can apply?

Similarly, we do not think that the Act works any *judicial* usurpation of properly executive functions. As should be apparent from our discussion of the Appointments Clause above, the power to appoint inferior officers such as independent counsel is not in itself an "executive" function in the constitutional sense, at least when Congress has exercised its power to vest the appointment of an inferior office in the "courts of Law." We note none-theless that under the Act the Special Division has no power to appoint an independent counsel *sua sponte;* it may only do so upon the specific request of the Attorney General, and the courts are specifically prevented from reviewing the Attorney General's decision not to seek appointment. In addition, once the court has appointed a counsel and defined his or her jurisdiction, it has no power to supervise or control the activities of the counsel. As we pointed out in our discussion of the Special Division in relation to Article III, the various powers delegated by the statute to the Division are not supervisory or administra-tive, nor are they functions that the Constitution requires be performed by officials within the Executive Branch. The Act does give a federal court the power to review the Attorney General's decision to remove an independent counsel, but in our view this is a function that is well within the traditional power of the Judiciary.

Justice KENNEDY took no part in the consideration or decision of this case.

Justice SCALIA, dissenting.

Article II, § 1, cl. 1, of the Constitution provides: "The executive Power shall be vested in a President of the United States." That is what this suit is about. Power. The allocation of power among Congress, the President, and the courts in such fashion as to preserve the equilibrium the Constitution sought to establish—so that "a gradual concentration of the several powers in the same department," The Federalist No. 51 (J. Madison), can effectively be resisted. Frequently an issue of this sort will come before the Court clad, so to speak, in sheep's clothing: the potential of the asserted principle to effect important change in the equilibrium of power is not immediately evident, and must be discerned by a careful and perceptive analysis. But this wolf comes as a wolf.

[B]y the application of this statute in the present case, Congress has effectively com-pelled a criminal investigation of a high-level appointee of the President in connection with his actions arising out of a bitter power dispute between the President and the Legislative Branch. Mr. Olson may or may not be guilty of a crime; we do not know. But we do know that the investigation of him has been commenced, not necessarily because the President or his authorized subordinates believe it is in the interest of the United States, in the sense that it warrants the diversion of resources from other efforts, and is worth the cost in money and in possible damage to other governmental interests; and not even, leaving aside those normally considered factors, because the President or his authorized subordinates necessarily believe that an investigation is likely to unearth a violation worth prosecuting; but only because the Attorney General cannot affirm, as Congress demands, that there are no reasonable grounds to believe that further investigation is warranted. The decisions regarding the scope of that further investigation, its duration, and, finally, whether or not prosecution should ensue, are likewise beyond the control of the President and his subor-dinates. If to describe this case is not to decide it, the concept of a government of separate and coordinate powers no longer has meaning.

To repeat, Article II, § 1, cl. 1, of the Constitution provides: "The executive Power shall be vested in a President of the United States." This does not mean *some of* the executive power, but *all of* the executive power. It seems to me, therefore, that the decision of the Court of Appeals invalidating the present statute must be upheld on fundamental separation-of-powers principles if the following two questions are answered affirmatively: (1) Is the conduct of a criminal prosecution (and of an investigation to decide whether to prosecute) the exercise of purely executive power? (2) Does the statute deprive the President of the United States of exclusive control over the exercise of that power? Surprising to say, the Court appears to concede an affirmative answer to both questions, but seeks to avoid the inevitable conclusion that since the statute vests some purely executive power in a person who is not the President of the United States it is void.

Governmental investigation and prosecution of crimes is a quintessentially executive function. As for the second question, whether the statute before us deprives the President of exclusive control over that quintessentially executive activity: *** That is indeed the whole object of the statute. *** [I]t is ultimately irrelevant *how much* the statute reduces Presidential control. *** It is not for us to determine, and we have never presumed to determine, how much of the purely executive powers of government must be within the full control of the President. The Constitution prescribes that they *all* are.

> **Take Note**
>
> Justice Scalia here advances the theory of the "Unitary Executive." What are the virtues of that view? What are the drawbacks?

The utter incompatibility of the Court's approach with our constitutional traditions can be made more clear, perhaps, by applying it to the powers of the other two branches. Is it conceivable that if Congress passed a statute depriving itself of less than full and entire control over some insignificant area of legislation, we would inquire whether the matter was "so central to the functioning of the Legislative Branch" as really to require complete control, or whether the statute gives Congress "sufficient control over the surrogate legislator to ensure that Congress is able to perform its constitutionally assigned duties"? Of course we would have none of that. *** Or to bring the point closer to home, consider a statute giving to non-Article III judges just a tiny bit of purely judicial power in a relatively insignificant field, with substantial control, though not total control, in the courts ***. We would say that our "constitutionally assigned duties" include complete control over all exercises of the judicial power.

Is it unthinkable that the President should have such exclusive power, even when alleged crimes by him or his close associates are at issue? No more so than that Congress should have the exclusive power of legislation, even when what is at issue is its own exemption from the burdens of certain laws. See Civil Rights Act of 1964, Title VII (prohibiting "employers," not defined to include the United States, from discriminating on the basis of race, color, religion, sex, or national origin). No more so than that this Court should have the exclusive power to pronounce the final decision on justiciable cases and controversies, even those pertaining to the constitutionality of a statute reducing the salaries of the Justices. See *United States v. Will*, 449 U.S. 200, 211-217 (1980). A system of separate and coordinate powers necessarily involves an acceptance of exclusive power that can theoretically be abused. *** While the separation of powers may prevent us from righting every wrong, it does so in order to ensure that we do not lose liberty. The checks against any branch's abuse of its exclusive powers are twofold: First, retaliation by one of the other branch's use of *its* exclusive powers: Congress, for example, can impeach the executive who willfully fails to enforce the laws ***. Second, and ultimately, there is the political check that the people will replace those in the political branches *** who are guilty of abuse. Political pressures produced special prosecutors—for Teapot Dome and for Watergate, for example—long before this statute created the independent counsel.

The Court has, nonetheless, replaced the clear constitutional prescription that the executive power belongs to the President with a "balancing test." What are the standards to determine how the balance is to be struck, that is, how much removal of Presidential power is too much? *** Once we depart from the text of the Constitution, just where short of that do we stop? The most amazing feature of the Court's opinion is that it does not even purport to give an answer. It simply announces, with no analysis, that the ability to control the decision whether to investigate and prosecute the President's closest advisers, and indeed the President himself, is not "so central to the functioning of the Executive Branch" as to be constitutionally required to be within the President's control. *** Evidently, the governing standard is to be what might be called the unfettered wisdom of a majority of this Court, revealed to an obedient people on a case-by-case basis. This is not only not the government of laws that the Constitution established; it is not a government of laws at all.

[T]he independent counsel is not an inferior officer because she is not subordinate to any officer in the Executive Branch (indeed, not even to the President). *** To be sure, it is not a *sufficient* condition for "inferior" officer status that one be subordinate to a principal officer. Even an officer who is subordinate to a department head can be a principal officer. *** But it is surely a *necessary* condition for inferior officer status that the officer be subordinate to another officer. *** Because appellant is not subordinate to another officer, she is not an "inferior" officer and her appointment other than by the President with the advice and consent of the Senate is unconstitutional.

[T]he restrictions upon the removal of the independent counsel also violate our established precedent dealing with that specific subject. *** Since our 1935 decision in _Humphrey's Executor_—which was considered by many at the time the product of an activist, anti-New Deal Court bent on reducing the power of President Franklin Roosevelt—it has been established that the line of permissible restriction upon removal of principal officers lies at the point at which the powers exercised by those officers are no longer purely executive. *** It has often been observed, correctly in my view, that the line between "purely executive" functions and "quasi-legislative" or "quasi-judicial" functions is not a clear one or even a rational one. But at least it permitted the identification of certain officers, and certain agencies, whose functions were entirely within the control of the President. *** Today, however, _Humphrey's Executor_ is swept into the dustbin of repudiated constitutional principles. *** "[O]ur present considered view" is simply that any executive officer's removal can be restricted, so long as the President remains "able to accomplish his constitutional role." There are now no lines. If the removal of a prosecutor, the virtual embodiment of the power to "take care that the laws be faithfully executed," can be restricted, what officer's removal cannot? This is an open invitation for Congress to experiment. What about a special Assistant Secretary of State, with responsibility for one very narrow area of foreign policy, who would not only have to be confirmed by the Senate but could also be removed only pursuant to certain carefully designed restrictions? Could this possibly render the President "[un]able to accomplish his constitutional role"? Or a special Assistant Secretary of Defense for Procurement? The possibilities are endless, and the Court does not understand what the separation of powers, what "[a]mbition ... counteract[ing] ambition," The Federalist No. 51 (J. Madison), is all about, if it does not expect Congress to try them.

> **Food for Thought**
>
> Do you agree that Congress is likely to use the power that the Court permits here to damage the Presidency? What other limits might there be on Congress's power to do so?

Under our system of government, the primary check against prosecutorial abuse is a political one. The prosecutors who exercise this awesome discretion are selected and can be removed by a President, whom the people have trusted enough to elect. Moreover, when crimes are not investigated and prosecuted fairly, nonselectively, with a reasonable sense of proportion, the President pays the cost in political damage to his administration. ***

That is the system of justice the rest of us are entitled to, but what of that select class consisting of present or former high-level Executive Branch officials? *** An independent counsel is selected, and the scope of his or her authority prescribed, by a panel of judges. What if they are politically partisan, as judges have been known to be, and select a prosecutor antagonistic to the administration, or even to the particular individual who has been selected for this special treatment? *** The independent counsel thus selected proceeds to assemble a staff. [I]n the nature of things this has to be done by finding lawyers who are willing to lay aside their current careers for an indeterminate amount of time, to take on a job that has no prospect of permanence and little prospect for promotion. One thing is certain, however: it involves investigating and perhaps prosecuting a particular individual.

> **Food for Thought**
>
> Justice Scalia here effectively predicted the controversy that would arise over Independent Counsel Kenneth Starr's investigation of President Clinton. Does subsequent history vindicate Justice Scalia's view? If so, as a matter of policy? Of constitutional law?

*** What would be the reaction if, in an area not covered by this statute, the Justice Department posted a public notice inviting applicants to assist in an investigation and possible prosecution of a certain prominent person? [T]o be sure, the investigation must relate to the area of criminal offense specified by the life-tenured judges. But [should] the independent counsel or his or her staff come up with something beyond that scope, nothing prevents him or her from asking the judges to expand his or her authority.

The mini-Executive that is the independent counsel, [operating] in an area where so little is law and so much is discretion, is intentionally cut off from the unifying influence of the Justice Department, and from the perspective that multiple responsibilities provide. What would normally be regarded as a technical violation (there are no rules defining such things), may in his or her small world assume the proportions of an indictable offense. What would normally be regarded as an investigation that has reached the level of pursuing such picayune matters that it should be concluded, may to him or her be an investigation that ought to go on for another year. How frightening it must be to have your own independent counsel and staff appointed, with nothing else to do but to investigate you until investigation is no longer worthwhile—with whether it is worthwhile not depending upon what such judgments usually hinge on, competing responsibilities. And to have that counsel and staff decide, with no basis for comparison, whether what you have done is bad enough, willful enough, and provable enough, to warrant an indictment. How admirable the constitutional system that provides the means to avoid such a distortion. And how unfortunate the judicial decision that has permitted it.

———————

Points for Discussion

a. The Appointments Clause

According to the Court's test, is the Deputy Secretary of Defense for War Planning a principal or inferior officer? If the latter, what does that suggest about the Court's test?

b. Functionalism vs. Formalism

The Court took a functionalist approach to the separation of powers issues presented, asking whether the arrangement that Congress created is inconsistent with the values that the separation of powers is designed to protect and a properly functioning governmental system. Justice Scalia, in contrast, took a formalist approach to the issues, asking whether the independent counsel exercises "executive" power and then concluding that the Constitution imposes rigid limits on Congress's power to limit the President's control over officials who exercise such power. But Justice Scalia also offered, in the final few paragraphs of his opinion, a functional response to the Court's argument. Who gave a more convincing assessment of the likely effect of the independent counsel regime on the operation of the separation of powers between Congress and the Executive Branch?

c. Need for an Independent Counsel

The Ethics in Government Act was a response to the Watergate scandal, and the independent counsel provisions were a specific response to President Nixon's termination of the first special prosecutor whom his Attorney General had appointed to investigate the scandal. In enacting the statute, Congress presumably concluded that the President faced a conflict of interest in deciding whether to permit investigation of wrong-doing by high-ranking Executive Branch officials, including the President.

How does Justice Scalia address the concern that an independent counsel is needed to prosecute government officials within the executive branch? Is his reasoning convincing? It apparently was persuasive, eventually, to Congress. The Ethics in Government Act expired in 1992. Congress renewed it in 1994, but then let it expire again in 1999, after independent counsels had pursued investigations of a number of executive branch officials, including President William Jefferson Clinton. Scholar Erwin Chemerinsky writes:

> "The ultimate question is whether the benefits in terms of independent investigations outweigh the costs with regard to the loss of accountability when there is a special prosecutor. After Watergate [when there was no independent counsel to investigate Nixon administration officials], the answer seemed clearly yes. Now after the Whitewater special prosecutor [who investigated President Clinton and other members of the Clinton administration] *** the answer to many seems clearly no. Not surprisingly, President Clinton is among those who have experienced this shift in views. The independent counsel law expired in 1992, and it was not renewed until 1994, when President Clinton took office and supported it. It is reported that subsequently President Clinton told [former Senator Majority Leader] Bob Dole, an opponent of renewing the Ethics in Government Act, "You were right and I was wrong on the independent counsel."

Erwin Chemerinsky, *Learning the Wrong Lessons from History: Why There Must be an Independent Counsel Law*, 5 WTR Widener L. Symp. J. 1, 9 (2000).

d. No Error or Harmless Error?

Did the Court conclude that no separation of powers violation had occurred or just that any separation of powers violation was so minor that it was harmless? Exactly what standard does the Court establish for application to future cases?

———————

Free Enterprise Fund v. Public Company Accounting Oversight Board

130 S.Ct. 3138 (2010)

Chief Justice ROBERTS delivered the opinion of the Court.

[The Sarbanes-Oxley Act of 2002, 116 Stat. 745, created a new five-member "Public Company Accounting Oversight Board" to supervise the accounting industry. The Board has five members, appointed to 5-year terms by the Securities and Exchange Commission (SEC). The Board has power to enforce the Act, the rules of the Board, and provisions of the securities laws relating to the preparation and issuance of audit reports and the obligations and liabilities of accountants. 15 U.S.C. § 7215(b)(1). The Board also may impose sanctions for violations, including revocation of a firm's registration and money penalties up to $15 million. *Id.* § 7215(c)(4).

The SEC has supervisory authority over the Board's functions, but can remove Board members only "for good cause shown," including willful violation of the Act, willful abuse of authority, or failing to enforce compliance with applicable rule and standards. *Id.* § 7217(d)(3). The Commissioners who make up the SEC have similar protection for their positions. On this point, the Court said: "The parties agree that the Commissioners cannot themselves be removed by the President except under the *Humphrey's Executor* standard of 'inefficiency, neglect of duty, or malfeasance in office,' 295 U.S. 602, 620 (1935) (internal quotation marks omitted), and we decide the case with that understanding."]

Our Constitution divided the "powers of the new Federal Government into three defined categories, Legislative, Executive, and Judicial." *INS v. Chadha*, 462 U.S. 919, 951 (1983). Article II vests "[t]he executive Power . . . in a President of the United States of America," who must "take Care that the Laws be faithfully executed." Art. II, § 1, cl. 1; *id.*, § 3. In light of "[t]he impossibility that one man should be able to perform all the great business of the State," the Constitution provides for executive officers to "assist the supreme Magistrate in discharging the duties of his trust." 30 Writings of George Washington 334 (J. Fitzpatrick ed.1939).

Since 1789, the Constitution has been understood to empower the President to keep these officers accountable—by removing them from office, if necessary. See generally *Myers v. United States*, 272 U.S. 52 (1926). This Court has determined, however, that this authority is not without limit. In *Humphrey's Executor v. United States*, 295 U.S. 602 (1935), we held that Congress can, under certain circumstances, create independent agencies run by principal officers appointed by the President, whom the President may not remove at will but only for good cause. Likewise, in *United States v. Perkins*, 116 U.S. 483 (1886), and *Morrison v. Olson*, 487 U.S. 654 (1988), the Court sustained similar restrictions on the power of principal executive officers—themselves responsible to the President—to remove their own inferiors. The parties do not ask us to reexamine any of these precedents, and we do not do so.

We are asked, however, to consider a new situation not yet encountered by the Court. The question is whether these separate layers of protection may be combined. May the President be restricted in his ability to remove a principal officer, who is in turn restricted in his ability to remove an inferior officer, even though that inferior officer determines the policy and enforces the laws of the United States?

We hold that such multilevel protection from removal is contrary to Article II's vesting of the executive power in the President. The President cannot "take Care that the Laws be faithfully executed" if he cannot oversee the faithfulness of the officers who execute them. Here the President cannot remove an officer who enjoys more than one level of good-cause protection, even if the President determines that the officer is neglecting his duties or discharging them improperly. That judgment is instead committed to another officer, who may or may not agree with the President's determination, and whom the President cannot remove simply because that officer disagrees with him. This contravenes the President's "constitutional obligation to ensure the faithful execution of the laws." *Morrison*, 487 U.S. at 693.

The removal of executive officers was discussed extensively in Congress when the first executive departments were created. The view that "prevailed, as most consonant to the text of the Constitution" and "to the requisite responsibility and harmony in the Executive Department," was that the executive power included a power to oversee executive officers through removal; because that traditional executive power was not "expressly taken away, it remained with the President." Letter from James Madison to Thomas Jefferson (June 30, 1789), 16 Documentary History of the First Federal Congress 893 (2004). "This Decision of 1789 provides contemporaneous and weighty evidence of the Constitution's meaning since many of the Members of the First Congress had taken part in framing that instrument." *Bowsher v. Synar*, 478 U.S. 714, 723-724 (1986). And it soon became the "settled and well understood construction of the Constitution." *Ex parte Hennen*, 38 U.S. 230 (1839).

As explained, we have previously upheld limited restrictions on the President's removal power [in *Perkins*, *Humphrey's Executor*, and *Morrison*]. In those cases, however, only one level of protected tenure separated the President from an officer exercising executive power. It was the President—or a subordinate he could remove at will—who decided whether the officer's conduct merited removal under the good-cause standard.

The Act before us does something quite different. It not only protects Board members from removal except for good cause, but withdraws from the President any decision on whether that good cause exists. That decision is vested instead in other tenured officers—the Commissioners—none of whom is subject to the President's direct control. The result is a Board that is not accountable to the President, and a President who is not responsible for the Board.

The added layer of tenure protection makes a difference. Without a layer of insulation between the Commission and the Board, the Commission could remove a Board member at any time, and therefore would be fully responsible for what the Board does. The President could then hold the Commission to account for its supervision of the Board, to the same extent that he may hold the Commission to account for everything else it does.

A second level of tenure protection changes the nature of the President's review. Now the Commission cannot remove a Board member at will. The President therefore cannot hold the Commission fully accountable for the Board's conduct, to the same extent that he may hold the Commission accountable for everything else that it does. The Commissioners are not responsible for the Board's actions. They are only responsible for their own determination of whether the Act's rigorous good-cause standard is met. And even if the President disagrees with their determination, he is powerless to intervene—unless that determination is so unreasonable as to constitute "inefficiency, neglect of duty, or malfeasance in office." *Humphrey's Executor*, 295 U.S., at 620.

This novel structure does not merely add to the Board's independence, but transforms it. Neither the President, nor anyone directly responsible to him, nor even an officer whose conduct he may review only for good cause, has full control over the Board. The President is stripped of the power our precedents have preserved, and his ability to execute the laws—by holding his subordinates accountable for their conduct—is impaired.

That arrangement is contrary to Article II's vesting of the executive power in the President.

> **Food for Thought**
>
> Why would Congress enact a provision that insulates the Board members from supervision in this manner? Do the possible benefits of insulating the Board members from political oversight come at any possible costs?

Without the ability to oversee the Board, or to attribute the Board's failings to those whom he *can* oversee, the President is no longer the judge of the Board's conduct. He is not the one who decides whether Board members are abusing their offices or neglecting their duties. He can neither ensure that the laws are faithfully executed, nor be held responsible for a Board member's breach of faith. This violates the basic principle that the President "cannot delegate ultimate responsibility or the active obligation to supervise that goes with it," because Article II "makes a single President responsible for the actions of the Executive Branch." *Clinton v. Jones*, 520 U.S. 681, 712-713 (1997) (BREYER, J., concurring in judgment).

Indeed, if allowed to stand, this dispersion of responsibility could be multiplied. If Congress can shelter the bureaucracy behind two layers of good-cause tenure, why not a third? At oral argument, the Government was unwilling to concede that even *five* layers between the President and the Board would be too many. The officers of such an agency— safely encased within a Matryoshka doll of tenure protections—would be immune from Presidential oversight, even as they exercised power in the people's name.

Perhaps an individual President might find advantages in tying his own hands. But the separation of powers does not depend on the views of individual Presidents, nor on whether "the encroached-upon branch approves the encroachment," *New York v. United States*, 505 U.S. 144, 182 (1992). The President can always choose to restrain himself in his dealings with subordinates. He cannot, however, choose to bind his successors by diminishing their powers, nor can he escape responsibility for his choices by pretending that they are not his own.

The diffusion of power carries with it a diffusion of accountability. The people do not vote for the "Officers of the United States." Art. II, § 2, cl. 2. They instead look to the President to guide the "assistants or deputies . . . subject to his superintendence." The Federalist No. 72, p. 487 (J. Cooke ed. 1961) (A. Hamilton). Without a clear and effective chain of command, the public cannot "determine on whom the blame or the punishment of a pernicious measure, or series of pernicious measures ought really to fall." *Id.*, No. 70, at 476 (same). That is why the Framers sought to ensure that "those who are employed in the execution of the law will be in their proper situation, and the chain of dependence be preserved; the lowest officers, the middle grade, and the highest, will depend, as they ought, on the President, and the President on the community." 1 Annals of Cong., at 499 (J. Madison).

By granting the Board executive power without the Executive's oversight, this Act subverts the President's ability to ensure that the laws are faithfully executed—as well as the public's ability to pass judgment on his efforts. The Act's restrictions are incompatible with the Constitution's separation of powers.

Petitioners' complaint argued that the Board's "freedom from Presidential oversight

Food for Thought

Isn't the Court's argument in this paragraph also an argument against *any* limits on the President's authority to remove any officer? If so, why doesn't the Court revisit *Humphrey's Executor* and *Morrison*?

and control" rendered it "and all power and authority exercised by it" in violation of the Constitution. We reject such a broad holding. Instead, we agree with the Government that the unconstitutional tenure provisions are severable from the remainder of the statute. *** The Sarbanes-Oxley Act remains "fully operative as a law" with these tenure restrictions excised.

Petitioners [also] argue that Board members are principal officers requiring Presidential appointment with the Senate's advice and consent. We held in *Edmond v. United States,* 520 U.S. 651 (1997), that "[w]hether one is an 'inferior' officer depends on whether he has a superior," and that "'inferior officers' are officers whose work is directed and supervised at some level" by other officers appointed by the President with the Senate's consent. In particular, we noted that "[t]he power to remove officers" at will and without cause "is a

> **Take Note**
>
> Is the standard that the Court announces here for distinguishing between principal and inferior officers the same standard that the Court applied in *Morrison*? Does it give sufficient guidance for making the distinction? Does it suggest that all officers except Heads of Departments are inferior officers?

powerful tool for control" of an inferior. *Id.*, at 664. As explained above, the statutory restrictions on the Commission's power to remove Board members are unconstitutional and void. Given that the Commission is properly viewed, under the Constitution, as possessing the power to remove Board members at will, and given the Commission's other oversight authority, we have no hesitation in concluding that under *Edmond* the Board members are inferior officers whose appointment Congress may permissibly vest in a "Hea[d] of Departmen[t]."

Justice BREYER, with whom Justice STEVENS, Justice GINSBURG, and Justice SOTO-MAYOR join, dissenting.

In answering the question presented, we cannot look to more specific constitutional text, such as the text of the Appointments Clause or the Presentment Clause, upon which the Court has relied in other separation-of-powers cases. That is because, with the exception of the general "vesting" and "take care" language, the Constitution is completely "silent with respect to the power of removal from office." *Ex parte Hennen,* 13 Pet. 230, 258 (1839); see also *Morrison v. Olson,* 487 U.S. 654, 723 (1988) (SCALIA, J., dissenting) ("There is, of course, no provision in the Constitution stating who may remove executive officers.").

Nor does history offer significant help. The President's power to remove Executive Branch officers "was not discussed in the Constitutional Convention." *Myers v. United States,* 272 U.S. 52, 109-110 (1926). The First Congress enacted federal statutes that limited the President's ability to *oversee* Executive Branch officials, including the Comptroller of the United States, federal district attorneys (precursors to today's United States Attorneys), and, to a lesser extent, the Secretary of the Treasury. But those statutes did not directly limit the President's authority to *remove* any of those officials—"a subject" that was "much disputed" during "the early history of this government," "and upon which a great diversity of opinion was entertained." *Hennen.* Scholars, like Members of this Court, have continued to disagree, not only about the inferences that should be drawn from the inconclusive historical record, but also about the nature of the original disagreement.

Nor does this Court's precedent fully answer the question presented. At least it does not clearly invalidate the provision in dispute. In *Myers*, the Court invalidated—for the first and only time—a congressional statute on the ground that it unduly limited the President's authority to remove an Executive Branch official. But soon thereafter the Court expressly disapproved most of *Myers'* broad reasoning. See *Humphrey's Executor*, 295 U.S., at 626-627. Moreover, the Court has since said that "the essence of the decision in *Myers* was the judgment that the Constitution prevents Congress from '*draw[ing] to itself* . . . the power to remove or the right to participate in the exercise of that power.' " *Morrison* (emphasis added). And that feature of the statute—a feature that would *aggrandize* the power of Congress—is not present here. Congress has not granted itself any role in removing the members of the Accounting Board.

When previously deciding this kind of nontextual question, the Court has emphasized the importance of examining how a particular provision, taken in context, is likely to function. *** [T]oday vast numbers of statutes governing vast numbers of subjects, concerned with vast numbers of different problems, provide for, or foresee, their execution or administration through the work of administrators organized within many different kinds of administrative structures, exercising different kinds of administrative authority, to achieve their legislatively mandated objectives. And, given the nature of the Government's work, it is not surprising that administrative units come in many different shapes and sizes. The functional approach required by our precedents recognizes this administrative complexity and, more importantly, recognizes the various ways presidential power operates within this context—and the various ways in which a removal provision might affect that power.

[We should] conclude that the "for cause" restriction before us will not restrict presidential power significantly. For one thing, the restriction directly limits, not the President's power, but the power of an already independent agency. The Court seems to have forgotten that fact when it identifies its central constitutional problem: According to the Court, the President "is powerless to intervene" if he has determined that the Board members' "conduct merit[s] removal" because "[t]hat decision is vested instead in other tenured officers—the Commissioners—none of whom is subject to the President's direct control." But so long as the President is *legitimately* foreclosed from removing the *Commissioners* except for cause (as the majority assumes), nullifying the Commission's power to remove Board members only for cause will not resolve the problem the Court has identified: The President will *still* be "powerless to intervene" by removing the Board members if the Commission reasonably decides not to do so.

In other words, the Court fails to show why *two* layers of "for cause" protection—Layer One insulating the Commissioners from the President, and Layer Two insulating the Board from the Commissioners—impose any more serious limitation upon the *President's* powers than *one* layer. Consider the four scenarios that might arise:

> 1. The President and the Commission both want to keep a Board member in office. Neither layer is relevant.

2. The President and the Commission both want to dismiss a Board member. Layer Two stops them both from doing so without cause. The President's ability to remove the Commission (Layer One) is irrelevant, for he and the Commission are in agreement.

3. The President wants to dismiss a Board member, but the Commission wants to keep the member. Layer One allows the Commission to make that determination notwithstanding the President's contrary view. Layer Two is irrelevant because the Commission does not seek to remove the Board member.

4. The President wants to keep a Board member, but the Commission wants to dismiss the Board member. Here, Layer Two *helps the President*, for it hinders the Commission's ability to dismiss a Board member whom the President wants to keep in place.

Thus, the majority's decision to eliminate only *Layer Two* accomplishes virtually nothing. And that is because a removal restriction's effect upon presidential power depends not on the presence of a "double-layer" of for-cause removal, as the majority pretends, but rather on the real-world nature of the President's relationship with the Commission. If the President confronts a Commission that seeks to *resist* his policy preferences—a distinct possibility when, as here, a Commission's membership must reflect both political parties, 15 U.S.C. § 78d(a)—the restriction on the *Commission's* ability to remove a Board member is either irrelevant (as in scenario 3) or may actually help the President (as in scenario 4). And if the President faces a Commission that seeks to implement his policy preferences, Layer One is irrelevant, for the President and Commission see eye to eye.

Points for Discussion

a. Differing Views of *Humphrey's Executor* and *Morrison v. Olson*?

Both the majority and dissent recognized that *Humphrey's Executor* and *Morrison* allow Congress to impose some restrictions on the President's ability to remove executive branch officials. Is it a fair inference that the majority was skeptical about the basis for *Humphrey's Executor* and *Morrison* and did not want to carry their principles further, whereas the dissent agreed with those decisions and saw no harm in extending them?

b. Functional Considerations

The dissent recommended that, when the Court is confronted with questions about the constitutionality of a statute that the text of the Constitution does not answer, the Court should consider how the statute "taken in context, is likely to function." Do you have confidence in the Court's ability to make such an assessment, and to create workable rules of constitutional law based on such an assessment? Conversely, is the Court's approach problematic because it did not dwell on such considerations?

E. Bills of Attainder

Article I, section 9, clause 3 provides that Congress cannot pass a "bill of attainder." Article I, section 10, clause 1 imposes the same prohibition on the states. As understood in modern times, a bill of attainder is a legislative act that imposes a forbidden type of punishment. The Supreme Court has said: "In deciding whether a statute inflicts forbidden punishment, we have recognized three necessary inquiries: (1) whether the challenged statute falls within the historical meaning of legislative punishment; (2) whether the statute, 'viewed in terms of the type and severity of burdens imposed, reasonably can be said to further nonpunitive legislative purposes'; and (3) whether the legislative record 'evinces a congressional intent to punish.' " *Selective Service System v. Minnesota Public Interest Research Group*, 468 U.S. 841, 852 (1984) (quoting *Nixon v. Administrator of General Services*, 433 U.S. 425, 473, 475-476, 478 (1977)). Impermissible legislative punishments historically have included the death penalty, imprisonment, banishment, confiscation of property, and bars to participating in specific employments and professions. *See id.* For example, suppose that Congress, following the attacks of September 11, 2001, had passed a law saying: "Osama bin Laden, when captured, shall be immediately put to death for his role in the attacks." This hypothetical law would be a bill of attainder, and it would be unconstitutional.

Bills of attainder, in a sense, violate the separation of powers. In passing a bill of attainder, Congress would be seeking to serve not only a legislative function, but also an executive and judicial function. In the example, Congress would be deciding that Bin Laden should face the prospect of punishment (instead of leaving this decision to the executive branch) and would be deciding what punishment he deserves (instead of leaving this decision to the judiciary). Bills of attainder, of course, also deprive the person being punished of important individual rights, such as due process of law. (Recall that Justice Powell thought that the exercise of legislative power in *Chadha* was tantamount to a bill of attainder.)

> **Food for Thought**
>
> Litigants often challenge federal and state laws as being unconstitutional bills of attainder. Between 2000 and 2010, over 1100 reported cases addressed the Bill of Attainder clauses in Article I, sections 9 and 10. The courts, however, very rarely have determined that legislation actually violates these clauses. Does this mean that the clauses are not important?

Perhaps no bill of attainder could raise more serious separation of power questions than one aimed against the President of the United States. Congress not only would be asserting executive power, but would be using it against the Chief Executive. The following case considers whether this extreme use of a bill of attainder occurred when Congress acted to take custody of President Richard Nixon's papers and tape recordings. In reading the case, consider how the Court decides whether Congress acted to punish President Nixon.

———————

Nixon v. Administrator of General Services

433 U.S. 425 (1977)

Mr. Justice BRENNAN delivered the opinion of the Court.

Title I of Pub. L. 93-526, 88 Stat. 1695, the Presidential Recordings and Materials Preservation Act (hereafter Act), directs the Administrator of General Services, official of the Executive Branch, to take custody of the Presidential papers and tape recordings of appellant, former President Richard M. Nixon, and promulgate regulations that (1) provide for the orderly processing and screening by Executive Branch archivists of such materials for the purpose of returning to appellant those that are personal and private in nature, and (2) determine the terms and conditions upon which public access may eventually be had to those materials that are retained. The question for decision is whether Title I is unconstitutional on its face as a violation of *** the Bill of Attainder Clause.

The materials at issue consist of some 42 million pages of documents and some 880 tape recordings of conversations. Upon his resignation, appellant directed Government archivists to pack and ship the materials to him in California. This shipment was delayed when the Watergate Special Prosecutor advised President Ford of his continuing need for the materials. At the same time, President Ford requested that the Attorney General give his opinion respecting ownership of the materials. The Attorney General advised that the historical practice of former Presidents and the absence of any governing statute to the contrary supported ownership in the appellant. ***

> **Make the Connection**
>
> In Chapter 5, we considered how President Nixon sought to invoke executive privilege to shield disclosure of tape recordings. This case is related. Congress passed the law at issue here because it was concerned that President Nixon might destroy some of his papers and tape recordings, including materials that might be relevant to the Watergate investigation.

[The Court first rejected former President Nixon's claim that the Act violated the separation of powers and his assertion of executive privilege.]

[Appellant's] argument is that Congress acted on the premise that he had engaged in "misconduct," was an "unreliable custodian" of his own documents, and generally was deserving of a "legislative judgment of blameworthiness." Thus, he argues, the Act is pervaded with the key features of a bill of attainder: a law that legislatively determines guilt and inflicts punishment upon an identifiable individual without provision of the protections of a judicial trial.

Appellant's argument relies almost entirely upon *United States v. Brown*, 381 U.S. 437 (1965), the Court's most recent decision addressing the scope of the Bill of Attainder Clause. It is instructive, therefore, to sketch the broad outline of that case. *Brown* invalidated § 504 of the Labor-Management Reporting and Disclosure Act of 1959, that made it a crime for a Communist Party member to serve as an officer of a labor union. After detailing the infamous history of bills of attainder, the Court found that the Bill of Attainder Clause was an important ingredient of the doctrine of "separation of powers," one of the organizing principles of our system of government.   381 U.S., at 442-443.   Just as Art. III confines the Judiciary to the task of adjudicating concrete "cases or controversies," so too the Bill of Attainder Clause was found to "reflect . . . the Framers' belief that the Legislative Branch is not so well suited as politically independent judges and juries to the task of ruling upon the blameworthiness of, and levying appropriate punishment upon, specific persons." *Id.* at 445.   <u>Brown</u> thus held that § 504 worked a bill of attainder by focusing upon easily identifiable members of a class— members of the Communist Party—and imposing on them the sanction of mandatory forfeiture of a job or office, long deemed to be punishment with the contemplation of the Bill of Attainder Clause.

In essence, he argues that <u>Brown</u> establishes that the Constitution is offended whenever a law imposes undesired consequences on an individual or on a class that is not defined at a proper level of generality.   The Act in question therefore is faulted for singling out appellant, as opposed to all other Presidents or members of the Government, for disfavored treatment.

Appellant's characterization of the meaning of a bill of attainder obviously proves far too much.   By arguing that an individual or defined group is attainted whenever he or it is compelled to bear burdens which the individual or group dislikes, appellant removes the anchor that ties the bill of attainder guarantee to realistic conceptions of classification and punishment.   His view would cripple the very process of legislating, for any individual or group that is made the subject of adverse legislation can complain that the lawmakers could and should have defined the relevant affected class at a greater level of generality.   Furthermore, every person or group made subject to legislation which he or it finds burdensome may subjectively feel, and can complain, that he or it is being subjected to unwarranted punishment.   However expansive the prohibition against bills of attainder, it surely was not intended to serve as a variant of the equal protection doctrine, invalidating every Act of Congress or the States that legislatively burdens some persons or groups but not all other plausible individuals.   In short, while the Bill of Attainder Clause serves as an important "bulwark against tyranny," *United States v. Brown,* 381 U.S., at 443, it does not do so by limiting Congress to the choice of legislating for the universe, or legislating only benefits, or not legislating at all.

Thus, in the present case, the Act's specificity—the fact that it refers to appellant by name—does not automatically offend the Bill of Attainder Clause.   Indeed, viewed in context, the focus of the enactment can be fairly and rationally understood.   It is true that Title I deals exclusively with appellant's papers.   But Title II casts a wider net by establishing a special commission to study and recommend appropriate legislation regarding the preservation of the records of future Presidents and all other federal officials.   In this light, Congress' action to preserve only appellant's records is easily explained by the fact that at the time of the Act's passage, only his materials demanded immediate attention.   The Presidential papers of all former Presidents from Hoover to Johnson were already housed in functioning Presidential libraries.   Congress had reason for concern solely with the preservation of appellant's materials, for he alone had entered into a depository agreement, the

Nixon-Sampson agreement, which by its terms called for the destruction of certain of the materials. Indeed, as the federal appellees argue, "appellant's depository agreement . . . created an imminent danger that the tape recordings would be destroyed if appellant, who had contracted phlebitis, were to die." In short, appellant constituted a legitimate class of one, and this provides a basis for Congress' decision to proceed with dispatch with respect to his materials while accepting the status of his predecessors' papers and ordering the further consideration of generalized standards to govern his successors.

Moreover, even if the specificity element were deemed to be satisfied here, the Bill of Attainder Clause would not automatically be implicated. Forbidden legislative punishment is not involved merely because the Act imposes burdensome consequences. Rather, we must inquire further whether Congress, by lodging appellant's materials in the custody of the General Services Administration pending their screening by Government archivists and the promulgation of further regulations, "inflict(ed) punishment" within the constitutional proscription against bills of attainder. *United States v. Lovett*, 328 U.S. 303, 315 (1946)

In England a bill of attainder originally connoted a parliamentary Act sentencing a named individual or identifiable members of a group to death. Article I, § 9, however, also proscribes enactments originally characterized as bills of pains and penalties, that is, legislative Acts inflicting punishment other than execution. Generally addressed to persons considered disloyal to the Crown or State, "pains and penalties" historically consisted of a wide array of punishments: commonly included were imprisonment, banishment, and the punitive confiscation of property by the sovereign. Our country's own experience with bills of attainder resulted in the addition of another sanction to the list of impermissible legislative punishments: a legislative enactment barring designated individuals or groups from participation in specified employments or vocations, a mode of punishment commonly employed against those legislatively branded as disloyal. See, e.g., *Cummings v. Missouri*, 71 U.S. (4 Wall.) 277, 323 (1867) (barring clergymen from ministry in the absence of subscribing to a loyalty oath); *United States v. Lovett* (barring named individuals from Government employment); *United States v. Brown* (barring Communist Party members from offices in labor unions).

Needless to say, appellant cannot claim to have suffered any of these forbidden deprivations at the hands of the Congress. While it is true that Congress ordered the General Services Administration to retain control over records that appellant claims as his property, § 105 of the Act makes provision for an award by the District Court of "just compensation." This undercuts even a colorable contention that the Government has punitively confiscated appellant's property, for the "owner (thereby) is to be put in the same position monetarily as he would have occupied if his property has not been taken." *United States v. Reynolds*, 397 U.S. 14, 16 (1970). Thus, no feature of the challenged Act falls within the historical meaning of legislative punishment.

But our inquiry is not ended by the determination that the Act imposes no punishment traditionally judged to be prohibited by the Bill of Attainder Clause. Our treatment of the scope of the Clause has never precluded the possibility that new burdens and deprivations might be legislatively fashioned that are inconsistent with the bill of attainder guarantee.

The Court, therefore, often has looked beyond mere historical experience and has applied a functional test of the existence of punishment, analyzing whether the law under challenge, viewed in terms of the type and severity of burdens imposed, reasonably can be said to further nonpunitive legislative purposes. Where such legitimate legislative purposes do not appear, it is reasonable to conclude that punishment of individuals disadvantaged by the enactment was the purpose of the decisionmakers.

Application of the functional approach to this case leads to rejection of appellant's argument that the Act rests upon a congressional determination of his blameworthiness and a desire to punish him. For, as noted previously, legitimate justifications for passage of the Act are readily apparent. First, in the face of the Nixon-Sampson agreement which expressly contemplated the destruction of some of appellant's materials, Congress stressed the need to preserve "[i]nformation included in the materials of former President Nixon [that] is needed to complete the prosecutions of Watergate-related crimes." H.R. Rep. No. 93-1507, p. 2 (1974). Second, again referring to the Nixon-Sampson agreement, Congress expressed its desire to safeguard the "public interest in gaining appropriate access to materials of the Nixon Presidency which are of general historical significance. The information in these materials will be of great value to the political health and vitality of the United States." *Ibid.* Indeed, these same objectives are stated in the text of the Act itself, § 104(a), where Congress instructs the General Services Administration to promulgate regulations that further these ends and at the same time protect the constitutional and legal rights of any individual adversely affected by the Administrator's retention of appellant's materials.

A third recognized test of punishment is strictly a motivational one: inquiring whether the legislative record evinces a congressional intent to punish. See, e.g., *United States v. Lovett*, 328 U.S., at 308-314. The District Court unequivocally found: "There is no evidence presented to us, nor is there any to be found in the legislative record, to indicate that Congress' design was to impose a penalty upon Mr. Nixon . . . as punishment for alleged past wrongdoings . . . . The legislative history leads to only one conclusion, namely, that the Act before us is regulatory and not punitive in character." We find no cogent reason for disagreeing with this conclusion.

————

Points for Discussion

a. Intent to Punish?

Why would Congress pass this law and single out President Nixon if it did not intend to punish him? Is the Court's definition of punishment unduly narrow?

b. Compensation

In 1998, President Nixon's estate and the United States finally reached a settlement in which the United States paid the estate $18 million for the confiscated papers and tape recordings, some of which may have been President Nixon's personal property. *See* Christopher Marquis, *Government Agrees to Pay Nixon Estate*, N.Y. Times, Jun. 13, 2000, at A18.

————

Executive Summary of This Chapter

The **non-delegation doctrine** says that Congress may not delegate its legislative authority to the executive branch. But Congress may give the executive branch discretion to promulgate rules and regulations so long as Congress guides the discretion with some "intelligible principle." *Whitman v. American Trucking* (2007).

Congress may exercise legislative power only by acting pursuant to the **Bicameralism and Presentment requirements** in Article I, § 7. *INS v. Chadha* (1983); *Clinton v. City of New York* (1998). Legislative power consists of actions that have "the purpose and effect of altering the legal rights, duties, and relations of persons outside of the legislative branch." *INS v. Chadha*.

In general, the President has the authority to **remove the heads of executive agencies** for any reason because the power to remove officials is incident to the power to appoint their replacements. *Myers v. United States* (1926). But this general power is qualified by Congress's power by statute to limit the President's power to remove to cases of good cause. Congress may restrict the President's power to remove in this fashion unless the "standard for removal by itself unduly trammels on executive authority." *Morrison v. Olson* (1988). In addition, Congress may not restrict the President's ability to remove a principal officer if that officer, in turn, is restricted in his ability to remove an inferior officer who is responsible for determining the policy and enforcing the laws of the United States. *Free Enterprise Fund v. Public Company Accounting Oversight Board* (2010). As a corollary to the foregoing rules, in general legislation cannot give executive powers to officials whom Congress can remove other than by impeachment and conviction. *Bowsher v. Synar* (1986).

The **Appointments Clause** permits Congress to vest in the courts the power of appointing inferior executive officers, such as prosecutors, and to give the courts some discretion in defining the nature and scope of the appointed officer's jurisdiction. *Morrison v. Olson* (1988). In addition, **Article III** permits federal judges to exercise **ministerial functions** not traditionally limited to the executive branch. *Morrison v. Olson* (1988).

In determining whether a law is a **bill of attainder**, the courts will consider precedent and a variety of factors, including (1) whether the challenged statute falls within the historical meaning of legislative punishment; (2) whether the statute furthers nonpunitive legislative purposes; and (3) whether the legislative record evinces an intent to punish. But a law is not a bill of attainder merely because it imposes burdens on only one person. *Nixon v. Admin. of General Services* (1977).

PART V: THE CONSTITUTION AND INDIVIDUAL RIGHTS

In the first six Chapters of this book, we considered what are conventionally known as the "structural" features of the Constitution—specifically, judicial review, federalism and the separation of powers. Many law schools bifurcate their constitutional law courses, focusing on structure in one course and on individual rights in the other. This book follows that basic approach. But it is important not to lose sight of the fact that the Framers viewed the Constitution's structural features as essential to preserving individual liberty, as well. With that caveat in mind, we turn directly to consideration of the Constitution's protections for individual rights.

CHAPTER 7

Introduction and Background

A. Early History

As we saw in Chapter 1, Anti-Federalist opponents of ratification of the Constitution were concerned that the federal government would become too powerful and pose a threat to individual liberties. To be sure, the Constitution as originally proposed did contain a few express limitations on federal authority. The most prominent among them were in Article I, § 9, which includes the Suspension Clause, which prohibits the suspension of habeas corpus except in cases of rebellion or invasion, and the prohibitions on bills of attainder and *ex post facto* laws.

> **FYI**
>
> An *ex post facto* law is a criminal law that purports to apply to conduct that occurred before the law's enactment. We considered bills of attainder in Chapter 6.

But the Constitution as originally proposed did not contain a more comprehensive group of provisions expressly guaranteeing individual liberties, such as a right to free speech and the freedom of the press. The omission of this guarantee—indeed, the absence of a complete Bill of Rights—was very controversial. At the Constitutional Convention, George Mason of Virginia and Elbridge Gerry of Massachusetts refused to sign the document for this reason. 2 *The Records of the Federal Convention of 1787* 646-47, 649 (Max Farrand, ed. 1911).

The Federalists initially responded to this objection during the ratification debates by asserting that a Bill of Rights was neither necessary nor a good idea. Speaking at the Pennsylvania ratifying convention on December 4, 1787, James Wilson, a former delegate to the Constitutional Convention, argued that the omission of a Bill of Rights was not a problem and, indeed, was a virtue. He explained:

> [A] bill of rights is by no means a necessary measure. In a government possessed of enumerated powers, such a measure would be not only unnecessary, but preposterous and dangerous. *** A bill of rights annexed to a constitution is an enumeration of the powers reserved. If we attempt an enumeration, every thing that is not enumerated is presumed to be given. The consequence is, that an imperfect enumeration would throw all implied power into the scale of the

government, and the rights of the people would be rendered incomplete. On the other hand, an imperfect enumeration of the powers of government reserves all implied power to the people; and by that means the constitution becomes incomplete. But of the two, it is much safer to run the risk on the side of the constitution; for an omission in the enumeration of the powers of government is neither so dangerous nor important.

2 *Elliot's Debates* 436 (1836). In other words, Federalists argued that the Constitution protects individual rights indirectly by limiting the powers of the federal government, and that the addition of a separate bill of rights might have suggested that the federal government's powers really were not truly limited. James Madison subsequently repeated these same arguments in The Federalist No. 84, which appeared in print on May 28, 1788. He addressed the omission of a Bill of Rights, stating: "I go further, and affirm that bills of rights, in the sense and to the extent in which they are contended for, are not only unnecessary in the proposed Constitution, but would even be dangerous. They would contain various exceptions to powers not granted; and, on this very account, would afford a colorable pretext to claim more than were granted."

The Federalists' arguments against a Bill of Rights have an important and easily recognized flaw. Although the federal government has only limited powers, Congress could still use some of these powers to impair the freedom of speech, freedom of the press, or other personal rights. For example, in the absence of any guarantee of rights, Congress could restrict the interstate distribution of newspapers using its plenary power to regulate interstate commerce. Or Congress could use its powers of taxation to make newspapers expensive and drive their publishers out of business. The same was true of other precious freedoms, such as the right to hold property and the right to fair process when accused of a crime.

The Federalists' arguments, it turned out, were not entirely convincing. Although the states, of course, did ratify the Constitution, four of them passed resolutions specifically urging the adoption of a Bill of Rights. *See* 2 Francis Newton Thorpe, *The Constitutional History of the United States* 198 (1902). James Madison took these resolutions seriously when he became a member of the House of Representatives. On June 8, 1789, Madison reversed his prior position from the ratification period and proposed a group of amendments to the Constitution that he specifically called the "Bill of Rights." 1 Annals of Congress 451-453. Congress debated, redrafted, and ultimately approved twelve of Madison's proposals and sent them to the states for ratification. By the end of 1791, the states had ratified numbers 3

> **FYI**
>
> Although some states promptly ratified the second of the twelve amendments approved by the first Congress, not enough states ratified it until 1992, more than 200 years later. It is now the Twenty-Seventh Amendment to the Constitution. It says: "No law, varying the compensation for the services of the Senators and Representatives, shall take effect, until an election of Representatives shall have intervened." The states have never ratified the first of the twelve amendments approved by the first Congress, which concerned the number of Representatives in the House.

through 12; they became the first ten Amendments to the Constitution, colloquially called the "Bill of Rights." The provisions of those amendments—and of several others, most prominently the Fourteenth Amendment—will be the focus of the remainder of this book.

> **Make the Connection**
>
> In *McCulloch v. Maryland* (in Chapter 3) and *U.S. Term Limits v. Thornton* and the cases concerning the Dormant Commerce Clause Doctrine (in Chapter 4), we saw that the Court has sometimes found implied limits on the authority of the states to act.

The original Constitution also did not contain many express limits on the authority of the states (as opposed to the federal government). In Chapter 4, we considered Article IV, § 4, which provides that the "Citizens of each State shall be entitled to all Privileges and Immunities of Citizens in the several States." As we saw, that provision has been interpreted to impose some modest limits on the states' ability to treat non-residents worse than their own residents. Perhaps more important—particularly in the first several decades of the Republic—Article I, § 10, cl. 1 prohibits the states from passing "any Bill of Attainder, *ex post facto* Law, or Law impairing the Obligation of Contracts." We will consider the last clause in this provision—the "Contract Clause"—in Chapter 18. But even though this provision was one of only a few express limitations on state authority, the Court in the early years interpreted its protections narrowly.

In *Calder v. Bull*, 3 U.S. 386 (1798), for example, the Supreme Court addressed a 1795 "law or resolution" of the Connecticut legislature that set aside a state court's 1793 ruling in a dispute over the interpretation of a will. The law directed the state court to conduct a new hearing on the matter, which it promptly did. On rehearing, the state court directed the party who had prevailed in the original judgment to forfeit the property that was the subject of the will. He sought review in the Supreme Court, contending that the Connecticut legislature's action amounted to an *ex post facto* law. The Court declined to grant relief to the plaintiff in error. In his opinion, Justice Chase explained (among other things) that *ex post facto* laws had been historically understood as retroactive criminal laws (as opposed to laws regulating property or contract). More important for present purposes, Justice Chase asserted in dicta that the Court had authority to invalidate such criminal laws because they were "manifestly unjust and oppressive." In Justice Chase's view, limits on state authority derived from natural law—the idea that certain principles that are inherent in nature and self-evidently true govern our rights, wholly aside from positive law. (This conception of rights had found voice, among other places, in the Declaration of Independence.) In a separate opinion, Justice Iredell rejected the natural-law approach, declaring that "some speculative jurists have held, that a legislative act against natural justice must, in itself, be

> **Make the Connection**
>
> As we turn to the Constitution's protections for individual rights, consider the extent to which the Court has—explicitly or implicitly—adopted Justice Chase's natural-law view or instead Justice Iredell's skepticism towards that view.

void; but I cannot think that, under such a government, any Court of Justice would possess a power to declare it so." In Justice Iredell's view, the Court is empowered to invalidate a law only when there is some positive constitutional restraint.

Twelve years later, the Court for the first time invalidated a state law. In 1795, the Georgia legislature passed a law that authorized the Governor to sell land in the western portion of the state to individual buyers; in return, the individual buyers who anticipated purchasing the land agreed to give members of the legislature an interest in the land. Peck purchased a tract of land shortly after it was sold by Georgia under the act, and in 1803 he conveyed it to Fletcher. At the time, neither party had knowledge of the graft that had tainted the original conveyance of the land. When the scandal broke, the Georgia legislature repealed the 1795 law and asserted ownership of any land conveyed under it. Fletcher brought suit against Peck for breach of covenant, claiming that Peck did not have clear title to the land in 1803.

In an opinion for a unanimous Court in *Fletcher v. Peck*, 10 U.S. 87 (1810), Chief Justice Marshall concluded that the rescinding legislation was invalid, on three grounds. First, he concluded that the 1795 Act was essentially a contract between the Georgia legislature and the purchasers of the land. Although "one legislature is competent to repeal any act which a former legislature was competent to pass," the Contract Clause limits the states' authority to impair the obligations of contracts. Second, he concluded that the law rescinding the original Act had "the effect of an *ex post facto* law," because it applied to transactions that had already taken place. Third, he suggested that, even aside from the provisions of Article I, § 10, the rescinding legislation was inconsistent with natural law. According to the Court, "Georgia was restrained, either by general principles which are common to our free institutions, or by the particular provisions of the constitution of the United States, from passing a law whereby the estate of the plaintiff in the premises so purchased could be constitutionally and legally impaired and rendered null and void."

Points for Discussion

a. Natural Law

Marcus Tullius Cicero, a Roman philosopher, gave the following classical description of natural law:

> [Natural law is a body of standards that are] universal, unchangeable, eternal, whose commands urge us to duty, and whose prohibitions restrain us from evil. *** This law cannot be contradicted by any other law, and is not liable either to derogation or abrogation. Neither the senate nor the people can give us any dispensation for not obeying this universal law of justice. It needs no other expositor and interpreter than our own conscience. It is not one thing at Rome, and another at Athens; one thing to-day, and another to-morrow; but in all times and nations this universal law must for ever reign, eternal and imperishable.

The Treatises of M.T. Cicero on the Nature of the Gods 360 (Thomas Francklin, trans. 1853). In other words, on this view there are universal "law-like standards" for right and wrong that never change, regardless of what statutes may say at any particular time and place. *See* Brian Bix, *Jurisprudence: Theory and Context* 63-64 (2d ed. 1999). These law-like standards constitute "natural law." Adherents to natural-law theory might conclude, for example, that murder is wrong, regardless of whether it is outlawed by any particular statute, and that murder will always be wrong. Are there rights—such as a right to be free from cruel and unusual punishment—to which all people are entitled *regardless* of what a particular statute or constitution might say?

> ### Food for Thought
>
> Even if natural law exists, does it follow that courts in the United States can or should use natural law to protect individual rights? Consider the view of Robert H. Bork, a leading critic of judges who stray from the original meaning of the Constitution: "I am far from denying that there is a natural law, but I do deny that we have given judges the authority to enforce it and that judges have greater access to that law than do the rest of us. Judges, like the rest of us, are apt to confuse their strongly held beliefs with the order of nature." Robert H. Bork, *The Tempting of America* 66 (1990). Do you agree?

Natural law is a profoundly important philosophical idea. Many prominent philosophers and political theorists—including John Locke, on whose work many of the Framers relied in the movement for independence and in crafting the Constitution—relied heavily on natural-law theories. But even assuming that there are principles of justice that inhere in nature, how do we—and, more important for our purposes, judges—find them? In his criticism of natural-law theories, Justice Iredell asserted: "The ideas of natural justice are regulated by no fixed standard: the ablest and the purest men have differed upon the subject; and all that the court could properly say, in such an event, would be, that the legislature (possessed of an equal right of opinion) had passed an act which, in the opinion of the judges, was inconsistent with abstract principles of natural justice." Do you agree that when judges rely on natural law, they effectively rely only on their own personal intuitions about right and wrong?

b. Positive Law

Justice Iredell did not believe that there were no limits on the ability of legislatures to act, but in his view those limits inhered only in positive law—law, that is, such as the Constitution, which had been affirmatively enacted through defined law-making processes. Reliance on positive law in theory limits judges to applying the judgments of authorized law-makers, rather than making the law themselves. As we will see in Chapters 8 and 11, however, a positive-law approach in the first half of the nineteenth century would presumably have required courts to recognize and uphold, at least in some circumstances, the institution of slavery. Reliance on natural law might, by contrast, have permitted courts to reject slavery. Does this suggest that the positive-law approach is flawed? Or merely that the original decision at the Constitutional Convention not to insist on the abolition of slavery was flawed? In this regard, keep in mind that many proponents of slavery in the years leading up to the Civil War themselves relied on conceptions of natural law to *defend* the institution.

In practice, as we will see, the competing approaches tend to blur. When, for example, the Court interprets the First Amendment to prohibit the criminalization of flag burning or the Due Process Clause to prohibit laws banning abortion—subjects we will consider in Chapters 14 and 8, respectively—is it relying on natural law or positive law? The constitutional text, after all, is usually quite vague and indeterminate. As a result, the process of interpretation of positive law sometimes resembles a natural-law approach. As you read the materials in the remainder of the book, consider whether it is possible always to identify whether a judge is pursuing one approach or the other.

———

Although there was debate in the early years over the extent to which natural-law principles applied, there was general agreement that the Constitution's limitations on state action had force, as well. However broadly the Court interpreted Article I, § 10's limitations on state authority, however, their application was still likely to be quite limited. The Bill of Rights, on the other hand, contained protections for individual rights with an apparently much wider sweep. But did the provisions of the first eight amendments—including the First Amendment's protections for speech and religious exercise and the Fourth, Fifth, Sixth, and Eighth Amendments' protections for criminal defendants—apply to the states, in addition to the federal government? The Court addressed that question in the case that follows.

———

Barron v. Baltimore

32 U.S. (7 Pet.) 243 (1833)

[Barron sued the City of Baltimore claiming that the City had destroyed the value of his wharf, which was on the Baltimore harbor, when it diverted streams while conducting street maintenance. He asserted that the work had left the water at his wharf too shallow to be used by most vessels. He claimed that the City's actions (which were authorized under state law) deprived him of his property without just compensation, in violation of the Fifth Amendment, which he argued "ought to be construed as to restrain the legislative power of a state, as well as that of the United States."]

Make the Connection

Can a city project that does not actually transfer title of property to the city amount to a "taking" of property within the meaning of the Fifth Amendment? We will consider this question—and "regulatory takings"—in Chapter 18.

MARSHALL, Ch. J. delivered the opinion of the court.

The question thus presented is, we think, of great importance, but not of much difficulty. The constitution was ordained and established by the people of the United States for themselves, for their own government, and not for the government of the individual states. Each state established a constitution for itself, and in that constitution, provided such limitations and restrictions on the powers of its particular government, as its judgment dictated. The people of the United States framed such a government for the United States as they supposed best adapted to their situation and best calculated to promote their interests. The powers they conferred on this government were to be exercised by itself; and the limitations on power, if expressed in general terms, are naturally, and, we think, necessarily, applicable to the government created by the instrument. They are limitations of power granted in the instrument itself; not of distinct governments, framed by different persons and for different purposes.

If these propositions be correct, the fifth amendment must be understood as restraining the power of the general government, not as applicable to the states. [But the] counsel for the plaintiff in error insists, that the constitution was intended to secure the people of the several states against the undue exercise of power by their respective state governments; as well as against that which might be attempted by their general government. [In] support of this argument he relies on the inhibitions contained in the tenth section of the first article. We think, that section affords a strong, if not a conclusive, argument in support of the opinion already indicated by the court. The preceding section contains restrictions which are obviously intended for the exclusive purpose of restraining the exercise of power by the departments of the general government. *** The ninth section having enumerated, in the nature of a bill of rights, the limitations intended to be imposed on the powers of the general government, the tenth proceeds to enumerate those which were to operate on the state legislatures. These restrictions are brought together in the same section, and are by express words applied to the states.

If the original constitution, in the ninth and tenth sections of the first article, draws this plain and marked line of discrimination between the limitations it imposes on the powers of the general government, and on those of the state; if, in every inhibition intended to act on state power, words are employed, which directly express that intent; some strong reason must be assigned for departing from this safe and judicious course, in framing the amendments, before that departure can be assumed. We search in vain for that reason. *** Had the framers of these amendments intended them to be limitations on the powers of the state governments, they would have imitated the framers of the original constitution, and have expressed that intention.

But it is universally understood, it is a part of the history of the day, that the great revolution which established the constitution of the United States, was not effected without immense opposition. Serious fears were extensively entertained, that those powers which the patriot statesmen [deemed essential to union] might be exercised in a manner dangerous to liberty. In almost every convention by which the constitution was adopted, amendments to guard against the abuse of power were recommended. These amendments demanded security against the apprehended encroachments of the general government—not against those of the local governments. In compliance with a sentiment thus generally expressed, to quiet fears thus extensively entertained, amendments were proposed by the required majority in congress, and adopted by the states. These amendments contain no expression indicating an intention to apply them to the state governments. This court cannot so apply them. *** We are, therefore, of opinion, that there is no repugnancy between the several acts of the general assembly of Maryland and the constitution of the United States.

————

Points for Discussion

a. Text and Original Meaning

Chief Justice Marshall concluded that the provisions of the Bill of Rights restrained the federal government, but not the states. He relied principally on text and the original meaning. Is his reasoning persuasive? Are there other indications in the ten amendments of the original meaning? The First Amendment states that "*Congress* shall make no law respecting an establishment of religion, or prohibiting the free exercise thereof ***" (emphasis added). Does this support Marshall's argument? Or does it instead suggest that the Framers knew how to limit a provision to the federal government when they wanted to, and that other provisions of the Bill of Rights—including the Takings Clause, which is phrased in the passive voice—therefore do not apply only to the federal government?

b. State Authority

The consequence of the Court's decision in *Barron* was that the Constitution imposed very few limits on the states' authority. To be sure, the states could adopt similar limitations in their own Constitutions, and indeed many did. But *Barron* also meant that states would, if they chose, be free to act as censors (in tension with the idea of free speech) and deny criminal defendants many of the protections that the Bill of Rights afforded to persons accused of federal crimes. Is it troubling that states could act oppressively, particularly towards unpopular individuals, even while, as a matter of constitutional principle, the federal government could not? If so, should the Court have decided <u>Barron</u> differently?

c. Natural Law

Does natural law prohibit the government from depriving a person of property without compensation? If so, does *Barron* implicitly reject the proposition that courts are to enforce natural-law rights?

————

In the years after <u>Barron</u>, federal constitutional challenges to state legislation had to rely on the limitations deriving from Article I, § 10, Article IV, the Dormant Commerce Clause Doctrine, and constitutional structure. In the five years after the end of the Civil War, however, Congress passed and the states ratified the Thirteenth, Fourteenth, and Fifteenth Amendments to the Constitution, which imposed new limits on the powers of the states. Together, these provisions are known as the "Reconstruction Amendments." We will consider two of those—the Thirteenth Amendment, which abolished slavery and involuntary servitude, and the Fifteenth Amendment, which ensured that the right to vote would "not be denied or abridged by the United States or by any State on account of race, color, or previous condition of servitude"—only briefly, principally in Chapter 13. The Fourteenth Amendment will be a central focus of the next few Chapters.

As we will see, the Fourteenth Amendment contains several profoundly important provisions. It makes all persons born or naturalized in the United States citizens both of the United States and the state in which they reside, thus overruling one of the holdings of the <u>Dred Scott</u> case, which we will consider in Chapter 11. In addition, it prohibits the states from abridging the privileges or immunities of citizens of the United States; it bars the states from depriving any person of life, liberty, or property without due process of law; and it prevents the states from denying equal protection of the laws to persons within their boundaries. And it confers on Congress the power to enforce its provisions by "appropriate legislation."

These provisions clearly were significant limitations on state authority. But just how sweeping were they? In Chapter 10, we will begin our consideration of the reach of the Equal Protection Clause. But what about the other provisions in Section 1 of the Fourteenth Amendment? Were the protections afforded by the Due Process Clause identical to those that the Fifth Amendment provides against federal action? Did the Privileges or Immunities Clause provide a different set of protections than those in the similarly (but not identically) worded provision in Article IV? Most important, did the protections afforded—either by one of the clauses, or by all of them working in tandem—to individual rights against state action parallel those afforded against federal action by the Bill of Rights?

The case that follows was the Court's first meaningful opportunity to address some of those questions.

B. Privileges or Immunities

Slaughter-House Cases

83 U.S. 36 (1873)

Mr. Justice MILLER delivered the opinion of the Court.

[In 1869, the Louisiana legislature passed a statute permitting the slaughtering of animals in New Orleans only in a slaughter-house owned by a corporation chartered by the statute. The statute required the corporation to permit independent butchers to slaughter their animals at its slaughter-house at a cost fixed by statute, but it also ordered all other slaughter-houses to close. The slaughter-house would be large enough to accommodate all butchers and to allow 500 animals to be slaughtered each day. Butchers aggrieved by the statutory monopoly brought suit challenging the constitutionality of the statute. Louisiana's Supreme Court upheld the law.]

It is not, and cannot be successfully controverted, that it is both the right and the duty of the legislative body—the supreme power of the State or municipality—to prescribe and determine the localities where the business of slaughtering for a great city may be conducted. To do this effectively it is indispensable that all persons who slaughter animals for food shall do it in those places and nowhere else.

The statute under consideration defines these localities and forbids slaughtering in any other. It does not, as has been asserted, prevent the butcher from doing his own slaughtering. On the contrary, the Slaughter-House Company is required, under a heavy penalty, to permit any person who wishes to do so, to slaughter in their houses; and they are bound to make ample provision for the convenience of all the slaughtering for the entire city. The butcher then is still permitted to slaughter, to prepare, and to sell his own meats; but he is required to slaughter at a specified place and to pay a reasonable compensation for the use of the accommodations furnished him at that place.

The wisdom of the monopoly granted by the legislature may be open to question, but it is difficult to see a justification for the assertion that the butchers are deprived of the right to labor in their occupation, or the people of their daily service in preparing food, or how this statute, with the duties and guards imposed upon the company, can be said to destroy the business of the butcher, or seriously interfere with its pursuit.

[Plaintiffs contend that the statute violates the Thirteenth Amendment and the Privileges or Immunities, Equal Protection, and Due Process Clauses of the Fourteenth Amendment.] This court is thus called upon for the first time to give construction to these articles. The most cursory glance at these articles discloses a unity of purpose, when taken in connection with the history of the times, which cannot fail to have an important bearing on any question of doubt concerning their true meaning. *** [U]ndoubtedly the overshadowing and efficient cause [of the Civil War] was African slavery. *** [O]n the most casual examination of the language of [the Reconstruction] amendments, no one can fail to be impressed with the one pervading purpose found in them all, lying at the foundation of each, and without which none of them would have been even suggested; we mean the freedom of the slave race, the security and firm establishment of that freedom, and the protection of the newly-made freeman and citizen from the oppressions of those who had formerly exercised unlimited dominion over him.

We do not say that no one else but the negro can share in this protection. *** Undoubtedly while negro slavery alone was in the mind of the Congress which proposed the thirteenth article, it forbids any other kind of slavery, now or hereafter. *** And so if other rights are assailed by the States which properly and necessarily fall within the protection of these articles, that protection will apply, though the party interested may not be of African descent. But what we do say, and what we wish to be understood is, that in any fair and just construction of any section or phrase of these amendments, it is necessary to look to the purpose which we have said was the pervading spirit of them all, the evil which they were designed to remedy, and the process of continued addition to the Constitution, until that purpose was supposed to be accomplished, as far as constitutional law can accomplish it.

The first section of the fourteenth article, to which our attention [is] specially invited, opens with a definition of citizenship—not only citizenship of the United States, but citizenship of the States. No such definition was previously found in the Constitution,

Make the Connection

We will discuss the _Dred Scott_ decision in Chapter 8, when we consider "substantive due process," and in Chapter 11, when we consider discrimination on the basis of race.

nor had any attempt been made to define it by act of Congress. *** [It] had been held by this court, in [the] _Dred Scott_ case, only a few years before the outbreak of the civil war, that a man of African descent, whether a slave or not, was not and could not be a citizen of a State or of the United States. [T]he first clause of the first section overturns the _Dred Scott_ decision by making _all persons_ born within the United States and subject to its jurisdiction citizens of the United States. That its main purpose was to establish the citizenship of the negro can admit of no doubt.

[T]he distinction between citizenship of the United States and citizenship of a State is clearly recognized and established. Not only may a man be a citizen of the United States without being a citizen of a State, but an important element is necessary to convert the former into the latter. He must reside within the State to make him a citizen of it, but it is only necessary that he should be born or naturalized in the United States to be a citizen of the Union. It is quite clear, then, that there is a citizenship of the United States, and a citizenship of a State, which are distinct from each other, and which depend upon different characteristics or circumstances in the individual.

We think this distinction and its explicit recognition in this amendment of great weight in this argument, because the next paragraph of this same section, which is the one mainly relied on by the plaintiffs in error, speaks only of privileges and immunities of citizens of the United States, and does not speak of those of citizens of the several States. *** The language is, "No State shall make or enforce any law which shall abridge the privileges or immunities of citizens of _the United States_." It is a little remarkable, if this clause was intended as a protection to the citizen of a State against the legislative power of his own State, that the word citizen of the State should be left out when it is so carefully used, and used in contradistinction to citizens of the United States, in the very sentence which precedes it. It is too clear for argument that the change in phraseology was adopted understandingly and with a purpose.

Of the privileges and immunities of the citizen of the United States, and of the privileges and immunities of the citizen of the State, and what they respectively are, we will presently consider; but we wish to state here that it is only the former which are placed by this clause under the protection of the Federal Constitution, and that the latter, whatever they may be, are not intended to have any additional protection by this paragraph of the amendment. [Article IV, § 2 provides:] "The citizens of each State shall be entitled to all the privileges and immunities of citizens of the several States." Fortunately we are not without judicial construction of this clause of the Constitution. The first and the leading case on the subject is that of _Corfield v. Coryell_, [6 Fed. Case

Take Note

The Court here misquotes the language of Article IV. Can you see how? Does the Court's language change the meaning of the provision?

546 (C.C.E.Dist. Pa. 1823),] decided by Mr. Justice Washington in the Circuit Court for the District of Pennsylvania in 1823. "The inquiry," he says, "is, what are the privileges and immunities of citizens of the several States? We feel no hesitation in confining these expressions to those privileges and immunities which are *fundamental;* which belong of right to the citizens of all free governments, and which have at all times been enjoyed by citizens of the several States which compose this Union, from the time of their becoming free, independent, and sovereign. What these fundamental principles are, it would be more tedious than difficult to enumerate. They may all, however, be comprehended under the following general heads: protection by the government, with the right to acquire and possess property of every kind, and to pursue and obtain happiness and safety, subject, nevertheless, to such restraints as the government may prescribe for the general good of the whole."

> **FYI**
>
> Until 1891, Justices of the Supreme Court were required to "ride circuit," which meant that they sat as judges on the courts of appeals for a significant part of each year. Justice Washington was riding circuit when he issued the opinion in *Corfield*. His opinion in this case was therefore not the opinion of the Supreme Court.

The description, when taken to include others not named, but which are of the same general character, embraces nearly every civil right for the establishment and protection of which organized government is instituted. They are, in the language of Judge Washington, those rights which [are] fundamental. Throughout his opinion, they are spoken of as rights belonging to the individual as a citizen of a State. They are so spoken of in the constitutional provision which he was construing. And they have always been held to be the class of rights which the State governments were created to establish and secure.

> **Food for Thought**
>
> If the Privileges and Immunities Clause of Article IV requires states only to treat non-residents the same as residents, what does it mean to say that it applies only to "fundamental rights"? If the rights are truly fundamental, can a state really deprive both its residents and non-residents of them?

The constitutional provision there alluded to did not create those rights, which it called privileges and immunities of citizens of the States. *** Nor did it profess to control the power of the State governments over the rights of its own citizens. Its sole purpose was to declare to the several States, that whatever those rights, as you grant or establish them to your own citizens, or as you limit or qualify, or impose restrictions on their exercise, the same, neither more nor less, shall be the measure of the rights of citizens of other States within your jurisdiction.

It would be the vainest show of learning to attempt to prove by citations of authority, that up to the adoption of the recent amendments, no claim or pretence was set up that those rights depended on the Federal government for their existence or protection, beyond the very few express limitations which the Federal Constitution imposed upon the States—such, for instance, as the prohibition against ex post facto laws, bills of attainder, and laws impairing the obligation of contracts. But with the exception of these and a few other restrictions, the entire domain of the privileges and immunities of citizens of the States, as above defined, lay within the constitutional and legislative power of the States, and without that of the Federal government. Was it the purpose of the fourteenth amendment, by the simple declaration that no State should make or enforce any law which shall abridge the privileges and immunities of *citizens of the United States*, to transfer the security and protection of all the civil rights which we have mentioned, from the States to the Federal government? And where it is declared that Congress shall have the power to enforce that article, was it intended to bring within the power of Congress the entire domain of civil rights heretofore belonging exclusively to the States?

All this and more must follow, if the proposition of the plaintiffs in error be sound. For not only are these rights subject to the control of Congress whenever in its discretion any of them are supposed to be abridged by State legislation, but that body may also pass laws in advance, limiting and restricting the exercise of legislative power by the States, in their most ordinary and usual functions, as in its judgment it may think proper on all such subjects. And still further, such a construction followed by the reversal of the judgments of the Supreme Court of Louisiana in these cases, would constitute this court a perpetual censor upon all legislation of the States, on the civil rights of their own citizens, with authority to nullify such as it did not approve as consistent with those rights, as they existed at the time of the adoption of this amendment. The argument we admit is not always the most conclusive which is drawn from the consequences urged against the adoption of a particular construction of an instrument. But when, as in the case before us, these consequences are so serious, so far-reaching and pervading, so great a departure from the structure and spirit of our institutions; when the effect is to fetter and degrade the State governments by subjecting them to the control of Congress, in the exercise of powers heretofore universally conceded to them of the most ordinary and fundamental character; when in fact it radically changes the whole theory of the relations of the State and Federal governments to each other and of both these governments to the people; the argument has a force that is irresistible, in the absence of language which expresses such a purpose too clearly to admit of doubt. We are convinced that no such results were intended by the Congress which proposed these amendments, nor by the legislatures of the States which ratified them.

Take Note

Section 5 of the Fourteenth Amendment gives Congress the power to enforce the Amendment's substantive provisions, including the Privileges or Immunities Clause in Section 1. Wasn't this authority conferred precisely to protect civil rights from state encroachment? In this sense, didn't the Reconstruction Amendments "radically change[] the whole theory of the relations" between the state and federal governments?

[Thus,] we may hold ourselves excused from defining the privileges and immunities of citizens of the United States which no State can abridge, until some case involving those privileges may make it necessary to do so. But lest it should be said that no such privileges and immunities are to be found if those we have been considering are excluded, we venture to suggest some which [owe] their existence to the Federal government, its

National character, its Constitution, or its laws. One of these is well described in the case of *Crandall v. Nevada*, 73 U.S. 35 (1867). It is said to be the right of the citizen of this great country, protected by implied guarantees of its Constitution, "to come to the seat of government to assert any claim he may have upon that government, to transact any business he may have with it, to seek its protection, to share its offices, to engage in administering its functions. He has the right of free access to its seaports, through which all operations of foreign commerce are conducted, to the subtreasuries, land offices, and courts of justice in the several States." Another privilege of a citizen of the United States is to demand the care and protection of the Federal government over his life, liberty, and property when on the high seas or within the jurisdiction of a foreign government. *** The right to peaceably assemble and petition for redress of grievances, the privilege of the writ of *habeas corpus*, are rights of the citizen guaranteed by the Federal Constitution. [One] of these privileges is conferred by the very article under consideration. It is that a citizen of the United States can, of his own volition, become a citizen of any State of the Union by a *bona fide* residence therein, with the same rights as other citizens of that State.

But it is useless to pursue this branch of the inquiry, since we are of opinion that the rights claimed by these plaintiffs in error, if they have any existence, are not privileges and immunities of citizens of the United States within the meaning of the clause of the fourteenth amendment under consideration.

[The Court also concluded that the challenged statute did not violate the Due Process or Equal Protection Clauses of the Fourteenth Amendment.]

Mr. Justice FIELD, [joined by Chief Justice CHASE, Justice SWAYNE, and Justice BRADLEY,] dissenting:

The question presented is *** nothing less than the question whether the recent amendments to the Federal Constitution protect the citizens of the United States against the deprivation of their common rights by State legislation. In my judgment the fourteenth amendment does afford such protection, and was so intended by the Congress which framed and the States which adopted it.

The amendment was adopted to obviate objections which had been raised and pressed with great force to the validity of the Civil Rights Act [of 1866], and to place the common rights of American citizens under the protection of the National government. *** The amendment does not attempt to confer any new privileges or immunities upon citizens, or to enumerate or define those already existing. It assumes that there are such privileges and immunities which belong of right to citizens as such, and ordains that they shall not be abridged by State legislation. If this inhibition has no reference to privileges and immunities of this character, but only refers, as held by the majority of the court in their opinion, to such privileges and immunities as were before its adoption specially designated in the Constitution or necessarily implied as belonging to citizens of the United States, it was a vain and idle enactment, which accomplished nothing, and most unnecessarily excited Congress and the people on its passage. With privileges and immunities thus designated or implied no State could ever have interfered by its laws, and no new constitutional provision was required to inhibit such interference. *** But if the amendment refers to the natural and inalienable rights which belong to all citizens, the inhibition has a profound significance and consequence.

What, then, are the privileges and immunities which are secured against abridgment by State legislation? *** The terms, privileges and immunities, are not new in the amendment; they were in the Constitution before the amendment was adopted. They are found in the second section of the fourth article; *** [the] privileges and immunities designated are those *which of right belong to the citizens of all free governments.* [*Corfield v. Coryell.*] *** What [Article IV] did for the protection of the citizens of one State against hostile and discriminating legislation of other States, the fourteenth amendment does for the protection of every citizen of the United States against hostile and discriminating legislation against him in favor of others, whether they reside in the same or in different States. If under the fourth article of the Constitution equality of privileges and immunities is secured between citizens of different States, under the fourteenth amendment the same equality is secured between citizens of the United States.

All monopolies in any known trade or manufacture are an invasion of these privileges, for they encroach upon the liberty of citizens to acquire property and pursue happiness ***. [F]reedom of pursuit has been always recognized as the common right of [Louisiana's] citizens. But were this otherwise, the fourteenth amendment secures the like protection to all citizens in that State against any abridgment of their common rights, as in other States. That amendment was intended to give practical effect to the declaration of 1776 of inalienable rights, rights which are the gift of the Creator, which the law does not confer, but only recognizes.

This equality of right, with exemption from all disparaging and partial enactments, in the lawful pursuits of life, throughout the whole country, is the distinguishing privilege of citizens of the United States. To them, everywhere, all pursuits, all professions, all avocations are open without other restrictions than such as are imposed equally upon all others of the same age, sex, and condition. The State may prescribe such regulations for every pursuit and calling of life as will promote the public health, secure the good order and advance the general prosperity of society, but when once prescribed, the pursuit or calling must be free to be followed by every citizen who is within the conditions designated, and will conform to the regulations. This is the fundamental idea upon which our institutions rest, and unless adhered to in the legislation of the country our government will be a republic only in name. The fourteenth amendment, in my judgment, makes it essential to the validity of the legislation of every State that this equality of right should be respected.

[I]t is to me a matter of profound regret that [the challenged Act's] validity is recognized by a majority of this court, for by it the right of free labor, one of the most sacred and imprescrip-

> **Make the Connection**
>
> In Justice Field's view, the Privileges or Immunities Clause requires equal treatment for persons who are similarly situated. If this view is correct, then in what way is that clause different from the Equal Protection Clause? We will consider the Equal Protection Clause in Chapters 10 and 11, and the relationship between Equal Protection and fundamental rights in Chapter 12.

tible rights of man, is violated. As stated by the Supreme Court of Connecticut [in *Norwich Gaslight Co. v. The Norwich City Gas Co.*, 25 Conn. 19 (1856),] grants of exclusive privileges, such as is made by the act in question, are opposed to the whole theory of free government, and it requires no aid from any bill of rights to render them void. That only is a free government, in the American sense of the term, under which the inalienable right of every citizen to pursue his happiness is unrestrained, except by just, equal, and impartial laws.

Mr. Justice BRADLEY, dissenting:

[T]here are certain fundamental rights which [the state] cannot infringe. *** I speak now of the rights of citizens of any free government. *** In this free country, the people of which inherited certain [rights] and privileges from their ancestors, citizenship means something. It has certain privileges and immunities attached to it which the government, whether restricted by express or implied limitations, cannot take away or impair. [And] these privileges and immunities attach as well to citizenship of the United States as to citizenship of the States.

The people of this country brought with them to its shores the rights of Englishmen; the rights which had been wrested from English sovereigns at various periods of the nation's history. *** A violation of one of the fundamental principles of [the unwritten English] constitution in the Colonies, namely, the principle that recognizes the property of the people as their own, and which, therefore, regards all taxes for the support of government as gifts of the people through their representatives, and regards taxation without representation as subversive of free government, was the origin of our own revolution. *** [T]he Declaration of Independence, which was the first political act of the American people in their independent sovereign capacity, [identified fundamental rights that] belong to the citizens of every free government.

But we are not bound to resort to implication, or to the constitutional history of England, to find an authoritative declaration of some of the most important privileges and immunities of citizens of the United States. It is in the Constitution itself. *** But even if the Constitution were silent, the fundamental privileges and immunities of citizens, as such, would be no less real and no less inviolable than they now are. It was not necessary to say in words that the citizens of the United States should have and exercise all the privileges of citizens; [t]heir very citizenship conferred these privileges, if they did not possess them before.

[Even admitting that] formerly the States were not prohibited from infringing any of the fundamental privileges and immunities of citizens of the United States, except in a few specified cases, that cannot be said now, since the adoption of the fourteenth amendment. In my judgment, it was the intention of the people of this country in adopting that amendment to provide National security against violation by the States of the fundamental rights of the citizen. *** If my views are correct with regard to what are the privileges and immunities of citizens, it follows conclusively that any law which establishes a sheer monopoly, depriving a large class of citizens of the privilege of pursuing a lawful employment, does abridge the privileges of those citizens.

Mr. Justice SWAYNE, dissenting:

By the Constitution, as it stood before the war, ample protection was given against oppression by the Union, but little was given against wrong and oppression by the States. That want was intended to be supplied by this amendment. Against the former this court has been called upon more than once to interpose. Authority of the same amplitude was intended to be conferred as to the latter. But this arm of our jurisdiction is, in these cases, stricken down by the judgment just given. Nowhere, than in this court, ought the will of the nation, as thus expressed, to be more liberally construed or more cordially executed. This determination of the majority seems to me to lie far in the other direction.

Points for Discussion

a. History, Context, and Federalism

The Court asserted that the Privileges or Immunities Clause should not be interpreted to "transfer the security and protection" of civil rights from the states to the federal government. But didn't the experience of slavery and the secession crisis that led to the Civil War suggest that the states might be inappropriate guardians of such rights? Is that history relevant in interpreting the Privileges or Immunities Clause—or, for that matter, the other provisions in the Reconstruction Amendments? Did the Reconstruction Amendments fundamentally change the original understanding of federalism?

b. What's Left?

Even before the ratification of the Fourteenth Amendment, states presumably were prohibited from depriving United States citizens of the various rights that come with national citizenship. (In this regard, recall *McCulloch v. Maryland*, which we discussed in Chapter 3, and *U.S. Term Limits v. Thornton*, which we considered in Chapter 4.) If this is true, then what, in the Court's view, did the Privileges or Immunities Clause add to the Constitution? Does Section 5 of the Fourteenth Amendment offer a hint for one possible answer?

c. History and Original Meaning

The principal author of the Fourteenth Amendment was Representative John Bingham. In a speech before the House of Representatives voted on the proposed amendment, Representative Bingham stated that the amendment was designed "to arm the Congress of the United States, by the consent of the people of the United States, with the power to enforce the bill of rights as it stands in the Constitution today." He also stated that it was intended to protect "by national law the privileges and immunities of all citizens of the Republic *and the inborn rights* of every person within its jurisdiction whenever the same shall be abridged or denied by the unconstitutional acts of any State." 39th Cong. Globe 1088-90 (1866) (emphasis added). Similarly, Senator Jacob Howard, the principal sponsor of the amendment in the Senate, explained in a floor speech that the proposed amendment was designed to protect "the personal rights guarantied and secured by the first eight amendments of the Constitution" and all of the fundamental rights described by Justice Washington in *Corfield v. Coryell*, which interpreted the phrase "privileges and immunities" in Article IV to refer to all fundamental natural-law rights. He then declared, "The great object of the first section of this amendment is, therefore, to restrain the power of the States and compel them at all times to respect these great fundamental guarantees." 39th Cong. Globe 2765-66 (1866). What is the relevance of this history to the question presented in the *Slaughter-House Cases*? What does it suggest about the Court's interpretation of the Privileges or Immunities Clause?

d. Another View of the Privileges or Immunities Clause

The traditional view of the Privileges or Immunities Clause is that the clause protects substantive rights but, under the interpretation advanced in the *Slaughter-House Cases*, the rights protected are only those rights already protected by federal law. The Clause, as interpreted, thus accomplishes very little. Professor John Harrison has challenged this entire view in a very influential article, arguing that the Clause instead promotes a specific kind of equality instead of protecting substantive rights. He explains his argument as follows:

> A *substantive* protection either prescribes or forbids a certain content of state law. An *equality-based* protection, by contrast, says nothing about the substance of the state's law; it instead requires that the law, whatever it is, be the same for all citizens. I argue that the Privileges or Immunities Clause is, with respect to everyday rights of state law, the latter kind of protection. The main point of the clause is to require that every state give the same privileges and immunities of state citizenship—the same positive law rights of property, contract, and so forth—to all of its citizens.

John Harrison, *Reconstructing the Privileges or Immunities Clause*, 101 Yale L.J. 1385 (1992). Harrison relies not only the legislative history of the Privileges or Immunities Clause, but also a careful examination of its text. What words in the Fourteenth Amendment support Harrison's view? On this view, what does the Equal Protection Clause add to the Fourteenth Amendment?

e. The Privileges or Immunities Clause in the Modern Era

The Court did not strike down any state laws under the Privileges or Immunities Clause in the century and a quarter after the Court's decision in the *Slaughter-House Cases*. In 1999, however, the Court held, in *Saenz v. Roe*, 526 U.S. 489 (1999), that a California law that limited the maximum welfare benefits available to residents who had been in the state for less than twelve months to the amount they would have received in their prior state of residence was invalid under the Clause. Justice Stevens, in his opinion for the Court, declared that the Privileges or Immunities Clause protects "the right of the newly arrived citizen to the same privileges and immunities enjoyed by other citizens of the same State," a right protected "not only by the new arrival's status as a state citizen, but also by her status as a citizen of the United States." Justice Stevens noted that the opinion in the *Slaughter-House Cases* explained that one of the privileges conferred by the Clause "is that a citizen of the United States can, of his own volition, become a citizen of any State of the Union by a *bona fide* residence therein, with the same rights as other citizens of that State." Because "[n]either the duration of respondents' California residence, nor the identity of their prior States of residence, [had] any relevance to their need for benefits," and because those factors did not "bear any relationship to the State's interest in making an equitable allocation of the funds to be distributed among its needy citizens," the Court invalidated the statute.

Was the Court's decision in *Saenz* merely an application of the *Slaughter-House* view of the meaning of the Privileges or Immunities Clause? Or did it signal a willingness to expand the reach of the Clause? The Court has not invalidated any other state laws under the Privileges or Immunities Clause since the decision in *Saenz*, but, as we will see in the next section, at least one Justice has urged the Court to revisit the *Slaughter-House* Court's interpretation of the Clause.

C. Incorporation

One possible interpretation of the Privileges or Immunities Clause would have been that it effectively applied to the states the protections for individual rights that the first eight Amendments afford against federal action. Indeed, there is substantial historical evidence that those who drafted and proposed the provision—particularly Congressman John Bingham, the Fourteenth Amendment's principal author—believed that it would "incorporate" the protections of the Bill of Rights, see, e.g., Richard L. Aynes, *On Misreading John Bingham and the Fourteenth Amendment*, 103 Yale L.J. 57 (1993), although the question is controversial, see Charles Fairman, *Does the Fourteenth Amendment Incorporate the Bill of Rights?*, 2 Stan. L. Rev. 5 (1949). Incorporation through the Privileges or Immunities Clause of the protections of the Bill of Rights would also help to minimize the difficulties of interpretation that would ensue if the Court were forced to define—without reference to the Bill of Rights—the privileges and immunities of national citizenship. But the Court has never accepted the view that the Privileges or Immunities Clause serves this function.

The Court has, however, looked to the Due Process Clause of the Fourteenth Amendment to play this role. The Due Process Clause prevents the states from denying any person "life, liberty, or property" without due process of law. On its face, this clause appears only to require a state to provide appropriate process—such as notice and an opportunity to be heard—when it seeks to deprive a person of an important interest. But the term "due process" has a deep historical pedigree—dating to English laws designed to implement Magna Carta's mandate that government action comply with the "law of the land"—and some commentators have argued that it traditionally embraced substantive, as well as procedural, rights. See, e.g., Frederick Mark Gedicks, *An Originalist Defense of Substantive Due Process: Magna Carta, Higher-Law Constitutionalism, and the Fifth Amendment*, 58 Emory L.J. 585 (2009). Others have vigorously disagreed. See, e.g., Raoul Berger, *Government by Judiciary: The Transformation of the Fourteenth Amendment* 221-44 (2d Ed. 1997).

In any event, beginning in the late nineteenth century, the Court began to hold that the Due Process Clause of the Fourteenth Amendment protected individuals against state action that would, if engaged in by the federal government, violate provisions in the Bill of Rights. In *Chicago, Burlington & Quincy R.R. Co. v. Chicago,* 166 U.S. 226 (1897), for example, the Court held that the Due Process Clause prohibited a state from taking private property for public use without just compensation, a form of protection (we saw in *Barron*) that is guaranteed against federal action by the Fifth Amendment. And in *Twining v. New Jersey,* 211 U.S. 78, 99 (1908), the Court stated that "it is possible that some of the personal rights safeguarded by the first eight Amendments against national action may also be safeguarded against state action, because a denial of them would be a denial of due process of law." But the Court also explicitly held during that era that some rights protected against federal action in the Bill of Rights did not apply to state action. See, e.g,. *Hurtado v. California,* 110 U.S. 516 (1884) (grand jury indictment requirement); *Minneapolis & St. Louis R.R. Co. v. Bombolis,* 241 U.S. 211 (1916) (right to a jury trial in a civil case).

In the middle of the twentieth century, the Court began a more systematic effort to define the scope of the rights protected by the Due Process Clause. In *Palko v. Connecticut,* 302 U.S. 319 (1937), for example, the Court concluded that a state law that permitted a state to appeal a judgment of acquittal of a criminal defendant—and thus permitted the state, after prevailing on appeal, to re-try the defendant for the same crime—did not violate the Due Process Clause of the Fourteenth Amendment, even though the Fifth Amendment provides that no person shall be "subject for the same offense to be twice put in jeopardy of life or limb." The Court reasoned that the mere inclusion of a right in the Bill of Rights does not require the conclusion that it is protected against state interference by the Due Process Clause. Instead, the Court declared that the Due Process Clause protects only those rights that are "implicit in the concept of ordered liberty," essential to "a fair and enlightened system of justice," and "so rooted in the traditions and conscience of our people as to be ranked as fundamental." On this view, some of the rights identified in the first eight amendments to the Constitution are protected against state interference by the Due Process Clause of the Fourteenth Amendment, but only because they are "implicit in the concept of ordered liberty," and not simply because they are enumerated in the Bill of Rights.

How does a Court go about deciding whether a right mentioned in the Bill of Rights—or, for that matter, a right not specifically enumerated in the Bill of Rights—is "implicit in the concept of ordered liberty"? This question divided the Court in the middle of the twentieth century. Would it make more sense to conclude that the Due Process Clause "incorporates" all of the rights mentioned in the first eight amendments and thus applies them against state action? The dueling opinions in the case that follows addressed these questions. As the notes after the case make clear, however, the majority's approach in *Adamson*—and the Court's specific holding in the case—is no longer the law.

————

Adamson v. California

332 U.S. 46 (1947)

Mr. Justice REED delivered the opinion of the Court.

The appellant [was] convicted [by] a jury in a Superior Court of the State of California of murder in the first degree [and sentenced to death.] *** The provisions of California law which were challenged in the state proceedings as invalid under the Fourteenth Amendment [permit] the failure of a defendant to explain or to deny evidence against him to be commented upon by court and by counsel and to be considered by court and jury. The defendant did not testify. [The prosecutor urged the jury to infer that the defendant was guilty because he failed to deny evidence offered against him. The court instructed the jury that this inference was permissible under California law.]

We shall assume, but without any intention thereby of ruling upon the issue, that state permission by law to the court, counsel and jury to comment upon and consider the failure of defendant [to testify] would infringe defendant's privilege against self-incrimination under the Fifth Amendment if this were a trial in a court of the United States under a similar law. Such an assumption does not determine appellant's rights under the Fourteenth Amendment. ***

[Appellant] contends that [the] privilege against self-incrimination, *** to its full scope under the Fifth Amendment, inheres in the right to a fair trial. A right to a fair trial is a right admittedly protected by the due process clause of the Fourteenth Amendment. *** The due process clause of the Fourteenth Amendment, however, does not draw all the rights of the federal Bill of Rights under its protection. That contention was made and rejected in *Palko v. Connecticut*, 302 U.S. 319, 323 [(1937)].

> **FYI**
>
> The Fifth Amendment provides that no person "shall be compelled in any criminal case to be a witness against himself." Putting aside the question whether the Fourteenth Amendment makes the privilege against self-incrimination applicable to state action, why was California law arguably in conflict with the privilege? How would an approach like California's affect a defendant's decision whether to testify in his own defense?

Palko held that such provisions of the Bill of Rights as were "implicit in the concept of ordered liberty" became secure from state interference by the clause. But it held nothing more.

For a state to require testimony from an accused is not necessarily a breach of a state's obligation to give a fair trial. *** California has prescribed a method for advising the jury in the search for truth. However sound may be the legislative conclusion that an accused should not be compelled in any criminal case to be a witness against himself, we see no reason why

> **Food for Thought**
>
> If the privilege against self-incrimination is not essential for a fair trial, why does the Fifth Amendment create such a privilege for federal criminal cases? Is there a coherent justification for the conclusion that the same practice that is considered unfair, as a matter of constitutional law, in federal cases is not unfair in state cases?

comment should not be made upon his silence. *** The purpose of due process is not to protect an accused against a proper conviction but against an unfair conviction. When evidence is before a jury that threatens conviction, it does not seem unfair to require him to choose between leaving the adverse evidence unexplained and subjecting himself to impeachment through disclosure of former crimes. Indeed, this is a dilemma with which any defendant may be faced.

Mr. Justice FRANKFURTER [concurring].

For historical reasons a limited immunity from the common duty to testify was written into the Federal Bill of Rights, and I am prepared to agree that, as part of that immunity, comment on the failure of an accused to take the witness stand is forbidden in federal prosecutions. *** But to suggest that such a limitation can be drawn out of "due process" in its protection of ultimate decency in a civilized society is to suggest that the Due Process Clause fastened fetters of unreason upon the States.

Between the incorporation of the Fourteenth Amendment into the Constitution and the beginning of the present membership of the Court—a period of 70 years—the scope of that Amendment was passed upon by 43 judges. Of all these judges, only one, who may respectfully be called an eccentric exception, ever indicated the belief that the Fourteenth Amendment was a shorthand summary of the first eight Amendments theretofore limiting only the Federal Government, and that due process incorporated those eight Amendments as restrictions upon the powers of the States. [The rest of those judges were] mindful of the relation of our federal system to a progressively democratic society and therefore duly regardful of the scope of authority that was left to the States even after the Civil War. And so they did not find that the Fourteenth Amendment, concerned as it was with matters fundamental to the pursuit of justice, fastened upon the States procedural arrangements which, in the language of Mr. Justice Cardozo, only those who are "narrow or provincial" would deem essential to "a fair and enlightened system of justice." *Palko v. Connecticut*, 302 U.S. 319, 325 (1937). To suggest that it is inconsistent with a truly free society to begin prosecutions without an indictment, to try petty civil cases without the paraphernalia of a common law jury, to take into consideration that one who has full opportunity to make a defense remains silent is, in de Tocqueville's phrase, to confound the familiar with the necessary.

The short answer to the suggestion that the [due process clause] was a way of saying that every State must thereafter initiate prosecutions through indictment by a grand jury, must have a trial by a jury of 12 in criminal cases, and must have trial by such a jury in common law suits where the amount in controversy exceeds $20, is that it is a strange way of saying it. *** Those reading the English language with the meaning which it ordinarily conveys, those conversant with the political and legal history of the concept of due process, those sensitive to the relations of the States to the central government as well as the relation of some of the provisions of the Bill of Rights to the process of justice, would hardly recognize the Fourteenth Amendment as a cover for the various explicit provisions of the first eight Amendments. *** The notion that the Fourteenth Amendment was a covert way of imposing upon the States all the rules which it seemed important to Eighteenth Century statesmen to write into the Federal Amendments, was rejected by judges who were themselves witnesses of the process by which the Fourteenth Amendment became part of the Constitution.

Remarks of a particular proponent of the Amendment, no matter how influential, are not to be deemed part of the Amendment. What was submitted for ratification was his proposal, not his speech. Thus, at the time of the ratification of the Fourteenth Amendment the constitutions of nearly half of the ratifying States did not have the rigorous requirements of the Fifth Amendment for instituting criminal proceedings through a grand jury. It could hardly have occurred to these States that by ratifying the Amendment they uprooted their established methods for prosecuting crime and fastened upon themselves a new prosecutorial system. *** As judges charged with the delicate task of subjecting the government of a continent to the Rule of Law we must be particularly mindful that it is "a constitution we are expounding," so that it should not be imprisoned in what are merely legal forms even though they have the sanction of the Eighteenth Century.

It may not be amiss to restate the pervasive function of the Fourteenth Amendment in exacting from the States observance of basic liberties. The Amendment neither comprehends the specific provisions by which the founders deemed it appropriate to restrict the federal government nor is it confined to them. The Due Process Clause of the Fourteenth Amendment has an independent potency, precisely as does the Due Process Clause of the Fifth Amendment in relation to the Federal Government. It ought not to require argument to reject the notion that due process of law meant one thing in the Fifth Amendment and another in the Fourteenth. The Fifth Amendment specifically [precludes] deprivation of "life, liberty, or property, without due process of law." Are Madison and his contemporaries in the framing of the Bill of Rights to be charged with writing into it a meaningless clause? To consider "due process of law" as merely a shorthand statement of other specific clauses in the same amendment is to attribute to the authors and proponents of this Amendment ignorance of, or indifference to, a historic conception which was one of the great instruments in the arsenal of constitutional freedom which the Bill of Rights was to protect and strengthen.

A construction which gives to due process no independent function but turns it into a summary of the specific provisions of the Bill of Rights would [tear] up by the roots much of the fabric of law in the several States, and would deprive the States of opportunity for reforms in legal process designed for extending the area of freedom. It would assume that no other abuses would reveal themselves in the course of time than those which had become manifest in 1791. Such a view not only disregards the historic meaning of "due process." It leads inevitably to a warped construction of specific provisions of the Bill of Rights to bring within their scope conduct clearly condemned by due process but not easily fitting into the pigeon-holes of the specific provisions. It seems pretty late in the day to suggest that a phrase so laden with historic meaning should be given an improvised content consisting of some but not all of the provisions of the first eight Amendments, selected on an undefined basis, with improvisation of content for the provisions so selected.

And so, [the] issue is not whether an infraction of one of the specific provisions of the first eight Amendments is disclosed by the record. The relevant question is whether the criminal proceedings which resulted in conviction deprived the accused of the due process of law. Judicial review of that guaranty of the Fourteenth Amendment inescapably imposes upon this Court an exercise of judgment upon the whole course of the proceedings in order to ascertain whether they offend those canons of decency and fairness which express the notions of justice of English-speaking peoples even toward those charged with the most heinous offenses. These standards of justice are not authoritatively formulated anywhere as though they were prescriptions in a pharmacopoeia. But neither does the application of the Due Process Clause imply that judges are wholly at large. The judicial judgment in applying the Due Process Clause must move within the limits of accepted notions of justice and is not to be based upon the idiosyncrasies of a merely personal judgment. *** An important safeguard against such merely individual judgment is an alert deference to the judgment of the State court under review.

Mr. Justice BLACK, [with whom Mr. Justice DOUGLAS joins,] dissenting.

[The Court asserts] a constitutional theory [that] this Court is endowed by the Constitution with boundless power under "natural law" periodically to expand and contract constitutional standards to conform to the Court's conception of what at a particular time constitutes "civilized decency" and "fundamental principles of liberty and justice." *** I think that [the] "natural law" theory of the Constitution upon which it relies [degrades] the constitutional safeguards of the Bill of Rights and simultaneously appropriate for this Court a broad power which we are not authorized by the Constitution to exercise.

My study of the historical events that culminated in the Fourteenth Amendment, and the expressions of those who sponsored and favored, as well as those who opposed its submission and passage, persuades me that one of the chief objects that the provisions of the Amendment's first section, separately, and as a whole, were intended to accomplish was to make the Bill of Rights applicable to the states. With full knowledge of the import of the _Barron_ decision, the framers and backers of the Fourteenth Amendment proclaimed its purpose to be to overturn the constitutional rule that case had announced.

I cannot consider the Bill of Rights to be an outworn 18th Century "strait jacket." Its provisions may be thought outdated abstractions by some. And it is true that they were designed to meet ancient evils. But they are the same kind of human evils that have emerged from century to century wherever excessive power is sought

> **FYI**
>
> Justice Black attached a lengthy appendix to his dissenting opinion containing, among other things, transcripts of the congressional debates concerning the Fourteenth Amendment. Justice Black relied in particular on statements in support of the proposed Fourteenth Amendment by Congressman Bingham, to whom Justice Black referred as "the Madison of the first section of the Fourteenth Amendment." For a sampling of the scholarly debate over the original meaning of the Fourteenth Amendment, compare William Crosskey, *Charles Fairman, "Legislative History," and the Constitutional Limitations on State Authority,* 22 U. Chi. L. Rev. 1 (1954), with Charles Fairman, *Does the Fourteenth Amendment Incorporate the Bill of Rights? The Original Understanding,* 2 Stan. L. Rev. 5 (1949) (disagreeing with Justice Black).

by the few at the expense of the many. In my judgment the people of no nation can lose their liberty so long as a Bill of Rights like ours survives and its basic purposes are conscientiously interpreted, enforced and respected so as to afford continuous protection against old, as well as new, devices and practices which might thwart those purposes. I fear to see the consequences of the Court's practice of substituting its own concepts of decency and fundamental justice for the language of the Bill of Rights as its point of departure in interpreting and enforcing that Bill of Rights. *** I would follow what I believe was the original purpose of the Fourteenth Amendment—to extend to all the people of the nation the complete protection of the Bill of Rights. To hold that this Court can determine what, if any, provisions of the Bill of Rights will be enforced, and if so to what degree, is to frustrate the great design of a written Constitution.

It is an illusory apprehension that literal application of some or all of the provisions of the Bill of Rights to the States would unwisely increase the sum total of the powers of this Court to invalidate state legislation. The Federal Government has not been harmfully burdened by the requirement that enforcement of federal laws affecting civil liberty conform literally to the Bill of Rights. Who would advocate its repeal? It must be conceded, of course, that the natural-law-due-process formula, which the Court today reaffirms, has been interpreted to limit substantially this Court's power to prevent state violations of the individual civil liberties guaranteed by the Bill of Rights. But this formula also has been used in the past and can be used in the future, to license this Court, in considering regulatory legislation, to roam at large in the broad expanses of policy and morals and to trespass, all too freely, on the legislative domain of the States as well as the Federal Government.

[Judicial review], of course, involves interpretation, and since words can have many meanings, interpretation obviously may result in contraction or extension of the original purpose of a constitutional provision thereby affecting policy. But to pass upon the constitutionality of statutes by looking to the particular standards enumerated in the Bill of Rights and other parts of the Constitution is one thing; to invalidate statutes because of application of "natural law" deemed to be above and undefined by the Constitution is another. "In the one instance, courts proceeding within clearly marked constitutional boundaries seek to execute policies written into the Constitution; in the other they roam at will in the limitless area of their own beliefs as to reasonableness and actually select policies, a responsibility which the Constitution entrusts to the legislative representatives of the people."

Mr. Justice MURPHY, with whom Mr. Justice RUTLEDGE concurs, dissenting.

While in substantial agreement with the views of Mr. Justice BLACK, I have one reservation and one addition to make. I agree that the specific guarantees of the Bill of Rights should be carried over intact into the first section of the Fourteenth Amendment. But I am not prepared to say that the latter is entirely and necessarily limited by the Bill of Rights. Occasions may arise where a proceeding falls so far short of conforming to fundamental standards of procedure as to warrant constitutional condemnation in terms of a lack of due process despite the absence of a specific provision in the Bill of Rights. That point, however, need not be pursued here inasmuch as the Fifth Amendment is explicit in its provision that no person shall be compelled in any criminal case to be a witness against himself. *** Accordingly, I would reverse the judgment below.

———————————

Points for Discussion

a. Selective or Total Incorporation?

In <u>Adamson</u>, the principal competing positions were advanced by Justices Frankfurter and Black. Justice Frankfurter concluded that the Due Process Clause of the Fourteenth Amendment affords rights that are "implicit in the concept of ordered liberty." Under this view, some of the same rights that the Bill of Rights provides against the federal government might apply against the states, but only because their recognition is essential to the notion of fundamental fairness embodied by the Due Process Clause. This approach is generally known as "selective incorporation," because in practice it would result in the application of some, but not all, of the prohibitions in the Bill of Rights to the states. Justice Black, in contrast, believed that the Due Process Clause incorporated all of the protections of the first eight amendments—nothing more, and nothing less. This approach is generally known as "total incorporation."

In the years after <u>Adamson</u>, the Court continued, at least as a formal matter, to interpret the Due Process Clause by asking which rights were "implicit in the concept of ordered liberty"—that is, by following the approach of selective incorporation. But increasingly, the Court—particularly the Warren Court in the 1960s—looked to the first eight amendments to give content to that standard. What resulted was an approach that claimed to be one of "selective incorporation"—that is, the view that the Due Process Clause incorporates some, but not all, of the rights identified in the first eight amendments, depending upon whether the right is necessary for fundamental fairness—but that in practice came close to Justice Black's total incorporation approach.

Indeed, in a series of decisions beginning a half-century before <u>Adamson</u> and continuing for several decades after the decision, the Court decided that the Due Process Clause incorporates virtually every provision in the first eight amendments. The Court has held, for example, that the Due Process Clause incorporates all of the substantive rights in the First Amendment, see e.g., *Everson v. Board of Education*, 330 U.S. 1 (1947) (establishment); *Cantwell v. Connecticut*, 310 U.S. 296 (1940) (free exercise); *Gitlow v. New York*, 268 U.S. 652 (1925) (speech); the Fourth Amendment, see, e.g., *Wolf v. Colorado*, 338 U.S. 25 (1949) (warrant requirement); the Fifth Amendment, see, e.g., *Benton v. Maryland*, 395 U.S. 784 (1969) (double jeopardy); *Chicago,*

> **Make the Connection**
>
> In Chapter 8, we will begin our consideration of the doctrine of "substantive due process," which holds that the Due Process Clause protects some substantive rights that cannot be abridged by government action regardless of the process that the government provides. When we do, keep in mind the debate over incorporation, and consider whether the process of incorporation itself is a form of "substantive due process."

Burlington & Quincy R.R. Co. v. Chicago, 166 U.S. 226 (1897) (takings); most of the substantive rights in the Sixth Amendment, see, e.g., *Gideon v. Wainwright*, 372 U.S. 335 (1963) (counsel); *Irvin v. Dowd*, 366 U.S. 717 (1961) (impartial jury); and the Eighth Amendment, see, e.g., *Robinson v. California*, 370 U.S. 660 (1962) (cruel and unusual punishment).

There are only two provisions in the first eight amendments that the Court has expressly determined are not incorporated, and those decisions, discussed above, pre-dated the Warren Court's more comprehensive approach to incorporation. See *Hurtado v. California*, 110 U.S. 516 (1884) (right to a grand jury indictment); *Minneapolis & St. Louis R.R. Co. v. Bombolis*, 241 U.S. 211 (1916) (right to a jury trial in civil cases). In addition, the Court has never decided whether the Third Amendment right not to have soldiers quartered in a home and the Eighth Amendment right not to be subject to excessive fines are incorporated.

b. Incorporation of the Privilege Against Self-Incrimination

Once the Warren Court had begun more aggressively to find that the Due Process Clause incorporated protections in the first eight amendments, it was only a matter of time before it reconsidered whether the Fourteenth Amendment incorporated the privilege against self-incrimination. In *Malloy v. Hogan*, 378 U.S. 1 (1964), the Court held that it did, and one year later, in *Griffin v. California*, 380 U.S. 609 (1965), the Court overruled the specific holding in <u>Adamson</u> and declared unconstitutional California's law permitting comment on the defendant's failure to testify.

c. Incorporation and the Judicial Role

Both Justices Frankfurter and Black claimed that their approaches were more consistent with the judicial role. Justice Frankfurter asserted that because total incorporation would impose more limits on state action (by expanding the number of individual rights that trump state action), that approach would empower judges to limit the ability of the democratic process to operate effectively in the states. Justice Black, by contrast, asserted that Justice Frankfurter's approach would give judges virtually standardless discretion to decide what rights are "implicit in the concept of ordered liberty." Which approach do you think is more consistent with the judicial role?

As we saw in Chapter 1, the Court in *District of Columbia v. Heller*, 554 U.S. 570 (2008), held for the first time that the Second Amendment protects an individual right to keep and bear arms unconnected with service in a state-regulated militia. Does the Fourteenth Amendment also limit the authority of the states to interfere with the right to keep and bear arms? The case that follows addresses that question.

McDonald v. City of Chicago

130 S.Ct. 3020 (2010)

Justice ALITO announced the judgment of the Court and delivered the opinion of the Court [except as stated in footnote 1].

[The City of Chicago and the Village of Oak Park, a Chicago suburb, have ordinances that ban or effectively ban private possession of handguns. Petitioners sought declarations that the bans violate the Second and Fourteenth Amendments. The Court of Appeals rejected those claims, relying on three cases—*United States v. Cruikshank,* 92 U.S. 542 (1876), *Presser v. Illinois,* 116 U.S. 252 (1886), and *Miller v. Texas,* 153 U.S. 535 (1894)— that the Court decided shortly after its decision in the *Slaughter-House Cases* and that held that the Second Amendment does not apply to the states, of its own force or through the Privileges or Immunities Clause of the Fourteenth Amendment. Petitioners urged the Court to overrule those decisions and to hold that the right to keep and bear arms is one of the "privileges or immunities of citizens of the United States."]

We see no need to reconsider that interpretation [of the Privileges or Immunities Clause] here.[1] For many decades, the question of the rights protected by the Fourteenth Amendment against state infringement has been analyzed under the Due Process Clause [and] not under the Privileges or Immunities Clause. We therefore decline to disturb the *Slaughter-House* holding. At the same time, however, this Court's decisions in *Cruikshank,* *Presser,* and *Miller* do not preclude us from considering whether the Due Process Clause of the Fourteenth Amendment makes the Second Amendment right binding on the States. [Those cases] all preceded the era in which the Court began the process of "selective incorporation" under the Due Process Clause, and we have never previously addressed the question whether the right to keep and bear arms applies to the States under that theory.

In the late 19th century, the Court began to consider whether the Due Process Clause prohibits the States from infringing rights set out in the Bill of Rights. Five features of the approach taken during the ensuing era should be noted. First, the Court viewed the due process question as entirely separate from the question whether a right was a privilege or immunity of national citizenship. *Twining v. New Jersey,* 211 U.S. 78, 99 (1908). Second, the Court explained that [w]hile it was "possible that some of the personal rights safeguarded by the first eight Amendments against National action [might] also be safeguarded against state action," [this] was "not because those rights are enumerated in the first eight Amendments." [*Id.*]. The Court used different formulations in describing the boundaries of due process. *** In *Snyder v. Massachusetts,* 291 U.S. 97, 105 (1934), the Court spoke of rights that are "so rooted in the traditions and conscience of our people as to be ranked as fundamental." And in *Palko v. Connecticut,* 302 U.S. 319 (1937), the Court famously said that due process protects those rights that are "the very essence of a scheme of ordered liberty" and essential to "a fair and enlightened system of justice."

---

[1] Justice Thomas did not join this paragraph of the Court's opinion.—*Eds.*

Third, in some cases decided during this era the Court "can be seen as having asked, when inquiring into whether some particular procedural safeguard was required of a State, if a civilized system could be imagined that would not accord the particular protection." *Duncan v. Louisiana*, 391 U.S. 145, 149, n. 14 (1968). *** Fourth, the Court during this era was not hesitant to hold that a right set out in the Bill of Rights failed to meet the test for inclusion within the protection of the Due Process Clause. The Court found that some such rights qualified, see, *e.g.*, *Gitlow v. New York*, 268 U.S. 652, 666 (1925) (freedom of speech and press), [but that] others did not, see, *e.g.*, *Hurtado v. California*, 110 U.S. 516 (1884) (grand jury indictment requirement). Finally, even when a right set out in the Bill of Rights was held to fall within the conception of due process, the protection or remedies afforded against state infringement sometimes differed from the protection or remedies provided against abridgment by the Federal Government.

An alternative theory regarding the relationship between the Bill of Rights and § 1 of the Fourteenth Amendment was championed by Justice Black. This theory held that § 1 of the Fourteenth Amendment totally incorporated all of the provisions of the Bill of Rights. See, *e.g.*, *Adamson v. California*, 332 U.S. 46, 71-72 (1947) (Black, J., dissenting). As Justice Black noted, the chief congressional proponents of the Fourteenth Amendment espoused the view that the Amendment made the Bill of Rights applicable to the States and, in so doing, overruled this Court's decision in *Barron*.

While Justice Black's ["total incorporation"] theory was never adopted, the Court eventually moved in that direction by initiating what has been called a process of "selective incorporation," *i.e.*, the Court began to hold that the Due Process Clause fully incorporates particular rights contained in the first eight Amendments. The decisions during this time [in the 1960s] abandoned three of the previously noted characteristics of the earlier period. The Court made it clear that the governing standard is not whether *any* "civilized system [can] be imagined that would not accord the particular protection." *Duncan*. Instead, the Court inquired whether a particular Bill of Rights guarantee is fundamental to *our* scheme of ordered liberty and system of justice. The Court also shed any reluctance to hold that rights guaranteed by the Bill of Rights met the requirements for protection under the Due Process Clause. The Court eventually incorporated almost all of the provisions of the Bill of Rights. Only a handful of the Bill of Rights protections remain unincorporated.

Finally, [the Court] decisively held that incorporated Bill of Rights protections "are all to be enforced against the States under the Fourteenth Amendment according to the same standards that protect those personal rights against federal encroachment." *Malloy v. Hogan*, 378 U.S. 1, 10 (1964). *** Employing this approach, the Court overruled earlier decisions in which it had held that particular Bill of Rights guarantees or remedies did not apply to the States. See, *e.g.*, *Mapp v. Ohio*, 367 U.S. 643 (1961) (exclusionary rule).

With this framework in mind, we now turn directly to the question whether the Second Amendment right to keep and bear arms is incorporated in the concept of due process. In answering that question, [we] must decide whether the right to keep and bear arms is fundamental to our scheme of ordered liberty, or as we have said in a related context, whether this right is "deeply rooted in this Nation's history and tradition," *Washington v. Glucksberg*, 521 U.S. 702, 721 (1997).

Our decision in *Heller* points unmistakably to the answer. Self-defense is a basic right, recognized by many legal systems from ancient times to the present day, and in *Heller*, we held that individual self-defense is "the *central component*" of the Second Amendment right. Explaining that "the need for defense of self, family, and property is most acute" in the home, we found that this right applies to handguns because they are "the most preferred firearm in the nation to 'keep' and use for protection of one's home and family."

Heller makes it clear that this right is "deeply rooted in this Nation's history and tradition." *Heller* explored the right's origins, noting that the 1689 English Bill of Rights explicitly protected a right to keep arms for self-defense, and that by 1765, Blackstone was able to assert that the right to keep and bear arms was "one of the fundamental rights of Englishmen." Blackstone's assessment was shared by the American colonists. *** The right to keep and bear arms was considered no less fundamental by those who drafted and ratified the Bill of Rights. *** Antifederalists and Federalists alike agreed that the right to bear arms was fundamental to the newly formed system of government. But those who were fearful that the new Federal Government would infringe traditional rights such as the right to keep and bear arms insisted on the adoption of the Bill of Rights as a condition for ratification of the Constitution. This is surely powerful evidence that the right was regarded as fundamental in the sense relevant here. This understanding persisted in the years immediately following the ratification of the Bill of Rights. In addition to the four States that had adopted Second Amendment analogues before ratification, nine more States adopted state constitutional provisions protecting an individual right to keep and bear arms between 1789 and 1820.

By the 1850's, the perceived threat that had prompted the inclusion of the Second Amendment in the Bill of Rights—the fear that the National Government would disarm the universal militia—had largely faded as a popular concern, but the right to keep and bear arms was highly valued for purposes of self-defense. Abolitionist authors wrote in support of the right. *** After the Civil War, many of the over 180,000 African Americans who served in the Union Army returned to the States of the old Confederacy, where systematic efforts were made to disarm them and other blacks. *** Congress concluded that legislative action was necessary. Its efforts to safeguard the right to keep and bear arms demonstrate that the right was still recognized to be fundamental.

The most explicit evidence of Congress' aim appears in § 14 of the Freedmen's Bureau Act of 1866, [which] explicitly guaranteed that "all the citizens," black and white, would have "the constitutional right to bear arms." [The Civil Rights Act of 1866] protected the same rights as enumerated in the Freedmen's Bureau bill. *** Congress, however, ultimately deemed these legislative remedies insufficient. Southern resistance, Presidential vetoes, and this Court's pre-Civil-War precedent persuaded Congress that a constitutional amendment was necessary to provide full protection for the rights of blacks. Today, it is generally accepted that the Fourteenth Amendment was understood to provide a constitutional basis for protecting the rights set out in the Civil Rights Act of 1866. [In addition, a] clear majority of [state constitutions in 1868] recognized the right to keep and bear arms as being among the foundational rights necessary to our system of Government. In sum, it is clear that the Framers and ratifiers of the Fourteenth Amendment counted the right to keep and bear arms among those fundamental rights necessary to our system of ordered liberty.

Municipal respondents' main argument is nothing less than a plea to disregard 50 years of incorporation precedent and return (presumably for this case only) to a bygone era. *** According to municipal respondents, if it is possible to imagine *any* civilized legal system that does not recognize a particular right, then the Due Process Clause does not make that right binding on the States. Therefore, the municipal respondents continue, because such countries as England, Canada, Australia, Japan, Denmark, Finland, Luxembourg, and New Zealand either ban or severely limit handgun ownership, it must follow that no right to possess such weapons is protected by the Fourteenth Amendment.

This line of argument is, of course, inconsistent with the long-established standard we apply in incorporation cases. And the present-day implications of municipal respondents' argument are stunning. *** [For example,] several of the countries that municipal respondents recognize as civilized have established state churches. If we were to adopt municipal respondents' theory, all of this Court's Establishment Clause precedents involving actions taken by state and local governments would go by the boards.

> **Make the Connection**
>
> We consider the Court's cases construing the Establishment Clause in Chapter 17.

Municipal respondents maintain that the Second Amendment differs from all of the other provisions of the Bill of Rights because it concerns the right to possess a deadly implement and thus has implications for public safety. *** The right to keep and bear arms, however, is not the only constitutional right that has controversial public safety implications. All of the constitutional provisions that impose restrictions on law enforcement and on the prosecution of crimes fall into the same category. *** Unless we turn back the clock or adopt a special incorporation test applicable only to the Second Amendment, municipal respondents' argument must be rejected. *** [We] hold that the Due Process Clause of the Fourteenth Amendment incorporates the Second Amendment right recognized in *Heller*.

Justice SCALIA, concurring.

I join the Court's opinion. Despite my misgivings about Substantive Due Process as an original matter, I have acquiesced in the Court's incorporation of certain guarantees in the Bill of Rights "because it is both long established and narrowly limited." *Albright v. Oliver,*

510 U.S. 266, 275 (1994) (SCALIA, J., concurring). *** I write separately only to respond to some aspects of Justice STEVENS' dissent.

Justice STEVENS begins with the odd assertion that "firearms have a fundamentally ambivalent relationship to liberty," since sometimes they are used to cause (or sometimes accidentally produce) injury to others. *** Justice STEVENS supplies neither a standard for how severe the impairment on others' liberty must be for a right to be disqualified, nor (of course) any method of measuring the severity.

Justice STEVENS next suggests that the Second Amendment right is not fundamental because *** owning a handgun is not "critical to leading a life of autonomy, dignity, or political equality." Who says? Deciding what is essential to an enlightened, liberty-filled life is an inherently political, moral judgment—the antithesis of an objective approach that reaches conclusions by applying neutral rules to verifiable evidence.

Justice STEVENS' final reason for rejecting incorporation of the Second Amendment [is that the] States' "right to experiment" with solutions to the problem of gun violence [is] at its apex here because "the best solution is far from clear." That is true of most serious social problems ***. The implication of Justice STEVENS' call for abstention is that if We The Court conclude that They The People's answers to a problem are silly, we are free to "interven[e]," but if we too are uncertain of the right answer, or merely think the States may be on to something, we can loosen the leash. *** I would not—and no judge should—presume to have that sort of omniscience, which seems to me far more "arrogant" than confining courts' focus to our own national heritage.

Justice THOMAS, concurring in part and concurring in the judgment.

I agree with [the plurality's] description of the right [to keep and bear arms as "funda-mental."] But I cannot agree that it is enforceable against the States through a clause that speaks only to "process." Instead, the right to keep and bear arms is a privilege of American citizenship that applies to the States through the Fourteenth Amendment's Privileges or Immunities Clause.

On its face, [the Clause] appears to grant the persons just made United States citizens [by the first Clause of the Fourteenth Amendment] a certain collection of rights—*i.e.*, privileges or immunities—attributable to that status. [But as] a consequence of this Court's marginalization of the Clause [in *Slaughter-House*], litigants seeking federal protection of fundamental rights turned to the remainder of § 1 in search of an alternative fount of such rights. They found one in a most curious place—that section's command that every State guarantee "due process" to any person before depriving him of "life, liberty, or property." [T]he Court has determined that the Due Process Clause [not only incorporates "funda-mental" rights mentioned in the Bill of Rights but also] applies rights against the States that are not mentioned in the Constitution at all ***. See, *e.g.*, *Lochner v. New York*, 198 U.S. 45 (1905); *Roe v. Wade*, 410 U.S. 113 (1973).

All of this is a legal fiction. The notion that a constitutional provision that guarantees only "process" before a person is deprived of life, liberty, or property could define the sub-stance of those rights strains credulity for even the most casual user of words. Moreover, this fiction is a particularly dangerous one. The one theme that links the Court's substantive due process precedents together is their lack of a guiding principle to distinguish "fundamental" rights that warrant protection from nonfundamental rights that do not. *** I cannot accept a theory of constitutional interpretation that rests on such tenuous footing. *** I believe the original meaning of the Fourteenth Amendment offers a superior alternative, and that a return to that meaning would allow this Court to enforce the rights the Fourteenth Amendment is designed to protect with greater clarity and predictability than the substantive due process framework has so far managed.

The evidence overwhelmingly demonstrates that the privileges and immunities of [U.S. citizens protected by Section 1 of the Fourteenth Amendment] included individual rights enumerated in the Constitution, including the right to keep and bear arms. [Several nineteenth-century] treaties through which the United States acquired territory from other sovereigns *** promised inhabitants of the newly acquired territories that they would enjoy all of the "rights," "privileges," and "immunities" of United States citizens, [and] identif[ied] liberties enumerated in the Constitution as [such] privileges and immunities ***.

Statements made by Members of Congress leading up to, and during, the debates on the Fourteenth Amendment point in the same direction. *** Representative John Bingham, the principal draftsman of § 1 [of the Fourteenth Amendment], emphasized [on the floor of the House] that § 1 was designed "to arm the Congress of the United States, by the consent of the people of the United States, with the power to enforce the bill of rights as it stands in the Constitution today." 39th Cong. Globe 1088 (1866). *** [While Bingham's original draft of § 1 was tabled for several months,] he delivered a second well-publicized speech, again arguing that a constitutional amendment was required to give Congress the power to enforce the Bill of Rights against the States.

By the time the debates on the Fourteenth Amendment resumed, Bingham had amended his draft of § 1 to include the text of the Privileges or Immunities Clause that was ultimately adopted. Senator Jacob Howard introduced the new draft on the floor of the Senate ***. [Howard explained that the protected rights] included "the privileges and immunities spoken of" in Article IV, § 2 [as described in *Corfield v. Coryell* and] "*the personal rights guaranteed and secured by the first eight amendments of the Constitution.*" [39 Cong. Globe 2765-66] (emphasis added). [T]hese well-circulated speeches indicate that § 1 was understood to enforce constitutionally declared rights against the States, and they provide no suggestion that any language in the section other than the Privileges or Immunities Clause would accomplish that task. ***

> **FYI**
>
> In *Corfield*, Justice Washington concluded that the Privileges and Immunities Clause of Article IV protected rights "which are, in their nature, fundamental." We briefly considered *Corfield* along with the *Slaughter-House Cases* earlier in this Chapter.

[The] ratifying public understood the Privileges or Immunities Clause to protect constitutionally enumerated rights, including the right to keep and bear arms. *** In the contentious years leading up to the Civil War, those who sought to retain the institution of slavery found that to do so, it was necessary to eliminate more and more of the basic liberties of slaves, free blacks, and white abolitionists. *** The overarching goal of pro-slavery forces was to repress the spread of abolitionist thought and the concomitant risk of a slave rebellion. *** The fear [of] rebellions led Southern legislatures to take particularly vicious aim at the rights of free blacks and slaves to speak or to keep and bear arms for their defense. *** After the Civil War, Southern anxiety about an uprising among the newly freed slaves peaked, [which led Southern states to prohibit blacks from possessing firearms and forcibly to disarm them].

The publicly circulated Report of the Joint Committee on Reconstruction extensively detailed these abuses, and statements by citizens indicate that they looked to the Committee to provide a federal solution to this problem, see, *e.g.*, 39th Cong. Globe 337 (remarks of Rep. Sumner) (introducing "a memorial from the colored citizens of the State of South Carolina" asking for, *inter alia*, "constitutional protection in keeping arms, in holding public assemblies, and in complete liberty of speech and of the press"). *** "Notwithstanding the provision in the Constitution of the United States, that the right to keep and bear arms shall not be abridged," [Frederick] Douglass explained that "the black man has never had the right either to keep or bear arms." Absent a constitutional amendment to enforce that right against the States, he insisted that "the work of the Abolitionists [wa]s not finished." This history confirms what the text of the Privileges or Immunities Clause most naturally suggests: Consistent with its command that "[n]o State shall . . . abridge" the rights of United States citizens, the Clause establishes a minimum baseline of federal rights, and the constitutional right to keep and bear arms plainly was among them.

My conclusion is contrary to this Court's precedents, which hold that the Second Amendment right to keep and bear arms is not a privilege of United States citizenship. *** I reject [the *Slaughter-House* Court's] understanding [of the Privileges or Immunities Clause]. There was no reason to interpret the Privileges or Immunities Clause as putting the Court to the extreme choice of interpreting the "privileges and immunities" of federal citizenship to mean either all those rights listed in *Corfield*, or almost no rights at all. *** The better view, in light of the States and Federal Government's shared history of recognizing certain inalienable rights in their citizens, is that the privileges and immunities of state and federal citizenship overlap. *** [In addition,] *Cruikshank* is not a precedent entitled to any respect. *** *Cruikshank*'s holding that blacks could look only to state governments for protection of their right to keep and bear arms enabled private forces, often with the assistance of local governments, to subjugate the newly freed slaves and their descendants through a wave of private violence designed to drive blacks from the voting booth and force them into peonage, an effective return to slavery.

In my view, the record makes plain that the Framers of the Privileges or Immunities Clause and the ratifying-era public understood—just as the Framers of the Second Amendment did—that the right to keep and bear arms was essential to the preservation of liberty. The record makes equally plain that they deemed this right necessary to include in the minimum baseline of federal rights that the Privileges or Immunities Clause established in the wake of the War over slavery.

Justice STEVENS, dissenting.

[T]he term "incorporation," like the term "unenumerated rights," is something of a misnomer. Whether an asserted substantive due process interest is explicitly named in one of the first eight Amendments to the Constitution or is not mentioned, the underlying inquiry is the same: We must ask whether the interest is "comprised within the term liberty." *Whitney v. California,* 274 U.S. 357, 373 (1927) (Brandeis, J., concurring). *** This Court's "selective incorporation" doctrine is not simply "related" to substantive due process; it is a subset thereof.

The question in this case [is] whether the particular right asserted by petitioners applies to the States because of the Fourteenth Amendment itself, standing on its own bottom. And to answer that question, we need to determine, first, the nature of the right that has been asserted and, second, whether that right is an aspect of Fourteenth Amendment "liberty." [T]he liberty interest petitioners have asserted is the "right to possess a functional, personal firearm, including a handgun, within the home." Complaint ¶ 34, App. 23. *** I would not foreclose the possibility that a particular plaintiff—say, an elderly widow who lives in a dangerous neighborhood and does not have the strength to operate a long gun—may have a cognizable liberty interest in possessing a handgun. But I cannot accept petitioners' broader submission.

First, firearms have a fundamentally ambivalent relationship to liberty. Just as they can help homeowners defend their families and property from intruders, they can help thugs and insurrectionists murder innocent victims. *** Hence, in evaluating an asserted right to be free from particular gun-control regulations, liberty is on both sides of the equation. *** Second, the right to possess a firearm of one's choosing is different in kind from the liberty interests we have recognized under the Due Process Clause. [I]t does not appear to be the case that the ability to own a handgun, or any particular type of firearm, is critical to leading a life of autonomy, dignity, or political equality.

Third, the experience of other advanced democracies, including those that share our British heritage, undercuts the notion that an expansive right to keep and bear arms is intrinsic to ordered liberty. Many of these countries place restrictions on the possession, use, and carriage of firearms far more onerous than the restrictions found in this Nation. *** While the "American perspective" must always be our focus, it is silly—indeed, arrogant—to think we have nothing to learn about liberty from the billions of people beyond our borders.

Fourth, the Second Amendment differs in kind from the Amendments that surround it ***. Notwithstanding the *Heller* Court's efforts to write the Second Amendment's preamble out of the Constitution, the Amendment still serves the structural function of protecting the States from encroachment by an overreaching Federal Government. *** The Second Amendment *** is directed at preserving the autonomy of the sovereign States, and its logic therefore "resists" incorporation by a federal court *against* the States.

Fifth, [the] States have a long and unbroken history of regulating firearms. *** This history of intrusive regulation is not surprising given that the very text of the Second

Amendment calls out for regulation, and the ability to respond to the social ills associated with dangerous weapons goes to the very core of the States' police powers. *** Finally, even apart from the States' long history of firearms regulation and its location at the core of their police powers, this is a quintessential area in which federalism ought to be allowed to flourish without this Court's meddling. *** Across the Nation, States and localities vary significantly in the patterns and problems of gun violence they face, as well as in the traditions and cultures of lawful gun use they claim. The city of Chicago, for example, faces a pressing challenge in combating criminal street gangs. Most rural areas do not. The city of Chicago has a high population density, which increases the potential for a gunman to inflict mass terror and casualties. Most rural areas do not. The city of Chicago offers little in the way of hunting opportunities. Residents of rural communities are, one presumes, much more likely to stock the dinner table with game they have personally felled. *** Given that relevant background conditions diverge so much across jurisdictions, the Court ought to pay particular heed to state and local legislatures' "right to experiment." *New State Ice Co. v. Liebmann*, 285 U.S. 262, 311 (1932) (Brandeis, J., dissenting). *** I respectfully dissent.

Justice BREYER, with whom Justice GINSBURG and Justice SOTOMAYOR join, dissenting.

Two years ago, in *Heller*, the Court rejected the pre-existing judicial consensus that the Second Amendment was primarily concerned with the need to maintain a "well regulated Militia." *** The Court based its conclusions almost exclusively upon its reading of history. But the relevant history in *Heller* was far from clear. *** [And since] *Heller*, historians, scholars, and judges have continued to express the view that the Court's historical account was flawed. *** At the least, where *Heller*'s historical foundations are so uncertain, why extend its applicability?

In my view, taking *Heller* as a given, the Fourteenth Amendment does not incorporate the Second Amendment right to keep and bear arms for purposes of private self-defense. *** The majority here, like that in *Heller*, relies almost exclusively upon history to make the necessary showing. But to do so for incorporation purposes is both wrong and dangerous. [O]ur society has historically made mistakes—for example, when considering certain 18th- and 19th-century property rights to be fundamental. And in the incorporation context, as elsewhere, history often is unclear about the answers. Accordingly, this Court, in considering an incorporation question, has never stated that the historical status of a right is the only relevant consideration. Rather, the Court has either explicitly or implicitly made clear in its opinions that the right in question has remained fundamental over time.

[T]here is no popular consensus that the private self-defense right described in *Heller* is fundamental. [E]very State regulates firearms extensively, and public opinion is sharply divided on the appropriate level of regulation. *** One side believes the right essential to protect the lives of those attacked in the home; the other side believes it essential to regulate the right in order to protect the lives of others attacked with guns. It seems unlikely that definitive evidence will develop one way or the other. And the appropriate level of firearm regulation has thus long been, and continues to be, a hotly contested matter of political debate.

Moreover, there is no reason here to believe that incorporation of the private self-defense right will further any other or broader constitutional objective. *** Unlike the First Amendment's rights of free speech, free press, assembly, and petition, the private self-defense right does not comprise a necessary part of the democratic process that the Constitution seeks to establish. Unlike the First Amendment's religious protections, the Fourth Amendment's protection against unreasonable searches and seizures, the Fifth and Sixth Amendments' insistence upon fair criminal procedure, and the Eighth Amendment's protection against cruel and unusual punishments, the private self-defense right does not significantly seek to protect individuals who might otherwise suffer unfair or inhumane treatment at the hands of a majority. Unlike the protections offered by many of these same Amendments, it does not involve matters as to which judges possess a comparative expertise, by virtue of their close familiarity with the justice system and its operation. And, unlike the Fifth Amendment's insistence on just compensation, it does not involve a matter where a majority might unfairly seize for itself property belonging to a minority.

Finally, incorporation of the right *will* work a significant disruption in the constitutional allocation of decisionmaking authority, thereby interfering with the Constitution's ability to further its objectives. *First*, on any reasonable accounting, the incorporation of the right recognized in *Heller* would amount to a significant incursion on a traditional and important area of state concern, altering the constitutional relationship between the States and the Federal Government. *** *Second*, determining the constitutionality of a particular state gun law requires finding answers to complex empirically based questions of a kind that legislatures are better able than courts to make. *** Government regulation of the right to bear arms normally embodies a judgment that the regulation will help save lives. The determination whether a gun regulation is constitutional would thus almost always require the weighing of the constitutional right to bear arms against the "primary concern of every government—a concern for the safety and indeed the lives of its citizens." *** *Third*, the ability of States to reflect local preferences and conditions—both key virtues of federalism—here has particular importance. *** States and local communities have historically differed about the need for gun regulation as well as about its proper level.

I can find much in the historical record that shows that some Americans in some places at certain times thought it important to keep and bear arms for private self-defense. [But the historical] record is insufficient to say that the right to bear arms for private self-defense, as explicated by *Heller*, is fundamental in the sense relevant to the incorporation inquiry. *** States and localities have consistently enacted firearms regulations, including regulations similar to those at issue here, throughout our Nation's history. Courts have repeatedly upheld such regulations. *** [N]othing in 18th-, 19th-, 20th-, or 21st-century history shows a consensus that the right to private armed self-defense, as described in *Heller*, is "deeply rooted in this Nation's history or tradition" or is otherwise "fundamental." *** With respect, I dissent.

———————————

Points for Discussion

a. The Second Amendment

In *Heller*, the Court concluded that the Second Amendment protects an individual right to keep and bear arms for self-defense. The dissenting Justices disagreed, reasoning that the Amendment was designed to protect the states from federal over-reaching. If the dissenters had prevailed, then there likely would not have been any argument about whether the Amendment's protections were incorporated by the Fourteenth Amendment, because it would make no sense to apply a structural protection for the states as a limit on state action. (Similarly, it would make no sense to incorporate the Tenth Amendment, which "reserve[s]" powers to the states.) How much of the debate between the majority and the dissenting Justices in *McDonald* was over the proper approach to incorporation, and how much was over whether *Heller* was correctly decided?

b. Due Process

As we have seen, the Court has held that the Due Process Clause incorporates most of the provisions in the Bill of Rights, including provisions that are addressed to substance rather than procedure. For example, the Court has held that the Due Process Clause incorporates the First Amendment right to free speech, which protects speech even if the government provides fair procedures before an act of censorship. See *Gitlow v. New York*, 268 U.S. 652, 666 (1925). Accordingly, the Court in *McDonald* cited not only "incorporation" precedents, but also "substantive due process" precedents, and Justice Stevens explicitly stated that the case was about substantive due process. Keep this in mind when we consider fundamental rights and the doctrine of substantive due process in Chapter 8.

c. Privileges or Immunities

The petitioners urged the Court to conclude that the Privileges or Immunities Clause "protects all of the rights set out in the Bill of Rights, as well as some others," but the Court noted that the petitioners were "unable to identify the Clause's full scope." Justice Thomas agreed with the petitioners that the incorporation doctrine should be anchored in the Privileges or Immunities Clause, rather than the Due Process Clause. He relied in significant part on the views of the Fourteenth Amendment's chief congressional sponsors. But Representative Bingham and Senator Howard not only declared that the Fourteenth Amendment would apply the Bill of Rights to the states, but also that it would protect *unenumerated* fundamental rights from state infringement. Representative Bingham declared that it would protect the "inborn rights" of all citizens, 39th Cong. Globe 2542 (1866), and Senator Howard argued that it would protect the (unenumerated) rights that Justice Washington declared fundamental in *Corfield v. Coryell*.

Would the logical consequence of Justice Thomas's approach be, as the petitioners argued, that the Fourteenth Amendment protects some unenumerated fundamental rights—including, perhaps, the right to an abortion and other rights that, as we will see in Chapter 8, the Court has declared are fundamental? In a portion of his opinion that has been omitted here, Justice Thomas stated, "Because this case does not involve an unenumerated right, it is not necessary to resolve the question whether the [Privileges or Immunities] Clause protects such rights." He declared, however, that the "mere fact that the Clause does not expressly list the rights it protects does not render it incapable of principled judicial application. *** To be sure, interpreting the Privileges or Immunities Clause may produce hard questions. But [I] believe those questions are more worthy of this Court's attention—and far more likely to yield discernable answers—than the substantive due process questions the Court has for years created on its own, with neither textual nor historical support." As we turn to the materials in the Chapters that follow, consider the implications of Justice Thomas's view.

Executive Summary of This Chapter

Some early decisions of the Supreme Court invalidating state laws were based in part on theories of **natural law**, which hold that there are principles inherent in the natural order that limit the power of governments to act. *Calder v. Bull* (1798); *Fletcher v. Peck* (1810). This approach contrasts with the view that the only limits on governmental power derive from **positive law**, such as the Constitution and other laws affirmatively enacted through defined law-making processes. Other early decisions upheld governmental actions without considering whether they violated natural law. *Barron v. Baltimore* (1833).

Before the ratification of the Fourteenth Amendment, the Court held that the provisions in the Bill of Rights protecting individual liberty applied only to actions by the federal government, not by the states. *Barron v. Baltimore* (1833). However, the Court eventually held, in a series of cases, that the Due Process Clause of the Fourteenth Amendment incorporated most of the provisions in the Bill of Rights, thus imposing their limits on the states, as well. *Wolf v. Colorado* (1949). This is known as the **incorporation doctrine**.

The Court has held that the **Privileges or Immunities Clause** of the Fourteenth Amendment limits the states from abridging only the privileges or immunities of national citizenship, not of state citizenship. *Slaughter-House Cases* (1873). This view was long thought to render the Privileges or Immunities Clause largely superfluous. More recently, however, the Court has held that the Clause prohibits a state from distinguishing among its citizens, for purposes of eligibility for welfare benefits, on the basis of how long they have been citizens. *Saenz v. Roe* (1999).

POINT-COUNTERPOINT

Is it too late to question the incorporation doctrine?

POINT: GREGORY E. MAGGS

The "incorporation doctrine" says that the Due Process Clause of the Fourteenth Amendment protects many of the rights in the first eight Amendments from state interference. We have seen arguments for and against this doctrine. Without rehashing the dispute, let's suppose a majority of the Supreme Court has considered the matter and has concluded that the incorporation doctrine is an incorrect interpretation of the Fourteenth Amendment. Is it too late now for the Court to abolish the doctrine, given decades of precedent holding that the Fourteenth Amendment forbids states to abridge the freedom of speech, to conduct unreasonable searches and seizures, to deny a right of counsel in criminal cases, and so forth?

The answer, in my view, draws on the familiar distinction between matters of principle and practical considerations. While the Court might disagree with the incorporation doctrine as a matter of principle, it still might decide that practical considerations preclude completely overruling the doctrine. Put simply, even if the doctrine is wrong, reversing course after all these years might work hardships on people who have come to rely on it. This notion that practical considerations may limit principles runs throughout our nation's history. The Declaration of Independence itself cautions that "all experience hath shewn that mankind are more disposed to suffer, while evils are sufferable than to right themselves by abolishing the forms to which they are accustomed."

But even if practical considerations would dissuade the Court from entirely abandoning the incorporation doctrine, the Court still would have room to question it. Most importantly, the Court could decide not to extend the doctrine further. For example, the Court has not yet held that the Fourteenth Amendment incorporates the right to a grand jury indictment or the right to a jury trial in civil cases. Although the logic of the doctrine may dictate including these rights, Justices who disagree with the doctrine could decline to extend it so far without unsettling any expectations.

In addition, even without overruling the whole doctrine, the Court might decide to keep or overrule parts of the doctrine based on practical considerations. For instance, the Justices might conclude that the incorporation of the Free Exercise Clause should not be overruled because many people have relied on it; they have built places of worship, attended seminaries, and so forth. On the other hand, the Court might perceive that people have relied less on the Establishment Clause, and thus be more inclined to reject cases incorporating it.

But what the Court should not do is decide whether to overrule incorporation doctrine precedents based on substantive views about the rights at issue. For example, while the

Justices might decide to preserve the right to counsel to avoid upsetting settled expectations, they should not decide to preserve this right merely because they consider it especially important and beneficial. That would be a question of policy, not practicality, and questions of policy are for others to decide.

———————————

COUNTERPOINT: PETER J. SMITH

Imagine that the legislature in the state in which you live enacts a statute that makes it a crime to question the divinity of Jesus Christ. The statute authorizes the police to search the home and private papers, without first obtaining a warrant, of any person who might possibly hold such beliefs. The statute also provides that a person convicted of violating the statute, after a trial with all of the procedural rights that we ordinarily expect criminal defendants to receive, shall be publicly flogged and then drawn and quartered. Imagine further that the statute is consistent with the state's constitution. Would the statute be constitutional? As we will see in later Chapters, it seems clearly to violate the Establishment, Free Exercise, and Speech clauses of the First Amendment; the Fourth Amendment's warrant requirement; and (probably) the Eighth Amendment's prohibition on cruel and unusual punishment. But in light of the Court's decision in *Barron v. Baltimore*, those provisions apply only to federal action. And the statute affords a defendant a fair trial before being deprived of life and liberty, in seeming compliance with the literal terms of the Due Process Clause of the Fourteenth Amendment. If not for the incorporation doctrine, therefore, the statute apparently would not violate the United States Constitution—a result that most people would find untenable. It is too late in the day, in other words, for abandonment of the incorporation doctrine.

This is not to say, however, that the incorporation doctrine is unassailable. The Due Process Clause of the Fourteenth Amendment, which seems on its face to promise only fair process, not substantive liberty, was an awkward textual anchor for the doctrine. And the process of selective incorporation is subject to criticism for lacking a clear standard for deciding which provisions in the Bill of Rights should apply to the states. But that does not mean that incorporation was misguided or illegitimate. There is ample historical evidence that the Framers of the Fourteenth Amendment intended the *Privileges or Immunities Clause* to incorporate at least the protections of the Bill of Rights; indeed, that clause, which seems to confer substantive liberties, is a natural vehicle for the incorporation of rights against the states. And the general terms of that clause also make clear by implication that the Framers were comfortable with the prospect that other actors—presumably the courts—would engage in a process of identifying and defining rights that are immune from state infringement.

As matters stand, however, the Court has chosen to base the incorporation of rights against the states on the Due Process Clause. And widespread acceptance of that choice tends to undermine the frequently expressed assertion that the doctrine of "substantive due process" is indefensible. As we will see in Chapter 9, the Court has interpreted the Due Process Clause to protect substantive liberties, wholly aside from the procedures that the state provides before depriving a person of them. If the Fourteenth Amendment is properly read to incorporate the protections for substantive liberty found in the Bill of Rights—such as the right to free speech—then the assertion that the Due Process Clause has nothing to do with "substance" falters. (We will return to this theme in the Point-Counterpoint after Part VI.) Incorporation, in other words, not only was defensible, but also strengthens the argument that the Due Process Clause protects substantive liberty, as well.

PART VI: DUE PROCESS

Introduction

There are two Due Process Clauses in the Constitution. The Fifth Amendment, which (we saw in Chapter 7) applies to the federal government, provides that no person shall be "deprived of life, liberty, or property, without due process of law," and the Fourteenth Amendment provides that no State shall "deprive any person of life, liberty, or property, without due process of law."

As you can see, the Due Process Clauses are as vague as they are majestic. They do not provide concrete definitions of "liberty" and "property," and they promise, somewhat tautologically, only that persons will not be denied the process that is due. But these constitutional provisions have a deep historical pedigree. Magna Carta, a charter that English nobility forced King John to sign in 1215 to guarantee certain rights to his subjects, originally provided protections against arbitrary imprisonment and seizure, and subsequent versions of the charter referred to due process explicitly: "No man of what state or condition he be, shall be put out of his lands or tenements nor taken,

Go Online

You can view Magna Carta at the website of the National Archives at http://www.archives.gov/exhibits/featured_documents/magna_carta/.

nor disinherited, nor put to death, without he be brought to answer by due process of law." At a minimum, this concept means that the government cannot arbitrarily imprison a person or seize his property without first providing notice and an opportunity to be heard. In the next two Chapters, we consider what else the concept means.

CHAPTER 8

Substantive Due Process

The Due Process Clauses in the United States Constitution are the source of a dizzying array of constitutional doctrines. For example, you have probably already seen in your class on Civil Procedure that the Court has tethered the constitutional requirements of notice before judgment and personal jurisdiction to the Due Process Clauses. And we saw in Chapter 7 how the Court has held that most of the protections in the Bill of Rights have been "incorporated" against state action by virtue of the Due Process Clause of the Fourteenth Amendment.

Notice that the Due Process Clauses refer to "liberty" and "property." Are the Clauses properly read to create and define rights inhering in those concepts? Or do they simply protect those concepts, elsewhere defined, from deprivation without adequate procedural protections, such as notice and an opportunity to be heard? In this Part, we will focus on two principal doctrines that respond to these questions. "Procedural due process," which we will consider in Chapter 9, refers to the government's obligation to provide adequate procedural protections before depriving a person of some important interest. There is little doubt that, if nothing else, the Clauses impose this obligation, although (as we will see) there is much debate about when that obligation is triggered and what procedural protections actually are "due" when it is. The (somewhat oxymoronically named) doctrine of "substantive due process," which we will consider in this Chapter, concerns the extent to which the "liberty" mentioned in the Due Process Clauses is protected from government deprivation, wholly aside from the fairness of the procedures that the government provides before the deprivation.

Although you might not have realized it at the time, we have already seen examples of both of these due process doctrines. Recall that the Court has held that the Due Process Clause of the Fourteenth Amendment "incorporates" most of the protections of the Bill of Rights. Some of those protections—such as the privilege against self-incrimination or the right to a trial by jury in a criminal case—seem quite clearly to be "procedural" in nature. When the Court held that those provisions of the Fifth and Sixth Amendments apply against the states through the force of the Due Process Clause, it effectively defined the process that is "due" when the state seeks to imprison or otherwise punish a person.

But other rights that the Court has held are incorporated through the Due Process Clause of the Fourteenth Amendment seem more like substantive forms of liberty than elaborations of the process that is due when the government seeks to deprive a person of liberty. As we will see in Chapters 14-17, for example, the First Amendment's rights of free speech and free exercise of religion cannot be abridged (except under rare circumstances) by state action, because those protections have been incorporated through the Due Process Clause. But those rights now exist against state action wholly aside from the fairness of the procedure that the state supplies before it seeks to abridge them. (The state cannot, for example, imprison you solely because it disagrees with your political views, even if it provides you with a fair trial to show what views you actually hold.) These incorporation decisions effectively defined the "liberty" mentioned in the Due Process Clause, and in that sense were a form of "substantive due process." In this Chapter, we consider just how far that doctrine extends.

As we saw in Chapter 7, the doctrine of incorporation was very controversial, at least for a time in the middle of the twentieth century. But even assuming that the Court was correct to conclude that the Due Process Clause applies the *explicit* protections for substantive liberty in the Bill of Rights—including the rights to free speech and free exercise of religion in the First Amendment—to state action, it does not necessarily follow that the Due Process Clause of the Fourteenth Amendment also protects forms of liberty that are *not* expressly enumerated in the constitutional text. Whether it does will be the focus of this Chapter.

———————————

A. Substantive Due Process and Economic Liberty

In Chapter 18, we will see that the Constitution provides some explicit protections for economic liberty. The Contract Clause limits the authority of states to "impair[] the Obligation of Contracts," and the Takings Clause imposes some constraints on the authority of the federal government (and, the Court has held, through incorporation the authority of the states) to take private property. Does the reference in the Due Process Clauses to "liberty" and "property" suggest broader protections for economic liberty?

The doctrine of substantive due process—and, in particular, the theory that the Due Process Clauses protect economic rights—is generally thought to have originated in the Court's infamous decision in *Dred Scott v. Sandford*, 60 U.S. 393 (1857). *See* David P. Currie, *The Constitution in the Supreme Court: Article IV and Federal Powers, 1836-64*, 1983 Duke L.J. 695, 735-36, and nn. 255-64. In that case, the Court considered the claim of a slave that he became free upon residing in the free state of Illinois and the free territory of Wisconsin, where he had been sent by his owner. In the course of its decision, the Court held that the Missouri Compromise, which abolished slavery in some of the territories, was unconstitutional. One part of its reasoning (the importance of which scholars debate) was the following:

> **Make the Connection**
>
> We will consider the Court's decision in *Dred Scott*, and in particular its role in the Constitution's evolution in its treatment of racial discrimination, in Chapter 11.

> [T]he rights of property are united with the rights of person, and placed on the same ground by the fifth amendment to the Constitution, which provides that no person shall be deprived of life, liberty, and property, without due process of law. And an act of Congress which deprives a citizen of the United States of his liberty or property, merely because he came himself or brought his property into a particular Territory of the United States, and who had committed no offence against the laws, could hardly be dignified with the name of due process of law.

Does this genesis of the doctrine of substantive due process taint it by association? Or are there good reasons to read the Due Process Clauses to protect (and define) a class of liberty and property that cannot be deprived even after a fair proceeding?

Lochner v. New York

198 U.S. 45 (1905)

Mr. Justice PECKHAM delivered the opinion of the Court.

[The New York legislature enacted a law that prohibited employees from working in a bakery more than ten hours a day and more than sixty hours a week. Lochner was convicted of permitting an employee to work more than sixty hours during one week of work. He defended on the ground that the statute violated the Due Process Clause of the Fourteenth Amendment.]

The statute necessarily interferes with the right of contract between the employer and employees, concerning the number of hours in which the latter may labor in the bakery of the employer. The general right to make a contract in relation to his business is part of the liberty of the individual protected by the 14th Amendment of the Federal Constitution. *** The right to purchase or to sell labor is part of the liberty protected by this amendment, unless there are circumstances which exclude the right. There are, however, certain powers, existing in the sovereignty of each state in the Union, somewhat vaguely termed police powers, the exact description and limitation of which have not been attempted by the courts. Those powers, broadly stated, and without, at present, any attempt at a more specific limitation, relate to the safety, health, morals, and general welfare of the public. ***

It must, of course, be conceded that there is a limit to the valid exercise of the police power by the state. [Otherwise] the 14th Amendment would have no efficacy and the legislatures of the states would have unbounded power, and it would be enough to say that any piece of legislation was enacted to conserve the morals, the health, or the safety of the people ***. [In] every case that comes before this court, therefore, where legislation of this character is concerned, and where the protection of the Federal Constitution is sought, the question necessarily arises: Is this a fair, reasonable, and appropriate exercise of the police power of the state, or is it an unreasonable, unnecessary, and arbitrary interference with the right of the individual to his personal liberty, or to enter into those contracts in relation to labor which may seem to him appropriate or necessary for the support of himself and his family? Of course the liberty of contract relating to labor includes both parties to it. The one has as much right to purchase as the other to sell labor.

This is not a question of substituting the judgment of the court for that of the legislature. If the act be within the power of the state it is valid, although the judgment of the court might be totally opposed to the enactment of such a law. But the question would still remain: Is it within the police power of the state? and that question must be answered by the court.

The question whether this act is valid as a labor law, pure and simple, may be dismissed in a few words. There is no reasonable ground for interfering with the liberty of person or the right of free contract, by determining the hours of labor, in the occupation of a baker. There is no contention that bakers as a class are not equal in intelligence and capacity to men in other trades or manual occupations, or that they are not able to assert their rights and care for themselves without the protecting arm of the state, interfering with their independence of judgment and of action. *** Viewed in the light of a purely labor law, with no reference whatever to the question of health, we think that a law like the one before us involves neither the safety, the morals, nor the welfare, of the public, and that the interest of the public is not in the slightest degree affected by such an act. The law must be upheld, if at all, as a law pertaining to the health of the individual engaged in the occupation of a baker. It does not affect any other portion of the public than those who are engaged in that occupation. Clean and wholesome bread does not depend upon whether the baker works but ten hours per day or only sixty hours a week. *** The mere assertion that the subject relates, though but in a remote degree, to the public health, does not necessarily render the enactment valid. The act must have a more direct relation, as a means to an end, and the end itself must be appropriate and legitimate, before an act can be held to be valid which interferes with the general right of an individual to be free in his person and in his power to contract in relation to his own labor.

> **Food for Thought**
>
> Do you agree with the Court that it is not substituting its judgment for that of the legislature? Does the Court defer at all to the legislature's judgments at issue here?

There is, in our judgment, no reasonable foundation for holding this to be necessary or appropriate as a health law to safeguard [the] health of the individuals who are following the trade of a baker. *** To the common understanding the trade of a baker has never been regarded as an unhealthy one. *** Some occupations are more healthy than others, but we think there are none which might not come under the power of the legislature to supervise and control the hours of working therein, if the mere fact that the occupation is not absolutely and perfectly healthy is to confer that right upon the legislative department of the government. *** There must be more than the mere fact of the possible existence of some small amount of unhealthiness to warrant legislative interference with liberty. It is unfortunately true that labor, even in any department, may possibly carry with it the seeds of unhealthiness. But are we all, on that account, at the mercy of legislative majorities? A printer, a tinsmith, a locksmith, a carpenter, a cabinetmaker, a dry goods clerk, a bank's, a lawyer's, or a physician's clerk, or a clerk in almost any kind of business, would all come under the power of the legislature, on this assumption. No trade, no occupation, no mode of earning one's living, could escape this all-pervading power, and the acts of the legislature in limiting the hours of labor in all employments would be valid, although such limitation might seriously cripple the ability of the laborer to support himself and his family.

It is also urged, pursuing the same line of argument, that it is to the interest of the state that its population should be strong and robust, and therefore any legislation which may be said to tend to make people healthy must be valid as health laws, enacted under the police power. *** Scarcely any law but might find shelter under such assumptions, and conduct, properly so called, as well as contract, would come under the restrictive sway of the legislature. Not only the hours of employees, but the hours of employers, could be regulated, and doctors, lawyers, scientists, all professional men, as well as athletes and artisans, could be forbidden to fatigue their brains and bodies by prolonged hours of exercise, lest the fighting strength of the state be impaired. We mention these extreme cases because the contention is extreme. *** Statutes of the nature of that under review, limiting the hours in which grown and intelligent men may labor to earn their living, are mere meddlesome interferences with the rights of the individual, and they are not saved from condemnation by the claim that they are passed in the exercise of the police power and upon the subject of the health of the individual whose rights are interfered with, unless there be some fair ground, reasonable in and of itself, to say that there is material danger to the public health, or to the health of the employees, if the hours of labor are not curtailed.

This interference on the part of the legislatures of the several states with the ordinary trades and occupations of the people seems to be on the increase. *** It is impossible for us to shut our eyes to the fact that many of the laws of this character, while passed under what is claimed to be the police power for the purpose of protecting the public health or welfare, are, in reality, passed from other motives. *** It seems to us that the real object and purpose [of the challenged law] were simply to regulate the hours of labor between the master and his employees (all being men, *Sui juris*), in a private business, not dangerous in any degree to morals, or in any real and substantial degree to the health of the employees. Under such circumstances the freedom of master and employee to contract with each other in relation to their employment, and in defining the same, cannot be prohibited or interfered with, without violating the Federal Constitution. *Reversed.*

Mr. Justice HOLMES dissenting.

This case is decided upon an economic theory which a large part of the country does not entertain. If it were a question whether I agreed with that theory, I should desire to study it further and long before making up my mind. But I do not conceive that to be my duty, because I strongly believe that my agreement or disagreement has nothing to do with the right of a majority to embody their opinions in law. It is settled by various decisions of this court that state constitutions and state laws may regulate life in many ways which we as legislators might think as injudicious, or if you like as tyrannical, as this, and which, equally with this, interfere with the liberty to contract. Sunday laws and usury laws are ancient examples. A more modern one is the prohibition of lotteries. The liberty of the citizen to do as he likes so long as he does not interfere with the liberty of others to do the same, which has been a shibboleth for some well-known writers, is interfered with by school laws, by the Post Office, by every state or municipal institution which takes his money for purposes thought desirable, whether he likes it or not. The 14th Amendment does not enact Mr. Herbert Spencer's Social Statics. [A] Constitution is not intended to embody a particular economic theory, whether of paternalism and the organic relation of the citizen to the state or of *laissez faire*. It is made for people of fundamentally differing views, and the accident of our finding certain opinions natural and familiar, or novel, and even shocking, ought not to conclude our judgment upon the question whether statutes embodying them conflict with the Constitution of the United States.

> **FYI**
>
> Herbert Spencer was a British biologist, philosopher, and libertarian who argued that evolutionary theory provided a guiding principle for human society. He coined the term the "survival of the fittest."

General propositions do not decide concrete cases. The decision will depend on a judgment or intuition more subtle than any articulate major premise. But I think that the proposition just stated, if it is accepted, will carry us far toward the end. Every opinion tends to become a law. I think that the word "liberty," in the 14th Amendment, is perverted when it is held to prevent the natural outcome of a dominant opinion, unless it can be said that a rational and fair man necessarily would admit that the statute proposed would infringe fundamental principles as they have been understood by the traditions of our people and our law. It does not need research to show that no such sweeping condemnation can be passed upon the statute before us. A reasonable man might think it a proper measure on the score of health. Men whom I certainly could not pronounce unreasonable would uphold it as a first installment of a general regulation of the hours of work. Whether in the latter aspect it would be open to the charge of inequality I think it unnecessary to discuss.

Mr. Justice HARLAN (with whom Mr. Justice WHITE and Mr. Justice DAY concurred) dissenting.

I take it to be firmly established that what is called the liberty of contract may, within certain limits, be subjected to regulations designed and calculated to promote the general welfare, or to guard the public health, the public morals, or the public safety. Granting, then, that there is a liberty of contract which cannot be violated even under the sanction of direct legislative enactment, but assuming [that] such liberty of contract is subject to such regulations as the state may reasonably prescribe for the common good and the well-being of society, what are the conditions under which the judiciary may declare such regulations to be in excess of legislative authority and void? [A] legislative enactment, Federal or state, is never to be disregarded or held invalid unless it be, beyond question, plainly and palpably in excess of legislative power. *** If there be doubt as to the validity of the statute, that doubt must therefore be resolved in favor of its validity, and the courts must keep their hands off, leaving the legislature to meet the responsibility for unwise legislation.

It is plain that this statute was enacted in order to protect the physical well-being of those who work in bakery and confectionery establishments. It may be that the statute had its origin, in part, in the belief that employers and employees in such establishments were not upon an equal footing, and that the necessities of the latter often compelled them to submit to such exactions as unduly taxed their strength. Be this as it may, the statute must be taken as expressing the belief of the people of New York that, as a general rule, and in the case of the average man, labor in excess of sixty hours during a week in such establishments may endanger the health of those who thus labor. Whether or not this be wise legislation it is not the province of the court to inquire. [I]n determining the question of power to interfere with liberty of contract, the court may inquire whether the means devised by the state are germane to an end which may be lawfully accomplished and have a real or substantial relation to the protection of health, as involved in the daily work of the persons, male and female, engaged in bakery and confectionery establishments. But when this inquiry is entered upon I find it impossible, in view of common experience, to say that there is here no real or substantial relation between the means employed by the state and the end sought to be accomplished by its legislation.

[Justice Harlan cited research that demonstrated that bakers were often sleep deprived because of the long hours that they worked; suffered from bronchial problems because they constantly inhaled flour; were susceptible to disease because of exposure to extremes of heat and cold; and had shorter average life expectancies.] There are many reasons of a weighty, substantial character, based upon the experience of mankind, in support of the theory that, all things considered, more than ten hours' steady work each day, from week to week, in a bakery or confectionery establishment, may endanger the health and shorten the lives of the workmen, thereby diminishing their physical and mental capacity to serve the state and to provide for those dependent upon them. If such reasons exist that ought to be the end of this case, for the state is not amenable to the judiciary, in respect of its legislative enactments, unless such enactments are plainly, palpably, beyond all question, inconsistent with the Constitution of the United States.

Points for Discussion

a. Substantive Due Process

The Court's approach in <u>Lochner</u> is referred to as substantive due process because it effectively concluded that there is a substantive component to the "liberty" protected by the Due Process Clause that cannot be deprived regardless of the adequacy of the process provided. Critics have chided the Court for ascribing substantive content to that term. Was that Justice Holmes's criticism? If the critics are correct, then is the Fourteenth Amendment's reference to "liberty" and "property" surplusage? Or do they refer to property and liberty established by state and federal common-law and statutory law? Without defining those terms, how does the Court even know if the Clause's protections are triggered?

b. Level of Scrutiny

What level of scrutiny did the Court apply to the challenged statute? Did it hold that a state categorically cannot regulate the number of hours that an employee can work, or instead that a state can do so only under certain circumstances? If the latter, then what might justify such state regulation? Contrast the Court's approach with Justice Harlan's approach. In his view, a state regulation must have a legitimate objective and a substantial relation to that objective. Even assuming that the Court's test is too searching, why should a statute that fails Justice Harlan's test violate the Due Process Clause? His proposed test, after all, does not turn on the procedure followed in enacting the law. Should the Due Process Clause impose any limits on state legislative or regulatory, as opposed to judicial, action?

c. Judicial Role

We saw in Chapter 2 that any time the Court invalidates a democratically enacted statute, it is presumptively acting in a counter-majoritarian fashion. Assuming (as most have) that the Court's approach in *Lochner* was problematic, is the problem that the Court was acing in such a fashion? That it was acting in that fashion in order to protect an unenumerated right? Or that the right that the Court chose to protect did not warrant constitutional protection?

––––––––––––––

In the three decades after *Lochner*, the Court invalidated almost 200 laws and regulations on the ground that they violated economic rights protected by the Due Process Clauses. Most of the invalidated regulation was progressive-era legislation, at the state and federal level, that protected workers or fixed prices. In *Adair v. United States*, 208 U.S. 161 (1908), for example, the Court struck down a federal law that protected the right of employees to organize unions, and in *Coppage v. Kansas*, 236 U.S. 1 (1915), the Court invalidated a similar state law. To be sure, the Court also upheld many such regulations during this period. But there remained significant support on the Court for *Lochner's* general approach; indeed, even in the cases that upheld state regulation, the reasoning did not always indicate a repudiation of *Lochner's* approach. In *Muller v. Oregon*, 208 U.S. 412 (1908), for example, the Court upheld an Oregon law that limited the number of hours per day that women could work in factories and laundries. But the Court's rationale in that case—that "inherent differences between the two sexes" justified the regulation notwithstanding the decision in *Lochner*—was based less on a relaxation of the scrutiny given to regulation of the workplace than it was on a paternalistic view of women.

And not even that rationale always prevailed. In *Adkins v. Children's Hospital*, 261 U.S. 525 (1923), the Court struck down a law enacted by Congress providing for minimum wages for women and children in the District of Columbia. Justice Sutherland, writing for the majority of the Court, declared that the law impermissibly interfered with the "freedom of contract included within the guaranties of the due process clause of the Fifth Amendment." The Court stated that it was "no longer open to question" that "the right to contract about one's affairs is a part of the liberty of the individual protected by this clause." The

Court continued: "Within this liberty are contracts of employment of labor. In making such contracts, generally speaking, the parties have an equal right to obtain from each other the best terms they can as the result of private bargaining." The law was inconsistent with this principle: "The law takes account of the necessities of only one party to the contract. It ignores the necessities of the employer by compelling him to pay not less than a certain sum, not only whether the employee is capable of earning it, but irrespective of the ability of his business to sustain the burden, generously leaving him, of course, the privilege of abandoning his business as an alternative for going on at a loss." Although the freedom of contract was "subject to a great variety of restraints," it was, the Court declared, "the general rule and restraint the exception, and the exercise of legislative authority to abridge it can be justified only by the existence of exceptional circumstances." Because the amount of the wage was unrelated to the employee's health, no such circumstances existed to justify the law. Chief Justice Taft and Justices Holmes and Sanford dissented.

In the 1930s, with the country facing the Great Depression, both the federal government and the states began more aggressively to regulate the market. Pressure built on the Court to change course, which it began to do in the case that follows.

> **Make the Connection**
>
> In Chapter 3, we considered how the Court changed course in its view of the scope of Congress's power to regulate pursuant to the Commerce Clause. The change that we considered there occurred simultaneously with the change that we take up here.

Nebbia v. New York

291 U.S. 502 (1934)

> **Take Note**
>
> As we saw in Chapter 3, Justice Roberts is the Justice whose "switch in time saved nine." There is a debate over whether Justice Roberts changed his view in 1937 in response to President Roosevelt's Court-packing plan. As you read his opinion here, issued three years before the announcement of the plan, consider what it suggests about the role that the plan played in influencing his views.

Mr. Justice ROBERTS delivered the opinion of the Court.

[In response to the rapid decline in the price of milk—and the resulting risk that farmers would not seek to produce it—the New York legislature created the Milk Control Board and gave it power to fix minimum and maximum retail prices for milk. The Board issued an order fixing nine cents as the price to be charged by a store for a quart of milk. Nebbia, the proprietor of a grocery store, was convicted of selling milk in violation of the Board's order after he sold a five-cent loaf of bread and two quarts of milk for eighteen cents. He defended on the ground that the Board's order violated the Fourteenth Amendment.]

Under our form of government the use of property and the making of contracts are normally matters of private and not of public concern. The general rule is that both shall be free of governmental interference. But neither property rights nor contract rights are absolute; for government cannot exist if the citizen may at will use his property to the detriment of his fellows, or exercise his freedom of contract to work them harm. Equally fundamental with the private right is that of the public to regulate it in the common interest. *** These correlative rights, that of the citizen to exercise exclusive dominion over property and freely to contract about his affairs, and that of the state to regulate the use of property and the conduct of business, are always in collision. *** But subject only to constitutional restraint the private right must yield to the public need.

The Fifth Amendment, in the field of federal activity, and the Fourteenth, as respects state action, do not prohibit governmental regulation for the public welfare. They merely condition the exertion of the admitted power, by securing that the end shall be accomplished by methods consistent with due process. And the guaranty of due process, as has often been held, demands only that the law shall not be unreasonable, arbitrary, or capricious, and that the means selected shall have a real and substantial relation to the object sought to be attained. It results that a regulation valid for one sort of business, or in given circumstances, may be invalid for another sort, or for the same business under other circumstances, because the reasonableness of each regulation depends upon the relevant facts.

So far as the requirement of due process is concerned, and in the absence of other constitutional restriction, a state is free to adopt whatever economic policy may reasonably be deemed to promote public welfare, and to enforce that policy by legislation adapted to its purpose. The courts are without authority either to declare such policy, or, when it is declared by the legislature, to override it. If the laws passed are seen to have a reasonable relation to a proper legislative purpose, and are neither arbitrary nor discriminatory, the requirements of due process are satisfied ***. Times without number we have said that the Legislature is primarily the judge of the necessity of such an enactment, that every possible presumption is in favor of its validity, and that though the court may hold views inconsistent with the wisdom of the law, it may not be annulled unless palpably in excess of legislative power.

The Constitution does not secure to any one liberty to conduct his business in such fashion as to inflict injury upon the public at large, or upon any substantial group of the people. Price control, like any other form of regulation, is unconstitutional only if arbitrary, discriminatory, or demonstrably irrelevant to the policy the Legislature is free to adopt, and hence an unnecessary and unwarranted interference with individual liberty. Tested by these considerations we find no basis in the due process clause of the Fourteenth Amendment for condemning the provisions of the Agriculture and Markets Law here drawn into question.

Mr. Justice McREYNOLDS, [joined by Mr. Justice VAN DEVANTER, Mr. Justice SUTHERLAND, and Mr. Justice BUTLER,] dissenting.

The statement by the court below that, "Doubtless the statute before us would be condemned by an earlier generation as a temerarious interference with the rights of property and contract [and] with the natural law of supply and demand," is obviously correct. ***
An end although apparently desirable cannot justify inhibited means. [The] Legislature cannot lawfully destroy guaranteed rights of one man with the prime purpose of enriching another, even if for the moment, this may seem advantageous to the public. And the adoption of any "concept of jurisprudence" which permits facile disregard of the Constitution as long interpreted and respected will inevitably lead to its destruction. Then, all rights will be subject to the caprice of the hour; government by stable laws will pass.

Points for Discussion

a. Level of Scrutiny

Did the Court in *Nebbia* conclude that no liberty protected by the Fourteenth Amendment was implicated by the challenged regulation? Or that the regulation permissibly abridged that liberty? Did it require "exceptional circumstances," as did the Court in *Adkins*? Or did it apply a more deferential level of scrutiny?

b. Sign of Change?

If indeed the Court's approach in *Nebbia* was different from its approach in *Adkins* and *Lochner*, why didn't the Court simply overrule those cases? If nothing else, Justice Roberts's papers make clear that he had concluded by 1936 that *Adkins* and *Lochner* were misguided. See Felix Frankfurter, *Mr. Justice Roberts*, 104 U. Pa. L. Rev. 311 (1955). In any event, there is little doubt that a majority of the Court was prepared formally to overrule *Adkins* and repudiate the *Lochner* approach.

West Coast Hotel Co. v. Parrish

300 U.S. 379 (1937)

Mr. Chief Justice HUGHES delivered the opinion of the Court.

[A Washington statute required the payment of minimum wages to women and minors. Respondent, an employee of West Coast Hotel, brought suit to recover the difference between the wages she received and those required under state law. West Coast Hotel defended on the ground that the statute violated the Fourteenth Amendment, as interpreted in *Adkins*. The state Supreme Court upheld the statute.]

We are of the opinion that this ruling of the state court demands on our part a reexamination of the *Adkins* Case. The importance of the question, in which many states having similar laws are concerned, the close division by which the decision in the *Adkins*

Case was reached, and the economic conditions which have supervened, and in the light of which the reasonableness of the exercise of the protective power of the state must be considered, make it not only appropriate, but we think imperative, that in deciding the present case the subject should receive fresh consideration.

In each case the violation alleged by those attacking minimum wage regulation for women is deprivation of freedom of contract. What is this freedom? The Constitution does not speak of freedom of contract. It speaks of liberty and prohibits the deprivation of liberty without due process of law. In prohibiting that deprivation, the Constitution does not recognize an absolute and uncontrollable liberty. Liberty in each of its phases has its history and connotation. But the liberty safeguarded is liberty in a social organization which requires the protection of law against the evils which menace the health, safety, morals, and welfare of the people. Liberty under the Constitution is thus necessarily subject to the restraints of due process, and regulation which is reasonable in relation to its subject and is adopted in the interests of the community is due process. This essential limitation of liberty in general governs freedom of contract in particular.

The minimum wage to be paid under the Washington statute is fixed after full consideration by representatives of employers, employees, and the public. It may be assumed that the minimum wage is fixed in consideration of the services that are performed in the particular occupations under normal conditions. Provision is made for special licenses at less wages in the case of women who are incapable of full service. The statement of Mr. Justice Holmes in the *Adkins* Case is pertinent: "This statute does not compel anybody to pay anything. It simply forbids employment at rates below those fixed as the minimum requirement of health and right living. It is safe to assume that women will not be employed at even the lowest wages allowed unless they earn them, or unless the employer's business can sustain the burden." 261 U.S. at 570. We think that the views thus expressed are sound and that the decision in the *Adkins* Case was a departure from the true application of the principles governing the regulation by the state of the relation of employer and employed. Those principles have been reenforced by our subsequent decisions. See *Nebbia v. New York*, 291 U.S. 502 (1934).

Make the Connection

The statute at issue here applied to women but not to men. Should the Court have found that the statute violated the Equal Protection Clause, on the ground that it discriminated against men or reflected a paternalistic view of women? We will consider such questions, and gender discrimination more generally, in Chapter 11.

What can be closer to the public interest than the health of women and their protection from unscrupulous and overreaching employers? And if the protection of women is a legitimate end of the exercise of state power, how can it be said that the requirement of the payment of a minimum wage fairly fixed in order to meet the very necessities of existence is not an admissible means to that end? The Legislature of the state was clearly entitled to consider the situation of women in employment, the fact that they are in the class receiving the least pay, that their bargaining power is relatively weak, and that they are the ready victims of those who would take advantage of their necessitous circumstances. The Legislature was entitled to adopt measures to reduce the evils of the "sweating system," the exploiting of workers at wages so low as to be insufficient to meet the bare cost of living, thus making their very helplessness the occasion of a most injurious competition. The adoption of similar requirements by many states evidences a deepseated conviction both as to the presence of the evil and as to the means adapted to check it. Legislative response to that conviction cannot be regarded as arbitrary or capricious and that is all we have to decide. Even if the wisdom of the policy be regarded as debatable and its effects uncertain, still the Legislature is entitled to its judgment.

There is an additional and compelling consideration which recent economic experience has brought into a strong light. The exploitation of a class of workers who are in an unequal position with respect to bargaining power and are thus relatively defenseless against the denial of a living wage is not only detrimental to their health and well being, but casts a direct burden for their support upon the community. What these workers lose in wages the taxpayers are called upon to pay. The bare cost of living must be met. We may take judicial notice of the unparalleled demands for relief which arose during the recent period of depression and still continue to an alarming extent despite the degree of economic recovery which has been achieved. *** The community is not bound to provide what is in effect a subsidy for unconscionable employers.

Our conclusion is that the case of *Adkins* should be, and it is, overruled. The judgment of the Supreme Court of the state of Washington is affirmed.

Mr. Justice SUTHERLAND [joined by Mr. Justice VAN DEVANTER, Mr. Justice McREYNOLDS, and Mr. Justice BUTLER, dissenting].

It is urged that the question involved should now receive fresh consideration, among other reasons, because of "the economic conditions which have supervened"; but the meaning of the Constitution does not change with the ebb and flow of economic events. We frequently are told in more general words that the Constitution must be construed in the light of the present. If by that it is meant that the Constitution is made up of living words that apply to every new condition which they include, the statement is quite true. But to say [that] the words of the Constitution mean today what they did not mean when written—that is, that they do not apply to a situation now to which they would have applied then—is to rob that instrument of the essential element which continues it in force as the people have made it until they, and not their official agents, have made it otherwise. *** The judicial function is that of interpretation; it does not include the power of amendment under the guise of interpretation. *** If the Constitution, intelligently and reasonably construed in the light of these principles, stands in the way of desirable legislation, the blame must rest upon that instrument, and not upon the court for enforcing it according to its terms. The remedy in that situation—and the only true remedy—is to amend the Constitution.

Points for Discussion

a. The Basis of the Decision

Did the Court depart from *Adkins* because that case simply interpreted the Constitution incorrectly? Or because circumstances had changed sufficiently—with the onset of the Great Depression—that the government's interest in regulating was suddenly substantially more compelling? If the latter, would the Court have overruled *Adkins*, or merely distinguished it?

b. Level of Scrutiny

Is the holding in *West Coast Hotel* that the liberty protected by the Due Process Clause does not embrace a freedom to contract? Or that the government may abridge that constitutionally protected freedom as long as the regulation reasonably relates to some legitimate governmental interest?

c. Parallel Developments

At the same time that the Court was deciding finally to depart from *Lochner*'s approach, the Court was beginning to recognize broad congressional power to regulate pursuant to the Commerce Clause. Recall from Chapter 3 that in *Jones & Laughlin Steel* and *Darby* the Court effectively applied the rational-basis test—essentially the same test that the Court applied in *West Coast Hotel*—to determine whether a statute fell within Congress's power to regulate pursuant to that clause. Recall as well that in early 1937 President Roosevelt announced his "Court-packing plan," which would have added a new seat on the Court for every Justice over age 70 who stayed on the bench, until the Court included fifteen members. If adopted, the plan would have enabled Roosevelt to dilute the votes of the members of the Court who were most committed to the *Lochner* line of cases (and to a narrow view of federal power). By the time of his proposal, the Court had already issued its decisions in *West Coast Hotel*, and two months after Roosevelt announced the proposal it issued its decision in *Jones & Laughlin Steel*.

———————————

The Court's decision in *West Coast Hotel* signaled that the Court would no longer searchingly review ordinary social and economic regulation. But did that mean that such regulation would not be subject to any scrutiny under the Due Process Clause at all? In *United States v. Carolene Products Co.*, 304 U.S. 144 (1938), the Court upheld a federal statute that prohibited the shipment in interstate commerce of skim milk mixed with some fat or oil other than milk fat. The Court rejected the defendant's argument that the statute violated the Due Process Clause of the Fifth Amendment, reasoning that "regulatory legislation affecting ordinary commercial transactions is not to be pronounced unconstitutional unless in the light of the facts made known or generally assumed it is of such a character as to preclude the assumption that it rests upon some rational basis within the knowledge and experience of the legislators." This approach came to be known as "rational-basis review." As we will see shortly, rational-basis review is a very deferential form of judicial scrutiny.

The Court noted, however, that such a deferential approach might not always be appropriate. In footnote 4 of the opinion—perhaps the most famous footnote in Supreme Court history—Justice Stone stated:

> There may be narrower scope for operation of the presumption of constitutionality when legislation appears on its face to be within a specific prohibition of the Constitution, such as those of the first ten Amendments, which are deemed equally specific when held to be embraced within the Fourteenth. It is unnecessary to consider now whether legislation which restricts those political processes which can ordinarily be expected to bring about repeal of undesirable legislation, is to be subjected to more exacting judicial scrutiny under the general prohibitions of the Fourteenth Amendment than are most other types of legislation. [The Court cited cases concerning "restrictions upon the right to vote," "restraints upon the dissemination of information," "interferences with political organizations," and "prohibition of peaceable assembly."] Nor need we enquire whether similar considerations enter into the review of statutes directed at particular religious, *Pierce v. Society of Sisters*, 268 U.S. 510 (1925), or national, *Meyer v. Nebraska*, 262 U.S. 390 (1923), or racial minorities; whether prejudice against discrete and insular minorities may be a special condition, which tends seriously to curtail the operation of those political processes ordinarily to be relied upon to protect minorities, and which may call for a correspondingly more searching judicial inquiry. Compare *McCulloch v. Maryland*, 4 Wheat. 316, 428 (1803).

Footnote 4 suggested that heightened judicial scrutiny might be warranted when regulation "restricts those political processes which can ordinarily be expected to bring about repeal of undesirable legislation." This has come be known as the "political process" rationale for heightened judicial scrutiny of regulation. Why might judicial intervention be more justified in such cases? Does the footnote 4 approach properly respond to the defects of the Court's approach in the *Lochner* era? Does it correctly identify those cases that call for more aggressive judicial intervention?

If nothing else, the Court made clear in subsequent cases that judicial scrutiny under the Due Process Clause would be quite deferential when ordinary social and economic regulation is at issue. Consider the case that follows.

Williamson v. Lee Optical Co.

348 U.S. 483 (1955)

Mr. Justice DOUGLAS delivered the opinion of the Court.

[An Oklahoma statute prohibited any person not licensed as an optometrist or ophthalmologist from fitting, duplicating, or replacing lenses without a written prescription from a licensed ophthalmologist or optometrist. After an optician challenged the provision, the District Court held that the ban on fitting without a prescription was not "reasonably and rationally related to the health and welfare of the people," and that the ban on duplication without a prescription was "neither reasonably necessary nor reasonably related to the end sought to be achieved."]

In practical effect, [the challenged statute] means that no optician can fit old glasses into new frames or supply a lens ***. The Oklahoma law may exact a needless, wasteful requirement in many cases. But it is for the legislature, not the courts, to balance the advantages and disadvantages of the new requirement. It appears that in many cases the optician can easily supply the new frames or new lenses without reference to the old written prescription. It also appears that many written prescriptions contain no directive data in regard to fitting spectacles to the face. But in some cases the directions contained in the prescription are essential, if the glasses are to be fitted so as to correct the particular defects of vision or alleviate the eye condition. The legislature might have concluded that the frequency of occasions when a prescription is necessary was sufficient to justify this regulation of the fitting of eyeglasses. Likewise, when it is necessary to duplicate a lens, a written prescription may or may not be necessary. But the legislature might have concluded that one was needed often enough to require one in every case. Or the legislature may have concluded that eye examinations were so critical, not only for correction of vision but also for detection of latent ailments or diseases, that every change in frames and every duplication of a lens should be accompanied by a prescription from a medical expert. To be sure, the present law does not require a new examination of the eyes every time the frames are changed or the lenses duplicated. *** But the law need not be in every respect logically consistent with its aims to be constitutional. It is enough that there is an evil at hand for correction, and that it might be thought that the particular legislative measure was a rational way to correct it.

> **Take Note**
>
> The Court offers a series of possible justifications for the law. Are they the ones that actually motivated the Oklahoma legislature? Does the Court require that the legislature even have thought of them? Can you think of any other reasons—including, perhaps, less admirable ones—why the legislature might have enacted the requirements in question?

The day is gone when this Court uses the Due Process Clause of the Fourteenth Amendment to strike down state laws, regulatory of business and industrial conditions, because they may be unwise, improvident, or out of harmony with a particular school of thought. [Reversed in relevant part.]

———————————

> **Make the Connection**
>
> In this Chapter and in Chapters 11 and 12, we will see some cases in which the Court applies (or at least purports to apply) rational-basis review and yet invalidates a challenged regulation. When you read those cases—including *Romer v. Evans* and *Cleburne v. Cleburne Living Center*—consider whether the Court is adhering to the form of rational-basis review that the Court applied in *Williamson*.

Points for Discussion

a. Rational-Basis Review

The Court in *Williamson* applied what has come to be known as "rational-basis review" to the challenged statute. Over the years, the Court has articulated the standard in various ways; but the "general rule is that legislation is presumed to be valid and will be sustained" if the regulation is "rationally related to a legitimate state interest." *City of Cleburne v. Cleburne Living Center*, 473 U.S. 432, 440 (1985). This is a highly deferential form of review, and it virtually always results in a conclusion that the challenged regulation is valid. The Court has stated, for example, that "[w]e have returned to the original constitutional proposition that courts do not substitute their social and economic beliefs for the judgment of legislative bodies, who are elected to pass laws," regardless of whether the laws are "wise or unwise." *Ferguson v. Skrupa*, 372 US. 726, 730-32 (1963).

Should the Court have any role to play in reviewing regulation for rationality? Why does such a requirement flow from the Due Process Clause? Conversely, is rational-basis review unduly deferential to legislative action? Does the Court's approach in *Williamson* amount effectively to judicial abdication?

b. "Legitimate Governmental Interest"

Notice that the Court in *Williamson* several times referred to what the legislature "*might have* concluded." Under rational-basis review, a court generally will not seek to determine the legislature's *actual* objective in enacting the challenged statute, but instead will judge it in light of *possible* objectives that the legislature might have sought to accomplish. See, e.g., *U.S. Railroad Retirement Board v. Fritz*, 449 U.S. 166 (1980). Indeed, courts will accept governmental interests that may well not have been on the minds of any of the legislators but that the government can articulate *post hoc* for the purposes of litigation. See, e.g., *Schweiker v. Wilson*, 450 U.S. 221 (1981).

Suppose that there had been strong evidence that the legislature had enacted the statute at issue in *Williamson* in order to create a monopoly for optometrists and ophthalmologists, after lobbyists for those professions showered the legislators with campaign contributions. Would it still be relevant that the statute arguably advances other legitimate governmental interests? Should the Court at least have inquired in *Williamson* whether the actual legislative objective was legitimate?

c. "Reasonably Related"

Even assuming that the statute at issue in *Williamson* was designed to serve the interests that the Court identified, it was not a particularly effective measure to accomplish those ends, as it was both under- and over-inclusive. It was under-inclusive because, to the extent that the statute was designed to promote frequent eye exams, it did not actually require optometrists and ophthalmologists to conduct such exams when they fitted, duplicated, or replaced lenses. And it was over-inclusive because, to the extent that the statute was designed to ensure proper medical guidance to opticians, the prescription requirement applied even when the optician was merely duplicating an existing pair of lenses, which presumably had been prepared on the basis of a prescription. Yet the Court stated that "the law need not be in every respect logically consistent with its aims to be constitutional." Under this approach, is it possible to imagine a state regulation that would fail this prong of the rational-basis test?

Perspective and Analysis

For the last seventy years, most commentators have criticized *Lochner* and the use of substantive due process to protect economic rights. Professor Richard Epstein, however, has argued for a return to *Lochner's* approach:

> *Lochner* may well have given *too much* scope to the police power ***. [The police power] does not sanction wholesale interference with financial arrangements, such as is mandated by a minimum-wage law. These statutes can impose heavy burdens upon both employer and employee for the benefit of parties who are strangers to the relationship—organized labor, for example, whose members are in competition with nonunion workers. To uphold minimum-wage legislation may be to invite, in the name of the police power, the very rent-seeking that any theory of limited government is designed to avoid.

Richard A. Epstein, *Toward a Revitalization of the Contract Clause*, 51 U. Chi. L. Rev. 703, 713-15, 734 (1984).

Are "economic" rights any different from other forms of liberty that we have come to prize? The following section takes up that question.

B. Substantive Due Process and Fundamental Rights

Notwithstanding the support of a few hearty commentators, *Lochner* has been subject to virtually universal condemnation. But what exactly was wrong with the decision and the approach that it embodied? Is it that any judicial protection of rights not enumerated in the Constitution is tantamount to impermissible judicial legislation that reflects the judges' individual policy preferences rather than constitutional law as actually embodied in the Constitution's text? Or is the problem with *Lochner* not that it involved judicial protection for unenumerated rights, but rather that "the Court chose the wrong values to enforce, wrong in the sense that complete laissez-faire capitalism was neither required by the historical understanding of 'liberty,' nor did it meaningfully enhance the freedom of the vast majority of Americans in the industrialized age"? Laurence H. Tribe & Michael C. Dorf, On Reading the Constitution 65-67 (1991). Or is the problem simply that most modern commentators have different values? Consider what the cases that follow suggest about the defect (if any) of *Lochner*.

1. Prelude

Lochner and the cases that we considered earlier in this Chapter concerned economic liberties, such as the freedom to contract. During the *Lochner* era, the Court also decided several cases that found protection in the Due Process Clauses for other forms of liberty, as well. In *Meyer v. Nebraska*, 262 U. S. 390 (1923), for example, the Court overturned the conviction of a parochial school teacher for violating a law prohibiting teaching in any language other than English. The Court stated that the liberty protected by the due process clause "denotes not merely freedom from bodily restraint but also the right of the individual to contract, to engage in any of the common occupations of life, to acquire useful knowledge, to marry, establish a home and bring up children, to worship God according to the dictates of his own conscience, and generally to enjoy those privileges long recognized at common law as essential to the orderly pursuit of happiness by free men." The Court held that the state had shown no justification for interference with "the calling of modern language teachers, with the opportunities of pupils to acquire knowledge, and with the power of parents to control the education of their own." The following case, also decided during the *Lochner* era, elaborated on this view of the Due Process Clause.

Pierce v. Society of the Sisters

268 U.S. 510 (1925)

Mr. Justice McREYNOLDS delivered the opinion of the Court.

[Two private schools in Oregon—one a parochial school and the other a non-parochial school—challenged an Oregon law that required children between 8 and 16 years old to attend public school.]

The inevitable practical result of enforcing the act under consideration would be destruction of appellees' primary schools, and perhaps all other private primary schools for normal children within the state of Oregon. Appellees are engaged in a kind of undertaking not inherently harmful, but long regarded as useful and meritorious. Certainly there is nothing in the present records to indicate that they have failed to discharge their obligations to patrons, students, or the state. And there are no peculiar circumstances or present emergencies which demand extraordinary measures relative to primary education.

Under the doctrine of *Meyer v. Nebraska*, 262 U. S. 390 (1923), we think it entirely plain that the Act of 1922 unreasonably interferes with the liberty of parents and guardians to direct the upbringing and education of children

> **Food for Thought**
>
> The plaintiffs in *Pierce* were private schools that were affected by the challenged law. But according to the Court, the "right" invaded by the statute belonged to the parents of the children that the schools hoped to enroll. Should the Court have concluded that these plaintiffs lacked standing to assert the rights of others? Or did the Court conclude that the schools have a protected right, as well?

under their control. As often heretofore pointed out, rights guaranteed by the Constitution may not be abridged by legislation which has no reasonable relation to some purpose within the competency of the state. The fundamental theory of liberty upon which all governments in this Union repose excludes any general power of the state to standardize its children by forcing them to accept instruction from public teachers only. The child is not the mere creature of the state; those who nurture him and direct his destiny have the right, coupled with the high duty, to recognize and prepare him for additional obligations.

Generally, it is entirely true, as urged by counsel, that no person in any business has such an interest in possible customers as to enable him to restrain exercise of proper power of the state upon the ground that he will be deprived of patronage. But the injunctions here sought are not against the exercise of any proper power. Appellees asked protection against arbitrary, unreasonable, and unlawful interference with their patrons and the consequent destruction of their business and property. Their interest is clear and immediate. *******

Points for Discussion

a. Level of Scrutiny

The Court appeared to hold that the Act had no reasonable relation to any legitimate state interest. What do you think the state's purpose was in enacting the statute? Is that purpose obviously illegitimate? If not, how could the statute fail the test that the Court proposed? Is the Court's real point that there are some rights that are simply beyond the competency of the state to regulate, regardless of how "reasonable" the regulation is? Or is it instead that it would take a much more compelling state interest to justify the abridgement of those rights?

b. Fundamental Right

What is the "fundamental theory of liberty" to which the Court referred? Where does it come from? Would this theory of liberty permit the state to require all children to receive schooling, regardless of the setting in which they receive it? If so, why is it problematic to require that all children be educated in public schools?

c. *Lochner* Redux?

Justice McReynolds wrote the opinion in *Pierce* (and *Meyer*) during the *Lochner* era. (Indeed, we saw earlier in this Chapter, in his dissent in *Nebbia* and his position in *West Coast Hotel*, that Justice McReynolds was deeply committed to the *Lochner* line of cases.) Is there a difference between concluding that the Due Process Clause protects economic liberties such as the freedom to contract, on the one hand, and other forms of personal liberty, such as the right to make choices about child-rearing, on the other? If *Lochner* is indefensible, then is *Pierce* necessarily indefensible, too?

Recall that the Court effectively overruled _Lochner_ in 1937 in _West Coast Hotel_. In so doing, did the Court also completely repudiate the view that the Due Process Clause protects some substantive definition of liberty wholly aside from the fairness of the process that precedes its deprivation?

In the case that follows, the Court relied on the Equal Protection Clause to invalidate a state law providing for the forced sterilization of felons convicted for the third time of crimes involving "moral turpitude." The Court had previously upheld a statute providing that "the health of the patient and the welfare of society may be promoted in certain cases by the sterilization of mental defectives" held in state institutions. In _Buck v. Bell_, 274 U.S. 200 (1927), Justice Holmes, writing for the Court, rejected the argument that forced sterilization can never be justified:

> We have seen more than once that the public welfare may call upon the best citizens for their lives. It would be strange if it could not call upon those who already sap the strength of the State for these lesser sacrifices, often not felt to be such by those concerned, in order to prevent our being swamped with incompetence. It is better for all the world, if instead of waiting to execute degenerate offspring for crime, or to let them starve for their imbecility, society can prevent those who are manifestly unfit from continuing their kind. *** Three generations of imbeciles are enough.

Justice Holmes rejected the petitioner's equal protection claim as the "usual last resort of constitutional arguments." We will consider the Equal Protection Clause, which generally speaking prohibits some forms of government classification, in Chapters 10-12. For the time being, consider whether the Court's conclusion in the case that follows is really about the government's general obligation to treat similarly situated persons the same, or is instead about individual liberty that cannot be abridged even when done even-handedly.

Skinner v. Oklahoma

316 U.S. 535 (1942)

Mr. Justice DOUGLAS delivered the opinion of the Court.

This case touches a sensitive and important area of human rights. Oklahoma deprives certain individuals of a right which is basic to the perpetuation of a race—the right to have offspring. [The Oklahoma Habitual Criminal Sterilization Act] defines an "habitual criminal" as a person who, having been convicted two or more times for crimes "amounting to felonies involving moral turpitude," is thereafter convicted of such a felony in Oklahoma and is sentenced to a term of imprisonment in an Oklahoma penal institution. Machinery is provided for the institution by the Attorney General of a proceeding against such a person in the Oklahoma courts for a judgment that such person shall be rendered sexually sterile. *** If [after notice and an opportunity to be heard] the court or jury finds that the defendant is an "habitual criminal" and that he "may be rendered sexually sterile without detriment to his or her general health," then the court "shall render judgment to the effect that said defendant be rendered sexually sterile." [The Act also] provides that "offenses arising out of the violation of the prohibitory laws, revenue acts, embezzlement, or political offenses, shall not come or be considered within the terms of this Act."

Food for Thought

Why do you think that Oklahoma made sterilization a punishment for larceny but not for embezzlement? Is a person guilty of larceny more blameworthy than a person guilty of embezzlement? Is the fact that embezzlement is usually considered a "white collar crime" important?

[Between 1926 and 1934, petitioner was convicted once of stealing chickens and twice of robbery with fire arms. In 1936, the Attorney General instituted proceedings against him, and the Oklahoma Supreme Court ultimately affirmed a judgment directing that the petitioner be sterilized.]

Several objections to the constitutionality of the Act have been pressed upon us. It is urged that the Act cannot be sustained as an exercise of the police power in view of the state of scientific authorities respecting inheritability of criminal traits. It is argued that due process is lacking because under this Act, unlike the act upheld in *Buck v. Bell*, 274 U.S. 200 (1927), the defendant is given no opportunity to be heard on the issue as to whether he is the probable potential parent of socially undesirable offspring. It is also suggested that the Act is penal in character and that the sterilization provided for is cruel and unusual punishment and violative of the Fourteenth Amendment. We pass those points without intimating an opinion on them, for there is a feature of the Act which clearly condemns it. That is its failure to meet the requirements of the equal protection clause of the Fourteenth Amendment.

We do not stop to point out all of the inequalities in this Act. A few examples will suffice. *** A clerk who appropriates over $20 from his employer's till and a stranger who steals the same amount are [both] guilty of felonies. If the latter repeats his act and is convicted three times, he may be sterilized. But the clerk is not subject to the pains and penalties of the Act no matter how large his embezzlements nor how frequent his convictions. *** Whether a particular act is larceny by fraud or embezzlement [turns] not on the intrinsic quality of the act but on when the felonious intent arose.

Take Note

Is the Court suggesting here that the state cannot provide different punishments for similar crimes? Is there an argument that robbery and embezzlement are different, and thus warrant different punishments, regardless of the amount taken?

[If] we had here only a question as to a State's classification of crimes, such as embezzlement or larceny, no substantial federal question would be raised. *** For a State is not constrained in the exercise of its police power to ignore experience which marks a class of offenders or a family of offenses for special treatment. Nor is it prevented by the equal protection clause from confining "its restrictions to those classes of cases where the need is deemed to be clearest." *Miller v. Wilson*, 236 U.S. 373, 384 (1915). ***

But [w]e are dealing here with legislation which involves one of the basic civil rights of man. Marriage and procreation are fundamental to the very existence and survival of the race. The power to sterilize, if exercised, may have subtle, far reaching and devastating effects. In evil or reckless hands it can cause races or types which are inimical to the dominant group to wither and disappear. There is no redemption for the individual whom the law touches. Any experiment which the State conducts is to his irreparable injury. He is forever deprived of a basic liberty. We mention these matters not to reexamine the scope of the police power of the States. We advert to them merely in emphasis of

> **Food for Thought**
>
> If the Constitution protects a "basic liberty" to reproduce, then why is the Equal Protection Clause relevant? Could the state avoid the defect that the Court finds here by providing for sterilization as a punishment for *all* crimes? If not, then what does that suggest about the Court's equal protection argument?

our view that strict scrutiny of the classification which a State makes in a sterilization law is essential, lest unwittingly or otherwise invidious discriminations are made against groups or types of individuals in violation of the constitutional guaranty of just and equal laws.

When the law lays an unequal hand on those who have committed intrinsically the same quality of offense and sterilizes one and not the other, it has made as invidious a discrimination as if it had selected a particular race or nationality for oppressive treatment. Sterilization of those who have thrice committed grand larceny with immunity for those who are embezzlers is a clear, pointed, unmistakable discrimination. Oklahoma makes no attempt to say that he who commits larceny by trespass or trick or fraud has biologically inheritable traits which he who commits embezzlement lacks. *** We have not the slightest basis for inferring that [Oklahoma's line between larceny by fraud and embezzlement] has any significance in eugenics nor that the inheritability of criminal traits follows the neat legal distinctions which the law has marked between those two offenses. *** The equal protection clause would indeed be a formula of empty words if such conspicuously artificial lines could be drawn. *** If such a classification were permitted, [a common-law distinction] could readily become a rule of human genetics. Reversed.

Mr. Chief Justice STONE concurring.

I concur in the result, but I am not persuaded that we are aided in reaching it by recourse to the equal protection clause. If Oklahoma may resort generally to the sterilization of criminals on the assumption that their propensities are transmissible to future generations by inheritance, I seriously doubt that the equal protection clause requires it to apply the measure to all criminals in the first instance, or to none.

*** I think the real question we have to consider is not one of equal protection, but whether the wholesale condemnation of a class to such an invasion of personal liberty, without opportunity to any individual to show that his is not the type of case which would justify resort to it, satisfies the demands of due process.

Although petitioner here was given a hearing to ascertain whether sterilization would be detrimental to his health, he was given none to discover whether his criminal tendencies are of an inheritable type. Undoubtedly a state may, after appropriate inquiry, constitutionally interfere with the personal liberty of the individual to prevent the transmission by inheritance of his socially injurious tendencies. *Buck v. Bell*, 274 U.S. 200 (1927). But until now we have not been called upon to say that it may do so without giving him a hearing and opportunity to challenge the existence as to him of the only facts which could justify so drastic a measure.

Mr. Justice JACKSON, concurring.

There are limits to the extent to which a legislatively represented majority may conduct biological experiments at the expense of the dignity and personality and natural powers of a minority—even those who have been guilty of what the majority define as crimes. But this Act falls down before reaching this problem, which I mention only to avoid the implication that such a question may not exist because not discussed. On it I would also reserve judgment.

————————

Points for Discussion

a. Historical Context

This case was decided in 1942, when the United States was beginning to learn about the extent of the atrocities that were being committed by the Nazis in Germany in the name of "eugenics" and the "science" of racial purity and superiority. Until this point, however, eugenics—that is, the "science" of improving the hereditary qualities of a race or breed by controlling reproduction—was not the subject of universal disapproval, and in fact had the support of prominent figures such as Woodrow Wilson. The Court made no reference in its opinion to events abroad. But would it have been appropriate for the Court to consider the Nazi example in construing the Constitution in 1942?

b. Other Possible Bases for the Decision

The Court appeared to indicate that it is not the enforced sterilization of criminals *per se* that is unconstitutional, but rather the different treatment accorded to persons convicted of similar crimes. Should the Court have concluded—as the petitioner argued—that sterilization is a cruel and unusual punishment in violation of the Eighth Amendment? Or that it violates a protected liberty interest in reproduction? Was the Court's decision really based on the Equal Protection Clause?

c. Precedent

The Court in <u>Skinner</u> did not purport to overrule <u>Buck</u>. Instead, it stated:

"In *Buck v. Bell*, the Virginia statute was upheld though it applied only to feebleminded persons in institutions of the State. But it was pointed out that "so far as the operations enable those who otherwise must be kept confined to be returned to the world, and thus open the asylum to others, the equality aimed at will be more nearly reached." <u>274 U.S. at 208</u>. Here there is no such saving feature. Embezzlers are forever free. Those who steal or take in other ways are not."

Is this a sensible ground for distinguishing _Buck_? Are Chief Justice Stone's grounds for distinguishing _Buck_ any more convincing?

d. Procedural vs. Substantive Due Process

Chief Justice Stone reasoned that the Oklahoma statute failed to accord adequate procedural protection to persons subject to the penalty of sterilization. We discuss arguments of this kind—usually called, somewhat redundantly, "procedural due process" arguments—in Chapter 9. Justice Jackson suggested that the statute might have been constitutionally problematic even if more process had been afforded, and wholly aside from any classifications that the statute created. There are hints of this view in the Court's opinion, as well. Putting aside for a moment the equal protection rationale, which view is a more defensible basis for the decision?

---

2. Contraception and Abortion

Skinner at least suggested that, notwithstanding the repudiation of _Lochner_, the Court might continue to interpret the Due Process Clauses to protect some substantive spheres of liberty. In the cases that follow, the Court considered claims of personal autonomy in intimate relationships.

Griswold v. Connecticut

381 U.S. 479 (1965)

Mr. Justice DOUGLAS delivered the opinion of the Court.

Appellant Griswold is Executive Director of the Planned Parenthood League of Connecticut. Appellant Buxton is a licensed physician and a professor at the Yale Medical School who served as Medical Director for the League at its Center in New Haven. *** They gave information, instruction, and medical advice to _married persons_ as to the means of preventing conception. *** [They were convicted and fined $100 as accessories to the violation of § 53-32 of the General Statutes of Connecticut, which provides: "Any person who uses any drug, medicinal article or instrument for the purpose of preventing conception shall be fined not less than fifty dollars or imprisoned not less than sixty days nor more than one year or be both fined and imprisoned." The state appellate courts affirmed the convictions notwithstanding appellants' claim that the statute as applied violated the Fourteenth Amendment.]

[W]e are met with a wide range of questions that implicate the Due Process Clause of the Fourteenth Amendment. Overtones of some arguments suggest that _Lochner v. New York_ should be our guide. But we decline that invitation as we did in _West Coast Hotel Co. v. Parrish_. We do not sit as a super-legislature to determine the wisdom, need, and propriety of laws that touch economic problems, business affairs, or social conditions. This law, however, operates directly on an intimate relation of husband and wife and their physician's role in one aspect of that relation.

The association of people is not mentioned in the Constitution nor in the Bill of Rights. The right to educate a child in a school of the parents' choice—whether public or private or parochial—is also not mentioned. Nor is the right to study any particular subject or any foreign language. Yet [b]y *Pierce v. Society of Sisters*, the right to educate one's children as one chooses is made applicable to the States by the force of the First and Fourteenth Amendments. By *Meyer v. State of Nebraska*, the same dignity is given the right to study the German language in a private school. In other words, the State may not, consistently with the spirit of the First Amendment, contract the spectrum of available knowledge. The right of freedom of speech and press includes not only the right to utter or to print, but the right to distribute, the right to receive, the right to read and freedom of inquiry, freedom of thought, and freedom to teach. *** Without those peripheral rights the specific rights would be less secure. And so we reaffirm the principle of the <u>Pierce</u> and the <u>Meyer</u> cases.

> **Take Note**
>
> Do you agree that in <u>Pierce</u> and <u>Meyer</u> the Court relied on the First Amendment as incorporated by the Fourteenth Amendment? If it did, is that a more defensible basis for those decisions than the more general claim that the "liberty" protected by the Due Process Clause includes the right to raise children or study foreign languages?

The foregoing cases suggest that specific guarantees in the Bill of Rights have penumbras, formed by emanations from those guarantees that help give them life and substance. Various guarantees create zones of privacy. The right of association contained in the penumbra of the First Amendment is one, as we have seen. The Third Amendment in its prohibition against the quartering of soldiers "in any house" in time of peace without the consent of the owner is another facet of that privacy. The Fourth Amendment explicitly affirms the "right of the people to be secure in their persons, houses, papers, and effects, against unreasonable searches and seizures." The Fifth Amendment in its Self-Incrimination Clause enables the citizen to create a zone of privacy which government may not force him to surrender to his detriment. The Ninth Amendment provides: "The enumeration in the Constitution, of certain rights, shall not be construed to deny or disparage others retained by the people." *** We have had many controversies over these penumbral rights of "privacy and repose." See, *e.g.*, *Skinner v. Oklahoma*, 316 U.S. 535, 541 (1942). These cases bear witness that the right of privacy which presses for recognition here is a legitimate one.

The present case, then, concerns a relationship lying within the zone of privacy created by several fundamental constitutional guarantees. And it concerns a law which, in forbidding the use of contraceptives rather than regulating their manufacture or sale, seeks to achieve its goals by means having a maximum destructive impact upon that relationship. Such a law cannot stand in light of the familiar principle, so often applied by this Court, that a "governmental purpose to control or prevent activities constitutionally subject to state regulation may not be achieved by means which sweep unnecessarily broadly and thereby invade the area of protected freedoms." *NAACP v. Alabama*, 377 U.S. 288, 307 (1964). Would we allow the police to search the sacred precincts of marital bedrooms for telltale signs of the use of contraceptives? The very idea is repulsive to the notions of privacy surrounding the marriage relationship.

We deal with a right of privacy older than the Bill of Rights—older than our political parties, older than our school system. Marriage is a coming together for better or for worse, hopefully enduring, and intimate to the degree of being sacred. It is an association that promotes a way of life, not causes; a harmony in living, not political faiths; a bilateral loyalty, not commercial or social projects. Yet it is an association for as noble a purpose as any involved in our prior decisions. [Reversed.]

Mr. Justice GOLDBERG, whom THE CHIEF JUSTICE and Mr. Justice BRENNAN join, concurring.

I agree with the Court that Connecticut's birth-control law unconstitutionally intrudes upon the right of marital privacy, and I join in its opinion and judgment. Although I have not accepted the view that "due process" as used in the Fourteenth Amendment includes all of the first eight Amendments ***, I do agree that the concept of liberty protects those personal rights that are fundamental, and is not confined to the specific terms of the Bill of Rights. My conclusion that the concept of liberty is not so restricted and that it embraces the right of marital privacy though that right is not mentioned explicitly in the Constitution is supported both by numerous decisions of this Court, referred to in the Court's opinion, and by the language and history of the Ninth Amendment. *** This Court, in a series of decisions, has held that the Fourteenth Amendment absorbs and applies to the States those specifics of the first eight amendments which express fundamental personal rights. The language and history of the Ninth Amendment reveal that the Framers of the Constitution believed that there are additional fundamental rights, protected from governmental infringement, which exist alongside those fundamental rights specifically mentioned in the first eight constitutional amendments.

The Ninth Amendment reads, "The enumeration in the Constitution, of certain rights, shall not be construed to deny or disparage others retained by the people." The Amendment is almost entirely the work of James Madison. It was introduced in Congress by him and passed the House and Senate with little or no debate and virtually no change in language. It was proffered to quiet expressed fears that a bill of specifically enumerated rights could not be sufficiently broad to cover all essential rights and that the specific mention of certain rights would be interpreted as a denial that others were protected. In presenting the proposed Amendment, Madison said:

> "It has been objected also against a bill of rights, that, by enumerating particular exceptions to the grant of power, it would disparage those rights which were not placed in that enumeration; and it might follow by implication, that those rights which were not singled out, were intended to be assigned into the hands of the General Government, and were consequently insecure. This is one of the most plausible arguments I have ever heard urged against the admission of a bill of rights into this system; but, I conceive, that it may be guarded against. I have attempted it, as gentlemen may see by turning to the last clause of [the proposed Ninth Amendment]." I Annals

of Congress 439 (Gales and Seaton ed. 1834).

While this Court has had little occasion to interpret the Ninth Amendment, "it cannot be presumed that any clause in the constitution is intended to be without effect." *Marbury v. Madison*, 1 Cranch 137, 174 (1803). *** To hold that a right so basic and fundamental and so deep-rooted in our society as the right of privacy in marriage may be infringed because that right is not guaranteed in so many words by the first eight amendments to the Constitution is to ignore the Ninth Amendment and to give it no effect whatsoever.

[I] do not mean to imply that the Ninth Amendment is applied against the States by the Fourteenth. Nor do I mean to state that the Ninth Amendment constitutes an independent source of rights protected from infringement by either the States or the Federal Government. Rather, [the] Ninth Amendment simply shows the intent of the Constitution's authors that other fundamental personal rights should not be denied such protection or disparaged in any other way simply because they are not specifically listed in the first eight constitutional amendments.

In determining which rights are fundamental, judges are not left at large to decide cases in light of their personal and private notions. Rather, they must look to the "traditions and collective conscience of our people" to determine whether a principle is "so rooted there as to be ranked as fundamental." *Snyder v. Massachusetts*, 291 U.S. 97, 105 (1934). The inquiry is whether a right involved is of such a character that it cannot be denied without violating those "fundamental principles of liberty and justice which lie at the base of all our civil and political institutions." *Powell v. State of Alabama*, 287 U.S. 45, 67 (1932).

> **Food for Thought**
>
> Does Justice Goldberg's opinion provide any real guidance in determining what rights should be deemed fundamental? Is it helpful to refer to "the traditions and collective conscience of our people" and "fundamental principles of liberty and justice"? Is the Court the most sensible institution to give content to such broad concepts?

> **Make the Connection**
>
> The level of scrutiny of the Connecticut law that Justice Goldberg urges here is known as "strict scrutiny," which generally requires the state to demonstrate that the challenged law or policy serves a compelling governmental interest and is narrowly tailored to advance that interest. We will consider strict scrutiny again when we discuss the Equal Protection Clause in Chapters 10-12.

I agree fully with the Court that, applying these tests, the right of privacy is a fundamental personal right, emanating "from the totality of the constitutional scheme under which we live." *** [W]here fundamental personal liberties are involved, *** "the State may prevail only upon showing a subordinating interest which is compelling," [and by showing that the] law is "necessary, and not merely rationally related to, the accomplishment of a permissible state policy." Although the Connecticut birth-control law obviously encroaches upon a fundamental personal liberty, the State [has not met this standard.]

Mr. Justice HARLAN, concurring in the judgment.

I fully agree with the judgment of reversal, but find myself unable to join the Court's opinion. The reason is that it seems to me to evince an approach to this case very much like that taken by my Brothers BLACK and STEWART in dissent, namely: the Due Process Clause of the Fourteenth Amendment does not touch this Connecticut statute unless the enactment is found to violate some right assured by the letter or penumbra of the Bill of Rights.

In my view, the proper constitutional inquiry in this case is whether this Connecticut statute infringes the Due Process Clause of the Fourteenth Amendment because the enactment violates basic values "implicit in the concept of ordered liberty," *Palko v. Connecticut,* 302 U.S. 319, 325 (1937). For reasons stated at length in my dissenting opinion in *Poe v. Ullman,* 367 US. 497 (1961), I believe that it does. While the relevant inquiry may be aided by resort to one or more of the provisions of the Bill of Rights, it is not dependent on them or any of their radiations. The Due Process Clause of the Fourteenth Amendment stands, in my opinion, on its own bottom.

> **FYI**
>
> We provide excerpts from Justice Harlan's dissenting opinion in *Poe v. Ullman* in the Points for Discussion after the case.

[Justices Black and Stewart rest on] the thesis that by limiting the content of the Due Process Clause of the Fourteenth Amendment to the protection of rights which can be found elsewhere in the Constitution, in this instance in the Bill of Rights, judges will thus be confined to "interpretation" of specific constitutional provisions, and will thereby be restrained from introducing their own notions of constitutional right and wrong into the "vague contours of the Due Process Clause." *Rochin v. People of State of California,* 342 U.S. 165, 170 (1952). While I could not more heartily agree that judicial "self restraint" is an indispensable ingredient of sound constitutional adjudication, I do submit that the formula suggested for achieving it is more hollow than real. "Specific" provisions of the Constitution, no less than "due process," lend themselves as readily to "personal" interpretations by judges whose constitutional outlook is simply to keep the Constitution in supposed "tune with the times." Judicial self-restraint *** will be achieved in this area, as in other constitutional areas, only by continual insistence upon respect for the teachings of history, solid recognition of the basic values that underlie our society, and wise appreciation of the great roles that the doctrines of federalism and separation of powers have played in establishing and preserving American freedoms.

Mr. Justice WHITE, concurring in the judgment.

An examination of the justification offered [for the statute] cannot be avoided by saying that the Connecticut anti-use statute invades a protected area of privacy and association or that it demands the marriage relationship. [S]uch statutes, if reasonably necessary for the effectuation of a legitimate and substantial state interest, and not arbitrary or capricious in application, are not invalid under the Due Process Clause.

The State claims but one justification for its anti-use statute. *** The statute is said to serve the State's policy against all forms of promiscuous or illicit sexual relationships, be they premarital or extramarital, concededly a permissible and legitimate legislative goal. *** I wholly fail to see how the ban on the use of contraceptives by married couples in any way reinforces the State's ban on illicit sexual relationships. *** Perhaps the theory is that the flat ban on use prevents married people from possessing contraceptives and without the ready availability of such devices for use in the marital relationship, there will be no or less temptation to use them in extramarital ones. *** At most the broad ban is of marginal utility to the declared objective. A statute limiting its prohibition on use to persons engaging in the prohibited relationship would serve the end posited by Connecticut in the same way, and with the same effectiveness, or ineffectiveness, as the broad anti-use statute under attack in this case. I find nothing in this record justifying the sweeping scope of this statute, with its telling effect on the freedoms of married persons, and therefore conclude that it deprives such persons of liberty without due process of law.

> **Take Note**
>
> What level of scrutiny does Justice White apply to this law? Under that level of scrutiny, does Justice White accord sufficient deference to the legislature's judgment?

Mr. Justice BLACK, with whom Mr. Justice STEWART joins, dissenting.

There is no single one of the graphic and eloquent strictures and criticisms fired at the policy of this Connecticut law either by the Court's opinion or by those of my concurring Brethren to which I cannot subscribe—except their conclusion that the evil qualities they see in the law make it unconstitutional. *** The Court talks about a constitutional "right of privacy" as though there is some constitutional provision or provisions forbidding any law ever to be passed which might abridge the "privacy" of individuals. But there is not. There are, of course, guarantees in certain specific constitutional provisions which are designed in part to protect privacy at certain times and places with respect to certain activities. Such, for example, is the Fourth Amendment's guarantee against "unreasonable searches and seizures." But I think it belittles that Amendment to talk about it as though it protects nothing but "privacy." *** "Privacy" is a broad, abstract and ambiguous concept which can easily be shrunken in meaning but which can also, on the other hand, easily be interpreted as a constitutional ban against many things other than searches and seizures. *** I like my privacy as well as the next one, but I am nevertheless compelled to admit that government has a right to invade it unless prohibited by some specific constitutional provision.

The due process argument which my Brothers HARLAN and WHITE adopt here is based, as their opinions indicate, on the premise that this Court is vested with power to invalidate all state laws that it considers to be arbitrary, capricious, unreasonable, or oppressive, or this Court's belief that a particular state law under scrutiny has no "rational or justifying" purpose, or is offensive to a "sense of fairness and justice." If these formulas based on "natural justice," or others which mean the same thing, are to prevail, they require judges to determine what is or is not constitutional on the basis of their own appraisal of what laws are unwise or unnecessary. The power to make such decisions is of course that of a legislative body.

The Ninth Amendment was *** passed, not to broaden the powers of this Court or any other department of "the General Government," but, as every student of history knows, to assure the people that the Constitution in all its provisions was intended to limit the Federal Government to the powers granted expressly or by necessary implication. *** This fact is perhaps responsible for the peculiar phenomenon that for a period of a century and a half no serious suggestion was ever made that the Ninth Amendment, enacted to protect state powers against federal invasion, could be used as a weapon of federal power to prevent state legislatures from passing laws they consider appropriate to govern local affairs. So far as I am concerned, Connecticut's law as applied here is not forbidden by any provision of the Federal Constitution as that Constitution was written, and I would therefore affirm.

Mr. Justice STEWART, whom Mr. Justice BLACK joins, dissenting.

I think this is an uncommonly silly law. As a practical matter, the law is obviously unenforceable, except in the oblique context of the present case. As a philosophical matter, I believe the use of contraceptives in the relationship of marriage should be left to personal and private choice, based upon each individual's moral, ethical, and religious beliefs. As a matter of social policy, I think professional counsel about methods of birth control should be available to all, so that each individual's choice can be meaningfully made. But we are not asked in this case to say whether we think this law is unwise, or even asinine. We are asked to hold that it violates the United States Constitution. And that I cannot do.

In the course of its opinion the Court refers to no less than six Amendments to the Constitution: the First, the Third, the Fourth, the Fifth, the Ninth, and the Fourteenth. But the Court does not say which of these Amendments, if any, it thinks is infringed by this Connecticut law. *** There is no claim that this law, duly enacted by the Connecticut Legislature, is unconstitutionally vague. There is no claim that the appellants were denied any of the elements of procedural due process at their trial, so as to make their convictions constitutionally invalid. And, as the Court says, the day has long passed since the Due

Process Clause was regarded as a proper instrument for determining "the wisdom, need, and propriety" of state laws.

As to the First, Third, Fourth, and Fifth Amendments, I can find nothing in any of them to invalidate this Connecticut law, even assuming that all those Amendments are fully applicable against the States. *** The Ninth Amendment, like its companion the Tenth, which this Court held "states but a truism that all is retained which has not been surrendered," *United States v. Darby*, 312 U.S. 100, 124 (1941), was framed by James Madison and adopted by the States simply to make clear that the adoption of the Bill of Rights did not alter the plan that the *Federal* Government was to be a government of express and limited powers, and that all rights and powers not delegated to it were retained by the people and the individual States. *** If, as I should surely hope, the law before us does not reflect the standards of the people of Connecticut, the people of Connecticut can freely exercise their true Ninth and Tenth Amendment rights to persuade their elected representatives to repeal it. That is the constitutional way to take this law off the books.

————————

Points for Discussion

a. "Penumbras": Justice Douglas's View

According to Justice Douglas, what is the constitutional source of the right that is protected in <u>Griswold</u>? According to his theory, is the right "enumerated" or "unenumerated"? How far do the penumbras of the rights that are enumerated in the Constitution extend?

b. Due Process: Justice Harlan's View

Even though the Constitution contains some provisions that protect privacy, is it an over-generalization to conclude from these provisions that the Constitution protects privacy as a general matter? In his concurrence in <u>Griswold</u>, Justice Harlan referred to his dissent in *Poe v. Ullman*, 367 U.S. 497 (1961), which involved a challenge to the same Connecticut statute at issue in <u>Griswold</u>. The Court in that case declined to reach the merits, concluding that, because there was no showing that the statute would actually be enforced against the plaintiffs, the case was not justiciable. Justice Harlan disagreed and accordingly reached the merits. He stated:

> Due process has not been reduced to any formula; its content cannot be determined by reference to any code. The best that can be said is that through the course of this Court's decisions it has represented the balance which our Nation, built upon postulates of respect for the liberty of the individual, has struck between that liberty and the demands of organized society. If the supplying of content to this Constitutional concept has of necessity been a rational process, it certainly has not been one where judges have felt free to roam where unguided speculation might take them. The balance of which I speak is the balance struck by this country, having regard to what history teaches are the traditions from which it developed as well as the traditions from which it broke. That tradition is a living thing. A decision of this Court which radically departs from it could not long survive, while a decision which builds on what has survived is likely to be sound. No formula could serve as a substitute, in this area, for judgment and restraint. This "liberty" is [a] rational continuum which, broadly speaking, includes a freedom from all substantial arbi-

trary impositions and purposeless restraints, and which also recognizes, what a reasonable and sensitive judgment must, that certain interests require particularly careful scrutiny of the state needs asserted to justify their abridgment.

I think the sweep of the Court's decisions, under both the Fourth and Fourteenth Amendments, amply shows that the Constitution protects the privacy of the home against all unreasonable intrusion of whatever character. *** [I]t is difficult to imagine what is more private or more intimate than a husband and wife's marital relations. [T]he intimacy of husband and wife is necessarily an essential and accepted feature of the institution of marriage, an institution which the State not only must allow, but which always and in every age it has fostered and protected. It is one thing when the State exerts its power either to forbid extra-marital sexuality altogether, or to say who may marry, but it is quite another when, having acknowledged a marriage and the intimacies inherent in it, it undertakes to regulate by means of the criminal law the details of that intimacy.

Since, as it appears to me, the statute marks an abridgment of important fundamental liberties protected by the Fourteenth Amendment, it will not do to urge in justification of that abridgment simply that the statute is rationally related to the effectuation of a proper state purpose. A closer scrutiny and stronger justification than that are required. *** [C]onclusive, in my view, is the utter novelty of this enactment. Although the Federal Government and many States have at one time or other had on their books statutes forbidding or regulating the distribution of contraceptives, none, so far as I can find, has made the *use* of contraceptives a crime. Indeed, a diligent search has revealed that no nation, including several which quite evidently share Connecticut's moral policy, has seen fit to effectuate that policy by the means presented here.

In Justice Harlan's view, the Due Process Clause protects liberty as defined by the nation's traditions, which he describes as "living." Does he mean by this that the meaning of "liberty" changes from generation to generation? Is it possible that the liberty that he found in *Poe* (and *Griswold*) will not be constitutionally protected in the future?

c. Due Process and the Role of the Ninth Amendment: Justice Goldberg's View

The Ninth Amendment states: "The enumeration in the Constitution of certain rights shall not be construed to deny or disparage others retained by the people." Justices Goldberg and Black disagreed on the weight and meaning of this Amendment. Justice Black asserted that the Amendment was never intended to create judicially enforceable rights. Did Justice Goldberg suggest that the Ninth Amendment itself creates enforceable rights? If not, what did he think it adds to the analysis? And if the Ninth Amendment does not itself create rights, where do they come from? Are they created by the limitation on federal powers?

Justice Stewart compared the Ninth Amendment to the Tenth Amendment, which we considered in Chapter 3, and he concluded that it was merely designed to confirm the enumeration. Is this a plausible reading of the Ninth Amendment's text? Conversely, for Justice Goldberg's view to be plausible, must he conclude that the Ninth Amendment applies to the states through the Fourteenth Amendment?

d. Contraception and Marriage

Griswold specifically addressed the rights of married persons to be free from governmental interference with their decisions regarding contraception. Indeed, Justices Douglas, Harlan, and White relied explicitly on the marital relationship in identifying the right at issue. In *Eisenstadt v. Baird*, 405 U.S. 438 (1972), decided seven years later, the Court invalidated a statute that permitted the distribution of contraceptives only to married— and thus not to unmarried—persons. Although the Court relied on the Equal Protection, rather than the Due Process, Clause, it suggested that the right at issue in *Griswold* did not exist solely by virtue of marriage:

> If under *Griswold* the distribution of contraceptives to married persons cannot be prohibited, a ban on distribution to unmarried persons would be equally impermissible. It is true that in *Griswold* the right of privacy in question inhered in the marital relationship. Yet the marital couple is not an independent entity with a mind and heart of its own, but an association of two individuals each with a separate intellectual and emotional makeup. If the right of privacy means anything, it is the right of the *individual*, married or single, to be free from unwarranted governmental intrusion into matters so fundamentally affecting a person as the decision whether to bear or beget a child.

Does the Court's decision in *Eisenstadt* suggest that *Griswold* was about more than simply *marital* privacy? Or was *Eisenstadt* an impermissible extension of *Griswold*?

———————————

Roe v. Wade

410 U.S. 113 (1973)

Mr. Justice BLACKMUN delivered the opinion of the Court.

[Texas law makes] it a crime to "procure an abortion," as therein defined, or to attempt one, except with respect to "an abortion procured or attempted by medical advice for the purpose of saving the life of the mother." Similar statutes are in existence in a majority of the States. [A woman alleging that she wished to terminate her pregnancy by an abortion performed by a licensed physician, and that she could not afford to travel to another jurisdiction in order to secure a legal abortion under safe conditions, filed suit to challenge the law. A separate action was instituted by a married couple who alleged that the woman suffered from a condition that made pregnancy dangerous to her health, that their physician had counseled them not to use birth control, and that they would wish to seek an abortion if she became pregnant. The Court first engaged in a lengthy discussion of the history of legal treatment of abortion, observing that it "perhaps is not generally appreciated that the restrictive criminal abortion laws in effect in a majority of States today are of relatively recent vintage. Those laws [derive] from statutory changes effected, for the most part, in the latter half of the 19th century." The Court then proceeded to the "main thrust" of the plaintiffs' argument.]

The Constitution does not explicitly mention any right of privacy. In a line of decisions, however, [the] Court has recognized that a right of personal privacy, or a guarantee of certain areas or zones of privacy, does exist under the Constitution. In varying contexts, the Court or individual Justices have, indeed, found at least the roots of that right in the First Amendment, *Stanley v. Georgia*, 394 U.S. 557, 564 (1969); in the Fourth and Fifth Amendments, *Terry v. Ohio*, 392 U.S. 1, 8-9 (1968); in the penumbras of the Bill of Rights, *Griswold v. Connecticut*, 381 U.S. 479, 484-485 (1965); in the Ninth Amendment, *id.* at 486; or in the concept of liberty guaranteed by the first section of the Fourteenth Amendment, see *Meyer v. Nebraska*, 262 U.S. 390, 399 (1923). These decisions make it clear that only personal rights that can be deemed "fundamental" or "implicit in the concept of ordered liberty," *Palko v. Connecticut*, 302 U.S. 319, 325 (1937), are included in this guarantee of personal privacy. They also make it clear that the right has some extension to activities relating to marriage, *Loving v. Virginia*, 388 U.S. 1, 12 (1967); procreation, *Skinner v. Oklahoma*, 316 U.S. 535, 541-542 (1942); contraception, *Eisenstadt v. Baird*, 405 U.S. 438, 453-454 (1972); family relationships, *Prince v. Massachusetts*, 321 U.S. 158, 166 (1944); and child rearing and education *Pierce v. Society of Sisters*, 268 U.S. 510, 535 (1925).

> **Take Note**
>
> This paragraph and the one that follows are among the most controversial in the history of the Court. What are the two steps in the Court's reasoning? Can the questions whether there is a general right of privacy and whether it is broad enough to embrace a right to have an abortion be decided so simply?

This right of privacy, whether it be founded in the Fourteenth Amendment's concept of personal liberty and restrictions upon state action, as we feel it is, or, as the District Court determined, in the Ninth Amendment's reservation of rights to the people, is broad enough to encompass a woman's decision whether or not to terminate her pregnancy. The detriment that the State would impose upon the pregnant woman by denying this choice altogether is apparent. Specific and direct harm medically diagnosable even in early pregnancy may be involved. Maternity, or additional offspring, may force upon the woman a distressful life and future. Psychological harm may be imminent. Mental and physical health may be taxed by child care. There is also the distress, for all concerned, associated with the unwanted child, and there is the problem of bringing a child into a family already unable, psychologically and otherwise, to care for it. In other cases, as in this one, the additional difficulties and continuing stigma of unwed motherhood may be involved. All these are factors the woman and her responsible physician necessarily will consider in consultation.

We, therefore, conclude that the right of personal privacy includes the abortion decision, but that this right is not unqualified and must be considered against important state interests in regulation. *** Where certain "fundamental rights" are involved, the Court has held that regulation limiting these rights may be justified only by a "compelling state interest," *Kramer v. Union Free School District, 395 U.S. 621, 627 (1969)*, and that legislative enactments must be narrowly drawn to express only the legitimate state interests at stake. *Griswold, 381 U.S., at 485.*

The appellee and certain amici argue that the fetus is a "person" within the language and meaning of the Fourteenth Amendment. *** If this suggestion of personhood is established, the appellant's case, of course, collapses, for the fetus' right to life would then be guaranteed specifically by the Amendment. *** The Constitution does not define "person" in so many words. Section 1 of the Fourteenth Amendment contains three references to "person." *** "Person" is [also] used in other places in the Constitution [b]ut in nearly all these instances, the use of the word is such that it has application only postnatally. All this *** persuades us that the word "person," as used in the Fourteenth Amendment, does not include the unborn.

> **Food for Thought**
>
> If the Court had accepted Texas's argument that the fetus is a "person" entitled to protection under the Fourteenth Amendment, would the provision in Texas law permitting abortions for the purpose of saving the life of the mother have been constitutional?

> **Take Note**
>
> Is the Court exercising judicial restraint in declining to decide when life begins? Or is the Court, in rejecting the theory advanced by Texas, effectively making just such a decision—or at least ruling out one possible view?

Texas [also] urges that, apart from the Fourteenth Amendment, life begins at conception and is present throughout pregnancy, and that, therefore, the State has a compelling interest in protecting that life from and after conception. When those trained in the respective disciplines of medicine, philosophy, and theology are unable to arrive at any consensus, the judiciary, at this point in the development of man's knowledge, is not in a position to speculate as to the answer. ***

[However, the] State does have an important and legitimate interest in preserving and protecting the health of the pregnant woman, whether she be a resident of the State or a non-resident who seeks medical consultation and treatment there, and [it] has still another important and legitimate interest in protecting the potentiality of human life. These interests are separate and distinct. Each grows in substantiality as the woman approaches term and, at a point during pregnancy, each becomes "compelling."

With respect to the State's important and legitimate interest in the health of the mother, the "compelling" point, in the light of present medical knowledge, is at approximately the end of the first trimester. This is so because of the now-established medical fact [that] until the end of the first trimester mortality in abortion may be less than mortality in normal childbirth. It follows that, from and after this point, a State may regulate the abortion procedure to the extent that the regulation reasonably relates to the preservation and protection of maternal health. *** This means, on the other hand, that, for the period of pregnancy prior to this "compelling" point, the attending physician, in consultation with his patient, is free to determine, without regulation by the State, that, in his medical judgment, the patient's pregnancy should be terminated. If that decision is reached, the judgment may be effectuated by an abortion free of interference by the State.

With respect to the State's important and legitimate interest in potential life, the "compelling" point is at viability. This is so because the fetus then presumably has the capability of meaningful life outside the mother's womb. State regulation protective of fetal life after viability thus has both logical and biological justifications. If the State is interested in protecting fetal life after viability, it may go so far as to proscribe abortion during that period, except when it is necessary to preserve the life or health of the mother.

Measured against these standards, [the Texas law] sweeps too broadly. The statute makes no distinction between abortions performed early in pregnancy and those performed later, and it limits to a single reason, "saving" the mother's life, the legal justification for the procedure. The statute, therefore, cannot survive the constitutional attack made upon it here.

> **Food for Thought**
>
> The Court rests its constitutional analysis in significant part on biological and medical realities. Does this mean that the scope of a woman's right to an abortion—and, conversely, the state's power to regulate abortion—will evolve over time as scientific understanding develops and medical technology advances? For example, what if techniques are invented to keep a fetus viable at any age? As a related point, does the Court explain why the life of a *viable* fetus must be subordinate to the *life or health* of the mother?

To summarize and to repeat: *** (a) For the stage prior to approximately the end of the first trimester, the abortion decision and its effectuation must be left to the medical judgment of the pregnant woman's attending physician. (b) For the stage subsequent to approximately the end of the first trimester, the State, in promoting its interest in the health of the mother, may, if it chooses, regulate the abortion procedure in ways that are reasonably related to maternal health. (c) For the stage subsequent to viability, the State in promoting its interest in the potentiality of human life may, if it chooses, regulate, and even proscribe, abortion except where it is necessary, in appropriate medical judgment, for the preservation of the life or health of the mother.

[Our] decision vindicates the right of the physician to administer medical treatment according to his professional judgment up to the points where important state interests provide compelling justifications for intervention. Up to those points, the abortion decision in all its aspects is inherently, and primarily, a medical decision, and basic responsibility for it must rest with the physician.

> **Take Note**
>
> What level of scrutiny does the Court apply in invalidating the Texas law? It refers to state interests that are "legitimate," important," and "compelling." Which of these does it require before the state can regulate the right to an abortion? And must any such regulation satisfy a "means" test, as well?

Mr. Justice STEWART, concurring.

In 1963, this Court, in *Ferguson v. Skrupa*, 372 U.S. 726 (1963), purported to sound the death knell for the doctrine of substantive due process ***. Barely two years later, in *Griswold*, the Court held a Connecticut birth control law unconstitutional. In view of what had been so recently said in *Skrupa*, the Court's opinion in *Griswold* understandably did its best to avoid reliance on the Due Process Clause of the Fourteenth Amendment as the ground for decision. Yet, the Connecticut law did not violate any provision of the Bill of Rights, nor any other specific provision of the Constitution. So it was clear to me then, and it is equally clear to me now, that the *Griswold* decision can be rationally understood only as a holding that the Connecticut statute substantively invaded the "liberty" that is protected by the Due Process Clause of the Fourteenth Amendment. As so understood, *Griswold* stands as one in a long line of pre- *Skrupa* cases decided under the doctrine of substantive due process, and I now accept it as such.

The Constitution nowhere mentions a specific right of personal choice in matters of marriage and family life, but the "liberty" protected by the Due Process Clause of the Fourteenth Amendment covers more than those freedoms explicitly named in the Bill of Rights. *** Several decisions of this Court make clear that freedom of personal choice in matters of marriage and family life is one of the liberties protected by the Due Process Clause of the Fourteenth Amendment. *** As recently as last Term, in *Eisenstadt v. Baird*, 405 U.S. 438 (1972), we recognized "the right of the individual, married or single, to be free from unwarranted governmental intrusion into matters so fundamentally affecting a person as the decision whether to bear or beget a child." That right necessarily includes the right of a woman to decide whether or not to terminate her pregnancy.

> **Take Note**
>
> Justice Stewart dissented in <u>Griswold</u>. Did he change his mind about the meaning of the Due Process Clause? Or did he just feel compelled to follow precedent? If the latter, is it an act consistent with the judicial role, or instead one in tension with it?

Mr. Justice REHNQUIST, dissenting.

I have difficulty in concluding, as the Court does, that the right of "privacy" is involved in this case. *** A transaction resulting in an [abortion] is not "private" in the ordinary usage of that word. *** If the Court means by the term "privacy" no more than that the claim of a person to be free from unwanted state regulation of consensual transactions may be a form of "liberty" protected by the Fourteenth Amendment, there is no doubt that similar claims have been upheld in our earlier decisions on the basis of that liberty. I agree with [Justice STEWART that "liberty"] embraces more than the rights found in the Bill of Rights. But that liberty is not guaranteed absolutely against deprivation, only against deprivation without due process of law. The test traditionally applied in the area of social and economic legislation is whether or not a law such as that challenged has a rational relation to a valid state objective. *Williamson v. Lee Optical Co.*, 348 U.S. 483, 491 (1955). [T]he Court's sweeping invalidation of any restrictions on abortion during the first trimester is impossible to justify under that standard, and the conscious weighing of competing factors that the Court's opinion apparently substitutes for the established test is far more appropriate to a legislative judgment than to a judicial one.

As in <u>Lochner</u> and similar cases applying substantive due process standards to economic and social welfare legislation, the adoption of the compelling state interest standard will inevitably require this Court to examine the legislative policies and pass on the wisdom of these policies in the very process of deciding whether a particular state interest put forward may or may not be "compelling." The decision here to break pregnancy into three distinct terms and to outline the permissible restrictions the State may impose in each one, for example, partakes more of judicial legislation than it does of a determination of the intent of the drafters of the Fourteenth Amendment.

The fact that a majority of the States reflecting, after all the majority sentiment in those States, have had restrictions on abortions for at least a century is a strong indication, it seems to me, that the asserted right to an abortion is not "so rooted in the traditions and conscience of our people as to be ranked as fundamental," *Snyder v. Massachusetts*, 291 U.S. 97, 105 (1934). Even today, when society's views on abortion are changing, the very existence of the debate is evidence that the "right" to an abortion is not so universally accepted as the appellant would have us believe.

To reach its result, the Court necessarily has had to find within the scope of the Fourteenth Amendment a right that was apparently completely unknown to the drafters of the Amendment. *** By the time of the adoption of the Fourteenth Amendment in 1868, there were at least 36 laws enacted by state or territorial legislatures limiting abortion. *** The only conclusion possible from this history is that the drafters did not intend to have the Fourteenth Amendment withdraw from the States the power to legislate with respect to this matter. ***

> **Food for Thought**
>
> As an originalist matter, does the fact that the framers or ratifiers of a constitutional provision expected it to permit a particular practice necessarily demonstrate that the practice is constitutional? If so, as we will see in Chapter 11, the Court's decision in *Brown v. Board of Education* that school segregation is unconstitutional might, as some have argued, be indefensible on originalist grounds. But some originalists have responded that there is a difference between the original "meaning" of a constitutional provision and the original "expected application" of the provision, and that only the former is binding. See Michael W. McConnell, *The Importance of Humility in Judicial Review*, 65 Ford. L. Rev. 1269, 1284 (1997); Jack M. Balkin, *Abortion and Original Meaning*, 24 Const. Comment. 291 (2007).

> **FYI**
>
> In *Doe v. Bolton*, 410 U.S. 179 (1973), the companion case to *Roe*, the Court invalidated a Georgia statute regulating abortions. Justice White's opinion was filed in response to both cases.

Mr. Justice WHITE, with whom Mr. Justice REHNQUIST joins, dissenting.

The Court apparently values the convenience of the pregnant woman more than the continued existence and development of the life or potential life that she carries. Whether or not I might agree with that marshaling of values, I can in no event join the Court's judgment because I find no constitutional warrant for imposing such an order of priorities on the people and legislatures of the States. In a sensitive area such as this, involving as it does issues over which reasonable men may easily and heatedly differ, I cannot accept the Court's exercise of its clear power of choice by interposing a constitutional barrier to state efforts to protect human life and by investing women and doctors with the constitutionally protected right to exterminate it. This issue, for the most part, should be left with the people and to the political processes the people have devised to govern their affairs.

[Justice DOUGLAS's concurring opinion is omitted.]

Points for Discussion

a. Due Process

In his opinion for the Court, Justice Blackmun declared that the right of privacy is "founded in the Fourteenth Amendment's concept of personal liberty"—that is, that the right is one protected by substantive due process. What does this mean for the "penumbras" approach that Justice Douglas advanced for the Court in *Griswold*? In fact, Justice Douglas issued a concurring opinion in *Roe* (and in a companion case) that asserted that the right at issue was "peripheral" to other rights specified in the Constitution. No other member of the Court joined his opinion.

b. The Trimester Framework

The Court determined that the right of a woman to choose an abortion depends on timing. Under *Roe*, in the first trimester of pregnancy, the state cannot ban abortion. In roughly the third trimester—the stage subsequent to "viability"—the state can prohibit abortion except where necessary to preserve the life or health of the mother. The Court also stated that in the second trimester, the state can regulate abortion "in ways that are reasonably related to maternal health." Where did this framework come from? Is it a sensible interpretation of the Due Process Clause? Is it the best interpretation?

c. Constitutional Interpretation or Judicial Legislation?

A familiar refrain in cases involving substantive due process claims is that the Court is engaging in so-called "judicial legislation." Concerns about "judicial activism" and the separation of powers are obviously not unique to Due Process Clause cases; recall, for instance, Justice Scalia's criticisms of the Dormant Commerce Clause Doctrine, which we considered in Chapter 4. Nor is reliance on the implications from broad constitutional text unusual; consider the Court's decisions in *New York v. United States* and *Printz v. United States*, which we considered in Chapter 3 and which concluded that "structural" postulates prohibit Congress from compelling the states to enact or administer federal regulatory programs.

Are *Griswold* and *Roe* any more problematic than the countless other instances in which the Court has interpreted vague constitutional provisions to be rights-creating? If so, why?

d. History and Debate

In a section of the opinion omitted here, the Court engaged in a lengthy discussion of the history of abortion, including philosophical, medical, and legal issues debated in the West over the last 2000 years. Why did the Court believe that this discussion was necessary to the constitutional analysis?

The debate over abortion obviously did not end with the Court's decision in *Roe*, as some of the Justices apparently believed that it would. Does the continuing debate tend to justify the Court's decision, or instead undermine it?

The Court's decision in *Roe* was not the last word on the subject. In the two decades after the decision, the Court decided many cases concerning the right to an abortion. But the Court continued to be divided; some members of the Court asserted that *Roe* should be overruled. See *Thornburgh v. American College of Obstetricians and Gynecologists*, 476 U.S. 747, 797 (1986) (White, J., dissenting). After several appointments to the Court by President Reagan, who had pledged to appoint Justices who would overrule *Roe*, many people believed that the Court was poised to do just that. And indeed, some of those Justices explicitly wrote in favor of overruling *Roe*. See *Webster v. Reproductive Health Services*, 492 U.S. 490 (1989) (Scalia, J., concurring in part and concurring in the judgment).

The Court, however, declined to do so in the case that follows. In it, the Court reviewed a Pennsylvania statute that limited the right to an abortion in several ways, including requiring a 24-hour waiting period before a woman could obtain an abortion; requiring spousal consent before a woman could obtain an abortion; requiring parental consent for minors who sought abortions; and requiring abortion clinics to report information to the state about abortions performed. (The statute also prohibited "sex-selection" abortions, but the petitioners did not challenge that section. Can you think of why they did not?)

Planned Parenthood of Southeastern Penn. v. Casey

505 U.S. 833 (1992)

Justice O'CONNOR, Justice KENNEDY, and Justice SOUTER announced the judgment of the Court and delivered the opinion of the Court with respect to Parts I, II, III, V-A, V-C, and VI, an opinion with respect to Part V-E, in which Justice STEVENS joins, and an opinion with respect to Parts IV, V-B, and V-D.

I

Liberty finds no refuge in a jurisprudence of doubt. Yet 19 years after our holding that the Constitution protects a woman's right to terminate her pregnancy in its early stages, that definition of liberty is still questioned. Joining the respondents as amicus curiae, the United States, as it has done in five other cases in the last decade, again asks us to overrule

Roe. *** After considering the fundamental constitutional questions resolved by *Roe*, principles of institutional integrity, and the rule of *stare decisis*, we are led to conclude this: the essential holding of *Roe v. Wade* should be retained and once again reaffirmed.

II

Constitutional protection of the woman's decision to terminate her pregnancy derives from the Due Process Clause of the Fourteenth Amendment. Although a literal reading of the Clause might suggest that it governs only the procedures by which a State may deprive persons of liberty, for at least 105 years, since *Mugler v. Kansas*, 123 U.S. 623, 660-661 (1887), the Clause has been understood to contain a substantive component as well, one "barring certain government actions regardless of the fairness of the procedures used to implement them." *Daniels v. Williams*, 474 U.S. 327, 331 (1986). As Justice Brandeis (joined by Justice Holmes) observed, "[d]espite arguments to the contrary which had seemed to me persuasive, it is settled that the due process clause of the Fourteenth Amendment applies to matters of substantive law as well as to matters of procedure. Thus all fundamental rights comprised within the term liberty are protected by the Federal Constitution from invasion by the States." *Whitney v. California*, 274 U.S. 357, 373 (1927) (concurring opinion).

It is tempting, as a means of curbing the discretion of federal judges, to suppose that liberty encompasses no more than those rights already guaranteed to the individual against federal interference by the express provisions of the first eight Amendments to the Constitution. But of course this Court has never accepted that view. *** It is a promise of the Constitution that there is a realm of personal liberty which the government may not enter. We have vindicated this principle before. Marriage is mentioned nowhere in the Bill of Rights and interracial marriage was illegal in most States in the 19th century, but the Court was no doubt correct in finding it to be an aspect of liberty protected against state interference by the substantive component of the Due Process Clause in *Loving v. Virginia*, 388 U.S. 1, 12 (1967). *** Neither the Bill of Rights nor the specific practices of States at the time of the adoption of the Fourteenth Amendment marks the outer limits of the substantive sphere of liberty which the Fourteenth Amendment protects. See U.S. Const., Amdt. 9. *** It is settled now, as it was when the Court heard arguments in *Roe v. Wade*, that the Constitution places limits on a State's right to interfere with a person's most basic decisions about family and parenthood, see *Eisenstadt*; *Loving*; *Griswold*; *Skinner*; *Pierce*; *Meyer*, as well as bodily integrity, see, *e.g.*, *Washington v. Harper*, 494 U.S. 210, 221-222 (1990).

> **Make the Connection**
>
> We will consider the Court's decision in *Loving* later in this Chapter, and again in Chapter 11, when we discuss the Equal Protection Clause.

The inescapable fact is that adjudication of substantive due process claims may call upon the Court in interpreting the Constitution to exercise that same capacity which by tradition courts always have exercised: reasoned judgment. Its boundaries are not susceptible of expression as a simple rule. That does not mean we are free to invalidate state policy choices with which we disagree; yet neither does it permit us to shrink from the duties of our office.

Men and women of good conscience can disagree, and we suppose some always shall disagree, about the profound moral and spiritual implications of terminating a pregnancy, even in its earliest stage. Some of us as individuals find abortion offensive to our most basic principles of morality, but that cannot control our decision. Our obligation is to define the liberty of all, not to mandate our own moral code. The underlying constitutional issue is whether the State can resolve these philosophic questions in such a definitive way that a woman lacks all choice in the matter, except perhaps in those rare circumstances in which the pregnancy is itself a danger to her own life or health, or is the result of rape or incest.

Our law affords constitutional protection to personal decisions relating to marriage, procreation, contraception, family relationships, child rearing, and education. *** These matters, involving the most intimate and personal choices a person may make in a lifetime, choices central to personal dignity and autonomy, are central to the liberty protected by the Fourteenth Amendment. At the heart of liberty is the right to define one's own concept of existence, of meaning, of the universe, and of the mystery of human life. Beliefs about these matters could not define the attributes of personhood were they formed under compulsion of the State.

> **Food for Thought**
>
> What does the penultimate sentence of this paragraph mean? What authority might support this conception of liberty?

[T]hough the abortion decision may originate within the zone of conscience and belief, it is more than a philosophic exercise. Abortion [is] an act fraught with consequences for others: for the woman who must live with the implications of her decision; for the persons who perform and assist in the procedure; for the spouse, family, and society which must confront the knowledge that these procedures exist, procedures some deem nothing short of an act of violence against innocent human life; and, depending on one's beliefs, for the life or potential life that is aborted. Though abortion is conduct, it does not follow that the State is entitled to proscribe it in all instances. That is because the liberty of the woman is at stake in a sense unique to the human condition and so unique to the law. The mother who carries a child to full term is subject to anxieties, to physical constraints, to pain that only she must bear. That these sacrifices have from the beginning of the human race been endured by woman with a pride that ennobles her in the eyes of others and gives to the infant a bond of love cannot alone be grounds for the State to insist she make

> **Food for Thought**
>
> The Court seems to suggest here that the Constitution protects a conception of liberty that is largely at odds with the visions that has been "dominant" in "our history and culture." Even assuming, as the Court states, that the Constitution protects unenumerated "fundamental rights," how can the Court define those rights to be largely in conflict with widely held views about the limits on personal liberty? Is the Court's approach consistent with Justice Harlan's approach in *Griswold* and *Poe*?

the sacrifice. Her suffering is too intimate and personal for the State to insist, without more, upon its own vision of the woman's role, however dominant that vision has been in the course of our history and our culture. The destiny of the woman must be shaped to a large extent on her own conception of her spiritual imperatives and her place in society.

While we appreciate the weight of the arguments [that] _Roe_ should be overruled, the reservations any of us may have in reaffirming the central holding of _Roe_ are outweighed by the explication of individual liberty we have given combined with the force of *stare decisis*. We turn now to that doctrine.

III

The obligation to follow precedent begins with necessity, and a contrary necessity marks its outer limit. [N]o judicial system could do society's work if it eyed each issue afresh in every case that raised it. Indeed, the very concept of the rule of law underlying our own Constitution requires such continuity over time that a respect for precedent is, by definition, indispensable. At the other extreme, a different necessity would make itself felt if a prior judicial ruling should come to be seen so clearly as error that its enforcement was for that very reason doomed.

Even when the decision to overrule a prior case is not, as in the rare, latter instance, virtually foreordained, it is common wisdom that the rule of *stare decisis* is not an "inexorable command," and certainly it is not such in every constitutional case. *** While [_Roe_] has engendered disapproval, it has not been unworkable. An entire generation has come of age free to assume _Roe_'s concept of liberty in defining the capacity of women to act in society, and to make reproductive decisions; no erosion of principle going to liberty or personal autonomy has left _Roe_'s central holding a doctrinal remnant; _Roe_ portends no developments at odds with other precedent for the analysis of personal liberty; and no changes of fact have rendered viability more or less appropriate as the point at which the balance of interests tips. Within the bounds of normal *stare decisis* analysis, then, and subject to the considerations on which it customarily turns, the stronger argument is for affirming _Roe_'s central holding, with whatever degree of personal reluctance any of us may have, not for overruling it.

In a less significant case, *stare decisis* analysis could, and would, stop at the point we have reached. But the sustained and widespread debate _Roe_ has provoked calls for some comparison between that case and others of comparable dimension that have responded to national controversies and taken on the impress of the controversies addressed. Only two such decisional lines from the past century present themselves for examination, and in each instance the result reached by the Court accorded with the principles we apply today.

The first example is that line of cases identified with *Lochner v. New York*, 198 U.S. 45 (1905). [By 1937, it] seemed unmistakable to most people [that] the interpretation of contractual freedom protected in [_Lochner_ and its progeny] rested on fundamentally false factual assumptions about the capacity of a relatively unregulated market to satisfy minimal levels of human welfare. *** The facts upon which the earlier case had premised a constitutional resolution of social controversy had proven to be untrue, and history's demonstration of their untruth not only justified but required the new choice of constitutional principle that *West Coast Hotel Co. v. Parrish*, 300 U.S. 379 (1937), announced.

The second comparison that 20th century history invites is with the cases employing the separate-but-equal rule for applying the Fourteenth Amendment's equal protection guarantee. They began with *Plessy v. Ferguson*, 163 U.S. 537 (1896), holding that legislatively mandated racial segregation in public transportation

> **Make the Connection**
>
> We will consider *Plessy* and *Brown* in Chapter 11.

works no denial of equal protection, rejecting the argument that racial separation enforced by the legal machinery of American society treats the black race as inferior. *** But [by 1954, when the Court decided *Brown v. Board of Education*, 347 U.S. 483 (1954), it was clear] that legally sanctioned segregation had just such an effect, to the point that racially separate public educational facilities were deemed inherently unequal.

> **Food for Thought**
>
> Was it really only the understanding of markets and the facts of economic life that changed in the three decades before 1937, or the understanding of the effects of segregation that changed in the half century before 1954, that explain the Court's decisions in *West Coast Hotel* and *Brown*? Don't social and moral shifts that made the old decisions unpalatable help to explain those decisions? Or even a change in the composition of the Court itself? How might a different view of these cases have affected the application of *stare decisis* to *Roe*?

West Coast Hotel and *Brown* each rested on facts, or an understanding of facts, changed from those which furnished the claimed justifications for the earlier constitutional resolutions. *** In constitutional adjudication as elsewhere in life, changed circumstances may impose new obligations, and the thoughtful part of the Nation could accept each decision to overrule a prior case as a response to the Court's constitutional duty. Because the cases before us present no such occasion it could be seen as no such response. Because neither the factual underpinnings of *Roe*'s central holding nor our understanding of it has changed ***, the Court could not pretend to be reexamining the prior law with any justification beyond a present doctrinal disposition to come out differently from the Court of 1973. To overrule prior law for no other reason than that would run counter to the view repeated in our cases, that a decision to overrule should rest on some special reason over and above the belief that a prior case was wrongly decided.

[O]verruling *Roe*'s central holding [would also] seriously weaken the Court's capacity to exercise the judicial power and to function as the Supreme Court of a Nation dedicated to the rule of law. *** As Americans of each succeeding generation are rightly told, the Court cannot buy support for its decisions by spending money and, except to a minor degree, it cannot independently coerce obedience to its decrees. The Court's power lies, rather, in its legitimacy, [which] depends on making legally principled decisions under circumstances in which their principled character is sufficiently plausible to be accepted by the Nation.

Where, in the performance of its judicial duties, the Court decides a case in such a way as to resolve the sort of intensely divisive controversy reflected in <u>Roe</u> and those rare, comparable cases, its decision has a dimension that the resolution of the normal case does not carry. It is the dimension present whenever the Court's interpretation of the Constitution calls the contending sides of a national controversy to end their national division by accepting a common mandate rooted in the Constitution. The Court is not asked to do this very often, having thus addressed the Nation only twice in our lifetime, in the decisions of <u>Brown</u> and <u>Roe</u>. But when the Court does act in this way, its decision requires an equally rare precedential force to counter the inevitable efforts to overturn it and to thwart its implementation. Some of those efforts may be mere unprincipled emotional reactions; others may proceed from principles worthy of profound respect. But whatever the premises of opposition may be, only the most convincing justification under accepted standards of precedent could suffice to demonstrate that a later decision overruling the first was anything but a surrender to political pressure, and an unjustified repudiation of the principle on which the Court staked its authority in the first instance. So to overrule under fire in the absence of the most compelling reason to reexamine a watershed decision would subvert the Court's legitimacy beyond any serious question. *** It is therefore imperative to adhere to the essence of <u>Roe</u>'s original decision, and we do so today.

> **Take Note**
>
> Is the Court suggesting here that it should use a heightened standard for departing from *stare decisis* whenever one of its previous decisions has proved controversial? Doesn't this approach simply entrench the very decisions about which a national dialogue is most likely to take place, and most likely to reveal the values that the Nation holds to be "fundamental"?

IV

From what we have said so far it follows that it is a constitutional liberty of the woman to have some freedom to terminate her pregnancy. We conclude that the basic decision in *Roe* was based on a constitutional analysis which we cannot now repudiate. The woman's liberty is not so unlimited, however, that from the outset the State cannot show its concern for the life of the unborn, and at a later point in fetal development the State's interest in life has sufficient force so that the right of the woman to terminate the pregnancy can be restricted.

We conclude the line should be drawn at viability, so that before that time the woman has a right to choose to terminate her pregnancy. *** Any judicial act of line-drawing may seem somewhat arbitrary, but *Roe* was a reasoned statement, elaborated with great care. [In addition,] the concept of viability, as we noted in *Roe*, is the time at which there is a realistic possibility of maintaining and nourishing a life outside the womb, so that the independent existence of the second life can in reason and all fairness be the object of state protection that now overrides the rights of the woman. *** The woman's right to terminate her pregnancy before viability is the most central principle of *Roe*. It is a rule of law and a component of liberty we cannot renounce.

Yet it must be remembered that *Roe* speaks with clarity in establishing not only the woman's liberty but also the State's "important and legitimate interest in potential life." *** A logical reading of the central holding in *Roe* itself, and a necessary reconciliation of the liberty of the woman and the interest of the State in promoting prenatal life, require, in our view, that we abandon the trimester framework as a rigid prohibition on all previability regulation aimed at the protection of fetal life. The trimester framework *** misconceives the nature of the pregnant woman's interest [and] in practice it undervalues the State's interest in potential life, as recognized in *Roe*. *** Not all burdens on the right to decide whether to terminate a pregnancy will be undue. In our view, the undue burden standard is the appropriate means of reconciling the State's interest with the woman's constitutionally protected liberty.

A finding of an undue burden is a shorthand for the conclusion that a state regulation has the purpose or effect of placing a substantial obstacle in the path of a woman seeking an abortion of a nonviable fetus. A statute with this purpose is invalid because the means chosen by the State to further the interest in potential life must be calculated to inform the woman's free choice, not hinder it. And a statute which, while furthering the interest in potential life or some other valid state interest, has the effect of placing a substantial obstacle in the path of a woman's choice cannot be considered a permissible means of serving its legitimate ends.

We give this summary: [T]hroughout pregnancy the State may take measures to ensure that the woman's choice is informed, and measures designed to advance this interest will not be invalidated as long as their purpose is to persuade the woman to choose childbirth over abortion. These measures must not be an undue burden on the right. As with any medical procedure, the State may enact regulations to further the health or safety of a woman seeking an abortion. Unnecessary health regulations that have the purpose or effect of presenting a substantial obstacle to a woman seeking an abortion impose an undue burden on the right. Regardless of whether exceptions are made for particular circumstances, a State may not prohibit any woman from making the ultimate decision to terminate her pregnancy before viability. [And] "subsequent to viability, the State in promoting its interest in the potentiality of human life may, if it chooses, regulate, and even proscribe, abortion except where it is necessary, in appropriate medical judgment, for the preservation of the life or health of the mother." <u>Roe</u>.

These principles control our assessment of the Pennsylvania statute [at issue in this case], and we now turn to the issue of the validity of its challenged provisions.

V

[Section V.A is omitted.]

B

Except in a medical emergency, the statute requires that at least 24 hours before performing an abortion a physician inform the woman of the nature of the procedure, the health risks of the abortion and of childbirth, and the "probable gestational age of the unborn child." *** In attempting to ensure that a woman apprehend the full consequences of her decision, the State furthers the legitimate purpose of reducing the risk that a woman may elect an abortion, only to discover later, with devastating psychological consequences, that her decision was not fully informed. *** [R]equiring that the woman be informed of the availability of information relating to fetal development and the assistance available should she decide to carry the pregnancy to full term is a reasonable measure to ensure an informed choice, one which might cause the woman to choose childbirth over abortion.

Whether the mandatory 24-hour waiting period is nonetheless invalid because in practice it is a substantial obstacle to a woman's choice to terminate her pregnancy is a closer question. The findings of fact by the District Court indicate that because of the distances many women must travel to reach an abortion provider, the practical effect will often be a delay of much more than a day because the waiting period requires that a woman seeking an abortion make at least two visits to the doctor. As a result, the District Court found that for those women who have the fewest financial resources, those who must travel long distances, and those who have difficulty explaining their whereabouts to husbands, employers, or others, the 24-hour waiting period will be "particularly burdensome." 744 F. Supp. 1323, 1352 (E.D. Pa. 1990).

These findings are troubling in some respects, but they do not demonstrate that the waiting period constitutes an undue burden. We do not doubt that, as the District Court held, the waiting period has the effect of "increasing the cost and risk of delay of abortions." *** Yet, as we have stated, under the undue burden standard a State is permitted to enact persuasive measures which favor childbirth over abortion, even if those measures do not further a health interest. *** A particular burden is not of necessity a substantial obstacle. Whether a burden falls on a particular group is a distinct inquiry from whether it is a substantial obstacle even as to the women in that group. And the District Court did not conclude that the waiting period is such an obstacle even for the women who are most burdened by it. Hence, on the record before us, and in the context of this facial challenge, we are not convinced that the 24-hour waiting period constitutes an undue burden.

C

Pennsylvania's abortion law provides, except in cases of medical emergency, that no physician shall perform an abortion on a married woman without receiving a signed statement from the woman that she has notified her spouse that she is about to undergo an abortion. The woman has the option of providing an alternative signed statement certifying that her husband is not the man who impregnated her; that her husband could not be located; that the pregnancy is the result of spousal sexual assault which she has reported; or that the woman believes that notifying her husband will cause him or someone else to inflict bodily injury upon her. A physician who performs an abortion on a married woman without receiving the appropriate signed statement will have his

Food for Thought

What weight, if any, should the Court accord the father's interest in the choice whether to carry a pregnancy to term? Is that right constitutionally protected? What would be the consequences of recognizing such a right?

or her license revoked, and is liable to the husband for damages.

The District Court [made] detailed findings of fact regarding the effect of this statute [including that mere] "notification of pregnancy is frequently a flashpoint for battering and violence within the family." These findings are supported by studies of domestic violence. *** In well-functioning marriages, spouses discuss important intimate decisions such as whether to bear a child. But there are millions of women in this country who are the victims of regular physical and psychological abuse at the hands of their husbands. Should these women become pregnant, they may have very good reasons for not wishing to inform their husbands of their decision to obtain an abortion. *** The spousal notification requirement is thus likely to prevent a significant number of women from obtaining an abortion.

We recognize that a husband has a "deep and proper concern and interest [in] his wife's pregnancy and in the growth and development of the fetus she is carrying." [But it] is an inescapable biological fact that state regulation with respect to the child a woman is carrying will have a far greater impact on the mother's liberty than on the father's. *** For the great many women who are victims of abuse inflicted by their husbands, or whose children are the victims of such abuse, a spousal notice requirement enables the husband to wield an effective veto over his wife's decision. [The] women most affected by this law—those who most reasonably fear the consequences of notifying their husbands that they are pregnant—are in the gravest danger.

The husband's interest in the life of the child his wife is carrying does not permit the State to empower him with this troubling degree of authority over his wife. *** A State may not give to a man the kind of dominion over his wife that parents exercise over their children. [The spousal notification requirement] embodies a view of marriage consonant with the common-law status of married women but repugnant to our present understanding of marriage and of the nature of the rights secured by the Constitution. Women do not lose their constitutionally protected liberty when they marry. [The spousal notification provision is invalid.]

D

We next consider the parental consent provision. Except in a medical emergency, an unemancipated young woman under 18 may not obtain an abortion unless she and one of her parents (or guardian) provides informed consent ***. Our cases establish, and we reaffirm today, that a State may require a minor seeking an abortion to obtain the consent of a parent or guardian, provided that there is an adequate judicial bypass procedure. *Ohio v. Akron Center for Reproductive Health*, 497 U.S., 502, 510-519 (1990).

FYI

A "judicial bypass procedure" permits a minor to seek judicial, rather than parental, consent for an abortion, for example when the pregnant minor's father is also the father of the fetus.

E

Under the recordkeeping and reporting requirements of the statute, every facility which performs abortions is required to file a report [including, for each abortion performed, the identity of the physician; the woman's age; the number of prior pregnancies and prior abortions she has had; gestational age; and similar information.] The collection of information with respect to actual patients is a vital element of medical research, and so it cannot be said that the requirements serve no purpose other than to make abortions more difficult. Nor do we find that the requirements impose a substantial obstacle to a woman's choice. At most they might increase the cost of some abortions by a slight amount. While at some point increased cost could become a substantial obstacle, there is no such showing on the record before us.

VI

Our Constitution is a covenant running from the first generation of Americans to us and then to future generations. *** Each generation must learn anew that the Constitution's written terms embody ideas and aspirations that must survive more ages than one. We accept our responsibility not to retreat from interpreting the full meaning of the covenant in light of all of our precedents. We invoke it once again to define the freedom guaranteed by the Constitution's own promise, the promise of liberty.

Justice STEVENS, concurring in part and dissenting in part.

[Justice Stevens would have concluded that the 24-hour waiting period required by the Pennsylvania statute was unconstitutional.] While there are well-established and consistently maintained reasons for the Commonwealth to view with skepticism the ability of minors to make decisions, none of those reasons applies to an adult woman's decision-making ability. *** Part of the constitutional liberty to choose is the equal dignity to which each of us is entitled. A woman who decides to terminate her pregnancy is entitled to the same respect as a woman who decides to carry the fetus to term. The mandatory waiting period denies women that equal respect.

Justice BLACKMUN, concurring in part, concurring in the judgment in part, and dissenting in part.

Three years ago, [four] Members of this Court appeared poised to [overrule *Roe*]. All that remained between the promise of *Roe* and the darkness [was] a single, flickering flame. *** But now, just when so many expected the darkness to fall, the flame has grown bright. I do not underestimate the significance of today's joint opinion. Yet I remain steadfast in my belief that the right to reproductive choice is entitled to the full protection afforded by this Court [in *Roe*]. And I fear for the darkness as four Justices anxiously await the single vote necessary to extinguish the light.

[C]ompelled continuation of a pregnancy infringes upon a woman's right to bodily integrity by imposing substantial physical intrusions and significant risks of physical harm. [In addition,] when the State restricts a woman's right to terminate her pregnancy, it deprives a woman of the right to make her own decision about reproduction and family planning—critical life choices that this Court long has deemed central to the right to privacy. A State's restrictions on a woman's right to terminate her pregnancy also implicate constitutional guarantees of gender equality. *** By restricting the right to terminate pregnancies, the State conscripts women's bodies into its service, forcing women to continue their pregnancies, suffer the pains of childbirth, and in most instances, provide years of maternal care. [The] assumption [that] women can simply be forced to accept the "natural" status and incidents of motherhood [appears] to rest upon a conception of women's role that has triggered the protection of the Equal Protection Clause.

Strict scrutiny of state limitations on reproductive choice still offers the most secure protection of the woman's right to make her own reproductive decisions, free from state coercion. [T]he _Roe_ framework is far more administrable, and far less manipulable, than the "undue burden" standard adopted by the joint opinion. [Applying this standard, Justice Blackmun would have concluded that the provisions requiring content-based counseling, a 24-hour delay, informed parental consent, and reporting of abortion-related information were unconstitutional.]

In one sense, the Court's approach is worlds apart from that of THE CHIEF JUSTICE and Justice SCALIA. And yet, in another sense, the distance between the two approaches is short— the distance is but a single vote. I am 83 years old. I cannot remain on this Court forever, and when I do step down, the confirmation process for my successor well may focus on the issue before us today. That, I regret, may be exactly where the choice between the two worlds will be made.

> **FYI**
>
> Justice Blackmun retired in 1994, two years after the decision in _Casey_. To fill his seat, President Clinton appointed Justice Breyer, who has generally followed the approach of the plurality in _Casey_.

Chief Justice REHNQUIST, with whom Justice WHITE, Justice SCALIA, and Justice THOMAS join, concurring in the judgment in part and dissenting in part.

In our view, authentic principles of *stare decisis* do not require that any portion of the reasoning in _Roe_ be kept intact. [Erroneous] decisions in such constitutional cases are uniquely durable, because correction through legislative action, save for constitutional amendment, is impossible. It is therefore our duty to reconsider constitutional interpretations that "depar[t] from a proper understanding" of the Constitution. [S]urely there is no requirement, in considering whether to depart from *stare decisis* in a constitutional case, that a decision be more wrong now than it was at the time it was rendered.

[The] joint opinion [argues that _Roe_] is exempt from reconsideration under established principles of *stare decisis* in constitutional cases [because the Court must] take special care not to be perceived as "surrendering to political pressure" and continued opposition. This is a truly novel principle, one which is contrary to both the Court's historical practice and to the Court's traditional willingness to tolerate criticism of its opinions. Under this principle, when the Court has ruled on a divisive issue, it is apparently prevented from overruling that decision for the sole reason that it was incorrect, unless opposition to the original decision has died away. ***

The end result of the joint opinion's paeans of praise for legitimacy is the enunciation of a brand new standard for evaluating state regulation of a woman's right to abortion—the "undue burden" standard. *** Despite the efforts of the joint opinion, the undue burden standard presents nothing more workable than the trimester framework which it discards today. Under the guise of the Constitution, this Court will still impart its own preferences on the States in the form of a complex abortion code.

[W]e think that the correct analysis is [as follows:] A woman's interest in having an abortion is a form of liberty protected by the Due Process Clause, but States may regulate abortion procedures in ways rationally related to a legitimate state interest. *** [Under this approach, the dissent would have concluded that all of the provisions in the Pennsylvania statute are constitutional.]

Justice SCALIA, with whom THE CHIEF JUSTICE, Justice WHITE, and Justice THOMAS join, concurring in the judgment in part and dissenting in part.

The States may, if they wish, permit abortion on demand, but the Constitution does not require them to do so. The permissibility of abortion, and the limitations upon it, are to be resolved like most important questions in our democracy: by citizens trying to persuade one another and then voting. [The issue in this case is] not whether the power of a woman to abort her unborn child is a "liberty" in the absolute sense; or even whether it is a liberty of great importance to many women. Of course it is both. The issue is whether it is a liberty protected by the Constitution of the United States. I am sure it is not. I reach that conclusion not because of anything so exalted as my views concerning the "concept of existence, of meaning, of the universe, and of the mystery of human life." Rather, I reach it [because] of two simple facts: (1) the Constitution says absolutely nothing about it, and (2) the longstanding traditions of American society have permitted it to be legally proscribed.

Beyond that brief summary of the essence of my position, I will not swell the United States Reports with repetition of what I have said before; and applying the rational basis test, I would uphold the Pennsylvania statute in its entirety. I must, however, respond to a few of the more outrageous arguments in today's opinion, which it is beyond human nature to leave unanswered.

[The joint opinion insists that the Court will apply "reasoned judgment."] The emptiness of the "reasoned judgment" that produced *Roe* is displayed in plain view by the fact that, after more than 19 years of effort by some of the brightest (and most determined) legal minds in the country, after more than 10 cases upholding abortion rights in this Court, and after dozens upon dozens of amicus briefs submitted in these and other cases, the best the Court can do to explain how it is that the word "liberty" must be thought to include the right to destroy human fetuses is to rattle off a collection of adjectives that simply decorate a value judgment and conceal a political choice.

[The joint opinion states,] "Liberty finds no refuge in a jurisprudence of doubt." One might have feared to encounter this august and sonorous phrase in an opinion defending the real *Roe v. Wade*, rather than the revised version fabricated today by the authors of the joint opinion. The shortcomings of *Roe* did not include lack of clarity: Virtually all regulation of abortion before the third trimester was invalid. But to come across this phrase in the joint opinion—which calls upon federal district judges to apply an "undue burden" standard as doubtful in application as it is unprincipled in origin—is really more than one should have to bear. *** Reason finds no refuge in this jurisprudence of confusion.

The Court's reliance upon *stare decisis* can best be described as contrived. It insists upon the necessity of adhering not to all of *Roe*, but only to what it calls the "central holding." It seems to me that *stare decisis* ought to be applied even to the doctrine of *stare decisis*, and I confess never to have heard of this new, keep-what-you-want-and-throw-away-the-rest version. ***

The Court's description of the place of *Roe* in the social history of the United States is unrecognizable. Not only did *Roe* not, as the Court suggests, resolve the deeply divisive issue of abortion; it did more than anything else to nourish it, by elevating it to the national level where it is infinitely more difficult to resolve. *** *Roe* fanned into life an issue that has inflamed our national politics in general, and has obscured with its smoke the selection of Justices to this Court in particular, ever since. And by keeping us in the abortion-umpiring business, it is the perpetuation of that disruption, rather than of any Pax Roeana, that the Court's new majority decrees.

I cannot agree with, indeed I am appalled by, the Court's suggestion that the decision whether to stand by an erroneous constitutional decision must be strongly influenced—against overruling, no less—by the substantial and continuing public opposition the decision has generated. *** But whether it would "subvert the Court's legitimacy" or not, the notion that we would decide a case differently from the way we otherwise would have in order to show that we can stand firm against public disapproval is frightening. *** In truth, I am as distressed as the Court is [about] the "political pressure" directed to the Court: the marches, the mail, the protests aimed at inducing us to change our opinions. *** The Court would profit, I think, from giving less attention to the fact of this distressing phenomenon, and more attention to the cause of it. That cause permeates today's opinion: a new mode of constitutional adjudication that relies not upon text and traditional practice to determine the law, but upon what the Court calls "reasoned judgment," which turns out to be nothing but philosophical predilection and moral intuition.

FYI

The unedited joint opinion takes up 58 pages in the U.S. Reports, and the entire document, including concurring and dissenting opinions, takes up 169 pages.

There is a poignant aspect to today's opinion. Its length, and what might be called its epic tone, suggest that its authors believe they are bringing to an end a troublesome era in the history of our Nation and of our Court.

There comes vividly to mind a portrait by Emanuel Leutze that hangs in the Harvard Law School: Roger Brooke Taney, painted in 1859, the 82d year of his life, the 24th of his Chief Justiceship, the second after his opinion in *Dred Scott*. *** There seems to be on his face, and in his deep-set eyes, an expression of profound sadness and disillusionment. *** I expect that two years earlier he, too, had thought himself "call[ing] the contending sides of national controversy to end their national division by accepting a common mandate rooted in the Constitution." It is no more realistic for us in this litigation, than it was for him in that, to think that an issue of the sort they both involved—an issue involving life and death, freedom and subjugation—can be "speedily and finally settled" by the Supreme Court. [B]y foreclosing all democratic outlet for the deep passions this issue arouses, by banishing the issue from the political forum that gives all participants, even the losers, the satisfaction of a fair hearing and an honest fight, by continuing the imposition of a rigid national rule instead of allowing for regional differences, the Court merely prolongs and intensifies the anguish. We should get out of this area, where we have no right to be, and where we do neither ourselves nor the country any good by remaining.

———————

Points for Discussion

a. The Role of *Stare Decisis*

Why does *stare decisis* play such a prominent role in the decision in *Casey*? In a portion of his dissent omitted here, Chief Justice Rehnquist stated that the joint opinion followed *Roe* even though it could not "bring itself to say that *Roe* was correct as an original matter." Is his characterization of the joint opinion correct? If so, does that undermine the plurality's approach? Would *stare decisis* have any force if it applied only to cases that were correctly decided?

The various opinions differed in their approaches to interpreting the Constitution. Does the force of *stare decisis* vary depending upon the interpretive methodology that the Court employs? For an originalist, can *stare decisis* vindicate a decision that is otherwise inconsistent with the original meaning? For a non-originalist, can *stare decisis* freeze constitutional meaning, ensuring that the Constitution does not "evolve"?

b. When Can a State Regulate Abortions?

After *Casey*, what types of restrictions can a state impose on the right to an abortion? Look carefully at the votes for each section of the joint opinion. Section IV, which announces the undue burden standard and the rejection of *Roe*'s trimester framework, attracted the votes of only three Justices. Is the undue burden standard now the governing standard? In decisions that do not command five votes for any one approach, generally only the most narrow ground for decision is entitled to binding force. What was the most narrow ground for the Court's conclusions for each challenged provision of the statute?

In assigning binding force to the various opinions in *Casey*, is it relevant that some of the Justices are no longer on the Court? (Since the decision, Chief Justice Rehnquist and Justices Blackmun and White have passed away, and Justices O'Connor, Stevens, and Souter retired.) If so, how?

c. "Undue Burden"

What exactly is an "undue burden"? Is Justice Scalia correct in suggesting that it is an empty standard that invites judges to impose their own views of public policy and morality? Does the plurality's application of the standard provide any guidance about its content, and about how it should be applied in the future? If so, does it rebut Justice Scalia's criticism or validate it?

d. Abortion and Gender Equality

Justice Stevens asserted in his separate opinion that the 24-hour waiting period was unconstitutional because it denied women equal "dignity" and "respect." Similarly, the plurality concluded that the spousal notification provision was invalid for this reason. Justice Blackmun went further, asserting that, as a general matter, restrictions on the right to an abortion presume that "women can simply be forced to accept the 'natural' status and incidents of motherhood," a "conception of women's role that has triggered the protection of the Equal Protection Clause."

If nothing else, it seems difficult to dispute that the most immediate burdens of laws restricting access to (or prohibiting) abortions fall on women, who have to carry a fetus to term. Should laws regulating abortion be viewed as a form of gender discrimination subject to heightened scrutiny under the Equal Protection Clause? The most immediate benefits are, of course, to the fetus. On this point, consider the argument that then-Judge Ginsburg advanced seven years before the decision in *Casey*:

> **Make the Connection**
>
> We will consider gender discrimination in Chapter 11.

> "The conflict, however, is not simply one between a fetus' interests and a woman's interests, narrowly conceived, nor is the overriding issue state versus private control of a woman's body for a span of nine months. Also in the balance is a woman's autonomous charge of her full life's course—as Professor Karst put it, her ability to stand in relation to man, society, and the state as an independent, self-sustaining, equal citizen."

Ruth Bader Ginsburg, *Some Thought on Autonomy and Equality in Relation to* Roe v. Wade, 63 N.C. L. Rev. 375, 383 (1985) (citing Kenneth L. Karst, *Foreword: Equal Citizenship Under the Fourteenth Amendment*, 91 Harv. L. Rev. 1, 57-59 (1977)). Do you agree that the availability of abortion enhances women's autonomy?

Casey, like *Roe* before it, did not succeed in ending political controversy over the subject of abortion, and states continued to seek to impose limits on abortion. In *Stenberg v. Carhart*, 530 U.S. 914 (2000), the Court, in a 5-4 decision, invalidated a Nebraska law that banned one form of "dilation and evacuation" abortions (often called "partial-birth abortions" by opponents of the procedure) without providing an exception in cases where necessary to preserve the mother's health. Justice Breyer, who wrote for the Court, accepted the District Court's finding that medical evidence demonstrated that the procedure was sometimes necessary to protect the health of the mother. Justice Breyer also noted that the law's definition of the banned procedure was sufficiently imprecise that it might be invoked to prosecute doctors who performed other procedures. Applying *Casey*'s undue burden standard, the Court invalidated the statute. Justices Stevens and Ginsburg wrote separately to express their support for the central holding of *Roe*. Justice O'Connor wrote separately to suggest that a more carefully drawn statute might survive scrutiny under the undue burden standard. And Justice Kennedy, who had been one of the authors of the joint opinion in *Casey*, dissented, as did Chief Justice Rehnquist and Justices Scalia and Thomas.

Not long after the Court's decision in *Stenberg*, Congress enacted a law banning the same procedure that was banned by the Nebraska statute at issue in *Stenberg*. The Court considered that statute in the case that follows.

————

Gonzales v. Carhart

550 U.S. 124 (2007)

Justice KENNEDY delivered the opinion of the Court.

These cases require us to consider the validity of the Partial-Birth Abortion Ban Act of 2003 (Act), 18 U.S.C. § 1531. *** The surgical procedure referred to as "dilation and evacuation" or "D & E" is the usual abortion method in [the second] trimester. *** The abortion procedure that was the impetus for the numerous bans on "partial-birth abortion," including the Act, is a variation of this standard D & E. [For] discussion purposes this D & E variation will be referred to as intact D & E. The main difference between the two procedures is that in intact D & E a doctor extracts the fetus intact or largely intact with only a few passes [of the forceps]. *** In an intact D & E procedure the doctor extracts the fetus in a way conducive to pulling out its entire body, instead of ripping it apart. [Intact D & E often involves the evacuation of the fetus's skull contents before the removal of the fetus from the patient.]

[The statute made it a crime for any physician knowingly to perform the banned procedure and "thereby [to kill] a human fetus," and provided that a person convicted under the statute could be fined or imprisoned for up to two years. The ban did "not apply to a partial-birth abortion that is necessary to save the life of a mother," but did not include an exception to protect the health of the mother. Physicians and abortion advocacy groups filed separate suits challenging the constitutionality of the statute on its face.]

In 2003, after this Court's decision in *Stenberg*, Congress passed the Act at issue here. The Act responded to *Stenberg* in two ways. First, Congress made factual findings. *** Congress found, among other things, that "[a] moral, medical, and ethical consensus exists that the practice of performing a partial-birth abortion [is] a gruesome and inhumane procedure that is never medically necessary and should be prohibited." Second, and more relevant here, the Act's language differs from that of the Nebraska statute struck down in *Stenberg*.

The principles set forth in the joint opinion in *Planned Parenthood of Southeastern Pa. v. Casey*, 505 U.S. 833 (1992), did not find support from all those who join the instant opinion. Whatever one's views concerning the <u>Casey</u> joint opinion, it is evident a premise central to its conclusion—that the government has a legitimate and substantial interest in preserving and promoting fetal life—would be repudiated were the Court now to affirm the judgments of the Courts of Appeals. *** We now apply [<u>Casey</u>'s] standard to the cases at bar.

The Act punishes "knowingly perform[ing]" a "partial-birth abortion." § 1531(a). It defines the unlawful abortion in explicit terms. First, the person performing the abortion must "vaginally delive[r] a living fetus." § 1531(b)(1)(A). *** Second, the Act's definition of partial-birth abortion requires the fetus to be delivered "until, in the case of a head-first presentation, the entire fetal head is outside the body of the mother, or, in the case of breech presentation, any part of the fetal trunk past the navel is outside the body of the mother." § 1531(b)(1)(A). *** Third, to fall within the Act, a doctor must perform an "overt act, other than completion of delivery, that kills the partially delivered living fetus." § 1531(b)(1)(B). *** Fourth, the Act contains scienter requirements concerning all the actions involved in the prohibited abortion.

A review of the statutory text discloses the limits of its reach. The Act prohibits intact D & E [and] does not prohibit the D & E procedure in which the fetus is removed in parts. *** [In contrast, the] statute in <u>Stenberg</u> prohibited "deliberately and intentionally delivering into the vagina a living unborn child, or a substantial portion thereof, for the purpose of performing a procedure that the person performing such procedure knows will kill the unborn child and does kill the unborn child." The Court concluded that this statute encompassed D & E because "D & E will often involve a physician pulling a 'substantial portion' of a still living fetus, say, an arm or leg, into the vagina prior to the death of the fetus." 530 U.S. at 939. Congress, it is apparent, responded to these concerns ***.

Under the principles accepted as controlling here, the Act, as we have interpreted it, would be unconstitutional "if its purpose or effect is to place a substantial obstacle in the path of a woman seeking an abortion before the fetus attains viability." *Casey*, 505 U.S. at 878. *** The question is whether the Act, measured by its text in this facial attack, imposes a substantial obstacle to late-term, but previability, abortions. The Act does not on its face impose a substantial obstacle, and we reject this [facial] challenge to its validity.

The Act proscribes a method of abortion in which a fetus is killed just inches before completion of the birth process. [Congress made findings that assert that the] Act expresses respect for the dignity of human life [and that Congress was concerned] with the effects on the medical community and on its reputation caused by the practice of partial-birth abortion. [See Congressional Findings (14), in notes following 18 U.S.C. § 1531.] There can be no doubt the government "has an interest in protecting the integrity and ethics of the medical profession."

<u>Casey</u> reaffirmed these governmental objectives. The government may use its voice and its regulatory authority to show its profound respect for the life within the woman.

*** [*Casey's*] premise, that the State, from the inception of the pregnancy, maintains its own regulatory interest in protecting the life of the fetus that may become a child, cannot be set at naught by interpreting *Casey's* requirement of a health exception so it becomes tantamount to allowing a doctor to choose the abortion method he or she might prefer. Where it has a rational basis to act, and it does not impose an undue burden, the State may use its regulatory power to bar certain procedures and substitute others, all in furtherance of its legitimate interests in regulating the medical profession in order to promote respect for life, including life of the unborn.

The Act's ban on abortions that involve partial delivery of a living fetus furthers the Government's objectives. No one would dispute that, for many, D & E is a procedure itself laden with the power to devalue human life. Congress could nonetheless conclude that the type of abortion proscribed by the Act requires specific regulation because it implicates additional ethical and moral concerns that justify a special prohibition. Congress determined that the abortion methods it proscribed had a "disturbing similarity to the killing of a newborn infant," and thus it was concerned with "draw[ing] a bright line that clearly distinguishes abortion and infanticide." The Court has in the past confirmed the validity of drawing boundaries to prevent certain practices that extinguish life and are close to actions that are condemned. *Washington v. Glucksberg*, 521 U.S. 702 (1997).

> **Make the Connection**
>
> We will consider the Court's decision in *Glucksberg*, which involved physician-assisted suicide, later in this chapter.

Respect for human life finds an ultimate expression in the bond of love the mother has for her child. The Act recognizes this reality as well. Whether to have an abortion requires a difficult and painful moral decision. While we find no reliable data to measure the phenomenon, it seems unexceptionable to conclude some women come to regret their choice to abort the infant life they once created and sustained. Severe depression and loss of esteem can follow. In a decision so fraught with emotional consequence some doctors may prefer not to disclose precise details of the means that will be used, confining themselves to the required statement of risks the procedure entails. *** It is, however, precisely this lack of information concerning the way in which the fetus will be killed that is of legitimate concern to the State. The State has an interest in ensuring so grave a choice is well informed. It is self-evident that a mother who comes to regret her choice to abort must struggle with grief more anguished and sorrow more profound when she learns, only after the event, what she once did not know: that she allowed a doctor to pierce the skull and vacuum the fast-developing brain of her unborn child, a child assuming the human form. *** In sum, we reject the contention that the congressional purpose of the Act was "to place a substantial obstacle in the path of a woman seeking an abortion."

[The] prohibition in the Act would be unconstitutional, under precedents we here assume to be controlling, if it "subject[ed] [women] to significant health risks." *** There is documented medical disagreement whether the Act's prohibition would ever impose significant health risks on women. *** The question becomes whether the Act can stand

Take Note

This is not the first time in this opinion that Justice Kennedy referred to precedent that the Court "assume[s]" to be controlling. Why does he use such an unusual verbal formulation?

when this medical uncertainty persists. The Court's precedents instruct that the Act can survive this facial attack. The Court has given state and federal legislatures wide discretion to pass legislation in areas where there is medical and scientific uncertainty. *** The law need not give abortion doctors unfettered choice in the course of their medical practice, nor should it elevate their status above other physicians in the medical community. Medical uncertainty does not foreclose the exercise of legislative power in the abortion context any more than it does in other contexts. The medical uncertainty over whether the Act's prohibition creates significant health risks provides a sufficient basis to conclude in this facial attack that the Act does not impose an undue burden.

[An as-applied challenge] is the proper manner to protect the health of the woman if it can be shown that in discrete and well-defined instances a particular condition has or is likely to occur in which the procedure prohibited by the Act must be used. In an as-applied challenge the nature of the medical risk can be better quantified and balanced than in a facial attack.

Justice THOMAS, with whom Justice SCALIA joins, concurring.

Make the Connection

Although the Court and Justice Thomas did not address the question, was the Act a valid exercise of Congress's power under the Commerce Clause? Is the connection between interstate commerce and abortion practices less attenuated than the relationship between interstate commerce and violence against women, which was at issue in *United States v. Morrison*? (We considered *Morrison* in Chapter 3.) Why do you suppose the respondents here chose not to attack the Act on these grounds?

I join the Court's opinion because it accurately applies current jurisprudence, including *Planned Parenthood of Southeastern Pa. v. Casey*, 505 U.S. 833 (1992). I write separately to reiterate my view that the Court's abortion jurisprudence, including *Casey* and *Roe v. Wade*, 410 U.S. 113 (1973), has no basis in the Constitution. I also note that whether the Act constitutes a permissible exercise of Congress' power under the Commerce Clause is not before the Court. The parties did not raise or brief that issue; it is outside the question presented; and the lower courts did not address it.

Justice GINSBURG, with whom Justice STEVENS, Justice SOUTER, and Justice BREYER join, dissenting.

Today's decision is alarming. It refuses to take *Casey* and *Stenberg* seriously. It tolerates, indeed applauds, federal intervention to ban nationwide a procedure found necessary and proper in certain cases by the American College of Obstetricians and Gynecologists (ACOG). It blurs the line, firmly drawn in *Casey*, between previability and postviability abortions. And, for the first time since *Roe*, the Court blesses a prohibition with no exception safeguarding a woman's health.

In *Stenberg*, we expressly held that a statute banning intact D & E was unconstitutional in part because it lacked a health exception. 530 U.S. at 930, 937. *** In 2003, a few years after our ruling in *Stenberg*, Congress passed the Partial-Birth Abortion Ban Act—without an exception for women's health.[4] The congressional findings on which the Partial-Birth Abortion Ban Act rests do not withstand inspection, as the lower courts have determined and this Court is obliged to concede. Many of the Act's recitations are incorrect. *** Congress claimed there was a medical consensus that the banned procedure is never necessary. But the evidence "very clearly demonstrate[d] the opposite." *Planned Parenthood Fed. of Am. v. Ashcroft*, 320 F.Supp.2d 957, 1025 [(N.D. CA 2004)]. Similarly, Congress found that "[t]here is no credible medical evidence that partial-birth abortions are safe or are safer than other abortion procedures." But the congressional record includes letters from numerous individual physicians stating that pregnant women's health would be jeopardized under the Act, as well as statements from nine professional associations.

In contrast to Congress, the District Courts made findings after full trials at which all parties had the opportunity to present their best evidence. *** Based on thoroughgoing review of the trial evidence and the congressional record, each of the District Courts to consider the issue rejected Congress' findings as unreasonable and not supported by the evidence. *** The District Courts' findings merit this Court's respect.

Today's ruling, the Court declares, advances [the] Government's "legitimate and substantial interest in preserving and promoting fetal life." But the Act scarcely furthers that interest: The law saves not a single fetus from destruction, for it targets only a *method* of performing abortion. *** Ultimately, the Court admits that "moral concerns" are at work, concerns that could yield prohibitions on any abortion. Notably, the concerns expressed are untethered to any ground genuinely serving the Government's interest in preserving life. [T]he Court invokes an anti-

> **Take Note**
>
> The Court deferred substantially to Congress's factual findings, whereas Justice Ginsburg asserted that the Court should defer to the trial courts' fact finding. Who is better suited to make findings about the nature of the banned procedure and the likely health effects of the ban?

abortion shibboleth for which it concededly has no reliable evidence: Women who have abortions come to regret their choices, and consequently suffer from "[s]evere depression and loss of esteem." *** The solution the Court approves [is] not to require doctors to inform women, accurately and adequately, of the different procedures and their attendant risks. Instead, the Court deprives women of the right to make an autonomous choice, even at the expense of their safety. *** This way of thinking reflects ancient notions about women's place in the family and under the Constitution—ideas that have long since been discredited.

---

[4] The Act's sponsors left no doubt that their intention was to nullify our ruling in *Stenberg*. See, e.g., 149 Cong. Rec. 5731 (2003) (statement of Sen. Santorum) ("Why are we here? We are here because the Supreme Court defended the indefensible. We have responded to the Supreme Court."). See also 148 Cong. Rec. 14273 (2002) (statement of Rep. Linder) (rejecting proposition that Congress has "no right to legislate a ban on this horrible practice because the Supreme Court says [it] cannot").

The Court's hostility to the right *Roe* and *Casey* secured is not concealed. Throughout, the opinion refers to obstetrician-gynecologists and surgeons who perform abortions not by the titles of their medical specialties, but by the pejorative label "abortion doctor." A fetus is described as an "unborn child," and as a "baby." *** And, most troubling, *Casey*'s principles, confirming the continuing vitality of "the essential holding of *Roe*," are merely "assume[d]" for the moment, rather than "retained" or "reaffirmed," *Casey*, 505 U.S. at 846.

> **Take Note**
>
> Justice Ginsburg suggested here that the Court chose loaded language used by opponents of abortion. Is it possible for the Court to choose "neutral" language to describe matters that are the subject of such intense debate?

The Court's allowance only of an "as-applied challenge in a discrete case" jeopardizes women's health and places doctors in an untenable position. Even if courts were able to carve-out exceptions through piecemeal litigation for "discrete and well-defined instances," women whose circumstances have not been anticipated by prior litigation could well be left unprotected. In treating those women, physicians would risk criminal prosecution, conviction, and imprisonment if they exercise their best judgment as to the safest medical procedure for their patients. The Court is thus gravely mistaken to conclude that narrow as-applied challenges are "the proper manner to protect the health of the woman."

[T]he Act, and the Court's defense of it, cannot be understood as anything other than an effort to chip away at a right declared again and again by this Court—and with increasing comprehension of its centrality to women's lives.

Points for Discussion

a. Federal Action and the Due Process Clause

The Court in *Roe* and *Casey* concluded that the right to an abortion derives from the Due Process Clause of the Fourteenth Amendment, which limits state action. *Carhart*, however, concerned the constitutionality of a *federal* statute. The Court did not specifically identify the provision of the Constitution on which the respondents' challenge was based. The Court of Appeals, however, declared that "the Due Process Clause of the Fifth Amendment is textually identical to the Due Process Clause of the Fourteenth Amendment, and both proscribe virtually identical governmental conduct." Should the Court interpret the Fifth Amendment's Due Process Clause to protect the same rights that it has held are protected by the Fourteenth Amendment's Due Process Clause?

b. Undue Burden

What does Justice Kennedy's approach in *Carhart* signal about the meaning of the undue burden test? Can Congress (or a state) ban any single procedure—without providing an exception for the health of the mother—as long as it leaves available some other procedure? What if there are government-imposed limits on the availability of that other procedure, as well?

c. The Future of the Right to an Abortion

The Court declared that Congress has a "legitimate and substantial interest in preserving and promoting fetal life" and a legitimate interest in "promot[ing] respect for life, including life of the unborn." The Court also noted, however, that the banned abortion procedure was challenged as imposing an undue burden on *pre*-viability abortions. Under *Roe* and *Casey*, does the government have a substantial (or compelling) interest in protecting actual fetal life *before* the point of viability? If not, then does *Carhart* signal that the Court now believes that the government can act to protect fetal life before viability? If so, what does that suggest about the enduring viability of *Roe* and *Casey*?

The Court also reasoned that the government has a legitimate interest in seeking to protect women from the psychological effects of the decision to have an abortion. Is there a logical stopping point for the implications of this concern? Wouldn't it justify bans on all forms of abortion, at all stages of pregnancy? Does the decision in *Carhart* signal that the Court is poised to overrule *Roe* and *Casey*? Or simply that the particular procedure at issue raised unique concerns?

————————

3. Marriage and Family

We began this section on fundamental rights by considering the Court's decision in *Pierce*, which held that the Due Process Clause protects the right of parents to direct the education and upbringing of their children. *Pierce*, then, concerned the parent-child relationship, which of course is an important part of the family relationship. Similarly, the Court in *Griswold* considered another aspect of the family relationship. Recall that in *Griswold*, the Justices who voted to invalidate Connecticut's ban on contraceptives all invoked the marriage relationship in giving content to the protected right. Justice Douglas referred to the "privacy surrounding the marriage relationship"; Justice Goldberg found a right of "marital privacy"; Justice White focused on the "freedom of married persons"; and Justice Harlan (in his separate opinion in *Poe*) was concerned with "intimacy" in the "institution of marriage."

To be sure, the Court made clear shortly after its decision in *Griswold* that its view of the liberty protected by the Due Process Clause extended to intimate relationships outside of marriage, as well. But clearly the Court has long viewed family relationships as particularly deserving of protection under the Due Process Clause. Just how far does this constitutional protection for marital or family relationships extend?

————————

Loving v. Virginia

388 U.S. 1 (1967)

Mr. Chief Justice WARREN delivered the opinion of the Court.

Make the Connection

The portion of *Loving v. Virgina* excerpted here concerns substantive due process. Another portion of the case, excerpted in Chapter 11, concerns equal protection.

This case presents a constitutional question never addressed by this Court: whether a statutory scheme adopted by the State of Virginia to prevent marriages between persons solely on the basis of racial classifications violates the Equal Protection and Due Process Clauses of the Fourteenth Amendment. For reasons which seem to us to reflect the central meaning of those constitutional commands, we conclude that these statutes cannot stand consistently with the Fourteenth Amendment.

In June 1958, two residents of Virginia, Mildred Jeter, a Negro woman, and Richard Loving, a white man, were married in the District of Columbia pursuant to its laws. Shortly after their marriage, the Lovings returned to Virginia and established their marital abode in Caroline County. [In October 1958, a grand jury in the Circuit Court of Caroline County] issued an indictment charging the Lovings with violating Virginia's ban on interracial marriages. [After the Lovings pleaded guilty, the trial judge suspended their one-year sentence] on the condition that the Lovings leave the State and not return to Virginia together for 25 years. [Five years later they challenged Virginia's anti-miscegenation statute, but the Supreme Court of Appeals of Virginia held that it was constitutional.]

FYI

At the time *Loving* was decided, Virginia was one of 16 states that had statutes prohibiting interracial marriages. The Virginia statute prohibited marriages between a "white person and a colored person."

In upholding the constitutionality of these provisions in the decision below, the Supreme Court of Appeals of Virginia referred to its 1955 decision in *Naim v. Naim*, 197 Va. 80, as stating the reasons supporting the validity of these laws. In *Naim*, the state court concluded that the State's legitimate purposes were "to preserve the racial integrity of its citizens," and to prevent "the corruption of blood," "a mongrel breed of citizens," and "the obliteration of racial pride,"

obviously an endorsement of the doctrine of White Supremacy. The court also reasoned that marriage has traditionally been subject to state regulation without federal intervention, and, consequently, the regulation of marriage should be left to exclusive state control by the Tenth Amendment.

[The Court first held that the Virginia law violated the Equal Protection Clause. We will consider that portion of the Court's opinion in Chapter 11.]

These statutes also deprive the Lovings of liberty without due process of law in violation of the Due Process Clause of the Fourteenth Amendment. The freedom to marry has long been recognized as one of the vital personal rights essential to the orderly pursuit of happiness by free men.

Marriage is one of the "basic civil rights of man," fundamental to our very existence and survival. *Skinner v. Oklahoma*, 316 U.S. 535, 541 (1942). To deny this fundamental freedom on so unsupportable a basis as the racial classifications embodied in these statutes, classifications so directly subversive of the principle of equality at the heart of the Fourteenth Amendment, is surely to deprive all the State's citizens of liberty without due process of law. The Fourteenth Amendment requires that the freedom of choice to marry not be restricted by invidious racial discriminations. Under our Constitution, the freedom to marry or not marry, a person of another race resides with the individual and cannot be infringed by the State. These convictions must be reversed.

————————

Points for Discussion

a. Due Process and Equal Protection

What was the basis for the Court's conclusion in the portion of the opinion excerpted here? As we will see in Chapter 11, the state presumptively violates the Equal Protection clause when it classifies on the basis of race, even when no constitutionally protected "right" is at issue; for example, it would violate the Equal Protection Clause to make driver's licenses available only to whites, even though there is no constitutional right to a driver's license. But the Court in *Loving* also stated that to deny the "fundamental freedom" to marry on the basis of an invidious racial classification "deprive[s] *all* the State's citizens of liberty without due process of law."

What is the scope of this right to marry? State-law restrictions on the right to marry, after all, are commonplace; virtually every state prohibits marriages between siblings, marriages involving a person younger than a certain age, and marriages to more than one person simultaneously. These prohibitions are plainly different from the one at issue in *Loving*, which involved an invidious racial classification, but they suggest that the "right" to marry is far from absolute. Just how far does the right extend?

b. Level of Scrutiny

What level of scrutiny did the Court apply to the Virginia statute? The Court stated that "the freedom to marry [a] person of another race [cannot] be infringed by the State," but did it mean that *no* state interest, no matter how compelling, could justify an infringement on the general freedom to marry? Was the Court applying strict scrutiny? Did it conclude that Virginia's interest in upholding the statute was illegitimate, and thus that the law was invalid? If so, does that mean that a state need advance only a legitimate—as opposed to a compelling—interest to justify regulation of marriage (absent invidious racial discrimination)? Should the Court apply strict scrutiny to all limitations on the right to marry?

c. Subsequent Developments

The Court addressed some of these questions in subsequent cases. In *Zablocki v. Red-hail*, 434 U.S. 374 (1978), the Court reviewed a Wisconsin statute that required a court's permission for a person who was already under an obligation to pay child support to obtain a marriage license. In order to be granted permission to marry, the individual had to show that he or she was paying the support and that the child was not likely in the future to be put in public charge. The Court invalidated the statute, relying in part on *Loving* and earlier Due Process cases. The Court observed that "[a]lthough *Loving* arose in the context of racial discrimination, prior and subsequent decisions of this Court confirm that the right to marry is of fundamental importance for all individuals." The Court acknowledged that "reasonable regulations that do not significantly interfere with decisions to enter into the marital relationship may legitimately be imposed," but concluded that more searching scrutiny was warranted for regulations, such as the one at issue, that "interfere directly and substantially with the right to marry." Although the Court assumed that the State's interests in counseling parents and providing for children were sufficiently important, the Court held that the ends employed by the State were not necessary to advancing those interests.

Are the rights protected in *Loving* and *Zablocki* uniquely related to the institution of marriage? Recall the Court's decision in *Pierce*, which involved parental rights. What protection does the Due Process Clause provide for other familial arrangements?

In *Moore v. City of East Cleveland*, 431 U.S. 494 (1977), the Court held that a city ordinance that used a narrow definition of family to dictate who could live together under one roof was unconstitutional as applied to a grandmother who shared a home with two grandsons who were not siblings. The Court rejected the city's argument that the Constitution's protections for family relationships extend only to nuclear families, concluding that regulations that "intrude on choices concerning family living arrangements" warrant heightened review. In a dissent, Justice Stewart asserted that equating the interests of a group of people who wish to live together with "the fundamental decisions to marry and to bear and raise children is to extend the limited substantive contours of the Due Process Clause beyond recognition."

The Court has also had occasion to revisit the Constitution's protection for parents' child-rearing decisions, an issue that the Court had long ago addressed in *Pierce*. In *Troxel v. Granville*, 530 U.S. 57 (2000), the Court reiterated that parents have a "fundamental" right "to make decisions concerning the care, custody, and control of their children." The Court held that a Washington statute that allowed the court to give visitation rights to anyone if it was found to be in the best interests of the child was unconstitutional as applied to the petitioner, a mother who sought to limit the extent to which her children's paternal grandparents could visit her children after their father died.

But surely the Constitution's protection for parental rights is not absolute; a parent does not have a right, for example, cavalierly and unnecessarily to subject his child to the risk of serious and imminent injury. How exactly does the Court define the scope of parental rights? In *Michael H. v. Gerald D.*, 491 U.S. 110 (1989), the Court refused to invalidate a California law that established a presumption, which could be rebutted under only very limited circumstances, that a child born to a married woman is a child of the marriage. The petitioner claimed that he was the father of a child in the care of the respondent because of an adulterous liaison that the petitioner had had with respondent's wife. Although blood tests established a 98% probability that he was in fact the biological father, the California courts, applying the statutory presumption, rejected his claim for paternity and visitation. The Court affirmed, but there was no one opinion that commanded a majority of the Court.

Justice Scalia, in a plurality opinion joined by Chief Justice Rehnquist and Justices O'Connor and Kennedy, began by stating that "[i]n an attempt to limit and guide interpretation" of the Due Process Clause, "we have insisted not merely that [an] interest denominated as a 'liberty' be 'fundamental' (a concept that, in isolation, is hard to objectify), but also that it be an interest traditionally protected by our society." Accordingly, to the plurality "the legal issue in the present case reduces to whether the relationship between persons in the situation of [the petitioner and the child's mother] has been treated as a protected family unit under the historic practices of our society, or whether on any other basis it has been accorded special protection." The plurality thought it "impossible to find that it has. In fact, quite to the contrary, our traditions have protected the marital family *** against the sort of claim [the petitioner] asserts." The plurality "found nothing in the older sources, nor in the older cases, addressing specifically the power of the natural father to assert parental rights over a child born into a woman's existing marriage with another man." Justice Scalia then asserted the following in a footnote:

> Justice BRENNAN [in dissent] criticizes our methodology in using historical traditions specifically relating to the rights of an adulterous natural father, rather than inquiring more generally "whether parenthood is an interest that historically has received our attention and protection." *** We do not understand why, having rejected our focus upon the societal tradition regarding the natural father's rights vis-à-vis a child whose mother is married to another man, Justice BRENNAN would choose to focus instead upon "parenthood." Why should the relevant category not be even more general—perhaps "family relationships"; or "personal relationships"; or even "emotional attachments in general"? Though the dissent has no basis for the level of generality it would select, we do: We refer to the most specific level at which a relevant tradition protecting, or denying protection to, the asserted right can be identified. If, for example, there were no societal tradition, either way, regarding the rights of the natural father of a child adulterously conceived, we would have to consult, and (if possible) reason from, the traditions regarding natural fathers in general. But there is such a more specific tradition, and it unqualifiedly denies protection to such a parent. *** Because [general traditions of the sort consulted by Justice BRENNAN] provide such imprecise guidance, they permit judges to dictate rather than discern the society's views. *** Although assuredly having the virtue (if it be that) of leaving judges free to decide as they think best when the unanticipated occurs, a rule of law that binds neither by text nor by any particular, identifiable tradition is no rule of law at all.

Justices O'Connor and Justice Kennedy joined all of Justice Scalia's opinion except for this footnote. Justice O'Connor wrote separately to make clear her view that Justice Scalia's "mode of historical analysis" for identifying liberty interests protected by the Due Process Clause "may be somewhat inconsistent with our past decisions in this area." She declined to "foreclose the unanticipated by the prior imposition of a single mode of historical analysis."

In dissent, Justice Brennan, joined by Justices Marshall and Blackmun, criticized the plurality's "pinched conception of the family." He would have concluded that the petitioner was entitled to more process than that offered by the statutory presumption before his claim of paternal rights could be rejected. Justice Brennan also responded to Justice Scalia's methodology for identifying liberty interests:

> Apparently oblivious to the fact that [tradition] can be as malleable and as elusive as "liberty" itself, the plurality pretends that tradition places a discernible border around the Constitution. The pretense is seductive; it would be comforting to believe that a search for "tradition" involves nothing more idiosyncratic or complicated than poring through dusty volumes on American history. *** [But] the plurality has not found the objective boundary that it seeks. Even if we could agree [on] the content and significance of particular traditions, we still would be forced to identify the point at which a tradition becomes firm enough to be relevant to our definition of liberty and the moment at which it becomes too obsolete to be relevant any longer. The plurality supplies no objective means by which we might make these determinations.

> It is ironic that an approach so utterly dependent on tradition is so indifferent to our precedents. *** Throughout our decisionmaking in this important area runs the theme that certain interests and practices—freedom from physical restraint, marriage, childbearing, childrearing, and others—form the core of our definition of "liberty." *** In deciding cases arising under the Due Process Clause, therefore, we have considered whether the concrete limitation under consideration impermissibly impinges upon one of these more generalized interests. Today's plurality, however, does not ask whether parenthood is an interest that historically has received our attention and protection; the answer to that question is too clear for dispute. Instead, the plurality asks whether the specific variety of parenthood under consideration—a natural father's relationship with a child whose mother is married to another man—has enjoyed such protection. *** If we had looked to tradition with such specificity in past cases, many a decision would have reached a different result. [See *Eisenstadt*; *Griswold*.]

> The plurality's interpretive method is more than novel; it is misguided. It ignores the good reasons for limiting the role of "tradition" in interpreting the Constitution's deliberately capacious language. In the plurality's constitutional universe, we may not take notice of the fact that the original reasons for the conclusive presumption of paternity are out of place in a world in which blood tests can prove virtually beyond a shadow of a doubt who sired a particular child and in which the fact of illegitimacy no longer plays the burdensome and stigmatizing role it once did. *** In construing the Fourteenth Amendment to offer shelter only to those interests specifically protected by historical practice, moreover, the plurality ignores the kind of society in which our Constitution exists. We are not an assimilative, homogeneous society, but a facilitative, pluralistic one, in which we must be willing to abide someone else's unfamiliar or even repellent practice because the same tolerant impulse protects our own idiosyncracies. Even if we can agree, therefore, that "family" and "parenthood" are part of the good life, it is absurd to assume that we can agree on the content of those terms and destructive to pretend that we do. In a community such as ours, "liberty" must include the freedom not to conform. The plurality today squashes this freedom by requiring specific approval from history before protecting anything in the name of liberty.

The document that the plurality construes today is unfamiliar to me. It is not the living charter that I have taken to be our Constitution; it is instead a stagnant, archaic, hidebound document steeped in the prejudices and superstitions of a time long past. *This* Constitution does not recognize that times change, does not see that sometimes a practice or rule outlives its foundations. I cannot accept an interpretive method that does such violence to the charter that I am bound by oath to uphold.

Points for Discussion

a. Defining "Family"

In each of these cases—*Moore*, *Troxel*, and *Michael H.*—the Court was required to define the "family" and the familial relationships that are protected by the Fourteenth Amendment. Is the plurality's approach in *Michael H.* consistent with the Court's approach in *Moore*? If not, which is more convincing? What are the implications of the two approaches for other questions about the scope of protection for familial rights? What are the implications for the judicial role in the answers to those questions?

b. Competing Rights

Even assuming that the Court can neatly define the scope of familial rights, how should the Court rule when a case involves *competing* claims of right? For example, although the Court in *Troxel* based its analysis on a consideration of the *mother's* rights, in his dissent Justice Stevens asserted that the *children's* rights were entitled to consideration, as well. (Indeed, one could have argued that the *grandparents* also had some interest.) Is the substantive protection afforded by the Due Process Clause the same for children as it is for adults? Do children have different or attenuated rights? The Court in *Michael H.* declined to take up a related issue—"whether a child has a liberty interest, symmetrical with that of her parent, in maintaining her filial relationship." How would you resolve these questions based on the cases discussed so far in this Chapter?

c. History and the Level of Generality Reprised

In *Michael H.*, Justices Scalia and Brennan debated the appropriate level of generality at which to identify fundamental rights. Justice Scalia reprised the debate, this time with Justice Stevens, in *McDonald v. City of Chicago*, 130 S.Ct. 3020 (2010). In Justice Stevens's view, "the liberty safeguarded by the Fourteenth Amendment is not merely preservative in nature but rather is a 'dynamic concept.' Its dynamism provides a central means through which the Framers enabled the Constitution to 'endure for ages to come,' *McCulloch v. Maryland*, 4 Wheat. 316, 415 (1819)." He asserted that the "judge who would outsource the interpretation of 'liberty' to historical sentiment has turned his back on a task the Constitution assigned to him and drained the document of its intended vitality."

Justice Stevens offered several reasons for rejecting a "rigid historical test" for determining rights protected by the Due Process Clause. First, he asserted that such an approach "would effect a major break from our case law," because "our substantive due process doctrine has never evaluated substantive rights in purely, or even predominantly, historical terms." Second and "[m]ore fundamentally," he asserted:

> [A] rigid historical methodology is unfaithful to *** the expansive principle Americans laid down when they ratified the Fourteenth Amendment and to the level of generality they chose when they crafted its language; it promises an objectivity it cannot deliver and masks the value judgments that pervade any analysis of what customs, defined in what manner, are sufficiently "rooted"; it countenances the most revolting injustices in the name of continuity, for we must never forget that not only slavery but also the subjugation of women and other rank forms of discrimination are part of our history; and it effaces this Court's distinctive role in saying what the law is, leaving the development and safekeeping of liberty to majoritarian political processes. It is judicial abdication in the guise of judicial modesty. ***

> Although Justice Scalia aspires to an "objective," "neutral" method of substantive due process analysis, his actual method is nothing of the sort. *** [H]istory is not an objective science, and [its] use can therefore "point in any direction the judges favor." *** [A] limitless number of subjective judgments may be smuggled into his historical analysis. Worse, they may be buried in the analysis. *** Justice Scalia's method invites not only bad history, but also bad constitutional law. *** The fact that we have a written Constitution does not consign this Nation to a static legal existence. [I]t is not fidelity to the Constitution to ignore its use of deliberately capacious language, in an effort to transform foundational legal commitments into narrow rules of decision.

Justice Stevens also rejected Justice Scalia's charge that his "dynamic" approach was a "license for unbridled judicial lawmaking." He acknowledged that his approach requires judges to "exercise judgment," because when "answering a constitutional question to which the text provides no clear answer, there is always some amount of discretion." But he asserted that there are several "constraints on the decisional process." First, he stated that "liberty" is "capable of being refined and delimited" by the "central values" of "[s]elf-determination, bodily integrity, freedom of conscience, intimate relationships, political equality, dignity and respect." Second, he stressed "respect for the democratic process": "If a particular liberty interest is already being given careful consideration in, and subjected to ongoing calibration by, the States, judicial enforcement may not be appropriate." Third, the Court can apply "both the doctrine of *stare decisis*—adhering to precedents, respecting reliance interests, prizing stability and order in the law—and the common-law method—taking cases and controversies as they present themselves, proceeding slowly and incrementally, building on what came before."

Justice Scalia responded by asserting that Justice Stevens's approach is "subjective," and that its claim that courts should "update" the Due Process Clause "basically means picking the rights we want to protect and discarding those we do not." In Justice Scalia's view, "[d]eciding what is essential to an enlightened, liberty-filled life is an inherently political, moral judgment—the antithesis of an objective approach that reaches conclusions by applying neutral rules to verifiable evidence." He acknowledged that "[h]istorical analysis can be difficult" and "sometimes requires *** making nuanced judgments about which evidence to consult and how to interpret it." But he asserted that "the question to be decided is not whether the historically focused method is a *perfect means* of restraining aristocratic judicial Constitution-writing; but whether it is the *best means available* in an imperfect world." In his view, it clearly is, because it is less subjective and more compatible with democracy:

> It is less subjective because it depends upon a body of evidence susceptible of reasoned analysis rather than a variety of vague ethico-political First Principles whose combined conclusion can be found to point in any direction the judges favor. *** Moreover, the methodological differences that divide historians, and the varying interpretive assumptions they bring to their work, are nothing compared to the differences among the American people (though perhaps not among graduates of prestigious law schools) with regard to the moral judgments Justice Stevens would have courts pronounce. *** And the Court's approach intrudes less upon the democratic process because the rights it acknowledges are those established by a constitutional history formed by democratic decisions; and the rights it fails to acknowledge are left to be democratically adopted or rejected by the people, with the assurance that their decision is not subject to judicial revision. Justice Stevens's approach, on the other hand, deprives the people of that power, since whatever the Constitution and laws may say, the list of protected rights will be whatever courts wish it to be.

Whose view do you find most convincing?

---

4. Sexuality

In *Eisenstadt v. Baird*, which we considered in our discussion of *Griswold*, the Court held that the state cannot prohibit the use of contraceptives by unmarried persons. If the Due Process Clause protects a right of intimate relations between unmarried persons, then how far does that right extend?

In *Bowers v. Hardwick*, 478 U.S. 186 (1986), the Court, in a 5-4 decision, upheld a Georgia statute that criminalized "sodomy"—defined as acts of oral or anal sex—as applied to the respondent's homosexual conduct. The Court began by declaring that "[t]he issue presented is whether the Federal Constitution confers a fundamental right upon homosexuals to engage in sodomy." Looking to historic prohibitions and the contemporaneous prevalence of anti-sodomy laws throughout the fifty states, the Court concluded that "homosexual sodomy" cannot be considered a fundamental right under the Due Process Clause. It distinguished *Griswold* and its progeny by noting that "no connection between family, marriage, or procreation [and] homosexual activity [has] been demonstrated." After concluding that the right to engage in "homosexual sodomy" is not fundamental, the Court applied rational-basis review to the statute. It rejected respondent's argument that the state's interest in advancing morality was an insufficient basis for the statute, stating that law in general "is constantly based on notions of morality, and if all laws representing essentially moral choices are to be invalidated under the Due Process Clause, courts will be very busy indeed." Chief Justice Burger concurred, stating that "proscriptions against sodomy have very 'ancient roots.' Decisions of individuals relating to homosexual conduct have been subject to state intervention throughout the history of Western civilization. Condemnation of those practices is firmly rooted in Judeo-Christian moral and ethical standards. *** To hold that the act of homosexual sodomy is somehow protected as a fundamental right would be to cast aside millennia of moral teaching."

Justice Blackmun, joined by Justices Brennan, Marshall, and Stevens, dissented. He declared: "[T]his case is about 'the most comprehensive of rights and the right most valued by civilized men,' namely, 'the right to be let alone.' *Olmstead v. United States,* 277 U.S. 438, 478 (1928) (Brandeis, J., dissenting). *** The Court claims that its decision today merely refuses to recognize a fundamental right to engage in homosexual sodomy; what the Court really has refused to recognize is the fundamental interest all individuals have in controlling the nature of their intimate associations with others."

The Court revisited the holding in *Bowers* in the case that follows.

Lawrence v. Texas

539 U.S. 558 (2003)

Justice KENNEDY delivered the opinion of the Court.

Liberty protects the person from unwarranted government intrusions into a dwelling or other private places. In our tradition the State is not omnipresent in the home. And there are other spheres of our lives and existence, outside the home, where the State should not be a dominant presence. Freedom extends beyond spatial bounds. Liberty presumes an autonomy of self that includes freedom of thought, belief, expression, and certain intimate conduct. The instant case involves liberty of the person both in its spatial and in its more transcendent dimensions.

The question before the Court is the validity of a Texas statute making it a crime for two persons of the same sex to engage in certain intimate sexual conduct. In Houston, Texas, officers of the Harris County Police Department were dispatched to a private residence in response to a reported weapons disturbance. They entered an apartment where one of the petitioners, John Geddes Lawrence, resided. *** The officers observed Lawrence and another man, Tyron Garner, engaging in a sexual act. The two petitioners were arrested, held in custody overnight, and charged and convicted before a Justice of the Peace. [The statute under which they were convicted prohibited "deviate sexual intercourse"—which the statute defined as oral or anal sex—"with another individual of the same sex."] The petitioners were adults at the time of the alleged offense. Their conduct was in private and consensual.

We conclude the case should be resolved by determining whether the petitioners were free as adults to engage in the private conduct in the exercise of their liberty under the Due Process Clause of the Fourteenth Amendment to the Constitution. For this inquiry we deem it necessary to reconsider the Court's holding in *Bowers*. [The court's statement of the issue in *Bowers*] discloses the Court's own failure to appreciate the extent of the liberty at stake. To say that the issue in *Bowers* was simply the right to engage in certain sexual conduct demeans the claim the individual put forward, just as it would demean a married couple were it to be said marriage is simply about the right to have sexual intercourse. The laws involved in <u>Bowers</u> and here are, to be sure, statutes that purport to do no more than prohibit a particular sexual act. Their penalties and purposes, though, have more far-reaching consequences, touching upon the most private human conduct, sexual behavior, and in the most private of places, the home. The statutes do seek to control a personal relationship that, whether or not entitled to formal recognition in the law, is within the liberty of persons to choose without being punished as criminals.

This, as a general rule, should counsel against attempts by the State, or a court, to define the meaning of the relationship or to set its boundaries absent injury to a person or abuse of an institution the law protects. It suffices for us to acknowledge that adults may choose to enter upon this relationship in the confines of their homes and their own private lives and still retain their dignity as free persons. When sexuality finds overt expression in intimate conduct with another person, the conduct can be but one element in a personal bond that is more enduring. The liberty protected by the Constitution allows homosexual persons the right to make this choice.

Food for Thought

Is the Court here articulating a libertarian vision of the Constitution? Recall that Justice Holmes criticized the Court in <u>Lochner</u> for concluding in effect that the Constitution "enact[s] Mr. Herbert Spencer's Social Statics." Does the Court here effectively conclude that the Constitution enacts John Stuart Mill's "On Liberty," which enunciated the "harm principle"—that is, the principle that "the only purpose for which power can be rightfully exercised over any member of a civilized community, against his will, is to prevent harm to others"?

Having misapprehended the claim of liberty there presented to it, and thus stating the claim to be whether there is a fundamental right to engage in consensual sodomy, the <u>Bowers</u> Court said: "Proscriptions against that conduct have ancient roots." *Id.* at 192 *** At the outset it should be noted that there is no longstanding history in this country of laws directed at homosexual conduct as a distinct matter. *** It was not until the 1970's that any State singled out same-sex relations for criminal prosecution, and only nine States have done so. [T]he historical grounds relied upon in <u>Bowers</u> are more complex than the majority opinion and the concurring opinion by Chief Justice Burger indicate. Their historical premises are not without doubt and, at the very least, are overstated.

It must be acknowledged, of course, that the Court in <u>Bowers</u> was making the broader point that for centuries there have been powerful voices to condemn homosexual conduct as immoral. The condemnation has been shaped by religious beliefs, conceptions of right and acceptable behavior, and respect for the traditional family. For many persons these are not trivial concerns but profound and deep convictions accepted as ethical and moral principles to which they aspire and which thus determine the course of their lives. These considerations do not answer the question before us, however. The issue is whether the majority may use the power of the State to enforce these views on the whole society through operation of the criminal law. "Our obligation is to define the liberty of all, not to mandate our own moral code." *Planned Parenthood of Southeastern Pa. v. Casey*, 505 U.S.

833, 850 (1992).

[W]e think that our laws and traditions in the past half century are of most relevance here. These references show an emerging awareness that liberty gives substantial protection to adult persons in deciding how to conduct their private lives in matters pertaining to sex. *** This emerging recognition should have been apparent when *Bowers* was decided.

Food for Thought

With which view of the Due Process Clause is the Court's emphasis on an "emerging awareness" consistent? With Justice Harlan's focus on "living" traditions? With Justice Scalia's focus on historical tradition at the highest level of specificity? At what point does an "emerging awareness" of a particular conception of liberty achieve the status of liberty protected by the Due Process Clause? Is there a way for the Court to recognize changing values and yet not be controlled by the whims of public opinion?

The sweeping references by Chief Justice Burger [in his concurring opinion in *Bowers*] to the history of Western civilization and to Judeo-Christian moral and ethical standards did not take account of other authorities pointing in an opposite direction. A committee advising the British Parliament recommended in 1957 repeal of laws punishing homosexual conduct [and] Parliament enacted the substance of those recommendations 10 years later. Of even more importance, almost five years before *Bowers* was decided the European Court of Human Rights *** held that the laws proscribing [consensual homosexual conduct] were invalid under the European Convention on Human Rights. *Dudgeon v. United Kingdom*, 45 Eur. Ct. H.R. (1981). Authoritative in all countries that are members of the Council of Europe (21 nations then, 45 nations now), the decision is at odds with the premise in *Bowers* that the claim put forward was insubstantial in our Western civilization.

Two principal cases decided after *Bowers* cast its holding into even more doubt. In *Planned Parenthood of Southeastern Pa. v. Casey*, 505 U.S. 833 (1992), [we] confirmed that our laws and tradition afford constitutional protection to personal decisions relating to marriage, procreation, contraception, family relationships, child rearing, and education. In explaining the respect the Constitution demands for the autonomy of the person in making these choices, we stated[:] "At the heart of liberty is the right to define one's own concept of existence, of meaning, of the universe, and of the mystery of human life. Beliefs about these matters could not define the attributes of personhood were they formed under compulsion of the State." Persons in a homosexual relationship may seek autonomy for these purposes, just as heterosexual persons do. The decision in *Bowers* would deny them this right.

The second post-*Bowers* case of principal relevance is *Romer v. Evans*, 517 U.S. 620 (1996). There the Court struck down class-based legislation directed at homosexuals as a violation of the Equal Protection Clause. *** As an alternative argument in this case, counsel

---

Make the Connection

We will consider *Romer*, and discrimination on the basis of sexual orientation, in Chapter 11.

for the petitioners and some amici contend that <u>Romer</u> provides the basis for declaring the Texas statute invalid under the Equal Protection Clause. That is a tenable argument, but we conclude the instant case requires us to address whether <u>Bowers</u> itself has continuing validity. Were we to hold the statute invalid under the Equal Protection Clause some might question whether a prohibition would be valid if drawn differently, say, to prohibit the conduct both between same-sex and different-sex participants.

Equality of treatment and the due process right to demand respect for conduct protected by the substantive guarantee of liberty are linked in important respects, and a decision on the latter point advances both interests. If protected conduct is made criminal and the law which does so remains unexamined for its substantive validity, its stigma might remain even if it were not enforceable as drawn for equal protection reasons. When homosexual conduct is made criminal by the law of the State, that declaration in and of itself is an invitation to subject homosexual persons to discrimination both in the public and in the private spheres. The central holding of <u>Bowers</u> has been brought in question by this case, and it should be addressed. Its continuance as precedent demeans the lives of homosexual persons.

The foundations of <u>Bowers</u> have sustained serious erosion from our recent decisions in <u>Casey</u> and <u>Romer</u>. When our precedent has been thus weakened, criticism from other sources is of greater significance. In the United States criticism of <u>Bowers</u> has been substantial and continuing, disapproving of its reasoning in all respects, not just as to its historical assumptions. The courts of five different States have declined to follow it in interpreting provisions in their own state constitutions parallel to the Due Process Clause of the Fourteenth Amendment. To the extent <u>Bowers</u> relied on values we share with a wider civilization, it should be noted that the reasoning and holding in <u>Bowers</u> have been rejected elsewhere. The European Court of Human Rights has [not followed] <u>Bowers</u> ***. The right the petitioners seek in this case has been accepted as an integral part of human freedom in many other countries. There has been no showing that in this country the governmental interest in circumscribing personal choice is somehow more legitimate or urgent.

The doctrine of *stare decisis* is essential to the respect accorded to the judgments of the Court and to the stability of the law. It is not, however, an inexorable command. [T]here has been no individual or societal reliance on <u>Bowers</u> of the sort that could counsel against overturning its holding once there are compelling reasons to do so. <u>Bowers</u> itself causes uncertainty, for the precedents before and after its issuance contradict its central holding. *** <u>Bowers</u> was not correct when it was decided, and it is not correct today. *** <u>Bowers v. Hardwick</u> should be and now is overruled.

> **Make the Connection**
>
> Justice Kennedy was one of the authors of the joint opinion in <u>Casey</u>, which included an extended discussion of the role of *stare decisis* in constitutional adjudication. Is his approach here consistent with the plurality's approach in <u>Casey</u>?

The present case does not involve minors. It does not involve persons who might be injured or coerced or who are situated in relationships where consent might not easily be refused. It does not involve public conduct or prostitution. It does not involve whether the government must give formal recognition to any relationship that homosexual persons seek to enter. The case does involve two adults who, with full and mutual consent from each other, engaged in sexual practices common to a homosexual lifestyle. The petitioners are entitled to respect for their private lives. The State cannot demean their existence or control their destiny by making their private sexual conduct a crime. Their right to liberty under the Due Process Clause gives them the full right to engage in their conduct without intervention of the government. *** The Texas statute furthers no legitimate state interest which can justify its intrusion into the personal and private life of the individual.

Justice O'CONNOR, concurring in the judgment.

The Court today overrules *Bowers v. Hardwick*, 478 U.S. 186 (1986). I joined <u>Bowers</u>, and do not join the Court in overruling it. Nevertheless, I agree with the Court that Texas' statute banning same-sex sodomy is unconstitutional. Rather than relying on the substantive component of the Fourteenth Amendment's Due Process Clause, as the Court does, I base my conclusion on the Fourteenth Amendment's Equal Protection Clause.

The statute at issue here makes sodomy a crime only if a person "engages in deviate sexual intercourse with another individual of the same sex." Tex. Penal Code Ann. § 21.06(a) (2003). Sodomy between opposite-sex partners, however, is not a crime in Texas. That is, Texas treats the same conduct differently based solely on the participants. *** The Texas statute makes homosexuals unequal in the eyes of the law by making particular conduct—and only that conduct—subject to criminal sanction.

Texas attempts to justify its law, and the effects of the law, by arguing that the statute satisfies rational basis review because it furthers the legitimate governmental interest of the promotion of morality. *** This case raises a different issue than <u>Bowers</u>: whether, under the Equal Protection Clause, moral disapproval is a legitimate state interest to justify by itself a statute that bans homosexual sodomy, but not heterosexual sodomy. It is not. Moral disapproval of this group, like a bare desire to harm the group, is an interest that is insufficient to satisfy rational basis review under the Equal Protection Clause. Indeed, we have never held that moral disapproval, without any other asserted state interest, is a sufficient rationale under the Equal Protection Clause to justify a law that discriminates among groups of persons. Moral disapproval of a group cannot be a legitimate governmental interest under the Equal Protection Clause because legal classifications must not be "drawn for the purpose of disadvantaging the group burdened by the law." *** Whether a sodomy law that is neutral both in effect and application would violate the substantive component of the Due Process Clause is an issue that need not be decided today. I am confident, however, that so long as the Equal Protection Clause requires a sodomy law to apply equally to the private con-

> **Food for Thought**
>
> Didn't the statute upheld in <u>Bowers</u>—which on its face applied both to heterosexual and homosexual conduct—continue to stand in Georgia? Is it relevant that the Georgia statute was, in practice, enforced only against homosexual conduct? If so, does it undermine Justice O'Connor's reasoning here? Or the Court's decision in <u>Bowers</u>?

sensual conduct of homosexuals and heterosexuals alike, such a law would not long stand in our democratic society.

A law branding one class of persons as criminal based solely on the State's moral disapproval of that class and the conduct associated with that class runs contrary to the values of the Constitution and the Equal Protection Clause, under any standard of review. I therefore concur in the Court's judgment that Texas' sodomy law banning "deviate sexual intercourse" between consenting adults of the same sex, but not between consenting adults of different sexes, is unconstitutional.

Justice SCALIA, with whom THE CHIEF JUSTICE and Justice THOMAS join, dissenting.

[In *Casey*,] when *stare decisis* meant preservation of judicially invented abortion rights, the widespread criticism of <u>Roe</u> was strong reason to reaffirm it. *** Today, however, the widespread opposition to <u>Bowers</u>, a decision resolving an issue as "intensely divisive" as the issue in <u>Roe</u>, is offered as a reason in favor of overruling it. *** [The Court today has] exposed <u>Casey</u>'s extraordinary deference to precedent for the result-oriented expedient that it is.

Having decided that it need not adhere to *stare decisis*, the Court still must establish that <u>Bowers</u> was wrongly decided and that the Texas statute, as applied to petitioners, is unconstitutional. *** We have held repeatedly, in cases the Court today does not overrule, that only fundamental rights qualify for [so-called] "heightened scrutiny" protection—that is, rights which are "deeply rooted in this Nation's history and tradition." *Washington v. Glucksberg*, 521 U.S. 702, 721 (1997) All other liberty interests may be abridged or abrogated pursuant to a validly enacted state law if that law is rationally related to a legitimate state interest.

[A]n "emerging awareness" is by definition not "deeply rooted in this Nation's history and tradition[s]." Constitutional entitlements do not spring into existence because some States choose to lessen or eliminate criminal sanctions on certain behavior. Much less do they spring into existence, as the Court seems to believe, because foreign nations decriminalize conduct. *** The Court's discussion of these foreign views (ignoring, of course, the many countries that have retained criminal prohibitions on sodomy) is therefore meaningless dicta. Dangerous dicta, however, since "this Court should not impose foreign moods, fads, or fashions on Americans." *Foster v. Florida*, 537 U.S. 990, n. (2002) (THOMAS, J., concurring in denial of certiorari).

I turn now to the ground on which the Court squarely rests its holding: the contention that there is no rational basis for the law here under attack. The Texas statute undeniably seeks to further the belief of its citizens that certain forms of sexual behavior are "immoral and unacceptable"—the same interest furthered by criminal laws against fornication, bigamy, adultery, adult incest, bestiality, and obscenity. <u>Bowers</u> held that this was a legitimate state interest. The Court today reaches the opposite conclusion. *** This effectively decrees the end of all morals legislation. If, as the Court asserts, the promotion of majoritarian sexual morality is not even a legitimate state interest, none of the above-mentioned laws can survive rational-basis review.

Today's opinion is the product of a Court, which is the product of a law-profession culture, that has largely signed on to the so-called homosexual agenda, by which I mean the agenda promoted by some homosexual activists directed at eliminating the moral opprobrium that has traditionally attached to homosexual conduct. *** Many Americans do not want persons who openly engage in homosexual conduct as partners in their business, as scoutmasters for their children, as teachers in their children's schools, or as boarders in their home. They view this as protecting themselves and their families from a lifestyle that they believe to be immoral and destructive. *** Let me be clear that I have nothing against homosexuals, or any other group, promoting their agenda through normal democratic means. [But] persuading one's fellow citizens is one thing, and imposing one's views in absence of democratic majority will is something else. *** What Texas has chosen to do is well within the range of traditional democratic action, and its hand should not be stayed through the invention of a brand-new "constitutional right" by a Court that is impatient of democratic change. It is indeed true that "later generations can see that laws once thought necessary and proper in fact serve only to oppress," and when that happens, later generations can repeal those laws. But it is the premise of our system that those judgments are to be made by the people, and not imposed by a governing caste that knows best.

> **Take Note**
>
> Justice Scalia defends the authority of the states to promote "majoritarian sexual morality." Couldn't the statute invalidated in *Loving*—which prohibited interracial marriage—have been defended on the same ground? (Indeed, wasn't it?) If the state can legislate majoritarian sexual morality to prohibit the conduct at issue here, then does that mean that the Court decided the substantive due process issue in *Loving* incorrectly, as well? If not, why are the two cases different?

[Justice THOMAS's dissenting opinion is omitted.]

Points for Discussion

a. Stating the Issue

The outcome in *Lawrence* turned in part on how the Court chose to frame the issue. Did the case involve the broad question whether government can interfere in personal relationships occurring within the home? Or did it instead involve the narrower question whether the state can prohibit "deviate" sexual acts? Framing it the first way practically guarantees that the case will fall into the sphere of liberty at issue in *Griswold* and *Casey*. Defining it the second way, by contrast, poses a more significant obstacle to petitioners' claim, particularly if the constitutional protection turns on whether the case involves a fundamental right that is deeply rooted in the Nation's history. Which is the more appropriate way to conceptualize the issue?

b. Level of Scrutiny

To what level of scrutiny did the Court subject the Texas statute? Was it heightened scrutiny, on the theory that the statute interferes with a fundamental right? The Court stated that the Texas statute furthered "no legitimate state interest." Does that suggest that the Court was applying rational-basis review? (Justice Scalia thought so.) Does it matter for purposes of this case?

c. Morality as a State Interest

What does it mean to say—as Justice O'Connor (and perhaps the Court) did—that moral disapproval alone is not a legitimate state interest under either the Equal Protection or Due Process Clause? If, for instance, a state passes a law against murder, must it seek a reason for the law outside of the moral disapproval most people feel towards this act of violence? Or is the point that we can conceive of other valid state interests served by the criminalization of murder?

Consider the perspective offered by Justice Blackmun in his dissent in *Bowers*: "Petitioner and the Court fail to see the difference between laws that protect public sensibilities and those that enforce private morality." Is this a valid distinction? Is the line between these types of laws clear? If people disagree as fundamentally about what is publicly acceptable as they do about what is privately acceptable, then does it make sense to allow the majority to dictate public sensibilities but not private sensibilities?

d. Same-Sex Marriage

Near the end of its opinion, the Court stated that the case did "not involve whether the government must give formal recognition to any relationship that homosexual persons seek to enter." In addition, in a portion of Justice O'Connor's separate opinion that has been omitted here, she asserted:

> That this law as applied to private, consensual conduct is unconstitutional under the Equal Protection Clause does not mean that other laws distinguishing between heterosexuals and homosexuals would similarly fail under rational basis review. *** Unlike the moral disapproval of same-sex relations—the asserted state interest in this case—other reasons exist to promote the institution of marriage beyond mere moral disapproval of an excluded group.

Justice Scalia responded:

> Today's opinion dismantles the structure of constitutional law that has permitted a distinction to be made between heterosexual and homosexual unions, insofar as formal recognition in marriage is concerned. If moral disapprobation of homosexual conduct is "no legitimate state interest" for purposes of proscribing that conduct ***, what justification could there possibly be for denying the benefits of marriage to homosexual couples exercising "[t]he liberty protected by the Constitution"?

Shortly after the Court's decision in *Lawrence*, the Massachusetts Supreme Judicial Court held that a ban on same-sex marriages violates the state's constitution. *Goodridge v. Department of Public Health*, 798 N.E.2d 941 (Mass. 2003). The Court cited *Lawrence* and echoed the Court's language, but it based its decision on state constitutional law. More recently, the California Supreme Court held that a state ban on same-sex marriages violated the state's Constitution, *In re Marriage Cases*, 183 P.3d 384 (Cal. 2008), though the decision was overturned by referendum. Does <u>Lawrence</u> compel the conclusion that prohibitions on same-sex marriages violate the United States Constitution, as well?

e. Equal Protection v. Due Process

The Court declined to rely on the Equal Protection Clause, reasoning that such a basis for decision would have suggested that the state could ban private sexual conduct as long as the ban applied equally to heterosexual and homosexual conduct. Is it a realistic fear—given the "emerging awareness" that the Constitution protects intimate sexual conduct—that states would have responded to such a decision by banning an entire class of sexual activity? Why couldn't the Court, as it had done in <u>Loving</u>, invalidate the statute under *both* the Due Process and Equal Protection Clauses?

Was the Court's reluctance to rely on the Equal Protection Clause more because of the Court's unwillingness to conclude that gays and lesbians are entitled to heightened judicial protection under that clause? Keep this question in mind when we take up the subject of Equal Protection—and specifically whether the Clause protects gays and lesbians from discrimination—in Chapter 11.

f. Reliance on Foreign Law

The Court cited a decision of the European Court of Human Rights and noted the approach that other countries have taken to the issue that confronted the Court. Did the Court treat these decisions as authoritative sources of the meaning of the United States Constitution? As persuasive authority? Is such reliance problematic? If so, why? Consider the views that follow.

Perspective and Analysis

Non-ornamental use of foreign decisions undermines the separation of powers and violates the constitutional rules against delegation of federal authority to bodies outside the control of the national government. *** Relying on decisions that interpret a wholly different document [from our Constitution] runs counter to the notion that judicial review derives from the Court's duty to enforce the Constitution. *** Foreign and international laws, other than treaties ratified by the United States, are not enumerated among the three kinds of law that can be "the supreme Law of the Land." Therefore, they should not be treated as outcome-determinative in constitutional adjudication.

Robert J. Delahunty & John Yoo, *Against Foreign Law*, 29 Harv. J. L. & Pub. Pol'y 291, 295-97, 313 (2005).

> ### Perspective and Analysis
>
> Foreign or international examples, both negative and positive, can [inform] the court's determination of appropriate measures to protect U.S. constitutional rights. *** Foreign practice and decisions can also be helpful in evaluating the justifications for government action. *** Foreign law can also help illustrate the possible consequences of different interpretive choices. *** Many of our constitutional rights and values—liberty, equal protection of the law, due process, freedom of expression—reflect not only specific decisions made in the United States, but also widely shared commitments of many Western democracies.
>
> **Vicki Jackson, "Yes Please, I'd love to Talk With You," Legal Affairs (July/August 2004), available at** http://www.legalaffairs.org/issues/July-August-2004/feature_jackson_julaug04.msp

———————

5. Life

In referring to "*life*, liberty, [and] property," do the Due Process Clauses protect a minimum level of personal safety, security, or quality of life? Consider the case that follows.

———————

DeShaney v. Winnebago County Dept. of Social Services

489 U.S. 189 (1989)

Chief Justice REHNQUIST delivered the opinion of the Court.

The facts of this case are undeniably tragic. [Notwithstanding indications of child abuse by his father, state officials declined to remove Joshua DeShaney from his father's custody.] In March 1984, [the father] beat 4-year-old Joshua so severely that he fell into a life-threatening coma. Emergency brain surgery revealed a series of hemorrhages caused by traumatic injuries to the head inflicted over a long period of time. Joshua did not die, but he suffered brain damage so severe that he is expected to spend the rest of his life confined to an institution for the profoundly retarded. [His father] was subsequently tried and convicted of child abuse. Joshua and his mother brought this action under 42 U.S.C. § 1983 [against] respondents Winnebago County, DSS, and various individual employees of DSS [alleging] that respondents had deprived Joshua of his liberty without due process of law [by] failing to intervene to protect him against a risk of violence at his father's hands of which they knew or should have known. The District Court granted summary judgment for respondents [and the Court of Appeals affirmed.]

[N]othing in the language of the Due Process Clause itself requires the State to protect the life, liberty, and property of its citizens against invasion by private actors. The Clause is phrased as a limitation on the State's power to act, not as a guarantee of certain minimal levels of safety and security. It forbids the State itself to deprive individuals of life, liberty, or property without "due process of law," but its language cannot fairly be extended to impose an affirmative obligation on the State to ensure that those interests do not come to harm through other means. Nor does history support such an expansive reading of the constitutional text. Like its counterpart in the Fifth Amendment, the Due Process Clause of the Fourteenth Amendment was intended to prevent government "from abusing [its] power, or employing it as an instrument of oppression." Its purpose was to protect the people from the State, not to ensure that the State protected them from each other. The Framers were content to leave the extent of governmental obligation in the latter area to the democratic political processes. Consistent with these principles, our cases have recognized that the Due Process Clauses generally confer no affirmative right to governmental aid, even where such aid may be necessary to secure life, liberty, or property interests of which the government itself may not deprive the individual. *** If the Due Process Clause does not require the State to provide its citizens with particular protective services, it follows that the State cannot be held liable under the Clause for injuries that could have been averted had it chosen to provide them. As a general matter, then, we conclude that a State's failure to protect an individual against private violence simply does not constitute a violation of the Due Process Clause.

> **Food for Thought**
>
> The majority notes that history reveals a purpose to limit the State's power to deprive individuals of life, liberty, and property. Today, however, many people rely on government services—including social security, welfare, and health care—to ensure "minimal levels of safety and security." Is increased reliance on the state and changed expectations an argument for reading the Due Process Clause more broadly than in the past? Or is it instead a reason *not* to expand the protections of the Clause, for fear of effectively making the State the insurer of everyone's well-being?

Petitioners contend, however, that even if the Due Process Clause imposes no affirmative obligation on the State to provide the general public with adequate protective services, such a duty may arise out of certain "special relationships" created or assumed by the State with respect to particular individuals. Petitioners argue that such a "special relationship" existed here because the State knew that Joshua faced a special danger of abuse at his father's hands, and specifically proclaimed, by word and by deed, its intention to protect him against that danger. Having actually undertaken to protect Joshua from this danger—which petitioners concede

> **Food for Thought**
>
> If the state is not required to provide a particular service, does it necessarily follow that, once it decides to provide it, the state has no obligation to avoid harms that flow from its provision of the service? Does the greater power always include the lesser power? For purposes of comparison, tort law generally imposes a duty on a person who voluntarily undertakes to protect another to act carefully. *See* Restatement (Second) of Torts § 323 (1965).

the State played no part in creating—the State acquired an affirmative "duty," enforceable through the Due Process Clause, to do so in a reasonably competent fashion. Its failure to discharge that duty, so the argument goes, was an abuse of governmental power that so "shocks the conscience" as to constitute a substantive due process violation.

We reject this argument. It is true that in certain limited circumstances the Constitution imposes upon the State affirmative duties of care and protection with respect to particular individuals. In *Estelle v. Gamble*, 429 U.S. 97 (1976), we recognized that the Eighth Amendment's prohibition against cruel and unusual punishment, made applicable to the States through the Fourteenth Amendment's Due Process Clause, requires the State to provide adequate medical care to incarcerated prisoners. *** In *Youngberg v. Romeo*, 457 U.S. 307 (1982), we extended this analysis beyond the Eighth Amendment setting holding that the substantive component of the Fourteenth Amendment's Due Process Clause requires the State to provide involuntarily committed mental patients with such services as are necessary to ensure their "reasonable safety" from themselves and others. *** The rationale for this principle is simple enough: when the State by the affirmative exercise of its power so restrains an individual's liberty that it renders him unable to care for himself, and at the same time fails to provide for his basic human needs—e.g., food, clothing, shelter, medical care, and reasonable safety—it transgresses the substantive limits on state action set by the Eighth Amendment and the Due Process Clause. The affirmative duty to protect arises not from the State's knowledge of the individual's predicament or from its expressions of intent to help him, but from the limitation which it has imposed on his freedom to act on his own behalf. In the substantive due process analysis, it is the State's affirmative act of restraining the individual's freedom to act on his own behalf—through incarceration, institutionalization, or other similar restraint of personal liberty—which is the "deprivation of liberty" triggering the protections of the Due Process Clause, not its failure to act to protect his liberty interests against harms inflicted by other means.

Petitioners concede that the harms Joshua suffered occurred not while he was in the State's custody, but while he was in the custody of his natural father, who was in no sense a state actor. While the State may have been aware of the dangers that Joshua faced in the free world, it played no part in their creation, nor did it do anything to render him any more vulnerable to them.

Judges and lawyers, like other humans, are moved by natural sympathy in a case like this to find a way for Joshua and his mother to receive adequate compensation for the grievous harm inflicted upon them. But before yielding to that impulse, it is well to remember once again that the harm was inflicted not by the State of

Food for Thought

How convincing is the Court's distinction here, given that Joshua is a child? Did Joshua actually have more freedom to act on his own behalf in his father's house than he would have in a state institution? Assuming that the Court is correct that ordinarily an affirmative duty to protect under the Due Process Clause arises only when the State limits an individual's freedom, should a different rule apply when the person at issue is a child who the state knows is the victim of abuse?

Wisconsin, but by Joshua's father. The most that can be said of the state functionaries in this case is that they stood by and did nothing when suspicious circumstances dictated a more active role for them. In defense of them it must also be said that had they moved too soon to take custody of the son away from the father, they would likely have been met with charges of improperly intruding into the parent-child relationship, charges based on the same Due Process Clause that forms the basis for the present charge of failure to provide adequate protection.

The people of Wisconsin may well prefer a system of liability which would place upon the State and its officials the responsibility for failure to act in situations such as the present one. They may create such a system, if they do not have it already, by changing the tort law of the State in accordance with the regular lawmaking process. But they should not have it thrust upon them by this Court's expansion of the Due Process Clause of the Fourteenth Amendment.

Justice BRENNAN, with whom Justice MARSHALL and Justice BLACKMUN join, dissenting.

In a constitutional setting that distinguishes sharply between action and inaction, one's characterization of the misconduct alleged [may] effectively decide the case. Thus, by leading off with a discussion (and rejection) of the idea that the Constitution imposes on the States an affirmative duty to take basic care of their citizens, the Court foreshadows—perhaps even preordains—its conclusion that no duty existed even on the specific facts before us. This initial discussion establishes the baseline from which the Court assesses the DeShaneys' claim ***. The Court's baseline is the absence of positive rights in the Constitution and a concomitant suspicion of any claim that seems to depend on such rights. From this perspective, the DeShaneys' claim is first and foremost about inaction (the failure, here, of respondents to take steps to protect Joshua), and only tangentially about action (the establishment of a state program specifically designed to help children like Joshua). *** I would begin from the opposite direction. I would focus first on the action that Wisconsin has taken with respect to Joshua and children like him, rather than on the actions that the State failed to take.

Wisconsin has established a child-welfare system specifically designed to help children like Joshua. Wisconsin law invites—indeed, directs—citizens and other governmental entities to depend on local departments of social services such as respondent to protect children from abuse. The specific facts before us bear out this view of Wisconsin's system of protecting children. Each time someone voiced a suspicion that Joshua was being abused, that information was relayed to the Department for investigation and possible action. Even more telling than these examples is the Department's control over the decision whether to take steps to protect a particular child from suspected abuse. While many different people contributed information and advice to this decision, it was up to the people at DSS to make the ultimate decision whether to disturb the family's current arrangements.

In these circumstances, a private citizen, or even a person working in a government agency other than DSS, would doubtless feel that her job was done as soon as she had reported her suspicions of child abuse to DSS. Through its child-welfare program, in other words, the State of Wisconsin has relieved ordinary citizens and governmental bodies other than the Department of any sense of obligation to do anything more than report their suspicions of child abuse to DSS. If DSS ignores or dismisses these suspicions, no one will step in to fill the gap. Wisconsin's child-protection program thus effectively confined Joshua DeShaney within the walls of Randy DeShaney's violent home until such time as DSS took action to remove him. *** Through its child-protection program, the State actively intervened in Joshua's life and, by virtue of this intervention, acquired ever more certain knowledge that Joshua was in grave danger. These circumstances, in my view, plant this case solidly within the tradition of cases like _Youngberg_ and _Estelle_.

I would allow Joshua and his mother the opportunity to show that respondents' failure to help him arose, not out of the sound exercise of professional judgment that we recognized in _Youngberg_ as sufficient to preclude liability, but from the kind of arbitrariness that we have in the past condemned.

Justice BLACKMUN, dissenting.

Like the antebellum judges who denied relief to fugitive slaves, the Court today claims that its decision, however harsh, is compelled by existing legal doctrine. On the contrary, the question presented by this case is an open one, and our Fourteenth Amendment precedents may be read more broadly or narrowly depending upon how one chooses to read them. Faced with the choice, I would adopt a "sympathetic" reading, one which comports with dictates of fundamental justice and recognizes that compassion need not be exiled from the province of judging.

Poor Joshua! Victim of repeated attacks by an irresponsible, bullying, cowardly, and intemperate father, and abandoned by respondents who placed him in a dangerous predicament and who knew or learned what was going on, and yet did essentially nothing except, as the Court revealingly observes, "dutifully recorded these incidents in [their] files." It is a sad commentary upon American life, and constitutional principles, [that] this child, Joshua DeShaney, now is assigned to live out the remainder of his life profoundly retarded. Joshua and his mother, as petitioners here, deserve—but now are denied by this Court—the opportunity to have the facts of their case considered in the light of the constitutional protection that 42 U.S.C. § 1983 is meant to provide.

───────────

Points for Discussion

a. The Nature of Liberty

What was the Court's theory of the form of liberty protected by the Due Process Clause? Consider Judge Posner's theory, which he offered in _Bowers v. DeVito_, 686 F.2d 616 (7th Cir. 1982). The case involved a tort suit by the administrator of the estate of a woman who was murdered by a man who had previously been committed to a state facility after being found not guilty of murder in a different case by reason of insanity. The plaintiff sued, among others, the state-employed physicians who had approved the release of the man before he committed the murder in question. The court affirmed the district court's grant of summary judgment. Judge Posner explained:

> There is a constitutional right not to be murdered by a state officer, for the state violates the Fourteenth Amendment when its officer, acting under color of state law, deprives a person of life without due process of law. But there is no constitutional right to be protected by the state against being murdered by criminals or madmen. *** The Constitution is a charter of negative liberties; it tells the state to let people alone; it does not require the federal government or the state to provide services, even so elementary a service as maintaining law and order.

Judge Posner acknowledged that "the line between action and inaction" is not always clear. But he declared that "the defendants in this case did not place Miss Bowers in a place or position of danger; they simply failed adequately to protect her, as a member of the public, from a dangerous man." Do you agree that the Constitution is a "charter of negative liberties"? Why was Judge Posner so certain that it is? Did the Court in *DeShaney* share this view?

b. A Slippery Slope?

Justice Blackmun asserted in dissent that the question presented was an open one. Assuming for a moment that the Due Process Clause could plausibly have been read either to permit or to prevent the petitioners' claims, which view of the Clause's protection makes more sense? What would have been the impact of Justice Brennan's and Blackmun's view on federal, state, and local governments? Would it have opened the door to suits against policemen, judges, and many other officials alleging that they provided inadequate protection for life and liberty? If so, such suits could be very costly for public servants and might affect their judgment while on the job, not to mention their willingness to take the job in the first place. Are these considerations relevant when the Court interprets the Constitution? Do you think that the Court implicitly considered them in *DeShaney*?

c. Judicial Oversight of the Provision of Government Services

Justice Brennan asserted that the petitioners should have had an opportunity to demonstrate that Joshua's injuries were the result not of professional judgment, but of arbitrary action by the government agency. Are the courts competent to draw such distinctions? What if, in its discretion, DSS had chosen not to give Joshua's case high priority because the agency had limited resources and was busy dealing with several even more pressing cases of child abuse? And if the constitutional defect is that the state failed to protect Joshua after affirmatively assuming an obligation to do so, why does it matter whether the failure to protect was because of what turned out ultimately to be a faulty prediction or instead was because of neglect or arbitrariness?

Yet is the Court's approach preferable? The Court asserted that the remedy for someone like Joshua lies with the democratic process—presumably, to change the law to require action from the state, or to permit suits for damages when it fails to provide adequate protection. Even if this approach might prevent some abuse, is this a satisfying resolution for the DeShaneys?

d. Equal Protection

In a footnote in its opinion, the Court stated, "The State may not, of course, selectively deny its protective services to certain disfavored minorities without violating the Equal Protection Clause." Under this view, if the state had failed to protect Joshua because of, say, his race or religion, he would have had a valid claim under the Equal Protection Clause. Yet even in such a case, it would still be the state's "inaction" that gave rise to the claim. Is this view consistent with the Court's insistence that the government has no affirmative obligation to act to protect its citizens? Or would the unconstitutional decision represent a form of "action" after all?

e. Substantive Due Process or Procedural Due Process?

The Court in *DeShaney* held that the substantive component of the Due Process Clause does not require the state to protect the well being of its citizens against the acts of other private citizens. In a portion of the opinion omitted here, the Court "decline[d] to consider" whether the state's child-protection statutes gave Joshua an "entitlement" to receive protective services of which he could not be deprived without adequate procedural protections. As we will see in Chapter 9, the Due Process Clause (not surprisingly) has a procedural component, which generally requires the state to give notice and some kind of hearing when it seeks to deprive a person of a "protected" liberty or property interest.

In *Town of Castle Rock v. Gonzales*, 545 U.S. 748 (2005), the Court confronted a claim that the town had violated the Due Process Clause when its police officers did not respond to the plaintiff's repeated reports over several hours that her estranged husband was violating the terms of a restraining order by kidnapping their children, whom he subsequently murdered. The respondent argued that the failure to respond had deprived her of a property interest because she had a legitimate expectation, based on the terms of the restraining order, that the police would respond to her calls. The Court rejected her claim, reasoning that because a "benefit is not a protected property or liberty

> **Make the Connection**
>
> We will consider the definition of "liberty" and "property" for purposes of the procedural due process doctrine in Chapter 9.

entitlement if government officials may grant it or deny it in their discretion," respondent did not enjoy a protected property interest in favorable police action.

———————————

6. Death

The Court in *Casey* and *Lawrence* stated that "[a]t the heart of liberty is the right to define one's own concept of existence, of meaning, of the universe, and of the mystery of human life." Does this definition of liberty embrace a right to define the circumstances under which a person may end his or her life?

———————————

Cruzan v. Director, Missouri Dep't of Health

497 U.S. 261 (1990)

Chief Justice REHNQUIST delivered the opinion of the Court.

Petitioner Nancy Beth Cruzan was rendered incompetent as a result of severe injuries sustained during an automobile accident. Lester and Joyce Cruzan, Nancy's parents and co-guardians, sought a court order directing the withdrawal of their daughter's artificial feeding and hydration equipment after it became apparent that she had virtually no chance of recovering her cognitive faculties. The Supreme Court of Missouri held that because there was no clear and convincing evidence of Nancy's desire to have life-sustaining treatment withdrawn under such circumstances, her parents lacked authority to effectuate such a request. We [affirm].

[T]he common-law doctrine of informed consent is viewed as generally encompassing the right of a competent individual to refuse medical treatment. This is the first case in which we have been squarely presented with the issue whether the United States Constitution grants what is in common parlance referred to as a "right to die." *** The principle that a competent person has a constitutionally protected liberty interest in refusing unwanted medical treatment may be inferred from our prior decisions. In *Jacobson v. Massachusetts*, 197 U.S. 11, 24-30 (1905), for instance, the Court balanced an individual's liberty interest in declining an unwanted smallpox vaccine against the State's interest in preventing disease. *** Just this Term, in the course of holding that a State's procedures for administering antipsychotic medication to prisoners were sufficient to satisfy due process concerns, we recognized that prisoners possess "a significant liberty interest in avoiding the unwanted administration of antipsychotic drugs under the Due Process Clause of the Fourteenth Amendment." *Washington v. Harper*, 494 U.S. 210, 221-222 (1990). *** Petitioners insist that under the general holdings of our cases, the forced administration of life-sustaining medical treatment, and even of artificially delivered food and water essential to life, would implicate a competent person's liberty interest. Although we think the logic of the cases discussed above would embrace such a liberty interest, the dramatic consequences involved in refusal of such treatment would inform the inquiry as to whether the deprivation of that interest is constitutionally permissible. But for purposes of this case, we assume that the United States Constitution would grant a competent person a constitutionally protected right to refuse lifesaving hydration and nutrition.

Missouri has in effect recognized that under certain circumstances a surrogate may act for the patient in electing to have hydration and nutrition withdrawn in such a way as to cause death, but it has established a procedural safeguard to assure that the action of the surrogate conforms as best it may to the wishes expressed by the patient while competent. Missouri requires that evidence of the incompetent's wishes as to the withdrawal of treatment be proved by clear and convincing evidence. The question, then, is whether the United States Constitution forbids the establishment of this procedural requirement by the State. We hold that it does not.

Whether or not Missouri's clear and convincing evidence requirement comports with the United States Constitution depends in part on what interests the State may properly seek to protect in this situation. Missouri relies on its interest in the protection and preservation of human life, and there can be no gainsaying this interest. As a general matter, the States—indeed, all civilized nations—demonstrate their commitment to life by treating homicide as a serious crime. Moreover, the majority of States in this country have laws imposing criminal penalties on one who assists another to commit suicide. We do not think a State is required to remain neutral in the face of an informed and voluntary decision by a physically able adult to starve to death.

> **Take Note**
>
> Missouri law did not prohibit a person who is dependent upon life support from withdrawing that support, or even from indicating in advance—for example, in a "living will"—her desire to do so should she become dependent upon life support. It only required clear proof of a person's wishes to withdraw life support. Can a state prohibit a person who *has* clearly expressed her intent—either contemporaneously or in a living will—not to be maintained by life support from withdrawing such support?

But in the context presented here, a State has more particular interests at stake. The choice between life and death is a deeply personal decision of obvious and overwhelming finality. We believe Missouri may legitimately seek to safeguard the personal element of this choice through the imposition of heightened evidentiary requirements. It cannot be disputed that the Due Process Clause protects an interest in life as well as an interest in refusing life-sustaining medical treatment. Not all incompetent patients will have loved ones available to serve as surrogate decisionmakers. And even where family members are present, "[t]here will, of course, be some unfortunate situations in which family members will not act to protect a patient." A State is entitled to guard against potential abuses in such situations.

In our view, Missouri has permissibly sought to advance these interests through the adoption of a "clear and convincing" standard of proof to govern such proceedings. *** The more stringent the burden of proof a party must bear, the more that party bears the risk of an erroneous decision. We believe that Missouri may permissibly place an increased risk of an erroneous decision on those seeking to terminate an incompetent individual's life-sustaining treatment.

> **Make the Connection**
>
> Is the Court's analysis of the parents' interests consistent with the Court's decisions, discussed earlier in this Chapter, about the Constitution's protections for family relationships? Does the protection afforded to choices by parents about child rearing vary depending upon the age of the child? Regardless, is there a difference for these purposes between a decision about how to raise a child and the decision at issue here?

Petitioners alternatively contend that Missouri must accept the "substituted judgment" of close family members even in the absence of substantial proof that their views reflect the views of the patient. *** No doubt is engendered by anything in this record but that Nancy Cruzan's mother and father are loving and caring parents. [But] we do not think the Due Process Clause requires the State to repose judgment on these matters with anyone but the patient herself. [T]here is no automatic assurance that the view of close family members will necessarily be the same as the patient's would have been had she been confronted with the prospect of her situation while competent.

Justice O'CONNOR, concurring.

Today's decision, holding only that the Constitution permits a State to require clear and convincing evidence of Nancy Cruzan's desire to have artificial hydration and nutrition withdrawn, does not preclude a future determination that the Constitution requires the States to implement the decisions of a patient's duly appointed surrogate. Nor does it prevent States from developing other approaches for protecting an incompetent individual's liberty interest in refusing medical treatment. [N]o national consensus has yet emerged on the best solution for this difficult and sensitive problem. Today we decide only that one State's practice does not violate the Constitution; the more challenging task of crafting appropriate procedures for safeguarding incompetents' liberty interests is entrusted to the "laboratory" of the States, in the first instance.

> **Take Note**
>
> Is Justice O'Connor's point here that if a national consensus emerges from the "laboratory," it will become a rule of constitutional dimension? If so, is that a sensible approach to this issue?

Justice SCALIA, concurring.

The various opinions in this case portray quite clearly the difficult, indeed agonizing, questions that are presented by the constantly increasing power of science to keep the human body alive for longer than any reasonable person would want to inhabit it. The States have begun to grapple with these problems through legislation.

I would have preferred that we announce, clearly and promptly, that the federal courts have no business in this field; that American law has always accorded the State the power to prevent, by force if necessary, suicide—including suicide by refusing to take appropriate measures necessary to preserve one's life; that the point at which life becomes "worthless," and the point at which the means necessary to preserve it become "extraordinary" or "inappropriate," are neither set forth in the Constitution nor known to the nine Justices of this Court any better than they are known to nine people picked at random from the Kansas City telephone directory; and hence, that even when it is demonstrated by clear and convincing evidence that a patient no longer wishes certain measures to be taken to preserve his or her life, it is up to the citizens of Missouri to decide, through their elected representatives, whether that wish will be honored. *** To determine that [a deprivation of liberty without due process of law] would not occur if Nancy Cruzan were forced to take nourishment against her will, it is unnecessary to reopen the historically recurrent debate over whether "due process" includes substantive restrictions. It is at least true that no "substantive due process" claim can be maintained unless the claimant demonstrates that the State has deprived him of a right historically and traditionally protected against state interference. *Michael H. v. Gerald D.*, 491 U.S. 110, 122 (1989); *Bowers v. Hardwick*, 478 U.S. 186, 192 (1986). That cannot possibly be established here. At common law in

England, a suicide [was] criminally liable. *** Case law at the time of the adoption of the Fourteenth Amendment generally held that assisting suicide was a criminal offense.

It seems to me [that] Justice BRENNAN's position ultimately rests upon the proposition that it is none of the State's business if a person wants to commit suicide. Justice STEVENS is explicit on the point ***. This is a view that some societies have held, and that our States are free to adopt if they wish. But it is not a view imposed by our constitutional traditions, in which the power of the State to prohibit suicide is unquestionable.

Are there, then, no reasonable and humane limits that ought not to be exceeded in requiring an individual to preserve his own life? There obviously are, but they are not set forth in the Due Process Clause. What assures us that those limits will not be exceeded is the same constitutional guarantee that is the source of most of our protection—what protects us, for example, from being assessed a tax of 100% of our income above the subsistence level, from being forbidden to drive cars, or from being required to send our children to school for 10 hours a day, none of which horribles are categorically prohibited by the Constitution. Our salvation is the Equal Protection Clause, which requires the democratic majority to accept for themselves and their loved ones what they impose on you and me. This Court need not, and has no authority to, inject itself into every field of human activity where irrationality and oppression may theoretically occur, and if it tries to do so it will destroy itself.

> **Make the Connection**
>
> In citing the Equal Protection Clause, is Justice Scalia suggesting here that the infirm or terminally ill—or perhaps the elderly, who are more likely to become infirm or terminally ill—do not need protection from majoritarian politics because we all recognize the possibility that we might one day be old or ill? Keep this view in mind when we consider, in Chapter 11, the groups accorded special protection under the Equal Protection Clause. As we will see in that Chapter, the Court has held that the Equal Protection Clause does not afford any special protection from legislation that classifies on the basis of age.

Justice BRENNAN, with whom Justice MARSHALL and Justice BLACKMUN join, dissenting.

The right to be free from medical attention without consent, to determine what shall be done with one's own body, is deeply rooted in this Nation's traditions, as the majority acknowledges. This right has long been "firmly entrenched in American tort law" and is securely grounded in the earliest common law. Anglo-American law starts with the premise of thorough-going self determination. It follows that each man is considered to be master of his own body, and he may, if he be of sound mind, expressly prohibit the performance of lifesaving surgery, or other medical treatment. *** Thus, freedom from unwanted medical attention is unquestionably among those principles "so rooted in the traditions and conscience of our people as to be ranked as fundamental." *Snyder v. Massachusetts*, 291 U.S. 97, 105 (1934).

The only state interest asserted here is a general interest in the preservation of life. But the State has no legitimate general interest in someone's life, completely abstracted from the interest of the person living that life, that could outweigh the person's choice to avoid medical treatment. *** [T]he State's general interest in life must accede to Nancy Cruzan's particularized and intense interest in self-determination in her choice of medical treatment.

Food for Thought

Does Chief Justice Rehnquist disagree with Justice Brennan that there is a fundamental right to reject medical care, or does he differ only in his view of the weight that should be accorded to the state's interests in limiting this right?

This is not to say that the State has no legitimate interests to assert here. As the majority recognizes, Missouri has [an] interest in providing Nancy Cruzan, now incompetent, with as accurate as possible a determination of how she would exercise her rights under these circumstances. [But] until Nancy's wishes have been determined, the only state interest that may be asserted is an interest in safe-guarding the accuracy of that determination. *** Missouri may constitutionally impose only those procedural requirements that serve to enhance the accuracy of a determination of Nancy Cruzan's wishes or are at least consistent with an accurate determination. The Missouri "safeguard" that the Court upholds today does not meet that standard. The determination needed in this context is whether the incompetent person would choose to live in a persistent vegetative state on life support or to avoid this medical treatment. Missouri's rule of decision imposes a markedly asymmetrical evidentiary burden. Only evidence of specific statements of treatment choice made by the patient when competent is admissible to support a finding that the patient, now in a persistent vegetative state, would wish to avoid further medical treatment. Moreover, this evidence must be clear and convincing. No proof is required to support a finding that the incompetent person would wish to continue treatment. *** Too few people execute living wills or equivalently formal directives for such an evidentiary rule to ensure adequately that the wishes of incompetent persons will be honored. While it might be a wise social policy to encourage people to furnish such instructions, no general conclusion about a patient's choice can be drawn from the absence of formalities.

Justice STEVENS, dissenting.

Choices about death touch the core of liberty. *** Our ethical tradition has long regarded an appreciation of mortality as essential to understanding life's significance. It may, in fact, be impossible to live for anything without being prepared to die for something.

Missouri asserts that its policy is related to a state interest in the protection of life. In my view, however, it is an effort to define life, rather than to protect it, that is the heart of Missouri's policy. Missouri insists, without regard to Nancy Cruzan's own interests, upon equating her life with the biological persistence of her bodily functions. *** But for patients like Nancy Cruzan, who have no consciousness and no chance of recovery, there is a serious question as to whether the mere persistence of their bodies is "life" as that word is commonly understood, or as it is used in both the Constitution and the Declaration of

Independence. The State's unflagging determination to perpetuate Nancy Cruzan's physical existence is comprehensible only as an effort to define life's meaning, not as an attempt to preserve its sanctity.

In my view, [the] best interests of the individual, especially when buttressed by the interests of all related third parties, must prevail over any general state policy that simply ignores those interests. Indeed, the only apparent secular basis for the State's interest in life is the policy's persuasive impact upon people other than Nancy and her family. *** However commendable may be the State's interest in human life, it cannot pursue that interest by appropriating Nancy Cruzan's life as a symbol for its own purposes.

————————

Points for Discussion

a. The Right to Die

What exactly is embraced by the "right to die"? Consider these possibilities: (1) The right to refuse medical treatment; (2) The right to refuse life support; (3) The right to withdraw life support once connected; (4) The right of a person who is terminally ill but who does not require life support to the assistance of a physician in ending his or her life; (5) The right of a terminally ill person who is not on life support to commit suicide; (6) The right of a healthy person to physician assistance in committing suicide; (7) The right of a healthy person to commit suicide.

Did the Court in *Cruzan* find that any of these actions is constitutionally protected? Is it possible that some are protected and that others are not? If so, is it because the state has a greater interest in regulating some than in regulating others, or instead because there simply is no liberty interest at all in some of these actions?

b. Competing Evidence and Competing Claims of Familial Rights

Nancy Cruzan's parents argued that their daughter wished to refuse medical treatment, and no one apparently contested this view. But what if her parents' evidence had been contradicted by evidence presented by her husband, who argued that she in fact wished to continue medical treatment and be kept alive? Are there any constitutional limits on the way that the state may referee these competing claims?

What if the patient had left a living will expressing her wishes that she not be maintained on life support, but her husband nevertheless wanted her to remain on life support? Are there any circumstances under which the wishes of a family member can trump the wishes of a terminally ill person?

c. Defining Life

Recall that the Court grappled in *Roe* with the general question of how to define life, and with the specific question of when life begins. In his dissent in *Cruzan*, Justice Stevens asserted that the state effectively (and impermissibly) sought to define life in erecting an obstacle to the termination of life support for a patient with "no consciousness and no chance of recovery." How (if at all) does Justice Stevens define "life"? Is his point that each individual gets to define his or her own life, and therefore the circumstances under which it should end? If so, is Justice Stevens in effect asserting (as Justice Scalia suggested that he was) that there is a constitutional right to commit suicide?

d. Meaning of the Opinion

A key sentence in the Court's opinion is: "[For] the purposes of this case, we assume that the United States Constitution would grant a competent person a constitutionally protected right to refuse lifesaving hydration and nutrition." The meaning of this sentence was disputed when the opinion came out, and remains so today.

One possibility is that the Court meant: "We *hold* that a competent person has the right to refuse lifesaving measures." Many commentators initially read the Court's decision in this way. *See, e.g.,* Linda Greenhouse, *Justices Find a Right to Die, but the Majority See Need for Clear Proof of Intent,* N.Y. Times, Jun. 26, 1990, at A1 ("Eight members of the Supreme Court, venturing for the first time into the sensitive 'right to die' issue, said in a ruling today that a person whose wishes are clearly known has a constitutional right to the discontinuance of life-sustaining treatment."). Under this interpretation, the Court decided both the substantive due process question of whether a right exists and the procedural due process question of whether the state could require clear and convincing evidence of an intent to exercise this right.

But another possibility is that the Court meant: "We *merely assume, without deciding,* that there is a constitutionally protected right to refuse lifesaving measures." *See, e.g.,* John E. Nowak & Ronald Rotunda, *Constitutional Law* 920 (6th ed. 2000) ("The majority opinion *** assumed for the purposes of the case (but did not decide) that the 'liberty' protected by the due process clauses *** included a right of mentally competent individuals to refuse live saving or life sustaining medical treatment. Even assuming that such a right existed, the majority found that the state could limit the ability to refuse such treatment ***."). Under this interpretation, the Court did not decide the substantive due process question, but concluded that no procedural due process violation occurred even if the substantive right did exist.

In reading the opinion, which meaning appears more likely? Did the Court give reasons for its conclusion that the Constitution protects a right to refuse lifesaving measures? Could the Court decide whether the procedural requirement for invoking the right was constitutional on the assumption that the right exists without actually determining whether the right exists? Which approach would have been more likely to gather eight votes? The Supreme Court has never clarified this ambiguity, as a careful reading of the following case will show.

Washington v. Glucksberg

521 U.S. 702 (1997)

Chief Justice REHNQUIST delivered the opinion of the Court.

The question presented in this case is whether Washington's prohibition against "caus[ing]" or "aid[ing]" a suicide offends the Fourteenth Amendment to the United States Constitution. We hold that it does not.

[W]e "ha[ve] always been reluctant to expand the concept of substantive due process because guideposts for responsible decision-making in this unchartered area are scarce and open-ended." *Collins v. Harker Heights,* 503 U.S. 115, 125 (1992). By extending constitutional protection to an asserted right or liberty interest, we, to a great extent, place the matter outside the arena of public debate and legislative action. We must therefore "exercise the utmost care whenever we are asked to break new ground in this field," lest the liberty protected by the Due Process Clause be subtly transformed into the policy preferences of the Members of this Court.

> **Food for Thought**
>
> Another provision of the statute challenged in this case addressed the circumstances that were at issue in *Cruzan,* by specifically providing that "withholding or withdrawal of life-sustaining treatment" at a patient's direction does not constitute suicide. Is this a clear or defensible line to draw? Is it constitutionally problematic to permit patients who are on life support to "pull the plug," but prohibit patients who are terminally ill but not on life support from ending their lives? If so, why?

Our established method of substantive-due-process analysis has two primary features: First, we have regularly observed that the Due Process Clause specially protects those fundamental rights and liberties which are, objectively, "deeply rooted in this Nation's history and tradition," and "implicit in the concept of ordered liberty," such that "neither liberty nor justice would exist if they were sacrificed," *Palko v. Connecticut,* 302 U.S. 319, 325, 326 (1937). Second, we have required in substantive-due-process cases a "careful description" of the asserted fundamental liberty interest. Our Nation's history, legal traditions, and practices thus provide the crucial "guideposts for responsible decisionmaking" that direct and restrain our exposition of the Due Process Clause. *** This approach tends to rein in the subjective elements that are necessarily present in due-process judicial review. In addition, by establishing a threshold requirement—that a challenged state action implicate a fundamental right—before requiring more than a reasonable relation to a legitimate state interest to justify the action, it avoids the need for complex balancing of competing interests in every case.

Turning to the claim at issue here, the [respondents, doctors and terminally ill patients to whom they provide care,] assert a "liberty to choose how to die" and a right to "control of one's final days," and describe the asserted liberty as "the right to choose a humane, dignified death" and "the liberty to shape death." *** The Washington statute at issue in this case prohibits "aid[ing] another person to attempt suicide," and, thus, the question before us is whether the "liberty" specially protected by the Due Process Clause includes a right to commit suicide which itself includes a right to assistance in doing so.

[We] are confronted with a consistent and almost universal tradition that has long rejected the asserted right, and continues explicitly to reject it today, even for terminally ill, mentally competent adults. To hold for respondents, we would have to reverse centuries of legal doctrine and practice, and strike down the considered policy choice of almost every State. Respondents contend, however, that the liberty interest they assert is consistent with this Court's substantive-due-process line of cases, if not with this Nation's history and practice. Pointing to *Casey* and *Cruzan*, respondents read our jurisprudence in this area as reflecting a general tradition of "self-sovereignty," and as teaching that the "liberty" protected by the Due Process Clause includes "basic and intimate exercises of personal autonomy." *** The right assumed in *Cruzan*, however, was not simply deduced from abstract concepts of personal autonomy. Given the common-law rule that forced medication was a battery, and the long legal tradition protecting the decision to refuse unwanted medical treatment, our assumption was entirely consistent with this Nation's history and constitutional traditions. The decision to commit suicide with the assistance of another may be just as personal and profound as the decision to refuse unwanted medical treatment, but it has never enjoyed similar legal protection. Indeed, the two acts are widely and reasonably regarded as quite distinct.

[Respondents also rely on *Casey*.] The Court's opinion in *Casey* described, in a general way and in light of our prior cases, those personal activities and decisions that this Court has identified as so deeply rooted in our history and traditions, or so fundamental to our concept of constitutionally ordered liberty, that they are protected by the Fourteenth Amendment. *** That many of the rights and liberties protected by the Due Process Clause sound in personal autonomy does not warrant the sweeping conclusion that any and all important, intimate, and personal decisions are so protected, and *Casey* did not suggest otherwise.

The history of the law's treatment of assisted suicide in this country has been and continues to be one of the rejection of nearly all efforts to permit it. That being the case, our decisions lead us to conclude that the asserted "right" to assistance in committing suicide is not a fundamental liberty interest protected by the Due Process Clause. The Constitution also requires, however, that Washington's assisted-suicide ban be rationally related to legitimate government interests. This requirement is unquestionably met here. *** Washington has an "unqualified interest in the preservation of human life." The State's prohibition on assisted suicide, like all homicide laws, both reflects and advances its commitment to this interest. *** Relatedly, all admit that suicide is a serious public-health problem, especially among persons in otherwise vulnerable groups. The State has an interest in preventing suicide, and in studying, identifying, and treating its causes.

The State also has an interest in protecting the integrity and ethics of the medical profession. [The] American Medical Association, like many other medical and physicians' groups, has concluded that "[p]hysician-assisted suicide is fundamentally incompatible with the physician's role as healer." And physician-assisted suicide could, it is argued, undermine the trust that is essential to the doctor-patient relationship by blurring the time-honored line between healing and harming. Next, the State has an interest in protecting vulnerable groups—including the poor, the elderly, and disabled persons—from abuse, neglect, and mistakes. *** The State's assisted-suicide ban reflects and reinforces its policy that the lives of terminally ill, disabled, and elderly people must be no less valued than the lives of the young and healthy, and that a seriously disabled person's suicidal impulses should be interpreted and treated the same way as anyone else's. Finally, the State may fear that permitting assisted suicide will start it down the path to voluntary and perhaps even involuntary euthanasia.

We need not weigh exactly the relative strengths of these various interests. They are unquestionably important and legitimate, and Washington's ban on assisted suicide is at least reasonably related to their promotion and protection. We therefore hold that [Washington's prohibition on assisted suicide] does not violate the Fourteenth Amendment, either on its face or "as applied to competent, terminally ill adults who wish to hasten their deaths by obtaining medication prescribed by their doctors." *** Throughout the Nation, Americans are engaged in an earnest and profound debate about the morality, legality, and practicality of physician-assisted suicide. Our holding permits this debate to continue, as it should in a democratic society.

Justice SOUTER, concurring in the judgment.

I conclude that the statute's application to the doctors has not been shown to be unconstitutional, but I write separately to give my reasons for analyzing the substantive due process claims as I do. *** My understanding of unenumerated rights [avoids] the absolutist failing of many older cases without embracing the opposite pole of equating reasonableness with past practice described at a very specific level. That understanding begins with a concept of "ordered liberty," comprising a continuum of rights to be free from "arbitrary impositions and purposeless restraints." [Justice Souter then quoted from Justice Harlan's dissent, excerpted earlier in this Chapter, in *Poe v. Ullman*, 367 U.S. 497 (1961).] This approach calls for a court to assess the relative "weights" or dignities of the contending interests, and to this extent the judicial method is familiar to the common law.

Common-law method is subject, however, to two important constraints in the hands of a court engaged in substantive due process review. First, such a court is bound to confine the values that it recognizes to those truly deserving constitutional stature, either to those expressed in constitutional text, or those exemplified by "the traditions from which [the Nation] developed" or revealed by contrast with "the traditions from which it broke."

The second constraint, again, simply reflects the fact that constitutional review, not judicial lawmaking, is a court's business here. *** It is no justification for judicial intervention merely to identify a reasonable resolution

> **Food for Thought**
>
> Justice Souter's approach clearly embraces the idea that constitutional protections can evolve to embrace new rights. How different is this approach from Chief Justice Rehnquist's approach? Does Chief Justice Rehnquist's opinion leave any room for a "living tradition" that would establish new fundamental rights over time?

of contending values that differs from the terms of the legislation under review. It is only when the legislation's justifying principle, critically valued, is so far from being commensurate with the individual interest as to be arbitrarily or pointlessly applied that the statute must give way.

Just as results in substantive due process cases are tied to the selections of statements of the competing interests, the acceptability of the results is a function of the good reasons for the selections made. It is here that the value of common-law method becomes apparent, for the usual thinking of the common law is suspicious of the all-or-nothing analysis that tends to produce legal petrification instead of an evolving boundary between the domains of old principles. Common-law method tends to pay respect instead to detail, seeking to understand old principles afresh by new examples and new counterexamples.

In my judgment, the importance of the individual interest here, as within that class of "certain interests" demanding careful scrutiny of the State's contrary claim, cannot be gainsaid. Whether that interest might in some circumstances, or at some time, be seen as "fundamental" to the degree entitled to prevail is not, however, a conclusion that I need draw here, for I am satisfied that the State's interests [are] sufficiently serious to defeat the present claim that its law is arbitrary or purposeless. [It] is enough to say that our examination of legislative reasonableness should consider the fact that the Legislature of the State of Washington is no more obviously at fault than this Court is in being uncertain about what would happen if respondents prevailed today. We therefore have a clear question about which institution, a legislature or a court, is relatively more competent to deal with an emerging issue as to which facts currently unknown could be dispositive. The answer has to be [that] the legislative process is to be preferred.

Justice O'CONNOR, concurring.

I join the Court's opinions because I agree that there is no generalized right to "commit suicide." But respondents urge us to address the narrower question whether a mentally competent person who is experiencing great suffering has a constitutionally cognizable interest in controlling the circumstances of his or her imminent death. I see no need to reach that question in the context of the facial challenges to the [Washington] laws at issue here. The parties and amici agree that [a] patient who is suffering from a terminal illness and who is experiencing great pain has no legal barriers to obtaining medication, from qualified physicians, to alleviate that suffering, even to the point of causing unconsciousness and hastening death. In this light, even assuming that we would recognize such an interest, I agree that the State's interests in protecting those who are not truly competent or facing imminent death, or those whose decisions to hasten death would not truly be voluntary, are sufficiently weighty to justify a prohibition against physician-assisted suicide.

Justice STEVENS, concurring in the [judgment].

Today, the Court decides that Washington's statute prohibiting assisted suicide is not invalid "on its face," that is to say, in all or most cases in which it might be applied. That holding, however, does not foreclose the possibility that some applications of the statute might well be invalid. *** A State, like Washington, that has authorized the death penalty, and thereby has concluded that the sanctity of human life does not require that it always be preserved, must acknowledge that there are situations in which an interest in hastening death is legitimate. Indeed, not only is that interest sometimes legitimate, I am also convinced that there are times when it is entitled to constitutional protection. *** In my judgment, [it] is clear that the so-called "unqualified interest in the preservation of human life," <u>Cruzan, 497 U.S., at 282</u>, is not itself sufficient to outweigh the interest in liberty that may justify the only possible means of preserving a dying patient's dignity and alleviating her intolerable suffering.

Justice BREYER, concurring in the [judgment].

I do not agree [with] the Court's formulation of [respondents'] claimed "liberty" interest [as] a "right to commit suicide with another's assistance." [I] would not reject the respondents' claim without considering a different formulation, for which our legal tradition may provide greater support. That formulation would use words roughly like a "right to die with dignity." But irrespective of the exact words used, at its core would lie personal control over the manner of death, professional medical assistance, and the avoidance of unnecessary and severe physical suffering ***. I do not believe, however, that this Court need or now should decide whether or a not such a right is "fundamental." That is because, in my view, the avoidance of severe physical pain (connected with death) would have to constitute an essential part of any successful claim and because, as Justice O'CONNOR points out, the laws before us do not force a dying person to undergo that kind of pain.

———————

Points for Discussion

a. Physician-Assisted Suicide and Federalism

As the Court predicted, the decision in this case allowed the debate over physician-assisted suicide to continue in the States. To date, only Oregon has adopted a law that allows this practice. In 2006, the United States Attorney General announced that physicians assisting patients to commit suicide pursuant to Oregon's Death with Dignity Act faced the loss of their federal licenses to prescribe drugs under the Controlled Substances Act. After doctors filed suit to enjoin the Attorney General from taking action, the Court rejected the Attorney General's view of the Controlled Substances Act while avoiding any implication that there is a "right" to physician-assisted suicide. *Gonzales v. Oregon*, 546 U.S. 243 (2006). Was the Attorney General's approach consistent with the Court's call for state experimentation on the question of the propriety of physician-assisted suicide? If not, is there some other justification for federal intervention?

b. Competing Approaches

Although Chief Justice Rehnquist and Justice Souter agreed on the outcome in the case, they disagreed on the reasoning. Justice Souter employed a "common-law" approach that he believed to be superior because of its focus on the relative importance of the contending interests—governmental and individual—at stake. By contrast, Chief Justice Rehnquist believed that his approach—which defines the liberty interest narrowly and focuses on tradition—was superior *precisely because* it "avoids the need for complex balancing of interests in every case."

What are the advantages and disadvantages of Justice Souter's more ad hoc, flexible approach? What are the advantages and disadvantages of Chief Justice Rehnquist's approach? Looking back at the substantive due process cases that we have considered in this Chapter, has one approach typically prevailed over the other? If so, why do you think that is?

c. Reconciling *Glucksberg* with *Lawrence*

The Court in *Glucksberg* stated that a right falls within the substantive reach of the Due Process Clause only if, after it has been "carefully described," it is "deeply rooted in the Nation's history and tradition." Is this approach consistent with the approach of the Court only six years later in *Lawrence v. Texas*, which we considered earlier in this Chapter? For an argument that it is not, see Yale Kamisar, *Foreword: Can* Glucksberg *Survive* Lawrence? *Another Look at the End of Life and Personal Autonomy*, 106 Mich. L. Rev. 1453 (2008).

d. Facial v. As-Applied Challenges

The Court treated respondents' claim as a facial challenge to the Washington statute. Justices O'Connor, Stevens, and Breyer indicated that they might be open to a properly argued as-applied challenge. Does that mean that, in their view, the right to assistance in committing suicide *is* a fundamental liberty interest under the Due Process Clause? Can you articulate what sort of as-applied challenge these Justices might have found convincing? Are there individual interests that might trump a state's ban on assisted suicide in some circumstances? What are they?

e. "Death With Dignity"

Justices Breyer, O'Connor, and Stevens all suggested that terminally ill people in severe pain might have a constitutional right to choose the manner of their death—to "die with dignity." But there is no suggestion in their opinions that people who are not terminally ill—including people in physical pain or those suffering from emotional and mental afflictions—enjoy a similar right. What justifies such a distinction? Are there historical justifications for this view, perhaps in the Nation's common-law traditions? Or are the Justices effectively applying the balancing test advocated by Justice Souter and weighing the interests of the patients against the interests of the State?

Executive Summary of this Chapter

Under the doctrine of **substantive due process**, the Court has held that the Due Process Clauses protect forms of liberty that the government cannot impair even after providing procedural protections. Although the Court held in the late nineteenth and early-twentieth centuries that the Due Process Clauses protect a **freedom to contract**, *Lochner v. New York* (1905); *Adkins v. Children's Hospital* (1923), the Court has since held that government regulation of social and economic matters is generally subject only to review for rationality, *West Coast Hotel Co. v. Parrish* (1936); *Williamson v. Lee Optical Co.* (1955).

Although the Court has abandoned the cases holding that economic liberty is entitled to heightened protection under the Due Process Clauses, the Court has held that the Clauses do protect **fundamental rights** regardless of the level of procedure that accompanies governmental efforts to impair them.

The Supreme Court has held that the Due Process Clauses protect various personal decisions concerning **intimate relationships**, **sex**, and **reproduction**. In particular, the government cannot prohibit the **use of contraceptives** by married couples, *Griswold v. Connecticut* (1965), or by unmarried couples, *Eisenstadt v. Baird* (1972). The government also cannot make it a crime to engage in **private, consensual sexual conduct**, including homosexual sex. *Lawrence v. Texas* (2003).

The Due Process Clauses also protect a woman's right to choose to have an **abortion**, at least under certain circumstances. *Roe v. Wade* (1973). The government may not prohibit a woman from choosing to terminate a pregnancy before viability, and the government may not impose an **undue burden** on that right. *Planned Parenthood of Southeastern Pennsylvania v. Casey* (1992). The government may, however, regulate or prohibit abortions after the time of viability, except where necessary to preserve the life or health of the mother. *Id.* The government may also prohibit certain abortion procedures, such as "intact D & E," to advance its interest in protecting the life of the fetus, as long as in doing so it does not impose an undue burden on the right to an abortion. *Gonzales v. Carhart* (2007).

The government also cannot use **sterilization** as a punishment for crime, at least when persons who commit similar crimes are exempt from that punishment. *Skinner v. Oklahoma* (1942).

The Supreme Court has held that the Due Process Clauses protect certain rights relating to marriage and family. **Marriage** is a fundamental right protected by the Due Process Clauses. *Loving v. Virginia* (1967). The state cannot limit the right to persons who choose to marry persons of the same race, *id.*, and cannot condition the right on a court's permission for persons who are under the obligation to pay child support, *Zablocki v. Redhail* (1978).

The Due Process Clauses also protect the "liberty of parents and guardians to direct the upbringing and education of children under their control." *Pierce v. Society of the Sisters* (1925); *Meyer v. Nebraska* (1923). This right embraces parental decisions about who can visit their children, *Troxel v. Granville* (2000), but does not limit the power of a state to establish a virtually unrebuttable presumption that a child born to a married woman is a child of the marriage, *Michael H. v. Gerald D.* (1989).

The Due Process Clauses do not impose an affirmative obligation on the government to guarantee a minimum level of personal security or safety. *DeShaney v. Winnebago County Dept. of Social Services* (1989). Nor do they prevent the government from insisting on clear evidence of an incompetent person's desire to have life-sustaining treatment withdrawn, *Cruzan v. Director, Missouri Dept. of Health* (1990), or from prohibiting persons (including doctors) from assisting others to commit suicide, *Washington v. Glucksberg* (1997).

Point-Counterpoint

Does the Constitution protect unenumerated rights?

POINT: PETER J. SMITH

The argument that the Constitution does not protect unenumerated rights has an appealing simplicity: the Framers would not have bothered to spell out some rights if others were entitled to the same judicial protection; and even if they thought that there were undefined rights that are entitled to protection, they would not have left it to unelected judges—and their largely unconstrained discretion—to decide what they are. But several uncontroversial propositions, when viewed together, suggest that the matter is substantially more complex.

First, there is general agreement that some rights that are not expressly defined in the Constitution's text nevertheless are properly implied from the enumeration of other rights. As we will see in Chapter 17, for example, there is little dispute that the First Amendment's explicit protections—for speech, religion, and so forth—also imply the existence of a "freedom of association," even though the Amendment nowhere mentions such a right. See, e.g., *Scales v. United States,* 367 U.S. 203, 229 (1961).

Second, most of the Constitution's express rights-granting provisions—such as the Due Process and Privileges or Immunities Clauses—are framed at very high levels of generality. As a result, the ordinary process of interpretation inevitably will lead to the identification of rights—such as the right, derived from the Due Process Clause, to insist that the government prove an allegation of criminal conduct beyond a reasonable doubt, *In re Winship,* 397 U.S. 358 (1970)—that are not explicitly mentioned in the constitutional text.

Once one accepts that expressly defined rights imply the existence of other rights, and that broadly defined rights necessarily entail the existence of specific (but not specifically defined) rights, one has essentially accepted the proposition that there are rights that the Constitution protects but that are not expressly enumerated in the document's text. Moreover, if such rights exist, they must be judicially enforceable, or it would be misleading to refer to them as "rights."

There are other reasons to conclude that the Constitution protects unenumerated rights. First, the Constitution's text in several places seems to presuppose that such rights exist. The Ninth Amendment makes the point explicitly, and the Privilege or Immunities Clause of the Fourteenth Amendment plainly protects something, even though it does not specifically enumerate what it is. Second, in other contexts, proponents of the view that the Constitution does not protect unenumerated rights see no problem with implying, from constitutional structure or general "postulates" that underlie the text, limits on the government's authority. In federalism cases such as *Printz v. United States,* 521 U.S. 898

(1997), and *Alden v. Maine*, 527 U.S. 706 (1999), for example, the Justices who are most skeptical of claims of unenumerated rights have nevertheless discovered unenumerated "immunities" that the states enjoy from federal regulation. If the Constitution is properly interpreted to protect these unenumerated states' rights, then it becomes more difficult to suggest that it does not also protect some unenumerated individual rights.

To be sure, concluding that the Constitution protects unenumerated rights does not tell us much about *which* rights it actually protects, and how to define them. There will always be disagreements at the margins about such questions of definition. But once we accept that there are rights that are not explicitly defined in the constitutional text but that nevertheless are entitled to judicial protection, the question simply becomes one of judgment. And that, of course, is what we ordinarily expect judges to exercise.

———

Counterpoint: Gregory E. Maggs

The Constitution does not secure unenumerated rights just because they may exist according to natural law or some political theory. Although the Supreme Court has decided otherwise, its decisions are incorrect as an originalist matter.

True, the Founders believed in natural-law rights. The Declaration of Independence, for instance, prominently appeals to the "Laws of Nature" in specifying how England had violated the rights of American colonists. But acknowledging that the Founders recognized natural law is different from concluding that the Constitution makes unenumerated rights judicially enforceable.

The text of the Constitution itself indicates that unenumerated natural-law rights are not protected. In Article I, §§ 9 & 10, the Constitution lists specific rights, including rights to be free from ex post facto laws, bills of attainder, suspensions of habeas corpus, and state impairments of contracts. The inclusion of these rights objectively indicates that similar rights, which are not enumerated, are not secured. Why list any rights if they are protected without enumeration based on a natural-law theory?

Additional support for this conclusion comes from a debate at the Constitutional Convention about whether to enumerate rights. Some delegates thought including an express prohibition against ex post facto laws was unnecessary because ex post facto laws are naturally void. But delegate Hugh Williamson disagreed, arguing: "Such a prohibitory clause is in the Constitution of N. Carolina, and tho it has been violated, it has done good there & may do good here, because the Judges can take hold of it." 2 The Records of the Federal Convention of 1787 at 376 (Max Farrand ed. 1911). Given that Williamson's view prevailed, a majority of the Convention presumably agreed that judges would enforce enumerated rights, but not unenumerated natural-law rights.

Subsequent events also confirm this was the original understanding. A major objection to ratification of the Constitution was the lack of enumerated rights. Opponents believed that only a listing of rights would guarantee their protection. The First Congress addressed their concern with the Bill of Rights, which would have been unnecessary if courts could enforce unenumerated rights. Why expressly provide for freedom of speech, protection against cruel and unusual punishment, and so forth if courts could enforce any natural-law rights? Also significant is that early court decisions did not enforce unenumerated natural-law rights.

Although the Constitution does not secure unenumerated rights based on natural-law, it does protect one limited kind of unenumerated rights: those arising because the federal government has limited powers. For example, in *United States v. Lopez*, 514 U.S. 549 (1995), the Supreme Court held that Congress lacks power to ban guns in school zones. This means that the defendant in the case had a correlative, although unenumerated, right against the federal government to possess a gun at school. The specific enumeration of other rights in the Constitution should not be construed to deny or disparage rights of this kind retained by the people because of our federal structure. See U.S. Const. amend. 9.

CHAPTER 9

Procedural Due Process

The Due Process Clauses in the Fifth and Fourteenth Amendments provide that persons are entitled to due process of law when the government seeks to deprive them of "life, liberty, or property." We saw in the last Chapter how the Court has struggled to define the liberty substantively protected by the Due Process Clauses. But whatever one's views about the Court's substantive due process doctrine, there is little doubt that the clauses provide *procedural* protections in at least some cases involving the deprivation of important interests. However, the Clauses themselves do not provide very much guidance about when exactly those protections are triggered, and what consequences flow when they are. These questions are the subject of extensive consideration in other courses in law school, including Administrative Law. What follows is a brief overview of the principal issues in cases involving procedural due process claims.

Point for Discussion

Procedural due process was a major concern at the time of the American Revolution. In the Declaration of Independence, the Second Continental Congress famously listed the American grievances against the Crown. Several of their complaints concerned unfair trials and biased tribunals. How should this history and context influence our understanding of the Fifth and Fourteenth Amendments?

Cleveland Board of Education v. Loudermill

470 U.S. 532 (1985)

Justice WHITE delivered the opinion of the Court.

In these cases we consider what pretermination process must be accorded a public employee who can be discharged only for cause. In 1979 the Cleveland Board of Education *** hired respondent James Loudermill as a security guard. On his job application, Loudermill stated that he had never been convicted of a felony. Eleven months later, as part of a routine examination of his employment records, the Board discovered that in fact Loudermill had been convicted of grand larceny in 1968. By letter dated November 3, 1980, the Board's Business Manager informed Loudermill that he had been dismissed because of his dishonesty in filling out the employment application. Loudermill was not afforded an opportunity to respond to the charge of dishonesty or to challenge his dismissal. On November 13, the Board adopted a resolution officially approving the discharge.

[Under Ohio law, Loudermill could be terminated only for cause. Pursuant to state law, he sought administrative review of his discharge. After a hearing before a referee, at which Loudermill argued that he had thought that his 1968 larceny conviction was for a misdemeanor rather than a felony, and oral arguments before the Cleveland Civil Service Commission, the Commission upheld the dismissal. Loudermill filed suit in federal court alleging that the applicable provision of Ohio law was unconstitutional on its face because it did not provide an employee an opportunity to respond to charges against him prior to removal. The Court consolidated Loudermill's case with another case presenting similar facts.]

Respondents' federal constitutional claim depends on their having had a property right in continued employment. If they did, the State could not deprive them of this property without due process. Property interests are not created by the Constitution, "they are created and their dimensions are defined by existing rules or understandings that stem from an independent source such as state law." *Board of Regents v. Roth*, 408 U.S. 564, 576-578 (1972) The Ohio statute plainly creates such an interest. Respondents were "classified civil service employees," Ohio Rev. Code Ann. § 124.11 (1984), entitled to retain their positions "during good behavior and efficient service," who could not be dismissed "except [for] misfeasance, malfeasance, or nonfeasance in office," § 124.34. The statute plainly supports the conclusion, reached by both lower courts, that respondents possessed property rights in continued employment.

[Petitioner] argues, however, that the property right is defined by, and conditioned on, the legislature's choice of procedures for its deprivation. The Board stresses that in addition to specifying the grounds for termination, the statute sets out procedures by which termination may take place. According to petitioner, "[t]o require additional procedures would in effect expand the scope of the property interest itself." [This] "bitter with the sweet" approach misconceives the constitutional guarantee. [T]he Due Process Clause provides that certain substantive rights—life, liberty, and property—cannot be deprived except pursuant to constitutionally adequate procedures. The categories of substance and procedure are distinct. Were the rule otherwise, the Clause would be reduced to a mere tautology. "Property" cannot be defined by the procedures provided for its deprivation any more than can life or liberty. The right to due process "is conferred, not by legislative grace, but by constitutional guarantee. While the legislature may elect not to confer a property interest in [public] employment, it may not constitutionally authorize the deprivation of such an interest, once conferred, without appropriate procedural safeguards." *Arnett v. Kennedy,* 416 U.S. 134, 167 (1974) (POWELL, J., concurring in part and concurring in result in part). *** In short, once it is determined that the Due Process Clause applies, "the question remains what process is due." *Morrissey v. Brewer,* 408 U.S. 471, 481 (1972). The answer to that question is not to be found in the Ohio statute.

An essential principle of due process is that a deprivation of life, liberty, or property "be preceded by notice and opportunity for hearing appropriate to the nature of the case." *Mullane v. Central Hanover Bank & Trust Co.,* 339 U.S. 306, 313 (1950). We have described "the root requirement" of the Due Process Clause as being "that an individual be given an opportunity for a hearing *before* he is deprived of any significant property interest." *Boddie v. Connecticut,* 401 U.S. 371, 379 (1971). This principle requires "some kind of a hearing" prior to the discharge of an employee who has a constitutionally protected property interest in his employment.

The need for some form of pretermination hearing [is] evident from a balancing of the competing interests at stake. These are the private interests in retaining employment, the governmental interest in the expeditious removal of unsatisfactory employees and the avoidance of administrative burdens, and the risk of an erroneous termination. See *Mathews v. Eldridge,* 424 U.S. 319, 335 (1976).

Take Note

The Court notes that pre-termination hearings are useful in these circumstances because the decision whether to terminate often turns on disputed factual questions and often involves the discretion of the decision-maker. Loudermill did not dispute at his termination hearings that he had been convicted for grand larceny. Is there any "fact" that the Commission might have found at a pre-termination hearing that would have affected its decision whether to terminate? (Was Loudermill terminated because he was an ex-felon?) And why might a pre-termination hearing for Loudermill have made it more likely that the employer would exercise its discretion not to terminate him?

First, the significance of the private interest in retaining employment cannot be gainsaid. We have frequently recognized the severity of depriving a person of the means of livelihood. While a fired worker may find employment elsewhere, doing so will take some time and is likely to be burdened by the questionable circumstances under which he left his previous job. *** Second, some opportunity for the employee to present his side of the case is recurringly of obvious value in reaching an accurate decision. Dismissals for cause will often involve factual disputes. Even where the facts are clear, the appropriateness or necessity of the discharge may not be; in such cases, the only meaningful opportunity to invoke the discretion of the decisionmaker is likely to be before the termination takes effect.

The cases before us illustrate these considerations. [G]iven the Commission's ruling we cannot say that [Loudermill's] discharge was mistaken. Nonetheless, in light of the referee's recommendation, neither can we say that a fully informed decisionmaker might not have exercised its discretion and decided not to dismiss him, notwithstanding its authority to do so. In any event, the termination involved arguable issues, and the right to a hearing does not depend on a demonstration of certain success.

The governmental interest in immediate termination does not outweigh these interests. [A]ffording the employee an opportunity to respond prior to termination would impose neither a significant administrative burden nor intolerable delays. Furthermore, the employer shares the employee's interest in avoiding disruption and erroneous decisions; and until the matter is settled, the employer would continue to receive the benefit of the employee's labors. It is preferable to keep a qualified employee on than to train a new one. A governmental employer also has an interest in keeping citizens usefully employed rather than taking the possibly erroneous and counterproductive step of forcing its employees onto the welfare rolls. Finally, in those situations where the employer perceives a significant hazard in keeping the employee on the job, it can avoid the problem by suspending with pay.

> **Food for Thought**
>
> Does the Court adequately state the government's interest in avoiding a pre-termination hearing in this case? What other costs might requiring a hearing impose on the government?

The foregoing considerations indicate that the pretermination "hearing," though necessary, need not be elaborate. We have pointed out that "[t]he formality and procedural requisites for the hearing can vary, depending upon the importance of the interests involved and the nature of the subsequent proceedings." *Boddie v. Connecticut,* 401 U.S., at 378. In general, "something less" than a full evidentiary hearing is sufficient prior to adverse administrative action. *Mathews v. Eldridge,* 424 U.S., at 343. Under state law, respondents were later entitled to a full administrative hearing and judicial review. The only question is what steps were required before the termination took effect.

> **FYI**
>
> In *Goldberg*, the Court held that a welfare beneficiary was entitled to a trial-type hearing before the termination of benefits. In what way does that context present "significantly different considerations than are present in the context of public employment"?

In only one case, *Goldberg v. Kelly,* 397 U.S. 254 (1970), has the Court required a full adversarial evidentiary hearing prior to adverse governmental action. [T]hat case presented significantly different considerations than are present in the context of public employment. Here, the pretermination hearing need not definitively resolve the propriety of the discharge. It should be an initial check against mistaken decisions—essentially, a determination of whether there are reasonable grounds to believe that the charges against the employee are true and support the proposed action.

The essential requirements of due process, and all that respondents seek or the Court of Appeals required, are notice and an opportunity to respond. The opportunity to present reasons, either in person or in writing, why proposed action should not be taken is a fundamental due process requirement. The tenured public employee is entitled to oral or written notice of the charges against him, an explanation of the employer's evidence, and an opportunity to present his side of the story. *** To require more than this prior to termination would intrude to an unwarranted extent on the government's interest in quickly removing an unsatisfactory employee.

Our holding rests in part on the provisions in Ohio law for a full post-termination hearing. *** We conclude that all the process that is due is provided by a pretermination opportunity to respond, coupled with post-termination administrative procedures as provided by the Ohio statute.

Justice MARSHALL, concurring in part and concurring in the judgment.

I write separately *** to reaffirm my belief that public employees who may be discharged only for cause are entitled, under the Due Process Clause of the Fourteenth Amendment, to more than respondents sought in this case. I continue to believe that *before the decision is made to terminate an employee's wages,* the employee is entitled to an opportunity to test the strength of the evidence "by confronting and cross-examining adverse witnesses and by presenting witnesses on his own behalf, whenever there are substantial disputes in testimonial evidence," *Arnett v. Kennedy,* 416 U.S. 134, 214 (1974) (MARSHALL, J., dissenting).

[T]he disruption caused by a loss of wages may be so devastating to an employee that, whenever there are substantial disputes about the evidence, additional pre-deprivation procedures are necessary to minimize the risk of an erroneous termination. *** By limiting the procedures due prior to termination of wages, the Court accepts an impermissibly high risk that a wrongfully discharged employee will be subjected to this often lengthy wait for vindication, and to the attendant and often traumatic disruptions to his personal and economic life. Considerable amounts of time may pass between the termination of wages and the decision in a post-termination evidentiary hearing ***. During this period the employee is left in limbo, deprived of his livelihood and of wages on which he may well depend for basic sustenance. In that time, his ability to secure another job might be hindered, either because of the nature of the charges against him, or because of the prospect that he will return to his prior public employment if permitted. *** Absent an interim source of wages, the employee might be unable to meet his basic, fixed costs, such as food, rent or mortgage payments. *** Given that so very much is at stake, I am unable to accept the Court's narrow view of the process due to a public employee before his wages are terminated, and before he begins the long wait for a public agency to issue a final decision in his case.

[Justice BRENNAN's separate opinion concurring in part and dissenting in part is omitted.]

Justice REHNQUIST, dissenting.

[I]n one legislative breath Ohio has conferred upon civil service employees such as respondents in these cases a limited form of tenure during good behavior, and prescribed the procedures by which that tenure may be terminated. *** We stated in *Board of Regents v. Roth,* 408 U.S. 564, 577 (1972): "Property interests, of course, are not created by the Constitution. Rather, they are created and their dimensions are defined by existing rules or understandings that stem from an independent source such as state law—rules or understandings that secure certain benefits and that support claims of entitlement to those benefits." We ought to recognize the totality of the State's definition of the property right in question, and not merely seize upon one of several paragraphs in a unitary statute to proclaim that in that paragraph the State has inexorably conferred upon a civil service employee something which it is powerless under the United States Constitution to qualify in the next paragraph of the statute. This practice ignores our duty under <u>Roth</u> to rely on state law as the source of property interests for purposes of applying the Due Process Clause of the Fourteenth Amendment. While it does not impose a federal definition of property, the Court departs from the full breadth of the holding in <u>Roth</u> by its selective choice from among the sentences the Ohio Legislature chooses to use in establishing and qualifying a right.

Having concluded by this somewhat tortured reasoning that Ohio has created a property right in the respondents in these cases, the Court naturally proceeds to inquire what process is "due" before the respondents may be divested of that right. This customary "balancing" inquiry conducted by the Court in these cases reaches a result that is quite unobjectionable, but it seems to me that it is devoid of any principles which will either instruct or endure. The balance is simply an ad hoc weighing which depends to a great extent upon how the Court subjectively views the underlying interests at stake. The results in previous cases and in these cases have been quite unpredictable. *** Every different set of facts will present a new issue on what process was due and when. One way to avoid this subjective and varying interpretation of the Due Process Clause in cases such as these is to hold that one who avails himself of government entitlements accepts the grant of tenure along with its inherent limitations.

———————

Points for Discussion

a. "Life, Liberty, or Property"

The Due Process Clauses require some process (that which is "due") only when the government deprives a person of "life, liberty, or property." The Court in <u>Loudermill</u> concluded that Mr. Loudermill, a public employee who could be fired only for cause, had a property interest in continued employment. How did the Court define "property"—or, for that matter, the companion terms "life" and "liberty"?

It seems clear that when a state takes a person's land in order to build a highway, it deprives him or her of property. Similarly, it seems plain that sending a person to prison as punishment for a crime involves the deprivation of liberty, and that sentencing a person to death as punishment for a crime involves the deprivation not only of liberty but also of life. In these instances, the Due Process Clauses require the government to accord some process to the person subject to the deprivation—in the case of the taking, a hearing to determine (at a minimum) the fair market value of the land, and in the case of criminal punishment, a hearing with the full protections of a criminal trial.

But the Due Process Clauses do not define the terms "life, liberty, [and] property." One can conceive of countless interests that people value—including their jobs, their reputations, and their government-provided benefits, such as health care or pension support. Does the "life, liberty, or property" protected by the Due Process Clauses embrace these important interests, as well, thus requiring some kind of hearing when the government takes action that impairs them?

For much of the twentieth century, the Court typically concluded that life, liberty, or property was at issue only when the government sought to deprive a person of a "right," rather than a "privilege." As (then state-court) Justice Holmes explained in a famous case involving a claim by a police officer that he was entitled to a hearing before he was fired for engaging in political activities, "The petitioner may have a constitutional right to talk politics, but he has no constitutional right to be a policeman." *McAuliffe v. New Bedford*, 29 N.E. 517 (Mass. 1892). Of course, on this view, the courts were still called upon to identify "rights"; but the approach typically freed the government from the obligation of providing a hearing whenever it sought to deprive a person of something to which, according to the courts, he was not entitled as a matter of right.

Two developments in the middle of the twentieth century led the Court to reconsider this approach. First, the Court developed the "unconstitutional conditions doctrine," which (at least sometimes) prevents the government from granting a privilege—that is, something to which a person is not entitled as a matter of constitutional right—only on the condition that the person forfeit a constitutional right. For example, the Court held that the government cannot condition the availability of unemployment compensation benefits on a person's willingness to work on the Sabbath, in violation of his genuinely held religious beliefs. *Sherbert v. Verner*, 374 U.S. 398 (1963). Second, the government increasingly provided important benefits, such as health care, welfare, disability

> **Make the Connection**
>
> We will consider the Court's decision in *Sherbert v. Verner*, and the free exercise of religion, in Chapter 17.

insurance, and retirement security, to many citizens as a matter of statutory entitlement, and many citizens relied on these benefits much as they relied on traditional sources of property. See Charles A. Reich, *The New Property*, 73 Yale L.J. 733 (1964). These developments stood in at least some tension with the right-privilege distinction.

In 1970, the Court held in *Goldberg v. Kelly*, 397 U.S. 254 (1970), that the government was required to provide an evidentiary hearing before terminating a welfare recipient's benefits. The Court held that "the extent to which procedural due process must be afforded to the recipient is influenced by the extent to which he may be condemned to suffer grievous loss, and depends upon whether the recipient's interest in avoiding that loss outweighs the governmental interest in summary adjudication." Because terminating benefits to welfare recipients threatened to leave them without any source of sustenance, the Court held that the Due Process Clause required a hearing, at which the recipients could attempt to demonstrate that they remained eligible for benefits, before the government could terminate their benefits. In *Goldberg*, the government did not dispute that welfare benefits are a form of property, and the Court thus had little occasion to define specifically the interests protected by the Clauses. The Court did, however, cite Professor Reich's view of the "new property," explaining that it "may be realistic today to regard welfare entitlements as more like 'property' than a 'gratuity,'" and that "[m]uch of the existing wealth in this country takes the form of rights that do not fall within traditional common-law concepts of property." 397 U.S. at 262 n.8.

Two years later, the Court addressed the question directly, in two cases that it decided on the same day. In *Board of Regents v. Roth*, 408 U.S. 564 (1972), a professor at a public university sued when he was fired after a fixed, one-year term of teaching. Under state law, a professor was guaranteed tenure after four years of teaching, and a non-tenured professor was granted an opportunity to review a termination decision only if he was dismissed during the academic year. Using the balancing test set out in *Goldberg*, the lower courts concluded that the professor's interest in continued employment outweighed the university's interest in dismissing him without a hearing. Declaring that it was necessary to look at "the nature of the interest at stake" before looking at the "weights" of the interests, however, the Supreme Court held that the state did not deprive the respondent of a protected property interest. The Court stated: "Property interests, of course, are not created by the Constitution. Rather they are created and their dimensions are defined by existing rules or understandings that stem from an independent source such as state law—rules or understandings that secure certain benefits and that support claims of entitlement to those benefits." The Court explained that "[t]o have a property interest in a benefit, a person clearly must have more than an abstract need or desire for it. He must have more than a unilateral expectation of it. He must, instead, have a legitimate claim of entitlement to it." Because the professor's contract did not include any provision for employment for the next year and no state statute or university rule guaranteed him continued employment, the Court concluded that he did not have a property interest in continued employment and, accordingly, that the Due Process Clause did not entitle him to a pre-termination hearing.

By contrast, in *Perry v. Sindermann*, 408 U.S. 593 (1972), a companion case to *Roth*, the Court held that a professor at a different public university had a property interest in his job that required the university to accord him a hearing prior to termination. Although the professor did not have formal tenure, he had been employed by the state college system for ten years under a series of one-year contracts. The Court held that this arrangement, coupled with the university's official employment policies, created a legitimate expectation of renewal tantamount to tenure, and accordingly that the university could not terminate respondent without providing notice and a hearing.

The Court elaborated on the "legitimate expectation" test in *Town of Castle Rock v. Gonzales*, 545 U.S. 748 (2005). In that case, the respondent, who sued for damages under 42 U.S.C. § 1983, claimed that Castle Rock violated the Due Process Clause when its police officers did not respond to her repeated reports that her estranged husband was violating the terms of a restraining order to protect their children. The husband subsequently kidnapped and murdered the children. Although a statement on the back of the restraining order informed law enforcement officials that they "shall use every reasonable means to enforce this restraining order," the Supreme Court found that this language, even when coupled with state domestic violence statutes, did not render the enforcement of restraining orders mandatory. Because a "benefit is not a protected property *** entitlement if government officials may grant it or deny it in their discretion," the Court held that the respondent did not enjoy a protected property interest in the hope that the police would arrest someone.

Property interests accordingly are created and defined by positive law, and not by the courts. (Indeed, it is this fact that led to the argument, rejected in <u>Loudermill</u>, that a person is not entitled to a hearing if the state, in creating a property interest, identifies the procedural rights that flow from the interest's termination.) In deciding whether a person has a protected property interest, therefore, a court must look to state or federal law—statutory or otherwise—to determine whether the person has some legally protected entitlement to the interest.

But the Court in <u>Roth</u> made clear that some *liberty* interests, unlike property interests, are defined by the Constitution, subject of course to the Court's interpretation. Accordingly, the government may have to accord notice and an opportunity to be heard when it deprives a person of any liberty interest protected in the Bill of Rights or any unenumerated interest that the Court has held is protected by the Constitution. Following this approach, the Court has concluded that the government must provide a hearing when it seeks, among other things, to institutionalize a person, *O'Connor v. Donaldson*, 422 U.S. 563 (1975), terminate a person's parental rights, *Santosky v. Kramer*, 455 U.S. 745 (1982), or discipline school children, *Ingraham v. Wright*, 430 U.S. 651 (1977) (corporal punishment); *Goss v. Lopez*, 419 U.S. 565 (1975) (suspension).

In light of this background, can you articulate why Loudermill had a protected interest in "continued employment"? Did Loudermill have both property and liberty interests in his job?

> ### Food for Thought
>
> Why has the Court concluded that the Constitution defines protected liberty interests, but leaves the definition of protected property interests to "independent sources," such as legislatively enacted or judicially developed state law?

b. "Due Process of Law"

If there is a deprivation of a protected interest, then to what process is the person entitled? The Due Process Clauses, of course, are notoriously vague, circularly requiring only that the government provide the process that is "due." In some cases, immediate government action, without any pre-action hearing, will be justified by some threat to public health or safety. See, e.g., *North American Cold Storage Co. v. Chicago*, 211 U.S. 306 (1908) (holding that government can seize and destroy rancid food without a pre-seizure hearing). But what about cases that do not involve such exigent circumstances? Is there one set of requirements that is always triggered by a deprivation, regardless of the nature of the deprivation or the particular protected interests at stake? After all, the Due Process Clauses are implicated by a large range of actions; must the government accord a full-blown trial-type hearing before it can fire an employee? Terminate welfare benefits? Suspend a child from school? The individuals subjected to these actions obviously would like to have ample opportunity to demonstrate why the government should not take the action after all. But requiring a judicial-type proceeding before the government can take countless actions could effectively slow government to a crawl—or lead the government not to create any entitlements in the first place.

There is no perfect formula to capture the Court's holdings in this area. In *Goldberg v. Kelly*, the Court stated, after balancing the interests of the welfare recipients with those of the government in the prompt termination of welfare benefits, that the hearing to which welfare recipients were entitled before the termination of their benefits did not have to "take the form of a judicial or quasi-judicial trial." But it nevertheless required notice, an opportunity for the recipient to be heard in person, an impartial decision-maker limited to a decision based on evidence in the record, and the right to cross-examine adverse witnesses and to use a lawyer. Six years later, however, in *Mathews v. Eldridge*, 424 U.S. 319 (1976), the Court concluded that recipients of disability benefits were not entitled to such a hearing before the termination of their benefits, when a post-termination hearing was available. The Court explained that "due process generally requires consideration of three distinct factors: First, the private interest that will be affected by the official action; second, the risk of an erroneous deprivation of such interest through the procedures used, and the probable value, if any, of additional or substitute procedural safeguards; and finally, the Government's interest, including the function involved and the fiscal and administrative burdens that the additional or substitute procedural requirement would entail." The Court concluded that the government interest outweighed the individual interest because requiring a full evidentiary hearing prior to termination would substantially increase the cost of the program, and because eligibility for disability benefits was not based on financial need. Can *Goldberg* and *Mathews* be reconciled? Which case was *Loudermill* more like?

In his dissent in *Loudermill*, then-Justice Rehnquist lamented that the Court's decisions in this area lack a principled pattern. In light of the cases described above, do you agree with his criticism?

Executive Summary of this Chapter

The Due Process Clauses ordinarily require **notice** and an **opportunity to be heard** when the government seeks to deprive a person of "life, liberty, or property." *Cleveland Board of Education v. Loudermill* (1985).

The procedural protections of the Clauses are triggered when the government deprives a person of a protected interest. The Constitution defines some liberty interests, which can include liberties accorded explicit protection (for example, in the Bill of Rights) and fundamental rights that the Court has concluded are implicit in the constitutional scheme. *Board of Regents v. Roth* (1972).

Property interests, on the other hand, are defined by independent sources of law, such as state common law or state or federal statutory law. Such independent sources of law create property interests when they create a **legitimate claim of entitlement** to continued possession. *Board of Regents v. Roth* (1972); *Perry v. Sindermann* (1972). A person does not have a legitimate claim of entitlement to a government benefit if the government may grant or deny it in its discretion. *Town of Castle Rock v. Gonzales* (2005).

Although the independent source of authority determines whether a person has a legitimate claim of entitlement, that source of law cannot define the procedures that must accompany a deprivation of the property interest. *Cleveland Board of Education v. Loudermill* (1985).

If there has been a deprivation of a protected interest, the Due Process Clauses typically require notice and some kind of hearing. In deciding exactly what process must be provided, particularly before the deprivation takes place, the Court applies a **balancing test** that considers three factors: (1) the private interest; (2) the risk of an erroneous deprivation and the probable value, if any, of additional or substitute procedural safeguards; and (3) the government's interest. *Mathews v. Eldridge* (1976).

Part VII: Equal Protection

Inscribed on the façade of the Supreme Court's majestic building in Washington, D.C., is the phrase, "Equal Justice Under Law." Americans have come to accept that this basic concept is essential to a just, democratic society. Yet the Constitution that was ratified in 1789—and the Bill of Rights, ratified in 1791—did not include any provision explicitly guaranteeing equal treatment under the laws other than the Privileges and Immunities Clause in Article IV. That provision, however, limits only certain kinds of discrimination by states against citizens of other states. It was not until 1868—after the nation had fought a bloody Civil War largely over the institution of slavery—that a general provision requiring some form of equal treatment under law became part of the Constitution.* The Fourteenth Amendment provides, in relevant part, that "No State shall [deny] to any person within its jurisdiction the equal protection of the laws." In the next two Chapters, we consider the meaning and application of this important provision.

---

* As we will see in Chapter 10, the Supreme Court subsequently ruled that the Due Process Clause of the Fifth Amendment includes an equal protection principle. See *Bolling v. Sharpe*, 347 U.S. 497 (1954). But the Court did not interpret the Fifth Amendment this way before ratification of the Fourteenth Amendment.

Introduction and Framework

A. Distinctions and Classifications

If equal treatment under the law is of exceeding importance, then so is the practical fact that government often must draw distinctions in order to govern sensibly, effectively, and fairly. Surely, for example, a public school teacher can award an "A" to a student who turns in an exceptional academic performance and a "C" to a student who has done mediocre work, even though those decisions distinguish between the students on the basis of their demonstrated academic ability. Similarly, although there might be debate over the wisdom of particular tax and social welfare policies, almost all would now agree that the government has power to impose a higher marginal tax rate on the wealthy than it imposes on the poor, or to award welfare benefits to the poor and not to the wealthy. But see *Knowlton v. Moore*, 178 U.S. 41, 110 (1900) (Brewer, J., dissenting from the Court's conclusion that a "progressive rate of tax can be validly imposed").

Indeed, one can find government distinctions and classifications wherever one turns. A city that wants to limit the number of sidewalk vendors on its streets might choose to grant licenses to operate sidewalk stands only to vendors who have already been engaged in business for a certain period of time. See *New Orleans v. Dukes*, 427 U.S. 297 (1976). The same city might decide to hire as police officers only those applicants who can, among other things, demonstrate competency with a firearm. And, to take an example familiar to virtually all students, the state can deny driver's licenses to all persons younger than, say, 16 years old, regardless of their demonstrated driving ability.

There would be serious (and fairly obvious) costs if the Equal Protection Clause prohibited these distinctions, even though each can be said to "discriminate" on some ground—in the examples above, on the basis respectively of academic ability, wealth, time in business, technical competence, and age. It is perhaps for this reason that Justice Oliver Wendell Holmes, one of our most famous jurists, ridiculed claims based on the Equal Protection Clause as "the last resort of constitutional arguments." *Buck v. Bell*, 274 U.S. 200, 208 (1927).

Yet the Clause must ban at least some forms of government discrimination. We have come to see, for example, that discrimination on the basis of race is dangerous and morally problematic; we can intuitively understand the difference between a rule denying driver's licenses to people younger than 16 years old and a rule denying licenses to persons because of the color of their skin. Indeed, as we will see in the first part of Chapter 11, classifications on the basis of race (other than affirmative action programs and remedial measures for past discrimination) are virtually always inconsistent with the Equal Protection Clause.

But outside of the context of race, whether a classification is presumptively problematic is sometimes a considerably more difficult question. May the government distinguish among persons on the basis of gender? National origin? Citizenship status? Sexual orientation? These questions have provoked serious debate and often divided the Court. At bottom, the question for our consideration is: if some government classifications are unobjectionable under the Equal Protection Clause and others are deeply problematic, then how do we distinguish between the defensible ones and the suspect ones?

One possibility would be to conclude that because the problem of racial discrimination was the principal motivation for the ratification of the Fourteenth Amendment, the Equal Protection Clause prohibits only classifications based on race. But the Clause does not, at least on its face, apply only to unequal treatment on the basis of race. And the Court has never accepted the view that the Clause is silent on all forms of discrimination other than racial discrimination.

Instead, the Court, at least in theory, subjects all challenged government classifications to some form of judicial review. In any case challenging a government classification, the Court assesses its constitutionality by considering the nature of the classification, the government's interest in the challenged regulation, and the relationship between the government's interest and the classification. But the "level of scrutiny" that the Court applies—the extent to which the Court insists on particularly weighty interests, accords deference to the government's judgment, and tolerates imperfect means to accomplish those ends—depends upon the basis for the classification. Under "strict scrutiny," the Court's most searching form of review, a law will be upheld only if it is "narrowly tailored" to advance a "compelling" government interest. Under "intermediate scrutiny," the Court will uphold a law only if it is "substantially related" to an "important" government interest. Finally, under the "rational-basis test" (also called "rationality review"), a law will be upheld if it is "rationally related" to a "legitimate" government interest. Unlike strict and intermediate scrutiny, rational-basis review is highly deferential.

> **Make the Connection**
>
> We saw a form of deferential rationality review in Chapter 3, when we considered *McCulloch v. Maryland* and the Court's test for federal legislation pursuant to the Necessary and Proper Clause. We also considered rational-basis review (and various forms of heightened scrutiny) in Chapter 8 when we considered the Court's cases concerning substantive due process and "fundamental rights."

But how does the Court know which level of scrutiny to apply to any given classification? The answer inheres in part in history, in part in contestable notions about the normative validity of certain bases of discrimination, and in part on political theory. Perhaps the Court's most famous attempt to identify when heightened scrutiny is warranted for a particular classification came in the famous footnote 4 of the Court's decision in *United States v. Carolene Products Co.*, 304 U.S. 144 (1938), which we considered in Chapter 8. In that case, the Court applied rational-basis review to a federal law that regulated the sale of milk. After declaring that ordinary regulatory legislation is entitled to a presumption of constitutionality, the Court stated in footnote 4:

> It is unnecessary to consider now whether legislation which restricts those political process-es which can ordinarily be expected to bring about repeal of undesirable legislation, is to be subjected to more exacting judicial scrutiny under the general prohibitions of the Fourteenth Amendment than are most other types of legislation. Nor need we enquire whether similar con-siderations enter into the review of statutes directed at particular religious, or national, or racial minorities; whether prejudice against discrete and insular minorities may be a special condition, which tends seriously to curtail the operation of those political processes ordinarily to be relied upon to protect minorities, and which may call for a correspondingly more searching judicial inquiry.

The Court's suggestion—that judicial intervention might be warranted, among other times, to protect "discrete and insular minorities" from the political process—has informed the Court as it has sought, over the last half-century, to determine which government classifica-tions are problematic. But note that the Court's approach in *Carolene Products* leaves many questions—including, significantly, who constitutes a "discrete and insular minority" not adequately protected by the political process—unanswered.

Perspective and Analysis

Professor John Hart Ely argued that the *Carolene Products* footnote suggested a "representation-reinforcement approach" to judicial review, including review under the Equal Protection Clause. Under that approach, Courts would intervene to invalidate actions by the elected branches only under certain circumstances:

> Our government cannot fairly be said to be "malfunctioning" simply because it some-times generates outcomes with which we disagree, however strongly ***. Malfunc-tion occurs when the *process* is undeserving of trust, when (1) the ins are choking off the channels of political change to ensure that they will stay in and the outs will stay out, or (2) though no one is actually denied a voice or a vote, representatives beholden to an effective majority are systematically disadvantaging some minority out of simple hostility or a prejudiced refusal to recognize commonalities of interest, and thereby denying that minority the protection afforded other groups by a representa-tive system.

John Hart Ely, Democracy and Distrust 103 (1980).

As we will see in Chapter 11, the Court has translated the *Carolene Products* approach into a sprawling body of doctrine. The Court applies "strict scrutiny" to classifications based on race and national origin, and "intermediate scrutiny" to classifications based on gender and the marital status of one's parents. Most other classifications are reviewed only for rationality. But various Justices have, over the years, contested an approach to review under the Equal Protection Clause that rigidly defines three "tiers" of scrutiny. They have instead suggested that judicial review should—and, in fact, does, as a matter of practice—

vary along a sliding scale depending upon the concerns raised by the particular basis for classification and the importance of the government interests advanced by the classification. As we explore the doctrine in the next two Chapters, consider the extent to which the Court has in practice, even if not in rhetoric, followed just such an approach.

————

B. To Whom Does the Obligation of Equal Protection Apply?

The Equal Protection Clause provides specifically that "[n]o *State*" shall deny any person equal protection of the laws. Does that mean that the federal government is free to discriminate on bases on which the states are forbidden to discriminate?

————

Bolling v. Sharpe

347 U.S. 497 (1954)

Mr. Chief Justice WARREN delivered the opinion of the Court.

[Petitioners, African-American school children, were refused admission to segregated public schools in the District of Columbia. They filed suit against the school board, alleging that such segregation deprived them of due process of law under the Fifth Amendment.]

> **Make the Connection**
>
> The Court decided *Bolling* on the same day that it decided *Brown v. Board of Education*, which addressed the constitutionality of segregation in education in the states. We will consider *Brown* in Chapter 11.

We have this day held that the Equal Protection Clause of the Fourteenth Amendment prohibits the states from maintaining racially segregated public schools. *** The Fifth Amendment, which is applicable in the District of Columbia, does not contain an equal protection clause as does the Fourteenth Amendment which applies only to the states. But the concepts of equal protection and due process, both stemming from our American ideal of fairness, are not mutually exclusive. The "equal protection of the laws" is a more explicit safeguard of prohibited unfairness than "due process of law," and, therefore, we do not imply that the two are always interchangeable phrases. But, as this Court has recognized, discrimination may be so unjustifiable as to be violative of due process.

Classifications based solely upon race must be scrutinized with particular care, since they are contrary to our traditions and hence constitutionally suspect. [*Korematsu v. United States*, 323 U.S. 214, 216 (1944); *Hirabayashi v. United*

> **Make the Connection**
>
> We will consider the Court's decision in *Korematsu* in Chapter 11.

States, 320 U.S. 81, 100 (1943).] As long ago as 1896, this Court declared the principle "that the constitution of the United States, in its present form, forbids, so far as civil and political rights are concerned, discrimination by the general government, or by the states, against any citizen because of his race." [*Gibson v. Mississippi*, 162 U.S. 565, 591 (1896).] And in *Buchanan v. Warley*, 245 U.S. 60 (1917), the Court held that a statute which limited the right of a property owner to convey his property to a person of another race was, as an unreasonable discrimination, a denial of due process of law.

Although the Court has not assumed to define "liberty" with any great precision, that term is not confined to mere freedom from bodily restraint. Liberty under law extends to the full range of conduct which the individual is free to pursue, and it cannot be restricted except for a proper governmental objective. Segregation in public education is not reasonably related to any proper governmental objective, and thus it imposes on Negro children of the District of Columbia a burden that constitutes an arbitrary deprivation of their liberty in violation of the Due Process Clause.

In view of our decision that the Constitution prohibits the states from maintaining racially segregated public schools, it would be unthinkable that the same Constitution would impose a lesser duty on the Federal Government. We hold that racial segregation in the public schools of the District of Columbia is a denial of the due process of law guaranteed by the Fifth Amendment to the Constitution.

Points for Discussion

a. Interpretation and Reverse Incorporation

In addition to the Equal Protection Clause, there is a Due Process Clause in the Fourteenth Amendment. If the concept of due process prohibits the government from discriminating on the basis of race (or any other ground that is "not reasonably related to any proper governmental objective"), then isn't the Equal Protection Clause redundant?

If nothing else, it seems clear that the Due Process Clause of the Fifth Amendment was not originally understood to prohibit racial discrimination. After all, the institution of slavery co-existed for over 60 years with the Due Process Clause, and the Court in the <u>Dred Scott</u> decision (which we will consider in Chapter 11) even concluded that a slave owner's interest in his slaves was *protected* by that Clause. By what process of interpretation, then, does the Court reach the conclusion that the Due Process Clause of the Fifth Amendment includes an equal protection component generally and prohibits racial discrimination specifically?

The Court's approach in <u>Bolling</u> is often considered an instance of "reverse incorporation." Just as the Court has held, as we saw in Chapter 7, that the Due Process Clause of the Fourteenth Amendment "incorporated" (most of) the protections of the Bill of Rights, the Court in <u>Bolling</u> effectively held that, presumably upon the ratification of the Fourteenth Amendment, the Due Process Clause of the Fifth Amendment incorporated the rights afforded by the Equal Protection Clause. Such an approach could hypothetically be justified on originalist grounds—if, for example, the ratifiers of the Fourteenth Amendment also understood that it would modify the reach of the Fifth Amendment. The originalist case, however, is a difficult one to advance, because there appears to have been no such understanding of the Fourteenth Amendment after its ratification. See, e.g., *La Belle Iron Works v. United States*, 256 U.S. 377, 392 (1921) (rejecting an equality-based challenge to federal action on the ground that "[t]he Fifth Amendment has no equal protection clause"). The Court in <u>Bolling</u> (and, we will see shortly, <u>Brown</u>) does not seem to have relied on an originalist approach, insisting instead that it would be "unthinkable" for the Constitution to permit the federal government to discriminate on the basis of race while forbidding the states from doing so. Is rejection of the "unthinkable" a generalizable basis for interpreting the Constitution?

<u>Bolling</u> was not the first case in which the Court suggested that there is an equal protection component to the Due Process Clause of the Fifth Amendment. In <u>Korematsu</u>, which the Court cited in <u>Bolling</u> and which we will consider in Chapter 11, the Court upheld the internment by military order during World War II of persons of Japanese descent. The Court stated, however, that "all legal restrictions which curtail the civil rights of a single racial group are immediately suspect"—including, presumably, restrictions, such as those at issue in the case, imposed by the federal government. The Court in <u>Korematsu</u>, however, did not specify what provision of the Constitution imposed limits on the federal government's ability to discriminate on the basis of race.

b. "Liberty" and Due Process

The Court declared in *Bolling* that liberty "cannot be restricted except for a proper governmental objective," and it concluded that segregation in the D.C. schools constituted "an arbitrary deprivation" of the school children's "liberty in violation of the Due Process Clause." Did the Court in *Bolling* rely on a theory of substantive due process, which we considered in Chapter 8? If, as some Justices have contended, the doctrine of substantive due process is illegitimate, does that mean that the Court's decision in *Bolling* necessarily was illegitimate, as well?

c. The Fifth Amendment vs. the Fourteenth Amendment

Are there any differences between the protection against discrimination provided by the Equal Protection Clause of the Fourteenth Amendment and the Due Process Clause of the Fifth Amendment? In <u>Bolling</u>, the Court stated that it was not "imply[ing] that [due process and equal protection] are always interchangeable phrases." In *Buckley v. Valeo*, 424 U.S. 1 (1976), however, the Supreme Court expressly declared that "[e]qual protection analysis in the Fifth Amendment area is the same as that under the Fourteenth Amendment." Would there be any justification for applying different standards to actions by the federal and state governments that discriminate on the basis of race?

This question has considerable history. In *Metro Broadcasting, Inc. v. F.C.C.*, 497 U.S. 547 (1990), the Supreme Court held that it owed deference to Congress, as a co-equal branch of government, in assessing the constitutionality of federal race-based affirmative action policies and would not subject them to strict scrutiny. Instead, the Court held that "benign race-conscious measures mandated by Congress—even if those measures are not 'remedial' in the sense of being designed to compensate victims of past governmental or societal discrimination—are constitutionally permissible to the extent that they serve important governmental objectives within the power of Congress and are substantially related to achievement of those objectives." *Id.* *at 564-565*. But just five years later, in *Adarand Constructors, Inc. v. Pena*, 515 U.S. 200, 227 (1995), the Supreme Court overruled *Metro Broadcasting*, holding that "all racial classifications, imposed by whatever federal, state, or local governmental actor, must be analyzed by a reviewing court under strict scrutiny." What might be the hazards of deferring to Congress when Congress classifies on the basis of race?

> **Make the Connection**
>
> We will consider the Court's decision in *Adarand*, and the constitutionality of affirmative action programs, in Chapter 11.

C. Rationality Review

As noted above, government classifications on bases that are not suspect are generally reviewed solely for rationality. Under this level of scrutiny, the Court asks whether the classification is rationally related to a legitimate government interest. As we saw in Chapter 8 when we considered the Court's review under the Due Process Clauses of social and economic regulation, this is a highly deferential form of review. Indeed, it is virtually always possible to articulate some legitimate interest served by a challenged government regulation. Otherwise, why would Congress or a state legislature enact the law?

But the simple fact that the government has not classified on some suspect basis, such as race or gender, does not mean that all government classifications are therefore fair or sensible. Just how aggressively should the courts review government classifications to avoid unfairness or arbitrariness?

Railway Express Agency v. People of State of New York

336 U.S. 106 (1949)

Mr. Justice DOUGLAS delivered the opinion of the Court.

[The Traffic Regulations of the City of New York prohibited the operation of "advertising vehicles"—vehicles that essentially served as moving billboards—but permitted the use of "business notices upon business delivery vehicles, so long as such vehicles [were] engaged in the usual business or regular work of the owner and not used merely or mainly for advertising." Appellant operated 1,900 trucks in New York City and sold the space on the exterior sides of these trucks for advertising for the most part unconnected with its own business. It was convicted and fined, and it appealed to challenge the constitutionality of the regulation.]

The Court of Special Sessions concluded that advertising on vehicles using the streets of New York City constitutes a distraction to vehicle drivers and to pedestrians alike and therefore affects the safety of the public in the use of the streets. [But it] is pointed out that the regulation draws the line between advertisements of products sold by the owner of the truck and general advertisements. It is argued that unequal treatment on the basis of such a distinction is not justified by the aim and purpose of the regulation. It is said, for example, that one of appellant's trucks carrying the advertisement of a commercial house would not cause any greater distraction of pedestrians and vehicle drivers than if the commercial house carried the same advertisement on its own truck. Yet the regulation allows the latter to do what the former is forbidden from doing. It is therefore contended that the classification which the regulation makes has no relation to the traffic problem since a violation turns not on what kind of advertisements are carried on trucks but on whose trucks they are carried.

That, however, is a superficial way of analyzing the problem ***. The local authorities may well have concluded that those who advertised their own wares on their trucks do not present the same traffic problem in view of the nature or extent of the advertising which they use. It would take a degree of omniscience which we lack to say that such is not the case. If that judgment is correct, the advertising displays that are exempt have less incidence on traffic than those of appellants.

> **Take Note**
>
> What level of scrutiny does the Court apply under the Equal Protection Clause? Is there a rational basis for believing that the challenged regulation furthers the government's interest in preventing distractions to motorists? How important can that interest be to the government when it permits advertisements on the side of other types of vehicles?

We cannot say that that judgment is not an allowable one. Yet if it is, the classification has relation to the purpose for which it is made and does not contain the kind of discrimination against which the Equal Protection Clause affords protection. [T]he fact that New York City sees fit to eliminate from traffic this kind of distraction but does not touch what may be even greater ones in a different category, such as the vivid displays on Times Square, is immaterial. It is no requirement of equal protection that all evils of the same genus be eradicated or none at all.

Mr. Justice JACKSON, concurring.

The burden should rest heavily upon one who would persuade us to use the due process clause to strike down a substantive law or ordinance. Even its provident use against municipal regulations frequently disables all government—state, municipal and federal—from dealing with the conduct in question because the requirement of due process is also applicable to State and Federal Governments. Invalidation of a statute or an ordinance on due process grounds leaves ungoverned and ungovernable conduct which many people find objectionable.

Invocation of the equal protection clause, on the other hand, does not disable any governmental body from dealing with the subject at hand. It merely means that the prohibition or regulation must have a broader impact. I regard it as a salutary doctrine that cities, states and the Federal Government must exercise their powers so as not to discriminate between their inhabitants except upon some reasonable differentiation fairly related to the object of regulation. This equality is not merely abstract justice. The framers of the Constitution knew, and we should not forget today, that there is no more effective practical guaranty against arbitrary and unreasonable government than to require that the principles of law which officials would impose upon a minority must be imposed generally. Conversely, nothing opens the door to arbitrary action so effectively as to allow those officials to pick and choose only a few to whom they will apply legislation and thus to escape the political retribution that might be visited upon them if larger numbers were affected. Courts can take no better measure to assure that laws will be just than to require that laws be equal in operation.

In this case, if the City of New York should assume that display of any advertising on vehicles tends and intends to distract the attention of persons using the highways and to increase the dangers of its traffic, I should think it fully within its constitutional powers to forbid it all. *** Instead of such general regulation of advertising, however, the City seeks to reduce the hazard only by saying that while some may, others may not exhibit such appeals. The same display, for example, advertising cigarettes, which this appellant is forbidden to carry on its trucks, may be carried on the trucks of a cigarette dealer and might on the trucks of this appellant if it dealt in cigarettes. And almost an identical advertisement, certainly one of equal size, shape, color and appearance, may be carried by this appellant if it proclaims its own offer to transport cigarettes. But it may not be carried so long as the message is not its own but a cigarette dealer's offer to sell the same cigarettes.

> **Take Note**
>
> What is the difference between advertising to serve one's "own commercial ends" and doing so for hire? Why would a city tolerate one while forbidding the other? Aren't both done to serve the self-interest of the operator of the vehicle?

The question in my mind comes to this. Where individuals contribute to an evil or danger in the same way and to the same degree, may those who do so for hire be prohibited, while those who do so for their own commercial ends but not for hire be allowed to continue? I think the answer has to be that the hireling may be put in a class by himself and may be dealt with differently than those who act on their own. But this is not merely because such a discrimination will enable the lawmaker to diminish the evil. That might be done by many classifications, which I should think wholly unsustainable. It is rather because there is a real difference between doing in self-interest and doing for hire, so that it is one thing to tolerate action from those who act on their own and it is another thing to permit the same action to be promoted for a price.

Points for Discussion

a. Under-Inclusiveness in Regulation

The challenged regulation in <u>Railway Express</u> distinguished between trucks whose sole purpose was to advertise and trucks that engaged in some business in addition to advertising. Of course, if the point of the regulation was, as the government argued, to promote traffic safety by eliminating distractions on the road, then the regulation was far from a comprehensive effort to achieve that end; there would still be many trucks on the road with advertising on the side, and thus there would still be many distractions.

To the extent that there was a problem with the regulation, therefore, it was not with the legitimacy of the government's interest in enacting the regulation—there is plainly a valid interest in promoting traffic safety—but was instead with the extent to which the government's chosen means advanced that interest. The regulation at issue was "under-inclusive," in that it failed to impose the same prohibition on others who were similarly situated, and thus failed completely to address the problem of distractions on the roads. <u>Railway Express</u> demonstrates that, at least when the Court is applying rational-basis review, under-inclusiveness does not mean that the regulation is not rationally related to the government's interest.

In what way was the distinction that the challenged regulation created "rational"? Should it have been enough that the regulation would remove at least some distractions from the road? Why shouldn't a court insist that the legislature treat all similarly situated parties the same? In thinking about this question, consider the implications of an approach that would have invalidated the regulation. If the city sought to promote traffic safety by eliminating distractions, would it also be required to eliminate signs on stores along the streets? To ban talking on a cell phone while driving? If not, who should draw lines of this sort—legislatures or courts?

b. Legitimate Government Interests

The Court in <u>Railway Express</u> treated as legitimate the government's assertion that the regulation was adopted for the purpose of ensuring traffic safety. Suppose that the appellant had offered evidence that the City had adopted the challenged regulation after large campaign contributions to City Council members by owners of conventional, street-side billboards, who did not want to be forced to compete with advertising vehicles. Would the government's assertion that the regulation promotes traffic safety still have qualified as a legitimate interest for purposes of rationality review?

As we saw in Chapter 8 when we considered the Court's decision in *Williamson v. Lee Optical Co.*, 348 U.S. 483 (1955), the answer is generally yes. The Court has repeatedly made clear that a challenged regulation will be upheld under the rational-basis test as long as the government can identify some plausible legitimate interest served by the regulation, even if it was not the "actual" purpose of the regulation and was instead devised by government lawyers defending the regulation in court. *See, e.g., United States Railroad Retirement Bd. v. Fritz*, 449 U.S. 166, 179 (1980) ("It is, of course, 'constitutionally irrelevant whether this reasoning in fact underlay the legislative decision,' because this Court has never insisted that a legislative body articulate its reasons for enacting a statute." (quoting *Flemming v. Nestor*, 363 U.S. 603, 612 (1960)).

Given that the Court will accept any conceivable legitimate interest offered, even if it was not the real purpose of the regulation, isn't rational-basis review in practice no meaningful review at all, and thus an abdication of the judicial role? On the other hand, how would a court determine the "actual" purpose of a regulation? And if the legislature can simply reenact the identical regulation and expressly assert a legitimate purpose, would it make any sense to permit courts to invalidate regulations because the "real" purpose was problematic?

New York City Transit Authority v. Beazer

440 U.S. 568 (1979)

Mr. Justice STEVENS delivered the opinion of the Court.

[The New York City Transit Authority ("TA") employs about 47,000 persons, many of them in positions potentially posing a danger to themselves or the general public. TA enforced a general policy against employing persons who use narcotic drugs. This included persons receiving methadone maintenance treatment for heroin addiction. Two former employees of TA who were dismissed while receiving methadone treatment and two others who were refused employment while receiving methadone treatment filed a class action challenging the policy. The District Court held that TA's blanket exclusion from employment of all persons undergoing methadone treatment violated the Equal Protection Clause of the Fourteenth Amendment, and the Court of Appeals affirmed.]

The Equal Protection Clause of the Fourteenth Amendment [announces] a fundamental principle: the State must govern impartially. General rules that apply evenhandedly to all persons within the jurisdiction unquestionably comply with this principle. Only when a governmental unit adopts a rule that has a special impact on less than all the persons subject to its jurisdiction does the question whether this principle is violated arise.

[The District Court upheld] rules requiring special supervision of methadone users to detect evidence of drug abuse, and excluding them from high-risk employment. [But] the District Court [concluded] that employment in nonsensitive jobs could not be denied to methadone users who had progressed satisfactorily with their treatment for one year, and who, when examined individually, satisfied TA's employment criteria.

[A]ny special rule short of total exclusion that TA might adopt is likely to be less precise—and will assuredly be more costly than the one that it currently enforces. If eligibility is marked at any intermediate point—whether after one year of treatment or later—the classification will inevitably discriminate between employees or applicants equally or almost equally apt to achieve full recovery. Even the District Court's opinion did not rigidly specify one year as a constitutionally mandated measure of the period of treatment that guarantees full recovery from drug addiction. The uncertainties associated with the rehabilitation of heroin addicts precluded it from identifying any bright line marking the point at which the risk of regression ends. [The District Court found that methadone is an effective cure for the physical aspects of heroin addiction, and that the risk of reversion to drug or alcohol abuse declines dramatically after the first few months of treatment, but that 20 to 30 percent of patients on methadone still revert to drug use.] By contrast, the "no drugs" policy now enforced by TA is supported by the legitimate inference that as long as a treatment program (or other drug use) continues, a degree of uncertainty persists. Accordingly, an employment policy that postpones eligibility until the treatment program has been completed, rather than accepting an intermediate point on an uncertain line, is rational. It is neither unprincipled nor invidious in the sense that it implies disrespect for the excluded subclass.

At its simplest, the District Court's conclusion was that TA's rule is broader than necessary to exclude those methadone users who are not actually qualified to work for TA. We may assume not only that this conclusion is correct but also that it is probably unwise for a large employer like TA to rely on a general rule instead of individualized consideration of every job applicant. But these assumptions concern matters of personnel policy that do not implicate the principle safeguarded by the Equal Protection Clause. As the District Court recognized, the special classification created by TA's rule serves the general objectives of safety and efficiency. Moreover, the exclusionary line challenged by respondents "is not one which is directed 'against' any individual or category of persons, but rather it represents a policy choice made by that branch of Government vested with the power to make such choices." Because it does not circumscribe a class of persons characterized by some unpopular trait or affiliation, it does not create or reflect any special likelihood of bias on the part of the ruling majority. Under these circumstances, it is of no constitutional significance that the degree of rationality is not as great with respect to certain ill-defined subparts of the classification as it is with respect to the classification as a whole.

No matter how unwise it may be for TA to refuse employment to individual car cleaners, track repairmen, or bus drivers simply because they are receiving methadone treatment, the Constitution does not authorize a federal court to interfere in that policy decision. [*Reversed.*]

> **Food for Thought**
>
> Is it clear that the challenged rule—which burdens current and former drug users—does not single out a class of persons "characterized by some unpopular trait or affiliation"? Would a rule that accords different treatment to alcoholics create a classification based on an unpopular trait? What consequences would flow from a conclusion that a classification did distinguish on such a basis?

Mr. Justice WHITE, with whom Mr. Justice MARSHALL joins, dissenting.

The question before us is the rationality of placing successfully maintained or recently cured persons in the same category as those just attempting to escape heroin addiction or who have failed to escape it, rather than in with the general population. The asserted justification for the challenged classification is the objective of a capable and reliable work force, and thus the characteristic in question is employability. "Employability," in this regard, does not mean that any particular applicant, much less every member of a given group of applicants, will turn out to be a model worker. Nor does it mean that no such applicant will ever become or be discovered to be a malingerer, thief, alcoholic, or even heroin addict. All employers take such risks. Employability, as the District Court used it in reference to successfully maintained methadone users, means only that the employer is no more likely to find a member of that group to be an unsatisfactory employee than he would an employee chosen from the general population.

Petitioners had every opportunity, but presented nothing to negative the employability of successfully maintained methadone users as distinguished from those who were unsuccessful. *** That 20% to 30% are unsuccessful after one year in a methadone program tells us nothing about the employability of the successful group, and it is the latter category of applicants that the District Court and the Court of Appeals held to be unconstitutionally burdened by the blanket rule disqualifying them from employment.

The District Court and the Court of Appeals were therefore fully justified in finding that petitioners could not reasonably have concluded that the protected group is less employable than the general population and that excluding it "[has] no rational relation to the demands of the jobs to be performed." *** Justification of the blanket exclusion is not furthered by the statement that "any special rule short of total exclusion is likely to be less precise" than the current rule. If the rule were narrowed as the District Court ordered, it would operate more precisely in at least one respect, for many employable persons would no longer be excluded.

Finally, even were the District Court wrong, and even were successfully maintained persons marginally less employable than the average applicant, the blanket exclusion of only these people, when but a few are actually unemployable and when many other groups have varying numbers of unemployable members, is arbitrary and unconstitutional. Many persons now suffer from or may again suffer from some handicap related to employability. But petitioners have singled out respondents—unlike ex-offenders, former alcoholics and mental patients, diabetics, epileptics, and those currently using tranquilizers, for example—for sacrifice to this at best ethereal and likely nonexistent risk of increased unemployability. Such an arbitrary assignment of burdens among classes that are similarly situated with respect to the proffered objectives is the type of invidious choice forbidden by the Equal Protection Clause.

> **Take Note**
>
> Justice White compares TA's policy to the hypothetical policy that the District Court held would have satisfied scrutiny under the Equal Protection Clause. Is it clear that the District Court's proposal would have been equally effective at furthering the TA's interests in safety and efficiency? If not, how would a Court decide when a policy impermissibly burdens some class of persons? If there is at least some danger in employing successfully maintained methadone users—that is, the danger that they might regress to heroin addiction—then what weight should the Court give to that danger in the analysis?

Points for Discussion

a. Over-Inclusiveness in Regulation

Unlike the regulation at issue in *Railway Express*, the regulation at issue in *Beazer* was challenged as *over*-inclusive. The problem was not that it failed to impose on one class of actors a burden that it imposed on others who were similarly situated, but instead that it imposed the burden on others who (at least arguably) were *not* similarly situated. The plaintiffs in *Beazer* argued that even if the government can refuse to employ drug users in certain jobs, because of the risk that their employment would pose to the public welfare, it could not refuse to hire persons undergoing methadone maintenance treatment for at least one year, because members of that class generally do not revert to illicit drug use. An over-inclusive regulation, in other words, regulates more people than necessary in order to accomplish the government's purpose.

Are over-inclusive regulations more problematic than under-inclusive ones? As the class of persons to whom a regulatory burden applies grows, do the protections of the political process increase or decrease?

b. The Point of Rationality Review

What is the objective of rationality review? Is it to "smoke out" classifications that were motivated by animus or prejudice against unpopular and thus politically powerless groups, as the Court implied? If so, how does the Court determine the "real" motivation for the regulation? Is the objective instead to prevent arbitrary regulation, as Justice White suggested? If so, should the Court defer to the legislature's judgment about the rationality of the regulation?

Consider the view that Justice Scalia expressed for the Court in holding that the District of Columbia's ban on handguns violated the Second Amendment:

> **Make the Connection**
>
> We considered the Court's decision in *District of Columbia v. Heller*, 554 U.S. 570 (2008), in Chapter 1.

> [R]ational-basis scrutiny is a mode of analysis we have used when evaluating laws under constitutional commands that are themselves prohibitions on irrational laws. In those cases, "rational basis" is not just the standard of scrutiny, but the very substance of the constitutional guarantee.

To which constitutional provisions was Justice Scalia referring?

c. Burden of Persuasion

Justice White stated in his dissent that the government "presented nothing to negative the employability of successfully maintained methadone users as distinguished from those who were unsuccessful." In his view, in other words, the government bore the burden of demonstrating that its classification was valid. But the Court traditionally has placed the burden on those challenging government regulation that is subject to rationality review to demonstrate that it is not rationally related to some legitimate government interest. Who should bear the burden of persuasion in equal protection cases?

In the two Chapters that follow, we will consider how the Court has addressed government classifications on a variety of bases. Some of the cases—such as those concerning discrimination on the basis of race and gender—will involve the application of heightened forms of scrutiny. Others—such as those concerning discrimination on the basis of age and wealth—involve the application of rational-basis review. As you read the cases—particularly those in the latter category—consider whether the Court has strictly adhered to the approach based on "tiers" of scrutiny, and whether the Court always applies rational-basis review in the same way that it did in the cases that we have just considered.

Executive Summary of this Chapter

The Equal Protection Clause of the Fourteenth Amendment imposes some limits on the ability of the states to engage in certain forms of discrimination. The Court has held that the Due Process Clause of the Fifth Amendment, which applies to the federal government, includes an equal protection component. *Bolling v. Sharpe* (1954). The same standards apply to evaluate state and federal action under the equal protection principle. *Buckley v. Valeo* (1976); *Adarand Constructors, Inc. v. Pena* (1995).

The Court generally reviews Equal Protection challenges to government classifications by considering the nature of the classification, the government's interest in the challenged regulation, and the relationship between the government's interest and the classification. The extent to which the Court insists on particularly weighty interests, accords deference to the government's judgment, and tolerates imperfect means to accomplish the government's ends depends upon which **level of scrutiny** the Court applies.

Under **strict scrutiny**, a law will be upheld only if it is "narrowly tailored" to advance a "compelling" government interest. *Adarand v. Pena* (1995). Under **intermediate scrutiny**, the Court will uphold a law only if it is "substantially related" to an "important" government interest. *United States v. Virginia* (1996). Under the **rational-basis test** (or **rationality review**), a law will be upheld if it is "rationally related" to a "legitimate" government interest. *New York City Transit Authority v. Beazer* (1979).

In deciding whether to apply a level of scrutiny more searching than rational-basis review, the Court sometimes considers whether the group disadvantaged by the challenged regulation is (1) a "discrete and insular" minority that is (2) the victim of societal prejudice and (3) unable to achieve adequate protection through the ordinary operation of the political process. *United States v. Carolene Products Co.* (1938).

Rational-basis review is highly deferential. When the Court applies rational-basis review, the fact that the challenged regulation is **under-inclusive**—that is, fails fully to address all manifestations of the problem that it is designed to remedy—generally will not be a sufficient basis for invalidation of the regulation. *Railway Express Agency v. New York* (1949). Similarly, the fact that a regulation is **over-inclusive**—that is, regulates more people than is arguably necessary to achieve its goal—is not generally a basis for invalidation under the rational-basis test. *New York City Transit Authority v. Beazer* (1979).

POINT-COUNTERPOINT

Was *Bolling v. Sharpe*, 347 U.S. 497 (1954), **correctly decided?**

POINT: GREGORY E. MAGGS

Our Constitution contains many great features. It establishes a democratic federal government in which powers are checked and balanced. It guarantees that all of the states will have a republican form of government. It bans slavery. It protects the freedom of speech and freedom of the press. The list could go on and on.

But any fair assessment of the Constitution must acknowledge that our Constitution also contains serious flaws. It does not require Congress to create any lower federal courts. It does not say whether states can secede from the Union. While the Constitution spells out how the federal government can enter treaties, it does not specify how the government can extricate itself from them. The Seventh Amendment guarantees a right to a jury trial in any civil case in which the value in controversy exceeds $20 without any provision to adjust this figure for inflation.

Very high among the list of flaws is the following defect: The Constitution contains no provision requiring the federal government to treat all persons equally. Although the Fourteenth Amendment has an Equal Protection Clause, by its own terms, this clause applies only to the states. Nothing comparable limits the federal government. But as a matter of policy, surely the federal government should not have the power to discriminate on the basis of race or otherwise deny the equal protection of laws.

This serious defect in the Constitution could have been remedied in two ways: legitimately or illegitimately. A legitimate way of addressing the problem would have been to use the procedures specified in Article V to amend the Constitution to add a federal Equal Protection Clause. Amendments have cured other defects in the Constitution: they have guaranteed a freedom of religion, they have banned slavery, they have given women the right to vote, and so forth. A properly adopted amendment similarly could have imposed an equal protection requirement on the federal government.

The Supreme Court, however, chose to remedy the problem in an illegitimate manner in <u>Bolling</u>. The Court simply declared by fiat that the federal government must provide equal protection. It cited no provision in the Constitution for this result. It simply said that any other result would be unthinkable. This decision was wrong because nothing in the Constitution gives the Supreme Court the power to amend the Constitution to remedy the document's shortcomings.

Some people might argue that ending racial discrimination is so important that any process to achieve that goal is warranted. In other words, in truly extreme cases, the ends can justify the means, however illegitimate the means otherwise might be. Maybe you could think of an outrageous hypothetical in which nearly everyone would concede this point. But *Bolling* was not such a case. Requiring the federal government to provide Equal Protection is not controversial. The Constitution could have been amended to achieve the same result.

————————

COUNTERPOINT: PETER J. SMITH

It is difficult to dispute that the Constitution as originally understood did not prohibit the federal government from discriminating on the basis of race; indeed, the original document expressly *precluded* Congress from banning the slave trade—a practice that actively institutionalized racial inequality—for 20 years. The original Constitution was indeed, as Professor Maggs notes, imperfect.

Was the Court's decision in *Bolling* an illegitimate attempt to remedy that serious imperfection? I believe that it was not, for three related reasons. First, the original document has been formally amended in ways that bear directly on the federal government's authority to discriminate on the basis of race. The Thirteenth Amendment applies to more than simply action by the states; it provides, categorically, that "[n]either slavery nor involuntary servitude *** *shall exist* within the United States ***." This language presumably would prevent Congress from enacting legislation mandating better protections for white workers than for African-American workers, and thereby replicating a system functionally equivalent to slavery. If this is true, then it is not a big leap to conclude that Congress is constrained, as a more general matter, from exercising its authority in a way that subordinates persons solely based on an arbitrary classification, such as race or national origin. And although the Fourteenth Amendment's provisions apply by their terms only to the states, their response to slavery and institutionalized discrimination can be read to embody a deeper constitutional anti-discrimination principle.

Second, even if we assume that the Reconstruction Amendments, standing alone, do not impose an equal protection principle on the federal government, it oversimplifies the nature of constitutional change—and threatens serious damage to the Constitution itself—to maintain that the only remedy for constitutional defects—including a defect so profound that it would permit our nation's government to discriminate on the basis of race—is to rely on the amendment process to cure constitutional imperfections. In practice, the amendment process is often as imperfect as the document it is designed to improve.

To see why, ask whether you think an amendment imposing the equal protection principle on the federal government would have been ratified by three-quarters of the states in 1954, when the Court decided *Bolling*. If you can think of 13 states (out of the 48 that were states at the time) that would not have ratified—because, for example, they were aggressively seeking to *preserve* segregation and institutionalized white supremacy—then you have your answer. (If you are wondering why the southern states ratified the Reconstruction Amendments, it was because they were forced to as a condition of reentry to the Union.) Then ask yourself whether you would consider our Constitution legitimate if the federal government were permitted to discriminate on the basis of race (or gender or other suspect grounds). Would you be comfortable living under a Constitution that, to take a timely example, permitted the federal government, in the name of national security, to prevent all persons of Arab descent from flying on planes or riding on trains and buses or attending sporting events?

Third, if the Court's decision in *Bolling* was wrong—because it failed properly to implement the original meaning of the Constitution, and because that meaning had never been changed pursuant to the formal amendment process—then the Court's decision in *Brown v. Board of Education of Topeka*, 347 U.S. 483 (1954), decided the same day, was almost certainly wrong, too. After all, virtually all commentators who have examined the question have concluded that the Framers of the Fourteenth Amendment did not understand it to prohibit segregated schools, and the Court in *Brown* very openly eschewed the original meaning in deciding whether segregation was constitutional.

Yet *Bolling* and *Brown* were a central reason why so many people today continue to find our Constitution a legitimate charter. I do not agree with Professor Maggs that the Court's decision in *Bolling* was wrong; but even if it was, it was a small price to pay to maintain a Constitution that we can continue to respect and admire—and, ultimately, follow.

CHAPTER 11

Status-Based Classifications

We saw in Chapter 10 how government regularly classifies on all sorts of bases, and how usually those classifications are defensible. Surely, for example, a state must be permitted to deny driver's licenses to children, or to accord different tax treatment to corporations and individuals. The Court reviews such classifications solely for rationality, a highly deferential standard that largely leaves the question of line-drawing to legislative (or at least non-judicial) action.

But some classifications are more problematic. The context in which the Fourteenth Amendment was ratified, for example, makes clear—if nothing else—that classifications based on race are suspect, and accordingly must be subjected to more searching scrutiny. Classifications based on race are suspect not merely because of history; race is an immutable characteristic, and (to borrow the _Carolene Products_ framework that we considered in Chapter 10) members of racial minorities historically have been the victims of societal prejudice and lacked significant electoral power. And race is rarely, if ever, a relevant characteristic for government decision-making. (Whether it is ever relevant will be the focus of our consideration of affirmative action programs later in this Chapter.) We begin this Chapter with a consideration of the constitutionality of government classifications on the basis of race.

Race plainly is not the only immutable characteristic that is arguably irrelevant to government decision-making. Are government decisions based on gender similarly suspect? What about decisions based on age, sexual orientation, disability, or other status-based characteristics? After our consideration of race-based classifications, we turn to these classifications. As you read the materials in this Chapter, pay close attention to (1) the process by which the Court identifies classifications that trigger heightened judicial scrutiny and (2) the variety of forms of scrutiny that the Court applies to such classifications.

A. Classifications Based on Race and National Origin

1. Historical Perspective: Pre-Reconstruction

As we saw in Chapter 1, slavery was a thorny issue at the Constitutional Convention. Several delegates from Northern states wanted the Constitution to prohibit it, but the Southern states sought to preserve the institution. The resulting compromise acknowledged, sometimes circumspectly and awkwardly, the institution of slavery, and in fact effectively preserved it for at least 20 years. Article I, § 2, cl. 3 treated slaves as three-fifths of a person for purposes of apportionment of Congress; Article I, § 9, cl. 1 prohibited Congress from ending the slave trade before 1808, and Article V prohibited the amendment of that provision before 1808; and Article IV, § 2, cl. 3 provided for the return of fugitive slaves. There was, of course, no equal protection clause in the original Constitution.

Laws permitting slavery—and protecting the rights of slaveholders—obviously classified, in the most invidious way, on the basis of race. It was therefore a stretch to argue that the Constitution as originally ratified and understood prohibited laws discriminating on the basis of race. The case that follows addressed the constitutional status of slaves and slavery before the Civil War. It is perhaps the Court's most infamous decision, and by most accounts it helped to precipitate the Civil War.

Dred Scott v. Sandford

60 U.S. 393 (1857)

Mr. Chief Justice TANEY delivered the opinion of the Court.

[Dred Scott, a slave owned by Dr. John Emerson, was taken from the slave state of Missouri to the free state of Illinois and later to the free territory of Wisconsin. In 1838, after Emerson married, he summoned Scott back to Missouri. Upon Emerson's death, Scott filed a diversity suit in federal court in Missouri against John Sandford, a citizen of New York and the administrator of Emerson's estate, for assault and imprisonment. Scott claimed that his residence in Illinois and later the Wisconsin territory made him a free person. In response, Sandford moved to dismiss on the ground that the court lacked jurisdiction. Sandford asserted that Scott was not a citizen, and therefore that there was no diversity of citizenship.]

The question is simply this: Can a negro, whose ancestors were imported into this country, and sold as slaves, become a member of the political community formed and brought into existence by the Constitution of the United States, and as such become entitled to all the rights, and privileges, and immunities, guaranteed by that instrument to the citizen? *** We think they are not, and that they are not included, and were not intended to be included, under the word "citizens" in the Constitution, and can therefore claim none of the rights and privileges which that instrument provides for and secures to citizens of the United States. On the contrary, they were at that time considered as a subordinate and inferior class of beings, who had been subjugated by the dominant race, and, whether emancipated or not, yet remained subject to their authority, and had no rights or privileges but such as those who held the power and the Government might choose to grant them. *** [N]o State can, by any act or law of its own, passed since the adoption of the Constitution, introduce a new member into the political community created by the Constitution of the United States. It cannot make him a member of this community by making him a member of its own.

[Because the Court concluded that Scott was not a "citizen" of the United States—regardless of whether he was ever a citizen of Missouri, under Missouri state laws—it held that the court lacked diversity jurisdiction. Notwithstanding the Court's conclusion that it lacked subject-matter jurisdiction over Scott's suit, it turned to the question whether Scott had become free by residing in the territories. In this inquiry, the Court addressed the constitutionality of the Missouri Compromise, which Congress had enacted in 1820 to abolish slavery in territories north of the 36° 30' latitude line, except within the boundaries of what became the state of Missouri.]

[T]he difficulty which meets us at the threshold of this part of the inquiry is, whether Congress was authorized to pass this law under any of the powers granted to it by the Constitution; for if the authority is not given by that instrument, it is the duty of this court to declare it void and inoperative, and incapable of conferring freedom upon any one who is held as a slave. ***

[T]he rights of property are united with the rights of person, and placed on the same ground by the fifth amendment to the Constitution, which provides that no person shall be deprived of life, liberty, and property, without due process of law. And an act of Congress which deprives a citizen of the United States of his liberty or property, merely because he came himself or brought his property into a particular Territory of the United States, and who had committed no offence against the laws, could hardly be dignified with the name of due process of law.

> ### Make the Connection
>
> Many commentators regard this passage as the birth of "substantive due process," which we considered in Chapter 8. Regardless of what one thinks of modern substantive due process doctrine, does this genesis—a conclusion that Congress lacks authority to regulate slavery because slaves are "property" of which a person cannot be deprived merely by transporting the slaves into a territory—render the doctrine problematic?

[T]he right of property in a slave is distinctly and expressly affirmed in the Constitution. The right to traffic in it, like an ordinary article of merchandise and property, was guarantied to the citizens of the United States, in every State that might desire it, for twenty years. And the Government in express terms is pledged to protect it in all future time, if the slave escapes from his owner.

FYI

The Court here is referring to Article I, § 9, cl. 1, which protected the slave trade until 1808, and Article IV, § 2, cl. 3, which provides that "No Person held to Service or Labour in one State, under the Laws thereof, escaping into another, shall, in Consequence of any Law or Regulation therein, be discharged from such Service or Labour, but shall be delivered up on Claim of the Party to whom such Service or Labour may be due." After the Civil War, the latter provision was superseded by the Thirteenth Amendment, which prohibits slavery.

This is done in plain words—too plain to be misunderstood. And no word can be found in the Constitution which gives Congress a greater power over slave property, or which entitles property of that kind to less protection than property of any other description. The only power conferred is the power coupled with the duty of guarding and protecting the owner in his rights. Upon these considerations, it is the opinion of the court that the [Missouri Compromise] is not warranted by the Constitution, and is therefore void; and that neither Dred Scott himself, nor any of his family, were made free by being carried into [a free territory]; even if they had been carried there by the owner, with the intention of becoming a permanent resident.

[Scott also contends] that he is made free by being taken to [the] State of Illinois, independently of his residence in the territory of the United States; and being so made free, he was not again reduced to a state of slavery by being brought back to Missouri. *** As Scott was a slave when taken into the State of Illinois by his owner, and was there held as such, and brought back in that character, his *status*, as free or slave, depended on the laws of Missouri, and not of Illinois.

[Before he had filed his federal suit, Scott had sued for freedom in Missouri state court, relying on the established principle of Missouri state law that once a slave became free by virtue of residence in a free state, he would remain free upon his return to Missouri. When his suit reached the Missouri Supreme Court in 1852, however, the Court reversed long-standing precedent, abandoned the principle of "once a free man, always a free man," and held that Scott was not a free man.]

Upon the whole, therefore, it is the judgment of this court, that it appears by the record before us that the plaintiff in error is not a citizen of Missouri, in the sense in which that word is used in the Constitution; and that the Circuit Court of the United States, for that reason, had no jurisdiction in the case, and could give no judgment in it. Its judgment for the defendant must, consequently, be reversed, and a mandate issued, directing the suit to be dismissed for want of jurisdiction.

[Justice CURTIS and Justice McLEAN dissented.]

Points for Discussion

a. Judicial Review and Judicial Restraint

The <u>Dred Scott</u> case was only the second time that the Court declared a federal statute unconstitutional. (The first, of course, was <u>Marbury</u>.) The Court's conclusion that the Missouri Compromise exceeded Congress's power was particularly striking in light of the Court's prior holding that it lacked subject-matter jurisdiction over the case.

Many accounts of the decision suggest that the Court initially planned to decide the case on the ground that the Missouri Supreme Court should have the final word on the content of Missouri law—specifically, on whether, under Missouri law, a slave who had lived in a free state remained a slave in Missouri. Pressure from President-elect James Buchanan and the sense that the political branches were unable to resolve the impasse over slavery, however, led the Court to attempt to put the question beyond the realm of ordinary politics. Is such a motivation ever a legitimate basis for a particular constitutional interpretation? If so, was it a legitimate basis in <u>Dred Scott</u>?

b. The Constitution and Slavery

As noted above, the Constitution acknowledged (and, at least for a time, explicitly preserved) the institution of slavery. Did the Constitution's recognition of slavery effectively compel the Court to conclude as it did in <u>Dred Scott</u>? Or did the Court have room—or even a moral obligation—to conclude otherwise?

c. State Law and Slavery

The Court's decision in <u>Dred Scott</u> left Scott's fate to Missouri law, which the Missouri Supreme Court had construed a few years before, in what was widely viewed as a partisan, aggressively pro-slavery decision, to retain as slaves even those who had lived in free states and territories. In that case—*Scott v. Emerson*, 15 Mo. 576 (1852)—the Court declared:

> As to the consequences of slavery, they are much more hurtful to the master than the slave. There is no comparison between the slave in the United States and the cruel, uncivilized negro in Africa. When the condition of our slaves is contrasted with the state of their miserable race in Africa; when their civilization, intelligence and instruction in religious truths are considered, and the means now employed to restore them to the country from which they have been torn, bearing with them the blessings of civilized life, we are almost persuaded, that the introduction of slavery amongst us was, in the providence of God, who makes the evil passions of men subservient to His own glory, a means of placing that unhappy race within the pale of civilized nations.

Was the United States Supreme Court in 1857 truly bound to interpret the Constitution to indulge this sort of reasoning?

————————————

2. Facial Discrimination Against Minorities

After the Civil War, Congress proposed, and the states ratified, the Thirteenth, Fourteenth, and Fifteenth Amendments. The Thirteenth Amendment outlawed slavery, and the first sentence of the Fourteenth Amendment, which provides that "All persons born or naturalized in the United States, and subject to the jurisdiction thereof, are citizens of the United States and the State wherein they reside," overruled *Dred Scott*.

The Equal Protection Clause of the Fourteenth Amendment—unlike Section 1 of the Fifteenth Amendment—does not refer explicitly to race; instead, it extends its protection to "any person" within the jurisdiction of the state. But whatever the scope of its application to classifications other than those based on race, there is little doubt that it imposes severe limits on the power of states to discriminate on the basis of race.

In this section, we consider state action that discriminates on its face against racial minorities. A state law or regulation discriminates on its face against racial minorities when the very terms of the provision treat members of one or more minority races differently from members of other races. Can such state action ever be justified?

———————

Strauder v. West Virginia

100 U.S. 303 (1879)

MR. JUSTICE STRONG delivered the opinion of the court.

The plaintiff in error, a colored man, was indicted for murder in the Circuit Court of Ohio County, in West Virginia, on the 20th of October, 1874, and upon trial was convicted and sentenced. [The grand and petit juries were constituted pursuant to a state law that provided: "All white male persons who are twenty-one years of age and who are citizens of this State shall be liable to serve as jurors, except as herein provided." The defendant challenged his conviction on the ground that blacks were excluded from jury service.]

It is to be observed that the [question] is not whether a colored man, when an indictment has been preferred against him, has a right to a grand or a petit jury composed in whole or in part of persons of his own race or color, but it is whether, in the composition or selection of jurors by whom he is to be indicted or tried, all persons of his race or color may be excluded by law, solely because of their race or color, so that by no possibility can any colored man sit upon the jury.

[The Fourteenth Amendment] is one of a series of constitutional provisions having a common purpose; namely, securing to a race recently emancipated, a race that through many generations had been held in slavery, all the civil rights that the superior race enjoy. *** The words of the amendment, it is true, are prohibitory, but they contain a necessary implication of a positive immunity, or right, most valuable to the colored race—the right to exemption from unfriendly legislation against them distinctively as colored, exemption from legal discriminations, implying inferiority in civil society, lessening the security of their enjoyment of the rights which others enjoy, and discriminations which are steps towards reducing them to the condition of a subject race.

That the West Virginia statute respecting juries—the statute that controlled the selection of the grand and petit jury in the case of the plaintiff in error—is such a discrimination ought not to be doubted. Nor would it be if the persons excluded by it were white men. If in those States where the colored people constitute a majority of the entire population a law should be enacted excluding all white men from jury service, thus denying to them the privilege of participating equally with the blacks in the administration of justice, we apprehend no one would be heard to claim that it would not be a denial to white men of the equal protection of the laws. Nor if a law should be passed excluding all naturalized Celtic Irishmen, would there by any doubt of its inconsistency with the spirit of the amendment. The very fact that colored people are singled out and expressly denied by a statute all right to participate in the administration of the law, as jurors, because of their color, though they are citizens, and may be in other respects fully qualified, is practically a brand upon them, affixed by the law, an assertion of their inferiority, and a stimulant to that race prejudice which is an impediment to securing to individuals of the race that equal justice which the law aims to secure to all others.

> **Make the Connection**
>
> When the Court decided *Strauder*, it had not yet held that (most of) the protections of the Bill of Rights were incorporated by the Fourteenth Amendment. Accordingly, the Court did not rely on the Sixth Amendment right to trial by jury. We considered the doctrine of incorporation in Chapter 7.

The right to a trial by jury is guaranteed to every citizen of West Virginia by the Constitution of that State, and the constitution of juries is a very essential part of the protection such a mode of trial is intended to secure. It is well known that prejudices often exist against particular classes in the community, which sway the judgment of jurors, and which, therefore, operate in some cases to deny to persons of those classes the full enjoyment of that protection which others enjoy. *** The framers of the constitutional amendment must have known full well the existence of such prejudice and its likelihood to continue against the manumitted slaves and their race, and that knowledge was doubtless a motive that led to the amendment.

In view of these considerations, it is hard to see why the statute of West Virginia should not be regarded as discriminating against a colored man when he is put upon trial for an alleged criminal offence against the State. It is not easy to comprehend how it can be said that while every white man is entitled to a trial by a jury selected from persons of his own race or color, or, rather, selected without discrimination

> **Take Note**
>
> Under the Court's reasoning, it seems clear that the exclusion of blacks from jury service violates the Equal Protection rights of those who are excluded. But the Court's holding is that the *defendant's* rights under the Clause also are violated by such exclusion. What leap must the Court make to reach that conclusion? Does the Court adequately explain that leap here?

against his color, and a negro is not, the latter is equally protected by the law with the former. Is not protection of life and liberty against race or color prejudice, a right, a legal right, under the constitutional amendment? And how can it be maintained that compelling a colored man to submit to a trial for his life by a jury drawn from a panel from which the State has expressly excluded every man of his race, because of color alone, however well qualified in other respects, is not a denial to him of equal legal protection?

We do not say that within the limits from which it is not excluded by the amendment a State may not prescribe the qualifications of its jurors, and in so doing make discriminations. It may confine the selection to males, to freeholders, to citizens, to persons within certain ages, or to persons having educational qualifications. We do not believe the Fourteenth Amendment was ever intended to prohibit this. *** Its aim was against discrimination because of race or color. As we have said more than once, its design was to protect an emancipated race, and to strike down all possible legal discriminations against those who belong to it.

[T]he statute of West Virginia, discriminating in the selection of jurors, as it does, against negroes because of their color, amounts to a denial of the equal protection of the laws to a colored man when he is put upon trial for an alleged offence against the State ***. The judgment of the Supreme Court of West Virginia will be reversed, and the case remitted with instructions to reverse the judgment of the Circuit Court.

[Justice FIELD's dissent, which was joined by Justice CLIFFORD, is omitted.]

————————

Points for Discussion

a. Equal Protection and Juries

The law at issue in <u>Strauder</u> discriminated on its face, categorically excluding non-whites from jury service. The Court held that a state may not categorically exclude persons from jury service solely because of their race. Jury selection, however, is a complicated process that usually involves the parties to the litigation, as well. Most states permit attorneys for the parties, in both civil and criminal cases, to exclude up to a certain number of prospective jurors without having to give a reason. Laws authorizing these "peremptory challenges" do not classify on the basis of race, but they certainly could be used (by attorneys for the government or for private parties) intentionally to exclude jurors because of their race unless some restrictions are placed on their use.

The Court has held that the use of peremptory challenges purposefully to exclude jurors of a particular race violates the Constitution. *Batson v. Kentucky*, 476 U.S. 79 (1986). The

Make the Connection

The Court has held that the prohibitions in the Fourteenth Amendment apply only to state, as opposed to private, action. How can racially discriminatory peremptory challenges by private litigants violate the Amendment? We will consider that question—and the Court's decision in <u>Edmonson</u>—in Chapter 19.

Court has held, moreover, that the prohibition applies not simply to peremptory challenges by prosecutors acting for the state, but also to the discriminatory use of challenges by criminal defendants, see *Georgia v. McCollum*, 505 U.S. 42 (1992), and civil litigants, see *Edmonson v. Leesville Concrete Co., Inc.*, 500 U.S. 614 (1991). The Court has also held that the Equal Protection Clause prohibits the use of peremptory challenges purposefully to exclude women from juries. See *J.E.B. v. Alabama ex rel. T.B.*, 511 U.S. 127 (1994).

b. Original Intent and Expected Application

The Court in <u>Strauder</u> declared that the "aim" of the Fourteenth Amendment "was to protect an emancipated race, and to strike down all possible legal discriminations against those who belong to it." But the Court also suggested that the Equal Protection Clause forbids *all* discrimination on the basis of race, regardless of which race is the victim of discrimination. Does the second conclusion necessarily follow from the first? If it does, then why was it so clear to the Court that the Equal Protection Clause does not protect against discrimination on the basis of gender? As we will see later in this Chapter, that view did not endure.

In Chapter 10, we saw that the Court has extended the equal protection principle to action by the federal government. The case that follows was the first case to do so, although it ultimately upheld the challenged federal action. The case arose as a challenge to the federal government's policy during World War II of internment of persons of Japanese descent, including American citizens.

Korematsu v. United States

323 U.S. 214 (1944)

Mr. Justice BLACK delivered the opinion of the Court.

The petitioner, an American citizen of Japanese descent, was convicted in a federal district court for remaining in San Leandro, California, a "Military Area," contrary to Civilian Exclusion Order No. 34 of the Commanding General of the Western Command, U.S. Army, which directed that after May 9, 1942, all persons of Japanese ancestry should be excluded from that area. No question was raised as to petitioner's loyalty to the United States.

It should be noted, to begin with, that all legal restrictions which curtail the civil rights of a single racial group are immediately suspect. That is not to say that all such restrictions are unconstitutional. It is to say that courts must subject them to the most rigid scrutiny. Pressing public necessity may sometimes justify the existence of such restrictions; racial antagonism never can.

[W]e are unable to conclude that it was beyond the war power of Congress and the Executive to exclude those of Japanese ancestry from the West Coast war area at the time they did. [E]xclusion from a threatened area [has] a definite and close relationship to the prevention of espionage and sabotage. The military authorities, charged with the primary responsibility of defending our shores, concluded that curfew provided inadequate protection and ordered exclusion. They did so *** in accordance with Congressional authority to the military to say who should, and who should not, remain in the threatened areas.

Take Note

Justice Black prided himself on being a strict constitutional textualist. Yet he did not cite a constitutional provision to support the assertion that "*all* legal restrictions" discriminating on the basis of race, including those imposed by the federal government, are suspect. What constitutional provision renders federal decisions that discriminate on the basis of race suspect?

Like curfew, exclusion of those of Japanese origin was deemed necessary because of the presence of an unascertained number of disloyal members of the group, most of whom we have no doubt were loyal to this country. It was because we could not reject the finding of the military authorities that it was impossible to bring about an immediate segregation of the disloyal from the loyal that we sustained [in *Hirabayashi v. United States*, 320 U.S. 81 (1943),] the validity of the curfew order as applying to the whole group. In the instant case, temporary exclusion of the entire group was rested by the military on the same ground. The judgment that exclusion of the whole group was for the same reason a military imperative answers the contention that the exclusion was in the nature of group punishment based on antagonism to those of Japanese origin. That there were members of the group who retained loyalties to Japan has been confirmed by investigations made subsequent to the exclusion. Approximately five thousand American citizens of Japanese ancestry refused to swear unqualified allegiance to the United States and to renounce allegiance to the Japanese Emperor, and several thousand evacuees requested repatriation to Japan.

FYI

Military officials promulgated the Order at issue here pursuant to authority delegated by the President in Executive Order 9066, which sought to prevent "espionage" and "sabotage" by authorizing military commanders to designate "military areas" from which "any or all persons" could be excluded. In addition to issuing Exclusion Order No. 34, which prohibited individuals of Japanese descent from *entering* the area, the Commanding General issued Proclamation No. 4, which prohibited the same individuals from *leaving* the area. To avoid violating these contradictory orders, persons of Japanese descent were forced to report to "Assembly Centers." Some detainees were eventually released but not allowed to return to the prohibited zones; others were shipped to "Relocation Centers," also known as internment camps.

[W]e are not unmindful of the hardships imposed by [the order] upon a large group of American citizens. But hardships are part of war, and war is an aggregation of hardships. All citizens alike, both in and out of uniform, feel the impact of war in greater or lesser measure. Citizenship has its responsibilities as well as its privileges, and in time of war the burden is always heavier. Compulsory exclusion of large groups of citizens from their homes, except under circumstances of direst emergency and peril, is inconsistent with our basic governmental institutions. But when under conditions of modern warfare our shores are threatened by hostile forces, the power to protect must be commensurate with the threatened danger.

Take Note

The Court assessed the constitutionality only of the exclusion order, but declined to review the detention order. Given the Court's reasoning in upholding the exclusion order, is there reason to think that the Court would have reached a different conclusion with respect to the detention order, if confronted with it?

We are [being] asked to pass at this time upon the whole subsequent detention program in both assembly and relocation centers ***. Since the petitioner has not been convicted of failing to report or to remain in an assembly or relocation center, we cannot in this case determine the validity of those separate provisions of the order. ***

Some of the members of the Court are of the view that evacuation and detention in an Assembly Center were inseparable. *** It is said that we are dealing here with the case of imprisonment of a citizen in a concentration camp solely because of his ancestry, without evidence or inquiry concerning his loyalty and good disposition towards the United States. Our task would be simple, our duty clear, were this a case involving the imprisonment of a loyal citizen in a concentration camp because of racial prejudice. Regardless of the true nature of the assembly and relocation centers—and we deem it unjustifiable to call them concentration camps with all the ugly connotations that term implies—we are dealing specifically with nothing but an exclusion order. Korematsu was not excluded from the Military Area because of hostility to him or his race. He was excluded because we are at war with the Japanese Empire, because the properly constituted military authorities feared an invasion of our West Coast and felt constrained to take proper security measures, because they decided that the military urgency of the situation demanded that all citizens of Japanese ancestry be segregated from the West Coast temporarily, and finally, because Congress, reposing its confidence in this time of war in our military leaders—as inevitably it must—determined that they should have the power to do just this. There was evidence of disloyalty on the part of some, the military authorities considered that the need for action was great, and time was short. We cannot—by availing ourselves of the calm perspective of hindsight—now say that at that time these actions were unjustified.

Mr. Justice FRANKFURTER, concurring.

[T]he validity of action under the war power must be judged wholly in the context of war. That action is not to be stigmatized as lawless because like action in times of peace would be lawless. To talk about a military order that expresses an allowable judgment of war needs by those entrusted with the duty of conducting war as "an unconstitutional order" is to suffuse a part of the Constitution with an atmosphere of unconstitutionality. *** If a military order such as that under review does not transcend the means appropriate for conducting war, such action by the military is as constitutional as would be any authorized action by the Interstate Commerce Commission within the limits of the constitutional power to regulate commerce. *** To find that the Constitution does not forbid the military measures now complained of does not carry with it approval of that which Congress and the Executive did. That is their business, not ours.

Mr. Justice MURPHY, dissenting.

This exclusion of "all persons of Japanese ancestry, both alien and non-alien," from the Pacific Coast area on a plea of military necessity in the absence of martial law *** goes over "the very brink of constitutional power" and falls into the ugly abyss of racism.

In dealing with matters relating to the prosecution and progress of a war, we must accord great respect and consideration to the judgments of the military authorities who are on the scene and who have full knowledge of the military facts. *** At the same time, however, it is essential that there be definite limits to military discretion, especially where martial law has not been declared. Individuals must not be left impoverished of their constitutional rights on a plea of military necessity that has neither substance nor support.

The judicial test of whether the Government, on a plea of military necessity, can validly deprive an individual of any of his constitutional rights is whether the deprivation is reasonably related to a public danger that is so "immediate, imminent, and impending" as not to admit of delay and not to permit the intervention of ordinary constitutional processes to alleviate the danger. [The challenged order] clearly does not meet that test.

It must be conceded that the military and naval situation in the spring of 1942 was such as to generate a very real fear of invasion of the Pacific Coast, accompanied by fears of sabotage and espionage in that area. *** But the exclusion, either temporarily or permanently, of all persons with Japanese blood in their veins has no such reasonable relation. And that relation is lacking because the exclusion order necessarily must rely for its reasonableness upon the assumption that all persons of Japanese ancestry may have a dangerous tendency to commit sabotage and espionage and to aid our Japanese enemy in other ways. It is difficult to believe that reason, logic or experience could be marshalled in support of such an assumption.

That this forced exclusion was the result in good measure of this erroneous assumption of racial guilt rather than bona fide military necessity is evidenced by the Commanding General's Final Report on the evacuation from the Pacific Coast area[, which] refers to all individuals of Japanese descent as "subversive," as belonging to "an enemy race" whose "racial strains are undiluted," and as constituting "over 112,000 potential enemies *** at large today" along the Pacific Coast. In support of this blanket condemnation of all persons of Japanese descent, however, no reliable evidence is cited to show that such individuals were generally disloyal, or had generally so conducted themselves in this area as to constitute a special menace to defense installations or war industries, or had otherwise by their behavior furnished reasonable ground for their exclusion as a group.

The main reasons relied upon by those responsible for the forced evacuation, therefore, [appear] to be largely an accumulation of much of the misinformation, half-truths and insinuations that for years have been directed against Japanese Americans by people with racial and economic prejudices ***. A military judgment based upon such racial and sociological considerations is not entitled to the great weight ordinarily given the judgments based upon strictly military considerations.

No one denies, of course, that there were some disloyal persons of Japanese descent on the Pacific Coast who did all in their power to aid their ancestral land. Similar disloyal activities have been engaged in by many persons of German, Italian and even more pioneer stock in our country. But to infer that examples of individual disloyalty prove group disloyalty and justify discriminatory action against the entire group is to deny that under our system of law individual guilt is the sole basis for deprivation of rights. *** To give constitutional sanction to that inference in this case, however well-intentioned may have been the military command on the Pacific Coast, is to adopt one of the cruelest of the rationales used by our enemies to destroy the dignity of the individual and to encourage and open the door to discriminatory actions against other minority groups in the passions of tomorrow.

> **FYI**
>
> At the time that the orders in question were issued, the United States was also at war with Nazi Germany, whose treatment of minority groups was well known. Is Justice Murphy's implicit comparison of the United States' internment policy to Nazi policy fair?

I dissent, therefore, from this legalization of racism. *** All residents of this nation are kin in some way by blood or culture to a foreign land. Yet they are primarily and necessarily a part of the new and distinct civilization of the United States. They must accordingly be treated at all times as the heirs of the American experiment and as entitled to all the rights and freedoms guaranteed by the Constitution.

Mr. Justice JACKSON, dissenting.

Korematsu was born on our soil, of parents born in Japan. The Constitution makes him a citizen of the United States by nativity and a citizen of California by residence. No claim is made that he is not loyal to this country. There is no suggestion that apart from the matter involved here he is not law-abiding and well disposed. Korematsu, however, has been convicted of an act not commonly a crime. It consists merely of being present in the state whereof he is a citizen, near the place where he was born, and where all his life he has lived.

A citizen's presence in the locality [was] made a crime only if his parents were of Japanese birth. Had Korematsu been one of four—the others being, say, a German alien enemy, an Italian alien enemy, and a citizen of American-born ancestors, convicted of treason but out on parole—only Korematsu's presence would have violated the order. The difference between their innocence and his crime would result, not from anything he did, said, or thought, different than they, but only in that he was born of different racial stock.

Now, if any fundamental assumption underlies our system, it is that guilt is personal and not inheritable. Even if all of one's antecedents had been convicted of treason, the

Constitution forbids its penalties to be visited upon him, for it provides that "no Attainder of Treason shall work Corruption of Blood, or Forfeiture except during the Life of the Person attained." Article III, § 3, cl. 2. But here is an attempt to make an otherwise innocent act a crime merely because this prisoner is the son of parents as to whom he had no choice, and belongs to a race from which there is no way to resign. If Congress in peace-time legislation should enact such a criminal law, I should suppose this Court would refuse to enforce it.

It would be impracticable and dangerous idealism to expect or insist that each specific military command in an area of probable operations will conform to conventional tests of constitutionality. When an area is so beset that it must be put under military control at all, the paramount consideration is that its measures be successful, rather than legal. *** But if we cannot confine military expedients by the Constitution, neither would I distort the Constitution to approve all that the military may deem expedient. [I] cannot say, from any evidence before me, that the orders of General DeWitt were not reasonably expedient military precautions, nor could I say that they were. But even if they were permissible military procedures, I deny that it follows that they are constitutional. If, as the Court holds, it does follow, then we may as well say that any military order will be constitutional and have done with it.

Much is said of the danger to liberty from the Army program for deporting and detaining these citizens of Japanese extraction. But a judicial construction of the due process clause that will sustain this order is a far more subtle blow to liberty than the promulgation of the order itself. A military order, however unconstitutional, is not apt to last longer than the military emergency. Even during that period a succeeding commander may revoke it all. But once a judicial opinion rationalizes such an order to show that it conforms to the Constitution, or rather rationalizes the Constitution to show that the Constitution sanctions such an order, the Court for all time has validated the principle of racial discrimination in criminal procedure and of transplanting American citizens. The principle then lies about like a loaded weapon ready for the hand of any authority that can bring forward a plausible claim of an urgent need. Every repetition imbeds that principle more deeply in our law and thinking and expands it to new purposes. *** A military commander may overstep the bounds of constitutionality, and it is an incident. But if we review and approve, that passing incident becomes the doctrine of the Constitution. There it has a generative power of its own, and all that it creates will be in its own image. Nothing better illustrates this danger than does the Court's opinion in this case.

I should hold that a civil court cannot be made to enforce an order which violates constitutional limitations even if it is a reasonable exercise of military authority. The courts can exercise only the judicial power, can apply only law, and must abide by the Constitution, or they cease to be civil courts and become instruments of military policy.

Of course the existence of a military power resting on force, so vagrant, so centralized, so necessarily heedless of the individual, is an inherent threat to liberty. But I would not lead people to rely on this Court for a review that seems to me wholly delusive. The military reasonableness of these orders can only be determined by military superiors. If the people ever let command of the war power fall into irresponsible and unscrupulous hands, the courts wield no power equal to its restraint. The chief restraint upon those who command the physical forces of the country, in the future as in the past, must be their responsibility to the political judgments of their contemporaries and to the moral judgments of history.

My duties as a justice as I see them do not require me to make a military judgment as to whether General De-Witt's evacuation and detention program was a reasonable military necessity. I do not suggest that the courts should have attempted to interfere with the Army in carrying out its task. But I do not think they may be asked to execute a military expedient that has no place in law under the Constitution. I would reverse the judgment and discharge the prisoner.

> **Take Note**
>
> Justice Jackson suggests that the Court should not "interfere" with the military in the execution of its responsibilities, but he also asserts that the Court should have reversed Korematsu's conviction. Are these positions reconcilable?

[Justice ROBERTS's dissenting opinion has been omitted.]

***

Points for Discussion

a. Understanding the Opinion

The Court stated that government discrimination on the basis of race or national origin is subject to "rigid" scrutiny. Since *Korematsu*, the Court has made clear that this level of scrutiny—now known as "strict scrutiny"—requires the government to demonstrate that the classification advances a "compelling" interest and is "narrowly tailored" to achieve the desired end—that is, could not be achieved through any less discriminatory means. Yet even assuming that the classification here advanced a compelling interest in preventing espionage and sabotage, was it narrowly tailored to achieve that end? Notice that it was both over-inclusive—in that all persons of Japanese descent were forced to relocate even though perhaps only a few were (or might have been) disloyal—and under-inclusive—because individuals not of Japanese descent who nevertheless might pose a danger (including persons of German and Italian descent) were not subject to the same harsh treatment. As Justice Murphy pointed out in his dissent, loyalty hearings and investigations could have been conducted for those of Japanese descent in the same manner as was done for those of German and Italian descent. Indeed, *Korematsu* is the only case decided since the ratification of the Fourteenth Amendment in which the Court applied strict scrutiny but upheld a racial classification that facially burdened racial minorities.

Accordingly, perhaps *Korematsu* is instead best understood as an example of the Court's deference to military decisions in times of war. Does the Court have a role to play in reviewing such decisions, particularly while the war is still in progress? If so, how much deference should the Court afford military decisions during times of war? If the Court does have a role to play, but the decision at issue in *Korematsu* was within the military's discretion, is it possible to conceive of a military war-time decision that the Court would second-guess?

b. Politics, the Military, and the Court

Justice Frankfurter, who agreed with the outcome of the case, stated: "To find that the Constitution does not forbid the military measures now complained of does not carry with it approval of that which Congress and the Executive did. That is their business, not ours." Do you agree?

c. Aftermath

In 1976, President Gerald Ford formally rescinded Executive Order No. 9066. Twelve years later, President Ronald Reagan signed the Civil Liberties Act of 1988. The Act's purpose, among other things, was to "(1) acknowledge the fundamental injustice of the evacuation, relocation, and internment of United States citizens and permanent resident aliens of Japanese ancestry during World War II;" and "(2) apologize on behalf of the people of the United States for the evacuation, relocation, and internment of [Japanese Americans]." The act also provided for reparations of $20,000 for each surviving detainee. What do these actions suggest about the validity of the Court's decision in *Korematsu*?

d. Alternatives to the Military Order

Assume, hypothetically, that everything that the military authorities believed and feared was in fact true: (1) the Japanese were preparing to attack the West Coast; (2) thousands of West Coast residents of Japanese ancestry were not loyal to the United States; and (3) among these thousands might be spies who were helping Japan. Recall also that in 1941, Japan had won devastating victories against the United States at Pearl Harbor and in the Philippines, and that the United States believed that Japan had benefited from the assistance of spies. How else could the United States have addressed the situation?

———

3. Discriminatory Application of Facially Neutral Laws

The provisions at issue in *Strauder* and *Korematsu* were facially discriminatory—that is, by their very terms they classified (and imposed burdens) on the basis of race. The Louisiana law at issue in *Strauder* excluded blacks (and other non-whites) from jury service, and the order at issue in *Korematsu* applied only to persons of Japanese descent. As *Korematsu* suggests, such facially discriminatory government actions are subject to strict scrutiny.

That is not to say, however, that laws that are facially *neutral*—that is, laws that by their terms do not classify on the basis of race—can never give rise to Equal Protection problems. Consider the case that follows.

———

Yick Wo v. Hopkins

118 U.S. 356 (1886)

MR. JUSTICE MATTHEWS delivered the opinion of the court.

[In 1880, San Francisco passed an ordinance requiring persons operating laundries in buildings not constructed either of brick or stone to petition for a permit from the Board of Supervisors. Of the 320 laundries in San Francisco when the ordinance was enacted, 310 were constructed of wood and 240 were owned and operated by persons of Chinese descent. The plaintiff in error, a Chinese immigrant who had been engaged in the laundry business for 22 years, and 200 other laundry operators of Chinese descent petitioned the Board for permission to continue operating their businesses in their wooden buildings. Their petitions were denied; yet all but one of the 81 petitions of laundry operators not of Chinese descent were granted. After he was fined and imprisoned for continuing to operate his laundry without a permit, Lee Yick sought a writ of *habeas corpus* in state court.]

> **FYI**
>
> The courts in this case mistakenly believed that the plaintiff in error's name was Yick Wo. In fact, his name was Lee Yick. Yick Wo was the name of Lee Yick's laundry business. *See* Gerald F. Uelman, *A Lawyer's Walking Tour of San Francisco*, 68 ABA J. 958 (1982).

[The provisions of the Fourteenth Amendment] are universal in their application, to all persons within the territorial jurisdiction, without regard to any differences of race, of color, or of nationality; and the equal protection of the laws is a pledge of the protection of equal laws. *** In the present cases, we are not obliged to reason from the probable to the actual, and pass upon the validity of the ordinances complained of, as tried merely by the opportunities which their terms afford, of unequal and unjust discrimination in their administration; for the cases present the ordinances in actual operation, and the facts shown establish an administration directed so exclusively against a particular class of persons as to warrant and require the conclusion that, whatever may have been the intent of the ordinances as adopted, they are applied by the public authorities charged with their administration, and thus representing the state itself, with a mind so unequal and oppressive as to amount to a practical denial by the state of that equal protection of the laws which is secured to the petitioners, as to all other persons, by the broad and benign provisions of the fourteenth amendment to the constitution of the United States. Though the law itself be fair on its face, and impartial in appearance, yet, if it is applied and administered by public authority with an evil eye and an unequal hand, so as practically to make unjust and illegal discriminations between persons in similar circumstances, material to their rights, the denial of equal justice is still within the prohibition of the constitution.

The present cases, as shown by the facts disclosed in the record, are within this class. It appears that both petitioners have complied with every requisite deemed by the law, or by the public officers charged with its administration, necessary for the protection of neighboring property from fire, or as a precaution against injury to the public health. No reason whatever, except the will of the supervisors, is assigned why they should not be permitted to carry on, in the accustomed manner, their harmless and useful occupation, on which they depend for a livelihood; and while this consent of the supervisors is withheld from them, and from 200 others who have also petitioned, all of whom happen to be Chinese subjects, 80 others, not Chinese subjects, are permitted to carry on the same business under similar conditions. *** No reason for [this discrimination] is shown, and the conclusion cannot be resisted that no reason for it exists except hostility to the race and nationality to which the petitioners belong, and which, in the eye of the law, is not justified. The discrimination is therefore illegal, and the public administration which enforces it is a denial of the equal protection of the laws, and a violation of the fourteenth amendment of the constitution. The imprisonment of the petitioners is therefore illegal, and they must be discharged.

> **Take Note**
>
> The Court holds that even though the San Francisco ordinance was facially neutral, the Board violated the Equal Protection Clause by administering it in a racially discriminatory manner. Was there an argument that the ordinance was motivated by a purpose to burden laundry owners of Chinese descent, and thus was invalid on its face? Is it possible for an ordinance that is race neutral on its face to violate the Equal Protection Clause's prohibition on racially discriminatory regulation, without any showing of discriminatory application?

Points for Discussion

a. Facially Neutral Laws and Discriminatory Application

Yick Wo stands for an uncontroversial proposition: discriminatory application of an otherwise facially neutral law triggers heightened scrutiny under the Equal Protection Clause. Indeed, this must be the case if the Equal Protection Clause is to have any serious force. There is little difference in practice, after all, between a statute expressly forbidding people of Chinese descent to receive permits and a statute that purportedly makes all applicants eligible but that is administered purposefully to deny permits to all applicants of Chinese descent.

But how does one demonstrate a case of discriminatory application? Are numbers or statistics enough? In *Yick Wo*, permits had been denied to all applicants of Chinese descent but granted to all but one of the white applicants (who, incidentally, was a woman). What if half of the applicants of Chinese descent had been granted permits, whereas all but one of the white applicants had received permits? What if two-thirds of the applicants of Chinese descent had received permits, and virtually all white applicants had?

b. Discretion

The discretion conferred on the Board of Supervisors was quite broad. The California Supreme Court had concluded that the ordinance vested the Board with discretion to grant or withhold permits "with a view to the protection of the public against the dangers of fire." (The permit requirement applied only to buildings made of wood.) But the United States

Supreme Court observed, in a portion of the opinion omitted above, that the ordinance "seem[s] intended to confer, and actually to confer, not a discretion to be exercised upon a consideration of the circumstances of each case, but a naked and arbitrary power to give or withhold consent, not only as to places, but as to persons ***."

On this view, the ordinance conferred authority that was so unbridled as to raise a serious risk of arbitrary application. Putting aside the Equal Protection Clause's limitation on discriminatory exercises of discretionary authority, is there an independent constitutional defect to standardless delegations of authority at the state and local level? Might such delegations violate the Due Process Clause of the Fourteenth Amendment? Or might they violate the Equal Protection Clause, even absent a showing of a pattern of discriminatory application, on the theory that they facilitate discrimination?

c. Scrutiny

The Court states that "no reason" is shown for the apparently discriminatory exercise of the permitting authority. What sort of reason would have justified the discrimination? Does the Court have in mind a reason that would demonstrate that the applicants' races in fact were not a basis for the determinations, or instead a reason that is so substantial that it would justify the Board's discrimination against applicants of Chinese descent?

---

4. Discriminatory Effect or Purpose

Yick Wo makes clear, among other things, that government action can be suspect even absent a law or regulation that is facially discriminatory. *Yick Wo* concerned the discriminatory application of a facially neutral law. But it is also the case that laws and regulations that are race-neutral on their face but that were motivated by a discriminatory purpose are subject to strict scrutiny and presumptively unconstitutional. Otherwise, legislatures could achieve discriminatory ends simply by enacting statutes that are certain to have a discriminatory effect but that do not mention race on their face at all.

Consider the case of *Gomillion v. Lightfoot*, 364 U.S. 339 (1960), which considered a challenge to an Alabama law that redefined the boundaries of the City of Tuskegee. The statute would have altered the shape of the city from "a square to an uncouth twenty-eight-sided figure" and would have resulted in the removal from the city of all but four or five of its 400 Negro voters while not removing a single white voter or resident. The Court concluded that the complaint, which recited these facts, "amply allege[d] a claim of racial discrimination," even though the statute was race-neutral on its face, because the conclusion "would be irresistible, tantamount for all practical purposes to a mathematical demonstration, that the legislation [was] solely concerned with segregating white and colored voters by fencing Negro citizens out of town so as to deprive them of their pre-existing municipal vote." In other words, because the statute had a racially discriminatory purpose, it triggered heightened scrutiny, even though it was race neutral on its face.

What is the constitutional status of laws that were *not* motivated by any discriminatory *purpose*, but that nevertheless have a demonstrable discriminatory *effect* or *impact*—that is, laws that disproportionately burden members of a particular racial group? The case that follows addresses that question.

Washington v. Davis

426 U.S. 229 (1976)

Mr. Justice WHITE delivered the opinion of the Court.

[Respondents alleged that a qualifying test administered to applicants for positions as police officers in the District of Columbia Metropolitan Police Department violated the Fifth Amendment because it excluded a disproportionately high number of African-American applicants.] [T]o be accepted by the Department and to enter an intensive 17-week training program, the police recruit was required to satisfy certain physical and character standards, to be a high school graduate or its equivalent, and to receive a grade of at least 40 out of 80 on "Test 21," which [was] "designed to test verbal ability, vocabulary, reading and comprehension."

[Respondents did not claim that the Police Department designed or administered Test 21 with any racially discriminatory purpose or intent. The Court of Appeals] declare[d] that lack of discriminatory intent in designing and administering Test 21 was irrelevant; the critical fact was rather that a far greater proportion of blacks—four times as many— failed the test than did whites. This disproportionate impact, standing alone and without regard to whether it indicated a discriminatory purpose, was held sufficient to establish a constitutional violation, absent proof by petitioners that the test was an adequate measure of job performance in addition to being an indicator of probable success in the training program, a burden which the court ruled petitioners had failed to discharge. *** But our cases have not embraced the proposition that a law or other official act, without regard to whether it reflects a racially discriminatory purpose, is unconstitutional [s]olely because it has a racially disproportionate impact.

This is not to say that the necessary discriminatory racial purpose must be express or appear on the face of the statute, or that a law's disproportionate impact is irrelevant in cases involving Constitution-based claims of racial discrimination. A statute, otherwise neutral on its face, must not be applied so as invidiously to discriminate on the basis of race. *Yick Wo v. Hopkins*, 118 U.S. 356 (1886). *** Necessarily, an invidious discriminatory purpose may often be inferred from the totality of the relevant facts, including the fact, if it is true, that the law bears more heavily on one race than another. *** Nevertheless, we have not held that a law, neutral on its face and serving ends otherwise within the power of government to pursue, is invalid under the Equal Protection Clause simply because it may affect a greater proportion of one race than of another. Disproportionate impact is not irrelevant, but it is not the sole touchstone of an invidious racial discrimination forbidden by the Constitution. Standing alone, it does not trigger the rule that racial classifications are to be subjected to the strictest scrutiny and are justifiable only by the weightiest of considerations.

As an initial matter, we have difficulty understanding how a law establishing a racially neutral qualification for employment is nevertheless racially discriminatory and denies "any person . . . equal protection of the laws" simply because a greater proportion of Negroes fail to qualify than members of other racial or ethnic groups. Had respondents, along with all others who had failed Test 21, whether white or black, brought an action claiming that the test denied each of them equal protection of the laws as compared with those who had passed with high enough scores to qualify them as police recruits, it is most unlikely that their challenge would have been sustained. Test 21, which is administered generally to prospective Government employees, concededly seeks to ascertain whether those who take it have acquired a particular level of verbal skill; and it is untenable that the Constitution prevents the Government from seeking modestly to upgrade the communicative abilities of its employees rather than to be satisfied with some lower level of competence, particularly where the job requires special ability to communicate orally and in writing. Respondents, as Negroes, could no more successfully claim that the test denied them equal protection than could white applicants who also failed. The conclusion would not be different in the face of proof that more Negroes than whites had been disqualified by Test 21. That other Negroes also failed to score well would, alone, not demonstrate that respondents individually were being denied equal protection of the laws by the application of an otherwise valid qualifying test being administered to prospective police recruits.

Nor on the facts of the case before us would the disproportionate impact of Test 21 warrant the conclusion that it is a purposeful device to discriminate against Negroes and hence an infringement of the constitutional rights of respondents as well as other black applicants. As we have said, the test is neutral on its face and rationally may be said to serve a purpose the Government is constitutionally empowered to pursue. *** A rule that a statute designed to serve neutral ends is nevertheless invalid, absent compelling justification, if in practice it benefits or burdens one race more than another would be far-reaching and would raise serious questions about, and perhaps invalidate, a whole range of tax, welfare, public service, regulatory, and licensing statutes that may be more burdensome to the poor and to the average black than to the more affluent white. *** The judgment of the Court of Appeals accordingly is reversed.

> **Take Note**
>
> The Court concludes that the qualifying test was not designed with a discriminatory purpose, and thus declines to subject it to strict scrutiny. What is the appropriate level of scrutiny for a neutral policy that is not motivated by a discriminatory purpose?

Mr. Justice STEVENS, concurring.

[T]he burden of proving a prima facie case [of discriminatory purpose] may well involve differing evidentiary considerations. *** Frequently the most probative evidence of intent will be objective evidence of what actually happened rather than evidence describing the subjective state of mind of the actor. For normally the actor is presumed to have intended the natural consequences of his deeds. This is particularly true in the case of governmental action which is frequently the product of compromise, of collective decisionmaking, and of mixed motivation. It is unrealistic, on the one hand, to require the victim of alleged discrimination to uncover the actual subjective intent of the decisionmaker or, conversely, to invalidate otherwise legitimate action simply because an improper motive affected the deliberation of a participant in the decisional process.

My point in making this observation is to suggest that the line between discriminatory purpose and discriminatory impact is not nearly as bright, and perhaps not quite as critical, as the reader of the Court's opinion might assume. I agree, of course, that a constitutional issue does not arise every time some disproportionate impact is shown. On the other hand, when the disproportion is as dramatic as in *Yick Wo v. Hopkins*, 118 U.S. 356 (1886), it really does not matter whether the standard is phrased in terms of purpose or effect. Therefore, although I accept the statement of the general rule in the Court's opinion, I am not yet prepared to indicate how that standard should be applied in the many cases which have formulated the governing standard in different language.

[Justice BRENNAN and Justice MARSHALL dissented from the Court's resolution of the respondents' claims under Title VII of the Civil Rights Act of 1964. They did not reach the constitutional issue.]

———————————

Points for Discussion

a. Constitutional Law and Statutory Law

In <u>Davis</u>, the Court held that a facially neutral law's discriminatory effect is not alone sufficient to establish an equal protection violation. Instead, a plaintiff must also demonstrate that the law was motivated by a discriminatory purpose. In a portion of the opinion that has been omitted here, the Court addressed respondents' claims that the qualifying test violated Title VII of the Civil Rights Act of 1964. Although the Court did not find a violation of that statute, the Court has held that some employment practices that have a disproportionate and negative effect on protected minorities violate Title VII. Accordingly, although "discriminatory impact" claims against government actors are not, without more, *constitutionally* cognizable, they are

> **Make the Connection**
>
> Section 5 of the Fourteenth Amendment gives Congress power to "enforce, by appropriate legislation," the substantive provisions of the Amendment. If facially neutral laws and practices that were not motivated by a discriminatory purpose do not violate Section 1 of the Fourteenth Amendment, then is Congress properly "enforc[ing]" the Fourteenth Amendment when it makes state and local actors liable for adopting such practices? We will consider Congress's authority to enforce the Reconstruction Amendments in Chapter 13.

sometimes cognizable under federal *statutory* law. See, e.g, *Griggs v. Duke Power Co.*, 401 U.S. 424 (1971).

b. Requiring Discriminatory Purpose

Consider the difficulty of proving discriminatory purpose. When the challenged policy was enacted legislatively, the problems are significant. A statute's legislative history is unlikely to be helpful: benign, non-discriminatory purposes can be articulated for almost any law; the legislators who voted for the law may have had widely varying motives; and even legislators motivated by discriminatory animus are unlikely to have openly declared their actual purpose. As Justice Stevens observed, it is unrealistic to expect potential plaintiffs to be able to gauge the "subjective state of mind" of multiple legislative actors. And although when executive or administrative action is challenged plaintiffs might be able to avoid the multiple-actor problem, the other obstacles remain.

In light of these problems of proof, is the Court's rejection in *Davis* of discriminatory effect claims satisfying? The answer may rest on one's view about the form of equality protected by the Equal Protection Clause. Does the Equal Protection clause require the government to treat individuals equally, or does it instead require the government to ensure equal results from its actions? In any event, what if the Police Department's use of the test—and the Court's view of the test's neutrality—in fact itself reflects unconscious racial prejudice?

c. Proving Discriminatory Purpose

Although it might be difficult to demonstrate a discriminatory purpose, it is not impossible. Often, those challenging government policies will rely on circumstantial evidence of purpose, which as a practical matter tends to be evidence of discriminatory effect. The Court's decision in *Yick Wo*, which we considered earlier in this Chapter, is a good example; in that case, all 200 petitioners of Chinese descent had their applications denied, and all but one of the petitioners who were not of Chinese descent had their applications approved. But most cases will not involve such clear evidence.

The Court has made clear since its decision in *Davis* that this form of circumstantial proof can substantiate a claim of discriminatory purpose. In *Hunter v. Underwood*, 471 U.S. 222 (1985), the Court invalidated a provision of the Alabama Constitution that disenfranchised all persons convicted of crimes involving "moral turpitude." The plaintiffs argued that the provision had been adopted in 1901 to disenfranchise blacks, and the Court agreed. The Court noted that the provision had disenfranchised about ten times as many blacks as whites; that at the Alabama Constitutional Convention in 1901 a "zeal for white supremacy ran rampant"; and that the crimes that qualified under the provision—including vagrancy, adultery, and wife beating—"were thought [at the time of the Convention] to be more commonly committed by blacks."

In most cases, however, it will be difficult to prove that a facially neutral law or policy was adopted for discriminatory reasons. In *Village of Arlington Heights v. Metropolitan Housing Development Corp.*, 429 U.S. 252 (1977), for example, the Court considered a challenge to a decision by a predominantly white Chicago suburb to deny a request from a non-profit developer, who hoped to build townhouse units that would be accessible to low-and moderate-income tenants, to rezone property from single-family to multiple-family use. The Court began by acknowledging that "[r]arely can it be said that a legislature or administrative body operating under a broad mandate made a decision motivated solely by a single concern, or even that a particular purpose was the 'dominant' or 'primary' one." The Court made clear that a person challenging government action under the Equal Protection Clause is not required to prove that "the challenged action rested solely on racially discriminatory purposes." Instead, the Court declared, "[w]hen there is a proof that a discriminatory purpose has been a motivating factor in the decision, this judicial deference is no longer justified." The Court then explained:

> Determining whether invidious discriminatory purpose was a motivating factor demands a sensitive inquiry into such circumstantial and direct evidence of intent as may be available. The impact of the official action—whether it "bears more heavily on one race than another"—may provide an important starting point. Sometimes a clear pattern, unexplainable on grounds other than race, emerges from the effect of the state action even when the governing legislation appears neutral on its face. The evidentiary inquiry is then relatively easy. But such cases are rare. Absent a pattern as stark as that in *Gomillion* or *Yick Wo*, impact alone is not determinative, and the Court must look to other evidence.

> The historical background of the decision is one evidentiary source, particularly if it reveals a series of official actions taken for invidious purposes. The specific sequence of events leading up the challenged decision also may shed some light on the decisionmaker's purposes. *** Departures from the normal procedural sequence also might afford evidence that improper purposes are playing a role. Substantive departures too may be relevant, particularly if the factors usually considered important by the decisionmaker strongly favor a decision contrary to the one reached. The legislative or administrative history may be highly relevant, especially where there are contemporary statements by members of the decisionmaking body, minutes of its meetings, or reports.

The Court went on to say that even if the plaintiff offered evidence that the government was motivated at least in part by a discriminatory purpose, the plaintiff would not automatically prevail: "Such proof would [have] shifted to the Village the burden of establishing that the same decision would have resulted even had the impermissible purpose not been considered. If this were established, the complaining party in a case of this kind no longer fairly could attribute the injury complained of to improper consideration of a discriminatory purpose." This inquiry was unnecessary, however, because the Court concluded that the respondents had failed to demonstrate a discriminatory purpose.

Does it make sense to validate government decisions motivated in part by a racially discriminatory purpose when the decision likely would have been the same absent the discriminatory animus? Or should the Court conclude that such government decisions are so tainted that they are constitutionally impermissible?

d. Justifying Policies with a Discriminatory Impact

Even if the discriminatory impact of the verbal skills test at issue in <u>Davis</u> did not render it subject to strict scrutiny, should the Police Department have been required to justify or explain the need for the test? What was the correlation between the test and good police work? Would it make sense to subject policies with a disparate racial impact to a level of scrutiny more searching than rational-basis review, even if not as searching as strict scrutiny?

e. Discriminatory Purpose and Discriminatory Effect

In <u>Davis</u>, the Court considered whether proof of discriminatory purpose was required in a case in which proof of discriminatory effect existed. Does that mean that proof of discriminatory purpose is sufficient, by itself, to establish an Equal Protection violation? In *Palmer v. Thompson*, 403 U.S. 217 (1971), the Court considered a decision by the City Council of Jackson, Mississippi, to close its swimming pools after a District Court ordered integration of the City's public recreational facilities. The plaintiffs contended that the decision was designed to prevent the pools from becoming integrated. The Court rejected the challenge. Justice Black, in a 5-4 opinion for the Court, stated that "no case in this Court has held that a legislative act may violate equal protection solely because of the motivations of the men who voted for it." He explained:

> [I]t is extremely difficult for a court to ascertain the motivation, or collection of different motivations, that lie behind a legislative enactment. Here, for example, petitioners have argued that the Jackson pools were closed because of ideological opposition to racial integration in swimming pools. Some evidence in the record appears to support this argument. On the other hand the courts below found that the pools were closed because the city council felt they could not be operated safely and economically on an integrated basis. There is substantial evidence in the record to support this conclusion. It is difficult or impossible for any court to determine the "sole" or "dominant" motivation behind the choices of a group of legislators. Furthermore, there is an element of futility in a judicial attempt to invalidate a law because of the bad motives of its supporters. If the law is struck down for this reason, rather than because of its facial content or effect, it would presumably be valid as soon as the legislature or relevant governing body repassed it for different reasons.
>
> It is true there is language in some of our cases interpreting the [Fourteenth Amendment] which may suggest that the motive or purpose behind a law is relevant to its constitutionality. But the focus in those cases was on the actual effect of the enactments, not upon the motivation which led the States to behave as they did. *** Here the record indicates only that Jackson once ran segregated public swimming pools and that no public pools are now maintained by the city. Moreover, there is no evidence in this record to show that the city is now covertly aiding the maintenance and operation of pools which are private in name only. It shows no state action affecting blacks differently from whites.

Justice White, who later wrote the Court's opinion in *Davis*, dissented, asserting that the decision to close the pools was "an expression of official policy that Negroes are unfit to associate with whites." Do *Davis* and *Palmer*, when viewed together, suggest that a facially neutral policy triggers strict scrutiny only when there is proof of *both* a discriminatory purpose *and* a discriminatory effect? If so, do you agree that there was no discriminatory effect in *Palmer*?

Hypothetical

A statistical study that examined 2,000 murder cases in Georgia in the 1970s found that defendants charged with killing white persons received the death penalty in 11% of cases, whereas defendants charged with killing black persons received the death penalty in only 1% of cases. In addition, the study found that the death penalty was assessed in 22% of cases involving black defendants and white victims; 8% of cases involving white defendants and white victims; and 1% of cases involving black defendants and black victims. Finally, the study found that prosecutors sought the death penalty in 70% of the cases involving black defendants and white victims, but only 32% of the cases involving white defendants and white victims and 15% of the cases involving black defendants and black victims. A black man sentenced to death in Georgia for killing a white police officer challenges his sentence, arguing that the death penalty was administered in a racially discriminatory manner. How should the Court rule? (These facts are drawn from *McCleskey v. Kemp*, 481 U.S. 279 (1987).)

———————

5. Race-Specific But Facially Symmetrical Laws

The cases that we have seen so far in this Chapter have involved challenges to laws that treated one class of persons defined by race differently than they treated others. What is the constitutional status of laws that are race-conscious but that purport to impose symmetrical obligations or burdens on persons of different races? Does a law that classifies on the basis of race but that treats members of different races the "same" violate the Equal Protection Clause? Perhaps the most well-known manifestations of this type of law are those laws that required "separate but equal" facilities for whites and blacks. In the following now-infamous case, *Plessy v. Ferguson*, the Court upheld such a law. *Plessy* has since been overruled, as we will see in the case that follows it, *Brown v. Board of Education*.

———————

Plessy v. Ferguson

163 U.S. 537 (1896)

Mr. Justice BROWN delivered the opinion of the Court.

This case turns upon the constitutionality of an act of the general assembly of the state of Louisiana, passed in 1890, providing for separate railway carriages for the white and colored races. The first section of the statute enacts "that all railway companies carrying passengers in their coaches in this state, shall provide equal but separate accommodations for the white, and colored races, by providing two or more passenger coaches for each passenger train, or by dividing the passenger coaches by a partition so as to secure separate accommodations ***. No person or persons shall be permitted to occupy seats in coaches, other than the ones assigned to them, on account of the race they belong to."

The petition for the writ of prohibition averred that petitioner was seven-eighths Caucasian and one-eighth African blood; that *** he took possession of a vacant seat in a coach where passengers of the white race were accommodated, and was ordered by the conductor to vacate said coach, and take a seat in another, assigned to persons of the colored race, and, having refused to comply with such demand, he was forcibly ejected, with the aid of a police officer, and imprisoned in the parish jail to answer a charge of having violated the above act.

The object of the [fourteenth] amendment was undoubtedly to enforce the absolute equality of the two races before the law, but, in the nature of things, it could not have been intended to abolish distinctions based upon color, or to enforce social, as distinguished from political, equality, or a commingling of the two races upon terms unsatisfactory to either. Laws permitting, and even requiring, their separation, in places where they are liable to be brought into contact, do not necessarily imply the inferiority of either race to the other, and have been generally, if not universally, recognized as within the competency of the state legislatures in the exercise of their police power. The most common instance of this is connected with the establishment of separate schools for white and colored children, which have been held to be a valid exercise of the legislative power even by courts of states where the political rights of the colored race have been longest and most earnestly enforced.

So far, then, as a conflict with the fourteenth amendment is concerned, the case reduces itself to the question whether the statute of Louisiana is a reasonable regulation, and with respect to this there must necessarily be a large discretion on the part of the legislature. [I]t is at liberty to act with reference to the established usages, customs, and traditions of the people, and with a view to the promotion of their comfort, and the preservation of the public peace and good order. Gauged by this standard, we cannot say that a law which authorizes or

> **Take Note**
>
> What level of scrutiny does the Court employ in evaluating the constitutionality of the Louisiana statute? If the test is mere reasonableness, did the Equal Protection Clause add anything to the Fourteenth Amendment, which also includes a Due Process Clause? And even assuming that standard, are you convinced that the end of preserving the "public peace and good order" is permissibly advanced by this law?

even requires the separation of the two races in public conveyances is unreasonable, or more obnoxious to the fourteenth amendment than the acts of congress requiring separate schools for colored children in the District of Columbia, the constitutionality of which does not seem to have been questioned, or the corresponding acts of state legislatures.

We consider the underlying fallacy of the plaintiff's argument to consist in the assumption that the enforced separation of the two races stamps the colored race with a badge of inferiority. If this be so, it is not by reason of anything found in the act, but solely because the colored race chooses to put that construction upon it. The argument necessarily assumes that if, as has been more than once the case, and is not unlikely to be so again, the colored race should become the dominant power in the state legislature, and should enact a law in precisely similar terms, it would thereby relegate the white race to an inferior position. We imagine that the white race, at least, would not acquiesce in this assumption. The argument also assumes that social prejudices may be overcome by legislation, and that equal rights cannot be secured to the negro except by an enforced commingling of the two races. We cannot accept this proposition. If the two races are to meet upon terms of social equality, it must be the result of natural affinities, a mutual appreciation of each other's merits, and a voluntary consent of individuals. *** Legislation is powerless to eradicate racial instincts, or to abolish distinctions based upon physical differences. *** If the civil and political rights of both races be equal, one cannot be inferior to the other civilly or politically. If one race be inferior to the other socially, the constitution of the United States cannot put them upon the same plane.

> **Food for Thought**
>
> The Court suggests here that government action cannot succeed when it challenges entrenched individual views. The same argument certainly could have been advanced in *Brown*, which follows, or in response to the Civil Rights Act of 1964, which we considered in Chapter 3. As you read about *Brown* and its long aftermath, consider what it suggests about the validity of the Court's assertion here.

Mr. Justice HARLAN dissenting.

It was said in argument that the statute of Louisiana does not discriminate against either race, but prescribes a rule applicable alike to white and colored citizens. But this argument does not meet the difficulty. Every one knows that the statute in question had its origin in the purpose, not so much to exclude white persons from railroad cars occupied by blacks, as to exclude colored people from coaches occupied by or assigned to white persons. *** The thing to accomplish was, under the guise of giving equal accommodation for whites and blacks, to compel the latter to keep to themselves while traveling in railroad passenger coaches. No one

> **Make the Connection**
>
> Justice John Marshall Harlan (1833-1911) dissented not only in *Plessy v. Ferguson*, 163 U.S. 537 (1896), but also in the *Civil Rights Cases*, which we will consider in Chapter 19. Harlan had been a colonel in the Union Army during the Civil War and a politician before joining the Supreme Court in 1877. While on the Court, Harlan taught constitutional law at the George Washington University for over two decades. His grandson, John Marshall Harlan II, was a Supreme Court Justice from 1955-1971.

would be so wanting in candor as to assert the contrary. *** If a white man and a black man choose to occupy the same public conveyance on a public highway, it is their right to do so; and no government, proceeding alone on grounds of race, can prevent it without infringing the personal liberty of each.

The white race deems itself to be the dominant race in this country. And so it is, in prestige, in achievements, in education, in wealth, and in power. So, I doubt not, it will continue to be for all time, if it remains true to its great heritage, and holds fast to the principles of constitutional liberty. But in view of the constitution, in the eye of the law, there is in this country no superior, dominant, ruling class of citizens. There is no caste here. Our constitution is color-blind, and neither knows nor tolerates classes among citizens. In respect of civil rights, all citizens are equal before the law. The humblest is the peer of the most powerful. The law regards man as man, and takes no account of his surroundings or of his color when his civil rights as guaranteed by the supreme law of the land are involved. It is therefore to be regretted that this high tribunal, the final expositor of the fundamental law of the land, has reached the conclusion that it is competent for a state to regulate the enjoyment by citizens of their civil rights solely upon the basis of race. In my opinion, the judgment this day rendered will, in time, prove to be quite as pernicious as the decision made by this tribunal in the _Dred Scott_ Case.

> **Food for Thought**
>
> Justice Harlan asserted that the Constitution is "color-blind." Yet the Thirteenth, Fourteenth, and Fifteenth Amendments give Congress the power to enforce their substantive provisions with "appropriate" legislation. Does Justice Harlan's view mean that Congress would have been prohibited, even in the years immediately after the amendments were ratified, from mandating affirmative action for black citizens who had suffered from slavery and institutionalized racism? Does it mean that Congress is prohibited from doing so today? We will take up these questions later in this Chapter and in Chapter 13.

Points for Discussion

a. Separate But Equal

The Court suggested in _Plessy_ that because the law was consistent with a formal notion of equality—in that on its face it imposed symmetrical burdens on people of different races—it was consistent with the Equal Protection Clause. The Court eventually repudiated this view. But even if the Court was correct that symmetrical laws are virtually by definition consistent with the Equal Protection Clause, was this law *designed* to apply—or did it *in fact* apply—equally to people of different races? Mr. Plessy, for example, was "seven-eighths Caucasian and one-eighth African blood." What does his assignment to the coach reserved for the "colored races" suggest about the operation of the statute?

b. Justice Harlan's Dissent

Justice Harlan was the lone dissenter in <u>Plessy</u>, but his opinion is regularly hailed today as visionary. He advanced a "color-blind" theory of the Equal Protection Clause, which holds that race is never an appropriate basis for government decision-making. We will consider this view in more detail shortly, when we turn to the constitutionality of public affirmative action programs. But it is important to note that Justice Harlan's regularly revered dissent was not as pure an endorsement of the color-blind Constitution as many choose to remember.

In a portion of the opinion that was omitted above, Justice Harlan stated that "[t]here is a race so different from our own that we do not permit those belonging to it to become citizens of the United States. *** I allude to the Chinese race." He then appeared to rely on the fact that the statute apparently permitted persons of Chinese descent to sit in the coaches reserved for whites, even though it did not permit blacks to do so, as a further ground for objecting to the statute. This was not the only time that Justice Harlan expressed this view. He joined Justice Fuller's dissent in *United States v. Wong Kim Ark*, 169 U.S. 649 (1898), an opinion that asserted that persons of Chinese descent but born in the United States did not become citizens notwithstanding the first clause of the Fourteenth Amendment. *See id. at 731* (Fuller, J., joined by Harlan, J., dissenting) (noting the danger of "the presence within our territory of large numbers of Chinese laborers, of a distinct race and religion, remaining strangers in the land, residing apart by themselves, tenaciously adhering to the customs and usages of their own country, unfamiliar with our institutions, and apparently incapable of assimilating with our people," and arguing that "[i]t is not to be admitted that the children of persons so situated become citizens by accident of birth"). *See generally* Gabriel J. Chin, *The Plessy Myth: Justice Harlan and the Chinese Cases*, 82 Iowa L. Rev. 151 (1996).

Do Justice Harlan's views about persons of Chinese descent suggest a defect in the theory of the color-blind Constitution? Or only in the consistency with which Justice Harlan followed it?

Brown v. Board of Education of Topeka

347 U.S. 483 (1954)

Mr. Chief Justice WARREN delivered the opinion of the Court.

These cases come to us from the States of Kansas, South Carolina, Virginia, and Delaware. [In] each of the cases, minors of the Negro race, through their legal representatives, seek the aid of the courts in obtaining admission to the public schools of their community on a nonsegregated basis. In each instance, they have been denied admission to schools attended by white children under laws requiring or permitting segregation according to race. *** In [all the cases but one], a three-judge federal district court denied relief to the plaintiffs on the so-called "separate but equal" doctrine announced by this Court in *Plessy* *v. Ferguson*, 163 U.S. 537 (1896).

The plaintiffs contend that segregated public schools are not "equal" and cannot be made "equal," and that hence they are deprived of the equal protection of the laws. Because of the obvious importance of the question presented, the Court took jurisdiction. Argument was heard in the 1952 Term, and reargument was heard this Term on certain questions propounded by the Court. Reargument was largely devoted to the circumstances surrounding the adoption of the Fourteenth Amendment in 1868. It covered exhaustively consideration of the Amendment in Congress, ratification by the states, then existing practices in racial segregation, and the views of proponents and opponents of the Amendment. This discussion and our own investigation convince us that, although these sources cast some light, it is not enough to resolve the problem with which we are faced. At best, they are inconclusive. The most avid proponents of the post-War Amendments undoubtedly intended them to remove all legal distinctions among "all persons born or naturalized in the United States." Their opponents, just as certainly, were antagonistic to both the letter and the spirit of the Amendments and wished them to have the most limited effect. What others in Congress and the state legislatures had in mind cannot be determined with any degree of certainty.

An additional reason for the inconclusive nature of the Amendment's history, with respect to segregated schools, is the status of public education at that time. In the South, the movement toward free common schools, supported by general taxation, had not yet taken hold. Education of white children was largely in the hands of private groups. Education of Negroes was almost nonexistent, and practically all of the race were illiterate. In fact, any education of Negroes was forbidden by law in some states. Today, in contrast, many Negroes have achieved outstanding success in the arts and sciences as well as in the business and professional world. It is true that public school education at the time of the Amendment had advanced further in the North, but the effect of the Amendment on Northern States was generally ignored in the congressional debates. Even in the North, the conditions of public education did not approximate those existing today. The curriculum was usually rudimentary; ungraded schools were common in rural areas; the school term was but three months a year in many states; and compulsory school attendance was virtually unknown. As a consequence, it is not surprising that there should be so little in the history of the Fourteenth Amendment relating to its intended effect on public education.

In [recent cases involving challenges to segregated public education], all on the graduate school level, inequality was found in that specific benefits enjoyed by white students were denied to Negro students of the same educational qualifications. In none of these cases was it necessary to re-examine the doctrine [of "separate but equal"] to grant relief to the Negro plaintiff. *** Here, [there] are findings below that the Negro and white schools involved have been equalized, or are being equalized, with respect to buildings, curricula, qualifications and salaries of teachers, and other "tangible" factors. Our decision, therefore, cannot turn on merely a comparison of these tangible factors in the Negro and white schools involved in each of the cases. We must look instead to the effect of segregation itself on public education.

In approaching this problem, we cannot turn the clock back to 1868 when the Amendment was adopted, or even to 1896 when *Plessy v. Ferguson* was written. We must consider public education in the light of its full development and its present place in American life throughout the Nation. Only in this way can it be determined if segregation in public schools deprives these plaintiffs of the equal protection of the laws.

Today, education is perhaps the most important function of state and local governments. Compulsory school attendance laws and the great expenditures for education both demonstrate our recognition of the importance of education to our democratic society. It is required in the performance of our most basic public responsibilities, even service in the armed forces. It is the very foundation of good citizenship. Today it is a principal instrument in awakening the child to cultural values, in preparing him for later professional training, and in helping him to adjust normally to his environment. In these days, it is doubtful that any child may reasonably be expected to succeed in life if he is denied the opportunity of an education. Such an opportunity, where the state has undertaken to provide it, is a right which must be made available to all on equal terms.

We come then to the question presented: Does segregation of children in public schools solely on the basis of race, even though the physical facilities and other "tangible" factors may be equal, deprive the children of the minority group of equal educational opportunities? We believe that it does.

In *Sweatt v. Painter*, 339 U.S. 629 (1950), in finding that a segregated law school for Negroes could not provide them equal educational opportunities, this Court relied in large part on "those qualities which are incapable of objective measurement but which make for greatness in a law school." In *McLaurin v. Oklahoma State Regents*, 339 U.S. 637 (1950), the Court, in requiring that a Negro admitted to a white graduate school be treated like all other students, again resorted to intangible considerations: "his ability to study, to engage in discussions and exchange views with other students, and, in general, to learn his profession." Such considerations apply with added force to children in grade and high schools. To separate them from others of similar age and qualifications solely because of their race generates a feeling of inferiority as to their status in the community that may affect their hearts and minds in a way unlikely ever to be undone. The effect of this separation on their educational opportunities was well stated by a finding in the Kansas case by a court which nevertheless felt compelled to rule against the Negro plaintiffs: "Segregation of white and colored children in public schools has a detrimental effect upon the colored children. The impact is greater when it has the sanction of the law; for the policy of separating the races is usually interpreted as denoting the inferiority of the negro group. A sense of inferiority affects the motivation of a child to learn. Segregation with the sanction of law, therefore, has a tendency to [retard] the educational and mental development of Negro children and to deprive them of some of the benefits they would receive in a racial[ly] integrated school system." Whatever may have been the extent of psychological knowledge at the time of

Plessy v. Ferguson, this finding is amply supported by modern authority.[11] Any language in *Plessy v. Ferguson* contrary to this finding is rejected.

We conclude that in the field of public education the doctrine of "separate but equal" has no place. Separate educational facilities are inherently unequal. Therefore, we hold that the plaintiffs and others similarly situated for whom the actions have been brought are, by reason of the segregation complained of, deprived of the equal protection of the laws guaranteed by the Fourteenth Amendment. *** In order that we may have the full assistance of the parties in formulating decrees, the cases will be restored to the docket, and the parties are requested to present further argument on [the appropriate remedy].

Points for Discussion

a. Public Education and Beyond

Did the Court in *Brown* expressly overrule *Plessy v. Ferguson*? Did it at least do so to the extent that *Plessy* was read to permit segregation in public education? In this regard, note that the Court suggested that the school context presented unique concerns. Shortly after the decision in *Brown*, the Court concluded, in a series of cases decided with terse, per curiam orders, that segregation in other public facilities—including municipal parks, *New Orleans City Park Improvement Ass'n v. Detiege*, 358 U.S. 54 (1958), buses, *Gayle v. Browder*, 352 U.S. 903 (1956), and golf courses, *Holmes v. City of Atlanta*, 350 U.S. 879 (1955)—was unconstitutional, as well.

b. Segregation and the Federal Government

We began our consideration of Equal Protection (in Chapter 10) with the Court's decision in *Bolling v. Sharpe*, which concluded that there is an equal protection component of the Due Process Clause of the Fifth Amendment that imposes limits on the federal government in much the same way that the Equal Protection Clause of the Fourteenth Amendment limits the states. The Court decided *Bolling* on the same day that it decided *Brown*.

c. The Fourteenth Amendment and the Original Meaning

The Supreme Court originally heard arguments in *Brown* in the October 1952 term, but the Court requested briefing and further argument on the original meaning of the Fourteenth Amendment. In its opinion, the Court determined that the original meaning was "inconclusive," and then appeared explicitly to eschew an originalist approach, declaring that "[i]n approaching this problem, we cannot turn the clock back to 1868 when the Amendment was adopted."

---

[11] K. B. Clark, Effect of Prejudice and Discrimination on Personality Development (Midcentury White House Conference on Children and Youth, 1950); Witmer and Kotinsky, Personality in the Making (1952), c. VI; Deutscher and Chein, The Psychological Effects of Enforced Segregation: A Survey of Social Science Opinion, 26 J. Psychol. 259 (1948); Chein, What are the Psychological Effects of Segregation Under Conditions of Equal Facilities?, 3 Int. J. Opinion and Attitude Res. 229 (1949); Brameld, Educational Costs, in Discrimination and National Welfare (MacIver, ed., 1949), 44-48; Frazier, The Negro in the United States (1949), 674-681. And see generally Myrdal, An American Dilemma (1944).

Others, however, have endeavored to discern the original meaning of the Fourteenth Amendment with respect to the question of segregated schools. Most commentators have concluded that the Fourteenth Amendment was not originally understood to prohibit segregated public schools. These scholars have generally noted that segregation in public schools was widespread, even in most parts of the North, immediately before the ratification of the Fourteenth Amendment, see Michael J. Klarman, Brown, *Originalism, and Constitutional Theory: A Response to Professor McConnell*, 81 Va. L. Rev. 1881 (1995), and that Republicans in Congress repeatedly reassured northern voters that the Amendment would have only a small impact on their states' laws, see Earl M. Maltz, *Originalism and the Segregation Decisions—A Response to Professor McConnell*, 13 Const. Comment. 223 (1996). In addition, these commentators have noted that, contemporaneously with the ratification of the Amendment, the same Republican members of Congress who supported the Amendment provided for segregated schools in the District of Columbia. *See* Raoul Berger, *Government By Judiciary* 117-34 (1977). *See generally* Alexander Bickel, *The Original Understanding and the Segregation Decision*, 69 Harv. L. Rev. 1 (1955).

Some, however, have argued that <u>Brown</u> was in fact consistent with the original meaning. Michael McConnell, for example, has relied on statements of members of Congress during debates over proposals to abolish segregation in public schools. These efforts did not succeed, but did ultimately culminate in the enactment of the Civil Rights Act of 1875, which prohibited some forms of public discrimination, though it did not require integrated schools. Michael W. McConnell, *Originalism and the Desegregation Decisions*, 81 Va. L. Rev. 947 (1995); see also Michael W. McConnell, *Segregation and the Original Understanding: A Reply to Professor Maltz*, 13 Const. Comment. 233 (1996). Robert Bork, a former judge, Supreme Court nominee, and legal scholar, has also argued that <u>Brown</u> was consistent with the original understanding. Consider his argument below.

Perspective and Analysis

"The ratifiers [of the Fourteenth Amendment] probably assumed that segregation was consistent with equality but they were not addressing segregation. The text itself demonstrates that the equality under law was the primary goal. By 1954, when <u>Brown</u> came up for decision, it had been apparent for some time that segregation rarely if ever produced equality. *** Since equality and segregation were mutually inconsistent, though the ratifiers did not understand that, both could not be honored."

Robert Bork, *The Tempting of America: The Political Seduction of the Law* 82 (1990).

Is Judge Bork's argument—which presumes that the Equal Protection Clause can today prohibit conduct that its ratifiers believed it would permit—consistent with your understanding of what originalism entails?

What does it mean for originalism if the Court's decision in <u>Brown</u> in fact was inconsistent with the original meaning? Does it make originalism more difficult to defend, or perhaps even illegitimate? Or does it instead reveal that the Constitution that we actually have is more difficult to defend or even illegitimate?

d. The Court's Rationale

Although they might strike us as odious, it is not self-evident that race-conscious laws that treat people of different races the same violate the Equal Protection Clause. What was the basis of the decision in <u>Brown</u> that the doctrine of separate but equal violated the Clause? The Court was surprisingly cryptic about it.

Was the principal justification for the Court's decision the recognition that segregation, which on its face applied equally to blacks and whites, in fact was designed to *subordinate* blacks? Even if this seemed, given the historical context, the obvious objective of segregated schools in many parts of the country *in 1954*, how should the Court determine *today* which race-conscious policies are designed to subordinate? (On this theory, is affirmative action constitutionally problematic?)

Was the justification for the Court's decision the sociological evidence presented in footnote 11, which (in the Court's view) demonstrated that racial segregation of children "generates a feeling of inferiority as to [minority children's] status in the community that may affect their hearts and minds in a way unlikely ever to be undone"? Under this view, segregation was problematic because it stigmatized black children, effectively treating them as inferior. If this was the basis of the Court's decision, what would be the constitutional status of separate schools if powerful sociological evidence emerges that single-race schools—for example, all-black-male schools in urban settings—in fact advance self-esteem and increase student performance?

Was the basis of the decision the fact that segregation was the product of a distorted political system in which blacks were largely excluded, or in which they at least lacked effective electoral strength? If so, would this mean that segregation would be constitutionally permissible as long as it is a product of a political system in which all groups are fairly represented?

Was the basis of the decision the instrumental view that integration in education produces good social results, because it teaches people to get along with others who are different than they are? (Recall that the Court emphasized the "importance of education to our democratic society.") If so, is this an appropriate way to interpret the Constitution?

Was the Court's decision based on the color-blind theory of the Constitution? This, after all, had been the basis of Justice Harlan's dissent in <u>Plessy</u>. But did the Court ever explicitly endorse this view in the opinion in <u>Brown</u>?

Or was the theory simply that by 1954 common experience had shown that separate facilities were invariably unequal facilities and that a condition of "separate but equal" was all but impossible? Subject only to a few possible exceptions, the reality was that schools that the government provided for white children were always in better condition than the corresponding schools that the government provided for black children, that white restrooms were invariably better equipped than black restrooms, and so forth. In this context, did it make any sense to tell states that they could segregate, so long as they treated races equally?

As we explore the cases that follow—particularly the cases on affirmative action—consider the implications of these various views of *Brown*'s rationale.

e. *Brown*'s Implementation

The Court concluded its opinion by requesting briefing on remedies for the constitutional defects of the policies in school districts at issue, remedies that likely would soon apply to countless other districts around the country. This was quite a delicate task, as it became clear almost immediately that *Brown* would face fierce resistance in some quarters.

One year after the decision in *Brown*, the Court announced the remedy. In *Brown v. Board of Education*, 349 U.S. 294 (1955) ("*Brown II*"), the Court acknowledged that "[f]ull implementation of [*Brown*] may require solution of varied local school problems." Accordingly, the Court declared that "[s]chool authorities have the primary responsibility for elucidating, assessing, and solving these problems," but emphasized that the courts that heard the initial challenges would "have to consider whether the action of school authorities constitutes good faith implementation of the governing constitutional principles." The Court instructed the lower courts to rely on equitable principles, which are "characterized by a practical flexibility in shaping its remedies and by a facility for adjusting and reconciling public and private needs." The Court stated that courts could "properly take into account the public interest in the elimination of [obstacles to integration] in a systematic and effective manner," but emphasized that "the vitality of these constitutional principles cannot be allowed to yield simply because of disagreement with them." The Court then ordered the school districts to make a "prompt and reasonable start toward full compliance" with *Brown*. The Court acknowledged the complexity of the task, but directed the lower courts to issue decrees "as are necessary and proper to admit to public schools on a racially nondiscriminatory basis with all deliberate speed the parties to these cases."

> **Make the Connection**
>
> Judicially supervised desegregation efforts often met massive resistance, particularly in the South. We considered the implications of such resistance in Chapter 2, when we discussed the Court's decision in *Cooper v. Aaron*.

The process of desegregation was a slow one. Some school districts did not adopt aggressive reforms to eliminate segregated schools, such as those that implemented "freedom of choice plans," which did not consolidate the formerly separate schools but permitted students to choose which school to attend. The Court held in *Green v. County School Board*, 391 U.S. 430 (1968), that such an approach failed to comply with *Brown II* in a district in which no white children had chosen to attend the schools formerly reserved for blacks and almost all of the district's black students remained in an all-black school. Other school districts eliminated *de jure* segregation—that is, segregation by law or official policy—but nevertheless retained schools that were segregated in fact, because school assignments were done by place of residence, and most neighborhoods remained segregated. The Court has made clear that "the Constitution is not violated by racial imbalance in the schools, without more," *Milliken v. Bradley*, 433 U.S. 267, 280, n. 14 (1977), but often it is difficult to tell whether the cause of segregation is official policy or instead simply *de facto* residential segregation.

In *Swann v. Charlotte-Mecklenburg Board of Education*, 402 U.S. 1 (1971), the Court unanimously affirmed a district court order requiring a large, urban school system in the South to redraw its district lines and bus elementary school students to schools not in their immediate neighborhoods in order to achieve a "unitary"—that is, formally de-segregated—school district. The Court accepted, at least in school systems with a history of *de jure* segregation, "a presumption against schools that are substantially disproportionate in their racial composition," and it declared that courts had the authority to use "frank—and sometimes drastic—gerrymandering of school districts and attendance zones" and to use busing plans.

The Court has, however, imposed some limits on district court discretion in overseeing the process of desegregation. Inter-district remedies—that is, remedies that apply both to districts that were segregated *de jure* and surrounding districts, such as a city and its suburban areas—are inappropriate "absent an inter-district violation." *Milliken v. Bradley*, 418 U.S. 717 (1974). District courts generally cannot order a district to raise taxes to finance a desegregation plan. *Missouri v. Jenkins*, 495 U.S. 33 (1990).

We will return to this line of cases later in this Chapter, when we consider the Court's decision in <u>Parents Involved in Community Schools v. Seattle School Dist. No. 1</u>. In your view, has the promise of <u>Brown</u> yet been fulfilled?

Loving v. Virginia

388 U.S. 1 (1967)

Mr. Chief Justice WARREN delivered the opinion of the Court.

[This case involved a challenge to a Virginia law that prohibited marriages between a "white person and a colored person." More detailed facts are recited in Chapter 8, where we considered the part of the opinion in which the Court relied on the Due Process Clause.]

In upholding the constitutionality of these provisions in the decision below, the Supreme Court of Appeals of Virginia [relied on its earlier decisions holding that] the State's legitimate purposes were "to preserve the racial integrity of its citizens," and to prevent "the corruption of blood," "a mongrel breed of citizens," and "the obliteration of racial pride," obviously an endorsement of the doctrine of White Supremacy.

[T]he State argues that the meaning of the Equal Protection Clause, as illuminated by the statements of the Framers, is only that state penal laws containing an interracial element as part of the definition of the offense must apply equally to whites and Negroes in the sense that members of each race are punished to the same degree. Thus, the State contends that, because its miscegenation statutes punish equally both the white and the Negro participants in an interracial marriage, these statutes, despite their reliance on racial classifications do not constitute an invidious discrimination based upon race. The second argument advanced by the State assumes the validity of its equal application theory. The argument is that, if the Equal Protection Clause does not outlaw miscegenation statutes because of their reliance on racial classifications, the question of constitutionality would thus become whether there was any rational basis for a State to treat interracial marriages differently from other marriages. On this question, the State argues, the scientific evidence is substantially in doubt and, consequently, this Court should defer to the wisdom of the state legislature in adopting its policy of discouraging interracial marriages.

Because we reject the notion that the mere "equal application" of a statute containing racial classifications is enough to remove the classifications from the Fourteenth Amendment's proscription of all invidious racial discriminations, we do not accept the State's contention that these statutes should be upheld if there is any possible basis for concluding that they serve a rational purpose. *** [W]e deal [here] with statutes containing racial classifications, and the fact of equal application does not immunize the statute from the very heavy burden of justification which the Fourteenth Amendment has traditionally required of state statutes drawn according to race.

The State argues that statements in the Thirty-ninth Congress about the time of the passage of the Fourteenth Amendment indicate that the Framers did not intend the Amendment to make unconstitutional state miscegenation laws. Many of the statements alluded to by the State concern the debates over the Freedmen's Bureau Bill, which President Johnson vetoed, and the Civil Rights Act of 1866, 14 Stat. 27, enacted over his veto. While these statements have some relevance to the intention of Congress in submitting the Fourteenth Amendment, it must be understood that they pertained to the passage of specific statutes and not to the broader, organic purpose of a constitutional amendment. As for the various statements directly concerning the Fourteenth Amendment, we have said in connection with a related problem, that although these historical sources "cast some light" they are not sufficient to resolve the problem; "at best, they are inconclusive." *Brown v. Board of Education of Topeka*, 347 U.S. 483, 489 (1954). See also *Strauder v. State of West Virginia*, 100 U.S. 303, 310 (1880).

> ## Food for Thought
>
> Is the Court's point here that the original meaning of the Fourteenth Amendment governs, but that the meaning is elusive with respect to this question? Or that the original meaning of the Amendment simply does not govern here?

[T]he Equal Protection Clause requires the consideration of whether the classifications drawn by any statute constitute an arbitrary and invidious discrimination. The clear and central purpose of the Fourteenth Amendment was to eliminate all official state sources of invidious racial discrimination in the States. *Slaughter-House Cases*, 16 Wall. 36, 71 (1873); *Strauder v. State of West Virginia*, 100 U.S. 303, 307-308 (1880); *Ex parte Virginia*, 100 U.S. 339, 344-345 (1880); *Shelley v. Kraemer*, 334 U.S. 1 (1948); *Burton v. Wilmington Parking Authority*, 365 U.S. 715 (1961). There can be no question but that Virginia's miscegenation statutes rest solely upon distinctions drawn according to race. The statutes proscribe generally accepted conduct if engaged in by members of different races. Over the years, this Court has consistently repudiated "[d]istinctions between citizens solely because of their ancestry" as being "odious to a free people whose institutions are founded upon the doctrine of equality." *Hirabayashi v. United States*, 320 U.S. 81, 100 (1943). At the very least, the Equal Protection Clause demands that racial classifications, especially suspect in criminal statutes, be subjected to the "most rigid scrutiny," *Korematsu v. United States*, 323 U.S. 214, 216 (1944), and, if they are ever to be upheld, they must be shown to be necessary to the accomplishment of some permissible state objective, independent of the racial discrimination which it was the object of the Fourteenth Amendment to eliminate.

There is patently no legitimate overriding purpose independent of invidious racial discrimination which justifies this classification. The fact that Virginia prohibits only interracial marriages involving white persons demonstrates that the racial classifications must stand on their own justification, as measures designed to maintain White Supremacy.[11] We have consistently denied the constitutionality of measures which restrict the rights of citizens on account of race. There can be no doubt that restricting the freedom to marry solely because of racial classifications violates the central meaning of the Equal Protection Clause.

Mr. Justice STEWART, concurring.

I have previously expressed the belief that "it is simply not possible for a state law to be valid under our Constitution which makes the criminality of an act depend upon the race of the actor." *McLaughlin v. State of Florida*, 379 U.S. 184, 198 (1964) (concurring opinion). Because I adhere to that belief, I concur in the judgment of the Court.

Points for Discussion

a. Theory of Equality

Why exactly did Virginia's ban on inter-racial marriages violate the Equal Protection Clause? Notice that the statute prevented white people from marrying black people, just as it prevented black people from marrying white people. If the Equal Protection Clause requires equality of treatment, rather than equality of result—which seemed to be the view

---

[11] Appellants point out that the State's concern in these statutes, as expressed in the words of the 1924 Act's title, "An Act to Preserve Racial Integrity," extends only to the integrity of the white race. While Virginia prohibits whites from marrying any nonwhite (subject to the exception for the descendants of Pocahontas), Negroes, Orientals, and any other racial class may intermarry without statutory interference. Appellants contend that this distinction renders Virginia's miscegenation statutes arbitrary and unreasonable even assuming the constitutional validity of an official purpose to preserve "racial integrity." We need not reach this contention because we find the racial classifications in these statutes repugnant to the Fourteenth Amendment, even assuming an even-handed state purpose to protect the "integrity" of all races.

of the Court in <u>Davis</u>, above—then why aren't laws that impose equal burdens on persons of different races constitutional? Does *Brown* provide the answer?

Was the problem with the statute at issue in <u>Loving</u> that it did not in fact impose such equal burdens? Consider footnote 11 to the Court's opinion, which seems to make clear that the statute in fact did not apply equally to persons of different races. Why didn't the Court simply rely on this ground to invalidate the statute? If it had, would it have in effect been suggesting that a more carefully drawn, but still race-conscious, statute that prohibited all inter-racial marriages would be permissible?

Is the point that all regulation that consciously distinguishes on the basis of race is constitutionally suspect, even if the law does not "burden" one race any more than it burdens any other race? Or was the Court's theory instead that the statute was so clearly designed to advance the cause of "white supremacy" that its purpose was therefore to *discriminate* on the basis of race? Or instead was the theory simply that, under the Equal Protection Clause, it is not enough for the government to treat *races* equally, but instead the government must also treat *persons* equally? If the law says that a white person may marry a white person but that a black person may not marry a white person, is the black person being treated equally? What view does the text of the Equal Protection Clause support?

b. Marriage and Race

In *Palmore v. Sidoti*, 466 U.S. 429 (1984), the Court held that a state court violated the Equal Protection Clause when it denied custody of a child to the mother because the mother, who was white, had married an African-American man. The state court had reasoned that the child would face stigmatization at school because she lived in a "racially mixed household." The Supreme Court acknowledged that it "would ignore reality to suggest that racial and ethnic prejudices do not exist or that all manifestations of those prejudices have been eliminated." But even if "[p]rivate biases [are] outside the reach of the law, [the] law cannot, directly or indirectly, give them effect." The Court concluded that the "effects of racial prejudice, however real, cannot justify a racial classification removing an infant child from the custody of its natural mother found to be an appropriate person to have such custody."

c. Are Race-Conscious but Facially Symmetrical Policies Ever Constitutional?

In *Johnson v. California*, 543 U.S. 499 (2005), the Court considered an unwritten policy that the California Department of Corrections (CDC) followed of assigning new inmates who had been transferred from another correctional facility to double cells, for a period of up to 60 days, based on the inmates' race. The CDC admitted that the chances of an inmate being assigned a cellmate of another race during this 60-day period were "petty close to zero percent." At the end of the 60-day period, inmates were assigned to cells without consideration of race. The state defended the policy on the ground that it was necessary to prevent violence caused by racial gangs; the state argued that the 60-day period of segregation enabled prison officials to determine whether new inmates posed a danger to others. The state argued that the policy should not be subject to strict scrutiny because it "neither benefit[ed] nor burden[ed] one group or individual more than any other group or individual," and thus did not have a discriminatory effect on persons of any particular race. The Court disagreed, holding that the policy was subject to strict scrutiny, although the Court did not decide whether the policy survived that level of scrutiny. Does the Court's decision in *Johnson* mean that race-conscious policies that are not motivated by a discriminatory purpose and that do not have a racially discriminatory effect are nevertheless always suspect?

----

6. Affirmative Action

The Court in <u>Loving</u> stated that the Equal Protection Clause forbids all "*invidious* racial discriminations" (emphasis added). Are there laws or government policies that classify on the basis of race but that are not invidious? This question has had significant salience for at least the last thirty years for the debate over race-based affirmative action. Affirmative action programs typically seek to give preference, in school admissions, hiring, or similar decisions, to members of certain disadvantaged or historically under-represented minority groups. Are such programs unconstitutional because they distribute benefits and burdens on the basis of race? Or is there a fundamental difference between policies that seek to exclude and those that seek to include—or, as Justice Stevens once put it, between "a 'No Trespassing' sign and a welcome mat"? *Adarand Constructors, Inc. v. Pena*, 515 U.S. 200, 245 (1995) (Stevens, J., dissenting). If the answer to these questions comes from the Court's decision in <u>Brown</u>—which, after all, many view as the paradigmatic statement of the Equal Protection Clause's commitment to racial equality—then which of the rationales that we discussed above for <u>Brown</u> should provide that answer?

In 1978, the Court held in *Regents of the University of California v. Bakke*, 438 U.S. 265 (1978), that a university may constitutionally consider race as one factor in its admissions process. The medical school at the University of California at Davis reserved 16 out of the 100 slots in each incoming class for disadvantaged members of certain minority groups. Allan Bakke, a white male, sued the university after he was rejected twice for admission, even though minorities with lower scores had been granted admission. The Court issued a fractured opinion. Justice Stevens, joined by Chief Justice Burger and Justices Stewart and Rehnquist, asserted that the set-aside system violated Title VI of the Civil Rights Act of 1964, which prohibits discrimination on the basis of race by institutions receiving federal funds; because of this conclusion, they did not reach the constitutional question. They would have affirmed an injunction preventing the University from considering race in admissions. Justice Brennan, joined by Justices White, Marshall, and Blackmun, found no statutory violation and urged the application of intermediate scrutiny for racial classifications that benefit minorities; under this standard, the four Justices would have upheld the affirmative action program. Finally, Justice Powell, who wrote only for himself but cast the deciding vote, concluded that strict scrutiny should apply, and that under that standard a quota system is unconstitutional. But he also declared that a public university may permissibly consider race as one factor in admissions in order to achieve a diverse student body. Justice Powell stated:

> Petitioner urges us to [hold] that discrimination against members of the white "majority" cannot be suspect if its purpose can be characterized as "benign." [But] the difficulties entailed in varying the level of judicial review according to a perceived "preferred" status of a particular racial or ethnic minority are intractable. [T]he white "majority" itself is composed of various minority groups, most of which can lay claim to a history of prior discrimination at the hands of the State and private individuals. *** Moreover, there are serious problems of justice connected with the idea of preference itself. First, it may not always be clear that a so-called preference is in fact benign. *** Second, preferential programs may only reinforce common stereotypes holding that certain groups are unable to achieve success without special protection based on a factor having no relationship to individual worth. Third, there is a measure of inequity in forcing innocent persons in respondent's position to bear the burdens of redressing grievances not of their making. *** When [classifications] touch upon an individual's race or ethnic background, he is entitled to a judicial determination that the burden he is asked to bear on that basis is precisely tailored to serve a compelling governmental interest.

> The State certainly has a legitimate and substantial interest in ameliorating, or eliminating where feasible, the disabling effects of identified discrimination. [But the goal of redressing] specific instances of racial discrimination [is] far more focused than the remedying of the effects of "societal discrimination," an amorphous concept of injury that may be ageless in its reach into the past. We have never approved a classification that aids persons perceived as members of relatively victimized groups at the expense of other innocent individuals in the absence of judicial, legislative, or administrative findings of constitutional or statutory violations. *** Without such findings of constitutional or statutory violations, it cannot be said that the government has any greater interest in helping one individual than in refraining from harming another.

> [The attainment of a diverse student body] clearly is a constitutionally permissible goal for an institution of higher education. *** As the interest of diversity is compelling in the context of a university's admissions program, the question remains whether the program's racial classification is necessary to promote this interest. *** [P]etitioner's argument that [the set-aside program] is the only effective means of serving the interest of diversity is seriously flawed. *** The diversity that furthers a compelling state interest encompasses a far broader array of qualifications and characteristics of which racial or ethnic origin is but a single though important element. Petitioner's special admissions program, focused *solely* on ethnic diversity, would hinder rather than further attainment of genuine diversity.

> The experience of other university admissions programs, which take race into account in achieving [educational diversity], demonstrates that the assignment of a fixed number of places to a minority group is not a necessary means toward that end. [Justice Powell cited Harvard College's policy, under which the race of an otherwise qualified applicant] "may tip the balance in his favor just as geographic origin or a life spent on a farm may tip the balance in other candidates' cases." In such an admissions program, race or ethnic background may be deemed a "plus" in a particular applicant's file, yet it does not insulate the individual from comparison with all other candidates for the available seats. *** This kind of program treats each applicant as an individual in the admissions process. *** [Whereas a] facial intent to discriminate [is] evident in petitioner's preference program, [no] such facial infirmity exists in an admissions program where race or ethnic background is simply one element—to be weighed fairly against other elements—in the selection process. *** And a court would not assume that a university, profess-

ing to employ a facially nondiscriminatory admissions policy, would operate it as a cover for the functional equivalent of a quota system.

Justice Powell's views were particularly important because he provided the fifth vote to invalidate the petitioner's admissions policy and the fifth vote for the view that universities can use race as a factor in the admissions process (and thus for dissolving the injunction precluding the University from considering race in admissions decisions).

In the years after *Bakke*, the Court continued to struggle with the constitutional status of affirmative action programs, unable to produce a majority for any one approach. The Court finally found five votes for one approach in the case that follows.

City of Richmond v. J. A. Croson Co.

488 U.S. 469 (1989)

Justice O'CONNOR announced the judgment of the Court and delivered the opinion of the Court with respect to Parts I, III-B, and IV, an opinion with respect to Part II, in which THE CHIEF JUSTICE and Justice WHITE join, and an opinion with respect to Parts III-A and V, in which THE CHIEF JUSTICE, Justice WHITE, and Justice KENNEDY join.

I

On April 11, 1983, the Richmond City Council adopted the Minority Business Utilization Plan (the Plan). The Plan required prime contractors to whom the city awarded construction contracts to subcontract at least 30% of the dollar amount of the contract to one or more Minority Business Enterprises (MBE's). *** The Plan defined an MBE as "[a] business at least fifty-one (51) percent of which is owned and controlled [by] minority group members," [who in turn were] defined as "[c]itizens of the United States who are Blacks, Spanish-speaking, Orientals, Indians, Eskimos, or Aleuts." *** The Plan authorized the Director of the Department of General Services [to] "allow waivers in those individual situations where a contractor can prove to the satisfaction of the director that the requirements herein cannot be achieved."

Proponents of the set-aside provision relied on a study which indicated that, while the general population of Richmond was 50% black, only 0.67% of the city's prime construction contracts had been awarded to minority businesses in the 5-year period from 1978 to 1983. *** There was no direct evidence of race discrimination on the part of the city in letting contracts or any evidence that the city's prime contractors had discriminated against minority-owned subcontractors.

[Respondent Croson, a mechanical plumbing and heating contractor, submitted a bid to install plumbing fixtures at the city jail. Although the city initially accepted Croson's bid, the company was unable to find MBE subcontractors that would work on the job for a price that respondent considered appropriate.] The city denied both Croson's request for a waiver and its suggestion that the contract price be raised. The city informed Croson that it had decided to rebid the project. [Croson filed suit arguing that the Richmond ordinance was unconstitutional.]

II

In [*Fullilove v. Klutznick*, 448 U.S. 448 (1980)], we upheld [a] minority set-aside [that Congress had created for certain contracts with the federal government]. The principal opinion in <u>*Fullilove*</u> [did] not employ "strict scrutiny" or any other traditional standard of equal protection review. [Instead, relying on Congress's remedial powers under Section 5 of the Fourteenth Amendment, the principal opinion concluded that the limited use of racial and ethnic criteria was a permissible means for Congress to carry out its objectives.]

> **Make the Connection**
>
> We will consider the scope of Congress's power to enforce the Fourteenth Amendment in Chapter 13.

That Congress may identify and redress the effects of society-wide discrimination does not mean that, *a fortiori,* the States and their political subdivisions are free to decide that such remedies are appropriate. Section 1 of the Fourteenth Amendment is an explicit *constraint* on state power, and the States must undertake any remedial efforts in accordance with that provision. [T]he Framers of the Fourteenth Amendment [desired] to place clear limits on the States' use of race as a criterion for legislative action, and to have the federal courts enforce those limitations.

III

A

The Richmond Plan denies certain citizens the opportunity to compete for a fixed percentage of public contracts based solely upon their race. To whatever racial group these citizens belong, their "personal rights" to be treated with equal dignity and respect are implicated by a rigid rule erecting race as the sole criterion in an aspect of public decision-making. Absent searching judicial inquiry into the justification for such race-based measures, there is simply no way of determining what classifications are "benign" or "remedial" and what classifications are in fact motivated by illegitimate notions of racial inferiority or simple racial politics. *** Classifications based on race carry a danger of stigmatic harm. Unless they are strictly reserved for remedial settings, they may in fact promote notions of racial inferiority and lead to a politics of racial hostility. [T]he standard of review under the Equal Protection Clause is not dependent on the race of those burdened or benefited by a particular classification.

In this case, blacks constitute approximately 50% of the population of the city of Richmond. Five of the nine seats on the city council are held by blacks. The concern that a political majority will more easily act to the disadvantage of a minority based on unwarranted assumptions or incomplete facts would seem to militate for, not against, the application of heightened judicial scrutiny in this case.

B

While there is no doubt that the sorry history of both private and public discrimination in this country has contributed to a lack of opportunities for black entrepreneurs, this observation, standing alone, cannot justify a rigid racial quota in the awarding of public contracts in Richmond, Virginia. [An] amorphous claim that there has been past discrimination in a particular industry cannot justify the use of an unyielding racial quota. *** While the States and their subdivisions may take remedial action when they possess evidence that their own spending practices are exacerbating a pattern of prior discrimination, they must identify that discrimination, public or private, with some specificity before they may use race-conscious relief.

[None] of the evidence presented by the city points to any identified discrimination in the Richmond construction industry. We, therefore, hold that the city has failed to demonstrate a compelling interest in apportioning public contracting opportunities on the basis of race. To accept Richmond's claim that past societal discrimination alone can serve as the basis for rigid racial preferences would be to open the door to competing claims for "remedial relief" for every disadvantaged group. The dream of a Nation of equal citizens in a society where race is irrelevant to personal opportunity and achievement would be lost in a mosaic of shifting preferences based on inherently unmeasurable claims of past wrongs. *** We think such a result would be contrary to both the letter and spirit of a constitutional provision whose central command is equality.

IV

[I]t is almost impossible to assess whether the Richmond Plan is narrowly tailored to remedy prior discrimination since it is not linked to identified discrimination in any way. We limit ourselves to two observations in this regard. First, there does not appear to have been any consideration of the use of race-neutral means [such as a program of city financing for small firms] to increase minority business participation in city contracting. Second, the 30% quota cannot be said to be narrowly tailored to any goal, except perhaps outright racial balancing. It rests upon the "completely unrealistic" assumption that minorities will choose a particular trade in lockstep proportion to their representation in the local population. *** Under Richmond's scheme, a successful black, Hispanic, or Oriental entrepreneur from anywhere in the country enjoys an absolute preference over other citizens based solely on their race. We think it obvious that such a program is not narrowly tailored to remedy the effects of prior discrimination.

V

Nothing we say today precludes a state or local entity from taking action to rectify the effects of identified discrimination within its jurisdiction. If the city of Richmond had evidence before it that nonminority contractors were systematically excluding minority businesses from subcontracting opportunities it could take action to end the discriminatory exclusion. Where there is a significant statistical disparity between the number of qualified minority contractors willing and able to perform a particular service and the number of such contractors actually engaged by the locality or the locality's prime contractors, an inference of discriminatory exclusion could arise. Under such circumstances, the city could act to dismantle the closed business system by taking appropriate measures against those who discriminate on the basis of race or other illegitimate criteria. In the extreme case, some form of narrowly tailored racial preference might be necessary to break down patterns of deliberate exclusion.

Justice STEVENS, concurring in part and concurring in the judgment.

I [do] not agree with the premise that seems to underlie today's decision, [that] a governmental decision that rests on a racial classification is never permissible except as a remedy for a past wrong. [I]nstead of engaging in a debate over the proper standard of review to apply in affirmative-action litigation, I believe it is more constructive to try to identify the characteristics of the advantaged and disadvantaged classes that may justify their disparate treatment. In this case that approach convinces me that, instead of carefully identifying the characteristics of the two classes of contractors that are respectively favored and disfavored by its ordinance, the Richmond City Council has merely engaged in the type of stereotypical analysis that is a hallmark of violations of the Equal Protection Clause. Whether we look at the class of persons benefited by the ordinance or at the disadvantaged class, the same conclusion emerges.

Justice SCALIA, concurring in the judgment.

I do not agree [with] Justice O'CONNOR's dictum suggesting that, despite the Fourteenth Amendment, state and local governments may in some circumstances discriminate on the basis of race in order (in a broad sense) "to ameliorate the effects of past discrimination." *** It is plainly true that in our society blacks have suffered discrimination immeasurably greater than any directed at other racial groups. But those who believe that racial preferences can help to "even the score" display, and reinforce, a manner of thinking by race that was the source of the injustice and that will, if it endures within our society, be the source of more injustice still. *** Racial preferences appear to "even the score" (in some small degree) only if one embraces the proposition that our society is appropriately viewed as divided into races, making it right that an injustice rendered in the past to a black man should be compensated for by discriminating against a white. Nothing is worth that embrace.

[Justice KENNEDY'S opinion concurring in part and concurring in the judgment is omitted.]

Justice MARSHALL, with whom Justice BRENNAN and Justice BLACKMUN join, dissenting.

It is a welcome symbol of racial progress when the former capital of the Confederacy acts forthrightly to confront the effects of racial discrimination in its midst. *** Richmond has two powerful interests in setting aside a portion of public contracting funds for minority-owned enterprises. The first is the city's interest in eradicating the effects of past racial discrimination. [The second] interest is the prospective one of preventing the city's own spending decisions from reinforcing and perpetuating the exclusionary effects of past discrimination. *** The more government bestows its rewards on those persons or businesses that were positioned to thrive during a period of private racial discrimination, the tighter the deadhand grip of prior discrimination becomes on the present and future.

In my judgment, Richmond's set-aside plan [is] substantially related to the interests it seeks to serve in remedying past discrimination and in ensuring that municipal contract procurement does not perpetuate that discrimination. [The plan] is limited to five years in duration, [contains] a waiver provision freeing from its subcontracting requirements those nonminority firms that demonstrate that they cannot comply with its provisions[, and affects only] 3% of overall Richmond area contracting.

A profound difference separates governmental actions that themselves are racist, and governmental actions that seek to remedy the effects of prior racism or to prevent neutral governmental activity from perpetuating the effects of such racism. *** Racial classifications "drawn on the presumption that one race is inferior to another or because they put the weight of government behind racial hatred and separatism" warrant the strictest judicial scrutiny because of the very irrelevance of these rationales. By contrast, racial classifications drawn for the purpose of remedying the effects of discrimination that itself was race based have a highly pertinent basis: the tragic and indelible fact that discrimination against blacks and other racial minorities in this Nation has pervaded our Nation's history and continues to scar our society.

In concluding that remedial classifications warrant no different standard of review under the Constitution than the most brutal and repugnant forms of state-sponsored racism, a majority of this Court signals that it regards racial discrimination as largely a phenomenon of the past, and that government bodies need no longer preoccupy themselves with rectifying racial injustice. I, however, do not believe this Nation is anywhere close to eradicating racial discrimination or its vestiges. In constitutionalizing its wishful thinking, the majority today does a grave disservice not only to those victims of past and present racial discrimination in this Nation whom government has sought to assist, but also to this Court's long tradition of approaching issues of race with the utmost sensitivity.

[Justice BLACKMUN's dissenting opinion is omitted.]

Points for Discussion

a. Individuals vs. Groups

Does the Equal Protection Clause protect only individuals, or does it instead pay attention to group rights? Justices O'Connor and Scalia suggested in *Croson* that its protections from discrimination on the basis of race are solely individualistic. It follows from this view that the government cannot deny a person a benefit solely on the basis of the person's race, regardless of the status of the group that benefits from the denial. Justice Marshall, in contrast, appeared to assert that the Clause's protections can be group-based as well as individualistic, and thus that policies that seek to protect disadvantaged racial groups are permissible. Which view do you find more compelling?

b. Affirmative Action and the Federal Government

After *Croson*, it appeared that state and federal efforts to use affirmative action in their public contracting programs might be subject to different levels of judicial scrutiny. In *Adarand Constructors, Inc. v. Pena*, 515 U.S. 200 (1995), however, the Court held, in a 5-4 decision, that "federal racial classifications, like those of a State, must serve a compelling governmental interest, and must be narrowly tailored to further that interest." Although the Court, under that standard, invalidated a set-aside program in federal contracting, it sought to "dispel the notion that strict scrutiny is 'strict in theory, but fatal in fact.' The unhappy persistence of both the practice and the lingering effects of racial discrimination against minority groups in this country is an unfortunate reality, and government is not disqualified from acting in response to it."

Justice Scalia concurred in part, asserting that "government can never have a 'compelling interest' in discriminating on the basis of race in order to 'make up' for past racial discrimination in the opposite direction." He declared that "under our Constitution, there can be no such thing as either a creditor or a debtor race. That concept is alien to the Constitution's focus upon the individual ***. In the eyes of government, we are just one race here. It is American."

Justice Thomas also concurred in part, writing separately to "express [his] disagreement with the premise underlying Justice Stevens' and Justice Ginsburg's dissents: that there is a racial paternalism exception to the principle of equal protection." In Justice Thomas's view, there is a "moral [and] constitutional equivalence between laws designed to subjugate a race and those that distribute benefits on the basis of race in order to foster some current notion of equality." He asserted that "[s]o-called 'benign' discrimination *** stamp[s] minorities with a badge of inferiority and may cause them to develop dependencies or to adopt an attitude that they are 'entitled' to preferences." To Justice Thomas, both affirmative action and "discrimination inspired by malicious prejudice" are "racial discrimination, plain and simple."

Justice Stevens dissented, asserting that "[t]here is no moral or constitutional equivalence between a policy that is designed to perpetuate a caste system and one that seeks to eradicate racial subordination. Invidious discrimination is an engine of oppression, subjugating a disfavored group to enhance or maintain the power of the majority." In contrast, he asserted, "[r]emedial race-based preferences reflect the opposite impulse: a desire to foster equality in society. No sensible conception of the Government's constitutional obligation to 'govern impartially' should ignore this distinction." Justice Ginsburg also dissented, contending that "[b]ias both conscious and unconscious, reflecting traditional and unexamined habits of thought, keeps up barriers that must come down if equal opportunity and nondiscrimination are ever genuinely to become this country's law and practice." She asserted that given the history of racial discrimination and its practical consequences, "Congress surely can conclude that a carefully designed affirmative action program may help to realize, finally, the 'equal protection of the laws' the Fourteenth Amendment has promised since 1868."

After *Adarand*, all government-sponsored affirmative action programs are subject to strict scrutiny. Are there any such programs that can survive that level of scrutiny? Note that *Croson* and *Adarand* both involved affirmative action programs in public contracting. Are there stronger constitutional arguments for affirmative action in the context of education? Recall that five Justices concluded in *Bakke* that there were. Did the view expressed by five Justices in *Bakke* that universities may take race into account in admissions decisions survive *Croson* and *Adarand*? Consider the two cases that follow, which the Court decided on the same day.

Grutter v. Bollinger

539 U.S. 306 (2003)

Justice O'CONNOR delivered the opinion of the Court.

This case requires us to decide whether the use of race as a factor in student admissions by the University of Michigan Law School is unlawful. *** The hallmark of [the Law School's admissions] policy is its focus on academic ability coupled with a flexible assessment of applicants' talents, experiences, and potential "to contribute to the learning of those around them." *** In reviewing an applicant's file, admissions officials must consider the applicant's undergraduate grade point average (GPA) and Law School Admission Test (LSAT) score because they are important (if imperfect) predictors of academic success in law school. [In addition, so-called] "soft variables" such as "the enthusiasm of recommenders, the quality of the undergraduate institution, the quality of the applicant's essay, and the areas and difficulty of undergraduate course selection" are all brought to bear in assessing an "applicant's likely contributions to the intellectual and social life of the institution."

The policy aspires to "achieve that diversity which has the potential to enrich everyone's education and thus make a law school class stronger than the sum of its parts." The policy does not restrict the types of diversity contributions eligible for "substantial weight" in the admissions process ***. The policy does, however, reaffirm the Law School's longstanding commitment [to] "racial and ethnic diversity with special reference to the inclusion of students from groups which have been historically discriminated against, like African-Americans, Hispanics and Native Americans, who without this commitment might not be represented in our student body in meaningful numbers." ***

Petitioner Barbara Grutter is a white Michigan resident who applied to the Law School in 1996 with a 3.8 GPA and 161 LSAT score. The Law School initially placed petitioner on a waiting list, but subsequently rejected her application. [She filed suit contending, among other things, that the admissions policy was inconsistent with the Equal Protection Clause.]

We have held that all racial classifications imposed by government "must be analyzed by a reviewing court under strict scrutiny." *Adarand Constructors, Inc. v. Peña*, 515 U.S. 200

(1995). *** Not every decision influenced by race is equally objectionable, and strict scrutiny is designed to provide a framework for carefully examining the importance and the sincerity of the reasons advanced by the governmental decisionmaker for the use of race in that particular context.

> **Take Note**
>
> The Court defers to the school's judgment that diversity is important and beneficial. Is this deference consistent with the Court's ordinary approach in cases involving strict scrutiny?

[W]e have never held that the only governmental use of race that can survive strict scrutiny is remedying past discrimination. Nor, since *Bakke*, have we directly addressed the use of race in the context of public higher education. Today, we hold that the Law School has a compelling interest in attaining a diverse student body. The Law School's educational judgment that such diversity is essential to its educational mission is one to which we defer. *** We have long recognized that, given the important purpose of public education and the expansive freedoms of speech and thought associated with the university environment, universities occupy a special niche in our constitutional tradition.

As part of its goal of "assembling a class that is both exceptionally academically qualified and broadly diverse," the Law School seeks to "enroll a 'critical mass' of minority students." The Law School's interest is not simply "to assure within its student body some specified percentage of a particular group merely because of its race or ethnic origin." *Bakke,* 438 U.S., at 307 (opinion of Powell, J.). That would amount to outright racial balancing, which is patently unconstitutional. Rather, the Law School's concept of critical mass is defined by reference to the educational benefits that diversity is designed to produce.

These benefits are substantial. As the District Court emphasized, the Law School's admissions policy promotes "cross-racial understanding," helps to break down racial stereotypes, and "enables [students] to better understand persons of different races." These benefits are "important and laudable," because "classroom discussion is livelier, more spirited, and simply more enlightening and interesting" when the students have "the greatest possible variety of backgrounds."

The Law School's claim of a compelling interest is further bolstered by its *amici,* who point to the educational benefits that flow from student body diversity. [N]umerous studies show that student body diversity promotes learning outcomes, and "better prepares students for an increasingly diverse workforce and society, and better prepares them as professionals." *** These benefits are not theoretical but real, as major American businesses have made clear that the skills needed in today's increasingly global marketplace can only be developed through exposure to widely diverse people, cultures, ideas, and viewpoints. *** What is more, high-ranking retired officers and civilian leaders of the United States military assert that, "[b]ased on [their] decades of experience," a "highly qualified, racially diverse officer corps [is] essential to the military's ability to fulfill its principal mission to provide national security."

Effective participation by members of all racial and ethnic groups in the civic life of our

Nation is essential if the dream of one Nation, indivisible, is to be realized. Moreover, universities, and in particular, law schools, represent the training ground for a large number of our Nation's leaders. [In] order to cultivate a set of leaders with legitimacy in the eyes of the citizenry, it is necessary that the path to leadership be visibly open to talented and qualified individuals of every race and ethnicity.

We [also] find that the Law School's admissions program bears the hallmarks of a narrowly tailored plan. As Justice Powell made clear in *Bakke*, *** universities cannot establish quotas for members of certain racial groups or put members of those groups on separate admissions tracks. *** Universities can, however, consider race or ethnicity more flexibly as a "plus" factor in the context of individualized consideration of each and every applicant.

The Law School's goal of attaining a critical mass of underrepresented minority students does not transform its program into a quota. *** "[S]ome attention to numbers," without more, does not transform a flexible admissions system into a rigid quota. [B]etween 1993 and 1998, the number of African-American, Latino, and Native-American students in each class at the Law School varied from 13.5 to 20.1 percent, a range inconsistent with a quota.

> **Take Note**
>
> What does it mean to say that the Law School seeks a "critical mass" of minority students? Doesn't it have to mean that there is some threshold below which the number of students cannot drop? If so, why isn't it tantamount to a quota?

That a race-conscious admissions program does not operate as a quota does not, by itself, satisfy the requirement of individualized consideration. When using race as a "plus" factor in university admissions, a university's admissions program must remain flexible enough to ensure that each applicant is evaluated as an individual and not in a way that makes an applicant's race or ethnicity the defining feature of his or her application. Here, the Law School engages in a highly individualized, holistic review of each applicant's file, giving serious consideration to all the ways an applicant might contribute to a diverse educational environment. *** There is no policy, either *de jure* or *de facto,* of automatic acceptance or rejection based on any single "soft" variable. Unlike the program at issue in *Gratz v. Bollinger,* 539 U.S. 244 (2003), [which is discussed below], the Law School awards no mechanical, predetermined diversity "bonuses" based on race or ethnicity. [And the] Law School does not [limit] in any way the broad range of qualities and experiences that may be considered valuable contributions to student body diversity.

Petitioner and the United States argue that the Law School's plan is not narrowly tailored because race-neutral means exist to obtain the educational benefits of student body diversity that the Law School seeks. We disagree. Narrow tailoring does not require exhaustion of every conceivable race-neutral alternative. Nor does it require a university to choose between maintaining a reputation for excellence or fulfilling a commitment to provide educational opportunities to members of all racial groups. Narrow tailoring does, however, require serious, good faith consideration of workable race-neutral alternatives that will achieve the diversity the university seeks.

[T]he Law School sufficiently considered workable race-neutral alternatives. The District Court took the Law School to task for failing to consider race-neutral alternatives such as "using a lottery system" or "decreasing the emphasis for all applicants on undergraduate GPA and LSAT scores." But these alternatives would require a dramatic sacrifice of diversity, the academic quality of all admitted students, or both. *** So too with the suggestion that the Law School simply lower admissions standards for all students, a drastic remedy that would require the Law School to become a much different institution and sacrifice a vital component of its educational mission. The United States advocates "percentage plans," recently adopted by public undergraduate institutions in Texas, Florida, and California, to guarantee admission to all students above a certain class-rank threshold in every high school in the State. The United States does not, however, explain how such plans could work for graduate and professional schools. Moreover, even assuming such plans are race-neutral, they may preclude the university from conducting the individualized assessments necessary to assemble a student body that is not just racially diverse, but diverse along all the qualities valued by the university. We are satisfied that the Law School adequately considered race-neutral alternatives currently capable of producing a critical mass without forcing the Law School to abandon the academic selectivity that is the cornerstone of its educational mission.

We are mindful, however, that "[a] core purpose of the Fourteenth Amendment was to do away with all governmentally imposed discrimination based on race." *Palmore v. Sidoti,* 466 U.S. 429, 432 (1984). Accordingly, race-conscious admissions policies must be limited in time. This requirement reflects that racial classifications, however compelling their goals, are potentially so dangerous that they may be employed no more broadly than the interest demands. Enshrining a permanent justification for racial preferences would offend this fundamental equal protection principle. *** It has been 25 years since Justice Powell first approved the use of race to further an interest in student body diversity in the context of public higher education. Since that time, the number of minority applicants with high grades and test scores has indeed increased. We expect that 25 years from now, the use of racial preferences will no longer be necessary to further the interest approved today.

> **Food for Thought**
>
> Is the Court suggesting here that the Constitution will mean something different in 25 years? Or does it mean that circumstances will have changed sufficiently in 25 years such that affirmative action will no longer survive strict scrutiny? If the latter, how does the Court know? Is it realistic to believe that affirmative action in education will end in the year 2028?

[Justice GINSBURG's concurring opinion and Justice SCALIA's opinion concurring in part and dissenting in part are omitted.]

Justice THOMAS, with whom Justice SCALIA joins [in relevant part], concurring in part and dissenting in part.

I believe blacks can achieve in every avenue of American life without the meddling of university administrators. *** No one would argue that a university could set up a lower general admissions standard and then impose heightened requirements only on black applicants. Similarly, a university may not maintain a high admissions standard and grant exemptions to favored races. The Law School, of its own choosing, and for its own purposes, maintains an exclusionary admissions system that it knows produces racially disproportionate results. Racial discrimination is not a permissible solution to the self-inflicted wounds of this elitist admissions policy.[4]

A majority of the Court has validated only two circumstances where "pressing public necessity" or a "compelling state interest" can possibly justify racial discrimination by state actors. First, the lesson of <u>Korematsu</u> is that national security constitutes a "pressing public necessity," though the government's use of race to advance that objective must be narrowly tailored. Second, the Court has recognized as a compelling state interest a government's effort to remedy past discrimination for which it is responsible. *Richmond v. J.A. Croson Co.,* 488 U.S. 469, 504 (1989). *** Where the Court has accepted only national security, and rejected even the best interests of a child, [see *Palmore v. Sidoti,* 466 U.S. 429 (1984),] as a justification for racial discrimination, I conclude that only those measures the State must take to provide a bulwark against anarchy, or to prevent violence, will constitute a "pressing public necessity."

Unlike the majority, I seek to define with precision the interest being asserted by the Law School before determining whether that interest is so compelling as to justify racial discrimination. *** The proffered interest that the majority vindicates today [is] not simply "diversity." Instead the Court upholds the use of racial discrimination as a tool to advance the Law School's interest in offering a marginally superior education while maintaining an elite institution. *** While legal education at a public university may be good policy or otherwise laudable, it is obviously not a pressing public necessity ***. Michigan [thus] has no compelling interest in having a law school at all, much less an *elite* one. Still, even assuming that a State may, under appropriate circumstances, demonstrate a cognizable interest in having an elite law school, Michigan has failed to do so here.

The only cognizable state interests vindicated by operating a public law school [are] the education of that State's citizens and the training of that State's lawyers. *** The Law School today, however, does precious little training of those attorneys who will serve the citizens of Michigan. [Less] than 16% of the Law School's graduating class elects to stay in Michigan after law school. *** It does not take a social scientist to conclude that it is precisely the Law School's status as an elite institution that causes it to be a waystation for the rest of the country's lawyers, rather than a training ground for those who will remain in Michigan. The Law School's decision to be an elite institution does little to advance the welfare of the people of Michigan or any cognizable interest of the State of Michigan.

With the adoption of different admissions methods, such as accepting all students who

---

[4] The Law School believes both that the educational benefits of a racially engineered student body are large and that adjusting its overall admissions standards to achieve the same racial mix would require it to sacrifice its elite status. If the Law School is correct that the educational benefits of "diversity" are so great, then achieving them by altering admissions standards should not compromise its elite status. The Law School's reluctance to do this suggests that the educational benefits it alleges are not significant or do not exist at all.

meet minimum qualifications, the Law School could achieve its vision of the racially aesthetic student body without the use of racial discrimination. [Indeed,] the Court ignores the fact that other top law schools have succeeded in meeting their aesthetic demands without racial discrimination. *** The sky has not fallen at Boalt Hall at the University of California, Berkeley, for example. Prior to [an amendment to the state Constitution that] bars the State from "grant[ing] preferential treatment [on] the basis of race [in] the operation of [public] education," Boalt Hall enrolled 20 blacks and 28 Hispanics in its first-year class for 1996. In 2002, without deploying express racial discrimination in admissions, Boalt's entering class enrolled 14 blacks and 36 Hispanics.

I must contest the notion that the Law School's discrimination benefits those admitted as a result of it. *** The Law School tantalizes unprepared students with the promise of a University of Michigan degree and all of the opportunities that it offers. These overmatched students take the bait, only to find that they cannot succeed in the cauldron of competition. Indeed, to cover the tracks of [supporters of affirmative action], this cruel farce of racial discrimination must continue—in selection for the Michigan Law Review and in hiring at law firms and for judicial clerkships—until the "beneficiaries" are no longer tolerated. While these students may graduate with law degrees, there is no evidence that they have received a qualitatively better legal education (or become better lawyers) than if they had gone to a less "elite" law school for which they were better prepared.

It is uncontested that each year, the Law School admits a handful of blacks who would be admitted in the absence of racial discrimination. Who can differentiate between those who belong and those who do not? The majority of blacks are admitted to the Law School because of discrimination, and because of this policy all are tarred as undeserving. This problem of stigma does not depend on determinacy as to whether those stigmatized are actually the "beneficiaries" of racial discrimination. When blacks take positions in the highest places of government, industry, or academia, it is an open question today whether their skin color played a part in their advancement. The question itself is the stigma—because either racial discrimination did play a role, in which case the person may be deemed "otherwise unqualified," or it did not, in which case asking the question itself unfairly marks those blacks who would succeed without discrimination.

Chief Justice REHNQUIST, with whom Justice SCALIA, Justice KENNEDY, and Justice THOMAS join, dissenting.

In practice, the Law School's program bears little or no relation to its asserted goal of achieving "critical mass." *** From 1995 through 2000, the Law School admitted between 1,130 and 1,310 students. Of those, between 13 and 19 were Native American, between 91 and 108 were African-American, and between 47 and 56 were Hispanic. *** [T]he correlation between the percentage of the Law School's pool of applicants who are members of the three minority groups and the percentage of the admitted applicants who are members of these same groups is far too precise to be dismissed as merely the result of the school paying "some attention to [the] numbers."

The Law School has offered no explanation for its actual admissions practices and, unexplained, we are bound to conclude that the Law School has managed its admissions program, not to achieve a "critical mass," but to extend offers of admission to members of selected minority groups in proportion to their statistical representation in the applicant pool. But this is precisely the type of racial balancing that the Court itself calls "patently unconstitutional."

[Justice KENNEDY's dissenting opinion is omitted.]

Gratz v. Bollinger

539 U.S. 244 (2003)

Chief Justice REHNQUIST delivered the opinion of the Court.

[Petitioners Jennifer Gratz and Patrick Hamacher were white students who were denied admission to the University of Michigan's College of Literature, Science, and the Arts (LSA). They filed suit to challenge the University's admission policies, pursuant to which the Office of Undergraduate Admissions used a "selection index" to award points to each applicant. The maximum score was 150 points, and all students with 100 points or more were admitted. Points were awarded based on high school grade point average, standardized test scores, academic quality of an applicant's high school, strength or weakness of high school curriculum, in-state residency, alumni relationship, personal essay, and personal achievement or leadership. In addition, African-American, Hispanic, and Native-American applicants were awarded 20 points for their membership in under-represented racial or ethnic minority groups. During the period in question, the University admitted virtually every qualified applicant from these groups.]

> **Make the Connection**
>
> Even if LSA did not have an affirmative action policy, there is no guarantee that the plaintiffs would have been admitted, as there may have been many other white students with stronger qualifications who were also denied admission under the policy. Should the Court have concluded that the plaintiffs lacked standing? We considered standing—and this question in particular—in Chapter 2.

We find that the University's policy [is] not narrowly tailored to achieve the interest in educational diversity that respondents claim justifies their program. *** The current LSA policy does not provide [individualized] consideration. The LSA's policy automatically distributes 20 points to every single applicant from an "underrepresented minority" group, as defined by the University. The only consideration that accompanies this distribution of points is a factual review of an application to determine whether an individual is a member of one of these minority groups. Moreover, unlike Justice Powell's example, where the race of a "particular black applicant" could be considered without being decisive, see *Bakke,* 438 U.S., at 317 the LSA's automatic distribution of 20 points has the effect of making "the factor of [race] decisive" for virtually every minimally qualified underrepresented minority applicant. *** Instead of considering how the differing backgrounds, experiences, and characteristics of students A, B, and C might benefit the University, admissions counselors reviewing LSA applications would simply award both A and B 20 points because their applications indicate that they are African-American, and student C, [whose "extraordinary artistic talent" rivaled that of Monet or Picasso,] would receive [only] up to 5 points for his "extraordinary talent" [under LSA's system].

We conclude, therefore, that because the University's use of race in its current freshman admissions policy is not narrowly tailored to achieve respondents' asserted compelling interest in diversity, the admissions policy violates the Equal Protection Clause of the Fourteenth Amendment.

Justice O'CONNOR, concurring.

Unlike the law school admissions policy the Court upholds today in [*Grutter*,] the procedures employed by the University of Michigan [do] not provide for a meaningful individualized review of applicants. [T]he Office of Undergraduate Admissions relies on the selection index to assign *every* underrepresented minority applicant the same, *automatic* 20-point bonus without consideration of the particular background, experiences, or qualities of each individual applicant. And this mechanized selection index score, by and large, automatically determines the admissions decision for each applicant. *** Although the Office of Undergraduate Admissions does assign 20 points to some "soft" variables other than race, the points available for other diversity contributions, such as leadership and service, personal achievement, and geographic diversity, are capped at much lower levels. Even the most outstanding national high school leader could never receive more than five points for his or her accomplishments ***. [T]he selection index, by setting up automatic, predetermined point allocations for the soft variables, ensures that the diversity contributions of applicants cannot be individually assessed. *** As a result, I join the Court's opinion reversing the decision of the District Court.

[Justice BREYER concurred in the judgment, joined Justice O'CONNOR's opinion "except insofar as it joins that of the Court," and joined Part I of Justice GINSBURG's dissenting opinion. Justice THOMAS's concurring opinion is omitted.]

Justice SOUTER, with whom Justice GINSBURG joins [in relevant part], dissenting.

The record does not describe a system with a quota like the one struck down in *Bakke*, which "insulate[d]" all nonminority candidates from competition from certain seats. *Bakke, supra*, at 317 (opinion of Powell, J.). *** The plan here, in contrast, lets all applicants compete for all places and values an applicant's offering for any place not only on grounds of race, but on grades, test scores, strength of high school, quality of course of study, residence, alumni relationships, leadership, personal character, socioeconomic disadvantage, athletic ability, and quality of a personal essay. [To be sure,] membership in an underrepresented minority is given a weight of 20 points on the 150-point scale. On the face of things, however, this assignment of specific points does not set race apart from all other weighted considerations. Nonminority students may receive 20 points for athletic ability, socioeconomic disadvantage, attendance at a socioeconomically disadvantaged or predominantly minority high school, or at the Provost's discretion; they may also receive

10 points for being residents of Michigan, 6 for residence in an underrepresented Michigan county, 5 for leadership and service, and so on.

The very nature of a college's permissible practice of awarding value to racial diversity means that race must be considered in a way that increases some applicants' chances for admission. Since college admission is not left entirely to inarticulate intuition, it is hard to see what is inappropriate in assigning some stated value to a relevant characteristic, whether it be reasoning ability, writing style, running speed, or minority race. *** Nor is it possible to say that the 20 points convert race into a decisive factor comparable to reserving minority places as in _Bakke._ Of course we can conceive of a point system in which the "plus" factor given to minority applicants would be so extreme as to guarantee every minority applicant a higher rank than every nonminority applicant in the university's admissions system. But petitioners do not have a convincing argument that the freshman admissions system operates this way.

> **Food for Thought**
>
> Do you agree with Justice Souter that the challenged policy is meaningfully different from the set-aside program invalidated in _Bakke_? At what point in his view would the "plus" factor approach become tantamount to a quota? Do you agree that it is "hard to see what is inappropriate" about giving someone 20 points solely because of his race, regardless of any other information about the person?

*** It suffices for me [that] there are no _Bakke_-like set-asides and that consideration of an applicant's whole spectrum of ability is no more ruled out by giving 20 points for race than by giving the same points for athletic ability or socioeconomic disadvantage.

[I]t seems especially unfair to treat the candor of the admissions plan as an Achilles' heel. In contrast to the college's forthrightness in saying just what plus factor it gives for membership in an underrepresented minority, it is worth considering the character of one alternative thrown up as preferable, because supposedly not based on race. Drawing on admissions systems used at public universities in California, Florida, and Texas, the United States contends that Michigan could get student diversity in satisfaction of its compelling interest by guaranteeing admission to a fixed percentage of the top students from each high school in Michigan. While there is nothing unconstitutional about such a practice, it nonetheless suffers from [the] disadvantage of deliberate obfuscation. The "percentage plans" are just as race conscious as the point scheme (and fairly so), but they get their racially diverse results without saying directly what they are doing or why they are doing it. In contrast, Michigan states its purpose directly and, if this were a doubtful case for me, I would be tempted to give Michigan an extra point of its own for its frankness. Equal protection cannot become an exercise in which the winners are the ones who hide the ball.

Justice GINSBURG, with whom Justice SOUTER joins, dissenting.

[T]he Court once again maintains that the same standard of review controls judicial inspection of all official race classifications. This insistence on "consistency" would be fitting were our Nation free of the vestiges of rank discrimination long reinforced by law. But we are not far distant from an overtly discriminatory past, and the effects of centuries of law-sanctioned inequality remain painfully evident in our communities and schools.

In the wake "of a system of racial caste only recently ended," *Adarand Constructors, Inc. v. Peña,* 515 U.S. 200, 273 (1995) (GINSBURG, J., dissenting), large disparities endure. Unemployment, poverty, and access to health care vary disproportionately by race. Neighborhoods and schools remain racially divided. African-American and Hispanic children are all too often educated in poverty-stricken and underperforming institutions. Adult African-Americans and Hispanics generally earn less than whites with equivalent levels of education. Equally credentialed job applicants receive different receptions depending on their race. Irrational prejudice is still encountered in real estate markets and consumer transactions. "Bias both conscious and unconscious, reflecting traditional and unexamined habits of thought, keeps up barriers that must come down if equal opportunity and non-discrimination are ever genuinely to become this country's law and practice." *Id.,* at 274.

In implementing [the instructions of the Equal Protection Clause], as I see it, government decisionmakers may properly distinguish between policies of exclusion and inclusion. Actions designed to burden groups long denied full citizenship stature are not sensibly ranked with measures taken to hasten the day when entrenched discrimination and its aftereffects have been extirpated. *** Our jurisprudence ranks race a "suspect" category, "not because [race] is inevitably an impermissible classification, but because it is one which usually, to our national shame, has been drawn for the purpose of maintaining racial inequality." *Norwalk Core v. Norwalk Redevelopment Agency,* 395 F.2d 920, 931-932 (C.A.2 1968). But where race is considered "for the purpose of achieving equality," no automatic proscription is in order.

Like other top-ranking institutions, the College has many more applicants for admission than it can accommodate in an entering class. Every applicant admitted under the current plan, petitioners do not here dispute, is qualified to attend the College. The racial and ethnic groups to which the College accords special consideration [historically] have been relegated to inferior status by law and social practice; their members continue to experience class-based discrimination to this day. There is no suggestion that the College adopted its current policy in order to limit or decrease enrollment by any particular racial or ethnic group, and no seats are reserved on the basis of race. *** The stain of generations of racial oppression is still visible in our society, and the determination to hasten its removal remains vital.

[Justice STEVENS dissented on the ground that petitioners lacked standing.]

————————

Points for Discussion

a. When Is Affirmative Action Permissible?

The Court in <u>Grutter</u> upheld a policy that gave some non-numerical advantage to minorities in order to achieve a "critical mass," but in <u>Gratz</u> invalidated a policy that awarded actual points on a numerical scale. Accordingly, an institution of higher education may sometimes constitutionally prefer minority applicants in order to advance the interest in diversity. Are you convinced that there is a meaningful difference between the types of admissions policies at issue in the two cases?

b. "Critical Mass"

How did the Law School (and the Court) define "critical mass"? If the admitted class would not have a critical mass of minority students absent an affirmative action program, then wouldn't the Law School's policy effectively operate to make the race of some admitted minority students dispositive? If so, how is that approach different in practice from the College's policy?

c. The Point of Affirmative Action

Isn't the whole point of affirmative action to give preference on the basis of race? After all, affirmative action would not be required in university admissions if race-neutral admissions policies could yield an optimally diverse class. Yet, as Justice Souter suggested, the import of the Court's decisions in *Grutter* and *Gratz* seems to be that affirmative action is permissible in higher education only when the school makes it seem as if race really doesn't matter. Is the Court's real point that a university is permitted to engage in race-based decision-making as long as it does not do so in a way that is too obvious?

d. Original Meaning of the Fourteenth Amendment

In March 1865, shortly before General Lee's surrender marked the end of the Civil War, Congress enacted the Freedmen's Bureau Act, 13 Stat. 507 (1865). Among other things, Congress charged the Bureau with providing relief and educational services to the freed slaves. Three years later, the Fourteenth Amendment was ratified. What does this suggest about the original understanding of race-conscious government policies designed to help disadvantaged minorities? See Eric Schnapper, *Affirmative Action and the Legislative History of the Fourteenth Amendment*, 71 Va. L. Rev. 753 (1985) (noting that around the time of ratification of the Fourteenth Amendment, Congress enacted a series of programs "whose benefits were expressly limited to blacks" and arguing that this history "strongly suggests that the framers of the amendment could not have intended it generally to prohibit affirmative action for blacks or other disadvantaged groups"). Is the Freedmen's Bureau Act arguably irrelevant in determining the original meaning of the Fourteenth Amendment, because it was enacted by Congress and the Fourteenth Amendment by its terms applies only to state governments? Is the Act irrelevant in determining the meaning of the Fourteenth Amendment, because its enactment predated the passage of the Amendment?

In any event, was Justice O'Connor's approach in *Grutter* originalist? Was Justice Thomas's? Does the "color-blind" vision of the Equal Protection Clause find support in the historical materials that we generally consult in determining the original meaning?

e. An Expiration Date on Affirmative Action?

Justice O'Connor suggested that affirmative action programs would no longer be constitutional in 25 years. Can constitutional rules have an expiration date? Or is the point that affirmative action will not be narrowly tailored in 25 years because of changes between now and then? What if nothing changes in those 25 years? Is the 25-year limit binding as a matter of *stare decisis*?

f. The Future of Affirmative Action Litigation

In his dissent in *Grutter*, Justice Scalia made the following prediction:

[Today's] split double header seems perversely designed to prolong the controversy and the litigation. Some future lawsuits will presumably focus on whether the discriminatory scheme in question contains enough evaluation of the applicant "as an individual," and sufficiently avoids "separate admissions tracks" ***. Some will focus on whether a university has [so] zealously pursued its "critical mass" as to make it an unconstitutional *de facto* quota system ***. Other lawsuits may focus on whether, in the particular setting at issue, any educational benefits flow from racial diversity. Still other suits may challenge the bona fides of the institution's expressed commitment to the educational benefits of diversity that immunize the discriminatory scheme in *Grutter*. (Tempting targets, one would suppose, will be those universities that talk the talk of multiculturalism and racial diversity in the courts but walk the walk of tribalism and racial segregation on their campuses—through minority-only student organizations, separate minority housing opportunities, separate minority student centers, even separate minority-only graduation ceremonies.) And still other suits may claim that the institution's racial preferences have gone below or above the mystical *Grutter*-approved "critical mass." Finally, litigation can be expected on behalf of minority groups intentionally short changed in the institution's composition of its generic minority "critical mass."

Do you agree that such suits are likely to follow? Who is likely to resolve them? If they reach the Supreme Court, how is it likely to decide them?

In answering the last question, consider the case that follows.

————————

Parents Involved in Community Schools v. Seattle School Dist. No. 1

551 U.S. 701 (2007)

Chief Justice ROBERTS announced the judgment of the Court, and delivered the opinion of the Court with respect to Parts I, II, III-A, and III-C, and an opinion with respect to Parts III-B and IV, in which Justices SCALIA, THOMAS, and ALITO join.

The school districts in these cases voluntarily adopted student assignment plans that rely upon race to determine which public schools certain children may attend. The Seattle school district classifies children as white or nonwhite; the Jefferson County school district as black or "other." In Seattle, this racial classification is used to allocate slots in oversubscribed high schools. In Jefferson County, [which embraces Louisville, Kentucky,] it is used to make certain elementary school assignments and to rule on transfer requests. In each case, the school district relies upon an individual student's race in assigning that student to a particular school, so that the racial balance at the school falls within a predetermined range based on the racial composition of the school district as a whole. Parents of students denied assignment to particular schools under these plans solely because of their race brought suit, contending that allocating children to different public schools on the basis of race violated the Fourteenth Amendment guarantee of equal protection.

[There are ten high schools in the Seattle School District, where white students constitute 41 percent of enrolled students and non-white students 59 percent. Incoming students rank the schools according to their preferences. If too many choose the same school, the District uses a series of "tiebreakers" to determine who will get to attend. If the school's racial composition deviates by more than 10% from the district's overall balance between white and non-white students, the race of the students who seek to attend is the second tiebreaker. In Jefferson County, where 34 percent of the students are black, the plan requires all non-magnet schools to maintain a black enrollment between 15 and 50 percent.]

III.A

It is well established that when the government distributes burdens or benefits on the basis of individual racial classifications, that action is reviewed under strict scrutiny. *Grutter v. Bollinger,* 539 U.S. 306, 326 (2003). [Our] prior cases, in evaluating the use of racial classifications in the school context, have recognized two interests that qualify as compelling. The first is the compelling interest of remedying the effects of past intentional discrimination. Yet the Seattle public schools have not shown that they were ever segregated by law, and were not subject to court-ordered desegregation decrees. The Jefferson County public schools were previously segregated by law and were subject to a desegregation decree entered in 1975. [But once] Jefferson County achieved unitary status, it had remedied the constitutional wrong that allowed race-based assignments. Any continued use of race must be justified on some other basis.

> **Definition**
>
> A school district achieved "unitary status" by eliminating *de jure* segregation and its vestiges, in compliance with the mandate of <u>Brown</u> and <u>Brown II</u>.

The second government interest we have recognized as compelling for purposes of strict scrutiny is the interest in diversity in higher education upheld in *Grutter,* 539 U.S., at 328. The specific interest found compelling in *Grutter* was student body diversity "in the context of higher education." *** The entire gist of the analysis in *Grutter* was that the admissions program at issue there focused on each applicant as an individual, and not simply as a member of a particular racial group. In the present cases, by contrast, race is not considered as part of a broader effort to achieve "exposure to widely diverse people, cultures, ideas, and viewpoints"; race, for some students, is determinative standing alone. The districts argue that other factors, such as student preferences, affect assignment decisions under their plans, but under each plan when race comes into play, it is decisive by itself. It is not simply one factor weighed with others in reaching a decision, as in *Grutter* ; it is *the* factor. *** Even when it comes to race, the plans here employ only a limited notion of diversity, viewing race exclusively in white/nonwhite terms in Seattle and black/"other" terms in Jefferson County.

B

Each school district argues that educational and broader socialization benefits flow from a racially diverse learning environment ***. The parties and their *amici* dispute whether racial diversity in schools in fact has a marked impact on test scores and other objective yardsticks or achieves intangible socialization benefits. The debate is not one we need to resolve, however, because it is clear that the racial classifications employed by the districts are not narrowly tailored to the goal of achieving the educational and social benefits asserted to flow from racial diversity. In design and operation, the plans are directed only to racial balance, pure and simple, an objective this Court has repeatedly condemned as illegitimate.

The plans are tied to each district's specific racial demographics, rather than to any pedagogic concept of the level of diversity needed to obtain the asserted educational benefits. [But the] districts offer no evidence that the level of racial diversity necessary to achieve the asserted educational benefits happens to coincide with the racial demographics of the respective school districts ***. This working backward to achieve a particular type of racial balance, rather than working forward from some demonstration of the level of diversity that provides the purported benefits, is a fatal flaw under our existing precedent. *** Accepting racial balancing as a compelling state interest would justify the imposition of racial proportionality throughout American society, contrary to our repeated recognition that "[a]t the heart of the Constitution's guarantee of equal protection lies the simple command that the Government must treat citizens as individuals, not as simply components of a racial, religious, sexual or national class." *** Racial balancing is not transformed from "patently unconstitutional" to a compelling state interest simply by relabeling it "racial diversity."

C

Food for Thought

Can you think of any race-neutral approaches that the school districts could take to achieve their goals? If so, do you think that they would be effective?

[The] minimal effect these classifications have on student assignments [suggests] that other means would be effective. Seattle's racial tiebreaker results, in the end, only in shifting a small number of students between schools. *** Similarly, Jefferson County's use of racial classifications has only a minimal effect on the assignment of students. *** Jefferson County estimates that the racial guidelines account for only 3 percent of assignments. [While] we do not suggest that *greater* use of race would be preferable, the minimal impact of the districts' racial classifications on school enrollment casts doubt on the necessity of using racial classifications. [The] districts have also failed to show that they considered methods other than explicit racial classifications to achieve their stated goals.

IV

In *Brown v. Board of Education,* 347 U.S. 483 (1954), [it] was not the inequality of the facilities but the fact of legally separating children on the basis of race on which the Court relied to find a constitutional [violation]. *** The parties and their *amici* debate which side is more faithful to the heritage of <u>Brown</u>, but the position of the plaintiffs in <u>Brown</u> was spelled out in their brief and could not have been clearer: "[T]he Fourteenth Amendment prevents states from according differential treatment to American children on the basis of their color or race." What do the racial classifications at issue here do, if not accord differential treatment on the basis of race? As counsel who appeared before this Court for the plaintiffs in <u>Brown</u> put it: "We have one fundamental contention which we will seek to develop in the course of this argument, and that contention is that no State has any authority under the equal-protection clause of the Fourteenth Amendment to use race as a factor in affording educational opportunities among its citizens." There is no ambiguity in that statement. And it was that position that prevailed in this Court ***.

Before <u>Brown</u>, schoolchildren were told where they could and could not go to school based on the color of their skin. The school districts in these cases have not carried the heavy burden of demonstrating that we should allow this once again—even for very different reasons. For schools that never segregated on the basis of race, such as Seattle, or that have removed the vestiges of past segregation, such as Jefferson County, the way "to achieve a system of determining admission to the public schools on a nonracial basis," *Brown II*, 349 U.S., at 300-301 is to stop assigning students on a racial basis. The way to stop discrimination on the basis of race is to stop discriminating on the basis of race.

Justice THOMAS, concurring.

Racial imbalance is not segregation. Although presently observed racial imbalance might result from past *de jure* segregation, racial imbalance can also result from any number of innocent private decisions, including voluntary housing choices. Because racial imbalance is not inevitably linked to unconstitutional segregation, it is not unconstitutional in and of itself. *** Although there is arguably a danger of racial imbalance in schools in Seattle and Louisville, there is no danger of resegregation.

Remediation of past *de jure* segregation is a one-time process involving the redress of a discrete legal injury inflicted by an identified entity. At some point, the discrete injury will be remedied, and the school district will be declared unitary. Unlike *de jure* segregation, there is no ultimate remedy for racial imbalance. Individual schools will fall in and out of balance in the natural course, and the appropriate balance itself will shift with a school district's changing demographics. Thus, racial balancing will have to take place on an indefinite basis—a continuous process with no identifiable culpable party and no discernable end point.

Most of the dissent's criticisms of today's result can be traced to its rejection of the color-blind Constitution. The dissent attempts to marginalize the notion of a color-blind Constitution by consigning it to me and Members of today's plurality. But I am quite comfortable in the company I keep. My view of the Constitution is Justice Harlan's view in *Plessy*: "Our Constitution is color-blind, and neither knows nor tolerates classes among citizens." *Plessy v. Ferguson*, 163 U.S. 537, 559 (1896) (dissenting opinion). And my view was the rallying cry for the lawyers who litigated <u>Brown</u>. See, *e.g.*, Brief for Appellants in

Brown v. Board of Education ("That the Constitution is color blind is our dedicated belief"). *** What was wrong in 1954 cannot be right today.

Justice KENNEDY, concurring in part and concurring in the judgment.

[P]arts of the opinion by THE CHIEF JUSTICE imply an all-too-unyielding insistence that race cannot be a factor in instances when, in my view, it may be taken into account. *** To the extent the plurality opinion suggests the Constitution mandates that state and local school authorities must accept the status quo of racial

> **Take Note**
>
> Justice Kennedy joined only part of Chief Justice Roberts's opinion. He was the fifth vote for those parts. As you read his opinion, consider what it suggests about the precedential effect of the Chief Justice's opinion.

isolation in schools, it is, in my view, profoundly mistaken. *** The statement by Justice Harlan that "[o]ur Constitution is color-blind" was most certainly justified in the context of his dissent in _Plessy_. [A]s an aspiration, Justice Harlan's axiom must command our assent. In the real world, it is regrettable to say, it cannot be a universal constitutional principle.

In the administration of public schools by the state and local authorities it is permissible to consider the racial makeup of schools and to adopt general policies to encourage a diverse student body, one aspect of which is its racial composition. If school authorities are concerned that the student-body compositions of certain schools interfere with the objective of offering an equal educational opportunity to all of their students, they are free to devise race-conscious measures to address the problem in a general way and without treating each student in different fashion solely on the basis of a systematic, individual typing by race.

School boards may pursue the goal of bringing together students of diverse backgrounds and races through other means, including strategic site selection of new schools; drawing attendance zones with general recognition of the demographics of neighborhoods; allocating resources for special programs; recruiting students and faculty in a targeted fashion; and tracking enrollments, performance, and other statistics by race. These mechanisms are race conscious but do not lead to different treatment based on a classification that tells each student he or she is to be defined by race, so it is unlikely any of them would demand strict scrutiny to be found permissible. *** Assigning to each student a personal designation according to a crude system of individual racial classifications is quite a different matter; and the legal analysis changes accordingly.

[I] agree that in the context of these plans, the small number of assignments affected suggests that the schools could have achieved their stated ends through different means. These include the facially race-neutral means set forth above or, if necessary, a more nuanced, individual evaluation of school needs and student characteristics that might include race as a component.

[The dissent raises the following question:] If it is legitimate for school authorities to work to avoid racial isolation in their schools, must they do so only by indirection and general policies? *** Why may the authorities not recognize the problem in candid fashion and solve it altogether through resort to direct assignments based on student racial classifications? So, the argument proceeds, if race is the problem, then perhaps race is the solution.

The argument ignores the dangers presented by individual classifications, dangers that are not as pressing when the same ends are achieved by more indirect means. When the government classifies an individual by race, it must first define what it means to be of a race. Who exactly is white and who is nonwhite? To be forced to live under a state-mandated racial label is inconsistent with the dignity of individuals in our society. And it is a label that an individual is powerless to change. Governmental classifications that command people to march in different directions based on racial typologies can cause a new divisiveness. The practice can lead to corrosive discourse, where race serves not as an element of our diverse heritage but instead as a bargaining chip in the political process. On the other hand race-conscious measures that do not rely on differential treatment based on individual classifications present these problems to a lesser degree.

This Nation has a moral and ethical obligation to fulfill its historic commitment to creating an integrated society that ensures equal opportunity for all of its children. A compelling interest exists in avoiding racial isolation, an interest that a school district, in its discretion and expertise, may choose to pursue. Likewise, a district may consider it a compelling interest to achieve a diverse student population. Race may be one component of that diversity, but other demographic factors, plus special talents and needs, should also be considered. What the government is not permitted to do, absent a showing of necessity not made here, is to classify every student on the basis of race and to assign each of them to schools based on that classification. Crude measures of this sort threaten to reduce children to racial chits valued and traded according to one school's supply and another's demand. *** The decision today should not prevent school districts from continuing the important work of bringing together students of different racial, ethnic, and economic backgrounds.

Justice STEVENS, dissenting.

There is a cruel irony in THE CHIEF JUSTICE's reliance on our decision in *Brown v. Board of Education,* 349 U.S. 294 (1955). The first sentence in the concluding paragraph of his opinion states: "Before <u>Brown</u>, schoolchildren were told where they could and could not go to school based on the color of their skin." *** THE CHIEF JUSTICE fails to note that it was only black schoolchildren who were so ordered; indeed, the history books do not tell stories of white children struggling to attend black schools. In this and other ways, THE CHIEF JUSTICE rewrites the history of one of this Court's most important decisions.

THE CHIEF JUSTICE rejects the conclusion that the racial classifications at issue here should be viewed differently than others, because they do not impose burdens on one race alone and do not stigmatize or exclude. The only justification for refusing to acknowledge the obvious importance of that difference is the citation of a few recent opinions—none of which even approached unanimity—grandly proclaiming that all racial classifications must be analyzed under "strict scrutiny." [This approach] obscures <u>Brown's</u> clear message. Perhaps the best example is provided by our approval of the decision of the Supreme Judicial

Court of Massachusetts in 1967 upholding a state statute mandating racial integration in that State's school system [through the allocation of students based on race]. See *School Comm. of Boston v. Board of Education*, 352 Mass. 693 (1967). Invoking our mandatory appellate jurisdiction,the Boston plaintiffs prosecuted an appeal in this Court. Our ruling on the merits simply stated that the appeal was "dismissed for want of a substantial federal question." *School Comm. of Boston v. Board of Education*, 389 U.S. 572 (1968) *(per curiam)*. That decision not only expressed our appraisal of the merits of the appeal, but it constitutes a precedent that the Court overrules today.

The Court has changed significantly since it decided *School Comm. of Boston* in 1968. It was then more faithful to *Brown* and more respectful of our precedent than it is today. It is my firm conviction that no Member of the Court that I joined in 1975 would have agreed with today's decision.

Justice BREYER, with whom Justice STEVENS, Justice SOUTER, and Justice GINSBURG join, dissenting.

A longstanding and unbroken line of legal authority tells us that the Equal Protection Clause permits local school boards to use race-conscious criteria to achieve positive race-related goals, even when the Constitution does not compel it. Because of its importance, I shall repeat what this Court said about the matter in *Swann v. Charlotte-Mecklenburg Bd. of Ed.*, 402 U.S. 1, 16 (1971). Chief Justice Burger, on behalf of a unanimous Court in a case of exceptional importance, wrote:

> **Make the Connection**
>
> We considered the line of cases to which Justice Breyer refers earlier in this Chapter, after our discussion of *Brown*.

> "School authorities are traditionally charged with broad power to formulate and implement educational policy and might well conclude, for example, that in order to prepare students to live in a pluralistic society each school should have a prescribed ratio of Negro to white students reflecting the proportion for the district as a whole. To do this as an educational policy is within the broad discretionary powers of school authorities."

The statement was not a technical holding in the case. But the Court set forth in *Swann* a basic principle of constitutional law—a principle of law that has found "wide acceptance in the legal culture." Thus, in *North Carolina Bd. of Ed. v. Swann*, 402 U.S. 43, 45 (1971), this Court [restated] the point. "[S]chool authorities," the Court said, "have wide discretion in formulating school policy, and [as] a matter of educational policy school authorities may well conclude that some kind of racial balance in the schools is desirable quite apart from any constitutional requirements." Then-Justice Rehnquist echoed this view in *Bustop, Inc. v. Los Angeles Bd. of Ed.*, 439 U.S. 1380, 1383 (1978)[:] "While I have the gravest doubts that [a state supreme court] was *required* by the United States Constitution to take the [race-conscious student assignment] action that it has taken in this case, I have very little doubt that it was *permitted* by that Constitution to take such action."

These statements nowhere suggest that this freedom is limited to school districts where court-ordered desegregation measures are also in effect. Indeed, in *McDaniel v. Barresi*, 402 U.S. 39, 40, n. 1 (1971), a case decided the same day as *Swann*, a group of parents challenged a race-conscious student assignment plan that the Clarke County School Board had *voluntarily* adopted as a remedy without a court order ***. The plan required that each elementary school in the district maintain 20% to 40% enrollment of African-American students, corresponding to the racial composition of the district. This Court upheld the plan, rejecting the parents' argument that "a person may not be *included* or *excluded* solely because he is a Negro or because he is white."

Swann is predicated upon a well-established legal view of the Fourteenth Amendment. That view understands the basic objective of those who wrote the Equal Protection Clause as forbidding practices that lead to racial exclusion. *** There is reason to believe that those who drafted an Amendment with this basic purpose in mind would have understood the legal and practical difference between the use of race-conscious criteria in defiance of that purpose, namely to keep the races apart, and the use of race-conscious criteria to further that purpose, namely to bring the races together. *** Sometimes Members of this Court have disagreed about the degree of leniency that the Clause affords to programs designed to include. But I can find no case in which this Court has followed Justice THOMAS' "colorblind" approach. And I have found no case that otherwise repudiated this constitutional asymmetry between that which seeks to *exclude* and that which seeks to *include* members of minority races. [N]o case—not *Adarand, Gratz, Grutter,* or any other— has ever held that the test of "strict scrutiny" means that all racial classifications—no matter whether they seek to include or exclude—must in practice be treated the same.

This context is *not* a context that involves the use of race to decide who will receive goods or services that are normally distributed on the basis of merit and which are in short supply. It is not one in which race-conscious limits stigmatize or exclude; the limits at issue do not pit the races against each other or otherwise significantly exacerbate racial tensions. They do not impose burdens unfairly upon members of one race alone but instead seek benefits for members of all races alike. The context here is one of racial limits that seek, not to keep the races apart, but to bring them together.

I believe that the law requires application here of a standard of review that is not "strict" in the traditional sense of that word ***. Nonetheless, [I conclude] that the plans before us pass both parts of the [conventional] strict scrutiny test. [T]he interest at stake possesses three essential elements. First, there is a historical and remedial element: an interest in setting right the consequences of prior conditions of segregation. *** Second, there is an educational element: an interest in overcoming the adverse educational effects produced by and associated with highly segregated schools. *** Third, there is a democratic element: an interest in producing an educational environment that reflects the "pluralistic society" in which our children will live. [It] is an interest in teaching children to engage in the kind of cooperation among Americans of all races that is necessary to make a land of three hundred million people one Nation. *** If an educational interest that combines these three elements is not "compelling," what is?

Several factors, taken together, [lead] me to conclude that the boards' use of race-conscious criteria in these plans passes even the strictest "tailoring" test. First, the race-conscious criteria at issue only help set the outer bounds of *broad* ranges. They constitute but one part of plans that depend primarily upon other, nonracial elements. [In] fact, the defining feature of both plans is greater emphasis upon student choice. In Seattle, for example, in more than 80% of all cases, that choice alone determines which high schools Seattle's ninth graders will attend. *** Second, [the] plans before us are *more narrowly tailored* than the race-conscious admission plans that this Court approved in *Grutter*. Here, race becomes a factor only in a fraction of students' non-merit-based assignments—not in large numbers of students' merit-based applications. Moreover, [d]isappointed students are not rejected from a State's flagship graduate program; they simply attend a different one of the district's many public schools, which in aspiration and in fact are substantially equal. *** Third, [each] plan is the product of a process that has sought to enhance student choice, while diminishing the need for mandatory busing.

Nor could the school districts have accomplished their desired aims (*e.g.,* avoiding forced busing, countering white flight, maintaining racial diversity) by other means. Nothing in the extensive history of desegregation efforts over the past 50 years gives the districts, or this Court, any reason to believe that another method is possible to accomplish these goals. The wide variety of different integration plans that school districts use throughout the Nation suggests that the problem of racial segregation in schools, including *de facto* segregation, is difficult to solve. The fact that many such plans have used explicitly racial criteria suggests that such criteria have an important, sometimes necessary, role to play.

The lesson of history [is] not that efforts to continue racial segregation are constitutionally indistinguishable from efforts to achieve racial integration. Indeed, it is a cruel distortion of history to compare Topeka, Kansas, in the 1950's to Louisville and Seattle in the modern day—to equate the plight of Linda Brown (who was ordered to attend a Jim Crow school) to the circumstances of Joshua McDonald (whose request to transfer to a school closer to home was initially declined). *** The last half-century has witnessed great strides toward racial equality, but we have not yet realized the promise of <u>Brown</u>. To invalidate the plans under review is to threaten the promise of <u>Brown</u>. The plurality's position, I fear, would break that promise. This is a decision that the Court and the Nation will come to regret.

———————

Points for Discussion

a. The Use of Race in School Assignments

After the Court's decision in <u>Parents Involved</u>, is there any use of race in the assignment of students to schools that can survive scrutiny? Notice that Justice Kennedy declined to join some sections of Chief Justice Roberts's opinion and suggested a greater willingness to permit race-conscious decision-making in this context. Is a narrowly drawn plan whose purpose is to avoid "racial isolation" and achieve "a diverse student population" constitutional?

Both Chief Justice Roberts and Justice Kennedy relied, in concluding that the plans were unconstitutional, in part on the availability of race-neutral means to achieve racial balance in schools. Suppose that a school district gives preference in school assignments to students from certain zip codes in which most of the district's minority population is concentrated, with the avowed purpose of achieving greater racial balance in schools. Such an approach would be race-neutral on its face, as it would apply equally to white students from the neighborhoods in question, but geography would be used quite intentionally as a proxy for race. Would such an approach survive scrutiny under the Court's approach? If so, why is it meaningfully different from the Seattle and Louisville plans?

b. The Role of Racial Identity

The various opinions disputed the utility and value of achieving "racial balance" in public schools. But even assuming that it is a desirable aim, the question of *when* a student population should be considered "racially balanced" is a difficult one. Seattle measured racial balance according to a binary "white/nonwhite" standard, and Jefferson County used a "black/other" standard. Such approaches are potentially problematic for at least two reasons. First, they appear to identify a significant percentage of the population only in contradistinction to one, perhaps arbitrarily defined, group. Second, they ignore the considerably more complex and rich set of racial and ethnic backgrounds that characterize the American population, particularly in the urban areas most likely to adopt plans such as those at issue in the case. Are such definitions of racial balance themselves problematic under the Fourteenth Amendment? Would an approach to racial balancing that explicitly considers other racial and ethnic groups avoid the problems of the challenged plans, or would it suffer from the same—or even a worse—defect as the plans at issue in <u>Parents Involved</u>?

c. Formal Strict Scrutiny versus Contextualized Strict Scrutiny

Traditionally, formal strict scrutiny is characterized as being "strict in theory, and fatal in fact." Gerald Gunther, *Foreword: In Search of Evolving Doctrine on a Changing Court: A Model for a Newer Equal Protection*, 86 Harv. L. Rev. 1, 8 (1972). But in <u>Grutter</u>, Justice O'Connor declared that "[c]ontext matters when reviewing race-based governmental action under the Equal Protection Clause," leading some commentators to believe that the Court was articulating a new, contextualized approach to strict scrutiny that examined historical circumstance and social conditions. The Ninth Circuit had applied this approach in upholding Seattle's student-assignment plan, and Justice Breyer would have applied it, as well. Is such an approach "strict scrutiny" in the conventional sense at all? If not, then to what types of classifications does it apply?

d. Competing Views of *Brown*

The competing opinions offer dramatically different views of the meaning of *Brown v. Board of Education*. To Chief Justice Roberts and Justice Thomas, *Brown* was, at its core, about the constitutional status of government actions that deviate from the color-blind ideal. To Justice Breyer, by contrast, *Brown* was about the status of government policies predicated on racial subordination or exclusion. Whose view is more faithful to the Court's decision in *Brown*? Whose view is more faithful to the original meaning of the Fourteenth Amendment? Is this a policy issue that the Justices should decide for themselves without reference to either the original meaning or precedent?

---

7. Race and Redistricting

As we will see in more detail in Chapter 13, there is a disturbing history of official attempts to deny the franchise to racial minorities. The Fifteenth Amendment sought to end these practices, but subtle forms of racial discrimination in voting persisted. Some states—particularly in the South—imposed various obstacles to the right to vote, including poll taxes and discriminatorily administered literacy tests. In addition, some states engaged in racial gerrymandering to dilute the strength of minority voters at the polls. See, e.g., *Gomillion v. Lightfoot*, 364 U.S. 339 (1960); *Rogers v. Lodge*, 458 U.S. 613 (1982).

> **Definition**
>
> A gerrymander is when legislative district lines are drawn to benefit a particular group. The term is derived from Elbridge Gerry, a founding father and the governor of Massachusetts, who was accused of manipulating district lines to benefit his political party.

Congress enacted the Voting Rights Act of 1965, codified as amended at 42 U.S.C. § 1973 *et seq.*, to prevent voting practices that burden disadvantaged minorities. Since that time, some state legislatures have sought to increase the voting power of minorities, particularly African Americans. The following case concerns the constitutionality of one means to that end.

Shaw v. Reno

509 U.S. 630 (1993)

Justice O'CONNOR delivered the opinion of the Court.

As a result of the 1990 census, North Carolina became entitled to a 12th seat in the United States House of Representatives. The General Assembly enacted a reapportionment plan that included one majority-black congressional district. After the Attorney General of the United States objected to the plan pursuant to § 5 of the Voting Rights Act of 1965 the General Assembly passed new legislation creating a second majority-black district. Appellants allege that the revised plan, which contains district boundary lines of dramatically irregular shape, constitutes an unconstitutional racial gerrymander.

[W]hat appellants object to is redistricting legislation that is so extremely irregular on its face that it rationally can be viewed only as an effort to segregate the races for purposes of voting, without regard for traditional districting principles and without sufficiently compelling justification. *** Appellants contend that redistricting legislation that is so bizarre on its face that it is "unexplainable on grounds other than race" demands the same close scrutiny that we give other state laws that classify citizens by race. Our voting rights precedents support that conclusion.

> **FYI**
>
> Section 5 of the Voting Rights Act of 1965 prohibits changes in election procedures in certain states or in certain parts of states (most of which are in the South and all of which had a history of discrimination on the basis of race in the administration of the franchise) until the new procedures have been approved by the United States Attorney General or the United States District Court for the District of Columbia. See 28 C.F.R. p.51, App. (listing jurisdictions that must seek preclearance).

A reapportionment plan that includes in one district individuals who belong to the same race, but who are otherwise widely separated by geographical and political boundaries, and who may have little in common with one another but the color of their skin, bears an uncomfortable resemblance to political apartheid. It reinforces the perception that members of the same racial group—regardless of their age, education, economic status, or the community in which they live—think alike, share the same political interests, and will prefer the same candidates at the polls. We have rejected such perceptions elsewhere as impermissible racial stereotypes. [Furthermore, when] a district obviously is created solely to effectuate the perceived common interests of one racial group, elected officials are more likely to believe that their primary obligation is to represent only the members of that group, rather than their constituency as a whole. This is altogether antithetical to our system of representative democracy.

For these reasons, we conclude that a plaintiff challenging a reapportionment statute under the Equal Protection Clause may state a claim by alleging that the legislation, though race-neutral on its face, rationally cannot be understood as anything other than an effort to separate voters into different districts on the basis of race, and that the separation lacks sufficient justification. *** We hold [that], on the facts of this case, appellants have stated a claim sufficient to defeat the state appellees' motion to dismiss.

Justice STEVENS argues that racial gerrymandering poses no constitutional difficulties when district lines are drawn to favor the minority, rather than the majority. We have made clear, however, that equal protection analysis "is not dependent on the race of those burdened or benefited by a particular classification." *City of Richmond v. J.A. Croson Co.,* 488 U.S. 469, 494 (1989) (plurality opinion). Indeed, racial classifications receive close scrutiny even when they may be said to burden or benefit the races equally. [The] very reason that the Equal Protection Clause demands strict scrutiny of all racial classifications is because without it, a court cannot determine whether or not the discrimination truly is "benign."

[A]ppellees assert that the deliberate creation of majority-minority districts is the most precise way—indeed the only effective way—to overcome the effects of racially polarized voting. This question [need] not be decided at this stage of the litigation. *** Today we hold only that appellants have stated a claim under the Equal Protection Clause by alleging that the North Carolina General Assembly adopted a reapportionment scheme so irrational on its face that it can be understood only as an effort to segregate voters into separate voting districts because of their race, and that the separation lacks sufficient justification. If the allegation of racial gerrymandering remains uncontradicted, the District Court further must determine whether the North Carolina plan is narrowly tailored to further a compelling governmental interest.

> **FYI**
>
> On remand, the district court held that the redistricting plan was narrowly tailored to serve the state's compelling interest in complying with the requirements of the Voting Rights Act. The Supreme Court reversed that decision, holding that the redistricting plan violated the Equal Protection Clause. See *Shaw v. Hunt,* 517 U.S. 899 (1996).

Justice WHITE, with whom Justice BLACKMUN and Justice STEVENS join, dissenting.

[T]he issue is whether the classification based on race discriminates against *anyone* by denying equal access to the political process. [I]t strains credulity to suggest that North Carolina's purpose in creating a second majority-minority district was to discriminate against members of the majority group by "impair[ing] or burden[ing their] opportunity [to] participate in the political process." The State has made no mystery of its intent, which was to respond to the Attorney General's objections by improving the minority group's prospects of electing a candidate of its choice. I doubt that this constitutes a discriminatory purpose as defined in the Court's equal protection cases—*i.e.,* an intent to aggravate "the unequal distribution of electoral power." But even assuming that it does, there is no question that appellants have not alleged the requisite discriminatory effects. Whites constitute roughly 76% of the total population and 79% of the voting age population in North Carolina. Yet, under the State's plan, they still constitute a voting majority in 10 (or 83%) of the 12 congressional districts. Though they might be dissatisfied at the prospect of casting a vote for a losing candidate—a lot shared by many, including a disproportionate number of minority voters—surely they cannot complain of discriminatory treatment. [The redistricting plan involves] an attempt to *equalize* treatment, and to provide minority voters with an effective voice in the political process. The Equal Protection Clause of the Constitution, surely, does not stand in the way.

Justice BLACKMUN, dissenting.

It is particularly ironic that the case in which today's majority chooses to abandon settled law and to recognize for the first time this "analytically distinct" constitutional claim is a challenge by white voters to the plan under which North Carolina has sent black representatives to Congress for the first time since Reconstruction.

Justice STEVENS, dissenting.

[This case gives] rise to three constitutional questions: Does the Constitution impose a requirement of contiguity or compactness on how the States may draw their electoral districts? Does the Equal Protection Clause prevent a State from drawing district boundaries for the purpose of facilitating the election of a member of an identifiable group of voters? And, finally, if the answer to the second question is generally "No," should it be different when the favored group is defined by race?

The first question is easy. There is no independent constitutional requirement of compactness or contiguity, and the Court's opinion (despite its many references to the shape of District 12) does not suggest otherwise. *** As for the second question, I believe that the Equal Protection Clause is violated when the State creates [uncouth] district boundaries [for] the sole purpose of making it more difficult for members of a minority group to win an election. The duty to govern impartially is abused when a group with power over the electoral process defines electoral boundaries solely to enhance its own political strength at the expense of any weaker group. That duty, however, is not violated when the majority acts to facilitate the election of a member of a group that lacks such power because it remains underrepresented in the state legislature—whether that group is defined by political affiliation, by common economic interests, or by religious, ethnic, or racial characteristics. The difference between constitutional and unconstitutional

> **Make the Connection**
>
> We will consider the constitutionality of "political gerrymanders"—that is, efforts to draw district lines for partisan purposes—in Chapter 12.

gerrymanders has nothing to do with whether they are based on assumptions about the groups they affect, but whether their purpose is to enhance the power of the group in control of the districting process at the expense of any minority group, and thereby to strengthen the unequal distribution of electoral power. [Finally, if] it is permissible to draw boundaries to provide adequate representation for rural voters, for union members, for Hasidic Jews, for Polish Americans, or for Republicans, it necessarily follows that it is permissible to do the same thing for members of the very minority group whose history in the United States gave birth to the Equal Protection Clause. A contrary conclusion could only be described as perverse.

Justice SOUTER, dissenting.

Unlike other contexts in which we have addressed the State's conscious use of race, electoral districting calls for decisions that nearly always require some consideration of race for legitimate reasons where there is a racially mixed population. As long as members of racial groups have the commonality of interest implicit in our ability to talk about concepts like "minority voting strength," and "dilution of minority votes," [which are important in cases interpreting the Voting Rights Act,] and as long as racial bloc voting takes place, legislators will have to take race into account in order to avoid dilution of minority voting strength in the districting plans they adopt. One need look no further than the Voting Rights Act to understand that this may be required, and we have held that race may constitutionally be taken into account in order to comply with that Act. *United Jewish Organizations of Williamsburgh, Inc. v. Carey*, 430 U.S. 144, 161-162 (1977).

A second distinction between districting and most other governmental decisions in which race has figured is that those other decisions using racial criteria characteristically occur in circumstances in which the use of race to the advantage of one person is necessarily at the obvious expense of a member of a different race. *** In districting, by contrast, the mere placement of an individual in one district instead of another denies no one a right or benefit provided to others. All citizens may register, vote, and be represented. In whatever district, the individual voter has a right to vote in each election, and the election will result in the voter's representation. *** It is true, of course, that one's vote may be more or less effective depending on the interests of the other individuals who are in one's district, and our cases recognize the reality that members of the same race often have shared interests. "Dilution" thus refers to the effects of districting decisions not on an individual's political power viewed in isolation, but on the political power of a group. *** Under our cases there is in general a requirement that in order to obtain relief under the Fourteenth Amendment, the purpose and effect of the districting must be to devalue the effectiveness of a voter compared to what, as a group member, he would otherwise be able to enjoy.

———————

Points for Discussion

a. Subsequent Developments

The Court in *Shaw* held that "bizarre" shapes for districts can demonstrate a prima facie case of racial gerrymandering. Several years after *Shaw*, the Court held that strict scrutiny is also warranted if the plaintiffs can demonstrate that race was a "predominant" factor in the drawing of district lines. *Bush v. Vera*, 517 U.S. 952 (1996); *Miller v. Johnson*, 515 U.S. 900 (1995). What kind of evidence is relevant to a determination that race was the "predominant" factor in districting?

The Court has also held, however, that government may use race as a factor in districting if the predominant factor in districting is political. *Easley v. Cromartie*, 532 U.S. 234 (2001). In *Cromartie*, the Court concluded that the legislature had considered race because African-American voters had voted overwhelmingly for Democrats, and thus that the legislative objective had been the permissible one of creating seats that were safe for candidates of one party. Is this a convincing distinction? We will consider the constitutionality of gerrymandering for political reasons in Chapter 12.

b. "Benign" and "Invidious" Uses of Race

Is there a meaningful difference between a redistricting plan that seeks to dilute the votes of blacks—by ensuring that no district has a very high concentration of black voters—and one that seeks to ensure that there are some districts in which blacks constitute a majority, or at least a strong plurality? Are some uses of race benign? If so, how can a court tell the benign uses from the invidious ones?

c. Individual or Group Rights?

As noted above, the affirmative action cases reveal that the Justices disagree about whether the Fourteenth Amendment protects individual or instead group rights. Regardless of whether it protects individual rights generally, is the context of voting sufficiently different that it could be said to protect group rights in that context? After all, doesn't it take a group of voters to elect a candidate? And wasn't the assumption of the legislators who unconstitutionally drew district lines in the 1960s to dilute the votes of African Americans, see, e.g., *Gomillion v. Lightfoot*, 364 U.S. 339 (1960), that blocs of voters act collectively in exercising the franchise?

d. Racial and Partisan Gerrymandering

The classic form of gerrymandering is the drawing of legislative district lines to benefit one political party over another. (Even in a state with an equal number of Democrats and Republicans and ten legislative seats, for example, a legislature could end up with nine Republican representatives by loading one district with Democrats and giving a slight majority to Republican voters in the other nine.) As this example suggests, and as we will see in Chapter 12 (and as we briefly noted in Chapter 2 when we considered *Baker v. Carr*, the political question doctrine case), part of the problem with gerrymandering is that it entrenches in power particular groups, even if they do not have clear majority voting power. There accordingly is not an easy political (as opposed to judicial) remedy for political gerrymandering. The same is true of gerrymandering plans that disadvantage voters who belong to racial minority groups. Is there a political remedy for racial gerrymandering plans that *benefit* members of minority groups?

B. Gender Classifications

In *Strauder v. West Virginia*, which the Court decided in the nineteenth century and which we considered earlier in this Chapter, the Court declared that a state may "prescribe the qualifications of its jurors, and in so doing make discriminations." Among other things, the Court stated, a state "may confine the selection to males." The Court did "not believe the Fourteenth Amendment was ever intended to prohibit this," because its "aim was against discrimination because of race or color."

For the first hundred years after the ratification of the Fourteenth Amendment, the Court adhered to this view that the Equal Protection Clause does not prevent discrimination on the basis of gender. Is it clear, either from the text of the Clause or from the history of its ratification, that it prevents only discrimination on the basis of race? As we will see in this section, the Court's view of the scope of the Equal Protection Clause's application has changed over time.

---

1. The Early View

The Court first addressed the Fourteenth Amendment's application to gender discrimination in *Bradwell v. People of the State of Ilinois*, 83 U.S. 130 (1872). Myra Bradwell sought a license to practice law in Illinois, but was refused based on the reasoning that as a married woman, she would not be bound by the contracts normally formed between attorney and client (a common-law rule no longer in existence). Mrs. Bradwell filed suit, claiming that she was entitled to the license under the Privileges or Immunities Clause of the Fourteenth Amendment. The Court rejected her claim, concluding that a right to practice law is not among the privileges protected by the Clause.

> **Take Note**
>
> *Bradwell* was argued (and decided) as a Privileges or Immunities case, rather than as an Equal Protection case. Why do you suppose that was?

In his concurring opinion, Justice Bradley addressed the permissibility of gender discrimination in natural-law terms. He stated:

> [The] civil law, as well as nature herself, has always recognized a wide difference in the respective spheres and destinies of man and woman. Man is, or should be, woman's protector and defender. The natural and proper timidity and delicacy which belongs to the female sex evidently unfits it for many of the occupations of civil life. The constitution of the family organization, which is founded in the divine ordinance, as well as in the nature of things, indicates the domestic sphere as that which properly belongs to the domain and functions of womanhood. The harmony, not to say identity, of interest and views which belong, or should belong, to the family institution is repugnant to the idea of a woman adopting a distinct and independent career from that of her husband. *** The paramount destiny and mission of woman are to fulfill the noble and benign offices of wife and mother. This is the law of the Creator. [I]n view of the peculiar characteristics, destiny, and mission of woman, it is within the province of the legislature to ordain what offices, positions, and callings shall be filled and discharged by men ***.

Women gradually gained political, social, and legal rights in the years after *Bradwell*, but these gains were largely the product of legislative action or constitutional amendment. (The Nineteenth Amendment, for example, prohibited discrimination on the basis of sex in the grant of the franchise.) Courts, however, continued to hold that laws discriminating on the basis of gender were consistent with the Constitution. Indeed, the Court in the early twentieth century was more likely to uphold laws that interfered with contractual relationships when they protected women, rather than all workers. Compare *Lochner v. New York*, 198 U.S. 45 (1905) (striking down a law limiting the number of hours a baker could work), with *Muller v. Oregon*, 208 U.S. 412 (1908) (upholding a law limiting the number of hours women could work in factories). The Court in <u>Muller</u> relied explicitly on women's "physical structure" and maternal obligations, which "place [them] at a disadvantage in the struggle for subsistence."

---

2. Heightened Scrutiny

Matters changed in the latter part of the twentieth century. In October 1971, the House of Representatives approved the Equal Rights Amendment, which provided, "Equality of rights under the law shall not be denied or abridged by the United States or by any State on account of sex." Before the Senate voted, the Court decided *Reed v. Reed*, 404 U.S. 71 (1971), which raised a challenge to a law that required courts, in deciding whom to appoint as administrators of estates of persons who died intestate, to prefer males to equally qualified females. The Court purported to apply rational-basis review, stating the question presented as "whether a difference in the sex of competing applicants for letters of administration bears a rational relationship to a state objective that is sought to be advanced by the operation" of the statute. But the Court nevertheless invalidated the statute. The Court noted that "the objective of reducing the workload on probate courts by eliminating one class of contests is not without some legitimacy." But the Court concluded that this interest was insufficient to justify the discrimination: "To give a mandatory preference to members of either sex over members of the other, merely to accomplish the elimination of hearings on the merits, is to make the very kind of arbitrary legislative choice forbidden by the Equal Protection Clause of the Fourteenth Amendment; and whatever may be said as to the positive values of avoiding intrafamily controversy, the choice in this context may not lawfully be mandated solely on the basis of sex."

Reed ushered in a new era of Equal Protection challenges to state discrimination on the basis of gender. In *Frontiero v. Richardson*, 411 U.S. 677 (1973), the Court considered a challenge to a federal law permitting men in the armed services automatically to claim their wives as dependents (and thus receive a greater allowance for housing and medical benefits), while permitting women in the service to receive such benefits only by proving that their husbands were dependent upon them for more than half of their support. Justice Brennan, writing for himself and three others, declared that classifications based on sex "are inherently suspect, and therefore must be subjected to strict judicial scrutiny." He reasoned that a "long and unfortunate history of sex discrimination," which traditionally was "rationalized by an attitude of 'romantic paternalism,'" "in practical effect [put] women, not on a pedestal, but in a cage." Justice Brennan contended that women continue to face pervasive discrimination, and that gender, "like race and national origin, is an immutable characteristic determined solely by birth." But there were not five votes for this view. Justice Stewart concurred in the judgment, stating his belief that the law was unconstitutional under the form of scrutiny applied in *Reed*. Justices Powell, Burger, and Blackmun also concurred in the judgment, asserting that the Court should not apply strict scrutiny before the nation decided finally on whether to ratify the Equal Rights Amendment. Justice Rehnquist was alone in dissent.

When the Court decided *Frontiero*, the Senate had already joined the House in passing the Equal Rights Amendment by the requisite majority, and 25 states had already ratified it. After the initial flurry of ratifications, however, the Amendment ran into political opposition. In 1976, when the Court decided the case that follows, the Amendment still had not achieved ratification in the requisite 38 states. (Indeed, in the end, only 35 states ratified the Equal Rights Amendment, and some of those later rescinded their ratification.)

————————————

Craig v. Boren

429 U.S. 190 (1976)

Mr. Justice BRENNAN delivered the opinion of the Court.

[Oklahoma law] prohibits the sale of "nonintoxicating" 3.2% beer to males under the age of 21 and to females under the age of 18. The question to be decided is whether such a gender-based differential constitutes a denial to males 18-20 years of age of the equal protection of the laws in violation of the Fourteenth Amendment.

To withstand constitutional challenge, previous cases establish that classifications by gender must serve important governmental objectives and must be substantially related to achievement of those objectives. Thus, in *Reed v. Reed*, 404 U.S. 71 (1971), the objectives of "reducing the workload on probate courts" and "avoiding intrafamily controversy" were deemed of insufficient importance to sustain use of an overt gender criterion in the appointment of administrators of intestate decedents' estates. Decisions following *Reed* similarly have rejected administrative ease and convenience as sufficiently important objectives to justify gender-based classifications. See, e. g., *Frontiero v. Richardson*, 411 U.S. 677, 690 (1973).

Reed has also provided the underpinning for decisions that have invalidated statutes employing gender as an inaccurate proxy for other, more germane bases of classification. Hence, "archaic and overbroad" generalizations concerning the financial position of servicewomen, *Frontiero*, and working women, *Weinberger v. Wiesenfeld*, 420 U.S. 636, 643 (1975), could not justify use of a gender line in determining eligibility for certain governmental entitlements. Similarly, increasingly outdated misconceptions concerning the role of females in the home rather than in the "marketplace and world of ideas" were rejected as loose-fitting characterizations incapable of supporting state statutory schemes that were premised upon their accuracy. *Stanton v. Stanton*, 421 U.S. 7 (1975). In light of the weak congruence between gender and the characteristic or trait that gender purported to represent, it was necessary that the legislatures choose either to realign their substantive laws in a gender-neutral fashion, or to adopt procedures for identifying those instances where the sex-centered generalization actually comported with fact.

In this case, too, "*Reed*, we feel is controlling." *Stanton*. *** We accept for purposes of discussion the District Court's identification of the objective underlying [the challenged statutes] as the enhancement of traffic safety. Clearly, the protection of public health and safety represents an important function of state and local governments. However, appellees' statistics in our view cannot support the conclusion that the gender-based distinction closely serves to achieve that objective ***. Even were this statistical evidence accepted as accurate, it nevertheless offers only a weak answer to the equal protection question presented here. The most focused and relevant of the statistical surveys, arrests of 18-20-year-olds for alcohol-related driving offenses, exemplifies the ultimate unpersuasiveness of this evidentiary record. Viewed in terms of the correlation between sex and the actual activity that Oklahoma seeks to regulate—driving while under the influence of alcohol—the statistics broadly establish that .18% of females and 2% of males in that age group were arrested for that offense. While such a disparity is not trivial in a statistical sense, it hardly can form the basis for employment of a gender line as a classifying device. Certainly if maleness is to serve as a proxy for drinking and driving, a correlation of 2% must be considered an unduly tenuous "fit." *** Moreover, the statistics exhibit a variety of other shortcomings that seriously impugn their value to equal protection analysis. Setting aside the obvious methodological problems,[14] the surveys do not adequately justify the salient features of Oklahoma's gender-based traffic-safety law. None purports to measure the use and dangerousness of 3.2% beer as opposed to alcohol generally, a detail that is of particular importance since, in light of its low alcohol level, Oklahoma apparently considers the 3.2% beverage to be "nonintoxicating."

[This analysis] illustrates that proving broad sociological propositions by statistics is a dubious business, and one that inevitably is in tension with the normative philosophy that underlies the Equal Protection Clause. Suffice to say that the showing offered by the appellees does not satisfy us that sex represents a legitimate, accurate proxy for the regulation of drinking and driving. In fact, when it is further recognized that Oklahoma's statute prohibits only the selling of 3.2% beer to young males and not their drinking the beverage once acquired (even after purchase by their 18-20-year-old female companions), the relationship between gender and traffic safety becomes far too tenuous to satisfy *Reed*'s requirement that the gender-based difference be substantially related to achievement of the statutory objective. We hold, therefore, that under *Reed*, Oklahoma's 3.2% beer statute invidiously discriminates against males 18-20 years of age.

Mr. Justice POWELL, concurring.

[I] find it unnecessary, in deciding this case, to read [*Reed*] as broadly as some of the

---

[14] The very social stereotypes that find reflection in age-differential laws are likely substantially to distort the accuracy of these comparative statistics. Hence "reckless" young men who drink and drive are transformed into arrest statistics, whereas their female counterparts are chivalrously escorted home. Moreover, the Oklahoma surveys, gathered under a regime where the age-differential law in question has been in effect, are lacking in controls necessary for appraisal of the actual effectiveness of the male 3.2% beer prohibition.

Court's language may imply. *** I view this as a relatively easy case. *** It seems to me that the statistics offered by appellees and relied upon by the District Court do tend generally to support the view that young men drive more, possibly are inclined to drink more, and for various reasons are involved in more accidents than young women. Even so, I am not persuaded that these facts and the inferences fairly drawn from them justify this classification based on a three-year age differential between the sexes, and especially one that it so easily circumvented as to be virtually meaningless. Putting it differently, this gender-based classification does not bear a fair and substantial relation to the object of the legislation.

Mr. Justice STEVENS, concurring.

There is only one Equal Protection Clause. It requires every State to govern impartially. It does not direct the courts to apply one standard of review in some cases and a different standard in other cases. *** I am inclined to believe that what has become known as the two-tiered analysis of equal protection claims does not describe a completely logical method of deciding cases, but rather is a method the Court has employed to explain decisions that actually apply a single standard in a reasonably consistent fashion.

In this case, the classification *** is objectionable because it is based on an accident of birth, because it is a mere remnant of the now almost universally rejected tradition of discriminating against males in this age bracket, and because, to the extent it reflects any physical difference between males and females, it is actually perverse. The question then is whether the traffic safety justification put forward by the State is sufficient to make an otherwise offensive classification acceptable. The classification is not totally irrational. For the evidence does indicate that there are more males than females in this age bracket who drive and also more who drink. Nevertheless, [it] is difficult to believe that the statute was actually intended to cope with the problem of traffic safety, since it has only a minimal effect on access to a not very intoxicating beverage and does not prohibit its consumption. Moreover, [the] legislation imposes a restraint on 100% of the males in the class allegedly because about 2% of them have probably violated one or more laws relating to the consumption of alcoholic beverages. It is unlikely that this law will have a significant deterrent effect either on that 2% or on the law-abiding 98%. But even assuming some such slight benefit, it does not seem to me that an insult to all of the young men of the State can be justified by visiting the sins of the 2% on the 98%.

Mr. Justice STEWART, concurring in the judgment.

The disparity created by these Oklahoma statutes amounts to total irrationality. For the statistics upon which the State now relies, whatever their other shortcomings, wholly fail to prove or even suggest that 3.2% beer is somehow more deleterious when it comes into the hands of a male aged 18-20 than of a female of like age. The disparate statutory treatment of the sexes here, without even a colorably valid justification or explanation, thus amounts to invidious discrimination. See *Reed*.

Mr. Justice REHNQUIST, dissenting.

Most obviously unavailable to support any kind of special scrutiny in this case is a history or pattern of past discrimination, such as was relied on by the plurality in <u>Frontiero</u> to support its invocation of strict scrutiny. There is no suggestion in the Court's opinion that males in this age group are in any way peculiarly disadvantaged, subject to systematic discriminatory treatment, or otherwise in need of special solicitude from the courts. *** [T]he Court's reliance on our previous sex-discrimination cases [thus] is ill-founded.

The Court's [proposed level of scrutiny] apparently comes out of thin air. The Equal Protection Clause contains no such language, and none of our previous cases adopt that standard. I would think we have had enough difficulty with the two standards of review which our cases have recognized [so] as to counsel weightily against the insertion of still another "standard" between those two. How is this Court to divine what objectives are important? How is it to determine whether a particular law is "substantially" related to the achievement of such objective, rather than related in some other way to its achievement? Both of the phrases used are so diaphanous and elastic as to invite subjective judicial preferences or prejudices relating to particular types of legislation, masquerading as judgments whether such legislation is directed at "important" objectives or, whether the relationship to those objectives is "substantial" enough.

The Oklahoma Legislature could have believed that 18-20-year-old males drive substantially more, and tend more often to be intoxicated than their female counterparts; that they prefer beer and admit to drinking and driving at a higher rate than females; and that they suffer traffic injuries out of proportion to the part they make up of the population. Under the appropriate rational-basis test for equal protection, it is neither irrational nor arbitrary to bar them from making purchases of 3.2% beer ***.

[Justice BLACKMUN's concurring opinion and Chief Justice BURGER's dissenting opinion are omitted.]

Points for Discussion

a. Heightened Scrutiny

Where did the form of scrutiny that the Court announced in <u>Craig</u> come from? Justice Brennan stated that "previous cases establish[ed]" this form of intermediate scrutiny for gender classifications. Is that an accurate statement of the law? If not, is the level of scrutiny that the Court announced otherwise defensible?

b. Gender Discrimination and the Original Meaning

Are there legitimate reasons to treat race and gender classifications differently? Considering the history of the Fourteenth Amendment and the Civil War, can you make an argument that race classifications should be more suspect? Conversely, can you make an originalist argument that gender discrimination is constitutionally suspect? (Consider former-Judge Bork's view of <u>Brown</u> and the original meaning, which we considered earlier in this Chapter.)

c. Constitutional Interpretation and Constitutional Amendment

Do you think that the Equal Rights Amendment, which was pending ratification when the Court decided <u>Reed</u>, <u>Frontiero</u>, and <u>Craig</u>, influenced the Court's interpretation in those cases of the Equal Protection Clause? If so, does this put the cart before the horse? Was Congress's (and many states') ratification of the proposed Amendment relevant to the meaning of the Equal Protection Clause? Did the proposed Amendment's ultimate failure demonstrate that the Court was wrong in these cases? Or did the Amendment fail in part because the Court offered the protection that the Amendment otherwise would have conferred?

———

United States v. Virginia

518 U.S. 515 (1996)

Justice GINSBURG delivered the opinion of the Court.

Founded in 1839, VMI is today the sole single-sex school among Virginia's 15 public institutions of higher learning. VMI's distinctive mission is to produce "citizen-soldiers," men prepared for leadership in civilian life and in military service. VMI pursues this mission through pervasive training of a kind not available anywhere else in Virginia. Assigning prime place to character development, VMI uses an "adversative method" modeled on English public schools and once characteristic of military instruction. VMI constantly endeavors to instill physical and mental discipline in its cadets and impart to them a strong moral code. The school's graduates leave VMI with heightened comprehension of their capacity to deal with duress and stress, and a large sense of accomplishment for completing the hazardous course. VMI has notably succeeded in its mission to produce leaders; among its alumni are military generals, Members of Congress, and business executives. *** Nevertheless, Virginia has elected to preserve exclusively for men the advantages and opportunities a VMI education affords.

Since [*Reed v. Reed*, 404 U.S. 71 (1971),] the Court has repeatedly recognized that neither federal nor state government acts compatibly with the equal protection principle when a law or official policy denies to women, simply because they are women, full citizenship stature—equal opportunity to aspire, achieve, participate in and contribute to society based on their individual talents and capacities. *** Without equating gender classifications, for all purposes, to classifications based on race or national origin, the Court, in post-<u>Reed</u> decisions, has carefully inspected official action that closes a door or denies opportunity to women (or to men). To summarize the Court's current directions for cases of official classification based on gender: Focusing on the differential treatment or denial of opportunity for which relief is sought, the reviewing court must determine whether the proffered justification is "exceedingly persuasive." The burden of justification is demanding and it rests entirely on the State. The State must show "at least that the [challenged] classification serves 'important governmental objectives and that the discriminatory means employed' are 'substantially related to the achievement of those objectives.'" The justification must be genuine, not hypothesized or invented post hoc in response to litigation. And it must not rely on overbroad generalizations about the different talents, capacities, or preferences of males and females.

Virginia [asserts] two justifications in defense of VMI's exclusion of women. First, the Commonwealth contends, "single-sex education provides important educational benefits," and the option of single-sex education contributes to "diversity in educational approaches." Second, the Commonwealth argues, "the unique VMI method of character development and leadership training," the school's adversative approach, would have to be modified were VMI to admit women. We consider these two justifications in turn.

Single-sex education affords pedagogical benefits to at least some students, Virginia emphasizes, and that reality is uncontested in this litigation. Similarly, it is not disputed that diversity among public educational institutions can serve the public good. But Virginia has not shown that VMI was established, or has been maintained, with a view to diversifying, by its categorical exclusion of women, educational opportunities within the Commonwealth. In cases of this genre, our precedent instructs that "benign" justifications proffered in defense of categorical exclusions will not be accepted automatically; a tenable justification must describe actual state purposes, not rationalizations for actions in fact differently grounded.

Neither recent nor distant history bears out Virginia's alleged pursuit of diversity through single-sex educational options. In 1839, when the Commonwealth established VMI, [higher education] was considered dangerous for women. In admitting no women, VMI followed the lead of the Commonwealth's flagship school, the University of Virginia, founded in 1819. *** Virginia eventually [in the late-nineteenth and early-twentieth centuries] provided for several women's seminaries and colleges. *** By the mid-1970's, all four schools had become coeducational. *** Debate concerning women's admission as undergraduates at the main university continued well past the [twentieth] century's midpoint. *** Ultimately, in 1970, "the most prestigious institution of higher education in Virginia," the University of Virginia, introduced coeducation and, in 1972, began to admit women on an equal basis with men.

Virginia describes the current absence of public single-sex higher education for women as "an historical anomaly." But the historical record indicates action more deliberate than anomalous: First, protection of women against higher education; next, schools for women far from equal in resources and stature to schools for men; finally, conversion of the separate schools to coeducation. *** In sum, we find no persuasive evidence in this record that VMI's male-only admission policy "is in furtherance of a state policy of diversity." *** A purpose genuinely to advance an array of educational options [is] not served by VMI's historic and constant plan—a plan to "affor[d] a unique educational benefit only to males." However "liberally" this plan serves the Commonwealth's sons, it makes no provision whatever for her daughters. That is not *equal* protection.

Virginia next argues that VMI's adversative method of training provides educational benefits that cannot be made available, unmodified, to women. Alterations to accommodate women would necessarily be "radical," so "drastic," Virginia asserts, as to transform, indeed "destroy," VMI's program. [It] is uncontested that women's admission would require accommodations, primarily in arranging housing assignments and physical training programs for female cadets. It is also undisputed, however, that "the VMI methodology could be used to educate women." 852 F.Supp., at 481. The District Court even allowed that some women may prefer it to the methodology a women's college might pursue. *** The parties, furthermore, agree that "some women can meet the physical standards [VMI] now impose[s] on men." 976 F.2d, at 896. *** In support of its initial judgment for Virginia, a judgment rejecting all equal protection objections presented by the United States, the District Court made "findings" on "gender-based developmental differences." These "findings" restate the opinions of Virginia's expert witnesses, opinions about typically male or typically female "tendencies." For example, "[m]ales tend to need an atmosphere of adversativeness," while "[f]emales tend to thrive in a cooperative atmosphere." [One expert maintained that] educational experiences must be designed "around the rule," [and] not "around the exception."

State actors controlling gates to opportunity, we have instructed, may not exclude qualified individuals based on "fixed notions concerning the roles and abilities of males and females." It may be assumed, for purposes of this decision, that most women would not choose VMI's adversative method. *** The issue, however, is not whether "women—or men—should be forced to attend VMI"; rather, the question is whether the Commonwealth can constitutionally deny to women who have the will and capacity, the training and attendant opportunities that VMI uniquely affords. The notion that admission of women would downgrade VMI's stature, destroy the adversative system and, with it, even the school, is a judgment hardly proved, a prediction hardly different from other "self-fulfilling prophecies" once routinely used to deny rights or opportunities. *** Women's successful entry into the federal military academies, and their participation in the Nation's military forces, indicate that Virginia's fears for the future of VMI may not be solidly grounded. The Commonwealth's justification for excluding all women from "citizen-soldier" training for which some are qualified, in any event, cannot rank as "exceedingly persuasive," as we have explained and applied that standard.

A proper remedy for an unconstitutional exclusion, we have explained, aims to "eliminate [so far as possible] the discriminatory effects of the past" and to "bar like discrimination in the future." [In the second phase of this litigation, Virginia proposed maintaining VMI's exclusionary policy and creating Virginia Women's Institute for Leadership (VWIL) as a separate program for women. VWIL is] different in kind from VMI and unequal in tangible and intangible facilities. *** VWIL affords women no opportunity to experience the rigorous military training for which VMI is famed. Instead, the VWIL program "deemphasize[s]" military education, and uses a "cooperative method" of education "which reinforces self-esteem." *** Virginia maintains that these methodological differences are "justified pedagogically," based on "important differences between men and women in learning and developmental needs," "psychological and sociological differences" Virginia describes as "real" and "not stereotypes." The Task Force charged with developing the leadership program for women *** "determined that [VMI's adversative method] would be wholly inappropriate for educating and training most women." As earlier stated, generalizations about "the way women are," estimates of what is appropriate for most women, no longer justify denying opportunity to women whose talent and capacity place them outside the average description.

In myriad respects other than military training, VWIL does not qualify as VMI's equal. VWIL's student body, faculty, course offerings, and facilities hardly match VMI's. Nor can the VWIL graduate anticipate the benefits associated with VMI's 157-year history, the school's prestige, and its influential alumni network. *** Virginia, in sum, while maintaining VMI for men only, has failed to provide any "comparable single-gender women's institution." Instead, the Commonwealth has created a VWIL program fairly appraised as a "pale shadow" of VMI in terms of the range of curricular choices and faculty stature, funding, prestige, alumni support and influence.

A prime part of the history of our Constitution [is] the story of the extension of constitutional rights and protections to people once ignored or excluded. VMI's story continued as our comprehension of "We the People" expanded. There is no reason to believe that the admission of women capable of all the activities required of VMI cadets would destroy the Institute rather than enhance its capacity to serve the "more perfect Union."

FYI

Justice Thomas did not participate in the decision of the case because his son was at the time attending VMI.

Chief Justice REHNQUIST, concurring in the judgment.

The Court defines the constitutional violation in these cases as "the categorical exclusion of women from an extraordinary educational opportunity afforded to men." [I] would not define the violation in this way; it is not the "exclusion of women" that violates the Equal Protection Clause, but the maintenance of an all-men school without providing any—much less a comparable—institution for women. Accordingly, the remedy should not necessarily require either the admission of women to VMI or the creation of a VMI clone for women. An adequate remedy in my opinion might be a demonstration by Virginia that its interest in educating men in a single-sex environment is matched by its interest in educating women in a single-sex institution. To demonstrate such, the Commonwealth does not need to create two institutions with the same number of faculty Ph.D.'s, similar SAT scores, or comparable athletic fields. *** It would be a sufficient remedy, I think, if the two institutions offered the same quality of education and were of the same overall caliber.

In the end, the women's institution Virginia proposes, VWIL, fails as a remedy, because it is distinctly inferior to the existing men's institution and will continue to be for the foreseeable future. *** I therefore ultimately agree with the Court that Virginia has not provided an adequate remedy.

Justice SCALIA, dissenting.

I have no problem with a system of abstract tests such as rational basis, intermediate, and strict scrutiny (though I think we can do better than applying strict scrutiny and intermediate scrutiny whenever we feel like it). *** But in my view the function of this Court is to preserve our society's values regarding (among other things) equal protection, not to revise them; to prevent backsliding from the degree of restriction the Constitution imposed upon democratic government, not to prescribe, on our own authority, progressively higher degrees. *** For that reason it is my view that, whatever abstract tests we may choose to devise, they cannot supersede—and indeed ought to be crafted so as to reflect—those constant and unbroken national traditions that embody the people's understanding of ambiguous constitutional texts. The all-male constitution of VMI comes squarely within such a governing tradition. *** Today, however, change is forced upon Virginia, and reversion to single-sex education is prohibited nationwide, not by democratic processes but by order of this Court. [This] is not the interpretation of a Constitution, but the creation of one.

To reject the Court's disposition today, however, it is not necessary to accept my view that the Court's made-up tests cannot displace longstanding national traditions as the primary determinant of what the Constitution means. It is only necessary to apply honestly the test the Court has been applying to sex-based classifications for the past two decades. *** Only the amorphous "exceedingly persuasive justification" phrase, and not the standard elaboration of intermediate scrutiny, can be made to yield this conclusion that VMI's single-sex composition is unconstitutional because there exist several women (or, one would have to conclude under the Court's reasoning, a single woman) willing and able to undertake VMI's program. Intermediate scrutiny has never required a least-restrictive-means analysis, but only a "substantial relation" between the classification and the state interests that it serves.

The Court's [application of a more searching level of scrutiny is] particularly out of place because it is perfectly clear that, if the question of the applicable standard of review for sex-based classifications were to be regarded as an appropriate subject for reconsideration, the stronger argument would be not for elevating the standard to strict scrutiny, but for reducing it to rational-basis review. *** It is hard to consider women a "discrete and insular minorit[y]" unable to employ the "political processes ordinarily to be relied upon" when they constitute a majority of the electorate. And the suggestion that they are incapable of exerting that political power smacks of the same paternalism that the Court so roundly condemns. Moreover, a long list of legislation proves the proposition false.

It is beyond question that Virginia has an important state interest in providing effective college education for its citizens. That single-sex instruction is an approach substantially related to that interest should be evident enough from the long and continuing history in this country of men's and women's colleges. ***

Under the constitutional principles announced and applied today, single-sex public education is unconstitutional. By going through the motions of applying a balancing test—asking whether the State has adduced an "exceedingly persuasive justification" for its sex-based classification—the Court creates the illusion that government officials in some future case will have a clear shot at justifying some sort of single-sex public education. [R]egardless of whether the Court's rationale leaves some small amount of room for lawyers to argue, it ensures that single-sex public education is functionally dead.

————————————

Points for Discussion

a. Level of Scrutiny

In his dissent, Justice Scalia suggested that the Court applied a different level of scrutiny than the intermediate scrutiny that the Court had applied in gender classification cases since *Craig v. Boren*. Do you agree that the Court's approach here was different? If so, in what way?

b. Separate but Equal?

The Court rejected the creation of VWIL as a remedy for gender discrimination at VMI, concluding that VWIL was a "pale shadow" of VMI. Chief Justice Rehnquist agreed, but suggested that the creation of an all-female institution that "offered the same quality of education and [was] of the same overall caliber" would eliminate the constitutional defect. Justice Scalia, in contrast, predicted that no public single-sex school would be able to survive the majority's decision. Given the Court's view—expressed here and in the affirmative action cases, which we considered earlier in this Chapter—about the importance of diversity in education, should equal, single-sex, parallel schools be a constitutionally acceptable approach to education? If so, how would the Court determine whether the parallel schools were in fact equal?

c. Gender Discrimination and the *Carolene Products* Test

Justice Scalia suggested in his dissent that, putting aside *stare decisis*, discrimination on the basis of gender should be subject only to rational-basis review, because women are in no meaningful sense a "minority" in need of judicial protection. Would this view have been correct in 1976, when the Court decided *Craig v. Boren*? Even if not, can't we today rely on the political process to protect women from discrimination?

Hypothetical

The City of Milwaukee, Wisconsin, relying on studies showing that girls tend to tune out in co-educational math and science classes, creates an all-girls Math and Science Academy and an all-boys magnet high school. The same faculty teach (on a rotating schedule) at both schools, which have comparable, state-of-the-art facilities. A boy who wishes to attend the Math and Science Academy sues, arguing that his exclusion on the basis of gender violates the Equal Protection Clause. How should the court rule? Would it matter if the all-boys school was a "Math and Science Academy," too?

---

3. Defining Gender Discrimination

The policy challenged in <u>Virginia</u> clearly classified on the basis of gender; women, after all, were categorically excluded from consideration for admission to VMI. But sometimes it is not as easy to tell whether a challenged policy "discriminates" against women or classifies on the basis of gender. The following case grappled with just such an issue.

Geduldig v. Aiello

417 U.S. 484 (1974)

Mr. Justice STEWART delivered the opinion of the Court.

California's disability insurance system is funded entirely from [mandatory] contributions deducted from the wages of participating employees. [The system pays benefits to persons in private employment who are temporarily unable to work because of disability not covered by workmen's compensation.] It is not every disabling condition, however, that triggers the obligation to pay benefits under the program. [Short-term disabilities are excluded, and no benefits are payable for any single disability beyond 26 weeks. The program] also excludes from coverage certain disabilities that are attributable to pregnancy. [Appellees challenged the constitutionality of this exclusion.]

We cannot agree that the exclusion of this disability from coverage amounts to invidious discrimination under the Equal Protection Clause. California does not discriminate with respect to the persons or groups which are eligible for disability insurance protection under the program. The classification challenged in this case relates to the asserted underinclusiveness of the set of risks that the State has selected to insure. Although California has created a program to insure most risks of employment disability, it has not chosen to insure all such risks, and this decision is reflected in the level of annual contributions exacted from participating employees. This Court has held that, consistently with the Equal Protection Clause, a State "may take one step at a time, addressing itself to the phase of the problem which seems most acute to the legislative mind. [The] legislature may select one phase of one field and apply a remedy there, neglecting the others." *Williamson v. Lee Optical Co.*, 348 U.S. 483, 489 (1955). Particularly with respect to social welfare programs, so long as the line drawn by the State is rationally supportable, the courts will not interpose their judgment as to the appropriate stopping point.

The District Court suggested that moderate alterations in [the] disability insurance program could be made to accommodate the substantial expense required to include normal pregnancy within the program's protection. The same can be said, however, with respect to the other expensive class of disabilities that are excluded from coverage—short-term disabilities. If the Equal Protection Clause were thought to compel disability payments for normal pregnancy, it is hard to perceive why it would not also compel payments for short-term disabilities suffered by participating employees. *** There is nothing in the Constitution, however, that requires the State to subordinate or compromise its legitimate interests solely to create a more comprehensive social insurance program than it already has.

The State has a legitimate interest in maintaining the self-supporting nature of its insurance program. Similarly, it has an interest in distributing the available resources in such a way as to keep benefit payments at an adequate level for disabilities that are covered, rather than to cover all disabilities inadequately. Finally, California has a legitimate concern in maintaining the contribution rate at a level that will not unduly burden participating employees, particularly low-income employees who may be most in need of the disability insurance.

These policies provide an objective and wholly noninvidious basis for the State's decision not to create a more comprehensive insurance program than it has. There is no evidence in the record that the selection of the risks insured by the program worked to discriminate against any definable group or class in terms of the aggregate risk protection derived by that group or class from the program.[4] There is no risk from which men are protected and women are not. Likewise, there is no risk from which women are protected and men are not.

Take Note	The appellee simply contends that, although she has received insurance protection equivalent to that provided all other participating employees, she has suffered discrimination because she encountered a risk that was outside the program's protection. For the reasons we have stated, we hold that this contention is not a valid one under the Equal Protection Clause of the Fourteenth Amendment.
The Court decided this case two years before it first accorded intermediate scrutiny to laws classifying on the basis of gender, in *Craig*. Would that development have made a difference in this case?	

Mr. Justice BRENNAN, with whom Mr. Justice DOUGLAS and Mr. Justice MARSHALL join, dissenting.

In my view, by singling out for less favorable treatment a gender-linked disability peculiar to women, the State has created a double standard for disability compensation: a

---

[4] The dissenting opinion to the contrary, this case is thus a far cry from cases like *Reed v. Reed*, 404 U.S. 71 (1971), and *Frontiero v. Richardson*, 411 U.S. 677 (1973), involving discrimination based upon gender as such. The California insurance program does not exclude anyone from benefit eligibility because of gender but merely removes one physical condition—pregnancy—from the list of compensable disabilities. While it is true that only women can become pregnant it does not follow that every legislative classification concerning pregnancy is a sex-based classification ***. Normal pregnancy is an objectively identifiable physical condition with unique characteristics. Absent a showing that distinctions involving pregnancy are mere pretexts designed to effect an invidious discrimination against the members of one sex or the other, lawmakers are constitutionally free to include or exclude pregnancy from the coverage of legislation such as this on any reasonable basis, just as with respect to any other physical condition. The lack of identity between the excluded disability and gender as such under this insurance program becomes clear upon the most cursory analysis. The program divides potential recipients into two groups—pregnant women and nonpregnant persons. While the first group is exclusively female, the second includes members of both sexes. The fiscal and actuarial benefits of the program thus accrue to members of both sexes.

limitation is imposed upon the disabilities for which women workers may recover, while men receive full compensation for all disabilities suffered, including those that affect only or primarily their sex, such as prostatectomies, circumcision, hemophilia, and gout. In effect, one set of rules is applied to females and another to males. Such dissimilar treatment of men and women, on the basis of physical characteristics inextricably linked to one sex, inevitably constitutes sex discrimination.

The State has clearly failed to meet [heightened scrutiny] in the present case. [When] a statutory classification is subject to strict judicial scrutiny, the State "must do more than show that denying (benefits to the excluded class) saves money." Moreover, California's legitimate interest in fiscal integrity could easily have been achieved through a variety of less drastic, sexually neutral means. *** The increased costs could be accommodated quite easily by making reasonable changes in the contribution rate, the maximum benefits allowable, and the other variables affecting the solvency of the program.

Points for Discussion

a. Defining Gender Discrimination

How does the majority opinion define gender discrimination? How does it differ from Justice Brennan's definition, which would explicitly include "dissimilar treatment of men and women [on] the basis of physical characteristics inextricably linked to one sex"? Does the majority disagree with Justice Brennan's view, or is the disagreement instead simply over whether pregnancy is equivalent to a physical characteristic?

In the majority's view, does gender discrimination exist only when a law separates *all* women from *all* men for purposes of determining treatment? Suppose, for example, that the state insurance program covered prostatectomies (i.e., the removal of a man's prostate) but did not cover hysterectomies (the removal of a woman's uterus). Would such a policy constitute gender discrimination subject to heightened review?

b. Disparate Impact

Was the appellees' claim essentially that the insurance program's coverage had a disparate impact on women? If so, recall that the Court held, in *Washington v. Davis*, that a showing of a disparate impact on a protected class, without a showing of discriminatory purpose, is not sufficient to constitute a violation of the Equal Protection Clause. Should the Court treat disparate impact claims differently when the affected group is defined by gender, on the ground that there are demonstrable and objectively definable differences between men and women? We will consider this question later in this Chapter.

---

4. Sex Differences and Stereotypes

The question for the Court in *Geduldig* was whether the insurance coverage scheme in fact discriminated on the basis of gender. Because the Court concluded that it did not, it had no occasion to consider whether differences between men and women justified the different treatment. Are differences between men and women ever an acceptable basis for different treatment by the government? Consider the cases that follow.

Orr v. Orr

440 U.S. 268 (1979)

Mr. Justice BRENNAN delivered the opinion of the Court.

[Mr. Orr, the appellant, challenged an Alabama divorce decree directing him to pay alimony to his ex-wife.] The question presented is the constitutionality of Alabama alimony statutes which provide that husbands, but not wives, may be required to pay alimony upon divorce.

The fact that the classification expressly discriminates against men rather than women does not protect it from scrutiny. *Craig v. Boren*, 429 U.S. 190 (1976). "To withstand scrutiny" under the Equal Protection Clause, "classifications by gender must serve important governmental objectives and must be substantially related to achievement of those objectives." *Califano v. Webster*, 430 U.S. 313, 316-317 (1977). We shall, therefore, examine the three governmental objectives that might arguably be served by Alabama's statutory scheme.

Appellant views the Alabama alimony statutes as effectively announcing the State's preference for an allocation of family responsibilities under which the wife plays a dependent role, and as seeking for their objective the reinforcement of that model among the State's citizens. We agree, as he urges, that prior cases settle that this purpose cannot sustain the statutes. *Stanton v. Stanton*, 421 U.S. 7, 10 (1975), held that the "old notio[n]" that "generally it is the man's primary responsibility to provide a home and its essentials," can no longer justify a statute that discriminates on the basis of gender. "No longer is the female destined solely for the home and the rearing of the family, and only the male for the marketplace and the world of ideas." If the statute is to survive constitutional attack, therefore, it must be validated on some other basis.

The opinion of the Alabama Court of Civil Appeals suggests other purposes that the statute may serve. Its opinion states that the Alabama statutes were "designed" for "the wife of a broken marriage who needs financial assistance." This may be read as asserting either of two legislative objectives. One is a legislative purpose to provide help for needy spouses, using sex as a proxy for need. The other is a goal of compensating women for past discrimination during marriage, which assertedly has left them unprepared to fend for themselves in the working world following divorce. We concede, of course, that assisting needy spouses is a legitimate and important governmental objective. We have also recognized "[r]eduction of the disparity in economic condition between men and women caused by the long history of discrimination against women [as] an important governmental objective." It only remains, therefore, to determine whether the classification at issue here is "substantially related to achievement of those objectives."

[E]ven if sex were a reliable proxy for need, and even if the institution of marriage did discriminate against women, these factors still would "not adequately justify the salient features of" Alabama's statutory scheme. Under the statute, individualized hearings at which the parties' relative financial circumstances are considered already occur. There is no reason, therefore, to use sex as a proxy for need. Needy males could be helped along with needy females with little if any additional burden on the State. In such circumstances, not even an administrative-convenience rationale exists to justify operating by generalization or proxy. Similarly, since individualized hearings can determine which women were in fact discriminated against vis-à-vis their husbands, as well as which family units defied the stereotype and left the husband dependent on the wife, Alabama's alleged compensatory purpose may be effectuated without placing burdens solely on husbands. Progress toward fulfilling such a purpose would not be hampered, and it would cost the State nothing more, if it were to treat men and women equally by making alimony burdens independent of sex.

> **Food for Thought**
>
> In light of the Court's reasoning, could a state divorce law survive scrutiny if it eliminated case-by-case adjudication of claims for alimony and instead simply automatically ordered the male spouse to pay a fixed percentage of his income to the female spouse? If not, then why did the Court choose to resolve the case on the grounds that it did?

> **FYI**
>
> On remand, the Alabama Court of Civil Appeals held that alimony could be awarded to husbands as well as to wives, curing the Equal Protection violation. But the court proceeded to order Mr. Orr to pay alimony to his wife. Was this result consistent with the Supreme Court's decision?

Legislative classifications which distribute benefits and burdens on the basis of gender carry the inherent risk of reinforcing the stereotypes about the "proper place" of women and their need for special protection. Thus, even statutes purportedly designed to compensate for and ameliorate the effects of past discrimination must be carefully tailored. Where, as here, the State's compensatory and ameliorative purposes are as well served by a gender-neutral classification as one that gender classifies and therefore carries with it the baggage of sexual stereotypes, the State cannot be permitted to classify on the basis of sex. [Reversed.]

[Justice BLACKMUN's concurring opinion is omitted.]

————————

Points for Discussion

a. Discrimination Against Men

The Court subjected the Alabama statute, which disadvantaged men, to the same level of scrutiny to which it subjects statutes that disadvantage women. In light of the reasons that the Court applies heightened scrutiny to gender classifications, do you agree that statutes that impose a heavier burden on men should be subjected to the same level of scrutiny? If in fact men enjoy disproportionate political power and historically women have been the victims of discrimination, then does it make sense to provide judicial protection to men who are burdened by legislative action? Or is the Court's point that statutes such as the one at issue in *Orr* in fact represent the institutionalization of invidious gender stereotypes, and thus in effect perpetuate discrimination against *women*?

b. The Relevance of Past Discrimination

The Court in *Orr* did not identify the circumstances under which a gender classification that is asserted to compensate for past discrimination can survive intermediate scrutiny. Several years earlier, however, in *Weinberger v. Wiesenfeld*, 420 U.S. 636 (1975), the Court invalidated a provision of the Social Security Act that provided for the payment of additional insurance benefits to women upon the death of their husbands, but did not provide comparable benefits to a man whose wife had died. Although the Court recognized that the government has a legitimate interest in helping women to overcome economic disadvantages, it noted that a "mere recitation of a benign, compensatory purpose is not an automatic shield which protects against any inquiry into the actual purposes underlying a statutory scheme." The Court concluded that Congress's purpose in enacting the provision was not to compensate women for past economic discrimination, but rather to provide a single mother with the choice to stay home with a child. Because widowers were deprived of this choice, the provision appeared driven by the assumption that women, but not men, should be (or at least more typically were) stay-at-home parents.

By contrast, in *Califano v. Webster*, 430 U.S. 313 (1977), the Court upheld a provision of the Social Security Act that allowed women to exclude from their computation of their average monthly wage three more lower-earning years than a similarly situated male wage earner. As with the provision at issue in *Weinberger*, the net effect was to provide higher benefits to women than to men. The Court distinguished *Weinberger* by noting that the clear purpose of the favorable treatment for women in the provision at issue was the "permissible one of redressing our society's longstanding disparate treatment of women," and that the provision "operated directly to compensate women for past economic discrimination." In the Court's view, the different treatment of the sexes was based upon real, calculable economic differences, rather than on mere gender stereotypes.

But since then, the Court has been skeptical of government arguments that gender classifications are warranted to provide a remedy for past discrimination against women. In *Mississippi Univ. for Women v. Hogan*, 458 U.S. 718 (1982), the Court, in an opinion by Justice O'Connor, declared unconstitutional the public university's policy of excluding men from its School of Nursing. The University had been founded as an all-women's school in

1884, and the School of Nursing had been established in 1971. Mississippi argued that continuing to deny men admission to the school served a compensatory purpose for past discrimination against women. But the Court, noting that women earn more than 90% of the nursing degrees in Mississippi and nationwide, concluded that "[r]ather than compensate for discriminatory barriers faced by women, MUW's policy of excluding males from admission to the School of Nursing tends to perpetuate the stereotyped view of nursing as an exclusively women's job."

———————

To be sure, some classifications on the basis of gender are based solely upon stereotypes that have historically disadvantaged women. But there are, of course, also real and important physiological differences between men and women. In *United States v. Virginia*, 518 U.S. 515 (1996), for example, Justice Ginsburg explained:

> The heightened review standard our precedent establishes does not make sex a proscribed classification. Supposed "inherent differences" are no longer accepted as a ground for race or national origin classifications. Physical differences between men and women, however, are enduring. *** "Inherent differences" between men and women, we have come to appreciate, remain cause for celebration, but not for denigration of the members of either sex or for artificial constraints on an individual's opportunity.

But, as it turns out, it is no easy task to identify the circumstances under which the government may take physiological differences between men and women into account. The next case is illustrative of the challenge.

———————

Michael M. v. Superior Court of Sonoma County

450 U.S. 464 (1981)

Justice REHNQUIST announced the judgment of the Court and delivered an opinion, in which THE CHIEF JUSTICE, Justice STEWART, and Justice POWELL joined.

Take Note

Justice Rehnquist wrote only for a plurality; Justice Blackmun, whose separate reasoning follows, provided the fifth vote to affirm the court below. After you have read both opinions, consider the extent to which Justice Rehnquist's reasoning has binding force.

The question presented in this case is whether California's "statutory rape" law [violates] the Equal Protection Clause of the Fourteenth Amendment. Section 261.5 [of the California Penal Code] defines unlawful sexual intercourse as "an act of sexual intercourse accomplished with a female not the wife of the perpetrator, where the female is under the age of 18 years." The statute thus makes men alone criminally liable for the act of sexual intercourse. [Petitioner, a 17-year-old male, was prosecuted for having sex with a 16-year-old female.]

Underlying [our] decisions is the principle that a legislature may not "make overbroad generalizations based on sex which are entirely unrelated to any differences between men and women or which demean the ability or social status of the affected class." But because the Equal Protection Clause does not "demand that a statute necessarily apply equally to all persons" or require "things which are different in fact [to] be treated in law as though they were the same," this Court has consistently upheld statutes where the gender classification is not invidious, but rather realistically reflects the fact that the sexes are not similarly situated in certain circumstances. As the Court has stated, a legislature may "provide for the special problems of women." *Weinberger v. Wiesenfeld*, 420 U.S. 636, 653 (1975).

Applying those principles to this case, the fact that the California Legislature criminalized the act of illicit sexual intercourse with a minor female is a sure indication of its intent or purpose to discourage that conduct. Precisely why the legislature desired that result is of course somewhat less clear. This Court has long recognized that "[i]nquiries into congressional motives or purposes are a hazardous matter," and the search for the "actual" or "primary" purpose of a statute is likely to be elusive. Here, for example, the individual legislators may have voted for the statute for a variety of reasons. Some legislators may have been concerned about preventing teenage pregnancies, others about protecting young females from physical injury or from the loss of "chastity," and still others about promoting various religious and moral attitudes towards premarital sex.

The justification for the statute offered by the State, and accepted by the Supreme Court of California, is that the legislature sought to prevent illegitimate teenage pregnancies. That finding, of course, is entitled to great deference. And although our cases establish that the State's asserted reason for the enactment of a statute may be rejected, if it "could not have been a goal of the legislation," this is not such a case. We are satisfied not only that the prevention of illegitimate pregnancy is at least one of the "purposes" of the statute, but also that the State has a strong interest in preventing such pregnancy. At the risk of stating the obvious, teenage pregnancies, which have increased dramatically over the last two decades, have significant social, medical, and economic consequences for both the mother and her child, and the State. Of particular concern to the State is that approximately half of all teenage pregnancies end in abortion. And of those children who are born, their illegitimacy makes them likely candidates to become wards of the State.

> **Take Note**
>
> If the "true" purpose of the statute was to protect the virtue and chastity of young women, then that purpose likely would not be sufficient under heightened scrutiny, as it arguably rests on archaic stereotypes about women. The Court concludes, however, that because there is at least one legitimate motive for the statute, it is irrelevant that other motives were impermissible. Is this consistent with the Court's approach in other cases involving gender classifications? What about the likelihood that the gender classification will itself perpetuate stereotypes?

We need not be medical doctors to discern that young men and young women are not similarly situated with respect to the problems and the risks of sexual intercourse. Only women may become pregnant, and they suffer disproportionately the profound physical, emotional and psychological consequences of sexual activity. The statute at issue here protects women from sexual intercourse at an age when those consequences are particularly severe.

The question thus boils down to whether a State may attack the problem of sexual intercourse and teenage pregnancy directly by prohibiting a male from having sexual intercourse with a minor female. *** We hold that such a statute is sufficiently related to the State's objectives to pass constitutional muster. Because virtually all of the significant harmful and inescapably identifiable consequences of teenage pregnancy fall on the young female, a legislature acts well within its authority when it elects to punish only the participant who, by nature, suffers few of the consequences of his conduct. It is hardly unreasonable for a legislature acting to protect minor females to exclude them from punishment. Moreover, the risk of pregnancy itself constitutes a substantial deterrence to young females. No similar natural sanctions deter males. A criminal sanction imposed solely on males thus serves to roughly "equalize" the deterrents on the sexes.

We are unable to accept petitioner's contention that the statute is impermissibly underinclusive and must, in order to pass judicial scrutiny, be broadened so as to hold the female as criminally liable as the male. It is argued that this statute is not necessary to deter teenage pregnancy because a gender-neutral statute, where both male and female would be subject to prosecution, would serve that goal equally well. The relevant inquiry, however, is not whether the statute is drawn as precisely as it might have been ***. In any event, we cannot say that a gender-neutral statute would be as effective as the statute California has chosen to enact. The State persuasively contends that a gender-neutral statute would frustrate its interest in effective enforcement. Its view is that a female is surely less likely to report violations of the statute if she herself would be subject to criminal prosecution. In an area already fraught with prosecutorial difficulties, we decline to hold that the Equal Protection Clause requires a legislature to enact a statute so broad that it may well be incapable of enforcement.

Justice STEWART, concurring.

The Constitution is violated when government, state or federal, invidiously classifies similarly situated people on the basis of the immutable characteristics with which they were born. Thus, detrimental racial classifications by government always violate the Constitution, for the simple reason that, so far as the Constitution is concerned, people of different races are always similarly situated. By contrast, while detrimental gender classifications by government often violate the Constitution, they do not always do so, for the reason that there are differences between males and females that the Constitution necessarily recognizes. [I]n certain narrow circumstances men and women are not similarly situated; in these circumstances a gender classification based on clear differences between the sexes is not invidious, and a legislative classification realistically based upon those differences is not unconstitutional.

Young women and men are not similarly situated with respect to the problems and risk associated with intercourse and pregnancy, and the statute is realistically related to the legitimate state purpose of reducing those problems and risks. In short, the Equal Protection Clause does not mean that the physiological differences between men and women must be disregarded. While those differences must never be permitted to become a pretext for invidious discrimination, no such discrimination is presented by this case. The Constitution surely does not require a State to pretend that demonstrable differences between men and women do not really exist.

Justice BLACKMUN, concurring in the judgment.

It is gratifying that the plurality recognizes that "teenage pregnancies *** have significant social, medical, and economic consequences for both the mother and her child, and the State." There have been times when I have wondered whether the Court was capable of this perception, particularly when it has struggled with the different but not unrelated problems that attend abortion issues. *** [I think the California statutory rape law] is a sufficiently reasoned and constitutional effort to control the problem at its inception.

Justice BRENNAN, with whom Justices WHITE and MARSHALL join, dissenting.

[T]he plurality opinion and Justices STEWART and BLACKMUN [place] too much emphasis on the desirability of achieving the State's asserted statutory goal—prevention of teenage pregnancy—and not enough emphasis on the fundamental question of whether the sex-based discrimination in the California statute is substantially related to the achievement of that goal. [E]ven assuming that prevention of teenage pregnancy is an important governmental objective and that it is in fact an objective of § 261.5, California still has the burden of proving that there are fewer teenage pregnancies under its gender-based statutory rape law than there would be if the law were gender neutral. To meet this burden, the State must show that because its statutory rape law punishes only males, and not females, it more effectively deters minor females from having sexual intercourse.

The State has not produced such evidence in this case. Moreover, there are at least two serious flaws in the State's assertion that law enforcement problems created by a gender-neutral statutory rape law would make such a statute less effective than a gender-based statute in deterring sexual activity. First, [t]here are now at least 37 States that have enacted gender-neutral statutory rape laws, [and] the laws of Arizona, Florida, and Illinois permit prosecution of both minor females and minor males for engaging in mutual sexual conduct. California has introduced no evidence that those States have been handicapped by the enforcement problems the plurality finds so persuasive. *** [Second, common sense] suggests that a gender-neutral statutory rape law is potentially a *greater* deterrent of sexual activity than a gender-based law, for the simple reason that a gender-neutral law subjects both men and women to criminal sanctions and thus arguably has a deterrent effect on twice as many potential violators. Even if fewer persons were prosecuted under the gender-neutral law, as the State suggests, it would still be true that twice as many persons would be *subject* to arrest. The State's failure to prove that a gender-neutral law would be a less effective deterrent than a gender-based law, like the State's failure to prove that a gender-neutral law would be difficult to enforce, should have led this Court to invalidate § 261.5.

Until very recently, no California court or commentator had suggested that the purpose of California's statutory rape law was to protect young women from the risk of pregnancy.

Indeed, the historical development of § 261.5 demonstrates that the law was initially enacted on the premise that young women, in contrast to young men, were to be deemed legally incapable of consenting to an act of sexual intercourse. Because their chastity was considered particularly precious, those young women were felt to be uniquely in need of the State's protection. In contrast, young men were assumed to be capable of making such decisions for themselves; the law therefore did not offer them any special protection.

It is perhaps because the gender classification in California's statutory rape law was initially designed to further these outmoded sexual stereotypes, rather than to reduce the incidence of teenage pregnancies, that the State has been unable to demonstrate a substantial relationship between the classification and its newly asserted goal. *** I would hold that § 261.5 violates the Equal Protection Clause of the Fourteenth Amendment.

Justice STEVENS, dissenting.

The question in this case is whether the difference between males and females justifies this statutory discrimination based entirely on sex. But the plurality surely cannot believe that the risk of pregnancy confronted by the female—any more than the risk of venereal disease confronted by males as well as females—has provided an effective deterrent to voluntary female participation in the risk-creating conduct. Yet the plurality's decision seems to rest on the assumption that the California Legislature acted on the basis of that rather fanciful notion.

The fact that the California Legislature has decided to apply its prohibition only to the male may reflect a legislative judgment that in the typical case the male is actually the more guilty party. Any such judgment must, in turn, assume that the decision to engage in the risk-creating conduct is always—or at least typically—a male decision. If that assumption is valid, the statutory classification should also be valid. But what is the support for the assumption? *** I think it is supported to some extent by traditional attitudes toward male-female relationships. But the possibility that such a habitual attitude may reflect nothing more than an irrational prejudice makes it an insufficient justification for discriminatory treatment that is otherwise blatantly unfair. For, as I read this statute, it requires that one, and only one, of two equally guilty wrongdoers be stigmatized by a criminal conviction.

———————

Points for Discussion

a. Identifying Stereotypes

The plurality in *Michael M.* concluded that the statute at issue was designed to prevent teen pregnancy; because the capacity to become pregnant is an uncontested physical difference between men and women, the plurality concluded that the statute permissibly treated men and women differently. Both Justices Brennan and Stevens, by contrast, concluded that the statute reflected archaic and invidious stereotypes about gender roles. Assuming that laws motivated by gender stereotypes should be invalidated, how does the Court know when a law is based on such stereotypes? Even putting aside the problem of identifying legislative motive, how does the Court determine that a particular view is an invidious stereotype, rather than a reflection of real differences?

b. Further Developments

Note that Justice Rehnquist wrote only for a plurality in *Michael M.* Since that decision, the Court has continued to struggle with classifications that purport to turn on differences between men and women. In *Nguyen v. INS*, 533 U.S. 53 (2001), for example, the Court upheld a statute that made it more difficult for a child born abroad out of wedlock to one United States parent to claim citizenship if the citizen parent was the father rather than the mother. The Court explained that the "distinction embodied in the statutory scheme here at issue is not marked by misconception and prejudice, nor does it show disrespect for either class. The difference between men and women in relation to the birth process is a real one." The Court concluded that Congress was justified in concluding that because a mother, unlike a father, must be present at the birth of the child, and because mothers are thus more likely to develop a relationship with the child, maternity—and thus citizenship—should be easier to demonstrate.

Justice O'Connor dissented, asserting that the law was based on a stereotypical view of women as more likely to establish and maintain a meaningful relationship with their children. In her view, a stereotype does not need to be disrespectful or devoid of empirical support in order to be an unconstitutional basis for a gender classification. Rather, she asserted that the Equal Protection Clause forbids any classification that "relies upon the simplistic outdated assumption that gender could be used as a proxy for other, more germane bases of classification." Which approach do you find more persuasive?

---

5. Purpose and Effect

Personnel Administrator of Massachusetts v. Feeney

442 U.S. 256 (1979)

Mr. Justice STEWART delivered the opinion of the Court.

This case presents a challenge to the constitutionality of the Massachusetts veterans' preference statute, Mass. Gen. Laws Ann., ch. 31, § 23, on the ground that it discriminates against women in violation of the Equal Protection Clause of the Fourteenth Amendment. Under ch. 31, § 23, all veterans who qualify for state civil service positions must be considered for appointment ahead of any qualifying nonveterans. The preference operates overwhelmingly to the advantage of males. [Ms. Feeney received the second highest score on a civil service examination for a job with the Board of Dental Examiners, and the third highest on a test for an Administrative Assistant position with a mental health center, but male veterans who had scored lower on the examinations received the positions.]

The [Massachusetts] veterans' preference statute [has long] defined the term "veterans" in gender-neutral language. *** Women who have served in official United States military units during wartime, then, have always been entitled to the benefit of the preference. [At the time, of the litigation, 98% of veterans in Massachusetts were male. Although 54% of the men appointed to civil service positions were veterans, only 1.8% of the women were.]

[As] was made clear in *Washington v. Davis*, 426 U.S. 229 (1976), and *Arlington Heights v. Metropolitan Housing Dev. Corp.*, 429 U.S. 252 (1977), even if a neutral law has a disproportionately adverse effect upon a racial minority, it is unconstitutional under the Equal Protection Clause only if that impact can be traced to a discriminatory purpose. *** Those principles apply with equal force to a case involving alleged gender discrimination.

The appellee has conceded that ch. 31, § 23, is neutral on its face. [Nor is the classification a covert form of gender discrimination.] Veteran status is not uniquely male. Although few women benefit from the preference, the *nonveteran* class is not substantially all female. To the contrary, significant numbers of nonveterans are men, and all nonveterans—male as well as female—are placed at a disadvantage. Too many men are affected by ch. 31, § 23, to permit the inference that the statute is but a pretext for preferring men over women.

The dispositive question, then, is whether the appellee has shown that a gender-based discriminatory purpose has, at least in some measure, shaped the Massachusetts veterans' preference legislation. *** "Discriminatory purpose" [implies] more than intent as volition or intent as awareness of consequences. It implies that the decisionmaker, in this case a state legislature, selected or reaffirmed a particular course of action at least in part "because of," not merely "in spite of," its adverse effects upon an identifiable group. Yet, nothing in the record demonstrates that this preference for veterans was originally devised or subsequently re-enacted because it would accomplish the collateral goal of keeping women in a stereotypic and pre-defined place in the Massachusetts Civil Service.

Veterans' hiring preferences represent an awkward—and, many argue, unfair—exception to the widely shared view that merit and merit alone should prevail in the employment policies of government. *** But the Fourteenth Amendment "cannot be made a refuge from ill-

> **Take Note**
>
> The Court concludes that the classification does not reflect a discriminatory purpose because it disadvantages many men, as well. If the class of persons benefited were *exclusively* male, would it matter that the disadvantaged class includes men as well as women? If the police force excluded all women from consideration, would the fact that many male applicants are also denied positions mean that there is no discrimination? If not, why is this case different?

> **Food for Thought**
>
> In the Court's view, who bears the burden of persuasion on the question of the state's purpose? Must the person challenging the law demonstrate that the state had a discriminatory purpose? Or should the showing that the law has a substantial disparate impact on women shift the burden to the state to demonstrate that it was enacted for *non*-discriminatory purposes?

CHAPTER 11 *Status-Based Classifications*

advised [laws]." The appellee [has] simply failed to demonstrate that the law in any way reflects a purpose to discriminate on the basis of sex.

Mr. Justice STEVENS, with whom Mr. Justice WHITE joins, concurring.

[F]or me the answer is largely provided by the fact that the number of males disadvantaged by Massachusetts' veterans' preference (1,867,000) is sufficiently large—and sufficiently close to the number of disadvantaged females (2,954,000)—to refute the claim that the rule was intended to benefit males as a class over females as a class.

Mr. Justice MARSHALL, with whom Mr. Justice BRENNAN joins, dissenting.

That a legislature seeks to advantage one group does not, as a matter of logic or of common sense, exclude the possibility that it also intends to disadvantage another. *** Absent an omniscience not commonly attributed to the judiciary, it will often be impossible to ascertain the sole or even dominant purpose of a given statute. *** Moreover, since reliable evidence of subjective intentions is seldom obtainable, resort to inference based on objective factors is generally unavoidable. To discern the purposes underlying facially neutral policies, this Court has therefore considered the degree, inevitability, and foreseeability of any disproportionate impact as well as the alternatives reasonably available.

Where the foreseeable impact of a facially neutral policy is so disproportionate, the burden should rest on the State to establish that sex-based considerations played no part in the choice of the particular legislative scheme. *** Clearly, that burden was not sustained here. The legislative history of the statute reflects the Commonwealth's patent appreciation of the impact the preference system would have on women, and an equally evident desire to mitigate that impact only with respect to certain traditionally female occupations. Until 1971, the statute and implementing civil service regulations exempted from operation of the preference any job requisitions "especially calling for women." In practice, this exemption, coupled with the absolute preference for veterans, has created a gender-based civil service hierarchy, with women occupying low-grade clerical and secretarial jobs and men holding more responsible and remunerative positions. *** Such a statutory scheme both reflects and perpetuates precisely the kind of archaic assumptions about women's roles which we have previously held invalid.

Food for Thought

Justice Marshall suggests that the state could have accomplished its (non-discriminatory) objective here—to recognize and reward veterans for their military service—through means that would not disproportionately affect women. Can you think of any such alternatives?

To survive challenge under the Equal Protection Clause, statutes reflecting gender-based discrimination must be substantially related to the achievement of important governmental objectives. *** In its present unqualified form, the veterans' preference statute precludes all but a small fraction of Massachusetts women from obtaining any civil service position also of interest to men. Given the range of alternatives available, this degree of preference is not constitutionally permissible.

Points for Discussion

a. Purpose v. Effects

Recall that in *Washington v. Davis*, which we considered earlier in this Chapter, the Court held that a facially neutral law that has a discriminatory effect on members of a racial minority does not violate the Equal Protection Clause absent a finding of discriminatory purpose. Does Justice Marshall quarrel with that conclusion here, in the context of gender discrimination? That is, does Justice Marshall suggest here that even absent a discriminatory purpose, discriminatory effects can be sufficient to invalidate an otherwise neutral classification? Or does he simply conclude that the statute is invalid because the effects are sufficient evidence of a discriminatory purpose? Assuming that *Davis*'s approach makes sense in the context of racial discrimination, does it make sense to apply that approach in the context of gender discrimination?

b. Ascertaining Discriminatory Purpose

If nothing else, the majority and the dissent appeared to agree that a law reflecting a purpose to discriminate against women must be subjected to heightened scrutiny. In what ways do they differ over the appropriate method for demonstrating such a purpose? When should a court infer a discriminatory purpose from the mere existence of disparate effects? And when, if ever, should indications of "subjective" legislative intent—such as the statements by one or two lawmakers that reflect discriminatory animus—be relevant?

c. Women and the Military

Is the real question in *Feeney* whether the one-time prohibition on women's serving in the military—and the present limits on the capacities in which women may serve—is itself an unconstitutional form of gender discrimination? Two years after the decision in *Feeney*, the Court held in *Rostker v. Goldberg*, 453 U.S. 57 (1981), that the Military Selective Service Act, which authorized the President to require the registration of males but not females, did not violate the Equal Protection component of the Due Process Clause of the Fifth Amendment. The Court emphasized the deference that the Court has applied to congressional judgments in matters of "national defense and military affairs" and the government's "important" interest in "raising and supporting armies." The Court reasoned that the "purpose of registration was to prepare for a draft of combat troops." Because "women are excluded from combat," Congress permissibly concluded that "they would not be needed in the event of a draft, and therefore decided not to register them." Do you agree with this decision? Does its validity turn on whether the exclusion of women from combat roles itself constitutes invidious discrimination?

If women can constitutionally be excluded from the draft (and, under current statutory law, from combat roles in the military), can there really be any constitutional objection to the classification at issue in *Feeney*? Or is there a difference between the exclusion of women from many forms of military service, on the one hand, and the conferral of benefits on a basis that largely reflects that exclusion, on the other? Conversely, should statutes like the one at issue in *Feeney* be relevant to the determination whether women can constitutionally be excluded from military service in the first place?

——————————

C. Other Classifications

So far, we have seen that a wide range of bases for government classifications receive only rational-basis review. We have also seen that classifications based on race or national origin are subject to strict scrutiny, and that classifications based on gender are subject to intermediate scrutiny. And as we will see in Chapters 14-17, the Constitution explicitly defines some other bases for classifications. The First Amendment, which protects both the "freedom of speech" and the "free exercise" of religion, clearly limits the government's authority to discriminate on the basis of a person's views or religious beliefs. (Indeed, sometimes the Court has even articulated these limits as inhering in the Equal Protection Clause. See, e.g, *Police Department of Chicago v. Mosley*, 408 U.S. 92 (1972).)

Are there other bases for classification that are subject to heightened scrutiny? Recall the Court's suggestion in *Carolene Products*, which we considered in Chapter 10, that "discrete and insular minorities" that face prejudice and have difficulty obtaining protection from ordinary political processes might be entitled to heightened judicial protection. Is this the proper test for identifying groups subject to heightened protection under the Equal Protection Clause? Either way, what other groups, if any, are deserving of such heightened judicial protection? The materials that follow address that question.

——————————

1. Alienage

Graham v. Richardson

403 U.S. 365 (1971)

Mr. Justice BLACKMUN delivered the opinion of the Court.

[Carmen Richardson was a lawfully admitted resident alien who had lived in Arizona for thirteen years. She was denied benefits under Arizona's disability insurance program because she was not a citizen and had not resided in Arizona for fifteen years. Elsie Leger was a lawfully admitted resident alien living and paying taxes in the state of Pennsylvania. After illness forced her to give up her employment, she applied for public assistance but was denied because she was not a citizen. Ms. Richardson and Mrs. Leger filed separate suits claiming that the denials violated the Equal Protection Clause.]

It has long been settled, and it is not disputed here, that the term "person" in [the Equal Protection Clause] encompasses lawfully admitted resident aliens as well as citizens of the United States and entitles both citizens and aliens to the equal protection of the laws of the State in which they reside. *Yick Wo v. Hopkins,* 118 U.S. 356, 369 (1886). Nor is it disputed that the Arizona and Pennsylvania statutes in question create two classes of needy persons, indistinguishable except with respect to whether they are or are not citizens of this country. Otherwise qualified United States citizens living in Arizona are entitled to federally funded categorical assistance benefits without regard to length of national residency, but aliens must have lived in this country for 15 years in order to qualify for aid. United States citizens living in Pennsylvania [may] be eligible for state-supported general assistance, but resident aliens as a class are precluded from that assistance.

Under traditional equal protection principles, a State retains broad discretion to classify as long as its classification has a reasonable basis. This is so in "the area of economics and social welfare." *Dandridge v. Williams,* 397 U.S. 471, 485 (1970). But the Court's decisions have established that classifications based on alienage, like those based on nationality or race, are inherently suspect and subject to close judicial scrutiny. Aliens as a class are a prime example of a "discrete and insular" minority (see *United States v. Carolene Products Co.,* 304 U.S. 144, 152-153 (1938)) for whom such heightened judicial solicitude is appropriate.

> **Food for Thought**
>
> Is discrimination on the basis of citizenship status tantamount to discrimination on the basis of national origin, which the Court subjects to strict scrutiny? If not, why is it different? Is alienage status immutable?

> **FYI**
>
> In *Crane v. New York,* 239 U.S. 195 (1915), the Court upheld a state statute prohibiting the employment of aliens on public works projects, reasoning that state employment is a privilege, not a right, that can be limited to citizens. In the early twentieth century, the Court also upheld state laws limiting the rights of aliens to own land and to exploit state natural resources. The Court refers to these holdings as the "special public-interest doctrine."

Arizona and Pennsylvania seek to justify their restrictions on the eligibility of aliens for public assistance solely on the basis of a State's "special public interest" in favoring its own citizens over aliens in the distribution of limited resources such as welfare benefits. It is true that this Court on occasion has upheld state statutes that treat citizens and noncitizens differently, the ground for distinction having been that such laws were necessary to protect special interests of the State or its citizens. ***

Whatever may be the contemporary vitality of the special public-interest doctrine, we conclude that a State's desire to preserve limited welfare benefits for its own citizens is inadequate to justify Pennsylvania's making noncitizens ineligible for public assistance, and Arizona's restricting benefits to citizens and longtime resident aliens. First, [this] Court now has rejected the concept that constitutional rights turn upon whether a governmental benefit is characterized as a "right" or as a "privilege." *Sherbert v. Verner*, 374 U.S. 398 (1963).

Second, as the Court recognized in *Shapiro v. Thompson*, 394 U.S. 618, 633 (1969), "[a] State has a valid interest in preserving the fiscal integrity of its programs. It may legitimately attempt to limit its expenditures, whether for public assistance, public education, or any other program. But a State may not accomplish such a purpose by invidious distinctions between classes of its citizens." Since an alien as well as a citizen is a "person" for equal protection purposes, a concern for fiscal integrity is no more compelling a justification for the questioned classification in these cases than it was in *Shapiro*.

> **Make the Connection**
>
> We briefly considered the "unconstitutional conditions doctrine" in Chapter 9, and we will consider *Sherbert* in Chapter 17, in our discussion of the Free Exercise of Religion.

> **FYI**
>
> In a section of the opinion that is omitted here, the Court concluded that the states' limitations on the eligibility of aliens for welfare benefits encroached upon federal authority over immigration and naturalization, on a theory of field preemption. (We considered preemption in Chapter 4.) Given this conclusion, was it necessary for the Court to address the equal protection claims?

We agree with the three-judge court in the Pennsylvania case that the "justification of limiting expenses is particularly inappropriate and unreasonable when the discriminated class consists of aliens. Aliens like citizens pay taxes and may be called into the armed forces." *** There can be no "special public interest" in tax revenues to which aliens have contributed on an equal basis with the residents of the State. Accordingly, we hold that a state statute that denies welfare benefits to resident aliens and one that denies them to aliens who have not resided in the United States for a specified number of years violates the Equal Protection Clause.

Points for Discussion

a. Level of Scrutiny

What level of scrutiny did the Court apply to the state statutes? The Court compared classifications based on citizenship status to those based on nationality and race, and declared that they are "inherently suspect and subject to close judicial scrutiny." But the Court did not make clear whether the state interest justifying the classification must be "compelling," and the Court did not discuss the required relationship between the state interest and the classification.

Two years later, in *Sugarman v. Dougall*, 413 U.S. 634 (1973), the Court applied strict scrutiny to invalidate a New York law that excluded non-citizens from permanent positions in the state's civil service. The Court acknowledged the state's "substantial" interest in "having an employee of undivided loyalty" in significant policy-making positions, but concluded that the statute covered mostly menial employees. Several years later, relying on the "policy-making" exception that the Court had suggested in <u>Sugarman</u>, the Court declined to apply strict scrutiny to a state policy excluding aliens from employment as state troopers. *Foley v. Connelie*, 435 U.S. 291 (1978). The Court declared that "to require every statutory exclusion of aliens to clear the high hurdle of 'strict scrutiny' [would] obliterate all the distinctions between citizens and aliens, and thus depreciate the historic values of citizenship." The Court noted that police officers "are clothed with authority to exercise an almost infinite variety of discretionary powers." The Court upheld the policy, concluding that "[i]n the enforcement and execution of the laws the police function is one where citizenship bears a rational relationship to the special demands of the particular position."

After <u>Graham</u>, <u>Sugarman</u>, and <u>Foley</u>, what is the appropriate level of scrutiny for classifications based upon citizenship status?

b. Defining the Political Community

The Court has struggled in many contexts with the states' efforts to define their political communities. It seems widely accepted that states can deny the right to vote to persons who are not citizens. Why is that denial less problematic than the denial at issue in <u>Graham</u>?

Is the amount of time that one spends in a community a relevant criteria in defining the political community? In <u>Graham</u>, the states sought to limit public benefits to those who were citizens, or at least (in the case of Arizona) to those who had been legal residents for a long time. In Chapter 7, we considered the Court's response to a state statute that limited newly arrived residents to the level of welfare benefits that they would have received in their prior states of residence. In <u>Saenz v. Roe</u>, the Court invalidated the statute, relying on the Privileges or Immunities Clause of the Fourteenth Amendment. Why didn't the Court rely on that provision in <u>Graham</u>? What limits, if any, should there be on the ability of the states to exclude persons from their political communities? Should those limits apply with equal force to the federal government?

c. Aliens Who Were Not Lawfully Admitted

Aliens who were not lawfully admitted to the United States plainly are "persons," they lack political power (indeed, they lack the right to vote), and they are often the targets of hostility. Can states withhold benefits from them? If so, why are such classifications different from the classifications at issue in <u>Graham</u>?

2. Parents' Marital Status

Clark v. Jeter

486 U.S. 456 (1988)

Justice O'CONNOR delivered the opinion of the Court.

Under Pennsylvania law, an illegitimate child must prove paternity before seeking support from his or her father, and a suit to establish paternity ordinarily must be brought within six years of an illegitimate child's birth. By contrast, a legitimate child may seek support from his or her parents at any time. [Ten years after her illegitimate daughter's birth, Cherlyn Clark filed a complaint on her daughter's behalf seeking to compel Gene Jeter, the alleged father, to pay support. Although a blood test demonstrated a 99.3% probability that Jeter was the father, the court entered judgment for Jeter based on the six-year statute of limitations.]

Between [the] extremes of rational basis review and strict scrutiny lies a level of intermediate scrutiny, which generally has been applied to discriminatory classifications based on sex or illegitimacy. To withstand intermediate scrutiny, a statutory classification must be substantially related to an important governmental objective. Consequently we have invalidated classifications that burden illegitimate children for the sake of punishing the illicit relations of their parents, because "visiting this condemnation on the head of an infant is illogical and unjust." *Weber v. Aetna Casualty & Surety Co.,* 406 U.S. 164, 175 (1972). Yet, in the seminal case concerning the child's right to support, this Court acknowledged that it might be appropriate to treat illegitimate children differently in the support context because of "lurking problems with respect to proof of paternity." *Gomez v. Perez,* 409 U.S. 535, 538 (1973).

[W]e conclude that Pennsylvania's 6-year statute of limitations violates the Equal Protection Clause. Even six years does not necessarily provide a reasonable opportunity to assert a claim on behalf of an illegitimate child. "The unwillingness of the mother to file a paternity action on behalf of her child, which could stem from her relationship with the natural father or [from] the emotional strain of having an illegitimate child, or even from the desire to avoid community and family disapproval, may continue years after the child is born. The problem may be exacerbated if, as often happens, the mother herself is a minor." *Mills v. Habluetzel,* 456 U.S. 91, 105 n.4 (1982) (O'CONNOR, J., concurring). Not all of these difficulties are likely to abate in six years. A mother might realize only belatedly "a loss of income attributable to the need to care for the child." Furthermore, financial difficulties are likely to increase as the child matures and incurs expenses for clothing, school, and medical care. Thus it is questionable whether a State acts reasonably when it requires most paternity and support actions to be brought within six years of an illegitimate child's birth.

We do not rest our decision on this ground, however, for it is not entirely evident that six years would necessarily be an unreasonable limitations period for child support actions involving illegitimate children. We are, however, confident that the 6-year statute of limitations is not substantially related to Pennsylvania's interest in avoiding the litigation of stale or fraudulent claims. In a number of circumstances, Pennsylvania permits the issue of paternity to be litigated more than six years after the birth of an illegitimate child. The statute itself permits a suit to be brought more than six years after the child's birth if it is brought within two years of a support payment made by the father. And in other types of suits, Pennsylvania places no limits on when the issue of paternity may be litigated. For example, the intestacy statute, 20 Pa. Cons. Stat. § 2107(3) (1982), permits a child born out of wedlock to establish paternity as long as "there is clear and convincing evidence that the man was the father of the child." Likewise, no statute of limitations applies to a father's action to establish paternity. [In addition, increasingly] sophisticated tests for genetic markers permit the exclusion of over 99% of those who might be accused of paternity, regardless of the age of the child. This scientific evidence is available throughout the child's minority.

We conclude that the Pennsylvania statute does not withstand heightened scrutiny under the Equal Protection Clause.

———————

Points for Discussion

a. Illegitimate Children as a Suspect Class

Are illegitimate children a "discrete and insular minority"? Are they the victims of societal prejudice? Is there reason to think that they will not be protected by the ordinary operation of the political process? And is the "status" of illegitimacy immutable? If so, then why doesn't the Court apply strict, as opposed to intermediate, scrutiny for classifications that burden people whose parents were not married?

Is the real concern with such classifications that they visit the "sins" of the parents on their children? In this regard, consider Article III, section 3, clause 2, which provides that "no Attainder of Treason shall work Corruption of Blood." Corruption of Blood was an old British practice by which the family of a person convicted of treason was prohibited from inheriting his property. Does this provision stand for the broader proposition that it is constitutionally suspect to punish children for the actions of their parents?

> **Make the Connection**
>
> We will consider this question in Chapter 12, when we discuss *Plyler v. Doe* and state efforts to deny public education to the children of illegal immigrants.

b. Application of Intermediate Scrutiny

Was the defect in the Pennsylvania statute invalidated in *Clark* that the state did not have an important interest? Or that the shorter statute of limitations was not sufficiently related to that interest? What other interests, if any, might justify classifying on the basis of a person's parents' marital status? Would an interest in upholding traditional family values and the sanctity of marriage be sufficiently important? Is there a countervailing state interest in granting men repose from the possibility of paternity suits?

---

3. Age

Massachusetts Bd. of Retirement v. Murgia

427 U.S. 307 (1976)

PER CURIAM

This case presents the question whether the provision of Mass.Gen.Laws Ann. c. 32, s 26(3)(a) (1969), that a uniformed state police officer "shall be retired [upon] his attaining age fifty," denies appellee police officer equal protection of the laws in violation of the Fourteenth Amendment. [Appellee, a police officer, was forced to retire on his 50th birthday, despite being in excellent physical and mental health. He brought suit claiming that his forced retirement violated the Equal Protection Clause.]

[S]trict scrutiny is not the proper test for determining whether the mandatory retirement provision denies appellee equal protection. [E]qual protection analysis requires strict scrutiny of a legislative classification only when the classification impermissibly interferes with the exercise of a fundamental right or operates to the peculiar disadvantage of a suspect class. Mandatory retirement at age 50 under the Massachusetts statute involves neither situation.

> **Make the Connection**
>
> We will discuss the relationship between the Equal Protection Clause and "fundamental rights" in Chapter 12.

This Court's decisions give no support to the proposition that a right of governmental employment per se is fundamental. *** Nor does the class of uniformed state police officers over 50 constitute a suspect class for purposes of equal protection analysis. [A] suspect class is one "saddled with such disabilities, or subjected to such a history of purposeful unequal treatment, or relegated to such a position of political powerlessness as to command extraordinary protection from the majoritarian political process." *San Antonio School District v. Rodriguez*, 411 U.S. 1, 16 (1973). While the treatment of the aged in this Nation has not been wholly free of discrimination, such persons, unlike, say, those who have been discriminated against on the basis of race or national origin, have not experienced a "history of purposeful

> **Take Note**
>
> The statute distinguishes between police officers who are older than 50 years and those who are younger than 50. Does the statute discriminate against the *elderly*? What if the statute excluded from service persons older than 40? Or persons older than 30? Conversely, what if it excluded only people older than 70? Would there be a stronger argument then that it burdened a suspect class?

unequal treatment" or been subjected to unique disabilities on the basis of stereotyped characteristics not truly indicative of their abilities. *** Even if the statute could be said to impose a penalty upon a class defined as the aged, it would not impose a distinction sufficiently akin to those classifications that we have found suspect to call for strict judicial scrutiny. Under the circumstances, it is unnecessary to subject the State's resolution of competing interests in this case to the degree of critical examination that our cases under the Equal Protection Clause recently have characterized as "strict judicial scrutiny."

We turn then to examine this state classification under the rational-basis standard. [T]he Massachusetts statute clearly meets the requirements of the Equal Protection Clause, for the State's classification rationally furthers the purpose identified by the State: Through mandatory retirement at age 50, the legislature seeks to protect the public by assuring physical preparedness of its uniformed police. Since physical ability generally declines with age, mandatory retirement at 50 serves to remove from police service those whose fitness for uniformed work presumptively has diminished with age. This clearly is rationally related to the State's objective. There is no indication that [the statute] has the effect of excluding from service so few officers who are in fact unqualified as to render age 50 a criterion wholly unrelated to the objective of the statute.

That the State chooses not to determine fitness more precisely through individualized testing after age 50 is not to say that the objective of assuring physical fitness is not rationally furthered by a maximum-age limitation. It is only to say that with regard to the interest of all concerned, the State perhaps has not chosen the best means to accomplish this purpose. But where rationality is the test, a State "does not violate the Equal Protection Clause merely because the classifications made by its laws are imperfect." *Dandridge v. Williams*, 397 U.S. 471, 485 (1970).

FYI
In addition to requiring retirement at age 50, the statute also required police officers to pass comprehensive physical examinations biennially until age 40, and then annually until age 50. In light of this requirement, what interest does the mandatory retirement age advance?

We do not make light of the substantial economic and psychological effects premature and compulsory retirement can have on an individual; nor do we denigrate the ability of elderly citizens to continue to contribute to society. *** We decide only that the system enacted by the Massachusetts Legislature does not deny appellee equal protection of the laws.

Mr. Justice MARSHALL, dissenting.

While depriving any government employee of his job is a significant deprivation, it is particularly burdensome when the person deprived is an older citizen. Once terminated, the elderly cannot readily find alternative employment. The lack of work is not only economically damaging, but emotionally and physically draining. Deprived of his status in the community and of the opportunity for meaningful activity, fearful of becoming dependent on others for his support, and lonely in his new-found isolation, the involuntarily retired person is susceptible to physical and emotional ailments as a direct consequence of his enforced idleness. Ample clinical evidence supports the conclusion that mandatory retirement poses a direct threat to the health and life expectancy of the retired person ***. Thus, an older person deprived of his job by the government loses not only his right to earn a living, but, too often, his health as well ***. Not only are the elderly denied important benefits when they are terminated on the basis of age, but the classification of older workers is itself one that merits judicial attention. Whether older workers constitute a "suspect" class or not, it cannot be disputed that they constitute a class subject to repeated and arbitrary discrimination in employment.

FYI

In 1967, Congress passed the Age Discrimination in Employment Act, 29 U.S.C. § 621(a), which prohibits discrimination on the basis of age in employment against persons who are at least 40 years old, except where age "is a bona fide occupational qualification reasonably necessary to the normal operation of the particular business." Does this legislation support Justice Marshall's view that the elderly are deserving of heightened judicial protection, or the Court's view that they are not?

Of course, [the] elderly are protected not only by certain anti-discrimination legislation, but by legislation that provides them with positive benefits not enjoyed by the public at large. Moreover, the elderly are not isolated in society, and discrimination against them is not pervasive but is centered primarily in employment. The advantage of a flexible equal protection standard, however, is that it can readily accommodate such variables. The elderly are undoubtedly discriminated against [when] legislation denies them an important benefit. [I] conclude that to sustain the legislation appellants must show a reasonably substantial interest and a scheme reasonably closely tailored to achieving that interest.

[I] agree that the purpose of the mandatory retirement law is legitimate, and indeed compelling[;] the Commonwealth has every reason to assure that its state police officers are of sufficient physical strength and health to perform their jobs. In my view, however, the means chosen, the forced retirement of officers at age 50, is so over-inclusive that it must fall. [T]he Commonwealth is in the position of already individually testing its police officers for physical fitness, conceding that such testing is adequate to determine the physical ability of an officer to continue on the job, and conceding that that ability may continue after age 50. In these circumstances, I see no reason at all for automatically terminating those officers who reach the age of 50; indeed, that action seems the height of irrationality.

Points for Discussion

a. Age as a Suspect Basis for Classification

Should age be a suspect basis for classification? Few people would dispute that the government should be able to draw distinctions that burden children because of their youth, such as a requirement that a person be at least sixteen years old to obtain a driver's license. But is it problematic when the government draws distinctions that burden the elderly? Are the elderly victims of prejudice who are not adequately protected by the political process?

Recall that Justice Scalia suggested in his separate opinion in *Cruzan v. Director, Missouri Department of Health*, which we considered in Chapter 8, that the elderly and infirm are protected by the Equal Protection Clause, "which requires the democratic majority to accept for themselves and their loved ones what they impose on you and me." Does the "golden rule," combined with the possibility that we may all be old one day, mean that there is no need for judicial protection for the elderly?

b. Tiers of Scrutiny

The Court concluded in *Murgia* that age is not a suspect basis for classification, and it accordingly subjected the challenged statute to rational-basis review. Justice Marshall urged a more nuanced approach to judicial scrutiny, one that would abandon the separate tiers of scrutiny and instead "accommodate" the various state and individual interests implicated by the state's regulation. What are the merits of such an approach? What are its drawbacks? The case that follows raises the same questions.

———

4. Disability

Cleburne v. Cleburne Living Center

473 U.S. 432 (1985)

Justice WHITE delivered the opinion of the Court.

A Texas city denied a special use permit for the operation of a group home for the mentally retarded, acting pursuant to a municipal zoning ordinance requiring permits for such homes. The Court of Appeals for the Fifth Circuit held that mental retardation is a "quasi-suspect" classification and that the ordinance violated the Equal Protection Clause because it did not substantially further an important governmental purpose. We hold that a lesser standard of scrutiny is appropriate, but conclude that under that standard the ordinance is invalid as applied in this case.

The general rule is that legislation is presumed to be valid and will be sustained if the classification drawn by the statute is rationally related to a legitimate state interest. *** [W]here individuals in the group affected by a law have distinguishing characteristics relevant to interests the State has the authority to implement, the courts have been very reluctant, as they should be in our federal system and with our respect for the separation of powers, to closely scrutinize legislative choices as to whether, how, and to what extent those interests should be pursued. In such cases, the Equal Protection Clause requires only a rational means to serve a legitimate end.

[W]e conclude for several reasons that the Court of Appeals erred in holding mental retardation a quasi-suspect classification calling for a more exacting standard of judicial review than is normally accorded economic and social legislation. First, it is undeniable, and it is not argued otherwise here, that those who are mentally retarded have a reduced ability to cope with and function in the everyday world. Nor are they all cut from the same pattern: as the testimony in this record indicates, they range from those whose disability is not immediately evident to those who must be constantly cared for. They are thus different, immutably so, in relevant respects, and the States' interest in dealing with and providing for them is plainly a legitimate one. How this large and diversified group is to be treated under the law is a difficult and often a technical matter, very much a task for legislators guided by qualified professionals and not by the perhaps ill-informed opinions of the judiciary. Heightened scrutiny inevitably involves substantive judgments about legislative decisions, and we doubt that the predicate for such judicial oversight is present where the classification deals with mental retardation.

Second, the distinctive legislative response, both national and state, to the plight of those who are mentally retarded demonstrates not only that they have unique problems, but also that the lawmakers have been addressing their difficulties in a manner that belies a continuing antipathy or prejudice and a corresponding need for more intrusive oversight by the judiciary. *** Third, the legislative response, which could hardly have occurred and survived without public support, negates any claim that the mentally retarded are politically powerless in the sense that they have no ability to attract the attention of the lawmakers.

Fourth, if the large and amorphous class of the mentally retarded were deemed quasi-suspect, it would be difficult to find a principled way to distinguish a variety of other groups who have perhaps immutable disabilities setting them off from others, who cannot themselves mandate the desired legislative responses, and who can claim some degree of prejudice from at least part of the public at large.

> **FYI**
>
> The Rehabilitation Act of 1973, 29 U.S.C. § 794, prohibits discrimination against persons with disabilities by federally funded programs, and several other federal statutes confer on the mentally retarded rights to equal educational opportunities and humane treatment facilities. Several years after the Court's decision in *Cleburne*, Congress enacted the Americans with Disabilities Act, 42 U.S.C. § 12101 et seq., which provides additional protections for the disabled in general and for the mentally retarded in particular. Do these statutes suggest that the mentally retarded are protected by the political process, or instead that government felt compelled to intervene to protect the mentally retarded from pervasive private prejudice and animus?

Our refusal to recognize the retarded as a quasi-suspect class does not leave them entirely unprotected from invidious discrimination. To withstand equal protection review, legislation that distinguishes between the mentally retarded and others must be rationally related to a legitimate governmental purpose. This standard, we believe, affords government the latitude necessary both to pursue policies designed to assist the retarded in realizing their full potential, and to freely and efficiently engage in activities that burden the retarded in what is essentially an incidental manner. The State may not rely on a classification whose relationship to an asserted goal is so attenuated as to render the distinction arbitrary or irrational.

The city does not require a special use permit [for] apartment houses, multiple dwellings, boarding and lodging houses, fraternity or sorority houses, dormitories, apartment hotels, hospitals, sanitariums, nursing homes for convalescents or the aged (other than for the insane or feebleminded or alcoholics or drug addicts), private clubs or fraternal orders, and other specified uses. *** May the city require the permit for [facilities for the mentally retarded] when other care and multiple-dwelling facilities are freely permitted? [T]he record does not reveal any rational basis for believing that [the home] would pose any special threat to the city's legitimate interests ***.

The District Court found that the City Council's insistence on the permit rested on several factors. First, the Council was concerned with the negative attitude of the majority of property owners located within 200 feet of the [facility], as well as with the fears of elderly residents of the neighborhood. But mere negative attitudes, or fear, unsubstantiated by factors which are properly cognizable in a zoning proceeding, are not permissible bases for treating a home for the mentally retarded differently from apartment houses, multiple dwellings, and the like. ***

Second, the Council [was] concerned that the facility was across the street from a junior high school, and it feared that the students might harass the occupants of the [home]. But the school itself is attended by about 30 mentally retarded students, and denying a permit based on such vague, undifferentiated fears is again permitting some portion of the community to validate what would otherwise be an equal protection violation. The other objection to the home's location was that it was located on "a five hundred year flood plain." This concern with the possibility of a flood, however, can hardly be based on a distinction between the [home] and, for example, nursing homes, homes for convalescents or the aged, or sanitariums or hospitals, any of which could be located on the [site] without obtaining a special use permit. The same may be said of another concern of the Council—doubts about the legal responsibility for actions which the mentally retarded might take. If there is no concern about legal responsibility with respect to other uses that would be permitted in the area, such as boarding and fraternity houses, it is difficult to believe that the groups of mildly or moderately mentally retarded individuals who would live at [the facility] would present any different or special hazard.

> **Take Note**
>
> The Court dismisses the reasons that the Council offered for the permit requirement. Is the Court's treatment of these interests consistent with rational-basis review?

Fourth, the Council was concerned with the size of the home and the number of people that would occupy it. [T]here would be no restrictions on the number of people who could occupy this home as a boarding house, nursing home, family dwelling, fraternity house, or dormitory. The question is whether it is rational to treat the mentally retarded differently. It is true that they suffer disability not shared by others; but why this difference warrants a density regulation that others need not observe is not at all apparent.

The short of it is that requiring the permit in this case appears to us to rest on an irrational prejudice against the mentally retarded, including those who would occupy the [facility] and who would live under the closely supervised and highly regulated conditions expressly provided for by state and federal law. The judgment of the Court of Appeals is affirmed insofar as it invalidates the zoning ordinance as applied to the [home].

Justice STEVENS, with whom THE CHIEF JUSTICE joins, concurring.

The Court of Appeals disposed of this case as if a critical question to be decided were which of three clearly defined standards of equal protection review should be applied to a legislative classification discriminating against the mentally retarded. In fact, our cases have not delineated three—or even one or two—such well-defined standards. Rather, our cases reflect a continuum of judgmental responses to differing classifications which have been explained in opinions by terms ranging from "strict scrutiny" at one extreme to "rational basis" at the other. I have never been persuaded that these so-called "standards" adequately explain the decisional process. Cases involving classifications based on alienage, illegal residency, illegitimacy, gender, age, or—as in this case—mental retardation do not fit well into sharply defined classifications.

In my own approach to these cases, I have always asked myself whether I could find a "rational basis" for the classification at issue. The term "rational," of course, includes a requirement that an impartial lawmaker could logically believe that the classification would serve a legitimate public purpose that transcends the harm to the members of the disadvantaged class. Thus, the word "rational—for me at least—includes elements of legitimacy and neutrality that must always characterize the performance of the sovereign's duty to govern impartially.

In every equal protection case, we have to ask certain basic questions. What class is harmed by the legislation, and has it been subjected to a "tradition of disfavor" by our laws? What is the public purpose that is being served by the law? What is the characteristic of the disadvantaged class that justifies the disparate treatment? In most cases the answer to these questions will tell us whether the statute has a "rational basis." The answers will result in the virtually automatic invalidation of racial classifications and in the validation of most economic classifications, but they will provide differing results in cases involving classifications based on alienage, gender, or illegitimacy. But that is not because we apply an "intermediate standard of review" in these cases; rather it is because the characteristics of these groups are sometimes relevant and sometimes irrelevant to a valid public purpose, or, more specifically, to the purpose that the challenged laws purportedly intended to serve.

Every law that places the mentally retarded in a special class is not presumptively irrational. The differences between mentally retarded persons and those with greater mental capacity are obviously relevant to certain legislative decisions. [But] the mentally retarded "have been subjected to a history of unfair and often grotesque mistreatment." [The record in this case] convinces me that this permit was required because of the irrational fears of neighboring property owners, rather than for the protection of the mentally retarded persons who would reside in respondent's home.

Justice MARSHALL, with whom Justice BRENNAN and Justice BLACKMUN join, concurring in the judgment in part and dissenting in part.

[The majority's discussion of the rational-basis test is] puzzling given that Cleburne's ordinance is invalidated only after being subjected to precisely the sort of probing inquiry associated with heightened scrutiny. To be sure, the Court does not label its handiwork heightened scrutiny, and perhaps the method employed must hereafter be called "second order" rational-basis review rather than "heightened scrutiny." But however labeled, the rational basis test invoked today is most assuredly not the rational-basis test of *Williamson v. Lee Optical of Oklahoma, Inc.*, 348 U.S. 483 (1955).

> **Make the Connection**
>
> We considered the Court's decisions in *Williamson* and *Lochner* in Chapter 8.

The refusal to acknowledge that something more than minimum rationality review is at work here is, in my view, unfortunate in at least two respects. The suggestion that the traditional rational-basis test allows this sort of searching inquiry creates precedent for this Court and lower courts to subject economic and commercial classifications to similar and searching "ordinary" rational-basis review—a small and regrettable step back toward the days of *Lochner*. Moreover, by failing to articulate the factors that justify today's "second order" rational-basis review, the Court provides no principled foundation for determining when more searching inquiry is to be invoked. Lower courts are thus left in the dark on this important question, and this Court remains unaccountable for its decisions employing, or refusing to employ, particularly searching scrutiny.

I have long believed the level of scrutiny employed in an equal protection case should vary with "the constitutional and societal importance of the interest adversely affected and the recognized invidiousness of the basis upon which the particular classification is drawn." When a zoning ordinance works to exclude the retarded from all residential districts in a community, these two considerations require that the ordinance be convincingly justified as substantially furthering legitimate and important purposes. First, the interest of the retarded in establishing group homes is substantial. The right to "establish a home" has long been cherished as one of the fundamental liberties embraced by the Due Process Clause. *** Second, the mentally retarded have been subject to a "lengthy and tragic history" [of] segregation and discrimination that can only be called grotesque.

> **Make the Connection**
>
> For some of the history on which Justice Marshall relies, recall the Court's decision in *Skinner v. Oklahoma* (and the decision in *Buck v. Bell*, which preceded it.) We considered those decisions in Chapter 8.

[Cleburne's] vague generalizations for classifying the "feeble-minded" with drug addicts, alcoholics, and the insane, and excluding them where the elderly, the ill, the boarder, and the transient are allowed, are not substantial or important enough to overcome the suspicion that the ordinance rests on impermissible assumptions or outmoded and perhaps invidious stereotypes.

[The Court points to] legislative action that is said to "beli[e] a continuing antipathy or prejudice." *** It is natural that evolving standards of equality come to be embodied in legislation. When that occurs, courts should look to the fact of such change as a source of guidance on evolving principles of equality. *** Moreover, even when judicial action *has* catalyzed legislative change, that change certainly does not eviscerate the underlying constitutional principle. The Court, for example, has never suggested that race-based classifications became any less suspect once extensive legislation had been enacted on the subject. For the retarded, just as for Negroes and women, much has changed in recent years, but much remains the same; out-dated statutes are still on the books, and irrational fears or ignorance, traceable to the prolonged social and cultural isolation of the retarded, continue to stymie recognition of the dignity and individuality of retarded people. Heightened judicial scrutiny of action appearing to impose unnecessary barriers to the retarded is required in light of increasing recognition that such barriers are inconsistent with evolving principles of equality embedded in the Fourteenth Amendment. *** In light of the scrutiny that should be applied here, Cleburne's ordinance sweeps too broadly to dispel the suspicion that it rests on a bare desire to treat the retarded as outsiders, pariahs who do not belong in the community.

Points for Discussion

a. Levels of Scrutiny

The Court's opinion in <u>Cleburne</u> was premised on the view that there are different tiers of scrutiny, and that the Court's role varies greatly depending upon which tier applies to a given government action. Justice Stevens, in contrast, urged the abandonment of an approach based on discrete tiers of scrutiny, offering a more searching (and perhaps literal) form of rational-basis review in its place. And Justice Marshall asserted that "[t]he formal label under which an equal protection claim is reviewed is less important than careful identification of the interest at stake and the extent to which society recognizes the classification as an invidious one," apparently suggesting that the Court should adopt a more flexible, sliding-scale approach to review under the Equal Protection Clause.

Which approach makes the most sense? Does the formal system of different levels of scrutiny limit the Court's authority to second-guess legislative and political judgments only to those circumstances in which it is most warranted? Or does it simply require arbitrary line-drawing in resolving the threshold question about what level of scrutiny a particular type of classification should receive? Has the tiered approach led to consistent and acceptable results? Conversely, are the more flexible approaches that Justice Stevens and Justice Marshall proposed likely to lead to judicial candor about the competing interests implicated in any given case? Or are they simply invitations for judicial legislation?

Regardless of the merits of the competing approaches, do you agree that the Court in

Cleburne adhered to the tiered system of review under the Equal Protection Clause?

b. Discrimination on the Basis of Mental Retardation or Disability

After *Cleburne*, what is the appropriate standard of review for state action that distinguishes between the mentally retarded and others? As a matter of constitutional law, can a state withhold driver's licenses from the mentally retarded? Can it refuse to hire the mentally retarded to serve in all sorts of civil service positions? Might rational bases exist for these actions? Does their constitutionality depend upon the government's actual motivation in taking them?

What about classifications that burden people with other physical disabilities? In *Board of Trustees of University of Alabama v. Garrett*, 531 U.S. 356 (2001), in which the Court considered Congress's power to enforce the Fourteenth Amendment, the Court stated, "the result of *Cleburne* is that States are not required by the Fourteenth Amendment to make special accommodations for *the disabled*, so long as their actions toward such individuals are rational." (Emphasis added.)

c. Rational Basis "With Bite"

Commentators have referred to the Court's approach in *Cleburne* as rational basis review "with bite"—an approach pursuant to which the Court is "less willing to supply justifying rationales by exercising its imagination," assesses the means "in terms of legislative purposes that have substantial basis in actuality, not merely in conjecture," and gauges the "reasonableness of questionable means on the basis of materials that are offered to the Court, rather than resorting to rationalizations created by perfunctory judicial hypothesizing." Gerald Gunther, *Foreword: In Search of Evolving Doctrine on a Changing Court: A Model for a Newer Equal Protection*, 86 Harv. L. Rev. 1 (1972). Is this approach preferable to the highly deferential form of rational-basis review that emerged post-1937? Is it at least appropriate for some forms of classifications, even if not all innocuous classifications?

Cleburne is not the only case in which the Court has purported to apply rational-basis review but in fact reviewed the challenged policy more searchingly. In *United States Department of Agriculture v. Moreno*, 413 U.S. 528 (1973), for example, the Court invalidated a provision of the Food Stamp Act of 1964 that excluded from participation in the program any household containing an individual unrelated to any other member of the household. The appellee shared an apartment with another woman on public assistance to whom she was not related, in order to save money on living expenses. The Court, in an opinion by Justice Brennan, concluded that the exclusion failed to satisfy rational-basis review. The Court reasoned that the classification (which treated persons living in group homes differently from people living in households only with family members) did not advance Congress's stated purpose in raising levels of nutrition in low-income households. Moreover, the Court concluded that the purpose suggested by the legislative history—that Congress sought "to prevent so-called 'hippies' and 'hippie communes' from participating in the food stamp program"—was insufficient, because the "bare congressional desire to harm a politically unpopular group cannot constitute a *legitimate* governmental interest." Justice Rehnquist, joined by Chief Justice Burger, dissented, reasoning that limiting assistance to households consisting of related individuals "provides a guarantee which is not provided by households containing unrelated individuals that the household exists for some purpose other than to collect federal food stamps." Did the classification at issue in *Moreno* warrant judicial scrutiny more searching than conventional rational- basis review?

---

5. Sexual Orientation

Romer v. Evans

517 U.S. 620 (1996)

Justice KENNEDY delivered the opinion of the Court.

The enactment challenged in this case is an amendment to the Constitution of the State of Colorado, adopted in a 1992 statewide referendum. The parties and the state courts refer to it as "Amendment 2," its designation when submitted to the voters. The impetus for the amendment [came] in large part from ordinances that had been passed in various Colorado municipalities [banning discrimination on the basis of sexual orientation]. Amendment 2 repeals these ordinances [and] prohibits all legislative, executive or judicial action at any level of state or local government designed to protect [homosexual] persons or gays and lesbians. The amendment reads [in relevant part]:

> "Neither the State of Colorado, through any of its branches or departments, nor any of its agencies, political subdivisions, municipalities or school districts, shall enact, adopt or enforce any statute, regulation, ordinance or policy whereby homosexual, lesbian or bisexual orientation, conduct, practices or relationships shall constitute or otherwise be the basis of or entitle any person or class of persons to have or claim any minority status, quota preferences, protected status or claim of discrimination."

[A gay municipal employee in Denver filed suit claiming that Amendment 2 was unconstitutional.]

The State's principal argument in defense of Amendment 2 is that it [does] no more than deny homosexuals special rights. This reading of the amendment's language is implausible. *** Homosexuals, by state decree, are put in a solitary class with respect to transactions and relations in both the private and governmental spheres. The amendment withdraws from homosexuals, but no others, specific legal protection from the injuries caused by discrimination, and it forbids reinstatement of these laws and policies. [A]mendment 2 bars homosexuals from securing protection against the injuries that [many municipal] public-accommodations laws address [and] nullifies specific legal protections for this targeted class in all transactions in housing, sale of real estate, insurance, health and welfare services, private education, and employment. Not confined to the private sphere, Amendment 2 also operates to repeal and forbid all laws or policies providing specific protection for gays or lesbians from discrimination by every level of Colorado government.

[W]e cannot accept the view that Amendment 2's prohibition on specific legal protections does no more than deprive homosexuals of special rights. To the contrary, the amendment imposes a special disability upon those persons alone. [Homosexuals] can obtain specific protection against discrimination only by enlisting the citizenry of Colorado to amend the State Constitution ***. This is so no matter how local or discrete the harm, no matter how public and widespread the injury. We find nothing special in the protections Amendment 2 withholds. These are protections taken for granted by most people either because they already have them or do not need them; these are protections against exclusion from an almost limitless number of transactions and endeavors that constitute ordinary civic life in a free society.

The Fourteenth Amendment's promise that no person shall be denied the equal protection of the laws must coexist with the practical necessity that most legislation classifies for one purpose or another, with resulting disadvantage to various groups or persons. We have attempted to reconcile the principle with the reality by stating that, if a law neither burdens a fundamental right nor targets a suspect class, we will uphold the legislative classification so long as it bears a rational relation to some legitimate end.

Amendment 2 fails, indeed defies, even this conventional inquiry. First, the amendment has the peculiar property of imposing a broad and undifferentiated disability on a single named group, an exceptional and, as we shall explain, invalid form of legislation. Second, its sheer breadth is so discontinuous with the reasons offered for it that the amendment seems inexplicable by anything but animus toward the class it affects; it lacks a rational relationship to legitimate state interests.

Taking the first point, even in the ordinary equal protection case calling for the most deferential of standards, we insist on knowing the relation between the classification adopted and the object to be attained. *** By requiring that the classification bear a rational relationship to an independent and legitimate legislative end, we ensure that classifications are not drawn for the purpose of disadvantaging the group burdened by the law.

Amendment 2 confounds this normal process of judicial review. It is at once too narrow and too broad. It identifies persons by a single trait and then denies them protection across the board. The resulting disqualification of a class of persons from the right to seek specific protection from the law is unprecedented in our jurisprudence. *** It is not within our constitutional tradition to enact laws of this sort. Central both to the idea of the rule of law and to our own Constitution's guarantee of equal protection is the principle that government and each of its parts remain open on impartial terms to all who seek its assistance. *** A law declaring that in general it shall be more difficult for

> **Take Note**
>
> The Court states that the purpose of rational-basis review is to ensure that classifications are not drawn for the purpose of "disadvantaging" the group "burdened" by the law. Isn't the group "burdened" by the law by definition "disadvantaged" by it? For example, a law permitting only persons younger than 50 years old to serve as police officers "advantages" people who are relatively young only because it excludes people who are relatively older. Isn't the point of rational-basis review simply to ensure that government classifications are not entirely arbitrary?

one group of citizens than for all others to seek aid from the government is itself a denial of equal protection of the laws in the most literal sense.

A second and related point is that laws of the kind now before us raise the inevitable inference that the disadvantage imposed is born of animosity toward the class of persons affected. "[I]f the constitutional conception of 'equal protection of the laws' means anything, it must at the very least mean that a bare [desire] to harm a politically unpopular group cannot constitute a *legitimate* governmental interest." *United States Department of Agriculture v. Moreno*, 413 U.S. 528, 534 (1973). *** Amendment 2, however, in making a general announcement that gays and lesbians shall not have any particular protections from the law, inflicts on them immediate, continuing, and real injuries that outrun and belie any legitimate justifications that may be claimed for it.

The primary rationale the State offers for Amendment 2 is respect for other citizens' freedom of association, and in particular the liberties of landlords or employers who have

> **Take Note**
>
> Is the Court's suggestion here that Colorado's asserted interests are not legitimate, or is it instead that the classification does not bear any rational relationship to those interests? Is either of those conclusions consistent with the Court's ordinary approach in cases applying rational-basis review? Is the Court applying rational-basis review?

personal or religious objections to homosexuality. Colorado also cites its interest in conserving resources to fight discrimination against other groups. The breadth of the amendment is so far removed from these particular justifications that we find it impossible to credit them. We cannot say that Amendment 2 is directed to any identifiable legitimate purpose or discrete objective. It is a status-based enactment divorced from any factual context from which we could discern a relationship to legitimate state interests; it is a classification of persons undertaken for its own sake, something the Equal Protection Clause does not permit.

We must conclude that Amendment 2 classifies homosexuals not to further a proper legislative end but to make them unequal to everyone else. This Colorado cannot do. A State cannot so deem a class of persons a stranger to its laws.

Justice SCALIA, with whom THE CHIEF JUSTICE and Justice THOMAS join, dissenting.

The Court has mistaken a Kulturkampf for a fit of spite. The constitutional amendment before us here is not the manifestation of a "bare [desire] to harm" homosexuals, but is rather a modest attempt by seemingly tolerant Coloradans to preserve traditional sexual mores against the efforts of a politically powerful minority to revise those mores through use of the laws. That objective, and the means chosen

> **Definition**
>
> The German word "Kulturkampf" literally means "conflict of cultures." Justice Scalia is suggesting that the Court has no business intervening in the culture wars. But does the mere fact that challenged legislation is the product of one side's victory in a public battle over values automatically immunize it from judicial scrutiny? Wasn't the law invalidated in *Loving*, which we considered earlier in this Chapter, a product of a "culture war," as well?

to achieve it, are not only unimpeachable under any constitutional doctrine hitherto pronounced (hence the opinion's heavy reliance upon principles of righteousness rather than judicial holdings); they have been specifically approved by [this] Court.

In holding that homosexuality cannot be singled out for disfavorable treatment, the Court contradicts a decision, unchallenged here, pronounced only 10 years ago, see *Bowers v. Hardwick,* 478 U.S. 186 (1986), and places the prestige of this institution behind the proposition that opposition to homosexuality is as reprehensible as racial or religious bias. Whether it is or not is *precisely* the cultural debate that gave rise to the Colorado constitutional amendment (and to the preferential laws against which the amendment was directed). Since the Constitution of the United States says nothing about this subject, it is left to be resolved by normal democratic means, including the democratic adoption of provisions in state constitutions. This Court has no business imposing upon all Americans the resolution favored by the elite class from which the Members of this institution are selected, pronouncing that "animosity" toward homosexuality [is] evil.

> **Make the Connection**
>
> Several years after the decision in *Romer*, the Court overruled *Bowers*, in *Lawrence v. Texas*. We considered *Lawrence* in Chapter 8.

[Amendment 2] prohibits *special treatment* of homosexuals, and nothing more. *** The only denial of equal treatment [the Court] contends homosexuals have suffered is this: They may not obtain *preferential* treatment without amending the State Constitution. That is to say, the principle underlying the Court's opinion is that one who is accorded equal treatment under the laws, but cannot as readily as others obtain *preferential* treatment under the laws, has been denied equal protection of the laws. If merely stating this alleged "equal protection" violation does not suffice to refute it, our constitutional jurisprudence has achieved terminal silliness.

> **Take Note**
>
> Colorado law (and the laws in many of the municipalities whose ordinances were repealed by Amendment 2) prohibited discrimination on many bases, including age, marital or family status, veterans' status, and even whether the person engaged in lawful behavior, such as smoking tobacco, in his spare time. In light of this, do you agree that the repealed ordinances' additional prohibition of discrimination on the basis of sexual orientation amounted to "special treatment"?

What [Colorado] has done is not only unprohibited, but eminently reasonable ***. The Court's opinion contains grim, disapproving hints that Coloradans have been guilty of "animus" or "animosity" toward homosexuality, as though that has been established as un-American. Of course it is our moral heritage that one should not hate any human being or class of human beings. But I had thought that one could consider certain conduct reprehensible—murder, for example, or polygamy, or cruelty to animals—and could exhibit even "animus" toward such conduct. Surely that is the only sort of "animus" at issue here: moral disapproval of homosexual conduct, the same sort of moral disapproval that produced the centuries-old criminal laws that we held constitutional in *Bowers*. The Colorado amendment does not, to speak entirely precisely, prohibit giving favored status to people who are *homosexuals;* they can be favored for many reasons—for example, because they are senior citizens or members of racial minorities. But it prohibits giving them favored status *because of their homosexual conduct*—that is, it prohibits favored status *for homosexuality.*

> But though Coloradans [are] *entitled* to be hostile toward homosexual conduct, the [Court's] portrayal of Coloradans as a society fallen victim to pointless, hate-filled "gay-bashing" is so false as to be comical. Colorado [was one of the first states to repeal its] anti-sodomy laws. But the society that eliminates criminal punishment for homosexual acts does not necessarily abandon the view that homosexuality is morally wrong and socially harmful; often, abo-

Take Note
Justice Scalia distinguishes between homosexuality as an orientation and homosexual "conduct." In his dissent in <u>Lawrence</u>, he advanced a similar view, referring not to homosexuals but instead to "persons who openly engage in homosexual conduct." There is, to be sure, continuing social debate over whether sexual orientation is biological or instead a choice. But if scientists were conclusively to demonstrate that sexual orientation is an immutable, biological characteristic, would Justice Scalia's view be tenable as a matter of constitutional law?

lition simply reflects the view that enforcement of such criminal laws involves unseemly intrusion into the intimate lives of citizens. *** Amendment 2 is designed to prevent piecemeal deterioration of the sexual morality favored by a majority of Coloradans, and is not only an appropriate means to that legitimate end, but a means that Americans have employed before. Striking it down is an act, not of judicial judgment, but of political will.

Points for Discussion

a. Sexual Orientation as a Suspect Basis for Classification

Under the <u>Carolene Products</u> test, are gays and lesbians a suspect class deserving of heightened judicial protection? Notice that Justice Scalia referred to gays and lesbians as a "politically powerful minority." Was he thereby suggesting that they do not meet the <u>Carolene Products</u> test?

Did the Court in <u>Romer</u> conclude that laws that discriminate on the basis of sexual orientation are subject to heightened scrutiny? What level of scrutiny did the Court apply?

b. Legitimate State Interests

The Court stated in <u>Romer</u> that the challenged Amendment was explainable only as a manifestation of animus towards gays and lesbians, and it suggested that animus is never a legitimate basis for a classification. But can this really be true? What about laws disadvantaging ex-felons, such as laws withholding from ex-felons the right to vote? To be sure, such laws might serve a variety of objectives, but assuming that they are based on animus towards ex-felons (and the acts that they committed), does that make them unconstitutional?

c. Same-Sex Marriage

Does the Court's decision in *Romer* suggest that state laws or constitutional provisions prohibiting same-sex marriage violate the Equal Protection Clause? In 2003, the Massachusetts Supreme Judicial Court invalidated state laws that limited the right to marry to opposite-sex couples. *Goodridge v. Department of Public Health*, 798 N.E.2d 941 (Mass. 2003). Although the Court relied on the state, rather than the federal, constitution, it cited the Supreme Court's decision in *Romer* (and the Court's decision in *Lawrence v. Texas*). In the wake of the decision in *Goodridge*, twenty-nine states approved amendments to their constitutions to limit the right to marry to opposite-sex couples. Since that time, the supreme courts in three states have held that so limiting marriage violates their states' constitutions. *Kerrigan v. Commissioner of Pub. Health*, 957 A.2d 407 (Conn. 2008); *In re Marriage Cases*, 183 P.3d 384 (Cal. 2008); *Varnum v. Brien*, 763 N.W.2d 862 (Iowa 2009). (The New Jersey Supreme Court similarly concluded that same-sex couples must receive legal treatment equal to opposite-sex couples, but it held that the state legislature was free to choose civil-union status rather than marital status for same-sex couples. *Lewis v. Harris*, 908 A.2d 196 (N.J. 2006).)

Voters in California responded to the state Supreme Court's decision in *In re Marriage Cases* by approving Proposition 8, which amended the state constitution to exclude same-sex couples from marriage. See CAL. CONST. art. I, § 7.5. A federal district court in California in 2010 invalidated Proposition 8, holding that it violates the Due Process and Equal Protection Clauses of the Fourteenth Amendment. *Perry v. Schwarzenegger*, 704 F.Supp.2d 921 (N.D. Cal. 2010). The court relied heavily on the Court's decisions in *Romer* and *Lawrence*. What are the strongest arguments for concluding that bans on same-sex marriage violate the federal Constitution? Is it relevant that several states have in recent years enacted legislation to permit same-sex marriages?

————————

Executive Summary of this Chapter

"[A]ll legal restrictions which curtail the civil rights of a single racial group are immediately suspect." *Korematsu v. United States* (1944). As such, laws, regulations, and policies that discriminate against racial minorities on the basis of race or national origin are subject to **strict scrutiny**—that is, they "must serve a **compelling governmental interest**, and must be **narrowly tailored** to further that interest." *Adarand Constructors, Inc. v. Pena* (1995). This rule applies to the states by the force of the Equal Protection Clause of the Fourteenth Amendment, *Strauder v. West Virginia* (1879), and to the federal government by the force of the Due Process Clause of the Fifth Amendment, *Bolling v. Sharpe* (1954).

Strict scrutiny applies to laws that discriminate on the basis of race or national origin on their face, *Strauder v. West Virginia* (1879), to laws that are motivated by discriminatory animus against persons based on their race or national origin, *Hunter v. Underwood*, 471 U.S. 222 (1985), and to the discriminatory application, based on race or national origin, of otherwise facially neutral laws, *Yick Wo v. Hopkins* (1886). "Standing alone," however, a racially disproportionate *impact* "does not trigger the rule that racial classifications are to be subjected to the strictest scrutiny and are justifiable only by the weightiest of considerations." *Washington v. Davis* (1976).

Laws that classify on the basis of race but are facially symmetrical—that is, laws that impose equal burdens on persons of different races—are also subject to strict scrutiny. Accordingly, laws prohibiting inter-racial marriage, *Loving v. Virginia* (1967), and laws providing for "separate but equal" public facilities, *Brown v. Board of Education of Topeka* (1954), are unconstitutional.

"[T]he standard of review under the Equal Protection Clause is not dependent on the race of those burdened or benefited by a particular classification." *City of Richmond v. J.A. Croson Co.* (1989). Accordingly, strict scrutiny applies to government consideration of race even when it is designed to benefit, rather than burden, racial minorities. *Adarand Constructors, Inc. v. Pena* (1995). This rule applies to affirmative action programs in government contracting, *City of Richmond v. J.A. Croson Co.* (1989), and school admissions, *Grutter v. Bollinger* (2003), and to legislative apportionment schemes for which race was a "predominant" factor in the drawing of district lines, *Shaw v. Reno* (1993); *Miller v. Johnson* (1995).

The Court has emphasized, however, that some race-conscious decision-making can satisfy strict scrutiny. In particular, because public institutions of higher education have a "compelling interest in attaining a diverse student body," admissions policies that seek to achieve a "critical mass" of minority students by considering race or ethnicity "flexibly as a 'plus' factor in the context of individualized consideration of each and every applicant" can survive strict scrutiny. *Grutter v. Bollinger* (2003). It is expected that, in the future, racial preferences will no longer be necessary, and therefore permissible, to further the government's interest in attaining a diverse student body. *Id.*

However, policies that "establish quotas for members of certain racial groups or put members of those groups on separate admissions tracks" fail strict scrutiny. *Gratz v. Bollinger* (2003). In addition, schools that have already achieved unitary status after desegregation efforts, or that were never segregated *de jure*, may not rely upon race to determine which schools children may attend. *Parents Involved in Community Schools v. Seattle School District No. 1* (2007).

Government decisions that classify on the basis of **gender** are subject to **intermediate scrutiny**. This level of scrutiny requires a justification that is "exceedingly persuasive" and will be upheld only if the government can demonstrate that "the [challenged] classification serves **important governmental objectives** and that the discriminatory means employed are **substantially related** to the achievement of those objectives." *United States v. Virginia* (1996). This rule applies both to laws that burden women, *id.*, and to laws that burden men, *Craig v. Boren* (1976). Neutral laws that were not motivated by discriminatory animus do not receive intermediate scrutiny simply because they have a disproportionate impact on persons of a particular gender. *Personnel Administrator of Massachusetts v. Feeney* (1979).

Laws and policies that distinguish between conditions that are uniquely associated with one sex do not on that basis alone necessarily trigger intermediate scrutiny. *Geduldig v. Aiello* (1974). Laws or policies that treat men and women differently because of "real" differences between the sexes might survive intermediate scrutiny, *Michael M. v. Superior Court of Sonoma County* (1981), but not if the lines are drawn based on mere gender stereotypes, *Orr v. Orr* (1979); *Mississippi Univ. for Women v. Hogan* (1982).

Classifications on the basis of **alienage** are subject to strict scrutiny. *Graham v. Richardson* (1971). However, policies excluding aliens from employment in "policy-making" positions are subject only to rational-basis review. *Foley v. Connelie* (1978).

Laws that discriminate on the basis of one's **parents' marital status** are subject to intermediate scrutiny. *Clark v. Jeter* (1988). Laws may classify on this basis in matters related to the establishment of paternity, but to survive intermediate scrutiny they must be substantially related to that end.

The elderly are not a suspect class. Accordingly, laws that classify on the basis of **age** are subject only to rational-basis review. *Massachusetts Board of Retirement v. Murgia* (1976).

Laws that discriminate on the basis of **disability** are subject to rational-basis review. In assessing such laws, however, the Court has sometimes applied a form of rational-basis review that is substantially more searching than the ordinary version of that approach. *Cleburne v. Cleburne Living Center* (1985).

It is not entirely clear what level of scrutiny applies to laws that discriminate on the basis of **sexual orientation**. The Court has, however, invalidated a state constitutional provision that prevented the government from extending its laws to protect persons from discrimination on the basis of sexual orientation. *Romer v. Evans* (1996). At least one member of the Court, moreover, has concluded that a law that criminalizes homosexual sex (but not heterosexual sex) violates the Equal Protection Clause. *Lawrence v. Texas* (2003).

CHAPTER 12

Equal Protection and Fundamental Rights

Introduction

We have now seen both the cases addressing "fundamental rights"—generally under the rubric of substantive due process, which we considered in Chapter 8—and the cases concerning equal protection, which we considered in Chapter 11. Although we have treated them as separate topics, in some of the cases that we saw the Court in fact relied on both concepts.

For example, in some of the fundamental rights cases that we considered in Chapter 8—such as the Court's decisions on constitutional protections for marital and family rights—the Court relied on the Equal Protection Clause, rather than (or in addition to) the Due Process Clause, to invalidate state laws that interfered with those rights. For instance, the Court's decision in _Loving v. Virginia_, which invalidated Virginia's ban on inter-racial marriages, was based both on the right to marry and the prohibition on state laws that discriminate on the basis of race. In _Skinner v. Oklahoma_, which invalidated a state law requiring the sterilization of persons convicted three times of crimes of moral turpitude, the Court seemed to rely both on the Equal Protection Clause—concluding that the statute's exemption of white-collar crimes amounted to unequal treatment—and the constitutional protection accorded to reproductive rights. And in _Lawrence v. Texas_, which invalidated Texas's ban on gay sex, Justice Kennedy's opinion for the Court relied on substantive due process, while Justice O'Connor's concurring opinion relied on the Equal Protection Clause.

In this Chapter, we explore the relationship between fundamental rights and the Equal Protection Clause more systematically. We defer until later Chapters the Court's treatment of laws that interfere with rights specifically identified in the Bill of Rights. In those cases, as we will see, the Court generally analyzes the challenged law according to the specific tests that apply to the specific right at issue. This Chapter, as did Chapter 8, concerns rights that are not specifically enumerated in the Constitution. Several questions will recur in the cases that follow, even if the Court does not always address them directly. First, if the Constitution (explicitly or implicitly) deems a right to be "fundamental," then isn't government largely precluded from abridging it (assuming it cannot satisfy heightened scrutiny) regardless of whether it abridges it only for some people? Phrased another way, if the government abridges a fundamental constitutional right, why is the Equal Protection Clause even relevant? (In Chapter 8, for example, we saw that in substantive due process cases the inquiry for the Court was generally whether a person had been denied an important right, not whether the right had been denied only to some class of individuals.)

Second, it is clear that the Equal Protection Clause sometimes prohibits state action even when the state does not abridge a fundamental right. For example, even if there is no constitutional right to a state-provided education—a question we will take up in this Chapter in *San Antonio Independent School District v. Rodriguez*—the state plainly cannot make education available only to citizens of one particular race.

But what if the state denies eligibility for a particular benefit based on membership in a class that is not "suspect" under the Court's Equal Protection cases? Are there some "benefits" that the state is not constitutionally obligated to provide, but that are sufficiently important that the state—once it decides to provide them—may not provide them *selectively* only to some classes of citizens?

As you read the cases that follow, keep these questions in mind.

————————————

A. The Franchise

One of the areas in which the interaction between fundamental rights and the equal protection principle has been most frequent is in matters related to the franchise. In this section, we consider two related issues: the right of citizens to vote, and "apportionment"—that is, the process by which elected officials draw the electoral maps that define the districts in which they will then seek office.

————————————

1. The Right to Vote

Law students are always surprised to learn that the Constitution does not explicitly protect an undifferentiated right to vote. To be sure, there are provisions of the Constitution that arguably recognize such a right. For example, the Guarantee Clause in Article IV provides that the United States shall guarantee the states a "Republican"—that is, representative—form of government. And the Fifteenth, Nineteenth, and Twenty-Sixth Amendments protect the "right" to vote against discrimination on the basis of race, gender, or (in some cases) age. But the Court has long suggested that the somewhat cryptic Guarantee Clause is non-justiciable, and the Amendments do not explicitly require the grant of the franchise; they seem to require only that, once a state grants the right to vote, the right may not be withheld selectively on one of the impermissible bases. Is it conceivable that the Constitution does not in fact protect a right to vote? The case that follows considers that question.

————————————

Harper v. Virginia State Bd. of Elections

383 U.S. 663 (1966)

Mr. Justice DOUGLAS delivered the opinion of the Court.

These are suits by Virginia residents to have declared unconstitutional Virginia's poll tax. *** While the right to vote in federal elections is conferred by Art. I, § 2 of the Constitution, the right to vote in state elections is nowhere expressly mentioned. It is argued that the right to vote in state elections is implicit, particularly by reason of the First Amendment and that it may not constitutionally be conditioned upon the payment of a tax or fee. We do not stop to canvass the relation between voting and political expression. For it is enough to say that once the franchise is granted to the electorate, lines may

> **FYI**
>
> The Twenty-Fourth Amendment, which was ratified in 1964, provides that the right to vote in elections for *federal* offices "shall not be denied or abridged by the United States or any State by reason of failure to pay any poll tax or other tax." It does not address the permissibility of poll taxes in elections for state offices. What does that suggest about the question presented here?

not be drawn which are inconsistent with the Equal Protection Clause of the Fourteenth Amendment. That is to say, the right of suffrage "is subject to the imposition of state standards which are not discriminatory and which do not contravene any restriction that Congress, acting pursuant to its constitutional powers, has imposed." *Lassiter v. Northampton County Board of Elections,* 360 U.S. 45, 51 (1959).

> **Take Note**
>
> The Court states that the "right to vote" in federal elections is conferred by Article I, § 2, cl. 1, which provides that "The House of Representatives shall be composed of Members chosen every second Year by the People of the several States, and the Electors in each State shall have the Qualifications requisite for Electors of the most numerous Branch of the State Legislature." But does that provision require the states to extend the franchise to *any particular portion* of the electorate? What if a state permits only college-educated adult males to vote for members of the state legislature?

We conclude that a State violates the Equal Protection Clause of the Fourteenth Amendment whenever it makes the affluence of the voter or payment of any fee an electoral standard. Voter qualifications have no relation to wealth nor to paying or not paying this or any other tax. Our cases demonstrate that the Equal Protection Clause of the Fourteenth Amendment restrains the States from fixing voter qualifications which invidiously discriminate.

Long ago in *Yick Wo v. Hopkins,* 118 U.S. 356, 370 (1886), the Court referred to "the political franchise of voting" as a "fundamental political right, because preservative of all rights." *** The Equal Protection Clause demands no less than substantially equal state legislative representation for all citizens, of all places as well as of all races. *Reynolds v. Sims,* 377 U.S. 533, 568 (1964). We say the same whether the citizen, otherwise qualified to vote, has $1.50 in his pocket or nothing at all, pays the fee or fails to pay it. The principle that denies the State the right to dilute a citizen's vote on account of his economic status or other such factors by analogy bars a system which excludes those unable to pay a fee to vote or who fail to pay.

It is argued that a State may exact fees from citizens for many different kinds of licenses; that if it can demand from all an equal fee for a driver's license, it can demand from all an equal poll tax for voting. But we must remember that the interest of the State, when it comes to voting, is limited to the power to fix qualifications. Wealth, like race, creed, or color, is not germane to one's ability to participate intelligently in the electoral process. Lines drawn on the basis of wealth or property, like those of race, are traditionally disfavored. To introduce wealth or payment of a fee as a measure of a voter's qualifications is to introduce a capricious or irrelevant factor.

Food for Thought

Does the Court invalidate the poll tax because it impermissibly discriminates among citizens on the basis of wealth? If that is a basis for invalidation, then are higher marginal tax rates for the wealthy, or fees for driver's licenses, also unconstitutional? Is the poll tax unconstitutional because there is a fundamental right to vote? If so, then why is the Equal Protection Clause relevant?

[The] Equal Protection Clause is not shackled to the political theory of a particular era. In determining what lines are unconstitutionally discriminatory, we have never been confined to historic notions of equality, any more than we have restricted due process to a fixed catalogue of what was at a given time deemed to be the limits of fundamental rights. Notions of what constitutes equal treatment for purposes of the Equal Protection Clause do change. *** See *Brown v. Board of Education*, 347 U.S. 483 (1954).

We have long been mindful that where fundamental rights and liberties are asserted under the Equal Protection Clause, classifications which might invade or restrain them must be closely scrutinized and carefully confined. Those principles apply here. For to repeat, wealth or fee paying has, in our view, no relation to voting qualifications; the right to vote is too precious, too fundamental to be so burdened or conditioned.

Mr. Justice BLACK, dissenting.

It should be pointed out at once that the Court's decision is to no extent based on a finding that the Virginia law as written or as applied is being used as a device or mechanism to deny Negro citizens of Virginia the right to vote on account of their color. Apparently the Court agrees with the District Court below [that] this record would not support any finding that the Virginia poll tax law the Court invalidates has any such effect. If the record could support a finding that the law as written or applied has such an effect, the law would of course be unconstitutional as a violation of the Fourteenth and Fifteenth Amendments ***.

All voting laws treat some persons differently from others in some respects. Some bar a person from voting who is under 21 years of age; others bar those under 18. Some bar convicted felons or the insane, and some have attached a freehold or other property qualification for voting. *** The equal protection cases carefully analyzed boil down to the principle that distinctions drawn and even discriminations imposed by state laws do not violate the Equal Protection Clause so long as these distinctions and discriminations are not "irrational," "irrelevant," "unreasonable," "arbitrary," or "invidious." *** State poll tax legislation can "reasonably," "rationally" and without an "invidious" or evil purpose to injure anyone be found to rest on a number of state policies including (1) the State's desire to collect its revenue, and (2) its belief that voters who pay a poll tax will be interested in furthering the State's welfare when they vote.

I can only conclude that the primary, controlling, predominate, if not the exclusive reason for declaring the Virginia law unconstitutional is the Court's deep-seated hostility and antagonism, which I share, to making payment of a tax a prerequisite to voting. *** [When] a "political theory" embodied in our Constitution becomes outdated, it seems to me that a majority of the nine members of this Court are not only without constitutional power but are far less qualified to choose a new constitutional political theory than the people of this country proceeding in the manner provided by Article V.

> **Make the Connection**
>
> If the poll tax does not violate the Fourteenth Amendment, can Congress really be said to be "enforcing" the Amendment by "appropriate legislation" if it prohibits the poll tax? We will consider this question—and Congress's power to enforce the provisions of the Reconstruction Amendments—in Chapter 13.

Moreover, the people, in § 5 of the Fourteenth Amendment, designated the governmental tribunal they wanted to provide additional rules to enforce the guarantees of that Amendment. The branch of Government they chose was not the Judicial Branch but the Legislative. I have no doubt at all that Congress has the power under § 5 to pass legislation to abolish the poll tax in order to protect the citizens of this country if it believes that the poll tax is being used as a device to deny voters equal protection of the laws. *** But for us to undertake in the guise of constitutional interpretation to decide the constitutional policy question of this case amounts, in my judgment, to a plain exercise of power which the Constitution has denied us but has specifically granted to Congress.

Mr. Justice HARLAN, whom Mr. Justice STEWART joins, dissenting.

The Court's analysis of the equal protection issue goes no further than to say that the electoral franchise is "precious" and "fundamental," and to conclude that "[t]o introduce wealth or payment of a fee as a measure of a voter's qualifications is to introduce a capricious or irrelevant factor." These are of course captivating phrases, but they are wholly inadequate to satisfy the standard governing adjudication of the equal protection issue: Is there a rational basis for Virginia's poll tax as a voting qualification? I think the answer to that question is undoubtedly "yes."

For example, it is certainly a rational argument that payment of some minimal poll tax promotes civic responsibility, weeding out those who do not care enough about public affairs to pay $1.50 or thereabouts a year for the exercise of the franchise. It is also arguable, indeed it was probably accepted as sound political theory by a large percentage of Americans through most of our history, that people with some property have a deeper stake in community affairs, and are consequently more responsible, more educated, more knowledgeable, more worthy of confidence, than those without means, and that the community and Nation would be better managed if the franchise were restricted to such citizens.

These viewpoints, to be sure, ring hollow on most contemporary ears. *** Property and poll-tax qualifications, very simply, are not in accord with current egalitarian notions of how a modern democracy should be organized. It is of course entirely fitting that legislatures should modify the law to reflect such changes in popular attitudes. However, it is all wrong, in my view, for the Court to adopt the political doctrines popularly accepted at a particular moment of our history and to declare all others to be irrational and invidious, barring them from the range of choice by reasonably minded people acting through the political process.

Points for Discussion

a. Level of Scrutiny

In their dissents, Justices Black and Harlan urged the Court to apply rational-basis review to the poll taxes in question (and, as a result, to uphold the constitutionality of the taxes). Although he obviously disagreed about the constitutionality of the taxes, Justice Douglas, writing for the Court, declared that wealth is a "capricious" and "irrelevant" factor in the grant of the franchise. Does this terminology indicate that Justice Douglas was in fact applying rational-basis review? Or was he applying some heightened level of scrutiny? If so, why?

b. Fundamental Rights and "Discrimination"

Did the Court invalidate the poll taxes because they abridged the right to vote, or because they classified voters on some impermissible basis? That is, did the Court conclude that the problem with the poll taxes was that they impaired the exercise of a fundamental right of some—any—voters, or did it conclude that the problem was that they treated different classes of citizens differently without an adequate justification? There is evidence for both conclusions. On the one hand, the Court described the right to vote as "fundamental"—and thus different from other state-conferred benefits, such as the right to drive a car. On the other hand, the Court declared that "[l]ines drawn on the basis of wealth or property, like those of race, are traditionally disfavored," suggesting that the problem with the poll taxes was that they discriminated on the basis of wealth.

Of course, if the right to vote is fundamental, it seems to follow that the right cannot be withheld from people who are poor, just as it cannot be withheld from people who were born in August or people who are too near-sighted to drive. But perhaps the right is not "fundamental" in the sense that the right to privacy in one's intimate relationships is fundamental, in that it can indeed be permissibly abridged in many ways—by, for example, rules that prohibit people who did not register 60 days before an election from voting. Yet even in that case, perhaps it is still sufficiently important that it cannot be withheld on the basis of wealth, which bears little relationship to the ability to vote responsibly. Assuming that the Court in *Harper* was correct to invalidate the poll taxes, which basis for decision do you find more compelling? Is it possible even to distinguish between the fundamental rights and equal protection approaches?

c. Assessing Burdens

The Court concluded its opinion in *Harper* by stating that "wealth or fee paying has [no] relation to voting qualifications; the right to vote is too precious, too fundamental to be so burdened or conditioned." As in other cases involving fundamental rights, the Court in *Harper* thus seemed to suggest that the relevant inquiry involved weighing the state's interest in the regulation against the burden imposed on the right.

How should a Court measure the burden in a case challenging a voting regulation? Is the question whether the regulation makes it more difficult for a particular class of voters to vote? Must the class of voters be a protected class under Equal Protection doctrine? If so, then why does it matter that the right to vote is fundamental? Or is it enough for one (or a few) voters to allege that their ability to vote has been substantially impaired?

In *Crawford v. Marion County Election Board,* 128 S. Ct. 1610 (2008), the Court considered a challenge to Indiana's "Voter ID" law, which required the presentation of photo identification issued by the government as a prerequisite to voting. The plaintiffs argued that the law imposed a substantial burden on elderly, disabled, poor, and minority voters, who are less likely to have the requisite forms of identification. The Court upheld the law, although no opinion attracted a majority of the Court. Justice Stevens, joined by Chief Justice Roberts and Justice Kennedy, noted that "evenhanded restrictions that protect the integrity and reliability of the electoral process itself" are not invidious and satisfy the standard set forth in *Harper.* Justice Stevens concluded that the state's interest in deterring voter fraud and promoting confidence in the electoral process were legitimate and important interests, and that the burden imposed on voters without photo IDs was not substantial—and plainly not sufficient to justify facial invalidation of the statute.

Justice Scalia, joined by Justices Thomas and Alito, asserted that "what petitioners view as the law's several light and heavy burdens are no more than the different *impacts* of the single burden that the law uniformly imposes on all voters. To vote in person in Indiana, *everyone* must have and present a photo identification that can be obtained for free." The law, he stated, thus "is a generally applicable, nondiscriminatory voting regulation." Accordingly, in Justice Scalia's view, a "voter complaining about [the] law's effect on him has no valid equal-protection claim because, without proof of discriminatory intent, a generally applicable law with disparate impact is not unconstitutional. [The] Fourteenth Amendment does not regard neutral laws as invidious ones, *even when their burdens purportedly fall disproportionately on a protected class. A fortiori* it does not do so when, as here, the classes complaining of disparate impact are not even protected."

After *Crawford,* what is the relevance of the Equal Protection Clause in assessing laws that are alleged to burden the right to vote?

Bush v. Gore

531 U.S. 98 (2000)

PER CURIAM.

On November 8, 2000, the day following the Presidential election, the Florida Division of Elections reported that petitioner Bush had received 2,909,135 votes, and respondent Gore had received 2,907,351 votes, a margin of 1,784 for Governor Bush. Because Governor Bush's margin of victory was less than "one-half of a percent [of] the votes cast," an automatic machine recount was conducted under [the Florida] election code, the results of which showed Governor Bush still winning the race but by a diminished margin. [Gore then sought manual recounts in four counties. After litigation, the Florida Supreme Court ordered the Florida Secretary of State to include in the certified election results the totals produced by the manual recounts if they were submitted by 5:00 pm on November 26. Some of the counties requested a brief extension, which the Secretary of State denied. The Secretary of State then certified Bush as the winner by 537 votes.]

On November 27, Vice President Gore, pursuant to Florida's contest provisions, filed a complaint in Leon County Circuit Court contesting the certification. He sought relief pursuant to [Fla. Stat.] § 102.168(3)(c), which provides that "[r]eceipt of a number of illegal votes or rejection of a number of legal votes sufficient to change or place in doubt the result of the election" shall be grounds for a contest. *** A "legal vote," as determined by the [Florida] Supreme Court, is "one in which there is a 'clear indication of the intent of the voter.'" [The Florida trial court held that Gore had not demonstrated a "reasonable probability" that the election results would have been different if not for the rejection of some legal votes, but on December 8 the Florida Supreme Court reversed.] Observing that the contest provisions vest broad discretion in the circuit judge to "provide any relief appropriate under such circumstances," § 102.168(8), the Supreme Court further held that the Circuit Court could order "the Supervisor of Elections and the Canvassing Boards, as well as the necessary public officials, in all counties that have not conducted a manual recount or tabulation of the undervotes [to] do so forthwith, said tabulation to take place in the individual counties where the ballots are located." [The Florida Supreme Court also directed the lower court to include in the certified results votes that had been counted during the manual recounts in Palm Beach and Miami-Dade Counties but that had not been accepted by the Secretary of State. A few hours later, the Florida trial court ordered manual recounts and set a deadline of December 10. The next morning, the Supreme Court granted Bush's petition for certiorari and granted a stay of the counting of votes.]

The individual citizen has no federal constitutional right to vote for electors for the President of the United States unless and until the state legislature chooses a statewide election as the means to implement its power to appoint members of the electoral college. *** History has now favored the voter, and in each of the several States the citizens themselves vote for Presidential electors. When the state legislature vests the right to vote for President in its people, the right to vote as the legislature has prescribed is fundamental; and one source of its fundamental nature lies in the equal weight accorded to each vote and the equal dignity owed to each voter. *** Equal protection applies as well to the manner of its exercise. Having once granted the right to vote on equal terms, the State may not, by later arbitrary and disparate treatment, value one person's vote over that of another. See, e.g., *Harper v. Virginia Bd. of Elections*, 383 U.S. 663 (1966).

The question before us [is] whether the recount procedures the Florida Supreme Court has adopted are consistent with its obligation to avoid arbitrary and disparate treatment of the members of its electorate. Much of the controversy seems to revolve around ballot cards designed to be perforated by a stylus but which, either through error or deliberate omission, have not been perforated with sufficient precision for a machine to register the perforations. In some cases a piece of the card—a chad—is hanging, say, by two corners. In other cases there is no separation at all, just an indentation. *** Florida's basic command for the count of legally cast votes is to consider the "intent of the voter." This is unobjectionable as an abstract proposition and a starting principle. The problem inheres in the absence of specific standards to ensure its equal application. The formulation of uniform rules to determine intent based on these recurring circumstances is practicable and, we conclude, necessary.

The want of those rules here has led to unequal evaluation of ballots in various respects. *** A monitor in Miami-Dade County testified at trial that he observed that three members of the county canvassing board applied different standards in defining a legal vote. And testimony at trial also revealed that at least one county changed its evaluative standards during the counting process. *** This is not a process with sufficient guarantees of equal treatment. The State Supreme Court ratified this uneven treatment. It mandated that the recount totals from [the counties in question] be included in the certified total. *** Yet each of the counties used varying standards to determine what was a legal vote. Broward County used a more forgiving standard than Palm Beach County, and uncovered almost three times as many new votes, a result markedly disproportionate to the difference in population between the counties. *** The recount process, in its features here described, is inconsistent with the minimum procedures necessary to protect the fundamental right of each voter in the special instance of a statewide recount under the authority of a single state judicial officer. Our consideration is limited to the present circumstances, for the problem of equal protection in election processes generally presents many complexities. *** When a court orders a statewide remedy, there must be at least some assurance that the rudimentary requirements of equal treatment and fundamental fairness are satisfied.

> **Food for Thought**
>
> The Court declares that its "consideration is limited to the present circumstances." Does that mean that the equal protection analysis in the decision will not serve as binding precedent in future controversies? If so, does the Court's decision itself satisfy the concept of equal protection on which its conclusion is based?

Upon due consideration of the difficulties identified to this point, it is obvious that the recount cannot be conducted in compliance with the requirements of equal protection and due process without substantial additional work. It would require not only the adoption (after opportunity for argument) of adequate statewide standards for determining what is a legal vote, and practicable procedures to implement them, but also orderly judicial review of any disputed matters that might arise.

The Supreme Court of Florida has said that the legislature intended the State's electors to "participat[e] fully in the federal electoral process," as provided in 3 U.S.C. § 5. That statute, in turn, requires that any controversy or contest that is designed to lead to a conclusive selection of electors be completed by December 12. That date is upon us, and there is no recount procedure in place under the State Supreme Court's order that comports with minimal constitutional standards. Because it is evident that any recount seeking to meet the December 12 date will be unconstitutional for the reasons we have discussed, we reverse the judgment of the Supreme Court of Florida ordering a recount to proceed.

None are more conscious of the vital limits on judicial authority than are the Members of this Court, and none stand more in admiration of the Constitution's design to leave the selection of the President to the people, through their legislatures, and to the political sphere. When contending parties invoke the process of the courts, however, it becomes our unsought responsibility to resolve the federal and constitutional issues the judicial system has been forced to confront. The judgment of the Supreme Court of Florida is reversed, and the case is remanded for further proceedings not inconsistent with this opinion.

Chief Justice REHNQUIST, with whom Justice SCALIA and Justice THOMAS join, concurring.

Article II, § 1, cl. 2 provides that "[e]ach State shall appoint, in such Manner as the *Legislature* thereof may direct," electors for President and Vice President. (Emphasis added.) Thus, the text of the election law itself, and not just its interpretation by the courts of the States, takes on independent significance. *** A significant departure from the legislative scheme for appointing Presidential electors presents a federal constitutional question.

Isolated sections of the [Florida election] code may well admit of more than one interpretation, but the general coherence of the legislative scheme may not be altered by judicial interpretation so as to wholly change the statutorily provided apportionment of responsibility among [the Secretary of State and the state circuit courts]. *** [T]he Florida Supreme Court's interpretation of the Florida election laws impermissibly distorted them beyond what a fair reading required, in violation of Article II.

Justice STEVENS, with whom Justice GINSBURG and Justice BREYER join, dissenting.

Admittedly, the use of differing substandards for determining voter intent in different counties employing similar voting systems may raise serious concerns. [But] "[t]he interpretation of constitutional principles must not be too literal. We must remember that the machinery of government would not work if it were not allowed a little play in its joints." *Bain Peanut Co. of Tex. v. Pinson*, 282 U.S. 499, 501 (1931) (Holmes, J.). If it were otherwise, Florida's decision to leave to each county the determination of what balloting system to employ—despite enormous differences in accuracy—might run afoul of equal protection. So, too, might the similar decisions of the vast majority of state legislatures to delegate to local authorities certain decisions with respect to voting systems and ballot design.

Even assuming that aspects of the remedial scheme might ultimately be found to violate the Equal Protection Clause, I could not subscribe to the majority's disposition of the case. *** Under their own reasoning, the appropriate course of action would be to remand to allow more specific procedures for implementing the legislature's uniform general standard to be established.

[T]he Florida Supreme Court [did not] make any substantive change in Florida electoral law. Its decisions were rooted in long-established precedent and were consistent with the relevant statutory provisions, taken as a whole. It did what courts do—it decided the case before it in light of the legislature's intent to leave no legally cast vote uncounted. *** What must underlie petitioners' entire federal assault on the Florida election procedures is an unstated lack of confidence in the impartiality and capacity of the state judges who would make the critical decisions if the vote count were to proceed. *** The endorsement of that position by the majority of this Court can only lend credence to the most cynical appraisal of the work of judges throughout the land. It is confidence in the men and women who administer the judicial system that is the true backbone of the rule of law. Time will one day heal the wound to that confidence that will be inflicted by today's decision. One thing, however, is certain. Although we may never know with complete certainty the identity of the winner of this year's Presidential election, the identity of the loser is perfectly clear. It is the Nation's confidence in the judge as an impartial guardian of the rule of law.

Justice SOUTER, with whom Justice BREYER joins, and with whom Justice STEVENS and Justice GINSBURG join as to all but Part III, dissenting.

[III] It is true that the Equal Protection Clause does not forbid the use of a variety of voting mechanisms within a jurisdiction, even though different mechanisms will have different levels of effectiveness in recording voters' intentions; local variety can be justified by concerns about cost, the potential value of innovation, and so on. But evidence in the record here suggests that a different order of disparity obtains under rules for determining a voter's intent that have been applied (and could continue to be applied) to identical types of ballots used in identical brands of machines and exhibiting identical physical characteristics (such as "hanging" or "dimpled" chads). I can conceive of no legitimate state interest served by these differing treatments of the expressions of voters' fundamental rights. The differences appear wholly arbitrary.

In deciding what to do about this, we should take account of the fact that electoral votes are due to be cast in six days. I would therefore remand the case to the courts of Florida with instructions to establish uniform standards for evaluating the several types of ballots that have prompted differing treatments, to be applied within and among counties when passing on such identical ballots in any further recounting (or successive recounting) that the courts might order. Unlike the majority, I see no warrant for this Court to assume that Florida could not possibly comply with this requirement before the date set for the meeting of electors, December 18. *** To recount these manually would be a tall order, but before this Court stayed the effort to do that the courts of Florida were ready to do their best to get that job done. There is no justification for denying the State the opportunity to try to count all disputed ballots now.

Justice GINSBURG, with whom Justice STEVENS joins, and with whom Justice SOUTER and Justice BREYER join as to Part I, dissenting.

[II] Ideally, perfection would be the appropriate standard for judging the recount. But we live in an imperfect world, one in which thousands of votes have not been counted. I cannot agree that the recount adopted by the Florida court, flawed as it may be, would yield a result any less fair or precise than the certification that preceded that recount. Even if there were an equal protection violation, I would agree with Justice STEVENS, Justice SOUTER, and Justice BREYER that the Court's concern about "the December 12 deadline" is misplaced. Time is short in part because of the Court's entry of a stay on December 9, several hours after an able circuit judge in Leon County had begun to superintend the recount process. More fundamentally, the Court's reluctance to let the recount go forward—despite its suggestion that "[t]he search for intent can be confined by specific rules designed to ensure uniform treatment"—ultimately turns on its own judgment about the practical realities of implementing a recount, not the judgment of those much closer to the process.

Justice BREYER, with whom Justice STEVENS and Justice GINSBURG join except as to Part I-A-1, and with whom Justice SOUTER joins as to Part I, dissenting.

[I-A-2] By halting the manual recount, and thus ensuring that the uncounted legal votes will not be counted under any standard, this Court crafts a remedy out of proportion to the asserted harm. And that remedy harms the very fairness interests the Court is attempting to protect. The manual recount would itself redress a problem of unequal treatment of ballots. ***

[II] Of course, the selection of the President is of fundamental national importance. But that importance is political, not legal. And this Court should resist the temptation unnecessarily to resolve tangential legal disputes, where doing so threatens to determine the outcome of the election. *** Justice Brandeis once said of the Court, "The most important thing we do is not doing." What it does today, the Court should have left undone. I would repair the damage done as best we now can, by permitting the Florida recount to continue under uniform standards.

————————

Points for Discussion

a. Counting the Votes (on the Court)

How many Justices concluded that the recount procedures violated the Equal Protection Clause? What was the rationale for this conclusion? Did the Court properly apply *Harper*'s test? Did any of the Justices conclude that the procedures did not violate Equal Protection? The Court's ruling on the Equal Protection issue has provoked strong but differing academic opinions. A leading article condemning the decision is Laurence H. Tribe, *Erog v. Hsub and its Disguises: Freeing Bush v. Gore from its Hall of Mirrors*, 115 Harv. L. Rev. 170 (2001), in which the author concludes that the skeptics of the decision are correct to proclaim "EQUAL PROTECTION, MY ASS!" For a response, see Nelson Lund, *"Equal Protection, My Ass!"? : Bush v. Gore and Laurence Tribe's Hall of Mirrors*, 19 Const. Comment. 543 (2002).

b. Elections and the Judicial Role

The Court's decision in <u>Bush v. Gore</u> effectively ended the recount in Florida, which resulted in George Bush's being certified the winner of Florida's electoral votes (and thus the Presidency). Did the Court properly intervene in this election dispute? Is there a difference between prospectively identifying constitutional standards for the exercise of the franchise and the administration of elections—as the Court did in <u>Harper</u>—and retrospectively reviewing the state's adherence to such standards?

Two days before the Court issued its decision in the case, it granted a stay of the recount, which prevented the counting of votes pending the Court's decision on the merits. Justice Stevens, joined by Justices Souter, Ginsburg, and Breyer, dissented from the order, arguing that Bush had failed to establish a likelihood of irreparable harm, a traditional prerequisite to the grant of a stay, because "[c]ounting every legally cast vote cannot constitute irreparable harm." Indeed, he asserted, "[p]reventing the recount from being completed will inevitably cast a cloud on the legitimacy of the election." Justice Scalia wrote separately to respond to Justice Stevens, asserting that the "counting of votes that are of questionable legality does in my view threaten irreparable harm to petitioner Bush, and to the country, by casting a cloud upon what he claims to be the legitimacy of his election." What do these competing views of irreparable harm suggest about the Justices' views of the judicial role in election disputes?

c. Equal Protection and Voting

What are the implications for voting practices of the Court's equal protection analysis? Can different counties in the same state (or precincts in the same county) use different vote-counting technologies? Must each precinct have the same voter-to-machine ratio? What should we (and lower courts entertaining challenges to election procedures) make of the Court's statement that its "consideration is limited to the present circumstances"?

d. Equal Protection and Remedies

If the defect under the Equal Protection Clause was that the recounts were being conducted in different counties pursuant to different standards, then why wasn't the remedy to require the counting of votes statewide pursuant to a uniform—even judicially declared—standard? Why was the only remedy for this problem not to count the votes at all?

After the Supreme Court's controversial decision to end the recount, a consortium of eight news organizations, including the *New York Times*, the *Wall Street Journal*, and the *Washington Post*, decided to undertake an unofficial recount. The consortium's systematic recounting process took 10 months. In the end, the consortium concluded: "Contrary to what many partisans of former Vice President Al Gore have charged, the United States Supreme Court did not award an election to Mr. Bush that otherwise would have been won by Mr. Gore. A close examination of the ballots found that Mr. Bush would have retained a slender margin over Mr. Gore if the Florida court's order to recount more than 43,000 ballots had not been reversed by the United States Supreme Court." Ford Fessenden and John M. Broder, *Study Finds Justices Did Not Cast the Deciding Vote*, N.Y. Times, Nov. 12, 2001, at A1. Does either the result of the consortium's recount or the duration of the recounting process affect your assessment of the Supreme Court's decision in this case?

---

2. Apportionment and Gerrymandering

Recall that in *Baker v. Carr*, 369 U.S. 186 (1962), which we considered in Chapter 2, the Court held that the Equal Protection Clause provides discoverable and manageable standards for use by lower courts in determining the constitutionality of a state legislative apportionment scheme. In the case that follows, the Court announced what those standards are.

Reynolds v. Sims

377 U.S. 533 (1964)

Mr. Chief Justice WARREN delivered the opinion of the Court.

[In 1961, Alabama voters brought a class-action lawsuit against state and political party officials responsible for conducting state elections, alleging that the apportionment of the Alabama legislature violated their rights under the Equal Protection Clause. The parties did not dispute that there were significant representative disparities among Alabama congressional districts that tended to favor rural areas over urban areas. For example, the largest district in the Alabama Senate had 46 times as many voters as the smallest, and the largest district in the state House of Representatives had 16 times as many voters as the smallest. The record demonstrated that approximately 25% of the state population could elect a majority of members in both houses. Although the Alabama Constitution required reapportionment every ten years, the legislature had not been reapportioned since 1901.]

Undeniably the Constitution of the United States protects the right of all qualified citizens to vote, in state as well as in federal elections. *** The right to vote freely for the candidate of one's choice is of the essence of a democratic society, and any restrictions on that right strike at the heart of representative government. And the right of suffrage can be denied by a debasement or dilution of the weight of a citizen's vote just as effectively as by wholly prohibiting the free exercise of the franchise.

[Our cases demonstrate that the] fundamental principle of representative government in this country is one of equal representation for equal numbers of people, without regard to race, sex, economic status, or place of residence within a State. Our problem, then, is to ascertain, in the instant cases, whether there are any constitutionally cognizable principles which would justify departures from the basic standard of equality among voters in the apportionment of seats in state legislatures.

> **Take Note**
>
> Alabama was not anomalous in its apportionment scheme. Yet the Court declares that "equal representation for equal numbers of people" is the "fundamental principle" governing state apportionment schemes. If actual state practice before _Reynolds_ regularly deviated from this principle, then how "fundamental" could it really be?

Legislators represent people, not trees or acres. Legislators are elected by voters, not farms or cities or economic interests. As long as ours is a representative form of government, and our legislatures are those instruments of government elected directly by and directly representative of the people, the right to elect legislators in a free and unimpaired fashion is a bedrock of our political system. *** It could hardly be gainsaid that a constitutional claim had been asserted by an allegation that certain otherwise qualified voters had been entirely prohibited from voting for members of their state legislature. And, if a State should provide that the votes of citizens in one part of the State should be given two times, or five times, or 10 times the weight of votes of citizens in another part of the State, it could hardly be contended that the right to vote of those residing in the disfavored areas had not been effectively diluted. *** The resulting discrimination against those individual voters living in disfavored areas is easily demonstrable mathematically. *** Two, five, or 10 of them must vote before the effect of their voting is equivalent to that of their favored neighbor.

Since legislatures are responsible for enacting laws by which all citizens are to be governed, they should be bodies which are collectively responsive to the popular will. With respect to the allocation of legislative representation, all voters, as citizens of a State, stand in the same relation regardless of where they live. Any suggested criteria for the differentiation of citizens are insufficient to justify any discrimination, as to the weight of their votes, unless relevant to the permissible purposes of legislative apportionment. *** Since the achieving of fair and effective representation for all citizens is concededly the basic aim of legislative apportionment, we conclude that the Equal Protection Clause guarantees the opportunity for equal participation by all voters in the election of state legislators.

We are told that the matter of apportioning representation in a state legislature is a complex and many-faceted one [and we] are cautioned about the dangers of entering into political thickets and mathematical quagmires. Our answer is this: a denial of constitutionally protected rights demands judicial protection; our oath and our office require no less of us. *** To the extent that a citizen's right to vote is debased, he is that much less a citizen. The fact that an individual lives here or there is not a legitimate reason for overweighting or diluting the efficacy of his vote. We hold that, as a basic constitutional standard, the Equal Protection Clause requires that the seats in both houses of a bicameral state legislature must be apportioned on a population basis. Simply stated, an individual's right to vote for state legislators is unconstitutionally impaired when its weight is in a substantial fashion diluted when compared with votes of citizens living in other parts of the State. [The current apportionment accordingly is constitutionally invalid.]

> **Food for Thought**
>
> Article IV, § 4 provides that the "United States shall guarantee to every State in this Union a Republican Form of Government." In common parlance, "republican" government means "representative" government. Wouldn't this be a more sensible basis for the Court's holding? The Court has traditionally avoided claims under the Guarantee Clause, however, usually concluding that they are not justiciable. See, e.g., *New York v. United States*, 505 U.S. 144, 183-86 (1992).

Much has been written since our decision in *Baker v. Carr* about the applicability of the so-called federal analogy to state legislative apportionment arrangements. *** Arising from unique historical circumstances, [the states' equal representation in the Senate] is based on the consideration that in establishing our type of federalism a group of formerly independent States bound themselves together under one national government. [A]t the time of the inception of the system of representation in the Federal Congress, a compromise between the larger and smaller States on this matter averted a deadlock in the Constitutional Convention which had threatened to abort the birth of our Nation. *** Since we find the so-called federal analogy inapposite to a consideration of the constitutional validity of state legislative apportionment schemes, we necessarily hold that the Equal Protection Clause requires both houses of a state legislature to be apportioned on a population basis.

> **Take Note**
>
> Most of the Equal Protection cases we have seen have involved claims of discrimination against minorities. Is the Court's holding in *Reynolds* designed to protect minorities? Or instead is it majorities who benefit from the decision?

By holding that as a federal constitutional requisite both houses of a state legislature must be apportioned on a population basis, we mean that the Equal Protection Clause requires that a State make an honest and good faith effort to construct districts, in both houses of its legislature, as nearly of equal population as is practicable. We realize that it is a practical impossibility to arrange legislative districts so that each one has an identical number of residents, or citizens, or voters. Mathematical exactness or precision is hardly a workable constitutional requirement. *** Lower courts can and assuredly will work out more concrete and specific standards for evaluating state legislative apportionment schemes in the context of actual litigation.

Mr. Justice HARLAN, dissenting.

Under the Court's ruling it is bound to follow that the legislatures in all but a few of the other [States] will meet the same fate. [The Court's decision has] the effect of placing basic aspects of state political systems under the pervasive overlordship of the federal judiciary.

[T]he Equal Protection Clause was never intended to inhibit the States in choosing any democratic method they pleased for the apportionment of their legislatures. *** I am unable to understand the Court's utter disregard of the second section [of the Fourteenth Amendment,] which expressly recognizes the States' power to deny "or in any way" abridge the right of their inhabitants to vote for "the members of the (State) Legislature," and its express provision of a remedy for such denial or abridgment. The comprehensive scope of the second section and its particular reference to the state legislatures preclude the suggestion that the first section was intended to have the result reached by the Court today.

Of the 23 loyal States which ratified the Amendment before 1870, five had constitutional provisions for apportionment of at least one house of their respective legislatures which wholly disregarded the spread of population. Ten more had constitutional provisions which gave primary emphasis to population, but which applied also other principles, such as partial ratios and recognition of political subdivisions, which were intended to favor sparsely settled areas. Can it be seriously contended that the legislatures of these States, almost two-thirds of those concerned, would have ratified an amendment which might render their own States' constitutions unconstitutional?

[A]fter the adoption of the [F]ourteenth [A]mendment, it was deemed necessary to adopt a [F]ifteenth ***. The [F]ourteenth [A]mendment had already provided that no State should make or enforce any law which should abridge the privileges or immunities of citizens of the United States. If suffrage was one of these privileges or immunities, why amend the Constitution to prevent its being denied on account of race, &c.? [U]nless one takes the highly implausible view that the Fourteenth Amendment controls methods of apportionment but leaves the right to vote itself unprotected, the conclusion is inescapable that the Court has, for purposes of these cases, relegated the Fifteenth and Nineteenth Amendments to the same limbo of constitutional anachronisms to which the second section of the Fourteenth Amendment has been assigned.

[The Court's decision gives] support to a current mistaken view of the Constitution and the constitutional function of this Court. This view, in a nutshell, is that every major social ill in this country can find its cure in some constitutional "principle." [This Court] does not serve its high purpose when it exceeds its authority, even to satisfy justified impatience with the slow workings of the political process. For when, in the name of constitutional interpretation, the Court adds something to the Constitution that was deliberately excluded from it, the Court in reality substitutes its view of what should be so for the amending process.

Points for Discussion

a. "One Person, One Vote"

The same term that it decided *Reynolds*, the Court applied the "one-person, one-vote" principle to districting for the United States House of Representatives. See *Wesberry v. Sanders*, 376 U.S. 1 (1964). Since that time, the Court has applied the principle to local governments, as well. See, e.g., *Avery v. Midland County*, 390 U.S. 474 (1968) (county commission).

The principle of one person, one vote requires that legislators (or other elected representatives) represent districts of equal sizes, so that no person's vote is worth "more" than any other's. Although the Court stated in *Reynolds* that it would not insist on "mathematical exactness," since that time it has tolerated only very small deviations from the principle of one person, one vote. See, e.g., *Karcher v. Daggett*, 462 U.S. 725 (1983) (invalidating districting for the House of Representatives with deviation among districts of 0.7 percent, where state could offer no justification for the deviation).

Does the one-person, one-vote principle apply to the United States Senate? If not, can it truly be a principle of constitutional importance?

b. Vote Dilution

Justice Harlan asserted in dissent in *Reynolds* that the Constitution does not prohibit the states from apportioning legislatures on principles other than one person, one vote, assuming that there is no invidious discrimination on the basis of race or gender. If Justice Harlan's view had prevailed, could a state conduct at-large elections for the state legislature—that is, eliminate individual districts and let the voters in the state choose from a slate to fill all of the legislative seats—and give some citizens—say, rural residents—ten votes to spread among candidates while giving other citizens only one? Could it give 100 votes to some citizens and only one to others? (The effect, of course, would be the same as the apportionment at issue in *Reynolds*.) Could it deny the vote to all urban residents or citizens who do not own property? Cf. *Harper v. Virginia State Bd. of Elections*, which we considered earlier in this chapter.

c. Remedies

Putting aside the question of the appropriate *standard* for apportionment, what *remedy* should a district court grant for a valid claim of unconstitutional apportionment? Can it order the state legislature to redraw the legislative map? Would such a remedy be consistent with *New York v. United States*, which we considered in Chapter 3? Can the district court draw the lines itself?

————

In Chapter 11, we considered the extent to which legislators may consider race when drawing the election map. In *Shaw v. Reno*, the Court concluded that strict scrutiny applies to the use of race in redistricting, even when race has been used to increase the likelihood that minority groups will be able to elect the candidate of their choice. Accordingly, claims of "racial gerrymandering"—the drawing of legislative district lines to benefit voters based on their race—not only are justiciable, but they also challenge a practice that is presumptively unconstitutional.

Does the same approach apply to efforts to draw electoral maps to benefit other definable groups? In *Davis v. Bandemer*, 478 U.S. 109 (1986), the Court considered a challenge by Indiana Democrats to a reapportionment plan passed by the Republican-controlled legislature and signed by the Republican Governor. The plaintiffs contended that the plan constituted an impermissible **political gerrymander** intended to disadvantage Democrats, but the Court rejected their challenge. A six-member majority of the Court, after considering the factors identified in *Baker v. Carr*, concluded that the claim was justiciable. But no standard for assessing the plaintiffs' claims received five votes. Justice White, joined by Justices Brennan, Marshall, and Blackmun, began by rejecting "any claim that the Constitution requires proportional representation or that legislatures in reapportioning must draw district lines to come as near as possible to allocating seats to the contending parties in proportion to what their anticipated statewide vote will be." In Justice White's view, plaintiffs could prevail only by proving both intentional discrimination against an identifiable political group and an actual discriminatory effect on that group. But he was unwilling to find the requisite effects in that case: "unconstitutional discrimination occurs only when the electoral system is arranged in a manner that will consistently degrade a voter's or a group of voters' influence on the political process as a whole."

Justice Powell, joined by Justice Stevens, agreed that the claim was justiciable, but proposed a multi-factored test for determining when a political gerrymander violates the Constitution: "The most important of these factors are the shapes of voting districts and adherence to established political subdivision boundaries. Other relevant considerations include the nature of the legislative procedures by which the apportionment law was adopted and legislative history reflecting contemporaneous legislative goals." In Justice Powell's view, "[n]o one factor should be dispositive."

Justice O'Connor, joined by Chief Justice Burger and Justice Rehnquist, wrote separately to assert that political gerrymandering claims should be non-justiciable: "[T]he legislative business of apportionment is fundamentally a political affair, and challenges to the manner in which an apportionment has been carried out—by the very parties that are responsible for this process—present a political question in the truest sense of the term." Justice O'Connor asserted that there is a "fundamental distinction between state action that inhibits an individual's right to vote and state action that affects the political strength of various groups that compete for leadership in a democratically governed community."

The Court had an opportunity in the case that follows to revisit the constitutionality (and justiciability) of political gerrymandering.

Vieth v. Jubelirer

541 U.S. 267 (2004)

Justice SCALIA announced the judgment of the Court and delivered an opinion, in which THE CHIEF JUSTICE, Justice O'CONNOR, and Justice THOMAS join.

Plaintiffs, registered Democrats who vote in Pennsylvania, brought suit *** to enjoin implementation of [legislation apportioning the state's federal congressional districts.] The complaint alleged, among other things, that the legislation *** constituted a political gerrymander, in violation of Article I and the Equal Protection Clause of the Fourteenth Amendment. [T]he complaint alleged that the districts [were] "meandering and irregular," and "ignor[ed] all traditional redistricting criteria, including the preservation of local government boundaries, solely for the sake of partisan advantage."

Over the dissent of three Justices, the Court held in *Davis v. Bandemer* that, since it was "not persuaded that there are no judicially discernible and manageable standards by which political gerrymander cases are to be decided," such cases *were* justiciable. The clumsy shifting of the burden of proof for the premise (the Court was "not persuaded" that standards do not exist, rather than "persuaded" that they do) was necessitated by the uncomfortable fact that the six-Justice majority could not discern what the judicially discernable standards might be. *** The lower courts have lived with that assurance of a standard (or more precisely, lack of assurance that there is no standard), coupled with that inability to specify a standard, for the past 18 years. In that time, they have considered numerous political gerrymandering claims; this Court has never revisited the unanswered question of what standard governs.

Nor can it be said that the lower courts have, over 18 years, succeeded in shaping the standard that this Court was initially unable to enunciate. They have simply applied the standard set forth in *Bandemer*'s four-Justice plurality opinion. This might be thought to prove that the four-Justice plurality standard has met the test of time—but for the fact that its application has almost invariably produced the same result (except for the incurring of attorney's fees) as would have obtained if the question were nonjusticiable: Judicial intervention has been refused. *** Lacking [judicially discernable and manageable standards], we must conclude that political gerrymandering claims are nonjusticiable and that *Bandemer* was wrongly decided.

Appellants' proposed standard retains the two-pronged framework of the *Bandemer* plurality—intent plus effect—but modifies the type of showing sufficient to satisfy each. To satisfy appellants' intent standard, a plaintiff must "show that the mapmakers acted with a *predominant intent* to achieve partisan advantage," which can be shown "by direct evidence or by circumstantial evidence that other neutral and legitimate redistricting criteria were subordinated to the goal of achieving partisan advantage," (emphasis added). *** Appellants contend that their intent test *must* be discernible and manageable because it has been borrowed from our racial gerrymandering cases. *** [However,] applying a "predominant intent" test to *racial* gerrymandering is easier and less disruptive. The Constitution clearly contemplates districting by political entities, see Article I, § 4, and unsurprisingly that turns out to be root-and-branch a matter of politics. By contrast, the purpose of segregating voters on the basis of race is not a lawful one, and is much more rarely encountered. *** [C]ourts might be justified in accepting a modest degree of unmanageability to enforce a constitutional command which (like the Fourteenth Amendment obligation to refrain from racial discrimination) is clear; whereas they are not justified in inferring a judicially enforceable constitutional obligation (the obligation not to apply *too much* partisanship in districting) which is both dubious and severely unmanageable.

[The effects prong of appellants' proposal is also flawed. A] person's politics is rarely as readily discernible—and *never* as permanently discernible—as a person's race. [This makes] it impossible to assess the effects of partisan gerrymandering, to fashion a standard for evaluating a violation, and finally to craft a remedy. *** Assuming, however, that the effects of partisan gerrymandering can be determined, appellants' test would invalidate the districting only when it prevents a majority of the electorate from electing a majority of representatives. *** Deny it as appellants may (and do), this standard rests upon the principle that groups (or at least political-action groups) have a right to proportional representation. But the Constitution contains no such principle. It guarantees equal protection of the law to persons, not equal representation in government to equivalently sized groups. *** Even if the standard were relevant, however, it is not judicially manageable.

<table>
<tr><td>

FYI

"Packing" a district means to fill it with a supermajority of a given group or party. "Cracking" involves the splitting of a group or party among several districts to deny that group or party a majority in any of those districts.

</td><td>

[And even] if we could identify a majority party, we would find it impossible to ensure that that party wins a majority of seats—unless we radically revise the States' traditional structure for elections. In any winner-take-all district system, there can be no guarantee, no matter how the district lines are drawn, that a majority of party votes statewide will produce a majority of seats for that party. *** Whether by reason of partisan districting or not, party constituents may always wind up "packed" in some districts and "cracked" throughout others.

</td></tr>
</table>

For many of the same reasons, we also reject the standard suggested by Justice Powell in *Bandemer.* *** It is essentially a totality-of-the-circumstances analysis, where all conceivable factors, none of which is dispositive, are weighed with an eye to ascertaining whether the particular gerrymander has gone too far—or, in Justice Powell's terminology, whether it is not "fair." "Fairness" does not seem to us a judicially manageable standard.

We turn next to consideration of the standards proposed by today's dissenters. We preface it with the observation that the mere fact that these four dissenters come up with three different standards—all of them different from the two proposed in *Bandemer* and the one proposed here by appellants—goes a long way to establishing that there is no constitutionally discernible standard.

Justice STEVENS's confidence that what courts have done with racial gerrymandering can be done with political gerrymandering rests in part upon his belief that "the same standards should apply." But in fact the standards are quite different. A purpose to discriminate on the basis of race receives the strictest scrutiny under the Equal Protection Clause, while a similar purpose to discriminate on the basis of politics does not. *** Justice STEVENS relies on *First Amendment cases* to suggest that politically discriminatory gerrymanders are subject to strict scrutiny under the *Equal Protection Clause*. *** Only an equal protection claim is before us in the present case—perhaps for the very good reason that a First Amendment claim, if it were sustained, would render unlawful *all* consideration of political affiliation in districting.

Justice SOUTER [proposes] a newly constructed standard loosely based in form on our Title VII cases and complete with a five-step prima facie test. *** While this five-part test seems eminently scientific, upon analysis one finds that each of the last four steps requires a quantifying judgment that is unguided and ill suited to the development of judicial standards. *** It does not solve [the] problem to break down the original unanswerable question (How much political motivation and effect is too much?) into four more discrete but equally unanswerable questions.

The criterion Justice BREYER proposes is nothing more precise than "the *unjustified* use of political factors to entrench a minority in power." While he invokes in passing the Equal Protection Clause, it should be clear to any reader that what constitutes *unjustified* entrenchment depends on his own theory of "effective government." While one must agree with Justice BREYER's incredibly abstract starting point that our Constitution sought to create a "basically democratic" form of government, that is a long and impassable distance away from the conclusion that the Judiciary may assess whether a group (somehow defined) has achieved a level of political power (somehow defined) commensurate with that to which they would be entitled absent *unjustified* political machinations (whatever that means).

Justice KENNEDY [concludes] that courts should continue to adjudicate such claims because a standard *may* one day be discovered. *** What are the lower courts to make of this pronouncement? We suggest that they must treat it as a reluctant fifth vote against justiciability at district and statewide levels—a vote that may change in some future case but that holds, for the time being, that this matter is nonjusticiable.

Eighteen years of essentially pointless litigation have persuaded us that <u>Bandemer</u> is incapable of principled application. We would therefore overrule that case, and decline to adjudicate these political gerrymandering claims.

Take Note

Justice Scalia says that "[w]e *would*" overrule <u>Bandemer</u>. Does the Court overrule it? Consider the opinions that follow.

Justice KENNEDY, concurring in the judgment.

I would not foreclose all possibility of judicial relief if some limited and precise rationale were found to correct an established violation of the Constitution in some redistricting cases. *** It is not in our tradition to foreclose the judicial process from the attempt to define standards and remedies where it is alleged that a constitutional right is burdened or denied. *** If suitable standards with which to measure the burden a gerrymander imposes on representational rights did emerge, hindsight would show that the Court prematurely abandoned the field. That is a risk the Court should not take. Instead, we should adjudicate only what is in the papers before us. *** Failing to show that the alleged classifications are unrelated to the aims of apportionment, appellants' evidence at best demonstrates only that the legislature adopted political classifications. That describes no constitutional flaw, at least under the governing Fourteenth Amendment standard.

Justice STEVENS, dissenting.

[I]n gerrymandered districts, instead of local groups defined by neutral criteria selecting their representatives, it is the architects of the districts who select the constituencies and, in effect, the representatives. *** But while political considerations may properly influence the decisions of our elected officials, when such decisions disadvantage members of a minority group—whether the minority is defined by its members' race, religion, or political affiliation—they must rest on a neutral predicate. [T]he Equal Protection Clause implements a duty to govern impartially that requires, at the very least, that every decision by the sovereign serve some nonpartisan public purpose.

[O]ur recent racial gerrymandering cases have examined the shape of the district and the purpose of the districting body to determine whether race, above all other criteria, predominated in the line-drawing process. *** In my view, the same standards should apply to claims of political gerrymandering, for the essence of a gerrymander is the same regardless of whether the group is identified as political or racial. *** Under my analysis, if no neutral criterion can be identified to justify the lines drawn, and if the only possible explanation for a district's bizarre shape is a naked desire to increase partisan strength, then no rational basis exists to save the district from an equal protection challenge. Such a narrow test would cover only a few meritorious claims, but it would preclude extreme abuses.

According to the complaint, Pennsylvania's 2002 redistricting plan splits "Montgomery County alone [into] six different congressional districts." The new District 6 "looms like a dragon descending on Philadelphia from the west, splitting up towns and communities throughout Montgomery and Bucks Counties." [The complaint] alleges that the districting plan was created "solely to effectuate the interests" of Republicans, and that the General Assembly relied "exclusively on a principle of maximum partisan advantage" when drawing the plan, "to the exclusion of all other criteria." *** Because this complaint states a claim under a judicially manageable standard for adjudicating partisan gerrymandering cases, I would reverse the judgment of the District Court and remand.

Justice SOUTER, with whom Justice GINSBURG joins, dissenting.

I would [preserve] *Davis*'s holding that political gerrymandering is a justiciable issue, but otherwise start anew. *** I would require the plaintiff to make out a prima facie case with five elements. First, the resident plaintiff would identify a cohesive political group to which he belonged, which would normally be a major party. *** Second, a plaintiff would need to show that the district of his residence paid little or no heed to those traditional districting principles whose disregard can be shown straightforwardly: contiguity, compactness, respect for political subdivisions, and conformity with geographic features like rivers and mountains. *** Third, the plaintiff would need to establish specific correlations between the district's deviations from traditional districting principles and the distribution of the population of his group. *** Fourth, a plaintiff would need to present the court with a hypothetical district including his residence, one in which the proportion of the plaintiff's group was lower (in a packing claim) or higher (in a cracking one) and which at the same time deviated less from traditional districting principles than the actual district. *** Fifth, and finally, the plaintiff would have to show that the defendants acted intentionally to manipulate the shape of the district in order to pack or crack his group. In substantiating claims of political gerrymandering under a plan devised by a single major party, proving intent should not be hard, once the third and fourth (correlation and cause) elements are established, politicians not being politically disinterested or characteristically naive. *** I would then shift the burden to the defendants to justify their decision by reference to objectives other than naked partisan advantage.

Justice BREYER, dissenting.

I start with a fundamental principle. "We the People," who "ordain[ed] and establish[ed]" the American Constitution, sought to create and to protect a workable form of government that is in its "principles, structure, and whole mass," basically democratic. [U]se of purely political boundary-drawing factors can amount to a serious, and remediable, abuse, namely, the *unjustified* use of political factors to entrench a minority in power. By entrenchment I mean a situation in which a party that enjoys only minority support among the populace has nonetheless contrived to take, and hold, legislative power. By *unjustified* entrenchment I mean that the minority's hold on power is purely the result of partisan manipulation and not other factors. *** Where unjustified entrenchment takes place, voters find it far more difficult to remove those responsible for a government they do not want; and [democratic] values are dishonored. *** Courts need not intervene often to prevent the kind of abuse I have described, because those harmed constitute a political majority, and a majority normally can work its political will. *** But we cannot always count on a severely gerrymandered legislature itself to find and implement a remedy. The party that controls the process has no incentive to change it.

———————

Points for Discussion

a. Justiciability

After the decision in *Vieth*, are claims challenging political gerrymanders under the Fourteenth Amendment justiciable?

b. Group v. Individual Rights

Does the Equal Protection Clause protect groups or individuals? Justice Scalia clearly believes that it protects individuals rather than conferring rights for membership in a particular group, defined by race, political affiliation, or any other common trait. The dissenters, in contrast, believe that the Clause offers protection based on group affiliation. Much turns on which view prevails. If the Clause confers group rights, then a claim that a definable group's voting strength has been impaired presumably is cognizable.

Even if the Equal Protection Clause ordinarily protects only individuals, should its application to the context of voting be different? After all, candidates can be elected in a majoritarian system only by receiving more votes, in the *aggregate*, than their opponents. Does the context of voting necessarily require reference to group rights?

c. Political Gerrymandering v. Racial Gerrymandering

Although in recent years cases involving racial gerrymandering have challenged districting that seeks to benefit, rather than harm, racial minorities, it was not too long ago that state legislatures drew district lines with the intent to impair—generally through dilution—the voting strength of racial minorities. The Court has made clear that such districting plans violate the Fourteenth Amendment. *See, e.g., Rogers v. Lodge,* 458 U.S. 613 (1982) (invalidating at-large voting system that was maintained for the invidious purpose of diluting the voting strength of African Americans). If claims challenging racial gerrymandering are justiciable, why isn't it clear that claims challenging political gerrymandering are, too?

In her separate opinion in <u>Bandemer</u>, which was decided before <u>Shaw v. Reno</u>, Justice O'Connor distinguished the Court's cases treating as justiciable claims of racial gerrymandering. She stated that "[a]s a matter of past history and present reality, there is a direct and immediate relationship between the racial minority's group voting strength in a particular community and the individual rights of its members to vote and to participate in the political process. In these circumstances, the stronger nexus between individual rights and group interests, and the greater warrant the Equal Protection Clause gives the federal courts to intervene for protection against racial discrimination, suffice to render racial gerrymandering claims justiciable." Doesn't this view acknowledge that sometimes the Equal Protection Clause protects group rights? How does Justice Scalia distinguish cases holding that claims of racial gerrymandering are justiciable?

d. Remedies and Institutional Logic

In a portion of Justice Scalia's opinion that was omitted above, he observed that "[p]olitical gerrymanders are not new to the American scene," and that "[i]t is significant that the Framers provided a remedy for such practices in the Constitution. Article I, § 4, while leaving in state legislatures the initial power to draw districts for federal elections, permitted Congress to 'make or alter' those districts if it wished." State legislatures draw the districts both for themselves and for Members of Congress. Why might it be significant that the Framers gave Congress the power to address gerrymandering? Is there any problem with relying on either state legislatures or Congress to fix political gerrymanders?

B. Welfare and Education

Dandridge v. Williams

397 U.S. 471 (1970)

Mr. Justice STEWART delivered the opinion of the Court.

[Maryland computed the standard of need for each eligible family under the federal Aid to Families with Dependent Children Program (AFDC) based on the number of children in the family and the circumstances under which the family lived. But the state imposed an upper limit on the total amount of money any one family unit was eligible to receive. In general, the standard of need increased with each additional person in the household, but the increments became proportionately smaller. The suit was filed by recipients who had large families—and whose standards of need thus substantially exceeded the maximum grants available—to enjoin Maryland's rule on the ground that it was in conflict with the Equal Protection Clause. The District Court held that the regulation "is invalid on its face for overreaching."]

Food for Thought

Does the fact that a state chooses to regulate "social or economic" matters automatically exempt it from heightened scrutiny under the Equal Protection Clause? Isn't the real question whether the challenged program discriminates on some impermissible basis? Is wealth or family size such a basis? And wouldn't regulation in this area be problematic if it abridged some fundamental right to which the Court has extended protection? Is there such a right here?

[Here] we deal with state regulation in the social and economic field, not affecting freedoms guaranteed by the Bill of Rights, and claimed to violate the Fourteenth Amendment only because the regulation results in some disparity in grants of welfare payments to the largest AFDC families. For this Court to approve the invalidation of state economic or social regulation as "overreaching" would be far too reminiscent of an era when the Court thought the Fourteenth Amendment gave it power to strike down state laws "because they may be unwise, improvident, or out of harmony with a particular school of thought." *Williamson v. Lee Optical Co.*, 348 U.S. 483 (1955). That era long ago passed into history. In the area of economics and social welfare, a State does not violate the Equal Protection Clause merely because the classifications made by its laws are imperfect. If the classification has some "reasonable basis," it does not offend the Constitution simply because the classification "is not made with mathematical nicety or because in practice it results in some inequality."

Under this long-established meaning of the Equal Protection Clause, it is clear that the Maryland Maximum grant regulation is constitutionally valid. We need not explore all the reasons that the State advances in justification of the regulation. It is enough that a solid foundation for the regulation can be found in the State's legitimate interest in encouraging employment and in avoiding discrimination between welfare families and the families of the working poor. By combining a limit on the recipient's grant with permission to retain money earned, without reduction in the amount of the grant, Maryland provides an incentive to seek gainful employment. And by keying the maximum family AFDC grants to the minimum wage a steadily employed head of a household receives, the State maintains some semblance of an equitable balance between families on welfare and those supported by an employed breadwinner.

[T]he intractable economic, social, and even philosophical problems presented by public welfare assistance programs are not the business of this Court. The Constitution may impose certain procedural safeguards upon systems of welfare administration, *Goldberg v. Kelly*, 397 U.S. 254 (1970), [but] the Constitution does not empower this Court to second-guess state officials charged with the difficult responsibility of allocating limited public welfare funds among the myriad of potential recipients.

> **Make the Connection**
>
> We considered the Court's decision in *Goldberg* in Chapter 9, in our unit on Procedural Due Process.

Mr. Justice HARLAN, concurring.

Except with respect to racial classifications, to which unique historical considerations apply, I believe the constitutional provisions assuring equal protection of the laws impose a standard of rationality of classification, long applied in the decisions of this Court, that does not depend upon the nature of the classification or interest involved. It is on this basis, and not because this case involves only interests in "the area of economics and social welfare," that I join the Court's constitutional holding.

[Justice DOUGLAS's dissent, which asserted that Maryland's rule was inconsistent with the federal Social Security Act, is omitted.]

Mr. Justice MARSHALL, whom Mr. Justice BRENNAN joins, dissenting.

[T]he operative effect [of the maximum grant regulation] is to create two classes of needy children and two classes of eligible families: those small families and their members who receive payments to cover their subsistence needs and those large families who do not. *** The class of individuals with respect to whom payments are actually made (the first four or five eligible dependent children in a family), is grossly underinclusive in terms of the class that the AFDC program was designed to assist, namely, all needy dependent children.

It is the individual interests here at stake that [most] clearly distinguish this case from the "business regulation" equal protection cases. AFDC support to needy dependent children provides the stuff that sustains those children's lives: food, clothing, shelter. And this Court has already recognized several times that when a benefit, even a "gratuitous" benefit, is necessary to sustain life, stricter constitutional standards, both procedural and substantive, are applied to the deprivation of that benefit.

The asserted state interests in the maintenance of the maximum grant regulation, on the other hand, are hardly clear. *** Maryland, with the encouragement and assistance of the Federal Government, has elected to provide assistance at a subsistence level for those in particular need—the aged, the blind, the infirm, and the unemployed and unemployable, and their children. The only question presented here is whether, having once undertaken such a program, the State may arbitrarily select from among the concededly eligible those to whom it will provide benefits. [To] the extent there is a legitimate state interest in encouraging heads of AFDC households to find employment, application of the maximum grant regulation [is] grossly underinclusive because it singles out and affects only large families. *** There is simply no indication whatever that heads of large families, as opposed to heads of small families, are particularly prone to refuse to seek or to maintain employment.

> **Make the Connection**
>
> Is under-inclusiveness a defect under rational-basis review? Recall the Court's discussion in the *Railway Express* case, which we considered in Chapter 10. Does this mean that Justice Marshall is applying something other than rational-basis review?

Appellees are not a gas company or an optical dispenser; they are needy dependent children and families who are discriminated against by the State. The basis of that discrimination—the classification of individuals into large and small families—is too arbitrary and too unconnected to the asserted rationale, the impact on those discriminated against—the denial of even a subsistence existence—too great, and the supposed interests served too contrived and attenuated to meet the requirements of the Constitution. In my view Maryland's maximum grant regulation is invalid under the Equal Protection Clause of the Fourteenth Amendment.

Points for Discussion

a. Level of Scrutiny and "Fundamental Rights"

The majority in *Dandridge* applied rational-basis review, implicitly suggesting that there is no fundamental right to welfare. Did Justice Marshall assert that there is in fact a constitutional right to welfare? If there is such a right, is the Equal Protection Clause a sensible textual basis for it? And if there is such a right, what is the proper level of scrutiny by which to review the regulation at issue in *Dandridge*?

b. Wealth and Classifications

The regulation at issue in *Dandridge* distinguished among poor families, not between rich and poor families. In light of this fact, did the case present the Court with an opportunity to decide whether the poor are a suspect class? The Court largely avoided the issue there, but the question was more squarely presented in the case that follows.

San Antonio Independent School Dist. v. Rodriguez

411 U.S. 1 (1973)

Mr. Justice POWELL delivered the opinion of the Court.

[At the time of this litigation, approximately 40% of Texas's state education budget came from local property taxes. Texas law also imposed a ceiling on the local property-tax rate that any locality could assess. Mexican-American parents whose children attended the public schools of Edgewood Independent School District in San Antonio, Texas, brought suit against various state officials challenging the funding scheme. Because Edgewood was in a district with low property values, it raised only $26 per student in local funds and spent $356 per student during the 1967-68 school year. In contrast, Alamo Heights Independent School District, which was also in San Antonio, raised substantially more money from property taxes and spent $594 per student. The District Court held that the funding scheme violated the Equal Protection Clause.]

Our task must be to ascertain whether [the] Texas system has been shown to discriminate on [the basis of wealth] and, if so, whether the resulting classification may be regarded as suspect. *** The individuals, or groups of individuals, who constituted the class discriminated against in our prior cases [involving the indigent] shared two distinguishing characteristics: because of their impecunity they were completely unable to pay for some desired benefit, and as a consequence, they sustained an absolute deprivation of a meaningful opportunity to enjoy that benefit. In *Griffin v. Illinois*, 351 U.S. 12 (1956), and its progeny, the Court invalidated state laws that prevented an indigent criminal defendant from acquiring a transcript, or an adequate substitute for a transcript, for use at several stages of the trial and appeal process. *** Likewise, [*Douglas v. California*, 372 U.S. 353 (1963), established] an indigent defendant's right to court-appointed counsel on direct appeal.

[N]either of the two distinguishing characteristics of wealth classifications can be found here. First, [there] is no basis on the record in this case for assuming that the poorest people—defined by reference to any level of absolute impecunity—are concentrated in the poorest districts. Second, [lack] of personal resources has not occasioned an absolute deprivation of the desired benefit. The argument here is not that the children in districts having relatively low assessable property values are receiving no public education; rather, it is that they are receiving a poorer quality education than that available to children in districts having more assessable wealth. [A]t least where wealth is involved, the Equal Protection Clause does not require absolute equality or precisely equal advantages.

> **Food for Thought**
>
> Is the Court suggesting here that "true" wealth classifications are suspect—that is, that classifications that actually single out the poor (and only the poor) are problematic—but that the challenged policy here is not such a classification?

[A]ppellees' suit asks this Court to extend its most exacting scrutiny to review a system that allegedly discriminates against a large, diverse, and amorphous class, unified only by the common factor of residence in districts that happen to have less taxable wealth than other districts. The system of alleged discrimination and the class it defines have none of the traditional indicia of suspectness: the class is not saddled with such disabilities, or subjected to such a history of purposeful unequal treatment, or relegated to such a position of political powerlessness as to command extraordinary protection from the majoritarian political process.

We thus conclude that the Texas system does not operate to the peculiar disadvantage of any suspect class. But [appellees] also assert that the State's system impermissibly interferes with the exercise of a "fundamental" right and that accordingly the prior decisions of this Court require the application of the strict standard of judicial review. *** In *Brown v. Board of Education*, 347 U.S. 483 (1954), a unanimous Court recognized that "education is perhaps the most important function of state and local governments." *** But the importance of a service performed by the State does not determine whether it must be regarded as fundamental for purposes of examination under the Equal Protection Clause. Education, of course, is not among the rights afforded explicit protection under our Federal Constitution. Nor do we find any basis for saying it is implicitly so protected.

It is appellees' contention, however, that education is distinguishable from other services and benefits provided by the State because it bears a peculiarly close relationship to other rights and liberties accorded protection under the Constitution. Specifically, they insist that education is itself a fundamental personal right because it is essential to the effective exercise of First Amendment freedoms and to intelligent utilization of the right to vote. *** That these may be desirable goals of a system of freedom of expression and of a representative form of government is not to be doubted. [But] they are not values to be implemented by judicial instruction into otherwise legitimate state activities.

Even if it were conceded that some identifiable quantum of education is a constitutionally protected prerequisite to the meaningful exercise of either right, *** no charge fairly could be made that [Texas's] system fails to provide each child with an opportunity to acquire the basic minimal skills necessary for the enjoyment of the rights of speech and of full participation in the political process. Furthermore, the logical limitations on appellees' nexus theory are difficult to perceive. How, for instance, is education to be distinguished from the significant personal interests in the basics of decent food and shelter? Empirical examination might well buttress an assumption that the ill-fed, ill-clothed, and ill-housed are among the most ineffective participants in the political process, and that they derive the least enjoyment from the benefits of the First Amendment. If so, appellees' thesis would cast serious doubt on the authority of *Dandridge v. Williams*. [In addition,] it would be difficult to imagine a case having a greater potential impact on our federal system than the one now before us, in which we are urged to abrogate systems of financing public education presently in existence in virtually every State.

The foregoing considerations buttress our conclusion that Texas' system of public school finance is an inappropriate candidate for strict judicial scrutiny. These same considerations are relevant to the determination whether that system, with its conceded imperfections, nevertheless bears some rational relationship to a legitimate state purpose. *** While assuring a basic education for every child in the State, [the Texas system of school financing] permits and encourages a large measure of participation in and control of each district's schools at the local level. *** Pluralism [affords] opportunity for experimentation, innovation, and a healthy competition for educational excellence. *** Moreover, if local taxation for local expenditures were an unconstitutional method of providing for education then it might be an equally impermissible means of providing other necessary services customarily financed largely from local property taxes, including local police and fire protection, public health and hospitals, and public utility facilities of various kinds. We perceive no justification for such a severe denigration of local property taxation and control as would follow from appellees' contentions.

In sum, to the extent that the Texas system of school financing results in unequal expenditures between children who happen to reside in different districts, we cannot say that such disparities are the product of a system that is so irrational as to be invidiously discriminatory. *** The constitutional standard under the Equal Protection Clause is whether the challenged state action rationally furthers a legitimate state purpose or interest. We hold that the Texas plan abundantly satisfies this standard.

[Justice STEWART's concurring opinion and Justice BRENNAN's dissenting opinion are omitted.]

Mr. Justice WHITE, with whom Mr. Justice DOUGLAS and Mr. Justice BRENNAN join, dissenting.

In [districts with low property values], the Texas system utterly fails to extend a realistic choice to parents because the property tax, which is the only revenue-raising mechanism extended to school districts, is practically and legally unavailable. *** In order to equal the [tax revenues of Alamo Heights, which taxes at a rate of 68¢ per $100 of assessed valuation,] Edgewood would be required to tax at the prohibitive rate of $5.76 per $100. But state law places a $1.50 per $100 ceiling on the maintenance tax rate, a limit that would surely be reached long before Edgewood attained an equal yield. Edgewood is thus precluded in law, as well as in fact, from achieving a yield even close to that of some other districts. *** If the State aims at maximizing local initiative and local choice, by permitting school districts to resort to the real property tax if they choose to do so, it utterly fails in achieving its purpose in districts with property tax bases so low that there is little if any opportunity for interested parents, rich or poor, to augment school district revenues. Requiring the State to establish only that unequal treatment is in furtherance of a permissible goal, without also requiring the State to show that the means chosen to effectuate that goal are rationally related to its achievement, makes equal protection analysis no more than an empty gesture. In my view, the parents and children in Edgewood, and in like districts, suffer from an invidious discrimination violative of the Equal Protection Clause.

> **Food for Thought**
>
> Justice White states that this case involves "invidious" discrimination. Must the plaintiffs demonstrate that the discrimination is intentional— that is, that the state intentionally deprived poor districts of adequate resources or mechanisms to secure adequate resources? Or is evidence of the discriminatory effects of the policy sufficient for Justice White?

Mr. Justice MARSHALL, with whom Mr. Justice DOUGLAS concurs, dissenting.

The Court today decides, in effect, that a State may constitutionally vary the quality of education which it offers its children in accordance with the amount of taxable wealth located in the school districts within which they reside. *** In my judgment, the right of every American to an equal start in life, so far as the provision of a state service as important as education is concerned, is far too vital to permit state discrimination on grounds as tenuous as those presented by this record. Nor can I accept the notion that it is sufficient to remit these appellees to the vagaries of the political process which, contrary to the majority's suggestion, has proved singularly unsuited to the task of providing a remedy for this discrimination. I, for one, am unsatisfied with the hope of an ultimate "political" solution sometime in the indefinite future while, in the meantime, countless children unjustifiably receive inferior educations that may affect their hearts and minds in a way unlikely ever to be undone.

It is an inescapable fact that if one district has more funds available per pupil than another district, the former will have greater choice in educational planning than will the latter. In this regard, I believe the question of discrimination in educational quality must be deemed to be an objective one that looks to what the State provides its children, not to what the children are able to do with what they receive. [The] Equal Protection Clause is not addressed to the minimal sufficiency but rather to the unjustifiable inequalities of state action. It mandates nothing less than that "all persons similarly circumstanced shall be treated alike."

[In addition, I cannot] accept the majority's labored efforts to demonstrate that fundamental interests, which call for strict scrutiny of the challenged classification, encompass only established rights which we are somehow bound to recognize from the text of the

Constitution itself. *** The task in every case should be to determine the extent to which constitutionally guaranteed rights are dependent on interests not mentioned in the Constitution. As the nexus between the specific constitutional guarantee and the nonconstitutional interest draws closer, the nonconstitutional interest becomes more fundamental and the degree of judicial scrutiny applied when the interest is infringed on a discriminatory basis must be adjusted accordingly. *** Education directly affects the ability of a child to exercise his First Amendment rights, both as a source and as a receiver of information and ideas, whatever interests he may pursue in life.

> **Take Note**
>
> Justice Marshall suggests that the Constitution protects not only the rights that it explicitly mentions but also those interests on which those rights are "dependent." Are you convinced that First Amendment rights, which we will consider in Chapters 14-17, depend upon access to public education? Even if not, can some of the Court's other decisions recognizing unenumerated rights, which we considered in Chapter 8, be justified on this ground?

Points for Discussion

a. Wealth Classifications

Should the Court treat the poor as a suspect class? Consider the framework that the Court suggested in its famous footnote in *United States v. Carolene Products Co.*, 304 U.S. 144, 152 n.4 (1938), which we considered in Chapters 8 and 10. There, the Court suggested that heightened scrutiny might be warranted when "prejudice against discrete and insular minorities may be a special condition, which tends seriously to curtail the operation of those political processes ordinarily to be relied upon to protect minorities." Are poor people a "discrete and insular minority" and the victims of prejudice? Poverty certainly is not immutable in the same sense that race and national origin are, but are the poor politically powerless? Are the existence of welfare programs and progressive taxation evidence to the contrary?

Did Justice White treat the poor as a suspect class? What level of scrutiny did he apply in his dissent? Was it rational-basis review or something else?

b. Education as a Fundamental Right

Did Justice Marshall suggest that the Constitution protects a fundamental right to a quality education? If so, what in his view is the source of that right? Is it the Equal Protection Clause? Is it implicit in other provisions of the Constitution, such as the First Amendment? Regardless of its constitutional source, if there is a fundamental right to a state-provided education, what level of scrutiny did Justice Marshall believe should apply to impairments of the right? Compare Susan H. Bitensky, *Theoretical Foundations for a Right to Education Under the United States Constitution*, 86 Nw. U. L. Rev. 550 (1992), with Gregory E. Maggs, *Innovation in Constitutional Law: The Right to Education and the Tricks of the Trade*, 86 Nw. U. L. Rev. 1038 (1992).

c. Is Equal Spending the Answer?

Even if the Supreme Court had concluded that everyone has a right to an equal education, would this conclusion necessarily have required all school districts to spend the same amount of money per student? Or are expenditures per pupil an incomplete measure of equality? A review of New York City's school districts found this startling result: "The amount of money spent per pupil is inversely related to academic performance, according to an analysis of spending in the city's 32 community school districts by The New York Times. The analysis *** found that the best schools spent the least per pupil and had the most crowded classrooms." John Tierney, *"Money Per Pupil" Is an Incomplete Response*, N.Y. Times, Jun. 21, 2000, at B4. What might explain this result? How should governments promote equality in education if not through spending equal amounts of money?

————————

If the Constitution does not protect a fundamental right to education, then presumably a state could constitutionally decline to provide it. But clearly it couldn't provide education to some but withhold it from others on the basis of their membership in a suspect class. Indeed, <u>Brown v. Board of Education</u> essentially held as much. But the Court has not recognized very many suspect classes. On what bases can a state withhold an education that it otherwise provides? The following case addresses whether a state can withhold an education from the children of illegal immigrants.

————————

Plyler v. Doe

457 U.S. 202 (1982)

Justice BRENNAN delivered the opinion of the Court.

The question presented by these cases is whether, consistent with the Equal Protection Clause of the Fourteenth Amendment, Texas may deny to undocumented school-age children the free public education that it provides to children who are citizens of the United States or legally admitted aliens. [Plaintiffs filed this class action on behalf of school-age children of Mexican origin who could not establish that they had been legally admitted into the United States.]

Persuasive arguments support the view that a State may withhold its beneficence from those whose very presence within the United States is the product of their own unlawful conduct. These arguments do not apply with the same force to classifications imposing disabilities on the minor *children* of such illegal entrants. [L]egislation directing the onus of a parent's misconduct against his children does not com-

> **Food for Thought**
>
> Article III of the Constitution prohibits Congress from effecting a "Corruption of Blood," which means to withhold from the children of condemned adults the right to inherit property. Does this principle, broadly construed, apply here?

port with fundamental conceptions of justice. *** It is thus difficult to conceive of a rational justification for penalizing these children for their presence within the United States. Yet that appears to be precisely the effect of [Texas law].

Public education is not a "right" granted to individuals by the Constitution. *San Antonio Independent School Dist. v. Rodriguez*, 411 U.S. 1 (1973). But neither is it merely some governmental "benefit" indistinguishable from other forms of social welfare legislation. [E]ducation has a fundamental role in maintaining the fabric of our society. We cannot ignore the significant social costs borne by our Nation when select groups are denied the means to absorb the values and skills upon which our social order rests. In addition to the pivotal role of education in sustaining our political and cultural heritage, denial of education to some isolated group of children poses an affront to one of the goals of the Equal Protection Clause: the abolition of governmental barriers presenting unreasonable obstacles to advancement on the basis of individual merit. Paradoxically, by depriving the children of any disfavored group of an education, we foreclose the means by which that group might raise the level of esteem in which it is held by the majority. *** By denying these children a basic education, we deny them the ability to live within the structure of our civic institutions, and foreclose any realistic possibility that they will contribute in even the smallest way to the progress of our Nation.

Undocumented aliens cannot be treated as a suspect class because their presence in this country in violation of federal law is not a "constitutional irrelevancy." Nor is education a fundamental right; a State need not justify by compelling necessity every variation in the manner in which education is provided to its population. [But in] determining the rationality of [Texas's education policy], we may appropriately take into account its costs to the Nation and to the innocent children who are its victims. In light of these countervailing costs, the discrimination [can] hardly be considered rational unless it furthers some substantial goal of the State.

We discern three colorable state interests that might support [the Texas policy.] First, appellants appear to suggest that the State may seek to protect itself from an influx of illegal immigrants. While a State might have an interest in mitigating the potentially harsh economic effects of sudden shifts in population, [the Texas policy] hardly offers an effective method of dealing with an urgent demographic or economic problem. *** The dominant incentive for illegal entry into the State of Texas is the availability of employment; few if any illegal immigrants come to this country, or presumably to the State of Texas, in order to avail themselves of a free education. [Second,] appellants suggest that undocumented children are appropriately singled out for exclusion because of the special burdens they impose on the State's ability to provide high-quality public education. [But] even if improvement in the quality of education were a likely result of barring some *number* of children from the schools of the State, the State must support its selection of *this* group as the appropriate target for exclusion.

Finally, appellants suggest that undocumented children are appropriately singled out because their unlawful presence within the United States renders them less likely than other children to remain within the boundaries of the State, and to put their education to productive social or political use within the State. Even assuming that such an interest is legitimate, it is an interest that is most difficult to quantify. The State has no assurance that any child, citizen or not, will employ the education provided by the State within the confines of the State's borders. It is difficult to understand precisely what the State hopes to achieve by promoting the creation and perpetuation of a subclass of illiterates within our boundaries, surely adding to the problems and costs of unemployment, welfare, and crime. If the State is to deny a discrete group of innocent children the free public education that it offers to other children residing within its borders, that denial must be justified by a showing that it furthers some substantial state interest. No such showing was made here.

[The separate concurring opinions of Justices MARSHALL, BLACKMUN, and POWELL are omitted.]

Chief Justice BURGER, with whom Justice WHITE, Justice REHNQUIST, and Justice O'CONNOR join, dissenting.

[T]he Court expressly—and correctly—rejects any suggestion that illegal aliens are a suspect class or that education is a fundamental right. Yet by patching together bits and pieces of what might be termed quasi-suspect-class and quasi-fundamental-rights analysis, the Court spins out a theory custom-tailored to the facts of these cases. * * * If ever a court was guilty of an unabashedly result-oriented approach, this case is a prime example.

[The] Equal Protection Clause does not preclude legislators from classifying among persons on the basis of factors and characteristics over which individuals may be said to lack "control." [A] state legislature is not barred from considering, for example, relevant differences between the mentally healthy and the mentally ill [simply] because these may be factors unrelated to individual choice or to any "wrongdoing." The Equal Protection Clause protects against arbitrary and irrational classifications, and against invidious discrimination stemming from prejudice and hostility; it is not an all-encompassing "equalizer" designed to eradicate every distinction for which persons are not "responsible."

The second strand of the Court's analysis rests on the premise that, although public education is not a constitutionally guaranteed right, "neither is it merely some governmental 'benefit' indistinguishable from other forms of social welfare legislation." Whatever meaning or relevance this opaque observation might have in some other context, it simply has no bearing on the issues at hand. * * * In *San Antonio Independent School Dist.*, [we] expressly rejected the proposition that state laws dealing with public education are subject to special scrutiny under the Equal Protection Clause. Moreover, the Court points to no meaningful way to distinguish between education and other governmental benefits in this context. Is the Court suggesting that education is more "fundamental" than food, shelter, or medical care? The Equal Protection Clause guarantees similar treatment of similarly situated persons, but it does not mandate a constitutional hierarchy of governmental services.

Once it is conceded—as the Court does—that illegal aliens are not a suspect class, and that education is not a fundamental right, our inquiry should focus on and be limited to whether the legislative classification at issue bears a rational relationship to a legitimate state purpose. * * * Without laboring what will undoubtedly seem obvious to many, it simply is not "irrational" for a state to conclude that it does not have the same responsibility to provide benefits for persons whose very presence in the state and this country is illegal as it does to provide for persons lawfully present. By definition, illegal aliens have no right whatever to be here, and the state may reasonably, and constitutionally, elect not to provide them with governmental services at the expense of those who are lawfully in the state.

Denying a free education to illegal alien children is not a choice I would make were I a legislator. Apart from compassionate considerations, the long-range costs of excluding any children from the public schools may well outweigh the costs of educating them. But that is not the issue; the fact that there are sound *policy* arguments against the Texas Legislature's choice does not render that choice an unconstitutional one. *** Today's [decision], I regret to say, present[s] yet another example of unwarranted judicial action which in the long run tends to contribute to the weakening of our political processes.

Points for Discussion

a. Level of Scrutiny

What level of scrutiny did the Court apply in *Plyler*? The Court purported to measure the rationality of the challenged policy, but it also seemed to require that the classification further a "substantial state interest." Rational-basis review, in contrast, typically requires only that the policy bear a rational relationship to some legitimate state interest. Is the Court effectively applying heightened scrutiny, as it does in the context of gender discrimination? If so, is it because of the group disadvantaged by the classification? Or because education is a uniquely important benefit?

The three concurring opinions (which have been omitted here) advanced varying rationales for invalidating the policy. Justice Marshall emphasized his view that "an individual's interest in education is fundamental." Justice Blackmun compared the absolute deprivation of education, as opposed to the arguably inferior education that nevertheless was provided in *Rodriguez*, to a denial of the right to vote, and he asserted that "the State must offer something more than a rational basis for its classification." Justice Powell wrote to "emphasize the unique character" of the case before the Court, substantially agreeing with the analysis of the majority.

Does it make sense to view challenged state regulation as falling along a continuum, rather than as falling into fixed categories (such as rational-basis review or strict scrutiny) that virtually pre-ordain the outcome? Recall Justice Marshall's and Justice Stevens's opinions in *Cleburne v. Cleburne Living Center*, which we considered in Chapter 11. Is the Court effectively adopting their suggested approach without actually saying so?

b. Immigration and the Constitution

The Constitution grants Congress the power to "establish an uniform Rule of Naturalization." Art. I., § 8, cl. 4. The Court has long held that there are strong reasons to conclude that Congress's authority over matters of immigration is not only plenary, but also exclusive:

> The Federal Government, representing as it does the collective interests of [the] states, is entrusted with full and exclusive responsibility for the conduct of affairs with foreign sovereignties. *** One of the most important and delicate of all international relationships, recognized immemorially as a responsibility of government, has to do with the protection of the just rights of a country's own nationals when those nationals are in another country. *** Legal imposition of distinct, unusual and extraordinary burdens and obligations upon aliens [thus] bears an inseparable relationship to the welfare and tranquility of all the states, and not merely to the welfare and tranquility of one.

Hines v. Davidowitz, 312 U.S. 52 (1941).

Could the Court have resolved *Plyler* on this basis, by concluding that the Texas policy in effect impermissibly attempted to regulate matters—the status and rights of aliens—that are within the exclusive authority of Congress? This approach might have answered Chief Justice Burger's contention that the Court was "weakening our political process," because the appropriate political process for resolving matters relating to aliens is the one at the national level, not the ones in the individual states. But there would also be problems with this approach. For example, if the Court had taken such an approach, would Congress then have had authority to withhold federal education funds from states that permit children of undocumented aliens to attend public school? If so, would that conclusion be consistent with the Court's frequent assertion that "[e]qual protection analysis in the Fifth Amendment area is the same as that under the Fourteenth Amendment"? *Buckley v. Valeo*, 424 U.S. 1 (1976).

> **Make the Connection**
>
> We considered the application of the equal protection principle to the federal government, and the Court's decision in *Bolling v. Sharpe*, in Chapter 10.

c. Parents and Children

> **Make the Connection**
>
> We considered discrimination on the basis of parents' marital status, and the Court's decision in *Clark v. Jeter*, in Chapter 11.

In treating illegitimate children as a suspect class under the Equal Protection Clause, the Court has reasoned that it is impermissible for a state to punish children for the actions of their parents. Do these cases provide support for the Court's conclusion in *Plyler*? Or would a better analogy be the state's presumed authority to deny welfare benefits to families—including families with children—as a result of the illegal actions of the parents? Cf. *Dandridge v. Williams*.

C. Access to the Courts

Dandridge and *Rodriguez* seem to stand for the proposition that wealth is not a suspect basis for classification under the Equal Protection Clause. Yet *Harper*, which we considered earlier in this Chapter, held that the state cannot condition the right to vote on the payment of a poll tax, because wealth "as a measure of a voter's qualifications" is "a capricious or irrelevant factor." The following case addresses whether a state can condition the availability of a civil appeal on the appellant's advance payment of costs. As you read the case, consider whether it is about wealth classifications, access to court, or instead something else.

M. L. B. v. S. L. J.

519 U.S. 102 (1996)

Justice GINSBURG delivered the opinion of the Court.

Petitioner M. L. B. and respondent S. L. J. are, respectively, the [unmarried] biological mother and father of two children. [After S. L. J. married respondent J. P. J., they] filed suit in Chancery Court in Mississippi, seeking to terminate the parental rights of M. L. B. and to gain court approval for adoption of the children by their stepmother, J. P. J. [T]he Chancellor [terminated] all parental rights of the natural mother [and] approved the adoption. *** Mississippi grants civil litigants a right to appeal, but conditions that right on prepayment of costs. *** Unable to pay $2,352.36, M. L. B. sought leave to appeal *in forma pauperis*. The Supreme Court of Mississippi denied her application.

> **Definition**
>
> *In forma pauperis* means "in the manner of a pauper" and describes the permission given to an indigent person to proceed without liability for court fees or costs.

[T]he Court's decisions concerning access to judicial processes reflect both equal protection and due process concerns. The equal protection concern relates to the legitimacy of fencing out would-be appellants based solely on their inability to pay [costs]. The due process concern homes in on the essential fairness of the state-ordered proceedings anterior to adverse state action. *** Nevertheless, "[m]ost decisions in this area [rest] on an equal protection framework," [for] due process does not independently require that the State provide a right to appeal. We place this case within the framework established by our past decisions in this area. In line with those decisions, we inspect the character and intensity of the individual interest at stake, on the one hand, and the State's justification for its exaction, on the other.

[T]he stakes for petitioner M. L. B.—forced dissolution of her parental rights—are large, "more substantial than mere loss of money." *** And the risk of error, Mississippi's experience shows, is considerable. [Mississippi] has, by statute, adopted a "clear and convincing proof" standard for parental status termination cases. Nevertheless, the Chancellor's termination order in this case simply recites statutory language; it describes no evidence, and otherwise details no reasons for finding M. L. B. "clear[ly] and convincing[ly]" unfit to be a parent.

> **Make the Connection**
>
> We considered the Constitution's protections for marriage and family in Chapter 8. If the petitioner's interest is in preserving a familial relationship, then isn't (substantive) Due Process a more appropriate basis for the Court's decision?

Mississippi urges, as the justification for its appeal cost prepayment requirement, the State's legitimate interest in offsetting the costs of its court system. But in the tightly circumscribed category of parental status termination cases, appeals are few, and not likely to impose an undue burden on the State. [W]e do not question the general rule [that] fee requirements ordinarily are examined only for rationality. The State's need for revenue to offset costs, in the mine run of cases, satisfies the rationality requirement. *** But our cases solidly establish two exceptions to that general rule. The basic right to participate in political processes as voters and candidates cannot be limited to those who can pay for a license. [See *Harper v. Virginia Bd. of Elections*, 383 U.S. 663, 664 (1966).] Nor may access to judicial processes in cases criminal or "quasi criminal in nature" turn on ability to pay. [See *Griffin v. Illinois*, 351 U.S. 12, 16 (1956) (invalidating Illinois rule that conditioned appeals from criminal convictions on the defendant's procurement of a transcript of trial proceedings).] [W]e place decrees forever terminating parental rights in the category of cases in which the State may not "bolt the door to equal justice." *** Accordingly, we reverse the judgment of the Supreme Court of Mississippi and remand the case for further proceedings not inconsistent with this opinion.

> **Food for Thought**
>
> Is this a case where the state is actively depriving a person of some important right, or instead a case where the state is simply declining to facilitate (or subsidize) a person's exercise of an important right? That is, does this case involve government action or government inaction? Should anything turn on that characterization?

Justice KENNEDY, concurring in the judgment.

[In my view,] due process is quite a sufficient basis for our holding. I acknowledge the authorities do not hold that an appeal is required, even in a criminal case; but given the existing appellate structure in Mississippi, the realities of the litigation process, and the fundamental interests at stake in this particular proceeding, the State may not erect a bar in the form of transcript and filing costs beyond this petitioner's means.

Justice THOMAS, with whom Justice SCALIA joins, and with whom THE CHIEF JUSTICE joins [in relevant part], dissenting.

If neither [the Due Process or Equal Protection] Clause affords petitioner the right to a free, civil-appeal transcript, I assume that no amalgam of the two does. The majority reaffirms that due process does not require an appeal. *** Due process has never compelled an appeal where, as here, its rigors are satisfied by an adequate hearing.

[W]e have regularly required more of an equal protection claimant than a showing that state action has a harsher effect on him or her than on others. *** I see no principled difference between a facially neutral rule that serves in some cases to prevent persons from availing themselves of state employment, or a state-funded education, or a state-funded abortion—each of which the State may, but is not required to, provide—and a facially neutral rule that prevents a person from taking an appeal that is available only because the State chooses to provide it.

Mississippi's requirement of prepaid transcripts in civil appeals seeking to contest the sufficiency of the evidence adduced at trial is facially neutral; it creates no classification. The transcript rule reasonably obliges would-be appellants to bear the costs of availing themselves of a service that the State chooses, but is not constitutionally required, to provide. Any adverse impact that the transcript requirement has on any person seeking to appeal arises not out of the State's action, but out of factors entirely unrelated to it.

> **Food for Thought**
>
> Anatole France, a French writer, once quipped, "The law, in its majestic equality, forbids the rich as well as the poor to sleep under bridges, to beg in the streets, and to steal bread." Is that the sense in which the state's rule here is "facially neutral"? Is there a sense in which it is not neutral at all?

Points for Discussion

a. Due Process v. Equal Protection

Does the Court base its decision on the Equal Protection Clause or the Due Process Clause? What if the underlying litigation had concerned a run-of-the-mill tort claim and the party who lost at trial was unable to appeal because of a cost-prepayment requirement? Would there be a constitutional problem then? If so, why? See *Pennzoil Co. v. Texaco, Inc.*, 481 U.S. 1, 7 & n. 6 (1987) (describing, but abstaining from deciding, a Due Process claim by oil giant Texaco that alleged that the company was effectively barred from appealing a massive tort judgment because the Texas courts would not stay the execution of a judgment lien, pending Texaco's appeal, unless Texaco secured a $13 billion bond).

b. Wealth and Access to the Courts

As we saw above, the Court in *Dandridge* and *Rodriguez* effectively held that the poor are not a suspect class, or at least that wealth classifications ordinarily will not receive strict scrutiny. Is *M.L.B.* consistent with *Dandridge* and *Rodriguez*?

Executive Summary of this Chapter

As we saw in Chapter 8, the Court sometimes relies on the Due Process Clause to identify and protect "fundamental rights." The Court also sometimes relies on the Equal Protection Clause to assess the constitutionality of regulations that selectively affect the exercise of important or fundamental rights.

Because the **right to vote** is "fundamental," a state violates the Equal Protection Clause when it denies the right to vote on the basis of wealth or the voter's failure to pay a poll tax. *Harper v. Virginia State Board of Elections* (1966). The Equal Protection Clause might also require uniform standards for counting votes during recounts. *Bush v. Gore* (2000).

The Equal Protection Clause requires electoral districts at the local, state, and federal level to be apportioned based on the principle of **one person, one vote**. *Reynolds v. Sims* (1964). A majority of the Court currently appears to hold the view that claims that district lines have been drawn solely for the sake of partisan advantage—that is, claims of **political gerrymandering**—are justiciable, but the Justices disagree about what standard the Equal Protection Clause requires the Court to apply to such claims. *Vieth v. Jubelirer* (2004).

A state does not violate the Equal Protection Clause when it limits the amount of welfare benefits that a large family may receive. *Dandridge v. Williams* (1970). Nor does a state violate the Equal Protection Clause when it creates a scheme that results in substantially less funding for poorer school districts than for wealthier school districts. *San Antonio Independent School District v. Rodriguez* (1973). These cases suggest that **classifications on the basis of wealth** are subject only to rational-basis review, and that there is no fundamental right to welfare or a free public school education.

A state does, however, violate the Equal Protection Clause when it denies a free public school education to undocumented children. *Plyler v. Doe* (1982). And a state violates the Equal Protection Clause when it conditions an indigent person's right to appeal an order terminating her parental rights on her ability to pre-pay the costs of the appeal. *M. L. B. v. S. L. J.* (1996).

PART VIII: LEGISLATIVE PROTECTION OF INDIVIDUAL RIGHTS

In Chapter 3, we considered Congress's affirmative powers under Article I of the Constitution. We paid particularly close attention to the power to regulate interstate commerce, the power to spend for the general welfare, and the power to tax. In addition, we saw that Congress has power under the Necessary and Proper Clause to select the means for carrying into execution not only the affirmative powers granted to Congress, but also "all other Powers vested by this Constitution in the Government of the United States, or in any Department or Officer thereof." In considering the scope of these powers, the principal question was whether particular constructions of the provisions granting those powers impermissibly encroached on the powers of the states; the limits on Congress's power, in other words, were a function of federalism.

In the last several Chapters, however, we have seen how the Constitution, through its rights-granting provisions, limits not only the power of the federal government but also the power of the state governments. Indeed, the Fourteenth Amendment, which has been our principal focus in the last six Chapters, is an express limitation on the power of the states; it prohibits states from abridging the privileges or immunities of citizens of the United States, depriving any person of life, liberty, or property without due process of law, or denying equal protection of the laws. At the same time that it limits the powers of the states, the Fourteenth Amendment (in Section 5) confers on Congress the power "to enforce, by appropriate legislation, the provisions of this article."

In a very important sense, therefore, the Fourteenth Amendment—and, indeed, the Thirteenth and Fifteenth Amendments, the other two "Reconstruction Amendments"—are about federalism, as well. But the balance that the Reconstruction Amendments contemplate between state and federal authority appears to be quite different from the balance created in 1789. In many respects this is unsurprising, particularly when one considers the historical background of the Amendments. The Thirteenth Amendment, which abolished slavery, was a sharp rebuke of the choice of Southern states before the Civil War to permit slavery. The Fourteenth Amendment was ratified three years after the Thirteenth, after it had become clear that the formal abolition of slavery had not stopped the former slave states from using legal means to subjugate Americans of African descent. And the Fifteenth Amendment was ratified two years after the Fourteenth, to prohibit those states from continuing to exclude former slaves from the political process to which they should have been welcomed upon the abolition of slavery. All three of the Reconstruction Amendments also authorized Congress to enforce their substantive provisions by "appropriate legislation." Viewed in

> **Definition**
>
> The "Reconstruction Amendments" acquired their name because they were adopted during the Reconstruction Era, in which the Union was reconstituted after the Civil War.

this context, it seems plain that the Reconstruction Amendments worked a significant change in the relationship between the states and the federal government.

But just how significant a change was it? Is Congress's power under those Amendments plenary, notwithstanding the limits imposed on its powers by the original provisions of the Constitution? Does the Tenth Amendment modify the Reconstruction Amendments, serving as a rule of construction that makes clear that Congress shall have only those powers necessary to enforce the Amendments' substantive provisions? Or, conversely, do the Reconstruction Amendments modify the Tenth, effectively legitimating the vast expansion of federal power that the Court permitted in the middle of the twentieth century? And can Congress, acting pursuant to its power to enforce the Reconstruction Amendments, effectively define new rights and provide them with legislative protection? Or is the notion of "appropriate" enforcement legislation limited by the Court's interpretation of the rights protected by the substantive provisions of the Amendments? As we will see, these last two questions are as much about the separation of powers as they are about federalism. Indeed, although our consideration of the Reconstruction Amendments thus far has been principally about individual rights rather than structural arrangements, federalism and the separation of powers will never be far from the surface in our discussion here of Congress's power under those Amendments.

> **Make the Connection**
>
> Recall that the Court in the *Slaughter-House Cases*, which we considered in Chapter 7, interpreted the Privileges or Immunities Clause of the Fourteenth Amendment narrowly, effectively concluding that the Amendment did not work a significant change in the balance between state and federal power. Keep that view in mind as you explore the materials in this Part.

CHAPTER 13

Congress's Power to Enforce the Reconstruction Amendments

A. The Thirteenth Amendment

On January 1, 1863, President Lincoln issued the Emancipation Proclamation, an executive order that famously declared that "all persons held as slaves" in the states engaged in "rebellion against the United States" were "thenceforward [and] forever free." The Proclamation, however, did not fully accomplish the objective of ending slavery. First, there was some doubt as to the legal validity of the order, issued unilaterally by the President pursuant to his authority as Commander in Chief, and by its terms applying only to states that did not (at the time) recognize the authority of the United States. Second, the Proclamation applied only to those slave states that were engaged in rebellion against the United States, and thus did not provide protection to slaves in the border slave states that had remained loyal to the United States or in states that had seceded but had since been brought under Union control. Third, the Confederate States ignored the Proclamation during the war, and even after the war had ended, the former slave states enacted so-called "Black Codes," which imposed severe restrictions on the former slaves' freedom, thereby creating a new legal institution nearly tantamount to slavery.

In response, Congress enacted, and the states ratified, the Thirteenth Amendment to abolish formally and finally the institution of slavery and its equivalents. The southern states were required to ratify it as a condition of re-entry to the Union.

U.S. Constitution, <u>Amendment XIII</u>

Section 1. Neither slavery nor involuntary servitude, except as a punishment for crime whereof the party shall have been duly convicted, shall exist within the United States, or any place subject to their jurisdiction.

Section 2. Congress shall have power to enforce this article by appropriate legislation.

The Thirteenth Amendment is the only provision in the Constitution (with the possible exception of the Treason Clause in Article III, § 3) that regulates private, as opposed to governmental, conduct. It does not merely forbid state legal regimes that tolerate slavery, but also any form of slavery or involuntary servitude—which "shall not exist within the United States."

At the time of its ratification, the Thirteenth Amendment was unique for another reason: it was the first provision added since the ratification of the original document that expressly conferred a new power on Congress. Note that Section 2 of the Amendment authorizes Congress to "enforce" Section 1 of the Amendment "by appropriate legislation." Because Section 1 of the Amendment prohibits private action, Congress presumably has at least some authority under Section 2 to regulate some forms of private action. What limits are there on the scope of that power?

In 1866, shortly after the ratification of the Thirteenth Amendment, Congress enacted the Civil Rights Act over the veto of President Andrew Johnson, who asserted that the Act was unconstitutional. The next case, decided more than 100 years after the enactment of that law, raised the question of the scope of Congress's power under Section 2 of the Thirteenth Amendment.

Jones v. Alfred H. Mayer Co.

392 U.S. 409 (1968)

Mr. Justice STEWART delivered the opinion of the Court.

In this case we are called upon to determine the scope and constitutionality of [part of the Civil Rights Act of 1866,] 42 U.S.C. § 1982, which provides that: "All citizens of the United States shall have the same right, in every State and Territory, as is enjoyed by white citizens thereof to inherit, purchase, lease, sell, hold, and convey real and personal property." [T]he petitioners [alleged] that the respondents had refused to sell them a home [for] the sole reason that petitioner Joseph Lee Jones is a Negro. Relying in part upon § 1982, the petitioners sought injunctive and other relief. The District Court sustained the respondents' motion to dismiss the complaint, and the Court of Appeals for the Eighth Circuit affirmed, concluding that § 1982 applies only to state action and does not reach private refusals to sell.

[The right to purchase and lease property] can be impaired as effectively by "those who place property on the market" as by the State itself. *** So long as a Negro citizen who wants to buy or rent a home can be turned away simply because he is not white, he cannot be said to enjoy "the same right [as] is enjoyed by white citizens [to] purchase [and] lease [real] and personal property." On its face, therefore, § 1982 appears to prohibit all discrimination against Negroes in the sale or rental of property—discrimination by private owners as well as discrimination by public authorities. [Our] examination of the relevant history [persuades] us that Congress meant exactly what it said.

The remaining question is whether Congress has power under the Constitution to *** prohibit all racial discrimination, private and public, in the sale and rental of property. Our starting point is the Thirteenth Amendment, for it was pursuant to that constitutional provision that Congress originally enacted what is now § 1982. *** As its text reveals, the Thirteenth Amendment "is not a mere prohibition of state laws establishing or upholding slavery, but an absolute declaration that slavery or involuntary servitude shall not exist in any part of the United States." *Civil Rights Cases,* 109 U.S. 3, 20 (1883). It has never been doubted, therefore, "that the power vested in Congress to enforce the article by appropriate legislation" [includes] the power to enact laws "direct and primary, operating upon the acts of individuals, whether sanctioned by state legislation or not."

If Congress has power under the Thirteenth Amendment to eradicate conditions that prevent Negroes from buying and renting property because of their race or color, then no federal statute calculated to achieve that objective can be thought to exceed the constitutional power of Congress simply because it reaches beyond state action to regulate the conduct of private individuals. The constitutional question in this case, therefore, comes to this: Does the authority of Congress to enforce the Thirteenth Amendment "by appropriate legislation" include the power to eliminate all racial barriers to the acquisition of real and personal property? We think the answer to that question is plainly yes.

"By its own unaided force and effect," the Thirteenth Amendment "abolished slavery, and established universal freedom." Whether or not the Amendment itself did any more than that—a question not involved in this case—it is at least clear that the Enabling Clause of that Amendment empowered Congress to do much more. For that clause clothed "Congress with power to pass *all laws necessary and proper for abolishing all badges and incidents of slavery in the United States.*" *Civil Rights Cases,* 109 U.S. at 20. *** Surely Congress has the power under the Thirteenth Amendment rationally to determine what are the badges and the incidents of slavery, and the authority to translate that determination into effective legislation. Nor can we say that the determination Congress has made is an irrational one. For this Court recognized long ago that, whatever else they may have encompassed, the badges and incidents of slavery—its "burdens and disabilities"—included restraints upon "those fundamental rights which are the essence of civil freedom, namely, the same right [to] inherit, purchase, lease, sell and convey property, as is enjoyed by white citizens." [*Civil Rights Cases.*] Just as the Black Codes, enacted after the Civil War to restrict the free exercise of those rights, were substitutes for the slave system,

> **Definition**
>
> The Court uses the term "badges and incidents of slavery" to capture the important idea that slavery was not merely a system in which slaves were owned as property. On the contrary, slaves lacked almost all civil and political rights enjoyed by non-slaves. They could not make contracts, marry, seek paid employment, and so forth. All of these disabilities are badges and incidents of slavery.

so the exclusion of Negroes from white communities became a substitute for the Black Codes. And when racial discrimination herds men into ghettos and makes their ability to buy property turn on the color of their skin, then it too is a relic of slavery.

Negro citizens, North and South, who saw in the Thirteenth Amendment a promise of freedom—freedom to "go and come at pleasure" and to "buy and sell when they please"—would be left with "a mere paper guarantee" if Congress were powerless to assure that a dollar in the hands of a Negro will purchase the same thing as a dollar in the hands of a white man. At the very least, the freedom that Congress is empowered to secure under the Thirteenth Amendment includes the freedom to buy whatever a white man can buy, the right to live wherever a white man can live. If Congress cannot say that being a free man means at least this much, then the Thirteenth Amendment made a promise the Nation cannot keep. [Reversed.]

[Justice DOUGLAS's concurring opinion is omitted.]

Mr. Justice HARLAN, whom Mr. Justice WHITE joins, dissenting.

I believe that the Court's construction of § 1982 as applying to purely private action is almost surely wrong, and at the least is open to serious doubt. The [issue] of the constitutionality of § 1982, as construed by the Court, [also presents] formidable difficulties. Moreover, the political processes of our own era have, since the date of oral argument in this case, given birth to [the Civil Rights Act of 1968, which contains] "fair housing" provisions which would at the end of this year make available to others, though apparently not to the petitioners themselves, the type of relief which the petitioners now seek. It seems to me that this latter factor so diminishes the public importance of this case that by far the wisest course would be for this Court to refrain from decision and to dismiss the writ as improvidently granted.

> **FYI**
>
> In 1865, all of the Southern former slave states adopted "Black Codes" that severely limited the civil, social, and political rights of former slaves. Among other things, the Codes typically defined the types of employment that blacks could hold and the terms under which they could hold their jobs, restrictions so severe in many cases that they amounted to a form of de facto slavery. Blacks were also denied the vote. In response to the Codes, Congress placed the South under military rule in 1866 to enforce "Reconstruction" and proposed the Fourteenth Amendment. For more information about the Black Codes and the reconstruction era, read Chapter 7 of the U.S. State Department's online Outline of U.S. History.

> **Take Note**
>
> Justice Harlan seems implicitly to suggest here that the Civil Rights Act of 1968's regulation of private housing arrangements was within Congress's authority to enact. If that is true—either under Section 2 of the Thirteenth Amendment or the Commerce Clause—then why isn't § 1982, as well?

Points for Discussion

a. The Thirteenth Amendment and Civil Rights Legislation

The Court concludes that Congress's power to enforce the Thirteenth Amendment includes the authority to eliminate the "badges and incident of slavery," which includes the power to enact civil rights legislation regulating certain types of private conduct. Recall that the Court held that provisions of the Civil Rights Act of 1964 that applied to private conduct were valid exercises of Congress's authority under the Commerce Clause. After *Jones*, isn't Section 2 of the Thirteenth Amendment a sufficient basis for all such legislation?

> **Make the Connection**
>
> We considered *Heart of Atlanta Motel* and *McClung*, and Congress's power under the Commerce Clause to enact the Civil Rights Act of 1964, in Chapter 3.

b. The Thirteenth Amendment and Protected Groups

Conversely, in discussing the "Black Codes" and pervasive discrimination against blacks in the mid-twentieth century, does *Jones* suggest that Congress's power to enforce the Thirteenth Amendment is considerably less robust when what is at issue is discrimination against persons other than African Americans? Section 1 of the Amendment plainly prohibits slavery, regardless of the race of the servant and the master. See *Slaughter-House Cases*, 83 U.S. 36, 72 (1872) ("Undoubtedly while negro slavery alone was in the mind of the Congress which proposed the thirteenth article, it forbids any other kind of slavery, now or hereafter."). But is the scope of *Congress's* power under *Section 2* broader when providing remedies for discrimination against African Americans due to their prior condition of servitude?

B. The Fourteenth and Fifteenth Amendments

President Johnson's veto of the Civil Rights Act of 1866 reflected concerns over the scope of Congress's power to enforce the Thirteenth Amendment. In response, Congress proposed the Fourteenth Amendment in June 1866, and it achieved the requisite number of state ratifications two years later. As we have seen in some detail, the Fourteenth Amendment included the Privileges or Immunities, Due Process, and Equal Protection Clauses. In addition, in February 1869, Congress passed the Fifteenth Amendment, which would prohibit denying or abridging the right to vote on the basis of race, and it reached the requisite number of state ratifications one year later. As did the Thirteenth Amendment, both Amendments expressly authorized Congress to enforce their substantive provisions.

> ### U.S. Constitution, <u>Amendment XIV</u>
>
> Section 5. The Congress shall have the power to enforce, by appropriate legislation, the provisions of this article.
>
> ### U.S. Constitution, <u>Amendment XV</u>
>
> Section 1. The right of citizens of the United States to vote shall not be denied or abridged by the United States or by any State on account of race, color, or previous condition of servitude.
>
> Section 2. The Congress shall have the power to enforce this article by appropriate legislation.

Unlike the Thirteenth Amendment, however, the Fourteenth and Fifteenth Amendments appear to address their substantive limitations only to the states. Indeed, the Court held shortly after the ratification of the Fourteenth Amendment that its provisions limit only state, and not private, action. (Accordingly, the Fourteenth Amendment does not prohibit, for example, a private employer from refusing to hire a person solely because of her race, although state and federal laws generally do prohibit such conduct.) Although (as some of the cases in Chapter 19 will make clear) the "state action doctrine" is controversial, it has important implications for the scope of Congress's power under the Fourteenth and Fifteenth Amendments. If those Amendments do not prohibit private action, can Congress invoke its power to enforce those Amendments to regulate private action?

> **Make the Connection**
>
> We will consider the Court's decision in the *Civil Rights Cases*, 109 U.S. 3, 20 (1883), and the state-action requirement, in Chapter 19.

United States v. Guest

383 U.S. 745 (1966)

Mr. Justice STEWART delivered the opinion of the Court.

The six defendants in this case were indicted by a United States grand jury in the Middle District of Georgia for criminal conspiracy in violation of 18 U.S.C. § 241 (1964 ed.), [which makes it a crime for "two or more persons [to] conspire to injure, oppress, threaten, or intimidate any citizen in the free exercise or enjoyment of any right or privilege secured to him by the Constitution or laws of the United States, or because of his having so exercised the same." Defendants were indicted for conspiring to deprive blacks of the right to use public state-owned and state-operated facilities in Athens, Georgia. The district court dismissed the indictment.]

[T]he indictment in the present case names no person alleged to have acted in any way under the color of state law. *** It is a commonplace that rights under the Equal Protection Clause itself arise only where there has been involvement of the State or of one acting under the color of its authority.

This is not to say, however, that the involvement of the State need be either exclusive or direct. In a variety of situations the Court has found state action of a nature sufficient to create rights under the Equal Protection Clause even though the participation of the State was peripheral, or its action was only one of several co-operative forces leading to the constitutional violation. See, e.g., *Shelley v. Kraemer*, 334 U.S. 1 (1948). This case, however, requires no determination of the threshold level that state action must attain in order to create rights under the Equal Protection Clause. This is so because, contrary to the argument of the litigants, the indictment in fact contains an express allegation of state involvement sufficient at least to require the denial of a motion to dismiss. One of the means of accomplishing the object of the conspiracy, according to the indictment, was "By causing the arrest of Negroes by means of false reports that such Negroes had committed criminal acts." [T]he allegation is broad enough to cover a charge of active connivance by agents of the State in the making of the "false reports," or other conduct amounting to official discrimination clearly sufficient to constitute denial of rights protected by the Equal Protection Clause. Although it is possible that a bill of particulars, or the proof if the case goes to trial, would disclose no co-operative action of that kind by officials of the State, the allegation is enough to prevent dismissal of this branch of the indictment. [Reversed and remanded.]

> **Make the Connection**
>
> We will discuss the Court's decision in *Shelley* in Chapter 19.

Mr. Justice CLARK, with whom Mr. Justice BLACK and Mr. Justice FORTAS join, concurring.

The Court's interpretation of the indictment clearly avoids the question whether Congress, by appropriate legislation, has the power to punish private conspiracies that interfere with Fourteenth Amendment rights, such as the right to utilize public facilities. [I]t is, I believe, both appropriate and necessary under the circumstances here to say that there now can be no doubt that the specific language of § 5 empowers the Congress to enact laws punishing all conspiracies—with or without state action—that interfere with Fourteenth Amendment rights.

Mr. Justice HARLAN, concurring in part and dissenting in part.

As a general proposition it seems to me very dubious that the Constitution was intended to create certain rights of private individuals as against other private individuals. The Constitutional Convention was called to establish a nation, not to reform the common law. Even the Bill of Rights, designed to protect personal liberties, was directed at rights against governmental authority, not other individuals. *** I would sustain this aspect of the indictment only on the premise that it sufficiently alleges state interference with [constitutional rights], and on no other ground.

Mr. Justice BRENNAN, with whom THE CHIEF JUSTICE and Mr. Justice DOUGLAS join, concurring in part and dissenting in part.

I do not agree [that] a conspiracy to interfere with the exercise of the right to equal utilization of state facilities is not, within the meaning of § 241, a conspiracy to interfere with the exercise of a "right [secured] by the Constitution" unless discriminatory conduct by state officers is involved in the alleged conspiracy. *** I believe that § 241 reaches [the private conspiracy alleged in the indictment], not because the Fourteenth Amendment of its own force prohibits such a conspiracy, but because § 241, as an exercise of congressional power under § 5 of that Amendment, prohibits *all* conspiracies to interfere with the exercise of a "right [secured] by the Constitution." [T]he right to use state facilities without discrimination on the basis of race is, within the meaning of § 241, a right created by, arising under and dependent upon the Fourteenth Amendment and hence is a right "secured" by that Amendment. ***

My view as to the scope of § 241 requires that I reach the question of constitutional power—whether § 241 or legislation indubitably designed to punish entirely private conspiracies to interfere with the exercise of Fourteenth Amendment rights constitutes a permissible exercise of the power granted to Congress by § 5 ***. A majority of the members of the Court expresses the view today that § 5 empowers Congress to enact laws punishing *all* conspiracies to interfere with the exercise of Fourteenth Amendment rights, whether or not state officers or others acting under the color of state law are implicated in the conspiracy. Although the Fourteenth Amendment itself, according to established doctrine, "speaks to the State or to those acting under the color of its authority," [§ 5] authorizes Congress to make laws that it concludes are reasonably necessary to protect a right created by and arising under that Amendment; and Congress is thus fully empowered to determine that punishment of private conspiracies interfering with the exercise of such a right is necessary to its full protection.

> **Take Note**
>
> Justice Brennan states that a majority of the Court agrees that Section 5 of the Fourteenth Amendment empowers Congress to punish private, as opposed to state, action. (Two other Justices joined Justice Clark's concurring opinion to that effect.) After the Court's decision in *Guest*, must the government, in a prosecution under 18 U.S.C. § 241, prove state involvement in the conspiracy?

Viewed in its proper perspective, § 5 of the Fourteenth Amendment appears as a positive grant of legislative power, authorizing Congress to exercise its discretion in fashioning remedies to achieve civil and political equality for all citizens. No one would deny that Congress could enact legislation directing state officials to provide Negroes with equal access to state schools, parks and other facilities owned or operated by the State. Nor could it be denied that Congress has the power to punish state officers who, in excess of their authority and in violation of state law, conspire to threaten, harass and murder Negroes for attempting to use these facilities. And I can find no principle of federalism nor word of the Constitution that denies Congress power to determine that in order adequately to protect the right to equal utilization of state facilities, it is also appropriate to punish other individuals—not state officers themselves and not acting in concert with state officers—who engage in the same brutal conduct for the same misguided purpose.

Points for Discussion

a. The Fourteenth Amendment and Private Conduct

As noted above (and explored in more detail in Chapter 19), the *Civil Rights Cases* held that Section 1 of the Fourteenth Amendment limits only state, as opposed to private, action. Assuming that the Court in that case properly interpreted the Fourteenth Amendment, does it follow that Congress cannot regulate purely private conduct pursuant to its authority to "enforce" Section 1 by "appropriate" legislation? Did the Court resolve that question in *Guest*? We will revisit this question later in this Chapter, when we consider the Court's decision in *United States v. Morrison*.

b. Other Sources of Authority

Would Congress's power to enforce the Thirteenth Amendment, which (we saw above) does apply to private action, be sufficient to prohibit private conspiracies of the type at issue in *Guest*, even if Congress lacks such power under Section 5 of the Fourteenth Amendment? How would 18 U.S.C. § 241 fare under the Court's approach in *Jones*?

The Thirteenth and Fourteenth Amendments are not the only conceivable sources of congressional authority to regulate private action to deprive individuals of constitutional rights. Recall that Congress enacted the Civil Rights Act of 1964 pursuant to its authority to regulate interstate commerce, and the Court upheld that assertion of authority in *Heart of Atlanta* and *McClung*.

Make the Connection

Recall that at least two Justices in *Heart of Atlanta* and *McClung* would have held that Congress had power to enact the provisions of the Civil Rights Act of 1964 that applied to places of public accommodations pursuant to its authority to enforce the Fourteenth Amendment. As you read the cases that follow, consider whether that view has prevailed.

Whatever limits exist on the scope of Congress's power to regulate *private* conduct pursuant to Section 5 of the Fourteenth Amendment, it clearly has power to create remedies for actual *state* violations of the substantive provisions of the Amendment. As the following case suggests, moreover, the Court has interpreted the enforcement provision of the Fifteenth Amendment in the same fashion that it has interpreted the analogous provision of the Fourteenth Amendment. What limits, if any, does the Constitution impose on Congress's power to regulate state action pursuant to those sources of authority?

South Carolina v. Katzenbach

383 U.S. 301 (1966)

Mr. Chief Justice WARREN delivered the opinion of the Court.

South Carolina [seeks] a declaration that selected provisions of the Voting Rights Act of 1965 violate the Federal Constitution. *** The Voting Rights Act was designed by Congress to banish the blight of racial discrimination in voting, which has infected the electoral process in parts of our country for nearly a century. *** Congress assumed the power to prescribe these remedies from § 2 of the Fifteenth Amendment, which authorizes the National Legislature to effectuate by "appropriate" measures the constitutional prohibition against racial discrimination in voting. We hold that the sections of the Act which are properly before us are an appropriate means for carrying out Congress' constitutional responsibilities and are consonant with all other provisions of the Constitution.

Before enacting the measure, Congress explored with great care the problem of racial discrimination in voting. The House and Senate Committees on the Judiciary each held hearings for nine days and received testimony from a total of 67 witnesses. *** Two points emerge vividly from the voluminous legislative history of the Act contained in the committee hearings and floor debates. First: Congress felt itself confronted by an insidious and pervasive evil which had been perpetuated in certain parts of our country through unremitting and ingenious defiance of the Constitution. Second: Congress concluded that the unsuccessful remedies which it had prescribed in the past would have to be replaced by sterner and more elaborate measures in order to satisfy the clear commands of the Fifteenth Amendment.

[B]eginning in 1890, the States of Alabama, Georgia, Louisiana, Mississippi, North Carolina, South Carolina, and Virginia enacted tests still in use which were specifically designed to prevent Negroes from voting. Typically, they made the ability to read and write a registration qualification and also required completion of a registration form. These laws were based on the fact that as of 1890 in each of the named States, more than two-thirds of the adult Negroes were illiterate while less than one-quarter of the adult whites were unable to read or write. At the same time, alternate tests were prescribed in all of the named States to assure that white illiterates would not be deprived of the franchise. These included grandfather clauses, property qualifications, "good character" tests, and the requirement that registrants "understand" or "interpret" certain matter. [D]iscriminatory application of voting tests [is] now the principal method used to bar Negroes from the polls.

FYI

The obstacles that states imposed to voting as a means of disenfranchising blacks often, if applied neutrally, would have excluded many poor white voters, as well. "Grandfather clauses" exempted voters from these obstacles to voting if their grandfathers had voted. Because blacks (but not whites) were wholly disenfranchised two generations before the imposition of these tests, the grandfather clauses permitted poor whites to vote but not blacks.

The heart of the [Voting Rights Act] is a complex scheme of stringent remedies aimed at areas where voting discrimination has been most flagrant. [Among other things, the Act created a formula defining the states and political subdivisions—mainly places with a history of voting discrimination—to which these new remedies would apply; suspended literacy tests and similar voting qualifications for a period of five years; suspended all new voting regulations pending review by federal authorities to determine whether their use would perpetuate voting discrimination; and broadly prohibited, in all jurisdictions, the use of voting rules to abridge exercise of the franchise on racial grounds.]

These provisions of the Voting Rights Act of 1965 are challenged on the fundamental ground that they exceed the powers of Congress and encroach on an area reserved to the States by the Constitution. *** The ground rules for resolving this question are clear. [As] against the reserved powers of the States, Congress may use any rational means to effectuate the constitutional prohibition of racial discrimination in voting. *** The Court [has] echoed [Chief Justice Marshall's language from *McCulloch v. Maryland*] in describing each of the Civil War Amendments: "Whatever legislation is appropriate, that is, adapted to carry out the objects the amendments have in view, whatever tends to enforce submission to the prohibitions they contain, and to secure to all persons the enjoyment of perfect equality of civil rights and the equal protection of the laws against State denial or invasion, if not prohibited, is brought within the domain of congressional power." *Ex parte Virginia*, 100 U.S. 339, 345-346 (1880).

> **Take Note**
>
> The Court declares here that Congress's power to enforce the Fifteenth Amendment authorizes it to prohibit state actions that themselves would not violate Section 1 of the Amendment. Can you articulate why some of the practices prohibited by the Act do not violate the Fifteenth Amendment? Can Congress really be said to "enforce" the Amendment when it prohibits conduct that the Amendment itself permits?

*** We therefore reject South Carolina's argument that Congress may appropriately do no more than to forbid violations of the Fifteenth Amendment in general terms—that the task of fashioning specific remedies or of applying them to particular localities must necessarily be left entirely to the courts.

South Carolina assails the temporary suspension of existing voting qualifications, reciting the rule laid down by *Lassiter v. Northampton County Bd. of Elections*, 360 U.S. 45 (1959), that literacy tests and related devices are not in themselves contrary to the Fifteenth Amendment. In that very case, however, the Court went on to say, "Of course a literacy test, fair on its face, may be employed to perpetuate that discrimination which the Fifteenth Amendment was designed to uproot." *Id.* at 53. The record shows that in most of the States covered by the Act, including South Carolina, various tests and devices have been instituted with the

> **Food for Thought**
>
> Under the Court's view of Congress's enforcement powers, is it necessary that the literacy tests have been adopted for discriminatory purposes or administered in a discriminatory fashion? Under the Court's test, could Congress ban *all* voter-qualification tests, even those adopted for benign and legitimate purposes?

purpose of disenfranchising Negroes, have been framed in such a way as to facilitate this aim, and have been administered in a discriminatory fashion for many years. Under these circumstances, the Fifteenth Amendment has clearly been violated.

The Act suspends literacy tests and similar devices for a period of five years from the last occurrence of substantial voting discrimination. *** Congress knew that continuance of the tests and devices in use at the present time, no matter how fairly administered in the future, would freeze the effect of past discrimination in favor of unqualified white registrants. Congress permissibly rejected the alternative of requiring a complete re-registration of all voters, believing that this would be too harsh on many whites who had enjoyed the franchise for their entire adult lives.

[The provision suspending new voting regulations pending scrutiny by federal authorities] may have been an uncommon exercise of congressional power, as South Carolina contends, but the Court has recognized that exceptional conditions can justify legislative measures not otherwise appropriate. Congress knew that some of the States covered by [the Act] had resorted to the extraordinary stratagem of contriving new rules of various kinds for the sole purpose of perpetuating voting discrimination in the face of adverse federal court decrees. Congress had reason to suppose that these States might try similar maneuvers in the future in order to evade the remedies for voting discrimination contained in the Act itself. Under the compulsion of these unique circumstances, Congress responded in a permissibly decisive manner.

After enduring nearly a century of widespread resistance to the Fifteenth Amendment, Congress has marshalled an array of potent weapons against the evil, with authority in the Attorney General to employ them effectively. We here hold that the portions of the Voting Rights Act properly before us are a valid means for carrying out the commands of the Fifteenth Amendment. Hopefully, millions of non-white Americans will now be able to participate for the first time on an equal basis in the government under which they live.

Mr. Justice BLACK, concurring [in part] and dissenting [in part].

I agree [that Section 2 of the Fifteenth Amendment] unmistakably gives Congress specific power to go further and pass appropriate legislation to protect [the] right to vote against any method of abridgement no matter how subtle. [I think, however, that the provision preventing a covered state from amending] its constitution or laws relating to voting without first trying to persuade the Attorney General of the United States or the Federal District Court for the District of Columbia that the new proposed laws do not have the purpose and will not have the effect of denying the right to vote to citizens on account of their race or color [is unconstitutional.]

[This provision], by providing that some of the States cannot pass state laws or adopt state constitutional amendments without first being compelled to beg federal authorities to approve their policies, so distorts our constitutional structure of government as to render any distinction drawn in the Constitution between state and federal power almost meaningless. One of the most basic premises upon which our structure of government was founded was that the Federal Government was to have certain specific and limited powers and no others, and all other power was to be reserved either "to the States respectively, or to the people." [If these premises] are to mean anything, they mean at least that the States have power to pass laws and amend their constitutions without first sending their officials hundreds of miles away to beg federal authorities to approve them. *** It is inconceivable to me that such a radical degradation of state power was intended in any of the provisions of our Constitution or its Amendments.

The proceedings of the original Constitutional Convention show beyond all doubt that the power to veto or negative state laws was denied Congress. *** The refusal to give Congress this extraordinary power to veto state laws was based on the belief that if such power resided in Congress the States would be helpless to function as effective governments. *** Since that time neither the Fifteenth Amendment nor any other Amendment to the Constitution has given the slightest indication of a purpose to grant Congress the power to veto state laws either by itself or its agents. Nor does any provision in the Constitution endow the federal courts with power to participate with state legislative bodies in determining what state policies shall be enacted into law. *** I would hold [the pre-clearance provision] invalid for the reasons stated above with full confidence that the Attorney General has ample power to give vigorous, expeditious and effective protection to the voting rights of all citizens.

Points for Discussion

a. The Reconstruction Amendments and Federalism

The Voting Rights Act of 1965, of course, is addressed to the issue of discrimination in the grant of the franchise. But South Carolina argued its challenge to the Act largely in the language of federalism. The Fourteenth and Fifteenth Amendments contain express limitations on state authority and expressly confer additional powers upon Congress. How helpful are our understandings of the system of federalism created by the original Constitution in interpreting the Reconstruction Amendments?

Justice Black appeared to assert that the Fifteenth Amendment should be read in light of the Tenth Amendment and principles of federalism. But the Fifteenth Amendment was ratified later in time, after an era in which federalism was thought to give inadequate protection to racial minorities. In light of this fact, would it be more appropriate to read the Tenth Amendment in light of the Fifteenth Amendment? Or does the inclusion of express, new powers in the Thirteenth, Fourteenth, and Fifteenth Amendments suggest an understanding that basic principles of federalism still prevailed and that the states would retain any powers not granted to Congress?

For example, we saw in Chapter 3 that the Court has held that Congress lacks authority to compel the states to enact or administer a federal regulatory program. See *New York v. United States*; *Printz v. United States*. Does the Voting Rights Act violate this principle? If so, does that principle limit Congress's power to enforce the Reconstruction Amendments? Can you think of reasons why it should not?

b. Selective Application

Some of the most stringent provisions of the Voting Rights Act apply only to states that had a history of discrimination in voting. Are there any limits on Congress's ability to apply legal norms to some states but not to others? Is there a risk that a majority of states will "gang up" on a small number of states? Or is the limited geographical application of some provisions of the Act evidence that it is more modest in scope, and thus more "appropriate" remedial legislation?

c. Purpose and Effect

Recall that the Court has held that state action that has a racially discriminatory *effect* is not unconstitutional absent evidence of a discriminatory *purpose*. Under the Court's decision in <u>Katzenbach</u>, does Congress have authority under Section 2 of the Fifteenth Amendment to prohibit practices that were not adopted with a discriminatory purpose but that nevertheless have a discriminatory effect? Can legislation be said to "enforce" the Amendment when it prohibits conduct that is permissible under the substantive provisions of the Amendment?

> **Make the Connection**
>
> We considered discriminatory purpose and effect, and the Court's decision in <u>Washington v. Davis</u>, in Chapter 11.

d. Is the Pre-Clearance Requirement Still Constitutional?

The Court in *Katzenbach* upheld Section 5 of the Voting Rights Act, which requires all changes in election procedures in states where racial discrimination in voting was most pronounced to be pre-cleared by a three-judge federal district court or the Attorney General. Specifically, Section 5 applied to all election changes in states that had used a forbidden test or device in November 1964 and had less than 50% voter registration or turnout in the 1964 Presidential election. Section 5 was designed to ensure that states and localities with a history of discrimination could not change their election procedures to abridge the right to vote on the basis of race. As originally enacted, Section 5 was to remain in effect for only five years, but Congress has extended the provision several times. The formula for determining which states are subject to the pre-clearance requirement has remained the same, but the pertinent date for assessing those criteria has moved from 1964 to 1972. Most recently, in 2006 Congress extended Section 5 for another 25 years. The 2006 extension retained 1972 as the last baseline year for triggering coverage under Section 5.

Does Congress's power to enforce the Fifteenth Amendment authorize it to require pre-clearance *indefinitely* in states that historically discriminated on the basis of race? In *Northwest Austin Municipal Utility District Number One v. Holder*, 129 S.Ct. 2504 (2009), a utility district in Texas, one of the states that is subject to the requirements under Section 5, filed suit seeking relief from the pre-clearance requirement. The Court acknowledged that the "historic accomplishments of the Voting Rights Act are undeniable," but it also noted that "[s]ome of the conditions that we relied upon in upholding this statutory scheme in *Katzenbach* [have] unquestionably improved." The Court continued:

Things have changed in the South. Voter turnout and registration rates now approach parity. Blatantly discriminatory evasions of federal decrees are rare. And minority candidates hold office at unprecedented levels. These improvements are no doubt due in significant part to the Voting Rights Act itself, and stand as a monument to its success. Past success alone, however, is not adequate justification to retain the preclearance requirements. It may be that these improvements are insufficient and that conditions continue to warrant preclearance under the Act. But the Act imposes current burdens and must be justified by current needs.

The Act also differentiates between the States, despite our historic tradition that all the States enjoy "equal sovereignty." Distinctions can be justified in some cases. *** But a departure from the fundamental principle of equal sovereignty requires a showing that a statute's disparate geographic coverage is sufficiently related to the problem that it targets. The evil that § 5 is meant to address may no longer be concentrated in the jurisdictions singled out for preclearance. The statute's coverage formula is based on data that is now more than 35 years old, and there is considerable evidence that it fails to account for current political conditions. For example, the racial gap in voter registration and turnout is lower in the States originally covered by § 5 than it is nationwide.

The Court noted that, in light of these changes, the Act's "preclearance requirements and its coverage formula raise serious constitutional questions." The Court declined to decide whether Section 5 of the Voting Rights Act was unconstitutional, however, because it concluded that a "bailout" provision in Section 5 allowed for the release of the utility district from the pre-clearance requirement. Justice Thomas concurred in the judgment in part and dissented in part, concluding that the "extensive pattern of discrimination that led the Court to previously uphold § 5 as enforcing the Fifteenth Amendment no longer exists." Accordingly, he would have held that the provision "can no longer be justified as an appropriate mechanism for enforcement of the Fifteenth Amendment."

———————————

There is little doubt that the enforcement clauses of the Fourteenth and Fifteenth Amendments empower Congress to create statutory remedies—such as criminal prohibitions or civil claims—for the violation of rights protected by the substantive clauses of those Amendments. Congress, for example, can authorize individuals to sue state officials who have violated their due process or equal protection rights. *See, e.g.,* 42 U.S.C. § 1983. And in *Katzenbach*, the Court suggested that Congress is not limited simply to providing remedies for actual violations of the Amendments. But just how far does Congress's enforcement power reach? Can Congress create remedies for state actions that, in Congress's view, are inconsistent with the values protected by the Amendments, but that the Court has already concluded do not actually violate the Amendments? If so, what is the necessary relationship between the Amendment's protections and Congress's remedy? Consider the cases that follow.

———————————

Katzenbach v. Morgan

384 U.S. 641 (1966)

Mr. Justice BRENNAN delivered the opinion of the Court.

These cases concern the constitutionality of § 4(e) of the Voting Rights Act of 1965. That law [provides] that no person who has successfully completed the sixth primary grade in a public school in, or a private school accredited by, the Commonwealth of Puerto Rico in which the language of instruction was other than English shall be denied the right to vote in any election because of his inability to read or write English. Appellees, registered voters in New York City, brought this suit to challenge the constitutionality of § 4(e) insofar as [it] prohibits the enforcement of the election laws of New York requiring an ability to read and write English as a condition of voting. *** We hold that, in the application challenged in these cases, § 4(e) is a proper exercise of the powers granted to Congress by § 5 of the Fourteenth Amendment ***.

The Attorney General of the State of New York argues that *** § 4(e) cannot be sustained as appropriate legislation to enforce the Equal Protection Clause unless the judiciary decides—even with the guidance of a congressional judgment—that the application of the English literacy requirement prohibited by § 4(e) is forbidden by the Equal Protection Clause itself. We disagree. *** A construction of § 5 that would require a judicial determination that the enforcement of the state law precluded by Congress violated the Amendment, as a condition of sustaining the congressional enactment, would depreciate both congressional resourcefulness and congressional responsibility for implementing the Amendment. It would confine the legislative power in this context to the insignificant role of abrogating only those state laws that the judicial branch was prepared to adjudge unconstitutional, or of merely informing the judgment of the judiciary by particularizing the "majestic generalities" of § 1 of the Amendment.

Thus our task in this case is not to determine whether the New York English literacy requirement as applied to deny the right to vote to a person who successfully completed the sixth grade in a Puerto Rican school violates the Equal Protection Clause. Accordingly, our decision in *Lassiter v. Northampton County Bd. of Election*, 360 U.S. 45 (1959), sustaining the North Carolina English literacy requirement as not in all circumstances prohibited by the first sections of the Fourteenth and Fifteenth Amendments, is inapposite. *Lassiter* did not present the question before us here: Without regard to whether the judiciary would find that the Equal Protection Clause itself nullifies New York's English literacy requirement as so applied, could Congress prohibit the enforcement of the state law by legislating under § 5 of the Fourteenth Amendment? In answering this question, our task is limited to determining whether such legislation is, as required by § 5, appropriate legislation to enforce the Equal Protection Clause.

By including § 5 the draftsmen sought to grant to Congress, by a specific provision applicable to the Fourteenth Amendment, the same broad powers expressed in the Necessary and Proper Clause, Art. I, s 8, cl. 18. The classic formulation of the reach of those powers was established by Chief Justice Marshall in *McCulloch v. Maryland*, 4 Wheat. 316, 421 (1819). *** Correctly viewed, § 5 is a positive grant of legislative power authorizing

Congress to exercise its discretion in determining whether and what legislation is needed to secure the guarantees of the Fourteenth Amendment. We therefore proceed to the consideration whether § 4(e) is "appropriate legislation" to enforce the Equal Protection Clause, that is, under the *McCulloch* standard, whether § 4(e) may be regarded as an enactment to enforce the Equal Protection Clause, whether it is "plainly adapted to that end" and whether it is not prohibited by but is consistent with "the letter and spirit of the constitution."[10]

There can be no doubt that § 4(e) may be regarded as an enactment to enforce the Equal Protection Clause. *** § 4(e) may be viewed as a measure to secure for the Puerto Rican community residing in New York nondiscriminatory treatment by government—both in the imposition of voting qualifications and the provision or administration of governmental services, such as public schools, public housing and law enforcement. Section 4(e) may be readily seen as "plainly adapted" to furthering these aims of the Equal Protection Clause. The practical effect of § 4(e) is to prohibit New York from denying the right to vote to large segments of its Puerto Rican community. *** This enhanced political power will be helpful in gaining nondiscriminatory treatment in public services for the entire Puerto Rican community. *** It was well within congressional authority to say that this need of the Puerto Rican minority for the vote warranted federal intrusion upon any state interests served by the English literacy requirement. It was for Congress, as the branch that made this judgment, to assess and weigh the various conflicting considerations—the risk or pervasiveness of the discrimination in governmental services, the effectiveness of eliminating the state restriction on the right to vote as a means of dealing with the evil, the adequacy or availability of alternative remedies, and the nature and significance of the state interests that would be affected by the nullification of the English literacy requirement as applied to residents who have successfully completed the sixth grade in a Puerto Rican school. It is not for us to review the congressional resolution of these factors. It is enough that we be able to perceive a basis upon which the Congress might resolve the conflict as it did. There plainly was such a basis to support § 4(e) in the application in question in this case.

The result is no different if we confine our inquiry to the question whether § 4(e) was merely legislation aimed at the elimination of an invidious discrimination in establishing voter qualifications. We are told that New York's English literacy requirement originated in the desire to provide an incentive for non-English speaking immigrants to learn the English language and in order to assure the intelligent exercise of the franchise. Yet Congress might well have questioned, in light of the many exemptions provided, and some evidence suggesting that prejudice played a prominent role in the enactment of the requirement, whether these were actually the interests being served. Congress might have also questioned whether denial of a right deemed so precious and fundamental in our society was a necessary or appropriate means of encouraging persons to learn English, or of furthering the goal of an intelligent exercise of the franchise. Finally, Congress might

---

[10] Contrary to the suggestion of the dissent, § 5 does not grant Congress power to exercise discretion in the other direction and to enact "statutes so as in effect to dilute equal protection and due process decisions of this Court." We emphasize that Congress' power under § 5 is limited to adopting measures to enforce the guarantees of the Amendment; § 5 grants Congress no power to restrict, abrogate, or dilute these guarantees. Thus, for example, an enactment authorizing the States to establish racially segregated systems of education would not be—as required by § 5—a measure "to enforce" the Equal Protection Clause since that clause of its own force prohibits such state laws.

well have concluded that as a means of furthering the intelligent exercise of the franchise, an ability to read or understand Spanish is as effective as ability to read English for those to whom Spanish-language newspapers and Spanish-language radio and television programs are available to inform them of election issues and governmental affairs. [It] was Congress' prerogative to weigh these competing considerations. Here again, it is enough that we perceive a basis upon which Congress might predicate a judgment that the application of New York's English literacy requirement *** constituted an invidious discrimination in violation of the Equal Protection Clause.

There remains the question whether the congressional remedies adopted in § 4(e) constitute means which are not prohibited by, but are consistent "with the letter and spirit of the constitution." [Appellees contend that § 4(e)] itself works an invidious discrimination in violation of the Fifth Amendment by prohibiting the enforcement of the English literacy requirement only for those educated in American-flag schools (schools located within United States jurisdiction) in which the language of instruction was other than English, and not for those educated in schools beyond the territorial limits of the United States in which the language of instruction was also other than English. *** Section 4(e) does not restrict or deny the franchise but in effect extends the franchise to persons who otherwise would be denied it by state law. *** [W]e are guided by the familiar [principle] that "reform may take one step at a time, addressing itself to the phase of the problem which seems most acute to the legislative mind." *Williamson v. Lee Optical Co.*, 348 U.S. 483, 489 (1955). *** [T]he congressional choice to limit the relief effected in § 4(e) may, for example, reflect Congress' greater familiarity with the quality of instruction in American-flag schools, a recognition of the unique historic relationship between the Congress and the Commonwealth of Puerto Rico, an awareness of the Federal Government's acceptance of the desirability of the use of Spanish as the language of instruction in Commonwealth schools, and the fact that Congress has fostered policies encouraging migration from the Commonwealth to the States. We have no occasion to determine in this case whether such factors would justify a similar distinction embodied in a voting-qualification law that denied the franchise to persons educated in non-American-flag schools. We hold only that the limitation on relief effected in § 4(e) does not constitute a forbidden discrimination since these factors might well have been the basis for the decision of Congress to go "no farther than it did."

[Justice DOUGLAS's concurring opinion is omitted.]

Mr. Justice HARLAN, whom Mr. Justice STEWART joins, dissenting.

Worthy as its purposes may be thought by many, I do not see how [§ 4(e)] can be sustained except at the sacrifice of fundamentals in the American constitutional system—the separation between the legislative and judicial function and the boundaries between federal and state political authority. *** Although § 5 [of the Fourteenth Amendment] most certainly does give to the Congress wide powers in the field of devising remedial legislation to effectuate the Amendment's prohibition on arbitrary state action, I believe the Court has confused the issue of how much enforcement power Congress possesses under § 5 with the distinct issue of what questions are appropriate for congressional determination and what questions are essentially judicial in nature. When recognized state violations of federal constitutional standards have occurred, Congress is of course empowered by § 5 to take appropriate remedial measures to redress and prevent the wrongs. But it is a judicial question whether the condition with which Congress has thus sought to deal is in truth an infringement of the Constitution, something that is the necessary prerequisite to bringing the § 5 power into play at all.

The question here is not whether the statute is appropriate remedial legislation to cure an established violation of a constitutional command, but whether there has in fact been an infringement of that constitutional command, that is, whether a particular state practice or, as here, a statute is so arbitrary or irrational as to offend the command of the Equal Protection Clause of the Fourteenth Amendment. That question is one for the judicial branch ultimately to determine. Were the rule otherwise, Congress would be able to qualify this Court's constitutional decisions under the Fourteenth and Fifteenth Amendments let alone those under other provisions of the Constitution, by resorting to congressional power under the Necessary and Proper Clause. In view of this Court's holding in *Lassiter* that an English literacy test is a permissible exercise of state supervision over its franchise, I do not think it is open to Congress to limit the effect of that decision as it has undertaken to do by § 4(e). In effect the Court reads § 5 of the Fourteenth Amendment as giving Congress the power to define the substantive scope of the Amendment. If that indeed be the true reach of § 5, then I do not see why Congress should not be able as well to exercise its § 5 "discretion" by enacting statutes so as in effect to dilute equal protection and due process decisions of this Court. In all such cases there is room for reasonable men to differ as to whether or not a denial of equal protection or due process has occurred, and the final decision is one of judgment. Until today this judgment has always been one for the judiciary to resolve.

I do not mean to suggest in what has been said that a legislative judgment of the type incorporated in § 4(e) is without any force whatsoever. *** To the extent "legislative facts" are relevant to a judicial determination, Congress is well equipped to investigate them, and such determinations are of course entitled to due respect. [See *South Carolina v. Katzenbach*; *Heart of Atlanta Motel, Inc. v. United States*, 379 U.S. 241 (1964).] But no such factual data provide a legislative record supporting § 4(e) by way of showing that Spanish-speaking citizens are fully as capable of making informed decisions in a New York election as are English-speaking citizens. Nor was there any showing whatever to support the Court's alternative argument that § 4(e) should be viewed as but a remedial measure designed to cure or assure against unconstitutional discrimination of other varieties *** to which Puerto Rican minorities might be subject in such communities as New York. *** Thus, we have here not a matter of giving deference to a congressional estimate, based on its determination of legislative facts, bearing upon the validity *vel non* of a statute, but rather what can at most be called a legislative announcement that Congress believes a state law to entail an unconstitutional deprivation of equal protection. Although this kind of declaration is of course entitled to the most respectful consideration, coming as it does from a concurrent branch and one that is knowledgeable in matters of popular political participation, I do not believe it lessens our responsibility to decide the fundamental issue of whether in fact the state enactment violates federal constitutional rights.

To hold, on this record, that § 4(e) overrides the New York literacy requirement seems to me tantamount to allowing the Fourteenth Amendment to swallow the State's constitutionally ordained primary authority in this field. For if Congress by what, as here, amounts to mere *ipse dixit* can set that otherwise permissible requirement partially at naught I see no reason why it could not also substitute its judgment for that of the States in other fields of their exclusive primary competence as well.

——————————————

After *Morgan*, can Congress create, define, and protect rights pursuant to its power to enforce the Fourteenth Amendment? The case that follows addresses this question directly.

——————————————

City of Boerne v. Flores

521 U.S. 507 (1997)

Justice KENNEDY delivered the opinion of the Court.

[The Archbishop of San Antonio applied for a building permit for construction to enlarge a church in the parish. City authorities, relying on a historic-preservation ordinance, denied the application. The Archbishop brought suit, relying on the Religious Freedom Restoration Act of 1993 (RFRA), 42 U.S.C. § 2000bb *et seq.* The City contended that the Act exceeded the scope of Congress's power under § 5 of the Fourteenth Amendment.]

Congress enacted RFRA in direct response to the Court's decision in *Employment Div., Dept. of Human Resources of Oregon v. Smith*, 494 U.S. 872 (1990), [which] held that neutral, generally applicable laws may be applied to religious practices even when not supported by a compelling governmental interest. *** RFRA prohibits "[g]overnment" from "substantially burden[ing]" a person's exercise of religion even if the burden results from a rule of general applicability unless the government can demonstrate [that] the burden "(1) is in furtherance of a compelling governmental interest; and (2) is the least restrictive means of furthering that compelling governmental interest."

> **Make the Connection**
>
> The Court's decision in *Smith* was by a narrow 5-4 margin, and it prompted great concern in Congress, which enacted RFRA "to restore the compelling interest test as set forth in [earlier cases] and to guarantee its application in all cases where free exercise of religion is substantially burdened." 42 U.S.C. § 2000bb(b). We will consider the Court's decision in *Smith*, and the First Amendment's protection for the free exercise of religion, in Chapter 17.

Legislation which deters or remedies constitutional violations can fall within the sweep of Congress' enforcement power even if in the process it prohibits conduct which is not itself unconstitutional and intrudes into "legislative spheres of autonomy previously reserved to the States." [See *South Carolina v. Katzenbach,* 383 U.S. 301, 308 (1966); *Katzenbach v. Morgan,* 384 U.S. 641 (1966).] Congress' power under § 5, however, extends only to "enforc[ing]" the provisions of the Fourteenth Amendment. The Court has described this power as "remedial." The design of the Amendment and the text of § 5 are inconsistent with the suggestion that Congress has the power to decree the substance of the Fourteenth Amendment's restrictions on the States. Legislation which alters the meaning of the Free Exercise Clause cannot be said to be enforcing the Clause. Congress does not enforce a constitutional right by changing what the right is.

> **Food for Thought**
>
> Congress acted to protect the free exercise of religion, a constitutional right that is included in the First Amendment. On what theory is Congress acting to enforce the *Fourteenth* Amendment when it seeks to provide protections for a right included in the *First* Amendment?

While the line between measures that remedy or prevent unconstitutional actions and measures that make a substantive change in the governing law is not easy to discern, and Congress must have wide latitude in determining where it lies, the distinction exists and must be observed. There must be a congruence and proportionality between the injury to be prevented or remedied and the means adopted to that end. Lacking such a connection, legislation may become substantive in operation and effect. History and our case law support drawing the distinction, one apparent from the text of the Amendment.

In February [1866], Republican Representative John Bingham of Ohio reported the following draft Amendment to the House of Representatives on behalf of the Joint Committee: "The Congress shall have power to make all laws which shall be necessary and proper to secure to the citizens of each State all privileges and immunities of citizens in the several States, and to all persons in the several States equal protection in the rights of life, liberty, and property." The proposal encountered immediate opposition, which continued through three days of debate. Members of Congress from across the political spectrum criticized the Amendment [on the ground that it] gave Congress too much legislative power at the expense of the existing constitutional structure. *** As a result of these objections, [the] Joint Committee [drafted a revised proposal under which] Congress' power was no longer plenary but remedial. Congress was granted the power to make the substantive constitutional prohibitions against the States effective.

There is language in our opinion in *Katzenbach v. Morgan,* 384 U.S. 641 (1966), which could be interpreted as acknowledging a power in Congress to enact legislation that expands the rights contained in § 1 of the Fourteenth Amendment. This is not a necessary interpretation, however, or even the best one. In *Morgan,* [the Court's] rationales for upholding § 4(e) rested on unconstitutional discrimination by

> **Take Note**
>
> The Court does not address the statements in *Morgan* suggesting that Congress has power to expand the class of protected rights beyond those identified by the Court in interpreting the Fourteenth Amendment. Is the Court effectively overruling *Morgan* without saying so?

New York and Congress' reasonable attempt to combat it.

If Congress could define its own powers by altering the Fourteenth Amendment's meaning, no longer would the Constitution be "superior paramount law, unchangeable by ordinary means." It would be "on a level with ordinary legislative acts, and, like other acts, [alterable] when the legislature shall please to alter it." *Marbury v. Madison,* 1 Cranch, at 177 Under this approach, it is difficult to conceive of a principle that would limit congressional power. Shifting legislative majorities could change the Constitution and effectively circumvent the difficult and detailed amendment process contained in Article V.

Respondent contends that RFRA is a proper exercise of Congress' remedial or preventive power. [He argues that it] prevents and remedies laws which are enacted with the unconstitutional object of targeting religious beliefs and practices. While preventive rules are sometimes appropriate remedial measures, there must be a congruence between the means used and the ends to be achieved. The appropriateness of remedial measures must be considered in light of the evil presented. Strong measures appropriate to address one harm may be an unwarranted response to another, lesser one.

Make the Connection

Although the Court held in *Smith* that neutral, generally applicable laws that burden the free exercise of religion do not violate the First Amendment, it has since made clear that laws that appear neutral on their face but in fact were enacted with the object of burdening particular religious practices must satisfy heightened scrutiny. See *Church of Lukumi Babalu Aye, Inc. v. Hialeah,* 508 U.S. 520, 533 (1993). We will consider these developments in Chapter 17.

A comparison between RFRA and the Voting Rights Act is instructive. In contrast to the record which confronted Congress and the Judiciary in the voting rights cases, RFRA's legislative record lacks examples of modern instances of generally applicable laws passed because of religious bigotry. [T]he emphasis of the hearings was on laws of general applicability which place incidental burdens on religion. *** Congress' concern was with the incidental burdens imposed, not the object or purpose of the legislation.

Regardless of the state of the legislative record, RFRA cannot be considered remedial, preventive legislation, if those terms are to have any meaning. RFRA is so out of proportion to a supposed remedial or preventive object that it cannot be understood as responsive to, or designed to prevent, unconstitutional behavior. It appears, instead, to attempt a substantive change in constitutional protections. Preventive measures prohibiting certain types of laws may be appropriate when there is reason to believe that many of the laws affected by the congressional enactment have a significant likelihood of being unconstitutional. *** RFRA is not so confined. Sweeping coverage ensures its intrusion at every level of government, displacing laws and prohibiting official actions of almost every description and regardless of subject matter. *** Any law is subject to challenge at any time by any individual who alleges a substantial burden on his or her free exercise of religion.

The stringent test RFRA demands of state laws reflects a lack of proportionality or congruence between the means adopted and the legitimate end to be achieved. *** Requiring a State to demonstrate a compelling interest and show that it has adopted the least restrictive means of achieving that interest is the most demanding test known to constitutional law. Laws valid under *Smith* would fall under RFRA without regard to whether they had the object of stifling or punishing free exercise. *** Simply put, RFRA is not designed to identify and counteract state laws likely to be unconstitutional because of their treatment of religion. In most cases, the state laws to which RFRA applies are not ones which will have been motivated by religious bigotry.

When the Court has interpreted the Constitution, it has acted within the province of the Judicial Branch, which embraces the duty to say what the law is. *Marbury* When the political branches of the Government act against the background of a judicial interpretation of the Constitution already issued, it must be understood that in later cases and controversies the Court will treat its precedents with the respect due them under settled principles, including *stare decisis,* and contrary expectations must be disappointed. RFRA was designed to control cases and controversies, such as the one before us; but as the provisions of the federal statute here invoked are beyond congressional authority, it is this Court's precedent, not RFRA, which must control.

[The separate concurring opinions of Justices STEVENS, SCALIA, O'CONNOR, SOUTER, and BREYER, which concerned the validity of the Court's holding in <u>Smith</u>, are omitted.]

Points for Discussion

a. Congruence and Proportionality

The Court emphasized in <u>Flores</u> that Congress has authority under Section 5 of the Fourteenth Amendment to prohibit some conduct that is not actually unconstitutional under the substantive provisions of the Amendment. But when Congress does so, there must be a "congruence and proportionality" between the violation and Congress's remedy. Is this a judicially manageable standard? How should the Court apply that standard? Does it give Congress sufficient guidance? Does it give Congress sufficient leeway to legislate prophylactically to prevent the violation of Fourteenth Amendment rights? Can that standard be reconciled with the Court's reasoning in *Morgan*?

b. Judicial Supremacy Redux?

In enacting RFRA, Congress effectively attempted to overrule a Supreme Court decision. Is the real point of the Court's decision in <u>Flores</u> that Congress simply lacks power to do so, regardless of which source of authority it invokes? Recall our discussion in Chapter 2 of the notion of judicial supremacy, and in particular of the Court's decisions in <u>Cooper v. Aaron</u> and <u>Dickerson v. United States</u>. Whatever one thinks about the general view that the Court's interpretation of the Constitution binds the other branches, is there any reason to argue that matters should be different under the Reconstruction Amendments? Consider the argument that follows.

Perspective and Analysis

[*City of Boerne's*] view of separation of powers *** seeks to exclude Congress from the process of constitutional lawmaking ***. We [propose a different model, under which] (1) Congress does not violate principles of separation of powers when it enacts Section 5 legislation premised on an understanding of the Constitution that differs from the Court's, and (2) Congress's action does not bind the Court, so that the Court remains free to invalidate Section 5 legislation that in the Court's view violates a constitutional principle requiring judicial protection.

Robert C. Post & Reva B. Siegel, *Legislative Constitutionalism and Section Five Power: Policentric Interpretation of the Family and Medical Leave Act*, 112 Yale L.J. 1943, 1946-47 (2003).

In Chapter 3, we considered the case that follows for its discussion of Congress's power under the Commerce Clause. The case involved a challenge to the Violence Against Women Act, 42 U.S.C. § 13981(a), which created a civil right of action for victims of gender-motivated violence against their attackers. In enacting the statute, Congress explicitly relied not only on the Commerce Clause, but also on its "affirmative power [under] section 5 of the Fourteenth Amendment to the Constitution." 42 U.S.C. § 13981(a). The government defended the Act as a valid exercise of that power.

United States v. Morrison

529 U.S. 598 (2000)

Chief Justice REHNQUIST delivered the opinion of the Court.

Petitioners' § 5 argument is founded on an assertion that there is pervasive bias in various state justice systems against victims of gender-motivated violence. This assertion is supported by a voluminous congressional record. Specifically, Congress received evidence that many participants in state justice systems are perpetuating an array of erroneous stereotypes and assumptions. Congress concluded that these discriminatory stereotypes often result in insufficient investigation and prosecution of gender-motivated crime, inappropriate focus on the behavior and credibility of the victims of that crime, and unacceptably lenient punishments for those who are actually convicted of gender-motivated violence. See H.R. Conf. Rep. No. 103-711, at 385-386; S.Rep. No. 103-138, at 38, 41-55; S.Rep. No. 102-197, at 33-35, 41, 43-47. Petitioners contend that this bias denies victims of gender-motivated violence the equal protection of the laws and that Congress therefore acted appropriately in enacting a private civil remedy against the perpetrators of gender-motivated violence to both remedy the States' bias and deter future instances of discrimination in the state courts.

As our cases have established, state-sponsored gender discrimination violates equal protection unless it serves "important governmental objectives and [the] discriminatory means employed" are "substantially related to the achievement of those objectives." *United States v. Virginia,* 518 U.S. 515, 533 (1996). However, the language and purpose of the Fourteenth Amendment place certain limitations on the manner in which Congress may attack discriminatory conduct. These limitations are necessary to prevent the Fourteenth Amendment from obliterating the Framers' carefully crafted balance of power between the States and the National Government. Foremost among these limitations is the time-honored principle that the Fourteenth Amendment, by its very terms, prohibits only state action.

> ### Make the Connection
>
> We discussed the Court's decision in *United States v. Virginia,* and the topic of gender discrimination, in Chapter 11.

Shortly after the Fourteenth Amendment was adopted, we decided two cases interpreting the Amendment's provisions, *United States v. Harris,* 106 U.S. 629 (1883), and the *Civil Rights Cases,* 109 U.S. 3 (1883). In *Harris,* the Court considered a challenge to § 2 of the Civil Rights Act of 1871. That section sought to punish "private persons" for "conspiring to deprive any one of the equal protection of the laws enacted by the State." 106 U.S., at 639. We concluded that this law exceeded Congress' § 5 power because the law was "directed exclusively against the action of private persons, without reference to the laws of the State, or their administration by her officers." *Id.,* at 640. *** We reached a similar conclusion in the *Civil Rights Cases.* In those consolidated cases, we held that the public accommodation provisions of the Civil Rights Act of 1875, which applied to purely private conduct, were beyond the scope of the § 5 enforcement power. 109 U.S., at 11.

> ### Food for Thought
>
> Why does the Court identify the Presidents who appointed the Justices who served on the Court in 1883? The five Presidents were all Republicans, the party that provided most of the support for Reconstruction. Is that fact relevant here? Should the Court consider the partisan identification of the Justices, let alone the partisan identification of the Presidents who appointed them, in deciding whether to adhere to their decisions?

The force of the doctrine of *stare decisis* behind these decisions stems not only from the length of time they have been on the books, but also from the insight attributable to the Members of the Court at that time. Every Member had been appointed by President Lincoln, Grant, Hayes, Garfield, or Arthur—and each of their judicial appointees obviously had intimate knowledge and familiarity with the events surrounding the adoption of the Fourteenth Amendment.

Petitioners [rely] on *United States v. Guest,* 383 U.S. 745 (1966), for the proposition that the rule laid down in the *Civil Rights Cases* is no

longer good law. In *Guest,* the Court reversed the construction of an indictment under 18 U.S.C. § 241, saying in the course of its opinion that "we deal here with issues of statutory construction, not with issues of constitutional power." 383 U.S., at 749. Three Members of the Court, in a separate opinion by Justice Brennan, expressed the view that the *Civil Rights Cases* were wrongly decided, and that Congress could under § 5 prohibit actions by private individuals. Three other Members of the Court, who joined the opinion of the Court, joined a separate opinion by Justice Clark which in two or three sentences stated the conclusion that Congress could "punis[h] all conspiracies—with or without state action— that interfere with Fourteenth Amendment rights." *Id.,* at 762. *** Though [these] Justices saw fit to opine on matters not before the Court in *Guest,* the Court had no occasion to revisit the *Civil Rights Cases* and *Harris,* having determined "the indictment [charging pri-
vate individuals with conspiring to deprive
blacks of equal access to state facilities] in fact
contain[ed] an express allegation of state
involvement." 383 U.S., at 756. *** To accept
petitioners' argument, moreover, one must add
to the three Justices joining Justice Brennan's
reasoned explanation for his belief that the *Civil
Rights Cases* were wrongly decided, the three
Justices joining Justice Clark's opinion who gave
no explanation whatever for their similar view.
This is simply not the way that reasoned constitutional adjudication proceeds.

> **Food for Thought**
>
> In *Guest,* which we considered ear-
> lier in this Chapter, a majority of
> the Justices signed Justice Stewart's
> opinion for the Court on the ques-
> tion of statutory construction. But a
> majority also expressed the view that
> Congress can regulate private con-
> duct pursuant to Section 5. What is
> the precedential value of the separate
> opinions? Does the Court here fairly
> dismiss them?

Petitioners alternatively argue that, unlike the situation in the *Civil Rights Cases,* here there has been gender-based disparate treatment by state authorities, whereas in those cases there was no indication of such state action. [But] prophylactic legislation under § 5 must have a "congruence and proportionality between the injury to be prevented or remedied and the means adopted to that end." *Florida Prepaid Postsecondary Ed. Expense Bd. v. College Savings Bank,* 527 U.S. 627, 639 (1999). Section 13981 is not aimed at proscribing discrimination by officials which the Fourteenth Amendment might not itself proscribe; it is directed not at any State or state actor, but at individuals who have committed criminal acts motivated by gender bias.

In the present cases, for example, § 13981 visits no consequence whatever on any Virginia public official involved in investigating or prosecuting Brzonkala's assault. The section is, therefore, unlike any of the § 5 remedies that we have previously upheld. [See *Katzenbach v. Morgan,* 384 U.S. 641 (1966); *South Carolina v. Katzenbach,* 383 U.S. 301 (1966).] Section 13981 is also different from these previously upheld remedies in that it applies uniformly throughout the Nation. *** By contrast, the § 5 remedy upheld in *Katzenbach v. Morgan* was directed only to the State where the evil found by Congress existed, and in *South Carolina v. Katzenbach,* the remedy was directed only to those States in which Congress found that there had been discrimination. For these reasons, we conclude that Congress' power under § 5 does not extend to the enactment of § 13981.

Justice BREYER, with whom Justice STEVENS joins, and with whom Justice SOUTER and Justice GINSBURG join as to Part I-A, dissenting.

[II]   Given my conclusion [that VAWA is a valid exercise of Congress's power under the Commerce Clause,] I need not consider Congress' authority under § 5 of the Fourteenth Amendment. Nonetheless, I doubt the Court's reasoning rejecting that source of authority. *** The Federal Government's argument [is] that Congress used § 5 to remedy the actions of *state actors,* namely, those States which, through discriminatory design or the discriminatory conduct of their officials, failed to provide adequate (or any) state remedies for women injured by gender-motivated violence—a failure that the States, and Congress, documented in depth. Neither *Harris* nor the *Civil Rights Cases* considered this kind of claim.

The Court responds directly to the relevant "state actor" claim by finding that the present law lacks "congruence and proportionality" to the state discrimination that it purports to remedy [because the law] is not "directed [at] any State or state actor." But why can Congress not provide a remedy against private actors? Those private actors, of course, did not themselves violate the Constitution. But this Court has held that Congress at least sometimes can enact remedial "[l]egislation [that] prohibits conduct which is not itself unconstitutional." *Flores*. The statutory remedy does not in any sense purport to "determine what constitutes a constitutional violation." [*Id.*] It intrudes little upon either States or private parties. It may lead state actors to improve their own remedial systems, primarily through example. It restricts private actors only by imposing liability for private conduct that is, in the main, already forbidden by state law. Why is the remedy "disproportionate"? And given the relation between remedy and violation—the creation of a federal remedy to substitute for constitutionally inadequate state remedies—where is the lack of "congruence"? *** Despite my doubts about the majority's § 5 reasoning, I need not, and do not, answer the § 5 question, which I would leave for more thorough analysis if necessary on another occasion.

Points for Discussion

a. State v. Private Conduct

The Violence Against Women Act authorized the victims of gender-motivated violence (whether male or female) to sue their attackers, even when those attackers were private citizens. Because of the state action doctrine, it is clear that such private attacks, however loathsome, do not violate the Fourteenth Amendment. In light of this fact, how did the plaintiff and the government defend the Act as a valid exercise of Section 5 authority? Was Congress responding to private conduct in creating the civil remedy? Or was it responding to state conduct? If the latter, what was the state conduct at issue? Did that conduct violate the Fourteenth Amendment?

b. State Acts v. State Omissions

> **Make the Connection**
>
> In *DeShaney v. Winnebago County Department of Social Services*, which we considered in Chapter 8 in our consideration of substantive due process, the Court held that the Due Process Clause does not impose an obligation on the states to protect their citizens from private violence. The Court reached a similar conclusion in *Town of Castle Rock v. Gonzales*, which we considered in Chapter 9 in our unit on procedural due process.

The government argued in *Morrison* that the states' failure to protect the victims of gender-motivated violence was a sufficient predicate for the exercise of Congress's Section 5 power. Can government inaction ever violate the Constitution? Even if the government generally has no affirmative constitutional obligation to act to protect individuals, is it possible that a systemic failure to act could itself be motivated by sexist views about the respective roles of men and women? If so, would that constitute a sufficient predicate for at least some remedy under Section 5?

c. Congruence and Proportionality

Under the Court's approach, can a remedy against *private* individuals ever be congruent and proportional to the injury inflicted by *state* actors? Should Congress ever have authority to create such remedies?

If nothing else, the test presumably permits Congress to regulate at least some state action that does not itself violate Section 1 of the Fourteenth Amendment. But how much? In *Tennesse v. Lane*, 541 U.S. 509 (2004), the Court held that Congress had authority under Section 5 to enact Title II of the Americans with Disabilities Act of 1990, 42 U.S.C § 12132, at least insofar as it required reasonable access to courts. That section provides that "no qualified individual with a disability shall, by reason of such disability, be excluded from participation in or be denied the benefits of the services, programs or activities of a public entity, or be subjected to discrimination by any such entity." In his opinion for the Court, Justice Stevens emphasized that the Due Process Clause of the Fourteenth Amendment guarantees a "right of access to the courts," and that Congress had enacted Title II "against a backdrop of pervasive unequal treatment" that led to the exclusion of disabled persons "from courthouses and court proceedings by reason of their disabilities." The Court reasoned that Congress's remedy for this "pattern of exclusion and discrimination"—Title II's requirement of program accessibility—was "congruent and proportional to its object of enforcing the right of access to the courts." The Court noted that the "unequal treatment of disabled persons in the administration of judicial services has a long history, and has persisted despite several legislative efforts to remedy the problem of disability discrimination." In addition, the Court stressed that Title II's remedy was "a limited one," requiring only "reasonable modifications" to existing facilities, a standard that permitted consideration of costs and other factors.

Chief Justice Rehnquist, joined by Justices Kennedy and Thomas, dissented, asserting that there was "nothing in the legislative record or statutory findings to indicate that disabled persons were systematically denied" the right of access to courts. Absent a constitutional violation, he reasoned, Congress could not act pursuant to Section 5 to impose the remedy in Title II. He also objected to the Court's decision to review Title II's constitutionality only as applied to a claim of right of access to the courts, stating that the "effect is to rig the congruence-and-proportionality test by artificially constricting the scope of the statute to closely mirror a recognized constitutional right."

In his separate dissent, Justice Scalia urged the Court to abandon the congruence and proportionality standard. He declared that the standard, "like all such flabby tests, is a standing invitation to judicial arbitrariness and policy-driven decisionmaking." He continued:

> Worse still, it casts this Court in the role of Congress's taskmaster. Under it, the courts (and ultimately this Court) must regularly check Congress's homework to make sure that it has identified sufficient constitutional violations to make its remedy congruent and proportional. As a general matter, we are ill advised to adopt or adhere to constitutional rules that bring us into constant conflict with a coequal branch of Government. And when conflict is unavoidable, we should not come to do battle with the United States Congress armed only with a test ("congruence and proportionality") that has no demonstrable basis in the text of the Constitution and cannot objectively be shown to have been met or failed.

Justice Scalia would have replaced the test with one that clearly prohibits Congress from going "*beyond* the provisions of the Fourteenth Amendment to proscribe, prevent, or 'remedy' conduct that does not *itself* violate any provision of the Fourteenth Amendment," because "[s]o-called 'prophylactic legislation' is reinforcement rather than enforcement." He declared, however, that "principally for reasons of *stare decisis*" he would continue to "apply the permissive *McCulloch* standard" applied in *Morgan* "to congressional measures designed to remedy racial discrimination by the States."

Do you agree that the congruence and proportionality test is effectively devoid of content? Or is it a sensible response to a constitutional text that itself calls for a judgment about whether particular legislation is "appropriate"?

Executive Summary of this Chapter

The **Thirteenth Amendment** prohibits slavery and involuntary servitude. The provision applies to both state action and private action. It also empowers Congress to enforce its provisions by "appropriate legislation." Pursuant to that power, Congress can pass laws that it rationally believes are necessary and proper for abolishing all of the "badges and incidents of slavery in the United States." *Jones v. Alfred H. Mayer Co.* (1968); *Civil Rights Cases* (1883) In exercising this power, Congress may prohibit some forms of private conduct. *Jones v. Alfred H. Mayer Co.* (1968).

The **Fourteenth and Fifteenth Amendments** include provisions empowering Congress to enforce their substantive provisions "by appropriate legislation." Pursuant to these sources of authority, Congress not only has power to outlaw state violations of the Amendments and provide for civil and criminal remedies for those violations, but also has power to act prophylactically to prevent violations of the Amendments. *South Carolina v. Katzenbach* (1966).

When Congress seeks to exercise those powers to regulate state conduct that does not violate the substantive provisions of the Amendments, however, there must be a **congruence and proportionality** between the injury to be prevented or remedied and the means adopted to that end. *City of Boerne v. Flores* (1997). Congressional efforts that seek to redefine the Amendments' substantive provisions exceed the scope of the enforcement powers. *Id.*

Because the substantive provisions of the Fourteenth Amendment prohibit only state, as opposed to private, action, *Civil Rights Cases* (1883) Congress's power under the Fourteenth Amendment to regulate private conduct is highly circumscribed. *United States v. Morrison* (2000); *United States v. Guest* (1966).

Point-Counterpoint

Should the Reconstruction Amendments be read in light of the Tenth Amendment?

POINT: Peter J. Smith

In the first 75 years of the nation's history, the phrase "the United States" was often used as a plural noun, suggesting that the union was in fact a collection of largely independent states. To be sure, there is, as we saw in Chapter 3, continuing debate over the extent to which this view was consistent with the original meaning of the Constitution. But even assuming that the Constitution's protections were as robust as proponents of serious limits on federal power assert, the events leading up to the Civil War—and in particular the southern states' repeated invocations of state sovereignty to defend their embrace of the institution of slavery—demonstrated that there were serious drawbacks to the conception of the United States as a loose union of independent states.

The Civil War itself was obviously the most immediate response to this problem, but the principal *legal* remedy was the ratification of the Reconstruction Amendments. It is difficult to overstate the transformative nature of their adoption. The original Constitution expressly imposed only a few limits on state authority—principally those included in Article I, section 10, and in the Supremacy Clause—and impliedly imposed only a few others—such as the bar on state taxation of federal instrumentalities that the Court announced in *McCulloch v. Maryland*, 17 U.S. (4 Wheat.) 316 (1819). (The Bill of Rights, as we saw in *Barron v Baltimore*, 32 U.S. (7 Pet.) 243 (1833), in Chapter 7, was not originally understood to limit state action.) In this scheme, the Tenth Amendment's rule of construction—that powers not granted to the United States expressly or by necessary implication remained with the states—stated a central structural principle.

The Reconstruction Amendments, in contrast, by their terms imposed substantial limits on state authority. The Equal Protection, Due Process, and Privileges or Immunities Clauses of the Fourteenth Amendment made clear that the states no longer had authority to engage in various forms of discrimination or to interfere with (at least some) individual rights. And the Amendments expressly authorized Congress to enforce their provisions "by appropriate legislation," language strongly reminiscent of the Necessary and Proper Clause, which itself had long been construed as a potent source of congressional authority.

In light of this history and text, it is inappropriate to read the Tenth Amendment as a limit on Congress's authority to enforce the Reconstruction Amendments. The Tenth Amendment—which was designed to confirm limits on federal authority and reiterate the breadth of state authority—seems singularly inapposite in interpreting provisions that were designed fundamentally to *alter* the relationship between the federal government and the states, and between the states and their citizens. Indeed, for this reason there is a strong argument that the *Tenth Amendment* should now be construed *in light of the Reconstruction Amendments*. At a minimum, however, the fact that the Reconstruction Amendments came later in time than did the Tenth Amendment suggests that their conception of the scope of state and federal authority should prevail with respect to matters within the scope of the Reconstruction Amendments.

———————————

COUNTERPOINT: GREGORY E. MAGGS

The Tenth Amendment says that the federal government has only the powers delegated to it in the Constitution. Congress, for example, cannot regulate non-economic intrastate activities that do not have a substantial effect on interstate commerce because nothing in the Constitution gives Congress this power. Therefore, Congress cannot regulate guns in schools or gender-motivated violence, or at least not as it tried to regulate these subjects in *United States v. Lopez*, 514 U.S. 549 (1995), and *United States v. Morrison*, 529 U.S. 598 (2000).

New amendments to the Constitution conceivably could declare that federalism is dead and that Congress has plenary legislative power. But the Thirteenth, Fourteenth, and Fifteenth Amendments do not do anything like this. Although they were added to the Constitution after the Tenth Amendment, their text and structure make clear that they were not intended to alter the principle that Congress may act only according to its delegated powers.

Consider what the Amendments say. They each include important new prohibitions, but they do not stop at that. Each also concludes by saying: "The Congress shall have power to enforce this article by appropriate legislation." Why were these words added? The Amendments evidently rest on the premise that Congress only has the powers granted by the Constitution, just as the Tenth Amendment says. The drafters of the Amendments understood that Congress would lack power to enforce them without newly delegated powers.

Contemporaneous court decisions and subsequent amendments to the Constitution confirm that the Thirteenth, Fourteenth, and Fifteenth Amendments did not undercut the Tenth Amendment. For example, in the *Civil Rights Cases*, 109 U.S. 3 (1883), the Supreme Court emphasized that the last section of the Fourteenth Amendment was added because otherwise Congress could not enforce the Equal Protection requirement. Similarly, the Sixteenth, Eighteenth, and Nineteenth Amendments also include sections granting additional powers to Congress. The Court and the drafters of the Amendments recognized that new grants of power were necessary because the Tenth Amendment's principles remained effective.

True, the prohibitions of the Thirteenth, Fourteenth, and Fifteenth Amendments strike deeply into what was formerly a sphere of state prerogative. But it would be an incorrect overgeneralization to conclude that because these Amendments reduced state power and increased federal power over certain subjects, they also decreased state power and increased federal power in additional respects. The Amendments go as far as they go, but no further.

While Congress may use its new power under the Thirteenth Amendment to enforce the prohibition on slavery, it cannot regulate all matters concerning race. Similarly, Congress can employ its power under the Fourteenth Amendment to pass laws preventing the states from denying anyone due process, but Congress cannot regulate all aspects of state government. And Congress can enforce the prohibition on discrimination in voting rights in the Fifteenth Amendment, but it cannot dictate all aspects of state elections. The Tenth Amendment continues to leave the powers not specifically granted in the Thirteenth, Fourteenth, and Fifteenth Amendments to the states.

PART IX: THE FIRST AMENDMENT

The First Amendment is the source of several of our most prized and fundamental rights: the freedom of speech, the press, and religion, and the rights to assemble and to petition the government for a redress of grievances.

> ### U.S. Constitution, <u>Amendment I</u>
>
> Congress shall make no law respecting an establishment of religion, or prohibiting the free exercise thereof; or abridging the freedom of speech, or of the press; or the right of the people peaceably to assemble, and to petition the Government for a redress of grievances.

There is a vast body of decisions interpreting the various provisions in the First Amendment. Many law schools have classes devoted solely to the First Amendment; indeed, many have separate classes for the freedom of speech and the freedom of religion. Our task here is to provide an overview of the doctrine that the Court has developed to govern all of these rights, in a book devoted to all of American constitutional law.

In the Chapters that follow, we focus on four discrete—but related—rights that the Court has protected under the First Amendment. In Chapter 14, we take up the freedom of speech. In Chapter 15, we consider the freedom of the press. In Chapter 16, we address the freedom of association, which the Court has held is essential to the rights expressly protected by the Amendment. And in Chapter 17, we discuss the "Religion Clauses"—that is, the prohibition on the "establishment" of religion and the protection for the free exercise of religion. Although we separately address each of these freedoms protected by the First Amendment, be mindful of the common themes in the Court's approach to those different freedoms.

CHAPTER 14

Freedom of Speech

Introduction

The freedom of speech as we now know it did not exist in the colonial era. For example, as a means of controlling public discourse, English laws required printers to obtain a license from the government. English laws also made "seditious libel"—the printing of words aimed at undermining government authority—a serious crime. Justice Hugo Black, a great champion of the freedom of speech, described some of this pre-Revolutionary history as follows:

> The obnoxious press licensing law of England, which was also enforced on the Colonies was due in part to the knowledge that exposure of the names of printers, writers and distributors would lessen the circulation of literature critical of the government. The old seditious libel cases in England show the lengths to which government had to go to find out who was responsible for books that were obnoxious to the rulers. John Lilburne was whipped, pilloried and fined for refusing to answer questions designed to get evidence to convict him or someone else for the secret distribution of books in England. Two Puritan Ministers, John Penry and John Udal, were sentenced to death on charges that they were responsible for writing, printing or publishing books. Before the Revolutionary War colonial patriots frequently had to conceal their authorship or distribution of literature that easily could have brought down on them prosecutions by English-controlled courts.

Talley v. California, 362 U.S. 60, 64-65 (1960).

Yet despite this history of oppression, the original Constitution contained no provision expressly guaranteeing a right of free speech. We saw in Chapter 7 how some delegates at the Constitutional Convention refused to sign the document because it did not include a Bill of Rights, 2 *The Records of the Federal Convention of 1787* 646-47, 649 (Max Farrand, ed. 1911), and how Anti-Federalist opponents of the Constitution demanded an express bill of rights to identify protected liberties, including the right to free speech.

Recall that the Federalists initially responded to this objection during the ratification debates by asserting that a Bill of Rights was neither necessary nor a good idea. As we have seen, the Federalists' arguments were not ultimately convincing, and several states, upon ratifying the Constitution, passed resolutions specifically urging the adoption of a Bill of Rights. *See* 2 Francis Newton Thorpe, *The Constitutional History of the United States* 198 (1902). By the end of 1791, the states had ratified the ten proposed amendments that we now call the "Bill of Rights."

The First Amendment says, in relevant part, that "Congress shall make no law ***
abridging the freedom of speech." Two aspects
of this language require comment. First, the
Amendment does not define "the freedom of
speech." Accordingly, many cases have arisen
over what the phrase means. Second, although
the Amendment refers to "Congress," the
Supreme Court has held that this provision
applies to the states through the Fourteenth
Amendment. *See* Grosjean v. American Press Co., 297 U.S. 233, 244 (1936).

> **Make the Connection**
>
> We addressed the "incorporation
> doctrine" in Chapter 7.

In this Chapter, we will consider how the Supreme Court has interpreted the First
Amendment's protection for the freedom of speech. If we were starting from scratch, one
possible view would be that the freedom of speech is "absolute"—that is, that no government interest can justify abridgment of the freedom in cases to which it extends. Justice
Black famously advanced this view, arguing that "the men who drafted our Bill of Rights
did all the 'balancing' that was to be done in this field." *Konigsberg v. State Bar of California,*
366 U.S. 36, 61 (1961) (Black, J., dissenting). But the Court has never accepted this
view. Instead, the Court has repeatedly stated that the freedom of speech is not absolute.
See, e.g., Virginia v. Black, 538 U.S. 343, 358 (2003). The government does not have to
allow a person to say anything he wishes, in any manner, at any place, at any time. On
the contrary, some regulation of speech is possible. So the basic question throughout
this Chapter is: What kind of government regulations are allowed, and what kinds are
not? Answering this question in a pragmatic fashion, the Supreme Court has adopted a
number of standards that essentially weigh the value of free speech against the importance
of governmental regulation. As you read the materials that follow, consider whether the
Court's tests properly accommodate these competing interests, and whether the Court has
properly applied those tests in its cases.

———————————

Points for Discussion

a. "*The* Freedom of Speech"

The First Amendment does not protect "freedom of speech"; it protects "*the* freedom of
speech." The use of a definite article (i.e., "the") before the word "freedom" has led some
to conclude that a freedom of speech pre-existed the First Amendment, and that the First
Amendment serves to preserve this freedom rather than to expand or otherwise redefine
it. For example, in an academic lecture, Justice John Paul Stevens said: "[T]he definite
article suggests that the draftsmen intended to immunize a previously identified category
or subset of speech. That category could not have been co-extensive with the category of
oral communications that are commonly described as 'speech' in ordinary usage. For it
is obvious that the Framers did not intend to provide constitutional protection for false
testimony under oath, or for oral contracts that are against public policy, such as wagers or
conspiracies ***." John Paul Stevens, *The Freedom of Speech: Address at the Inaugural Ralph*

Gregory Elliot First Amendment Lecture, 102 Yale L.J. 1293, 1296 (1993). What implications would this theory have for interpreting the First Amendment?

b. A Debate over the Original Meaning of "Freedom of Speech"

A common view of American history is that the Framers protected the freedom of speech because they knew first hand the value of being able to express dissenting opinions. The Framers had felt oppressed by England before the Revolution, and they wanted to secure complete freedom for their descendents. According to this view, we are to understand the freedom of speech as a right, at a minimum, to be free from the many kinds of restrictions that England had placed on the colonists during the colonial period. Writing for the Court, for example, Justice Scalia has asserted:

> The First Amendment's guarantee of "the freedom of speech, or of the press" prohibits a wide assortment of government restraints upon expression, but the core abuse against which it was directed was the scheme of licensing laws implemented by the monarch and Parliament to contain the "evils" of the printing press in 16th- and 17-century England.

Thomas v. Chicago Park District, 534 U.S. 316, 320 (2002).

The late Leonard W. Levy, a renowned scholar of constitutional history, has contested this account of the original meaning of the freedom of speech. In a lengthy book describing the freedom of speech in the newly formed United States, he writes:

> The persistent image of colonial America as a society in which freedom of expression was cherished is an hallucination of sentiment that ignores history. The evidence provides little comfort for the notion that the colonies hospitably received advocates of obnoxious or detestable ideas on matters that counted. *** The American people simply did not understand that freedom of thought and expression means equal freedom for the other fellow, especially the one with hated ideas.

Leonard W. Levy, *Legacy of Suppression: Freedom of Speech and Press in Early American History* 18 (1960). How would Levy's alternative view, if accepted, affect interpretation of the First Amendment from an originalist perspective?

c. What Counts as "Speech"?

There is little doubt that the First Amendment's protection for the freedom of speech extends to a person's attempt to give a speech on a soap box, or to a pamphlet that a person publishes to convince the public that the President has made an unwise decision. But what else counts as "speech" under the First Amendment? As it turns out, there is no easy answer to this question.

What speeches and pamphlets have in common is their use in conveying a message. Does this mean that every act that conveys a message counts as speech? Music often conveys a message, as do symbolic acts, such as bowing one's head and holding one's right fist above the head, or even the burning of a flag or a draft card at a protest rally. These acts have an obvious expressive content. And, as we will see, the First Amendment is principally concerned with expression. But many other acts that do not seem principally expressive—such as the assassination of a political leader—also make a statement, and sometimes are committed in large part for that purpose. Surely such acts are not immune from punishment simply because they contain an expressive element.

As you read the cases in this Chapter, consider whether it is possible to discern a test for when a particular act that conveys a message counts as "speech" within the meaning of the First Amendment.

d. The Theory of the Freedom of Speech

What is the basic theory of the First Amendment's protection for the freedom of speech? One possibility, suggested by the history recounted above, is that the freedom of speech is designed to ensure that government remains accountable and responsive to the will of the people. These ends are obviously substantially undermined by prohibitions on criticism of the government.

Another possibility is that the freedom of speech aids in the quest for the truth by creating a robust marketplace of ideas. As Justice Brandeis famously stated, "freedom to think as you will and to speak as you think are means indispensable to the discovery and spread of political truth." *Whitney v. California*, 274 U.S. 357, 375 (1927) (Brandeis, J., concurring). On this view, speech is protected because the expression of every possible view permits individuals to assess the relative merits of competing views and to decide which view is worthy of adherence. As Justice Holmes put it, "the ultimate good desired is better reached by free trade in ideas—[the] best test of truth is the power of the thought to get itself accepted in the competition of the market, and that truth is the only ground upon which their wishes safely can be carried out." *Abrams v. United States*, 250 U.S. 616, 630 (1919) (Holmes, J., dissenting).

On both of these views—the "government accountability" theory and the "market-place of ideas" theory—the freedom of speech is largely instrumental—that is, it is important because it permits the advancement of *other* important goals. Is there a value to the freedom of speech—to the ability to express oneself freely—wholly aside from its potential to enhance the democratic process or aid in the search for truth?

As you read the materials in this Chapter, consider which theory (or theories) of the First Amendment the Court embraces, and the implications of those choices for First Amendment doctrines.

A. General Principles and Rules for Regulating Speech

In interpreting the First Amendment, the Supreme Court has developed a number of distinct doctrines and rules. These doctrines and rules basically fall into two general categories. Some concern the various types of regulations that the government wants to impose on speech. Others focus on the kinds of speech that the government wants to regulate. This Chapter's organization follows this same division.

In this section, we consider the following types of governmental regulations on speech: (1) content-based restrictions; (2) reasonable time, place, and manner restrictions; (3) generally applicable regulations that incidentally affect expression; (4) prior restraints; (5) vague or overbroad restrictions; and (6) unconstitutional conditions. In section B, we take up doctrines and rules pertaining to particular classes of speech.

---

1. Content-Based Restrictions

The first general principle concerns **content-based restrictions** on speech. A content-based restriction on speech is a restraint based on the content of what is being said. For example, in *Boos v. Barry*, 485 U.S. 312 (1988), the Supreme Court considered the constitutionality of a District of Columbia statute making it unlawful to "display [any] placard" within 500 feet of an embassy if the placard was "designed [to] bring into public odium any foreign government [or] to bring into public disrepute political, social, or economic acts, views, or purposes of any foreign government." The Court concluded that this statute was a content-based restriction on speech because it prohibited only placards that contained messages critical of foreign governments, while permitting ones that contained supportive messages. For example, under the statute, a person could permissibly hold a sign outside the United Kingdom's embassy saying, "Princess Diana, Forever in our Hearts, May She Rest in Peace," but could not display a placard saying, "Unite Ireland! British Oppressors Out of Belfast Now!"

A "freedom" of speech that nevertheless allowed the government to restrict the content of what people may say would not be much of a freedom at all. (Recall automaker Henry Ford's famous joke that his customers could buy the Model-T in any color they want, "so long as it is black.") And if the government could ban unpopular speech—and if the First Amendment protected only the expression of popular views—then there really wouldn't be any *need* for the First Amendment, as the majority would be unlikely to ban views that they hold and wish to express.

For this reason, the Supreme Court subjects content-based restrictions to strict scrutiny: The government may enforce a content-based restriction on speech in a public forum only if the regulation is necessary to serve a compelling state interest and the regulation is narrowly drawn to achieve that end. As we have seen elsewhere in this book, strict scrutiny is the most searching form of review that the Court applies, and challenged government actions rarely survive such judicial inquiries.

> **Make the Connection**
>
> We saw strict scrutiny, among other places, in Chapter 8, in our consideration of fundamental rights, and in Chapter 11, in our consideration of discrimination on the basis of race and national origin.

Note that a regulation need not discriminate among competing *viewpoints* in order to be considered content based. To be sure, such regulations constitute a particularly pernicious form of content-based restriction: a law that prohibits statements supporting Republican (but not Democratic) candidates for public office not only is based on the content of the proscribed speech—manners concerning electoral politics—but is also based on the particular viewpoint that the speaker expresses. But the Court has made clear that a regulation that "does not favor either side of a political controversy" nevertheless imposes a content-based restriction if it prohibits "public discussion of an entire topic." *Consolidated Edison Co. v. Public Service Comm'n*, 447 U.S. 530, 537 (1980). Accordingly, a law that prohibits statements in favor of *any* candidate for political office, regardless of political party, is also content based and thus is subject to strict scrutiny.

In *Boos v. Barry*, the Supreme Court struck down the District of Columbia law regarding placards outside of embassies. The law, as explained, was clearly a content-based restriction. The District of Columbia argued that the law served to protect the dignity of foreign diplomats. Without deciding whether this was a compelling interest, the Court concluded that the law was not narrowly tailored to achieve the government's goal, because there were other ways to protect the dignity of ambassadors without banning negative messages. *See id.* at 329.

In contrast, government regulations that affect speech but that do not single out disfavored speech based upon its content do not generally trigger such searching scrutiny. For example, a law that prohibits the use of megaphones on residential streets does not single out particular messages—based solely on their content—for disfavored treatment. Instead, it applies regardless of the message conveyed by the user of the megaphone—it applies, that is, equally to a person announcing a sale at the local general store, a person trying to get people to attend a political rally sponsored by the mayor, and a person seeking to register voters to oppose the current mayor. Such "content-neutral" regulations do not run the same risk of government censorship as do content-based restrictions, and they accordingly raise fewer concerns. But they nevertheless impose some burdens on the ability of individuals to convey their messages. Accordingly, as we will see, they are permitted if they are narrowly tailored to serve a significant governmental interest and leave open ample alternative channels for communication.

Such "time, place, and manner" restrictions directly regulate expressive activities but are generally thought to be reasonable regulations of those activities. It is also possible (and, indeed, not uncommon) for a generally applicable, content-neutral regulation that is not limited in its application to expressive activities nevertheless to impose burdens on expressive activities. For example, the creation of a no-parking zone in a downtown area might affect the business of a bookstore located in the area. Such regulations do not generally have as their aim the suppression (or even the regulation) of expressive activities protected by the First Amendment, but they might nevertheless have some effect on such activities. Although the Court's cases in this area are not easy to summarize, the Court generally will uphold such regulations if they further "an important or substantial governmental interest; if the governmental interest is unrelated to the suppression of free expression; and if the incidental restriction on alleged First Amendment freedoms is no greater than is essential to the furtherance of that interest." *United States v. O'Brien*, 391 U.S. 367 (1968).

Content-neutral regulations, in other words, are subject to a less searching level of scrutiny than are content-based regulations. Given the different levels of scrutiny triggered by the different types of government regulation, the threshold question—whether the challenged regulation is content based or instead content neutral—takes on great significance in cases concerning the freedom of speech. But as the cases that follow demonstrate, that question is not always easy to answer.

————————————

What should a court consider in deciding whether a challenged regulation is content based? Is the language of the regulation the only relevant consideration? (In *Boos v. Barry*, for example, it was clear on the face of the statute that its application turned on the content of the message on the placard.) Is the legislature's motive in enacting the regulation relevant? In the following case, the Court considered the legislature's motive for regulating the speech in question. As you read the case, consider whether the legislature's motive was relevant because it was not clear on the statute's face whether it was content based, or instead because it suggested that a statute that *was* content based on its face nevertheless should not be treated as such.

————————————

Renton v. Playtime Theatres, Inc.

475 U.S. 41 (1986)

Justice REHNQUIST delivered the opinion of the Court.

In May 1980, the Mayor of Renton, a city of approximately 32,000 people located just south of Seattle, suggested to the Renton City Council that it consider the advisability of enacting zoning legislation dealing with adult entertainment uses. No such uses existed in the city at that time. Upon the Mayor's suggestion, the City Council referred the matter to the city's Planning and Development Committee. The Committee held public hearings, reviewed the experiences of Seattle and other cities, and received a report from the City Attorney's Office advising as to developments in other cities. The City Council, meanwhile, adopted Resolution No. 2368, which imposed a moratorium on the licensing of "any business [which] has as its primary purpose the selling, renting or showing of sexually explicit materials." The resolution contained a clause explaining that such businesses "would have a severe impact upon surrounding businesses and residences."

In April 1981, acting on the basis of the Planning and Development Committee's recommendation, the City Council enacted Ordinance No. 3526. The ordinance prohibited any "adult motion picture theater" from locating within 1,000 feet of any residential zone, single- or multiple-family dwelling, church, or park, and within one mile of any school. The term "adult motion picture theater" was defined as "[a]n enclosed building used for presenting motion picture films, video cassettes, cable television, or any other such visual media, distinguished or characteri[zed] by an emphasis on matter depicting, describing or relating to 'specified sexual activities' or 'specified anatomical areas' [for] observation by patrons therein."

In early 1982, respondents acquired two existing theaters in downtown Renton, with the intention of using them to exhibit feature-length adult films. The theaters were located within the area proscribed by Ordinance No. 3526. At about the same time, respondents filed [a] lawsuit challenging the ordinance on First and Fourteenth Amendment grounds, and seeking declaratory and injunctive relief. While the federal action was pending, the City Council amended the ordinance in several respects, adding a statement of reasons for its enactment and reducing the minimum distance from any school to 1,000 feet. [The lower courts held that the ordinance did not violate the First Amendment.]

In our view, the resolution of this case is largely dictated by our decision in *Young v. American Mini Theatres, Inc.,* 427 U.S. 50 (1976). There, although five Members of the Court did not agree on a single rationale for the decision, we held that the city of Detroit's zoning ordinance, which prohibited locating an adult theater within 1,000 feet of any two other "regulated uses" or within 500 feet of any residential zone, did not violate the First and Fourteenth Amendments. The Renton ordinance, like the one in <u>American Mini Theatres</u>, does not ban adult theaters altogether, but merely provides that such theaters may not be located within 1,000 feet of any residential zone, single- or multiple-family dwelling, church, park, or school. The ordinance is therefore properly analyzed as a form of time, place, and manner regulation.

Describing the ordinance as a time, place, and manner regulation is, of course, only the first step in our inquiry. This Court has long held that regulations enacted for the purpose of restraining speech on the basis of its content presumptively violate the First Amendment. See *Carey v. Brown,* 447 U.S. 455, 462-463 & n. 7 (1980); *Police Dept. of Chicago v. Mosley,* 408 U.S. 92, 95, 98-99 (1972). On the other hand, so-called "content-neutral" time, place, and manner regulations are acceptable so long as they are designed to serve a substantial governmental interest and do not unreasonably limit alternative avenues of communication. *See Clark v. Community for Creative Non-Violence,* 468 U.S. 288, 293 (1984).

At first glance, the Renton ordinance, like the ordinance in <u>American Mini Theatres</u>, does not appear to fit neatly into either the "content-based" or the "content-neutral" category. To be sure, the ordinance treats theaters that specialize in adult films differently from other kinds of theaters. Nevertheless, as the District Court concluded, the Renton ordinance is aimed not at the *content* of the films shown at "adult motion picture theatres," but rather at the *secondary effects* of such theaters on the surrounding community. The District Court found that the City Council's *"predominate* concerns" were with the secondary effects of adult theaters, and not with the content of adult films themselves. ***

The District Court's finding as to "predominate" intent, left undisturbed by the Court

> **Take Note**
>
> We will consider "time, place, and manner" regulations in the section that follows. For now, note that such regulations trigger a form of scrutiny less searching than strict scrutiny only if they are content neutral. How does the Court go about deciding whether the ordinance at issue here is content neutral?

of Appeals, is more than adequate to establish that the city's pursuit of its zoning interests here was unrelated to the suppression of free expression. The ordinance by its terms is designed to prevent crime, protect the city's retail trade, maintain property values, and generally "protec[t] and preserv[e] the quality of [the city's] neighborhoods, commercial districts, and the quality of urban life," not to suppress the expression of unpopular views. As Justice POWELL observed in *American Mini Theatres*, "[i]f [the city] had been concerned with restricting the message purveyed by adult theaters, it would have tried to close them or restrict their number rather than circumscribe their choice as to location." 427 U.S. at 82, n. 4.

In short, the Renton ordinance is completely consistent with our definition of "content-neutral" speech regulations as those that "are *justified* without reference to the content of the regulated speech." *Virginia Pharmacy Board v. Virginia Citizens Consumer Council, Inc.*, 425 U.S. 748, 771 (1976) (emphasis added). The ordinance does not contravene the fundamental principle that underlies our concern about "content-based" speech regulations: that "government may not grant the use of a forum to people whose views it finds acceptable, but deny use to those wishing to express less favored or more controversial views." *Mosley*, 408 U.S., at 95-96.

The appropriate inquiry in this case, then, is whether the Renton ordinance is designed to serve a substantial governmental interest and allows for reasonable alternative avenues of communication. [The Court then answered both questions in the affirmative.]

Justice BLACKMUN concurs in the result.

Justice BRENNAN, with whom Justice MARSHALL joins, dissenting.

The fact that adult movie theaters may cause harmful "secondary" land-use effects may arguably give Renton a compelling reason to regulate such establishments; it does not mean, however, that such regulations are content neutral. Because the ordinance imposes special restrictions on certain kinds of speech on the basis of content, I cannot simply accept, as the Court does, Renton's claim that the ordinance was not designed to suppress the content of adult movies.

The ordinance discriminates on its face against certain forms of speech based on content. Movie theaters specializing in "adult motion pictures" may not be located within 1,000 feet of any residential zone, single- or multiple-family dwelling, church, park, or school. Other motion picture theaters, and other forms of "adult entertainment," such as bars, massage parlors, and adult bookstores, are not subject to the same restrictions. This selective treatment strongly suggests that Renton was interested not in controlling the "secondary effects" associated with adult businesses, but in discriminating against adult theaters based on the content of the films they exhibit.

Rather than speculate about Renton's motives for adopting such measures, our cases require the conclusion that the ordinance, like any other content-based restriction on speech, is constitutional "only if the [city] can show that [it] is a precisely drawn means of serving a compelling [governmental] interest." *Consolidated Edison Co. v. Public Service*

Comm'n of N.Y., 447 U.S. 530, 540 (1980). Only this strict approach can insure that cities will not use their zoning powers as a pretext for suppressing constitutionally protected expression.

Points for Discussion

a. Secondary Effects

In *Renton*, much turned on the Court's characterization of the challenged ordinance. If the ordinance was content based, it would be subject to strict scrutiny and thus would likely be invalid. The challenged ordinance on its face provided disfavored treatment only to theaters that showed one type of film. Doesn't that mean by definition that it was a content-based regulation?

In concluding that it was not, the Court's theory appeared to be that the City of Renton did not care what an adult theater might show on its screens; it cared only about the "secondary effects" of the presence of theaters showing such films. Are these considerations entirely distinct? Aren't most content-based restrictions on speech imposed because of a fear of the consequences of the speech? Consider the Court's discussion in *Boos v. Barry*, 485 U.S. 312 (1988):

> Listeners' reactions to speech are not the type of "secondary effects" we referred to in *Renton*. To take an example factually close to *Renton*, if the ordinance there was justified by the city's desire to prevent the psychological damage it felt was associated with viewing adult movies, then analysis of the measure as a content-based statute would have been appropriate. The hypothetical regulation targets the direct impact of a particular category of speech, not a secondary feature that happens to be associated with that type of speech.

Can you articulate the distinction between "listeners' reactions" and "secondary effects"? Suppose a city council bans the display of political bumper stickers on cars. It justifies the ban as follows: "When we banned the political bumper stickers, it was not because of their political content; we just thought that people seeing them might vote for our opponents. We were worried about this secondary effect." Would that argument be successful? If not, why was the ordinance in *Renton* different?

b. Content-Based Regulation and Municipal Zoning

In *City of Los Angeles v. Alameda Books, Inc.*, 535 U.S. 425, 448 (2002), Justice O'Connor suggested, in a plurality opinion joined by three other Justices, that *Renton's* reasoning should be confined to the zoning context:

> The Court [in *Renton*] appeared to recognize [that] the designation ["content neutral"] was something of a fiction, which, perhaps, is why it kept the phrase in quotes. After all, whether a statute is content neutral or content based is something that can be determined on the face of it; if the statute describes speech by content then it is content based. *** The fiction that this sort of ordinance is content neutral [is] perhaps more confusing than helpful ***. It is also not a fiction that has commanded our consistent adherence. See *Thomas v. Chicago Park Dist.*, 534 U.S. 316, 322, and n. 2 (2002) (suggesting that a licensing scheme targeting only those businesses

purveying sexually explicit speech is not content neutral). These ordinances are content based, and we should call them so.

Nevertheless, [the] central holding of *Renton* is sound: A zoning restriction that is designed to decrease secondary effects and not speech should be subject to intermediate rather than strict scrutiny. [Z]oning regulations do not automatically raise the specter of impermissible content discrimination, even if they are content based, because they have a prima facie legitimate purpose: to limit the negative externalities of land use. As a matter of common experience, these sorts of ordinances are more like a zoning restriction on slaughterhouses and less like a tax on unpopular newspapers. The zoning context provides a built-in legitimate rationale, which rebuts the usual presumption that content-based restrictions are unconstitutional.

Is there a reason to treat the zoning context differently? If so, does that suggest that the "secondary effects" rationale will have little application outside of that context?

Congress has long regulated television broadcasters. (In Chapter 15, we will consider what special rules, if any, should apply in this context, given the First Amendment's protection for the freedom of the press.) Can Congress tell cable operators what stations they must carry? Does it matter how Congress defines those stations? The following case considers these questions.

Turner Broadcasting System, Inc. v. F.C.C.

512 U.S. 622 (1994)

Justice KENNEDY announced the judgment of the Court and delivered the opinion of the Court, except as to Part III-B.

Sections 4 and 5 of the Cable Television Consumer Protection and Competition Act of 1992 require cable television systems to devote a portion of their channels to the transmission of local broadcast television stations. This case presents the question whether these provisions abridge the freedom of speech or of the press, in violation of the First Amendment.

At the heart of the First Amendment lies the principle that each person should decide for himself or herself the ideas and beliefs deserving of expression, consideration, and adherence. Our political system and cultural life rest upon this ideal. Government action that stifles speech on account of its message, or that requires the utterance of a particular message favored by the Government, contravenes this essential right. Laws of this sort pose the inherent risk that the Government seeks not to

> **Take Note**
>
> In this passage, the Court explains why content-based restrictions on speech are problematic. On which theory (or theories) of the First Amendment's protections does the Court rely?

advance a legitimate regulatory goal, but to suppress unpopular ideas or information or manipulate the public debate through coercion rather than persuasion. These restrictions "rais[e] the specter that the Government may effectively drive certain ideas or viewpoints from the marketplace." *Simon & Schuster, Inc. v. Members of State Crime Victims Bd.*, 502 U.S. 105, 116 (1991).

For these reasons, the First Amendment, subject only to narrow and well-understood exceptions, does not countenance governmental control over the content of messages expressed by private individuals. Our precedents thus apply the most exacting scrutiny to regulations that suppress, disadvantage, or impose differential burdens upon speech because of its content. Laws that compel speakers to utter or distribute speech bearing a particular message are subject to the same rigorous scrutiny. In contrast, regulations that are unrelated to the content of speech are subject to an intermediate level of scrutiny, see *Clark v. Community for Creative Non-Violence*, 468 U.S. 288, 293 (1984), because in most cases they pose a less substantial risk of excising certain ideas or viewpoints from the public dialogue.

Deciding whether a particular regulation is content based or content neutral is not always a simple task. We have said that the "principal inquiry in determining content neutrality [is] whether the government has adopted a regulation of speech because of [agreement or] disagreement with the message it conveys." *Ward v. Rock Against Racism*, 491 U.S. 781, 791 (1989). The purpose, or justification, of a regulation will often be evident on its face. See *Frisby v. Schultz*, 487 U.S. 474, 481 (1988). But while a content-based purpose may be sufficient in certain circumstances to show that a regulation is content based, it is not necessary to such a showing in all cases. Cf. *Simon & Schuster*, 502 U.S., at 117 ("[I]llicit legislative intent is not the *sine qua non* of a violation of the First Amendment") (quoting *Minneapolis Star & Tribune, supra*, 460 U.S. 575, 592 (1993)). Nor will the mere assertion of a content-neutral purpose be enough to save a law which, on its face, discriminates based on content.

> **Take Note**
>
> Is the Court's statement here of the role of government motive in determining whether a regulation is content based consistent with the Court's approach in *Renton*?

As a general rule, laws that by their terms distinguish favored speech from disfavored speech on the basis of the ideas or views expressed are content based. See, *e.g.*, *Burson v. Freeman*, 504 U.S. 191, 197 (1992) ("Whether individuals may exercise their free-speech rights near polling places depends entirely on whether their speech is related to a political campaign"); *Boos v. Barry*, 485 U.S. 312, 318-319 (1988) (plurality opinion) (whether municipal ordinance permits individuals to "picket in front of a foreign embassy depends entirely upon whether their picket signs are critical of the foreign government or not"). By contrast, laws that confer benefits or impose burdens on speech without reference to the ideas or views expressed are in most instances content neutral. See, *e.g.*, *Members of City Council of Los Angeles v. Taxpayers for Vincent*, 466 U.S. 789, 804 (1984) (ordinance prohibiting the posting of signs on public property "is neutral—indeed it is silent—concerning any speaker's point of view"); *Heffron v. International Soc. for Krishna Consciousness, Inc.*, 452

U.S. 640, 649 (1981) (State Fair regulation requiring that sales and solicitations take place at designated locations "applies evenhandedly to all who wish to distribute and sell written materials or to solicit funds").

Insofar as they pertain to the carriage of full-power broadcasters, the must-carry rules, on their face, impose burdens and confer benefits without reference to the content of speech. Although the provisions interfere with cable operators' editorial discretion by compelling them to offer carriage to a certain minimum number of broadcast stations, the extent of the interference does not depend upon the content of the cable operators' programming. The rules impose obligations upon all operators, save those with fewer than 300 subscribers, regardless of the programs or stations they now offer or have offered in the past. Nothing in the Act imposes a restriction, penalty, or burden by reason of the views, programs, or stations the cable operator has selected or will select. The number of channels a cable operator must set aside depends only on the operator's channel capacity; hence, an operator cannot avoid or mitigate its obligations under the Act by altering the programming it offers to subscribers.

The must-carry provisions also burden cable programmers by reducing the number of channels for which they can compete. But, again, this burden is unrelated to content, for it extends to all cable programmers irrespective of the programming they choose to offer viewers. And finally, the privileges conferred by the must-carry provisions are also unrelated to content. The rules benefit all full power broadcasters who request carriage—be they commercial or noncommercial, independent or network affiliated, English or Spanish language, religious or secular. The aggregate effect of the rules is thus to make every full power commercial and noncommercial broadcaster eligible for must-carry, provided only that the broadcaster operates within the same television market as a cable system.

It is true that the must-carry provisions distinguish between speakers in the television programming market. But they do so based only upon the manner in which speakers transmit their messages to viewers, and not upon the messages they carry: Broadcasters, which transmit over the airwaves, are favored, while cable programmers, which do not, are disfavored. Cable operators, too, are burdened by the carriage obligations, but only because they control access to the cable conduit. So long as they are not a subtle means of exercising a content preference, speaker distinctions of this nature are not presumed invalid under the First Amendment.

That the must-carry provisions, on their face, do not burden or benefit speech of a particular content does not end the inquiry. Our cases have recognized that even a regulation neutral on its face may be content based if its manifest purpose is to regulate speech because of the message it conveys. Appellants contend, in this regard, that the must-carry regulations are content based because Congress' purpose in enacting them was to promote speech of a favored content. We do not agree. Our review of the Act and its various findings persuades us that Congress' overriding objective in enacting must-carry was not to favor programming of a particular subject matter, viewpoint, or format, but rather to preserve access to free television programming for the 40 percent of Americans without cable.

In unusually detailed statutory findings, Congress explained that because cable systems and broadcast stations compete for local advertising revenue, and because cable operators have a vested financial interest in favoring their affiliated programmers over broadcast stations, cable operators have a built-in "economic incentive [to] delete, reposition, or not carry local broadcast signals." Congress concluded that absent a requirement that cable systems carry the signals of local broadcast stations, the continued availability of free local broadcast television would be threatened. Congress sought to avoid the elimination of broadcast television because, in its words, "[s]uch programming [is] free to those who own television sets and do not require cable transmission to receive broadcast television signals," and because "[t]here is a substantial governmental interest in promoting the continued availability of such free television programming, especially for viewers who are unable to afford other means of receiving programming." [The challenged provisions thus] are designed to guarantee the survival of a medium that has become a vital part of the Nation's communication system, and to ensure that every individual with a television set can obtain access to free television programming. This overriding congressional purpose is unrelated to the content of expression disseminated by cable and broadcast speakers.

> **Food for Thought**
>
> The Court here relies heavily on Congress's findings in assessing the legislative motives that led to enactment of the challenged provisions. In a challenge under the First Amendment, should the Court defer to such findings? Or should the Court instead view them skeptically?

The design and operation of the challenged provisions confirm that the purposes underlying the enactment of the must-carry scheme are unrelated to the content of speech. The rules, as mentioned, confer must-carry rights on all full power broadcasters, irrespective of the content of their programming. They do not require or prohibit the carriage of particular ideas or points of view. They do not penalize cable operators or programmers because of the content of their programming. They do not compel cable operators to affirm points of view with which they disagree. They do not produce any net decrease in the amount of available speech. And they leave cable operators free to carry whatever programming they wish on all channels not subject to must-carry requirements.

[Because the Court concluded that the challenged provisions were content neutral, it declared that they should be upheld if they further "an important or substantial governmental interest; if the governmental interest is unrelated to the suppression of free expression; and if the incidental restriction on alleged First Amendment freedoms is no greater than is essential to the furtherance of that interest." The Justices could not agree on whether the Act actually furthered these interests, and therefore they decided to remand the case.]

[The separate opinions of Justices BLACKMUN, STEVENS, O'CONNOR, and GINSBURG are omitted.]

————————

Points for Discussion

a. Content Based or Content Neutral?

The challenged provisions required cable operators to carry local broadcast stations, even if they would otherwise have chosen to carry different stations that broadcast different programs. What was the Court's rationale in concluding that these provisions were content neutral? Can you make an argument that the provisions were content based?

b. Surviving Intermediate Scrutiny

The Court concluded that because the challenged provisions were content neutral, they should be subject to intermediate scrutiny. On remand, how might the government attempt to show that the must-carry provisions advance substantial governmental interests? Can the government rely on Congress's findings, or must it do more?

The cases that we have considered so far have largely turned on the sometimes-thorny question whether the challenged regulation was content based or instead content neutral. Once the Court concludes that a regulation is content based, however, it is well established that it is consistent with the First Amendment only if it survives strict scrutiny (subject to exceptions that we will consider in the second half of this chapter). The following case is an example of how the Court applies strict scrutiny to content-based regulations.

Republican Party of Minnesota v. White

536 U.S. 765 (2002)

Justice SCALIA delivered the opinion of the Court.

The question presented in this case is whether the First Amendment permits the Minnesota Supreme Court to prohibit candidates for judicial election in that State from announcing their views on disputed legal and political issues.

Since Minnesota's admission to the Union in 1858, the State's Constitution has provided for the selection of all state judges by popular election. Since 1912, those elections have been nonpartisan. Since 1974, they have been subject to a legal restriction which states that a "candidate for a judicial office, including an incumbent judge," shall not "announce his or her views on disputed legal or political issues." This prohibition, promulgated by the Minnesota Supreme Court and based on Canon 7(B) of the 1972 American Bar Association (ABA) Model Code of Judicial Conduct, is known as the "announce clause." Incumbent judges who violate it are subject to discipline, including removal, censure, civil penalties, and suspension without pay. Lawyers who run for judicial office also must comply with the announce clause. Those who violate it are subject to, *inter alia,* disbarment, suspension, and probation.

In 1996, one of the petitioners, Gregory Wersal, ran for associate justice of the Minnesota Supreme Court. In the course of the campaign, he distributed literature criticizing several Minnesota Supreme Court decisions on issues such as crime, welfare, and abortion. Wersal withdrew from the election after a complaint was filed with the Minnesota Lawyers Professional Responsibility Board. *** In 1998, Wersal ran again for the same office. Early in that race, he sought an advisory opinion from the Lawyers Board with regard to whether it planned to enforce the announce clause. The Lawyers Board responded equivocally, stating that, although it had significant doubts about the constitutionality of the provision, it was unable to answer his question because he had not submitted a list of the announcements he wished to make. Shortly thereafter, Wersal filed this lawsuit in Federal District Court against respondents, seeking, *inter alia,* a declaration that the announce clause violates the First Amendment and an injunction against its enforcement. ***

As the Court of Appeals recognized, the announce clause both prohibits speech on the basis of its content and burdens a category of speech that is "at the core of our First Amendment freedoms"—speech about the qualifications of candidates for public office. The Court of Appeals concluded that the proper test to be applied to determine the constitutionality of such a restriction is what our cases have called strict scrutiny; the parties do not dispute that this is correct. Under the strict-scrutiny test, respondents have the burden to prove that the announce clause is (1) narrowly tailored to serve (2) a compelling state interest. *E.g., Eu v. San Francisco County Democratic Central Comm.,* 489 U.S. 214, 222 (1989). In order for respondents to show that the announce clause is narrowly tailored, they must demonstrate that it does not "unnecessarily circumscrib[e] protected expression." *Brown v. Hartlage,* 456 U.S. 45, 54 (1982).

> **Take Note**
>
> The parties agreed that the challenged rule imposed a content-based restriction on speech. Note that it applied to all candidates for judicial office, regardless of their views. Can you articulate why the rule was content based?

The Court of Appeals concluded that respondents had established two interests as sufficiently compelling to justify the announce clause: preserving the impartiality of the state judiciary and preserving the appearance of the impartiality of the state judiciary. Respondents reassert these two interests before us, arguing that the first is compelling because it protects the due process rights of litigants, and that the second is compelling because it preserves public confidence in the judiciary. Respondents are rather vague, however, about what they mean by "impartiality." Indeed, although the term is used throughout the Eighth Circuit's opinion, the briefs, the Minnesota Code of Judicial Conduct, and the ABA Codes of Judicial Conduct, none of these sources bothers to define it. Clarity on this point is essential before we can decide whether impartiality is indeed a compelling state interest, and, if so, whether the announce clause is narrowly tailored to achieve it.

One meaning of "impartiality" in the judicial context—and of course its root meaning—is the lack of bias for or against either *party* to the proceeding. Impartiality in this sense assures equal application of the law. That is, it guarantees a party that the judge who hears his case will apply the law to him in the same way he applies it to any other party.

This is the traditional sense in which the term is used. It is also the sense in which it is used in the cases cited by respondents and *amici* for the proposition that an impartial judge is essential to due process. *Tumey v. Ohio,* 273 U.S. 510, 523, 531-534 (1927) (judge violated due process by sitting in a case in which it would be in his financial interest to find against one of the parties); *Aetna Life Ins. Co. v. Lavoie,* 475 U.S. 813, 822-825 (1986) (same).

We think it plain that the announce clause is not narrowly tailored to serve impartiality (or the appearance of impartiality) in this sense. Indeed, the clause is barely tailored to serve that interest *at all,* inasmuch as it does not restrict speech for or against particular *parties,* but rather speech for or against particular *issues.* To be sure, when a case arises that turns on a legal issue on which the judge (as a candidate) had taken a particular stand, the party taking the opposite stand is likely to lose. But not because of any bias against that party, or favoritism toward the other party. *Any* party taking that position is just as likely to lose. The judge is applying the law (as he sees it) evenhandedly.

It is perhaps possible to use the term "impartiality" in the judicial context (though this is certainly not a common usage) to mean lack of preconception in favor of or against a particular *legal view.* This sort of impartiality would be concerned, not with guaranteeing litigants equal application of the law, but rather with guaranteeing them an equal chance to persuade the court on the legal points in their case. Impartiality in this sense may well be an interest served by the announce clause, but it is not a *compelling* state interest, as strict scrutiny requires. A judge's lack of predisposition regarding the relevant legal issues in a case has never been thought a necessary component of equal justice, and with good reason. For one thing, it is virtually impossible to find a judge who does not have preconceptions about the law. As then-Justice REHNQUIST observed of our own Court: "Since most Justices come to this bench no earlier than their middle years, it would be unusual if they had not by that time formulated at least some tentative notions that would influence them in their interpretation of the sweeping clauses of the Constitution and their interaction with one another. It would be not merely unusual, but extraordinary, if they had not at least given opinions as to constitutional issues in their previous legal careers." *Laird v. Tatum,* 409 U.S. 824, 835 (1972). Indeed, even if it were possible to select judges who did not have preconceived views on legal issues, it would hardly be desirable to do so. "Proof that a Justice's mind at the time he joined the Court was a complete *tabula rasa* in the area of constitutional adjudication would be evidence of lack of qualification, not lack of bias." *Ibid.* The Minnesota Constitution positively forbids the selection to courts of general jurisdiction of judges who are impartial in the sense of having no views on the law. Minn. Const., Art. VI, § 5 ("Judges of the supreme court, the court of appeals and the district court shall be learned in the law"). And since avoiding judicial preconceptions on legal issues is neither possible nor desirable, pretending otherwise by attempting to preserve the "appearance" of that type of impartiality can hardly be a compelling state interest either.

A third possible meaning of "impartiality" (again not a common one) might be described as open-mindedness. This quality in a judge demands, not that he have no preconceptions on legal issues, but that he be willing to consider views that oppose his preconceptions, and remain open to persuasion, when the issues arise in a pending case. *** Respondents argue that the announce clause serves the interest in open-mindedness, or at least in the appearance of open-mindedness, because it relieves a judge from pressure to rule a certain way in order to maintain consistency with statements the judge has previously made. ***

The short of the matter is this: In Minnesota, a candidate for judicial office may not say "I think it is constitutional for the legislature to prohibit same-sex marriages." He may say the very same thing, however, up until the very day before he declares himself a candidate, and may say it repeatedly (until litigation is pending) after he is elected. As a means of pursuing the objective of open-mindedness that respondents now articulate, the announce clause is so woefully underinclusive as to render belief in that purpose a challenge to the credulous.

The Minnesota Supreme Court's canon of judicial conduct prohibiting candidates for judicial election from announcing their views on disputed legal and political issues violates the First Amendment. [Reversed.]

Justice O'CONNOR, concurring.

I join the opinion of the Court but write separately to express my [concern that,] even aside from what judicial candidates may say while campaigning, the very practice of electing judges undermines [the interest in an impartial judiciary.]

Justice KENNEDY, concurring.

I agree with the Court that Minnesota's prohibition on judicial candidates' announcing their legal views is an unconstitutional abridgment of the freedom of speech. *** I adhere to my view, however, that content-based speech restrictions that do not fall within any traditional exception should be invalidated without inquiry into narrow tailoring or compelling government interests. The speech at issue here does not come within any of the exceptions to the First Amendment recognized by the Court.

[Justice STEVENS's dissent is omitted.]

Justice GINSBURG, with whom Justice STEVENS, Justice SOUTER, and Justice BREYER join, dissenting.

All parties to this case agree that, whatever the validity of the Announce Clause, the State may constitutionally prohibit judicial candidates from pledging or promising certain results. *** Uncoupled from the Announce Clause, the ban on pledges or promises is easily circumvented. By prefacing a campaign commitment with the caveat, "although I cannot promise anything," or by simply avoiding the language of promises or pledges altogether, a candidate could declare with impunity how she would decide specific issues. Semantic sanitizing of the candidate's commitment would not, however, diminish its pernicious effects on actual and perceived judicial impartiality. To use the Court's example, a candidate who campaigns by saying, "If elected, I will vote to uphold the legislature's power to prohibit same-sex marriages," will feel scarcely more pressure to honor that statement than the candidate who stands behind a podium and tells a throng of cheering supporters: "I think it is constitutional for the legislature to prohibit same-sex marriages." Made during a campaign, both statements contemplate a quid pro quo between candidate and voter.

Both effectively "bind [the candidate] to maintain that position after election." And both convey the impression of a candidate prejudging an issue to win votes.

By targeting statements that do not technically constitute pledges or promises but nevertheless "publicly [make] known how [the candidate] would decide" legal issues, the Announce Clause prevents this end run around the letter and spirit of its companion provision. No less than the pledges or promises clause itself, the Announce Clause is an indispensable part of Minnesota's effort to maintain the health of its judiciary, and is therefore constitutional for the same reasons.

Points for Discussion

a. Compelling State Interest

The majority and dissent disagreed about whether the Minnesota law serves a compelling state interest. Did they disagree about whether the state has a compelling interest in having a judiciary that is (and is perceived to be) impartial? Or did they just disagree about whether the challenged rule advances that interest? Assuming it is the latter, why is it clear that the state has a compelling interest in an impartial judiciary? Is the answer contained in the First Amendment, or in some other provision of the Constitution? If not, is the conclusion that a particular interest is "compelling" simply a matter of opinion? If so, is that why Justice Kennedy urged the Court to abandon interest-balancing in this context?

b. Narrowly Tailored

The Court explained that a content-based regulation in which the state has a compelling interest will survive strict scrutiny only if it does not "unnecessarily circumscribe protected expression." This formulation of the narrow-tailoring test makes clear that the challenged regulation cannot abridge more (or at least much more) speech than is necessary to achieve the government's compelling interest. How does the Court know when a regulation "unnecessarily" abridges speech?

c. Content-Based Regulation

Why did the parties agree that the challenged rule was a content-based restriction on speech? Did the law prohibit announcements only with respect to certain legal issues and not others? (Is that a pre-requisite to a finding that a regulation is content based?) Could the state successfully have argued that it was not concerned about the speech itself but instead about the secondary effects of the speech? If not, why not?

Hypothetical

After public outrage over several highly publicized instances in which persons convicted of crimes profited by writing books about their crimes, the state legislature enacted a statute that required publishers that published books by persons accused or convicted of a crime to deposit in an escrow account all income from works describing those crimes. Funds in the account were then made available to crime victims who obtained civil judgments against the convicted authors. A publisher of a tell-all book by a person convicted of a crime has challenged the law under the First and Fourteenth Amendments. How should the Court rule?

2. Reasonable Time, Place, and Manner Restrictions

The second general principle is that the government may impose **reasonable restrictions on the time, place, or manner of speech,** even in public forums, if the restrictions: (1) are content neutral; (2) are narrowly tailored to serve a significant governmental interest; and (3) leave open ample alternative channels for communication of the information. The Supreme Court devised this rule as a means of balancing free speech rights against important public needs, recognizing that allowing anyone to speak at any time and in any manner might be intolerable.

The case of *Kovacs v. Cooper*, 336 U.S. 77 (1949), is a classic example of this approach. The City of Trenton, New Jersey, enacted an ordinance generally barring sound-amplification devices from its streets. The Supreme Court held that the city could apply this ordinance to prohibit a truck from playing music and announcements from loud speakers on city roads. The regulation was content neutral because it applied to all sound amplification, regardless of the message being broadcast. The regulation also served significant government interests in promoting safety and controlling noise pollution. Justice Reed explained: "On the business streets of cities like Trenton, with its more than 125,000 people, such distractions would be dangerous to traffic at all hours useful for the dissemination of information, and in the residential thoroughfares the quiet and tranquility so desirable for city dwellers would likewise be at the mercy of advocates of particular religious, social or political persuasions." Finally, the prohibition restricted only one of many different ways of communicating with the public.

How different from strict scrutiny is this form of review for time, place, and manner restrictions? Consider the case that follows.

Ward v. Rock Against Racism

491 U.S. 781 (1989)

Justice KENNEDY delivered the opinion of the Court.

FYI

You can view the Naumburg Acoustic Bandshell here.

In the southeast portion of New York City's Central Park, about 10 blocks upward from the park's beginning point at 59th Street, there is an amphitheater and stage structure known as the Naumburg Acoustic Bandshell. The bandshell faces west across the remaining width of the park. In close proximity to the bandshell, and lying within the directional path of its sound, is a grassy open area called the Sheep Meadow. The city has designated the Sheep Meadow as a quiet area for passive recreations like reclining, walking, and reading. Just beyond the park, and also within the potential sound range of the bandshell, are the apartments and residences of Central Park West.

This case arises from the city's attempt to regulate the volume of amplified music at the bandshell so the performances are satisfactory to the audience without intruding upon those who use the Sheep Meadow or live on Central Park West and in its vicinity. The city's regulation requires bandshell performers to use sound-amplification equipment and a sound technician provided by the city. The challenge to this volume control technique comes from the sponsor of a rock concert. ***

Over the years, the city received numerous complaints about excessive sound amplification at respondent's concerts from park users and residents of areas adjacent to the park. *** The city considered various solutions to the sound-amplification problem. The idea of a fixed decibel limit for all performers using the bandshell was rejected because the impact on listeners of a single decibel level is not constant, but varies in response to changes in air temperature, foliage, audience size, and like factors. The city also rejected the possibility of employing a sound technician to operate the equipment provided by the various sponsors of bandshell events, because the city's technician might have had difficulty satisfying the needs of sponsors while operating unfamiliar, and perhaps inadequate, sound equipment. Instead, the city concluded that the most effective way to achieve adequate but not excessive sound amplification would be for the city to furnish high quality sound equipment and retain an independent, experienced sound technician for all performances at the bandshell. After an extensive search the city hired a private sound company capable of meeting the needs of all the varied users of the bandshell.

Music is one of the oldest forms of human expression. From Plato's discourse in the Republic to the totalitarian state in our own times, rulers have known its capacity to appeal to the intellect and to the emotions, and have censored musical compositions to serve the needs of the state. The Constitution prohibits any like attempts in our own legal order. Music, as a form of expression and communication, is protected under the First Amendment. In the case before us the performances apparently consisted of remarks by speakers, as well as rock music, but the case has been presented as one in which the constitutional challenge is to the city's regulation of the musical aspects of the concert; and, based on the principle we have stated, the city's guideline must meet the demands of the First Amendment. The parties do not appear to dispute that proposition.

Food for Thought

It is not difficult to see why some musical performances are protected as speech under the First Amendment; consider, for example, songs parodying the government or encouraging listeners to donate money for relief efforts. But why is all music—even music without lyrics—protected? Why does any form of "expression," as opposed to any form of "communication," count as "speech"?

Our cases make clear [that] even in a public forum the government may impose reasonable restrictions on the time, place, or manner of protected speech, provided the restrictions "are justified without reference to the content of the regulated speech, that they are narrowly tailored to serve a significant governmental interest, and that they leave open ample alternative channels for communication of the information." *Clark v. Community for Creative Non-Violence,* 468 U.S. 288, 293 (1984). We consider these requirements in turn.

The principal inquiry in determining content neutrality, in speech cases generally and in time, place, or manner cases in particular, is whether the government has adopted a regulation of speech because of disagreement with the message it conveys. The government's purpose is the controlling consideration. A regulation that serves purposes unrelated to the content of expression is deemed neutral, even if it has an incidental effect on some speakers or messages but not others. See *Renton v. Playtime Theatres, Inc.,* 475 U.S. 41, 47-48 (1986). *** The principal justification for the sound-amplification guideline is the city's desire to control noise levels at bandshell events, in order to retain the character of the Sheep Meadow and its more sedate activities, and to avoid undue intrusion into residential areas and other areas of the park. This justification for the guideline "ha[s] nothing to do with content," *Boos v. Barry,* 485 U.S. 312, 320 (1988), and it satisfies the requirement that time, place, or manner regulations be content neutral.

The only other justification offered below was the city's interest in "ensur[ing] the quality of sound at Bandshell events." Respondent urges that this justification is not content neutral because it is based upon the quality, and thus the content, of the speech being regulated. In respondent's view, the city is seeking to assert artistic control over performers at the bandshell by enforcing a bureaucratically determined, value-laden conception of good sound. That all performers who have used the city's sound equipment have been completely satisfied is of no moment, respondent argues, because "[t]he First Amendment does not permit and cannot tolerate state control of artistic expression merely because the State claims that [its] efforts will lead to 'top-quality' results."

While respondent's arguments that the government may not interfere with artistic judgment may have much force in other contexts, they are inapplicable to the facts of this case. The city has disclaimed in express terms any interest in imposing its own view of appropriate sound mix on performers. To the contrary, as the District Court found, the city requires its sound technician to defer to the wishes of event sponsors concerning sound mix. On this record, the city's concern with sound quality extends only to the clearly content-neutral goals of ensuring adequate sound amplification and avoiding the volume problems associated with inadequate sound mix. Any governmental attempt to serve purely esthetic goals by imposing subjective standards of acceptable sound mix on performers would raise serious First Amendment concerns, but this case provides us with no opportunity to address those questions. As related above, the District Court found that the city's equipment and its sound technician could meet all of the standards requested by the performers, including [respondent].

The city's regulation is also "narrowly tailored to serve a significant governmental interest." *Community for Creative Non-Violence,* 468 U.S., at 293. Despite respondent's protestations to the contrary, it can no longer be doubted that government "ha[s] a substantial interest in protecting its citizens from unwelcome noise." *City Council of Los Angeles v. Taxpayers for Vincent,* 466 U.S. 789, 806 (1984). This interest is perhaps at its greatest when government seeks to protect "the well-being, tranquility, and privacy of the home," *Frisby v. Schultz,* 487 U.S. 474, 484 (1988) (quoting *Carey v. Brown,* 447 U.S. 455, 471 (1980)), but it is by no means limited to that context, for the government may act to protect even such traditional public forums as city streets and parks from excessive noise. *Kovacs v. Cooper,* 336 U.S. 77, 86-87 (1988) (opinion of Reed, J.).

We think it also apparent that the city's interest in ensuring the sufficiency of sound amplification at bandshell events is a substantial one. The record indicates that inadequate sound amplification has had an adverse [effect] on the ability of some audiences to hear and enjoy performances at the bandshell. The city enjoys a substantial interest in ensuring the ability of its citizens to enjoy whatever benefits the city parks have to offer, from amplified music to silent meditation.

The city's second content-neutral justification for the guideline, that of ensuring "that the sound amplification [is] sufficient to reach all listeners within the defined concert-ground," also supports the city's choice of regulatory methods. By providing competent sound technicians and adequate amplification equipment, the city eliminated the problems of inexperienced technicians and insufficient sound volume that had plagued some bandshell performers in the past. No doubt this concern is not applicable to respondent's concerts, which apparently were characterized by more-than-adequate sound amplification. But that fact is beside the point, for the validity of the regulation depends on the relation it bears to the overall problem the government seeks to correct, not on the extent to which it furthers the government's interests in an individual case. Here, the regulation's effectiveness must be judged by considering all the varied groups that use the bandshell, and it is valid so long as the city could reasonably have determined that its interests overall would be served less effectively without the sound-amplification guideline than with it. Considering these proffered justifications together, therefore, it is apparent that the guideline directly furthers the city's legitimate governmental interests and that those interests would have been less well served in the absence of the sound-amplification guideline.

The final requirement, that the guideline leave open ample alternative channels of communication, is easily met. Indeed, in this respect the guideline is far less restrictive than regulations we have upheld in other cases, for it does not attempt to ban any particular manner or type of expression at a given place or time. Rather, the guideline continues to permit expressive activity in the bandshell, and has no effect on the quantity or content of that expression beyond regulating the extent of amplification. That the city's limitations on volume may reduce to some degree the potential audience for respondent's speech is of no consequence, for there has been no showing that the remaining avenues of communication are inadequate.

The city's sound-amplification guideline is narrowly tailored to serve the substantial and content-neutral governmental interests of avoiding excessive sound volume and providing sufficient amplification within the bandshell concert ground, and the guideline leaves open ample channels of communication. Accordingly, it is valid under the First Amendment as a reasonable regulation of the place and manner of expression.

Justice BLACKMUN concurs in the result.

Justice MARSHALL, with whom Justice BRENNAN and Justice STEVENS join, dissenting.

No one can doubt that government has a substantial interest in regulating the barrage of excessive sound that can plague urban life. Unfortunately, the majority plays to our shared impatience with loud noise to obscure the damage that it does to our First Amendment rights. Until today, a key safeguard of free speech has been government's obligation to adopt the least intrusive restriction necessary to achieve its goals. ***

Government's interest in avoiding loud sounds cannot justify giving government total control over sound equipment, any more than its interest in avoiding litter could justify a ban on handbill distribution. In both cases, government's legitimate goals can be effectively and less intrusively served by directly punishing the evil—the persons responsible for excessive sounds and the persons who litter. Indeed, the city concedes that it has an ordinance generally limiting noise but has chosen not to enforce it.[5]

———

Points for Discussion

a. Reasonable Restrictions

As described above, reasonable time, place, and manner restrictions are permissible if they are content neutral, are narrowly tailored to serve a substantial state interest, and leave open ample alternative means of communication. *Ward* concerned a challenge to regulations about sound amplification at a city bandshell. Would the First Amendment have prevented the city from demolishing the bandshell and replacing it with a ball field? If not, then how could the challenged regulation, which *permitted* concerts in the space,

———

[5] Significantly, the National Park Service relies on the very methods of volume control rejected by the city—monitoring sound levels on the perimeter of an event, communicating with event sponsors, and, if necessary, turning off the power. In light of the Park Service's "experienc[e] with thousands of events over the years," the city's claims that these methods of monitoring excessive sound are ineffective and impracticable are hard to accept.

not be a reasonable restriction? Doesn't the greater power here to get rid of the bandshell necessarily include the lesser power to regulate sound amplification at the bandshell?

b. Position of the Dissent

The dissent agreed that the government has a substantial interest in controlling noise, but concluded that it cannot advance that interest by actually asserting control over amplification equipment and thus over private expression itself. Does this view provide an answer to the "greater-includes-the-lesser" argument in favor of the challenged regulation? If you were arguing the case for the plaintiffs, what analogy might you offer to support this view?

Hypothetical

After receiving many complaints about the unsightliness of signs and advertisements on telephone poles and along sidewalks, the Los Angeles City Council adopted an ordinance that prohibits the posting of any signs on public property. A candidate for elected public office has filed a lawsuit alleging that the ordinance prevents him from promoting his candidacy and seeking a declaration that the ordinance violates the First and Fourteenth Amendments. At the same time, the City Council of Ladue, a suburb of St. Louis, adopted an ordinance that prohibits the display of all signs (other than "for sale" signs or signs displaying a house's street address) on residential property. A person who wants to display a sign stating "End the War" filed a suit seeking to enjoin enforcement of the ordinance on the ground that it violates the First and Fourteenth Amendments. The Supreme Court has decided to review both ordinances. How should the Court rule in the two cases?

---

3. Generally Applicable Regulations that Incidentally Affect Expression

As we have just seen, time, place, and manner restrictions directly regulate expressive activities: limitations on the permissible volume at which trucks can broadcast messages or musicians can amplify their music at public concerts, to take the examples we have just considered, by design apply to activities that are squarely protected by the First Amendment. But it is also possible for a government regulation that is *not* directed at protected expressive activities nevertheless to affect those activities. In this section, we consider how the Court reviews challenges to such regulations.

As a general matter, the Court will uphold a regulation that incidentally affects speech if "it furthers an important or substantial governmental interest; if the governmental interest is unrelated to the suppression of free expression; and if the incidental restriction on alleged First Amendment freedoms is no greater than is essential to the furtherance of that interest." *United States v. O'Brien*, 391 U.S. 367 (1968). This test, however, is more easily stated than applied, as the following cases demonstrate.

————————

United States v. O'Brien

391 U.S. 367 (1968)

Mr. Chief Justice WARREN delivered the opinion of the Court.

On the morning of March 31, 1966, David Paul O'Brien and three companions burned their Selective Service registration certificates on the steps of the South Boston Courthouse. A sizable crowd, including several agents of the Federal Bureau of Investigation, witnessed the event. Immediately after the burning, members of the crowd began attacking O'Brien and his companions. An FBI agent ushered O'Brien to safety inside the courthouse. After he was advised of his right to counsel and to silence, O'Brien stated to FBI agents that he had burned his registration certificate because of his beliefs, knowing that he was violating federal law. He produced the charred remains of the certificate, which, with his consent, were photographed.

> **FYI**
>
> Some opponents of the war in Vietnam burned their draft cards as a means of protesting the United States' involvement in the war.

For this act, O'Brien was indicted, tried, convicted, and sentenced in the United States District Court for the District of Massachusetts. He did not contest the fact that he had burned the certificate. He stated in argument to the jury that he burned the certificate publicly to influence others to adopt his antiwar beliefs, as he put it, "so that other people would reevaluate their positions with Selective Service, with the armed forces, and reevaluate their place in the culture of today, to hopefully consider my position."

[A 1965 Amendment to the Universal Military Training and Service Act of 1948 made it an offense knowingly to destroy or mutilate a selective service registration certificate, also known as a draft card. Prior to enactment of the Amendment, regulations required registrants to keep their certificates in their "personal possession at all times."] O'Brien first argues that the 1965 Amendment is unconstitutional as applied to him because his act of burning his registration certificate was protected "symbolic speech" within the First Amendment. His argument is that the freedom of expression which the First Amendment guarantees includes all modes of "communication of ideas by conduct," and that his conduct is within this definition because he did it in "demonstration against the war and against the draft."

We cannot accept the view that an apparently limitless variety of conduct can be labeled "speech" whenever the person engaging in the conduct intends thereby to express an idea. However, even on the assumption that the alleged communicative element in O'Brien's conduct is sufficient to bring into play the First Amendment, it does not necessarily follow that the destruction of a registration certificate is constitutionally protected activity. This Court has held that when "speech" and "nonspeech" elements are combined in the same course of conduct, a sufficiently important governmental interest in regulating the nonspeech element can justify incidental limitations on First Amendment freedoms. To characterize the quality of the governmental interest which must appear, the Court has employed a variety of descriptive terms: compelling; substantial; subordinating; paramount; cogent; strong. Whatever imprecision inheres in these terms, we think it clear that a government regulation is sufficiently justified if it is within the constitutional power of the Government; if it furthers an important or substantial governmental interest; if the governmental interest is unrelated to the suppression of free expression; and if the incidental restriction on alleged First Amendment freedoms is no greater than is essential to the furtherance of that interest. We find that the 1965 Amendment to § 12(b)(3) of the Universal Military Training and Service Act meets all of these requirements, and consequently that O'Brien can be constitutionally convicted for violating it.

> **Make the Connection**
>
> We will consider the extent to which "expressive conduct" is protected by the First Amendment later in this Chapter, when we discuss the Court's treatment of a law prohibiting flag burning.

The power of Congress to classify and conscript manpower for military service is "beyond question." *Lichter v. United States*, 334 U.S. 742, 755-758 (1948). Pursuant to this power, Congress may establish a system of registration for individuals liable for training and service, and may require such individuals within reason to cooperate in the registration system. The issuance of certificates indicating the registration and eligibility classification of individuals is a legitimate and substantial administrative aid in the functioning of this system. And legislation to insure the continuing availability of issued certificates serves a legitimate and substantial purpose in the system's administration.

O'Brien's argument to the contrary is necessarily premised upon his unrealistic characterization of Selective Service certificates. He essentially adopts the position that such certificates are so many pieces of paper designed to notify registrants of their registration or classification, to be retained or tossed in the wastebasket according to the convenience or taste of the registrant. Once the registrant has received notification, according to this view, there is no reason for him to retain the certificates. O'Brien notes that most of the information on a registration certificate serves no notification purpose at all; the registrant hardly needs to be told his address and physical characteristics. We agree that the registration certificate contains much information of which the registrant needs no notification. This circumstance, however, does not lead to the conclusion that the certificate serves no purpose, but that, like the classification certificate, it serves purposes in addition to initial notification. Many of these purposes would be defeated by the certificates' destruction or mutilation. Among these are:

1. The registration certificate serves as proof that the individual described thereon has registered for the draft. The classification certificate shows the eligibility classification of a named but undescribed individual. Voluntarily displaying the two certificates is an easy and painless way for a young man to dispel a question as to whether he might be delinquent in his Selective Service obligations. Correspondingly, the availability of the certificates for such display relieves the Selective Service System of the administrative burden it would otherwise have in verifying the registration and classification of all suspected delinquents. * * *

2. The information supplied on the certificates facilitates communication between registrants and local boards, simplifying the system and benefiting all concerned. To begin with, each certificate bears the address of the registrant's local board, an item unlikely to be committed to memory. Further, each card bears the registrant's Selective Service number, and a registrant who has his number readily available so that he can communicate it to his local board when he supplies or requests information can make simpler the board's task in locating his file. Finally, a registrant's inquiry, particularly through a local board other than his own, concerning his eligibility status is frequently answerable simply on the basis of his classification certificate; whereas, if the certificate were not reasonably available and the registrant were uncertain of his classification, the task of answering his questions would be considerably complicated.

3. Both certificates carry continual reminders that the registrant must notify his local board of any change of address, and other specified changes in his status. The smooth functioning of the system requires that local boards be continually aware of the status and whereabouts of registrants, and the destruction of certificates deprives the system of a potentially useful notice device.

4. The regulatory scheme involving Selective Service certificates includes clearly valid prohibitions against the alteration, forgery, or similar deceptive misuse of certificates. The destruction or mutilation of certificates obviously increases the difficulty of detecting and tracing abuses such as these. Further, a mutilated certificate might itself be used for deceptive purposes.

The many functions performed by Selective Service certificates establish beyond doubt that Congress has a legitimate and substantial interest in preventing their wanton and unrestrained destruction and assuring their continuing availability by punishing people who knowingly and wilfully destroy or mutilate them. And we are unpersuaded that the pre-existence of the nonpossession regulations in any way negates this interest.

[B]oth the governmental interest and the operation of the 1965 Amendment are limited to the noncommunicative aspect of O'Brien's conduct. The governmental interest and the scope of the 1965 Amendment are limited to preventing harm to the smooth and efficient functioning of the Selective Service System. When O'Brien deliberately rendered unavailable his registration certificate, he wilfully frustrated this governmental interest. For this noncommunicative impact of his conduct, and for nothing else, he was convicted. The case at bar is therefore unlike one where the alleged governmental interest in regulating conduct arises in some measure because the communication allegedly integral to the conduct is itself thought to be harmful. In *Stromberg v. People of State of California*, 283 U.S. 359 (1931), for example, this Court struck down a statutory phrase which punished people who expressed their "opposition to organized government" by displaying "any flag, badge, banner, or device." Since the statute there was aimed at suppressing communication it could not be sustained as a regulation of noncommunicative conduct. [Here,] a sufficient governmental interest has been shown to justify O'Brien's conviction.

O'Brien finally argues that the 1965 Amendment is unconstitutional as enacted because what he calls the "purpose" of Congress was "to suppress freedom of speech." We reject this argument because under settled principles the purpose of Congress, as O'Brien uses that term, is not a basis for declaring this legislation unconstitutional. It is a familiar principle of constitutional law that this Court will not strike down an otherwise constitutional statute on the basis of an alleged illicit legislative motive. *** Inquiries into congressional motives or purposes are a hazardous matter. When the issue is simply the interpretation of legislation, the Court will look to statements by legislators for guidance as to the purpose of the legislature, because the benefit to sound decision-making in this circumstance is thought sufficient to risk the possibility of misreading Congress' purpose. It is entirely a different matter when we are asked to void a statute that is, under well-settled criteria, constitutional on its face, on the basis of what fewer than a handful of Congressmen said about it. What motivates one legislator to make a speech about a statute is not necessarily what motivates scores of others to enact it, and the stakes are sufficiently high for us to eschew guesswork. We decline to void essentially on the ground that it is unwise legislation which Congress had the undoubted power to enact and which could be reenacted in its exact form if the same or another legislator made a "wiser" speech about it. *** Accordingly, we [reinstate] the judgment and sentence of the District Court.

Mr. Justice HARLAN, concurring.

I wish to make explicit my understanding that [the Court's decision] does not foreclose consideration of First Amendment claims in those rare instances when an "incidental" restriction upon expression, imposed by a regulation which furthers an "important or substantial" governmental interest and satisfies the Court's other criteria, in practice has the effect of entirely preventing a "speaker" from reaching a significant audience with whom he could not otherwise lawfully communicate. This is not such a case, since O'Brien manifestly could have conveyed his message in many ways other than by burning his draft card.

[Justice DOUGLAS's dissenting opinion is omitted.]

Points for Discussion

a. "Incidental Limitations on First Amendment Freedoms"

Is it clear that the statute prohibiting the destruction of a draft card imposed only an "incidental" limitation on O'Brien's ability to express his opposition to the war? After all, it prohibited the *exact* expressive conduct in which he engaged to protest the war. Is the point that O'Brien's conduct only tangentially conveyed a message, and thus was not entitled to robust protection under the First Amendment? Or that he could have found some other way to protest the war and thus communicate his message? We will consider the conundrum posed by "expressive conduct" later in this Chapter.

b. "Unrelated to the Suppression of Free Expression"

The O'Brien test applies, by its terms, only when the government's interest is "unrelated to the suppression of free expression." Accordingly, O'Brien scrutiny does not apply to content-based regulations. Could the government prohibit the burning of a draft card if "done for the specific purpose of protesting the draft"? Or would such a statute be content based and thus subject to strict scrutiny?

Is it clear that the *actual* statute at issue was content neutral? Suppose that upon receiving his draft card in the mail, O'Brien, upset by being drafted, threw his draft card in the trash. If the government had somehow learned of this act—for example, when O'Brien responded to a routine summons to the local draft board—do you think that he would have been prosecuted under the 1965 Amendment to the Universal Military Training and Service Act of 1948? If not, what does that suggest about whether the statute was "related to the suppression of free expression"?

c. The O'Brien Test and Reasonable Time, Place, or Manner Restrictions

Is there a difference between the O'Brien test and the test for time, place, and manner restrictions? Both require that the challenged regulation be content neutral, supported by a substantial governmental interest, and narrowly tailored to avoid burdening more expression than is necessary. In *Clark v. Community for Creative Non-Violence,* 468 U.S. 288 (1984), the Court suggested that the inquiries are essentially the same.

Under the O'Brien test, content-neutral laws that have an incidental effect on activities protected under the First Amendment are subject to an intermediate form of scrutiny. In the case that follows, consider whether (1) the challenged law was in fact content neutral and (2) whether, if so, the Court properly concluded that it was constitutionally valid.

Barnes v. Glen Theatre, Inc.

501 U.S. 560 (1991)

> **Take Note**
>
> Chief Justice Rehnquist's opinion was joined only by Justices O'Connor and Kennedy.

Chief Justice REHNQUIST delivered the opinion of the Court.

Respondents are two establishments in South Bend, Indiana, that wish to provide totally nude dancing as entertainment, and individual dancers who are employed at these establishments. They claim that the First Amendment's guarantee of freedom of expression prevents the State of Indiana from enforcing its public indecency law to prevent this form of dancing. [That law, Ind.Code § 35-45-4-1 (1988), makes it a misdemeanor for any person to "knowingly or intentionally, in a public place *** [appear] in a state of nudity with the intent to arouse the sexual desires of the person or another person." We] hold that the Indiana statutory requirement that the dancers in the establishments involved in this case must wear pasties and G-strings does not violate the First Amendment.

Several of our cases contain language suggesting that nude dancing of the kind involved here is expressive conduct protected by the First Amendment. *Schad v. Mount Ephraim,* 452 U.S. 61, 66 (1981). *** These statements support the conclusion of the Court of Appeals that nude dancing of the kind sought to be performed here is expressive conduct within the outer perimeters of the First Amendment, though we view it as only marginally so. This, of course, does not end our inquiry. We must determine [whether] the Indiana statute is an impermissible infringement of that protected activity.

Indiana, of course, has not banned nude dancing as such, but has proscribed public nudity across the board. The Supreme Court of Indiana has construed the Indiana statute to preclude nudity in what are essentially places of public accommodation such as the Glen Theatre and the Kitty Kat Lounge.

Applying the four-part *O'Brien* [test], we find that Indiana's public indecency statute is justified despite its incidental limitations on some expressive activity. The public indecency statute is clearly within the constitutional power of the State and furthers substantial governmental interests. It is impossible to discern, other than from the text of the statute, exactly what governmental interest the Indiana legislators had in mind when they enacted this statute, for Indiana does not record legislative history, and the State's highest court has not shed additional light on the statute's purpose. Nonetheless, the statute's purpose of protecting societal order and morality is clear from its text and history. Public indecency statutes of this sort are of ancient origin and presently exist in at least 47 States. Public indecency, including nudity, was a criminal offense at common law, and [p]ublic nudity was considered an act *malum in se.* *Le Roy v. Sidley,* 1 Sid. 168, 82 Eng.Rep. 1036 (K.B.1664). Public indecency statutes such as the one before us reflect moral disapproval of people appearing in the nude among strangers in public places.

> **Definition**
>
> An act *malum in se* is an act that is wrong in and of itself, wholly aside from whether it is formally prohibited by law.

The traditional police power of the States is defined as the authority to provide for the public health, safety, and morals, and we have upheld such a basis for legislation. *** Thus, the public indecency statute furthers a substantial government interest in protecting order and morality.

This interest is unrelated to the suppression of free expression. *** It can be argued, of course, that almost limitless types of conduct—including appearing in the nude in public—are "expressive," and in one sense of the word this is true. People who go about in the nude in public may be expressing something about themselves by so doing. But the court rejected this expansive notion of "expressive conduct" in *O'Brien* ***.

Respondents contend that even though prohibiting nudity in public generally may not be related to suppressing expression, prohibiting the performance of nude dancing is related to expression because the State seeks to prevent its erotic message. Therefore, they reason that the application of the Indiana statute to the nude dancing in this case violates the First Amendment ***. But we do not think that when Indiana applies its statute to the nude dancing in these nightclubs it is proscribing nudity because of the erotic message conveyed by the dancers. Presumably numerous other erotic performances are presented at these establishments and similar clubs without any interference from the State, so long as the performers wear a scant amount of clothing. Likewise, the requirement that the dancers don pasties and G-strings does not deprive the dance of whatever erotic message it conveys; it simply makes the message slightly less graphic. The perceived evil that Indiana seeks to address is not erotic dancing, but public nudity. The appearance of people of all shapes, sizes and ages in the nude at a beach, for example, would convey little if any erotic message, yet the State still seeks to prevent it. Public nudity is the evil the State seeks to prevent, whether or not it is combined with expressive activity.

The statutory prohibition is not a means to some greater end, but an end in itself. It is without cavil that the public indecency statute is "narrowly tailored"; Indiana's requirement that the dancers wear at least pasties and G-strings is modest, and the bare minimum necessary to achieve the State's purpose.

Justice SCALIA, concurring in the judgment.

In my view, [the] challenged regulation must be upheld, not because it survives some lower level of First Amendment scrutiny, but because, as a general law regulating conduct and not specifically directed at expression, it is not subject to First Amendment scrutiny at all. *** On its face, [Indiana's] law is not directed at expression in particular. *** The intent to convey a "message of eroticism" (or any other message) is not a necessary element of the statutory offense of public indecency; nor does one commit that statutory offense by conveying the most explicit "message of eroticism," so long as he does not [engage in public nudity] in the process. *** Were it the case that Indiana *in practice* targeted only expressive nudity, while turning a blind eye to nude beaches and unclothed purveyors of hot dogs and machine tools, it might be said that what posed as a regulation of conduct in general was in reality a regulation of only communicative conduct. Respondents have adduced no evidence of that.

The dissent confidently asserts that the purpose of restricting nudity in public places in general is to protect nonconsenting parties from offense; and argues that since only consenting, admission-paying patrons see respondents dance, that purpose cannot apply and the only remaining purpose must relate to the communicative elements of the performance. Perhaps the dissenters believe that "offense to others" *ought* to be the only reason for restricting nudity in public places generally, but there is no basis for thinking that our society has ever shared that Thoreauvian "you-may-do-what-you-like-so-long-as-it-does-not-injure-someone-else" beau ideal—much less for thinking that it was written into the

Constitution. The purpose of Indiana's nudity law would be violated, I think, if 60,000 fully consenting adults crowded into the Hoosier Dome to display their genitals to one another, even if there were not an offended innocent in the crowd. Our society prohibits, and all human societies have prohibited, certain activities not because they harm others but because they are considered, in the traditional phrase, *"contra bonos mores,"* i.e., immoral. In American society, such prohibitions have included, for example, sadomasochism, cock-fighting, bestiality, suicide, drug use, prostitution, and sodomy. While there may be great diversity of view on whether various of these prohibitions should exist (though I have found few ready to abandon, in principle, all of them), there is no doubt that, absent specific constitutional protection for the conduct involved, the Constitution does not prohibit them simply because they regulate "morality." See *Bowers v. Hardwick*, 478 U.S. 186 (1986). The purpose of the Indiana statute, as both its text and the manner of its enforcement demonstrate, is to enforce the traditional moral belief that people should not expose their private parts indiscriminately, regardless of whether those who see them are disedified. Since that is so, the dissent has no basis for positing that, where only thoroughly edified adults are present, the purpose must be repression of communication.

Since the Indiana regulation is a general law not specifically targeted at expressive conduct, its application to such conduct does not in my view implicate the First Amendment. The First Amendment explicitly protects "the freedom of speech [and] of the press"—oral and written speech—not "expressive conduct." When any law restricts speech, even for a purpose that has nothing to do with the suppression of communication, *** we insist that it meet the high, First-Amendment standard of justification. But virtually *every* law restricts conduct, and virtually *any* prohibited conduct can be performed for an expressive purpose—if only expressive of the fact that the actor disagrees with the prohibition. It cannot reasonably be demanded, therefore, that every restriction of expression incidentally produced by a general law regulating conduct pass normal First Amendment scrutiny, or even—as some of our cases have suggested, see, *e.g., United States v. O'Brien*, 391 U.S. 367, 377 (1968)—that it be justified by an "important or substantial" government interest. Nor do our holdings require such justification: We have never invalidated the application of a general law simply because the conduct that it reached was being engaged in for expressive purposes and the government could not demonstrate a sufficiently important state interest.

This is not to say that the First Amendment affords no protection to expressive conduct. Where the government prohibits conduct *precisely because of its communicative attributes,* we hold the regulation unconstitutional. See, *e.g., Texas v. Johnson*, 491 U.S. 397 (1989) [(burning flag)]; *Tinker v. Des Moines Independent Community School Dist.*, 393 U.S. 503 (1969) (wearing black arm bands). In each of the foregoing cases, we explicitly found that suppressing communication was the object of the regulation of conduct. Where that has not been the case, however—where suppression of communicative use of the conduct was merely the incidental effect of forbidding the conduct for other reasons—we have allowed the regulation to stand. *O'Brien*, 391 U.S., at 377. *** Such a regime ensures that the government does not act to suppress communication, without requiring that all conduct-restricting regulation (which means in effect all regulation) survive an enhanced level of scrutiny.

Justice SOUTER, concurring in the judgment.

I agree with the plurality and the dissent that an interest in freely engaging in the nude dancing at issue here is subject to a degree of First Amendment protection. *** I nonetheless write separately to rest my concurrence in the judgment, not on the possible sufficiency of society's moral views to justify the limitations at issue, but on the State's substantial interest in combating the secondary effects of adult entertainment establishments of the sort typified by respondents' establishments.

In my view, the interest asserted by petitioners in preventing prostitution, sexual assault, and other criminal activity, although presumably not a justification for all applications of the statute, is sufficient under *O'Brien* to justify the State's enforcement of the statute against the type of adult entertainment at issue here. *** The type of entertainment respondents seek to provide is plainly of the same character as that at issue in *Renton v. Playtime Theatres, Inc.,* 475 U.S. 41 (1986). It therefore is no leap to say that live nude dancing of the sort at issue here is likely to produce the same pernicious secondary effects as the adult films displaying "specified anatomical areas" at issue in *Renton.* *** Because the State's interest in banning nude dancing results from a simple correlation of such dancing with other evils, rather than from a relationship between the other evils and the expressive component of the dancing, the interest is unrelated to the suppression of free expression.

Justice WHITE, with whom Justice MARSHALL, Justice BLACKMUN, and Justice STEVENS join, dissenting.

Both the plurality and Justice SCALIA in his opinion concurring in the judgment overlook a fundamental and critical aspect of our cases upholding the States' exercise of their police powers. None of the cases they rely upon, including *O'Brien* and *Bowers*, involved anything less than truly *general* proscriptions on individual conduct. *** By contrast, in this case Indiana does not suggest that its statute applies to, or could be applied to, nudity wherever it occurs, including the home. We do not understand the plurality or Justice SCALIA to be suggesting that Indiana could constitutionally enact such an intrusive prohibition, nor do we think such a suggestion would be tenable ***. As a result, the plurality and Justice SCALIA's simple references to the State's general interest in promoting societal order and morality are not sufficient justification for a statute which concededly reaches a significant amount of protected expressive activity.

Legislators do not just randomly select certain conduct for proscription; they have reasons for doing so and those reasons illuminate the purpose of the law that is passed. Indeed, a law may have multiple purposes. The purpose of forbidding people to appear nude in parks, beaches, hot dog stands, and like public places is to protect others from offense. But that could not possibly be the purpose of preventing nude dancing in theaters and barrooms since the viewers are exclusively consenting adults who pay money to see these dances. The purpose of the proscription in these contexts is to protect the viewers from what the State believes is the harmful message that nude dancing communicates.

In arriving at its conclusion, the plurality concedes that nude dancing conveys an erotic message and concedes that the message would be muted if the dancers wore pasties and G-strings. Indeed, the emotional or erotic impact of the dance is intensified by the nudity of the performers. *** The sight of a fully clothed, or even a partially clothed, dancer generally will have a far different impact on a spectator than that of a nude dancer, even if the same dance is performed. The nudity is itself an expressive component of the dance, not merely incidental "conduct."

This being the case, it cannot be that the statutory prohibition is unrelated to expressive conduct. Since the State permits the dancers to perform if they wear pasties and G-strings but forbids nude dancing, it is precisely because of the distinctive, expressive content of the nude dancing performances at issue in this case that the State seeks to apply the statutory prohibition. It is only because nude dancing performances may generate emotions and feelings of eroticism and sensuality among the spectators that the State seeks to regulate such expressive activity, apparently on the assumption that creating or emphasizing such thoughts and ideas in the minds of the spectators may lead to increased prostitution and the degradation of women. But generating thoughts, ideas, and emotions is the essence of communication.

That fact dictates the level of First Amendment protection to be accorded the performances at issue here. *** Content based restrictions "will be upheld only if narrowly drawn to accomplish a compelling governmental interest." *** The plurality and Justice SOUTER do not go beyond saying that the state interests asserted here are important and substantial. But even if there were compelling interests, the Indiana statute is not narrowly drawn. If the State is genuinely concerned with prostitution and associated evils, *** it can adopt restrictions that do not interfere with the expressiveness of nonobscene nude dancing performances. *** Banning an entire category of expressive activity, however, generally does not satisfy the narrow tailoring requirement of strict First Amendment scrutiny.

Points for Discussion

a. Content Neutral or Content Based?

Part of the disagreement between the dissent, on the one hand, and the plurality and Justice Scalia, on the other, was over whether Indiana's public indecency law's application to the nude dancing establishments was "unrelated to the suppression of free expression"— that is, content neutral. Assuming a state can ban nudity in public generally—which the dissent did not seem to question—is it clear that the application of such a ban to nude dancing has nothing to do with the expressive elements of the dancing? What was the dissent's reasoning in asserting that it does? What was the plurality's response?

b. Conduct v. Speech

Another source of disagreement in the case was the extent to which nude dancing falls within the scope of the First Amendment at all. The plurality conceded that it does, although "only marginally so," and Justice Souter and the four dissenters likewise concluded that it is an activity protected by the First Amendment. In what way is nude dancing a form of "expression"? What is the "message" that is communicated by nude dancing? In what way does the "message" it communicates differ from the message that dancing while fully clothed communicates? For that matter, in what way does the message communicated by nude dancing differ from the "message" communicated by walking down a public street in the nude?

Clearly not all conduct is protected by the First Amendment. But it seems just as clear that some conduct contains strong expressive elements. Justice Scalia, for example, cited *Tinker v. Des Moines Independent Community School Dist.*, 393 U.S. 503 (1969). In that case, the Court held that a school policy forbidding the wearing of black arm bands—which some students had done as a form of protest against the Vietnam War—violated the First Amendment. There was little doubt that the wearing of the arm bands—whatever one thinks of the message—was a means (and apparently a potent one, given the school's response) of conveying a message.

Can you articulate a test for identifying when "conduct" contains sufficiently strong expressive elements that it is entitled to protection under the First Amendment? We will consider this question further later in this chapter.

c. The *O'Brien* Test and Laws of General Applicability

In his separate opinion, Justice Scalia asserted that content-neutral laws of general applicability should not be subject to scrutiny under the First Amendment at all, even when they incidentally burden expression. He has expressed a similar view in the context of the First Amendment's protection for the free exercise of religion, and in that context a majority of the Court agreed. See *Employment Div., Dept. of Human Resources of Ore. v. Smith*, 494 U.S. 872 (1990). What are the virtues of such an approach? What are the costs?

> **Make the Connection**
>
> We will consider the First Amendment's protection for the free exercise of religion, and the Court's decision in *Smith*, in Chapter 17.

4. Prior Restraints

A **prior restraint on speech** is an executive or judicial order prohibiting a communication before it has occurred. See *Alexander v. United States*, 509 U.S. 544, 550 (1993). For example, in *Nebraska Press Association v. Stuart*, 427 U.S. 539 (1976), a state court was worried that pretrial publicity might frustrate the ability of a defendant charged with a triple murder to receive a fair trial. To address this concern, the state court issued an injunction barring the press from publishing accounts of the defendant's alleged confession and other facts. This order was a prior restraint because it blocked the publication of speech (i.e., news reports) before it occurred.

The Court has long held that the First Amendment provides more protection against prior restraints on speech than it does against subsequent liability for speech. For example,

FYI

The general counsel of *The New York Times* summarized the case that follows in this way: "In 1971, the Pentagon Papers—the Defense Department's top-secret study of the growth of United States military involvement in Vietnam—were leaked by a government official to *The New York Times*. On June 13 of that year, the newspaper began publishing articles based on the documents. When the government learned of this, the Department of Justice asked for a temporary restraining order, which was granted." The following litigation ensued.

the Supreme Court has held that the First Amendment would not allow a state to enjoin a publisher in advance from publishing a "malicious, scandalous and defamatory newspaper, magazine or other periodical," *Near v. Minnesota ex rel. Olson*, 283 U.S. 697, 707 (1931), even if the state could constitutionally provide a remedy for libel after publication, id. at 714. The Supreme Court has explained its concern over prior restraints concisely: "It is always difficult to know in advance what an individual will say, and the line between legitimate and illegitimate speech is often so finely drawn that the risks of freewheeling censorship are formidable." *Southeastern Promotions, Ltd. v. Conrad*, 420 U.S. 546, 558-559 (1975).

The following case is a leading decision on the issue of whether the prohibition on prior restraints is absolute. As you read the various opinions in the case, consider whether there are any exceptions to the rule against prior restraints, and if so when they can be applied.

New York Times Co. v. United States

403 U.S. 713 (1971)

PER CURIAM.

We granted certiorari in these cases in which the United States seeks to enjoin the New York Times and the Washington Post from publishing the contents of a classified study entitled "History of U.S. Decision-Making Process on Viet Nam Policy."

"Any system of prior restraints of expression comes to this Court bearing a heavy presumption against its constitutional validity." *Bantam Books, Inc. v. Sullivan*, 372 U.S. 58, 70 (1963). The Government "thus carries a heavy burden

Definition

Per curiam means by the court. *Black's Law Dictionary* (8th ed. 2004). In this case, a majority of the Supreme Court agreed on the ultimate judgment in the case, but the individual justices in the majority could not agree on the reasoning. They therefore issued an opinion for the Court, and then wrote separate concurring opinions offering their different reasons for the judgment.

of showing justification for the imposition of such a restraint." *Organization for a Better Austin v. Keefe*, 402 U.S. 415, 419 (1971). The District Court for the Southern District of New York in the New York Times case, and the District Court for the District of Columbia and the Court of Appeals for the District of Columbia Circuit, in the Washington Post case held that the Government had not met that burden. We agree. So ordered.

Mr. Justice BLACK, with whom Mr. Justice DOUGLAS joins, concurring.

> ### Make the Connection
>
> We will consider the freedom of the press, and the extent to which that protection is different from the freedom of speech, in Chapter 15.

In seeking injunctions against these newspapers and in its presentation to the Court, the Executive Branch seems to have forgotten the essential purpose and history of the First Amendment. *** Both the history and language of the First Amendment support the view that the press must be left free to publish news, whatever the source, without censorship, injunctions, or prior restraints.

*** In my view, far from deserving condemnation for their courageous reporting, the New York Times, the Washington Post, and other newspapers should be commended for serving the purpose that the Founding Fathers saw so clearly. In revealing the workings of government that led to the Vietnam war, the newspapers nobly did precisely that which the Founders hoped and trusted they would do.

The Government's case here is based on premises entirely different from those that guided the Framers of the First Amendment. *** [T]he Government argues in its brief that in spite of the First Amendment, "[t]he authority of the Executive Department to protect the nation against publication of information whose disclosure would endanger the national security stems from two interrelated sources: the constitutional power of the President over the conduct of foreign affairs and his authority as Commander-in-Chief."

In other words, we are asked to hold that despite the First Amendment's emphatic command, the Executive Branch, the Congress, and the Judiciary can make laws enjoining publication of current news and abridging freedom of the press in the name of "national security." The Government does not even attempt to rely on any act of Congress. *** To find that the President has "inherent power" to halt the publication of news by resort to the courts would wipe out the First Amendment and destroy the fundamental liberty and security of the very people the Government hopes to make "secure." No one can read the history of the adoption of the First Amendment without being convinced beyond any doubt that it was injunctions like those sought here that Madison and his collaborators intended to outlaw in this Nation for all time.

> ### Make the Connection
>
> We considered the President's "inherent" constitutional powers, and the President's powers over foreign affairs and as Commander in Chief, in Chapter 5.

Mr. Justice DOUGLAS, with whom Mr. Justice BLACK joins, concurring.

The dominant purpose of the First Amendment was to prohibit the widespread practice of governmental suppression of embarrassing information. It is common knowledge that the First Amendment was adopted against the widespread use of the common law of seditious libel to punish the dissemination of material that is embarrassing to the powers-that-be. See T. Emerson, The System of Freedom of Expression, c. V (1970); Z. Chafee, Free Speech in the United States, c. XIII (1941). The present cases will, I think, go down in history as the most dramatic illustration of that principle. A debate of large proportions goes on in the Nation over our posture in Vietnam. That debate antedated the disclosure of the contents of the present documents. The latter are highly relevant to the debate in progress.

Secrecy in government is fundamentally anti-democratic, perpetuating bureaucratic errors. Open debate and discussion of public issues are vital to our national health. On public questions there should be "uninhibited, robust, and wide-open" debate. *New York Times Co. v. Sullivan*, 376 U.S. 254, 269-270 (1964).

Mr. Justice BRENNAN, concurring.

The error that has pervaded these cases from the outset was the granting of any injunctive relief whatsoever, interim or otherwise. The entire thrust of the Government's claim throughout these cases has been that publication of the material sought to be enjoined "could," or "might," or "'may" prejudice the national interest in various ways. But the First Amendment tolerates absolutely no prior judicial restraints of the press predicated upon surmise or conjecture that untoward consequences may result. Our cases, it is true, have indicated that there is a single, extremely narrow class of cases in which the First Amendment's ban on prior judicial restraint may be overridden. Our cases have thus far indicated that such cases may arise only when the Nation "is at war," *Schenck v. United States*, 249 U.S. 47, 52 (1919), during which times "[n]o one would question but that a government might prevent actual obstruction to its recruiting service or the publication of the sailing dates of transports or the number and location of troops." *Near v. Minnesota ex rel. Olson*, 283 U.S. 697, 716 (1931). Even if the present world situation were assumed to be tantamount to a time of war, or if the power of presently available armaments would justify even in peacetime the suppression of information that would set in motion a nuclear holocaust, in neither of these actions has the Government presented or even alleged that publication of items from or based upon the material at issue would cause the happening of an event of that nature. [O]nly governmental allegation and proof that publication must inevitably, directly, and immediately cause the occurrence of an event kindred to imperiling the safety of a transport already at sea can support even the issuance of an interim restraining order. In no event may mere conclusions be sufficient: for if the Executive Branch seeks judicial aid in preventing publication, it must inevitably submit the basis upon which that aid is sought to scrutiny by the judiciary. And therefore, every restraint issued in this case, whatever its form, has violated the First Amendment—and not less so because that restraint was justified as necessary to afford the courts an opportunity to examine the claim more thoroughly. Unless and until the Government has clearly made out its case, the First Amendment commands that no injunction may issue.

Mr. Justice WHITE, with whom Mr. Justice STEWART joins, concurring.

I concur in today's judgments, but only because of the concededly extraordinary protection against prior restraints enjoyed by the press under our constitutional system. I do not say that in no circumstances would the First Amendment permit an injunction against publishing information about government plans or operations. Nor, after examining the materials the Government characterizes as the most sensitive and destructive, can I deny that revelation of these documents will do substantial damage to public interests. Indeed, I am confident that their disclosure will have that result. But I nevertheless agree that the United States has not satisfied the very heavy burden that it must meet to warrant an injunction against publication in these cases, at least in the absence of express and appropriately limited congressional authorization for prior restraints in circumstances such as these.

The Government's position is simply stated: The responsibility of the Executive for the conduct of the foreign affairs and for the security of the Nation is so basic that the President is entitled to an injunction against publication of a newspaper story whenever he can convince a court that the information to be revealed threatens "grave and irreparable" injury to the public interest; and the injunction should issue whether or not the material to be published is classified, whether or not publication would be lawful under relevant criminal statutes enacted by Congress, and regardless of the circumstances by which the newspaper came into possession of the information.

At least in the absence of legislation by Congress, based on its own investigations and findings, I am quite unable to agree that the inherent powers of the Executive and the courts reach so far as to authorize remedies having such sweeping potential for inhibiting publications by the press. Much of the difficulty inheres in the "grave and irreparable danger" standard suggested by the United States. If the United States were to have judgment under such a standard in these cases, our decision would be of little guidance to other courts in other cases, for the material at issue here would not be available from the Court's opinion or from public records, nor would it be published by the press. Indeed, even today where we hold that the United States has not met its burden, the material remains sealed in court records and it is properly not discussed in today's opinions. Moreover, because the material poses substantial dangers to national interests and because of the hazards of criminal sanctions, a responsible press may choose never to publish the more sensitive materials. To sustain the Government in these cases would start the courts down a long and hazardous road that I am not willing to travel, at least without congressional guidance and direction.

Mr. Justice MARSHALL, concurring.

It would [be] utterly inconsistent with the concept of separation of powers for this Court to use its power of contempt to prevent behavior that Congress has specifically declined to prohibit. There would be a similar damage to the basic concept of these co-equal branches of Government if when the Executive Branch has adequate authority granted by Congress to protect "national security" it can choose instead to invoke the contempt power of a court to enjoin the threatened conduct. The Constitution provides that Congress shall make laws, the President execute laws, and courts interpret laws. *Youngstown Sheet & Tube*

Co. v. Sawyer, 343 U.S. 579 (1952). ***

Mr. Chief Justice BURGER, dissenting.

In these cases, the imperative of a free and unfettered press comes into collision with another imperative, the effective functioning of a complex modern government and specifically the effective exercise of certain constitutional powers of the Executive. Only those who view the First Amendment as an absolute in all circumstances—a view I respect, but reject—can find such cases as these to be simple or easy.

Mr. Justice HARLAN, with whom THE CHIEF JUSTICE and Mr. Justice BLACKMUN join, dissenting.

With all respect, I consider that the Court has been almost irresponsibly feverish in dealing with these cases. Both the Court of Appeals for the Second Circuit and the Court of Appeals for the District of Columbia Circuit rendered judgment on June 23. The New York Times' petition for certiorari, its motion for accelerated consideration thereof, and its application for interim relief were filed in this Court on June 24 at about 11 a.m. The application of the United States for interim relief in the Post case was also filed here on June 24 at about 7:15 p.m. This Court's order setting a hearing before us on June 26 at 11 a.m., a course which I joined only to avoid the possibility of even more peremptory action by the Court, was issued less than 24 hours before. The record in the Post case was filed with the Clerk shortly before 1 p.m. on June 25; the record in the Times case did not arrive until 7 or 8 o'clock that same night. The briefs of the parties were received less than two hours before argument on June 26.

This frenzied train of events took place in the name of the presumption against prior restraints created by the First Amendment. Due regard for the extraordinarily important and difficult questions involved in these litigations should have led the Court to shun such a precipitate timetable. *** Forced as I am to reach the merits of these cases, I dissent from the opinion and judgments of the Court. Within the severe limitations imposed by the time constraints under which I have been required to operate, I can only state my reasons in telescoped form, even though in different circumstances I would have felt constrained to deal with the cases in the fuller sweep indicated above.

> **FYI**
>
> The Court issued its decision in this case on June 30, 1971, four days after the argument.

It is plain to me that the scope of the judicial function in passing upon the activities of the Executive Branch of the Government in the field of foreign affairs is very narrowly restricted. This view is, I think, dictated by the concept of separation of powers upon which our constitutional system rests. *** *See United States v. Curtiss-Wright Export Corp.*, 299 U.S. 304, 319-321 (1936), collecting authorities.

From this constitutional primacy in the field of foreign affairs, it seems to me that certain conclusions necessarily follow. *** The power to evaluate [what President Washington called] the "pernicious influence" of premature disclosure [of sensitive materials related to foreign affairs] is not [lodged] in the Executive alone. I agree that, in performance of its duty to protect the values of the First Amendment against political pressures, the judiciary must review the initial Executive determination to the point of satisfying itself that the subject matter of the dispute does lie within the proper compass of the President's foreign relations power. *** Moreover the judiciary may properly insist that the determination that disclosure of the subject matter would irreparably impair the national security be made by the head of the Executive Department concerned—here the Secretary of State or the Secretary of Defense—after actual personal consideration by that officer. This safeguard is required in the analogous area of executive claims of privilege for secrets of state. But in my judgment the judiciary may not properly go beyond these two inquiries and redetermine for itself the probable impact of disclosure on the national security.

Even if there is some room for the judiciary to override the executive determination, it is plain that the scope of review must be exceedingly narrow. I can see no indication in the opinions of either the District Court or the Court of Appeals in the Post litigation that the conclusions of the Executive were given even the deference owing to an administrative agency, much less that owing to a co-equal branch of the Government operating within the field of its constitutional prerogative.

Mr. Justice BLACKMUN, dissenting.

The First Amendment [is] only one part of an entire Constitution. Article II of the great document vests in the Executive Branch primary power over the conduct of foreign affairs and places in that branch the responsibility for the Nation's safety. Each provision of the Constitution is important, and I cannot subscribe to a doctrine of unlimited absolutism for the First Amendment at the cost of downgrading other provisions. *** What is needed here is a weighing, upon properly developed standards, of the broad right of the press to print and of the very narrow right of the Government to prevent. Such standards are not yet developed. The parties here are in disagreement as to what those standards should be. But even the newspapers concede that there are situations where restraint is in order and is constitutional. ***

I strongly urge, and sincerely hope, that these two newspapers will be fully aware of their ultimate responsibilities to the United States of America. Judge Wilkey, dissenting in the District of Columbia case, after a review of only the affidavits before his court (the basic papers had not then been made available by either party), concluded that there were a number of examples of documents that, if in the possession of the Post, and if published, "could clearly result in great harm to the nation," and he defined "harm" to mean "the death of soldiers, the destruction of alliances, the greatly increased difficulty of negotiation with our enemies, the inability of our diplomats to negotiate ***." I, for one, have now been able to give at least some cursory study not only to the affidavits, but to the material itself. I regret to say that from this examination I fear that Judge Wilkey's statements have possible foundation. *** I hope that damage has not already been done. If, however, damage has been done, and if, with the Court's action today, these newspapers proceed to publish the critical documents and there results therefrom [the consequences that Judge Wilkey feared,] to which list I might add the factors of prolongation of the war and of further delay in the freeing of United States prisoners, then the Nation's people will know where the responsibility for these sad consequences rests.

Points for Discussion

a. Prior Restraint on Publication vs. Punishment After Publication

If releasing classified documents would violate a federal criminal law, would the First Amendment bar the government from prosecuting the newspapers for publishing the Pentagon Papers? The Court did not reach this question. But in omitted portions of the opinions excerpted above, four justices mentioned this issue. Why would subsequent prosecution differ from prior restraint? Why wouldn't a federal law prohibiting the publication of sensitive government documents itself violate the First Amendment?

In any event, wouldn't a person who is willing to violate a federal statute prohibiting the communication of certain information, even though the statute authorizes punishment for the disclosure, also be willing to violate a judicial order prohibiting the communication of the same information? In thinking about this question, consider the relative status of laws and judicial orders. If the person believes that the statute prohibiting the communication violates the First Amendment, on its face or as applied, then he can assert such a defense in the course of the prosecution. And if he is correct, then the First Amendment defense will shield him from punishment. Is the same true of judicial orders? Can a court punish a person who violates a judicial order, even if the order turns out to have been an unconstitutional prior restraint?

b. Justifying Prior Restraints

How many Justices concluded that prior restraints are permissible under at least some circumstances? In the view of those Justices, when is a prior restraint justified? Do those circumstances exist only when the President or an officer of the Executive Branch seeks the restraint, or might they also apply when a state official, such as a prosecutor or Governor, seeks a restraint?

Hypothetical

In World War II, Allied Forces devised an elaborate plan, Operation Over-lord, for launching an amphibious invasion of France to fight the occupying Nazi forces. The success of the plan depended to a large extent on keeping the exact date and location of the invasion secret from the German forces. Tens of thou-sands of lives were at stake in the immediate battle, and failure by the Allies may have changed the outcome of the war. We now know, of course, that the Allies planned the invasion for June 6, 1944, also known as "D-Day." Suppose that the *New York Times* had learned the details of the invasion in advance. Would a court have had authority to enjoin the newspaper from publishing this information? Or would such a prior restraint have violated the First Amendment?

5. Vague or Overbroad Restrictions

We will see later in this chapter that some kinds of speech do not have full protection under the First Amendment. The government, for example, may pass laws restricting libel, fighting words, and obscenity. But if not artfully phrased, a legislature's attempts to regulate these kinds of speech may suffer from two common problems in the First Amendment area.

First, the government might pass a law that is **overbroad**, meaning that it reaches both protected and unprotected speech. For example, the federal Child Pornography Preven-tion Act of 1996 outlawed possession not only of actual pictures of children, but also of "any visual depiction, including any photograph, film, video, picture, or computer or computer-generated image or picture" that "is, or appears to be, of a minor engaging in sexually explicit conduct." The Supreme Court held that this statute violated the First Amendment because it was overbroad. It concluded that, although the government may regulate actual child pornography and obscenity, it cannot ban any image merely because it appears to involve children. "Pictures of what appear to be 17-year-olds engaging in sexu-ally explicit activity," the Court said, "do not in every case contravene community standards [of obscenity]." See *Ashcroft v. Free Speech Coalition*, 535 U.S. 234 (2002).

Second, the government might enact a law that suffers from **vagueness**, meaning that the law does not make clear to a reasonable person what it prohibits and what it does not. For example, a Nevada Supreme Court rule prohibited a lawyer from making extrajudicial statements to the media that would have a "substantial likelihood of materially prejudicing" a pending case, but the prohibition was subject to an exception allowing the lawyer to "state without elaboration [the] general nature of [the] defense." The Supreme Court recognized that a state court may, consistently with the First Amendment, limit what lawyers can say about a pending case, but it nevertheless held that the challenged rule was void for vagueness. The Court said: "A lawyer seeking to avail himself of [the exception] must guess at its contours. The right to explain the 'general' nature of the defense without 'elaboration' provides insufficient guidance because 'general' and 'elaboration' are both classic terms of degree." *Gentile v. State Bar of Nevada*, 501 U.S. 1030, 1048-49 (1991).

A special and important procedural rule applies to lawsuits claiming that a law violates the First Amendment because of overbreadth or vagueness. In general, when claiming that a law is unconstitutional, a plaintiff can assert either an "**as-applied challenge**" or a "**facial challenge**" to the law. In an as-applied challenge, the plaintiff claims that the law is unconstitutional as applied to the facts of his or her case. In a typical facial challenge, by contrast, the plaintiff claims that the law is "invalid *in toto*—and therefore incapable of any valid application." *Steffel v. Thompson*, 415 U.S. 452, 474 (1974).

> **Make the Connection**
>
> We briefly considered the difference between as-applied and facial challenges in Chapter 3, when we considered cases concerning the scope of Congress's power under the Commerce Clause.

In the First Amendment context, however, the standard for facial challenges on the ground of overbreadth and vagueness is relaxed. The Supreme Court has held that any law that is "substantially overbroad" in its application to protected speech may be invalidated on its face. *Members of City Council of Los Angeles v. Taxpayers for Vincent*, 466 U.S. 789, 800 (1984). In other words, the plaintiff does not have to show that the law is unconstitutional in every case, or even that it would be unconstitutional as applied to the facts of his or her case. Similarly, a plaintiff can challenge a law on its face as being void for vagueness if the law "fails to draw reasonably clear lines between" what is permitted or not, *Smith v. Goguen*, 415 U.S. 566, 569 (1974), or if the law "encourages arbitrary enforcement by failing to describe with sufficient particularity" what is permitted and what is not, *Kolender v. Lawson*, 461 U.S. 352 (1983). The standards for facial challenges are relaxed because an overbroad or vague law may have a "**chilling effect**" on protected speech; unless the law's constitutionality is clarified, speakers worried about liability under the laws may censor their speech more than is constitutionally required. See *Law Students Civil Rights Research Council, Inc. v. Wadmond*, 401 U.S 154, 158-159 (1971).

The two cases that follow concern the doctrines of vagueness and overbreadth.

NAACP v. Button

371 U.S. 415 (1963)

Mr. Justice BRENNAN delivered the opinion of the Court.

The NAACP was formed in 1909 and incorporated under New York law as a nonprofit membership corporation in 1911. It maintains its headquarters in New York and presently has some 1,000 active unincorporated branches throughout the Nation. *** The basic aims and purposes of NAACP are to secure the elimination of all racial barriers which deprive Negro citizens of the privileges and burdens of equal citizenship rights in the United States. To this end the Association engages in extensive educational and lobbying activities. It also devotes much of its funds and energies to an extensive program of assisting certain kinds of litigation on behalf of its declared purposes. For more than 10 years, the Virginia Conference has concentrated upon financing litigation aimed at ending racial segregation in the public schools of the Commonwealth.

The members of the legal staff of the Virginia Conference and other NAACP or Defense Fund lawyers called in by the staff to assist are drawn into litigation in various ways. One is for an aggrieved Negro to apply directly to the Conference or the legal staff for assistance. His application is referred to the Chairman of the legal staff. The Chairman, with the concurrence of the President of the Conference, is authorized to agree to give legal assistance in an appropriate case. In litigation involving public school segregation, the procedure tends to be different. Typically, a local NAACP branch will invite a member of the legal staff to explain to a meeting of parents and children the legal steps necessary to achieve desegregation. The staff member will bring printed forms to the meeting authorizing him, and other NAACP or Defense Fund attorneys of his designation, to represent the signers in legal proceedings to achieve desegregation. On occasion, blank forms have been signed by litigants, upon the understanding that a member or members of the legal staff, with or without assistance from other NAACP lawyers, or from the Defense Fund, would handle the case. It is usual, after obtaining authorizations, for the staff lawyer to bring into the case the other staff members in the area where suit is to be brought, and sometimes to bring in lawyers from the national organization or the Defense Fund. In effect, then, the prospective litigant retains not so much a particular attorney as the "firm" of NAACP and Defense Fund lawyers, which has a corporate reputation for expertness in presenting and arguing the difficult questions of law that frequently arise in civil rights litigation.

Statutory regulation of unethical and nonprofessional conduct by attorneys has been in force in Virginia since 1849. These provisions outlaw, inter alia, solicitation of legal business in the form of "running" or "capping." Prior to 1956, however, no attempt was made to proscribe under such regulations the activities of the NAACP, which had been carried on openly for many years in substantially the manner described. In 1956, however, the legislature amended, by the addition of Chapter 33, the provisions of the Virginia Code forbidding

> **Definition**
>
> The terms "running" and "capping" describe the act of soliciting clients for a legal practice, usually in personal injury cases.

solicitation of legal business by a "runner" or "capper" to include, in the definition of "runner" or "capper," an agent for an individual or organization which retains a lawyer in connection with an action to which it is not a party and in which it has no pecuniary right or liability. The Virginia Supreme Court of Appeals held that the chapter's purpose "was to strengthen the existing statutes to further control the evils of solicitation of legal business ***." The court held that the activities of NAACP, the Virginia Conference, the Defense Fund, and the lawyers furnished by them, fell within, and could constitutionally be proscribed by, the chapter's expanded definition of improper solicitation of legal business, and also violated Canons 35 and 47 of the American Bar Association's Canons of Professional Ethics, which the court had adopted in 1938. Specifically the court held that, under the expanded definition, such activities on the part of NAACP, the Virginia Conference, and the Defense Fund constituted "fomenting and soliciting legal business in which they are not parties and have no pecuniary right or liability, and which they channel to the enrichment of certain lawyers employed by them, at no cost to the litigants and over which the litigants have no control." ***

Petitioner challenges the decision of the Supreme Court of Appeals on many grounds. But we reach only one: that Chapter 33 as construed and applied abridges the freedoms of the First Amendment, protected against state action by the Fourteenth. More specifically, petitioner claims that the chapter infringes the right of the NAACP and its members and lawyers to associate for the purpose of assisting persons who seek legal redress for infringements of their constitutionally guaranteed and other rights. ***

> **Make the Connection**
>
> We consider the First Amendment's protection for the freedom of association in Chapter 16.

We meet at the outset the contention that "solicitation" is wholly outside the area of freedoms protected by the First Amendment. To this contention there are two answers. The first is that a State cannot foreclose the exercise of constitutional rights by mere labels. The second is that abstract discussion is not the only species of communication which the Constitution protects; the First Amendment also protects vigorous advocacy, certainly of lawful ends, against governmental intrusion. In the context of NAACP objectives, litigation is not a technique of resolving private differences; it is a means for achieving the lawful objectives of equality of treatment by all government, federal, state and local, for the members of the Negro community in this country. It is thus a form of political expression. Groups which find themselves unable to achieve their objectives through the ballot frequently turn to the courts. Just as it was true of the opponents of New Deal legislation during the 1930's, for example, no less is it true of the Negro minority today. And under the conditions of modern government, litigation may well be the sole practicable avenue open to a minority to petition for redress of grievances.

*** If the line drawn by the decree between the permitted and prohibited activities of the NAACP, its members and lawyers is an ambiguous one, we will not presume that the statute curtails constitutionally protected activity as little as possible. For standards of permissible statutory vagueness are strict in the area of free expression. See *Smith v. Cali-*

fornia, 361 U.S. 147, 151 (1959). Furthermore, the instant decree may be invalid if it prohibits privileged exercises of First Amendment rights whether or not the record discloses that the petitioner has engaged in privileged conduct. For in appraising a statute's inhibitory effect upon such rights, this Court has not hesitated to take into account possible applications of the statute in other factual contexts besides that at bar. *Thornhill v. Alabama*, 310 U.S. 88, 97-98 (1940). It makes no difference that the instant case was not a criminal prosecution and not based on a refusal to comply with a licensing requirement. The objectionable quality of vagueness and overbreadth does not depend upon absence of fair notice to a criminally accused or upon unchanneled delegation of legislative powers, but upon the danger of tolerating, in the area of First Amendment freedoms, the existence of a penal statute susceptible of sweeping and improper application. Cf. *Marcus v. Search Warrant*, 367 U.S. 717, 733 (1961). These freedoms are delicate and vulnerable, as well as supremely precious in our society. The threat of sanctions may deter their exercise almost as potently as the actual application of sanctions. Cf. *Smith v. California*, 361 U.S. at 151-154. Because First Amendment freedoms need breathing space to survive, government may regulate in the area only with narrow specificity. *Cantwell v. Connecticut*, 310 U.S. 296, 311 (1940).

We read the decree of the Virginia Supreme Court of Appeals in the instant case as proscribing any arrangement by which prospective litigants are advised to seek the assistance of particular attorneys. No narrower reading is plausible. We cannot accept the reading suggested on behalf of the Attorney General of Virginia on the second oral argument that the Supreme Court of Appeals construed Chapter 33 as proscribing control only of the actual litigation by the NAACP after it is instituted. In the first place, upon a record devoid of any

> **Food for Thought**
>
> What does the Court mean when it says that First Amendment freedoms "need breathing space"? Does that mean that the government is effectively prohibited from regulating not only those activities protected by the Amendment, but also other actions that are not themselves protected but are closely linked to actions that are?

evidence of interference by the NAACP in the actual conduct of litigation, or neglect or harassment of clients, the court nevertheless held that petitioner, its members, agents and staff attorneys had practiced criminal solicitation. Thus, simple referral to or recommendation of a lawyer may be solicitation within the meaning of Chapter 33. In the second place, the decree does not seem to rest on the fact that the attorneys were organized as a staff and paid by petitioner. The decree expressly forbids solicitation on behalf of "any particular attorneys" in addition to attorneys retained or compensated by the NAACP. In the third place, although Chapter 33 purports to prohibit only solicitation by attorneys or their "agents," it defines agent broadly as anyone who "represents" another in his dealings with a third person. Since the statute appears to depart from the common-law concept of the agency relationship and since the Virginia court did not clarify the statutory definition, we cannot say that it will not be applied with the broad sweep which the statutory language imports.

We conclude that under Chapter 33, as authoritatively construed by the Supreme Court of Appeals, a person who advises another that his legal rights have been infringed and refers him to a particular attorney or group of attorneys (for example, to the Virginia Conference's legal staff) for assistance has committed a crime, as has the attorney who knowingly renders assistance under such circumstances. There thus inheres in the statute the gravest danger of smothering all discussion looking to the eventual institution of litigation on behalf of the rights of members of an unpopular minority. Lawyers on the legal staff or even mere NAACP members or sympathizers would understandably hesitate, at an NAACP meeting or on any other occasion, to do what the decree purports to allow, namely, acquaint "persons with what they believe to be their legal rights and *** (advise) them to assert their rights by commencing or further prosecuting a suit ***." For if the lawyers, members or sympathizers also appeared in or had any connection with any litigation supported with NAACP funds contributed under the provision of the decree by which the NAACP is not prohibited "from contributing money to persons to assist them in commencing or further prosecuting such suits," they plainly would risk (if lawyers) disbarment proceedings and, lawyers and nonlawyers alike, criminal prosecution for the offense of "solicitation," to which the Virginia court gave so broad and uncertain a meaning. It makes no difference whether such prosecutions or proceedings would actually be commenced. It is enough that a vague and broad statute lends itself to selective enforcement against unpopular causes. We cannot close our eyes to the fact that the militant Negro civil rights movement has engendered the intense resentment and opposition of the politically dominant white community of Virginia; litigation assisted by the NAACP

> **Take Note**
>
> In this paragraph, the Court explains that a vague or overbroad statute may be challenged even if it has not been applied to protected speech. What reason does the Court give for this rule?

has been bitterly fought. In such circumstances, a statute broadly curtailing group activity leading to litigation may easily become a weapon of oppression, however evenhanded its terms appear. Its mere existence could well freeze out of existence all such activity on behalf of the civil rights of Negro citizens.

It is apparent, therefore, that Chapter 33 as construed limits First Amendment freedoms. As this Court said in *Thomas v. Collins*, 323 U.S. 516, 537 (1945), "Free trade in ideas means free trade in the opportunity to persuade to action, not merely to describe facts." *** [T]he Association and its members were advocating lawful means of vindicating legal rights.

*** However valid may be Virginia's interest in regulating the traditionally illegal practices of barratry, maintenance and champerty, that interest does not justify the prohibition of the NAACP activities disclosed by this record. Malicious intent was of the essence of the common-law offenses of fomenting or stirring up litigation. And whatever may be or may have been true of suits against government in other

> **Definition**
>
> Barratry is "[v]exatious incitement to litigation," while maintenance and champerty consist of assisting in the litigation of a case in which one has no legal interest. *Black's Law Dictionary* (8th ed. 2004). Why would a state ban the latter practices?

countries, the exercise in our own, as in this case, of First Amendment rights to enforce constitutional rights through litigation, as a matter of law, cannot be deemed malicious. Even more modern, subtler regulations of unprofessional conduct or interference with professional relations, not involving malice, would not touch the activities at bar; regulations which reflect hostility to stirring up litigation have been aimed chiefly at those who urge recourse to the courts for private gain, serving no public interest. Hostility still exists to stirring up private litigation where it promotes the use of legal machinery to oppress: as, for example, to sow discord in a family; to expose infirmities in land titles, as by hunting up claims of adverse possession; to harass large companies through a multiplicity of small claims; or to oppress debtors as by seeking out unsatisfied judgments. For a member of the bar to participate, directly or through intermediaries, in such misuses of the legal process is conduct traditionally condemned as injurious to the public. And beyond this, for a lawyer to attempt to reap gain by urging another to engage in private litigation has also been condemned: that seems to be the import of Canon 28, which the Virginia Supreme Court of Appeals has adopted as one of its Rules.

We conclude that although the petitioner has amply shown that its activities fall within the First Amendment's protections, the State has failed to advance any substantial regulatory interest, in the form of substantive evils flowing from petitioner's activities, which can justify the broad prohibitions which it has imposed. Nothing that this record shows as to the nature and purpose of NAACP activities permits an inference of any injurious intervention in or control of litigation which would constitutionally authorize the application of Chapter 33 to those activities. A fortiori, nothing in this record justifies the breadth and vagueness of the Virginia Supreme Court of Appeals' decree. Reversed.

Mr. Justice HARLAN, whom Mr. Justice CLARK and Mr. Justice STEWART join, dissenting.

In my opinion the litigation program of the NAACP, as shown by this record, falls within an area of activity which a State may constitutionally regulate. (Whether it was wise for Virginia to exercise that power in this instance is not, of course, for us to say.) ***

The regulation before us has its origins in the long-standing common-law prohibitions of champerty, barratry, and maintenance, the closely related prohibitions in the Canons of Ethics against solicitation and intervention by a lay intermediary, and statutory provisions forbidding the unauthorized practice of law. The Court recognizes this formidable history, but puts it aside in the present case on the grounds that there is here no element of malice or of pecuniary gain, that the interests of the NAACP are not to be regarded as substantially different from those of its members, and that we are said to be dealing here with a matter that transcends mere legal ethics—the securing of federally guaranteed rights. But these distinctions are too facile. They do not account for the full scope of the State's legitimate interest in regulating professional conduct. For although these professional standards may have been born in a desire to curb malice and self-aggrandizement by those who would use clients and the courts for their own pecuniary ends, they have acquired a far broader significance during their long development.

Points for Discussion

a. Vagueness or Overbreadth?

Did the law at issue in *Button* violate the First Amendment because it was vague or because it was overbroad? Or did it suffer from both defects? Can you articulate why the law was arguably vague and overbroad?

b. Litigation as a Protected Activity

Former Judge Patricia Wald has written that *Button* is one of the Warren Court's most important decisions because it "recognized public interest litigation as a valid form of political advocacy." Patricia Wald *et al., Remembering a Constitutional Hero*, 43 N.Y.L. Sch. L. Rev. 13, 32 (1999). Public interest litigation has brought about many very important changes since the 1950s. If the states could have regulated lawyers as Virginia had sought to regulate them in this case, much of this public interest litigation might not have occurred. Is the First Amendment right at stake in public interest litigation the right to free speech? The freedom of association? Or the right to petition the government for the redress of grievances?

c. State Regulation of Lawyers and the First Amendment

Does state regulation of lawyers' solicitation of clients in more mundane cases violate the First Amendment? The Court's decisions in this area do not admit of easy synthesis, but the short answer is "sometimes." The Court has invalidated some such restrictions on the ground that they violate the freedom of speech, see, e.g., *Shapero v. Kentucky Bar Assn.*, 486 U.S. 466 (1988); *Zauderer v. Office of Disciplinary Counsel of Supreme Court of Ohio*, 471 U.S. 626 (1985); *In re R.M.J.*, 455 U.S. 191, 202 (1982), but upheld others against First Amendment challenges, see *Florida Bar v. Went For It, Inc.*, 515 U.S. 618 (1995). These cases concern the doctrine of "commercial speech," which we will consider later in this Chapter.

Schad v. Borough of Mount Ephraim

452 U.S. 61 (1981)

Justice WHITE delivered the opinion of the Court.

In 1973, appellants began operating an adult bookstore in the commercial zone in the Borough of Mount Ephraim in Camden County, N. J. The store sold adult books, magazines, and films. Amusement licenses shortly issued permitting the store to install coin-operated devices by virtue of which a customer could sit in a booth, insert a coin, and watch an adult film. In 1976, the store introduced an additional coin-operated mechanism permitting the customer to watch a live dancer, usually nude, performing behind a glass panel. Complaints were soon filed against appellants charging that the bookstore's exhibition of live dancing violated § 99-15B of Mount Ephraim's zoning ordinance, which described the permitted uses in a commercial zone, in which the store was located, as follows:

> (1) Offices and banks; taverns; restaurants and luncheonettes for sit-down dinners only and with no drive-in facilities; automobile sales; retail stores, such as but not limited to food, wearing apparel, millinery, fabrics, hardware, lumber, jewelry, paint, wallpaper, appliances, flowers, gifts, books, stationery, pharmacy, liquors, cleaners, novelties, hobbies and toys; repair shops for shoes, jewels, clothes and appliances; barbershops and beauty salons; cleaners and laundries; pet stores; and nurseries. Offices may, in addition, be permitted to a group of four (4) stores or more without additional parking, provided the offices do not exceed the equivalent of twenty percent (20%) of the gross floor area of the stores.

> (2) Motels.

Mount Ephraim Code § 99-15B(1), (2) (1979). Section 99-4 of the Borough's code provided that "[a]ll uses not expressly permitted in this chapter are prohibited."

Appellants were found guilty in the Municipal Court and fines were imposed. *** Appellants appealed to this Court. Their principal claim is that the imposition of criminal penalties under an ordinance prohibiting all live entertainment, including nonobscene, nude dancing, violated their rights of free expression guaranteed by the First and Fourteenth Amendments of the United States Constitution. ***

As the Mount Ephraim Code has been construed by the New Jersey courts—a construction that is binding upon us—"live entertainment," including nude dancing, is "not a permitted use in any establishment" in the Borough of Mount Ephraim. By excluding live entertainment throughout the Borough, the Mount Ephraim ordinance prohibits a wide range of expression that has long been held to be within the protections of the First and Fourteenth Amendments. Entertainment, as well as political and ideological speech, is protected; motion pictures, programs broadcast by radio and television, and live entertainment, such as musical and dramatic works fall within the First Amendment guarantee. Nor may an entertainment program be prohibited solely because it displays the nude human figure. "[N]udity alone" does not place otherwise protected material outside the mantle of the First Amendment. *Jenkins v. Georgia*, 418 U.S. 153 (1974). Furthermore, as the state courts in this case recognized, nude dancing is not without its First Amendment protections from official regulation.

Whatever First Amendment protection should be extended to nude dancing, live or on film, however, the Mount Ephraim ordinance prohibits all live entertainment in the Borough: no property in the Borough may be principally used for the commercial production of plays, concerts, musicals, dance, or any other form of live entertainment. Because appellants' claims are rooted in the First Amendment, they are entitled to rely on the impact of the ordinance on the expressive activities of others as well as their own. "Because overbroad laws, like vague ones, deter privileged activit[ies], our cases firmly establish appellant's standing to raise an overbreadth challenge." *Grayned v. City of Rockford*, 408 U.S. 104, 114 (1972).

The power of local governments to zone and control land use is undoubtedly broad and its proper exercise is an essential aspect of achieving a satisfactory quality of life in both urban and rural communities. But the zoning power is not infinite and unchallengeable; it "must be exercised within constitutional limits." *Moore v. East Cleveland*, 431 U.S. 494, 514 (1977) (STEVENS, J., concurring in judgment). ***

In this [case], Mount Ephraim has not adequately justified its substantial restriction of protected activity. None of the justifications asserted in this Court was articulated by the state courts and none of them withstands scrutiny. First, the Borough contends that permitting live entertainment would conflict with its plan to create a commercial area that caters only to the "immediate needs" of its residents and that would enable them to purchase at local stores the few items they occasionally forgot to buy outside the Borough. No evidence was introduced below to support this assertion, and it is difficult to reconcile this characterization of the Borough's commercial zones with the provisions of the ordinance. Section 99-15A expressly states that the purpose of creating commercial zones was to provide areas for "local and *regional* commercial operations." (Emphasis added.) The range of permitted uses goes far beyond providing for the "immediate needs" of the residents. Motels, hardware stores, lumber stores, banks, offices, and car showrooms are permitted in commercial zones. The list of permitted "retail stores" is nonexclusive, and it includes such services as beauty salons, barbershops, cleaners, and restaurants. Virtually the only item or service that may not be sold in a commercial zone is entertainment, or at least live entertainment. The Borough's first justification is patently insufficient.

Second, Mount Ephraim contends that it may selectively exclude commercial live entertainment from the broad range of commercial uses permitted in the Borough for reasons normally associated with zoning in commercial districts, that is, to avoid the problems that may be associated with live entertainment, such as parking, trash, police protection, and medical facilities. The Borough has presented no evidence, and it is not immediately apparent as a matter of experience, that live entertainment poses problems of this nature more significant than those associated with various permitted uses; nor does it appear that the Borough's zoning authority has arrived at a defensible conclusion that unusual problems are presented by live entertainment. We do not find it self-evident that a theater, for example, would create greater parking problems than would a restaurant. Even less apparent is what unique problems would be posed by exhibiting live nude dancing in connection with the sale of adult books and films, particularly since the bookstore is licensed to exhibit nude dancing on films. It may be that some forms of live entertainment would create problems that are not associated with the commercial uses presently permitted in Mount Ephraim. Yet this ordinance is not narrowly drawn to respond to what might be the distinctive problems arising from certain types of live entertainment, and it is not clear that a more selective approach would fail to address those unique problems if any there are. The Borough has not established that its interests could not be met by restrictions that are less intrusive on protected forms of expression.

> **Food for Thought**
>
> In this passage, the Court explains why the Borough's restrictions are overbroad. How could they have been rewritten to survive this challenge?

Accordingly, the convictions of these appellants are infirm, and the judgment of the Appellate Division of the Superior Court of New Jersey is reversed and the case is remanded for further proceedings not inconsistent with this opinion.

Justice STEVENS, concurring in the judgment.

The difficulty in this case is that we are left to speculate as to the Borough's reasons for proceeding against appellants' business, and as to the justification for the distinction the Borough has drawn between live and other forms of entertainment. While a municipality need not persuade a federal court that its zoning decisions are correct as a matter of policy, when First Amendment interests are implicated it must at least be able to demonstrate that a uniform policy in fact exists and is applied in a content-neutral fashion. Presumably, municipalities may regulate expressive activity—even protected activity—pursuant to narrowly drawn content-neutral standards; however, they may not regulate protected activity when the only standard provided is the unbridled discretion of a municipal official. Compare *Saia v. New York*, 334 U.S. 558 (1948), with *Kovacs v. Cooper*, 336 U.S. 77 (1949) Because neither the text of the zoning ordinance nor the evidence in the record indicates that Mount Ephraim applied narrowly drawn content-neutral standards to the appellants' business, for me this case involves a criminal prosecution of appellants simply because one of their employees has engaged in expressive activity that has been assumed, *arguendo*, to be protected by the First Amendment. Accordingly, and without endorsing the overbreadth analysis employed by the Court, I concur in its judgment.

Chief Justice BURGER, with whom Justice REHNQUIST joins, dissenting.

The Court depicts Mount Ephraim's ordinance as a ban on live entertainment. But, in terms, it does not mention any kind of entertainment. As applied, it operates as a ban on nude dancing in appellants' "adult" bookstore, and for that reason alone it is here. Thus, the issue *in the case that we have before us* is not whether Mount Ephraim may ban traditional live entertainment, but whether it may ban nude dancing, which is used as the "bait" to induce customers into the appellants' bookstore. When, and if, this ordinance is used to prevent a high school performance of "The Sound of Music," for example, the Court can deal with that problem.

> **Definition**
>
> "The Sound of Music" is a wholesome musical drama in which an Austrian family and their lovely governess oppose the Nazis' rise to power in the 1930s. A film version made in 1965 won 5 Oscars.

Points for Discussion

a. Overbreadth

The Court concluded that the challenged ordinance was overbroad because it prohibited an entire class of expressive activities. In reaching this conclusion, the Court considered the other possible applications of the ordinance, regardless of whether the Borough had authority to prohibit live, nude dancing. With which feature of the overbreadth doctrine, as described above, did the dissent disagree? Does it make sense for the Court to invalidate a statute that could constitutionally have been applied to the person raising the challenge?

b. Nude Dancing and the First Amendment

Did the Court conclude that live, nude dancing is protected by the First Amendment? Did it need to decide that question, in light of its conclusion that the zoning ordinance was overbroad? As we have seen, ten years after the Court's decision in *Schad*, a divided Court in *Barnes v. Glen Theatre, Inc.*, 501 U.S. 560 (1991), upheld an Indiana statute that prohibited nudity in public places as applied to an establishment very similar to the one that brought the challenge in *Schad*. A majority of the Court, however, agreed that nude dancing "is expressive conduct" under the First Amendment, although the Justices disagreed about the extent of protection that the First Amendment offers that activity and the constitutionality of the statute as applied in the case. Does the Court's decision in *Barnes* strengthen or undermine the Court's conclusion in *Schad*?

---

6. Unconstitutional Conditions

As we saw in Chapter 3, the government sometimes uses conditional spending to accomplish ends that it cannot achieve through direct regulation. For example, in *South Dakota v. Dole*, 483 U.S. 203 (1987), Congress threatened to withhold certain federal highway funds unless states set the drinking age at 21. A long-standing question is whether and how the First Amendment limits Congress's spending power. For example, suppose that the First Amendment plainly would prevent Congress from passing a statute barring an individual from discussing a particular topic. May the government use conditional spending to accomplish the same objective—by stating, in effect, "You will receive a payment from the government unless you discuss the particular topic"?

The Supreme Court has addressed this issue with two doctrines. On the one hand, the **unconstitutional conditions** doctrine says that the "the government 'may not deny a benefit to a person on a basis that infringes his constitutionally protected *** freedom of speech' even if he has no entitlement to that benefit." *Board of Commissioners, Wabaunsee County v. Umbehr*, 518 U.S. 668, 674 (1996) (quoting *Perry v. Sindermann*, 408 U.S. 593, 597 (1972)). For example, in *Umbehr*, the Supreme Court held that a county violated the free speech rights of a trash hauler. The trash hauler had an at-will employment contract, and the county board fired him after he made critical statements about the board. The Court held that even though the county did not have to hire the trash hauler, and even though he could be fired for

> **Make the Connection**
>
> We briefly considered the unconstitutional conditions doctrine, and the Court's decision in *Sindermann*, in Chapter 9, on Procedural Due Process.

essentially no reason at all, it could not fire him for criticizing the government. The county, in other words, could not condition his continued employment on his willingness to refrain from criticizing the government.

On the other hand, as we will see in the following case, the Supreme Court has said: "The Government can, without violating the Constitution, **selectively fund a program** to encourage certain activities it believes to be in the public interest, without at the same time funding an alternative program which seeks to deal with the problem in another way." *Rust v. Sullivan*, 500 U.S. 173, 194 (1991). The funding of the program may be conditional. For example, in *United States v. American Library Association*, 539 U.S. 194 (2003), the federal government gave libraries subsidies to provide internet access to their patrons. But the subsidies came only on the condition that the libraries agree to install internet filters to block pornography. The Supreme Court held that this restriction did not violate the Constitution, explaining that the government could choose not to provide subsidies for pornography.

Are these two doctrines in tension? Consider the case that follows.

————————

Rust v. Sullivan

500 U.S. 173 (1991)

Chief Justice REHNQUIST delivered the opinion of the Court.

In 1970, Congress enacted Title X of the Public Health Service Act (Act), 84 Stat. 1506, as amended, 42 U.S.C. §§ 300-399a-6, which provides federal funding for family-planning services. The Act authorizes the Secretary to "make grants to and enter into contracts with public or nonprofit private entities to assist in the establishment and operation of voluntary family planning projects which shall offer a broad range of acceptable and effective family planning methods and services." § 300(a). Grants and contracts under Title X must "be made in accordance with such regulations as the Secretary may promulgate." § 300a-4(a). Section 1008 of the Act, however, provides that "[n]one of the funds appropriated under this subchapter shall be used in programs where abortion is a method of family planning." § 300a-6. That restriction was intended to ensure that Title X funds would "be used only to support preventive family planning services, population research, infertility services, and other related medical, informational, and educational activities." H.R. Conf. Rep. No. 91-1667, p. 8 (1970). [The Secretary promulgated regulations prohibiting recipients of Title X funds from, among other things, discussing abortion with their clients and patients.]

Petitioners contend that the regulations violate the First Amendment by impermissibly discriminating based on viewpoint because they prohibit "all discussion about abortion as a lawful option—including counseling, referral, and the provision of neutral and accurate information about ending a pregnancy—while compelling the clinic or counselor to provide information that promotes continuing a pregnancy to term." They assert that the regulations violate the "free speech rights of private health care organizations that receive

Title X funds, of their staff, and of their patients" by impermissibly imposing "viewpoint-discriminatory conditions on government subsidies" and thus "penaliz[e] speech funded with non-Title X monies." Because "Title X continues to fund speech ancillary to pregnancy testing in a manner that is not evenhanded with respect to views and information about abortion, it invidiously discriminates on the basis of viewpoint." Relying on *Regan v. Taxation with Representation of Wash.,* 461 U.S. 540 (1983), and *Arkansas Writers' Project, Inc. v. Ragland,* 481 U.S. 221, 234 (1987), petitioners also assert that while the Government may place certain conditions on the receipt of federal subsidies, it may not "discriminate invidiously in its subsidies in such a way as to 'ai[m] at the suppression of dangerous ideas.'" <u>*Regan, supra,* 461 U.S., at 548</u> (quoting *Cammarano v. United States,* 358 U.S. 498, 513 (1959)).

There is no question but that the statutory prohibition contained in § 1008 is constitutional. In *Maher v. Roe,* 432 U.S. 464 (1977), we upheld a state welfare regulation under which Medicaid recipients received payments for services related to childbirth, but not for nontherapeutic abortions. The Court rejected the claim that this unequal subsidization worked a violation of the Constitution. We held that the government may "make a value judgment favoring childbirth over abortion, [and] implement that judgment by the allocation of public funds." <u>*Id.,* 432 U.S., at 474</u>. Here the Government is exercising the authority it possesses under <u>*Maher*</u> and *Harris v. McRae,* 448 U.S. 297 (1980), to subsidize family planning services which will lead to conception and childbirth, and declining to "promote or encourage abortion." The Government can, without violating the Constitution, selectively fund a program to encourage certain activities it believes to be in the public interest, without at the same time funding an alternative program which seeks to deal with the problem in another way. In so doing, the Government has not discriminated on the basis of viewpoint; it has merely chosen to fund one activity to the exclusion of the other. "[A] legislature's decision not to subsidize the exercise of a fundamental right does not infringe the right." *Regan, supra,* 461 U.S., at 549. See also *Buckley v. Valeo,* 424 U.S. 1 (1976). "A refusal to fund protected activity, without more, cannot be equated with the imposition of a 'penalty' on that activity." <u>*McRae,* 448 U.S., at 317, n.19</u>. "There is a basic difference between direct state interference with a protected activity and state encouragement of an alternative activity consonant with legislative policy." <u>*Maher,* 432 U.S., at 475</u>.

The challenged regulations implement the statutory prohibition by prohibiting counseling, referral, and the provision of information regarding abortion as a method of family planning. They are designed to ensure that the limits of the federal program are observed. The Title X program is designed not for prenatal care, but to encourage family planning. A doctor who wished to offer prenatal care to a project patient who became pregnant could properly be prohibited from doing so because such service is outside the scope of the federally funded program. The regulations prohibiting abortion counseling and referral are of the same ilk; "no

> **Take Note**
>
> The Court explains here why the restrictions imposed on recipients of the federal funds do not violate the First Amendment. Is there a difference between declining to spend federal funds to subsidize a particular activity and providing funds only on the condition that the recipients refrain from discussing certain matters with patients?

funds appropriated for the project may be used in programs where abortion is a method of family planning," and a doctor employed by the project may be prohibited in the course of his project duties from counseling abortion or referring for abortion. This is not a case of the Government "suppressing a dangerous idea," but of a prohibition on a project grantee or its employees from engaging in activities outside of the project's scope.

To hold that the Government unconstitutionally discriminates on the basis of viewpoint when it chooses to fund a program dedicated to advance certain permissible goals, because the program in advancing those goals necessarily discourages alternative goals, would render numerous Government programs constitutionally suspect. When Congress established a National Endowment for Democracy to encourage other countries to adopt democratic principles, 22 U.S.C. § 4411(b), it was not constitutionally required to fund a program to encourage competing lines of political philosophy such as communism and fascism. Petitioners' assertions ultimately boil down to the position that if the government chooses to subsidize one protected right, it must subsidize analogous counterpart rights. But the Court has soundly rejected that proposition. Within far broader limits than petitioners are willing to concede, when the Government appropriates public funds to establish a program it is entitled to define the limits of that program.

Justice BLACKMUN, with whom Justice MARSHALL joins, with whom Justice STEVENS joins as to Parts II and III, and with whom Justice O'CONNOR joins as to Part I, dissenting.

[II]

Until today, the Court never has upheld viewpoint-based suppression of speech simply because that suppression was a condition upon the acceptance of public funds. Whatever may be the Government's power to condition the receipt of its largess upon the relinquishment of constitutional rights, it surely does not extend to a condition that suppresses the recipient's cherished freedom of speech based solely upon the content or viewpoint of that speech. ***

Nothing in the Court's opinion in *Regan v. Taxation with Representation of Washington,* 461 U.S. 540 (1983), can be said to challenge this long-settled understanding. In *Regan,* the Court upheld a content-neutral provision of the Internal Revenue Code, 26 U.S.C. § 501(c)(3), that disallowed a particular tax-exempt status to organizations that "attempt[ed] to influence legislation," while affording such status to veterans' organizations irrespective of their lobbying activities. [T]he Court explained: "The case would be different if Congress were to discriminate invidiously in its subsidies in such a way as to "ai[m] at the suppression of dangerous ideas. ... We find no indication that the statute was intended to suppress any ideas or any demonstration that it has had that effect." 461 U.S., at 548. The separate concurrence in *Regan* joined the Court's opinion precisely "[b]ecause 26 U.S.C. § 501's discrimination between veterans' organizations and charitable organizations is not based on the content of their speech." 461 U.S., at 551.

It cannot seriously be disputed that the counseling and referral provisions at issue in the present cases constitute content-based regulation of speech. Title X grantees may provide counseling and referral regarding any of a wide range of family planning and other topics, save abortion.

The regulations are also clearly viewpoint based. While suppressing speech favorable to abortion with one hand, the Secretary compels antiabortion speech with the other. For example, the Department of Health and Human Services' own description of the regulations makes plain that "Title X projects are *required* to facilitate access to prenatal care and social services, including adoption services, that might be needed by the pregnant client to promote her well-being and that of her child, while making it abundantly clear that the project is not permitted to promote abortion by facilitating access to abortion through the referral process." 53 Fed. Reg. 2927 (1988) (emphasis added).

> **Take Note**
>
> Justice Blackmun asserts here that the challenged regulations are both content based and viewpoint based. Can you articulate the difference between content-based and viewpoint-based restrictions? Would it be possible for a challenged regulation in this context to be content based but not viewpoint based? Would that make the regulations any more likely to be upheld?

Moreover, the regulations command that a project refer for prenatal care each woman diagnosed as pregnant, irrespective of the woman's expressed desire to continue or terminate her pregnancy. 42 CFR § 59.8(a)(2) (1990). If a client asks directly about abortion, a Title X physician or counselor is required to say, in essence, that the project does not consider abortion to be an appropriate method of family planning. § 59.8(b)(4). Both requirements are antithetical to the First Amendment. See *Wooley v. Maynard*, 430 U.S. 705, 714 (1977).

> **FYI**
>
> In *Wooley*, the Court held that New Hampshire could not compel a person who sought to register a car to use a license plate that said, "Live Free or Die." The Court reasoned that such compulsion violated the "right to refrain from speaking," by effectively requiring the appellees "to use their private property as a 'mobile billboard' for the State's ideological message."

The regulations pertaining to "advocacy" are even more explicitly viewpoint based. These provide: "A Title X project may not *encourage, promote or advocate* abortion as a method of family planning." § 59.10 (emphasis added). They explain: "This requirement prohibits actions to *assist* women to obtain abortions or *increase* the availability or accessibility of abortion for family planning purposes." § 59.10(a) (emphasis added). The regulations do not, however, proscribe or even regulate anti-abortion advocacy. These are clearly restrictions aimed at the suppression of "dangerous ideas."

The Court concludes that the challenged regulations do not violate the First Amendment rights of Title X staff members because any limitation of the employees' freedom of expression is simply a consequence of their decision to accept employment at a federally funded project. But it has never been sufficient to justify an otherwise unconstitutional condition upon public employment that the employee may escape the condition by relinquishing his or her job. It is beyond question "that a government may not require an individual to relinquish rights guaranteed him by the First Amendment as a condition of public employment." *Abood v. Detroit Bd. of Ed.*, 431 U.S. 209, 234 (1977). *** Under the majority's reasoning, the First Amendment could be read to tolerate *any* governmental restriction upon an employee's speech so long as that restriction is limited to the funded workplace. This is a dangerous proposition, and one the Court has rightly rejected in the past.

Finally, it is of no small significance that the speech the Secretary would suppress is truthful information regarding constitutionally protected conduct of vital importance to the listener. One can imagine no legitimate governmental interest that might be served by suppressing such information. Concededly, the abortion debate is among the most divisive and contentious issues that our Nation has faced in recent years. "But freedom to differ is not limited to things that do not matter much. That would be a mere shadow of freedom. The test of its substance is the right to differ as to things that touch the heart of the existing order." *West Virginia Bd. of Ed. v. Barnette,* 319 U.S. 624, 642 (1943).

————————

Points for Discussion

a. The "Gag Rule"

Many critics of the <u>Rust</u> decision have referred to the Reagan Administration's regulations implementing § 1008 as the "gag rule." *Get Rid of the Gag Rule*, N.Y. Times, Jul. 13, 1991, at 1:20. Is this moniker an appropriate nickname for the regulations? Has the government prevented anyone from speaking about any subject? What could a doctor who wished to have unfettered discretion to discuss abortion with her patients have done to avoid the restrictions imposed by the regulations? Would that be a realistic option?

b. Executive Suspension

Although the Supreme Court upheld the regulations implementing the conditional spending program, President Clinton (on his first day in office) ordered the Secretary of Health and Human Services to suspend their enforcement. See The Title X "Gag Rule," Memorandum from President William J. Clinton to Secretary of Health and Human Services, 58 Fed. Reg. 7455 (1993). Was this action within the President's power? Does it matter that the challenged regulations were themselves promulgated by the Secretary of Health and Human Services in a prior Administration?

c. Withholding Funds from Organizations Based upon their Views

Can a state university withhold funds that it gives to some groups from religious student groups, on the ground that it has limited funds and does not want to fund religious organizations? In *Rosenberger v. Rector and Visitors of University of Virginia*, 515 U.S. 819 (1995), the Court held that scarcity of funds does not permit a public university to discriminate on the basis of viewpoint. Is this decision consistent with <u>Rust</u>? Is this decision consistent with the Establishment Clause?

d. Government Speech

In *Rosenberger v. Rector and Visitors of University of Virginia*, 515 U.S. 819 (1995), described above, the state argued that <u>Rust</u> stands for the proposition that "content-based funding decisions are both inevitable and lawful." Writing for the Court, Justice Kennedy disagreed, stating that in <u>Rust</u>, "the government did not create a program to encourage private speech but instead used private speakers to transmit specific information pertaining to its own program." He continued:

Make the Connection

We will consider the Establishment Clause, and the limits that it imposes on state involvement in, and state aid to, religion, in Chapter 17.

> We recognized [in <u>Rust</u>] that when the government appropriates public funds to promote a particular policy of its own it is entitled to say what it wishes. When the government disburses public funds to private entities to convey a governmental message, it may take legitimate and appropriate steps to ensure that its message is neither garbled nor distorted by the grantee. It does not follow, however, [that] viewpoint-based restrictions are proper when the [government] does not itself speak or subsidize transmittal of a message it favors but instead expends funds to encourage a diversity of views from private speakers.

Do you agree that the Court's decision in <u>Rust</u> turned on the fact that the government itself was seeking to speak? Didn't the challenged regulations simply prohibit the doctors and other program participants from communicating a message that they might otherwise have thought was appropriate?

What is the status of "government speech" under the First Amendment? Does the government have the same right to communicate a message that private actors enjoy? In *Pleasant Grove City, Utah v. Summum*, 129 S.Ct. 1125 (2009), the Court held that a city's decision to place a donated monument in a public park—and to refuse to place in the park a monument that a different group wished to donate to communicate a different message—was a form of government speech and thus not subject to scrutiny under the Free Speech Clause of the First Amendment. The Court reasoned:

> The Free Speech Clause restricts government regulation of private speech; it does not regulate government speech. Indeed, it is not easy to imagine how government could function if it lacked this freedom. "If every citizen were to have a right to insist that no one paid by public funds express a view with which he disagreed, debate over issues of great concern to the public would be limited to those in the private sector, and the process of government as we know it radically transformed." *Keller v. State Bar of Cal.*, 496 U.S. 1, 12-13 (1990). *** A government entity may exercise this same freedom to express its views when it receives assistance from private sources for the purpose of delivering a government-controlled message.

When the government provides funds to private actors who then speak (or refrain from speaking)—or when private actors donate monuments designed to express a particular point of view—how can the Court tell whether it is the government or instead the private actor who is speaking?

B. Categories of Speech

In the previous materials, we considered doctrines that the Supreme Court has developed for analyzing different types of regulations that the federal and state governments have attempted to place on speech. Most of those doctrines require a reviewing court to consider whether the governmental interests advanced by the regulation justify the interference with the freedom of speech. Recall that Justice Black believed that such balancing is inappropriate when a law abridges the freedom of speech—in essence, that the First Amendment's reference to "no law" means what it says. Would that view mean that the government simply cannot regulate in any fashion that impairs expression or communication?

Our intuition tells us that this cannot always be the case, at least as a matter of existing practice, and that there must be some categories of speech that are beyond the protection of the First Amendment. Indeed, in our legal culture we routinely permit prosecution and conviction for many forms of speech. For example, false statements under oath can be punished as perjury, even though those statements clearly count as "speech" within the general understanding of the term. The same is true of speech soliciting a bribe—such as when a public official says, "I will vote for this bill if you give me $10,000"—and blackmail—such as when a person says, "Give me $10,000 or I will tell your wife that you're having an affair."

In a famous passage in *Chaplinsky v. State of New Hampshire*, 315 U.S. 568 (1942), which we will consider later in this section, the Court declared:

> Allowing the broadest scope to the language and purpose of the Fourteenth Amendment, it is well understood that the right of free speech is not absolute at all times and under all circumstances. There are certain well-defined and narrowly limited classes of speech, the prevention and punishment of which has never been thought to raise any Constitutional problem. These include the lewd and obscene, the profane, the libelous, and the insulting or "fighting" words—those which by their very utterance inflict injury or tend to incite an immediate breach of the peace. It has been well observed that such utterances are no essential part of any exposition of ideas, and are of such slight social value as a step to truth that any benefit that may be derived from them is clearly outweighed by the social interest in order and morality.

As we will see, the Court has frequently quoted this language when deciding whether to exclude a particular category of speech from the protection of the First Amendment.

But it is easier to note that some categories of speech have long been treated as beyond the protection of the First Amendment than it is to develop a coherent theory about *why* those categories are excluded from protection—and thus why *other* categories might be, as well. Indeed, in light of what we have seen about the danger of content-based regulation, it seems particularly important to develop such a coherent (and perhaps limiting) theory for when the Court can declare that an entire category of speech, defined by its content, is beyond the protection of the First Amendment.

So how exactly does the Court identify exceptions to the general rule against content-based restrictions? Are those categories excluded from protection because of some historical tradition that declines to treat such utterances as "speech"? Are they excluded because the speech itself is dangerous or of low value? Are they excluded because the government's interest in regulating such speech is so strong that it essentially always justifies regulation? Or is there simply no coherent theory that can explain the exclusion of certain categories of speech from the protection of the First Amendment?

We explore these questions in the materials that follow in this section. The materials are organized by category of speech. These categories include: (1) incitement and advocacy of crime; (2) defamation, (3) obscenity; (4) symbolic conduct; (5) provocative speech; (6) commercial speech; (7) campaign contributions and expenditures; and (8) the speech of public employees.

As you read these materials, consider how the Court goes about deciding whether a particular category of speech should be subject to distinctive rules, whether such an inquiry is itself consistent with the First Amendment, and, if so, whether the Court has done a good job in identifying those categories and the special rules that apply.

---

1. Incitement and Advocacy of Crime

In what circumstances does the First Amendment permit the government to punish a person merely for advocating the commission of crimes (without actually committing them)? This question has a long and frequently discussed history, at least in part because it was one of the first questions that the Court decided respecting the freedom of speech. The Court concisely summarized much of this history in the following excerpt from *Dennis v. United States*, 341 U.S. 494 (1951):

> No important case involving free speech was decided by this Court prior to *Schenck v. United States*, 249 U.S. 47 (1919). *** That case involved a conviction under the Criminal Espionage Act, 40 Stat. 217 (1917).
>
> The question the Court faced was whether the evidence was sufficient to sustain the conviction. Writing for a unanimous Court, Justice Holmes stated that the "question in every case is whether the words used are used in such circumstances and are of such a nature as to create a clear and present danger that they will bring about the substantive evils that Congress has a right to prevent." 249 U.S. at 52. *** The charge was causing and attempting to cause insubordination in the military forces and obstruct recruiting. The objectionable document denounced conscription and its most inciting sentence was, "You must do your share to maintain, support and uphold the rights of the people of this country." *Id.* at 51. Fifteen thousand copies were printed and some circulated. This insubstantial gesture toward insubordination in 1917 during war was held to be a clear and present danger of bringing about the evil of military insubordination.

FYI

The Criminal Espionage Act of 1917 was enacted during World War I. The Act imposed severe criminal penalties for spying, interfering with the draft, encouraging disloyalty, and other acts thought to harm the war effort.

In several later cases involving convictions under the Criminal Espionage Act, the nub of the evidence the Court held sufficient to meet the "clear and present danger" test enunciated in *Schenck* was as follows: *Frohwerk v. United States*, 249 U.S. 204 (1919)—publication of twelve newspaper articles attacking the war; *Debs v. United States*, 249 U.S. 211 (1919)—one speech attacking the United States' participation in the war; *Abrams v. United States*, 250 U.S. 616 (1919)—circulation of copies of two different socialist circulars attacking the war; *Schaefer v. United States*, 251 U.S. 466 (1920)—publication of a German-language newspaper with allegedly false articles, critical of capitalism and the war; *Pierce v. United States*, 252 U.S. 239 (1920)—circulation of copies of a four-page pamphlet written by a clergyman, attacking the purposes of the war and United States' participation therein. ***

The rule we deduce from these cases is that where an offense is specified by a statute in nonspeech or nonpress terms, a conviction relying upon speech or press as evidence of violation may be sustained only when the speech or publication created a "clear and present danger" of attempting or accomplishing the prohibited crime, e. g., interference with enlistment. ***

The next important case before the Court in which free speech was the crux of the conflict was *Gitlow v. New York*, 268 U.S. 652 (1925). There New York had made it a crime to advocate "the necessity or propriety of overthrowing . . . organized government by force." The evidence of violation of the statute was that the defendant had published a Manifesto attacking the Government and capitalism. The convictions were sustained, Justices Holmes and Brandeis dissenting. The majority refused to apply the "clear and present danger" test to the specific utterance. Its reasoning was as follows: The "clear and present danger" test was applied to the utterance itself in *Schenck* because the question was merely one of sufficiency of evidence under an admittedly constitutional statute. *Gitlow*, however, presented a different question. There a legislature had found that a certain kind of speech was, itself, harmful and unlawful. The constitutionality of such a state statute had to be adjudged by this Court just as it determined the constitutionality of any state statute, namely, whether the statute was "reasonable." Since it was entirely reasonable for a state to attempt to protect itself from violent overthrow, the statute was perforce reasonable. The only question remaining in the case became whether there was evidence to support the conviction, a question which gave the majority no difficulty. *** This approach was emphasized in *Whitney v. California*, 274 U.S. 357 (1927), where the Court was confronted with a conviction under the California Criminal Syndicalist statute. The Court sustained the conviction ***.

> **Definition**
>
> The term "criminal syndicalism" refers to a radical political doctrine that "advocates or teaches the use of illegal methods to change industrial or political control," such as workers taking over factories by force. *Black's Law Dictionary* (8th ed. 2008).

The cases discussed in this excerpt from *Dennis* arose under a variety of circumstances. The earliest cases were decided while (or shortly after) the United States was involved in World War I. The cases from the 1920s—*Gitlow* and *Whitney*—involved statutes that were enacted in response to the perceived "Red Scare," the fear that radicals would import the Russian Revolution to American shores. And *Dennis* involved a prosecution under the Smith Act of 1940, which made it a crime to conspire to overthrow the government of the United States by force and violence, and which was increasingly used against communist sympathizers at the beginning of the Cold War. In all of these cases, the Court permitted the conviction of the defendants on the basis of their authorship or distribution of leaflets, pamphlets, and the like that advocated the overthrow of the government, or on the basis of their membership in organizations, such as the Communist Party, that espoused similar aims.

In virtually all of the cases described in <u>Dennis</u> (and in <u>Dennis</u> itself), there were strong dissents (or at least separate concurring opinions). The most enduring were Justice Holmes's dissent in <u>Abrams</u> and Justice Brandeis's concurrence in <u>Whitney</u>. In *Abrams*, which permitted a conviction for the distribution of a pamphlet calling on workers in factories to stop making ammunition and to "unite in the fight against capitalism," Justice Holmes stated in dissent:

> It is only the present danger of immediate evil or an intent to bring it about that warrants Congress in setting a limit to the expression of opinion where private rights are not concerned. Congress certainly cannot forbid all effort to change the mind of the country. *** In this case sentences of twenty years imprisonment have been imposed for the publishing of two leaflets that I believe the defendants had as much right to publish as the Government has to publish the Constitution of the United States now vainly invoked by them. Even if I am technically wrong and enough can be squeezed from these poor and puny anonymities to turn the color of legal litmus paper, [the] most nominal punishment seems to me all that possibly could be inflicted, unless the defendants are to be made to suffer not for what the indictment alleges but for the creed that they avow ***.

> Persecution for the expression of opinions seems to me perfectly logical. If you have no doubt of your premises or your power and want a certain result with all your heart you naturally express your wishes in law and sweep away all opposition. To allow opposition by speech seems to indicate that you think the speech impotent, as when a man says that he has squared the circle, or that you do not care whole heartedly for the result, or that you doubt either your power or your premises. But when men have realized that time has upset many fighting faiths, they may come to believe even more than they believe the very foundations of their own conduct that the ultimate good desired is better reached by free trade in ideas—that the best test of truth is the power of the thought to get itself accepted in the competition of the market, and that truth is the only ground upon which their wishes safely can be carried out. That at any rate is the theory of our Constitution. It is an experiment, as all life is an experiment. *** While that experiment is part of our system I think that we should be eternally vigilant against attempts to check the expression of opinions that we loathe and believe to be fraught with death, unless they so imminently threaten immediate interference with the lawful and pressing purposes of the law that an immediate check is required to save the country.

250 U.S. at 628-30 (Holmes, J., dissenting)

Justice Holmes was not the only Justice who advanced a different view of the First Amendment. In <u>Whitney</u>, which involved the conviction of Anita Whitney, the niece of Justice Stephen Field and a member of the Communist Party who was arrested after giving a speech criticizing race-based lynching, Justice Brandeis stated the following in his separate opinion:

> Those who won our independence believed that the final end of the state was to make men free to develop their faculties, and that in its government the deliberative forces should prevail over the arbitrary. They valued liberty both as an end and as a means. *** They believed that

freedom to think as you will and to speak as you think are means indispensable to the discovery and spread of political truth; that without free speech and assembly discussion would be futile; that with them, discussion affords ordinarily adequate protection against the dissemination of noxious doctrine; that the greatest menace to freedom is an inert people; that public discussion is a political duty; and that this should be a fundamental principle of the American government. They recognized the risks to which all human institutions are subject. But they knew that order cannot be secured merely through fear of punishment for its infraction; that it is hazardous to discourage thought, hope and imagination; that fear breeds repression; that repression breeds hate; that hate menaces stable government; that the path of safety lies in the opportunity to discuss freely supposed grievances and proposed remedies; and that the fitting remedy for evil counsels is good ones. Believing in the power of reason as applied through public discussion, they eschewed silence coerced by law—the argument of force in its worst form. Recognizing the occasional tyrannies of governing majorities, they amended the Constitution so that free speech and assembly should be guaranteed.

Fear of serious injury cannot alone justify suppression of free speech and assembly. Men feared witches and burnt women. It is the function of speech to free men from the bondage of irrational fears. To justify suppression of free speech there must be reasonable ground to fear that serious evil will result if free speech is practiced. There must be reasonable ground to believe that the danger apprehended is imminent. There must be reasonable ground to believe that the evil to be prevented is a serious one. *** But even advocacy of violation, however reprehensible morally, is not a justification for denying free speech where the advocacy falls short of incitement and there is nothing to indicate that the advocacy would be immediately acted on.

274 U.S. at 375-76 (Brandeis, J., concurring).

————————————

Points for Discussion

a. Theory of the First Amendment

The cases about the government's power to punish the advocacy of crime provide a stark context in which to discern the basic theory (or theories) of the First Amendment. On which theory did the Court rely from World War I until the 1950s? What was Justice Holmes's theory of the First Amendment? Was it different from Justice Brandeis's theory? What are the costs of the Court's approach from this era? What are the costs of Justices Holmes's and Brandeis's approaches?

b. War and Exigent Circumstances

Does the First Amendment by necessity permit greater government regulation of speech advocating its overthrow during times of stress or war? If so, how can we determine when such times exist, and whether circumstances are sufficiently exigent to justify such regulation?

————————————

In the case that follows, the Court developed the modern test for when the government can punish a person for advocating the commission of a crime or inciting violence.

_____

Brandenburg v. Ohio

395 U.S. 444 (1969)

PER CURIAM.

The appellant, a leader of a Ku Klux Klan group, was convicted under the Ohio Criminal Syndicalism statute for "advocat[ing] *** the duty, necessity, or propriety of crime, sabotage, violence, or unlawful methods of terrorism as a means of accomplishing industrial or political reform" and for "voluntarily assembl[ing] with any society, group, or assemblage of persons formed to teach or advocate the doctrines of criminal syndicalism." Ohio Rev. Code Ann. § 2923.13. He was fined $1,000 and sentenced to one to 10 years' imprisonment. ***

The record shows that a man, identified at trial as the appellant, telephoned an announcer-reporter on the staff of a Cincinnati television station and invited him to come to a Ku Klux Klan "rally" to be held at a farm in Hamilton County. With the cooperation of the organizers, the reporter and a cameraman attended the meeting and filmed the events. Portions of the films were later broadcast on the local station and on a national network.

The prosecution's case rested on the films and on testimony identifying the appellant as the person who communicated with the reporter and who spoke at the rally. The State also introduced into evidence several articles appearing in the film, including a pistol, a rifle, a shotgun, ammunition, a Bible, and a red hood worn by the speaker in the films.

One film showed 12 hooded figures, some of whom carried firearms. They were gathered around a large wooden cross, which they burned. No one was present other than the participants and the newsmen who made the film. Most of the words uttered during the scene were incomprehensible when the film was projected, but scattered phrases could be understood that were derogatory of Negroes and, in one instance, of Jews. Another scene on the same film showed the appellant, in Klan regalia, making a speech. The speech, in full, was as follows:

> "This is an organizers' meeting. We have had quite a few members here today which are— we have hundreds, hundreds of members throughout the State of Ohio. I can quote from a newspaper clipping from the Columbus, Ohio Dispatch, five weeks ago Sunday morning. The Klan has more members in the State of Ohio than does any other organization. We're not a revengent organization, but if our President, our Congress, our Supreme Court, continues to suppress the white, Caucasian race, it's possible that there might have to be some revengeance taken. We are marching on Congress July the Fourth, four hundred thousand strong. From there we are dividing into two groups, one group to march on St. Augustine, Florida, the other group to march into Mississippi. Thank you."

The second film showed six hooded figures one of whom, later identified as the appellant, repeated a speech very similar to that recorded on the first film. The reference to the possibility of "revengeance" was omitted, and one sentence was added: "Personally, I believe the nigger should be returned to Africa, the Jew returned to Israel." Though some of the figures in the films carried weapons, the speaker did not.

The Ohio Criminal Syndicalism Statute was enacted in 1919. From 1917 to 1920, identical or quite similar laws were adopted by 20 States and two territories. In 1927, this Court sustained the constitutionality of California's Criminal Syndicalism Act, the text of which is quite similar to that of the laws of Ohio. *Whitney v. California*, 274 U.S. 357 (1927). The Court upheld the statute on the ground that, without more, "advocating" violent means to effect political and economic change involves such danger to the security of the State that the State may outlaw it. But *Whitney* has been thoroughly discredited by later decisions. See *Dennis v. United States*, 341 U.S. 494, 507 (1951). These later decisions have fashioned the principle that the constitutional guarantees of free speech and free press do not permit a State to forbid or proscribe advocacy of the use of force or of law violation except where such advocacy is directed to inciting or producing imminent lawless action and is likely to incite or produce such action. As we said in *Noto v. United States*, 367 U.S. 290, 297-298 (1961), "the mere abstract teaching *** of the moral propriety or even moral necessity for a resort to force and violence, is not the same as preparing a group for violent action and steeling it to such action." A statute which fails to draw this distinction impermissibly intrudes upon the freedoms guaranteed by the First and Fourteenth Amendments. It sweeps within its condemnation speech which our Constitution has immunized from governmental control.

> **Take Note**
>
> In this passage, the Court specifies the standard for when the government may restrict advocacy of crime. In what way does the standard differ from the approach of the older cases?

Measured by this test, Ohio's Criminal Syndicalism Act cannot be sustained. The Act punishes persons who "advocate or teach the duty, necessity, or propriety" of violence "as a means of accomplishing industrial or political reform"; or who publish or circulate or display any book or paper containing such advocacy; or who "justify" the commission of violent acts "with intent to exemplify, spread or advocate the propriety of the doctrines of criminal syndicalism"; or who "voluntarily assemble" with a group formed "to teach or advocate the doctrines of criminal syndicalism." Neither the indictment nor the trial judge's instructions to the jury in any way refined the statute's bald definition of the crime in terms of mere advocacy not distinguished from incitement to imminent lawless action.

Accordingly, we are here confronted with a statute which, by its own words and as applied, purports to punish mere advocacy and to forbid, on pain of criminal punishment, assembly with others merely to advocate the described type of action. Such a statute falls within the condemnation of the First and Fourteenth Amendments. The contrary teaching of *Whitney v. California* cannot be supported, and that decision is therefore overruled.

———————————

Points for Discussion

a. Incitement of Imminent Lawless Action

The Court in <u>Brandenburg</u> held that the government may restrict advocacy of crime only where "advocacy is directed to inciting or producing imminent lawless action and is likely to incite or produce such action." As a practical matter, how would the government know when advocacy of crime is "likely to incite" lawless action? Is it ever possible for the mere delivery of a speech, authorship of a book or pamphlet, or membership in an organization to satisfy that standard?

b. Crime and Speech

The Court in <u>Brandenburg</u> did not go so far as to hold that a person can *never* be punished for his speech, even if a person could constitutionally be punished for actually engaging in conduct, such as armed insurrection or mob violence, that the state legitimately has criminalized. Should the Court have done so, on the ground that any other approach effectively chills some speech?

Or did the Court go too far in <u>Brandenburg</u>, and perhaps even in its older "clear and present danger" cases? Robert Bork, for example, has argued that the First Amendment provides *no* protection for speech advocating the violation of the law. See Robert H. Bork, *Neutral Principles and Some First Amendment Problems*, 47 Ind. L. J. 1 (1971). On this view, is advocacy of crime unprotected because of the strong government interest in preventing crime, or because such speech simply isn't worthy of protection? Would the speeches of Martin Luther King, Jr., regularly have subjected him to criminal punishment for advocating "crime," in the form of civil disobedience?

---

2. Defamation

Under the tort law of most states, a person may incur liability for libel or slander by making "a false and defamatory statement concerning another." Restatement (Second) of the Law of Torts § 558. A statement is "defamatory if it tends so to harm the reputation of another as to lower him in the estimation of the community or to deter third persons from associating or dealing with him." Id. § 559. The tort of libel generally consists of the "publication of defamatory matter by written or printed words," while the tort of slander typically consists of "the publication of defamatory matter by spoken words." Id. § 568.

Imposing liability for defamatory statements is, in some senses, a limitation on the freedom of speech. For example, in one case (fortunately not involving either of the co-authors of this textbook), a court required a professor to pay $50,000 in damages for saying that one of his colleagues was "a liar, deceitful, absolutely useless, and does not have a Ph.D., and was a fraud ***." Raymond U v. Duke University, 371 S.E.2d 701, 709 (N.C. App. 1988). Judgments like this one certainly limit the freedom of people to say whatever they think about other people, and they are imposed and enforced by courts, which are clearly governmental actors.

The Supreme Court has held that the First Amendment does not absolutely bar the imposition of tort liability for defamatory statements. See *Beauharnais v. People of State of Illinois*, 343 U.S. 250, 266 (1952). But the First Amendment does impose some important restrictions. Two of the most important are as follows. First, a **public official, political candidate, or public figure** may not recover in tort for a defamatory statement relating to his official conduct unless the statement was both false and made with "actual malice." See *New York Times Co. v. Sullivan*, 376 U.S. 254 (1964), which follows. Second, a private figure may not recover for a defamatory statement regarding **a matter of public concern** unless the statement was both false and made knowingly or at least negligently. See *Gertz v. Robert Welch, Inc.*, 418 U.S. 323 (1974).

To understand these two rules, several terms require explanation. The Supreme Court has said that "actual malice" is "a term of art denoting deliberate or reckless falsification." *Masson v. New Yorker Magazine, Inc.*, 501 U.S. 496, 499 (1991). The term "public offi-cial" includes "at the very least *** those among the hierarchy of government employees who have, or appear to the public to have, substantial responsibility for or control over the conduct of governmental affairs." *Rosenblatt v. Baer*, 383 U.S. 75 (1966). The Court in *Rosenblatt* also stated that a public official is a person who holds a position of such "apparent importance that the public has an independent interest in the qualifications and performance of the person who holds it." A "public figure" is generally someone, such as a movie star or other celebrity, who has voluntarily become the subject of public attention; the term does not include a person who has merely become "involved in or associated with a matter that attracts public attention," like a mere criminal suspect. *Wolston v. Reader's Digest Ass'n, Inc.*, 443 U.S. 157, 167 (1979). The term "matter of public concern" does not have a precise definition, but the Supreme Court has said that the term refers to "something that is a subject of legitimate news interest; that is, a subject of general interest and of value and concern to the public at the time of publication." *City of San Diego v. Roe*, 543 U.S. 77, 83-84 (2004).

Points for Discussion

a. Competing Interests

The rules reflect an attempt to strike a balance between the interest in protecting reputations and the interest in free speech. In thinking about this balance, consider these two questions.

First, if the First Amendment protects the freedom of speech, why should a state be allowed to impose *any* liability for statements a person might make, even if they are defamatory? One commentator writes:

> No matter how much it values speech, [a] civilized society cannot refuse to protect reputation. Some form of libel law is as essential to the health of the commonweal and the press as it is to the victims of defamation. Without libel law, the credibility of the press would be at the mercy of the least scrupulous among it, and public discourse would have no necessary anchor in truth.

David A. Anderson, *Is Libel Law Worth Reforming*, 140 U. Penn. L. Rev. 487, 490 (1991). Can you think of hypothetical examples of negative consequences that might flow from the abolition of libel laws? Do you agree that prohibitions on defamation, regardless of their desirability, are consistent with the First Amendment? Does it matter that libel laws were common at the time that the First Amendment was ratified?

Second, on the other hand, why should the First Amendment restrict tort liability for defamatory statements at all? For example, should a newspaper be able to publish an editorial falsely implicating an innocent government scientist in terrorist attacks, absolutely ruin his career, but then escape liability if the scientist cannot show that the newspaper acted with actual malice? Cf. *Hatfill v. New York Times*, 532 F.3d 312 (4th Cir. 2008) (similar facts). What policies could justify excusing this real harm to an individual? Are these policies of constitutional significance? Could a newspaper escape tort liability if one of its reporters negligently ran over a pedestrian on the way to interview someone for a news story? Why is defamation different?

b. Matter of Public Concern

What is a matter of public concern? Can it be anything that, if included in a newspaper, will attract public attention? Doesn't the very fact that it was in a newspaper by definition guarantee that it will be, even if it wasn't before, a matter of public concern?

c. Public Figures

If in fact the interest in free speech is paramount, why are First Amendment limits on liability for defamation limited to cases involving "public figures"? Is speech about public figures more valuable than speech about people that no one has heard of? Are courts capable of applying principled standards to distinguish public figures from everyone else?

––––––––––––––––––

As you read the case that follows, consider whether the Court satisfactorily answered the questions that we have just raised.

––––––––––––––––––

New York Times Co. v. Sullivan

376 U.S. 254 (1964)

Mr. Justice BRENNAN delivered the opinion of the Court.

We are required in this case to determine for the first time the extent to which the constitutional protections for speech and press limit a State's power to award damages in a libel action brought by a public official against critics of his official conduct.

Respondent L. B. Sullivan is one of the three elected Commissioners of the City of Montgomery, Alabama. He testified that he was "Commissioner of Public Affairs and the duties are supervision of the Police Department, Fire Department, Department of Cemetery and Department of Scales." He brought this civil libel action against the four individual petitioners, who are Negroes and Alabama clergymen, and against petitioner the New York Times Company, a New York corporation which publishes the New York Times, a daily newspaper. A jury in the Circuit Court of Montgomery County awarded him damages of $500,000, the full amount claimed, against all the petitioners, and the Supreme Court of Alabama affirmed.

Respondent's complaint alleged that he had been libeled by statements in a full-page advertisement that was carried in the New York Times on March 29, 1960. Entitled "Heed Their Rising Voices," the advertisement began by stating that "As the whole world knows by now, thousands of Southern Negro students are engaged in widespread non-violent demonstrations in positive affirmation of the right to live in human dignity as guaranteed by the U.S. Constitution and the Bill of Rights." It went on to charge that "in their efforts to uphold these guarantees, they are being met by an unprecedented wave of terror by those who would deny and negate that document which the whole world looks upon as setting the pattern for modern freedom. ***" Succeeding paragraphs purported to illustrate the "wave of terror" by describing certain alleged events. The text concluded with an appeal for funds for three purposes: support of the student movement, "the struggle for the right-to-vote," and the legal defense of Dr. Martin Luther King, Jr., leader of the movement, against a perjury indictment then pending in Montgomery.

Of the 10 paragraphs of text in the advertisement, the third and a portion of the sixth were the basis of respondent's claim of libel. They read as follows:

> Third paragraph: "In Montgomery, Alabama, after students sang 'My Country, 'Tis of Thee' on the State Capitol steps, their leaders were expelled from school, and truckloads of police armed with shotguns and tear-gas ringed the Alabama State College Campus. When the entire student body protested to state authorities by refusing to re-register, their dining hall was padlocked in an attempt to starve them into submission."

> Sixth paragraph: "Again and again the Southern violators have answered Dr. King's peaceful protests with intimidation and violence. They have bombed his home almost killing his wife and child. They have assaulted his person. They have arrested him seven times—for 'speeding,' 'loitering' and similar 'offenses.' And now they have charged him with 'perjury'—a felony under which they could imprison him for ten years. ***"

Although neither of these statements mentions respondent by name, he contended that the word "police" in the third paragraph referred to him as the Montgomery Commissioner who supervised the Police Department, so that he was being accused of "ringing" the campus with police. He further claimed that the paragraph would be read as imputing to the police, and hence to him, the padlocking of the dining hall in order to starve the students into submission. As to the sixth paragraph, he contended that since arrests are ordinarily made by the police, the statement "They have arrested (Dr. King) seven times" would be read as referring to him; he further contended that the "They" who did the arresting would be equated with the "They" who committed the other described acts and with the 'Southern violators.' Thus, he argued, the paragraph would be read as accusing the Montgomery police, and hence him, of answering Dr. King's protests with "intimidation and violence," bombing his home, assaulting his person, and charging him with perjury. Respondent and six other Montgomery residents testified that they read some or all of the statements as referring to him in his capacity as Commissioner.

It is uncontroverted that some of the statements contained in the two paragraphs were not accurate descriptions of events which occurred in Montgomery. Although Negro students staged a demonstration on the State Capital steps, they sang the National Anthem and not "My Country, 'Tis of Thee." Although nine students were expelled by the State Board of Education, this was not for leading the demonstration at the Capitol, but for demanding service at a lunch counter in the Montgomery County Courthouse on another day. Not the entire student body, but most of it, had protested the expulsion, not by refusing to register, but by boycotting classes on a single day; virtually all the students did register for the ensuing semester. The campus dining hall was not padlocked on any occasion, and the only students who may have been barred from eating there were the few who had neither signed a preregistration application nor requested temporary meal tickets. Although the police were deployed near the campus in large numbers on three occasions, they did not at any time "ring" the campus, and they were not called to the campus in connection with the demonstration on the State Capitol steps, as the third paragraph implied. Dr. King had not been arrested seven times, but only four; and although he claimed to have been assaulted some years earlier in connection with his arrest for loitering outside a courtroom, one of the officers who made the arrest denied that there was such an assault.

On the premise that the charges in the sixth paragraph could be read as referring to him, respondent was allowed to prove that he had not participated in the events described. Although Dr. King's home had in fact been bombed twice when his wife and child were there, both of these occasions antedated respondent's tenure as Commissioner, and the police were not only not implicated in the bombings, but had made every effort to apprehend those who were. Three of Dr. King's four arrests took place before respondent became Commissioner. Although Dr. King had in fact been indicted (he was subsequently acquitted) on two counts of perjury, each of which carried a possible five-year sentence, respondent had nothing to do with procuring the indictment.

Approximately 394 copies of the edition of the Times containing the advertisement were circulated in Alabama. Of these, about 35 copies were distributed in Montgomery County. The total circulation of the Times for that day was approximately 650,000 copies.

Under Alabama law as applied in this case, a publication is "libelous per se" if the words "tend to injure a person *** in his reputation" or to "bring [him] into public contempt"; the trial court stated that the standard was met if the words are such as to "injure him in his public office, or impute misconduct to him in his office, or want of official integrity, or want of fidelity to a public trust ***." The jury must find that the words were published "of and concerning" the plaintiff, but where the plaintiff is a public official his place in the governmental hierarchy is sufficient evidence to support a finding that his reputation has been affected by statements that reflect upon the agency of which he is in charge. Once "libel per se" has been established, the defendant has no defense as to stated facts unless he can persuade the jury that they were true in all their particulars. His privilege of "fair comment" for expressions of opinion depends on the truth of the facts upon which the comment is based. Unless he can discharge the burden of proving truth, general damages are presumed, and may be awarded without proof of pecuniary injury. A showing of actual malice is apparently a prerequisite to recovery of punitive damages, and the defendant may in any event forestall a punitive award by a retraction meeting the statutory requirements. Good motives and belief in truth do not negate an inference of malice, but are relevant only in mitigation of punitive damages if the jury chooses to accord them weight.

The question before us is whether this rule of liability, as applied to an action brought by a public official against critics of his official conduct, abridges the freedom of speech and of the press that is guaranteed by the First and Fourteenth Amendments.

Respondent relies heavily, as did the Alabama courts, on statements of this Court to the effect that the Constitution does not protect libelous publications. Those statements do not foreclose our inquiry here. None of the cases sustained the use of libel laws to impose sanctions upon expression critical of the official conduct of public officials. *** In the only previous case that did present the question of constitutional limitations upon the power to award damages for libel of a public official, the Court was equally divided and the question was not decided. *Schenectady Union Pub. Co. v. Sweeney*, 316 U.S. 642 (1942). In deciding the question now, we are compelled by neither precedent nor policy to give any more weight to the epithet "libel" than we have to other "mere labels" of state law. *N.A.A.C.P. v. Button*, 371 U.S. 415 (1963). Like insurrection, contempt, advocacy of unlawful acts, breach of the peace, obscenity, solicitation of legal business, and the various other formulae for the repression of expression that have been challenged in this Court, libel can claim no talismanic immunity from constitutional limitations. It must be measured by standards that satisfy the First Amendment.

The general proposition that freedom of expression upon public questions is secured by the First Amendment has long been settled by our decisions. The constitutional safeguard, we have said, "was fashioned to assure unfettered interchange of ideas for the bringing about of political and social changes desired by the people." *Roth v. United States*, 354 U.S. 476, 484 (1957). ***

Thus we consider this case against the background of a profound national commitment to the principle that debate on public issues should be uninhibited, robust, and wide-open, and that it may well include vehement, caustic, and sometimes unpleasantly sharp attacks on government and public officials. The present advertisement, as an expression of grievance and protest on one of the major public issues of our time, would seem clearly to qualify for the constitutional protection. The question is whether it forfeits that protection by the falsity of some of its factual statements and by its alleged defamation of respondent.

Authoritative interpretations of the First Amendment guarantees have consistently refused to recognize an exception for any test of truth—whether administered by judges, juries, or administrative officials—and especially one that puts the burden of proving truth on the speaker. The constitutional protection does not turn upon "the truth, popularity, or social utility of the ideas and beliefs which are offered." <u>N.A.A.C.P. v. Button, 371 U.S. at 445</u>. As Madison said, "Some degree of abuse is inseparable from the proper use of every thing; and in no instance is this more true than in that of the press." 4 Elliot's Debates on the Federal Constitution (1876), p. 571. ***

A rule compelling the critic of official conduct to guarantee the truth of all his factual assertions—and to do so on pain of libel judgments virtually unlimited in amount—leads to a comparable "self-censorship." Allowance of the defense of truth, with the burden of proving it on the defendant, does not mean that only false speech will be deterred. Even courts accepting this defense as an adequate safeguard have recognized the difficulties of adducing legal proofs that the alleged libel was true in all its factual particulars. Under such a rule, would-be critics of official conduct may be deterred from voicing their criticism, even though it is believed to be true and even though it is in fact true, because of doubt whether it can be proved in court or fear of the expense of having to do so. They tend to make only statements which "steer far wider of the unlawful zone." *Speiser v. Randall*, 357 U.S. 513, 526 (1958). The rule thus dampens the vigor and limits the variety of public debate. It is inconsistent with the First and Fourteenth Amendments.

> **Take Note**
>
> The Court here declares that a rule permitting judgments by public figures in defamation cases unless the critic can demonstrate the truth of the statements is insufficient under the First Amendment. Is this because the First Amendment protects even untrue statements? Is it because courts (and juries) are ill-suited to determine the truth? Or is it because a truth standard would tend to chill true speech, even though false speech is not protected?

The constitutional guarantees require, we think, a federal rule that prohibits a public official from recovering damages for a defamatory falsehood relating to his official conduct unless he proves that the statement was made with "actual malice"—that is, with knowledge that it was false or with reckless disregard of whether it was false or not. *** We conclude that such a privilege is required by the First and Fourteenth Amendments.

Applying these standards, we consider that the proof presented to show actual malice lacks the convincing clarity which the constitutional standard demands, and hence that it would not constitutionally sustain the judgment for respondent under the proper rule of law. *** Even assuming that [the individual petitioners] could constitutionally be found to have authorized the use of their names on the advertisement, there was no evidence whatever that they were aware of any erroneous statements or were in any way reckless in that regard. *** We think the evidence against the Times supports at most a finding of negligence in failing to discover the misstatements, and is constitutionally insufficient to show the recklessness that is required for a finding of actual malice.

We also think the evidence was constitutionally defective in another respect: it was incapable of supporting the jury's finding that the allegedly libelous statements were made "of and concerning" respondent. *** There was no reference to respondent in the advertisement, either by name or official position. [The Supreme Court of Alabama relied] on the bare fact of respondent's official position. *** Raising as it does the possibility that a good-faith critic of government will be penalized for his criticism, the proposition relied on by the Alabama courts strikes at the very center of the constitutionally protected area of free expression. We hold that such a proposition may not constitutionally be utilized to establish that an otherwise impersonal attack on governmental operations was a libel of an official responsible for those operations. Since it was relied on exclusively here, and there was no other evidence to connect the statements with respondent, the evidence was constitutionally insufficient to support a finding that the statements referred to respondent. [Reversed.]

Mr. Justice BLACK, with whom Mr. Justice DOUGLAS joins, concurring.

I base my vote to reverse on the belief that the First and Fourteenth Amendments not merely "delimit" a State's power to award damages to "public officials against critics of their official conduct" but completely prohibit a State from exercising such a power. *** The requirement that malice be proved provides at best an evanescent protection for the right critically to discuss public affairs and certainly does not measure up to the sturdy safeguard embodied in the First Amendment. Unlike the Court, therefore, I vote to reverse exclusively on the ground that the Times and the individual defendants had an absolute, unconditional constitutional right to publish in the Times advertisement their criticisms of the Montgomery agencies and officials. *** This Nation, I suspect, can live in peace without libel suits based on public discussions of public affairs and public officials. But I doubt that a country can live in freedom where its people can be made to suffer physically or financially for criticizing their government, its actions, or its officials. *** An unconditional right to say what one pleases about public affairs is what I consider to be the minimum guarantee of the First Amendment.

Mr. Justice GOLDBERG, with whom Mr. Justice DOUGLAS joins, concurring in the result.

In my view, the First and Fourteenth Amendments to the Constitution afford to the citizen and to the press an absolute, unconditional privilege to criticize official conduct despite the harm which may flow from excesses and abuses. *** This is not to say that the Constitution protects defamatory statements directed against the private conduct of a public official or private citizen. *** Purely private defamation has little to do with the political ends of a self-governing society. The imposition of liability for private defamation does not abridge the freedom of public speech or any other freedom protected by the First Amendment. This, of course, cannot be said "where public officials are concerned or where public matters are involved. ***"

———————

Points for Discussion

a. The Importance of *Sullivan*

Professor Harry Kalven Jr., a noted scholar of the First Amendment, predicted that *New York Times v. Sullivan* would "prove to be the best and most important" decision that the Supreme Court "has ever produced in the realm of Freedom of Speech." Harry Kalven Jr., *The New York Times Case: A Note on "The Central Meaning of the First Amendment,"* 1964

Sup. Ct. Rev. 191, 193-94. He correctly anticipated that the rule of the case would expand from protecting speech about public officials to protecting speech about other matters in the public interest. *Id.* at 221. Why is the right of newspapers to publish false stories without fearing tort liability so important?

b. The Theory of *Sullivan*

Did the Court in *Sullivan* conclude that all false and defamatory speech is nevertheless speech, and thus entitled to protection under the First Amendment? Or did it instead conclude that, although false and defamatory speech is outside of the protection of the First Amendment, the interests served by the Amendment require some limits on the authority of courts to impose liability for such speech? And if the latter, did the Court simply attempt to strike a balance between First Amendment interests and the individual interest in reputation?

In *Gertz v. Robert Welch, Inc.*, 418 U.S. 323 (1974), mentioned above, the Court held that a private figure may not recover for a defamatory statement regarding a matter of public concern unless the statement was both false and made knowingly or at least negligently, a lesser standard than the one that the Court announced in *Sullivan*. Two things about the Court's decision in *Gertz* are particularly notable here. First, the Court stated:

> Under the First Amendment there is no such thing as a false idea. However pernicious an opinion may seem, we depend for its correction not on the conscience of judges and juries but on the competition of other ideas. But there is no constitutional value in false statements of fact. Neither the intentional lie nor the careless error materially advances society's interest in "uninhibited, robust, and wide-open" debate on public issues. They belong to that category of utterances which "are no essential part of any exposition of ideas, and are of such slight social value as a step to truth that any benefit that may be derived from them is clearly outweighed by the social interest in order and morality." *Chaplinsky v. New Hampshire*, 315 U.S. 568, 572 (1942).

Second, the Court in *Gertz* declared that the *Sullivan* standard was not "justified solely by reference to the interest of the press and broadcast media in immunity from liability," but instead "states an accommodation between this concern and the limited state interest present in the context of libel actions brought by public persons." The Court then declared that a different "balance between the needs of the press and the individual's claim to compensation for wrongful injury" should apply for statements about private figures on matters of public concern. The Court noted that "[p]ublic officials and public figures usually enjoy significantly greater access to the channels of effective communication and hence have a more realistic opportunity to counteract false statements than private individuals normally enjoy," whereas "private individuals will [likely] lack effective opportunities for rebuttal." In addition, the Court stated that, by virtue of their positions, public officials and public figures "must accept certain necessary consequences of [their] involvement in public affairs" and effectively have "voluntarily exposed themselves to increased risk of injury from defamatory falsehood concerning them." In contrast, "[n]o such assumption is justified with respect to a private individual."

Is it appropriate for the Court to permit some liability for speech based on, as the

Court in *Gertz* described it, an explicit "accommodation of the competing values at stake in defamation suits"? Doesn't the First Amendment strike a balance in favor of speech? Or, conversely, would it make more sense for the Court simply to conclude that the First Amendment has nothing to say about defamation claims, which were historically considered appropriate notwithstanding their chilling effect on speech?

c. Limiting *Sullivan*

Sullivan and related cases make clear that the First Amendment requires special rules for the imposition of tort liability in cases involving statements about public officials and public figures and in cases involving claims by private figures arising from statements on matters of public concern. Does the First Amendment impose any limits on the authority of a court to impose liability for a statement about a private figure on a matter of private concern? In *Dun & Bradstreet, Inc. v. Greenmoss Builders, Inc.*, 472 U.S. 749 (1985), the Court held that a state rule permitting the recovery of presumed and punitive damages in defamation cases—that is, permitting recovery without a showing of actual harm and damages—absent a showing of actual malice did not violate the First Amendment when the defamatory statements were about a private figure and did not involve matters of public concern. The Court applied the "approach approved in *Gertz* and balance[d] the State's interest in compensating private individuals for injury to their reputation against the First Amendment interest in protecting this type of expression." The Court noted that the state interest in protecting the reputation of private figures was "identical to the one weighed in *Gertz*," but that "speech on matters of purely private concern is of less First Amendment concern" than the speech on matters of public concern at issue in *Gertz*. The Court also reasoned that the common-law rule permitting the award of damages even absent proof of actual damage "furthers the state interest in providing remedies for defamation by ensuring that those remedies are effective." The Court concluded: "In light of the reduced constitutional value of speech involving no matters of public concern, we hold that the state interest adequately supports awards of presumed and punitive damages—even absent a showing of 'actual malice.'" Justice Brennan, joined by three other Justices, dissented, asserting (among other things) that "unrestrained presumed and punitive damages" rules violate the First Amendment.

Does the Court's decision in *Dun & Bradstreet* mean that the First Amendment imposes no limits on the states' authority to permit liability for defamatory statements about private figures on matters of private concern?

d. Extending <u>*Sullivan*</u>

As we noted above, the Court eventually extended <u>*Sullivan*</u> to cases involving public figures (not just public officials) and to cases involving claims by private figures arising from speech on matters of public concern. Does the approach in <u>*Sullivan*</u> also apply to tort claims other than those sounding in defamation?

In *Hustler Magazine, Inc. v. Falwell*, 485 U.S. 46 (1988), Jerry Falwell, a prominent minister and televangelist, sued a magazine after it published a parody depicting Falwell having a drunken sexual encounter with his mother in an outhouse. Falwell asserted claims for invasion of privacy, libel, and intentional infliction of emotional distress. The jury found against him on the first two claims, but in his favor on the last one. The Supreme Court reversed. The Court noted that, historically, "graphic depictions and satirical cartoons have played a prominent role in public and political debate." Relying on *Sullivan*, the Court held that "public figures and public officials may not recover for the tort of intentional infliction of emotional distress by reason of publications such as the one here at issue without showing in addition that the publication contains a false statement of fact which was made with 'actual malice' ***." If the Court had reached the opposite conclusion, would public figures be able effectively to recover for injured reputations by asserting claims for intentional infliction of emotional distress?

----

3. Obscenity

The Supreme Court has held that the First Amendment does not protect "obscenity." See *Roth v. United States,* 354 U.S. 476 (1957), which we consider below. The government, therefore, can regulate and even ban obscene materials, including those that might appear in magazines, movies, internet sites, and so forth. From this principle, two key questions arise: What is obscenity? And why does it receive no First Amendment protection?

> **FYI**
>
> Justice Potter Stewart once famously quipped that although obscenity might be difficult to define, "I know it when I see it." *Jacobellis v. Ohio,* 378 U.S. 184, 197 (1964) (Stewart, J., concurring).

Obscenity is notoriously hard to define. But since 1973, the basic test has remained the same. The Supreme Court has said:

> The basic guidelines for the trier of fact must be: (a) whether the average person, applying contemporary community standards would find that the work, taken as a whole, appeals to the prurient interest; (b) whether the work depicts or describes, in a patently offensive way, sexual conduct specifically defined by the applicable state law; and (c) whether the work, taken as a whole, lacks serious literary, artistic, political, or scientific value.

Miller v. California, 413 U.S. 15, 24 (1973). The word "prurient" is an adjective meaning "[c]haracterized by or arousing inordinate or unusual sexual desire." *Black's Law Dictionary* (8th ed. 2008). Note, then, that under the Court's test for obscenity, the material in question must both arouse (*i.e.*, appeal to the prurient interest) and disgust (*i.e.*, be "offensive"). Is this a sensible or manageable test?

The Supreme Court has relied on historical and originalist arguments, among others, in concluding that the First Amendment does not protect obscenity. In *Roth*, the Court explained that the history reveals "the rejection of obscenity as utterly without redeeming social importance." And as Justice Scalia has concisely put it: "There is no doubt, for example, that laws against [obscenity] do not violate 'the freedom of speech' to which the First Amendment refers; they existed and were universally approved in 1791." *McIntyre v. Ohio Elections Com'n*, 514 U.S. 334, 372 (1995) (Scalia, J., dissenting). But see Eric M. Freedman, *A Lot More Comes into Focus When You Remove the Lens Cap*, 81 Iowa L. Rev. 883, 898 (1996) (doubting claims that "prior to 1791, the American colonies recognized sexually explicit materials as an exception to their normal rules protecting freedom of speech").

As you read the materials that follow, consider whether the Court has properly excluded obscenity from the protection of the First Amendment, and whether the Court's test for identifying obscenity is sensible and manageable.

————

Roth v. United States

354 U.S. 476 (1957)

Mr. Justice BRENNAN delivered the opinion of the Court.

The constitutionality of a criminal obscenity statute is the question in each of these cases. In *Roth*, the primary constitutional question is whether the federal obscenity statute[1] violates the provision of the First Amendment that "Congress shall make no law *** abridging the freedom of speech, or of the press ***." In *Alberts*, [a companion case,] the primary constitutional question is whether the obscenity provisions of the California Penal Code[2] invade the freedoms of speech and press as they may be incorporated in the liberty protected from state action by the Due Process Clause of the Fourteenth Amendment.

Roth conducted a business in New York in the publication and sale of books, photographs and magazines. He used circulars and advertising matter to solicit sales. He was convicted by a jury in the District Court for the Southern District of New York upon 4 counts of a 26-count indictment charging him with mailing obscene circulars and advertising, and an obscene book, in violation of the federal obscenity statute. *** Alberts conducted a mail-order business from Los Angeles. He was convicted by the Judge of the Municipal Court of the Beverly Hills Judicial District (having waived a jury trial) under a misdemeanor complaint which charged him with lewdly keeping for sale obscene and indecent books, and with writing, composing and publishing an obscene advertisement of

---

[1] The federal obscenity statute provided, in pertinent part: "Every obscene, lewd, lascivious, or filthy book, pamphlet, picture, paper, letter, writing, print, or other publication of an indecent character; and [e]very written or printed card, letter, circular, book, pamphlet, advertisement, or notice of any kind giving information, directly or indirectly, where, or how, or from whom, or by what means any of such mentioned matters, articles, or things may be obtained or made, *** whether sealed or unsealed *** [i]s declared to be nonmailable matter and shall not be conveyed in the mails or delivered from any post office or by any letter carrier. Whoever knowingly deposits for mailing or delivery, anything declared by this section to be nonmailable, or knowingly takes the same from the mails for the purpose of circulating or disposing thereof, or of aiding in the circulation or disposition thereof, shall be fined not more than $5,000 or imprisoned not more than five years, or both." 18 U.S.C. § 1461. ***

[2] "Every person who wilfully and lewdly, either: *** 3. Writes, composes, stereotypes, prints, publishes, sells, distributes, keeps for sale, or exhibits any obscene or indecent writing, paper, or book; or designs, copies, draws, engraves, paints, or otherwise prepares any obscene or indecent picture or print; or molds, cuts, casts, or otherwise makes any obscene or indecent figure; or ***, 4. Writes, composes, or publishes any notice or advertisement of any such writing, paper, book, picture, print or figure; *** is guilty of a misdemeanor ***." West's Cal. Penal Code Ann., 1955 § 311.

them, in violation of the California Penal Code. ***

The dispositive question is whether obscenity is utterance within the area of protected speech and press. Although this is the first time the question has been squarely presented to this Court, either under the First Amendment or under the Fourteenth Amendment, expressions found in numerous opinions indicate that this Court has always assumed that obscenity is not protected by the freedoms of speech and press.

The guaranties of freedom of expression in effect in 10 of the 14 States which by 1792 had ratified the Constitution, gave no absolute protection for every utterance. Thirteen of the 14 States provided for the prosecution of libel, and all of those States made either blasphemy or profanity, or both, statutory crimes. As early as 1712, Massachusetts made it criminal to publish "any filthy, obscene, or profane song, pamphlet, libel or mock sermon" in imitation or mimicking of religious services. Acts and Laws of the Province of Mass. Bay, c. CV, § 8 (1712), Mass. Bay Colony Charters & Laws 399 (1814). Thus, profanity and obscenity were related offenses.

In light of this history, it is apparent that the unconditional phrasing of the First Amendment was not intended to protect every utterance. This phrasing did not prevent this Court from concluding that libelous utterances are not within the area of constitutionally protected speech. *Beauharnais v. People of State of Illinois*, 343 U.S. 250, 266 (1952). At the time of the adoption of the First Amendment, obscenity law was not as fully developed as libel law, but there is sufficiently contemporaneous evidence to show that obscenity, too, was outside the protection intended for speech and press.

The protection given speech and press was fashioned to assure unfettered interchange of ideas for the bringing about of political and social changes desired by the people. *** All ideas having even the slightest redeeming social importance—unorthodox ideas, controversial ideas, even ideas hateful to the prevailing climate of opinion—have the full protection of the guaranties, unless excludable because they encroach upon the limited area of more important interests. But implicit in the history of the First Amendment is the rejection of obscenity as utterly without redeeming social importance. This rejection for that reason is mirrored in the universal judgment that obscenity should be restrained, reflected in the international agreement of over 50 nations, in the obscenity laws of all of the 48 States, and in the 20 obscenity laws enacted by the Congress from 1842 to 1956. This is the same judgment expressed by this Court in *Chaplinsky v. New Hampshire*, 315 U.S. 568, 571-572 (1942):

> *** There are certain well-defined and narrowly limited classes of speech, the prevention and punishment of which have never been thought to raise any Constitutional problem. These include the lewd and obscene ***. It has been well observed that such utterances are no essential part of any exposition of ideas, and are of such slight social value as a step to truth that any benefit that may be derived from them is clearly outweighed by the social interest in order and morality ***.

We hold that obscenity is not within the area of constitutionally protected speech or press.

It is strenuously urged that these obscenity statutes offend the constitutional guaranties because they punish incitation to impure sexual *thoughts*, not shown to be related to any overt antisocial conduct which is or may be incited in the persons stimulated to such *thoughts*. *** However, sex and obscenity are not synonymous. Obscene material is material which deals with sex in a manner appealing to prurient interest.[20] The portrayal of sex, e.g., in art, literature and scientific works, is not itself sufficient reason to deny material the constitutional protection of freedom of speech and press. Sex, a great and mysterious motive force in human life, has indisputably been a subject of absorbing interest to mankind through the ages; it is one of the vital problems of human interest and public concern.

> **Take Note**
>
> The Court decides that the First Amendment does not protect obscenity. But it then gives obscenity a somewhat narrow definition. Although the definition of obscenity has varied over time, this basic approach to obscenity has not. Does the Court's approach mean that courts will repeatedly be called upon to decide what depictions of sex sufficiently appeal to the "prurient interest" to fall outside the scope of the First Amendment's protection?

The fundamental freedom of speech and press have contributed greatly to the development and well-being of our free society and are indispensable to its continued growth. Ceaseless vigilance is the watchword to prevent their erosion by Congress or by the States. The door barring federal and state intrusion into this area cannot be left ajar; it must be kept tightly closed and opened only the slightest crack necessary to prevent encroachment upon more important interests. It is therefore vital that the standards for judging obscenity safeguard the protection of freedom of speech and press for material which does not treat sex in a manner appealing to prurient interest.

The early leading standard of obscenity allowed material to be judged merely by the effect of an isolated excerpt upon particularly susceptible persons. *Regina v. Hicklin*, (1868) L.R. 3 Q.B. 360. Some American courts adopted this standard but later decisions have rejected it and substituted this test: whether to the average person, applying contemporary community standards, the dominant theme of the material taken as a whole appeals to prurient interest. The *Hicklin* test, judging obscenity by the effect of isolated passages upon the most susceptible persons, might well encompass material legitimately treating with sex, and so it must be rejected as unconstitutionally restrictive of the freedoms of speech and press. On the other hand, the substituted standard provides safeguards adequate to withstand the charge of constitutional infirmity. Both trial courts below sufficiently followed the proper standard. Both courts used the proper definition of obscenity. [Affirmed.]

[Justice HARLAN'S dissenting opinion is omitted.]

Mr. Justice DOUGLAS, with whom Mr. Justice BLACK concurs, dissenting.

When we sustain these convictions, we make the legality of a publication turn on the purity of thought which a book or tract instills in the mind of the reader. I do not think

---

[20] I.e., material having a tendency to excite lustful thoughts. Webster's New International Dictionary (Unabridged, 2d ed., 1949) defines prurient, in pertinent part, as follows: "Itching; longing; uneasy with desire or longing; of persons, having itching, morbid, or lascivious longings; of desire, curiosity, or propensity, lewd."

we can approve that standard and be faithful to the command of the First Amendment, which by its terms is a restraint on Congress and which by the Fourteenth is a restraint on the States.

Any test that turns on what is offensive to the community's standards is too loose, too capricious, too destructive of freedom of expression to be squared with the First Amendment. Under that test, juries can censor, suppress, and punish what they don't like, provided the matter relates to "sexual impurity" or has a tendency "to excite lustful thoughts." This is community censorship in one of its worst forms. It creates a regime where in the battle between the literati and the Philistines, the Philistines are certain to win.

I can understand (and at times even sympathize) with programs of civic groups and church groups to protect and defend the existing moral standards of the community. *** When speech alone is involved, I do not think that government, consistently with the First Amendment, can become the sponsor of any of these movements. I do not think that government, consistently with the First Amendment, can throw its weight behind one school or another. Government should be concerned with antisocial conduct, not with utterances. Thus, if the First Amendment guarantee of freedom of speech and press is to mean anything in this field, it must allow protests even against the moral code that the standard of the day sets for the community. In other words, literature should not be suppressed merely because it offends the moral code of the censor. *** [T]he test that suppresses a cheap tract today can suppress a literary gem tomorrow. All it need do is to incite a lascivious thought or arouse a lustful desire. The list of books that judges or juries can place in that category is endless.

I would give the broad sweep of the First Amendment full support. I have the same confidence in the ability of our people to reject noxious literature as I have in their capacity to sort out the true from the false in theology, economics, politics, or any other field.

Points for Discussion

a. Examples

The Court says that the "portrayal of sex, e.g., in art, literature and scientific works," is not necessarily obscenity. Can you think of specific examples of such portrayals that are not obscene? Are you confident that your peers would share your assessment?

What does count as obscenity? In *Miller v. California*, 413 U.S. 15, 25 (1973), the Court suggested that a state could define obscenity to include "[p]atently offensive representations or descriptions of ultimate sexual acts, normal or perverted, actual or simulated" and "[p]atently offensive representation or descriptions of masturbation, excretory functions, and lewd exhibition of the genitals." How would you decide what is "patently offensive"? Can you think of books that contain descriptions or movies that contain scenes that fall within these tests for obscenity but that nevertheless should be protected as valuable speech under the First Amendment?

b. The Court's Reasoning

Although the Supreme Court had previously suggested in dicta that the Constitution does not protect obscenity, *Roth* was the first case in which the Court actually decided the issue. What reasoning did the Court use to reach its decision? If the Court applied this reasoning in all First Amendment cases, what other types of speech or expression would be beyond the protection of the First Amendment?

c. Excluding Categories of Speech from First Amendment Protection

Doesn't the Court have to "weigh" the value of speech in order to decide that it and other similar speech is not worthy of protection under the First Amendment? Are you confident that the Court can identify categories of speech that are beyond the protection of the First Amendment without, in the process, effectively acting as a censor itself? Note, in this regard, that the statutes at issue in *Roth* and the companion case were quintessentially content-based regulations.

Consider the test that the Court established in *Miller*, which requires the Court to determine "whether the work, taken as a whole, lacks serious literary, artistic, political, or scientific value." How does a court make such an assessment? Would that inquiry be acceptable for other categories of speech?

d. Vagueness and Overbreadth

Even if obscenity is not protected by the First Amendment, didn't the statutes at issue in *Roth* and the companion case suffer from problems of vagueness and overbreadth, which we considered earlier in this Chapter? Can you formulate an argument that the Court should have invalidated the convictions on those grounds? Is the Court's own test for obscenity itself subject to attack on those grounds?

Although Justice Brennan wrote the opinion in *Roth*, he subsequently changed his mind about the viability of the Court's obscenity doctrine because of the Court's inability to formulate a workable standard. Consider the view that he expressed in dissent in *Paris Adult Theatre I v. Slaton*, 413 U.S. 49 (1973), a companion case to *Miller v. California*, 413 U.S. 15, 25 (1973):

> Our experience with the *Roth* approach has certainly taught us that the outright suppression of obscenity cannot be reconciled with the fundamental principles of the First and Fourteenth Amendments. For we have failed to formulate a standard that sharply distinguishes protected from unprotected speech, and out of necessity, we have resorted to [an] approach [that] resolves cases as between the parties, but offers only the most obscure guidance to legislation, adjudication by other courts, and primary conduct. *** It comes as no surprise that judicial attempts to follow our lead conscientiously have often ended in hopeless confusion.
>
> Of course, the vagueness problem would be largely of our own creation if it stemmed primarily from our failure to reach a consensus on any one standard. But after 16 years of experimentation and debate I am reluctantly forced to the conclusion that none of the available formulas, including the one announced today, can reduce the vagueness to a tolerable level while at the same time striking an acceptable balance between the protections of the First and Fourteenth Amendments, on the one hand, and on the other the asserted state interest

in regulating the dissemination of certain sexually oriented materials. Any effort to draw a constitutionally acceptable boundary on state power must resort to such indefinite concepts as "prurient interest," "patent offensiveness," "serious literary value," and the like. The meaning of these concepts necessarily varies with the experience, outlook, and even idiosyncrasies of the person defining them. Although we have assumed that obscenity does exist and that we "know it when (we) see it," *Jacobellis v. Ohio*, 378 U.S., at 197 (Stewart, J., concurring), we are manifestly unable to describe it in advance except by reference to concepts so elusive that they fail to distinguish clearly between protected and unprotected speech.

Is the problem that any test that is clear and workable would also run the risk of permitting the banning of material that is entitled to First Amendment protection under any theory of the Amendment?

New York v. Ferber

458 U.S. 747 (1982)

Justice WHITE delivered the opinion of the Court.

At issue in this case is the constitutionality of a New York criminal statute which prohibits persons from knowingly promoting sexual performances by children under the age of 16 by distributing material which depicts such performances.

This case arose when Paul Ferber, the proprietor of a Manhattan bookstore specializing in sexually oriented products, sold two films to an undercover police officer. The films are devoted almost exclusively to depicting young boys masturbating. Ferber was indicted on two counts of violating § 263.10 and two counts of violating § 263.15, the two New York laws controlling dissemination of child pornography. After a jury trial, Ferber was acquitted of the two counts of promoting an obscene sexual performance, but found guilty of the two counts under § 263.15, which did not require proof that the films were obscene. Ferber's convictions were affirmed without opinion by the Appellate Division of the New York State Supreme Court. The New York Court of Appeals reversed, holding that § 263.15 violated the First Amendment. ***

[This] Court squarely held in *Roth v. United States*, 354 U.S. 476 (1957), that "obscenity is not within the area of constitutionally protected speech or press." The Court recognized that "rejection of obscenity as utterly without redeeming social importance" was implicit in the history of the First Amendment ***. *Roth* was followed by 15 years during which this Court struggled with "the intractable obscenity problem." *Interstate Circuit, Inc. v. Dallas*, 390 U.S. 676, 704 (1968) (opinion of Harlan, J.). Despite considerable vacillation over the proper definition of obscenity, a majority of the Members of the Court remained firm in the position that "the States have a legitimate interest in prohibiting dissemination or exhibition of obscene material when the mode of dissemination carries with it a significant danger of offending the sensibilities of unwilling recipients or of exposure to juveniles." *Miller v. California*, 413 U.S. 15, 18-19 (1973).

Throughout this period, we recognized "the inherent dangers of undertaking to regulate any form of expression." Consequently, our difficulty was not only to assure that statutes designed to regulate obscene materials sufficiently defined what was prohibited, but also to devise substantive limits on what fell within the permissible scope of regulation. In *Miller*, a majority of the Court agreed that a "state offense must also be limited to works which, taken as a whole, appeal to the prurient interest in sex, which portray sexual conduct in a patently offensive way, and which, taken as a whole, do not have serious literary, artistic, political, or scientific value." *Id., at 24*. Over the past decade, we have adhered to the guidelines expressed in *Miller*, which subsequently has been followed in the regulatory schemes of most States.

The *Miller* standard, like its predecessors, was an accommodation between the State's interests in protecting the "sensibilities of unwilling recipients" from exposure to pornographic material and the dangers of censorship inherent in unabashedly content-based laws. Like obscenity statutes, laws directed at the dissemination of child pornography run the risk of suppressing protected expression by allowing the hand of the censor to become unduly heavy. For the following reasons, however, we are persuaded that the States are entitled to greater leeway in the regulation of pornographic depictions of children.

First. It is evident beyond the need for elaboration that a State's interest in "safeguarding the physical and psychological well-being of a minor" is "compelling." *Globe Newspaper Co. v. Superior Court*, 457 U.S. 596, 607 (1982). "A democratic society rests, for its continuance, upon the healthy, well-rounded growth of young people into full maturity as citizens." *Prince v. Massachusetts*, 321 U.S. 158, 168 (1944). Accordingly, we have sustained legislation aimed at protecting the physical and emotional well-being of youth even when the laws have operated in the sensitive area of constitutionally protected rights. In *Prince*, the Court held that a statute prohibiting use of a child to distribute literature on the street was valid notwithstanding the statute's effect on a First Amendment activity. In *Ginsberg v. New York*, 390 U.S. 629 (1968), we sustained a New York law protecting children from exposure to nonobscene literature. Most recently, we held that the Government's interest in the "well-being of its youth" justified special treatment of indecent broadcasting received by adults as well as children. *FCC v. Pacifica Foundation*, 438 U.S. 726 (1978).

The prevention of sexual exploitation and abuse of children constitutes a government objective of surpassing importance. *** Suffice it to say that virtually all of the States and the United States have passed legislation proscribing the production of or otherwise combating "child pornography." The legislative judgment, as well as the judgment found in the relevant literature, is that the use of children as subjects of pornographic materials is harmful to the physiological, emotional, and mental health of the child. That judgment, we think, easily passes muster under the First Amendment.

Second. The distribution of photographs and films depicting sexual activity by juveniles is intrinsically related to the sexual abuse of children in at least two ways. First, the materials produced are a permanent record of the children's participation and the harm to the child is exacerbated by their circulation. Second, the distribution network for child pornography must be closed if the production of material which requires the sexual exploitation of children is to be effectively controlled. Indeed, there is no serious contention that the legislature was unjustified in believing that it is difficult, if not impossible, to halt the exploitation of children by pursuing only those who produce the photographs and movies. While the production of pornographic materials is a low-profile, clandestine industry, the need to market the resulting products requires a visible apparatus of distribution. The most expeditious if not the only practical method of law enforcement may be to dry up the market for this material by imposing severe criminal penalties on persons selling, advertising, or otherwise promoting the product. Thirty-five States and Congress have concluded that restraints on the distribution of pornographic materials are required in order to effectively combat the problem, and there is a body of literature and testimony to support these legislative conclusions.

Respondent does not contend that the State is unjustified in pursuing those who distribute child pornography. Rather, he argues that it is enough for the State to prohibit the distribution of materials that are legally obscene under the *Miller* test. While some States may find that this approach properly accommodates its interests, it does not follow that the First Amendment prohibits a State from going further. The *Miller* standard, like all general definitions of what may be banned as obscene, does not reflect the State's particular and more compelling interest in prosecuting those who promote the sexual exploitation of children. Thus, the question under the *Miller* test of whether a work, taken as a whole, appeals to the prurient interest of the average person bears no connection to the issue of whether a child has been physically or psychologically harmed in the production of the work. Similarly, a sexually explicit depiction need not be "patently offensive" in order to have required the sexual exploitation of a child for its production. In addition, a work which, taken on the whole, contains serious literary, artistic, political, or scientific value may nevertheless embody the hardest core of child pornography. "It is irrelevant to the child [who has been abused] whether or not the material [has] a literary, artistic, political or social value." Memorandum of Assemblyman Lasher in Support of § 263.15. We therefore cannot conclude that the *Miller* standard is a satisfactory solution to the child pornography problem.

Third. The advertising and selling of child pornography provide an economic motive for and are thus an integral part of the production of such materials, an activity illegal throughout the Nation. "It rarely has been suggested that the constitutional freedom for speech and press extends its immunity to speech or writing used as an integral part of conduct in violation of a valid criminal statute." *Giboney v. Empire Storage & Ice Co.*, 336 U.S. 490, 498 (1949). We note that were the statutes outlawing the employment of children in these films and photographs fully effective, and the constitutionality of these laws has not been questioned, the First Amendment implications would be no greater than that presented by laws against distribution: enforceable production laws would leave no child pornography to be marketed.

Fourth. The value of permitting live performances and photographic reproductions of children engaged in lewd sexual conduct is exceedingly modest, if not *de minimis*. We consider it unlikely that visual depictions of children performing sexual acts or lewdly exhibiting their genitals would often constitute an important and necessary part of a literary performance or scientific or educational work. As a state judge in this case observed, if it were necessary for literary or artistic value, a person over the statutory age who perhaps looked younger could be utilized. Simulation outside of the prohibition of the statute could provide another alternative. Nor is there any question here of censoring a particular literary theme or portrayal of sexual activity. The First Amendment interest is limited to that of rendering the portrayal somewhat more "realistic" by utilizing or photographing children.

Fifth. Recognizing and classifying child pornography as a category of material outside the protection of the First Amendment is not incompatible with our earlier decisions. *** "[I]t is the content of [an] utterance that determines whether it is a protected epithet or an unprotected 'fighting comment.' " See *Chaplinsky v. New Hampshire*, 315 U.S. 568 (1942). Leaving aside the special considerations when public officials are the target, *New York Times Co. v. Sullivan*, 376 U.S. 254 (1964), a libelous publication is not protected by the Constitution. *Beauharnais v. Illinois*, 343 U.S. 250 (1952). Thus, it is not rare that a content-based classification of speech has been accepted because it may be appropriately generalized that within the confines of the given classification, the evil to be restricted so overwhelmingly outweighs the expressive interests, if any, at stake, that no process of case-by-case adjudication is required. When a definable class of material, such as that covered by § 263.15, bears so heavily and pervasively on the welfare of children engaged in its production, we think the balance of competing interests is clearly struck and that it is permissible to consider these materials as without the protection of the First Amendment.

> **Make the Connection**
>
> We will consider the "fighting words" doctrine, and the Court's decision in *Chaplinsky*, later in this Chapter. We considered the libel cases earlier in this Chapter.

There are, of course, limits on the category of child pornography which, like obscenity, is unprotected by the First Amendment. As with all legislation in this sensitive area, the conduct to be prohibited must be adequately defined by the applicable state law, as written or authoritatively construed. Here the nature of the harm to be combated requires that the state offense be limited to works that *visually* depict sexual conduct by children below a specified age. The category of "sexual conduct" proscribed must also be suitably limited and described.

The test for child pornography is separate from the obscenity standard enunciated in *Miller*, but may be compared to it for the purpose of clarity. The *Miller* formulation is adjusted in the following respects: A trier of fact need not find that the material appeals to the prurient interest of the average person; it is not required that sexual conduct portrayed be done so in a patently offensive manner; and the material at issue need not be considered as a whole. We note that the distribution of descriptions or other depictions of sexual conduct, not otherwise obscene, which do not involve live performance or photographic or other visual reproduction of live performances, retains First Amendment protection. As with obscenity laws, criminal responsibility may not be imposed without some element of scienter on the part of the defendant.

We hold that § 263.15 sufficiently describes a category of material the production and distribution of which is not entitled to First Amendment protection. It is therefore clear that there is nothing unconstitutionally "underinclusive" about a statute that singles out this category of material for proscription.[18]

Reversed and remanded.

[The separate opinions of four Justices, either concurring or concurring in the judgment, are omitted.]

―――――――――

Points for Discussion

a. Obscenity v. Child Pornography

The opinion makes clear that child pornography and obscenity are two separate categories of speech, though neither is protected by the First Amendment. Was this distinction necessary for deciding the case? Given the facts of the case, could the Court have held that the child pornography at issue was obscene?

b. Defining Child Pornography

What exactly is the Court's definition of child pornography? Would Vladmir Nabokov's famous novel *Lolita*, which is about a man who becomes obsessed with, and has a sexual relationship with, a twelve-year-old girl, count as child pornography, such that a state could ban its sale and possession? Could a state ban Stanley Kubrick's critically acclaimed film adaptation of the novel?

c. Virtual Child Pornography

How would the Court's theory for why child pornography is not protected apply to computer-generated virtual child pornography? In *Ashcroft v. Free Speech Coalition,* 535 U.S. 234, 251 (2002), the Supreme Court held that the First Amendment prohibits the government from banning non-obscene, virtual child pornography. But in *United States v. Williams,* 553 U.S. 285, 300 (2008), the Court held that the government may punish a person for distributing virtual child pornography as though it were real child pornography. What is the distinction between the two cases?

―――――――――

---

[18] *** Today, we hold that child pornography as defined in § 263.15 is unprotected speech subject to content-based regulation. Hence, it cannot be underinclusive or unconstitutional for a State to do precisely that.

4. Symbolic Conduct

The First Amendment explicitly protects only "speech." The Amendment, for example, does not mention marching in a parade, participating in a sit-down strike, burning a flag or other emblem, wearing an arm band as a sign of protest, and other forms of expressive conduct. A question thus arises whether these activities count as "speech." Can the government regulate these communicative activities without violating the First Amendment?

The Supreme Court has concluded that conduct may be "sufficiently imbued with elements of communication to fall within the scope of the First and Fourteenth Amendments." *Spence v. Washington*, 418 U.S. 405, 409 (1974). For example, in *Tinker v. Des Moines Independent Community School Dist.*, 393 U.S. 503 (1969), the Court held that a school regulation prohibiting students from wearing arm bands violated the First Amendment. The school had adopted the regulation only after learning that a group of students had decided to wear the arm bands to protest the Vietnam War. The Court concluded that the school had acted "to punish petitioners for a silent, passive expression of opinion, unaccompanied by any disorder or disturbance on the part of petitioners," and that "undifferentiated fear or apprehension of disturbance is not enough" to justify such a content-based regulation of expressive activity. Accordingly, when the government seeks to regulate "conduct" *because of* the expressive elements of that conduct, the Court applies searching scrutiny.

But we have also already seen important cases in which the Court seemed to conclude that expressive conduct receives less protection than other speech. In *United States v. O'Brien*, 391 U.S. 367 (1968), which we considered earlier in this Chapter, the Court noted that "when 'speech' and 'nonspeech' elements are combined in the same course of conduct, a sufficiently important governmental interest in regulating the nonspeech element can justify incidental limitations on First Amendment freedoms." Under the Court's approach in *O'Brien*, the government may regulate expressive conduct if four conditions are met: (1) the regulation is within the constitutional power of the Government; (2) the regulation furthers an important or substantial governmental interest; (3) the governmental interest is unrelated to the suppression of free expression; and (4) the incidental restriction on alleged First Amendment freedoms is no greater than is essential to the furtherance of that interest. Significantly, the *O'Brien* test is not strict scrutiny; under the test, the government does not need to have a compelling interest to regulate expressive conduct, but instead merely must advance an important or substantial interest.

Does the *O'Brien* test apply to all government attempts to regulate "expressive conduct"? By its own terms, it requires, at a minimum, that the governmental interest in the regulation be "unrelated to the suppression of free expression"—that is, that the regulation not be content based, and thus not be directed at the suppression of the very message expressed by the regulated conduct. As you read the following case, consider (1) whether the government's interest in the challenged regulation makes the case more like *Tinker* or instead more like *O'Brien*, and (2) whether a distinction between "conduct" and "speech" is a useful device in assessing claims under the First Amendment.

———————

Texas v. Johnson

491 U.S. 397 (1989)

Justice BRENNAN delivered the opinion of the Court.

After publicly burning an American flag as a means of political protest, Gregory Lee Johnson was convicted of desecrating a flag in violation of Texas law. This case presents the question whether his conviction is consistent with the First Amendment. We hold that it is not.

While the Republican National Convention was taking place in Dallas in 1984, respondent Johnson participated in a political demonstration dubbed the "Republican War Chest Tour." As explained in literature distributed by the demonstrators and in speeches made by them, the purpose of this event was to protest the policies of the Reagan administration and of certain Dallas-based corporations. The demonstrators marched through the Dallas streets, chanting political slogans and stopping at several corporate locations to stage "die-ins" intended to dramatize the consequences of nuclear war. On several occasions they spray-painted the walls of buildings and overturned potted plants, but Johnson himself took no part in such activities. He did, however, accept an American flag handed to him by a fellow protestor who had taken it from a flagpole outside one of the targeted buildings.

The demonstration ended in front of Dallas City Hall, where Johnson unfurled the American flag, doused it with kerosene, and set it on fire. While the flag burned, the protestors chanted: "America, the red, white, and blue, we spit on you." After the demonstrators dispersed, a witness to the flag burning collected the flag's remains and buried them in his backyard. No one was physically injured or threatened with injury, though several witnesses testified that they had been seriously offended by the flag burning.

Of the approximately 100 demonstrators, Johnson alone was charged with a crime. The only criminal offense with which he was charged was the desecration of a venerated object in violation of Tex. Penal Code Ann. § 42.09(a)(3) (1989).[1] [The Texas Court of Criminal Appeals reversed the conviction on the ground that it violated the First Amendment.]

The First Amendment literally forbids the abridgment only of "speech," but we have long recognized that its protection does not end at the spoken or written word. While we have rejected "the view that an apparently limitless variety of conduct can be labeled 'speech' whenever the person engaging in the conduct intends thereby to express an idea," *United States v. O'Brien,* 391 U.S. 367, 376 (1968), we have acknowledged that conduct may be "sufficiently imbued with elements of communication to fall within the scope of the First and Fourteenth Amendments," *Spence v. Washington,* 418 U.S. 405, 409 (1974).

In deciding whether particular conduct possesses sufficient communicative elements

---

[1] Texas Penal Code Ann. § 42.09 (1989) provides in full: "§ 42.09. Desecration of Venerated Object. (a) A person commits an offense if he intentionally or knowingly desecrates: (1) a public monument; (2) a place of worship or burial; or (3) a state or national flag. (b) For purposes of this section, 'desecrate' means deface, damage, or otherwise physically mistreat in a way that the actor knows will seriously offend one or more persons likely to observe or discover his action. (c) An offense under this section is a Class A misdemeanor."

to bring the First Amendment into play, we have asked whether "[a]n intent to convey a particularized message was present, and [whether] the likelihood was great that the message would be understood by those who viewed it." 418 U.S., at 410-411. Hence, we have recognized the expressive nature of students' wearing of black armbands to protest American military involvement in Vietnam, *Tinker v. Des Moines Independent Community School Dist.,* 393 U.S. 503, 505 (1969); of a sit-in by blacks in a "whites only" area to protest segregation, *Brown v. Louisiana,* 383 U.S. 131, 141-142 (1966); of the wearing of American military uniforms in a dramatic presentation criticizing American involvement in Vietnam, *Schacht v. United States,* 398 U.S. 58 (1970); and of picketing about a wide variety of causes, see, *e.g., Food Employees v. Logan Valley Plaza, Inc.,* 391 U.S. 308, 313-314 (1968).

Especially pertinent to this case are our decisions recognizing the communicative nature of conduct relating to flags. Attaching a peace sign to the flag, *Spence, supra,* at 409-410; refusing to salute the flag, *West Virginia Board of Education v. Barnette,* 319 U.S. 624, 632 (1943); and displaying a red flag, *Stromberg v. California,* 283 U.S. 359, 368-369 (1931), we have held, all may find shelter under the First Amendment. That we have had little difficulty identifying an expressive element in conduct relating to flags should not be surprising. The very purpose of a national flag is to serve as a symbol of our country; it is, one might say, "the one visible manifestation of two hundred years of nationhood." *Smith v. Goguen,* 415 U.S. 566, 603 (1974) (REHNQUIST, J., dissenting). Thus, we have observed:

"[T]he flag salute is a form of utterance. Symbolism is a primitive but effective way of communicating ideas. The use of an emblem or flag to symbolize some system, idea, institution, or personality, is a short cut from mind to mind. Causes and nations, political parties, lodges and ecclesiastical groups seek to knit the loyalty of their followings to a flag or banner, a color or design." *Barnette, supra,* at 632.

[A]lthough we have recognized that where "'speech' and 'nonspeech' elements are combined in the same course of conduct, a sufficiently important governmental interest in regulating the nonspeech element can justify incidental limitations on First Amendment freedoms," *O'Brien, supra,* at 376, we have limited the applicability of *O'Brien's* relatively lenient standard to those cases in which "the governmental interest is unrelated to the suppression of free expression." *Id.* at 377. In stating, moreover, that *O'Brien's* test "in the last analysis is little, if any, different from the standard applied to time, place, or manner restrictions," *Clark v. Community for Creative Non-Violence,* 468 U.S. 288, 298 (1984), we have highlighted the requirement that the governmental interest in question be unconnected to expression in order to come under *O'Brien's* less demanding rule.

Take Note

Beginning here, the Court reviews the interests that Texas claims to have in the enforcement of its law. How does the Court decide whether these interests are sufficient? Does it measure them against the standard from *O'Brien*? If not, what level of scrutiny does it apply?

Texas claims that its interest in preventing breaches of the peace justifies Johnson's conviction for flag desecration. However, no disturbance of the peace actually occurred or threatened to occur because of Johnson's burning of the flag. *** The State's position, therefore, amounts to a claim that an audience that takes serious offense at particular expression is necessarily likely to disturb the peace and that the expression may be prohibited on this basis. Our precedents do not countenance such a presumption. On the contrary, they recognize that a principal "function of free speech under our system of government is to invite dispute. It may indeed best serve its high purpose when it induces a condition of unrest, creates dissatisfaction with conditions as they are, or even stirs people to anger." *Terminiello v. Chicago,* 337 U.S. 1, 4 (1949). ***

Thus, we have not permitted the government to assume that every expression of a provocative idea will incite a riot, but have instead required careful consideration of the actual circumstances surrounding such expression, asking whether the expression "is directed to inciting or producing imminent lawless action and is likely to incite or produce such action." *Brandenburg v. Ohio,* 395 U.S. 444, 447 (1969). To accept Texas' arguments that it need only demonstrate "the potential for a breach of the peace," and that every flag burning necessarily possesses that potential, would be to eviscerate our holding in *Brandenburg.* This we decline to do. *** We thus conclude that the State's interest in maintaining order is not implicated on these facts.

The State also asserts an interest in preserving the flag as a symbol of nationhood and national unity. *** We [are] persuaded that this interest is related to expression in the case of Johnson's burning of the flag. The State, apparently, is concerned that such conduct will lead people to believe either that the flag does not stand for nationhood and national unity, but instead reflects other, less positive concepts, or that the concepts reflected in the flag do not in fact exist, that is, that we do not enjoy unity as a Nation. These concerns blossom only when a person's treatment of the flag communicates some message, and thus are related "to the suppression of free expression" within the meaning of *O'Brien.* We are thus outside of *O'Brien's* test altogether.

It remains to consider whether the State's interest in preserving the flag as a symbol of nationhood and national unity justifies Johnson's conviction. *** Johnson was prosecuted because he knew that his politically charged expression would cause "serious offense." If he had burned the flag as a means of disposing of it because it was dirty or torn, he would not have been convicted of flag desecration under this Texas law: federal law designates burning as the preferred means of disposing of a flag "when it is in such condition that it is no longer a fitting emblem for display," 36 U.S.C. § 176(k), and Texas has no quarrel with this means of disposal. The Texas law is thus not aimed at protecting the physical integrity of the flag in all circumstances, but is designed instead to protect it only against impairments that would cause serious offense to others.

Whether Johnson's treatment of the flag violated Texas law thus depended on the likely communicative impact of his expressive conduct. *** Johnson's political expression [thus] was restricted because of the content of the message he conveyed. We must therefore subject the State's asserted interest in preserving the special symbolic character of the flag to "the most exacting scrutiny." *Boos v. Barry,* 485 U.S. 312, 321 (1988).

Texas argues that its interest in preserving the flag as a symbol of nationhood and national unity survives this close analysis. Quoting extensively from the writings of this Court chronicling the flag's historic and symbolic role in our society, the State emphasizes the "special place" reserved for the flag in our Nation. The State's argument is not that it has an interest simply in maintaining the flag as a symbol of *something,* no matter what it symbolizes; indeed, if that were the State's position, it would be difficult to see how that interest is endangered by highly symbolic conduct such as Johnson's. Rather, the State's claim is that it has an interest in preserving the flag as a symbol of *nationhood* and *national unity,* a symbol with a determinate range of meanings. According to Texas, if one physically treats the flag in a way that would tend to cast doubt on either the idea that nationhood and national unity are the flag's referents or that national unity actually exists, the message conveyed thereby is a harmful one and therefore may be prohibited.

If there is a bedrock principle underlying the First Amendment, it is that the government may not prohibit the expression of an idea simply because society finds the idea itself offensive or disagreeable. *** We have not recognized an exception to this principle even where our flag has been involved. In *Street v. New York,* 394 U.S. 576 (1969), we held that a State may not criminally punish a person for uttering words critical of the flag. Rejecting the argument that the conviction could be sustained on the ground that Street had "failed to show the respect for our national symbol which may properly be demanded of every citizen," we concluded that "the constitutionally guaranteed 'freedom to be intellectually ... diverse or even contrary,' and the 'right to differ as to things that touch the heart of the existing order,' encompass the freedom to express publicly one's opinions about our flag, including those opinions which are defiant or contemptuous." *Id., at 593,* quoting *Barnette,* 319 U.S., at 642. Nor may the government, we have held, compel conduct that would evince respect for the flag. "To sustain the compulsory flag salute we are required to say that a Bill of Rights which guards the individual's right to speak his own mind, left it open to public authorities to compel him to utter what is not in his mind." *Id., at 634.*

There is, moreover, no indication—either in the text of the Constitution or in our cases interpreting it—that a separate juridical category exists for the American flag alone. Indeed, we would not be surprised to learn that the persons who framed our Constitution and wrote the Amendment that we now construe were not known for their reverence for the Union Jack. The First Amendment does not guarantee that other concepts virtually sacred to our Nation as a whole—such as the principle that discrimination on the basis of race is odious and destructive—will go unquestioned in the marketplace of ideas. See *Brandenburg v. Ohio,* 395 U.S. 444 (1969). We decline, therefore, to create for the flag an exception to the joust of principles protected by the First Amendment.

It is not the State's ends, but its means, to which we object. It cannot be gainsaid that there is a special place reserved for the flag in this Nation, and thus we do not doubt that the government has a legitimate interest in making efforts to "preserv[e] the national flag as an unalloyed symbol of our country." *Spence,* 418 U.S., at 412. We reject the suggestion, urged at oral argument by counsel for Johnson, that the government lacks "any state interest whatsoever" in regulating the manner in which the flag may be displayed. Congress has, for example, enacted precatory regulations describing the proper treatment of the flag, see 36 U.S.C. §§ 173-177, and we cast no doubt on the legitimacy of its interest in making such recommendations. To say that the government has an interest in encouraging proper treatment of the flag, however, is not to say that it may criminally punish a person for burning a flag as a means of political protest. "National unity as an end which officials may foster by persuasion and example is not in question. The problem is whether under our Constitution compulsion as here employed is a permissible means for its achievement." _Barnette, 319 U.S., at 640_. *Affirmed*.

Justice KENNEDY, concurring.

I write not to qualify the words Justice BRENNAN chooses so well, for he says with power all that is necessary to explain our ruling. I join his opinion without reservation, but with a keen sense that this case, like others before us from time to time, exacts its personal toll.

The hard fact is that sometimes we must make decisions we do not like. We make them because they are right, right in the sense that the law and the Constitution, as we see them, compel the result. And so great is our commitment to the process that, except in the rare case, we do not pause to express distaste for the result, perhaps for fear of undermining a valued principle that dictates the decision. This is one of those rare cases.

Our colleagues in dissent advance powerful arguments why respondent may be convicted for his expression, reminding us that among those who will be dismayed by our holding will be some who have had the singular honor of carrying the flag in battle. And I agree that the flag holds a lonely place of honor in an age when absolutes are distrusted and simple truths are burdened by unneeded apologetics.

With all respect to those views, I do not believe the Constitution gives us the right to rule as the dissenting Members of the Court urge, however painful this judgment is to announce. Though symbols often are what we ourselves make of them, the flag is constant in expressing beliefs Americans share, beliefs in law and peace and that freedom which sustains the human spirit. The case here today forces recognition of the costs to which those beliefs commit us. It is poignant but fundamental that the flag protects those who hold it in contempt.

For all the record shows, this respondent was not a philosopher and perhaps did not even possess the ability to comprehend how repellent his statements must be to the Republic itself. But whether or not he could appreciate the enormity of the offense he gave, the fact remains that his acts were speech, in both the technical and the fundamental meaning of the Constitution. So I agree with the Court that he must go free.

Chief Justice REHNQUIST, with whom Justice WHITE and Justice O'CONNOR join, dissenting.

In holding this Texas statute unconstitutional, the Court ignores Justice Holmes' familiar aphorism that "a page of history is worth a volume of logic." *New York Trust Co. v. Eisner,* 256 U.S. 345, 349 (1921). For more than 200 years, the American flag has occupied a unique position as the symbol of our Nation, a uniqueness that justifies a governmental prohibition against flag burning in the way respondent Johnson did here.

The flag symbolizes the Nation in peace as well as in war. It signifies our national presence on battleships, airplanes, military installations, and public buildings from the United States Capitol to the thousands of county courthouses and city halls throughout the country. Two flags are prominently placed in our courtroom. Countless flags are placed by the graves of loved ones each year on what was first called Decoration Day, and is now called Memorial Day. The flag is traditionally placed on the casket of deceased members of the Armed Forces, and it is later given to the deceased's family. 10 U.S.C. §§ 1481, 1482. Congress has provided that the flag be flown at half-staff upon the death of the President, Vice President, and other government officials "as a mark of respect to their memory." 36 U.S.C. § 175(m).

The American flag, then, throughout more than 200 years of our history, has come to be the visible symbol embodying our Nation. It does not represent the views of any particular political party, and it does not represent any particular political philosophy. The flag is not simply another "idea" or "point of view" competing for recognition in the marketplace of ideas. Millions and millions of Americans regard it with an almost mystical reverence regardless of what sort of social, political, or philosophical beliefs they may have. I cannot agree that the First Amendment invalidates the Act of Congress, and the laws of 48 of the 50 States, which make criminal the public burning of the flag.

In *Chaplinsky v. New Hampshire*, 315 U.S. 568 (1942), a unanimous Court said:

"Allowing the broadest scope to the language and purpose of the Fourteenth Amendment, it is well understood that the right of free speech is not absolute at all times and under all circumstances. There are certain well-defined and narrowly limited classes of speech, the prevention and punishment of which have never been thought to raise any Constitutional problem. These include the lewd and obscene, the profane, the libelous, and the insulting or 'fighting' words— those which by their very utterance inflict injury or tend to incite an immediate breach of the peace. It has been well observed that such utterances are no essential part of any exposition of ideas, and are of such slight social value as a step to truth that any benefit that may be derived from them is clearly outweighed by the social interest in order and morality." *Id.*, at 571-572.

Here it may equally well be said that the public burning of the American flag by Johnson was no essential part of any exposition of ideas, and at the same time it had a tendency to incite a breach of the peace. Johnson was free to make any verbal denunciation of the flag that he wished; indeed, he was free to burn the flag in private. He could publicly burn other symbols of the Government or effigies of political leaders. He did lead a march through the streets of Dallas, and conducted a rally in front of the Dallas City Hall. He engaged in a "die-in" to protest nuclear weapons. He shouted out various slogans during the march ***. For none of these acts was he arrested or prosecuted; it was only when he proceeded to burn publicly an American flag stolen from its rightful owner that he violated the Texas statute.

Johnson's public burning of the flag *** obviously did convey [his] bitter dislike of his country. But his act *** conveyed nothing that could not have been conveyed and was not conveyed just as forcefully in a dozen different ways. As with "fighting words," so with flag burning, for purposes of the First Amendment: It is "no essential part of any exposition of ideas, and [is] of such slight social value as a step to truth that any benefit that may be derived from [it] is clearly outweighed" by the public interest in avoiding a probable breach of the peace.

The Court decides that the American flag is just another symbol, about which not only must opinions pro and con be tolerated, but for which the most minimal public respect may not be enjoined. The government may conscript men into the Armed Forces where they must fight and perhaps die for the flag, but the government may not prohibit the public burning of the banner under which they fight. I would uphold the Texas statute as applied in this case.

Justice STEVENS, dissenting.

The value of the flag as a symbol cannot be measured. Even so, I have no doubt that the interest in preserving that value for the future is both significant and legitimate. Conceivably that value will be enhanced by the Court's conclusion that our national commitment to free expression is so strong that even the United States as ultimate guarantor of that freedom is without power to prohibit the desecration of its unique symbol. But I am unpersuaded. The creation of a federal right to post bulletin boards and graffiti on the Washington Monument might enlarge the market for free expression, but at a cost I would not pay. Similarly, in my considered judgment, sanctioning the public desecration of the flag will tarnish its value—both for those who cherish the ideas for which it waves and for those who desire to don the robes of martyrdom by burning it. That tarnish is not justified by the trivial burden on free expression occasioned by requiring that an available, alternative mode of expression—including uttering words critical of the flag, see *Street v. New York*, 394 U.S. 576 (1969)—be employed.

Respondent was prosecuted because of the method he chose to express his dissatisfaction with those policies. Had he chosen to spray-paint *** his message of dissatisfaction on the facade of the Lincoln Memorial, there would be no question about the power of the Government to prohibit his means of expression. The prohibition would be supported by the legitimate interest in preserving the quality of an important national asset. Though the asset at stake in this case is intangible, given its unique value, the same interest supports a prohibition on the desecration of the American flag.

Points for Discussion

a. Comparison to *O'Brien*

How does this case differ from *United States v. O'Brien*? Note that both involved "symbolic conduct" that led to criminal punishment. Why did the Court permit O'Brien's conviction for his conduct but prohibit the state from punishing Johnson?

b. Reasoning by Analogy

Justice Stevens suggested in his dissent that the statute under which Johnson was convicted was no different from a statute prohibiting a person from spray-painting a message on the Lincoln Memorial. Is there a difference between convicting a person under an anti-graffiti ordinance for spray-painting a message critical of the government on the side of a government building, on the one hand, and convicting Johnson under Texas's flag desecration law, on the other?

In answering this question, consider whether it would have violated the Texas statute if Johnson had been camping in the wilderness, became lost, and burned a flag—the only cloth he had other than his clothes—in order to stay warm. If such an act would not have run afoul of the Texas statute, what does it say about whether the statute was directed at a particular message? Is the same true of an ordinance prohibiting all graffiti on public buildings?

c. Carving Out a Category for Flag Desecration

In his dissent, Chief Justice Rehnquist acknowledged that there is an expressive element to flag burning of the sort at issue in *Johnson*, but he urged the Court to treat it as a category of expression that, like obscenity, is outside the scope of First Amendment protection. Do you agree that the Court should exclude this form of symbolic conduct—or any other forms of symbolic conduct—from the protection of the First Amendment? What considerations are relevant in deciding whether to create such a category of expression? Are you satisfied that any such considerations argue here for exclusion?

d. Response by Congress

Congress responded to *Texas v. Johnson* by passing the Flag Protection Act of 1989. This federal act prohibited knowingly mutilating, defacing, defiling, burning, or trampling on a flag, without regard to whether the conduct might offend someone else. How is that different from the Texas law? Is the difference enough to make the federal law constitutional? The Court concluded that it was not. *See United States v. Eichman*, 496 U.S. 310 (1990). Can you make an argument that the Act should have survived scrutiny under the principles announced in *Johnson*?

Since the Court's decision in *Eichman*, Congress has on several occasions considered a proposed constitutional amendment that provides: "The Congress shall have power to prohibit the physical desecration of the flag of the United States." Although the House of Representatives has passed the Amendment by the requisite super-majority vote several times, the Senate has not, although it fell only one vote short one of the times that it considered it. Do you think that it would be a good idea to amend the Constitution to prohibit this form of conduct?

5. Provocative Speech

Can the government prohibit a person from saying something, not because the government specifically disapproves of the speech, but instead because the words might offend others and possibly lead to violence or other disruption? The answer is not so clear. We have already seen—in *Texas v. Johnson*, the flag desecration case—how the First Amendment imposes limits on the government's ability to criminalize expressive conduct solely because it might tend to offend others. How far do those limits extend? Can the government act when the offense is likely to be so great that it might provoke a violent response?

In this section, we consider several categories of offensive and provocative speech. We consider speech that is likely to provoke the listener to respond with violence against the speaker, otherwise known as "fighting words"; profanity; hate speech; and threats. As you read the materials that follow, consider whether these are separate categories that ought to be treated by their own distinctive rules, or instead whether there are broader themes that justify uniform treatment.

In the following case, the Supreme Court held that the First Amendment does not protect "insulting or 'fighting' words—those which by their very utterance inflict injury or tend to incite an immediate breach of the peace." Although the Court has never overruled the case, in no subsequent case has the Supreme Court upheld a government restriction on fighting words. As you read the case, consider whether it remains viable today, and whether, in light of the Court's decision in *Brandenburg*, it adds anything to the doctrine.

Chaplinsky v. State of New Hampshire

315 U.S. 568 (1942)

Mr. Justice MURPHY delivered the opinion of the Court.

Appellant, a member of the sect known as Jehovah's Witnesses, was convicted in the municipal court of Rochester, New Hampshire, for violation of Chapter 378, Section 2, of the Public Laws of New Hampshire: "No person shall address any offensive, derisive or annoying word to any other person who is lawfully in any street or other public place, nor call him by any offensive or derisive name, nor make any noise or exclamation in his presence and hearing with intent to deride, offend or annoy him, or to prevent him from pursuing his lawful business or occupation."

The complaint charged that appellant "with force and arms, in a certain public place in said city of Rochester, to wit, on the public sidewalk on the easterly side of Wakefield Street, near unto the entrance of the City Hall, did unlawfully repeat, the words following, addressed to the complainant, that is to say, 'You are a God damned racketeer' and 'a damned Fascist and the whole government of Rochester are Fascists or agents of Fascists' the same being offensive, derisive and annoying words and names."

There is no substantial dispute over the facts. Chaplinsky was distributing the literature of his sect on the streets of Rochester on a busy Saturday afternoon. Members of the local citizenry complained to the City Marshal, Bowering, that Chaplinsky was denouncing all religion as a "racket." Bowering told them that Chaplinsky was lawfully engaged, and then warned Chaplinsky that the crowd was getting restless. Some time later a disturbance occurred and the traffic officer on duty at the busy intersection started with Chaplinsky for the police station, but did not inform him that he was under arrest or that he was going to be arrested. On the way they encountered Marshal Bowering who had been advised that a riot was under way and was therefore hurrying to the scene. Bowering repeated his earlier warning to Chaplinsky who then addressed to Bowering the words set forth in the complaint.

Chaplinsky's version of the affair was slightly different. He testified that when he met Bowering, he asked him to arrest the ones responsible for the disturbance. In reply Bowering cursed him and told him to come along. Appellant admitted that he said the words charged in the complaint with the exception of the name of the Deity.

Allowing the broadest scope to the language and purpose of the Fourteenth Amendment, it is well understood that the right of free speech is not absolute at all times and under all circumstances. There are certain well-defined and narrowly limited classes of speech, the prevention and punishment of which has never been thought to raise any Constitutional problem. These include the lewd and obscene, the profane, the libelous, and the insulting or "fighting" words—those which by their very utterance inflict injury or tend to incite an immediate breach of the peace. It has been well observed that such utterances are no essential part of any exposition of ideas, and are of such slight social value as a step to truth that any benefit that may be derived from them is clearly outweighed by the social interest in order and morality. "Resort to epithets or personal abuse is not in any proper sense communication of information or opinion safeguarded by the Constitution, and its punishment as a criminal act would raise no question under that instrument." *Cantwell v. Connecticut*, 310 U.S. 296, 309, 310 (1940).

The state statute here challenged comes to us authoritatively construed by the highest court of New Hampshire. *** On the authority of its earlier decisions, the state court declared that the statute's purpose was to preserve the public peace, no words being "forbidden except such as have a direct tendency to cause acts of violence by the person to whom, individually, the remark is addressed." It was further said: "The word 'offensive' is not to be defined in terms of what a particular addressee thinks. *** The test is what men of common intelligence would understand would be words likely to cause an average addressee to fight. *** The English language has a number of words and expressions which by general consent are 'fighting words' when said without a disarming smile. *** Such words, as ordinary men know, are likely to cause a fight. ***"

We are unable to say that the limited scope of the statute as thus construed contravenes the constitutional right of free expression. It is a statute narrowly drawn and limited to define and punish specific conduct lying within the domain of state power, the use in a public place of words likely to cause a breach of the peace. This conclusion necessarily disposes of appellant's contention that the statute is so vague and indefinite as to render a conviction thereunder a violation of due process. A statute punishing verbal acts, carefully drawn so as not unduly to impair liberty of expression, is not too vague for a criminal law.

Nor can we say that the application of the statute to the facts disclosed by the record substantially or unreasonably impinges upon the privilege of free speech. Argument is unnecessary to demonstrate that the appellations "damn racketeer" and "damn Fascist" are epithets likely to provoke the average person to retaliation, and thereby cause a breach of the peace. Affirmed.

Points for Discussion

a. Understanding the Decision

The Court gives several distinct reasons for concluding that fighting words lack First Amendment protection. Can you identify them? Is the Court's reasoning consistent with other cases that we have seen? Note that the Court cited *Chaplinsky* in *Roth v. United States*, which concluded that obscenity is not protected by the First Amendment, and Chief Justice Rehnquist cited it in his dissent in *Texas v. Johnson*, the flag-burning case.

b. Alternative Rationale

Could the Supreme Court have reached the same conclusion by a different method of reasoning? For example, could the Court have said that Chaplinsky's words were protected by the First Amendment, but that New Hampshire could impose reasonable restrictions on the time, place, and manner in which Chaplinsky uttered them? Consider the following suggestion by Judge Richard Posner: "[W]hile the First Amendment surely prevents the government from interfering with the dissemination of offensive ideas, it is less clear why it should be thought to privilege their dissemination by means that show an intent not to persuade, but instead to incite a violent reaction either from ordinarily peaceable people or from extremists at the other end of the political spectrum ***." *Church of American Knights of Ku Klux Klan v. City of Gary, Indiana*, 334 F.3d 676, 684 (7th Cir. 2003). Do you agree that the New Hampshire statute would survive scrutiny as a reasonable time, place, and manner restriction? Was it content neutral?

Regardless of the Court's reasoning in 1942, is the "fighting words" exception really just a specific application today of the *Brandenburg* doctrine about incitement? In the Court's view, aren't fighting words just an invitation to engage in assault and battery?

c. Fighting Words

Putting aside the problems of vagueness, which the Court in *Chaplinsky* rejected, do you agree that there are words or epithets that are "likely to provoke the average person to retaliation"? To *physical* retaliation? Under the Court's view of the First Amendment, is it not just sticks and stones that lead to broken bones, but also words?

The Court did not purport in *Chaplinsky* to define what counts as fighting words, other than to conclude that calling someone a "damn racketeer" and "damn Fascist" apparently counts. The case that followed concerned more colorful language. Even if profanity is not alone always enough to amount to fighting words, should profanity simply be considered another category outside of the protection of the First Amendment?

————————

Cohen v. California

403 U.S. 15 (1971)

Mr. Justice HARLAN delivered the opinion of the Court.

This case may seem at first blush too inconsequential to find its way into our books, but the issue it presents is of no small constitutional significance. Appellant Paul Robert Cohen was convicted in the Los Angeles Municipal Court of violating that part of California Penal Code § 415 which prohibits "maliciously and willfully disturb[ing] the peace or quiet of any neighborhood or person [by] offensive conduct ***." He was given 30 days' imprisonment. The facts upon which his conviction rests are detailed in the opinion of the Court of Appeal of California, Second Appellate District, as follows:

> On April 26, 1968, the defendant was observed in the Los Angeles County Courthouse in the corridor outside of division 20 of the municipal court wearing a jacket bearing the words "Fuck the Draft" which were plainly visible. There were women and children present in the corridor. The defendant was arrested. The defendant testified that he wore the jacket knowing that the words were on the jacket as a means of informing the public of the depth of his feelings against the Vietnam War and the draft.

> The defendant did not engage in, nor threaten to engage in, nor did anyone as the result of his conduct in fact commit or threaten to commit any act of violence. The defendant did not make any loud or unusual noise, nor was there any evidence that he uttered any sound prior to his arrest.

The conviction quite clearly rests upon the asserted offensiveness of the words Cohen used to convey his message to the public. The only "conduct" which the State sought to punish is the fact of communication. Thus, we deal here with a conviction resting solely upon "speech," not upon any separately identifiable conduct which allegedly was intended by Cohen to be perceived by others as expressive of particular views but which, on its face, does not necessarily convey any message and hence arguably could be regulated without effectively repressing Cohen's ability to express himself. *Cf. United States v. O'Brien*, 391 U.S. 367 (1968). Further, the State certainly lacks power to punish Cohen for the underlying content of the message the inscription conveyed. At least so long as there is no showing of an intent to incite disobedience to or disruption of the draft, Cohen could not, consistently with the First and Fourteenth Amendments, be punished for asserting the evident position on the inutility or immorality of the draft his jacket reflected.

Appellant's conviction, then, rests squarely upon his exercise of the "freedom of speech" protected from arbitrary governmental interference by the Constitution and can be justified, if at all, only as a valid regulation of the manner in which he exercised that freedom, not as a permissible prohibition on the substantive message it conveys. ***

This Court has *** held that the States are free to ban the simple use, without a demonstration of additional justifying circumstances, of so-called "fighting words," those personally abusive epithets which, when addressed to the ordinary citizen, are, as a matter of common knowledge, inherently likely to provoke violent reaction. *Chaplinsky v. New Hampshire,* 315 U.S. 568 (1942). While the four-letter word displayed by Cohen in relation to the draft is not uncommonly employed in a personally provocative fashion, in this instance it was clearly not "directed to the person of the hearer." *Cantwell v. Connecticut,* 310 U.S. 296, 309 (1940). No individual actually or likely to be present could reasonably have regarded the words on appellant's jacket as a direct personal insult. Nor do we have here an instance of the exercise of the State's police power to prevent a speaker from intentionally provoking a given group to hostile reaction. There is, as noted above, no showing that anyone who saw Cohen was in fact violently aroused or that appellant intended such a result.

Finally, in arguments before this Court much has been made of the claim that Cohen's distasteful mode of expression was thrust upon unwilling or unsuspecting viewers, and that the State might therefore legitimately act as it did in order to protect the sensitive from otherwise unavoidable exposure to appellant's crude form of protest. Of course, the mere presumed presence of unwitting listeners or viewers does not serve automatically to justify curtailing all speech capable of giving offense. While this Court has recognized that government may properly act in many situations to prohibit intrusion into the privacy of the home of unwelcome views and ideas which cannot be totally banned from the public dialogue, e.g., *Rowan v. United States Post Office Dept.,* 397 U.S. 728 (1970), we have at the same time consistently stressed that "we are often 'captives' outside the sanctuary of the home and subject to objectionable speech." *Id.* at 738. The ability of government, consonant with the Constitution, to shut off discourse solely to protect others from hearing it is, in other words, dependent upon a showing that substantial privacy interests are being invaded in an essentially intolerable manner. Any broader view of this authority would effectively empower a majority to silence dissidents simply as a matter of personal predilections.

In this regard, persons confronted with Cohen's jacket were in a quite different posture than, say, those subjected to the raucous emissions of sound trucks blaring outside their residences. Those in the Los Angeles courthouse could effectively avoid further bombardment of their sensibilities simply by averting their eyes. ***

Against this background, the issue flushed by this case stands out in bold relief. It is whether California can excise, as "offensive conduct," one particular scurrilous epithet from the public discourse, either upon the theory of the court below that its use is inherently likely to cause violent reaction or upon a more general assertion that the States, acting as guardians of public morality, may properly remove this offensive word from the public vocabulary.

We have been shown no evidence that substantial numbers of citizens are standing ready to strike out physically at whoever may assault their sensibilities with execrations like that uttered by Cohen. There may be some persons about with such lawless and violent proclivities, but that is an insufficient base upon which to erect, consistently with constitutional values, a governmental power to force persons who wish to ventilate their dissident views into avoiding particular forms of expression. The argument amounts to little more than the self-defeating proposition that to avoid physical censorship of one who has not sought to provoke such a response by a hypothetical coterie of the violent and lawless, the States may more appropriately effectuate that censorship themselves.

Admittedly, it is not so obvious that the First and Fourteenth Amendments must be taken to disable the States from punishing public utterance of this unseemly expletive in order to maintain what they regard as a suitable level of discourse within the body politic. We think, however, that examination and reflection will reveal the shortcomings of a contrary viewpoint. *** The constitutional right of free expression is powerful medicine in a society as diverse and populous as ours. It is designed and intended to remove governmental restraints from the arena of public discussion, putting the decision as to what views shall be voiced largely into the hands of each of us, in the hope that use of such freedom will ultimately produce a more capable citizenry and more perfect polity and in the belief that no other approach would comport with the premise of individual dignity and choice upon which our political system rests. See *Whitney v. California*, 274 U.S. 357, 375-377 (1927) (Brandeis, J., concurring).

To many, the immediate consequence of this freedom may often appear to be only verbal tumult, discord, and even offensive utterance. These are, however, within established limits, in truth necessary side effects of the broader enduring values which the process of open debate permits us to achieve. That the air may at times seem filled with verbal cacophony is, in this sense not a sign of weakness but of strength. We cannot lose sight of the fact that, in what otherwise might seem a trifling and annoying instance of individual distasteful abuse of a privilege, these fundamental societal values are truly implicated.

Against this perception of the constitutional policies involved, we discern certain more particularized considerations that peculiarly call for reversal of this conviction. First, the principle contended for by the State seems inherently boundless. How is one to distinguish this from any other offensive word? Surely the State has no right to cleanse public debate to the point where it is grammatically palatable to the most squeamish among us. Yet no readily ascertainable general principle exists for stopping short of that result were we to affirm the judgment below. For, while the particular four-letter word being litigated here is perhaps more distasteful than most others of its genre, it is nevertheless often true that one man's vulgarity is another's lyric. Indeed, we think it is largely because governmental officials cannot make principled distinctions in this area that the Constitution leaves matters of taste and style so largely to the individual.

Additionally, we cannot overlook the fact, because it is well illustrated by the episode involved here, that much linguistic expression serves a dual communicative function: it conveys not only ideas capable of relatively precise, detached explication, but otherwise inexpressible emotions as well. In fact, words are often chosen as much for their emotive as their cognitive force. We cannot sanction the view that the Constitution, while solicitous of the cognitive content of individual speech has little or no regard for that emotive function which practically speaking, may often be the more important element of the overall message sought to be communicated.

Finally, and in the same vein, we cannot indulge the facile assumption that one can forbid particular words without also running a substantial risk of suppressing ideas in the process. Indeed, governments might soon seize upon the censorship of particular words as a convenient guise for banning the expression of unpopular views.

It is, in sum, our judgment that, absent a more particularized and compelling reason for its actions, the State may not, consistently with the First and Fourteenth Amendments, make the simple public display here involved of this single four-letter expletive a criminal offense. Because that is the only arguably sustainable rationale for the conviction here at issue, the judgment below must be reversed.

Mr. Justice BLACKMUN, with whom THE CHIEF JUSTICE and Mr. Justice BLACK join.

Cohen's absurd and immature antic, in my view, was mainly conduct and little speech. *** Further, the case appears to me to be well within the sphere of *Chaplinsky v. New Hampshire*, 315 U.S. 568 (1942), where Mr. Justice Murphy, a known champion of First Amendment freedoms, wrote for a unanimous bench. As a consequence, this Court's agonizing over First Amendment values seem misplaced and unnecessary.

———————————————

Points for Discussion

a. The Value of Words

The Court in *Cohen* gave several reasons why the state could not punish the defendant for the words on his jacket. Can you articulate those reasons? Under the Court's reasoning, are there *any* words that are so offensive or likely to cause the listener to fight that the state can ban their use? If so, what are they? How can the court identify which words are proscribable and which are not?

b. Comparing *Cohen* and *Chaplinsky*

In the Court's view, *Cohen*, unlike *Chaplinksy*, did not involve "words likely to cause an average addressee to fight." But *Chaplinsky* also gave other rationales for banning fighting words, namely that they formed "no essential part of any exposition of ideas" and that "by their very utterance [they] inflict injury." Was the same true for the words on Cohen's jacket? If not, is it because the words at issue in *Cohen* were different in kind, or instead because the Court in *Chaplinsky* under-valued the importance of the words at issue there?

———————————————

Hypothetical

Pursuant to a federal statute prohibiting "obscene, indecent, or profane" language on the airwaves, the Federal Communications Commission adopted a policy to impose penalties for "fleeting expletives"—that is, the occasional utterance of expletives during a live broadcast. A television network ordered to pay a substantial fine under the policy challenged the order as violating the First Amendment. How should the Court rule? (We will consider special rules that apply to television broadcasters in Chapter 15, when we take up the freedom of the press.)

———————

Can the government ban "hate speech"—that is, speech that communicates hatred on the basis of race or some other status-based criterion—that is likely to cause the listener to fight? The Court took up that question in the case that follows.

———————

R.A.V. v. City of St. Paul, Minn.

505 U.S. 377 (1992)

Justice SCALIA delivered the opinion of the Court.

In the predawn hours of June 21, 1990, petitioner and several other teenagers allegedly assembled a crudely made cross by taping together broken chair legs. They then allegedly burned the cross inside the fenced yard of a black family that lived across the street from the house where petitioner was staying. Although this conduct could have been punished under any of a number of laws, one of the two provisions under which respondent city of St. Paul chose to charge petitioner (then a juvenile) was the St. Paul Bias-Motivated Crime Ordinance, which provides:

> Whoever places on public or private property a symbol, object, appellation, characterization or graffiti, including, but not limited to, a burning cross or Nazi swastika, which one knows or has reasonable grounds to know arouses anger, alarm or resentment in others on the basis of race, color, creed, religion or gender commits disorderly conduct and shall be guilty of a misdemeanor.

Petitioner moved to dismiss this count on the ground that the St. Paul ordinance was substantially overbroad and impermissibly content based and therefore facially invalid under the First Amendment. ***

In construing the St. Paul ordinance, we are bound by the construction given to it by the Minnesota court. Accordingly, we accept the Minnesota Supreme Court's authoritative statement that the ordinance reaches only those expressions that constitute "fighting words" within the meaning of *Chaplinsky v. New Hampshire,* 315 U.S. 568, 572 (1942). Petitioner and his *amici* urge us to modify the scope of the *Chaplinsky* formulation, thereby invalidating the ordinance as "substantially overbroad," *Broadrick v. Oklahoma,* 413 U.S. 601, 610 (1973). We find it unnecessary to consider this issue. Assuming, *arguendo,* that all of the expression reached by the ordinance is proscribable under the "fighting words" doctrine, we nonetheless conclude that the ordinance is facially unconstitutional in that it prohibits otherwise permitted speech solely on the basis of the subjects the speech addresses.

The First Amendment generally prevents government from proscribing speech, see, *e.g., Cantwell v. Connecticut,* 310 U.S. 296, 309-311 (1940), or even expressive conduct, see, *e.g., Texas v. Johnson,* 491 U.S. 397, 406 (1989), because of disapproval of the ideas expressed. Content-based regulations are presumptively invalid. *Simon & Schuster, Inc. v. Members of N.Y. State Crime Victims Bd.,* 502 U.S. 105, 115 (1991). From 1791 to the present, however, our society, like other free but civilized societies, has permitted restrictions upon the content of speech in a few limited areas, which are "of such slight social value as a step to truth that any benefit that may be derived from them is clearly outweighed by the social interest in order and morality." <u>*Chaplinsky,* 315 U.S., at 572</u>. We have recognized that "the freedom of speech" referred to by the First Amendment does not include a freedom to disregard these traditional limitations. See, *e.g., Roth v. United States,* 354 U.S. 476 (1957) (obscenity); *Beauharnais v. Illinois,* 343 U.S. 250 (1952) (defamation); <u>*Chaplinsky v. New Hampshire, supra*</u> ("'fighting' words"). Our decisions since the 1960s have narrowed the scope of the traditional categorical exceptions for defamation, but a limited categorical approach has remained an important part of our First Amendment jurisprudence.

We have sometimes said that these categories of expression are "not within the area of constitutionally protected speech," *Roth v. United States,* 354 U.S. 476, 483 (1957), or that the "protection of the First Amendment does not extend" to them, *Bose Corp. v. Consumers Union of United States, Inc.,* 466 U.S. 485, 504 (1984). Such statements must be taken in context, however ***. What they mean is that these areas of speech can, consistently with the First Amendment, be regulated *because of their constitutionally proscribable content* (obscenity, defamation, etc.)—not that they are categories of speech entirely invisible to the Constitution, so that they may be made the vehicles for content discrimination unrelated to their distinctively proscribable content. Thus, the government may proscribe libel; but it may not make the further content discrimination of proscribing *only* libel critical of the government.

Our cases surely do not establish the proposition that the First Amendment imposes no obstacle whatsoever to regulation of particular instances of such proscribable expression, so that the government "may regulate [them] freely." That would mean that a city council could enact an ordinance prohibiting only those legally obscene works that contain criticism of the city government or, indeed, that do not include endorsement of the city government. Such a simplistic, all-or-nothing-at-all approach to First Amendment protection is at odds with common sense and with our jurisprudence as well. It is not true that "fighting words" have at most a "*de minimis*" expressive content, or that their content is in *all respects* "worthless and undeserving of constitutional protection"; sometimes they are quite expressive indeed. We have not said that they constitute "*no* part of the expression of ideas," but only that they constitute "no *essential* part of any exposition of ideas." Chaplinsky, 315 U.S., at 572 (emphasis added).

The proposition that a particular instance of speech can be proscribable on the basis of one feature (*e.g.,* obscenity) but not on the basis of another (*e.g.,* opposition to the city government) is commonplace and has found application in many contexts. We have long held, for example, that nonverbal expressive activity can be banned because of the action it entails, but not because of the ideas it expresses—so that burning a flag in violation of an ordinance against outdoor fires could be punishable, whereas burning a flag in violation of an ordinance against dishonoring the flag is not. See Johnson, 491 U.S., at 406-407. Similarly, we have upheld reasonable "time, place, or manner" restrictions, but only if they are "justified without reference to the content of the regulated speech." *Ward v. Rock Against Racism,* 491 U.S. 781, 791 (1989) (internal quotation marks omitted). And just as the power to proscribe particular speech on the basis of a noncontent element (*e.g.,* noise) does not entail the power to proscribe the same speech on the basis of a content element; so also, the power to proscribe it on the basis of *one* content element (*e.g.,* obscenity) does not entail the power to proscribe it on the basis of *other* content elements.

The concurrences describe us as setting forth a new First Amendment principle that prohibition of constitutionally proscribable speech cannot be "underinclusiv[e]"—a First Amendment "absolutism" whereby "[w]ithin a particular 'proscribable' category of expression, [a] government must either proscribe all speech or no speech at all." That easy target is of the concurrences' own invention. In our view, the First Amendment imposes not an "underinclusiveness" limitation but a "content discrimination" limitation upon a State's prohibition of proscribable speech. There is no problem whatever, for example, with a State's prohibiting obscenity (and other forms of proscribable expression) only in certain media or markets, for although that prohibition would be "underinclusive," it would not discriminate on the basis of content.

Even the prohibition against content discrimination that we assert the First Amendment requires is not absolute. It applies differently in the context of proscribable speech than in the area of fully protected speech. *** When the basis for the content discrimination consists entirely of the very reason the entire class of speech at issue is proscribable, no significant danger of idea or viewpoint discrimination exists. Such a reason, having been adjudged neutral enough to support exclusion of the entire class of speech from First Amendment protection, is also neutral enough to form the basis of distinction within the class. To illustrate: A State might choose to prohibit only that obscenity which is the most patently offensive *in its prurience*—i.e., that which involves the most lascivious displays of sexual activity. But it may not prohibit, for example, only that obscenity which includes offensive *political* messages. And the Federal Government can criminalize only those threats of violence that are directed against the President, see 18 U.S.C. § 871—since the reasons why threats of violence are outside the First Amendment (protecting individuals from the fear of violence, from the disruption that fear engenders, and from the possibility that the threatened violence will occur) have special force when applied to the person of the President. See *Watts v. United States*, 394 U.S. 705, 707 (1969). But the Federal Government may not criminalize only those threats against the President that mention his policy on aid to inner cities.

Another valid basis for according differential treatment to even a content-defined subclass of proscribable speech is that the subclass happens to be associated with particular "secondary effects" of the speech, so that the regulation is "justified without reference to the content of the ... speech," *Renton v. Playtime Theatres, Inc.*, 475 U.S. 41, 48 (1986). A State could, for example, permit all obscene live performances except those involving minors. Moreover, since words can in some circumstances violate laws directed not against speech but against conduct (a law against treason, for example, is violated by telling the enemy the Nation's defense secrets), a particular content-based subcategory of a proscribable class of speech can be swept up incidentally within the reach of a statute directed at conduct rather than speech. Thus, for example, sexually derogatory "fighting words," among other words, may produce a violation of Title VII's general prohibition against sexual discrimination in employment practices. Where the government does not target conduct on the basis of its expressive content, acts are not shielded from regulation merely because they express a discriminatory idea or philosophy. [In addition,] it may not even be necessary to identify any particular "neutral" basis, so long as the nature of the content discrimination is such that there is no realistic possibility that official suppression of ideas is afoot.

Applying these principles to the St. Paul ordinance, we conclude that, even as narrowly construed by the Minnesota Supreme Court, the ordinance is facially unconstitutional. Although the phrase in the ordinance, "arouses anger, alarm or resentment in others," has been limited by the Minnesota Supreme Court's construction to reach only those symbols or displays that amount to "fighting words," the remaining, unmodified terms make clear that the ordinance applies only to "fighting words" that insult, or provoke violence, "on the basis of race, color, creed, religion or gender." Displays containing abusive invective, no matter how vicious or severe, are permissible unless they are addressed to one of the specified disfavored topics. Those who wish to use "fighting words" in connection with other ideas—to express hostility, for example, on the basis of political affiliation, union membership, or homosexuality—are not covered. The First Amendment does not permit St. Paul to impose special prohibitions on those speakers who express views on disfavored subjects.

In its practical operation, moreover, the ordinance goes even beyond mere content discrimination, to actual viewpoint discrimination. Displays containing some words—odious racial epithets, for example—would be prohibited to proponents of all views. But "fighting words" that do not themselves invoke race, color, creed, religion, or gender—aspersions upon a person's mother, for example—would seemingly be usable *ad libitum* in the placards of those arguing in favor of racial, color, etc., tolerance and equality, but could not be used by those speakers' opponents. One could hold up a sign saying, for example, that all "anti-Catholic bigots" are misbegotten; but not that all "papists" are, for that would insult and provoke violence "on the basis of religion." St. Paul has no such authority to license one side of a debate to fight freestyle, while requiring the other to follow Marquis of Queensberry rules.

*** Justice STEVENS suggests that [the ordinance] is directed, [not] to speech of a particular content, but to particular "injur[ies]" that are "qualitatively different" from other injuries. This is wordplay. What makes the anger, fear, sense of dishonor, etc., produced by violation of this ordinance distinct from the anger, fear, sense of dishonor, etc., produced by other fighting words is nothing other than the fact that it is caused by a distinctive idea, conveyed by a distinctive message. The First Amendment cannot be evaded that easily.

The content-based discrimination reflected in the St. Paul ordinance comes within neither any of the specific exceptions to the First Amendment prohibition we discussed earlier nor a more general exception for content discrimination that does not threaten censorship of ideas. It assuredly does not fall within the exception for content discrimination based on the very reasons why the particular class of speech at issue (here, fighting words) is proscribable. *** St. Paul has not singled out an especially offensive mode of expression—it has not, for example, selected for prohibition only those fighting words that communicate ideas in a threatening (as opposed to a merely obnoxious) manner. Rather, it has proscribed fighting words of whatever manner that communicate messages of racial, gender, or religious intolerance. Selectivity of this sort creates the possibility that the city is seeking to handicap the expression of particular ideas.

St. Paul [argues that], even if the ordinance regulates expression based on hostility towards its protected ideological content, this discrimination is nonetheless justified because it is narrowly tailored to serve compelling state interests. Specifically, they assert that the ordinance helps to ensure the basic human rights of members of groups that have historically been subjected to discrimination, including the right of such group members to live in peace where they wish. We do not doubt that these interests are compelling, and that the ordinance can be said to promote them. But [the ordinance's content discrimination is not] reasonably necessary to achieve St. Paul's compelling interests ***. An ordinance not limited to the favored topics, for example, would have precisely the same beneficial effect. In fact the only interest distinctively served by the content limitation is that of displaying the city council's special hostility towards the particular biases thus singled out. That is precisely what the First Amendment forbids. The politicians of St. Paul are entitled to express that hostility—but not through the means of imposing unique limitations upon speakers who (however benightedly) disagree.

Justice WHITE, with whom Justice BLACKMUN and Justice O'CONNOR join, and with whom Justice STEVENS joins except as to Part I-A, concurring in the judgment.

This Court's decisions have plainly stated that expression falling within certain limited categories so lacks the values the First Amendment was designed to protect that the Constitution affords no protection to that expression. *** Thus, [this] Court has long held certain discrete categories of expression [including child pornography, obscenity, and some forms of libel] to be proscribable on the basis of their content. *** All of these categories are content based. But the Court has held that the First Amendment does not apply to them because their expressive content is worthless or of de minimis value to society. *Chaplinsky v. New Hampshire*, 315 U.S. 568, 571-572 (1942). We have not departed from this principle, emphasizing repeatedly that, "within the confines of [these] given classification[s], the evil to be restricted so overwhelmingly outweighs the expressive interests, if any, at stake, that no process of case-by-case adjudication is required." *New York v. Ferber*, 458 U.S. 747, 763-764 (1982). This categorical approach has provided a principled and narrowly focused means for distinguishing between expression that the government may regulate freely and that which it may regulate on the basis of content only upon a showing of compelling need.

It is inconsistent to hold that the government may proscribe an entire category of speech because the content of that speech is evil, but that the government may not treat a subset of that category differently without violating the First Amendment; the content of the subset is by definition worthless and undeserving of constitutional protection. *** Fighting words are not a means of exchanging views, rallying supporters, or registering a protest; they are directed against individuals to provoke violence or to inflict injury. *Chaplinsky*, 315 U.S., at 572. Therefore, a ban on all fighting words or on a subset of the fighting words category would restrict only the social evil of hate speech, without creating the danger of driving viewpoints from the marketplace. *** Any contribution of [the Court's] holding to First Amendment jurisprudence is surely a negative one, since it necessarily signals that expressions of violence, such as the message of intimidation and racial hatred conveyed by burning a cross on someone's lawn, are of sufficient value to outweigh the social interest in order and morality that has traditionally placed such fighting words outside the First Amendment.

In a second break with precedent, the Court refuses to sustain the ordinance even though it would survive under the strict scrutiny applicable to other protected expression. *** The Court expressly concedes that [St. Paul's] interest is compelling and is promoted by the ordinance. Nevertheless, the Court treats strict scrutiny analysis as irrelevant to the constitutionality of the legislation. *** Under the majority's view, a narrowly drawn, content-based ordinance could never pass constitutional muster if the object of that legislation could be accomplished by banning a wider category of speech. This appears to be a general renunciation of strict scrutiny review, a fundamental tool of First Amendment analysis.

[The Court also creates an exception to] its newly announced First Amendment rule: Content-based distinctions may be drawn within an unprotected category of speech if the basis for the distinctions is "the very reason the entire class of speech at issue is proscribable." *** The exception swallows the majority's rule. Certainly, it should apply to the St. Paul ordinance ***. A prohibition on fighting words [is] a ban on a class of speech that conveys an overriding message of personal injury and imminent violence, a message that is at its ugliest when directed against groups that have long been the targets of discrimination. Accordingly, the ordinance falls within the first exception to the majority's theory.

Although I disagree with the Court's analysis, I do agree with its conclusion: The St. Paul ordinance is unconstitutional. *** Although the ordinance as construed reaches categories of speech that are constitutionally unprotected, it also criminalizes a substantial amount of expression that—however repugnant—is shielded by the First Amendment. *** The mere fact that expressive activity causes hurt feelings, offense, or resentment does not render the expression unprotected. *** The ordinance is therefore fatally overbroad and invalid on its face. *** I join the judgment, but not the folly of the opinion.

Justice BLACKMUN, concurring in the judgment.

I fear that the Court has been distracted from its proper mission by the temptation to decide the issue over "politically correct speech" and "cultural diversity," neither of which is presented here. ***

I see no First Amendment values that are compromised by a law that prohibits hood-lums from driving minorities out of their homes by burning crosses on their lawns, but I see great harm in preventing the people of Saint Paul from specifically punishing the race-based fighting words that so prejudice their community. I concur in the judgment, however, because I agree with Justice WHITE that this particular ordinance reaches beyond fighting words to speech protected by the First Amendment.

Justice STEVENS, with whom Justice WHITE and Justice BLACKMUN join as to Part I, concurring in the judgment.

[W]hile the Court rejects the "all-or-nothing-at-all" nature of the categorical approach, it promptly embraces an absolutism of its own: Within a particular "proscribable" category of expression, the Court holds, a government must either proscribe *all* speech or no speech at all. *** This new absolutism in the prohibition of content-based regulations severely contorts the fabric of settled First Amendment law.

Our First Amendment decisions have created a rough hierarchy in the constitutional protection of speech. Core political speech occupies the highest, most protected posi-tion; commercial speech and nonobscene, sexually explicit speech are regarded as a sort of second-class expression; obscenity and fighting words receive the least protection of all. Assuming that the Court is correct that this last class of speech is not wholly "unprotected," it certainly does not follow that fighting words and obscenity receive the *same* sort of protection afforded core political speech. Yet in ruling that proscribable speech cannot be regulated based on subject matter, the Court does just that.

Although I agree with much of Justice WHITE's analysis, I do not join Part I-A of his opinion because I have reservations about the "categorical approach" to the First Amend-ment. *** Admittedly, the categorical approach to the First Amendment has some appeal: Either expression is protected or it is not—the categories create safe harbors for govern-ments and speakers alike. But this approach sacrifices subtlety for clarity and is, I am convinced, ultimately unsound. As an initial matter, the concept of "categories" fits poorly with the complex reality of expression. Few dividing lines in First Amendment law are straight and unwavering, and efforts at categorization inevitably give rise only to fuzzy boundaries. Our definitions of "obscenity" *** illustrate this all too well. *** Moreover, [the] history of the categorical approach is largely the history of narrowing the categories of unprotected speech. *** This evolution, I believe, indicates that the categorical approach is unworkable and the quest for absolute categories of "protected" and "unprotected" speech ultimately futile.

Unlike the Court, I do not believe that all content-based regulations are equally infirm and presumptively invalid; unlike Justice WHITE, I do not believe that fighting words are wholly unprotected by the First Amendment. To the contrary, I believe our decisions establish a more complex and subtle analysis, one that considers the content and context of the regulated speech, and the nature and scope of the restriction on speech. Applying this analysis and assuming, *arguendo*, (as the Court does) that the St. Paul ordinance is *not* overbroad, I conclude that such a selective, subject-matter regulation on proscribable speech is constitutional.

[T]he ordinance (by hypothesis) regulates *only* fighting words. *** By hypothesis, then, the St. Paul ordinance restricts speech in confrontational and potentially violent situations. *** Significantly, the St. Paul ordinance regulates speech not on the basis of its subject matter or the viewpoint expressed, but rather on the basis of the *harm* the speech causes. [J]ust as the ordinance would prohibit a Muslim from hoisting a sign claiming that all Catholics were misbegotten, so the ordinance would bar a Catholic from hoisting a similar sign attacking Muslims.

Finally, it is noteworthy that the St. Paul ordinance is, as construed by the Court today, quite narrow. The St. Paul ordinance does not ban all "hate speech," nor does it ban, say, all cross burnings or all swastika displays. Rather it only bans a subcategory of the already narrow category of fighting words. Such a limited ordinance leaves open and protected a vast range of expression on the subjects of racial, religious, and gender equality. *** Taken together, these several considerations persuade me that the St. Paul ordinance is not an unconstitutional content-based regulation of speech. Thus, were the ordinance not overbroad, I would vote to uphold it.

Points for Discussion

a. Content-Based Restrictions on Unprotected Speech

In *New York v. Ferber*, 458 U.S. 747, 765 n.18 (1982), which we discussed above, the Supreme Court held that "child pornography [is] unprotected speech subject to content-based regulation. Hence, it cannot be underinclusive or unconstitutional for a State to do precisely that." But in *R.A.V.*, although the court recognized that fighting words are unprotected speech, it concluded that fighting words cannot be subjected to content-based restrictions. Does this inconsistency call *Ferber* into doubt, or is there an explanation for it? Logically speaking, if a particular category of speech is unprotected, should the government be able to impose content-based restrictions on it? Does the greater power here include the lesser power?

b. Solving All Problems at Once

In other First Amendment cases, the Court has said that the government "need not deal with every problem at once." *Denver Area Educational Telecommunications Consortium, Inc. v. F.C.C.*, 518 U.S. 727, 757 (1996). Was the Court effectively saying in *R.A.V.* that, if a state wants to ban fighting words, it must ban them in all contexts at once? Must a state address the problems of fighting words concerning "political affiliation, union membership, or homosexuality" at the same time that it addresses the problem of fighting words concerning "race, color, creed, religion or gender?" What if only some of the problems have actually arisen in the state?

c. Threats

When one person threatens another—particularly when he does so in words—he communicates a message. Are threats protected speech, or are they instead outside of the protection of the First Amendment? In *R.A.V.*, the Court suggested that they were not. And, indeed, in *Watts v. United States*, 394 U.S. 705 (1969), which involved a statute (18 U.S.C. § 871) that criminalizes threats of violence directed against the President, the Court implied that genuine threats are not protected speech. The petitioner had been convicted for stating, "I have already received my draft classification as 1-A and I have got to report for my physical this Monday coming. I am not going. If they ever make me carry a rifle the first man I want to get in my sights is L.B.J. *** They are not going to make me kill my black brothers." In its brief opinion, the Court reversed the petitioner's conviction. The Court stated:

> Certainly the statute under which petitioner was convicted is constitutional on its face. The Nation undoubtedly has a valid, even an overwhelming, interest in protecting the safety of its Chief Executive and in allowing him to perform his duties without interference from threats of physical violence. Nevertheless, a statute such as this one, which makes criminal a form of pure speech, must be interpreted with the commands of the First Amendment clearly in mind. What is a threat must be distinguished from what is constitutionally protected speech.

The Court reversed the petitioner's conviction because "the statute initially requires the Government to prove a true 'threat.' We do not believe that the kind of political hyperbole indulged in by petitioner fits within that statutory term." Does the Court's decision mean that all genuine threats are simply beyond the protection of the First Amendment? If so, why? And if they are unprotected speech, after *R.A.V.* can the government decide to criminalize only some threats, defined by the content of the threats?

In *Virginia v. Black*, 538 U.S. 343 (2003), the Court considered a Virginia statute that made it a crime to burn a cross with "the intent to intimidate a person or group of persons." The Court first traced the history of cross burning and noted that it is a "symbol of hate" that is often used to convey a message of intimidation. The Court then declared, citing *Watts*, that the First Amendment "permits a State to ban a 'true threat,'" which it defined as a statement "where the speaker means to communicate a serious expression of an intent to commit an act of unlawful violence to a particular individual or group of individuals." The Court noted that "a prohibition on true threats 'protect[s] individuals from the fear of violence' and 'from the disruption that fear engenders,' in addition to protecting people 'from the possibility that the threatened violence will occur.'" The Court also stated that "some cross burnings fit within this meaning of intimidating speech."

The Court also disagreed with the conclusion of the Supreme Court of Virginia, which had relied on *R.A.V.*, that "even if it is constitutional to ban cross burning in a content-neutral manner, the Virginia cross-burning statute is unconstitutional because it discriminates on the basis of content and viewpoint." The Court reasoned that, under *R.A.V.*, the government can engage in content discrimination in banning a subset of speech in an unprotected category when "the basis for the content discrimination consists entirely of the very reason the entire class of speech at issue is proscribable." The Court then stated:

> The First Amendment permits Virginia to outlaw cross burnings done with the intent to intimidate because burning a cross is a particularly virulent form of intimidation. Instead of prohibiting all intimidating messages, Virginia may choose to regulate this subset of intimidating messages in light of cross burning's long and pernicious history as a signal of impending violence. Thus, just as a State may regulate only that obscenity which is the most obscene due to its prurient content, so too may a State choose to prohibit only those forms of intimidation that are most likely to inspire fear of bodily harm.

The Court, however, invalidated a provision of the statute that treated any cross burning as "prima facie evidence of an intent to intimidate a person or group of persons," reasoning that the provision "strips away the very reason why a State may ban cross burning with the intent to intimidate" and instead "permits the Commonwealth to arrest, prosecute, and convict a person based solely on the fact of cross burning itself." Justice O'Connor reasoned that "a burning cross is not always intended to intimidate," but instead sometimes "is a statement of ideology, a symbol of group solidarity." Accordingly, the provision "chill[ed] constitutionally protected political speech because of the possibility that the Commonwealth [would] prosecute—and potentially convict—somebody engaging only in lawful political speech at the core of what the First Amendment is designed to protect."

Do you agree that cross burning should sometimes be considered a form of protected speech? And if not, is it because it is a "true threat" or instead for some other reason?

---

6. Commercial Speech

Commercial speech consists of advertising and other business communications. Until 1976, the Court viewed commercial speech as a category of speech entirely outside the protection of the First Amendment. See, e.g., *Valentine v. Chrestensen*, 316 U.S. 52 (1942) (stating that although government may not "unduly burden or proscribe" the freedom of communicating information and disseminating opinion on public streets, "the Constitution imposes no such restraint on government as respects purely commercial advertising"); *Breard v. Alexandria*, 341 U.S. 622 (1951) (upholding conviction for violation of an ordinance prohibiting door-to-door solicitation of magazine subscriptions because of the "commercial feature" of the act).

In *Virginia State Bd. of Pharmacy v. Virginia Citizens Consumer Council, Inc.*, 425 U.S. 748 (1976), however, the Court invalidated a Virginia law prohibiting pharmacists from advertising the prices of prescription drugs. The Court concluded that commercial speech—that is, speech that "does no more than propose a commercial transaction"—is protected by the First Amendment. The Court noted that "speech does not lose its First Amendment protection because money is spent to project it, as in a paid advertisement of one form or another. Speech likewise is protected even though it is carried in a form that is 'sold' for profit," as occurs with books and movies. The Court also noted that the "consumer's interest in the free flow of commercial information *** may be as keen, if not keener by far, than his interest in the day's most urgent political debate." The Court stated that "[s]o long as we preserve a predominantly free enterprise economy, the allocation of our resources in large measure will be made through numerous private economic decisions. It is a matter of public interest that those decisions, in the aggregate, be intelligent and well informed. To this end, the free flow of commercial information is indispensable." The Court concluded:

> [T]he State's protectiveness of its citizens rests in large measure on the advantages of their being kept in ignorance. *** There is, of course, an alternative to this highly paternalistic approach. That alternative is to assume that this information is not in itself harmful, that people will perceive their own best interests if only they are well enough informed, and that the best means to that end is to open the channels of communication rather than to close them.

The Court in *Virginia State Board of Pharmacy* did not identify a level of scrutiny for reviewing claims that the government has impermissibly regulated commercial speech. The Court did observe, however, that "[s]ome forms of commercial speech regulation are surely permissible." Most important, the Court noted that "[u]ntruthful speech, commercial or otherwise, has never been protected for its own sake," and that the First Amendment "does not prohibit the State from insuring that the stream of commercial information flow cleanly as well as freely." The Court stated, moreover, that

> [t]he truth of commercial speech [may] be more easily verifiable by its disseminator than [news] reporting or political commentary ***. Also, [s]ince advertising is the Sine qua non of commercial profits, there is little likelihood of its being chilled by proper regulation and forgone entirely. Attributes such as these, the greater objectivity and hardiness of commercial speech, may make it less necessary to tolerate inaccurate statements for fear of silencing the speaker.

The Court therefore suggested that commercial speech might be subject to greater regulation than other forms of speech.

Several years after the Court's decision in *Virginia State Board of Pharmacy*, the Court settled on an approach for reviewing regulations of commercial speech. Under the leading case of *Central Hudson Gas & Electric Corp. v. Public Service Comm'n of New York,* 447 U.S. 557 (1980), the Supreme Court divided commercial speech into two categories. First, commercial speech that concerns an unlawful activity or that is fraudulent or misleading has no First Amendment protection. For example, the government may completely prohibit businesses from discussing the formation of horizontal price-fixing conspiracies that would violate the antitrust laws. *See North Texas Speciality Physicians v. FTC,* 528 F.3d 346, 372 (5th Cir. 2008). Second, regulation of other commercial speech is reviewed by a test similar to *O'Brien* scrutiny. The government may regulate it if the government has a substantial interest, the regulation directly furthers the interest, and the regulation restrains speech only to the extent necessary to further the interest. Note that, under this test, a compelling governmental interest is not required. The Court, however, has struggled to apply this standard, and several Justices on the current Court have urged the Court to abandon it.

Points for Discussion

a. Protecting Commercial Speech

What is the Court's rationale for protecting commercial speech? Is it that protection is necessary to preserve the marketplace of ideas? That the First Amendment embodies a general principle against government paternalism? That consumers, as "listeners," have a First Amendment right to *receive* the information? Or is it that the courts have no way to distinguish between commercial speech and other forms of speech? What do these various rationales suggest about the extent of the protection that the Court should provide to commercial speech?

b. Limits on Protection for Commercial Speech

Do you agree that commercial speech is more readily "verifiable," and less subject to a chilling effect, than other forms of speech? If so, is this an argument for a lower level of scrutiny under the First Amendment for commercial speech regulations, or instead an argument that commercial speech should not be protected at all?

In the years after the Court announced the *Central Hudson* standard, the Court struggled to apply it consistently. For example, in *Posadas de Puerto Rico Associates v. Tourism Co. of Puerto Rico*, 478 U.S. 328 (1986), the Court upheld the constitutionality of a Puerto Rico statute and regulations restricting advertising of casino gambling. The Court reasoned that Puerto Rico had a substantial interest in protecting the health, safety, and welfare of its citizens, and that the legislature's belief that advertising for casino gambling would increase the demand for the product—and thus potentially lead to an "increase in local crime, the fostering of prostitution, the development of corruption, and the infiltration of organized crime"—was a "reasonable one." The Court rejected the appellant's contention that the ban was impermissibly under-inclusive because advertising for other forms of gambling—including horse racing, cockfighting, and the lottery—was legal. The Court reasoned that the legislature permissibly concluded that "the risks associated with casino gambling were significantly greater than those associated with the more traditional kinds of gambling in Puerto Rico." The Court also stated that "the greater power to completely ban casino gambling necessarily includes the lesser power to ban advertising of casino gambling."

> **FYI**
>
> Puerto Rico is a self-governing, unincorporated territory of the United States. 28 U.S.C. § 1258(2) specifically authorizes an appeal to the Supreme Court from a decision of the Supreme Court of Puerto Rico "where is drawn in question the validity of a statute of the Commonwealth of Puerto Rico on the ground of its being repugnant to the Constitution, treaties, or laws of the United States, and the decision is in favor of its validity."

Many commentators read the Court's opinion in *Posadas*, which seemed to apply a more deferential version of intermediate scrutiny than it applies in other contexts, to suggest, at a minimum, that the government has more leeway to regulate commercial speech that promotes traditional "vices." Less than ten years later, however, the Court in *Rubin v. Coors Brewing Co.*, 514 U.S. 476 (1995), squarely rejected the government's argument that "legislatures have broader latitude to regulate speech that promotes socially harmful activities, such as alcohol consumption, than they have to regulate other types of speech." The Court in *Rubin* held that a federal statute prohibiting beer labels from displaying alcoholic content violated the First Amendment.

One year after the Court's decision in *Rubin*, it decided the case that follows. As you will see, although the Court was unanimous in invalidating the challenged laws—a pair of Rhode Island statutes prohibiting the advertising of the price of alcoholic beverages except by tags and signs in liquor stores—the Justices divided sharply on the rationale and on the appropriate level of scrutiny.

———

44 Liquormart, Inc. v. Rhode Island

517 U.S. 484 (1996)

[This case involved a challenge to two Rhode Island laws that together prohibited advertising of the price of alcoholic beverages "in any manner whatsoever," except by tags or signs inside liquor stores. Among other things, the laws thus banned advertisements in print and broadcast media stating a price for alcoholic beverages. The plaintiffs were discount liquor retailers that wanted to advertise their low prices for alcoholic beverages but had previously been fined for print advertisements that implied (without identifying) low prices for alcoholic beverages. The state argued that the statutes advanced its interest in reducing alcohol consumption. Justice Stevens announced the judgment of the Court, but no opinion commanded a majority.]

Justice STEVENS [joined by Justice KENNEDY and Justice GINSBURG].

Advertising has been a part of our culture throughout our history. *** In accord with the role that commercial messages have long played, the law has developed to ensure that advertising provides consumers with accurate information about the availability of goods and services. *** On the basis of [the principles announced in *Virginia Bd. of Pharmacy*], our early cases uniformly struck down several broadly based bans on truthful, nonmisleading commercial speech, each of which served ends unrelated to consumer protection. *** At the same time, our early cases recognized that the State may regulate some types of commercial advertising more freely than other forms of protected speech. Specifically, we explained that the State may require commercial messages to "appear in such a form, or include such additional information, warnings, and disclaimers, as are necessary to prevent its being deceptive," *Virginia Bd. of Pharmacy*, 425 U.S., at 772, n. 24, and that it may restrict some forms of aggressive sales practices that have the potential to exert "undue influence" over consumers, see *Bates v. State Bar of Ariz.*, 433 U.S. 350, 366 (1977). *** Our decision [in *Central Hudson Gas & Elec. Corp. v. Public Serv. Comm'n of N.Y.*, 447 U.S.

557 (1980),] acknowledged the special features of commercial speech but identified the serious First Amendment concerns that attend blanket advertising prohibitions that do not protect consumers from commercial harms.

Rhode Island errs in concluding that *all* commercial speech regulations are subject to a similar form of constitutional review simply because they target a similar category of expression. The mere fact that messages propose commercial transactions does not in and of itself dictate the constitutional analysis that should apply to decisions to suppress them.

When a State regulates commercial messages to protect consumers from misleading, deceptive, or aggressive sales practices, or requires the disclosure of beneficial consumer information, the purpose of its regulation is consistent with the reasons for according constitutional protection to commercial speech and therefore justifies less than strict review. However, when a State entirely prohibits the dissemination of truthful, nonmisleading commercial messages for reasons unrelated to the preservation of a fair bargaining process, there is far less reason to depart from the rigorous review that the First Amendment generally demands. ***

Sound reasons justify reviewing the latter type of commercial speech regulation more carefully. Most obviously, complete speech bans, unlike content-neutral restrictions on the time, place, or manner of expression, see *Kovacs v. Cooper*, 336 U.S. 77, 89 (1949), are particularly dangerous because they all but foreclose alternative means of disseminating certain information.

> **Take Note**
>
> Justice Stevens suggests here that bans on the "dissemination of truthful, nonmisleading commercial messages for reasons unrelated to the preservation of a fair bargaining process" should receive "the rigorous review that the First Amendment generally demands." Does this mean that he believes that strict scrutiny should apply to such regulations? If so, is there a conceivable argument that the challenged laws would survive scrutiny?

The special dangers that attend complete bans on truthful, nonmisleading commercial speech cannot be explained away by appeals to the "commonsense distinctions" that exist between commercial and noncommercial speech. *Virginia Bd. of Pharmacy*, 425 U.S., at 771, n. 24. Regulations that suppress the truth are no less troubling because they target objectively verifiable information, nor are they less effective because they aim at durable messages. As a result, neither the "greater objectivity" nor the "greater hardiness" of truthful, nonmisleading commercial speech justifies reviewing its complete suppression with added deference. *Ibid.*

It is the State's interest in protecting consumers from "commercial harms" that provides "the typical reason why commercial speech can be subject to greater governmental regulation than noncommercial speech." *Cincinnati v. Discovery Network, Inc.*, 507 U.S. 410, 426 (1993). Yet bans that target truthful, nonmisleading commercial messages rarely protect consumers from such harms. Instead, such bans often serve only to obscure an "underlying governmental policy" that could be implemented without regulating speech. *Central Hudson*, 447 U.S., at 566, n. 9. In this way, these commercial speech bans not only hinder consumer choice, but also impede debate over central issues of public policy.

Precisely because bans against truthful, nonmisleading commercial speech rarely seek to protect consumers from either deception or overreaching, they usually rest solely on the offensive assumption that the public will respond "irrationally" to the truth. The First Amendment directs us to be especially skeptical of regulations that seek to keep people in the dark for what the government perceives to be their own good. That teaching applies equally to state attempts to deprive consumers of accurate information about their chosen products ***.

Take Note

Justices Kennedy, Souter, and Ginsburg joined the next four paragraphs of Justice Stevens's opinion.

In this case, there is no question that Rhode Island's price advertising ban constitutes a blanket prohibition against truthful, nonmisleading speech about a lawful product. There is also no question that the ban serves an end unrelated to consumer protection. Accordingly, we must review the price advertising ban with "special care," *Central Hudson*, 447 U.S., at 566, n. 9, mindful that speech prohibitions of this type rarely survive constitutional review.

The State argues that the price advertising prohibition should nevertheless be upheld because it directly advances the State's substantial interest in promoting temperance, and because it is no more extensive than necessary. *** [T]he State bears the burden of showing not merely that its regulation will advance its interest, but also that it will do so "to a material degree." The need for the State to make such a showing is particularly great given the drastic nature of its chosen means—the wholesale suppression of truthful, nonmisleading information. Accordingly, we must determine whether the State has shown that the price advertising ban will *significantly* reduce alcohol consumption.

We can agree that common sense supports the conclusion that a prohibition against price advertising, like a collusive agreement among competitors to refrain from such advertising, will tend to mitigate competition and maintain prices at a higher level than would prevail in a completely free market. Despite the absence of proof on the point, we can even agree with the State's contention that it is reasonable to assume that demand, and hence consumption throughout the market, is somewhat lower whenever a higher, noncompetitive price level prevails. However, [the] State has presented no evidence to suggest that its speech prohibition will *significantly* reduce marketwide consumption. Indeed, the District Court's considered and uncontradicted finding on this point is directly to the contrary. Moreover, the evidence suggests that the abusive drinker will probably not be deterred by a marginal price increase, and that the true alcoholic may simply reduce his purchases of other necessities. *** [A]ny conclusion that elimination of the ban would significantly increase alcohol consumption would require us to engage in the sort of "speculation or conjecture" that is an unacceptable means of demonstrating that a restriction on commercial speech directly advances the State's asserted interest.

The State also cannot satisfy the requirement that its restriction on speech be no more extensive than necessary. It is perfectly obvious that alternative forms of regulation that would not involve any restriction on speech would be more likely to achieve the State's goal of promoting temperance. As the State's own expert conceded, higher prices can be maintained either by direct regulation or by increased taxation. Per capita purchases could be limited as is the case with prescription drugs. Even educational campaigns focused on the problems of excessive, or even moderate, drinking might prove to be more effective. As a result, even under the less than strict standard that generally applies in commercial speech cases, the State has failed to establish a "reasonable fit" between its abridgment of speech and its temperance goal. It necessarily follows that the price advertising ban cannot survive the more stringent constitutional review that *Central Hudson* itself concluded was appropriate for the complete suppression of truthful, nonmisleading commercial speech.

> **Take Note**
>
> Justices Kennedy, Thomas, and Ginsburg joined the next three paragraphs of Justice Stevens's opinion.

Relying on the *Central Hudson* analysis set forth in *Posadas de Puerto Rico Associates v. Tourism Co. of P. R.*, 478 U.S. 328 (1986), and *United States v. Edge Broadcasting Co.*, 509 U.S. 418 (1993), Rhode Island [argues] that, because expert opinions as to the effectiveness of the price advertising ban "go both ways," the Court of Appeals correctly concluded that the ban constituted a "reasonable choice" by the legislature. The State next contends that precedent requires us to give particular deference to that legislative choice because the State could, if it chose, ban the sale of alcoholic beverages outright. Finally, the State argues that deference is appropriate because alcoholic beverages are so-called "vice" products. *** The reasoning in *Posadas* does support the State's argument, but, on reflection, we are now persuaded that *Posadas* erroneously performed the First Amendment analysis. *** [W]e conclude that a state legislature does not have the broad discretion to suppress truthful, nonmisleading information for paternalistic purposes that the *Posadas* majority was willing to tolerate.

We also cannot accept the State's second contention, which is premised entirely on the "greater-includes-the-lesser" reasoning [in] *Posadas*, [because that argument] is inconsistent with both logic and well-settled doctrine. *** [W]e think it quite clear that banning speech may sometimes prove far more intrusive than banning conduct. *** The text of the First Amendment makes clear that the Constitution presumes that attempts to regulate speech are more dangerous than attempts to regulate conduct.

Finally, we find unpersuasive the State's contention that [the] price advertising ban should be upheld because it targets commercial speech that pertains to a "vice" activity. *** Our decision last Term striking down an alcohol-related advertising restriction effectively rejected the very contention respondents now make. See *Rubin v. Coors Brewing Co.*, 514 U.S. 476, 478, 482 n.2 (1995). *** Moreover, the scope of any "vice" exception to the protection afforded by the First Amendment would be difficult, if not impossible, to define.

Justice SCALIA, concurring in part and concurring in the judgment.

I share Justice THOMAS's discomfort with the *Central Hudson* test, which seems to me to have nothing more than policy intuition to support it. I also share Justice STEVENS's aversion towards paternalistic governmental policies that prevent men and women from hearing facts that might not be good for them. On the other hand, it would also be paternalism for us to prevent the people of the States from enacting laws that we consider paternalistic, unless we have good reason to believe that the Constitution itself forbids them. I will take my guidance as to what the Constitution forbids, with regard to a text as indeterminate as the First Amendment's preservation of "the freedom of speech," and where the core offense of suppressing particular political ideas is not at issue, from the long accepted practices of the American people. The briefs and arguments of the parties in the present case provide no illumination on *** the state legislative practices prevalent at the time the First Amendment was adopted [and] at the time the Fourteenth Amendment was adopted.

Since I do not believe we have before us the wherewithal to declare *Central Hudson* wrong—or at least the wherewithal to say what ought to replace it—I must resolve this case in accord with our existing jurisprudence, which all except Justice THOMAS agree would prohibit the challenged regulation.

Justice THOMAS, concurring [in part] and concurring in the judgment.

In cases such as this, in which the government's asserted interest is to keep legal users of a product or service ignorant in order to manipulate their choices in the marketplace, the balancing test adopted in *Central Hudson* should not be applied, in my view. Rather, such an "interest" is *per se* illegitimate and can no more justify regulation of "commercial" speech than it can justify regulation of "noncommercial" speech. *** Faulting the State for failing to show that its price advertising ban decreases alcohol consumption "significantly," as Justice STEVENS does, seems to imply that if the State had been more successful at keeping consumers ignorant and thereby decreasing their consumption, then the restriction might have been upheld. This contradicts *Virginia Bd. of Pharmacy*'s rationale for protecting "commercial" speech in the first instance.

Both Justice STEVENS and Justice O'CONNOR appear to adopt a stricter, more categorical interpretation of the fourth prong of *Central Hudson* than that suggested in some of our other opinions, one that could, as a practical matter, go a long way toward the position I take. *** [Their] opinions would appear to commit the courts to striking down restrictions on speech whenever a direct regulation (i.e., a regulation involving no restriction on speech regarding lawful activity at all) would be an equally effective method of dampening demand by legal users. But it would seem that directly banning a product (or rationing it, taxing it, controlling its price, or otherwise restricting its sale in specific ways) would virtually always be at least as effective in discouraging consumption as merely restricting advertising regarding the product would be, and thus virtually all restrictions with such a purpose would fail the fourth prong of the *Central Hudson* test. *** I welcome this outcome; but, rather than "applying" the fourth prong of *Central Hudson* to reach the inevitable result that all or most such advertising restrictions must be struck down, I would adhere to the doctrine adopted in *Virginia Bd. of Pharmacy* [that] all attempts to dissuade legal choices by citizens by keeping them ignorant are impermissible.

Justice O'CONNOR, with whom THE CHIEF JUSTICE, Justice SOUTER, and Justice

BREYER join, concurring in the judgment.

I agree with the Court that Rhode Island's price-advertising ban is invalid. I would resolve this case more narrowly, however, by applying our established *Central Hudson* test to determine whether this commercial speech regulation survives First Amendment scrutiny.

Rhode Island's regulation [is] more extensive than necessary to serve the State's interest. *** Rhode Island offers one, and only one, justification for its ban on price advertising. Rhode Island says that the ban is intended to keep alcohol prices high as a way to keep consumption low. *** The fit between Rhode Island's method and this particular goal is not reasonable. *** The State has other methods at its disposal—methods that would more directly accomplish this stated goal without intruding on sellers' ability to provide truthful, nonmisleading information to customers. *** A [sales] tax, for example, is not normally very difficult to administer and would have a far more certain and direct effect on prices, without any restriction on speech. The principal opinion suggests further alternatives ***. The ready availability of such alternatives—at least some of which would far more effectively achieve Rhode Island's only professed goal, at comparatively small additional administrative cost—demonstrates that the fit between ends and means is not narrowly tailored. *** Because Rhode Island's regulation fails even the less stringent standard set out in *Central Hudson*, nothing here requires adoption of a new analysis for the evaluation of commercial speech regulation.

---

a. Level of Scrutiny

The Justices in *44 Liquormart* divided over the proper level of scrutiny for restrictions on commercial speech. Justices Stevens, Kennedy, and Ginsburg apparently would have applied strict scrutiny to prohibitions on the "dissemination of truthful, nonmisleading commercial messages for reasons unrelated to the preservation of a fair bargaining process." Justice Thomas would have gone even further, subjecting such regulations to a rule of *per se* invalidity. Justice Scalia concluded that the law was invalid under the Court's precedents, but would have preferred the Court to apply an originalist approach. He did not say what standard such an approach likely would produce for commercial speech regulation, because the Court had no evidence of historic legislative practices before it. And Justices O'Connor, Souter, and Breyer and Chief Justice Rehnquist concluded that the *Central Hudson* test was the appropriate level of scrutiny. What level of scrutiny should the Court apply to regulations of commercial speech? Does it matter whether the regulated speech is "truthful" and "non-misleading"? Are courts competent to determine when in fact speech is "truthful" or "non-misleading"?

In its verbal formulation, the *Central Hudson* test sounds very much like the other forms of intermediate scrutiny that we have seen in this Chapter, including the test for reasonable time, place, and manner restrictions, see *Ward v. Rock Against Racism*, 491 U.S. 781 (1989), and the test for generally applicable laws that incidentally burden expression, see *United States v. O'Brien*, 391 U.S. 367 (1968). Is that test sufficiently protective of commercial speech? Conversely, is it too protective? More important, is the *Central Hudson* test still the appropriate standard for commercial speech regulation after *44 Liquormart*? In fact, the Court has applied the *Central Hudson* test in cases decided since *44 Liquormart*, see, *e.g.*, *Thompson v. Western States Med. Ctr.*, 535 U.S. 357 (2002), though some Justices have continued to express the view that the Court should abandon the test, see *id.* (Thomas, J., concurring). What test should replace the *Central Hudson* test, if the Court does abandon it?

b. Identifying Commercial Speech

The Court in *Virginia State Board of Pharmacy* defined commercial speech as a communication that "does no more than propose a commercial transaction." Even assuming that commercial speech should receive a different degree of protection under the First Amendment than other forms of speech, is that the appropriate test for what counts as commercial speech? And if it is the appropriate test, does it provide sufficient guidance for distinguishing between commercial speech and other forms of speech? Suppose, for example, that an athletic apparel company broadcasts a television commercial that consists simply of girls, dressed in the company's athletic apparel, stating, "I am an athlete," and ends with a depiction of the company's logo. Would such an advertisement be commercial speech? After all, it would be designed (among other things) to encourage prospective customers to buy the company's products. Would it be problematic to say that the government can regulate the content of such an advertisement?

c. Commercial Speech and the Original Meaning

Is there an originalist argument for giving commercial speech less protection than other forms of speech? Judge Alex Kozinski and Stuart Banner note that "[t]he argument would go like this: The Framers evidenced absolutely no interest in protecting commercial speech, so it would be a gross misinterpretation of the first amendment to construe it to afford commercial speech the same level of protection as political speech." In their view, however, "this argument proves too much. The Framers never expressed an interest in protecting literature either, but the idea that the first amendment protects artistic expression is not one that attracts much opposition." Alex Kozkinski & Stuart Banner, *Who's Afraid of Commercial Speech?*, 76 Va. L. Rev. 627 (1990). They argue that the same is true for proselytizing, nude dancing, and so forth. Ultimately, they reason, there is little in the text or history of the First Amendment to suggest that commercial speech should be treated differently from political speech.

What inference about the original meaning should be drawn given this lack of evidence? Is the problem that the only clear evidence we have of the First Amendment's original meaning provides clues of its meaning only at a very high level of generality?

---

7. Campaign Contributions and Expenditures

Candidates running for political office usually must spend large amounts of money for television, radio, internet, and other advertising. Restricting these expenditures would hamper their ability to convey their political messages to potential voters, a very important form of free speech. But permitting unfettered campaign spending might also permit wealthy or well-financed candidates effectively to swamp the messages of less well-financed candidates.

Of course, spending money is only half of what a candidate ordinarily must do in order to get out his message. In order to spend money on campaigning, most candidates (all but the very wealthy) must first obtain the funds from contributors. Accordingly, limits on campaign contributions affect candidates' ability to convey their political messages, as well. But if contributions are totally unregulated, political candidates in effect might be unduly influenced—"bought"—by wealthy donors. In light of these competing interests, can the government regulate campaign spending and contributions?

The Court developed two rules in the case that follows. The first is that the First Amendment generally prohibits the federal government from regulating how much money a political candidate is permitted to spend. The second is that the First Amendment generally permits the government to impose reasonable restrictions on the right to contribute to a political campaign. In reading the case, try to identify the Court's rationale for each rule.

Buckley v. Valeo

424 U.S. 1 (1976)

PER CURIAM.

Take Note

What follows is only a brief excerpt from an extremely long opinion touching upon numerous issues. We briefly considered this case in Chapter 5, when we discussed the Constitution's provisions for the appointment of officers of the United States.

These appeals present constitutional challenges to the key provisions of the Federal Election Campaign Act of 1971 (Act), and related provisions of the Internal Revenue Code of 1954, all as amended in 1974. [The Act imposed a variety of restrictions on campaign contributions and expenditures. Among the most important were limitations prohibiting individuals from contributing more than $25,000 in a single year or more than $1,000 to any single candidate for an election campaign and from spending more than $1,000 a year "relative to a clearly identified candidate." The Act also restricted candidates' use of personal and family resources in their campaigns and limited the amount that they could spend on a campaign for federal office. The plaintiffs, who included political candidates and political parties, challenged the contribution and spending limitations under the First Amendment.]

The Act's contribution and expenditure limitations operate in an area of the most fundamental First Amendment activities. Discussion of public issues and debate on the qualifications of candidates are integral to the operation of the system of government established by our Constitution. The First Amendment affords the broadest protection to such political expression in order "to assure (the) unfettered interchange of ideas for the bringing about of political and social changes desired by the people." *Roth v. United States*, 354 U.S. 476, 484 (1957). Although First Amendment protections are not confined to "the exposition of ideas," *Winters v. New York*, 333 U.S. 507, 510 (1948), "there is practically universal agreement that a major purpose of that Amendment was to protect the free discussion of governmental affairs [of] course includ(ing) discussions of candidates." *Mills v. Alabama*, 384 U.S. 214, 218 (1966). This no more than reflects our "profound national commitment to the principle that debate on public issues should be uninhibited, robust, and wide-open," *New York Times Co. v. Sullivan*, 376 U.S. 254, 270 (1964). In a republic where the people are sovereign, the ability of the citizenry to make informed choices among candidates for office is essential, for the identities of those who are elected will inevitably shape the course that we follow as a nation. As the Court observed in *Monitor Patriot Co. v. Roy*, 401 U.S. 265, 272 (1971), "it can hardly be doubted that the constitutional guarantee has its fullest and most urgent application precisely to the conduct of campaigns for political office."

The First Amendment protects political association as well as political expression. The constitutional right of association explicated in *NAACP v. Alabama*, 357 U.S. 449, 460 (1958), stemmed from the Court's recognition that "[e]ffective advocacy of both public and private points of view, particularly controversial ones, is undeniably enhanced by group association." Subsequent decisions have made clear that the First and Fourteenth Amendments guarantee "freedom to associate with others for the common advancement of political beliefs and ideas," a freedom that encompasses "[t]he right to associate with the political party of one's choice." *Kusper v. Pontikes*, 414 U.S. 51, 56, 57 (1973), quoted in *Cousins v. Wigoda*, 419 U.S. 477, 487 (1975).

> **Make the Connection**
>
> We will consider the First Amendment's protection for the freedom of association in Chapter 16.

It is with these principles in mind that we consider the primary contentions of the parties with respect to the Act's limitations upon the giving and spending of money in political campaigns. Those conflicting contentions could not more sharply define the basic issues before us. Appellees contend that what the Act regulates is conduct, and that its effect on speech and association is incidental at most. Appellants respond that contributions and expenditures are at the very core of political speech, and that the Act's limitations thus constitute restraints on First Amendment liberty that are both gross and direct.

In upholding the constitutional validity of the Act's contribution and expenditure provisions on the ground that those provisions should be viewed as regulating conduct, not speech, the Court of Appeals relied upon *United States v. O'Brien*, 391 U.S. 367 (1968). *** We cannot share the view that the present Act's contribution and expenditure limitations are comparable to the restrictions on conduct upheld in *O'Brien*. The expenditure of money simply cannot be equated with such conduct as destruction of a draft card. Some forms of communication made possible by the giving and spending of money involve speech alone, some involve conduct primarily, and some involve a combination of the two. Yet this Court has never suggested that the dependence of a communication on the expenditure of money operates itself to introduce a nonspeech element or to reduce the exacting scrutiny required by the First Amendment. ***

Even if the categorization of the expenditure of money as conduct were accepted, the limitations challenged here would not meet the *O'Brien* test because the governmental interests advanced in support of the Act involve "suppressing communication." The interests served by the Act include restricting the voices of people and interest groups who have money to spend and reducing the overall scope of federal election campaigns. Although the Act does not focus on the ideas expressed by persons or groups subject to its regulations, it is aimed in part at equalizing the relative ability of all voters to affect electoral outcomes by placing a ceiling on expenditures for political expression by citizens and groups. Unlike *O'Brien*, where the Selective Service System's administrative interest in the preservation of draft cards was wholly unrelated to their use as a means of communication, it is beyond dispute that the interest in regulating the alleged "conduct" of giving or spending money "arises in some measure because the communication allegedly integral to the conduct is itself thought to be harmful." 391 U.S., at 382.

Nor can the Act's contribution and expenditure limitations be sustained, as some of the parties suggest, by reference to the constitutional principles reflected in such decisions as *** *Kovacs v. Cooper*, 336 U.S. 77 (1949). Those cases stand for the proposition that the government may adopt reasonable time, place, and manner regulations, which do not discriminate among speakers or ideas, in order to further an important governmental interest unrelated to the restriction of communication. *** The critical difference between this case and [the] time, place, and manner cases is that the present Act's contribution and expenditure limitations impose direct quantity restrictions on political communication and association by persons, groups, candidates, and political parties in addition to any reasonable time, place, and manner regulations otherwise imposed.

A restriction on the amount of money a person or group can spend on political communication during a campaign necessarily reduces the quantity of expression by restricting the number of issues discussed, the depth of their exploration, and the size of the audience reached. This is because virtually every means of communicating ideas in today's mass society requires the expenditure of money. The distribution of the humblest handbill or leaflet entails printing, paper, and circulation costs. Speeches and rallies generally necessitate hiring a hall and publicizing the event. The electorate's increasing dependence on television, radio, and other mass media for news and information has made these expensive modes of communication indispensable instruments of effective political speech.

The expenditure limitations contained in the Act represent substantial rather than merely theoretical restraints on the quantity and diversity of political speech. The $1,000 ceiling on spending "relative to a clearly identified candidate" would appear to exclude all citizens and groups except candidates, political parties, and the institutional press from any significant use of the most effective modes of communication. Although the Act's limitations on expenditures by campaign organizations and political parties provide substantially greater room for discussion and debate, they would have required restrictions in the scope of a number of past congressional and Presidential campaigns and would operate to constrain campaigning by candidates who raise sums in excess of the spending ceiling.

By contrast with a limitation upon expenditures for political expression, a limitation upon the amount that any one person or group may contribute to a candidate or political committee entails only a marginal restriction upon the contributor's ability to engage in free communication. A contribution serves as a general expression of support for the candidate and his views, but does not communicate the underlying basis for the support. The quantity of communication by the contributor does not increase perceptibly with the size of his contribution, since the expression rests solely on the undifferentiated, symbolic act of contributing. At most, the size of the contribution provides a very rough index of the intensity of the contributor's support for the candidate. A limitation on the amount of money a person may give to a candidate or campaign organization thus involves little direct restraint on his political communication, for it permits the symbolic expression of support evidenced by a contribution but does not in any way infringe the contributor's freedom to discuss candidates and issues. While contributions may result in political expression if spent by a candidate or an association to present views to the voters, the transformation of contributions into political debate involves speech by someone other than the contributor.

Given the important role of contributions in financing political campaigns, contribution restrictions could have a severe impact on political dialogue if the limitations prevented candidates and political committees from amassing the resources necessary for effective advocacy. There is no indication, however, that the contribution limitations imposed by the Act would have any dramatic adverse effect on the funding of campaigns and political associations. The overall effect of the Act's contribution ceilings is merely to require candidates and political committees to raise funds from a greater number of persons and to compel people who would otherwise contribute amounts greater than the statutory limits to expend such funds on direct political expression, rather than to reduce the total amount of money potentially available to promote political expression.

In sum, although the Act's contribution and expenditure limitations both implicate fundamental First Amendment interests, its expenditure ceilings impose significantly more severe restrictions on protected freedoms of political expression and association than do its limitations on financial contributions.

[T]he primary First Amendment problem raised by the Act's contribution limitations is their restriction of one aspect of the contributor's freedom of political association. *** Yet [even] a "'significant interference' with protected rights of political association" may be sustained if the State demonstrates a sufficiently important interest and employs means closely drawn to avoid unnecessary abridgment of associational freedoms.

It is unnecessary to look beyond the Act's primary purpose to limit the actuality and appearance of corruption resulting from large individual financial contributions in order to find a constitutionally sufficient justification for the $1,000 contribution limitation. ***

To the extent that large contributions are given to secure a political quid pro quo from current and potential office holders, the integrity of our system of representative democracy is undermined. Although the scope of such pernicious practices can never be reliably ascertained, the deeply disturbing examples surfacing after the 1972 election demonstrate that the problem is not an illusory one. Of almost equal concern as the danger of actual quid pro quo arrangements is the impact of the appearance of corruption stemming from public awareness of the opportunities for abuse inherent in a regime of large individual financial contributions.

Appellants contend that the contribution limitations must be invalidated because bribery laws and narrowly drawn disclosure requirements constitute a less restrictive means of dealing with "proven and suspected quid pro quo arrangements." But laws making criminal the giving and taking of bribes deal with only the most blatant and specific attempts of those with money to influence governmental action. *** Congress was surely entitled to conclude that disclosure was only a partial measure, and that contribution ceilings were a necessary legislative concomitant to deal with the reality or appearance of corruption ***. We find that, under the rigorous standard of review established by our prior decisions, the weighty interests served by restricting the size of financial contributions to political candidates are sufficient to justify the limited effect upon First Amendment freedoms caused by the $1,000 contribution ceiling.

The Act's expenditure ceilings impose direct and substantial restraints on the quantity of political speech. *** We find that the governmental interest in preventing corruption and the appearance of corruption is inadequate to justify [the Act's limits on expenditures "relative to a clearly identified candidate."] *** [The] parties defending [the limits] contend that it is necessary to prevent would-be contributors from avoiding the contribution limitations by the simple expedient of paying directly for media advertisements or for other portions of the candidate's campaign activities. *** Yet such controlled or coordinated expenditures are treated as contributions rather than expenditures under the Act. *** By contrast, [the provision at issue] limits expenditures for express advocacy of candidates made totally independently of the candidate and his campaign. *** The absence of prearrangement and coordination of an expenditure with the candidate or his agent not only undermines the value of the expenditure to the candidate, but also alleviates the danger that expenditures will be given as a quid pro quo for improper commitments from the candidate. *** While the independent expenditure ceiling thus fails to serve any substantial governmental interest in stemming the reality or appearance of corruption in the electoral process, it heavily burdens core First Amendment expression.

It is argued, however, that the ancillary governmental interest in equalizing the relative ability of individuals and groups to influence the outcome of elections serves to justify the limitation on express advocacy of the election or defeat of candidates ***. But the concept that government may restrict the speech of some elements of our society in order to enhance the relative voice of others is wholly foreign to the First Amendment, which was designed "to secure 'the widest possible dissemination of information from diverse and antagonistic sources,'" and "to assure unfettered interchange of ideas for the bringing about of political and social changes desired by the people." *Sullivan*, 376 U.S., at 266, 269. The First Amendment's protection against governmental abridgment of free expression cannot properly be made to depend on a person's financial ability to engage in public discussion. *** [W]e conclude that [the] independent expenditure limitation is unconstitutional under the First Amendment.

The Act also sets limits on expenditures by a candidate "from his personal funds, or the personal funds of his immediate family, in connection with his campaigns during any calendar year." *** The candidate, no less than any other person, has a First Amendment right to engage in the discussion of public issues and vigorously and tirelessly to advocate his own election and the election of other candidates. *** The primary governmental interest served by the Act—the prevention of actual and apparent corruption of the political process—does not support the limitation on the candidate's expenditure of his own personal funds. *** Indeed, the use of personal funds reduces the candidate's dependence on outside contributions and thereby counteracts the coercive pressures and attendant risks of abuse to which the Act's contribution limitations are directed. *** The ancillary interest in equalizing the relative financial resources of candidates competing for elective office [is] clearly not sufficient to justify the provision's infringement of fundamental First Amendment rights. First, the limitation may fail to promote financial equality among candidates. A candidate who spends less of his personal resources on his campaign may nonetheless outspend his rival as a result of more successful fundraising efforts. *** Second, and more fundamentally, the First Amendment simply cannot tolerate [the Act's] restriction upon the freedom of a candidate to speak without legislative limit on behalf of his own candidacy. We therefore hold that the restriction on a candidate's personal expenditures is unconstitutional.

[The Act] places limitations on overall campaign expenditures by candidates seeking nomination for election and election to federal office. *** No governmental interest that has been suggested is sufficient to justify the restriction on the quantity of political expression imposed by [these limits]. *** The interest in alleviating the corrupting influence of large contributions is served by the Act's contribution limitations and disclosure provisions ***. The interest in equalizing the financial resources of candidates competing for federal office is no more convincing a justification for restricting the scope of federal election campaigns. Given the limitation on the size of outside contributions, the financial resources available to a candidate's campaign, like the number of volunteers recruited, will normally vary with the size and intensity of the candidate's support. There is nothing invidious, improper, or unhealthy in permitting such funds to be spent to carry the candidate's message to the electorate.

The campaign expenditure ceilings appear to be designed primarily to serve the governmental interests in reducing the allegedly skyrocketing costs of political campaigns. *** The First Amendment denies government the power to determine that spending to promote one's political views is wasteful, excessive, or unwise. In the free society ordained by our Constitution it is not the government, but the people individually as citizens and candidates and collectively as associations and political committees who must retain control over the quantity and range of debate on public issues in a political campaign.

Mr. Chief Justice BURGER, concurring in part and dissenting in part.

I agree fully with that part of the Court's opinion that holds unconstitutional the limitations the Act puts on campaign expenditures ***. Yet when it approves similarly stringent limitations on contributions, the Court ignores the reasons it finds so persuasive in the context of expenditures. For me contributions and expenditures are two sides of the same First Amendment coin.

By limiting campaign contributions, the Act restricts the amount of money that will be spent on political activity and does so directly. Appellees argue, as the Court notes, that these limits will "act as a brake on the skyrocketing cost of political campaigns." *** Limiting contributions, as a practical matter, will limit expenditures and will put an effective ceiling on the amount of political activity and debate that the Government will permit to take place. The argument that the ceiling is not, after all, very low as matters now stand gives little comfort for the future, since the Court elsewhere notes the rapid inflation in the cost of political campaigning.

Mr. Justice WHITE, concurring in part and dissenting in part.

I am [in] agreement with the Court's judgment upholding the limitations on contributions. I dissent, however, from the Court's view that the expenditure limitations [violate] the First Amendment. *** Since the contribution and expenditure limitations are neutral as to the content of speech and are not motivated by fear of the consequences of the political speech of particular candidates or of political speech in general, this case depends on whether the nonspeech interests of the Federal Government in regulating the use of money in political campaigns are sufficiently urgent to justify the incidental effects that the limitations visit upon the First Amendment interests of candidates and their supporters.

The Court [accepts] the congressional judgment that the evils of unlimited contributions are sufficiently threatening to warrant restriction regardless of the impact of the limits on the contributor's opportunity for effective speech and in turn on the total volume of the candidate's political communications by reason of his inability to accept large sums from those willing to give. The congressional judgment, which I would also accept, was that other steps must be taken to counter the corrosive effects of money in federal election campaigns. One of these steps is [the Act's limits on expenditures in support of a candidate]. *** It would make little sense to me, and apparently made none to Congress, to limit the amounts an individual may give to a candidate or spend with his approval but fail to limit the amounts that could be spent on his behalf. Yet the Court permits the former while striking down the latter limitation. *** I would take the word of those who know that limiting independent expenditures is essential to prevent transparent and widespread evasion of the contribution limits.

The Court also rejects Congress' judgment [that] the federal interest in limiting total campaign expenditures by individual candidates justifies the incidental effect on their opportunity for effective political speech. *** In this posture of the case, there is no sound basis for invalidating the expenditure limitations, so long as the purposes they serve are legitimate and sufficiently substantial, which in my view they are. In the first place, expenditure ceilings reinforce the contribution limits and help eradicate the hazard of corruption. [In addition,] expenditure limits have their own potential for preventing the corruption of federal elections themselves. [T]he corrupt use of money by candidates is as much to be feared as the corrosive influence of large contributions. *** I have little doubt in addition that limiting the total that can be spent will ease the candidate's understandable obsession with fundraising, and so free him and his staff to communicate in more places and ways unconnected with the fundraising function. *** It is also important to restore and maintain public confidence in federal elections. It is critical to obviate or dispel the impression that federal elections are purely and simply a function of money, that federal offices are bought and sold or that political races are reserved for those who have the facility and the stomach for doing whatever it takes to bring together those interests, groups, and individuals that can raise or contribute large fortunes in order to prevail at the polls.

The ceiling on candidate expenditures represents the considered judgment of Congress that elections are to be decided among candidates none of whom has overpowering advantage by reason of a huge campaign war chest. At least so long as the ceiling placed upon the candidates is not plainly too low, elections are not to turn on the difference in the amounts of money that candidates have to spend. This seems an acceptable purpose and the means chosen a common-sense way to achieve it.

I also disagree with the Court's judgment that [the Act's limit on the amount of money that a candidate or his family may spend on his campaign] violates the Constitution. Although it is true that this provision does not promote any interest in preventing the corruption of candidates, the provision [helps] to assure that only individuals with a modicum of support from others will be viable candidates. This in turn would tend to discourage any notion that the outcome of elections is primarily a function of money. Similarly, [the limit] tends to equalize access to the political arena, encouraging the less wealthy, unable to bankroll their own campaigns, to run for political office.

[Justice MARSHALL's, REHNQUIST's, and BLACKMUN'S separate opinions concurring in part and dissenting in part have been omitted.]

Points for Discussion

a. Campaign Finance Laws and Level of Scrutiny

What level of scrutiny did the Court apply to the challenged provisions? Are statutory limitations on contributions to and expenditures by political campaigns content based? Did Congress impose similar limits on contributions to charitable organizations or expenditures by companies to promote their business? If the limitations were content based, what does that suggest about the appropriate level of scrutiny? Assuming they were content based, is there something distinct about the regulated category of speech that justifies distinctive rules?

What government interests were advanced by the expenditure and contribution limitations? The per curiam opinion found that the "Act's primary purpose to limit the actuality and appearance of corruption resulting from large individual financial contributions" was a "sufficient justification for the $1,000 contribution limitation." Is that interest compelling? Wouldn't the criminalization of bribery and graft advance that interest without placing such a burden on expression? Conversely, why wasn't that interest sufficient to justify the limits on individuals' expenditures, as well?

b. Inequality

If candidates can spend as much money as they want, but are limited in how much money they can receive, are all candidates treated equally? Or are incumbents favored because they have an advantage, based on name-recognition, in raising contributions from a large number of people and an advantage, based on incumbency itself, in raising contributions from those with interests in pending and future legislation? And aren't rich candidates systematically favored over poor candidates because they can spend their own money? (If you belonged to a minority party, would you want to nominate a wealthy candidate or one who would have to raise funds from donations?) Is inequality of this kind a concern of the First Amendment?

c. *Buckley*'s Theory of the First Amendment

At the beginning of this Chapter, we suggested several visions of the theory of the First Amendment. On which theory did the Court rely in *Buckley*? Does the decision promote the marketplace of ideas, or instead make it more likely that only one or a few ideas will be available in that marketplace? Does the decision promote the ideal of accountable government, or does it instead make it more likely that electoral checks will *not* operate effectively?

d. Distinction Between Contributions and Expenditures

Although the Supreme Court continues to conclude that the government has more leeway to regulate campaign contributions than it does to regulate campaign expenditures, see, e.g., *Nixon v. Shrink Missouri Government PAC*, 528 U.S. 377 (2000), some of the Justices disagree with that approach. Justice Thomas writes:

> [U]nlike the *Buckley* Court, I believe that contribution limits infringe as directly and as seriously upon freedom of political expression and association as do expenditure limits. The protections of the First Amendment do not depend upon so fine a line as that between spending money to support a candidate or group and giving money to the candidate or group to spend for the same purpose. In principle, people and groups give money to candidates and other groups for the same reason that they spend money in support of those candidates and groups: because they share social, economic, and political beliefs and seek to have those beliefs affect governmental policy.

Colorado Republican Federal Campaign Comm. v. Federal Election Comm'n, 518 U.S. 604 (1996) (Thomas, J., concurring in part and dissenting in part). If the Court adopted this view, what alternatives would be available to Congress to limit the influence of rich donors who make large campaign contributions?

————

After the decision in <u>Buckley</u>, federal law allowed candidates for federal office to spend an unlimited amount of money on their own campaigns, but limited how much money they may receive in campaign contributions from donors. In addition, the decision in <u>Buckley</u> opened the door to other significant expenditures, at least if they did not relate to a clearly identified candidate. After the decision in <u>Buckley</u>, did Congress have any authority to limit certain types of independent expenditures? In particular, after <u>Buckley</u>, does the First Amendment prevent Congress from limiting the influence of corporations and unions in the federal elections process?

In 2003, in *McConnell v. Federal Election Comm'n*, 540 U.S. 93 (2003), the Court upheld a provision of federal law prohibiting corporations and unions from using their general treasury funds to make independent expenditures for speech defined as an "electioneering communication" or for speech expressly advocating the election or defeat of a candidate. 2 U.S.C. § 441b. The Court revisited that holding in the case that follows.

————

Citizens United v. Federal Election Commission

130 S.Ct. 876 (2010)

Justice KENNEDY delivered the opinion of the Court.

Citizens United is a nonprofit corporation [with] an annual budget of about $12 million. Most of its funds are from donations by individuals; but, in addition, it accepts a small portion of its funds from for-profit corporations. In January 2008, Citizens United released a film entitled *Hillary: The Movie*, [a] 90-minute documentary about then-Senator Hillary Clinton, who was a candidate in the Democratic Party's 2008 Presidential primary elections. *** *Hillary* was released in theaters and on DVD, but Citizens United wanted to increase distribution by making it available through video-on-demand. [To] promote the film, it produced two 10-second ads and one 30-second ad for *Hillary*. Each ad includes a short (and, in our view, pejorative) statement about Senator Clinton, followed by the name of the movie and the movie's Website address. Citizens United desired to promote the video-on-demand offering by running advertisements on broadcast and cable television.

Before the Bipartisan Campaign Reform Act of 2002 (BCRA), federal law prohibited—and still does prohibit—corporations and unions from using general treasury funds to make direct contributions to candidates or independent expenditures that expressly advocate the election or defeat of a candidate, through any form of media, in connection with certain qualified federal elections. 2 U.S.C. § 441b (2000 ed.). BCRA amended § 441b to prohibit any "electioneering communication" as well. 2 U.S.C. § 441b(b)(2) (2006 ed.). An electioneering communication is defined as "any broadcast, cable, or satellite communication" that "refers to a clearly identified candidate for Federal office" and is made within 30 days of a primary or 60 days of a general election. § 434(f)(3)(A). *** Corporations and unions are barred from using their general treasury funds for express advocacy or electioneering communications. They may establish, however, a "separate segregated fund" (known as a political action committee, or PAC) for these purposes. 2 U.S.C. § 441b(b)(2). The moneys received by the segregated fund are limited to donations from stockholders and employees of the corporation or, in the case of unions, members of the union. *Ibid.*

Citizens United wanted to make *Hillary* available through video-on-demand within 30 days of the 2008 primary elections. It feared, however, that both the film and the ads would be covered by § 441b's ban on corporate-funded independent expenditures, thus subjecting the corporation to civil and criminal penalties under § 437g. In December 2007, Citizens United sought declaratory and injunctive relief against the FEC [arguing that the ban violated the First Amendment. A three-judge district court impaneled under BCRA granted the FEC's motion for summary judgment.]

[*Hillary*,] in essence, is a feature-length negative advertisement that urges viewers to vote against Senator Clinton for President. In light of historical footage, interviews with persons critical of her, and voiceover narration, the film would be understood by most viewers as an extended criticism of Senator Clinton's character and her fitness for the office of the Presidency. *** [T]he film qualifies as the functional equivalent of express advocacy [against a specific candidate, and thus falls within § 441b].

The law before us is an outright ban, backed by criminal sanctions. Section 441b makes it a felony for all corporations—including nonprofit advocacy corporations—either to expressly advocate the election or defeat of candidates or to broadcast electioneering communications within 30 days of a primary election and 60 days of a general election. *** Section 441b is a ban on corporate speech notwithstanding the fact that a PAC created by a corporation can still speak. A PAC is a separate association from the corporation. So the PAC exemption from § 441b's expenditure ban does not allow corporations to speak. Even if a PAC could somehow allow a corporation to speak, [the] option to form PACs does not alleviate the First Amendment problems with § 441b. PACs are burdensome alternatives; they are expensive to administer and subject to extensive regulations. *** This might explain why fewer than 2,000 of the millions of corporations in this country have PACs. *** Section 441b's prohibition on corporate independent expenditures is thus a ban on speech.

[N]ot until 1947 did Congress first prohibit independent expenditures by corporations and labor unions in § 304 of the Labor Management Relations Act 1947 (codified at 2 U.S.C. § 251 (1946 ed., Supp. I)). *** For almost three decades thereafter, the Court did not reach the question whether restrictions on corporate and union expenditures are constitutional.

In *Buckley v. Valeo*, 424 U.S. 1 (1976), the Court [invalidated an independent expenditure ban, 18 U.S.C. § 608(e) (1970 ed., Supp. V), that applied to individuals as well as corporations and labor unions. The Court in _Buckley_ did not consider a different provision of the Federal Election Campaign Act, 18 U.S.C. § 610, that banned corporate and union independent expenditures.] Had § 610 been challenged in the wake of _Buckley_, however, it could not have been squared with the reasoning and analysis of that precedent. Notwithstanding this precedent, Congress recodified § 610's corporate and union expenditure ban at 2 U.S.C. § 441b four months after _Buckley_ was decided. Section 441b is the independent expenditure restriction challenged here.

Less than two years after _Buckley_, *First Nat. Bank of Boston v. Bellotti*, 435 U.S. 765 (1978), *** struck down a state-law prohibition on corporate independent expenditures related to referenda issues. *** [T]he reasoning and holding of *Bellotti* [rested] on the principle that the Government lacks the power to ban corporations from speaking. _Bellotti_ did not address the constitutionality of the State's [separate] ban on corporate independent expenditures to support candidates. In our view, however, that restriction would have been unconstitutional under _Bellotti_'s central principle: that the First Amendment does not allow political speech restrictions based on a speaker's corporate identity.

Take Note

Some of the cases that we have seen so far in this Chapter involved protected speech by corporations. See, e.g., *New York Times Co. v. Sullivan*, 376 U.S. 254 (1964). In what way did the First Amendment claims in those cases differ from the claim in this case?

Thus the law stood until *Austin v. Michigan Chamber of Commerce*, 494 U.S. 652 (1990). *** There, the Michigan Chamber of Commerce sought to use general treasury funds to run a newspaper ad supporting a specific candidate. Michigan law, however, prohibited corporate independent expenditures that supported or opposed any candidate for state office. *** The Court sustained the speech prohibition. To bypass _Buckley_ and _Bellotti_, the _Austin_ Court *** found a compelling governmental interest in preventing "the corrosive and distorting effects of immense aggregations of wealth that are accumulated with the help of the corporate form and that have little or no correlation to the public's support for the corporation's political ideas."

As for _Austin_'s antidistortion rationale, the Government does little to defend it. And with good reason, for the rationale cannot support § 441b. If the First Amendment has any force, it prohibits Congress from fining or jailing citizens, or associations of citizens, for simply engaging in political speech. If the antidistortion rationale were to be accepted, however, it would permit Government to ban political speech simply because the speaker is an association that has taken on the corporate form. *** If _Austin_ were correct, the Government could prohibit a corporation from expressing political views in media beyond those presented here, such as by printing books.

Austin sought to defend the antidistortion rationale as a means to prevent corporations from obtaining "an unfair advantage in the political marketplace" by using "resources amassed in the economic marketplace." 494 U.S., at 659. But _Buckley_ rejected the premise that the Government has an interest "in equalizing the relative ability of individuals and groups to influence the outcome of elections." <u>424 U.S., at 48</u>. *** The rule that political speech cannot be limited based on a speaker's wealth is a necessary consequence of the premise that the First Amendment generally prohibits the suppression of political speech based on the speaker's identity.

> ### Food for Thought
>
> Where does the principle that the government may not suppress speech based on the speaker's identity come from? Is such regulation necessarily tantamount to content-based regulation? If not, why is it problematic?

Austin's antidistortion rationale would produce the dangerous, and unacceptable, consequence that Congress could ban political speech of media corporations. Media corporations are now exempt from § 441b's ban on corporate expenditures. See 2 U.S.C. §§ 431(9)(B)(i), 434(f)(3)(B)(i). Yet media corporations accumulate wealth with the help of the corporate form, the largest media corporations have "immense aggregations of wealth," and the views expressed by media corporations often "have little or no correlation to the public's support" for those views. Thus, under the Government's reasoning, wealthy media corporations could have their voices diminished to put them on par with other media entities. *** The law's exception for media corporations is, on its own terms, all but an admission of the invalidity of the antidistortion rationale.

There is simply no support for the view that the First Amendment, as originally understood, would permit the suppression of political speech by media corporations. *** The First Amendment [was] understood as a response to the repression of speech and the press that had existed in England and the heavy taxes on the press that were imposed in the colonies. *** The Framers may have been unaware of certain types of speakers or forms of communication, but that does not mean that those speakers and media are entitled to less First Amendment protection than those types of speakers and media that provided the means of communicating political ideas when the Bill of Rights was adopted.

[T]he Government falls back on the argument that corporate political speech can be banned in order to prevent corruption or its appearance. In *Buckley*, the Court found this interest "sufficiently important" to allow limits on contributions but did not extend that reasoning to expenditure limits. [W]e now conclude that independent expenditures, including those made by corporations, do not give rise to corruption or the appearance of corruption. *** [I]ndependent expenditures do not lead to, or create the appearance of, *quid pro quo* corruption. In fact, there is only scant evidence that independent expenditures even ingratiate. Ingratiation and access, in any event, are not corruption.

If elected officials succumb to improper influences from independent expenditures; if they surrender their best judgment; and if they put expediency before principle, then surely there is cause for concern. *** The remedies enacted by law, however, must comply with the First Amendment; and, it is our law and our tradition that more speech, not less, is the governing rule. *** Here Congress has created categorical bans on speech that are asymmetrical to preventing *quid pro quo* corruption.

Austin should be and now is overruled. We return to the principle established in *Buckley* and *Bellotti* that the Government may not suppress political speech on the basis of the speaker's corporate identity. *** Section 441b's restrictions on corporate independent expenditures are therefore invalid and cannot be applied to *Hillary*. Given our conclusion we are further required to overrule the part of *McConnell* that upheld [BCRA's] extension of § 441b's restrictions on corporate independent expenditures.

[The Court rejected the petitioner's challenge to BCRA's disclaimer provision, which requires televised electioneering communications funded by anyone other than a candidate to identify clearly who is responsible for the communication, 2 U.S.C. § 441d(d)(2), and BCRA's disclosure provision, which requires any person who spends more than $10,000 on electioneering communications within a calendar year to file a statement with the FEC identifying the person making the expenditure, the amount of the expenditure, the election to which the communication was directed, and the names of certain contributors, 2 U.S.C. § 434(f)(1) & (2). The Court concluded, "Disclaimer and disclosure requirements may burden the ability to speak, but they 'impose no ceiling on campaign-related activities,' and 'do not prevent anyone from speaking.'"[2]]

[Chief Justice ROBERTS's concurring opinion is omitted.]

Justice SCALIA, with whom Justice ALITO joins, and with whom Justice THOMAS joins in part, concurring.

I write separately to address Justice STEVENS' [dissent, which] purports to show that today's decision is not supported by the original understanding of the First Amendment. The dissent attempts this demonstration, however, in splendid isolation from the text of the First Amendment. It never shows why "the freedom of speech" that was the right of Englishmen did not include the freedom to speak in association with other individuals, including association in the corporate form.

Instead of taking this straightforward approach to determining the Amendment's meaning, the dissent embarks on a detailed exploration of the Framers' views about the "role of corporations in society." The Framers didn't like corporations, the dissent concludes, and therefore it follows (as night the day) that corporations had no rights of free speech. Of course the Framers' personal affection or disaffection for corporations is relevant only insofar as it can be thought to be reflected in the understood meaning of the text they enacted—not, as the dissent suggests, as a freestanding substitute for that text.

[In any event, despite] the corporation-hating quotations the dissent has dredged up, it is far from clear that by the end of the 18th century corporations were despised. If so, how came there to be so many of them? *** There were approximately 335 charters issued to business corporations in the United States by the end of the 18th century. [W]hat seems like a small number by today's standards surely does not indicate the relative importance of corporations when the Nation was considerably smaller. *** Even if we thought it proper to apply the dissent's approach of excluding from First Amendment

---

[2] Justice Thomas joined all of the Court's opinion except the part upholding the disclaimer and disclosure requirements, which he concluded "abridge the right to anonymous speech." —*Eds.*

coverage what the Founders disliked, and even if we agreed that the Founders disliked founding-era corporations; modern corporations might not qualify for exclusion. Most of the Founders' resentment towards corporations was directed at the state-granted monopoly privileges that individually chartered corporations enjoyed. Modern corporations do not have such privileges, and would probably have been favored by most of our enterprising Founders—excluding, perhaps, Thomas Jefferson and others favoring perpetuation of an agrarian society. Moreover, [a]t the time of the founding, religious, educational, and literary corporations were incorporated under general incorporation statutes, much as business corporations are today. *** Were all of these silently excluded from the protections of the First Amendment?

The dissent says that when the Framers "constitutionalized the right to free speech in the First Amendment, it was the free speech of individual Americans that they had in mind." That is no doubt true. All the provisions of the Bill of Rights set forth the rights of individual men and women—not, for example, of trees or polar bears. But the individual person's right to speak includes the right to speak *in association with other individual persons.* Surely the dissent does not believe that speech by the Republican Party or the Democratic Party can be censored because it is not the speech of "an individual American." It is the speech of many individual Americans, who have associated in a common cause, giving the leadership of the party the right to speak on their behalf. The association of individuals in a business corporation is no different—or at least it cannot be denied the right to speak on the simplistic ground that it is not "an individual American."

[The First Amendment] is written in terms of "speech," not speakers. Its text offers no foothold for excluding any category of speaker, from single individuals to partnerships of individuals, to unincorporated associations of individuals, to incorporated associations of individuals—and the dissent offers no evidence about the original meaning of the text to support any such exclusion.

> **Food for Thought**
>
> How helpful is the text of the First Amendment in resolving the question in this case? The Court, for example, has consistently held that the Amendment limits the action of the President and other executive officials, even though the text refers only to "Congress." Is there reason to think that the text is clearer with respect to the question at issue here?

We are therefore simply left with the question whether the speech at issue in this case is "speech" covered by the First Amendment. No one says otherwise. A documentary film critical of a potential Presidential candidate is core political speech, and its nature as such does not change simply because it was funded by a corporation.

Justice STEVENS, with whom Justice GINSBURG, Justice BREYER, and Justice SOTO-MAYOR join, concurring in part and dissenting in part.

Pervading the Court's analysis is the ominous image of a "categorical ba[n]" on corporate speech. *** This characterization is highly misleading, and needs to be corrected. *** Under BCRA, any corporation's "stockholders and their families and its executive or administrative personnel and their families" can pool their resources [in a PAC] to finance electioneering communications. 2 U.S.C. § 441b(b)(4)(A)(i). A significant and growing number of corporations avail themselves of this option; during the most recent election cycle, corporate and union PACs raised nearly a billion dollars. Administering a PAC entails some administrative burden, but so does complying with the disclaimer, disclosure, and reporting requirements that the Court today upholds, and no one has suggested that the burden is severe for a sophisticated for-profit corporation. *** [T]he majority's incessant talk of a "ban" aims at a straw man.

The second pillar of the Court's opinion is its assertion that "the Government cannot restrict political speech based on the speaker's . . . identity." *** Apart perhaps from measures designed to protect the press, [the text of the First Amendment] might seem to permit no distinctions of any kind. Yet in a variety of contexts, we have held that speech can be regulated differentially on account of the speaker's identity, when identity is understood in categorical or institutional terms. The Government routinely places special restrictions on the speech rights of students, prisoners, members of the Armed Forces, foreigners, and its own employees. When such restrictions are justified by a legitimate governmental interest, they do not necessarily raise constitutional problems.

> **Make the Connection**
>
> We will consider the speech of government employees later in this Chapter.

The same logic applies to this case with additional force because it is the identity of corporations, rather than individuals, that the Legislature has taken into account. *** Campaign finance distinctions based on corporate identity tend to be less worrisome [because] the "speakers" are not natural persons, much less members of our political community, and the governmental interests are of the highest order. Furthermore, when corporations, as a class, are distinguished from noncorporations, as a class, there is a lesser risk that regulatory distinctions will reflect invidious discrimination or political favoritism.

A third fulcrum of the Court's opinion is the idea that *Austin* and *McConnell* are radical outliers, "aberration[s]," in our First Amendment tradition. The Court has it exactly backwards. It is today's holding that is the radical departure from what had been settled First Amendment law. *** To the extent that the Framers' views are discernible and relevant to the disposition of this case, they would appear to cut strongly against the majority's position.

This is not only because the Framers and their contemporaries conceived of speech more narrowly than we now think of it, but also because they held very different views about the nature of the First Amendment right and the role of corporations in society. Those few corporations that existed at the founding were authorized by grant of a special legislative charter. *** Corporations were created, supervised, and conceptualized as quasi-public entities, "designed to serve a social function for the state." The individualized charter mode of incorporation reflected the "cloud of disfavor under which corporations labored" in the early years of this Nation. Thomas Jefferson famously fretted that corporations would subvert the Republic. General incorporation statutes, and widespread acceptance of business corporations as socially useful actors, did not emerge until the 1800's.

The Framers thus took it as a given that corporations could be comprehensively regulated in the service of the public welfare. Unlike our colleagues, they had little trouble distinguishing corporations from human beings, and when they constitutionalized the right to free speech in the First Amendment, it was the free speech of individual Americans that they had in mind. While individuals might join together to exercise their speech rights, business corporations, at least, were plainly not seen as facilitating such associational or expressive ends. In light of these background practices and understandings, it seems to me implausible that the Framers believed "the freedom of speech" would extend equally to all corporate speakers, much less that it would preclude legislatures from taking limited measures to guard against corporate capture of elections.

In fairness, our campaign finance jurisprudence has never attended very closely to the views of the Framers, whose political universe differed profoundly from that of today. [But] in light of the Court's effort to cast itself as guardian of ancient values, it pays to remember that nothing in our constitutional history dictates today's outcome. To the contrary, [a] century of more recent history puts to rest any notion that today's ruling is faithful to our First Amendment tradition. At the federal level, the express distinction between corporate and individual political spending on elections stretches back to 1907, when Congress passed the Tillman Act banning all corporate contributions to candidates.

In the Court's view, _Buckley_ and _Bellotti_ decisively rejected the possibility of distinguishing corporations from natural persons in the 1970's. [But it] is implausible to think, as the majority suggests, that _Buckley_ covertly invalidated FECA's separate corporate and union campaign expenditure restriction, even though that restriction had been on the books for decades before _Buckley_ and would remain on the books, undisturbed, for decades after. [And] _Bellotti_ ruled, in an explicit limitation on the scope of its holding, that "our consideration of a corporation's right to speak on issues of general public interest implies no comparable right in the quite different context of participation in a political campaign for election to public office." 435 U.S., at 788, n. 26. *** The _Bellotti_ Court confronted a dramatically different factual situation from the one that confronts us in this case: a state statute that barred business corporations' expenditures on some referenda but not others. *** _Bellotti_ thus involved a _viewpoint-discriminatory_ statute, created to effect a particular policy outcome. *** _Austin_ and _McConnell_, then, sit perfectly well with _Bellotti_.

[I] come at last to the interests that are at stake. Undergirding the majority's approach to the merits is the claim that the only "sufficiently important governmental interest in preventing corruption or the appearance of corruption" is one that is "limited to *quid pro quo* corruption." [But corruption] operates along a spectrum, and the majority's apparent belief that *quid pro quo* arrangements can be neatly demarcated from other improper influences does not accord with the theory or reality of politics. It certainly does not accord with the record Congress developed in passing BCRA, a record that stands as a remarkable testament to the energy and ingenuity with which corporations, unions, lobbyists, and politicians may go about scratching each other's backs—and which amply supported Congress' determination to target a limited set of especially destructive practices. *** Starting today, corporations with large war chests to deploy on electioneering may find democratically elected bodies becoming much more attuned to their interests.

The majority seems oblivious to the simple truth that laws such as [§ 441b] do not merely pit the anticorruption interest against the First Amendment, but also pit competing First Amendment values against each other. *** The Court's blinkered and aphoristic approach to the First Amendment may well promote corporate power at the cost of the individual and collective self-expression the Amendment was meant to serve.

At bottom, the Court's opinion is [a] rejection of the common sense of the American people, who have recognized a need to prevent corporations from undermining self-government since the founding, and who have fought against the distinctive corrupting potential of corporate electioneering since the days of Theodore Roosevelt. It is a strange time to repudiate that common sense. While American democracy is imperfect, few outside the majority of this Court would have thought its flaws included a dearth of corporate money in politics.

Points for Discussion

a. Theory of the First Amendment

What is the Court's theory of the First Amendment? Is the Court concerned with the corporate speaker's right to communicate or with the public's right to hear the speaker's message? Is there a difference? If so, does Justice Stevens have a different vision of the First Amendment?

b. The Reach of the Ban on Corporate Speech

Many advocacy organizations from across the political spectrum—including the Sierra Club, the National Rifle Association, and the American Civil Liberties Union—are organized as non-profit corporations. The provision at issue in *Citizens United* thus prohibited such organizations from expressly advocating the election or defeat of a candidate within 60 days of an election (or 30 days of a primary election). Does this fact strengthen the Court's conclusion, or instead justify Congress's decision to limit corporate independent expenditures?

c. State of the Union Address

At the 2010 State of the Union address, President Obama criticized the Court's decision in *Citizens United*, saying: "With all due deference to the separation of powers, last week the Supreme Court reversed a century of law that I believe will open the floodgates for special interests—including foreign corporations—to spend without limit in our elections." Justice Alito, who was in the audience, appeared to mouth the words, "Not true." Who was correct? Was either comment inappropriate?

---

8. Speech of Public Employees

Suppose that an employee makes comments that his or her employer does not like. For example, the employee might criticize the employer's management style or say negative things about his co-workers' performance. If the employer is a private business, the employer generally may fire the employee for these comments without violating the First Amendment. As we will see in Chapter 19, under the state action doctrine, the First Amendment applies to government institutions and officials, but does not apply to non-state actors like private businesses.

When the employer is the government, the situation is more complicated. Under the First Amendment, the government generally cannot take adverse actions against individuals based upon the content of their speech. In addition, as we saw in the first part of this Chapter, "the government 'may not deny a benefit to a person on a basis that infringes his constitutionally protected *** freedom of speech' even if he has no entitlement to that benefit." *Board of Commissioners, Wabaunsee County v. Umbehr*, 518 U.S. 668, 674 (1996). The Court thus has, at least as a matter of theory, rejected the absolutist premise behind Justice Holmes's famous statement, in a case upholding the termination of a police officer for engaging in political activities, that the "petitioner may have a constitutional right to talk politics, but he has no constitutional right to be a policeman." *McAuliffe v. New Bedford*, 29 N.E. 517 (Mass. 1892).

Yet the government—like a private employer—needs some ability to control the speech and conduct of its employees. The Supreme Court balanced these competing concerns in *Connick v. Myers*, 461 U.S. 138 (1983). In that case, a district attorney fired an assistant district attorney after she prepared and distributed a questionnaire soliciting the views of other staff on office morale, confidence in supervisors, and other subjects. The assistant district attorney claimed that her firing violated the First Amendment. In assessing her claim, the Supreme Court drew a distinction. Adverse personnel actions based upon speech about private concerns generally do not implicate the First Amendment. But if an employee speaks on matters of public concern, the government may take an adverse action only if the government's needs as an employer exceed the employee's interest in free speech. The Court pursued this balancing approach in other cases, as well. *See, e.g.*, *Pickering v. Board of Ed. of Township High School Dist. 205, Will Cty.*, 391 U.S. 563, 568 (1968).

In the following case, the Supreme Court further refined this test. It held that speech about matters of public concern is protected only if the employee is speaking in a private capacity. In reading the case, think carefully about what this new limitation means.

———————————

Garcetti v. Ceballos

547 U.S. 410 (2006)

Justice KENNEDY delivered the opinion of the Court.

It is well settled that "a State cannot condition public employment on a basis that infringes the employee's constitutionally protected interest in freedom of expression." *Connick v. Myers,* 461 U.S. 138, 142 (1983). The question presented by the instant case is whether the First Amendment protects a government employee from discipline based on speech made pursuant to the employee's official duties.

Respondent Richard Ceballos has been employed since 1989 as a deputy district attorney for the Los Angeles County District Attorney's Office. During the period relevant to this case, Ceballos was a calendar deputy in the office's Pomona branch, and in this capacity he exercised certain supervisory responsibilities over other lawyers. In February 2000, a defense attorney contacted Ceballos about a pending criminal case. The defense attorney said there were inaccuracies in an affidavit used to obtain a critical search warrant. The attorney informed Ceballos that he had filed a motion to traverse, or challenge, the warrant, but he also wanted Ceballos to review the case. According to Ceballos, it was not unusual for defense attorneys to ask calendar deputies to investigate aspects of pending cases.

After examining the affidavit and visiting the location it described, Ceballos determined the affidavit contained serious misrepresentations. The affidavit called a long driveway what Ceballos thought should have been referred to as a separate roadway. Ceballos also questioned the affidavit's statement that tire tracks led from a stripped-down truck to the premises covered by the warrant. His doubts arose from his conclusion that the roadway's composition in some places made it difficult or impossible to leave visible tire tracks.

Ceballos spoke on the telephone to the warrant affiant, a deputy sheriff from the Los Angeles County Sheriff's Department, but he did not receive a satisfactory explanation for the perceived inaccuracies. He relayed his findings to his supervisors, petitioners Carol Najera and Frank Sundstedt, and followed up by preparing a disposition memorandum. The memo explained Ceballos' concerns and recommended dismissal of the case. On March 2, 2000, Ceballos submitted the memo to Sundstedt for his review. ***

Despite Ceballos' concerns, Sundstedt decided to proceed with the prosecution, pending disposition of the defense motion to traverse. The trial court held a hearing on the motion. Ceballos was called by the defense and recounted his observations about the affidavit, but the trial court rejected the challenge to the warrant.

Ceballos claims that in the aftermath of these events he was subjected to a series of retaliatory employment actions. The actions included reassignment from his calendar deputy position to a trial deputy position, transfer to another courthouse, and denial of a promotion. [Ceballos claimed that the petitioners violated the First and Fourteenth Amendments by retaliating against him based on his memo of March 2.]

The Court has made clear that public employees do not surrender all their First Amendment rights by reason of their employment. Rather, the First Amendment protects a public employee's right, in certain circumstances, to speak as a citizen addressing matters of public concern. See, *e.g. Pickering v. Board of Ed. of Township High School Dist. 205, Will Cty.*, 391 U.S. 563, 568 (1968).

Pickering provides a useful starting point in explaining the Court's doctrine. There the relevant speech was a teacher's letter to a local newspaper addressing issues including the funding policies of his school board. "The problem in any case," the Court stated, "is to arrive at a balance between the interests of the teacher, as a citizen, in commenting upon matters of public concern and the interest of the State, as an employer, in promoting the efficiency of the public services it performs through its employees." Id. at 568. The Court found the teacher's speech "neither [was] shown nor can be presumed to have in any way either impeded the teacher's proper performance of his daily duties in the classroom or to have interfered with the regular operation of the schools generally." Id. at 568. Thus, the Court concluded that "the interest of the school administration in limiting teachers' opportunities to contribute to public debate is not significantly greater than its interest in limiting a similar contribution by any member of the general public." Id. at 573.

Pickering and the cases decided in its wake identify two inquiries to guide interpretation of the constitutional protections accorded to public employee speech. The first requires determining whether the employee spoke as a citizen on a matter of public concern. If the answer is no, the employee has no First Amendment cause of action based on his or her employer's reaction to the speech. See Connick, 461 U.S. at 147. If the answer is yes, then the possibility of a First Amendment claim arises. The question becomes whether the relevant government entity had an adequate justification for treating the employee differently from any other member of the general public. See Pickering, 391 U.S., at 568. This consideration reflects the importance of the relationship between the speaker's expressions and employment. A government entity has broader discretion to restrict speech when it acts in its role as employer, but the restrictions it imposes must be directed at speech that has some potential to affect the entity's operations.

When a citizen enters government service, the citizen by necessity must accept certain limitations on his or her freedom. Government employers, like private employers, need a significant degree of control over their employees' words and actions; without it, there would be little chance for the efficient provision of public services. Public employees, moreover, often occupy trusted positions in society. When they speak out, they can express views that contravene governmental policies or impair the proper performance of governmental functions.

Food for Thought

The government can speak only through the individuals who work for it. Does the government have an independent interest in controlling its own speech? If so, is that interest protected by the First Amendment, or is it merely an interest relevant to determining whether the government has violated the Amendment?

At the same time, the Court has recognized that a citizen who works for the government is nonetheless a citizen. The First Amendment limits the ability of a public employer to leverage the employment relationship to restrict, incidentally or intentionally, the liberties employees enjoy in their capacities as private citizens. So long as employees are speaking as citizens about matters of public concern, they must face only those speech restrictions that are necessary for their employers to operate efficiently and effectively. *See, e.g., Connick,* 461 U.S. at 147 ("Our responsibility is to ensure that citizens are not deprived of fundamental rights by virtue of working for the government").

With these principles in mind we turn to the instant case. Respondent Ceballos believed the affidavit used to obtain a search warrant contained serious misrepresentations. He conveyed his opinion and recommendation in a memo to his supervisor. That Ceballos expressed his views inside his office, rather than publicly, is not dispositive. Employees in some cases may receive First Amendment protection for expressions made at work. See, *e.g., Givhan v. Western Line Consol. School Dist.,* 439 U.S. 410, 414 (1979). Many citizens do much of their talking inside their respective workplaces, and it would not serve the goal of treating public employees like "any member of the general public," *Pickering,* 391 U.S., at 573, to hold that all speech within the office is automatically exposed to restriction.

The memo concerned the subject matter of Ceballos' employment, but this, too, is nondispositive. The First Amendment protects some expressions related to the speaker's job. As the Court noted in *Pickering:* "Teachers are, as a class, the members of a community most likely to have informed and definite opinions as to how funds allotted to the operation of the schools should be spent. Accordingly, it is essential that they be able to speak out freely on such questions without fear of retaliatory dismissal." 391 U.S., at 572. The same is true of many other categories of public employees.

The controlling factor in Ceballos' case is that his expressions were made pursuant to his duties as a calendar deputy. That consideration—the fact that Ceballos spoke as a prosecutor fulfilling a responsibility to advise his supervisor about how best to proceed with a pending case—distinguishes Ceballos' case from those in which the First Amendment provides protection against discipline. We hold that when public employees make statements pursuant to their official duties, the employees are not speaking as citizens for First Amendment purposes, and the Constitution does not insulate their communications from employer discipline.

Ceballos wrote his disposition memo because that is part of what he, as a calendar deputy, was employed to do. It is immaterial whether he experienced some personal gratification from writing the memo; his First Amendment rights do not depend on his job satisfaction. The significant point is that the memo was written pursuant to Ceballos' official duties. Restricting speech that owes its existence to a public employee's professional responsibilities does not infringe any liberties the employee might have enjoyed as a private citizen. It simply reflects the exercise of employer control over what the employer itself has commissioned or created. * * *

Justice STEVENS, dissenting.

The proper answer to the question "whether the First Amendment protects a government employee from discipline based on speech made pursuant to the employee's official duties," is "Sometimes," not "Never." Of course a supervisor may take corrective action when such speech is "inflammatory or misguided." But what if it is just unwelcome speech because it reveals facts that the supervisor would rather not have anyone else discover?[2]

Justice SOUTER, with whom Justice STEVENS and Justice GINSBURG join, dissenting.

I agree with the majority that a government employer has substantial interests in effectuating its chosen policy and objectives, and in demanding competence, honesty, and judgment from employees who speak for it in doing their work. But I would hold that private and public interests in addressing official wrongdoing and threats to health and safety can outweigh the government's stake in the efficient implementation of policy, and when they do public employees who speak on these matters in the course of their duties should be eligible to claim First Amendment protection.

Justice BREYER, dissenting.

> **FYI**
>
> In *Brady*, the Court held that prosecutors must disclose to the defense evidence that is material to guilt or punishment.

[In this case, the] respondent, a government lawyer, complained of retaliation, in part, on the basis of speech contained in his disposition memorandum that he says fell within the scope of his obligations under *Brady v. Maryland*, 373 U.S. 83 (1963). The facts present two special circumstances that together justify First Amendment review.

First, the speech at issue is professional speech—the speech of a lawyer. Such speech is subject to independent regulation by canons of the profession. Those canons provide an obligation to speak in certain instances. And where that is so, the government's own interest in forbidding that speech is diminished. *** Second, the Constitution itself here imposes speech obligations upon the government's professional employee. A prosecutor has a constitutional obligation to learn of, to preserve, and to communicate with the defense about exculpatory and impeachment evidence in the government's possession. ***

Where professional and special constitutional obligations are both present, the need to protect the employee's speech is augmented, the need for broad government authority to control that speech is likely diminished, and administrable standards are quite likely available. Hence, I would find that the Constitution mandates special protection of employee speech in such circumstances. Thus I would apply the *Pickering* balancing test here.

---

[2] See, *e.g., Branton v. Dallas*, 272 F.3d 730 (5th Cir. 2001) (police internal investigator demoted by police chief after bringing the false testimony of a fellow officer to the attention of a city official); *Miller v. Jones*, 444 F.3d 929, 936 (7th Cir. 2006) (police officer demoted after opposing the police chief's attempt to "us[e] his official position to coerce a financially independent organization into a potentially ruinous merger"); *Delgado v. Jones*, 282 F.3d 511 (7th Cir. 2002) (police officer sanctioned for reporting criminal activity that implicated a local political figure who was a good friend of the police chief); *Herts v. Smith*, 345 F.3d 581 (8th Cir. 2003) (school district official's contract was not renewed after she gave frank testimony about the district's desegregation efforts); *Kincade v. Blue Springs*, 64 F.3d 389 (8th Cir. 1995) (engineer fired after reporting to his supervisors that contractors were failing to complete dam-related projects and that the resulting dam might be structurally unstable); *Fox v. District of Columbia*, 83 F.3d 1491, 1494 (D.C. Cir. 1996) (D.C. Lottery Board security officer fired after informing the police about a theft made possible by "rather drastic managerial ineptitude").

Points for Discussion

a. Official Capacity v. Private Capacity

Under the Court's approach in <u>Garcetti</u>, public employees' statements pursuant to their official duties are not protected by the First Amendment. How does the Court tell whether a particular statement was made in that capacity? Suppose, for example, that Mr. Ceballos had talked to a reporter or sent a letter to the editor of a local newspaper at the same time that he prepared the memo in question, and that he had then been fired. Would he have been fired for speaking in his capacity as a private citizen or in his official capacity? How would a court make that determination?

b. Whistleblowers

Does the Court's decision in <u>Garcetti</u> make it more difficult for "whistleblowers" publicly to disclose government wrongdoing? If so, is the Court's decision consistent with the theory that the First Amendment is designed to ensure, among other things, the means for citizens to hold their government accountable for bad decision-making and wrongdoing?

Hypothetical

Most law school deans are professors who serve in the role of dean at the pleasure of the university president. The president of the university, in other words, can ask a dean at any time to step down and assume a non-leadership position on the faculty. Suppose that the dean of the law school at a state university writes a well-researched but controversial law review article on a sensitive political topic. Unhappy with what the dean has written, and fearing condemnation by donors, the president of the university asks the dean to step down. Has the university president violated the dean's First Amendment rights?

---

9. Other Categories?

In this section, we have considered whether there are categories of speech, defined by their content, that are outside of the protection of the First Amendment. Are there other such categories that the Court has not yet identified? If so, how will the Court go about identifying them? Consider the case that follows.

United States v. Stevens

130 S.Ct. 1577 (2010)

Chief Justice ROBERTS delivered the opinion of the Court.

18 U.S.C. § 48 establishes a criminal penalty of up to five years in prison for anyone who knowingly "creates, sells, or possesses a depiction of animal cruelty," if done "for commercial gain" in interstate or foreign commerce. § 48(a). A depiction of "animal cruelty" is defined as one "in which a living animal is intentionally maimed, mutilated, tortured, wounded, or killed," if that conduct violates federal or state law where "the creation, sale, or possession takes place." § 48(c)(1). In what is referred to as the "exceptions clause," the law exempts from prohibition any depiction "that has serious religious, political, scientific, educational, journalistic, historical, or artistic value." § 48(b).

The legislative background of § 48 focused primarily on the interstate market for "crush videos." According to the House Committee Report on the bill, such videos feature the intentional torture and killing of helpless animals, including cats, dogs, monkeys, mice, and hamsters. H.R.Rep. No. 106-397, p. 2 (1999). Crush videos often depict women slowly crushing animals to death "with their bare feet or while wearing high heeled shoes," sometimes while "talking to the animals in a kind of dominatrix patter" over "[t]he cries and squeals of the animals, obviously in great pain." *Ibid.* Apparently these depictions "appeal to persons with a very specific sexual fetish who find them sexually arousing or otherwise exciting." *Id.,* at 2-3. The acts depicted in crush videos are typically prohibited by the animal cruelty laws enacted by all 50 States and the District of Columbia. But crush videos rarely disclose the participants' identities, inhibiting prosecution of the underlying conduct.

This case, however, involves an application of § 48 to depictions of animal fighting. *** Respondent Robert J. Stevens ran a business, "Dogs of Velvet and Steel," and an associated Web site, through which he sold videos of pit bulls engaging in dogfights and attacking other animals. Among these videos were Japan Pit Fights and Pick-A-Winna: A Pit Bull Documentary, which include contemporary footage of dogfights in Japan (where such conduct is allegedly legal) as well as footage of American dogfights from the 1960's and 1970's. A third video, Catch Dogs and Country Living, depicts the use of pit bulls to hunt wild boar, as well as a "gruesome" scene of a pit bull attacking a domestic farm pig. On the basis of these videos, Stevens was indicted on three counts of violating § 48. Stevens moved to dismiss the indictment, arguing that § 48 is facially invalid under the First Amendment. [The Court of Appeals held that Section 48 was facially invalid.]

The Government's primary submission is that § 48 necessarily complies with the Constitution because the banned depictions of animal cruelty, as a class, are categorically unprotected by the First Amendment. We disagree.

"[A]s a general matter, the First Amendment means that government has no power to restrict expression because of its message, its ideas, its subject matter, or its content." *Ashcroft v. American Civil Liberties Union,* 535 U.S. 564, 573 (2002). Section 48 explicitly regulates expression based on content: The statute restricts "visual [and] auditory depiction[s]," such as photographs, videos, or sound recordings, depending on whether they depict conduct in which a living animal is intentionally harmed. As such, § 48 is "'presumptively invalid,' and the Government bears the burden to rebut that presumption." *United States v. Playboy Entertainment Group, Inc.*, 529 U.S. 803, 817 (2000) (quoting *R.A.V. v. St. Paul*, 505 U.S. 377, 382 (1992)).

"From 1791 to the present," however, the First Amendment has "permitted restrictions upon the content of speech in a few limited areas" ***. *Id.*, at 382-383. These "historic and traditional categories long familiar to the bar"—including obscenity, defamation, fraud, incitement, and speech integral to criminal conduct—are "well-defined and narrowly limited classes of speech, the prevention and punishment of which have never been thought to raise any Constitutional problem." *Chaplinsky v. New Hampshire*, 315 U.S. 568, 571-572 (1942).

The Government argues that "depictions of animal cruelty" should be added to the list. *** As the Government notes, the prohibition of animal cruelty itself has a long history in American law, starting with the early settlement of the Colonies. But we are unaware of any similar tradition excluding *depictions* of animal cruelty from "the freedom of speech" codified in the First Amendment, and the Government points us to none. The Government contends that *** categories of speech may be exempted from the First Amendment's protection without any long-settled tradition of subjecting that speech to regulation. Instead, the Government *** proposes that a claim of categorical exclusion should be considered under a simple balancing test: "Whether a given category of speech enjoys First Amendment protection depends upon a categorical balancing of the value of the speech against its societal costs." Brief for United States 8.

As a free-floating test for First Amendment coverage, that sentence is startling and dangerous. The First Amendment's guarantee of free speech does not extend only to categories of speech that survive an ad hoc balancing of relative social costs and benefits. The First Amendment itself reflects a judgment by the American people that the benefits of its restrictions on the Government outweigh the costs. Our Constitution forecloses any attempt to revise that judgment simply on the basis that some speech is not worth it.

To be fair to the Government, its view did not emerge from a vacuum. As the Government correctly notes, this Court has often *described* historically unprotected categories of speech as being "of such slight social value as a step to truth that any benefit that may be derived from them is clearly outweighed by the social interest in order and morality." R.A.V., 505 U.S. at 383 (quoting Chaplinsky, 315 U.S. at 572). In *New York v. Ferber*, 458 U.S. 747 (1982), we noted that within these categories of unprotected speech, "the evil to be restricted so overwhelmingly outweighs the expressive interests, if any, at stake, that no process of case-by-case adjudication is required," because "the balance of competing interests is clearly struck." The Government derives its proposed test from these descriptions in our precedents.

But such descriptions are just that—descriptive. They do not set forth a test that may be applied as a general matter to permit the Government to imprison any speaker so long as his speech is deemed valueless or unnecessary, or so long as an ad hoc calculus of costs and benefits tilts in a statute's favor.

When we have identified categories of speech as fully outside the protection of the First Amendment, it has not been on the basis of a simple cost-benefit analysis. In *Ferber*, for example, we classified child pornography as such a category. We noted that the State of New York had a compelling interest in protecting children from abuse, and that the value of using children in these works (as opposed to simulated conduct or adult actors) was *de minimis*. But our decision did not rest on this "balance of competing interests" alone. *Id.*, at 764. We made clear that [the] market for child pornography was "intrinsically related" to the underlying abuse, and was therefore "an integral part of the production of such materials, an activity illegal throughout the Nation." *Id.*, at 759. As we noted, "[i]t rarely has been suggested that the constitutional freedom for speech and press extends its immunity to speech or writing used as an integral part of conduct in violation of a valid criminal statute." *Id.*, at 761-762 (quoting *Giboney v. Empire Storage & Ice Co.*, 336 U.S. 490, 498 (1949)). *Ferber* thus grounded its analysis in a previously recognized, long-established category of unprotected speech ***.

> **FYI**
>
> *Giboney* involved the application of a state antitrust law to a union that was picketing—and thus engaged in expressive activity—as a means to restrain trade.

Our decisions in *Ferber* and other cases cannot be taken as establishing a freewheeling authority to declare new categories of speech outside the scope of the First Amendment. Maybe there are some categories of speech that have been historically unprotected, but have not yet been specifically identified or discussed as such in our case law. But if so, there is no evidence that "depictions of animal cruelty" is among them. We need not foreclose the future recognition of such additional categories to reject the Government's highly manipulable balancing test as a means of identifying them.

Because we decline to carve out from the First Amendment any novel exception for § 48, we review Stevens's First Amendment challenge under our existing doctrine. [The Court concluded that Section 48 creates "a criminal prohibition of alarming breadth" and is "substantially overbroad, and therefore invalid under the First Amendment."]

[Justice ALITO's dissenting opinion is omitted.]

Points for Discussion

a. Identifying Excluded Categories

According to the Court, what is the appropriate test for determining if a category of speech is excluded from the protection of the First Amendment? Is it based only on history? If so, do the other categories of speech that the Court has excluded obviously satisfy the test?

b. Child Pornography and Animal Cruelty

The Court stated that its conclusion in <u>Ferber</u> that non-obscene child pornography is outside of the protection of the First Amendment was "grounded" in the excluded category of speech used as an "integral part of conduct in violation of a valid criminal statute." Do you agree that this was the basis of the Court's decision in <u>Ferber</u>? Even if it was, in what way does that distinguish it from this case? After all, just as the related criminal "conduct" in <u>Ferber</u> was the actual exploitation of children (rather than the distribution of the videos that chronicled the exploitation), the statute in *Stevens* applied only to videos that depicted animal cruelty that violates state or federal law. Is this a fair basis for treating "crush videos" differently?

c. "Crush Videos" and Obscenity

The statute at issue in *Stevens* exempted from the prohibition any depiction "that has serious religious, political, scientific, educational, journalistic, historical, or artistic value," a standard that Congress obviously based on the Court's obscenity doctrine. Why wasn't this exemption sufficient to protect the statute from a First Amendment challenge?

Executive Summary of This Chapter

Basic Ideas

The First Amendment says, in part, that "Congress shall make no law *** abridging the freedom of speech." The amendment does not define "the freedom of speech."

The Supreme Court has said in many cases that the freedom is not absolute. See, e.g., *Virginia v. Black*, 538 U.S. 343, 358 (2003). On the contrary, some regulation of speech is possible. The central question therefore is: What kind of government regulations are allowed, and what kinds are not? In answering this question, the Supreme Court has adopted a number of standards that essentially weigh the value of free speech against the importance of governmental regulations.

Although the First Amendment refers to "Congress," the Supreme Court has held that the protection of freedom of speech applies to the states through the Fourteenth Amendment under the incorporation doctrine. *Grosjean v. American Press Co.*, 297 U.S. 233, 244 (1936).

In interpreting the First Amendment, the Supreme Court has developed a number of distinct doctrines and rules. These doctrines and rules basically fall into two general categories. Some concern the types of regulation that the government wants to impose on speech. Others focus on the kinds of speech that the government wants to regulate.

Types of Regulations on Speech

The Supreme Court subjects **content-based restrictions** to strict scrutiny: The government may enforce a content-based restriction on speech that does not fall into a recognized exception only if the regulation is necessary to serve a compelling state interest and the regulation is narrowly drawn to achieve that end. *Renton v. Playtime Theatres*, Inc., 475

U.S. 41 (1986); *Turner Broadcasting System, Inc. v. F.C.C.*, 512 U.S. 622 (1994); *Republican Party of Minnesota v. White*, 536 U.S. 765 (2002).

The government may impose **reasonable restrictions on the time, place, or manner of speech**, even in public forums, if the restrictions (1) are content neutral; (2) are narrowly tailored to serve a significant governmental interest; and (3) leave open ample alternative channels for communication of the information. *Ward v. Rock Against Racism*, 491 U.S. 781, 791 (1989).

The government may enforce a **generally applicable regulation**, even when it incidentally burdens expressive activities, if "it furthers an important or substantial governmental interest; if the governmental interest is unrelated to the suppression of free expression; and if the incidental restriction on alleged First Amendment freedoms is no greater than is essential to the furtherance of that interest." *United States v. O'Brien*, 391 U.S. 367 (1968).

A **prior restraint on speech** is an executive or judicial order prohibiting a communication before it has occurred. The First Amendment provides more protection against prior restraints on speech than it does against subsequent liability for speech. Although the Court has suggested that the First Amendment does not absolutely bar prior restraints, and that exceptions might exist, it has not fully specified what these exceptions might be. *New York Times Co. v. United States*, 403 U.S. 713 (1971).

A law regulating speech is **overbroad** if it reaches both protected and unprotected speech. A law is **vague** if it does not make clear to a reasonable person what it prohibits and what it does not. In the First Amendment context, overbroad and vague laws may be challenged either **as applied** to the actual facts of a particular case or **on their face** without regard to the particular facts. The standards for facial challenges are relaxed because overbroad or vague laws may have a **chilling effect** on protected speech; unless the constitutionality is clarified, speakers worried about liability under the laws may censor their speech more than is constitutionally required. *NAACP v. Button*, 371 U.S. 415 (1963); *Schad v. Borough of Mount Ephraim*, 452 U.S. 61 (1981).

The **unconstitutional conditions** doctrine says that the government may not grant or deny benefits to a person based on whether the person engages in speech protected by the First Amendment. But the government can **selectively fund programs** and does not have to pay for all speech. *Rust v. Sullivan*, 500 U.S. 173, 194 (1991).

Categories of Speech

The First Amendment does not allow the government to proscribe **advocacy of crime** except where such advocacy is directed to inciting or producing imminent lawless action and is likely to incite or produce such action. *Brandenburg v. Ohio*, 395 U.S. 444 (1969).

The First Amendment does not absolutely prohibit liability for defamatory statements. Generally speaking, a plaintiff may recover for the torts of slander and libel. *Beauharnais v. People of State of Illinois*, 343 U.S. 250, 266 (1952). But the First Amendment does impose some important restrictions. First, a **public official, political candidate, or public figure** may not recover in tort for a defamatory statement unless the statement was both false and made with actual malice. *New York Times Co. v. Sullivan*, 376 U.S. 254 (1964). Second, a private figure may not recover for a defamatory statement regarding **a matter of public concern** unless the statement was both false and made with at least negligence. A statement is made with **actual malice** if it is deliberately false or if the speaker was reckless with regard to its falsity. A "**public figure**" is generally someone, like a movie star or other celebrity, who has voluntarily become the subject of public attention. A "**matter of public concern**" is something that has significant news value.

The First Amendment does not protect **obscenity**. *Roth v. United States*, 354 U.S. 476 (1957). Whether speech is obscene depends on the following factors:

> (a) whether the average person, applying contemporary community standards would find that the work, taken as a whole, appeals to the prurient interest; (b) whether the work depicts or describes, in a patently offensive way, sexual conduct specifically defined by the applicable state law; and (c) whether the work, taken as a whole, lacks serious literary, artistic, political, or scientific value.

Miller v. California, 413 U.S. 15, 24 (1973) (internal quotation marks and citations omitted). The First Amendment also does not protect **child pornography**, regardless of whether it is obscene. *New York v. Ferber*, 458 U.S. 747 (1982).

The First Amendment protects **expressive conduct** if it is "sufficiently imbued with elements of communication." *Spence v. Washington*, 418 U.S. 405 (1974). The government may regulate expressive conduct if four conditions are met: (1) the regulation is within the constitutional power of the Government; (2) the regulation furthers an important or substantial governmental interest; (3) the governmental interest is unrelated to the suppression of free expression; and (4) the incidental restriction on alleged First Amendment freedoms is no greater than is essential to the furtherance of that interest. *United States v. O'Brien*, 391 U.S. 367 (1968). Government regulation of conduct that is directed at the expressive elements of the conduct, however, fails the third factor of the test and accordingly is subject to strict scrutiny. *Texas v. Johnson*, 491 U.S. 397 (1989).

The First Amendment does not protect **fighting words**, which are words "which by their very utterance inflict injury or tend to incite an immediate breach of the peace." *Chaplinsky v. State of New Hampshire*, 315 U.S. 568 (1942). Words that are merely offensive and not likely to provoke a fight are not fighting words. *Cohen v. California*, 403 U.S. 15 (1971). The government may not impose certain content-based restrictions on fighting words. *R.A.V. v. City of St. Paul, Minn.*, 505 U.S. 377 (1992).

Commercial speech consists of advertising and other business communications. Under the leading case of *Central Hudson Gas & Electric Corp. v. Public Service Comm'n of New York*, 447 U.S. 557 (1980), the Supreme Court has divided commercial speech into two categories. First, commercial speech that concerns an unlawful activity or that is fraudulent or misleading has no First Amendment protection. Second, other commercial speech may be regulated if the government has a substantial interest, the regulation directly furthers the interest, and the regulations restrain speech only to the extent necessary to further the interest. *Posadas de Puerto Rico Associates v. Tourism Co. of Puerto Rico*, 478 U.S. 328 (1986).

The First Amendment applies to **campaign financing**. It prohibits the government from regulating how much money a political candidate can spend, but permits the government to regulate campaign contributions to avoid corruption or the appearance of corruption. *Buckley v. Valeo*, 424 U.S. 1 (1976). The First Amendment also prohibits the government from limiting the right of corporations to spend money to support candidates for political office. *Citizens United v. Federal Election Comm'n*, 130 S.Ct. 876 (2010).

The First Amendment also applies to some speech of **government employees**. The government may take adverse personnel actions based on speech about private concerns. But if an employee speaks on matters of public concern, the government may take an adverse action only if the government's needs as an employer exceed the employee's interest in free speech. *Connick v. Myers*, 461 U.S. 138 (1983). In addition, speech about matters of public concern is protected only if the employee is speaking in a private capacity. *Garcetti v. Ceballos*, 547 U.S. 410 (2006).

Chapter 15

Freedom of the Press

Introduction

Before the Revolution, John Hancock, John Adams, and other dissidents published articles in newspapers and journals criticizing British rule over the colonies. Through their articles, they helped to spread revolutionary ideas. In writing their missives, these authors typically used pseudonyms to conceal their identities. They feared imprisonment for the content of their writing because a general freedom of the press did not exist. *See* Clyde Augustus Duniway, *The Development of Freedom of the Press in Massachusetts* 123 (1906).

In Virginia, after the royal governor dissolved the House of Burgesses (the colonial legislature), a number of revolutionary figures held a series of meetings called the Virginia Conventions. At the convention held in June of 1776, the members adopted the Virginia Declaration of Rights. This document, drafted principally by George Mason, later influenced both the Declaration of Independence and the Bill of Rights. In addition to addressing various other liberties, the document announced that "the Freedom of the Press is one of the great Bulwarks of Liberty, and can never be restrained but by despotick Governments."

The original Constitution contained no mention of a freedom of the press. During the ratification period, Anti-Federalists criticized the Constitution for this omission. One of the leading Anti-Federalists, writing under the pseudonym Federal Farmer, argued: "All parties apparently agree, that the freedom of the press is a fundamental right, and ought not to be restrained by any taxes, duties, or in any manner whatever. Why should not the people, in adopting a federal constitution, declare this, even if there are only doubts about it." Federal Farmer, No. 16 (Jan. 20, 1788) (reprinted in *The Complete Anti-Federalist* (Herbert J. Storing ed. 1981), and *The Founders' Constitution* (Philip B. Kurland & Ralph Lerner eds. 1986)). Although this sentiment did not prevent ratification of the Constitution, it did prevail when Congress and the states added the Bill of Rights. The First Amendment provides in part that "Congress shall make no law *** abridging the freedom of speech, or of the press." The Supreme Court has held that the prohibition against abridging the freedom of the press applies not just to Congress, but also to the states under the incorporation doctrine. *Gitlow v. People of State of New York*, 268 U.S. 652, 666 (1925); *Near v. Minnesota*, 283 U.S. 697, 707 (1931).

Points for Discussion

a. Freedom of the Press and Freedom of Speech

Is there a difference between the freedom of "the press" and the freedom of "speech"? Are the protections that the First Amendment affords for the press and speech duplicative? When "the press" publishes views that are critical of the government, isn't it—or the publisher or journalist responsible for the content of the article—engaging in the act of "speech"? Does the separate inclusion of a specific freedom of the press suggest that the press is entitled to even greater protection for its "speech" than ordinary citizens?

b. Meaning of "Press"

A "metonymy" is a figure of speech in which the name of one thing stands for another thing associated with it. For example, in the phrase "the White House opposes the legislation," the term "White House" is a metonymy for the President. When the First Amendment refers to the freedom "of the press," the term "press" clearly is, at a minimum, a metonymy for those who traditionally used printing presses, such as the publishers of books, magazines, and newspapers. But does the term "press" also extend to publishers who use non-print media, such as radio and television broadcasters? Does the term include journalists as well as publishers? Does it also include internet bloggers? The Supreme Court has never answered these questions in any detail. As the following cases will show, the Court generally has viewed the freedom of the press to be coextensive with the freedom of speech. Because (as we will see later in this Part) everyone enjoys the freedom of speech, the Court generally has not had to make distinctions between "the press" and others who seek to disseminate their views through non-traditional means. Should any special rules apply to the press?

————————

A. Applicability of General Laws to the Press

In a variety of cases, members of the press have claimed that the First Amendment grants them special exemptions from the operation of generally applicable laws. As the cases that follow demonstrate, this issue involves competing considerations. On the one hand, enforcing general laws sometimes has the effect of impeding the work of journalists. For example, in the following case, *Branzburg v. Hayes*, 408 U.S. 665 (1972), reporters sought to avoid giving testimony before a grand jury about what their sources had told them. They feared that the sources might refuse to talk to them in the future if they could not speak confidentially. On the other hand, attempting to recognize exceptions for the press might prove a very difficult judicial task. Courts would have to decide who counts as "the press" and whether there are any exceptions to the general sweep of the term. Perhaps to avoid these difficult questions, the Supreme Court has held that "generally applicable laws do not offend the First Amendment simply because their enforcement against the press has incidental effects on its ability to gather and report the news." *Cohen v. Cowles Media Co.,* 501 U.S. 663 (1991), which we consider below. This conclusion, however, does not mean that the press *must* be treated the same as everyone else. On the contrary, Congress and the states can use legislation to grant the media exemptions from general laws. As you read the following case, consider whether the Constitution itself should be interpreted to exempt "the press" from the impact of some generally applicable laws.

Branzburg v. Hayes

408 U.S. 665 (1972)

Opinion of the Court by Mr. Justice WHITE, announced by THE CHIEF JUSTICE.

The issue in these cases is whether requiring newsmen to appear and testify before state or federal grand juries abridges the freedom of speech and press guaranteed by the First Amendment. We hold that it does not.

The writ of certiorari in No. 70-85, *Branzburg v. Hayes and Meigs*, brings before us two judgments of the Kentucky Court of Appeals, both involving petitioner Branzburg, a staff reporter for the Courier-Journal, a daily newspaper published in Louisville, Kentucky.

On November 15, 1969, the Courier-Journal carried a story under petitioner's by-line describing in detail his observations of two young residents of Jefferson County synthesizing hashish from marihuana, an activity which, they asserted, earned them about $5,000 in three weeks. The article included a photograph of a pair of hands working above a laboratory table on which was a substance identified by the caption as hashish. The article stated that petitioner had promised not to reveal the identity of the two hashish makers. Petitioner was shortly subpoenaed by the Jefferson County grand jury; he appeared, but refused to identify the individuals he had seen possessing marihuana or the persons he had seen making hashish from marihuana. ***

The second case involving petitioner Branzburg arose out of his later story published on January 10, 1971, which described in detail the use of drugs in Frankfort, Kentucky. The article reported that in order to provide a comprehensive survey of the "drug scene" in Frankfort, petitioner had "spent two weeks interviewing several dozen drug users in the capital city" and had seen some of them smoking marihuana. A number of conversations with and observations of several unnamed drug users were recounted. Subpoenaed to appear before a Franklin County grand jury "to testify in the matter of violation of statutes concerning use and sale of drugs," petitioner Branzburg moved to quash the summons; the motion was denied ***.

In re Pappas, No. 70-94, originated when petitioner Pappas, a television newsman-photographer working out of the Providence, Rhode Island, office of a New Bedford, Massachusetts, television station, was called to New Bedford on July 30, 1970, to report on civil disorders there which involved fires and other turmoil. He intended to cover a Black Panther news conference at that group's headquarters in a boarded-up store. Petitioner found the streets around the store barricaded, but he ultimately gained entrance to the area and recorded and photographed a prepared statement read by one of the Black Panther leaders at about 3 p.m. He then asked for and received permission to re-enter the area. Returning at about 9 o'clock, he was allowed to enter and remain inside Panther headquarters. As a condition of entry, Pappas agreed not to disclose anything he saw or heard inside the store except an anticipated police raid, which Pappas, "on his own," was free to photograph and report as he wished. Pappas stayed inside the headquarters for about three hours, but there was no police raid, and petitioner wrote no story and did not otherwise reveal what had occurred in the store while he was there. Two months later, petitioner was summoned before the Bristol County Grand Jury and appeared, answered questions as to his name, address, employment, and what he had seen and heard outside Panther headquarters, but refused to answer any questions about what had taken place inside headquarters while he was there, claiming that the First Amendment afforded him a privilege to protect confidential informants and their information. * * *

<u>United States v. Caldwell</u>, No. 70-57, arose from subpoenas issued by a federal grand jury in the Northern District of California to respondent Earl Caldwell, a reporter for the New York Times assigned to cover the Black Panther Party and other black militant groups. A subpoena duces tecum was served on respondent on February 2, 1970, ordering him to appear before the grand jury to testify and to bring with him notes and tape recordings of interviews given him for publication by officers and spokesmen of the Black Panther Party concerning the aims, purposes, and activities of that organization. * * * Respondent and his employer, the New York Times, moved to quash on the ground that the unlimited breadth of the subpoenas and the fact that Caldwell would have to appear in secret before the grand jury would destroy his working relationship with the Black Panther Party and "suppress vital First Amendment freedoms [by] driving a wedge of distrust and silence between the news media and the militants." * * *

> **Definition**
>
> A *subpoena duces tecum* is a "subpoena ordering the witness to appear in court and to bring specified documents, records, or things." *Black's Law Dictionary* (9th ed. 2009).

Petitioners Branzburg and Pappas and respondent Caldwell press First Amendment claims that may be simply put: that to gather news it is often necessary to agree either not to identify the source of information published or to publish only part of the facts revealed, or both; that if the reporter is nevertheless forced to reveal these confidences to a grand jury, the source so identified and other confidential sources of other reporters will be measurably deterred from furnishing publishable information, all to the detriment of the free flow of information protected by the First Amendment. Although the newsmen in these cases do not claim an absolute privilege against official interrogation in all circumstances, they assert that the reporter should not be forced either to appear or to testify before a grand jury or at trial until and unless sufficient grounds are

> **Practice Pointer**
>
> The journalists did not assert an absolute privilege in this case, but instead asserted only a qualified privilege. Why do you think they made that choice?

shown for believing that the reporter possesses information relevant to a crime the grand jury is investigating, that the information the reporter has is unavailable from other sources, and that the need for the information is sufficiently compelling to override the claimed invasion of First Amendment interests occasioned by the disclosure. Principally relied upon are prior cases emphasizing the importance of the First Amendment guarantees to individual development and to our system of representative government, decisions requiring that official action with adverse impact on First Amendment rights be justified by a public interest that is "compelling" or "paramount," and those precedents establishing the principle that justifiable governmental goals may not be achieved by unduly broad means having an unnecessary impact on protected rights of speech, press, or association. The heart of the claim is that the burden on news gathering resulting from compelling reporters to disclose confidential information outweighs any public interest in obtaining the information.

We do not question the significance of free speech, press, or assembly to the country's welfare. Nor is it suggested that news gathering does not qualify for First Amendment protection; without some protection for seeking out the news, freedom of the press could be eviscerated. But these cases involve no intrusions upon speech or assembly, no prior restraint or restriction on what the press may publish, and no express or implied command that the press publish what it prefers to withhold. No exaction or tax for the privilege of publishing, and no penalty, civil or criminal, related to the content of published material is at issue here. The use of confidential sources by the press is not forbidden or restricted; reporters remain free to seek news from any source by means within the law. No attempt is made to require the press to publish its sources of information or indiscriminately to disclose them on request.

The sole issue before us is the obligation of reporters to respond to grand jury subpoenas as other citizens do and to answer questions relevant to an investigation into the commission of crime. Citizens generally are not constitutionally immune from grand jury subpoenas; and neither the First Amendment nor any other constitutional provision protects the average citizen from disclosing to a grand jury information that he has received in confidence. The claim is [that] reporters are exempt from these obligations ***.

It is clear that the First Amendment does not invalidate every incidental burdening of the press that may result from the enforcement of civil or criminal statutes of general applicability. Under prior cases, otherwise valid laws serving substantial public interests may be enforced against the press as against others, despite the possible burden that may be imposed. The Court has emphasized that "[t]he publisher of a newspaper has no special immunity from the application of general laws. He has no special privilege to invade the rights and liberties of others." *Associated Press v. NLRB*, 301 U.S. 103, 132-133 (1937). It was there held that the Associated Press, a news-gathering and disseminating organization, was not exempt from the requirements of the National Labor Relations Act. The holding was reaffirmed in *Oklahoma Press Publishing Co. v. Walling*, 327 U.S. 186, 192-193 (1946), where the Court rejected the claim that applying the Fair Labor Standards Act to a newspaper publishing business would abridge the freedom of press guaranteed by the First Amendment. *Associated Press v. United States*, 326 U.S. 1 (1945), similarly overruled assertions that the First Amendment precluded application of the Sherman Act to a news-gathering and disseminating organization. Likewise, a newspaper may be subjected to nondiscriminatory forms of general taxation. *Grosjean v. American Press Co.*, 297 U.S. 233, 250 (1936).

The prevailing view is that the press is not free to publish with impunity everything and anything it desires to publish. Although it may deter or regulate what is said or published, the press may not circulate knowing or reckless falsehoods damaging to private reputation without subjecting itself to liability for damages, including punitive damages, or even criminal prosecution. See *New York Times Co. v. Sullivan*, 376 U.S. 254, 279-280 (1964). A newspaper or a journalist may also be punished for contempt of court, in appropriate circumstances. *Craig v. Harney*, 331 U.S. 367, 377-378 (1947).

It has generally been held that the First Amendment does not guarantee the press a constitutional right of special access to information not available to the public generally. In *Zemel v. Rusk*, 381 U.S. 1, 16-17 (1965), for example, the Court sustained the Government's refusal to validate passports to Cuba even though that restriction "render[ed] less than wholly free the flow of information concerning that country." The ban on travel was held constitutional, for "[t]he right to speak and publish does not carry with it the unrestrained right to gather information."

Despite the fact that news gathering may be hampered, the press is regularly excluded from grand jury proceedings, our own conferences, the meetings of other official bodies gathered in executive session, and the meetings of private organizations. Newsmen have no constitutional right of access to the scenes of crime or disaster when the general public is excluded, and they may be prohibited from attending or publishing information about trials if such restrictions are necessary to assure a defendant a fair trial before an impartial tribunal. In *Sheppard v. Maxwell*, 384 U.S. 333 (1966), for example, the Court reversed a state court conviction where the trial court failed to adopt "stricter rules governing the use of the courtroom by newsmen, as Sheppard's counsel requested," neglected to insulate witnesses from the press, and made no "effort to control the release of leads, information, and gossip to the press by police officers, witnesses, and the counsel for both sides." *Id., at 358*. "[T]he trial court might well have proscribed extrajudicial statements by any lawyer, party, witness, or court official which divulged prejudicial matters." *Id., at 361*.

> **Make the Connection**
>
> Does the First Amendment impose limits on the ability of the government—and the courts in particular—to exclude the press from its proceedings? Could the government declare that all criminal trials will occur in secrecy, without permitting members of the press to attend? We will take up this question later in this Chapter when we consider the Court's decision in *Richmond Newspapers, Inc. v. Virginia*.

It is thus not surprising that the great weight of authority is that newsmen are not exempt from the normal duty of appearing before a grand jury and answering questions relevant to a criminal investigation. ***

A number of States have provided newsmen a statutory privilege of varying breadth, but the majority have not done so, and none has been provided by federal statute. Until now the only testimonial privilege for unofficial witnesses that is rooted in the Federal Constitution is the Fifth Amendment privilege against compelled self-incrimination. We are asked to create another by interpreting the First Amendment to grant newsmen a testimonial privilege that other citizens do not enjoy. This we decline to do. Fair and effective law enforcement aimed at providing security for the person and property of the individual is a fundamental function of government, and the grand jury plays an important, constitutionally mandated role in this process. On the records now before us, we perceive no basis for holding that the public interest in law enforcement and in ensuring effective grand jury proceedings is insufficient to override the consequential, but uncertain, burden on news gathering that is said to result from insisting that reporters, like other citizens, respond to relevant questions put to them in the course of a valid grand jury investigation or criminal trial.

> **FYI**
>
> The privilege against self-incrimination is typically addressed in the course on Criminal Procedure. We did, however, consider it briefly in Chapter 7, when we discussed the incorporation doctrine and the Court's decision in *Adamson v. California*.

Mr. Justice STEWART, with whom Mr. Justice BRENNAN and Mr. Justice MARSHALL join, dissenting.

The reporter's constitutional right to a confidential relationship with his source stems from the broad societal interest in a full and free flow of information to the public. It is this basic concern that underlies the Constitution's protection of a free press because the guarantee is "not for the benefit of the press so much as for the benefit of all of us." *Time, Inc. v. Hill*, 385 U.S. 374, 389 (1967).

Enlightened choice by an informed citizenry is the basic ideal upon which an open society is premised, and a free press is thus indispensable to a free society. Not only does the press enhance personal self-fulfillment by providing the people with the widest possible range of fact and opinion, but it also is an incontestable precondition of self-government. The press "has been a mighty catalyst in awakening public interest in governmental affairs, exposing corruption among public officers and employees and generally informing the citizenry of public events and occurrences ***." *Estes v. Texas*, 381 U.S. 532, 539 (1965). As private and public aggregations of power burgeon in size and the pressures for conformity necessarily mount, there is obviously a continuing need for an independent press to disseminate a robust variety of information and opinion through reportage, investigation, and criticism, if we are to preserve our constitutional tradition of maximizing freedom of choice by encouraging diversity of expression.

A corollary of the right to publish must be the right to gather news. The full flow of information to the public protected by the free-press guarantee would be severely curtailed if no protection whatever were afforded to the process by which news is assembled and disseminated. *** The right to gather news implies, in turn, a right to a confidential relationship between a reporter and his source. This proposition follows as a matter of simple logic once three factual predicates are recognized: (1) newsmen require informants to gather news; (2) confidentiality—the promise or understanding that names or certain aspects of communications will be kept off the record—is essential to the creation and maintenance of a news-gathering relationship with informants; and (3) an unbridled subpoena power—the absence of a constitutional right protecting, in any way, a confidential relationship from compulsory process—will either deter sources from divulging information or deter reporters from gathering and publishing information.

It is obvious that informants are necessary to the news-gathering process as we know it today. If it is to perform its constitutional mission, the press must do far more than merely print public statements or publish prepared handouts. Familiarity with the people and circumstances involved in the myriad background activities that result in the final product called "news" is vital to complete and responsible journalism, unless the press is to be a captive mouthpiece of "newsmakers."

Points for Discussion

a. Rationale

The Court acknowledged the journalists' argument that if "forced to respond to subpoenas and identify their sources or disclose other confidences, their informants will refuse or be reluctant to furnish newsworthy information in the future." Why did the Court conclude that this argument was insufficient to justify a journalist's privilege not to testify before a grand jury? Did the Court conclude that there is a "privilege," but that it was overcome by "the public interest in law enforcement and in ensuring effective grand jury proceedings"? Or did it conclude that there is no privilege at all, regardless of the circumstances surrounding the subpoena?

b. Constitutional Privileges

The Court stated that "the only testimonial privilege for unofficial witnesses that is rooted in the Federal Constitution is the Fifth Amendment privilege against compelled self-incrimination," and it declined to "create" another. Two years after the Court's decision in *Branzburg*, the Court held in *United States v. Nixon* that the Constitution protects an "executive privilege," which permits the President (at least under certain circumstances) to protect confidential communications from disclosure. Does the Court's subsequent decision in *Nixon* suggest a greater willingness of the Court to find implied evidentiary privileges from more general constitutional text? Is the argument for a journalist's privilege to protect confidential sources stronger than the argument for executive privilege, or weaker?

> **Make the Connection**
>
> We discussed the Court's decision in *Nixon* in Chapter 5, during our consideration of the federal executive power.

c. Legislation

Congress and the states presumably have authority to enact legislation that would create an evidentiary privilege giving journalists the right not to disclose information about their sources. The privilege would be similar to the attorney-client privilege, which protects confidential communications between lawyers and their clients from disclosure. Would creating a journalist's privilege be a good idea? How exactly would you phrase the legislation? In particular, how would you define a "journalist" or describe the kinds of communications to which the privilege would apply? Would it be a qualified privilege or an absolute one?

d. Journalists' Ethics

Should journalists make promises of confidentiality to their sources when they do not have the lawful power to keep these promises? If a journalist has promised confidentiality to a source, should the journalist refuse to testify before a grand jury even if it means spending time in jail on charges of contempt? Judith Miller, a former *New York Times* reporter, thought that going to prison was the proper course. A judge jailed her after she refused to answer questions about her sources of information in writing about the CIA's decision to send Joe Wilson, the husband of a CIA employee, Valerie Plame, to Africa to investigate the potential sale of uranium to Iraq. Upon her release from prison, Miller said: "I went to jail to preserve the time-honored principle that a journalist must respect a promise not to reveal the identity of a confidential source. *** I am leaving jail today because my source has now voluntarily and personally released me from my promise of confidentiality regarding our conversations relating to the Wilson-Plame matter." Neil A. Lewis & Scott Shane, *Reporter Who Was Jailed Testifies in Libby Case*, N.Y. Times, Jan. 31, 2007, at A1. Did Miller owe an obligation to anyone other than her source?

Zurcher v. Stanford Daily

436 U.S. 547 (1978)

Mr. Justice WHITE delivered the opinion of the Court.

Late in the day on Friday, April 9, 1971, officers of the Palo Alto Police Department and of the Santa Clara County Sheriff's Department responded to a call from the director of the Stanford University Hospital requesting the removal of a large group of demonstrators who had seized the hospital's administrative offices and occupied them since the previous afternoon. After several futile efforts to persuade the demonstrators to leave peacefully, more drastic measures were employed. The demonstrators had barricaded the doors at both ends of a hall adjacent to the administrative offices. The police chose to force their way in at the west end of the corridor. As they did so, a group of demonstrators emerged through the doors at the east end and, armed with sticks and clubs, attacked the group of nine police officers stationed there. One officer was knocked to the floor and struck repeatedly on the head; another suffered a broken shoulder. All nine were injured. There were no police photographers at the east doors, and most bystanders and reporters were on the west side. The officers themselves were able to identify only two of their assailants, but one of them did see at least one person photographing the assault at the east doors.

On Sunday, April 11, a special edition of the Stanford Daily (Daily), a student newspaper published at Stanford University, carried articles and photographs devoted to the hospital protest and the violent clash between demonstrators and police. The photographs carried the byline of a Daily staff member and indicated that he had been at the east end of the hospital hallway where he could have photographed the assault on the nine officers. The next day, the Santa Clara County District Attorney's Office secured a warrant from the Municipal Court for an immediate search of the Daily's offices for negatives, film, and pictures showing the events and occurrences at the hospital on the evening of April 9. The warrant issued on a finding of "just, probable and reasonable cause for believing that: Negatives and photographs and films, evidence material and relevant to the identity of the perpetrators of felonies, to wit, Battery on a Peace Officer, and Assault with Deadly Weapon, will be located [on the premises of the Daily]." The warrant affidavit contained no allegation or indication that members of the Daily staff were in any way involved in unlawful acts at the hospital.

The search pursuant to the warrant was conducted later that day by four police officers and took place in the presence of some members of the Daily staff. The Daily's photographic laboratories, filing cabinets, desks, and wastepaper baskets were searched. Locked drawers and rooms were not opened. The officers apparently had opportunity to read notes and correspondence during the search; but, contrary to claims of the staff, the officers denied that they had exceeded the limits of the warrant. They had not been advised by the staff that the areas they were searching contained confidential materials. The search revealed only the photographs that had already been published on April 11, and no materials were removed from the Daily's office.

A month later the Daily and various members of its staff, respondents here, brought a civil action in the United States District Court for the Northern District of California seeking declaratory and injunctive relief under 42 U.S.C. § 1983 against the police officers who conducted the search, the chief of police, the district attorney and one of his deputies, and the judge who had issued the warrant. The complaint alleged that the search of the Daily's office had deprived respondents under color of state law of rights secured to them by the First, Fourth, and Fourteenth Amendments of the United States Constitution.

The issue here is how the Fourth Amendment is to be construed and applied to the "third party" search, the recurring situation where state authorities have probable cause to believe that fruits, instrumentalities, or other evidence of crime is located on identified property but do not then have probable cause to believe that the owner or possessor of the property is himself implicated in the crime that has occurred or is occurring. [Addressing this Fourth Amendment issue, the Court reasoned that "the State's interest in enforcing the criminal law and recovering evidence is the same whether the third party is culpable or not" and that "[t]he critical element in a reasonable search is not that the owner of the property is suspected of crime but that there is reasonable cause to believe that the specific 'things' to be searched for and seized are located on the property to which entry is sought." The Court therefore held that the premises of a third-party could be searched upon a showing of probable cause. The Court then turned to the First Amendment.]

The District Court held, and respondents assert here, that whatever may be true of third-party searches generally, where the third party is a newspaper, there are additional factors derived from the First Amendment that justify a nearly *per se* rule forbidding the search warrant and permitting only the subpoena *duces tecum*. The general submission is that searches of newspaper offices for evidence of crime reasonably believed to be on the premises will seriously threaten the ability of the press to gather, analyze, and disseminate news. This is said to be true for several reasons: First, searches will be physically disruptive to such an extent that timely publication will be impeded. Second, confidential sources of information will dry up, and the press will also lose opportunities to cover various events because of fears of the participants that press files will be readily available to the authorities. Third, reporters will be deterred from recording and preserving their recollections for future use if such information is subject to seizure. Fourth, the processing of news and its dissemination will be chilled by the prospects that searches will disclose internal editorial deliberations. Fifth, the press will resort to self-censorship to conceal its possession of information of potential interest to the police.

> **Take Note**
>
> What exactly do the respondents claim is prohibited by the First Amendment? Do they argue that they can withhold relevant evidence from the police or the prosecutor? Or simply that the police may not obtain that evidence during a search pursuant to a warrant?

It is true that the struggle from which the Fourth Amendment emerged "is largely a history of conflict between the Crown and the press," *Stanford v. Texas*, 379 U.S. 476, 482 (1965), and that in issuing warrants and determining the reasonableness of a search, state and federal magistrates should be aware that "unrestricted power of search and seizure could also be an instrument for stifling liberty of expression." *Marcus v. Search Warrant*, 367 U.S. 717, 729 (1961). Where the materials sought to be seized may be protected by the First Amendment, the requirements of the Fourth Amendment must be applied with "scrupulous exactitude." *Stanford v. Texas*, 379 U.S., at 485. "A seizure reasonable as to one type of material in one setting may be unreasonable in a different setting or with respect to another kind of material." *Roaden v. Kentucky*, 413 U.S. 496, 501 (1973). Hence, in *Stanford v. Texas*, the Court invalidated a warrant authorizing the search of a private home for all books, records, and other materials relating to the Communist Party, on the ground that whether or not the warrant would have been sufficient in other contexts, it authorized the searchers to rummage among and make judgments about books and papers and was the functional equivalent of a general warrant, one of the principal targets of the Fourth Amendment. Where presumptively protected materials are sought to be seized, the warrant requirement should be administered to leave as little as possible to the discretion or whim of the officer in the field.

Neither the Fourth Amendment nor the cases requiring consideration of First

Amendment values in issuing search warrants, however, call for imposing the regime ordered by the District Court. Aware of the long struggle between Crown and press and desiring to curb unjustified official intrusions, the Framers took the enormously important step of subjecting searches to the test of reasonableness and to the general rule requiring search warrants issued by neutral magistrates. They nevertheless did not forbid warrants where the press was involved, did not require special showings that subpoenas would be impractical, and did not insist that the owner of the place to be searched, if connected with the press, must be shown to be implicated in the offense being investigated. Further, the prior cases do no more than insist that the courts apply the warrant requirements with particular exactitude when First Amendment interests would be endangered by the search. As we see it, no more than this is required where the warrant requested is for the seizure of criminal evidence reasonably believed to be on the premises occupied by a newspaper. Properly administered, the preconditions for a warrant—probable cause, specificity with respect to the place to be searched and the things to be seized, and overall reasonableness—should afford sufficient protection against the harms that are assertedly threatened by warrants for searching newspaper offices.

> ### Food for Thought
>
> The Court sees no reason to believe that the prospect of searches pursuant to properly issued warrants will affect journalistic decisions or cause sources to refuse to talk to the press. Do you agree? Can you think of any hypothetical searches in which a newspaper's journalistic decisions might be affected?

There is no reason to believe, for example, that magistrates cannot guard against searches of the type, scope, and intrusiveness that would actually interfere with the timely publication of a newspaper. Nor, if the requirements of specificity and reasonableness are properly applied, policed, and observed, will there be any occasion or opportunity for officers to rummage at large in newspaper files or to intrude into or to deter normal editorial and publication decisions. The warrant issued in this case authorized nothing of this sort. Nor are we convinced, any more than we were in *Branzburg v. Hayes*, 408 U.S. 665 (1972), that confidential sources will disappear and that the press will suppress news because of fears of warranted searches. Whatever incremental effect there may be in this regard if search warrants, as well as subpoenas, are permissible in proper circumstances, it does not make a constitutional difference in our judgment.

Mr. Justice STEWART, with whom Mr. Justice MARSHALL joins, dissenting.

It seems to me self-evident that police searches of newspaper offices burden the freedom of the press. The most immediate and obvious First Amendment injury caused by such a visitation by the police is physical disruption of the operation of the newspaper. Policemen occupying a newsroom and searching it thoroughly for what may be an extended period of time will inevitably interrupt its normal operations, and thus impair or even temporarily prevent the processes of newsgathering, writing, editing, and publishing. By contrast, a subpoena would afford the newspaper itself an opportunity to locate whatever material might be requested and produce it.

But there is another and more serious burden on a free press imposed by an unannounced police search of a newspaper office: the possibility of disclosure of information received from confidential sources, or of the identity of the sources themselves. Protection of those sources is necessary to ensure that the press can fulfill its constitutionally designated function of informing the public, because important information can often be obtained only by an assurance that the source will not be revealed. *Branzburg v. Hayes,* 408 U.S. 665, 725-736 (dissenting opinion). And the Court has recognized that "without some protection for seeking out the news, freedom of the press could be eviscerated." *Pell v. Procunier,* 417 U.S. 817, 833 (1974).

Today the Court does not question the existence of this constitutional protection, but says only that it is not "convinced [that] confidential sources will disappear and that the press will suppress news because of fears of warranted searches." This facile conclusion seems to me to ignore common experience. It requires no blind leap of faith to understand that a person who gives information to a journalist only on condition that his identity will not be revealed will be less likely to give that information if he knows that, despite the journalist's assurance his identity may in fact be disclosed. And it cannot be denied that confidential information may be exposed to the eyes of police officers who execute a search warrant by rummaging through the files, cabinets, desks, and wastebaskets of a newsroom. Since the indisputable effect of such searches will thus be to prevent a newsman from being able to promise confidentiality to his potential sources, it seems obvious to me that a journalist's access to information, and thus the public's will thereby be impaired.

A search warrant allows police officers to ransack the files of a newspaper, reading each and every document until they have found the one named in the warrant, while a subpoena would permit the newspaper itself to produce only the specific documents requested. A search, unlike a subpoena, will therefore lead to the needless exposure of confidential information completely unrelated to the purpose of the investigation. The knowledge that police officers can make an unannounced raid on a newsroom is thus bound to have a deterrent effect on the availability of confidential news sources. The end result, wholly inimical to the First Amendment, will be a diminishing flow of potentially important information to the public.

Points for Discussion

a. Comparison to *Branzburg v. Hayes*

Zurcher and *Branzburg* both held that the press does not have any exemption from generally applicable laws. In which case do you think the press had a stronger argument for seeking an exception? Given the decision in *Branzburg*, does the majority's view in *Zurcher* necessarily follow?

b. Federal Legislation

Congress responded to the *Zurcher* decision by enacting the Privacy Protection Act of

1980, 42 U.S.C. § 2000aa, which restricts the ability of the police to search newsrooms for evidence of crimes committed by third-parties. Subject to various exceptions, the act makes it "unlawful for a government officer or employee, in connection with the investigation or prosecution of a criminal offense, to search for or seize any work product materials possessed by a person reasonably believed to have a purpose to disseminate to the public a newspaper, book, broadcast, or other similar form of public communication, in or affecting interstate or foreign commerce." One exception is for when "there is probable cause to believe that the person possessing such materials has committed or is committing the criminal offense to which the materials relate." Does this statute address all of the concerns expressed by Justice Stewart in *Zurcher*?

Cohen v. Cowles Media Co.

501 U.S. 663 (1991)

Justice WHITE delivered the opinion of the Court.

During the closing days of the 1982 Minnesota gubernatorial race, Dan Cohen, an active Republican associated with Wheelock Whitney's Independent-Republican gubernatorial campaign, approached reporters from the St. Paul Pioneer Press Dispatch (Pioneer Press) and the Minneapolis Star and Tribune (Star Tribune) and offered to provide documents relating to a candidate in the upcoming election. Cohen made clear to the reporters that he would provide the information only if he was given a promise of confidentiality. Reporters from both papers promised to keep Cohen's identity anonymous and Cohen turned over copies of two public court records concerning Marlene Johnson, the Democratic-Farmer-Labor candidate for Lieutenant Governor. The first record indicated that Johnson had been charged in 1969 with three counts of unlawful assembly, and the second that she had been convicted in 1970 of petit theft. Both newspapers interviewed Johnson for her explanation and one reporter tracked down the person who had found the records for Cohen. As it turned out, the unlawful assembly charges arose out of Johnson's participation in a protest of an alleged failure to hire minority workers on municipal construction projects, and the charges were eventually dismissed. The petit theft conviction was for leaving a store without paying for $6 worth of sewing materials. The incident apparently occurred at a time during which Johnson was emotionally distraught, and the conviction was later vacated.

> **FYI**
>
> Negative information about a candidate released just before an election is sometimes called an "October Surprise" because elections generally occur at the start of November. Do you recall any famous October surprises? *See* Carey Goldberg, *The Tipster: Maine Lawyer Delights in Leaking Bush's Arrest*, N.Y. Times, Nov. 4, 2000, at A14 (describing how a lawyer active in the Democratic Party revealed news just before the 2000 election that presidential candidate George W. Bush was convicted of drunk driving in 1976).

After consultation and debate, the editorial staffs of the two newspapers independently decided to publish Cohen's name as part of their stories concerning Johnson. In their stories, both papers identified Cohen as the source of the court records, indicated his connection to the Whitney campaign, and included denials by Whitney campaign officials of any role in the matter. The same day the stories appeared, Cohen was fired by his employer.

[Cohen sued the newspapers' publishers, claiming that they had violated their promises of confidentiality. A jury awarded him $200,000, concluding that the promises were enforceable on a theory of promissory estoppel. The Minnesota Supreme Court vacated the judgment, concluding that "in this case enforcement of the promise of confidentiality under a promissory estoppel theory would violate defendants' First Amendment rights."]

Respondents rely on the proposition that "if a newspaper lawfully obtains truthful information about a matter of public significance then state officials may not constitutionally punish publication of the information, absent a need to further a state interest of the highest order." *Smith v. Daily Mail Publishing Co.,* 443 U.S. 97, 103 (1979). That proposition is unexceptionable, and it has been applied in various cases that have found insufficient the asserted state interests in preventing publication of truthful, lawfully obtained information.

This case, however, is not controlled by this line of cases but, rather, by the equally well-established line of decisions holding that generally applicable laws do not offend the First Amendment simply because their enforcement against the press has incidental effects on its ability to gather and report the news. As the cases relied on by respondents recognize, the truthful information sought to be published must have been lawfully acquired. The press may not with impunity break and enter an office or dwelling to gather news. Neither does the First Amendment relieve a newspaper reporter of the obligation shared by all citizens to respond to a grand jury subpoena and answer questions relevant to a criminal investigation, even though the reporter might be required to reveal a confidential source. *Branzburg v. Hayes,* 408 U.S. 665 (1972). The press, like others interested in publishing, may not publish copyrighted material without obeying the copyright laws. See *Zacchini v. Scripps-Howard Broadcasting Co.,* 433 U.S. 562, 576-579 (1977). Similarly, the media must obey the National Labor Relations Act, *Associated Press v. NLRB,* 301 U.S. 103 (1937), and the Fair Labor Standards Act, *Oklahoma Press Publishing Co. v. Walling,* 327 U.S. 186, 192-193 (1946); may not restrain trade in violation of the antitrust laws, *Associated Press v. United States,* 326 U.S. 1 (1945); and must pay non-discriminatory taxes, *Murdock v. Pennsylvania,* 319 U.S. 105, 112 (1943). It is, therefore, beyond dispute that "[t]he publisher of a newspaper has no special immunity from the application of general laws. He has no special privilege to invade the rights and liberties of others." *Associated Press v. NLRB, supra,* 301 U.S., at 132-133. Accordingly, enforcement of such general laws against the press is not subject to stricter scrutiny than would be applied

> **Take Note**
>
> The Court announces here the rule that the press is subject to generally applicable laws notwithstanding the First Amendment. From the cases we have seen so far, are there any exceptions to this general rule? Does the First Amendment impose any limits on the application of generally applicable rules to the press?

to enforcement against other persons or organizations.

There can be little doubt that the Minnesota doctrine of promissory estoppel is a law of general applicability. It does not target or single out the press. Rather, insofar as we are advised, the doctrine is generally applicable to the daily transactions of all the citizens of Minnesota. The First Amendment does not forbid its application to the press. *** Accordingly, the judgment of the Minnesota Supreme Court is reversed, and the case is remanded for further proceedings not inconsistent with this opinion.

Justice BLACKMUN, with whom Justice MARSHALL and Justice SOUTER join, dissenting.

*** I regard our decision in *Hustler Magazine, Inc. v. Falwell,* 485 U.S. 46 (1988), to be precisely on point. There, we found that the use of a claim of intentional infliction of emotional distress to impose liability for the publication of a satirical critique violated the First Amendment. There was no doubt that Virginia's tort of intentional infliction of emotional distress was "a law of general applicability" unrelated to the suppression of speech. Nonetheless, a unanimous Court found that, when used to penalize the expression of opinion, the law was subject to the strictures of the First Amendment. In applying that principle, we concluded that "public figures and public officials may not recover for the tort of intentional infliction of emotional distress by reason of publications such as the one here at issue without showing in addition that the publication contains a false statement of fact which was made with 'actual malice,'" as defined by *New York Times Co. v. Sullivan,* 376 U.S. 254 (1964). In so doing, we rejected the argument that Virginia's interest in protecting its citizens from emotional distress was sufficient to remove from First Amendment protection a "patently offensive" expression of opinion.

> **Make the Connection**
>
> We considered some of the limits that the First Amendment imposes on common-law rights of action—and in particular claims for defamation—in Chapter 14, when we considered *New York Times v. Sullivan*.

*** I perceive no meaningful distinction between a statute that penalizes published speech in order to protect the individual's psychological well being or reputational interest and one that exacts the same penalty in order to compensate the loss of employment or earning potential. Certainly, our decision in *Hustler* recognized no such distinction.

Justice SOUTER, with whom Justice MARSHALL, Justice BLACKMUN, and Justice O'CONNOR join, dissenting.

*** [G]eneral laws [that] entail effects on the content of speech, like the one in question, may of course be found constitutional, but only, as Justice Harlan observed,

> when [such effects] have been found justified by subordinating valid governmental interests, a prerequisite to constitutionality which has necessarily involved a weighing of the governmental interest involved. *** Whenever, in such a context, these constitutional protections are asserted against the exercise of valid governmental powers a reconciliation must be effected, and that perforce requires an appropriate weighing of the respective interests involved.

Konigsberg v. State Bar of California, 366 U.S. 36, 51 (1961). Because I believe the State's interest in enforcing a newspaper's promise of confidentiality insufficient to outweigh the interest in unfettered publication of the information revealed in this case, I respectfully dissent.

Points for Discussion

a. Defamation vs. Promissory Estoppel

Is there a meaningful difference between a claim that a newspaper's publication of information damaged a person's reputation or emotional psyche, on the one hand, and a claim that a newspaper's publication of information violated a promise not to disclose that information, on the other? If so, what is the difference? Is it sufficient to justify different rules under the First Amendment? Didn't the decisions in *Sullivan* and *Falwell*, which we considered in Chapter 14, favor the press because they involved public figures, and thus called for the application of a special rule? Was the same true in *Cohen*? Does it turn on whether Mr. Cohen was a public figure?

b. Rules vs. Standards

Justice Souter's dissent calls for a balancing of interests—specifically, the balancing of the need for the general enforcement of laws against the needs of the media. What might be the benefits of a balancing test in comparison to the categorical rule adopted by the Court? Would a balancing test have any drawbacks?

B. Requiring the Press to Provide Media Access to Others

The freedom of the press is often justified as a means to an end. If the media are free to publish whatever they wish, the reasoning goes, all good ideas will be heard. This logic, however, rests on an assumption that the press actually will use its freedom to promote all ideas. There is a significant question whether this assumption accords with reality. Over forty years ago, Professor Jerome Barron (later the dean of the George Washington University Law School) addressed this issue in a highly influential article. He observed that:

> Our constitutional theory is in the grip of a romantic conception of free expression, a belief that the "marketplace of ideas" is freely accessible. But if ever there were a self-operating marketplace of ideas, it has long ceased to exist. The mass media's development of an antipathy to ideas requires legal intervention if novel and unpopular ideas are to be assured a forum—unorthodox points of view which have no claim on broadcast time and newspaper space as a matter of right are in poor position to compete with those aired as a matter of grace.

Jerome Barron, *Access to the Press—A New First Amendment Right*, 80 Harv. L. Rev. 1641, 1641 (1967).

The following two landmark cases involved government regulations that attempted to require "balance" in what the press publishes. The regulations at issue did not prohibit media outlets from saying anything. But they each required (or attempted to require) publishers to devote some of their news content to opposing views. The Supreme Court upheld the regulation in the case of radio programming, but not newspaper publishing. In reading the two cases, attempt to discern what justifies the difference in results.

———————

Red Lion Broadcasting Co. v. F.C.C.

395 U.S. 367 (1969)

Mr. Justice WHITE delivered the opinion of the Court.

The Federal Communications Commission has for many years imposed on radio and television broadcasters the requirement that discussion of public issues be presented on broadcast stations, and that each side of those issues must be given fair coverage. This is known as the fairness doctrine, which originated very early in the history of broadcasting and has maintained its present outlines for some time. It is an obligation whose content has been defined in a long series of FCC rulings in particular cases, and which is distinct from the statutory requirement of § 315 of the Communications Act that equal time be allotted all qualified candidates for public office. Two aspects of the fairness doctrine, relating to personal attacks in the context of controversial public issues and to political editorializing, were codified more precisely in the form of FCC regulations in 1967. The two cases before us now, which were decided separately below, challenge the constitutional and statutory bases of the doctrine and component rules. [One] involves the application of the fairness doctrine to a particular broadcast, and [the other] arises as an action to review the FCC's 1967 promulgation of the personal attack and political editorializing regulations, which were laid down after the Red Lion litigation had begun.

The Red Lion Broadcasting Company is licensed to operate a Pennsylvania radio station, WGCB. On November 27, 1964, WGCB carried a 15-minute broadcast by the Reverend Billy James Hargis as part of a "Christian Crusade" series. A book by Fred J. Cook entitled "Goldwater—Extremist on the Right" was discussed by Hargis, who said that Cook had been fired by a newspaper for making false charges against city officials; that Cook had then worked for a Communist-affiliated publication; that he had defended Alger Hiss and attacked J. Edgar Hoover and the Central Intelligence Agency; and that he had now written a "book to smear and destroy Barry Goldwater." When Cook heard of the broadcast he concluded that he had been personally attacked and demanded free reply time, which the station refused. After an exchange of letters among Cook, Red Lion,

> **FYI**
>
> Senator Barry Goldwater of Arizona was the Republican nominee for president in the 1964 election. One of his famous quotations from the campaign was: "I would remind you that extremism in the defense of liberty is no vice! And let me remind you also that moderation in the pursuit of justice is no virtue!"

and the FCC, the FCC declared that the Hargis broadcast constituted a personal attack on Cook [and] that Red Lion had failed to meet its obligation under the fairness doctrine ***.

Before 1927, the allocation of frequencies was left entirely to the private sector, and the result was chaos. It quickly became apparent that broadcast frequencies constituted a scarce resource whose use could be regulated and rationalized only by the Government. Without government control, the medium would be of little use because of the cacophony of competing voices, none of which could be clearly and predictably heard. Consequently, the Federal Radio Commission was established to allocate frequencies among competing applicants in a manner responsive to the public "convenience, interest, or necessity."

Make the Connection

Is Congress's charge to the Commission (later the FCC) to distribute licenses in a manner consistent with public "convenience, interest, or necessity," 47 U.S.C. § 303 & § 303(r), consistent with the non-delegation doctrine? We briefly addressed that doctrine—and the Court's decision to uphold the delegation of authority to the FCC—in Chapter 6.

Very shortly thereafter the Commission expressed its view that the "public interest requires ample play for the free and fair competition of opposing views, and the commission believes that the principle applies [to] all discussions of issues of importance to the public." *Great Lakes Broadcasting Co.*, 3 F.R.C. Ann. Rep. 32, 33 (1929), rev'd on other grounds, 37 F.2d 993 (D.C. Cir. 1929), *cert. dismissed*, 281 U.S. 706 (1930). ***

There is a twofold duty laid down by the FCC's decisions and described by the 1949 Report on Editorializing by Broadcast Licensees, 13 F.C.C. 1246 (1949). The broadcaster must give adequate coverage to public issues, *United Broadcasting Co.*, 10 F.C.C. 515 (1945), and coverage must be fair in that it accurately reflects the opposing views. *New Broadcasting Co.,* 6 P & F Radio Reg. 258 (1950). This must be done at the broadcaster's own expense if sponsorship is unavailable. *Cullman Broadcasting Co.*, 25 P & F Radio Reg. 895 (1963). Moreover, the duty must be met by programming obtained at the licensee's own initiative if available from no other source. *John J. Dempsey*, 6 P & F Radio Reg. 615 (1950). ***

When a personal attack has been made on a figure involved in a public issue both [FCC doctrine, established case by case, and] the 1967 regulations [require] that the individual attacked himself be offered an opportunity to respond. Likewise, where one candidate is endorsed in a political editorial, the other candidates must themselves be offered reply time to use personally or through a spokesman. These obligations differ from the general fairness requirement that issues be presented, and presented with coverage of competing views, in that the broadcaster does not have the option of presenting the attacked party's side himself or choosing a third party to represent that side. But insofar as there is an obligation of the broadcaster to see that both sides are presented, and insofar as that is an affirmative obligation, the personal attack doctrine and regulations do not differ from the preceding fairness doctrine. The simple fact that the attacked men or unendorsed candidates may respond themselves or through agents is not a critical distinction, and indeed, it is not unreasonable for the FCC to conclude that the objective of adequate presentation of all sides may best be served by allowing those most closely affected to make the response, rather than leaving the response in the hands of the station which has attacked their candidacies, endorsed their opponents, or carried a personal attack upon them.

The broadcasters challenge the fairness doctrine and its specific manifestations in the personal attack and political editorial rules on conventional First Amendment grounds, alleging that the rules abridge their freedom of speech and press. Their contention is that the First Amendment protects their desire to use their allotted frequencies continuously to broadcast whatever they choose, and to exclude whomever they choose from ever using that frequency. No man may be prevented from saying or publishing what he thinks, or from refusing in his speech or other utterances to give equal weight to the views of his opponents. This right, they say, applies equally to broadcasters.

Although broadcasting is clearly a medium affected by a First Amendment interest, *United States v. Paramount Pictures, Inc.*, 334 U.S. 131, 166 (1948), differences in the characteristics of new media justify differences in the First Amendment standards applied to them. For example, the ability of new technology to produce sounds more raucous than those of the human voice justifies restrictions on the sound level, and on the hours and places of use, of sound trucks so long as the restrictions are reasonable and applied without discrimination. *Kovacs v. Cooper*, 336 U.S. 77 (1949).

> **Food for Thought**
>
> Do you agree that the regulation at issue here is analogous to an ordinance limiting the volume at which (or the places in which) "sound trucks" may amplify certain messages? Wouldn't the proper analogy be an ordinance requiring sound trucks to play not only their chosen message (at whatever volume) but also messages with which the sound truck operator disagrees?

Just as the Government may limit the use of sound-amplifying equipment potentially so noisy that it drowns out civilized private speech, so may the Government limit the use of broadcast equipment. The right of free speech of a broadcaster, the user of a sound truck, or any other individual does not embrace a right to snuff out the free speech of others.

When two people converse face to face, both should not speak at once if either is to be clearly understood. But the range of the human voice is so limited that there could be meaningful communications if half the people in the United States were talking and the other half listening. Just as clearly, half the people might publish and the other half read. But the reach of radio signals is incomparably greater than the range of the human voice and the problem of interference is a massive reality. The lack of know-how and equipment may keep many from the air, but only a tiny fraction of those with resources and intelligence can hope to communicate by radio at the same time if intelligible communication is to be had, even if the entire radio spectrum is utilized in the present state of commercially acceptable technology.

It was this fact, and the chaos which ensued from permitting anyone to use any frequency at whatever power level he wished, which made necessary the enactment of the Radio Act of 1927 and the Communications Act of 1934, as the Court has noted at length before. *National Broadcasting Co. v. United States*, 319 U.S. 190, 210-214 (1943). It was this reality which at the very least necessitated first the division of the radio spectrum into portions reserved respectively for public broadcasting and for other important radio uses such as amateur operation, aircraft, police, defense, and navigation; and then the subdivision of each portion, and assignment of specific frequencies to individual users or groups of users. Beyond this, however, because the frequencies reserved for public broadcasting were limited in number, it was essential for the Government to tell some applicants that they could not broadcast at all because there was room for only a few.

Where there are substantially more individuals who want to broadcast than there are frequencies to allocate, it is idle to posit an unabridgeable First Amendment right to broadcast comparable to the right of every individual to speak, write, or publish. If 100 persons want broadcast licenses but there are only 10 frequencies to allocate, all of them may have the same "right" to a license; but if there is to be any effective communication by radio, only a few can be licensed and the rest must be barred from the airwaves. It would be strange if the First Amendment, aimed at protecting and furthering communications, prevented the Government from making radio communication possible by requiring licenses to broadcast and by limiting the number of licenses so as not to overcrowd the spectrum.

> **Make the Connection**
>
> In Chapter 14, we considered the "unconstitutional conditions" doctrine. Is the Court's suggestion here—that the government can compel broadcasters to present views with which they disagree because the broadcasters have no "right" to their broadcast licenses—consistent with that doctrine?

By the same token, as far as the First Amendment is concerned those who are licensed stand no better than those to whom licenses are refused. A license permits broadcasting, but the licensee has no constitutional right to be the one who holds the license or to monopolize a radio frequency to the exclusion of his fellow citizens. There is nothing in the First Amendment which prevents the Government from requiring a licensee to share his frequency with others and to conduct himself as a proxy or fiduciary with obligations to present those views and voices which are representative of his community and which would otherwise, by necessity, be barred from the airwaves.

This is not to say that the First Amendment is irrelevant to public broadcasting. On the contrary, it has a major role to play as the Congress itself recognized in § 326, which forbids FCC interference with "the right of free speech by means of radio communication." Because of the scarcity of radio frequencies, the Government is permitted to put restraints on licensees in favor of others whose views should be expressed on this unique medium. But the people as a whole retain their interest in free speech by radio and their collective right to have the medium function consistently with the ends and purposes of the First Amendment. It is the right of the viewers and listeners, not the right of the broadcasters, which is paramount.

> **Take Note**
>
> The Court suggests here that the First Amendment protects the "right of the viewers and listeners, not the right of the broadcasters." Is this consistent with the view of the First Amendment that we saw in Chapter 14? Is it a sensible view of the First Amendment's protections for speech and the press?

It is the purpose of the First Amendment to preserve an uninhibited marketplace of ideas in which truth will ultimately prevail, rather than to countenance monopolization of that market, whether it be by the Government itself or a private licensee. It is the right of the public to receive suitable access to social, political, esthetic, moral, and other ideas and experiences which is crucial here. That right may not constitutionally be abridged either by Congress or by the FCC.

Rather than confer frequency monopolies on a relatively small number of licensees, in a Nation of 200,000,000, the Government could surely have decreed that each frequency should be shared among all or some of those who wish to use it, each being assigned a portion of the broadcast day or the broadcast week. The ruling and regulations at issue here do not go quite so far. They assert that under specified circumstances, a licensee must offer to make available a reasonable amount of broadcast time to those who have a view different from that which has already been expressed on his station. The expression of a political endorsement, or of a personal attack while dealing with a controversial public issue, simply triggers this time sharing. As we have said, the First Amendment confers no right on licensees to prevent others from broadcasting on "their" frequencies and no right to an unconditional monopoly of a scarce resource which the Government has denied others the right to use.

It is strenuously argued, however, that if political editorials or personal attacks will trigger an obligation in broadcasters to afford the opportunity for expression to speakers who need not pay for time and whose views are unpalatable to the licensees, then broadcasters will be irresistibly forced to self-censorship and their coverage of controversial public issues will be eliminated or at least rendered wholly ineffective. Such a result would indeed be a serious matter, for should licensees actually eliminate their coverage of controversial issues, the purposes of the doctrine would be stifled.

At this point, however, as the Federal Communications Commission has indicated, that possibility is at best speculative. The communications industry, and in particular the networks, have taken pains to present controversial issues in the past, and even now they do not assert that they intend to abandon their efforts in this regard. It would be better if the FCC's encouragement were never necessary to induce the broadcasters to meet their responsibility. And if experience with the administration of those doctrines indicates that they have the net effect of reducing rather than enhancing the volume and quality of coverage, there will be time enough to reconsider the constitutional implications. The fairness doctrine in the past has had no such overall effect.

In view of the scarcity of broadcast frequencies, the Government's role in allocating those frequencies, and the legitimate claims of those unable without governmental assistance to gain access to those frequencies for expression of their views, we hold the regulations and ruling at issue here are both authorized by statute and constitutional.

———

Points for Discussion

a. The Fairness Doctrine

Did the Supreme Court, in referring to the rights of "viewers and listeners," suggest in <u>Red Lion</u> that the First Amendment *required* the fairness doctrine, or instead only that the fairness doctrine did not violate the First Amendment? Note that the FCC decided to abolish the fairness doctrine in 1989, a decision that was upheld in subsequent litigation. See *Syracuse Peace Council v. FCC*, 867 F.2d 654, 665 (D.C. Cir. 1989). Would the fairness doctrine, which applied only to the "broadcast spectrum," be constitutional in an era when most people watch cable television and a large number of people obtain their news from numerous sources on the internet?

b. Theories of First Amendment Protection

What is the purpose of the First Amendment's protections for the press (and for speech)? One common theory is that it promotes democracy by enabling the electorate to become informed. See, e.g., Owen Fiss, *Free Speech and Social Structure*, 71 Iowa L. Rev. 1405 (1986). Is <u>Red Lion</u> based on this view of the First Amendment? If so, in what way?

Hypothetical

Rush Limbaugh has been the most popular radio talk show host in America since the late 1980s. Millions of listeners tune in to his 3-hour radio program every day to hear his conservative commentary. In 1993, Congress considered enacting a statute to reinstate the fairness doctrine. Opponents dubbed the proposed legislation the "Hush Rush" bill. *The Hush Rush Law*, Wall St. J., Sept. 1, 1993, at A14. They reasoned that no radio station could afford to deliver Limbaugh's program every day if the station also had to broadcast a 3-hour program espousing contrary (and presumably less popular) views. Commentators predicted that radio stations "would certainly eliminate [Rush's program] rather than carve out three additional hours for a liberal political show." *"Fairness" Not Fair to Electronic Media*, South Fl. Sun-Sent., Oct. 19, 1993, at 1E. If the purpose of recreating the fairness doctrine was to silence Rush Limbaugh, would the law be constitutional under <u>Red Lion</u>? What if the purpose was to diversify the marketplace of ideas, but the likely effect was to silence Limbaugh and similar programs?

The Court in <u>Red Lion</u> upheld the fairness doctrine as applied to a radio station. Does the First Amendment permit its application to newspapers, as well? The following case considered that question.

Miami Herald Publishing Co. v. Tornillo

418 U.S. 241 (1974)

Mr. Chief Justice BURGER delivered the opinion of the Court.

The issue in this case is whether a state statute granting a political candidate a right to equal space to reply to criticism and attacks on his record by a newspaper violates the guarantees of a free press. In the fall of 1972, appellee, Executive Director of the Classroom Teachers Association, apparently a teachers' collective-bargaining agent, was a candidate for the Florida House of Representatives. On September 20, 1972, and again on September 29, 1972, appellant printed editorials critical of appellee's candidacy. In response to these editorials appellee demanded that appellant print verbatim his replies, defending the role of the Classroom Teachers Association and the organization's accomplishments for the citizens of Dade County. Appellant declined to print the appellee's replies and appellee brought suit in Circuit Court, Dade County, seeking declaratory and injunctive relief and actual and punitive damages in excess of $5,000. The action was premised on Florida Statute § 104.38 (1973), a "right of reply" statute which provides that if a candidate for nomination or election is assailed regarding his personal character or official record by any newspaper, the candidate has the right to demand that the newspaper print, free of cost to the candidate, any reply the candidate may make to the newspaper's charges. The reply must appear in as conspicuous a place and in the same kind of type as the charges which prompted the reply, provided it does not take up more space than the charges. Failure to comply with the statute constitutes a first-degree misdemeanor.

> **Make the Connection**
>
> We considered vagueness as a ground for facial invalidation of a statute under the First Amendment, and the constitutional status of defamatory speech, in Chapter 14.

Appellant contends the statute is void on its face because it purports to regulate the content of a newspaper in violation of the First Amendment. Alternatively it is urged that the statute is void for vagueness since no editor could know exactly what words would call the statute into operation. It is also contended that the statute fails to distinguish between critical comment which is and which is not defamatory.

The appellee and supporting advocates of an enforceable right of access to the press vigorously argue that government has an obligation to ensure that a wide variety of views reach the public.[8] The contentions of access proponents will be set out in some detail. It is urged that at the time the First Amendment to the Constitution was ratified in 1791 as part of our Bill of Rights the press was broadly representative of the people it was serving. While many of the newspapers were intensely partisan and narrow in their views, the press collectively presented a broad range of opinions to readers. Entry into publishing was inexpensive; pamphlets and books provided meaningful alternatives to the organized press for the expression of unpopular ideas and often treated events and expressed views not covered by conventional newspapers. A true marketplace of ideas existed in which there was relatively easy access to the channels of communication.

[8] *See generally* Jerome Barron, *Access to the Press—A New First Amendment Right*, 80 Harv. L. Rev. 1641 (1967).

Access advocates submit that although newspapers of the present are superficially similar to those of 1791 the press of today is in reality very different from that known in the early years of our national existence. In the past half century a communications revolution has seen the introduction of radio and television into our lives, the promise of a global community through the use of communications satellites, and the spectre of a "wired" nation by means of an expanding cable television network with two-way capabilities. The printed press, it is said, has not escaped the effects of this revolution. Newspapers have become big business and there are far fewer of them to serve a larger literate population. Chains of newspapers, national newspapers, national wire and news services, and one-newspaper towns, are the dominant features of a press that has become noncompetitive and enormously powerful and influential in its capacity to manipulate popular opinion and change the course of events. Major metropolitan newspapers have collaborated to establish news services national in scope. Such national news organizations provide syndicated "interpretive reporting" as well as syndicated features and commentary, all of which can serve as part of the new school of "advocacy journalism."

The elimination of competing newspapers in most of our large cities, and the concentration of control of media that results from the only newspaper's being owned by the same interests which own a television station and a radio station, are important components of this trend toward concentration of control of outlets to inform the public.

The result of these vast changes has been to place in a few hands the power to inform the American people and shape public opinion. Much of the editorial opinion and commentary that is printed is that of syndicated columnists distributed nationwide and, as a result, we are told, on national and world issues there tends to be a homogeneity of editorial opinion, commentary, and interpretive analysis. The abuses of bias and manipulative reportage are, likewise, said to be the result of the vast accumulations of unreviewable power in the modern media empires. In effect, it is claimed, the public has lost any ability to respond or to contribute in a meaningful way to the debate on issues. The monopoly of the means of communication allows for little or no critical analysis of the media except in professional journals of very limited readership.

The obvious solution, which was available to dissidents at an earlier time when entry into publishing was relatively inexpensive, today would be to have additional newspapers. But the same economic factors which have caused the disappearance of vast numbers of metropolitan newspapers, have made entry into the marketplace of ideas served by the print media almost impossible. It is urged that the claim of newspapers to be "surrogates for the public" carries with it a concomitant fiduciary obligation to account for that stewardship. From this premise it is reasoned that the only effective way to insure fairness and accuracy and to provide for some accountability is for government to take affirmative action. The First Amendment interest of the public in being informed is said to be in peril because the "marketplace of ideas" is today a monopoly controlled by the owners of the market.

However much validity may be found in these arguments, at each point the implementation of a remedy such as an enforceable right of access necessarily calls for some mechanism, either governmental or consensual. If it is governmental coercion, this at once brings about a confrontation with the express provisions of the First Amendment and the judicial gloss on that Amendment developed over the years.

The Court foresaw the problems relating to government-enforced access as early as its decision in *Associated Press v. United States*, 326 U.S. 1 (1945). There it carefully contrasted the private "compulsion to print" called for by the Association's bylaws with the provisions of the District Court decree against appellants which "does not compel AP or its members to permit publication of anything which their 'reason' tells them should not be published." *Id.*, at 20. In *Branzburg v. Hayes*, 408 U.S. 665, 681 (1972), we emphasized that the cases then before us "involve no intrusions upon speech or assembly, no prior restraint or restriction on what the press may publish, and no express or implied command that the press publish what it prefers to withhold." In *Columbia Broadcasting System, Inc. v. Democratic National Committee*, 412 U.S. 94, 117 (1973), the plurality opinion [noted]:

> The power of a privately owned newspaper to advance its own political, social, and economic views is bounded by only two factors: first, the acceptance of a sufficient number of readers— and hence advertisers—to assure financial success; and, second, the journalistic integrity of its editors and publishers.

[Beginning] with <u>Associated Press</u>, the Court has expressed sensitivity as to whether a restriction or requirement constituted the compulsion exerted by government on a newspaper to print that which it would not otherwise print. The clear implication has been that any such compulsion to publish that which " 'reason' tells them should not be published" is unconstitutional. A responsible press is an undoubtedly desirable goal, but press responsibility is not mandated by the Constitution and like many other virtues it cannot be legislated.

Appellee's argument that the Florida statute does not amount to a restriction of appellant's right to speak because "the statute in question here has not prevented the Miami Herald from saying anything it wished" begs the core question. Compelling editors or publishers to publish that which "reason tells them should not be published" is what is at issue in this case. The Florida statute operates as a command in the same sense as a statute or regulation forbidding appellant to publish specified matter. Governmental restraint on publishing need not fall into familiar or traditional patterns to be subject to constitutional limitations on governmental powers. *Grosjean v. American Press Co.*, 297 U.S. 233, 244-245 (1936). The Florida statute exacts a penalty on the basis of the content of a newspaper. The first phase of the penalty resulting from the compelled printing of a reply is exacted in terms of the cost in printing and composing time and materials and in taking up space that could be devoted to other material the newspaper may have preferred to print. It is correct, as appellee contends, that a newspaper is not subject to the

Take Note

The Court explains in these passages how the Florida statute imposes a burden on newspapers and, consequently, why the statute might chill protected speech. Is the Court's point that a regulation *mandating* the inclusion of particular content is tantamount to a regulation *prohibiting* the inclusion of other content? Or that any government interference with editorial choices are suspect, regardless of whether it mandates coverage or prohibits coverage?

finite technological limitations of time that confront a broadcaster but it is not correct to say that, as an economic reality, a newspaper can proceed to infinite expansion of its column space to accommodate the replies that a government agency determines or a statute commands the readers should have available.

Faced with the penalties that would accrue to any newspaper that published news or commentary arguably within the reach of the right-of-access statute, editors might well conclude that the safe course is to avoid controversy. Therefore, under the operation of the Florida statute, political and electoral coverage would be blunted or reduced. Government-enforced right of access inescapably "dampens the vigor and limits the variety of public debate." *New York Times Co. v. Sullivan*, 376 U.S. 254, 279 (1964). *******

Even if a newspaper would face no additional costs to comply with a compulsory access law and would not be forced to forgo publication of news or opinion by the inclusion of a reply, the Florida statute fails to clear the barriers of the First Amendment because of its intrusion into the function of editors. A newspaper is more than a passive receptacle or conduit for news, comment, and advertising. The choice of material to go into a newspaper, and the decisions made as to limitations on the size and content of the paper, and treatment of public issues and public officials—whether fair or unfair—constitute the exercise of editorial control and judgment. It has yet to be demonstrated how governmental regulation of this crucial process can be exercised consistent with First Amendment guarantees of a free press as they have evolved to this time. Accordingly, the judgment of the Supreme Court of Florida is reversed.

Points for Discussion

a. Newspapers and Broadcasters

The Supreme Court oddly did not cite <u>Red Lion</u> in <u>Tornillo</u>, even though the two cases involved similar issues. Are the two cases inconsistent or are they distinguishable?

b. Theory of the First Amendment's Protections

What theory of the First Amendment's protections did the Court advance in <u>Tornillo</u>? Did the court reject the "marketplace of ideas" theory that seemed central to the Court's decision in <u>Red Lion</u>? Or did the Court simply conclude that the challenged statute did not ultimately advance that theory of the First Amendment? If the former, what interests did the Court think that the First Amendment serves?

C. Press Access to Government Proceedings

Newspapers and broadcast media cannot publish informed accounts of important developments unless their reporters have access to the sources of the news. Does the freedom of the press guarantee journalists a right of access to government proceedings, to crime and accident scenes, and to other places where news is made? The Supreme Court has not attempted to give a general answer to this question. Instead, the Court has given some context-specific answers. The following case considers whether the media have a right to attend criminal trials.

————————————

Richmond Newspapers, Inc. v. Virginia

448 U.S. 555 (1980)

Take Note

This is a plurality opinion. Consider what that means for the analysis contained in this opinion and in those by the other Justices.

Mr. Chief Justice BURGER announced the judgment of the Court and delivered an opinion, in which Mr. Justice WHITE and Mr. Justice STEVENS joined.

[Stevenson was tried and convicted in state court in Virginia in July 1976 of second-degree murder, but the Virginia Supreme Court reversed after concluding that a bloodstained shirt purportedly belonging to Stevenson had been improperly admitted into evidence. Stevenson was retried in the same court, but the second trial ended in a mistrial in May 1978 when a juror asked to be excused after trial had begun and no alternate was available. A third trial one month later in the same court also ended in a mistrial, apparently because a prospective juror had read about the previous trials in a newspaper and had told other prospective jurors about the case before the retrial began.]

Stevenson was tried in the same court for a fourth time beginning on September 11, 1978. Present in the courtroom when the case was called were appellants Wheeler and McCarthy, reporters for appellant Richmond Newspapers, Inc. Before the trial began, counsel for the defendant moved that it be closed to the public [on the ground that persons who observed the prior trials might shuffle information "back and forth when we have a recess as to what—who testified to what."] The trial judge, who had presided over two of the three previous trials, asked if the prosecution had any objection to clearing the courtroom. The prosecutor stated he had no objection and would leave it to the discretion of the court. Presumably [relying on] Va. Code § 19.2-266 (Supp.1980), the trial judge then [ordered] "that the Courtroom be kept clear of all parties except the witnesses when they testify." The record does not show that any objections to the closure order were made by anyone present at the time, including appellants Wheeler and McCarthy.

Later that same day, however, appellants sought a hearing on a motion to vacate the closure order. The trial judge granted the request and scheduled a hearing to follow the close of the day's proceedings. When the hearing began, the court ruled that the hearing was to be treated as part of the trial; accordingly, he again ordered the reporters to leave the courtroom, and they complied.

At the closed hearing, counsel for appellants observed that no evidentiary findings had been made by the court prior to the entry of its closure order and pointed out that the court had failed to consider any other, less drastic measures within its power to ensure a fair trial. Counsel for appellants argued that constitutional considerations mandated that before ordering closure, the court should first decide that the rights of the defendant could be protected in no other way.

Counsel for defendant Stevenson pointed out that this was the fourth time he was standing trial. He also referred to "difficulty with information between the jurors," and stated that he "didn't want information to leak out," be published by the media, perhaps inaccurately, and then be seen by the jurors. Defense counsel argued that these things, plus the fact that "this is a small community," made this a proper case for closure. The court denied the motion to vacate and ordered the trial to continue the following morning "with the press and public excluded."

What transpired when the closed trial resumed the next day was disclosed in the following manner by an order of the court entered September 12, 1978:

> [I]n the absence of the jury, the defendant by counsel made a Motion that a mistrial be declared, which motion was taken under advisement. At the conclusion of the Commonwealth's evidence, the attorney for the defendant moved the Court to strike the Commonwealth's evidence on grounds stated to the record, which Motion was sustained by the Court. And the jury having been excused, the Court doth find the accused NOT GUILTY of Murder, as charged in the Indictment, and he was allowed to depart.

[The newspapers appealed the denial of their motion. The Court considered the possibility that the case was now moot because the trial was over. But the Court decided to grant review on grounds that "it is reasonably foreseeable that other trials may be closed by other judges" and "criminal trials will be of sufficiently short duration that a closure order" will evade review.]

We have found nothing to suggest that the presumptive openness of the trial, which English courts were later to call "one of the essential qualities of a court of justice," *Daubney v. Cooper*, 10 B. & C. 237, 240, 109 Eng. Rep. 438, 440 (K. B. 1829), was not also an attribute of the judicial systems of colonial America. In Virginia, for example, such records as there are of early criminal trials indicate that they were open, and nothing to the contrary has been cited. *See* A. Scott, Criminal Law in Colonial Virginia 128-129 (1930); Reinsch, The English Common Law in the Early American Colonies, in 1 Select Essays in Anglo-American Legal History 367, 405 (1907). *** In some instances, the openness of trials was explicitly recognized as part of the fundamental law of the Colony. The 1677 Concessions and Agreements of West New Jersey, for example, provided:

> That in all publick courts of justice for tryals of causes, civil or criminal, any person or persons,

inhabitants of the said Province may freely come into, and attend the said courts, and hear and be present, at all or any such tryals as shall be there had or passed, that justice may not be done in a corner nor in any covert manner." Reprinted in Sources of Our Liberties 188 (R. Perry ed. 1959). See also 1 B. Schwartz, The Bill of Rights: A Documentary History 129 (1971).

The Pennsylvania Frame of Government of 1682 also provided "[t]hat all courts shall be open ***," Sources of Our Liberties, *supra*, at 217; 1 Schwartz, *supra*, at 140, and this declaration was reaffirmed in § 26 of the Constitution adopted by Pennsylvania in 1776. See 1 Schwartz, *supra*, at 271.

As we have shown, and as was shown in both the Court's opinion and the dissent in *Gannett Co. v. DePasquale*, 443 U.S. 368, 384, 386, n. 15 (1979), the historical evidence demonstrates conclusively that at the time when our organic laws were adopted, criminal trials both here and in England had long been presumptively open. The question is whether anyone else can insist on a public trial if the defendant waives that right. This is no quirk of history; rather, it has long been recognized as an indispensable attribute of an Anglo-American trial. Both Hale in the 17th century and Blackstone in the 18th saw the importance of openness to the proper functioning of a trial; it gave assurance that the proceedings were conducted fairly to all concerned, and it discouraged perjury, the misconduct of participants, and decisions based on secret bias or partiality. *See, e. g.*, M. Hale, The History of the Common Law of England 343-345 (6th ed. 1820); 3 W. Blackstone, Commentaries *372-*373. *** From this unbroken, uncontradicted history, supported by reasons as valid today as in centuries past, we are bound to conclude that a presumption of openness inheres in the very nature of a criminal trial under our system of justice.

> **FYI**
>
> The Sixth Amendment guarantees a right to a "public trial." In *Gannett*, however, the Court concluded that this right belongs only to the accused criminal defendant. The Court held that the press and members of the public have no right under the Sixth Amendment to attend criminal trials. In what way is the claim here different?

The First Amendment, in conjunction with the Fourteenth, prohibits governments from "abridging the freedom of speech, or of the press; or the right of the people peaceably to assemble, and to petition the Government for a redress of grievances." These expressly guaranteed freedoms share a common core purpose of assuring freedom of communication on matters relating to the functioning of government. Plainly it would be difficult to single out any aspect of government of higher concern and importance to the people than the manner in which criminal trials are conducted; as we have shown, recognition of this pervades the centuries-old history of open trials and the opinions of this Court.

The Bill of Rights was enacted against the backdrop of the long history of trials being presumptively open. Public access to trials was then regarded as an important aspect of the process itself; the conduct of trials "before as many of the people as chuse to attend" was regarded as one of "the inestimable advantages of a free English constitution of government." 1 Journals 106, 107. In guaranteeing freedoms such as those of speech and press, the First Amendment can be read as protecting the right of everyone to attend trials so as to give meaning to those explicit guarantees. "[T]he First Amendment goes beyond protection of the press and the self-expression of individuals to prohibit government from limiting the stock of information from which members of the public may draw." *First National Bank of Boston v. Bellotti*, 435 U.S. 765, 783 (1978). Free speech carries with it some freedom to listen. "In a variety of contexts this Court has referred to a First Amendment right to 'receive information and ideas.'" *Kleindienst v. Mandel*, 408 U.S. 753, 762 (1972). What this means in the context of trials is that the First Amendment guarantees of speech and press, standing alone, prohibit government from summarily closing courtroom doors which had long been open to the public at the time that Amendment was adopted. "For the First Amendment does not speak equivocally. [It] must be taken as a command of the broadest scope that explicit language, read in the context of a liberty-loving society, will allow." *Bridges v. California*, 314 U.S. 252, 263 (1941).

It is not crucial whether we describe this right to attend criminal trials to hear, see, and communicate observations concerning them as a "right of access" or a "right to gather information," for we have recognized that "without some protection for seeking out the news, freedom of the press could be eviscerated." *Branzburg v. Hayes*, 408 U.S. 665, 681 (1972). The explicit, guaranteed rights to speak and to publish concerning what takes place at a trial would lose much meaning if access to observe the trial could, as it was here, be foreclosed arbitrarily.

The State argues that the Constitution nowhere spells out a guarantee for the right of the public to attend trials, and that accordingly no such right is protected. The possibility that such a contention could be made did not escape the notice of the Constitution's draftsmen; they were concerned that some important rights might be thought disparaged because not specifically guaranteed. It was even argued that because of this danger no Bill of Rights should be adopted. See, *e. g.*, The Federalist No. 84 (A. Hamilton). In a letter to Thomas Jefferson in October 1788, James Madison [stated] that "there is great reason to fear that a positive declaration of some of the most essential rights could not be obtained in the requisite latitude." 5 Writings of James Madison 271 (G. Hunt ed. 1904).[15]

> **Make the Connection**
>
> The plurality here compares the right to attend criminal trials to other unenumerated rights that the Court has recognized. Is the Court's approach here consistent with the approach that it took in other cases involving unenumerated rights that we considered in Chapter 8?

Notwithstanding the appropriate caution against reading into the Constitution rights not explicitly defined, the Court has acknowledged that certain unarticulated rights are implicit in enumerated guarantees. For example, the rights of association and of privacy, the right to be presumed innocent, and the right to be judged by a standard of proof beyond a reasonable doubt in a criminal trial, as well as the right to travel,

---

[15] Madison's comments in Congress also reveal the perceived need for some sort of constitutional "saving clause," which, among other things, would serve to foreclose application to the Bill of Rights of the maxim that the affirmation of particular rights implies a negation of those not expressly defined. See 1 Annals of Cong. 438-440 (1789). See also, e.g., 2 J. Story, Commentaries on the Constitution of the United States 651 (5th ed. 1891). Madison's efforts, culminating in the Ninth Amendment, served to allay the fears of those who were concerned that expressing certain guarantees could be read as excluding others.

appear nowhere in the Constitution or Bill of Rights. Yet these important but unarticulated rights have nonetheless been found to share constitutional protection in common with explicit guarantees. The concerns expressed by Madison and others have thus been resolved; fundamental rights, even though not expressly guaranteed, have been recognized by the Court as indispensable to the enjoyment of rights explicitly defined.

We hold that the right to attend criminal trials is implicit in the guarantees of the First Amendment; without the freedom to attend such trials, which people have exercised for centuries, important aspects of freedom of speech and "of the press could be eviscerated." *Branzburg*, 408 U.S., at 681.

Having concluded there was a guaranteed right of the public under the First and Fourteenth Amendments to attend the trial of Stevenson's case, we return to the closure order challenged by appellants. Despite the fact that this was the fourth trial of the accused, the trial judge made no findings to support closure; no inquiry was made as to whether alternative solutions would have met the need to ensure fairness; there was no recognition of any right under the Constitution for the public or press to attend the trial. [T]here exist in the context of the trial itself various tested alternatives to satisfy the constitutional demands of fairness. There was no suggestion that any problems with witnesses could not have been dealt with by their exclusion from the courtroom or their sequestration during the trial. Nor is there anything to indicate that sequestration of the jurors would not have guarded against their being subjected to any improper information. All of the alternatives admittedly present difficulties for trial courts, but none of the factors relied on here was beyond the realm of the manageable. Absent an overriding interest articulated in findings, the trial of a criminal case must be open to the public. *** *Reversed.*

> **Take Note**
>
> Note that the plurality's conclusion here appears to extend the right to attend trials not only to the press, but also to the public. Does that suggest that the First Amendment's protection for the freedom of the press is not central to the resolution of the case? Whatever the weight of the public's general interest in open trials, does the press have a special claim of access to criminal trials?

Mr. Justice BRENNAN, with whom Mr. Justice MARSHALL joins, concurring in the judgment.

Gannett Co. v. DePasquale, 443 U.S. 368 (1979), held that the Sixth Amendment right to a public trial was personal to the accused, conferring no right of access to pretrial proceedings that is separately enforceable by the public or the press. The instant case raises the question whether the First Amendment, of its own force and as applied to the States through the Fourteenth Amendment, secures the public an independent right of access to trial proceedings. Because I believe that the First Amendment—of itself and as applied to the States through the Fourteenth Amendment—secures such a public right of access, I agree with those of my Brethren who hold that, without more, agreement of the trial judge and the parties cannot constitutionally close a trial to the public.

Secrecy is profoundly inimical to [the] demonstrative purpose of the trial process.

Open trials assure the public that procedural rights are respected, and that justice is afforded equally. Closed trials breed suspicion of prejudice and arbitrariness, which in turn spawns disrespect for law. Public access is essential, therefore, if trial adjudication is to achieve the objective of maintaining public confidence in the administration of justice.

But the trial is more than a demonstrably just method of adjudicating disputes and protecting rights. It plays a pivotal role in the entire judicial process, and, by extension, in our form of government. *** While individual cases turn upon the controversies between parties, or involve particular prosecutions, court rulings impose official and practical consequences upon members of society at large. Moreover, judges bear responsibility for the vitally important task of construing and securing constitutional rights. Thus, so far as the trial is the mechanism for judicial factfinding, as well as the initial forum for legal decisionmaking, it is a genuine governmental proceeding. *** It follows that the conduct of the trial is pre-eminently a matter of public interest. More importantly, public access to trials acts as an important check, akin in purpose to the other checks and balances that infuse our system of government. ***

Since in the present case the trial judge appears to have given no recognition to the right of representatives of the press and members of the public to be present at the Virginia murder trial over which he was presiding, the judgment under review must be reversed. ***

Mr. Justice BLACKMUN, concurring in the judgment.

My opinion and vote in partial dissent last Term in *Gannett Co. v. DePasquale*, 443 U.S. 368, 406 (1979), compels my vote to reverse the judgment of the Supreme Court of Virginia. The Court, however, has eschewed the Sixth Amendment route. The plurality turns to other possible constitutional sources and invokes a veritable potpourri of them— the Speech Clause of the First Amendment, the Press Clause, the Assembly Clause, the Ninth Amendment, and a cluster of penumbral guarantees recognized in past decisions. This course is troublesome, but it is the route that has been selected and, at least for now, we must live with it. ***

Having said all this, and with the Sixth Amendment set to one side in this case, I am driven to conclude, as a secondary position, that the First Amendment must provide some measure of protection for public access to the trial. The opinion in partial dissent in <u>Gannett</u> explained that the public has an intense need and a deserved right to know about the administration of justice in general; about the prosecution of local crimes in particular; about the conduct of the judge, the prosecutor, defense counsel, police officers, other public servants, and all the actors in the judicial arena; and about the trial itself. See 443 U.S., at 413, and n.2, 414, 428-429, 448. It is clear and obvious to me, on the approach the Court has chosen to take, that, by closing this criminal trial, the trial judge abridged these First Amendment interests of the public.

Mr. Justice REHNQUIST, dissenting.

For the reasons stated in my separate concurrence in *Gannett Co. v. DePasquale*, 443 U.S. 368, 403 (1979), I do not believe that either the First or Sixth Amendment, as made applicable to the States by the Fourteenth, requires that a State's reasons for denying public access to a trial, where both the prosecuting attorney and the defendant have consented to an order of closure approved by the judge, are subject to any additional constitutional review at our hands. And I most certainly do not believe that the Ninth Amendment confers upon us any such power to review orders of state trial judges closing trials in such situations.

The issue here is not whether the "right" to freedom of the press conferred by the First Amendment to the Constitution overrides the defendant's "right" to a fair trial conferred by other Amendments to the Constitution; it is instead whether any provision in the Constitution may fairly be read to prohibit what the trial judge in the Virginia state-court system did in this case. Being unable to find any such prohibition in the First, Sixth, Ninth, or any other Amendment to the United States Constitution, or in the Constitution itself, I dissent.

———————————

Points for Discussion

a. Views of the Justices

On what ground did the plurality decision rest? Why did the concurrences agree with the result but not the rationale? Was their dispute with the Court's interpretive methodology? Or simply with the particular provisions of the Constitution on which the plurality relied? How was the dissent's position different from the positions expressed in the other opinions?

Consider the following hypothetical case: A prominent businessman and supporter of the mayor is implicated in a bribery scandal. He is indicted by a prosecutor who is loyal to the mayor. Shortly after the mayor is defeated in an election but before the new mayor takes office, an elected trial judge from the outgoing mayor's party enters an order announcing his plan to hold a closed trial. The local newspaper challenges the order, arguing that the judge might direct a judgment of acquittal to ensure that the businessman is protected by the double jeopardy provision of the Fifth Amendment. How would the claim be resolved under the Court's approach? Under the dissent's approach? Would we need to know other facts, as well?

b. Right of Access to Prisons

In *Pell v. Procunier*, 417 U.S. 817 (1974), the Supreme Court rejected a claim by journalists that they had a constitutional right to interview a particular inmate in a prison. In what ways is a prison different from a criminal trial?

———————————

Executive Summary of This Chapter

The First Amendment expressly prohibits Congress from abridging the **freedom of the press**. The Supreme Court has held that this prohibition also applies to the states under the incorporation doctrine. *Gitlow v. People of State of New York*, 268 U.S. 652, 666 (1925).

One question is whether the freedom of the press gives the press (e.g., newspapers, radio and television news producers, journalists, etc.) **special rights or special exemptions from generally applicable laws** beyond the free speech rights generally enjoyed by everyone. The Supreme Court has answered this question in the negative by holding that "generally applicable laws do not offend the First Amendment simply because their enforcement against the press has incidental effects on its ability to gather and report the news." *Cohen v. Cowles Media Co.*, 501 U.S. 663 (1991). Cases in this chapter provide several illustrations. The freedom of the press does not give journalists a right to refuse to appear and testify before grand juries. *Branzburg v. Hayes*, 408 U.S. 665 (1972). The freedom of the press does not immunize newspaper offices from search warrants or exempt newspaper offices from complying with otherwise lawful subpoenas to turn over evidence of crimes. *Zurcher v. Stanford Daily*, 436 U.S. 547 (1978). And the freedom of the press does not prevent the enforcement of a reporter's promises to a source under the doctrine of promissory estoppel. *Cohen*.

A second question is whether the freedom of the press prevents the government from requiring news providers to give outsiders **access to their media** (e.g., column space in a newspaper or airtime during a radio or television broadcast). The Supreme Court's answer to this question has depended upon the context. The Court has held that the freedom of the press does not prevent the government from requiring radio and television broadcasters to discuss public issues and to give fair coverage to each side of the issues. *Red Lion Broadcasting Co. v. F.C.C.*, 395 U.S. 367 (1969). But the Court has held that the government cannot require a newspaper to give political candidates space to reply to criticism printed in a newspaper. *Miami Herald Publishing Co. v. Tornillo*, 418 U.S. 241 (1974). A possible rationale for why the government may require broadcasters to publish contrary views but not newspapers is that anyone can start a newspaper but the number of radio and television stations is limited because the airwaves can physically carry only so many radio and television broadcasts.

A third question is whether the freedom of the press gives the media **special rights of access to government proceedings**. The Supreme Court has not announced a general rule with respect to this issue. But a plurality of the Court concluded that the First Amendment gives the press, and the general public, a right to attend criminal trials. *Richmond Newspapers, Inc. v. Virginia*, 448 U.S. 555 (1980).

CHAPTER 16

Freedom of Association

Introduction

The text of the Constitution does not expressly mention a "freedom of association." So what is this freedom and where does it come from? The Supreme Court offered a concise explanation in *Roberts v. U.S. Jaycees*, 468 U.S. 609, 617-618 (1984):

> Our decisions have referred to constitutionally protected "freedom of association" in two distinct senses. In one line of decisions, the Court has concluded that choices to enter into and maintain certain intimate human relationships must be secured against undue intrusion by the State because of the role of such relationships in safeguarding the individual freedom that is central to our constitutional scheme. In this respect, freedom of association receives protection as a fundamental element of personal liberty. In another set of decisions, the Court has recognized a right to associate for the purpose of engaging in those activities protected by the First Amendment—speech, assembly, petition for the redress of grievances, and the exercise of religion. The Constitution guarantees freedom of association of this kind as an indispensable means of preserving other individual liberties.

In other words, the Supreme Court has developed two distinct "freedom of association" doctrines. Under the first doctrine, freedom of association is a fundamental right, protected under the theory of substantive due process. This freedom of association may encompass, for example, "a right to maintain certain familial relationships, including association among members of an immediate family and association between grandchildren and grandparents." *Overton v. Bazzetta*, 539 U.S. 126, 131 (2003). In recent years, the Supreme Court has said fairly little about the freedom of association protected by the Due Process Clauses, perhaps because of continuing controversy over the concept of substantive due process. *Collins v. Harker Heights*, 503 U.S. 115, 125 (1992) ("As a general matter, the Court has always been reluctant to expand the concept of substantive due process because guideposts for responsible decisionmaking in this unchartered area are scarce and open-ended.").

> **Make the Connection**
>
> We addressed the doctrine of substantive due process—the idea that the Due Process Clauses in the Fifth and Fourteenth Amendments confer substantive rights (as opposed to procedural rights)—and protected rights of family and intimate association in Chapter 8.

Under the second doctrine, the Court has treated the protection of freedom of association as a necessary means for securing rights guaranteed by the First Amendment. The reasoning behind this doctrine is as follows: The First Amendment protects freedom of speech. The government therefore must allow a dissenter to speak. But a single voice speaking alone often goes unheard. Therefore, if the government can prevent a dissenter from associating with others—say, at a rally or in a parade—the government effectively could stifle the dissenter's message. The First Amendment, accordingly, must protect the dissenter's freedom to associate with others who may wish to express similar views.

The idea that speakers can propagate ideas more effectively when they act with others is not new. Recounting American history, the Supreme Court has said:

> [T]he practice of persons sharing common views banding together to achieve a common end is deeply embedded in the American political process. The 18th-century *** pamphleteers were early examples of this phenomen[on] and the *Federalist Papers* were perhaps the most significant and lasting example. The tradition of volunteer committees for collective action has manifested itself in myriad community and public activities; in the political process it can focus on a candidate or on a ballot measure. Its value is that by collective effort individuals can make their views known, when, individually, their voices would be faint or lost.

Citizens Against Rent Control/Coalition for Fair Housing v. City of Berkeley, 454 U.S. 290, 294 (1981). Thus, even though the Constitution does not expressly mention a freedom of association, recognition of such a right appears to be consistent with the original understanding of what freedom of speech requires. *See* Robert H. Bork, *Neutral Principles and Some First Amendment Problems*, 47 Ind. L.J. 1, 17 (1971) (arguing that deriving "secondary rights" in this manner "is essential to the interpretation of the first amendment"). In any event, the Court has consistently accorded it protection.

In this Chapter, we are concerned with the freedom of association that derives from the First Amendment. We will consider three main issues: (1) the extent to which the government may penalize a person for being a member of a group; (2) the extent to which the government may force a group or organization to divulge the identities of its members; and (3) the extent to which the government may force groups to associate with individuals with whom they do not wish to associate.

———————————

Points for Discussion

a. Freedom of Association and Religion

The justification that we considered above for a derivative First Amendment right of freedom of association is based primarily on the need to protect the freedom of speech and assembly. Can you construct an argument that freedom of association is also necessary if the First Amendment is to provide meaningful protection for the free exercise of *religion*? *See Salvation Army v. Department of Community Affairs*, 919 F.2d 183, 198-201 (3d Cir. 1990) (discussing the constitutional right to associate for religious purposes). We will consider the freedom of religion in Chapter 17.

b. Activity Not Protected by the First Amendment

In the quotation from *Roberts* above, the Supreme Court indicated that protecting freedom of association is "an indispensable means of preserving" First Amendment rights. A corollary of this logic is that the Court will not recognize a right of association when the association is not a means of engaging in conduct protected by the First Amendment. A good illustration of this corollary appears in *City of Chicago v. Morales*, 527 U.S. 41 (1999). The City of Chicago enacted an ordinance that prohibits "criminal street gang members" from loitering in public places. Although the Supreme Court invalidated the ordinance on other grounds, it concluded that the ordinance did not violate the freedom of association. It stated:

> The ordinance does not prohibit speech. Because the term "loiter" is defined as remaining in one place "with no apparent purpose," it is also clear that it does not prohibit any form of conduct that is apparently intended to convey a message. By its terms, the ordinance is inapplicable to assemblies that are designed to demonstrate a group's support of, or opposition to, a particular point of view. Its impact on the social contact between gang members and others does not impair the First Amendment "right of association" that our cases have recognized.

Id. at 53. In other words, the gang members' First Amendment freedom of association was not impaired because loitering is not an activity protected by the First Amendment. Can you make an argument that all decisions about whom to associate with implicate First Amendment values, even when the activities that the individuals engage in together do not communicate a message?

c. Protecting Association as an End in Itself?

The Supreme Court has treated the freedom of association largely instrumentally, as a means to secure the rights expressly protected by the First Amendment. Do you agree that the freedom of association is not an end in itself, but merely a means to ensure protection of other rights? See David Cole, *Hanging with the Wrong Crowd: Of Gangs, Terrorists, and the Right of Association*, 1999 Sup. Ct. Rev. 203 (arguing that freedom of association should be seen as an end in itself, and not just a means to other ends).

––––––––––––

A. Penalizing Individuals for Joining Groups

In general, the government cannot impose civil or criminal liability on a person merely because he or she has decided to associate with others. As the court explained in *Scales v. United States*, 367 U.S. 203, 229 (1961), allowing the government to prohibit group memberships would raise "a real danger that legitimate political expression or association would be impaired." For example, suppose a number of students at a state university want to debate politics. The First Amendment clearly would prohibit the university from forbidding any of the individual students to speak on political matters. So too, the First Amendment must prevent the university from forbidding the students to form and join a political debating society at which they argue politics with each other. Debates cannot occur unless the students can form the society and thus have debating partners.

This general rule, however, has an important exception. The government does not have to permit individuals to associate with each other for the purpose of undertaking unlawful activities that are not themselves protected by the First Amendment. Because bank robbery is illegal, for example, the government can outlaw conspiracies to commit bank robbery. This exception may apply even when a group is political in nature. In *Scales*, for example, the Court upheld the conviction of an individual for his membership in a communist party organization where evidence showed that he specifically intended to accomplish the criminal aims of the organization, namely, the overthrow of the U.S. government "by resort to violence." *Id.* at 229. In a different case decided the same day, however, the Court reversed the conviction of an individual who had joined a communist organization but who did not advocate or intend illegal action. See *Noto v. United States*, 367 U.S. 290, 299 (1961).

The federal and state governments have generally taken to heart the rule that they cannot ban membership in groups that do not have illegal purposes, and accordingly have rarely enacted laws that expressly seek to accomplish that end. But what is the constitutional status of a law that does not directly ban membership in a group that engages in protected First Amendment activities, but still indirectly discourages individuals from joining the group? For example, imagine a state law that provides: "Membership in political debating societies on state university campuses is permitted. But if any member of a political debating society shall make a slanderous remark, all members of the debating society will be jointly and severally liable." This law surely would discourage membership in the political debating society because few potential members would want to risk incurring vicarious liability for the slanderous remarks of another.

The following case suggests that such a law would be unconstitutional. Although the state may impose liability on a person who commits slander, it may not impose this liability on others merely because they associated with the person.

————

NAACP v. Claiborne Hardware Co.

458 U.S. 886 (1982)

Justice STEVENS delivered the opinion of the Court.

In March 1966, black citizens of Port Gibson, Miss., and other areas of Claiborne County presented white elected officials with a list of particularized demands for racial equality and integration. The complainants did not receive a satisfactory response and, at a local National Association for the Advancement of Colored People (NAACP) meeting at the First Baptist Church, several hundred black persons voted to place a boycott on white merchants in the area. On October 31, 1969, several of the merchants filed suit in state court to recover losses caused by the boycott and to enjoin future boycott activity. ***

The complaint [named] two corporations and 146 individuals as defendants: the NAACP, a New York membership corporation; Mississippi Action for Progress (MAP), a Mississippi corporation that implemented the federal "Head Start" program; Aaron Henry, the President of the Mississippi State Conference of the NAACP; Charles Evers, the Field Secretary of the NAACP in Mississippi; and 144 other individuals who had participated in the boycott. The complaint sought injunctive relief and an attachment of property, as well as damages. ***

[The Mississippi Supreme Court held that most of the defendants, including the NAACP, were jointly and severally liable under Mississippi law for the tort of malicious interference with the plaintiffs' businesses.] After reviewing the chancellor's recitation of the facts, the court quoted the following finding made by the trial court:

> In carrying out the agreement and design [of the boycott], certain of the defendants, acting for all others, engaged in acts of physical force and violence against the persons and property of certain customers and prospective customers. Intimidation, threats, social ostracism, vilification, and traduction were some of the devices used by the defendants to achieve the desired results. Most effective, also, was the stationing of guards ("enforcers," "deacons," or "black hats") in the vicinity of white-owned businesses. Unquestionably, the evidence shows that the volition of many black persons was overcome out of sheer fear, and they were forced and compelled against their personal wills to withhold their trade and business intercourse from the complainants.

On the basis of this finding, the court concluded that the entire boycott was unlawful. "If any of these factors—force, violence, or threats—is present, then the boycott is illegal regardless of whether it is primary, secondary, economical, political, social or other." ***

The First Amendment *** restricts the ability of the State to impose liability on an individual solely because of his association with another. In *Scales v. United States*, 367 U.S. 203, 229 (1961), the Court noted that a "blanket prohibition of association with a group having both legal and illegal aims" would present "a real danger that legitimate political expression or association would be impaired." The Court suggested that to punish association with such a group, there must be "clear proof that a defendant 'specifically intend[s] to accomplish [the aims of the organization] by resort to violence.' " *Ibid.* (quoting *Noto v. United States*, 367 U.S. 290, 299 (1961)). Moreover, in *Noto* the Court emphasized that this intent must be judged "according to the strictest law," for "otherwise there is a danger that one in sympathy with the legitimate aims of such an organization, but not specifically intending to accomplish them by resort to violence, might be punished for his adherence to lawful and constitutionally protected purposes, because of other and unprotected purposes which he does not necessarily share." *Id.* at 299-300.

In *Healy v. James*, 408 U.S. 169 (1972), the Court applied these principles in a non-criminal context. In that case the Court held that a student group could not be denied recognition at a state-supported college merely because of its affiliation with a national organization associated with disruptive and violent campus activity. It noted that "the Court has consistently disapproved governmental action imposing criminal sanctions or denying rights and privileges solely because of a citizen's association with an unpopular organization." *Id., at 185-186.* The Court stated that "it has been established that 'guilt by association alone, without [establishing] that an individual's association poses the threat feared by the Government,' is an impermissible basis upon which to deny First Amendment rights." <u>Id., at 186</u> (quoting *United States v. Robel*, 389 U.S. 258, 265 (1967)) "The government has the burden of establishing a knowing affiliation with an organization possessing unlawful aims and goals, and a specific intent to further those illegal aims." <u>408 U.S., at 186</u>.

The principles announced in <u>Scales</u>, <u>Noto</u>, and <u>Healy</u> are relevant to this case. Civil liability may not be imposed merely because an individual belonged to a group, some members of which committed acts of violence. For liability to be imposed by reason of association alone, it is necessary to establish that the group itself possessed unlawful goals and that the individual held a specific intent to further those illegal aims.

[Reversed.]

———————————

Points for Discussion

a. An Individual's Liability for Belonging to an Organization

A significant part of the Court's discussion in *Claiborne Hardware* is addressed to the problem under the First Amendment of "guilt by association"—that is, the imposition of criminal liability on one person solely because of the actions of a person with whom he associates. Isn't imposing guilt by association problematic wholly aside from any First Amendment concerns? Doesn't the imposition of criminal liability for actions taken by another (and not fairly attributed to the defendant) violate basic notions of Due Process, under which the government must demonstrate beyond a reasonable doubt that the defendant committed the charged offense? Does it matter whether the Court grounds a presumption against guilt by association in the First Amendment or instead in the Due Process Clause? Did it matter in this case, where the guilt by association had been imposed on an organization, rather than on an individual?

b. An Organization's Liability for Acts of its Members

Another portion of the Court's opinion, not quoted above, addressed the issue of whether the NAACP as an organization could be liable because of the acts of some of its members. The Court said: "To impose liability without a finding that the NAACP authorized—either actually or apparently—or ratified unlawful conduct would impermissibly burden the rights of political association that are protected by the First Amendment." What might happen to an organization like the NAACP if it were held liable for the acts of some (or any) of its members? Can you articulate why those consequences might raise particular concerns under the First Amendment?

———————————

The preceding case concerned the possibility that imposing civil liability on members of a group might discourage membership in the group. A state law also could discourage membership in groups by denying legal or other privileges to persons who belong to groups or who refuse to provide information about them. The following case addresses the constitutionality of such a law.

———————————

Baird v. State Bar of Arizona

401 U.S. 1 (1971)

Mr. Justice BLACK announced the judgment of the Court and delivered an opinion in which Mr. Justice DOUGLAS, Mr. Justice BRENNAN, and Mr. Justice MARSHALL join.

This is one of two cases now before us from two different States in which applicants have been denied admission to practice law solely because they refused to answer questions about their personal beliefs or their affiliations with organizations that advocate certain ideas about government. Sharp conflicts and close divisions have arisen in this Court concerning the power of States to refuse to permit applicants to practice law in cases where bar examiners have been suspicious about applicants' loyalties and their views on Communism and revolution. This has been an increasingly divisive and bitter issue for some years, especially since Senator Joseph McCarthy from Wisconsin stirred up anti-Communist feelings and fears by his "investigations" in the early 1950's. One applicant named Raphael Konigsberg was denied admission in California and this Court reversed. *Konigsberg v. State Bar*, 353 U.S. 252 (1957). The State nevertheless denied him admission a second time, and this Court then affirmed by a 5-to-4 decision. 366 U.S. 36 (1961). An applicant named Rudolph Schware was denied admission in New Mexico and this Court reversed, with five Justices agreeing on one opinion, three Justices on another opinion, and one not participating. *Schware v. Board of Bar Examiners*, 353 U.S. 232 (1957). In another case an applicant named George Anastaplo was denied admission in Illinois on grounds similar to those involved in <u>Konigsberg</u> and <u>Schware</u>, and the denial was affirmed by a 5-to-4 margin. *In re Anastaplo*, 366 U.S. 82 (1961). With sharp divisions in this Court, our docket and those of the Courts of Appeals have been filled for years with litigation involving inquisitions about beliefs and associations and refusals to let people practice law and hold public or even private jobs solely because public authorities have been suspicious of their ideas. Usually these denials of employment have not been based on any overt acts of misconduct or lawlessness, and the litigation has continued to raise serious questions of alleged violations of the First Amendment and other guarantees of the Bill of Rights.

The foregoing cases and others contain thousands of pages of confusing formulas, refined reasonings, and puzzling holdings that touch on the same suspicions and fears about citizenship and loyalty. However we have concluded the best way to handle this case is to narrate its simple facts and then relate them to the 45 words that make up the First Amendment.

These are the facts. The petitioner, Sara Baird, graduated from law school at Stanford University in California in 1967. So far as the record shows there is not now and never has been a single mark against her moral character. She has taken the examination prescribed by Arizona, and the answer of the State admits that she satisfactorily passed it. Among the questions she answered was No. 25, which called on her to reveal all organizations with which she had been associated since she reached 16 years of age. This question she answered to the satisfaction of the Arizona Bar Committee. *** In addition, however, she was asked [in question 27] to state whether she had ever been a member of the Communist Party or any organization "that advocates overthrow of the United States Government by force or violence." When she refused to answer this question, the Committee declined to process her application further or recommend her admission to the bar. The Arizona Supreme Court then denied her petition for an order to the Committee to show cause why she should not be admitted to practice law. We granted certiorari.

In Arizona it is perjury to answer the bar committee's questions falsely, and perjury is punishable as a felony. In effect this young lady was asked by the State to make a guess as to whether any organization to which she ever belonged "advocates overthrow of the United States Government by force or violence." There may well be provisions of the Federal Constitution other than the First Amendment that would protect an applicant to a state bar from being subjected to a question potentially so hazardous to her liberty. But whether or not there are other provisions that protect her, we think the First Amendment does so here.

> **Food for Thought**
>
> In what way might answering Question 27 have been "hazardous to [Baird's] liberty"? Does the answer to that question help to identify another provision of the Constitution that might give Baird a right to decline to answer?

The First Amendment's protection of association prohibits a State from excluding a person from a profession or punishing him solely because he is a member of a particular political organization or because he holds certain beliefs. *United States v. Robel*, 389 U.S. 258, 266 (1967). Similarly, when a State attempts to make inquiries about a person's beliefs or associations, its power is limited by the First Amendment. Broad and sweeping state inquiries into these protected areas, as Arizona has engaged in here, discourage citizens from exercising rights protected by the Constitution.

When a State seeks to inquire about an individual's beliefs and associations a heavy burden lies upon it to show that the inquiry is necessary to protect a legitimate state interest. Of course Arizona has a legitimate interest in determining whether petitioner has the qualities of character and the professional competence requisite to the practice of law. But here petitioner has already supplied the Committee with extensive personal and professional information to assist its determination. By her answers to questions other than No. 25, and her listing of former employers, law school professors, and other references, she has made available to the Committee the information relevant to her fitness to practice law. And whatever justification may be offered, a State may not inquire about a man's views or associations solely for the purpose of withholding a right or benefit because of what he believes.

Much has been written about the application of the First Amendment to cases where penalties have been imposed on people because of their beliefs. Some of what has been written is reconcilable with what we have said here and some of it is not. Without detailed reference to all prior cases, it is sufficient to say we hold that views and beliefs are immune from bar association inquisitions designed to lay a foundation for barring an applicant from the practice of law. Clearly Arizona has engaged in such questioning here.

> **Take Note**
>
> Justice Black concludes here that the First Amendment precluded Arizona from asking Question 27 because the question improperly delved into Sara Baird's views and beliefs. Justice Black, however, was joined by only three other Justices. What is the rule that emerges from this case?

The practice of law is not a matter of grace, but of right for one who is qualified by his learning and his moral character. This record is wholly barren of one word, sentence, or paragraph that tends to show this lady is not morally and professionally fit to serve honorably and well as a member of the legal profession. It was error not to process her application and not to admit her to the Arizona Bar. The judgment of the Arizona Supreme Court is reversed and the case remanded for further proceedings not inconsistent with this opinion.

Mr. Justice STEWART, concurring in judgment.

The Court has held that under some circumstances simple inquiry into present or past Communist Party membership of an applicant for admission to the Bar is not as such unconstitutional. *Konigsberg v. State Bar*, 366 U.S. 36 (1957); *In re Anastaplo*, 366 U.S. 82 (1961). Question 27, however, goes further and asks applicants whether they have ever belonged to any organization "that advocates overthrow of the United States Government by force or violence." Our decisions have made clear that such inquiry must be confined to knowing membership to satisfy the First and Fourteenth Amendments. It follows from these decisions that mere membership in an organization can never, by itself, be sufficient ground for a State's imposition of civil disabilities or criminal punishment. Such membership can be quite different from knowing membership in an organization advocating the overthrow of the Government by force or violence, on the part of one sharing the specific intent to further the organization's illegal goals.

> **Take Note**
>
> Justice Stewart concludes here that Arizona could not ask Question 27 because it did not ask whether Sara Baird "knowingly" belonged to an organization that advocates the overthrow of the United States Government by force or violence. Why does the phrasing of the question matter?

There is a further constitutional infirmity in Arizona's Question 27. The respondent State Bar is the agency entrusted with the administration of the standards for admission to practice law in Arizona. And the respondent's explanation of its purpose in asking the question makes clear that the question must be treated as an inquiry into political beliefs. For the respondent explicitly states that it would recommend denial of admission solely because of an applicant's beliefs that the respondent found objectionable. Yet the First and Fourteenth Amendments bar a State from acting against any person merely because of his beliefs.

Mr. Justice BLACKMUN, with whom THE CHIEF JUSTICE, Mr. Justice HARLAN, and Mr. Justice WHITE join, dissenting.

In my view, applicant Baird vastly overstates her case. *** No one is in a better position to know the aim and purpose and advocacy of an organization than a member. Certainly the Committee and the Arizona Supreme Court, which have other things to do, are not equipped for the task of checking out the identity of every named organization, especially one which might follow the standard of the less said and known, the better. And Mrs. Baird would place this burden on the Committee by submitting partial answers. She gives the appearance of playing a game. The importance of the subject deserves better than that.

————

Points for Discussion

a. The Holding

In a companion case, *Law Students Civil Rights Research Council v. Wadmond*, 401 U.S. 154 (1971), the Supreme Court found no constitutional defect with a question that asked bar applicants if they had ever belonged to an organization that they "knew was advocating or teaching that the government of the United States or any state or any political subdivision thereof should be overthrown or overturned by force." Justice Stewart wrote the majority opinion, and Justice Black wrote a dissent. What does that suggest about the governing rule?

b. The Rationale

How does the rationale in Justice Black's opinion for the plurality differ from the rationale in Justice Stewart's concurrence in judgment? Which opinion is more consistent with the analysis in *NAACP v. Claiborne Hardware*? If the state can deny a person a valuable benefit (such as bar membership) for knowingly belonging to an organization that merely advocates—but does not necessarily take actions to bring about—the overthrow of the government, then isn't the government effectively punishing that person for her views? Is Justice Stewart's view that the government *can* punish people for holding such views, as long as it is sure that the person actually *does* hold the views? If so, then what role, if any, did he believe the freedom of association played in the analysis? If so, is it consistent with the Court's decision in *Brandenburg v. Ohio*, 395 U.S. 444 (1969), which we considered in Chapter 14?

————

B. Disclosure of Membership Lists

May the government require a private group to divulge the identities of its members, or would required disclosure violate the members' freedom of association? This question does not have an easy answer. The following case concludes that the government may require disclosure, but only if the government has a compelling interest in knowing the identities of the group's members.

NAACP v. State of Alabama ex rel. Patterson

357 U.S. 449 (1958)

Mr. Justice HARLAN delivered the opinion of the Court.

> **Definition**
>
> The term *ex rel.* (an abbreviation for the Latin *ex relatione*) means "by or on the relation of." In some cases, the government litigates upon the invitation of a private person, called the relator. In other cases, a private party conducts the litigation on behalf of the government. (We saw an example of this in *McCulloch v. Maryland* in Chapter 3.) In this case, John Patterson, the Alabama Attorney General, litigated on behalf of the state government of Alabama.

We review [a] judgment of civil contempt entered against petitioner, the National Association for the Advancement of Colored People, in the courts of Alabama. The question presented is whether Alabama, consistently with the Due Process Clause of the Fourteenth Amendment, can compel petitioner to reveal to the State's Attorney General the names and addresses of all its Alabama members and agents, without regard to their positions or functions in the Association. The judgment of contempt was based upon petitioner's refusal to comply fully with a court order requiring in part the production of membership lists. Petitioner's claim is that the order, in the circumstances shown by this record, violated rights assured to petitioner and its members under the Constitution.

Alabama has a statute similar to those of many other States which requires a foreign corporation, except as exempted, to qualify before doing business by filing its corporate charter with the Secretary of State and designating a place of business and an agent to receive service of process. The statute imposes a fine on a corporation transacting intrastate business before qualifying and provides for criminal prosecution of officers of such a corporation. The National Association for the Advancement of Colored People is a nonprofit membership corporation organized under the laws of New York. Its purposes, fostered on a nationwide basis, are those indicated by its name, and it operates through chartered affiliates which are independent unincorporated associations, with membership therein equivalent to membership in petitioner. The first Alabama affiliates were chartered in 1918. Since that time the aims of the Association have been advanced through activities of its affiliates, and in 1951 the Association itself opened a regional office in Alabama, at which it employed two supervisory persons and one clerical worker. The Association has never complied with the qualification statute, from which it considered itself exempt.

In 1956 the Attorney General of Alabama brought an equity suit in the State Circuit Court, Montgomery County, to enjoin the Association from conducting further activities within, and to oust it from, the State. Among other things the bill in equity alleged that the Association had opened a regional office and had organized various affiliates in Alabama; had recruited members and solicited contributions within the State; had given financial support and furnished legal assistance to Negro students seeking admission to the state university; and had supported a Negro boycott of the bus lines in Montgomery to compel the seating of passengers without regard to race. The bill recited that the Association, by continuing to do business in Alabama without complying with the qualification statute, was "causing irreparable injury to the property and civil rights of the residents and citizens of the State of Alabama for which criminal prosecution and civil actions at law afford no adequate relief." On the day the complaint was filed, the Circuit Court issued ex parte an order restraining the Association, *pendente lite*, from engaging in further activities within the State and forbidding it to take any steps to qualify itself to do business therein.

> **Definition**
>
> The Latin term *pendente lite* means "during the litigation."

Petitioner demurred to the allegations of the bill and moved to dissolve the restraining order. It contended that its activities did not subject it to the qualification requirements of the statute and that in any event what the State sought to accomplish by its suit would violate rights to freedom of speech and assembly guaranteed under the Fourteenth Amendment to the Constitution of the United States. Before the date set for a hearing on this motion, the State moved for the production of a large number of the Association's records and papers, including bank statements, leases, deeds, and records containing the names and addresses of all Alabama "members" and "agents" of the Association. It alleged that all such documents were necessary for adequate preparation for the hearing, in view of petitioner's denial of the conduct of intrastate business within the meaning of the qualification statute. Over petitioner's objections, the court ordered the production of a substantial part of the requested records, including the membership lists, and postponed the hearing on the restraining order to a date later than the time ordered for production.

*** Thereafter petitioner filed its answer to the bill in equity. It admitted its Alabama activities substantially as alleged in the complaint and that it had not qualified to do business in the State. Although still disclaiming the statute's application to it, petitioner offered to qualify if the bar from qualification made part of the restraining order were lifted, and it submitted with the answer an executed set of the forms required by the statute. However petitioner did not comply with the production order, and for this failure was adjudged in civil contempt and fined $10,000. The contempt judgment provided that the fine would be subject to reduction or remission if compliance were forthcoming within five days but otherwise would be increased to $100,000. [When the NAACP did not comply with the production order, the court held it in contempt.]

We thus reach petitioner's claim that the production order in the state litigation trespasses upon fundamental freedoms protected by the Due Process Clause of the Fourteenth Amendment. Petitioner argues that in view of the facts and circumstances shown in the record, the effect of compelled disclosure of the membership lists will be to abridge the rights of its rank-and-file members to engage in lawful association in support of their common beliefs. It contends that governmental action which, although not directly suppressing association, nevertheless carries this consequence, can be justified only upon some overriding valid interest of the State.

Effective advocacy of both public and private points of view, particularly controversial ones, is undeniably enhanced by group association, as this Court has more than once recognized by remarking upon the close nexus between the freedoms of speech and assembly. *De Jonge v. Oregon*, 299 U.S. 353, 364 (1937); *Thomas v. Collins*, 323 U.S. 516, 530 (1945). It is beyond debate that freedom to engage in association for the advancement of beliefs and ideas is an inseparable aspect of the "liberty" assured by the Due Process Clause of the Fourteenth Amendment, which embraces freedom of speech. Of course, it is immaterial whether the beliefs sought to be advanced by association pertain to political, economic, religious or cultural matters, and state action which may have the effect of curtailing the freedom to associate is subject to the closest scrutiny.

The fact that Alabama, so far as is relevant to the validity of the contempt judgment presently under review, has taken no direct action to restrict the right of petitioner's members to associate freely, does not end inquiry into the effect of the production order. See *American Communications Ass'n v. Douds*, 339 U.S. 382, 402 (1950). In the domain of these indispensable liberties, whether of speech, press, or association, the decisions of this Court recognize that abridgement of such rights, even though unintended, may inevitably follow from varied forms of governmental action. Thus in <u>Douds</u>, the Court stressed that the legislation there challenged, which on its face sought to regulate labor unions and to secure stability in interstate commerce, would have the practical effect "of discouraging" the exercise of constitutionally protected political rights, and it upheld that statute only after concluding that the reasons advanced for its enactment were constitutionally sufficient to justify its possible deterrent effect upon such freedoms. ***

We think that the production order, in the respects here drawn in question, must be regarded as entailing the likelihood of a substantial restraint upon the exercise by petitioner's members of their right to freedom of association. Petitioner has made an uncontroverted showing that on past occasions revelation of the identity of its rank-and-file members has exposed these members to economic reprisal, loss of employment, threat of physical coercion, and other manifestations of public hostility. Under these circumstances, we think it apparent that compelled disclosure of petitioner's Alabama membership is likely to affect adversely the ability of petitioner and its members to pursue their collective effort to foster beliefs which they admittedly have the right to advocate, in that it may induce members to withdraw from the Association and dissuade others from joining it because of fear of exposure of their beliefs shown through their associations and of the consequences of this exposure.

We turn to the final question whether Alabama has demonstrated an interest in obtaining the disclosures it seeks from petitioner which is sufficient to justify the deterrent effect which we have concluded these disclosures may well have on the free exercise by petitioner's members of their constitutionally protected right of association. Such a "subordinating interest of the State must be compelling," *Sweezy v. New Hampshire*, 354 U.S. 234, 265 (1957) (concurring opinion). It is not of moment that the State has here acted solely through its judicial branch, for whether legislative or judicial, it is still the application of state power which we are asked to scrutinize.

*** During the course of a hearing before the Alabama Circuit Court on a motion of petitioner to set aside the production order, the State Attorney General presented at length, under examination by petitioner, the State's reason for requesting the membership lists. The exclusive purpose was to determine whether petitioner was conducting intrastate business in violation of the Alabama foreign corporation registration statute, and the membership lists were expected to help resolve this question. The issues in the litigation commenced by Alabama by its bill in equity were whether the character of petitioner and its activities in Alabama had been such as to make petitioner subject to the registration statute, and whether the extent of petitioner's activities without qualifying suggested its permanent ouster from the State. Without intimating the slightest view upon the merits of these issues, we are unable to perceive that the disclosure of the names of petitioner's rank-and-file members has a substantial bearing on either of them. As matters stand in the state court, petitioner (1) has admitted its presence and conduct of activities in Alabama since 1918; (2) has offered to comply in all respects with the state qualification statute, although preserving its contention that the statute does not apply to it; and (3) has apparently complied satisfactorily with the production order, except for the membership lists, by furnishing the Attorney General with varied business records, its charter and statement of purposes, the names of all of its directors and officers, and with the total number of its Alabama members and the amount of their dues. These last items would not on this record appear subject to constitutional challenge and have been furnished, but whatever interest the State may have in obtaining names of ordinary members has not been shown to be sufficient to overcome petitioner's constitutional objections to the production order.

We hold that the immunity from state scrutiny of membership lists which the Association claims on behalf of its members is here so related to the right of the members to pursue their lawful private interests privately and to associate freely with others in so doing as to come within the protection of the Fourteenth Amendment. And we conclude that Alabama has fallen short of showing a controlling justification for the deterrent effect on the free enjoyment of the right to associate which disclosure of membership lists is likely to have. Accordingly, the judgment of civil contempt and the $100,000 fine which resulted from petitioner's refusal to comply with the production order in this respect must fall.

Reversed.

————————————

Points for Discussion

a. Substantial Burden on the Freedom of Association

Notice that this case arose at a time when the NAACP was a central figure in efforts to challenge segregation in the South, and particularly in Alabama. The Court appeared to give weight to this fact. In concluding that disclosure of the organization's membership lists would impose a substantial burden on the freedom of association, the Court noted that "on past occasions revelation of the identity of its rank-and-file members has exposed these members to economic reprisal, loss of employment, threat of physical coercion, and other manifestations of public hostility." Does the Court's reliance on these circumstances suggest that state requests for the membership lists of private organizations under different circumstances are not as likely to impose a substantial restraint on the freedom of association?

Consider the Court's treatment of disclosure requirements in other contexts. Federal election laws require political campaigns to disclose a list of their contributors. Litigants challenged this requirement in *Buckley v. Valeo*, 424 U.S. 1 (1976). Relying on *NAACP v. Alabama ex rel. Patterson*, the litigants argued that requiring disclosure of the names of contributors violates the freedom of association. The Supreme Court, however, upheld the federal law. The Court explained:

> There could well be a case, similar to those before the Court in *NAACP v. Alabama* ***, where the threat to the exercise of First Amendment rights is so serious and the state interest furthered by disclosure so insubstantial that the Act's requirements cannot be constitutionally applied. But no appellant in this case has tendered record evidence of the sort proffered in *NAACP v. Alabama*. Instead, appellants primarily rely on "the clearly articulated fears of individuals, well experienced in the political process." At best they offer the testimony of several minor-party officials that one or two persons refused to make contributions because of the possibility of disclosure. On this record, the substantial public interest in disclosure identified by the legislative history of this Act outweighs the harm generally alleged.

Id. at 71-72. What is the government's interest in requiring disclosure of the identities of campaign contributors? Does the reasoning in the passage leave open the possibility that a litigant might succeed in challenging the required disclosure of the identities of campaign contributors in the future?

In *Citizens United v. Federal Election Comm'n*, 130 S.Ct. 876 (2010), which we considered in Chapter 14, the Court upheld federal statutory provisions requiring (1) televised electioneering communications funded by anyone other than a candidate to include a disclaimer identifying the person or entity that was responsible for the content and funding of the advertisement and (2) a person or entity who spends more than $10,000 on electioneering communications within a calendar year to file a disclosure statement with the Federal Election Commission identifying the person making the expenditure, the amount of the expenditure, the election to which the communication was directed, and the names of certain contributors. The Court reasoned that the requirements were justified by a "governmental interest in providing information to the electorate," and that "disclosure is a less restrictive alternative to more comprehensive regulations of speech." The Court concluded by noting that the "transparency" fostered by disclosure and disclaimer requirements "enables the electorate to make informed decisions and give proper weight to different speakers and messages."

b. The State's Interest

What interest did the state assert as a reason for requiring disclosure? Did the Court conclude that the state's interest in requiring disclosure was not compelling, or that the request for disclosure did not sufficiently advance that interest? If the former, what sorts of state interests in disclosure would count as compelling?

C. Freedom Not to Associate with Others

Does the freedom of association include not only a freedom to associate with others but also **a freedom to choose not to associate** with others? In other words, may the government tell an organization that it must accept members that the organization does not want to admit? If so, may the organization object to members based on race, sex, sexual orientation, or other such factors? The Supreme Court addressed this question in the leading case of *Roberts v. United States Jaycees*, 468 U.S. 609 (1984).

In *Roberts*, the state of Minnesota sued the Jaycees, a national organization of young men interested in business, claiming that the Jaycees' refusal to admit women violated the state's anti-discrimination laws. In deciding the case, the Court established (or at least clarified) three important principles. First, the freedom of association generally gives an organization a right to choose its members. Second, the government may regulate this freedom if the state has "compelling state interests *** that cannot be achieved through means significantly less restrictive of associational freedoms." *Id.* at 623. But third, the government may not prohibit an organization from discriminating in its selection of members if the regulation would significantly affect the organization's "intimate association" or "expressive activity." *Id.*

Applying these factors to the case, the Court recognized that the Jaycees in general had a right to decide who could join their organization and who could not. But the Court held that preventing discrimination against women was a compelling state interest. And the Court concluded that the Jaycees could not object to the anti-discrimination law because the Jaycees, as a very large organization, could not claim that discrimination was necessary for intimate association (given the large size of the organization), and because the Jaycees did not claim that having women members would affect any message they wished to convey. The Court thus held that the state could apply the anti-discrimination legislation to the organization.

The Supreme Court applied the *Roberts* standard in the following three cases. In the first, the Court considered whether anti-discrimination legislation, even if it otherwise advances a compelling governmental interest, would impair an organization's expressive activities.

Hurley v. Irish-American Gay, Lesbian and Bisexual Group of Boston

515 U.S. 557 (1995)

Justice SOUTER delivered the opinion of the Court.

The issue in this case is whether Massachusetts may require private citizens who organize a parade to include among the marchers a group imparting a message the organizers do not wish to convey. We hold that such a mandate violates the First Amendment.

[The South Boston Allied War Veterans Council is an unincorporated association of individuals elected from various South Boston veterans groups. Every year since 1947, the Council has held a parade in Boston on March 17 to celebrate St. Patrick's Day. The Council obtains a permit from the City of Boston to conduct the parade. The Council allows numerous groups to join the parade, which has included as many as 20,000 marchers. More than one million spectators typically watch the parade. In 1992 and 1993, the Irish-American Gay, Lesbian and Bisexual Group of Boston (GLIB) asked the Council for permission to join the parade, but in both years the Council denied the request.]

In 1993, after the Council had again refused to admit GLIB to the upcoming parade, the organization and some of its members filed this suit against the Council, the individual petitioner John J. "Wacko" Hurley, and the city of Boston, alleging violations of the State and Federal Constitutions and of the state public accommodations law, which prohibits "any distinction, discrimination or restriction on account [of] sexual orientation [relative] to the admission of any person to, or treatment in any place of public accommodation, resort or amusement." Mass. Gen. Laws § 272:98 (1992). After finding that "[f]or at least the past 47 years, the Parade has traveled the same basic route along the public streets of South Boston, providing entertainment, amusement, and recreation to participants and spectators alike," the state trial court ruled that the parade fell within the statutory definition of a public accommodation, which includes "any place [which] is open to and accepts or solicits the patronage of the general public and, without limiting the generality of this definition, whether or not it be . . . (6) a boardwalk or other public highway [or] (8) a place of public amusement, recreation, sport, exercise or entertainment," Mass. Gen. Laws § 272:92A (1992). The court found that the Council had no written criteria and employed no particular procedures for

> **Take Note**
>
> The trial court interpreted the Massachusetts statute to require the Council to associate with GLIB. For this reason, the Council argued that the statute was unconstitutional. Is there any argument that the exclusion itself violated the Constitution? Was the defendant a state (or instead a private) actor?

admission, voted on new applications in batches, had occasionally admitted groups who simply showed up at the parade without having submitted an application, and did "not generally inquire into the specific messages or views of each applicant." The court consequently rejected the Council's contention that the parade was "private" (in the sense of being exclusive), holding instead that "the lack of genuine selectivity in choosing participants and sponsors demonstrates that the Parade is a public event." It found the parade to be "eclectic," containing a wide variety of "patriotic, commercial, political, moral, artistic, religious, athletic, public service, trade union, and eleemosynary themes," as well as conflicting messages. While noting that the Council had indeed excluded the Ku Klux Klan and ROAR (an antibusing group), it attributed little significance to these facts, concluding ultimately that "[t]he only common theme among the participants and sponsors is their public involvement in the Parade." [The Massachusetts Supreme Judicial Court affirmed.]

*** Real "[p]arades are public dramas of social relations, and in them performers define who can be a social actor and what subjects and ideas are available for communication and consideration." S. Davis, Parades and Power: Street Theatre in Nineteenth-Century Philadelphia 6 (1986). Hence, we use the word "parade" to indicate marchers who are making some sort of collective point, not just to each other but to bystanders along the way. Indeed, a parade's dependence on watchers is so extreme that nowadays, as with Bishop Berkeley's celebrated tree, "if a parade or demonstration receives no media coverage, it may as well not have happened." Parades are thus a form of expression, not just motion, and the inherent expressiveness of marching to make a point explains our cases involving protest marches. In *Gregory v. Chicago,* 394 U.S. 111, 112 (1969), for example, petitioners had taken part in a procession to express their grievances to the city government, and we held that such a "march, if peaceful and orderly, falls well within the sphere of conduct protected by the First Amendment." Similarly, in *Edwards v. South Carolina,* 372 U.S. 229, 235 (1963), where petitioners had joined in a march of protest and pride, carrying placards and singing The Star Spangled Banner, we held that the activities "reflect an exercise of these basic constitutional rights in their most pristine and classic form."

The protected expression that inheres in a parade is not limited to its banners and songs, however, for the Constitution looks beyond written or spoken words as mediums of expression. Noting that "[s]ymbolism is a primitive but effective way of communicating ideas," *West Virginia Bd. of Ed. v. Barnette,* 319 U.S. 624, 632 (1943), our cases have recognized that the First Amendment shields such acts as saluting a flag (and refusing to do so), id. at 632, wearing an armband to protest a war, *Tinker v. Des Moines Independent Community School Dist.,* 393 U.S. 503, 505-506 (1969), displaying a red flag, *Stromberg v. California,* 283 U.S. 359, 369 (1931), and even "[m]arching, walking or parading" in uniforms displaying the swastika, *National Socialist Party of America v. Skokie,* 432 U.S. 43 (1977). As some of these examples show, a narrow, succinctly articulable message is not a condition of constitutional

> **Make the Connection**
>
> We considered the status of symbolic conduct under the First Amendment in Chapter 14.

protection, which if confined to expressions conveying a "particularized message" would never reach the unquestionably shielded painting of Jackson Pollock, music of Arnold

Schöenberg, or Jabberwocky verse of Lewis Carroll.

Not many marches, then, are beyond the realm of expressive parades, and the South Boston celebration is not one of them. Spectators line the streets; people march in costumes and uniforms, carrying flags and banners with all sorts of messages (*e.g.,* "England get out of Ireland," "Say no to drugs"); marching bands and pipers play; floats are pulled along; and the whole show is broadcast over Boston television. To be sure, we agree with the state courts that in spite of excluding some applicants, the Council is rather lenient in admitting participants. But a private speaker does not forfeit constitutional protection simply by combining multifarious voices, or by failing to edit their themes to isolate an exact message as the exclusive subject matter of the speech. Nor, under our precedent, does First Amendment protection require a speaker to generate, as an original matter, each item featured in the communication. Cable operators, for example, are engaged in protected speech activities even when they only select programming originally produced by others. *Turner Broadcasting System, Inc. v. FCC,* 512 U.S. 622, 636 (1994). For that matter, the presentation of an edited compilation of speech generated by other persons is a staple of most newspapers' opinion pages, which, of course, fall squarely within the core of First Amendment security, *Miami Herald Publishing Co. v. Tornillo,* 418 U.S. 241, 258 (1974), as does even the simple selection of a paid noncommercial advertisement for inclusion in a daily paper, see *New York Times v. Sullivan,* 376 U.S. 254, 265-266 (1964). The selection of contingents to make a parade is entitled to similar protection.

Respondents' participation as a unit in the parade was equally expressive. GLIB was formed for the very purpose of marching in it, as the trial court found, in order to celebrate its members' identity as openly gay, lesbian, and bisexual descendants of the Irish immigrants, to show that there are such individuals in the community, and to support the like men and women who sought to march in the New York parade. The organization distributed a fact sheet describing the members' intentions, and the record otherwise corroborates the expressive nature of GLIB's participation. In 1993, members of GLIB marched behind a shamrock-strewn banner with the simple inscription "Irish American Gay, Lesbian and Bisexual Group of Boston." GLIB understandably seeks to communicate its ideas as part of the existing parade, rather than staging one of its own.

Petitioners disclaim any intent to exclude homosexuals as such, and no individual member of GLIB claims to have been excluded from parading as a member of any group that the Council has approved to march. Instead, the disagreement goes to the admission of GLIB as its own parade unit carrying its own banner. Since every participating unit affects the message conveyed by the private organizers, the state courts' application of the statute produced an order essentially requiring petitioners to alter the expressive content of their parade. Although the state courts spoke of the parade as a place of public accommodation, once the expressive character of both the parade and the marching GLIB contingent is understood, it becomes apparent that the state courts' application of the statute had the effect of declaring the sponsors' speech itself to be the public accommodation. Under this approach any contingent of protected individuals with a message would have the right to participate in petitioners' speech, so that the communication produced by the private organizers would be shaped by all those protected by the law who wished to join in with some expressive demonstration of their own. But this use of the State's power violates the fundamental rule of protection under the First Amendment, that a speaker has the autonomy to choose the content of his own message.

Petitioners' claim to the benefit of this principle of autonomy to control one's own speech is as sound as the South Boston parade is expressive. Rather like a composer, the Council selects the expressive units of the parade from potential participants, and though the score may not produce a particularized message, each contingent's expression in the Council's eyes comports with what merits celebration on that day. Even if this view gives the Council credit for a more considered judgment than it actively made, the Council clearly decided to exclude a message it did not like from the communication it chose to make, and that is enough to invoke its right as a private speaker to shape its expression by speaking on one subject while remaining silent on another. The message it disfavored is not difficult to identify. Although GLIB's point (like the Council's) is not wholly articulate, a contingent marching behind the organization's banner would at least bear witness to the fact that some Irish are gay, lesbian, or bisexual, and the presence of the organized marchers would suggest their view that people of their sexual orientations have as much claim to unqualified social acceptance as heterosexuals and indeed as members of parade units orga-nized around other identifying characteristics. The parade's organizers may not believe these facts about Irish sexuality to be so, or they may object to unqualified social acceptance of gays and lesbians or have some other reason for wishing to keep GLIB's message out of the parade. But whatever the reason, it boils down to the choice of a speaker not to propound a particular point of view, and that choice is pre-sumed to lie beyond the government's power to control.

> **Take Note**
>
> In this passage, the Court explains why requiring the parade organizers to include GLIB would affect the pa-rade organizers' speech. In *Roberts v. United States Jaycees*, by contrast, the Court held that the state could pre-vent the private organization from discriminating. In what ways were the two cases different?

Our holding today rests not on any particular view about the Council's message but on the Nation's commitment to protect freedom of speech. Disapproval of a private speaker's statement does not legitimize use of the Commonwealth's power to compel the speaker to alter the message by including one more acceptable to others. Accordingly, the judgment of the Supreme Judicial Court is reversed, and the case is remanded for proceedings not inconsistent with this opinion.

————————

Points for Discussion

a. Pattern of Argumentation

The three principles explained in *Roberts v. United States Jaycees* give rise to a pattern of argumentation apparent in this case and others like it. The parade organizers argued that they had a First Amendment right to choose not to associate with GLIB. GLIB responded that the freedom not to associate was not absolute, and that the state had a compelling interest in preventing discrimination. But the parade organizers replied that even if the state ordinarily has a compelling interest in preventing discrimination, in this case—unlike in *Roberts*—the discrimination was integral to their expressive activity. The Court in *Roberts* agreed with the persons who had been excluded; the Court in *Hurley* agreed with the organization.

Doesn't every organization convey some message—even if only implicitly—by its membership choices? For example, a private school that chose in 1955 to accept students of all races plainly made a statement about the importance of racial integration, as did a private school at that time that chose to accept only white children. If these actions are therefore "expressive," then was the Court's decision in *Roberts* correct? If not, was the Court's decision in *Hurley* nevertheless correct?

b. Condoning Discrimination

In *Hurley*, the Supreme Court essentially held that the First Amendment permits an organization to discriminate against a group based on the group's views on sexual orientation. Is allowing this kind of discrimination objectionable? Is it inconsistent with the spirit of the Fourteenth Amendment? (Recall that the Court has held that the Fourteenth Amendment applies only to state, as opposed to private, action.) Or is it an unfortunate but necessary consequence of protecting free speech?

In answering these questions, does it help to consider how you might respond to the converse set of circumstances? That is, should the organizers of a Gay Pride march have to include in their parade a religious group known for its opposition to homosexuality?

c. Discrimination against a Group's Members

In this case, the parade organization expressed a willingness to allow individual members of GLIB to join the parade, just not GLIB as a group. Suppose the facts had been different and that the parade organizers had decided to exclude any members of GLIB—or, for that matter, any person who was homosexual—from marching. Under those circumstances, could Massachusetts have enforced its anti-discrimination laws to require the parade organizers to include the gay marchers? If so, would the parade organizers nevertheless have been permitted to refuse to allow any members of the Ku Klux Klan to join in its parade? If so, why would the organizers have the right to exclude racists but not to exclude gays?

In *Hurley*, the Court unanimously concluded that a private organization's parade involves a quintessential form of expressive activity and thus cannot be regulated by anti-discrimination legislation. Can the state apply such legislation to groups that do not engage in expressive activity as obvious as a parade?

Boy Scouts of America v. Dale

530 U.S. 640 (2000)

Justice REHNQUIST delivered the opinion of the Court.

Petitioners are the Boy Scouts of America and the Monmouth Council, a division of the Boy Scouts of America (collectively, Boy Scouts). The Boy Scouts is a private, not-for-profit organization engaged in instilling its system of values in young people. The Boy Scouts asserts that homosexual conduct is inconsistent with the values it seeks to instill. Respondent is James Dale, a former Eagle Scout whose adult membership in the Boy Scouts was revoked when the Boy Scouts learned that he is an avowed homosexual and gay rights activist. The New Jersey Supreme Court held that New Jersey's public accommodations law requires that the Boy Scouts readmit Dale. This case presents the question whether applying New Jersey's public accommodations law in this way violates the Boy Scouts' First Amendment right of expressive association. We hold that it does.

Dale applied for adult membership in the Boy Scouts in 1989. The Boy Scouts approved his application for the position of assistant scoutmaster of Troop 73. Around the same time, Dale left home to attend Rutgers University. After arriving at Rutgers, Dale first acknowledged to himself and others that he is gay. He quickly became involved with, and eventually became the co-president of, the Rutgers University Lesbian/Gay Alliance. In 1990, Dale attended a seminar addressing the psychological and health needs of lesbian and gay teenagers. A newspaper covering the event interviewed Dale about his advocacy of homosexual teenagers' need for gay role models. In early July 1990, the newspaper published the interview and Dale's photograph over a caption identifying him as the co-president of the Lesbian/Gay Alliance.

Later that month, Dale received a letter from Monmouth Council Executive James Kay revoking his adult membership. Dale wrote to Kay requesting the reason for Monmouth Council's decision. Kay responded by letter that the Boy Scouts "specifically forbid membership to homosexuals."

In 1992, Dale filed a complaint against the Boy Scouts in the New Jersey Superior Court. The complaint alleged that the Boy Scouts had violated New Jersey's public accommodations statute and its common law by revoking Dale's membership based solely on his sexual orientation. New Jersey's public accommodations statute prohibits, among other things, discrimination on the basis of sexual orientation in places of public accommodation. N.J. Stat. Ann. §§ 10:5-4 and 10:5-5 (West Supp. 2000). *** The New Jersey Supreme Court [held] that the Boy Scouts was a place of public accommodation subject to the public accommodations law, that the organization was not exempt from the law under any of its express exceptions, and that the Boy Scouts violated the law by revoking Dale's membership based on his avowed homosexuality. *** [The New Jersey Supreme Court rejected the Boy Scouts' claim that applying the public accommodations law to the Boy Scouts would violate the Boy Scouts' First Amendment right of freedom of association.]

In *Roberts v. United States Jaycees,* 468 U.S. 609, 622 (1984), we observed that "implicit in the right to engage in activities protected by the First Amendment" is "a corresponding right to associate with others in pursuit of a wide variety of political, social, economic, educational, religious, and cultural ends." This right is crucial in preventing the majority from imposing its views on groups that would rather express other, perhaps unpopular, ideas. Government actions that may unconstitutionally burden this freedom may take many forms, one of which is "intrusion into the internal structure or affairs of an association" like a "regulation that forces the group to accept members it does not desire." <u>Id., at 623</u>. Forcing a group to accept certain members may impair the ability of the group to express those views, and only those views, that it intends to express. Thus, "[f]reedom of association [plainly] presupposes a freedom not to associate." <u>Ibid</u>.

The forced inclusion of an unwanted person in a group infringes the group's freedom of expressive association if the presence of that person affects in a significant way the group's ability to advocate public or private viewpoints. But the freedom of expressive association, like many freedoms, is not absolute. We have held that the freedom could be overridden "by regulations adopted to serve compelling state interests, unrelated to the suppression of ideas, that cannot be achieved through means significantly less restrictive of associational freedoms." <u>Ibid</u>.

To determine whether a group is protected by the First Amendment's expressive associational right, we must determine whether the group engages in "expressive association." The First Amendment's protection of expressive association is not reserved for advocacy groups. But to come within its ambit, a group must engage in some form of expression, whether it be public or private.

The record reveals the following. The Boy Scouts is a private, nonprofit organization. According to its mission statement:

> It is the mission of the Boy Scouts of America to serve others by helping to instill values in young people and, in other ways, to prepare them to make ethical choices over their lifetime in achieving their full potential.

The values we strive to instill are based on those found in the Scout Oath and Law:

Scout Oath

On my honor I will do my best
To do my duty to God and my country
and to obey the Scout Law;
To help other people at all times;
To keep myself physically strong,
mentally awake, and morally straight.

Scout Law

A Scout is:

Trustworthy.	Obedient.
Loyal.	Cheerful.
Helpful.	Thrifty.
Friendly.	Brave.
Courteous.	Clean.
Kind.	Reverent.

Thus, the general mission of the Boy Scouts is clear: "[T]o instill values in young people." The Boy Scouts seeks to instill these values by having its adult leaders spend time with the youth members, instructing and engaging them in activities like camping, archery, and fishing. During the time spent with the youth members, the scoutmasters and assistant scoutmasters inculcate them with the Boy Scouts' values—both expressly and by example. It seems indisputable that an association that seeks to transmit such a system of values engages in expressive activity.

> **Food for Thought**
>
> In *Hurley*, there was little doubt that the parade was a form of expressive activity, and that the parade's message was conveyed to people—one million spectators—outside of the parade itself. Is the Court suggesting here that the Boy Scouts' expressive activity is similarly intended to convey a message to persons outside of the organization? Or instead that the message is intended for persons—specifically, the Scouts themselves—*inside* the organization? If the latter, is this distinction relevant?

Given that the Boy Scouts engages in expressive activity, we must determine whether the forced inclusion of Dale as an assistant scoutmaster would significantly affect the Boy Scouts' ability to advocate public or private viewpoints. This inquiry necessarily requires us first to explore, to a limited extent, the nature of the Boy Scouts' view of homosexuality.

The values the Boy Scouts seeks to instill are "based on" those listed in the Scout Oath and Law. The Boy Scouts explains that the Scout Oath and Law provide "a positive moral code for living;" they are a list of "do's" rather than "don'ts." The Boy Scouts asserts that homosexual conduct is inconsistent with the values embodied in the Scout Oath and Law, particularly with the values represented by the terms "morally straight" and "clean."

Obviously, the Scout Oath and Law do not expressly mention sexuality or sexual orientation. And the terms "morally straight" and "clean" are by no means self-defining. Different people would attribute to those terms very different meanings. For example, some people may believe that engaging in homosexual conduct is not at odds with being "morally straight" and "clean." And others may believe that engaging in homosexual conduct is contrary to being "morally straight" and "clean." The Boy Scouts says it falls within the latter category.

The New Jersey Supreme Court analyzed the Boy Scouts' beliefs and found that the "exclusion of members solely on the basis of their sexual orientation is inconsistent with Boy Scouts' commitment to a diverse and 'representative' membership [and] contradicts Boy Scouts' overarching objective to reach 'all eligible youth.'" The court concluded that the exclusion of members like Dale "appears antithetical to the organization's goals and philosophy." But our cases reject this sort of inquiry; it is not the role of the courts to reject a group's expressed values because they disagree with those values or find them internally inconsistent. See *Democratic Party of United States v. Wisconsin ex rel. La Follette*, 450 U.S. 107, 124 (1981) ("[A]s is true of all expressions of First Amendment freedoms, the courts may not interfere on the ground that they view a particular expression as unwise or irrational"); see also *Thomas v. Review Bd. of Indiana Employment Security Div.*, 450 U.S. 707, 714 (1981) ("[R]eligious beliefs need not be acceptable, logical, consistent, or comprehensible to others in order to merit First Amendment protection.").

The Boy Scouts asserts that it "teach[es] that homosexual conduct is not morally straight," Brief for Petitioners 39, and that it does "not want to promote homosexual conduct as a legitimate form of behavior," Reply Brief for Petitioners 5. We accept the Boy Scouts' assertion. We need not inquire further to determine the nature of the Boy Scouts' expression with respect to homosexuality. ***

Take Note

> Here the Court defers to the Boy Scouts' assertion about the message that it wants to convey. Is this approach consistent with the Court's decisions in *Roberts* and *Hurley*, or should the Court have delved more deeply into the sincerity of the Boy Scouts' position?

We must then determine whether Dale's presence as an assistant scoutmaster would significantly burden the Boy Scouts' desire to not "promote homosexual conduct as a legitimate form of behavior." As we give deference to an association's assertions regarding the nature of its expression, we must also give deference to an association's view of what would impair its expression. That is not to say that an expressive association can erect a shield against antidiscrimination laws simply by asserting that mere acceptance of a member from a particular group would impair its message. But here Dale, by his own admission, is one of a group of gay Scouts who have "become leaders in their community and are open and honest about their sexual orientation." Dale was the co-president of a gay and lesbian organization at college and remains a gay rights activist. Dale's presence in the Boy Scouts would, at the very least, force the organization to send a message, both to the youth members and the world, that the Boy Scouts accepts homosexual conduct as a legitimate form of behavior.

Hurley v. Irish-American Gay, Lesbian and Bisexual Group of Boston, Inc., 515 U.S. 557 (1995), is illustrative on this point. There we [held that Massachusetts could not require the organizers of a private St. Patrick's Day parade to include among the marchers an Irish-American gay, lesbian, and bisexual group, GLIB.] We observed:

> [T]he presence of the organized marchers would suggest their view that people of their sexual orientations have as much claim to unqualified social acceptance as heterosexuals . . . . The parade's organizers may [object] to unqualified social acceptance of gays and lesbians or have some other reason for wishing to keep GLIB's message out of the parade. [W]hatever the reason, it boils down to the choice of a speaker not to propound a particular point of view, and that choice is presumed to lie beyond the government's power to control.

515 U.S., at 574-575.

Here, we have found that the Boy Scouts believes that homosexual conduct is inconsistent with the values it seeks to instill in its youth members; it will not "promote homosexual conduct as a legitimate form of behavior." Reply Brief for Petitioners 5. As the presence of GLIB in Boston's St. Patrick's Day parade would have interfered with the parade organizers' choice not to propound a particular point of view, the presence of Dale as an assistant scoutmaster would just as surely interfere with the Boy Scouts' choice not to propound a point of view contrary to its beliefs. [Reversed.]

Justice STEVENS, with whom Justice SOUTER, Justice GINSBURG, and Justice BREYER join, dissenting.

[T]he right to associate does not mean "that in every setting in which individuals exercise some discrimination in choosing associates, their selective process of inclusion and exclusion is protected by the Constitution." *New York State Club Assn., Inc. v. City of New York*, 487 U.S. 1, 13 (1988). For example, we have routinely and easily rejected assertions of this right by expressive organizations with discriminatory membership policies, such as private schools, law firms, and labor organizations. In fact, until today, we have never once found a claimed right to associate in the selection of members to prevail in the face of a State's antidiscrimination law. To the contrary, we have squarely held that a State's antidiscrimination law does not violate a group's right to associate simply because the law conflicts with that group's exclusionary membership policy.

Several principles are made perfectly clear by *Jaycees*. First, to prevail on a claim of expressive association in the face of a State's antidiscrimination law, it is not enough simply to engage in *some kind* of expressive activity. *** Second, it is not enough to adopt an openly avowed exclusionary membership policy. *** Third, it is not sufficient merely to articulate *some* connection between the group's expressive activities and its exclusionary policy. *** The relevant question is whether the mere inclusion of the person at issue would "impose any serious burden," "affect in any significant way," or be "a substantial restraint upon" the organization's "shared goals," "basic goals," or "collective effort to foster beliefs." Accordingly, it is necessary to examine what, exactly, are BSA's shared goals and the degree to which its expressive activities would be burdened, affected, or restrained by including homosexuals.

*** The evidence before this Court makes it exceptionally clear that BSA has, at most, simply adopted an exclusionary membership policy and has no shared goal of disapproving of homosexuality. BSA's mission statement and federal charter say nothing on the matter; its official membership policy is silent; its Scout Oath and Law—and accompanying definitions—are devoid of any view on the topic; its guidance for Scouts and Scoutmasters on sexuality declare that such matters are "not construed to be Scouting's proper area," but are the province of a Scout's parents and pastor; and BSA's posture respecting religion tolerates a wide variety of views on the issue of homosexuality. Moreover, there is simply no evidence that BSA otherwise teaches anything in this area, or that it instructs Scouts on matters involving homosexuality in ways not conveyed in the Boy Scout or Scoutmaster Handbooks. In short, Boy Scouts of America is simply silent on homosexuality. There is no shared goal or collective effort to foster a belief about homosexuality at all—let alone one that is significantly burdened by admitting homosexuals.

Surely there are instances in which an organization that truly aims to foster a belief at odds with the purposes of a State's antidiscrimination laws will have a First Amendment right to association that precludes forced compliance with those laws. But that right *** is an implicit right designed to protect the enumerated rights of the First Amendment, not a license to act on any discriminatory impulse. To prevail in asserting a right of expressive association as a defense to a charge of violating an antidiscrimination law, the organization must at least show it has adopted and advocated an unequivocal position inconsistent with a position advocated or epitomized by the person whom the organization seeks to exclude. If this Court were to defer to whatever position an organization is prepared to assert in its briefs, there would be no way to mark the proper boundary between genuine exercises of the right to associate, on the one hand, and sham claims that are simply attempts to insulate nonexpressive private discrimination, on the other hand.

The majority's argument relies exclusively on *Hurley v. Irish-American Gay, Lesbian and Bisexual Group of Boston, Inc.*, 515 U.S. 557 (1995). *** Though *Hurley* has a superficial similarity to the present case, a close inspection reveals a wide gulf between that case and the one before us today. First, it was critical to our analysis that GLIB was actually conveying a message by participating in the parade—otherwise, the parade organizers could hardly claim that they were being forced to include any unwanted message at all. *** Second, we found it relevant that GLIB's message "would likely be perceived" as the parade organizers' own speech. *** Dale's inclusion in the Boy Scouts is nothing like the case in *Hurley*. His participation sends no cognizable message to the Scouts or to the world. Unlike GLIB, Dale did not carry a banner or a sign; he did not distribute any factsheet; and he expressed no intent to send any message. If there is any kind of message being sent, then, it is by the mere act of joining the Boy Scouts. Such an act does not constitute an instance of symbolic speech under the First Amendment.

Unfavorable opinions about homosexuals "have ancient roots." *Bowers v. Hardwick,* 478 U.S. 186, 192 (1986). *** That such prejudices are still prevalent and that they have caused serious and tangible harm to countless members of the class New Jersey seeks to protect are established matters of fact that neither the Boy Scouts nor the Court disputes. That harm can only be aggravated by the creation of a constitutional shield for a policy that is itself the product of a habitual way of thinking about strangers. As Justice Brandeis so wisely advised, "we must be ever on our guard, lest we erect our prejudices into legal principles."

Points for Discussion

a. Burdening Expressive Activity

The Court concludes that, on these facts, inclusion of Dale as an adult member of the Boy Scouts would "significantly burden" the Boy Scouts' right to control the content of its own speech. Can you imagine a hypothetical situation in which including Dale would not significantly burden the Boy Scouts' speech?

b. Limits on the Freedom of Association

If the Boy Scouts engage in expressive activity because of its desire to "transmit its values" to its members, then does a large business similarly engage in expressive activity if it requires its employees to act in a "morally straight" way? If so, are employers immune from state anti-discrimination laws, as well? Similarly, are the members of a country club engaging in expression when they decide to limit membership only to white men? If not, why are those associations different from the Boy Scouts?

c. Understanding the Dissent

Did the dissent object to the content of the Boy Scouts' asserted message, disagree about the sincerity of the message, or both? Should the freedom of association under the First Amendment turn on either consideration? Or did the dissent conclude that the Boy Scouts was not engaged in expressive activity at all?

––––––––––––

In the following case, the question was not whether an organization had a right to exclude homosexuals, but instead a right to exclude *those who discriminate against* homosexuals. Again, the answer turned on whether the regulation affected the expressive activity of regulated organizations.

––––––––––––

Rumsfeld v. Forum for Academic and Institutional Rights, Inc.

547 U.S. 47 (2006)

Chief Justice ROBERTS delivered the opinion of the Court.

When law schools began restricting the access of military recruiters to their students because of disagreement with the Government's policy on homosexuals in the military, Congress responded by enacting the Solomon Amendment. See 10 U.S.C.A. § 983 (Supp. 2005). That provision specifies that if any part of an institution of higher education denies military recruiters access equal to that provided other recruiters, the entire institution would lose certain federal funds. *** Respondent Forum for Academic and Institutional Rights, Inc. (FAIR), is an association of law schools and law faculties. Its declared mission is "to promote academic freedom, support educational institutions in opposing discrimination and vindicate the rights of institutions of higher education." FAIR members have adopted policies expressing their opposition to discrimination based on, among other factors, sexual orientation. They would like to restrict military recruiting on their campuses because they object to the policy Congress has adopted with respect to homosexuals in the military. See 10 U.S.C. § 654.[1] The Solomon Amendment, however, forces institutions to choose between enforcing their nondiscrimination policy against military recruiters in this way and continuing to receive specified federal funding. [FAIR challenged the policy on the ground that it violated the First Amendment. The District Court rejected the claim, but the Court of Appeals for the Third Circuit reversed and ordered the District Court to enter a preliminary injunction against enforcement of the Solomon Amendment.]

––––––––––––

[1] Under this policy, a person generally may not serve in the Armed Forces if he has engaged in homosexual acts, stated that he is a homosexual, or married a person of the same sex. Respondents do not challenge that policy in this litigation.

Some of this Court's leading First Amendment precedents have established the principle that freedom of speech prohibits the government from telling people what they must say. In *West Virginia Bd. of Ed. v. Barnette,* 319 U.S. 624, 642 (1943), we held unconstitutional a state law requiring schoolchildren to recite the Pledge of Allegiance and to salute the flag. And in *Wooley v. Maynard,* 430 U.S. 705, 717 (1977), we held unconstitutional another that required New Hampshire motorists to display the state motto—"Live Free or Die"—on their license plates.

The Solomon Amendment does not require any similar expression by law schools. Nonetheless, recruiting assistance provided by the schools often includes elements of speech. For example, schools may send e-mails or post notices on bulletin boards on an employer's behalf. Law schools offering such services to other recruiters must also send e-mails and post notices on behalf of the military to comply with the Solomon Amendment. As FAIR points out, these compelled statements of fact ("The U.S. Army recruiter will meet interested students in Room 123 at 11 a.m."), like compelled statements of opinion, are subject to First Amendment scrutiny.
*** This sort of recruiting assistance, however, is a far cry from the compelled speech in *Barnette* and *Wooley.* The Solomon Amendment, unlike the laws at issue in those cases, does not dictate the content of the speech at all, which is only "compelled" if, and to the extent, the school provides such speech for other recruiters. There is nothing in this case approaching a Government-mandated pledge or motto that the school must endorse.

> **Make the Connection**
>
> This portion of the Court's opinion provides a helpful overview of several First Amendment doctrines. We considered those doctrines in Chapter 14, in the unit on freedom of speech.

The compelled speech to which the law schools point is plainly incidental to the Solomon Amendment's regulation of conduct, and "it has never been deemed an abridgment of freedom of speech or press to make a course of conduct illegal merely because the conduct was in part initiated, evidenced, or carried out by means of language, either spoken, written, or printed." *Giboney v. Empire Storage & Ice Co.,* 336 U.S. 490, 502 (1949). Congress, for example, can prohibit employers from discriminating in hiring on the basis of race. The fact that this will require an employer to take down a sign reading "White Applicants Only" hardly means that the law should be analyzed as one regulating the employer's speech rather than conduct. See *R.A.V. v. St. Paul,* 505 U.S. 377, 389 (1992) ("[W]ords can in some circumstances violate laws directed not against speech but against conduct"). Compelling a law school that sends scheduling e-mails for other recruiters to send one for a military recruiter is simply not the same as forcing a student to pledge allegiance, or forcing a Jehovah's Witness to display the motto "Live Free or Die," and it trivializes the freedom protected in *Barnette* and *Wooley* to suggest that it is.

Our compelled-speech cases are not limited to the situation in which an individual must personally speak the government's message. We have also in a number of instances limited the government's ability to force one speaker to host or accommodate another speaker's message. See *Hurley v. Irish-American Gay, Lesbian and Bisexual Group of Boston,*

Inc., 515 U.S. 557, 566 (1995); *Miami Herald Publishing Co. v. Tornillo,* 418 U.S. 241, 258 (1974) (right-of-reply statute violates editors' right to determine the content of their newspapers). Relying on these precedents, the Third Circuit concluded that the Solomon Amendment unconstitutionally compels law schools to accommodate the military's message "[b]y requiring schools to include military recruiters in the interviews and recruiting receptions the schools arrange."

In this case, accommodating the military's message does not affect the law schools' speech, because the schools are not speaking when they host interviews and recruiting receptions. Unlike a parade organizer's choice of parade contingents, a law school's decision to allow recruiters on campus is not inherently expressive. Law schools facilitate recruiting to assist their students in obtaining jobs. A law school's recruiting services lack the expressive quality of a parade, a newsletter, or the editorial page of a newspaper; its accommodation of a military recruiter's message is not compelled speech because the accommodation does not sufficiently interfere with any message of the school.

> **Take Note**
>
> In this passage, the Court distinguishes *Hurley.* In the Court's view, why are the two cases different? Can you think of hypothetical facts that would make the differences seem less significant?

Having rejected the view that the Solomon Amendment impermissibly regulates *speech,* we must still consider whether the expressive nature of the *conduct* regulated by the statute brings that conduct within the First Amendment's protection. [W]e have extended First Amendment protection only to conduct that is inherently expressive. [See, e.g., *United States v. O'Brien,* 391 U.S. 367, 377 (1968); *Texas v. Johnson,* 491 U.S. 397, 406 (1989).] [T]he conduct regulated by the Solomon Amendment is not inherently expressive. Prior to the adoption of the Solomon Amendment's equal-access requirement, law schools "expressed" their disagreement with the military by treating military recruiters differently from other recruiters. But these actions were expressive only because the law schools accompanied their conduct with speech explaining it. *** An observer who sees military recruiters interviewing away from the law school has no way of knowing whether the law school is expressing its disapproval of the military, all the law school's interview rooms are full, or the military recruiters decided for reasons of their own that they would rather interview someplace else. *** The expressive component of a law school's actions is not created by the conduct itself but by the speech that accompanies it. The fact that such explanatory speech is necessary is strong evidence that the conduct at issue here is not so inherently expressive that it warrants protection under *O'Brien.* If combining speech and conduct were enough to create expressive conduct, a regulated party could always transform conduct into "speech" simply by talking about it.

The Solomon Amendment does not violate law schools' freedom of speech, but the First Amendment's protection extends beyond the right to speak. We have recognized a First Amendment right to associate for the purpose of speaking, which we have termed a "right of expressive association." See, *e.g., Boy Scouts of America v. Dale,* 530 U.S. 640, 644 (2000). The reason we have extended First Amendment protection in this way is clear: The right to speak is often exercised most effectively by combining one's voice with the voices of others. See *Roberts v. United States Jaycees,* 468 U.S. 609, 622 (1984). If the government were free to restrict individuals' ability to join together and speak, it could essentially silence views that the First Amendment is intended to protect.

FAIR argues that the Solomon Amendment violates law schools' freedom of expressive association. According to FAIR, law schools' ability to express their message that discrimination on the basis of sexual orientation is wrong is significantly affected by the presence of military recruiters on campus and the schools' obligation to assist them. Relying heavily on our decision in *Dale,* the Court of Appeals agreed.

In *Dale,* we held that the Boy Scouts' freedom of expressive association was violated by New Jersey's public accommodations law, which required the organization to accept a homosexual as a scoutmaster. *** The Solomon Amendment, however, does not similarly affect a law school's associational rights. To comply with the statute, law schools must allow military recruiters on campus and assist them in whatever way the school chooses to assist other employers. Law schools therefore "associate" with military recruiters in the sense that they interact with them. But recruiters are not part of the law school. Recruiters are, by definition, outsiders who come onto campus for the limited purpose of trying to hire students—not to become members of the school's expressive association. This distinction is critical. Unlike the public accommodations law in *Dale,* the Solomon Amendment does not force a law school "to accept members it does not desire." The law schools *say* that allowing military recruiters equal access impairs their own expression by requiring them to associate with the recruiters, but just as saying conduct is undertaken for expressive purposes cannot make it symbolic speech, so too a speaker cannot "erect a shield" against laws requiring access "simply by asserting" that mere association "would impair its message." 530 U.S., at 653.

FAIR correctly notes that the freedom of expressive association protects more than just a group's membership decisions. For example, we have held laws unconstitutional that require disclosure of membership lists for groups seeking anonymity, *Brown v. Socialist Workers '74 Campaign Comm. (Ohio),* 459 U.S. 87, 101-102 (1982), or impose penalties or withhold benefits based on membership in a disfavored group, *Healy v. James,* 408 U.S. 169, 180-184 (1972). Although these laws did not directly interfere with an organization's composition, they made group membership less attractive, raising the same First Amendment concerns about affecting the group's ability to express its message.

The Solomon Amendment has no similar effect on a law school's associational rights. Students and faculty are free to associate to voice their disapproval of the military's message; nothing about the statute affects the composition of the group by making group membership less desirable. The Solomon Amendment therefore does not violate a law school's First Amendment rights. A military recruiter's mere presence on campus does not violate a law school's right to associate, regardless of how repugnant the law school considers the recruiter's message.

In this case, FAIR has attempted to stretch a number of First Amendment doctrines well beyond the sort of activities these doctrines protect. The law schools object to having to treat military recruiters like other recruiters, but that regulation of conduct does not violate the First Amendment.

Points for Discussion

a. Decision to Litigate

The Supreme Court's decision was unanimous. (Justice Alito, who was not yet on the Court when it was argued, did not participate in the decision.) Was it responsible for law schools (including the George Washington University Law School, where both authors of this textbook teach) to have brought a lawsuit that, according to the Court, "attempted to stretch a number of First Amendment doctrines well beyond the sort of activities these doctrines protect"? For one view on this question, see *Army 8, Yale 0*, Wall St. J., Mar. 7, 2006, at A12 (editorial regarding the "complete rout of the other-worldly professors who had challenged the law"). On the other hand, is there an argument that the Court was unduly stingy in construing *Hurley* and *Dale*?

b. Freedom of Association and Discrimination

Hurley, *Dale*, and *Forum for Academic and Institutional Rights* all involved claims that sought to challenge policies—by private or public actors—excluding people on the basis of their sexual orientation. In each case, the opponents of such policies lost. Would the cases have been any different if the challenged policies excluded people on the basis of race, instead of on the basis of sexual orientation? If so, why?

c. Conditional Spending

This case involved conditional spending. Under the Solomon Amendment, law schools must follow the conditions imposed or lose certain federal funds for their universities. Could the Court have analyzed this case under principles of conditional spending developed in cases like *South Dakota v. Dole*, 483 U.S. 203 (1987), without addressing the First Amendment? What would have been the likely outcome of a claim that the law exceeded Congress's power under the General Welfare Clause?

> **Make the Connection**
>
> We discussed Congress's power to spend, Congress's power to impose conditions upon the recipients of federal funds, and the Court's decision in *Dole* in Chapter 3.

Executive Summary of This Chapter

The Supreme Court has developed two distinct **freedom of association** doctrines. Under one doctrine, freedom of association is a right of substantive due process. This freedom of association encompasses rights such as the right to maintain familial relationships. Under the other doctrine, the Court has treated protection of freedom of association as a necessary means for securing rights guaranteed by the First Amendment. The theory is that associating with others may strengthen the ability to communicate. This Chapter concerns the latter doctrine.

Civil or Criminal Liability for Associating with Others

In general, the government cannot impose civil or criminal liability on a person merely because he or she has decided to associate with others. This general rule, however, has an important exception. The government does not have to allow individuals to associate with each other for the purpose of undertaking unlawful activities. *Scales v. United States*, 367 U.S. 203, 229 (1961).

The government may not discourage membership in a group by imposing vicarious liability on non-culpable group members, *NAACP v. Claiborne Hardware Co.*, 458 U.S. 886 (1982), or by denying legal or other privileges to persons who belong to groups or who refuse to provide information about them, *Baird v. State Bar of Arizona*, 401 U.S. 1 (1971).

Disclosure of Membership Lists

The government may require a group to disclose its membership only if the government has a compelling interest in knowing the identities of the group's members. *NAACP v. State of Alabama ex rel. Patterson*, 357 U.S. 449 (1958); *Buckley v. Valeo*, 424 U.S. 1 (1976).

Freedom Not to Associate with Others

The freedom of association generally gives an organization a right to choose its members. The government, however, may pass laws that regulate this freedom if the state has a compelling interest that cannot be achieved through means significantly less restrictive of associational freedoms. But government regulations may not prohibit an organization from discriminating in its membership if the regulations would significantly affect "intimate association" or "expressive activity." *Roberts v. United States Jaycees*, 468 U.S. 609 (1984).

The Supreme Court has held that a state may prevent a large group of businessmen from excluding women where the exclusion of women would not affect the group's message. *Roberts v. United States Jaycees*, 468 U.S. 609 (1984). Similarly, the Court has held that the federal government may prevent law schools from excluding military recruiters where the presence of military recruiters would not affect the law schools' expressive activities. *Rumsfeld v. Forum for Academic and Institutional Rights, Inc.*, 547 U.S. 47 (2006).

But the Supreme Court has held that a state may not prevent the organizers of a parade from excluding a gay-rights group where inclusion of the group would affect the parade organizer's message. *Hurley v. Irish-American Gay, Lesbian and Bisexual Group of Boston*, 515 U.S. 557 (1995). Similarly, a state may not prevent the Boy Scouts from excluding a homosexual scout leader where his inclusion would affect the Boy Scouts' expressive activity. *Boy Scouts of America v. Dale*, 530 U.S. 640 (2000).

CHAPTER 17

Freedom of Religion

The original Constitution addressed freedom of religion in just one clause. Article VI, clause 3 says that "no religious Test shall ever be required as a Qualification to any Office or public Trust under the United States." This clause has a clear purpose. As Justice Joseph Story explained in his influential treatise on constitutional law, "It is easy to foresee, that without some prohibition of religious tests, a successful sect, in our country, might, by once possessing power, pass test-laws, which would secure to themselves a monopoly of all the offices of trust and profit, under the national government." 3 Joseph Story, *Commentaries on the Constitution of the United States* § 1843 (1833).

The First Amendment substantially augments the protection of religious freedom. The Amendment begins by saying: "Congress shall make no law respecting an establishment of religion, or prohibiting the free exercise thereof ***." The two clauses in this phrase have become known, respectively, as the **Establishment Clause** and the **Free Exercise Clause**. Although on their faces these clauses refer only to Congress, the Supreme Court has held that the Due Process Clause of the Fourteenth Amendment makes both of these clauses applicable to the states, as well. See *Cantwell v. Connecticut*, 310 U.S. 296, 303 (1940). This Chapter considers the meaning and application of these two clauses.

> **Make the Connection**
>
> The incorporation doctrine, which makes certain provisions of the Bill of Rights applicable to the states, is addressed in Chapter 7.

A. The Establishment Clause

At the time of the Revolution, twelve of the thirteen colonies had established religions or churches. See *Engel v. Vitale*, 370 U.S. 421, 428 (1962). Justice Scalia has described some of what the establishment of religion in these colonies customarily entailed:

> Typically, attendance at the state church was required; only clergy of the official church could lawfully perform sacraments; and dissenters, if tolerated, faced an array of civil disabilities. Thus, for example, in the Colony of Virginia, where the Church of England had been established, ministers were required by law to conform to the doctrine and rites of the Church of England;

and all persons were required to attend church and observe the Sabbath, were tithed for the public support of Anglican ministers, and were taxed for the costs of building and repairing churches.

Lee v. Weisman, 505 U.S. 577, 640-641 (1992) (Scalia, J., dissenting) (citations omitted).

The Supreme Court has held that the Establishment Clause prohibits all of these practices: "Neither a state nor the Federal Government can *** force nor influence a person to go to or to remain away from church against his will or force him to profess a belief or disbelief in any religion. No person can be punished for entertaining or professing religious beliefs or disbeliefs, for church attendance or non-attendance ***." *Everson v. Board of Education of Ewing Township,* 330 U.S. 1, 15-16 (1947).

More difficult questions concern the extent to which the government may take other actions pertaining to religion. The following sections consider two broad topics: government aid to religious institutions and religion within government institutions. Most modern Establishment Clause challenges involve one of these topics.

———————————

Points for Discussion

a. The "Separation of Church and State"

In *Reynolds v. United States,* 98 U.S. 145, 164 (1878), the Supreme Court asserted that the First Amendment implements the "separation of church and state." This phrase, which the Supreme Court has used many times since *Reynolds,* refers to a civic ideal in which the government and religion operate in separate spheres: the government is secular, and the clergy and their congregations have no formal political authority. The Supreme Court has recognized that the mere invocation of the phrase "separation of church and state" cannot answer all questions that arise under the Establishment Clause, but the Court still views the phrase as "a useful figure of speech." See *Lynch v. Donnelly,* 465 U.S. 668, 673 (1984).

> **FYI**
>
> *Reynolds* involved a Mormon's Free Exercise challenge to a federal law banning polygamy.

In *Reynolds,* the Supreme Court relied on a now-famous letter that Thomas Jefferson wrote to a religious congregation in 1802. In the letter, Jefferson stated:

> Believing with you that religion is a matter which lies solely between man and his God, that he owes account to none other for his faith or his worship, that the legislative powers of government reach actions only, and not opinions, I contemplate with sovereign reverence that act of the whole American people which declared that their legislature should "make no law respecting an establishment of religion, or prohibiting the free exercise thereof," *thus building a wall of separation between Church and State.*

Letter from Thomas Jefferson to Danbury Baptist Association, reprinted in 5 *The Founders' Constitution* 58 (Philip B. Kurland & Ralph Lerner eds. 1987) (emphasis added).

More than 150 years before Jefferson articulated his view, Roger Williams, a Christian clergyman who had been exiled from Salem, Massachusetts, for resisting the establishment of a state church, helped to found the colony of Rhode Island as a place where religious minorities could live in peace and tolerance. In 1644, a few years before the colony obtained a royal charter ensuring religious liberty, Williams warned about the risks of creating an opening "in the hedge, or wall of separation, between the garden of the church and the wilderness of the world."

James Madison advanced a similar view in his famous "Memorial and Remonstrance," which he wrote in 1785 to oppose a Bill (proposed by Patrick Henry) in the Virginia legislature to impose a tax to support "teachers of the Christian religion." After providing a robust defense of the freedom of religion, he argued:

> Who does not see that the same authority which can establish Christianity, in exclusion of all other Religions, may establish with the same ease any particular sect of Christians, in exclusion of all other Sects? That the same authority which can force a citizen to contribute three pence only of his property for the support of any one establishment, may force him to conform to any other establishment in all cases whatsoever? *** Whilst we assert for ourselves a freedom to embrace, to profess and to observe the Religion which we believe to be of divine origin, we cannot deny an equal freedom to those whose minds have not yet yielded to the evidence which has convinced us. ***

> During almost fifteen centuries has the legal establishment of Christianity been on trial. What have been its fruits? More or less in all places, pride and indolence in the Clergy, ignorance and servility in the laity, in both, superstition, bigotry and persecution. *** Rulers who wished to subvert the public liberty, may have found an established Clergy convenient auxiliaries. A just Government instituted to secure & perpetuate it needs them not. Such a Government will be best supported by protecting every Citizen in the enjoyment of his Religion with the same equal hand which protects his person and his property; by neither invading the equal rights of any Sect, nor suffering any Sect to invade those of another.

This view—sometimes called "separationism" because of its central premise that there ought to be a separation between church and state—thus has a significant historical pedigree. Some scholars have asserted, moreover, that the Establishment Clause incorporated this view, and thus that the Clause not only prohibits the government from establishing an official church but also prohibits the government from, among other things, preferring religion over non-religion. See, e.g., Douglas Laycock, *"Nonpreferential" Aid to Religion: A False Claim About Original Intent*, 27 Wm & Mary L. Rev. 875 (1986).

Not everyone shares the view, however, that the Establishment Clause requires an absolute separation of church and state. In 1985, then-Justice William Rehnquist asserted in a lengthy dissent in *Wallace v. Jaffree*, 472 U.S. 38 (1985), that the Clause does not require "neutrality on the part of government between religion and irreligion." Instead, he concluded, after an extensive review of the drafting history of the Establishment Clause and early government practice, that the Clause merely "forbade establishment of a national religion, and forbade preference among religious sects or denominations." Accordingly, he reasoned that the Clause does not prohibit the government from "providing nondiscriminatory aid to religion." Justice Rehnquist's opinion, with his support for these assertions, appears later in this Chapter. His view is typically referred to as "non-preferentialism," because it asserts that the Establishment Clause requires only that the government not prefer one religion over another, not that the government be neutral between religion and non-religion.

In an influential book, Professor Phillip Hamburger reaches a similar conclusion. See Phillip Hamburger, *Separation of Church and State* (2002). He argues that the Establishment Clause was originally intended only to prevent the government from discriminating based on religion. See *id.* at 14. A desire for separation of church and state, he contends, arose much later in United States history, based on "ideals of individual independence, fears of Catholicism, and various types of specialization." *Id.* Hamburger concluded: "Americans gradually transformed their understanding of religious liberty. Increasingly, Americans conceived their freedom to require an independence from churches and they feared the demands of one church in particular. To limit such threats, Americans called for a separation of church and state, and eventually the U.S. Supreme Court gave their new conception of religious liberty the force of law." *Id.* at 17.

Despite this criticism, the ideal of separation of church and state remains an important influence in the Supreme Court's interpretation of the Establishment Clause. Does the historical ambiguity mean that originalism cannot answer which view better captures the meaning of the Establishment Clause? If originalism is the appropriate approach, what weight should be given to the views of figures such as Jefferson, Madison, and Williams? As we consider the cases in this section, consider the extent to which the Supreme Court has accepted the pure view of separation.

b. Who Is Protected By the Establishment Clause?

Most of the provisions in the Bill of Rights are designed to protect minority rights against majoritarian incursion. The protections in the Fourth, Fifth, Sixth, and Eighth Amendments, for example, serve to ensure that unpopular persons—that is, persons accused of crimes—receive process that an angry majority might otherwise be reluctant to provide. Similarly, as we saw in Chapter 14, the Free Speech Clause of the First Amendment protects dissenters and others with unpopular views from retribution by the majority. Indeed, the provisions in the Bill of Rights typically matter only because they provide minority protections; the majority, after all, rarely needs protection from the majoritarian political process.

Is the Establishment Clause such a provision, as well? If so, whom does it protect? Those who support the separationist view generally assert that the Establishment Clause protects several groups: (1) adherents of minority religions, who would face ostracism and coercion if adherents of the dominant religion could impose their religious views by law; (2) those who do not subscribe to any religion or hold any religious beliefs, for much the same reason; and (3) religious institutions and organizations, such as organized churches, which would inevitably be corrupted by the political process and the resulting desire to attain and consolidate power. See, e.g., James Madison, Memorial and Remonstrance, reprinted in *Everson v. Board of Education of Ewing Township*, 330 U.S. 1, 67 (1947)

Whom does the Establishment Clause protect under the non-preferentialist view, which Justice Rehnquist advanced in the excerpt above and which (we will see in this Chapter) has become increasingly popular on the Court? Does it protect adherents of minority religions, on the theory that they can receive the same aid from the government that adherents of the dominant religion can receive? Does it protect religious organizations, by giving them access to government aid and the public square? What is its view of the rights of non-believers? As you read the materials in this Chapter, consider the justifications for and implications of the competing views of the Establishment Clause.

c. Application of the Establishment Clause to the States

Although the Supreme Court has squarely held that the Establishment Clause applies to the states as a result of the clause's incorporation by the Due Process Clause of the Fourteenth Amendment, *Cantwell v. Connecticut,* 310 U.S. 296, 303 (1940), some Justices in recent years have expressed a willingness to revisit the issue. Justice Clarence Thomas articulated this view in a separate opinion in *Elk Grove Unified School Dist. v. Newdow,* 542 U.S. 1, 45 (2004) (Thomas, J., concurring in judgment):

> As a textual matter, [the Establishment] Clause probably prohibits Congress from establishing a national religion. *But see* P. Hamburger, *Separation of Church and State* 106, n. 40 (2002). Perhaps more importantly, the Clause made clear that Congress could not interfere with state establishments, notwithstanding any argument that could be made based on Congress' power under the Necessary and Proper Clause. *See* A. Amar, *The Bill of Rights* 36-39 (1998).

> Nothing in the text of the Clause suggests that it reaches any further. The Establishment Clause does not purport to protect individual rights. By contrast, the Free Exercise Clause plainly protects individuals against congressional interference with the right to exercise their religion, and the remaining Clauses within the First Amendment expressly disable Congress from "abridging [particular] *freedom[s].*" (Emphasis added.) This textual analysis is consistent with the prevailing view that the Constitution left religion to the States. *See, e.g.,* 2 J. Story, *Commentaries on the Constitution of the United States* § 1873 (5th ed. 1891); *see also* Amar, *The Bill of Rights,* at 32-42; *id.,* at 246-257. History also supports this understanding: At the founding, at least six States had established religions, see McConnell, *The Origins and Historical Understanding of Free Exercise of Religion,* 103 Harv. L.Rev. 1409, 1437 (1990). Nor has this federalism point escaped the notice of Members of this Court. *See, e.g., Zelman v. Simmons-Harris,* 536 U.S. 639, 677-680 (2002) (THOMAS, J., concurring); *Lee v. Weisman,* 505 U.S. 577, 641 (1992) (SCALIA, J., dissenting).

> Quite simply, the Establishment Clause is best understood as a federalism provision—it protects state establishments from federal interference but does not protect any individual right. These two features independently make incorporation of the Clause difficult to understand. The best argument in favor of incorporation would be that, by disabling Congress from establishing a national religion, the Clause protected an individual right, enforceable against the Federal Government, to be free from coercive federal establishments. ***

Under Justice Thomas's view, the Establishment Clause would prohibit Congress from establishing a national church or religion, but it would not impose any limits on the authority of the states to do the same. Accordingly, under this view, a bill today similar to the 1785 Bill in Virginia to impose a tax to support "teachers of the Christian religion," which prompted Madison to write his "Memorial and Remonstrance," would not violate the Establishment Clause, notwithstanding the doctrine of incorporation. Does the fact that many states had established churches or religions before the ratification of the Constitution support Justice Thomas's conclusion, or does it shed light on the reasons why the First Amendment was proposed and ratified?

Consider the competing view, which Justice Brennan expressed in a concurring opinion in *School Dist. of Abington Twp. v. Schempp*, 374 U.S. 203 (1963):

> It has been suggested, with some support in history, that [incorporation of the Establishment Clause] is conceptually impossible because the Framers meant the Establishment Clause also to foreclose any attempt by Congress to disestablish the existing official state churches. Whether or not such was the understanding of the Framers and whether such a purpose would have inhibited the absorption of the Establishment Clause at the threshold of the Nineteenth Century are questions not dispositive of our present inquiry. For it is clear on the record of history that the last of the formal state establishments was dissolved more than three decades before the Fourteenth Amendment was ratified, and thus the problem of protecting official state churches from federal encroachments could hardly have been any concern of those who framed the post-Civil War Amendments. Any such objective of the First Amendment, having become historical anachronism by 1868, cannot be thought to have deterred the absorption of the Establishment Clause to any greater degree than it would, for example, have deterred the absorption of the Free Exercise Clause. That no organ of the Federal Government possessed in 1791 any power to restrain the interference of the States in religious matters is indisputable. It is equally plain, on the other hand, that the Fourteenth Amendment created a panoply of new federal rights for the protection of citizens of the various States [including] freedom from such state governmental involvement in the affairs of religion as the Establishment Clause had originally foreclosed on the part of Congress.

> It has also been suggested that [the Establishment Clause is not incorporated] because that clause is not one of the provisions of the Bill of Rights which in terms protects a "freedom" of the individual. The fallacy in this contention, I think, is that it underestimates the role of the Establishment Clause as a coguarantor, with the Free Exercise Clause, of religious liberty. The Framers did not entrust the liberty of religious beliefs to either clause alone.

> Finally, it has been contended that absorption of the Establishment Clause is precluded by the absence of any intention on the part of the Framers of the Fourteenth Amendment to circumscribe the residual powers of the States to aid religious activities and institutions in ways which fell short of formal establishments. *** Even if we assume that the draftsmen of the Fourteenth Amendment saw no immediate connection between its protections against state action infringing personal liberty and the guarantees of the First Amendment, it is certainly too late in the day to suggest that their assumed inattention to the question dilutes the force of these constitutional guarantees in their application to the States. It is enough to conclude that the religious liberty embodied in the Fourteenth Amendment would not be viable if the Constitution were interpreted to forbid only establishments ordained by Congress.

Was Justice Brennan suggesting that the understanding of the states' role in matters of religion had changed between 1791 and 1868 such that the Establishment principle held by the Supreme Court to be incorporated by the Fourteenth Amendment is different from the principle in the original First Amendment? Or was he suggesting that the meaning of the Establishment principle has evolved since its incorporation in 1868?

The majority of the cases that follow in this Part involve challenges to state, as opposed to federal, laws. As you read them, consider what the results would have been if the Supreme Court had accepted Justice Thomas's view of the reach of the Establishment Clause.

---

1. Government Aid to Religious Institutions

To what extent does the Establishment Clause prevent the federal and state governments from providing aid to religious institutions? Although the Supreme Court has addressed this question in many cases, a simple answer has not emerged. The Court has concluded that some forms of aid are permissible, but that other forms are not. Exactly what distinguishes the two categories, however, remains unsettled.

Consider, for example, cases involving governmental aid to parochial schools (i.e., private schools with a religious affiliation). On the one hand, the Supreme Court has said that the government cannot supplement the salary of teachers in parochial schools, *Lemon v. Kurtzman*, 403 U.S. 602 (1971), or conduct classes in parochial schools, *School District of the City of Grand Rapids v. Ball*, 473 U.S. 373 (1985). Under current doctrine, these actions violate the Establishment Clause. On the other hand, the Supreme Court has held that the government may provide tax credits to parents for tuition paid to parochial schools, *Mueller v. Allen*, 463 U.S. 388 (1983), loan textbooks to parochial schools, *Board of Education v. Allen*, 392 U.S. 236 (1968), and reimburse the cost of transportation to parochial schools, *Everson v. Board of Education of Ewing Township*, 330 U.S. 1 (1947). Under current doctrine, these actions do not violate the Establishment Clause. As

> **For More Information**
>
> For lists of more examples of cases that have upheld and struck down governmental programs under the Establishment Clause, see *Van Orden v. Perry*, 545 U.S. 677, 685 nn. 3 & 4 (2005) (plurality opinion).

Chief Justice William Rehnquist aptly put it: "Our cases, Januslike, point in two directions in applying the Establishment Clause." *Van Orden v. Perry*, 545 U.S. 677, 685 (2005) (plurality opinion).

> **Definition**
>
> Januslike means like the Roman god Janus, who had two faces looking in opposite directions.

In the following case, the Court announced at least two principles. First, the Court, echoing the separationist view described above, declared that the Establishment Clause "was intended to erect 'a wall of separation between Church and State'" and thus that "[n]o tax in any amount, large or small, can be levied to support any religious activities or institutions ***." Second, the Court announced what might be called a general neutrality principle. This principle states that the Establishment Clause "requires the state to be a neutral in its relations with groups of religious believers and non-believers." The government may provide benefits to religious believers if it does so in a neutral fashion—that is, if, generally speaking, it does not favor religious individuals or organizations over the non-religious. As you read the case, ask yourself whether (1) these principles are sensible interpretations of the Establishment Clause, (2) they are reconcilable, and (3) the Court applied them correctly in the case.

————————

Everson v. Board of Education of Ewing Township

330 U.S. 1 (1947)

Mr. Justice BLACK delivered the opinion of the Court.

A New Jersey statute authorizes its local school districts to make rules and contracts for the transportation of children to and from schools. The [appellee] acting pursuant to this statute authorized reimbursement to parents of money expended by them for the bus transportation of their children on regular busses operated by the public transportation system. Part of this money was for the payment of transportation of some children in the community to Catholic parochial schools. These church schools give their students, in addition to secular education, regular religious instruction conforming to the religious tenets and modes of worship of the Catholic Faith. The superintendent of these schools is a Catholic priest.

The appellant, in his capacity as a district taxpayer, filed suit in a State court challenging the right of the Board to reimburse parents of parochial school students. He contended that the statute and the resolution passed pursuant to it violated both the State and the Federal Constitutions. ***[2]

> **Make the Connection**
>
> Under current standing doctrine, which we discussed in Chapter 2, did the plaintiff in this suit have standing? What was his injury? Should that be a cognizable injury under Article III? We consider this question later in this chapter.

A large proportion of the early settlers of this country came here from Europe to escape the bondage of laws which compelled them to support and attend government favored churches. The centuries immediately before and contemporaneous with the colonization of America had been filled with turmoil, civil strife, and persecutions, generated in large part by established sects determined to maintain their absolute political and religious supremacy. With the power of government supporting them, at various times and places, Catholics had persecuted Protestants, Protestants had persecuted Catholics, Protestant sects had persecuted other Protestant sects, Catholics of one shade of belief had persecuted

---

[2] Although the township resolution authorized reimbursement only for parents of public and Catholic school pupils, appellant does not allege, nor is there anything in the record which would offer the slightest support to an allegation, that there were any children in the township who attended or would have attended, but for want of transportation, any but public and Catholic schools.

Catholics of another shade of belief, and all of these had from time to time persecuted Jews. In efforts to force loyalty to whatever religious group happened to be on top and in league with the government of a particular time and place, men and women had been fined, cast in jail, cruelly tortured, and killed. Among the offenses for which these punishments had been inflicted were such things as speaking disrespectfully of the views of ministers of government-established churches, nonattendance at those churches, expressions of non-belief in their doctrines, and failure to pay taxes and tithes to support them.

These practices of the old world were transplanted to and began to thrive in the soil of the new America. The very charters granted by the English Crown to the individuals and companies designated to make the laws which would control the destinies of the colonials authorized these individuals and companies to erect religious establishments which all, whether believers or non-believers, would be required to support and attend. An exercise of this authority was accompanied by a repetition of many of the old world practices and persecutions. Catholics found themselves hounded and proscribed because of their faith; Quakers who followed their conscience went to jail; Baptists were peculiarly obnoxious to certain dominant Protestant sects; men and women of varied faiths who happened to be in a minority in a particular locality were persecuted because they steadfastly persisted in worshipping God only as their own consciences dictated. And all of these dissenters were compelled to pay tithes and taxes to support government-sponsored churches whose ministers preached inflammatory sermons designed to strengthen and consolidate the established faith by generating a burning hatred against dissenters.

These practices became so commonplace as to shock the freedom-loving colonials into a feeling of abhorrence. The imposition of taxes to pay ministers' salaries and to build and maintain churches and church property aroused their indignation. It was these feelings which found expression in the First Amendment. No one locality and no one group throughout the Colonies can rightly be given entire credit for having aroused the sentiment that culminated in adoption of the Bill of Rights' provisions embracing religious liberty. But Virginia, where the established church had achieved a dominant influence in political affairs and where many excesses attracted wide public attention, provided a great stimulus and able leadership for the movement. The people there, as elsewhere, reached the conviction that individual religious liberty could be achieved best under a government which was stripped of all power to tax, to support, or otherwise to assist any or all religions, or to interfere with the beliefs of any religious individual or group.

Go Online

For more history of this struggle for religious freedom in Virginia and for images and transcripts of Madison's and Jefferson's documents, visit the Library of Congress's online exhibition on Religion and the Founding of the American Republic.

The movement toward this end reached its dramatic climax in Virginia in 1785-86 when the Virginia legislative body was about to renew Virginia's tax levy for the support of the established church. Thomas Jefferson and James Madison led the fight against this tax. Madison wrote his great Memorial and Remonstrance against the law. In it, he eloquently argued that a true religion did not need the support of law; that no person, either believer or non-believer, should be taxed to support a religious institution of any kind; that the best interest of a society required that the minds of men always be wholly free; and that cruel persecutions were the inevitable result of government-established religions. Madison's Remonstrance received strong support throughout Virginia, and the Assembly postponed consideration of the proposed tax measure until its next session. When the proposal came up for consideration at that session, it not only died in committee, but the Assembly enacted the famous "Virginia Bill for Religious Liberty" originally written by Thomas Jefferson. The preamble to that Bill stated among other things that

> Almighty God hath created the mind free; that all attempts to influence it by temporal punishments, or burthens, or by civil incapacitations, tend only to beget habits of hypocrisy and meanness, and are a departure from the plan of the Holy author of our religion who being Lord both of body and mind, yet chose not to propagate it by coercions on either . . . ; that to compel a man to furnish contributions of money for the propagation of opinions which he disbelieves, is sinful and tyrannical; that even the forcing him to support this or that teacher of his own religious persuasion, is depriving him of the comfortable liberty of giving his contributions to the particular pastor, whose morals he would make his pattern. ***

And the statute itself enacted

> That no man shall be compelled to frequent or support any religious worship, place, or ministry whatsoever, nor shall be enforced, restrained, molested, or burthened, in his body or goods, nor shall otherwise suffer on account of his religious opinions or belief. . . .

This Court has previously recognized that the provisions of the First Amendment, in the drafting and adoption of which Madison and Jefferson played such leading roles, had the same objective and were intended to provide the same protection against governmental intrusion on religious liberty as the Virginia statute. *Reynolds v. United States*, 98 U.S. 145, 164 (1878). Prior to the adoption of the Fourteenth Amendment, the First Amendment did not apply as a restraint against the states. Most of them did soon provide similar constitutional protections for religious liberty. But some states persisted for about half a century in imposing restraints upon the free exercise of religion and in discriminating against particular religious groups. In recent years, so far as the provision against the establishment of a religion is concerned, the question has most frequently arisen in connection with proposed state aid to church schools and efforts to carry on religious teachings in the public schools in accordance with the tenets of a particular sect. Some churches have either sought or accepted state financial support for their schools. Here again the efforts to obtain state aid or acceptance of it have not been limited to any one particular faith. The state courts, in the main, have remained faithful to the language of their own constitutional provisions designed to protect religious freedom and to separate religious and governments. Their decisions, however, show the difficulty in drawing the line between tax legislation which provides funds for the welfare of the general public and that which is designed to support institutions which teach religion.

The "establishment of religion" clause of the First Amendment means at least this: Neither a state nor the Federal Government can set up a church. Neither can pass laws which aid one religion, aid all religions, or prefer one religion over another. Neither can force nor influence a person to go to or to remain away from church against his will or force him to profess a belief or disbelief in any religion. No person can be punished for entertaining or professing religious beliefs or disbeliefs, for church attendance or non-attendance. No tax in any amount, large or small, can be levied to support any religious activities or institutions, whatever they may be called, or whatever form they may adopt to teach or practice religion. Neither a state nor the Federal Government can, openly or secretly, participate in the affairs of any religious organizations or groups and vice versa. In the words of Jefferson, the clause against establishment of religion by law was intended to erect "a wall of separation between Church and State." _Reynolds v. United States_, 98 U.S. at 164.

> **Take Note**
>
> The Court here announces a series of principles that derive from the Establishment Clause. How many of these principles are implicated by the practice challenged in this case? Assuming that not all are, is most of this passage simply dicta? Or is it essential to the Court's reasoning and interpretation of the First Amendment?

We must consider the New Jersey statute in accordance with the foregoing limitations imposed by the First Amendment. *** New Jersey cannot consistently with the "establishment of religion" clause of the First Amendment contribute tax-raised funds to the support of an institution which teaches the tenets and faith of any church. On the other hand, other language of the amendment commands that New Jersey cannot hamper its citizens in the free exercise of their own religion. Consequently, it cannot exclude individual Catholics, Lutherans, Mohammedans, Baptists, Jews, Methodists, Non-believers, Presbyterians, or the members of any other faith, because of their faith, or lack of it, from receiving the benefits of public welfare legislation. While we do not mean to intimate that a state could not provide transportation only to children attending public schools, we must be careful, in protecting the citizens of New Jersey against state-established churches, to be sure that we do not inadvertently prohibit New Jersey from extending its general State law benefits to all its citizens without regard to their religious belief.

Measured by these standards, we cannot say that the First Amendment prohibits New Jersey from spending tax raised funds to pay the bus fares of parochial school pupils as a part of a general program under which it pays the fares of pupils attending public and other schools. It is undoubtedly true that children are helped to get to church schools. There is even a possibility that some of the children might not be sent to the church schools if the parents were compelled to pay their children's bus fares out of their own pockets when transportation to a public school would have been paid for by the State. The same possibility exists where the state requires a local transit company to provide reduced fares to school children including those attending parochial schools, or where a municipally owned transportation system undertakes to carry all school children free of charge. Moreover, state-paid policemen, detailed to protect children going to and from church schools from the very real hazards of traffic, would serve much the same purpose and accomplish much the same result as state provisions intended to guarantee free transportation of a kind which the state deems to be best for the school children's welfare. And parents might refuse to risk their children to the serious danger of traffic accidents going to and from parochial schools, the approaches to which were not protected by policemen. Similarly, parents

> **Take Note**
>
> In this passage, the Court states a test of neutrality between religion and non-religion. In what way is the law in this case neutral? Is there an argument that it is not neutral? Is the challenged policy different in any meaningful way from a policy that provides police and fire protection to religious institutions?

might be reluctant to permit their children to attend schools which the state had cut off from such general government services as ordinary police and fire protection, connections for sewage disposal, public highways and sidewalks. Of course, cutting off church schools from these services, so separate and so indisputably marked off from the religious function, would make it far more difficult for the schools to operate. But such is obviously not the purpose of the First Amendment. That Amendment requires the state to be a neutral in its relations with groups of religious believers and non-believers; it does not require the state to be their adversary. State power is no more to be used so as to handicap religions, than it is to favor them.

The First Amendment has erected a wall between church and state. That wall must be kept high and impregnable. We could not approve the slightest breach. New Jersey has not breached it here.

Mr. Justice JACKSON, [joined by Mr. Justice FRANKFURTER,] dissenting.

I find myself, contrary to first impressions, unable to join in this decision. I have a sympathy, though it is not ideological, with Catholic citizens who are compelled by law to pay taxes for public schools, and also feel constrained by conscience and discipline to support other schools for their own children. Such relief to them as this case involves is not in itself a serious burden to taxpayers and I had assumed it to be as little serious in principle. Study of this case convinces me otherwise. The Court's opinion marshals every argument in favor of state aid and puts the case in its most favorable light, but much of its reasoning confirms my conclusions that there are no good grounds upon which to support the present legislation. In fact, the undertones of the opinion, advocating complete and uncompromising separation of Church from State, seem utterly discordant with its conclusion yielding support to their commingling in educational matters. ***

It seems to me that the basic fallacy in the Court's reasoning, which accounts for its failure to apply the principles it avows, is in ignoring the essentially religious test by which beneficiaries of this expenditure are selected. A policeman protects a Catholic, of course— but not because he is a Catholic; it is because he is a man and a member of our society. The fireman protects the Church school—but not because it is a Church school; it is because it is property, part of the assets of our society. Neither the fireman nor the policeman has to ask before he renders aid "Is this man or building identified with the Catholic Church." But before these school authorities draw a check to reimburse for a student's fare they must ask just that question, and if the school is a Catholic one they may render aid because it is such, while if it is of any other faith or is run for profit, the help must be withheld. To consider the converse of the Court's reasoning will best disclose its fallacy. That there is no parallel between police and fire protection and this plan of reimbursement is apparent from the incongruity of the limitation of this Act if applied to police and fire service. Could we sustain an Act that said police shall protect pupils on the way to or from public schools and Catholic schools but not while going to and coming from other schools, and firemen shall extinguish a blaze in public or Catholic school buildings but shall not put out a blaze in Protestant Church schools or private schools operated for profit? That is the true analogy to the case we have before us and I should think it pretty plain that such a scheme would not be valid.

> **Take Note**
>
> Is Justice Jackson's objection to the challenged statute that it is not neutral between religion and *non*-religion, or that it is not neutral among *different* religions? Under Justice Jackson's reasoning, what would be the constitutional status of a law that used taxpayer funds to pay for bus transportation to all schools, public and private, secular and religious of any denomination? As you consider this question, note that Justice Jackson also joined Justice Rutledge's opinion, which follows.

Mr. Justice RUTLEDGE, with whom Mr. Justice FRANKFURTER, Mr. Justice JACKSON and Mr. Justice BURTON agree, dissenting.

Believers of all faiths, and others who do not express their feeling toward ultimate issues of existence in any creedal form, pay the New Jersey tax. When the money so raised is used to pay for transportation to religious schools, the Catholic taxpayer to the extent of his proportionate share pays for the transportation of Lutheran, Jewish and otherwise religiously affiliated children to receive their non-Catholic religious instruction. Their parents likewise pay proportionately for the transportation of Catholic children to receive Catholic instruction. Each thus contributes to "the propagation of opinions which he disbelieves" in so far as their religions differ, as do others who accept no creed without regard to those differences. Each thus pays taxes also to support the teaching of his own religion, an exaction equally forbidden since it denies "the comfortable liberty" of giving one's contribution to the particular agency of instruction he approves.

New Jersey's action therefore exactly fits the type of exaction and the kind of evil at which Madison and Jefferson struck. Under the test they framed it cannot be said that the cost of transportation is no part of the cost of education or of the religious instruction given. That it is a substantial and a necessary element is shown most plainly by the continuing and increasing demand for the state to assume it. Nor is there pretense that it relates only to the secular instruction given in religious schools or that any attempt is or could be made toward allocating proportional shares as between the secular and the religious instruction. It is precisely because the instruction is religious and relates to a particular faith, whether one or another, that parents send their children to religious schools *** . And the very purpose of the state's contribution is to defray the cost of conveying the pupil to the place where he will receive not simply secular, but also and primarily religious, teaching and guidance.

Points for Discussion

a. Identifying the Rule

Which one of the Establishment Clause principles that the Court announced in *Everson* governed the outcome of the case? Did the policy authorizing reimbursement to parents permit the use of tax funds "to support any religious activities or institutions"? If so, in what way? And if so, then why was the policy nevertheless consistent with the Constitution?

The Court declared that the policy was constitutional because it was consistent with the "neutrality principle." Where did this rule come from? Is it based on the history that the Court discussed earlier in the opinion? Is it based on a political or philosophical theory about the role of government in matters of conscience? If so, do you agree with that theory? Or is it based on other Clauses in the Constitution (or even in the First Amendment)?

b. Satisfying the Rule of Neutrality

The Court held in *Everson* that a local board of education does not violate the rule of neutrality when it pays for transporting children to schools, even if some of the schools are private Catholic schools. Yet, as Justice Jackson observed, the policy (at least in practice) paid costs *only* for children attending public schools and Catholic schools; children (if any) attending other private religious schools were not covered. Does this suggest that the policy was not neutral towards religion and non-religion? Or only that it was not neutral among religions? If the latter, is that a defect under the Establishment Clause? Under the Equal Protection Clause? Under the Free Exercise Clause?

Even if the policy had paid transportation costs to *all* schools, including private religious schools of all denominations, is there an argument that the policy was nevertheless inconsistent with the Establishment Clause? Justice Rutledge asserted that the policy was unconstitutional because it effectively provided a government subsidy for religious instruction. In his view, what exactly was wrong with such a subsidy? Did he reject the rule of neutrality as insufficient under the Establishment Clause, or did he simply think that the rule was not satisfied in this case? Would his view require the conclusion that a state cannot provide police or fire protection for religious institutions? If not, why was this case different?

Assuming that the Court was correct in its conclusion that the challenged policy was neutral, what sorts of policies would fail the Court's test? Can you think of hypothetical examples of policies that would provide payment for transportation to Catholic schools but that would not be neutral?

c. Other Forms of Aid to Parochial Schools

How important was the fact that the aid at issue in *Everson* was provided to individuals rather than to the religious schools themselves? Obviously, the aid benefitted the schools, in that it made it more likely that students would choose to enroll. But is such aid different in kind from aid provided directly to religious institutions?

For example, could a public school board of education pay for the costs of field trips taken by students at religious schools if it also pays for the cost of field trips taken at public schools? Would such a law be "neutral"? If so, is neutrality enough? The Supreme Court initially held that a board of education could not pay for field trips even under a neutral policy. In *Wolman v. Walter*, 433 U.S. 229, 253-254 (1977), the Court explained:

> [A]lthough a trip may be to a location that would be of interest to those in public schools, it is the individual teacher who makes a field trip meaningful. The experience begins with the study and discussion of the place to be visited; it continues on location with the teacher pointing out items of interest and stimulating the imagination; and it ends with a discussion of the experience. The field trips are an integral part of the educational experience, and where the teacher works within and for a sectarian institution, an unacceptable risk of fostering of religion is an inevitable byproduct.

Accordingly, the Court concluded in *Wolman* that neutrality is not enough to satisfy scrutiny under the Establishment Clause; the governmental action also must not "foster" religion. But the Court overruled *Wolman* in *Mitchell v. Helms*, 530 U.S. 793 (2000). In *Mitchell*, the Court held that a policy permitting the use of public funds to pay for library books, computers, laboratory equipment, and other educational items at religious schools did not violate the Establishment Clause. The plurality opinion asserted that neutral aid to religious schools is permissible so long as no "religious indoctrination that occurs in those schools could reasonably be attributed to governmental action." *Id.* at 809.

How can a court tell whether public funds provided to religious institutions are used for "religious indoctrination"? Assuming that the religious institution has other, non-governmental sources of funds, isn't all of the money fungible? That is, doesn't any government aid to a religious institution free up the institution's other funds to be used for religious indoctrination?

d. Dissatisfaction with Neutrality

To the extent that the dissenters in *Everson* disagreed with the neutrality principle, the source of their disagreement was the conviction that the principle did not *adequately constrain* the power of government to subsidize religious practice. As we will see in the materials that follow, however, in more recent years several members of the Supreme Court have disagreed with the neutrality principle on the ground that it *unduly* constrains the power of the government to affirm and support religious practices.

Justice Scalia, writing for himself and two others, recently expressed his opposition to the neutrality principle in a dissenting opinion in *McCreary County, Ky. v. American Civil Liberties Union of Ky.*, 545 U.S. 844, 888-891 (2005), which held that a display of the Ten Commandments in a courthouse violates the Establishment Clause:

> Presidents continue to conclude the Presidential oath with the words "so help me God." Our legislatures, state and national, continue to open their sessions with prayer led by official

> **Make the Connection**
>
> We will consider the Ten Commandments cases—*McCreary* and *Van Orden v. Perry*, 545 U.S. 677 (2005), a companion case—later in this Chapter.

chaplains. The sessions of this Court continue to open with the prayer "God save the United States and this Honorable Court." Invocation of the Almighty by our public figures, at all levels of government, remains commonplace. Our coinage bears the motto, "IN GOD WE TRUST." And our Pledge of Allegiance contains the acknowledgment that we are a Nation "under God." ***

> With all of this reality (and much more) staring it in the face, how can the Court *possibly* assert that the "First Amendment mandates governmental neutrality between . . . religion and nonreligion," and that "[m]anifesting a purpose to favor [adherence] to religion generally," is unconstitutional? Who says so? Surely not the words of the Constitution. Surely not the history and traditions that reflect our society's constant understanding of those words. *** Nothing stands behind the Court's assertion that governmental affirmation of the society's belief in God is unconstitutional except the Court's own say-so, citing as support only the unsubstantiated say-so of earlier Courts going back no further than the mid-20th century. *** And [the Court's practice] is discredited because the Court has not had the courage (or the foolhardiness) to apply the neutrality principle consistently.

Is it clear that "history and tradition" demonstrate that the neutrality principle is incorrect? One commentator has argued that Justice Scalia "selectively [drew] upon the historical record to give the appearance of a historical consensus that did not exist," holding out as "unambiguous evidence of a universally understood original meaning actions that, in fact, many of the Framers themselves strongly condemned as unconstitutional":

> For instance, James Madison—who originally proposed the Establishment Clause—fought the First Congress's decision to hire a legislative chaplain, and condemned it as "a palpable violation [of] Constitutional principles." Similarly, Thomas Jefferson refused to issue Thanksgiving prayers because he understood them to violate the Establishment Clause's prohibition against governmental "recommendation" of religion. Madison also refused during his early years in office to issue calls for Thanksgiving prayer. Later, during the politically contentious War of 1812, he did issue such calls, but he subsequently confessed that his doing so had violated the Constitution. *** [T]he text, historical antecedents, drafting history, and debate surrounding the adoption of the Establishment Clause all provide compelling, though perhaps not conclusive, evidence that the clause was intended and originally understood to preclude government preference for particular religions or for religion over nonreligion, as the Court has long understood.

Thomas B. Colby, *A Constitutional Hierarchy of Religions? Justice Scalia, the Ten Commandments, and the Establishment Clause*, 100 Nw. U. L. Rev. 1097 (2006). There remains, in other words, substantial debate about the neutrality rule announced in *Everson*.

————————

After the decision in *Everson*, the Supreme Court struggled to reconcile the neutrality principle with the principle that the government should not use tax funds to support religion. In the following landmark case, the Court attempted to address this difficulty by devising a multi-factor analysis for deciding whether a law violates the Establishment Clause. The case created the so-called **_Lemon_ test**, by which the courts consider (1) whether the challenged law has a secular purpose; (2) whether the principal or primary effect of the law is to advance or inhibit religion; and (3) whether the law excessively entangles the government and religion. The *Lemon* test quickly became the operative standard in Establishment Clause cases. In the two and a half decades that followed the decision, about 2000 state and federal cases applied the *Lemon* test. As you read the case, consider whether the test sensibly implements Establishment Clause principles.

Lemon v. Kurtzman

403 U.S. 602 (1971)

Mr. Chief Justice BURGER delivered the opinion of the Court.

These two appeals raise questions as to Pennsylvania and Rhode Island statutes providing state aid to church-related elementary and secondary schools. *** The Rhode Island Salary Supplement Act was enacted in 1969. It rests on the legislative finding that the quality of education available in nonpublic elementary schools has been jeopardized by the rapidly rising salaries needed to attract competent and dedicated teachers. The Act authorizes state officials to supplement the salaries of teachers of secular subjects in nonpublic elementary schools by paying directly to a teacher an amount not in excess of 15% of his current annual salary. As supplemented, however, a nonpublic school teacher's salary cannot exceed the maximum paid to teachers in the State's public schools, and the recipient must be certified by the state board of education in substantially the same manner as public school teachers.

The Pennsylvania Nonpublic Elementary and Secondary Education Act was passed in 1968 in response to a crisis that the Pennsylvania Legislature found existed in the State's nonpublic schools due to rapidly rising costs. *** The statute authorizes appellee state Superintendent of Public Instruction to "purchase" specified "secular educational services" from nonpublic schools. Under the "contracts" authorized by the statute, the State directly reimburses nonpublic schools solely for their actual expenditures for teachers' salaries, textbooks, and instructional materials. A school seeking reimbursement must maintain prescribed accounting procedures that identify the "separate" cost of the "secular educational service." *** Reimbursement is limited to courses "presented in the curricula of the public schools." It is further limited "solely" to courses in the following "secular" subjects: mathematics, modern foreign languages, physical science, and physical education. Textbooks and instructional materials included in the program must be approved by the state Superintendent of Public Instruction. Finally, the statute prohibits reimbursement for any course that contains "any subject matter expressing religious teaching, or the morals or forms of worship of any sect."

Food for Thought

Before reading further, ask yourself how you would attempt to defend these programs based on the principles announced in *Everson v. Board of Education*. In what way were Rhode Island and Pennsylvania arguably acting neutrally in supplementing or reimbursing the teachers' salaries? Even if the laws were neutral, was there anything else wrong with them?

Candor compels acknowledgment [that] we can only dimly perceive the lines of demarcation in this extraordinarily sensitive area of constitutional law. The language of the Religion Clauses of the First Amendment is at best opaque, particularly when compared with other portions of the Amendment. Its authors did not simply prohibit the establishment of a state church or a state religion, an area history shows they regarded as very important and fraught with great dangers. Instead they commanded that there should be "no law respecting an establishment of religion." A law may be one "respecting" the forbidden objective while falling short of its total realization. *** A given law might not establish a state religion but nevertheless be one "respecting" that end in the sense of being a step that could lead to such establishment and hence offend the First Amendment.

In the absence of precisely stated constitutional prohibitions, we must draw lines with reference to the three main evils against which the Establishment Clause was intended to afford protection: "sponsorship, financial support, and active involvement of the sovereign in religious activity." *Walz v. Tax Commission*, 397 U.S. 664, 668 (1970).

Every analysis in this area must begin with consideration of the cumulative criteria developed by the Court over many years. Three such tests may be gleaned from our cases. First, the statute must have a secular legislative purpose; second, its principal or primary effect must be one that neither advances nor inhibits religion, *Board of Education v. Allen*, 392 U.S. 236, 243 (1968); finally, the statute must not foster "an excessive government entanglement with religion." *Walz, supra, at 674*.

Inquiry into the legislative purposes of the Pennsylvania and Rhode Island statutes affords no basis for a conclusion that the legislative intent was to advance religion. On the contrary, the statutes themselves clearly state that they are intended to enhance the quality of the secular education in all schools covered by the compulsory attendance laws. There is no reason to believe the legislatures meant anything else. A State always has a legitimate concern for maintaining minimum standards in all schools it allows to operate. *** The legislatures of Rhode Island and Pennsylvania have concluded that secular and religious education are identifiable and separable. In the abstract we have no quarrel with this conclusion.

The two legislatures, however, have also recognized that church-related elementary and secondary schools have a significant religious mission and that a substantial portion of their activities is religiously oriented. They have therefore sought to create statutory restrictions designed to guarantee the separation between secular and religious educational functions and to ensure that State financial aid supports only the former. *** We need not decide whether these legislative precautions restrict the principal or primary effect of the programs to the point where they do not offend the Religion Clauses, for we conclude that the cumulative impact of the entire relationship arising under the statutes in each State involves excessive entanglement between government and religion.

In order to determine whether the government entanglement with religion is excessive, we must examine the character and purposes of the institutions that are benefited, the nature of the aid that the State provides, and the resulting relationship between the government and the religious authority. Mr. Justice Harlan, in a separate opinion in *Walz*, echoed the classic warning as to "programs, whose very nature is apt to entangle the state in details of administration." Here we find that both statutes foster an impermissible degree of entanglement.

The church schools involved in the program are located close to parish churches. This understandably permits convenient access for religious exercises since instruction in faith and morals is part of the total educational process. The school buildings contain identifying religious symbols such as crosses on the exterior and crucifixes, and religious paintings and statues either in the classrooms or hallways. Although only approximately 30 minutes a day are devoted to direct religious instruction, there are religiously oriented extracurricular activities. Approximately two-thirds of the teachers in these schools are nuns of various religious orders. Their dedicated efforts provide an atmosphere in which religious instruction and religious vocations are natural and proper parts of life in such schools. ***

The dangers and corresponding entanglements are enhanced by the particular form of aid that the Rhode Island Act provides. *** The Rhode Island Roman Catholic elementary schools are under the general supervision of the Bishop of Providence and his appointed representative, the Diocesan Superintendent of Schools. In most cases, each individual parish, however, assumes the ultimate financial responsibility for the school, with the parish priest authorizing the allocation of parish funds. *** Religious authority necessarily pervades the school system.

The schools are governed by the standards set forth in a "Handbook of School Regulations," which has the force of synodal law in the diocese. It emphasizes the role and importance of the teacher in parochial schools: "The prime factor for the success or the failure of the school is the spirit and personality, as well as the professional competency, of the teacher . . . ." The Handbook also states that: "Religious formation is not confined to formal courses; nor is it restricted to a single subject area." Finally, the Handbook advises teachers to stimulate interest in religious vocations and missionary work. Given the mission of the church school, these instructions are consistent and logical.

We need not and do not assume that teachers in parochial schools will be guilty of bad faith or any conscious design to evade the limitations imposed by the statute and the First Amendment. We simply recognize that a dedicated religious person, teaching in a school affiliated with his or her faith and operated to inculcate its tenets, will inevitably experience great difficulty in remaining religiously neutral. Doctrines and faith are not inculcated or advanced by neutrals. With the best of intentions such a teacher would find it hard to make a total separation between secular teaching and religious doctrine. What would appear to some to be essential to good citizenship might well for others border on or constitute instruction in religion. Further difficulties are inherent in the combination of religious discipline and the possibility of disagreement between teacher and religious authorities over the meaning of the statutory restrictions.

There is another area of entanglement in the Rhode Island program that gives concern. The statute excludes teachers employed by nonpublic schools whose average per-pupil expenditures on secular education equal or exceed the comparable figures for public schools. In the event that the total expenditures of an otherwise eligible school exceed this norm, the program requires the government to examine the school's records in order to determine how much of the total expenditures is attributable to secular education and how much to religious activity. This kind of state inspection and evaluation of the religious content of a religious organization is fraught with the sort of entanglement that the Constitution forbids. It is a relationship pregnant with dangers of excessive government direction of church schools and hence of churches. [W]e cannot ignore here the danger that pervasive modern governmental power will ultimately intrude on religion and thus conflict with the Religion Clauses.

Food for Thought

Who is the "separation" between church and state designed to benefit? Those who practice minority religions or no religion at all? Those who follow the dominant religion (or one of the dominant religions)? Religious institutions themselves? Or is it designed to protect all of them? What does the Court's analysis here suggest about this question?

The Pennsylvania statute also provides state aid to church-related schools for teachers' salaries. The complaint describes an educational system that is very similar to the one existing in Rhode Island. According to the allegations, the church-related elementary and secondary schools are controlled by religious organizations, have the purpose of propagating and promoting a particular religious faith, and conduct their operations to fulfill that purpose. Since this complaint was dismissed for failure to state a claim for relief, we must accept these allegations as true for purposes of our review.

As we noted earlier, the very restrictions and surveillance necessary to ensure that teachers play a strictly non-ideological role give rise to entanglements between church and state. The Pennsylvania statute, like that of Rhode Island, fosters this kind of relationship. Reimbursement is not only limited to courses offered in the public schools and materials approved by state officials, but the statute excludes "any subject matter expressing religious teaching, or the morals or forms of worship of any sect." In addition, schools seeking reimbursement must maintain accounting procedures that require the State to establish the cost of the secular as distinguished from the religious instruction.

The Pennsylvania statute, moreover, has the further defect of providing state financial aid directly to the church-related schools. This factor distinguishes both *Everson* and *Allen*, for in both those cases the Court was careful to point out that state aid was provided to the student and his parents—not to the church-related school. In *Walz*, the Court warned of the dangers of direct payments to religious organizations:

FYI

In *Allen*, the Court upheld a New York law that required school districts to purchase and loan textbooks to students enrolled in public, private, and parochial schools.

> Obviously a direct money subsidy would be a relationship pregnant with involvement and, as with most governmental grant programs, could encompass sustained and detailed administrative relationships for enforcement of statutory or administrative standards ***.

A broader base of entanglement of yet a different character is presented by the divisive political potential of these state programs. In a community where such a large number of pupils are served by church-related schools, it can be assumed that state assistance will entail considerable political activity. Partisans of parochial schools, understandably concerned with rising costs and sincerely dedicated to both the religious and secular educational missions of their schools, will inevitably champion this cause and promote political action to achieve their goals. Those who oppose state aid, whether for constitutional, religious, or fiscal reasons, will inevitably respond and employ all of the usual political campaign techniques to prevail. Candidates will be forced to declare and voters to choose. It would be unrealistic to ignore the fact that many people confronted with issues of this kind will find their votes aligned with their faith. *** The potential for political divisiveness related to religious belief and practice is aggravated in these two statutory programs by the need for continuing annual appropriations and the likelihood of larger and larger demands as costs and populations grow.

Finally, nothing we have said can be construed to disparage the role of church-related elementary and secondary schools in our national life. Their contribution has been and is enormous. Nor do we ignore their economic plight in a period of rising costs and expanding need. Taxpayers generally have been spared vast sums by the maintenance of these educational institutions by religious organizations, largely by the gifts of faithful adherents.

The merit and benefits of these schools, however, are not the issue before us in these cases. The sole question is whether state aid to these schools can be squared with the dictates of the Religion Clauses. Under our system the choice has been made that government is to be entirely excluded from the area of religious instruction and churches excluded from the affairs of government. The Constitution decrees that religion must be a private matter for the individual, the family, and the institutions of private choice, and that while some involvement and entanglement are inevitable, lines must be drawn.

Points for Discussion

a. Understanding the *Lemon* Test

The Court described three factors for deciding whether a government action (including a policy or statute) violates the Establishment Clause. The first factor is whether the action has a secular (i.e., non-religious) legislative purpose. In *Everson*, the purpose of reimbursing transportation fares was to enable children to travel to school where they could be educated. Phrased as such, the policy appeared to have a secular purpose. (Can you think of a way to characterize the purpose of the policy that suggests that it was not entirely secular?) By contrast, if a city announced that it would subsidize bus fares to services at a church, mosque, or synagogue, it seems clear that the policy would not have a secular purpose.

The second factor asks whether the principal or primary effect of the policy is one that neither advances nor inhibits religion. In *Board of Education v. Allen*, 392 U.S. 236

(1968), cited in *Lemon*, the Court upheld a New York statute requiring school districts to loan textbooks to all students, regardless of whether they were enrolled in public or private schools, including private parochial schools. The Court there explained: "The express purpose of [the statute] was stated by the New York Legislature to be furtherance of the educational opportunities available to the young. Appellants have shown us nothing about the necessary effects of the statute that is contrary to its stated purpose. The law merely makes available to all children the benefits of a general program to lend school books free of charge." Id. at 243. Should the Court simply defer to such a statement of legislative purpose? How would this factor have been applied if the New York statute had required school districts to buy and distribute Bibles to all school children? (Would it have mattered in which class—say, history or theology—the students were using the Bibles?)

The third factor asks whether the statute fosters "an excessive government entanglement with religion." In *Walz v. Tax Commission*, 397 U.S. 664 (1970), the Court upheld a New York law that provided a tax exemption for property used exclusively for religious purposes. The Court observed that any tax policy would entangle government and churches to some extent. Without the exemption, the government would benefit fiscally from the churches; with the exemption, the government might have to monitor the use of the property to ensure that the exemption was properly claimed. The Court said: "In analyzing either alternative the questions are whether the involvement is excessive, and whether it is a continuing one calling for official and continuing surveillance leading to an impermissible degree of entanglement." The Court ultimately concluded that the entanglement was not excessive: "The exemption creates only a minimal and remote involvement between church and state and far less than taxation of churches." How can a Court determine what counts as "excessive" in this context?

b. Criticism of the *Lemon* Test

Critics maintain that the *Lemon* test is problematic for two reasons. First, the parts of the test are rather vague and open-ended. For example, how does a court know when governmental entanglement with religion is "excessive"? And how does the Court determine whether the "principal" or "primary" effect of a policy is to advance or inhibit religion, when most controversial policies have both secular and religious implications? Second, perhaps even more troubling, the second and third factors tend in practice to point in opposite directions. Dean Jesse Choper elaborates on this problem in the context of aid to religious schools:

> The Court began with a critical premise: the mission of church related elementary and secondary schools is to teach religion, and all subjects either are, or carry the potential of being, permeated with religion. Therefore, if the government were to help fund any subjects in these schools, the effect would aid religion unless public officials monitored the situation to see to it that those courses were not infused with religious doctrine. But if public officials did engage in adequate surveillance—this is the other horn of the dilemma—there would be excessive entanglement between government and religion, the image being government spies regularly or periodically sitting in the classes conducted in parochial schools.

Jesse H. Choper, *The Establishment Clause and Aid to Parochial Schools—An Update*, 75 Cal. L. Rev. 5 (1987). Does this suggest that the Court should abandon the *Lemon* test? Or is ambiguity and nuance inevitable in this area of the law, given the Court's adherence both to the principle that the government should not spend tax money to support religion and to the neutrality principle?

c. The Elusive Death of the *Lemon* Test

Criticism of the *Lemon* test seems to have influenced the Supreme Court. In recent years, the Supreme Court has not consistently followed the *Lemon* test. But it has not formally overruled *Lemon* or abandoned its test, either.

In *Lee v. Weisman,* 505 U.S. 577, 586-587 (1992), which we consider below, the Supreme Court declined to apply the *Lemon* test in determining whether a clergyman's benediction at a high school graduation violated the Establishment Clause. But the following year, in *Lamb's Chapel v. Center Moriches Union Free School Dist.,* 508 U.S. 384 (1993), the Court applied the test to determine whether allowing a church to use school facilities for showing a film violated the Establishment Clause. The citation of *Lemon* caused Justice Scalia to write the following statement in his concurrence in the judgment:

> Like some ghoul in a late-night horror movie that repeatedly sits up in its grave and shuffles abroad, after being repeatedly killed and buried, *Lemon* stalks our Establishment Clause jurisprudence once again, frightening the little children and school attorneys of Center Moriches Union Free School District. Its most recent burial, only last Term, was, to be sure, not fully six feet under: Our decision in *Lee v. Weisman,* 505 U.S. 577, 586-587 (1992), conspicuously avoided using the supposed "test" but also declined the invitation to repudiate it. Over the years, however, no fewer than five of the currently sitting Justices have, in their own opinions, personally driven pencils through the creature's heart (the author of today's opinion repeatedly), and a sixth has joined an opinion doing so.
>
> The secret of the *Lemon* test's survival, I think, is that it is so easy to kill. It is there to scare us (and our audience) when we wish it to do so, but we can command it to return to the tomb at will. When we wish to strike down a practice it forbids, we invoke it, see, *e.g., Aguilar v. Felton,* 473 U.S. 402 (1985) (striking down state remedial education program administered in part in parochial schools); when we wish to uphold a practice it forbids, we ignore it entirely, see *Marsh v. Chambers,* 463 U.S. 783 (1983) (upholding state legislative chaplains). Sometimes, we take a middle course, calling its three prongs "no more than helpful signposts," *Hunt v. McNair,* 413 U.S. 734, 741 (1973). Such a docile and useful monster is worth keeping around, at least in a somnolent state; one never knows when one might need him.

In Justice Scalia's view, what is most problematic about the *Lemon* test? Is it the way that the Court has applied it? Or is it the test itself?

––––––––––––

The *Lemon* test did not resolve the tension between the competing principles that the Court announced in *Everson,* but instead merely incorporated it. (Notice that a law violates the second prong of the test if its principal or primary effect is *either* to "advance *or* inhibit religion.") It thus is unsurprising that in the years after the decision in *Lemon,* the Court continued to struggle with challenges to government policies that conferred financial benefits on religious institutions. For example, in *Mueller v. Allen,* 463 U.S. 388 (1983), the Court considered the constitutionality of a Minnesota law that permitted taxpayers to deduct expenses incurred for tuition, textbooks, and transportation for the education of their children. Because the law permitted parents to deduct (among other things) the cost of tuition and other expenses incurred in sending children to private religious schools, it had the practical effect of conferring a financial benefit on those schools. The Court, however, applied the *Lemon* test and upheld the law. The Court concluded that the primary effect of the policy was not to advance "the sectarian aims of the nonpublic schools." The Court stressed that the deduction was "available for educational expenses incurred by *all* parents, including those whose children attend public schools and those whose children attend non-sectarian private schools or sectarian private schools." In addition, the Court reasoned that "by channeling whatever assistance it may provide to parochial schools through individual parents, Minnesota has reduced the Establishment Clause objections to which its action is subject," because "under Minnesota's arrangement public funds become available only as a result of numerous, private choices of individual parents of school-age children." Justice Marshall, joined by three others, dissented, asserting that the Establishment Clause "prohibits a State from subsidizing religious education, whether it does so directly or indirectly," and thus forbids "any tax benefit, including the tax deduction at issue here, which subsidizes tuition payments to sectarian schools."

Twelve years later, in *Rosenberger v. Rector and Visitors of the University of Virginia*, 515 U.S. 819 (1995), the Court considered a public university's refusal to use funds derived from student activities fees to pay printing costs for the newspaper of an evangelical Christian student group, Wide Awake Productions ("WAP"), even though the University authorized payment for printing costs for other student-authored publications. WAP challenged the exclusion as a violation of its freedom of speech. The state defended the exclusion on the ground that it would violate the Establishment Clause to use the funds, which it said were tantamount to tax revenues, to support sectarian proselytizing. The Court rejected this claim and held that the exclusion constituted impermissible viewpoint discrimination in violation of WAP's freedom of speech.

> **Make the Connection**
>
> We briefly considered the Court's decision in *Rosenberger*, and its view of the freedom of speech, in Chapter 14.

Writing for the Court, Justice Kennedy stated:

The governmental program here is neutral toward religion. There is no suggestion that the University created it to advance religion or adopted some ingenious device with the purpose of aiding a religious cause. The object of the [student activities fund] is to open a forum for speech and to support various student enterprises, including the publication of newspapers, in recognition of the diversity and creativity of student life. *** The neutrality of the program distinguishes the student fees from a tax levied for the direct support of a church or group of churches.

Government neutrality is apparent in the State's overall scheme in a further meaningful respect. *** The University has taken pains to disassociate itself from the private speech involved in this case. *** We do not confront a case where, even under a neutral program that includes nonsectarian recipients, the government is making direct money payments to an institution or group that is engaged in religious activity. *** It does not violate the Establishment Clause for a public university to grant access to its facilities on a religion-neutral basis to a wide spectrum of student groups ***. There is no difference in logic or principle, and no difference of constitutional significance, between a school using its funds to operate a facility to which students have access, and a school paying a third-party contractor to operate the facility on its behalf. The latter occurs here. *** [Moreover, by] paying outside printers, the University in fact attains a further degree of separation from the student publication, for it avoids the duties of supervision, escapes the costs of upkeep, repair, and replacement attributable to student use, and has a clear record of costs.

Justice Souter, joined by Justices Stevens, Ginsburg, and Breyer, dissented. He would have concluded that providing funds to the religious student group to publish their newspaper would violate the Establishment Clause, and thus that the University was justified in withholding its funds. Justice Souter noted that WAP's newspaper contained "nothing other than the preaching of the word, which (along with the sacraments) is what most branches of Christianity offer those called to the religious life." He then declared, "Using public funds for the direct subsidization of preaching the word is categorically forbidden under the Establishment Clause, and if the Clause was meant to accomplish nothing else, it was meant to bar this use of public money." Justice Souter reasoned that the mere fact that a funding program is neutral, "in the formal sense that it makes funds available on an evenhanded basis to secular and sectarian applicants alike, *** does not alone satisfy the requirements of the Establishment Clause. *** [W]henever affirmative government aid ultimately benefits religion, the Establishment Clause requires some justification beyond evenhandedness on the government's part ***." He then sought to explain the relative importance of the separation principle and the neutrality principle:

> [T]he relationship between the prohibition on direct aid and the requirement of evenhandedness when affirmative government aid does result in some benefit to religion reflects the relationship between basic rule and marginal criterion. At the heart of the Establishment Clause stands the prohibition against direct public funding, but that prohibition does not answer the questions that occur at the margins of the Clause's application. Is any government activity that provides any incidental benefit to religion likewise unconstitutional? Would it be wrong to put out fires in burning churches, wrong to pay the bus fares of students on the way to parochial schools, wrong to allow a grantee of special education funds to spend them at a religious college? These are the questions that call for drawing lines, and it is in drawing them that evenhandedness becomes important. However the Court may in the past have phrased its line-drawing test, the question whether such benefits are provided on an evenhanded basis has been relevant, for the question addresses one aspect of the issue whether a law is truly neutral with respect to religion (that is, whether the law either "advance[s] [or] inhibit[s] religion." *** In the doubtful cases (those not involving direct public funding), where there is initially room for argument about a law's effect, evenhandedness serves to weed out those laws that impermissibly advance religion by channelling aid to it exclusively. Evenhandedness is therefore a prerequisite to further enquiry into the constitutionality of a doubtful law, but evenhandedness goes no further. It does not guarantee success under Establishment Clause scrutiny.

Justice Souter also disagreed with the Court's suggestion that funding for WAP's publication was permissible because the University paid the funds directly to the printer: "The formalism of distinguishing between payment to Wide Awake so it can pay an approved bill and payment of the approved bill itself cannot be the basis of a decision of constitutional law. If this indeed were a critical distinction, the Constitution would permit a State to pay all the bills of any religious institution ***."

The decisions in *Mueller* and *Rosenberger* suggest that the Court has increasingly relied on the neutrality principle over the "no support" (or separation) principle. That trend continued in the case that follows, one of the Court's most important recent decisions about the limits that the Establishment Clause imposes on the ability of government to provide aid that benefits religious institutions. The case involved the constitutionality of a program providing parents with vouchers that could be used to cover the cost of tuition at private schools, including religious schools. As you read the case, consider what it suggests about the Court's likely approach in the future to questions that arise in this area.

———————

Zelman v. Simmons-Harris

536 U.S. 639 (2002)

Chief Justice REHNQUIST delivered the opinion of the Court.

There are more than 75,000 children enrolled in the Cleveland City School District. The majority of these children are from low-income and minority families. Few of these families enjoy the means to send their children to any school other than an inner-city public school. For more than a generation, however, Cleveland's public schools have been among the worst performing public schools in the Nation. *** It is against this backdrop that Ohio enacted, among other initiatives, its Pilot Project Scholarship Program, Ohio Rev.Code Ann. §§ 3313.974-3313.979. *** The program [provides] tuition aid for students in kindergarten through third grade, expanding each year through eighth grade, to attend a participating public or private school of their parent's choosing. *** Any private school, whether religious or nonreligious, may participate in the program and accept program students so long as the school is located within the boundaries of a covered district and meets statewide educational standards. *** Any public school located in a school district adjacent to the covered district may also participate in the program [and is] eligible to receive a $2,250 tuition grant for each program student accepted in addition to the full amount of per-pupil state funding attributable to each additional student. *** Tuition aid is distributed to parents according to financial need. *** If parents choose a private school, checks are made payable to the parents who then endorse the checks over to the chosen school. § 3313.979.

The program has been in operation within the Cleveland City School District since the 1996-1997 school year. In the 1999-2000 school year, 56 private schools participated in the program, 46 (or 82%) of which had a religious affiliation. None of the public schools in districts adjacent to Cleveland have elected to participate. More than 3,700 students participated in the scholarship program, most of whom (96%) enrolled in religiously affiliated schools. [Ohio taxpayers filed this suit seeking to enjoin the program on the ground that it violated the Establishment Clause.]

The Establishment Clause of the First Amendment, applied to the States through the

Fourteenth Amendment, prevents a State from enacting laws that have the "purpose" or "effect" of advancing or inhibiting religion. *Agostini v. Felton,* 521 U.S. 203, 222-223 (1997). There is no dispute that the program challenged here was enacted for the valid secular purpose of providing educational assistance to poor children in a demonstrably failing public school system. Thus, the question presented is whether the Ohio program nonetheless has the forbidden "effect" of advancing or inhibiting religion.

> **Take Note**
>
> The Court's statement of the test under the Establishment Clause omits the third prong of the *Lemon* test—whether the challenged policy fosters an excessive entanglement between church and state. In *Agostini,* a five-Justice majority treated this factor as an aspect of the inquiry into the second factor—the effects of the challenged policy. Do you agree with the Court's reasoning in that case that the considerations relevant to assessing whether an entanglement is "excessive" are similar to the considerations used to determine the challenged policy's "effect"?

To answer that question, our decisions have drawn a consistent distinction between government programs that provide aid directly to religious schools and programs of true private choice, in which government aid reaches religious schools only as a result of the genuine and independent choices of private individuals. *** Three times we have confronted Establishment Clause challenges to neutral government programs that provide aid directly to a broad class of individuals, who, in turn, direct the aid to religious schools or institutions of their own choosing. Three times we have rejected such challenges.

In *Mueller v. Allen,* 463 U.S. 388 (1983), we rejected an Establishment Clause challenge to a Minnesota program authorizing tax deductions for various educational expenses, including private school tuition costs, even though the great majority of the program's beneficiaries (96%) were parents of children in religious schools. We began by focusing on the class of beneficiaries, [which] included "*all* parents," including parents with "children [who] attend nonsectarian private schools or sectarian private schools," 463 U.S., at 397. *** Then, viewing the program as a whole, we emphasized the principle of private choice, noting that public funds were made available to religious schools "only as a result of numerous, private choices of individual parents of school-age children." 463 U.S., at 399-400. [We] thus found it irrelevant to the constitutional inquiry that the vast majority of beneficiaries were parents of children in religious schools ***.

In *Witters v. Washington Dept. of Servs. for Blind,* 474 U.S. 481 (1986) we used identical reasoning to reject an Establishment Clause challenge to a vocational scholarship program that provided tuition aid to a student studying at a religious institution to become a pastor. *** Finally, in *Zobrest v. Catalina Foothills School Dist.,* 509 U.S. 1 (1993) we applied *Mueller* and *Witters* to reject an Establishment Clause challenge to a federal program that permitted sign-language interpreters to assist deaf children enrolled in religious schools.

Mueller, Witters, and *Zobrest* thus make clear that where a government aid program is neutral with respect to religion, and provides assistance directly to a broad class of citizens who, in turn, direct government aid to religious schools wholly as a result of their own genuine and independent private choice, the program is not readily subject to challenge under the Establishment Clause. A program that shares these features permits government aid to reach religious institutions only by way of the deliberate choices of numerous individual recipients. The incidental advancement of a religious mission, or the perceived endorsement of a religious message, is reasonably attributable to the individual recipient, not to the government, whose role ends with the disbursement of benefits. *** It is precisely for these reasons that we have never found a program of true private choice to offend the Establishment Clause.

We believe that the program challenged here is a program of true private choice [and] thus constitutional. [The] Ohio program is neutral in all respects toward religion. It is part of a general and multifaceted undertaking by the State of Ohio to provide educational opportunities to the children of a failed school district. It confers educational assistance directly to a broad class of individuals defined without reference to religion, *i.e.,* any parent of a school-age child who resides in the Cleveland City School District. The program permits the participation of *all* schools within the district, religious or nonreligious. Adjacent public schools also may participate and have a financial incentive to do so. Program benefits are available to participating families on neutral terms, with no reference to religion.

There are no "financial incentives" that "skew" the program toward religious schools. *** The program here in fact creates financial *dis*incentives for religious schools, with private schools receiving only half the government assistance given to community schools and one-third the assistance given to magnet schools. Adjacent public schools, should any choose to accept program students, are also eligible to receive two to three times the state funding of a private religious school. [In addition, parents] that choose to participate in the scholarship program and then to enroll their children in a private school (religious or nonreligious) must copay a portion of the school's tuition. Families that choose a community school, magnet school, or traditional public school pay nothing. Although such features of the program are not necessary to its constitutionality, they clearly dispel the claim that the program "creates [financial] incentives for parents to choose a sectarian school." *Zobrest,* 509 U.S., at 10.

> **Food for Thought**
>
> As the Court noted, over 80% of the private schools participating in the challenged program had a religious affiliation, and over 90% of the students participating used the vouchers to attend religious schools. In light of this fact, can you make an argument that the program was not in fact "neutral" toward religion?

Respondents suggest that even without a financial incentive for parents to choose a religious school, the program creates a "public perception that the State is endorsing religious practices and beliefs." But [no] reasonable observer would think a neutral program of private choice, where state aid reaches religious schools solely as a result of the numerous independent decisions of private individuals, carries with it the *imprimatur* of government endorsement. *** Any objective observer familiar with the full history and context of the

Ohio program would reasonably view it as one aspect of a broader undertaking to assist poor children in failed schools, not as an endorsement of religious schooling in general.

There also is no evidence that the program fails to provide genuine opportunities for Cleveland parents to select secular educational options for their school-age children. Cleveland schoolchildren enjoy a range of educational choices: They may remain in public school as before, remain in public school with publicly funded tutoring aid, obtain a scholarship and choose a religious school, obtain a scholarship and choose a nonreligious private school, enroll in a community school, or enroll in a magnet school. That 46 of the 56 private schools now participating in the program are religious schools does not condemn it as a violation of the Establishment Clause.

Justice SOUTER speculates that because more private religious schools currently participate in the program, the program itself must somehow discourage the participation of private nonreligious schools. *** It is true that 82% of Cleveland's participating private schools are religious schools, but it is also true that 81% of private schools in Ohio are religious schools. To attribute constitutional significance to this figure, moreover, would lead to the absurd result that a neutral school-choice program might be permissible in some parts of Ohio, such as Columbus, where a lower percentage of private schools are religious schools, but not in inner-city Cleveland, where Ohio has deemed such programs most sorely needed, but where the preponderance of religious schools happens to be greater.

Respondents and Justice SOUTER claim that even if we do not focus on the number of participating schools that are religious schools, we should attach constitutional significance to the fact that 96% of scholarship recipients have enrolled in religious schools. [But the] constitutionality of a neutral educational aid program simply does not turn on whether and why, in a particular area, at a particular time, most private schools are run by religious organizations, or most recipients choose to use the aid at a religious school. [In any event, the] 96% figure upon which respondents and Justice SOUTER rely discounts entirely (1) the more than 1,900 Cleveland children enrolled in alternative community schools, (2) the more than 13,000 children enrolled in alternative magnet schools, and (3) the more than 1,400 children enrolled in traditional public schools with tutorial assistance. Including some or all of these children in the denominator of children enrolled in nontraditional schools during the 1999-2000 school year drops the percentage enrolled in religious schools from 96% to under 20%.

In sum, the Ohio program is entirely neutral with respect to religion. It provides benefits directly to a wide spectrum of individuals, defined only by financial need and residence in a particular school district. It permits such individuals to exercise genuine choice among options public and private, secular and religious. The program is therefore a program of true private choice. In keeping with an unbroken line of decisions rejecting challenges to similar programs, we hold that the program does not offend the Establishment Clause.

Justice O'CONNOR, concurring.

These cases are different from prior indirect aid cases in part because a significant portion of the funds appropriated for the voucher program reach religious schools without restrictions on the use of these funds. The share of public resources that reach religious schools is not, however, as significant as respondents suggest. *** Even if one assumes that all voucher students came from low-income families and that each voucher student used up the entire $2,250 voucher, at most $8.2 million of public funds flowed to religious schools under the voucher program in 1999-2000. [In contrast,] the State spent over $1 million more—$9.4 million—on students in community schools than on students in religious private schools because per-pupil aid to community schools is more than double the per-pupil aid to private schools under the voucher program. Moreover, the amount spent on religious private schools is minor compared to the $114.8 million the State spent on students in the Cleveland magnet schools.

Although $8.2 million is no small sum, it pales in comparison to the amount of funds that federal, state, and local governments already provide religious institutions. Religious organizations may qualify for exemptions from the federal corporate income tax, the corporate income tax in many States, and property taxes in all 50 States ***. In addition, the Federal Government provides individuals, corporations, trusts, and estates a tax deduction for charitable contributions to qualified religious groups [and] tax credits for educational expenses, many of which are spent on education at religious schools. [These tax policies] confer a significant relative benefit on religious institutions. [In addition, federal] dollars also reach religiously affiliated organizations through public health programs such as Medicare and Medicaid, through educational programs such as the Pell Grant program, and the G.I. Bill of Rights, and through childcare programs ***. A significant portion of the funds appropriated for these programs reach religiously affiliated institutions, typically without restrictions on its subsequent use. *** Against this background, the support that the Cleveland voucher program provides religious institutions is neither substantial nor atypical of existing government programs.

> **Food for Thought**
>
> Justice O'Connor suggests here that the program is permissible because the government routinely provides various forms of aid to religious institutions. If in fact the Establishment Clause was designed to prevent such direct aid, is it convincing to note that the government has been systematically engaged in the provision of such aid?

There is little question in my mind that the Cleveland voucher program is neutral as between religious schools and nonreligious schools. *** In looking at the voucher program, all the choices available to potential beneficiaries of the government program should be considered. *** That inquiry requires an evaluation of all reasonable educational options Ohio provides the Cleveland school system, regardless of whether they are formally made available in the same section of the Ohio Code as the voucher program. *** I am persuaded that the Cleveland voucher program affords parents of eligible children genuine nonreligious options and is consistent with the Establishment Clause.

[Justice THOMAS's concurring opinion is omitted.]

Justice SOUTER, with whom Justice STEVENS, Justice GINSBURG, and Justice BREYER join, dissenting.

The applicability of the Establishment Clause to public funding of benefits to religious schools was settled in *Everson v. Board of Ed. of Ewing,* 330 U.S. 1 (1947), which inaugurated the modern era of establishment doctrine. The Court stated the principle in words from which there was no dissent: "No tax in any amount, large or small, can be levied to support any religious activities or institutions, whatever they may be called, or whatever form they may adopt to teach or practice religion." The Court has never in so many words repudiated this statement, let alone, in so many words, overruled *Everson*

Today, however, the majority holds that the Establishment Clause is not offended by Ohio's Pilot Project Scholarship Program, under which students may be eligible to receive as much as $2,250 in the form of tuition vouchers transferable to religious schools. In the city of Cleveland the overwhelming proportion of large appropriations for voucher money must be spent on religious schools if it is to be spent at all, and will be spent in amounts that cover almost all of tuition. The money will thus pay for eligible students' instruction not only in secular subjects but in religion as well, in schools that can fairly be characterized as founded to teach religious doctrine and to imbue teaching in all subjects with a religious dimension. Public tax money will pay at a systemic level for teaching the covenant with Israel and Mosaic law in Jewish schools, the primacy of the Apostle Peter and the Papacy in Catholic schools, the truth of reformed Christianity in Protestant schools, and the revelation to the Prophet in Muslim schools, to speak only of major religious groupings in the Republic. *** It is only by ignoring *Everson* that the majority can claim to rest on traditional law in its invocation of neutral aid provisions and private choice to sanction the Ohio law. It is, moreover, only by ignoring the meaning of neutrality and private choice themselves that the majority can even pretend to rest today's decision on those criteria.

Neutrality in this sense refers, of course, to evenhandedness in setting eligibility as between potential religious and secular recipients of public money. *** In order to apply the neutrality test, then, it makes sense to focus on a category of aid that may be directed to religious as well as secular schools, and ask whether the scheme favors a religious direction. Here, one would ask whether the voucher provisions, allowing for as much as $2,250 toward private school tuition (or a grant to a public school in an adjacent district), were written in a way that skewed the scheme toward benefiting religious schools. *** This, however, is not what the majority asks. The majority looks not to the provisions for tuition vouchers, but to every provision for educational opportunity. *** The illogic is patent. [T]he majority's reasoning would find neutrality in a scheme of vouchers available for private tuition in districts with no secular private schools at all. "Neutrality" as the majority employs the term is, literally, verbal and nothing more.

The majority addresses the issue of choice the same way it addresses neutrality, by asking whether recipients or potential recipients of voucher aid have a choice of public schools among secular alternatives to religious schools. [But the] majority's view that all educational choices are comparable for purposes of choice [ignores] the whole point of the choice test: it is a criterion for deciding whether indirect aid to a religious school is legitimate because it passes through private hands that can spend or use the aid in a secular school. The question is whether the private hand is genuinely free to send the money in either a secular direction or a religious one. The majority now has transformed this question about private choice in channeling aid into a question about selecting from examples of state spending (on education) including direct spending on magnet and community public schools that goes through no private hands and could never reach a religious school under any circumstance. When the choice test is transformed from where to spend the money to where to go to school, it is cut loose from its very purpose. [I]f the majority wishes to claim that choice is a criterion, it must define choice in a way that can function as a criterion with a practical capacity to screen something out.

If, contrary to the majority, we ask the right question about genuine choice to use the vouchers, the answer shows that something is influencing choices in a way that aims the money in a religious direction ***. Evidence shows [that] almost two out of three families using vouchers to send their children to religious schools did not embrace the religion of those schools. The families made it clear they had not chosen the schools because they wished their children to be proselytized in a religion not their own, or in any religion, but because of educational opportunity. *** The [fact that] 96.6% [of students participating in the program enrolled in religious schools] reflects [the] fact that too few nonreligious school desks are available and few but religious schools can afford to accept more than a handful of voucher students. [For] the overwhelming number of children in the voucher scheme, the only alternative to the public schools is religious.

I do not dissent merely because the majority has misapplied its own law, for even if I assumed *arguendo* that the majority's formal criteria were satisfied on the facts, today's conclusion would be profoundly at odds with the Constitution. *** [First, the] scale of the aid to religious schools approved today is unprecedented, both in the number of dollars and in the proportion of systemic school expenditure supported. *** [The] majority makes no pretense that substantial amounts of tax money are not systematically underwriting religious practice and indoctrination.

[Second,] every objective underlying the prohibition of religious establishment is betrayed by this scheme ***. [The first, respect for freedom of conscience,] has simply been lost in the majority's formalism. As for the second objective, to save religion from its own corruption, Madison wrote of the "experience [that] ecclesiastical establishments, instead of maintaining the purity and efficacy of Religion, have had a contrary operation." Memorial and Remonstrance ¶ 7, reprinted in *Everson, 330 U.S., at 67.* In [the] 21st century, the risk is one of "corrosive secularism" to religious schools, and the specific threat is to the primacy of the schools' mission to educate the children of the faithful according to the unaltered precepts of their faith.

The risk is already being realized. In Ohio, for example, a condition of receiving government money under the program is that participating religious schools may not "discriminate on the basis [of] religion," Ohio Rev. Code Ann. § 3313.976(A)(4), which means the school may not give admission preferences to children who are members of the patron faith; children of a parish are generally consigned to the same admission lotteries as non-believers. *** Indeed, a separate condition that "[t]he school [not] teach hatred of any person or group on the basis [of] religion," § 3313.976(A)(6), could be understood (or subsequently broadened) to prohibit religions from teaching traditionally legitimate articles of faith as to the error, sinfulness, or ignorance of others, if they want government money for their schools. *** For perspective on this foot-in-the-door of religious regulation, it is well to remember that the money has barely begun to flow. *** When government aid goes up, so does reliance on it; the only thing likely to go down is independence. *** A day will come when religious schools will learn what political leverage can do, just as Ohio's politicians are now getting a lesson in the leverage exercised by religion.

Increased voucher spending is not, however, the sole portent of growing regulation of religious practice in the school, for state mandates to moderate religious teaching may well be the most obvious response to the third concern behind the ban on establishment, its inextricable link with social conflict. *Everson*, 330 U.S., at 8-11. As appropriations for religious subsidy rise, competition for the money will tap sectarian religion's capacity for discord. *** [I]t is enough to say that the intensity of the expectable friction can be gauged by realizing that the scramble for money will energize not only contending sectarians, but taxpayers who take their liberty of conscience seriously. Religious teaching at taxpayer expense simply cannot be cordoned from taxpayer politics, and every major religion currently espouses social positions that provoke intense opposition. [Such views] have been safe in the sectarian pulpits and classrooms of this Nation not only because the Free Exercise Clause protects them directly, but because the ban on supporting religious establishment has protected free exercise, by keeping it relatively private. With the arrival of vouchers in religious schools, that privacy will go, and along with it will go confidence that religious disagreement will stay moderate.

[The dissenting opinions of Justice BREYER and Justice STEVENS have been omitted.]

Points for Discussion

a. The Test for Government Aid to Religious Institutions

After *Zelman*, what is the test for determining the constitutionality of government aid to religious institutions? Is neutrality the rule? If so, how is neutrality determined? What else, if anything, must be true for neutral policies to survive scrutiny? What is the status of the "no support" (or separation) principle?

Did the Court apply the *Lemon* test in *Zelman*? If so, did it apply the same test that we have seen in prior cases? Consider Justice O'Connor's view that the Court's approach involved a "refinement" of the *Lemon* test:

> The Court's opinion in [this case] focuses on a narrow question related to the *Lemon* test: how to apply the primary effects prong in indirect aid cases? *** What the Court clarifies in [this

case] is that the Establishment Clause [requires] that state aid flowing to religious organizations through the hands of beneficiaries must do so only at the direction of those beneficiaries.

Do you agree that this is the import of the Court's decision? If so, do you agree that it represents simply a "refinement" of the *Lemon* test? What did Justice Souter think was the appropriate test?

b. "True Private Choice"

How important to the Court's conclusion was the ability of the voucher recipients to choose which school to attend? Consider this view:

> *Zelman* represents the most recent and dramatic move away from Separationism. By holding in no uncertain terms that the Cleveland school voucher program satisfies constitutional requirements, the Supreme Court has opened the door for a wide range of relationships, once thought impermissible, between government and religious institutions. The key to these new relationships, the Court held, is the concept of "true," "genuine," and "independent" private choice to partake of services offered by religious entities.

Ira C. Lupu & Robert W. Tuttle, Zelman's *Future: Vouchers, Sectarian Providers, and the Next Round of Constitutional Battles*, 78 Notre Dame L. Rev. 917 (2003).

Do you agree that the recipients' choice under the challenged program was "genuine"? The Court reasoned that it was genuine because, at least as a formal matter, there were non-religious schools—including community and magnet schools—to which the parents could send their children. But was the parents' choice really unfettered? Again, consider the view of Professors Lupu and Tuttle:

> Parents might prefer School A over School B on grounds of academic quality, value emphasis, and/or physical safety, but prefer B over A because of the religious teaching at A. Parents in such circumstances are squeezed by the set of trade-offs presented to them. The comparative quality or safety of the various schools may generate pressure on parents to send their children to religious schools, calling into question the "genuineness" of their choice of a particular religious element to their child's education. The Court's opinion, however, evinces no concern for their plight.

Is there an argument that the voucher program effectively *coerced* parents—at least, that is, parents hoping to find better educational options for their children—to send their children to religious schools?

————————

> **Hypothetical**
>
> Imagine that Congress recently enacted the "Level Playing Field Act," which provides that "faith-based" providers of social services—such as drug-addiction treatment programs and welfare programs administered by churches and other religious organizations—are eligible to compete for (and receive) federal funds. The Act protects the "right of religious organizations to maintain their religious identities while providing social services" funded by the government and permits those organizations to "provide a preference in hiring to persons who share their religious beliefs." There is no provision in the Act forbidding participating faith-based organizations to engage in religious proselytizing or instruction in the programs funded by the government. A suit has been filed challenging the program under the Establishment Clause. How should the Court rule?

A Note on Standing and Establishment Clause Challenges

We noted in our consideration of *Everson* that the plaintiff had filed the challenge "in his capacity as a district taxpayer." The plaintiff presumably objected to the government's decision to use tax revenues to pay the cost of transportation to religious schools. But is this a cognizable injury under the Court's Article III standing doctrine, which we considered in Chapter 2? Recall that the Court has "repeatedly held that an asserted right to have the Government act in accordance with law is not sufficient, standing alone, to confer jurisdiction on a federal court." *Allen v. Wright*, 468 U.S. 737 (1984). In addition, the Court has held that, as a general matter, the interest of a federal taxpayer in seeing that government funds are spent in accordance with the Constitution does not constitute a cognizable "injury in fact." *Frothingham v. Mellon*, 262 U.S. 447, 488 (1923). Should matters be any different when the challenge alleges that government spending violates the Establishment Clause?

In *Flast v. Cohen*, 392 U.S. 83 (1968) the Court held that "a taxpayer will have standing [when] he alleges that congressional action under the taxing and spending clause is in derogation of those constitutional provisions which operate to restrict the exercise of the taxing and spending power." The Court concluded that the Establishment Clause was such a provision:

> Our history vividly illustrates that one of the specific evils feared by those who drafted the Establishment Clause and fought for its adoption was that the taxing and spending power would be used to favor one religion over another or to support religion in general. *** The Establishment Clause was designed as a specific bulwark against such potential abuses of governmental power, and that clause of the First Amendment operates as a specific constitutional limitation upon the exercise by Congress of the taxing and spending power.

Many Establishment Clause challenges—including most of those that we have considered so far in this Chapter—have been maintained on the basis of taxpayer standing under the theory announced in *Flast*.

More recently, however, the Court has questioned the consistency of *Flast* with its standing doctrine more generally. In *Hein v. Freedom From Religion Foundation, Inc.*, 551 U.S. 587 (2007), the Court held that a taxpayer lacked standing to challenge the President's expenditure of funds from a general appropriation for day-to-day activities. Writing for himself and Chief Justice Roberts and Justice Kennedy, Justice Alito concluded that *Flast* authorized taxpayer standing only in suits challenging *specific* congressional appropriations of funds for activities that are alleged to violate the Establishment Clause. Because the claim in *Hein* was to an executive decision to spend funds without any specific congressional direction that they be spent for those purposes, Justice Alito found *Flast* inapposite and accordingly declined to reconsider it. Justice Scalia, joined by Justice Thomas, asserted in his opinion concurring in the judgment that *Flast* is inconsistent with the Court's standing doctrine and should be overruled. Justice Souter, joined by Justices Stevens, Ginsburg, and Breyer, asserted in dissent that *Flast* was correct and authorized standing in the case.

Under Justice Alito's or Justice Scalia's approach in *Hein*—under which taxpayer standing will be either more difficult or impossible to establish—is it likely that there will be *any* plaintiff with standing to challenge government programs that provide direct aid to religious organizations? If not, what does that suggest about the various approaches in *Hein*? About the future of Establishment Clause litigation itself?

————

2. Religion In Governmental Institutions

Visit the U.S. Supreme Court to hear an oral argument in December and you will pass a large Christmas tree in the main hall on your way into the courtroom. After sitting down, you might study the elaborate frieze encircling the top of the courtroom. In the frieze, you can see a depiction of Moses with the Ten Commandments and other religious images. The Court's marshal will announce the start of the day's sessions by stating, "God save this Honorable Court!" If the Court is admitting new attorneys to its bar, the Clerk of Court may ask them to take an oath of admission, which they may accomplish by solemnly swearing to conduct themselves uprightly.

Does the Establishment Clause permit these religious displays in a public courthouse? The answer to this question, under decisions of the Supreme Court, appears to be yes. Religion is not completely banned in government institutions. But surely there are *some* limits on the ability of government to engage in religious activities. After all, if nothing else, Congress cannot create a national church. That prohibition, moreover, presumably extends beyond a formal congressional declaration creating such a church to other actions promoting religion. The difficult task, therefore, is to determine precisely what limits the Establishment Clause imposes on the government's ability to promote religion or engage in religious activities or displays.

The Supreme Court has held that the Establishment Clause does not bar all religious activities—including prayer—in public institutions. The Court has occasionally permitted some such activities, outside of the public primary and secondary school context, if they are deeply embedded in the history and tradition of the country. In addition, the Court has held that the Establishment Clause does not prevent the display of religious symbols on government property if the symbols have a secular purpose and do not amount to an endorsement of a particular religion or religion in general. Determining when that standard is satisfied, however, has proved to be no easy task.

The Court has also had many opportunities to decide how the Establishment Clause applies to religious acts in public schools. The Establishment Clause bars prayer in public schools if the prayer is an official or approved part of school activities. Indeed, official prayer is banned in schools whether the students say the prayer or merely hear the prayer, whether the prayer is denominational or non-denominational, whether the prayer is silent or spoken, and whether student participation in the prayer is voluntary or involuntary. The following cases explore these rules.

We begin with the Court's decisions concerning religious activities in public schools. As you read them, consider whether there is something special about schools, or instead whether this context should be considered paradigmatic.

––––––––––––––––

As with the cases we saw in our unit on government funding for religious activities, the Court's decisions concerning religious activities in public schools have often revealed competing visions of the scope and meaning of the Establishment Clause. For example, in *Illinois ex rel. McCollum v. Board of Education*, 333 U.S. 203 (1948), the Court invalidated a local school board's policy of permitting teachers employed by private religious groups "to come weekly into the school buildings during the regular hours set apart for secular teaching, and then and there for a period of thirty minutes substitute their religious teaching for the secular education provided under the compulsory education law." Classes were offered "by Protestant teachers, Catholic priests, and a Jewish rabbi" and "conducted in the regular classrooms of the school building. Students who did not choose to take the religious instruction were not released from public school duties; they were required to leave their classrooms and go to some other place in the school building for pursuit of their secular studies. On the other hand, students who were released from secular study for the religious instructions were required to be present at the religious classes." Writing for the Court, Justice Black reasoned that the policy violated the Establishment Clause because it amounted to "a utilization of the tax-established and tax-supported public school system to aid religious groups to spread their faith." Justice Black also concluded that the policy impermissibly "afford[ed] sectarian groups an invaluable aid in that it help[ed] to provide pupils for their religious classes through use of the state's compulsory public school machinery." Both of these features of the policy, Justice Black concluded, were inconsistent with the principle of separation of church and state. Only Justice Reed dissented.

The Court's decision in *McCollum* provoked a strong reaction in many parts of the country. Four years later, the Court in *Zorach v. Clauson*, 343 U.S. 306 (1952), upheld a public school policy permitting the release of children from school during school hours to attend sectarian classes outside the public schools. The Court concluded that the challenged policy did not violate the Establishment Clause. Writing for the Court, Justice Douglas first observed that, under the program, "[n]o one is forced to go to the religious classroom and no religious exercise or instruction is brought to the classrooms of the public schools. A student need not take religious instruction. He is left to his own desires as to the manner or time of his religious devotions, if any." Justice Douglas declared that "[t]here cannot be the slightest doubt that the First Amendment reflects the philosophy that Church and State should be separated." But, he asserted, "[w]e would have to press the concept of separation of Church and State [to] extremes to condemn the present law on constitutional grounds," because such a conclusion also perhaps would require school officials to deny permission to religious students who asked to be excused for the observance of religious holiday or other reasonable accommodations. Justice Douglas rejected this view of separation, declaring:

> We are a religious people whose institutions presuppose a Supreme Being. We guarantee the freedom to worship as one chooses. We make room for as wide a variety of beliefs and creeds as the spiritual needs of man deem necessary. We sponsor an attitude on the part of government that shows no partiality to any one group and that lets each flourish according to the zeal of its adherents and the appeal of its dogma. When the state encourages religious instruction or cooperates with religious authorities by adjusting the schedule of public events to sectarian needs, it follows the best of our traditions. For it then respects the religious nature of our people and accommodates the public service to their spiritual needs. To hold that it may not would be to find in the Constitution a requirement that the government show a callous indifference to religious groups. That would be preferring those who believe in no religion over those who do believe. Government may not finance religious groups nor undertake religious instruction nor blend secular and sectarian education nor use secular institutions to force one or some religion on any person. *** The government must be neutral when it comes to competition between sects. *** It may not coerce anyone to attend church, to observe a religious holiday, or to take religious instruction. But it can close its doors or suspend its operations as to those who want to repair to their religious sanctuary for worship or instruction. No more than that is undertaken here.

Justice Douglas distinguished *McCollum* by noting that in that case "the classrooms were used for religious instruction and the force of the public school was used to promote that instruction," whereas in *Zorach* "the public schools do no more than accommodate their schedules to a program of outside religious instruction."

Justice Black dissented, finding no meaningful difference between the challenged policy and the policy at issue in *McCollum*, which he read to stand for the proposition that the state cannot "constitutionally manipulate the compelled classroom hours of its compulsory school machinery so as to channel children into sectarian classes." Justice Jackson also dissented, reasoning that the challenged program was impermissibly "founded upon a use of the State's power of coercion." He stated:

> Stripped to its essentials, the plan has two stages, first, that the State compel each student to yield a large part of his time for public secular education and, second, that some of it be "released" to him on condition that he devote it to sectarian religious purposes. No one suggests that the Constitution would permit the State directly to require this "released" time to be spent

"under the control of a duly constituted religious body." This program accomplishes that forbidden result by indirection. If public education were taking so much of the pupils' time as to injure the public or the students' welfare by encroaching upon their religious opportunity, simply shortening everyone's school day would facilitate voluntary and optional attendance at Church classes. But that suggestion is rejected upon the ground that if they are made free many students will not go to the Church. Hence, they must be deprived of freedom for this period, with Church attendance put to them as one of the two permissible ways of using it. *** Here schooling is more or less suspended during the "released time" so the nonreligious attendants will not forge ahead of the churchgoing absentees. But it serves as a temporary jail for a pupil who will not go to Church. It takes more subtlety of mind than I possess to deny that this is governmental constraint in support of religion. It is as unconstitutional, in my view, when exerted by indirection as when exercised forthrightly.

Justice Jackson found the Court's attempt to distinguish *McCollum* "trivial, almost to the point of cynicism." He concluded by declaring, "The wall which the Court was professing to erect [in *McCollum*] between Church and State has become even more warped and twisted than I expected," and he warned that the "day that this country ceases to be free for irreligion it will cease to be free for religion—except for the sect that can win political power."

The decisions in *McCollum* and *Zorarch* reflect competing visions of the Establishment Clause. How should the Court apply the principles in those decisions to policies requiring or permitting prayer in school? Consider the cases that follow.

Engel v. Vitale

370 U.S. 421 (1962)

Mr. Justice BLACK delivered the opinion of the Court.

The respondent Board of Education of Union Free School District No. 9, New Hyde Park, New York, acting in its official capacity under state law, directed the School District's principal to cause the following prayer to be said aloud by each class in the presence of a teacher at the beginning of each school day: "Almighty God, we acknowledge our dependence upon Thee, and we beg Thy blessings upon us, our parents, our teachers and our Country."

This daily procedure was adopted on the recommendation of the State Board of Regents, a governmental agency created by the State Constitution to which the New York Legislature has granted broad supervisory, executive, and legislative powers over the State's public school system. These state officials composed the prayer which they recommended and published as a part of their "Statement on Moral and Spiritual Training in the Schools," saying: "We believe that this Statement will be subscribed to by all men and women of good will, and we call upon all of them to aid in giving life to our program."

Shortly after the practice of reciting the Regents' prayer was adopted by the School District, the parents of ten pupils brought this action in a New York State Court insisting that use of this official prayer in the public schools was contrary to the beliefs, religions, or religious practices of both themselves and their children. Among other things, these parents challenged the constitutionality of both the state law authorizing the School District to direct the use of prayer in public schools and the School District's regulation ordering the recitation of this particular prayer on the ground that these actions of official governmental agencies violate [the First and Fourteenth Amendments.] The New York Court of Appeals *** sustained an order of the lower state courts which had upheld the power of New York to use the Regents' prayer as a part of the daily procedures of its public schools so long as the schools did not compel any pupil to join in the prayer over his or his parents' objection. ***

> **Take Note**
>
> Before this case came to the Supreme Court, the New York courts concluded that no student could be compelled to recite the challenged prayer. One of the questions for the Supreme Court, therefore, was whether the "voluntary" nature of the prayer eliminated any concerns under the Establishment Clause.

We think that by using its public school system to encourage recitation of the Regents' prayer, the State of New York has adopted a practice wholly inconsistent with the Establishment Clause. There can, of course, be no doubt that New York's program of daily classroom invocation of God's blessings as prescribed in the Regents' prayer is a religious activity. It is a solemn avowal of divine faith and supplication for the blessings of the Almighty. ***

It is a matter of history that this very practice of establishing governmentally composed prayers for religious services was one of the reasons which caused many of our early colonists to leave England and seek religious freedom in America. The *Book of Common Prayer*, which was created under governmental direction and which was approved by Acts of Parliament in 1548 and 1549, set out in minute detail the accepted form and content of prayer and other religious ceremonies to be used in the established, tax-supported Church of England. The controversies over the Book and what should be its content repeatedly threatened to disrupt the peace of that country as the accepted forms of prayer in the established church changed with the views of the particular ruler that happened to be in control at the time. Powerful groups representing some of the varying religious views of the people struggled among themselves to impress their particular views upon the Government and obtain amendments of the Book more suitable to their respective notions of how religious services should be conducted in order that the official religious establishment would advance their particular religious beliefs. Other groups, lacking the necessary political power to influence the Government on the matter, decided to leave England and its established church and seek freedom in America from England's governmentally ordained and supported religion.

It is an unfortunate fact of history that when some of the very groups which had most strenuously opposed the established Church of England found themselves sufficiently in control of colonial governments in this country to write their own prayers into law, they passed laws making their own religion the official religion of their respective colonies. Indeed, as late as the time of the Revolutionary War, there were established churches in at least eight of the thirteen former colonies and established religions in at least four of the other five. But the successful Revolution against English political domination was shortly followed by intense opposition to the practice of establishing religion by law. This opposition crystallized rapidly into an effective political force in Virginia where the minority religious groups such as Presbyterians, Lutherans, Quakers and Baptists had gained such strength that the adherents to the established Episcopal Church were actually a minority themselves. In 1785-1786, those opposed to the established Church, led by James Madison and Thomas Jefferson, who, though themselves not members of any of these dissenting religious groups, opposed all religious establishments by law on grounds of principle, obtained the enactment of the famous "Virginia Bill for Religious Liberty" by which all religious groups were placed on an equal footing so far as the State was concerned. Similar though less far-reaching legislation was being considered and passed in other States.

By the time of the adoption of the Constitution, our history shows that there was a widespread awareness among many Americans of the dangers of a union of Church and State. These people knew, some of them from bitter personal experience that one of the greatest dangers to the freedom of the individual to worship in his own way lay in the Government's placing its official stamp of approval upon one particular kind of prayer or one particular form of religious services. They knew the anguish, hardship and bitter strife that could come when zealous religious groups struggled with one another to obtain the Government's stamp of approval from each King, Queen, or Protector that came to temporary power. The Constitution was intended to avert a part of this danger by leaving the government of this country in the hands of the people rather than in the hands of any monarch. But this safeguard was not enough. Our Founders were no more willing to let the content of their prayers and their privilege of praying whenever they pleased be influenced by the ballot box than they were to let these vital matters of personal conscience depend upon the succession of monarchs. The First Amendment was added to the Constitution to stand as a guarantee that neither the power nor the prestige of the Federal Government would be used to control, support or influence the kinds of prayer the American people can say—that the people's religions must not be subjected to the pressures of government for change each time a new political administration is elected to office. Under that Amendment's prohibition against governmental establishment of religion, as reinforced by the provisions of the Fourteenth Amendment, government in this country, be it state or federal, is without power to prescribe by law any particular form of prayer which is to be used as an official prayer in carrying on any program of governmentally sponsored religious activity.

There can be no doubt that New York's state prayer program officially establishes the religious beliefs embodied in the Regents' prayer. The respondents' argument to the contrary, which is largely based upon the contention that the Regents' prayer is "nondenominational" and the fact that the program, as modified and approved by state courts, does not require all pupils to recite the prayer but permits those who wish to do so to remain silent or be excused from the room, ignores the essential nature of the program's constitutional defects. Neither the fact that the prayer may be denominationally neutral nor the fact that its observance on the part of the students is voluntary can serve to free it from the limitations of the Establishment Clause, as it might from the Free Exercise Clause, of the First Amendment, both of which are operative against the States by virtue of the Fourteenth Amendment. Although these two clauses may in certain instances overlap, they forbid two quite different kinds of governmental encroachment upon religious freedom. The Establishment Clause, unlike the Free Exercise Clause, does not depend upon any showing of direct governmental compulsion and is violated by the enactment of laws which establish an official religion whether those laws operate directly to coerce nonobserving individuals or not. This is not to say, of course, that laws officially prescribing a particular form of religious worship do not involve coercion of such individuals. When the power, prestige and financial support of government is placed behind a particular religious belief, the indirect coercive pressure upon religious minorities to conform to the prevailing officially approved religion is plain. But the purposes underlying the Establishment Clause go much further than that. Its first and most immediate purpose rested on the belief that a union of government and religion tends to destroy government and to degrade religion. *** Another purpose of the Establishment Clause rested upon an awareness of the historical fact that governmentally established religions and religious persecutions go hand in hand. *** It was in large part to get completely away from this sort of systematic religious persecution that the Founders brought into being our Nation, our Constitution, and our Bill of Rights with its prohibition against any governmental establishment of religion. The New York laws officially prescribing the Regents' prayer are inconsistent both with the purposes of the Establishment Clause and with the Establishment Clause itself.

It has been argued that to apply the Constitution in such a way as to prohibit state laws respecting an establishment of religious services in public schools is to indicate a hostility toward religion or toward prayer. Nothing, or course, could be more wrong. *** It is neither sacrilegious nor antireligious to say that each separate government in this country should stay out of the business of writing or sanctioning official prayers and leave that purely religious function to the people themselves and to those the people choose to look to for religious guidance. [Reversed.]

Mr. Justice STEWART, dissenting.

With all respect, I think the Court has misapplied a great constitutional principle. I cannot see how an "official religion" is established by letting those who want to say a prayer say it. On the contrary, I think that to deny the wish of these school children to join in reciting this prayer is to deny them the opportunity of sharing in the spiritual heritage of our Nation.

————————

Points for Discussion

a. Scope of the Decision

In response to hearing that the Supreme Court had banned school prayer in *Engel*, someone quipped in disbelief: "As long as there are math tests, there will be prayer in school." (Perhaps your personal educational experience confirms this truth.) The observation, although offered as humor, raises important questions about the exact scope and theory of the Court's decision. The Court held that New York had violated the Establishment Clause even though the state had not mandated that students join in the Regents' prayer. Does the Court's decision mean that all voluntary prayer in school is unconstitutional? In other words, if a student in a public middle school said a prayer before an algebra test, would that violate the Establishment Clause? Or does the decision bar only government-authorized or approved prayer?

b. Reach of the Decision

The prayer at issue in *Engel* had been composed and approved by the state. One year after *Engel*, the Court held in *School Dist. of Abington Twp. v. Schempp*, 374 U.S. 203 (1963), that the Establishment Clause also prohibits state laws and policies "requiring the selection and reading at the opening of the school day of verses from the Holy Bible and the recitation of the Lord's Prayer by the students in unison." The challenged Pennsylvania law required that "[a]t least ten verses from the Holy Bible" be read each day, though it permitted children to be excused from the reading upon the written request of their parents. The Court held that the law was unconstitutional because the prayers were "prescribed as part of the curricular activities of students who are required by law to attend school" and were "held in the school buildings under the supervision and with the participation of teachers employed in those schools." The Court emphasized that "[n]othing we have said here indicates that such study of the Bible or of religion, when presented objectively as part of a secular program of education, may not be effected consistently with the First Amendment," but the Court concluded that the "exercises here do not fall into those categories."

c. Theory of the Decision

The Court's insistence that the Regents' prayer was unconstitutional even though students could abstain is particularly notable in light of an earlier, seminal First Amendment case. In *West Virginia State Board of Education v. Barnette*, 319 U.S. 624 (1943), the Court concluded that the state could not require students to salute the flag and recite the pledge of allegiance. The Court reasoned:

> To sustain the compulsory flag salute we are required to say that a Bill of Rights which guards the individual's right to speak his own mind, left it open to public authorities to compel him to utter what is not in his mind. *** Struggles to coerce uniformity of sentiment in support of some end thought essential to their time and country have been waged by many good as well as by evil men. [As] first and moderate methods to attain unity have failed, those bent on its accomplishment must resort to an ever-increasing severity. *** Those who begin coercive elimination of dissent soon find themselves exterminating dissenters. Compulsory unification of opinion achieves only the unanimity of the graveyard.

> It seems trite but necessary to say that the First Amendment to our Constitution was designed to avoid these ends by avoiding these beginnings. There is no mysticism in the American concept of the State or of the nature or origin of its authority. We set up government by consent of the governed, and the Bill of Rights denies those in power any legal opportunity to coerce that consent. Authority here is to be controlled by public opinion, not public opinion by authority. *** If there is any fixed star in our constitutional constellation, it is that no official, high or petty, can prescribe what shall be orthodox in politics, nationalism, religion, or other

matters of opinion or force citizens to confess by word or act their faith therein. If there are any circumstances which permit an exception, they do not now occur to us.

If coercion was the defect of the policy at issue in *Barnette*, under which students were required to recite the pledge of allegiance, then why wasn't the defect of the Regents' prayer addressed by the New York Court's decision that the prayer was optional? Is there a difference between the pledge of allegiance (which in 1943 did not include the phrase "under God") and the prayer at issue in *Engel*? Was coercion the only defect in *Engel*?

> ### Make the Connection
>
> We will consider the extent to which claims under the Establishment Clause require a showing of governmental coercion later in this section, when we consider the Court's decision in *Lee v. Weisman*.

In response to *Engel*, some states and school districts eliminated public prayers but left a time in the day for school children to pray silently if they so chose. In the following case, the Supreme Court considered whether providing a "moment of silence" in schools violates the Constitution.

Wallace v. Jaffree

472 U.S. 38 (1985)

Justice STEVENS delivered the opinion of the Court.

[Alabama Code § 16-1-20, as initially enacted in 1978, provided: "At the commencement of the first class each day in the first through the sixth grades in all public schools, the teacher in charge of the room in which each such class is held shall announce that a period of silence, not to exceed one minute in duration, shall be observed for meditation, and during any such period silence shall be maintained and no activities engaged in." Alabama Code § 16-1-20 (Supp.1984). Three years later, the Alabama legislature enacted a statute authorizing teachers to provide a period of silence "for meditation or voluntary prayer," during which "no other activities shall be engaged in." Alabama Code § 16-1-20.1 (Supp.1984) And in 1982, the legislature authorized teachers to lead "willing students" in a prescribed prayer to "Almighty God *** the Creator and Supreme Judge of the world." Alabama Code § 16-1-20.2 (Supp.1984).

Appellee Ishmael Jaffree, the father of three children in Alabama public schools, brought a lawsuit claiming that the statutes violated the Establishment Clause. In an earlier order, the Supreme Court summarily affirmed the court of appeals' conclusion, based on *School Dist. Abington v. Schempp*, 374 U.S. 203 (1963), that the 1982 statute was unconstitutional. *See Wallace v. Jaffree*, 466 U.S. 924 (1984). Before the Supreme Court, appellee did not argue that § 16-1-20 was unconstitutional, leaving only his claim that § 16-1-20.1, which authorized a period of silence for meditation or voluntary prayer, violated the Establishment Clause.]

When the Court has been called upon to construe the breadth of the Establishment Clause, it has examined the criteria developed over a period of many years. Thus, in *Lemon v. Kurtzman,* 403 U.S. 602 (1971), we [announced a three-factor test]: "First, the statute must have a secular legislative purpose; second, its principal or primary effect must be one that neither advances nor inhibits religion; finally, the statute must not foster 'an excessive government entanglement with religion.'"

It is the first of these three criteria that is most plainly implicated by this case. As the District Court correctly recognized, no consideration of the second or third criteria is necessary if a statute does not have a clearly secular purpose. For even though a statute that is motivated in part by a religious purpose may satisfy the first criterion, the First Amendment requires that a statute must be invalidated if it is entirely motivated by a purpose to advance religion.

> ### Food for Thought
>
> We have regularly noted in this book the difficulty of determining the motivation or purpose of a multi-member legislative body. Yet the *Lemon* test requires the Court to discern a legislative purpose. Is this a problem with the *Lemon* test? Or is the problem unavoidable in this context, where legislative purpose must be a relevant—and sometimes dispositive—criterion? Even if legislative purpose is relevant here, is evidence of the views of one legislator sufficient?

The sponsor of the bill that became § 16-1-20.1, Senator Donald Holmes, inserted into the legislative record—apparently without dissent—a statement indicating that the legislation was an "effort to return voluntary prayer" to the public schools. Later Senator Holmes confirmed this purpose before the District Court. In response to the question whether he had any purpose for the legislation other than returning voluntary prayer to public schools, he stated: "No, I did not have no other purpose in mind." The State did not present evidence of *any* secular purpose.

We must, therefore, conclude that the Alabama Legislature *** enacted § 16-1-20.1 [for] the sole purpose of expressing the State's endorsement of prayer activities for one minute at the beginning of each schoolday. The addition of "or voluntary prayer" indicates that the State intended to characterize prayer as a favored practice. Such an endorsement is not consistent with the established principle that the government must pursue a course of complete neutrality toward religion.

The importance of that principle does not permit us to treat this as an inconsequential case involving nothing more than a few words of symbolic speech on behalf of the political majority. For whenever the State itself speaks on a religious subject, one of the questions that we must ask is "whether the government intends to convey a message of endorsement or disapproval of religion." The well-supported concurrent findings of the District Court and the Court of Appeals—that § 16-1-20.1 was intended to convey a message of state approval of prayer activities in the public schools—make it unnecessary, and indeed inappropriate, to evaluate the practical significance of the addition of the words "or voluntary prayer" to the statute. Keeping in mind, as we must, "both the fundamental place held by the Establishment Clause in our constitutional scheme and the myriad, subtle ways in which Establishment Clause values can be eroded," *Lynch v. Donnelly,* 465 U.S. 668, 694 (1984) (O'CONNOR, J., concurring), we conclude that § 16-1-20.1 violates the First Amendment.

Justice O'CONNOR, concurring in the judgment.

*** It once appeared that the Court had developed a workable standard by which to identify impermissible government establishments of religion. *See Lemon v. Kurtzman,* 403 U.S. 602 (1971). Under the now familiar *Lemon* test, statutes must have both a secular legislative purpose and a principal or primary effect that neither advances nor inhibits religion, and in addition they must not foster excessive government entanglement with religion. Despite its initial promise, the *Lemon* test has proved problematic. The required inquiry into "entanglement" has been modified and questioned, *see Mueller v. Allen,* 463 U.S. 388, 403, n. 11 (1983), and in one case we have upheld state action against an Establishment Clause challenge without applying the *Lemon* test at all. *Marsh v. Chambers,* 463 U.S. 783 (1983). The author of *Lemon* himself apparently questions the test's general applicability. *See Lynch v. Donnelly,* 465 U.S. 668, 679 (1984). ***

Perhaps because I am new to the struggle, I am not ready to abandon all aspects of the *Lemon* test. I do believe, however, that the standards announced in *Lemon* should be reexamined and refined in order to make them more useful in achieving the underlying purpose of the First Amendment. *** Last Term, I proposed a refinement of the *Lemon* test with this goal in mind. *Lynch v. Donnelly, 465 U.S., at 687-689* (concurring opinion). [I] suggested that the religious liberty protected by the Establishment Clause is infringed when the government makes adherence to religion relevant to a person's standing in the political community. Direct government action endorsing

> **Make the Connection**
>
> We will consider the Court's decision in *Lynch* later in this Chapter.

religion or a particular religious practice is invalid under this approach because it "sends a message to nonadherents that they are outsiders, not full members of the political community, and an accompanying message to adherents that they are insiders, favored members of the political community." *Id., at 688.* Under this view, *Lemon*'s inquiry as to the purpose and effect of a statute requires courts to examine whether government's purpose is to endorse religion and whether the statute actually conveys a message of endorsement.

The endorsement test is useful because of the analytic content it gives to the *Lemon*-mandated inquiry into legislative purpose and effect. In this country, church and state must necessarily operate within the same community. Because of this coexistence, it is inevitable that the secular interests of government and the religious interests of various sects and their adherents will frequently intersect, conflict, and combine. A statute that ostensibly promotes a secular interest often has an incidental or even a primary effect of helping or hindering a sectarian belief. Chaos would ensue if every such statute were invalid under the Establishment Clause. For example, the State could not criminalize murder for fear that it would thereby promote the Biblical command against killing. The task for the Court is to sort out those statutes and government practices whose purpose and effect go against the grain of religious liberty protected by the First Amendment.

The endorsement test does not preclude government from acknowledging religion or from taking religion into account in making law and policy. It does preclude government from conveying or attempting to convey a message that religion or a particular religious belief is favored or preferred. Such an endorsement infringes the religious liberty of the nonadherent, for "[w]hen the power, prestige and financial support of government is placed behind a particular religious belief, the indirect coercive pressure upon religious minorities to conform to the prevailing officially approved religion is plain." *Engel v. Vitale,* 370 U.S., at 431. At issue today is whether state moment of silence statutes in general, and Alabama's moment of silence statute in particular, embody an impermissible endorsement of prayer in public schools.

*** The sole purpose reflected in the official history is "to return voluntary prayer to our public schools." Nor does anything in the legislative history contradict an intent to encourage children to choose prayer over other alternatives during the moment of silence. *** In light of the legislative history and the findings of the courts below, I agree with the Court that the State intended § 16-1-20.1 to convey a message that prayer was the endorsed activity during the state-prescribed moment of silence. ***

Chief Justice BURGER, dissenting.

Some who trouble to read the opinions in these cases will find it ironic—perhaps even bizarre—that on the very day we heard arguments in the cases, the Court's session opened with an invocation for Divine protection. Across the park a few hundred yards away, the House of Representatives and the Senate regularly open each session with a prayer. These legislative prayers are not just one minute in duration, but are extended, thoughtful invocations and prayers for Divine guidance. They are given, as they have been since 1789, by clergy appointed as official chaplains and paid from the Treasury of the United States. Congress has also provided chapels in the Capitol, at public expense, where Members and others may pause for prayer, meditation—or a moment of silence.

*** The Alabama Legislature has no more "endorsed" religion than a state or the Congress does when it provides for legislative chaplains, or than this Court does when it opens each session with an invocation to God. ***

Justice REHNQUIST, dissenting.

It is impossible to build sound constitutional doctrine upon a mistaken understanding of constitutional history, but unfortunately the Establishment Clause has been expressly freighted with Jefferson's misleading metaphor [of "a wall of separation between church and State"] for nearly 40 years. Thomas Jefferson was of course in France at the time the constitutional Amendments known as the Bill of Rights were passed by Congress and ratified by the States. [The letter in which he stated the wall metaphor] was a short note of courtesy, written 14 years after the Amendments were passed by Congress. He would seem to any detached observer as a less than ideal source of contemporary history as to the meaning of the Religion Clauses of the First Amendment. [In contrast,] James Madison [was] present in the United States, and he was a leading Member of the First Congress. But when we turn to the record of the proceedings in the First Congress leading up to the adoption of the Establishment Clause of the Constitution, including Madison's significant contributions thereto, we see a far different picture of its purpose than the highly simplified "wall of separation between church and State."

The language Madison proposed for what ultimately became the Religion Clauses of the First Amendment was this: "The civil rights of none shall be abridged on account of religious belief or worship, nor shall any national religion be established, nor shall the full and equal rights of conscience be in any manner, or on any pretext, infringed." *** [During the floor debate on a Select Committee's revision of the proposal, Madison stated] that "he apprehended the meaning of the words to be, that Congress should not establish a religion, and enforce the legal observation of it by law, nor compel men to worship God in any manner contrary to their conscience." 1 Annals of Cong. 730. [In response to concerns that this language might "be taken in such latitude as to be extremely hurtful to the cause of religion," Madison emphasized the word "national" before the word "religion."] "He believed that the people feared one sect might obtain a pre-eminence, or two combine together, and establish a religion to which they would compel others to conform. He thought that if the word 'national' was introduced, it would point the amendment directly to the object it was intended to prevent." *Id.*, at 731.

The following week, without any apparent debate, the House voted to alter the language of the Religion Clauses to read "Congress shall make no law establishing religion, or to prevent the free exercise thereof, or to infringe the rights of conscience." *Id.*, at 766. The floor debates in the Senate were secret, and therefore not reported in the Annals. *** The House refused to accept the Senate's changes in the Bill of Rights and asked for a conference; the version which emerged from the conference was that which ultimately found its way into the Constitution as a part of the First Amendment.

On the basis of the record of these proceedings in the House of Representatives, James Madison was undoubtedly the most important architect among the Members of the House of the Amendments which became the Bill of Rights, but it was James Madison speaking as an advocate of sensible legislative compromise, not as an advocate of incorporating the Virginia Statute of Religious Liberty into the United States Constitution. During the ratification debate in the Virginia Convention, Madison had actually opposed the idea of any Bill of Rights. His sponsorship of the Amendments in the House was obviously not that of a zealous believer in the necessity of the Religion Clauses, but of one who felt it might do some good, could do no harm, and would satisfy those who had ratified the Constitution on the condition that Congress propose a Bill of Rights. His original language "nor shall any national religion be established" obviously does not conform to the "wall of separation" between church and State idea which latter-day commentators have ascribed to him. His explanation on the floor of the meaning of his language *** is of the same ilk.

It seems indisputable from these glimpses of Madison's thinking, as reflected by actions on the floor of the House in 1789, that he saw the Amendment as designed to prohibit the establishment of a national religion, and perhaps to prevent discrimination among sects. He did not see it as requiring neutrality on the part of government between religion and irreligion. Thus the Court's opinion in *Everson*—while correct in bracketing Madison and Jefferson together in their exertions in their home State leading to the enactment of the Virginia Statute of Religious Liberty—is totally incorrect in suggesting that Madison carried these views onto the floor of the United States House of Representatives when he proposed the language which would ultimately become the Bill of Rights.

None of the other Members of Congress who spoke during the [congressional] debate expressed the slightest indication that they thought the language before them from the Select Committee, or the evil to be aimed at, would require that the Government be absolutely neutral as between religion and irreligion. The evil to be aimed at, so far as those who spoke were concerned, appears to have been the establishment of a national church, and perhaps the preference of one religious sect over another; but it was definitely not concerned about whether the Government might aid all religions evenhandedly.

The actions of the First Congress *** confirm the view that Congress did not mean that the Government should be neutral between religion and irreligion. *** On the day after the House of Representatives voted to adopt the form of the First Amendment Religion Clauses which was ultimately proposed and ratified, Representative Elias Boudinot proposed a resolution asking President George Washington to issue a Thanksgiving Day Proclamation. Boudinot said he "could not think of letting the session pass over without offering an opportunity to all the citizens of the United States of joining with one voice, in returning to Almighty God their sincere thanks for the many blessings he had poured down upon them." 1 Annals of Cong. 914 (1789). *** George Washington responded [by issuing a proclamation that recommended that the day "be devoted by the people of these States to the service of that great and glorious Being who is the beneficent author of all the good that was, that is, or that will be" and that "we may then unite in most humbly offering our prayers and supplications to the great Lord and Ruler of Nations, and beseech Him to pardon our national and other transgressions."] John Adams [and] James Madison also issued Thanksgiving Proclamations ***.

[In the nineteenth century, Congress on several occasions appropriated money for the aid of religion.] It would seem from this evidence that the Establishment Clause of the First Amendment had acquired a well-accepted meaning: it forbade establishment of a national religion, and forbade preference among religious sects or denominations. *** The Establishment Clause did not require government neutrality between religion and irreligion nor did it prohibit the Federal Government from providing nondiscriminatory aid to religion. There is simply no historical foundation for the proposition that the Framers intended to build the "wall of separation" that was constitutionalized in *Everson*.

Notwithstanding the absence of a historical basis for this theory of rigid separation, the wall idea might well have served as a useful albeit misguided analytical concept, had it led this Court to unified and principled results in Establishment Clause cases. The opposite, unfortunately, has been true; in the 38 years since *Everson* our Establishment Clause cases have been neither principled nor unified. *** Whether due to its lack of historical support or its practical unworkability, the *Everson* "wall" has proved all but useless as a guide to sound constitutional adjudication. *** But the greatest injury of the "wall" notion is its mischievous diversion of judges from the actual intentions of the drafters of the Bill of Rights. *** [The "wall" metaphor] should be frankly and explicitly abandoned.

[T]he *Lemon* test has no more grounding in the history of the First Amendment than does the wall theory upon which it rests. The three-part test represents a determined effort to craft a workable rule from a historically faulty doctrine; but the rule can only be as sound as the doctrine it attempts to service. *** [N]othing in the Establishment Clause requires government to be strictly neutral between religion and irreligion, nor does that Clause prohibit Congress or the States from pursuing legitimate secular ends through nondiscriminatory sectarian means.

It would come as much of a shock to those who drafted the Bill of Rights as it will to a large number of thoughtful Americans today to learn that the Constitution, as construed by the majority, prohibits the Alabama Legislature from "endorsing" prayer. George Washington himself, at the request of the very Congress which passed the Bill of Rights, proclaimed a day of "public thanksgiving and prayer, to be observed by acknowledging with grateful hearts the many and signal favors of Almighty God." History must judge whether it was the Father of his Country in 1789, or a majority of the Court today, which has strayed from the meaning of the Establishment Clause.

[The concurring opinion of Justice POWELL and the dissenting opinion of Justice WHITE are omitted.]

———————

Points for Discussion

a. Religious Purpose

In this case, the Alabama statute expressly made the moment of silence a time for "voluntary prayer," and the state acknowledged that the purpose was to encourage prayer. Would the case have come out differently if the statute merely provided for "a moment of silence for reflection" without mentioning prayer and if the legislative history also did not say anything about prayer? For example, every year on September 11, many schools and public institutions hold a moment of silence in memory of the victims of the terrorist attacks of 2001. Certainly many people use this time for prayer. Is this moment of silence unconstitutional?

b. Justice O'Connor's Proposed Endorsement Test

The Supreme Court has not replaced the *Lemon* test with an endorsement test such as the one that Justice O'Connor proposed in her separate opinion. But the Court in subsequent cases has recognized endorsement as a factor relevant to determining the constitutionality of actions challenged under the Establishment Clause. In *County of Allegheny v. ACLU*, 492 U.S. 573, 593-94 (1989), the Court said:

> Whether the key word is "endorsement," "favoritism," or "promotion," the essential principle remains the same. The Establishment Clause, at the very least, prohibits government from appearing to take a position on questions of religious belief or from "making adherence to a religion relevant in any way to a person's standing in the political community." *Lynch v. Donnelly,* 465 U.S., at 687 (O'CONNOR, J., concurring).

c. Non-Preferentialism

Justice Rehnquist asserted that the Establishment Clause does not require neutrality "between religion and irreligion" and does not prohibit "nondiscriminatory aid to religion." He thus rejected the separation principle that the Court had announced in *Everson*, and proposed in its place a principle that merely forbids the government from preferring one religion to another. What is the source of this principle? Are you convinced by Justice Rehnquist's historical argument? If Madison's views are largely dispositive, then isn't it also important that he concluded that presidential Thanksgiving proclamations invoking God violate the Establishment Clause? See *Lee v. Weisman*, 505 U.S. 577 (1992) (Souter, J., concurring). Also, is it possible for the government to endorse or provide aid to religion generally without preferring some religions to others?

In the previous two cases, schools provided time for students to pray at school during the school day. Is the Establishment Clause violated if schools offer, and students hear, non-denominational prayers at graduation ceremonies?

Lee v. Weisman

505 U.S. 577 (1992)

Justice KENNEDY the opinion of the Court.

Deborah Weisman graduated from Nathan Bishop Middle School, a public school in Providence, at a formal ceremony in June 1989. She was about 14 years old. For many years it has been the policy of the Providence School Committee and the Superintendent of Schools to permit principals to invite members of the clergy to give invocations and benedictions at middle school and high school graduations. Many, but not all, of the principals elected to include prayers as part of the graduation ceremonies. Acting for himself and his daughter, Deborah's father, Daniel Weisman, objected to any prayers at Deborah's middle school graduation, but to no avail. The school principal, petitioner Robert E. Lee, invited a rabbi to deliver prayers at the graduation exercises for Deborah's class. Rabbi Leslie Gutterman, of the Temple Beth El in Providence, accepted.[*]

*** It is beyond dispute that, at a minimum, the Constitution guarantees that government may not coerce anyone to support or participate in religion or its exercise, or otherwise act in a way which "establishes a [state] religion or religious faith, or tends to do so." *Lynch v. Donnelly*, 465 U.S. 668, 678 (1984). The State's involvement in the school prayers challenged today violates these central principles.

That involvement is as troubling as it is undenied. A school official, the principal, decided that an invocation and a benediction should be given; this is a choice attributable to the State, and from a constitutional perspective it is as if a state statute decreed that the prayers must occur. The principal chose the religious participant, here a rabbi, and that choice is also attributable to the State. The reason for the choice of a rabbi is not disclosed by the record, but the potential for divisiveness over the choice of a particular member of the clergy to conduct the ceremony is apparent.

The State's role did not end with the decision to include a prayer and with the choice of a clergyman. Principal Lee provided Rabbi Gutterman with a copy of the "Guidelines for Civic Occasions," and advised him that his prayers should be nonsectarian. Through these means the principal directed and controlled the content of the prayers. Even if the only sanction for ignoring the instructions were that the rabbi would not be invited back, we think no religious representative who valued his or her continued reputation and effectiveness in the community would incur the State's displeasure in this regard. It is a cornerstone principle of our Establishment Clause jurisprudence that "it is no part of the business of government to compose official prayers for any group of the American people to recite as a part of a religious program carried on by government," *Engel v. Vitale*, 370 U.S. 421, 425 (1962), and that is what the school officials attempted to do.

Petitioners argue, and we find nothing in the case to refute it, that the directions for the content of the prayers were a good-faith attempt by the school to ensure that the sectarianism which is so often the flashpoint for religious animosity be removed from the graduation ceremony. The concern is understandable, as a prayer which uses ideas or images

---

[*] Rabbi Gutterman's invocation was as follows: "God of the Free, Hope of the Brave: For the legacy of America where diversity is celebrated and the rights of minorities are protected, we thank You. May these young men and women grow up to enrich it. For the liberty of America, we thank You. May these new graduates grow up to guard it. For the political process of America in which all its citizens may participate, for its court system where all may seek justice we thank You. May those we honor this morning always turn to it in trust. For the destiny of America we thank You. May the graduates of Nathan Bishop Middle School so live that they might help to share it. May our aspirations for our country and for these young people, who are our hope for the future, be richly fulfilled." In his benediction, he stated: "O God, we are grateful to You for having endowed us with the capacity for learning which we have celebrated on this joyous commencement. Happy families give thanks for seeing their children achieve an important milestone. Send Your blessings upon the teachers and administrators who helped prepare them. The graduates now need strength and guidance for the future, help them to understand that we are not complete with academic knowledge alone. We must each strive to fulfill what You require of us all: To do justly, to love mercy, to walk humbly. We give thanks to You, Lord, for keeping us alive, sustaining us and allowing us to reach this special, happy occasion."—*Eds.*

identified with a particular religion may foster a different sort of sectarian rivalry than an invocation or benediction in terms more neutral. The school's explanation, however, does not resolve the dilemma caused by its participation. The question is not the good faith of the school in attempting to make the prayer acceptable to most persons, but the legitimacy of its undertaking that enterprise at all when the object is to produce a prayer to be used in a formal religious exercise which students, for all practical purposes, are obliged to attend.

The degree of school involvement here made it clear that the graduation prayers bore the imprint of the State and thus put school-age children who objected in an untenable position. We turn our attention now to consider the position of the students, both those who desired the prayer and she who did not.

As we have observed before, there are heightened concerns with protecting freedom of conscience from subtle coercive pressure in the elementary and secondary public schools. Our decisions in *Engel v. Vitale, 370 U.S. 421 (1962)*, and *School Dist. Abington v. Schempp, 374 U.S. 203 (1963)*, recognize, among other things, that prayer exercises in public schools carry a particular risk of indirect coercion. The concern may not be limited to the context of schools, but it is most pronounced there. What to most believers may seem nothing more than a reasonable request that the nonbeliever respect their religious practices, in a school context may appear to the nonbeliever or dissenter to be an attempt to employ the machinery of the State to enforce a religious orthodoxy.

We need not look beyond the circumstances of this case to see the phenomenon at work. The undeniable fact is that the school district's supervision and control of a high school graduation ceremony places public pressure, as well as peer pressure, on attending students to stand as a group or, at least, maintain respectful silence during the invocation and benediction. This pressure, though subtle and indirect, can be as real as any overt compulsion. Of course, in our culture standing or remaining silent can signify adherence to a view or simple respect for the views of others. And no doubt some persons who have no desire to join a prayer have little objection to standing as a sign of respect for those who do. But for the dissenter of high school age, who has a reasonable perception that she is being forced by the State to pray in a manner her conscience will not allow, the injury is no less real. There can be no doubt that for many, if not most, of the students at the graduation, the act of standing or remaining silent was an expression of participation in the rabbi's prayer. That was the very point of the religious exercise. It is of little comfort to a dissenter, then, to be told that for her the act of standing or remaining in silence signifies mere respect, rather than participation. What matters is that, given our social conventions, a reasonable dissenter in this milieu could believe that the group exercise signified her own participation or approval of it.

Finding no violation under these circumstances would place objectors in the dilemma of participating, with all that implies, or protesting. We do not address whether that choice is acceptable if the affected citizens are mature adults, but we think the State may not, consistent with the Establishment Clause, place primary and secondary school children in this position. Research in psychology supports the common assumption that adolescents are often susceptible to pressure from their peers towards conformity, and that the influence is strongest in matters of social convention. Brittain, Adolescent Choices and Parent-Peer Cross-Pressures, 28 Am. Sociological Rev. 385 (June 1963); Clasen & Brown, The Multidimensionality of Peer Pressure in Adolescence, 14 J. of Youth and Adolescence 451 (Dec.1985); Brown, Clasen, & Eicher, Perceptions of Peer Pressure, Peer Conformity Dispositions, and Self-Reported Behavior Among Adolescents, 22 Developmental Psychology 521 (July 1986). To recognize that the choice imposed by the State constitutes an unacceptable constraint only acknowledges that the government may no more use social pressure to enforce orthodoxy than it may use more direct means.

> **Food for Thought**
>
> We will see later in this Chapter that the Court has upheld the practice of prayer at legislative sessions. *Marsh v. Chambers,* 463 U.S. 783, 790 (1983). Does the Court's discussion here suggest a reason to treat such practices differently? Or are the "pressures" on a non-believing, elected member of the legislature at least as great, if not greater?

There was a stipulation in the District Court that attendance at graduation and promotional ceremonies is voluntary. Petitioners and the United States, as *amicus,* made this a center point of the case, arguing that the option of not attending the graduation excuses any inducement or coercion in the ceremony itself. The argument lacks all persuasion. Law reaches past formalism. And to say a teenage student has a real choice not to attend her high school graduation is formalistic in the extreme. True, Deborah could elect not to attend commencement without renouncing her diploma; but we shall not allow the case to turn on this point. Everyone knows that in our society and in our culture high school graduation is one of life's most significant occasions. A school rule which excuses attendance is beside the point. Attendance may not be required by official decree, yet it is apparent that a student is not free to absent herself from the graduation exercise in any real sense of the term "voluntary," for absence would require forfeiture of those intangible benefits which have motivated the student through youth and all her high school years. Graduation is a time for family and those closest to the student to celebrate success and express mutual wishes of gratitude and respect, all to the end of impressing upon the young person the role that it is his or her right and duty to assume in the community and all of its diverse parts.

The [school district and the United States contend] that the prayers are an essential part of these ceremonies because for many persons an occasion of this significance lacks meaning if there is no recognition, however brief, that human achievements cannot be understood apart from their spiritual essence. [This argument] fails to acknowledge that what for many of Deborah's classmates and their parents was a spiritual imperative was for Daniel and Deborah Weisman religious conformance compelled by the State. *** The essence of the Government's position is that with regard to a civic, social occasion of this importance it is the objector, not the majority, who must take unilateral and private action to avoid compromising religious scruples, hereby electing to miss the graduation exercise. This turns conventional First Amendment analysis on its head. It is a tenet of the First Amendment that the State cannot require one of its citizens to forfeit his or her rights and benefits as the price of resisting conformance to state-sponsored religious practice. To say that a student must remain apart from the ceremony at the opening invocation and closing benediction is to risk compelling conformity in an environment analogous to the classroom setting, where we have said the risk of compulsion is especially high.

We do not hold that every state action implicating religion is invalid if one or a few citizens find it offensive. People may take offense at all manner of religious as well as nonreligious messages, but offense alone does not in every case show a violation. We know too that sometimes to endure social isolation or even anger may be the price of conscience or nonconformity. But, by any reading of our cases, the conformity required of the student in this case was too high an exaction to withstand the test of the Establishment Clause. The prayer exercises in this case are especially improper because the State has in every practical sense compelled attendance and participation in an explicit religious exercise at an event of singular importance to every student, one the objecting student had no real alternative to avoid. *** *Affirmed.*

Justice BLACKMUN, with whom Justice STEVENS and Justice O'CONNOR join, concurring.

I join the Court's opinion today because I find nothing in it inconsistent with the essential precepts of the Establishment Clause developed in our precedents. The Court holds that the graduation prayer is unconstitutional because the State "in effect required participation in a religious exercise." Although our precedents make clear that proof of government coercion is not necessary to prove an Establishment Clause violation, it is sufficient. Government pressure to participate in a religious activity is an obvious indication that the government is endorsing or promoting religion.

But it is not enough that the government restrain from compelling religious practices: It must not engage in them either. The Court repeatedly has recognized that a violation of the Establishment Clause is not predicated on coercion. The Establishment Clause proscribes public schools from "conveying or attempting to convey a message that religion or a particular religious belief is *favored* or *preferred*," *County of Allegheny v. American Civil Liberties Union, Greater Pittsburgh Chapter*, 492 U.S. 573, 593 (1989), even if the schools do not actually "impos[e] pressure upon a student to participate in a religious activity." *Board of Ed. of Westside Community Schools (Dist. 66) v. Mergens*, 496 U.S. 226, 261 (1990) (KENNEDY, J., concurring in part and concurring in judgment).

There is no doubt that attempts to aid religion through government coercion jeopardize freedom of conscience. Even subtle pressure diminishes the right of each individual to choose voluntarily what to believe. *** Our decisions have gone beyond prohibiting coercion, however, because the Court has recognized that "the fullest possible scope of religious liberty" entails more than freedom from coercion. *** The mixing of government and religion can be a threat to free government, even if no one is forced to participate. When the government puts its *imprimatur* on a particular religion, it conveys a message of exclusion to all those who do not adhere to the favored beliefs. A government cannot be premised on the belief that all persons are created equal when it asserts that God prefers some.

It is these understandings and fears that underlie our Establishment Clause jurisprudence. We have believed that religious freedom cannot exist in the absence of a free democratic government, and that such a government cannot endure when there is fusion between religion and the political regime. We have believed that religious freedom cannot thrive in the absence of a vibrant religious community and that such a community cannot prosper when it is bound to the secular. And we have believed that these were the animating principles behind the adoption of the Establishment Clause. To that end, our cases have prohibited government endorsement of religion, its sponsorship, and active involvement in religion, whether or not citizens were coerced to conform.

Justice SOUTER, with whom Justice STEVENS and Justice O'CONNOR join, concurring.

Since *Everson* we have consistently held the [Establishment] Clause applicable no less to governmental acts favoring religion generally than to acts favoring one religion over others. *** Some have challenged this precedent by reading the Establishment Clause to permit "nonpreferential" state promotion of religion. The challengers argue that, as originally understood by the Framers, "[t]he Establishment Clause did not require government neutrality between religion and irreligion nor did it prohibit the Federal Government from providing nondiscriminatory aid to religion." *Wallace v. Jaffree,* 472 U.S. 38, 106 (1985) (REHNQUIST, J., dissenting). While a case has been made for this position, it is not so convincing as to warrant reconsideration of our settled law; indeed, I find in the history of the Clause's textual development a more powerful argument supporting the Court's jurisprudence following *Everson* ***

> **Go Online**
>
> In the full text of his opinion, Justice Souter provided a detailed account of the drafting history of the Establishment Clause. You can read his discussion, in Section I.B of his opinion, here.

While [this history is], for me, sufficient to reject the nonpreferentialist position, one further concern animates my judgment. In many contexts, including this one, nonpreferentialism requires some distinction between "sectarian" religious practices and those that would be, by some measure, ecumenical enough to pass Establishment Clause muster. Simply by requiring the enquiry, nonpreferentialists invite the courts to engage in comparative theology. I can hardly imagine a subject less amenable to the competence of the federal judiciary, or more deliberately to be avoided where possible. *** Nor does it solve the problem to say that the State should promote a "diversity" of religious views; that position would necessarily compel the government and, inevitably, the courts to make wholly inappropriate judgments about the number of religions the State should sponsor and the relative frequency with which it should sponsor each.

Petitioners rest most of their argument on a theory that, whether or not the Establishment Clause permits extensive nonsectarian support for religion, it does not forbid the state to sponsor affirmations of religious belief that coerce neither support for religion nor participation in religious observance. *** But we could not adopt that reading without abandoning our settled law, a course that, in my view, the text of the Clause would not readily permit. *** Over the years, this Court has declared the invalidity of many noncoercive state laws and practices conveying a message of religious endorsement. For example, [in] *Wallace v. Jaffree*, 472 U.S. 38 (1985), we struck down a state law requiring a moment of silence in public classrooms not because the statute coerced students to participate in prayer (for it did not), but because the manner of its enactment "convey[ed] a message of state approval of prayer activities in the public schools." *** Our precedents may not always have drawn perfectly straight lines. They simply cannot, however, support the position that a showing of coercion is necessary to a successful Establishment Clause claim.

[Petitioners also cannot] easily square that claim with the constitutional text. The First Amendment forbids not just laws "respecting an establishment of religion," but also those "prohibiting the free exercise thereof." Yet laws that coerce nonadherents to "support or participate in any religion or its exercise" would virtually by definition violate their right to religious free exercise. Thus, a literal application of the coercion test would render the Establishment Clause a virtual nullity ***.

Petitioners contend that because the early Presidents included religious messages in their inaugural and Thanksgiving Day addresses, the Framers could not have meant the Establishment Clause to forbid noncoercive state endorsement of religion. The argument ignores the fact, however, that *** President Jefferson, for example, steadfastly refused to issue Thanksgiving proclamations of any kind, in part because he thought they violated the Religion Clauses. *** He accordingly construed the Establishment Clause to forbid not simply state coercion, but also state endorsement, of religious belief and observance. *** During his first three years in office, James Madison also refused to call for days of thanksgiving and prayer, though later, amid the political turmoil of the War of 1812, he did so on four separate occasions. Upon retirement, in an essay condemning as an unconstitutional "establishment" the use of public money to support congressional and military chaplains, he concluded that "[r]eligious proclamations by the Executive recommending thanksgivings & fasts are shoots from the same root with the legislative acts reviewed."

To be sure, the leaders of the young Republic engaged in some of the practices that separationists like Jefferson and Madison criticized. The First Congress did hire institutional chaplains, and Presidents Washington and Adams unapologetically marked days of "public thanksgiving and prayer." Yet in the face of the separationist dissent, those practices prove, at best, that the Framers simply did not share a common understanding of the Establishment Clause, and, at worst, that they, like other politicians, could raise constitutional ideals one day and turn their backs on them the next. *** Sometimes the National Constitution fared no better. Ten years after proposing the First Amendment, Congress passed the Alien and Sedition Acts, measures patently unconstitutional by modern standards. If the early Congress's political actions were determinative, and not merely relevant, evidence of constitutional meaning, we would have to gut our current First Amendment doctrine to make room for political censorship.

While the Establishment Clause's concept of neutrality is not self-revealing, our recent cases have invested it with specific content: the State may not favor or endorse either religion generally over nonreligion or one religion over others. *** [T]he government's sponsorship of prayer at the graduation ceremony is most reasonably understood as an official endorsement of religion and, in this instance, of theistic religion.

Petitioners would deflect this conclusion by arguing that graduation prayers are no different from Presidential religious proclamations and similar official "acknowledgments" of religion in public life. But religious invocations in Thanksgiving Day addresses and the like, rarely noticed, ignored without effort, conveyed over an impersonal medium, and directed at no one in particular, inhabit a pallid zone worlds apart from official prayers delivered to a captive audience of public school students and their families. When public school officials, armed with the State's authority, convey an endorsement of religion to their students, they strike near the core of the Establishment Clause. However "ceremonial" their messages may be, they are flatly unconstitutional.

Justice SCALIA, with whom THE CHIEF JUSTICE, Justice WHITE, and Justice THOMAS join, dissenting.

In holding that the Establishment Clause prohibits invocations and benedictions at public-school graduation ceremonies, the Court—with nary a mention that it is doing so—lays waste a tradition that is as old as public-school graduation ceremonies themselves, and that is a component of an even more longstanding American tradition of nonsectarian prayer to God at public celebrations generally. As its instrument of destruction, the bulldozer of its social engineering, the Court invents a boundless, and boundlessly manipulable, test of psychological coercion ***. Today's opinion shows more forcefully than volumes of argumentation why our Nation's protection, that fortress which is our Constitution, cannot possibly rest upon the changeable philosophical predilections of the Justices of this Court, but must have deep foundations in the historic practices of our people. The history and tradition of our Nation are replete with public ceremonies featuring prayers of thanksgiving and petition. Illustrations of this point have been amply provided in our prior opinions, see, *e.g., Lynch v. Donnelly,* 465 U.S. 668, 673 (1984); *Marsh v. Chambers,* 463 U.S. 783, 790 (1983) ***.

From our Nation's origin, prayer has been a prominent part of governmental ceremonies and proclamations. The Declaration of Independence, the document marking our birth as a separate people, "appeal[ed] to the Supreme Judge of the world for the rectitude of our intentions" and avowed "a firm reliance on the protection of divine Providence." In his first inaugural address, after swearing his oath of office on a Bible, George Washington deliberately made a prayer a part of his first official act as President:

> "[I]t would be peculiarly improper to omit in this first official act my fervent supplications to that Almighty Being who rules over the universe, who presides in the councils of nations, and whose providential aids can supply every human defect, that His benediction may consecrate to the liberties and happiness of the people of the United States a Government instituted by themselves for these essential purposes." Inaugural Addresses of the Presidents of the United States, S.Doc. 101-10, p. 2 (1989).

Our national celebration of Thanksgiving likewise dates back to President Washington. [Our] tradition of Thanksgiving Proclamations—with their religious theme of prayerful gratitude to God—has been adhered to by almost every President. *** The other two branches of the Federal Government also have a long-established practice of prayer at public events. [C]ongressional sessions have opened with a chaplain's prayer ever since the First Congress. And this Court's own sessions have opened with the invocation "God save the United States and this Honorable Court" since the days of Chief Justice Marshall. In addition to this general tradition of prayer at public ceremonies, there exists a more specific tradition of invocations and benedictions at public school graduation exercises. By one account, the first public high school graduation ceremony took place in Connecticut in July 1868—the very month, as it happens, that the Fourteenth Amendment (the vehicle by which the Establishment Clause has been applied against the States) was ratified—when "15 seniors from the Norwich Free Academy marched in their best Sunday suits and dresses into a church hall and waited through majestic music and long prayers."

The Court presumably would separate graduation invocations and benedictions from other instances of public "preservation and transmission of religious beliefs" on the ground that they involve "psychological coercion." [But a] few citations of "[r]esearch in psychology" that have no particular bearing upon the precise issue here cannot disguise the fact that the Court has gone beyond the realm where judges know what they are doing. The Court's argument that state officials have "coerced" students to take part in the invocation and benediction at graduation ceremonies is, not to put too fine a point on it, incoherent.

The Court's notion that a student who simply *sits* in "respectful silence" during the invocation and benediction (when all others are standing) has somehow joined—or would somehow be perceived as having joined—in the prayers is nothing short of ludicrous. We indeed live in a vulgar age. But surely "our social conventions" have not coarsened to the point that anyone who does not stand on his chair and shout obscenities can reasonably be deemed to have assented to everything said in his presence. Since the Court does not dispute that students exposed to prayer at graduation ceremonies retain (despite "subtle coercive pressures") the free will to sit, there is absolutely no basis for the Court's decision. It is fanciful enough to say that "a reasonable dissenter," standing head erect in a class of bowed heads, "could believe that the group exercise signified her own participation or approval of it." It is beyond the absurd to say that she could entertain such a belief while pointedly declining to rise.

But let us assume the very worst, that the nonparticipating graduate is "subtly coerced" ... to stand! Even that [does] not remotely establish a "participation" (or an "appearance of participation") in a religious exercise. [I]f it is a permissible inference that one who is standing is doing so simply out of respect for the prayers of others that are in progress, then how can it possibly be said that a "reasonable dissenter could believe that the group exercise signified her own participation or approval"? *** I may add, moreover, that maintaining respect for the religious observances of others is a fundamental civic virtue that government (including the public schools) can and should cultivate—so that even if it were the case that the displaying of such respect might be mistaken for taking part in the prayer, I would deny that the dissenter's interest in avoiding *even the false appearance of participation* constitutionally trumps the government's interest in fostering respect for religion generally.

The deeper flaw in the Court's opinion does not lie in its wrong answer to the question whether there was state-induced "peer-pressure" coercion; it lies, rather, in the Court's making violation of the Establishment Clause hinge on such a precious question. The coercion that was a hallmark of historical establishments of religion was coercion of religious orthodoxy and of financial support *by force of law and threat of penalty.* *** The Establishment Clause was adopted to prohibit such an establishment of religion at the federal level (and to protect state establishments of religion from federal interference). I will further acknowledge for the sake of argument that, as some scholars have argued, by 1790 the term "establishment" had acquired an additional meaning—"financial support of religion generally, by public taxation"—that reflected the development of "general or multiple" establishments, not limited to a single church. But that would still be an establishment coerced *by force of law.* And I will further concede that our constitutional tradition, from the Declaration of Independence and the first inaugural address of Washington, quoted earlier, down to the present day, has, with a few aberrations, see *Church of Holy Trinity v. United States,* 143 U.S. 457 (1892), ruled out of order government-sponsored endorsement of religion—even when no legal coercion is present, and indeed even when no ersatz, "peer-pressure" psycho-coercion is present—where the endorsement is sectarian, in the sense of specifying details upon which men and women who believe in a benevolent, omnipotent Creator and Ruler of the world are known to differ (for example, the divinity of Christ). But there is simply no support for the proposition that the officially sponsored nondenominational invocation and benediction read by Rabbi Gutterman—with no one legally coerced to recite them—violated the Constitution of the United States. To the contrary, they are so characteristically American they could have come from the pen of George Washington or Abraham Lincoln himself.

> **Food for Thought**
>
> Justice Scalia suggests here that the Establishment Clause was designed, among other things, to "protect state establishments of religion from federal interference." On this view, would incorporation of the Establishment Clause make any sense? Would it mean that states can in fact establish state churches and coerce religious orthodoxy? For a more detailed account of this view, see Akhil R. Amar, *The Bill of Rights as a Constitution,* 100 Yale L.J. 1131, 1157 (1991).

Thus, while I have no quarrel with the Court's general proposition that the Establishment Clause "guarantees that government may not coerce anyone to support or participate in religion or its exercise," I see no warrant for expanding the concept of coercion beyond acts backed by threat of penalty—a brand of coercion that, happily, is readily discernible to those of us who have made a career of reading the disciples of Blackstone rather than of Freud. The Framers were indeed opposed to coercion of religious worship by the National Government; but, as their own sponsorship of nonsectarian prayer in public events demonstrates, they understood that "[s]peech is not coercive; the listener may do as he likes." *American Jewish Congress v. Chicago,* 827 F.2d 120, 132 (1987) (Easterbrook, J., dissenting).

The Court relies on our "school prayer" cases. But whatever the merit of those cases, they do not support, much less compel, the Court's psycho-journey. In the first place, *Engel* and *Schempp* do not constitute an exception to the rule, distilled from historical practice, that public ceremonies may include prayer; rather, they simply do not fall within the scope of the rule (for the obvious reason that school instruction is not a public ceremony). Second, we have made clear our understanding that school prayer occurs within a framework in which legal coercion to attend school (*i.e.*, coercion under threat of penalty) provides the ultimate backdrop. [O]ur school prayer cases turn in part on the fact that the classroom is inherently an instructional setting, and daily prayer there—where parents are not present to counter "the students' emulation of teachers as role models and the children's susceptibility to peer pressure," *Edwards v. Aguillard*, 482 U.S. 578, 584 (1987)—might be thought to raise special concerns regarding state interference with the liberty of parents to direct the religious upbringing of their children ***. Voluntary prayer at graduation—a one-time ceremony at which parents, friends, and relatives are present—can hardly be thought to raise the same concerns.

Given the odd basis for the Court's decision, invocations and benedictions will be able to be given at public school graduations next June, as they have for the past century and a half, so long as school authorities make clear that anyone who abstains from screaming in protest does not necessarily participate in the prayers. All that is seemingly needed is an announcement, or perhaps a written insertion at the beginning of the graduation program, to the effect that, while all are asked to rise for the invocation and benediction, none is compelled to join in them, nor will be assumed, by rising, to have done so. That obvious fact recited, the graduates and their parents may proceed to thank God, as Americans have always done, for the blessings He has generously bestowed on them and on their country.

The reader has been told much in this case about the personal interest of Mr. Weisman and his daughter, and very little about the personal interests on the other side. They are not inconsequential. Church and state would not be such a difficult subject if religion were, as the Court apparently thinks it to be, some purely personal avocation that can be indulged entirely in secret, like pornography, in the privacy of one's room. For most believers it is *not* that, and has never been. Religious men and women of almost all denominations have felt it necessary to acknowledge and beseech the blessing of God as a people, and not just as individuals ***. One can believe in the effectiveness of such public worship, or one can deprecate and deride it. But the longstanding American tradition of prayer at official ceremonies displays with unmistakable clarity that the Establishment Clause does not forbid the government to accommodate it.

I must add one final observation: The Founders of our Republic knew the fearsome potential of sectarian religious belief to generate civil dissension and civil strife. And they also knew that nothing, absolutely nothing, is so inclined to foster among religious believers of various faiths a toleration—no, an affection—for one another than voluntarily joining in prayer together, to the God whom they all worship and seek. Needless to say, no one should be compelled to do that, but it is a shame to deprive our public culture of the opportunity, and indeed the encouragement, for people to do it voluntarily. *** To deprive our society of that important unifying mechanism, in order to spare the nonbeliever what seems to me the minimal inconvenience of standing or even sitting in respectful nonparticipation, is as senseless in policy as it is unsupported in law.

Points for Discussion

a. A Question of Tolerance?

Erwin Griswold, the dean of Harvard Law School and later the Solicitor General of the United States, asserted that although religious believers in the majority should respect the views of a non-believer in the minority, a non-believer should reciprocate. In his view, so long as prayers are voluntary, the non-believer "too has the opportunity to be tolerant. He [should allow] the majority of the group to follow their own tradition, perhaps coming to understand and respect what they feel is significant to them." Erwin Griswold, *Absolute in the Dark: A Discussion of the Approach of the Supreme Court to Constitutional Questions*, 8 Utah L. Rev. 167, 177 (1963) (quoted in Erwin Chemerinsky, *Constitutional Law: Principles and Policies* 1221 (3d ed. 2006)). In *Lee*, Justice Kennedy answered this line of reasoning by saying: "What to most believers may seem nothing more than a reasonable request that the nonbeliever respect their religious practices, in a school context may appear to the nonbeliever or dissenter to be an attempt to employ the machinery of the State to enforce a religious orthodoxy." If the believer and non-believer see the matter in different ways, must the non-believer's view prevail? What, if anything, does the Establishment Clause tell us about the answer to this question?

b. Non-Preferentialism and Non-Sectarianism

At the beginning of this Chapter, we considered several different views of the Establishment Clause. Recall that one view, which the Court appeared to endorse in *Everson* and subsequent cases, is sometimes called "separationism." Under this view, the Establishment Clause requires a firm separation between church and state. Another view, which then-Justice Rehnquist advanced in his dissent in *Wallace* and which Justice Scalia arguably advanced in his dissent in *Lee*, is usually called "non-preferentialism." Under this view, the government need not remain neutral as between religion and non-religion, but instead merely must refrain from preferring one religion over another.

The school in *Lee* argued that the graduation prayer was permissible because it was non-sectarian and non-denominational. The school thus advanced a non-preferentialist view of the Establishment Clause. The Court concluded that even such prayers are impermissible in this context, in part because they (by definition) do not include, at the very least, the views of those who adhere to no religion at all. The Court therefore advanced a separationist view of the Establishment Clause.

If the Court had reached the opposite conclusion—if, for example, it had accepted the non-preferentialist view of the Establishment Clause—then how would it have determined whether a challenged prayer in fact was non-sectarian and non-denominational? Is it clear that the prayer at issue in *Lee* was truly non-sectarian and non-denominational? Did it, for example, embrace the views of adherents of religions, such as some forms of Hinduism, that believe that there is more than one God? What religions "count" for these purposes? Should courts be engaged in such an inquiry?

c. Prayer in School and Free Speech

The foregoing cases show that the government may not require or approve official prayer on public school grounds.   Does this mean that government also may (or must) ban all voluntary prayer or religious speech on school grounds?   Or would such a ban itself violate the First Amendment?   In *Good News Club v. Milford*, 533 U.S. 98 (2001), a public school allowed various community groups to use its building after school hours, but prohibited the petitioner from using the school because it was a religious organization. The Supreme Court held that the ban violated the First Amendment's protection for the freedom of speech because the ban constituted viewpoint discrimination, and that such discrimination was not required to avoid violating the Establishment Clause.   See also *Rosenberger v. Rector and Visitors of the University of Virginia*, 515 U.S. 819 (1995), which we considered earlier in this Chapter.

d. Student-Led Prayer at School Events

In *Lee*, the prayer at an official school event was led by a member of the clergy.   In *Santa Fe Independent School District v. Doe*, 530 U.S. 290 (2000), the Court considered a public high school's program authorizing the student body to vote each year on whether to choose a student to deliver, before each varsity football game, a "brief invocation and/or message [to] solemnize the event," and to vote on who the student should be.   The program replaced an earlier program under which a student "chaplain" led prayers before each football game.   (That program was enjoined after the Court's decision in *Lee*.)   The Court held that the program violated the Establishment Clause, concluding that the "specific purpose of the policy was to preserve a popular state-sponsored religious practice."   The Court rejected the argument that the program was valid because it simply permitted the private speech of students rather than official speech, noting that the program was "authorized by a government policy," took place "on governmental property at government-sponsored school-related events," and relied on a "majoritarian process" that guaranteed "by definition [that] minority candidates will never prevail and that their views will be effectively silenced."

Everyone who has read or seen Jerome Lawrence's and Robert Edwin Lee's play *Inherit the Wind*, which recounted the "Scopes trial" and the legal battle over Tennessee's "monkey law," knows that many states once banned the teaching in public schools of the theory of evolution.   In *Epperson v. Arkansas*, 393 U.S. 97 (1968), the Court held that an Arkansas law forbidding the teaching of evolution in public schools and universities violated the First and Fourteenth Amendments.   The Court began by asserting the rule of neutrality:

> Government in our democracy, state and national, must be neutral in matters of religious theory, doctrine, and practice.   It may not be hostile to any religion or to the advocacy of [non]-religion; and it may not aid, foster, or promote one religion or religious theory against another or even against the militant opposite.   The First Amendment mandates governmental neutrality between religion and religion, and between religion and nonreligion.

The Court then invalidated the statute as a violation of that rule:

> [T]here can be no doubt that Arkansas has sought to prevent its teachers from discussing the theory of evolution because it is contrary to the belief of some that the Book of Genesis must be the exclusive source of doctrine as to the origin of man. No suggestion has been made that Arkansas' law may be justified by considerations of state policy other than the religious views of some of its citizens. It is clear that fundamentalist sectarian conviction was and is the law's reason for existence. Its antecedent, Tennessee's "monkey law," candidly stated its purpose: to make it unlawful "to teach any theory that denies the story of the Divine Creation of man as taught in the Bible, and to teach instead that man has descended from a lower order of animals." Perhaps the sensational publicity attendant upon the Scopes trial induced Arkansas to adopt less explicit language. It eliminated Tennessee's reference to "the story of the Divine Creation of man" as taught in the Bible, but there is no doubt that the motivation for the law was the same: to suppress the teaching of a theory which, it was thought, "denied" the divine creation of man.

> Arkansas' law cannot be defended as an act of religious neutrality. Arkansas did not seek to excise from the curricula of its schools and universities all discussion of the origin of man. The law's effort was confined to an attempt to blot out a particular theory because of its supposed conflict with the Biblical account, literally read.

In the decades after the Court's decision in *Epperson*, several states sought to include in their public school curricula consideration of "creationism"—that is, the study of the Biblical account of the creation of the earth and all of its species—alongside consideration of the theory of evolution. Do such policies satisfy the rule of neutrality that the Court enforced in *Epperson*? The case that follows addresses that question.

Edwards v. Aguillard

482 U.S. 578 (1987)

Justice BRENNAN delivered the opinion of the Court.

The question for decision is whether Louisiana's "Balanced Treatment for Creation-Science and Evolution-Science in Public School Instruction" Act (Creationism Act), La.Rev. Stat.Ann. §§ 17:286.1-17:286.7, is facially invalid as violative of the Establishment Clause of the First Amendment. The Creationism Act forbids the teaching of the theory of evolution in public schools unless accompanied by instruction in "creation science." § 17:286.4A. No school is required to teach evolution or creation science. If either is taught, however, the other must also be taught. The theories of evolution and creation science are statutorily defined as "the scientific evidences for [creation or evolution] and inferences from those scientific evidences." §§ 17.286.3(2) and (3). Appellees, who include parents of children attending Louisiana public schools, Louisiana teachers, and religious leaders, challenged the constitutionality of the Act ***.

The Court has applied [the three-pronged *Lemon* test] to determine whether legislation comports with the Establishment Clause. *** *Lemon's* first prong focuses on the purpose that animated adoption of the Act. *** In this case, appellants have identified no clear secular purpose for the Louisiana Act. True, the Act's stated purpose is to protect academic freedom. La.Rev.Stat.Ann. § 17:286.2. *** While the Court is normally deferential to a State's articulation of a secular purpose, it is required that the statement of such purpose be sincere and not a sham. [R]equiring schools to teach creation science with evolution does not advance academic freedom. The Act does not grant teachers a flexibility that they did not already possess to supplant the present science curriculum with the presentation of theories, besides evolution, about the origin of life. Furthermore, the goal of basic "fairness" is hardly furthered by the Act's discriminatory preference for the teaching of creation science and against the teaching of evolution.

> **Take Note**
>
> The Court asserts that the Act creates a "discriminatory preference" in favor of creation science. Can you articulate in what way the Act "discriminates" against the teaching of evolution? Do you agree that the statute "discriminates"?

If the Louisiana Legislature's purpose was solely to maximize the comprehensiveness and effectiveness of science instruction, it would have encouraged the teaching of all scientific theories about the origins of humankind. But under the Act's requirements, teachers who were once free to teach any and all facets of this subject are now unable to do so. *** Thus we agree with the Court of Appeals' conclusion that the Act does not serve to protect academic freedom, but has the distinctly different purpose of discrediting "evolution by counterbalancing its teaching at every turn with the teaching of creationism." 765 F.2d, at 1257.

[W]e need not be blind in this case to the legislature's preeminent religious purpose in enacting this statute. There is a historic and contemporaneous link between the teachings of certain religious denominations and the teaching of evolution. [See *Epperson v. Arkansas*, 393 U.S. 97 (1968).] The preeminent purpose of the Louisiana Legislature was clearly to advance the religious viewpoint that a supernatural being created humankind. *** The legislative history [reveals] that the term "creation science," as contemplated by the legislature that adopted this Act, embodies the religious belief that a supernatural creator was responsible for the creation of humankind.

Furthermore, it is not happenstance that the legislature required the teaching of a theory that coincided with this religious view. The legislative history documents that the Act's primary purpose was to change the science curriculum of public schools in order to provide persuasive advantage to a particular religious doctrine that rejects the factual basis of evolution in its entirety. The sponsor of the Creationism Act, Senator Keith, explained during the legislative hearings that his disdain for the theory of evolution resulted from the support that evolution supplied to views contrary to his own religious beliefs. [He] repeatedly stated that scientific evidence supporting his religious views should be included in the public school curriculum to redress the fact that the theory of evolution incidentally coincided with what he characterized as religious beliefs antithetical to his own. The legislation therefore sought to alter the science curriculum to reflect endorsement of a religious view that is antagonistic to the theory of evolution.

> **Food for Thought**
>
> The Court relies heavily on the views expressed by the sponsor of the bill in the state senate. Is it appropriate to put such heavy reliance on the views of one legislator? Isn't it possible that other members of the legislature voted for the bill for entirely different reasons? If so, can you think of any secular reasons that one might have had for supporting the bill?

[Accordingly,] the Creationism Act is designed *either* to promote the theory of creation science which embodies a particular religious tenet by requiring that creation science be taught whenever evolution is taught *or* to prohibit the teaching of a scientific theory disfavored by certain religious sects by forbidding the teaching of evolution when creation science is not also taught. The Establishment Clause, however, "forbids *alike* the preference of a religious doctrine *or* the prohibition of theory which is deemed antagonistic to a particular dogma." *Epperson*, 393 U.S. at 106-107 (emphasis added). Because the primary purpose of the Creationism Act is to advance a particular religious belief, the Act endorses religion in violation of the First Amendment.

We do not imply that a legislature could never require that scientific critiques of prevailing scientific theories be taught. [T]eaching a variety of scientific theories about the origins of humankind to schoolchildren might be validly done with the clear secular intent of enhancing the effectiveness of science instruction. But because the primary purpose of the Creationism Act is to endorse a particular religious doctrine, the Act furthers religion in violation of the Establishment Clause.

[Justice POWELL'S concurring opinion and Justice WHITE's opinion concurring in the judgment are omitted.]

Justice SCALIA, with whom THE CHIEF JUSTICE joins, dissenting.

I doubt whether [the] "purpose" requirement of *Lemon* is a proper interpretation of the Constitution; but even if it were, I could not agree with the Court's assessment that the requirement was not satisfied here. *** We have relatively little information upon which to judge the motives of those who supported the Act. *** Nevertheless, there is ample evidence that the majority is wrong in holding that the Balanced Treatment Act is without secular purpose. *** Senator Keith and his witnesses testified essentially: (1) There are two and only two scientific explanations for the beginning of life—evolution and creation science. *** Since there are only two possible explanations of the origin of life, any evidence that tends to disprove the theory of evolution necessarily tends to prove the theory of creation science, and vice versa. (2) The body of scientific evidence supporting creation science is as strong as that supporting evolution. *** Evolution is not a scientific "fact," since it cannot actually be observed in a laboratory. Rather, evolution is merely a scientific theory or "guess" [and] a very bad guess at that. (3) Students exposed to [creation science] better understand the current state of scientific evidence about the origin of life. (4) Although creation science is educationally valuable and strictly scientific, it is now being censored from or misrepresented in the public schools. (5) The censorship of creation science [deprives] students of knowledge of one of the two scientific explanations for the origin of life and leads them to believe that evolution is proven fact; thus, their education suffers and they are wrongly taught that science has proved their religious beliefs false.

> **Food for Thought**
>
> Does the question whether the enacting legislature had a secular purpose turn on the validity of the evidence on which the legislature relied? Must creation science be a "legitimate" science in order to attribute the secular purpose that Justice Scalia says existed? If so, are courts competent to make such judgments?

We have no way of knowing, of course, how many legislators believed the testimony of Senator Keith and his witnesses. But in the absence of evidence to the contrary, we have to assume that many of them did. Given that assumption, the Court today plainly errs in holding that the Louisiana Legislature passed the Balanced Treatment Act for exclusively religious purposes.

I can only attribute [the Court's rejection of this legislative history and the Act's stated purpose] to an intellectual predisposition created by the facts and the legend of *Scopes v. State*, 154 Tenn. 105 (1927)—an instinctive reaction that any governmentally imposed requirements bearing upon the teaching of evolution must be a manifestation of Christian fundamentalist repression. In this case, however, it seems to me the Court's position is the repressive one. The people of Louisiana, including those who are Christian fundamentalists, are quite entitled, as a secular matter, to have whatever scientific evidence there may be against evolution presented in their schools, just as Mr. Scopes was entitled to present whatever scientific evidence there was for it. *** Because I believe that the Balanced Treatment Act had a secular purpose, which is all the first component of the *Lemon* test requires, I would reverse the judgment of the Court of Appeals and remand for further consideration.

I have to this point assumed the validity of the *Lemon* "purpose" test. In fact, however, I think [it] is "a constitutional theory [that] has no basis in the history of the amendment it seeks to interpret, is difficult to apply and yields unprincipled results." *Wallace v. Jaffree*, 472 U.S., at 112 (REHNQUIST, J., dissenting). *** Our cases interpreting and applying the purpose test have made such a maze of the Establishment Clause that even the most conscientious governmental officials can only guess what motives will be held unconstitutional.

But the difficulty of knowing what vitiating purpose one is looking for is as nothing compared with the difficulty of knowing how or where to find it. For while it is possible to discern the objective "purpose" of a statute (*i.e.,* the public good at which its provisions appear to be directed), or even the formal motivation for a statute where that is explicitly set forth (as it was, to no avail, here), discerning the subjective motivation of those enacting the statute is, to be honest, almost always an impossible task. The number of possible motivations, to begin with, is not binary, or indeed even finite. *** To look for *the sole purpose* of even a single legislator is probably to look for something that does not exist. *** Putting that problem aside, however, where ought we to look for the individual legislator's purpose? *** Legislative histories can be contrived and sanitized, favorable media coverage orchestrated, and postenactment recollections conveniently distorted. [And we] must still confront the question (yet to be addressed in any of our cases) how *many* of them must have the invalidating intent. Because there are no good answers to these questions, this Court has recognized [that] determining the subjective intent of legislators is a perilous enterprise.

In the past we have attempted to justify our embarrassing Establishment Clause jurisprudence on the ground that it "sacrifices clarity and predictability for flexibility." *Committee for Public Education & Religious Liberty v. Regan,* 444 U.S. 646, 662 (1980). *** I think it time that we sacrifice some "flexibility" for "clarity and predictability." Abandoning *Lemon*'s purpose test [would] be a good place to start.

———

Points for Discussion

a. Teaching Creationism

The Court in *Epperson* invalidated a state law prohibiting the teaching of the theory of evolution. Is a statute requiring the teaching of creationism equivalent, for Establishment Clause purposes, to a statute banning the teaching of evolution? Could a state constitutionally enact a statute that permits, but does not require, science teachers to teach creationism? (Can you articulate how such a statute would be different from the statute at issue in *Edwards*?) Similarly, in the absence of any statutory guidance, could a teacher in a public school science class constitutionally teach his or her students that the account in Genesis, and not the theory of evolution, explains the origin of the human species? If not, then how could the statute at issue in *Edwards* be constitutional?

b. Purpose and the *Lemon* Test

The Court in *Edwards* considered only the first prong of the *Lemon* test, invalidating the statute as lacking a valid secular purpose. Justice Scalia asserted that (at least) this prong of the *Lemon* test should be abandoned. Do you agree that it is usually impossible to determine the "actual" purpose that motivated a legislature to enact a statute? Even if you agree with Justice Scalia that the inquiry is fraught with difficulties, is there an argument that the inquiry nevertheless is essential in the Establishment Clause context?

c. Teaching "Intelligent Design"

After the decision in *Edwards*, advocates of teaching creationism in public schools began an effort to encourage the teaching of the theory of "intelligent design," which posits that there are natural systems that cannot be adequately explained by undirected natural forces and that thus must be the product of design by some intelligent agent. Does the teaching in public schools of the theory of intelligent design—either alone or alongside the theory of evolution—violate the Establishment Clause? The only court to address the question concluded that it does. See *Kitzmiller v. Dover Area School District,* 400 F. Supp. 2d 707 (M.D. Pa. 2005). Do you agree?

So far, the cases that we have considered in this section have involved the public school context. Is that context unique? Or do the rules that the Court has announced for religious activities in public schools apply equally to governmental actions outside of the school context?

Marsh v. Chambers

463 U.S. 783 (1983)

Chief Justice BURGER delivered the opinion of the Court.

The Nebraska Legislature begins each of its sessions with a prayer offered by a chaplain who is chosen biennially by the Executive Board of the Legislative Council and paid out of public funds. Robert E. Palmer, a Presbyterian minister, has served as chaplain since 1965 at a salary of $319.75 per month for each month the legislature is in session.

Ernest Chambers is a member of the Nebraska Legislature and a taxpayer of Nebraska. Claiming that the Nebraska Legislature's chaplaincy practice violates the Establishment Clause of the First Amendment, he brought this action under 42 U.S.C. § 1983, seeking to enjoin enforcement of the practice. ***

The opening of sessions of legislative and other deliberative public bodies with prayer is deeply embedded in the history and tradition of this country. From colonial times through the founding of the Republic and ever since, the practice of legislative prayer has coexisted with the principles of disestablishment and religious freedom. In the very courtrooms in which the United States District Judge and later three Circuit Judges heard and decided this case, the proceedings opened with an announcement that concluded, "God save the United States and this Honorable Court." The same invocation occurs at all sessions of this Court.

The tradition in many of the colonies was, of course, linked to an established church, but the Continental Congress, beginning in 1774, adopted the traditional procedure of opening its sessions with a prayer offered by a paid chaplain. See *e.g.,* 1 J. of the Continental Cong. 26 (1774). Although prayers were not offered during the Constitutional Convention, the First Congress, as one of its early items of business, adopted the policy of selecting a chaplain to open each session with prayer. Thus, on April 7, 1789, the Senate appointed a committee "to take under consideration the manner of electing Chaplains." J. of the Sen. 10. On April 9, 1789, a similar committee was appointed by the House of Representatives. On April 25, 1789, the Senate elected its first chaplain, J. of the Sen. 16;

the House followed suit on May 1, 1789, J. of the H.R. 26. A statute providing for the payment of these chaplains was enacted into law on Sept. 22, 1789. 2 Annals of Cong. 2180; 1 Stat. 71.

On Sept. 25, 1789, three days after Congress authorized the appointment of paid chaplains, final agreement was reached on the language of the Bill of Rights, J. of the Sen. 88; J. of the H.R. 121. Clearly the men who wrote the First Amendment Religion Clause did not view paid legislative chaplains and opening prayers as a violation of that Amendment, for the practice of opening sessions with prayer has continued without interruption ever since that early session of Congress. It has also been followed consistently in most of the states, including Nebraska, where the institution of opening legislative sessions with prayer was adopted even before the State attained statehood. Nebraska Journal of the Council at the First Regular Session of the General Assembly 16 (Jan. 22, 1855).

Standing alone, historical patterns cannot justify contemporary violations of constitutional guarantees, but there is far more here than simply historical patterns. In this context, historical evidence sheds light not only on what the draftsmen intended the Establishment Clause to mean, but also on how they thought that Clause applied to the practice authorized by the First Congress—their actions reveal their intent. An act "passed by the first Congress assembled under the Constitution, many of whose members had taken part in framing that instrument, [is] contemporaneous and weighty evidence of its true meaning." *Wisconsin v. Pelican Ins. Co.,* 127 U.S. 265, 297 (1888).

Food for Thought

The First Congress passed the Bill of Rights and submitted it to the states for ratification. Is it possible that the Bill of Rights prohibits some of the actions in which the First Congress engaged? If the original meaning is the touchstone of constitutional meaning, should the Court consider what members of the First Congress intended, or should it instead consider what the words would objectively have meant to the ratifiers? And is there a difference between how the drafters and ratifiers *expected* a provision to apply and how it *does* apply to modern circumstances?

No more is Nebraska's practice of over a century, consistent with two centuries of national practice, to be cast aside. It can hardly be thought that in the same week Members of the First Congress voted to appoint and to pay a Chaplain for each House and also voted to approve the draft of the First Amendment for submission to the States, they intended the Establishment Clause of the Amendment to forbid what they had just declared acceptable. In applying the First Amendment to the states through the Fourteenth Amendment, it would be incongruous to interpret that clause as imposing more stringent First Amendment limits on the States than the draftsmen imposed on the Federal Government.

This unique history leads us to accept the interpretation of the First Amendment draftsmen who saw no real threat to the Establishment Clause arising from a practice of prayer similar to that now challenged. We conclude that legislative prayer presents no more potential for establishment than the provision of school transportation, *Everson v. Board of*

Education, 330 U.S. 1 (1946), beneficial grants for higher education, *Tilton v. Richardson,* 403 U.S. 672 (1971), or tax exemptions for religious organizations, *Walz v. Tax Comm'n,* 397 U.S. 664, 678 (1970).

Justice BRENNAN, with whom Justice MARSHALL joins, dissenting.

The most commonly cited formulation of prevailing Establishment Clause doctrine is found in *Lemon v. Kurtzman,* 403 U.S. 602 (1971):

> "First, the statute [at issue] must have a secular legislative purpose; second, its principal or primary effect must be one that neither advances nor inhibits religion; finally, the statute must not foster 'an excessive government entanglement with religion.' "

That the "purpose" of legislative prayer is preeminently religious rather than secular seems to me to be self-evident. "To invoke Divine guidance on a public body entrusted with making the laws," is nothing but a religious act. Moreover, whatever secular functions legislative prayer might play—formally opening the legislative session, getting the members of the body to quiet down, and imbuing them with a sense of seriousness and high purpose—could so plainly be performed in a purely nonreligious fashion that to claim a secular purpose for the prayer is an insult to the perfectly honorable individuals who instituted and continue the practice.

The "primary effect" of legislative prayer is also clearly religious. *** More importantly, invocations in Nebraska's legislative halls explicitly link religious belief and observance to the power and prestige of the State. "[T]he mere appearance of a joint exercise of legislative authority by Church and State provides a significant symbolic benefit to religion in the minds of some by reason of the power conferred." *Larkin v. Grendel's Den,* 459 U.S. 116 (1982).

Finally, there can be no doubt that the practice of legislative prayer leads to excessive "entanglement" between the State and religion. <u>Lemon</u> pointed out that "entanglement" can take two forms: First, a state statute or program might involve the state impermissibly in monitoring and overseeing religious affairs. In the case of legislative prayer, the process of choosing a "suitable" chaplain, whether on a permanent or rotating basis, and insuring that the chaplain limits himself or herself to "suitable" prayers, involves precisely the sort of supervision that agencies of government should if at all possible avoid.

Second, excessive "entanglement" might arise out of "the divisive political potential" of a state statute or program. *** In this case, this second aspect of entanglement is also clear. The controversy between Senator Chambers and his colleagues, which had reached the stage of difficulty and rancor long before this lawsuit was brought, has split the Nebraska Legislature precisely on issues of religion and religious conformity. The record in this case also reports a series of instances, involving legislators other than Senator Chambers, in which invocations by Reverend Palmer and others led to controversy along religious lines. And in general, the history of legislative prayer has been far more eventful—and divisive—than a hasty reading of the Court's opinion might indicate.

Justice STEVENS, dissenting.

In a democratically elected legislature, the religious beliefs of the chaplain tend to reflect the faith of the majority of the lawmakers' constituents. Prayers may be said by a Catholic priest in the Massachusetts Legislature and by a Presbyterian minister in the Nebraska Legislature, but I would not expect to find a Jehovah's Witness or a disciple of Mary Baker Eddy or the Reverend Moon serving as the official chaplain in any state legislature. Regardless of the motivation of the majority that exercises the power to appoint the chaplain, it seems plain to me that the designation of a member of one religious faith to serve as the sole official chaplain of a state legislature for a period of 16 years constitutes the preference of one faith over another in violation of the Establishment Clause of the First Amendment.

———————————

Points for Discussion

a. School Prayer and Legislative Prayer

Although the Supreme Court held in *Marsh* that Nebraska can begin its legislative sessions with a prayer, we have also seen that it has concluded that the Establishment Clause bars almost all kinds of official authorized or approved prayers in public elementary and secondary schools. The Court decided the seminal case concerning prayer in schools— *Engel v. Vitale*—more than twenty years before it decided *Marsh*. The majority in *Marsh*, however, did not cite *Engel* in its opinion. Should the Court in *Marsh* have concluded that *Engel* was controlling?

Was there anything in the Court's opinion in *Engel* or its progeny to suggest that the school context is unique? For example, are schools different because they teach impressionable children? Or because school attendance is generally mandatory? Or because schools form a traditional melting pot for society? Consider the view that Justice Brennan expressed in *Edwards v. Aguillard*, several years after the decision in *Marsh*:

> The Court has been particularly vigilant in monitoring compliance with the Establishment Clause in elementary and secondary schools. Families entrust public schools with the education of their children, but condition their trust on the understanding that the classroom will not purposely be used to advance religious views that may conflict with the private beliefs of the student and his or her family. Students in such institutions are impressionable and their attendance is involuntary. The State exerts great authority and coercive power through mandatory attendance requirements, and because of the students' emulation of teachers as role models and the children's susceptibility to peer pressure.

Edwards v. Aguillard, 482 U.S. 578 (1987).

Did the Court in *Marsh* have an obligation to specify that schools are in fact different? If you conclude that there is no meaningful difference between the school context and the legislative context, does that mean that the school cases were decided incorrectly? Or was it *Marsh* that was decided incorrectly? In any event, if evidence emerged that prayer was common in public schools as a matter of history and tradition, would the decision in *Marsh* require the Court to overrule *Engel*?

b. The Rule of *Marsh*

The Court stated in *Marsh* that legislative prayers are "deeply embedded in the history and tradition of this country." Does this language suggest that any religious activities in governmental institutions that have a long history and tradition are constitutional under the Establishment Clause? Must the tradition extend to the time before the First Amendment (or Fourteenth Amendment, in the case of actions by the states) was ratified? Are history and tradition relevant because they help us to determine the original meaning of the Establishment Clause? Or are they relevant because, regardless of the original meaning of the Clause, a consistently observed tradition can become constitutional simply by virtue of its repetition?

What history and traditions should the Court consider in deciding the constitutionality of practices under the Establishment Clause? Consider Justice Souter's view in *Lee v. Weisman*, which we considered earlier in this Chapter:

> To be sure, the leaders of the young Republic engaged in some of the practices that separationists like Jefferson and Madison criticized. The First Congress did hire institutional chaplains, and Presidents Washington and Adams unapologetically marked days of "public thanksgiving and prayer." Yet in the face of the separationist dissent, those practices prove, at best, that the Framers simply did not share a common understanding of the Establishment Clause, and, at worst, that they, like other politicians, could raise constitutional ideals one day and turn their backs on them the next. *** Ten years after proposing the First Amendment, Congress passed the Alien and Sedition Acts, measures patently unconstitutional by modern standards. If the early Congress's political actions were determinative, and not merely relevant, evidence of constitutional meaning, we would have to gut our current First Amendment doctrine to make room for political censorship.

Lee v. Weisman, 505 U.S. 577 (1992) (Souter, J., concurring). Can the Court tell the difference between history that shows the exception and history that shows the rule?

c. History v. the *Lemon* Test

Chief Justice Burger's opinion resolved this case based upon the original meaning (or perhaps intent) of the Establishment Clause, and he did not attempt to apply the *Lemon* test (which, you might recall, he had authored). Justice Brennan, by contrast, relied on the *Lemon* test. Was his application of the *Lemon* test correct? If the *Lemon* test produces results that are inconsistent with history, tradition, or the original expected application of the Establishment Clause, is the *Lemon* test problematic?

d. Separationism vs. Non-Preferentialism

Justice Brennan's dissent in *Marsh* advanced the classic view of separationism—that is, he asserted that the Establishment Clause prohibits the government from preferring religion over non-religion. Justice Stevens's dissent, by contrast, rejected the practice as inconsistent with even a non-preferentialist view—that is, he asserted that the Establishment Clause at least requires the government to refrain from preferring one religion over another. Which view of the Establishment Clause did Chief Justice Burger advance?

e. The Continuing Vitality of <u>Marsh</u>

In *McCreary County, Kentucky v. American Civil Liberties Union, Kentucky*, 545 U.S. 844 (2005), which we will consider later in this Chapter, the Court held that a public display of the Ten Commandments violated the Establishment Clause. In his opinion for the Court, Justice Souter stated:

> At least since *Everson v. Board of Ed. of Ewing*, 330 U.S. 1 (1947), it has been clear that Establishment Clause doctrine lacks the comfort of categorical absolutes. In special instances we have found good reason to hold governmental action legitimate even where its manifest purpose was presumably religious. See, *e.g.*, *Marsh v. Chambers*, 463 U.S. 783 (1983) (upholding legislative prayer despite its religious nature). No such reasons present themselves here.

Does this suggest that the approach of the Court in <u>Marsh</u> is confined to "special" (and thus presumably rare) instances? Or are similar examples of religion in governmental institutions—such as the friezes, oaths, and prayers at the Supreme Court described at the start of this section—so clearly unproblematic that they are seldom litigated?

———————

The cases that we have considered so far in this section have concerned religious activities by government or government actors. The following cases concern a particular manifestation of this phenomenon: the placement of religious symbols on government property. As you will see, the early cases apply the <u>Lemon</u> test, while the later cases are less likely to do so. But it is still possible to discern rules from the cases. For the most part, the Court has held that religious symbols are permissible if they have a secular purpose and do not endorse a specific religion or religion in general. As you read the cases, consider (1) whether this is a sensible approach and (2) whether the Court has faithfully and consistently followed this approach.

———————

Lynch v. Donnelly

465 U.S. 668 (1984)

THE CHIEF JUSTICE delivered the opinion of the Court.

Each year, in cooperation with the downtown retail merchants' association, the City of Pawtucket, Rhode Island, erects a Christmas display as part of its observance of the Christmas holiday season. The display is situated in a park owned by a nonprofit organization and located in the heart of the shopping district. The display is essentially like those to be found in hundreds of towns or cities across the Nation—often on public grounds—during the Christmas season. The Pawtucket display comprises many of the figures and decorations traditionally associated with Christmas, including, among other things, a Santa Claus house, reindeer pulling Santa's sleigh, candy-striped poles, a Christmas tree, carolers, cutout figures representing such characters as a clown, an elephant, and a teddy bear, hundreds of colored lights, a large banner that reads "SEASONS GREETINGS," and the crèche at issue here. All components of this display are owned by the City.

The crèche, which has been included in the display for 40 or more years, consists of the traditional figures, including the Infant Jesus, Mary and Joseph, angels, shepherds, kings, and animals, all ranging in height from 5" to 5'. In 1973, when the present crèche was acquired, it cost the City $1365; it now is valued at $200. The erection and dismantling of the crèche costs the City about $20 per year; nominal expenses are incurred in lighting the crèche. No money has been expended on its maintenance for the past 10 years.

Respondents, Pawtucket residents and individual members of the Rhode Island affiliate of the American Civil Liberties Union, and the affiliate itself, brought this action [claiming that] the crèche in the display violates the Establishment Clause which is binding on the states through the Fourteenth Amendment. ***

This Court has explained that the purpose of the Establishment and Free Exercise Clauses of the First Amendment is "to prevent, as far as possible, the intrusion of either [the church or the state] into the precincts of the other." *Lemon v. Kurtzman*, 403 U.S. 602, 614 (1971). At the same time, however, the Court has recognized that "total separation is not possible in an absolute sense. Some relationship between government and religious organizations is inevitable." *Ibid*. In every Establishment Clause case, we must reconcile the inescapable tension between the objective of preventing unnecessary intrusion of either the church or the state upon the other, and the reality that, as the Court has so often noted, total separation of the two is not possible.

There is an unbroken history of official acknowledgment by all three branches of government of the role of religion in American life from at least 1789. *** Beginning in the early colonial period long before Independence, a day of Thanksgiving was celebrated as a religious holiday to give thanks for the bounties of Nature as gifts from God. *** Executive Orders and other official announcements of Presidents and of the Congress have proclaimed both Christmas and Thanksgiving National Holidays in religious terms. And, by Acts of Congress, it has long been the practice that federal employees are released from duties on these National Holidays, while being paid from the same public revenues that provide the compensation of the Chaplains of the Senate and the House and the military services. Thus, it is clear that Government has long recognized—indeed it has subsidized—holidays with religious significance. Other examples of reference to our religious heritage are found in the statutorily prescribed national motto "In God We Trust," 36 U.S.C. § 186, which Congress and the President mandated for our currency, see 31 U.S.C. § 324, and in the language "One nation under God," as part of the Pledge of Allegiance to the American flag. *** Art galleries supported by public revenues display religious paintings of the 15th and 16th centuries, predominantly inspired by one religious faith. *** One cannot look at even this brief resume without finding that our history is pervaded by expressions of religious beliefs ***. Equally pervasive is the evidence of accommodation of all faiths and all forms of religious expression, and hostility toward none.

This history may help explain why the Court consistently has declined to take a rigid, absolutist view of the Establishment Clause. *** Rather than mechanically invalidating all governmental conduct or statutes that confer benefits or give special recognition to religion in general or to one faith—as an absolutist approach would dictate—the Court has scrutinized challenged legislation or official conduct to determine whether, in reality, it establishes a religion or religious faith, or tends to do so. In each case, the inquiry calls for line drawing; no fixed, *per se* rule can be framed.

In the line-drawing process we have often found it useful to inquire whether the challenged law or conduct has a secular purpose, whether its principal or primary effect is to advance or inhibit religion, and whether it creates an excessive entanglement of government with religion. <u>Lemon</u>. But, we have repeatedly emphasized our unwillingness to be confined to any single test or criterion in this sensitive area. *** We did not, for example, consider that analysis relevant in *Marsh v. Chambers,* 463 U.S. 783 (1983). ***

The District Court inferred from the religious nature of the crèche that the City has no secular purpose for the display. In so doing, it rejected the City's claim that its reasons for including the crèche are essentially the same as its reasons for sponsoring the display as a whole. The District Court plainly erred by focusing almost exclusively on the crèche. When viewed in the proper context of the Christmas Holiday season, it is apparent that, on this record, there is insufficient evidence to establish that the inclusion of the crèche is a purposeful or surreptitious effort to express some kind of subtle governmental advocacy of a particular religious message. In a pluralistic society a variety of motives and purposes are implicated. The City, like the Congresses and Presidents, however, has principally taken note of a significant historical religious event long celebrated in the Western World. The crèche in the display depicts the historical origins of this traditional event long recognized as a National Holiday.

Take Note

The Court concludes here that the display of the crèche has the legitimate secular purpose of celebrating and depicting the origins of Christmas. Must the Court rely, in reaching this conclusion, on the premise that Christmas is not a religious holiday? If so, do you agree? By contrast, if the Court views Christmas as a religious holiday, then how can official governmental celebration of the holiday have a secular purpose?

The narrow question is whether there is a secular purpose for Pawtucket's display of the crèche. The display is sponsored by the City to celebrate the Holiday and to depict the origins of that Holiday. These are legitimate secular purposes. The District Court's inference, drawn from the religious nature of the crèche, that the City has no secular purpose was, on this record, clearly erroneous.

The District Court found that the primary effect of including the crèche is to confer a substantial and impermissible benefit on religion in general and on the Christian faith in particular. Comparisons of the relative benefits to religion of different forms of governmental support are elusive and difficult to make. But to conclude that the primary effect of including the crèche is to advance religion in violation of the Establishment Clause would require that we view it as more beneficial to and more an endorsement of religion, for example, than expenditure of large sums of public money for textbooks supplied throughout the country to students attending church-sponsored schools, *Board of Education v. Allen,* 392 U.S. 236 (1968); expenditure of public funds for transportation of students to church-sponsored schools, *Everson v. Board of Education,* 330 U.S. 1 (1947); federal grants for college buildings of church-sponsored institutions of higher education combining secular and religious education, *Tilton v. Richardson,* 403 U.S. 672 (1971); noncategorical grants to church-sponsored colleges and universities, *Roemer v. Board of Public Works,* 426 U.S. 736 (1976); and the tax exemptions for church properties sanctioned in *Walz v. Tax Commission,* 397 U.S. 664, 671 (1970). It would also require that we view it as more of an endorsement of religion than the Sunday Closing Laws upheld in *McGowan v. Maryland,* 366 U.S. 420 (1961); the release time program for religious training in *Zorach v. Clauson,* 343 U.S. 306, 314, 315 (1952); and the legislative prayers upheld in <u>Marsh</u>.

> **Food for Thought**
>
> Most (though not all) of the cases that the Court cites here involved government aid to religious institutions, rather than religious displays by government institutions. Is there a difference in the way that those types of activities appear to "endorse" religion?

We are unable to discern a greater aid to religion deriving from inclusion of the crèche than from these benefits and endorsements previously held not violative of the Establishment Clause. What was said about the legislative prayers in <u>Marsh</u> and implied about the Sunday Closing Laws in <u>McGowan</u> is true of the City's inclusion of the crèche: its "reason or effect merely happens to coincide or harmonize with the tenets of [some] religions."

The dissent asserts some observers may perceive that the City has aligned itself with the Christian faith by including a Christian symbol in its display and that this serves to advance religion. We can assume, *arguendo*, that the display advances religion in a sense; but our precedents plainly contemplate that on occasion some advancement of religion will result from governmental action. *** Here, whatever benefit to one faith or religion or to all religions, is indirect, remote and incidental; display of the crèche is no more an advancement or endorsement of religion than the Congressional and Executive recognition of the origins of the Holiday itself as "Christ's Mass," or the exhibition of literally hundreds of religious paintings in governmentally supported museums.

The District Court found that there had been no administrative entanglement between religion and state resulting from the City's ownership and use of the crèche. But it went on to hold that some political divisiveness was engendered by this litigation. Coupled with its finding of an impermissible sectarian purpose and effect, this persuaded the court that there was "excessive entanglement." The Court of Appeals expressly declined to accept the District Court's finding that inclusion of the crèche has caused political divisiveness along religious lines, and noted that this Court has never held that political divisiveness alone was sufficient to invalidate government conduct.

Entanglement is a question of kind and degree. In this case, however, there is no reason to disturb the District Court's finding on the absence of administrative entanglement. There is no evidence of contact with church authorities concerning the content or design of the exhibit prior to or since Pawtucket's purchase of the crèche. No expenditures for maintenance of the crèche have been necessary; and since the City owns the crèche, now valued at $200, the tangible material it contributes is *de minimis*. In many respects the display requires far less ongoing, day-to-day interaction between church and state than religious paintings in public galleries. There is nothing here, of course, like the "comprehensive, discriminating, and continuing state surveillance" or the "enduring entanglement" present in *Lemon*.

We are satisfied that the City has a secular purpose for including the crèche, that the City has not impermissibly advanced religion, and that including the crèche does not create excessive entanglement between religion and government.

The display engenders a friendly community spirit of good will in keeping with the season. *** It would be ironic [if] the inclusion of a single symbol of a particular historic religious event, as part of a celebration acknowledged in the Western World for 20 centuries, and in this country by the people, by the Executive Branch, by the Congress, and the courts for two centuries, would so "taint" the City's exhibit as to render it violative of the Establishment Clause. To forbid the use of this one passive symbol—the crèche—at the very time people are taking note of the season with Christmas hymns and carols in public schools and other public places, and while the Congress and Legislatures open sessions with prayers by paid chaplains would be a stilted over-reaction contrary to our history and to our holdings. If the presence of the crèche in this display violates the Establishment Clause, a host of other forms of taking official note of Christmas, and of our religious heritage, are equally offensive to the Constitution. *** Any notion that these symbols pose a real danger of establishment of a state church is far-fetched indeed.

We hold that, notwithstanding the religious significance of the crèche, the City of Pawtucket has not violated the Establishment Clause of the First Amendment.

Justice O'CONNOR, concurring.

The Establishment Clause prohibits government from making adherence to a religion relevant in any way to a person's standing in the political community. Government can run afoul of that prohibition in two principal ways. One is excessive entanglement with religious institutions ***. The second and more direct infringement is government endorsement or disapproval of religion. Endorsement sends a message to nonadherents that they are outsiders, not full members of the political community, and an accompanying message to adherents that they are insiders, favored members of the political community. Disapproval sends the opposite message.

Our prior cases have used the three-part [*Lemon* test] as a guide to detecting these two forms of unconstitutional government action. It has never been entirely clear, however, how the three parts of the test relate to the principles enshrined in the Establishment Clause. Focusing on institutional entanglement and on endorsement or disapproval of religion clarifies the *Lemon* test as an analytical device.

In this case, as even the District Court found, there is no institutional entanglement.

*** The central issue [is] whether Pawtucket has endorsed Christianity by its display of the crèche. To answer that question, we must examine both what Pawtucket intended to communicate in displaying the crèche and what message the City's display actually conveyed. The purpose and effect prongs of the *Lemon* test represent these two aspects of the meaning of the City's action. *** The purpose prong [asks] whether government's actual purpose is to endorse or disapprove of religion. The effect prong asks whether, irrespective of government's actual purpose, the practice under review in fact conveys a message of endorsement or disapproval.

Applying that formulation to this case, I would find that Pawtucket did not intend to convey any message of endorsement of Christianity or disapproval of non-Christian religions. The evident purpose of including the crèche in the larger display was not promotion of the religious content of the crèche but celebration of the public holiday through its traditional symbols. Celebration of public holidays, which have cultural significance even if they also have religious aspects, is a legitimate secular purpose.

Focusing on the evil of government endorsement or disapproval of religion makes clear that the effect prong of the *Lemon* test is properly interpreted not to require invalidation of a government practice merely because it in fact causes, even as a primary effect, advancement or inhibition of religion. *** What is crucial is that a government practice not have the effect of communicating a message of government endorsement or disapproval of religion. It is only practices having that effect, whether intentionally or unintentionally, that make religion relevant, in reality or public perception, to status in the political community.

Pawtucket's display of its crèche, I believe, does not communicate a message that the government intends to endorse the Christian beliefs represented by the crèche. Although the religious and indeed sectarian significance of the crèche, as the district court found, is not neutralized by the setting, the overall holiday setting changes what viewers may fairly understand to be the purpose of the display—as a typical museum setting, though not neutralizing the religious content of a religious painting, negates any message of endorsement of that content. The display celebrates a public holiday, and no one contends that declaration of that holiday is understood to be an endorsement of religion. The holiday itself has very strong secular components and traditions. Government celebration of the holiday, which is extremely common, generally is not understood to endorse the religious content of the holiday, just as government celebration of Thanksgiving is not so understood. The crèche is a traditional symbol of the holiday that is very commonly displayed along with purely secular symbols, as it was in Pawtucket.

These features combine to make the government's display of the crèche in this particular physical setting no more an endorsement of religion than such governmental "acknowledgments" of religion as legislative prayers of the type approved in *Marsh v. Chambers*, 463 U.S. 783 (1983), government declaration of Thanksgiving as a public holiday, printing of "In God We Trust" on coins, and opening court sessions with "God save the United States and this honorable court." Those government acknowledgments of religion serve, in the only ways reasonably possible in our culture, the legitimate secular purposes of solemnizing public occasions, expressing confidence in the future, and encouraging the recognition of what is worthy of appreciation in society. For that reason, and because of their history and ubiquity, those practices are not understood as conveying government approval of particular religious beliefs. The display of the crèche likewise *** cannot fairly be understood to convey a message of government endorsement of religion.

Justice BRENNAN, with whom Justice MARSHALL, Justice BLACKMUN and Justice STEVENS join, dissenting.

Applying the three-part [*Lemon*] test to Pawtucket's crèche, I am persuaded that the City's inclusion of the crèche in its Christmas display simply does not reflect a "clearly secular purpose." *** Plainly, the City's interest in celebrating the holiday and in promoting both retail sales and goodwill are fully served by the elaborate display of Santa Claus, reindeer, and wishing wells that are already a part of Pawtucket's annual Christmas display. More importantly, the nativity scene, unlike every other element of the Hodgson Park display, reflects a sectarian exclusivity that the avowed purposes of celebrating the holiday season and promoting retail commerce simply do not encompass. To be found constitutional, Pawtucket's seasonal celebration must at least be non-denominational and not serve to promote religion. The inclusion of a distinctively religious element like the crèche, however, demonstrates that a narrower sectarian purpose lay behind the decision to include a nativity scene. That the crèche retained this religious character for the people and municipal government of Pawtucket is suggested by the Mayor's testimony at trial in which he stated that for him, as well as others in the City, the effort to eliminate the nativity scene from Pawtucket's Christmas celebration "is a step towards establishing another religion, non-religion that it may be." Plainly, the City and its leaders understood that the inclusion of the crèche in its display would serve the wholly religious purpose of "keep[ing] 'Christ in Christmas.' " From this record, therefore, it is impossible to say *** that a wholly secular goal predominates.

The "primary effect" of including a nativity scene in the City's display [is] to place the government's imprimatur of approval on the particular religious beliefs exemplified by the crèche. Those who believe in the message of the nativity receive the unique and exclusive benefit of public recognition and approval of their views. For many, the City's decision to include the crèche as part of its extensive and costly efforts to celebrate Christmas can only mean that the prestige of the government has been conferred on the beliefs associated with the crèche, thereby providing "a significant symbolic benefit to religion." *Larkin v. Grendel's Den, Inc.,* 459 U.S., at 125. The effect on minority religious groups, as well as on those who may reject all religion, is to convey the message that their views are not similarly worthy of public recognition nor entitled to public support.

Finally, it is evident that Pawtucket's inclusion of a crèche as part of its annual Christmas display does pose a significant threat of fostering "excessive entanglement." *** [A]fter today's decision, *** Jews and other non-Christian groups *** can be expected to press government for inclusion of their symbols, and faced with such requests, government will have to become involved in accommodating the various demands. More importantly, although no political divisiveness was apparent in Pawtucket prior to the filing of respondents' lawsuit, that act, as the District Court found, unleashed powerful emotional reactions which divided the City along religious lines.

The Court, by focusing on the holiday "context" in which the nativity scene appeared, seeks to explain away the clear religious import of the crèche ***. The effect of the crèche, of course, must be gauged not only by its inherent religious significance but also by the overall setting in which it appears. But it blinks reality to claim, as the Court does, that by including such a distinctively religious object as the crèche in its Christmas display, Pawtucket has done no more than make use of a "traditional" symbol of the holiday, and has thereby purged the crèche of its religious content and conferred only an "incidental and indirect" benefit on religion. *** [E]ven in the context of Pawtucket's seasonal celebration, the crèche retains a specifically Christian religious meaning. *** It is the chief symbol of the characteristically Christian belief that a divine Savior was brought into the world and that the purpose of this miraculous birth was to illuminate a path toward salvation and redemption. For Christians, that path is exclusive, precious and holy. But for those who do not share these beliefs, the symbolic re-enactment of the birth of a divine being who has been miraculously incarnated as a man stands as a dramatic reminder of their differences with Christian faith. *** To be so excluded on religious grounds by one's elected government is an insult and an injury that, until today, could not be countenanced by the Establishment Clause.

The Court also attempts to justify the crèche by entertaining a beguilingly simple, yet faulty syllogism. *** The Court apparently believes that once it finds that the designation of Christmas as a public holiday is constitutionally acceptable, it is then free to conclude that virtually every form of governmental association with the celebration of the holiday is also constitutional. The vice of this dangerously superficial argument is that it overlooks the fact that the Christmas holiday in our national culture contains both secular and sectarian elements. To say that government may recognize the holiday's traditional, secular elements of giftgiving, public festivities and community spirit, does not mean that government may indiscriminately embrace the distinctively sectarian aspects of the holiday.

> ### Make the Connection
>
> Does the government have an obligation, under the Free Exercise Clause of the First Amendment, to accommodate people who observe Christmas? We will consider questions of this sort later in this Chapter.

When government decides to recognize Christmas day as a public holiday, it does no more than accommodate the calendar of public activities to the plain fact that many Americans will expect on that day to spend time visiting with their families, attending religious services, and perhaps enjoying some respite from pre-holiday activities. *** Because it is clear that the celebration of Christmas has both secular and sectarian elements, it may well be that by taking note of the holiday, the government is simply seeking to serve [wholly] secular goals [such as] promoting goodwill and a common day of rest ***. If public officials go further and participate in the *secular* celebration of Christmas—by, for example, decorating public places with such secular images as wreaths, garlands or Santa Claus figures—they move closer to the limits of their constitutional power but nevertheless remain within the boundaries set by the Establishment Clause. But when those officials participate in or appear to endorse the distinctively religious elements of this otherwise secular event, they encroach upon First Amendment freedoms. For it is at that point that the government brings to the forefront the theological content of the holiday, and places the prestige, power and financial support of a civil authority in the service of a particular faith.

The inclusion of a crèche in Pawtucket's otherwise secular celebration of Christmas clearly violates these principles. Unlike such secular figures as Santa Claus, reindeer and carolers, a nativity scene represents far more than a mere "traditional" symbol of Christmas. The essence of the crèche's symbolic purpose and effect is to prompt the observer to experience a sense of simple awe and wonder appropriate to the contemplation of one of the central elements of Christian dogma—that God sent His son into the world to be a Messiah. Contrary to the Court's suggestion, the crèche is far from a mere representation of a "particular historic religious event." It is, instead, best understood as a mystical re-creation of an event that lies at the heart of Christian faith.

The Court's opinion [also] asserts, without explanation, that Pawtucket's inclusion of a crèche in its annual Christmas display poses no more of a threat to Establishment Clause values than [other] official "acknowledgments" of religion. *** [T]he Court has never comprehensively addressed the extent to which government may acknowledge religion by, for example, incorporating religious references into public ceremonies and proclamations, and I do not presume to offer a comprehensive approach. Nevertheless, it appears from our prior decisions that at least three principles [may] be identified. First, although the government may not be compelled to do so by the Free Exercise Clause, it may, consistently with the Establishment Clause, act to accommodate to some extent the opportunities of individuals to practice their religion. *** [F]or me that principle would justify government's decision to declare December 25th a public holiday.

Second, our cases recognize that while a particular governmental practice may have derived from religious motivations and retain certain religious connotations, it is nonetheless permissible for the government to pursue the practice when it is continued today solely for secular reasons. *** Thanksgiving Day, in my view, fits easily within this principle, for despite its religious antecedents, the current practice of celebrating Thanksgiving is unquestionably secular and patriotic. *** Finally, we have noted that government cannot be completely prohibited from recognizing in its public actions the religious beliefs and practices of the American people as an aspect of our national history and culture. While I remain uncertain about these questions, I would suggest that such practices as the designation of "In God We Trust" as our national motto, or the references to God contained in the Pledge of Allegiance can best be understood [as] a form a "ceremonial deism," protected from Establishment Clause scrutiny chiefly because they have lost through rote repetition any significant religious content. Moreover, these references are uniquely suited to serve such wholly secular purposes as solemnizing public occasions, or inspiring commitment to meet some national challenge in a manner that simply could not be fully served in our culture if government were limited to purely non-religious phrases. The practices by which the government has long acknowledged religion are therefore probably necessary to serve certain secular functions, and that necessity, coupled with their long history, gives those practices an essentially secular meaning.

The crèche fits none of these categories. Inclusion of the crèche is not necessary to accommodate individual religious expression. *** Nor is the inclusion of the crèche necessary to serve wholly secular goals; it is clear that the City's secular purposes of celebrating the Christmas holiday and promoting retail commerce can be fully served without the crèche. And the crèche, because of its unique association with Christianity, is clearly more sectarian than those references to God that we accept in ceremonial phrases or in other contexts that assure neutrality.

The Court today [insists] that Pawtucket has done nothing more than include a "traditional" symbol of Christmas in its celebration of this national holiday, thereby muting the religious content of the crèche. But the City's action should be recognized for what it is: a coercive, though perhaps small, step toward establishing the sectarian preferences of the majority at the expense of the minority, accomplished by placing public facilities and funds in support of the religious symbolism and theological tidings that the crèche conveys.

[Justice BLACKMUN's dissenting opinion is omitted.]

Points for Discussion

a. Neutrality

The dispute in <u>Lynch</u> was over whether the inclusion of a crèche—a scene depicting the birth of Jesus Christ—in the town's Christmas display violated the Establishment Clause. Do you agree that the City had a secular purpose for including this symbol in the display?

Do you agree that the inclusion of the crèche did not "impermissibly advance" religion (to use the majority's approach) or "endorse" religion (to use Justice O'Connor's approach)? In answering those questions, from whose perspective should we view the display? From the perspective of an observant Christian who celebrates both the religious and secular aspects of Christmas? From the perspective of someone who celebrates the secular aspects of Christmas but not the religious aspects? From the perspective of someone who is not Christian and does not celebrate the holiday in any of its aspects?

b. Non-Preferentialism

In his dissent, Justice Brennan criticized the Court for, in his view, failing to adhere to the rule of separation. But regardless of the Court's adherence to that rule, did the Court at least ensure that the City did not prefer one religious denomination over others? After all, even the non-preferentialist view—which a majority of the Court has never explicitly adopted—generally prohibits the government from discriminating among different religious sects. *Wallace v. Jaffree*, 472 U.S. 38 (1985) (Rehnquist, J., dissenting). Didn't the challenged display prefer Christianity over all other religions?

c. Subsequent Developments

After the Supreme Court's decision in <u>Lynch</u>, lawsuits continued regarding municipal holiday decorations. Some disputes concerned the degree to which displays conveyed secular, as opposed to non-secular, messages. Judge Frank Easterbrook, unsettled by the view that <u>Lynch</u> requires this kind of analysis, wrote: "It would be appalling to conduct litigation under the Establishment Clause as if it were a trademark case, with experts testifying about whether one display is really like another, and witnesses testifying that they were offended—but would have been less so were the crèche five feet closer to the jumbo candy cane." *American Jewish Congress v. City of Chicago*, 827 F.2d 120, 130 (7th Cir. 1987) (Easterbrook, J., dissenting).

Two years later, in *County of Allegheny v. American Civil Liberties Union*, 492 U.S. 573 (1989), a divided Court allowed a city to display a menorah because it was accompanied by a Christmas tree and a sign extolling liberty, but did not allow the city to display a crèche because it was unaccompanied by other religious and non-secular symbols. Does this case suggest that Judge Easterbrook's apprehensions have come to pass? Does the case suggest a way that municipalities may display religious symbols without violating the Constitution?

———

Hypothetical

Every day, public schools throughout the United States request students to stand and recite the Pledge of Allegiance, which states: "I pledge allegiance to the flag of the United States of America and to the republic for which it stands, one nation under God, indivisible, with liberty and justice for all." The pledge dates to the late nineteenth century, but the phrase "under God" did not become part of the pledge until 1954. In *Elk Grove Unified School Dist. v. Newdow*, 542 U.S. 1 (2004), the father of an elementary school student sued, claiming that a public school's practice of having a teacher lead the pledge violated the Establishment Clause. The Supreme Court granted certiorari in the case, but did not reach the merits of the constitutional claim because it held that the father lacked standing to bring the challenge. (Justice Antonin Scalia recused himself from <u>Newdow</u> because he had previously made a public speech in which he specifically criticized the lower court decision holding that the pledge was unconstitutional. See Linda Greenhouse, *Supreme Court to Consider Case on "Under God" in Pledge to Flag*, N.Y. Times, Oct. 15, 2003, at A1.) If the question had properly been before the Court, what would have been the best arguments on both sides of the constitutional issue?

———

In addition to litigation over holiday displays, the Supreme Court in several cases has addressed the question whether government institutions may display the Ten Commandments, a set of moral imperatives found in the Bible at Exodus 20:2–17 and Deuteronomy 5:6–21. As it turns out, this question has no single answer. The Court has held that schools may not display the Ten Commandments, reasoning that the Commandments "are undeniably a sacred text in the Jewish and Christian faiths." *Stone v. Graham,* 449 U.S. 39 (1980) *(per curiam).* But the Court has issued dueling opinions about the constitutionality of displays of the Ten Commandments on government property. As you read the following two cases, which were decided on the same day, consider what principles govern the Court's analysis, whether the cases can be reconciled, and whether they are consistent with the cases that we have already seen.

Go Online

The books of Exodus and Deuteronomy do not enumerate the Ten Commandments, but instead describe various obligations in narrative prose. Based on this prose, Jewish, Catholic, and Protestant religious orders identify and list the Ten Commandments in different ways. For more information on this subject, see this informative article in the Catholic Encyclopedia.

McCreary County, Kentucky v. American Civil Liberties Union of Kentucky

545 U.S. 844 (2005)

Justice SOUTER delivered the opinion of the Court.

[In 1999, two counties in Kentucky put up in their courthouses large, gold-framed copies of an abridged text of the King James version of the Ten Commandments. After lawsuits were filed to challenge the displays under the Establishment Clause,] the legislative body of each County authorized a second, expanded display, by nearly identical resolutions reciting that the Ten Commandments are "the precedent legal code upon which the civil and criminal codes [of] Kentucky are founded," and stating several grounds for taking that position: that "the Ten Commandments are codified in Kentucky's civil and criminal laws"; that the Kentucky House of Representatives had in 1993 "voted unanimously [to] adjourn 'in remembrance and honor of Jesus Christ, the Prince of Ethics' "; and that the "Founding Father[s] [had an] explicit understanding of the duty of elected officials to publicly acknowledge God as the source of America's strength and direction."

As directed by the resolutions, the Counties expanded the displays of the Ten Commandments in their locations [to include] eight other documents in smaller frames, each either having a religious theme or excerpted to highlight a religious element. [After a District Court issued an injunction prohibiting the revised displays, the counties installed new displays consisting of] nine framed documents of equal size, one of them setting out the Ten Commandments explicitly identified as the "King James Version" at Exodus 20:3-17 [and] quoted at greater length than before. *** Assembled with the Commandments are framed copies of the Magna Carta, the Declaration of Independence, the Bill of Rights, the lyrics of the Star Spangled Banner, the Mayflower Compact, the National Motto, the Preamble to the Kentucky Constitution, and a picture of Lady Justice. The collection is entitled "The Foundations of American Law and Government Display" and each document comes with a statement about its historical and legal significance.

Ever since *Lemon* summarized the three familiar considerations for evaluating Establishment Clause claims, looking to whether government action has "a secular legislative purpose" has been a common, albeit seldom dispositive, element of our cases. The touchstone for our analysis is the principle that the "First Amendment mandates governmental neutrality between religion and religion, and between religion and nonreligion." *Epperson v. Arkansas*, 393 U.S. 97, 104 (1968); *Everson v. Board of Ed. of Ewing*, 330 U.S. 1, 15-16 (1947). When the government acts with the ostensible and predominant purpose of advancing religion, it violates that central Establishment Clause value of official religious neutrality, there being no neutrality when the government's ostensible object is to take sides. ***

Despite the intuitive importance of official purpose to the realization of Establishment Clause values, the Counties ask us to abandon *Lemon*'s purpose test, or at least to truncate any enquiry into purpose here. [A]ccording to them, true "purpose" is unknowable, and its search merely an excuse for courts to act selectively and unpredictably in picking out evidence of subjective intent. The assertions are as seismic as they are unconvincing.

Examination of purpose is [a] key element of a good deal of constitutional doctrine, *e.g.*, *Washington v. Davis*, 426 U.S. 229 (1976). *** [S]crutinizing purpose does make practical sense, as in Establishment Clause analysis, where an understanding of official objective emerges from readily discoverable fact, without any judicial psychoanalysis of a drafter's heart of hearts. *** The cases with findings of a predominantly religious purpose point to the straightforward nature of the test. In *Wallace v. Jaffree*, 472 U.S. 38, 58-60 (1985), for example, we inferred purpose from a change of wording from an earlier statute to a later one, each dealing with prayer in schools. And in *Edwards v. Aguillard*, 482 U.S. 578, 586-588 (1987), we relied on a statute's text and the detailed public comments of its sponsor, when we sought the purpose of a state law requiring creationism to be taught alongside evolution. In other cases, the government action itself bespoke the purpose, as in *School Dist. of Abington Township v. Schempp*, 374 U.S. 203 (1963), where the object of required Bible study in public schools was patently religious. *** In each case, the government's action was held unconstitutional only because openly available data supported a commonsense conclusion that a religious objective permeated the government's action.

The Counties would read the cases as if the purpose enquiry were so naive that any transparent claim to secularity would satisfy it ***. [T]he Court often does accept governmental statements of purpose, in keeping with the respect owed in the first instance to such official claims. But in those unusual cases where the claim was an apparent sham, or the secular purpose secondary, the unsurprising results have been findings of no adequate secular object, as against a predominantly religious one. *** [The Counties also] argue that purpose in a case like this one should be inferred, if at all, only from the latest news about the last in a series of governmental actions, however close they may all be in time and subject. But the world is not made brand new every morning, and the Counties are simply asking us to ignore perfectly probative evidence; they want an absentminded objective observer, not one presumed to be familiar with the history of the government's actions and competent to learn what history has to show. The Counties' position just bucks common sense: reasonable observers have reasonable memories, and our precedents sensibly forbid an observer "to turn a blind eye to the context in which [the] policy arose."

[T]he Commandments [are] a central point of reference in the religious and moral history of Jews and Christians. They proclaim the existence of a monotheistic god (no other gods). They regulate details of religious obligation (no graven images, no sabbath breaking, no vain oath swearing). And they unmistakably rest even the universally accepted prohibitions (as against murder, theft, and the like) on the sanction of the divinity proclaimed at the beginning of the text. Displaying that text is thus different from a symbolic depiction, like tablets with 10 roman numerals, which could be seen as alluding to a general notion of law, not a sectarian conception of faith. Where the text is set out, the insistence of the religious message is hard to avoid in the absence of a context plausibly suggesting a message going beyond an excuse to promote the religious point of view.

[There was no such context for the original exhibits here.] [A]t the [original] ceremony for posting the framed Commandments in Pulaski County, the county executive was accompanied by his pastor, who testified to the certainty of the existence of God. The reasonable observer could only think that the Counties meant to emphasize and celebrate the Commandments' religious message. [The second version of the exhibits included] a series of American historical documents with theistic and Christian references ***. The display's unstinting focus was on religious passages, showing that the Counties were posting the Commandments precisely because of their sectarian content. That demonstration of the government's objective was enhanced by serial religious references and the accompanying resolution's claim about the embodiment of ethics in Christ. Together, the display and resolution presented an indisputable, and undisputed, showing of an impermissible purpose. Today, the Counties make no attempt to defend their undeniable objective, but instead hopefully describe version two as "dead and buried." Their refusal to defend the second display is understandable, but the reasonable observer could not forget it.

> **Take Note**
>
> The Court here considers the original exhibits (which were no longer on display) to determine the purpose behind the current exhibits. Given that, as the Court acknowledges, there are plausible secular motives to support posting the Ten Commandments in public buildings under some circumstances, does it make sense to consider the purpose that motivated the posting of the *original* versions of the exhibits?

[After mounting the third display, the counties] cited several new purposes ***, including a desire "to educate the citizens of the county regarding some of the documents that played a significant role in the foundation of our system of law and government." *** These new statements of purpose were presented only as a litigating position, there being no further authorizing action by the Counties' governing boards. And although repeal of the earlier county authorizations would not have erased them from the record of evidence bearing on current purpose, the extraordinary resolutions for the second display passed just months earlier were not repealed or otherwise repudiated. Indeed, the sectarian spirit of the common resolution found enhanced expression in the third display, which quoted more of the purely religious language of the Commandments than the first two displays had done. No reasonable observer could swallow the claim that the Counties had cast off the objective so unmistakable in the earlier displays.

Nor did the selection of posted material suggest a clear theme that might prevail over evidence of the continuing religious object. In a collection of documents said to be "foundational" to American government, it is at least odd to include a patriotic anthem, but to omit the Fourteenth Amendment ***. And it is no less baffling to leave out the original Constitution of 1787 while quoting the 1215 Magna Carta even to the point of its declaration that "fish-weirs shall be removed from the Thames." If an observer found these choices and omissions perplexing in isolation, he would be puzzled for a different reason when he read the Declaration of Independence seeking confirmation for the Counties' posted explanation that the Ten Commandments' "influence is clearly seen in the Declaration"; in fact the observer would find that the Commandments are sanctioned as divine imperatives, while the Declaration of Independence holds that the authority of government to enforce the law derives "from the consent of the governed." If the observer had not thrown up his hands, he would probably suspect that the Counties were simply reaching for any way to keep a religious document on the walls of courthouses constitutionally required to embody religious neutrality.

[W]e do not decide that the Counties' past actions forever taint any effort on their part to deal with the subject matter. We hold only that purpose needs to be taken seriously under the Establishment Clause and needs to be understood in light of context; an implausible claim that governmental purpose has changed should not carry the day in a court of law any more than in a head with common sense. Nor do we have occasion here to hold that a sacred text can never be integrated constitutionally into a governmental display on the subject of law, or American history. We do not forget, and in this litigation have frequently been reminded, that our own courtroom frieze was deliberately designed in the exercise of governmental authority so as to include the figure of Moses holding tablets exhibiting a portion of the Hebrew text of the later, secularly phrased Commandments; in the company of 17 other lawgivers, most of them secular figures, there is no risk that Moses would strike an observer as evidence that the National Government was violating neutrality in religion.

[The principle of neutrality] responds to one of the major concerns that prompted adoption of the Religion Clauses. The Framers and the citizens of their time intended not only to protect the integrity of individual conscience in religious matters, but to guard against the civic divisiveness that follows when the government weighs in on one side of religious debate; nothing does a better job of roiling society, a point that needed no explanation to the descendants of English Puritans and Cavaliers (or Massachusetts Puritans and Baptists).

The dissent, however, puts forward a limitation on the application of the neutrality principle, with citations to historical evidence said to show that the Framers understood the ban on establishment of religion as sufficiently narrow to allow the government to espouse submission to the divine will. *** But the dissent's argument for the original understanding is flawed from the outset by its failure to consider the full range of evidence showing what the Framers believed. The dissent is certainly correct in putting forward evidence that some of the Framers thought some endorsement of religion was compatible with the establishment ban ***. [But] there is also evidence supporting the proposition that the Framers intended the Establishment Clause to require governmental neutrality in matters of religion, including neutrality in statements acknowledging religion. The very language of the Establishment Clause represented a significant departure from early drafts that merely prohibited a single national religion, and the final language instead "extended [the] prohibition to state support for 'religion' in general." See *Lee v. Weisman,* 505 U.S. 577, 614-615 (1992) (SOUTER, J., concurring). The historical record, moreover, is complicated beyond the dissent's account by the writings and practices of figures no less influential than Thomas Jefferson and James Madison. Jefferson, for example, refused to issue Thanksgiving Proclamations because he believed that they violated the Constitution. And Madison, whom the dissent claims as supporting its thesis, criticized Virginia's general assessment tax not just because it required people to donate "three pence" to religion, but because "it is itself a signal of persecution. It degrades from the equal rank of Citizens all those whose opinions in Religion do not bend to those of the Legislative authority."

[The dissent also says] that the deity the Framers had in mind was the God of monotheism, with the consequence that government may espouse a tenet of traditional monotheism. This is truly a remarkable view. Other Members of the Court have dissented on the ground that the Establishment Clause bars nothing more than governmental preference for one religion over another, *e.g., Wallace,* 472 U.S., at 98-99 (REHNQUIST, J., dissenting), but at least religion has previously been treated inclusively. Today's dissent, however, apparently means that government should be free to approve the core beliefs of a favored religion over the tenets of others, a view that should trouble anyone who prizes religious liberty. *** We are centuries away from the St. Bartholomew's Day massacre and the treatment of heretics in early Massachusetts, but the divisiveness of religion in current public life is inescapable. This is no time to deny the prudence of understanding the Establishment Clause to require the Government to stay neutral on religious belief, which is reserved for the conscience of the individual.

FYI

In the St. Bartholomew's Day massacre, a mob of French Catholics killed thousands of French Protestants over a period of several days in 1572. The treatment of heretics in early Massachusetts is famously chronicled in Arthur Miller's play *The Crucible.*

[The Court affirmed the district court's grant of a preliminary injunction against the challenged displays.]

Justice O'CONNOR, concurring.

Given the history of this particular display of the Ten Commandments, the Court correctly finds an Establishment Clause violation. The purpose behind the counties' display is relevant because it conveys an unmistakable message of endorsement to the reasonable observer. It is true that many Americans find the Commandments in accord with their personal beliefs. But we do not count heads before enforcing the First Amendment. Nor can we accept the theory that Americans who do not accept the Commandments' validity are outside the First Amendment's protections. There is no list of approved and disapproved beliefs appended to the First Amendment—and the Amendment's broad terms ("free exercise," "establishment," "religion") do not admit of such a cramped reading. It is true that the Framers lived at a time when our national religious diversity was neither as robust nor as well recognized as it is now. They may not have foreseen the variety of religions for which this Nation would eventually provide a home. They surely could not have predicted new religions, some of them born in this country. But they did know that line-drawing between religions is an enterprise that, once begun, has no logical stopping point. *** The Religion Clauses, as a result, protect adherents of all religions, as well as those who believe in no religion at all.

Justice SCALIA, with whom THE CHIEF JUSTICE and Justice THOMAS join, and with whom Justice KENNEDY joins as to Parts II and III, dissenting.

[O]ne model of the relationship between church and state [is the] model spread across Europe by the armies of Napoleon, and reflected in the Constitution of France, which begins, "France is [a] secular Republic." Religion is to be strictly excluded from the public forum. This is not, and never was, the model adopted by America. *** George Washington added to the form of Presidential oath prescribed by Art. II, § 1, cl. 8, of the Constitution, the concluding words "so help me God." The Supreme Court under John Marshall opened its sessions with the prayer, "God save the United States and this Honorable Court." The First Congress instituted the practice of beginning its legislative sessions with a prayer. The same week that Congress submitted the Establishment Clause as part of the Bill of Rights for ratification by the States, it enacted legislation providing for paid chaplains in the House and Senate. The day after the First Amendment was proposed, the same Congress that had proposed it requested the President to proclaim "a day of public thanksgiving and prayer, to be observed, by acknowledging, with grateful hearts, the many signal favours of Almighty God." H.R. Jour., 1st Cong., 1st Sess., 123 (1826 ed.). *** And of course the First Amendment itself accords religion (and no other manner of belief) special constitutional protection.

These actions of our First President and Congress and the Marshall Court were not idiosyncratic; they reflected the beliefs of the period. Those who wrote the Constitution believed that morality was essential to the well-being of society and that encouragement of religion was the best way to foster morality. *** Nor have the views of our people on this matter significantly changed. Presidents continue to conclude the Presidential oath with the words "so help me God." Our legislatures, state and national, continue to open their sessions with prayer led by official chaplains. The sessions of this Court continue to open with the prayer "God save the United States and this Honorable Court." Invocation of the

Almighty by our public figures, at all levels of government, remains commonplace. Our coinage bears the motto, "IN GOD WE TRUST." And our Pledge of Allegiance contains the acknowledgment that we are a Nation "under God." As one of our Supreme Court opinions rightly observed, "We are a religious people whose institutions presuppose a Supreme Being." *Zorach v. Clauson*, 343 U.S. 306, 313 (1952).

With all of this reality (and much more) staring it in the face, how can the Court *possibly* assert that the "First Amendment mandates governmental neutrality between [religion] and nonreligion," and that "[m]anifesting a purpose to favor [adherence] to religion generally," is unconstitutional? Who says so? Surely not the words of the Constitution. Surely not the history and traditions that reflect our society's constant understanding of those words. *** Nothing stands behind the Court's assertion that governmental affirmation of the society's belief in God is unconstitutional except the Court's own say-so, citing as support only the unsubstantiated say-so of earlier Courts going back no further than the mid-20th century. *** And it is, moreover, a thoroughly discredited say-so. It is discredited [because] a majority of the Justices on the current Court (including at least one Member of today's majority) have, in separate opinions, repudiated the brain-spun "*Lemon* test" that embodies the supposed principle of neutrality between religion and irreligion. And it is discredited because the Court has not had the courage (or the foolhardiness) to apply the neutrality principle consistently.

Besides appealing to the demonstrably false principle that the government cannot favor religion over irreligion, today's opinion suggests that the posting of the Ten Commandments violates the principle that the government cannot favor one religion over another. That is indeed a valid principle where public aid or assistance to religion is concerned, see *Zelman v. Simmons-Harris*, 536 U.S. 639, 652 (2002), or where the free exercise of religion is at issue, but it necessarily applies in a more limited sense to public acknowledgment of the Creator. If religion in the public forum had to be entirely nondenominational, there could be no religion in the public forum at all. One cannot say the word "God," or "the Almighty," one cannot offer public supplication or thanksgiving, without contradicting the beliefs of some people that there are many gods, or that God or the gods pay no attention to human affairs. With respect to public acknowledgment of religious belief, it is entirely clear from our Nation's historical practices that the Establishment Clause permits this disregard of polytheists and believers in unconcerned deities, just as it permits the disregard of devout atheists.

Historical practices [demonstrate] that there is a distance between the acknowledgment of a single Creator and the establishment of a religion. *** The three most popular religions in the United States, Christianity, Judaism, and Islam—which combined account for 97.7% of all believers—are monotheistic. All of them, moreover (Islam included), believe that the Ten Commandments were given by God to Moses, and are divine prescriptions for a virtuous life. Publicly honoring the Ten Commandments is thus indistinguishable, insofar as discriminating against other religions is concerned, from publicly honoring God. Both practices are recognized across such a broad and diverse range of the population—from Christians to Muslims—that they cannot be reasonably understood as a government endorsement of a particular religious viewpoint.

*** I must respond to Justice STEVENS' assertion [in his dissent in *Van Orden v. Perry*, 545 U.S. 677, 719, n. 18 (2005), the companion case,] that I would "marginaliz[e] the belief systems of more than 7 million Americans" who adhere to religions that are not monotheistic. Surely that is a gross exaggeration. The beliefs of those citizens are entirely protected by the Free Exercise Clause, and by those aspects of the Establishment Clause that do not relate to government acknowledgment of the Creator. Invocation of God despite their beliefs is permitted not because nonmonotheistic religions cease to be religions recognized by the Religion Clauses of the First Amendment, but because governmental invocation of God is not an establishment. Justice STEVENS fails to recognize that in the context of public acknowledgments of God there are legitimate *competing* interests: On the one hand, the interest of that minority in not feeling "excluded"; but on the other, the interest of the overwhelming majority of religious believers in being able to give God thanks and supplication *as a people*, and with respect to our national endeavors. Our national tradition has resolved that conflict in favor of the majority.

Acknowledgment of the contribution that religion has made to our Nation's legal and governmental heritage partakes of a centuries-old tradition. *** Display of the Ten Commandments is well within the mainstream of this practice of acknowledgment. *** The Supreme Court Building itself includes depictions of Moses with the Ten Commandments in the Courtroom and on the east pediment of the building ***. Similar depictions of the Decalogue appear on public buildings and monuments throughout our Nation's Capital. The frequency of these displays testifies to the popular understanding that the Ten Commandments are a foundation of the rule of law, and a symbol of the role that religion played, and continues to play, in our system of government.

─────────

Van Orden v. Perry

545 U.S. 677 (2005)

Chief Justice REHNQUIST announced the judgment of the Court and delivered an opinion, in which Justice SCALIA, Justice KENNEDY, and JUSTICE THOMAS join.

> **Take Note**
>
> This case does not have a majority opinion.

The 22 acres surrounding the Texas State Capitol contain 17 monuments and 21 historical markers commemorating the "people, ideals, and events that compose Texan identity."[1] Tex. H. Con. Res. 38, 77th Leg., Reg.Sess. (2001). The monolith challenged here stands 6-feet high and 3 1/2-feet wide. It is located to the north of the Capitol building, between the Capitol and the Supreme Court building. Its primary content is the text of the Ten

──────────

[1] The monuments are: Heroes of the Alamo, Hood's Brigade, Confederate Soldiers, Volunteer Fireman, Terry's Texas Rangers, Texas Cowboy, Spanish-American War, Texas National Guard, Ten Commandments, Tribute to Texas School Children, Texas Pioneer Woman, The Boy Scouts' Statue of Liberty Replica, Pearl Harbor Veterans, Korean War Veterans, Soldiers of World War I, Disabled Veterans, and Texas Peace Officers.

Commandments. An eagle grasping the American flag, an eye inside of a pyramid, and two small tablets with what appears to be an ancient script are carved above the text of the Ten Commandments. Below the text are two Stars of David and the superimposed Greek letters Chi and Rho, which represent Christ. The bottom of the monument bears the inscription "PRESENTED TO THE PEOPLE AND YOUTH OF TEXAS BY THE FRATERNAL ORDER OF EAGLES OF TEXAS 1961." *** The Eagles paid the cost of erecting the monument, the dedication of which was presided over by two state legislators.

Go Online

You can view the actual monolith at issue in this case here.

Our cases, Januslike, point in two directions in applying the Establishment Clause. One face looks toward the strong role played by religion and religious traditions throughout our Nation's history. *** The other face looks toward the principle that governmental intervention in religious matters can itself endanger religious freedom.

This case, like all Establishment Clause challenges, presents us with the difficulty of respecting both faces. Our institutions presuppose a Supreme Being, yet these institutions must not press religious observances upon their citizens. One face looks to the past in acknowledgment of our Nation's heritage, while the other looks to the present in demanding a separation between church and state. Reconciling these two faces requires that we neither abdicate our responsibility to maintain a division between church and state nor evince a hostility to religion by disabling the government from in some ways recognizing our religious heritage ***.

These two faces are evident in representative cases both upholding and invalidating laws under the Establishment Clause. Over the last 25 years, we have sometimes pointed to *Lemon v. Kurtzman*, 403 U.S. 602 (1971), as providing the governing test in Establishment Clause challenges. Yet [m]any of our recent cases simply have not applied the *Lemon* test. *** Whatever may be the fate of the *Lemon* test in the larger scheme of Establishment Clause jurisprudence, we think it not useful in dealing with the sort of passive monument that Texas has erected on its Capitol grounds. Instead, our analysis is driven both by the nature of the monument and by our Nation's history.

In this case we are faced with a display of the Ten Commandments on government property outside the Texas State Capitol. Such acknowledgments of the role played by the Ten Commandments in our Nation's heritage are common throughout America. We need only look within our own Courtroom. Since 1935, Moses has stood, holding two tablets that reveal portions of the Ten Commandments written in Hebrew, among other lawgivers in the south frieze. [In addition,] a large statue of Moses holding the Ten Commandments, alongside a statue of the Apostle Paul, has overlooked the rotunda of the Library of Congress' Jefferson Building since 1897. And the Jefferson Building's Great Reading Room contains a sculpture of a woman beside the Ten Commandments with a quote above her from the Old Testament (Micah 6:8). A medallion with two tablets depicting the Ten Commandments decorates the floor of the National Archives. Inside the Department of Justice, a statue entitled "The Spirit of Law" has two tablets representing the Ten Commandments lying at its feet. In front of the Ronald Reagan Building is another sculpture that includes a depiction of the Ten Commandments. So too a 24-foot-tall sculpture, depicting, among other things, the Ten Commandments and a cross, stands outside the federal courthouse that houses both the Court of Appeals and the District Court for the District of Columbia. ***

Of course, the Ten Commandments are religious—they were so viewed at their inception and so remain. The monument, therefore, has religious significance. According to Judeo-Christian belief, the Ten Commandments were given to Moses by God on Mt. Sinai. But Moses was a lawgiver as well as a religious leader. And the Ten Commandments have an undeniable historical meaning, as the foregoing examples demonstrate. Simply having religious content or promoting a message consistent with a religious doctrine does not run afoul of the Establishment Clause. See <u>Lynch v. Donnelly, 465 U.S., at 680, 687</u>.

There are, of course, limits to the display of religious messages or symbols. For example, we held unconstitutional a Kentucky statute requiring the posting of the Ten Commandments in every public schoolroom. *Stone v. Graham*, 449 U.S. 39 (1980) *(per curiam)*. *** As evidenced by *Stone's* almost exclusive reliance upon two of our school prayer cases, <u>id., at 41-42</u> (citing *School Dist. of Abington Township v. Schempp*, 374 U.S. 203 (1963), and *Engel v. Vitale*, 370 U.S. 421 (1962)), it stands as an example of the fact that we have "been particularly vigilant in monitoring compliance with the Establishment Clause in elementary and secondary schools," *Edwards v. Aguillard*, 482 U.S. 578, 583-584 (1987). ***

The placement of the Ten Commandments monument on the Texas State Capitol grounds is a far more passive use of those texts than was the case in *Stone*, where the text confronted elementary school students every day. *** The monument is therefore also quite different from the prayers involved in *Schempp* and *Lee v. Weisman*. Texas has treated its Capitol grounds monuments as representing the several strands in the State's political and legal history. The inclusion of the Ten Commandments monument in this group has a dual significance, partaking of both religion and government. We cannot say that Texas' display of this monument violates the Establishment Clause of the First Amendment.

Justice SCALIA, concurring.

I join the opinion of THE CHIEF JUSTICE because I think it accurately reflects our current Establishment Clause jurisprudence—or at least the Establishment Clause jurisprudence we currently apply some of the time. I would prefer to reach the same result by adopting an Establishment Clause jurisprudence that is in accord with our Nation's past and present practices, and that can be consistently applied—the central relevant feature of which is that there is nothing unconstitutional in a State's favoring religion generally, honoring God through public prayer and acknowledgment, or, in a nonproselytizing manner, venerating the Ten Commandments.

Justice THOMAS, concurring.

This case would be easy if the Court were willing to abandon the inconsistent guide-posts it has adopted for addressing Establishment Clause challenges, and return to the original meaning of the Clause. I have previously suggested that the Clause's text and history "resis[t] incorporation" against the States. See *Elk Grove Unified School Dist. v. Newdow*, 542 U.S. 1, 45-46 (2004) (opinion concurring in judgment). If the Establishment Clause does not restrain the States, then it has no application here, where only state action is at issue.

Even if the Clause is incorporated, or if the Free Exercise Clause limits the power of States to establish religions, our task would be far simpler if we returned to the original meaning of the word "establishment" than it is under the various approaches this Court now uses. The Framers understood an establishment "necessarily [to] involve actual legal coercion." *Newdow*, 542 U.S. at 52 (THOMAS, J., concurring in judgment). *** There is no question that, based on the original meaning of the Establishment Clause, the Ten Commandments display at issue here is constitutional. In no sense does Texas compel petitioner Van Orden to do anything. The only injury to him is that he takes offense at seeing the monument as he passes it on his way to the Texas Supreme Court Library. He need not stop to read it or even to look at it, let alone to express support for it or adopt the Commandments as guides for his life. The mere presence of the monument along his path involves no coercion and thus does not violate the Establishment Clause.

Returning to the original meaning would do more than simplify our task. It also would avoid the pitfalls present in the Court's current approach to such challenges. This Court's precedent elevates the trivial to the proverbial "federal case," by making benign signs and postings subject to challenge. Yet even as it does so, the Court's precedent attempts to avoid declaring all religious symbols and words of longstanding tradition unconstitutional, by counterfactually declaring them of little religious significance. Even when the Court's cases recognize that such symbols have religious meaning, they adopt an unhappy compromise that fails fully to account for either the adherent's or the nonadherent's beliefs, and provides no principled way to choose between them. Even worse, the incoherence of the Court's decisions in this area renders the Establishment Clause impenetrable and incapable of consistent application. *** While the Court correctly rejects the challenge to the Ten Commandments monument on the Texas Capitol grounds, a more fundamental rethinking of our Establishment Clause jurisprudence remains in order.

Justice BREYER, concurring in the judgment.

If the relation between government and religion is one of separation, but not of mutual hostility and suspicion, one will inevitably find difficult borderline cases. And in such cases, I see no test-related substitute for the exercise of legal judgment. *** While the Court's prior tests provide useful guideposts—and might well lead to the same result the Court reaches today, see, *e.g., Lemon v. Kurtzman*, 403 U.S. 602, 612-613 (1971)—no exact formula can dictate a resolution to such fact-intensive cases.

The case before us is a borderline case. *** On the one hand, the Commandments' text undeniably has a religious message, invoking, indeed emphasizing, the Deity. On the other hand, focusing on the text of the Commandments alone cannot conclusively resolve this case. Rather, to determine the message that the text here conveys, we must examine how the text is *used*. And that inquiry requires us to consider the context of the display.

In certain contexts, a display of the tablets of the Ten Commandments can convey not simply a religious message but also a secular moral message (about proper standards of social conduct). And in certain contexts, a display of the tablets can also convey a historical message (about a historic relation between those standards and the law)—a fact that helps to explain the display of those tablets in dozens of courthouses throughout the Nation, including the Supreme Court of the United States.

Here the tablets have been used as part of a display that communicates not simply a religious message, but a secular message as well. The circumstances surrounding the display's placement on the capitol grounds and its physical setting suggest that the State itself intended the latter, nonreligious aspects of the tablets' message to predominate. And the monument's 40-year history on the Texas state grounds indicates that that has been its effect.

The group that donated the monument, the Fraternal Order of Eagles, a private civic (and primarily secular) organization, while interested in the religious aspect of the Ten Commandments, sought to highlight the Commandments' role in shaping civic morality as part of that organization's efforts to combat juvenile delinquency. The Eagles' consultation with a committee composed of members of several faiths in order to find a nonsectarian text underscores the group's ethics-based motives. The tablets, as displayed on the monument, prominently acknowledge that the Eagles donated the display, a factor which, though not sufficient, thereby further distances the State itself from the religious aspect of the Commandments' message.

The physical setting of the monument, moreover, suggests little or nothing of the sacred. The monument sits in a large park containing 17 monuments and 21 historical markers, all designed to illustrate the "ideals" of those who settled in Texas and of those who have lived there since that time. The setting does not readily lend itself to meditation or any other religious activity. But it does provide a context of history and moral ideals. It (together with the display's inscription about its origin) communicates to visitors that the State sought to reflect moral principles, illustrating a relation between ethics and law that the State's citizens, historically speaking, have endorsed. That is to say, the context suggests that the State intended the display's moral message—an illustrative message reflecting the historical "ideals" of Texans—to predominate.

If these factors provide a strong, but not conclusive, indication that the Commandments' text on this monument conveys a predominantly secular message, a further factor is determinative here. As far as I can tell, 40 years passed in which the presence of this monument, legally speaking, went unchallenged (until the single legal objection raised by petitioner). And I am not aware of any evidence suggesting that this was due to a climate of intimidation. Hence, those 40 years suggest more strongly than can any set of formulaic tests that few individuals, whatever their system of beliefs, are likely to have understood the monument as amounting, in any significantly detrimental way, to a government effort to favor a particular religious sect, primarily to promote religion over nonreligion, to "engage in" any "religious practic[e]," to "compel" any "religious practic[e]," or to "work deterrence" of any "religious belief." *School Dist. of Abington Township v. Schempp,* 374 U.S. 203, 305 (1963) (Goldberg, J., concurring).

This display has stood apparently uncontested for nearly two generations. That experience helps us understand that as a practical matter of *degree* this display is unlikely to prove divisive. And this matter of degree is, I believe, critical in a borderline case such as this one.

Justice STEVENS, with whom Justice GINSBURG joins, dissenting.

The sole function of the monument on the grounds of Texas' State Capitol is to display the full text of one version of the Ten Commandments. The monument is not a work of art and does not refer to any event in the history of the State. It is significant because, and only because, it communicates the [message of the monument's text]. *** The message transmitted by Texas' chosen display is quite plain: This State endorses the divine code of the "Judeo-Christian" God.

In my judgment, at the very least, the Establishment Clause has created a strong presumption against the display of religious symbols on public property. *** Government's obligation to avoid divisiveness and exclusion in the religious sphere is compelled by the Establishment and Free Exercise Clauses, which together erect a wall of separation between church and state. This metaphorical wall protects principles long recognized and often recited in this Court's cases. The first and most fundamental of these principles, one that a majority of this Court today affirms, is that the Establishment Clause demands religious neutrality—government may not exercise a preference for one religious faith over another. This essential command, however, is not merely a prohibition against the government's differentiation among religious sects. We have repeatedly reaffirmed that neither a State nor the Federal Government "can constitutionally pass laws or impose requirements which aid all religions as against non-believers, and neither can aid those religions based on a belief in the existence of God as against those religions founded on different beliefs." *Torcaso v. Watkins,* 367 U.S. 488, 495 (1961).

In restating this principle, I do not discount the importance of avoiding an overly strict interpretation of the metaphor so often used to define the reach of the Establishment Clause. *** The wall that separates the church from the State does not prohibit the government from acknowledging the religious beliefs and practices of the American people, nor does it require governments to hide works of art or historic memorabilia from public view just because they also have religious significance.

This case, however, is not about historic preservation or the mere recognition of religion. *** The monolith displayed on Texas Capitol grounds cannot be discounted as a passive acknowledgment of religion, nor can the State's refusal to remove it upon objection be explained as a simple desire to preserve a historic relic. *** When the Ten Commandments monument was donated to the State of Texas in 1961, it was not for the purpose of commemorating a noteworthy event in Texas history, signifying the Commandments' influence on the development of secular law, or even denoting the religious beliefs of Texans at that time. To the contrary, the donation was only one of over a hundred largely identical monoliths, and of over a thousand paper replicas, distributed to state and local governments throughout the Nation over the course of several decades. This ambitious project was the work of the Fraternal Order of Eagles, a well-respected benevolent organization *** motivated by a desire to "inspire the youth" and curb juvenile delinquency by providing children with a "code of conduct or standards by which to govern their actions."

Though the State of Texas may genuinely wish to combat juvenile delinquency, and may rightly want to honor the Eagles for their efforts, it cannot effectuate these admirable purposes through an explicitly religious medium. The State may admonish its citizens not to lie, cheat, or steal, to honor their parents, and to respect their neighbors' property ***. The message at issue in this case, however, is fundamentally different from either a bland admonition to observe generally accepted rules of behavior or a general history lesson.

The reason this message stands apart is that the Decalogue is a venerable religious text. *** For many followers, the Commandments represent the literal word of God as spoken to Moses and repeated to his followers after descending from Mount Sinai. The message conveyed by the Ten Commandments thus cannot be analogized to an appendage to a common article of commerce ("In God we Trust") or an incidental part of a familiar recital ("God save the United States and this honorable Court"). Thankfully, the plurality does not attempt to minimize the religious significance of the Ten Commandments. Attempts to secularize what is unquestionably a sacred text defy credibility and disserve people of faith.

The profoundly sacred message embodied by the text inscribed on the Texas monument is emphasized by the especially large letters that identify its author: "I AM the LORD thy God." It commands present worship of Him and no other deity. It directs us to be guided by His teaching in the current and future conduct of all of our affairs. It instructs us to follow a code of divine law, some of which has informed and been integrated into our secular legal code ("Thou shalt not kill"), but much of which has not ("Thou shalt not make to thyself any graven images .... Thou shalt not covet"). Moreover, despite the Eagles' best efforts to choose a benign nondenominational text, the Ten Commandments display projects not just a religious, but an inherently sectarian, message. There are many distinctive versions of the Decalogue, ascribed to by different religions and even different denominations within a particular faith; to a pious and learned observer, these differences may be of enormous religious significance. In choosing to display this version of the Commandments, Texas tells the observer that the State supports this side of the doctrinal religious debate.

Even if, however, the message of the monument, despite the inscribed text, fairly could be said to represent the belief system of all Judeo-Christians, it would still run afoul of the Establishment Clause by prescribing a compelled code of conduct from one God, namely a Judeo-Christian God, that is rejected by prominent polytheistic sects, such as Hinduism, as well as nontheistic religions, such as Buddhism. And, at the very least, the text of the Ten Commandments impermissibly commands a preference for religion over irreligion. *** [A]llowing the seat of government to serve as a stage for the propagation of an unmistakably Judeo-Christian message of piety would have the tendency to make nonmonotheists and nonbelievers "feel like [outsiders] in matters of faith, and [strangers] in the political community."

The plurality relies heavily on the fact that our Republic was founded, and has been governed since its nascence, by leaders who spoke then (and speak still) in plainly religious rhetoric. *** [But] when public officials deliver public speeches, we recognize that their words are not exclusively a transmission from the government because those oratories have embedded within them the inherently personal views of the speaker as an individual member of the polity. The permanent placement of a textual religious display on state property is different in kind; it amalgamates otherwise discordant individual views into a collective statement of government approval.

The plurality's reliance on early religious statements and proclamations made by the Founders is also problematic ***. Notably absent from their historical snapshot is the fact that Thomas Jefferson refused to issue the Thanksgiving proclamations that Washington had so readily embraced based on the argument that to do so would violate the Establishment Clause. THE CHIEF JUSTICE and Justice SCALIA disregard the substantial debates that took place regarding the constitutionality of the early proclamations and acts they cite, and paper over the fact that Madison more than once repudiated the views attributed to him by many ***. [In addition,] many of the Framers understood the word "religion" in the Establishment Clause to encompass only the various sects of Christianity. *** The original understanding of the type of "religion" that qualified for constitutional protection under the Establishment Clause likely did not include those followers of Judaism and Islam who are among the preferred "monotheistic" religions Justice SCALIA has embraced in his *McCreary County* opinion. *** Justice SCALIA's inclusion of Judaism and Islam is a laudable act of religious tolerance, but it is one that is unmoored from the Constitution's history and text, and moreover one that is patently arbitrary in its inclusion of some, but exclusion of other (*e.g.*, Buddhism), widely practiced non-Christian religions.

A reading of the First Amendment dependent on either of the purported original meanings expressed above would eviscerate the heart of the Establishment Clause. It would replace Jefferson's "wall of separation" with a perverse wall of exclusion—Christians inside, non-Christians out. It would permit States to construct walls of their own choosing—Baptists inside, Mormons out; Jewish Orthodox inside, Jewish Reform out. A Clause so understood might be faithful to the expectations of some of our Founders, but it is plainly not worthy of a society whose enviable hallmark over the course of two centuries has been the continuing expansion of religious pluralism and tolerance.

It is our duty, therefore, to interpret the [Establishment Clause] *** not by merely asking what those words meant to observers at the time of the founding, but instead by deriving from the Clause's text and history the broad principles that remain valid today. *** The principle that guides my analysis is neutrality. *** As religious pluralism has expanded, so has our acceptance of what constitutes valid belief systems. *** The Establishment Clause thus [prohibits] Texas from displaying the Ten Commandments monument the plurality so casually affirms.

[Justice O'CONNOR'S dissenting opinion has been omitted.]

Justice SOUTER, with whom Justice STEVENS and Justice GINSBURG join, dissenting.

The Ten Commandments constitute a religious statement, [their] message is inherently religious, and [the] purpose of singling them out in a display is clearly the same. *** Thus, a pedestrian happening upon the monument at issue here needs no training in religious doctrine to realize that the statement of the Commandments, quoting God himself, proclaims that the will of the divine being is the source of obligation to obey the rules, including the facially secular ones. In this case, moreover, the text is presented to give particular prominence to the Commandments' first sectarian reference, "I am the Lord thy God." That proclamation is centered on the stone and written in slightly larger letters than the subsequent recitation. *** What follows, of course, are the rules against other gods, graven images, vain swearing, and Sabbath breaking.

Nothing on the monument, in fact, detracts from its religious nature, and the plurality does not suggest otherwise. It would therefore be difficult to miss the point that the government of Texas is telling everyone who sees the monument to live up to a moral code because God requires it, with both code and conception of God being rightly understood as the inheritances specifically of Jews and Christians.

Points for Discussion

a. Reconciling *McCreary County* and *Van Orden*

Four of the five Justices who agreed that the display in *McCreary County* violated the Establishment Clause dissented in *Van Orden*; only Justice Breyer was on the winning side in both cases, although he did not join Chief Justice Rehnquist's opinion in *Van Orden*. What was Justice Breyer's reasoning in concluding that the displays in *McCreary County* were unconstitutional, but that the monument in *Van Orden* was not?

Was it the context in which the Commandments were displayed? If so, then why wasn't the inclusion in the final version of the Kentucky displays of other, secular documents sufficient to render them constitutional? Was it instead that the Kentucky displays were of recent vintage? If so, does that mean essentially that any already-existing displays are likely to survive challenge but that newly created ones will not? What would be the basis of such a rule?

b. The Test Under the Establishment Clause

After *McCreary* and *Van Orden*, what is the test for determining the constitutionality of religious displays on government property? Is neutrality still the governing principle? (How many Justices subscribed to that view in the two cases?) Is the proper test the one announced in *Lemon*? Note that Justice Souter based his opinion in *McCreary* on the purpose of the displays, which of course is the first prong of the traditional inquiry under *Lemon*. But in *Van Orden*, Chief Justice Rehnquist (who did not write for a majority) did not appear to apply the test. Is the proper test simply a multi-factored inquiry of the sort applied by Justice Breyer, or the "endorsement" test applied by Justice O'Connor in her separate opinion in *Lynch*? If so, are those approaches preferable to the *Lemon* test?

c. Legal Advice

Suppose that you are counsel to a local government. The government wants to display a religious symbol—perhaps the Ten Commandments, perhaps something else—without violating the Establishment Clause. What practical steps could you advise the government to take?

d. The Supreme Court

At the beginning of this section, we described various manifestations of religion that one might encounter on an ordinary day at the Supreme Court. Having read the cases in this section, can you explain why the Court's Christmas tree, its frieze depicting Moses and the Ten Commandments, and its customary prayer to save the Court are consistent with the Establishment Clause? Do you agree with this conclusion?

B. The Free Exercise Clause

Many colonists came to the United States from England because they wanted freedom to practice their religions. At the time, England was notorious for suppressing practices outside of the established Church of England (also called the Anglican Church). Justice Story reminded his readers

> that the laws of England merely tolerated protestant dissenters [i.e., protestants who were not Anglicans] in their public worship upon certain conditions, at once irritating and degrading; that the test and corporation acts excluded them from public and corporate offices, both of trust and profit, *** in common with Turks, Jews, heretics, papists, and other sectaries; that to deny the Trinity, however conscientiously disbelieved, was a public offence, punishable by fine and imprisonment; and that, in the rear of all these disabilities and grievances, came the long list of acts against papists, by which they were reduced to a state of political and religious slavery, and cut off from some of the dearest privileges of mankind.

3 Joseph Story, *Commentaries on the Constitution of the United States* § 1872 (1833).

The First Amendment responds to such practices. It provides: "Congress shall make no law respecting an establishment of religion, *or prohibiting the free exercise thereof ***.*" What exactly is the scope of that provision? The answer is not perfectly clear, at least in part because the Court has decided many fewer Free Exercise Clause cases than Establishment Clause cases. But certain principles are widely accepted.

First, the government cannot punish people solely for holding certain religious beliefs. It clearly would violate the Free Exercise Clause for the government to require all persons to renounce a belief in a particular conception of God. Similarly, the government plainly cannot outlaw worship, such as by making it a crime to attend services at, say, a Jewish temple or a Catholic church. As a corollary to these principles, the government cannot punish the expression of religious doctrines it believes to be false. For example, in *United States v. Ballard*, 322 U.S. 78, 86-88 (1944), the Court reviewed a mail fraud indictment of the widow and son of the founder of the "I am" religion after they claimed that they had power to cure diseases. The Court held that the jury could not be permitted to determine the truth or falsity of the defendants' representations about their ability to cure diseases.

Second, the government cannot impose special disabilities on the basis of religious belief or religious status. Accordingly, the Court invalidated a state constitutional provision that excluded ministers from serving as legislators or delegates to the state's constitutional convention. *McDaniel v. Paty*, 435 U.S. 618 (1978). Similarly, in *Torcaso v. Watkins*, 367 U.S. 488 (1961), the Court invalidated a provision in the Maryland Constitution that required state officials to declare their belief in the existence of God. The Court reasoned that the government cannot force a person to "profess a belief or disbelief in any religion."

Together, these cases stand for the principle that the "freedom to hold religious beliefs and opinions is absolute." *Braunfeld v. Brown*, 366 U.S. 599, 603 (1961). But government action seeking to interfere directly with the "freedom to believe," *Cantwell v. Connecticut*, 310 U.S. 296 (1940), is rare. Instead, most cases arising under the Free Exercise Clause involve claims that government regulations of conduct interfere with the ability to practice one's religion. Sometimes the claim is that a law prohibits conduct that a person's religion requires. The first Supreme Court decision involving the Free Exercise Clause, for example, involved a claim that a law prohibiting polygamy abridged a Mormon's right to exercise his religion, which he claimed required him to marry more than one woman. See *Reynolds v. United States*, 98 U.S. 145 (1878) (rejecting challenge). Other times, the claim is that a law requires conduct that a person's religion forbids. For example, in *United States v. Lee*, 455 U.S. 252 (1982), the Court considered (and rejected) a claim by Amish employees that the imposition of Social Security taxes interfered with their free exercise rights because the payment of taxes violated their religious beliefs.

These cases require the Supreme Court to mediate between competing principles. On the one hand, the Free Exercise Clause guarantees that individuals generally may practice their religions freely. In general, they should have an unburdened right to pray, fast, sing hymns, keep kosher, tithe, attend religious services, and so forth. On the other hand, the Free Exercise Clause cannot mean that individuals may take any actions that they choose in the name of religion. The government, for example, must be able to criminalize murder and theft even if a person might claim that he engages in these acts out of religious obligation. Indeed, as the Supreme Court has said, "the very concept of ordered liberty precludes allowing every person to make his own standards on matters of conduct in which society as a whole has important interests." *Wisconsin v. Yoder*, 406 U.S. 205, 215-216 (1972).

The current standard, developed in *Employment Division, Dept. of Human Resources of Oregon v. Smith*, 494 U.S. 872 (1990), and *Church of the Lukumi Babalu Aye, Inc. v. City of Hialeah*, 508 U.S. 520 (1993), is as follows: The government may enforce a law that burdens a particular religious practice only if (1) the law is both neutral and of general applicability; or (2) the government has a compelling interest for imposing the burden and the law is narrowly tailored to advance that interest. A law is not neutral if the object of the law is to infringe upon or restrict practices because of their religious motivation. A law lacks general applicability if it is underinclusive, applying to religious practices but not to similar non-religious practices.

By way of example, contrast two hypothetical laws. The first bars the consumption of all alcoholic beverages (as some counties in the United States still do) for the purpose of reducing alcoholism, domestic violence, and drunk driving. This law may have an effect on religious practices; for example, a Catholic church could not use wine in a communion service. But under current doctrine, the law would not violate the Free Exercise Clause because it would be neutral (given its secular purposes) and of general application (given that it applies to all consumption of alcoholic beverages). The second bans the consumption of wine only in churches, in order to discourage Catholic congregations from settling in an area. This second law is neither neutral—because its purpose is to burden religious practice—nor of general application—because it bans the consumption of wine in only limited (and religious) contexts.

In the cases that follow, we explore the path that the Supreme Court took to arrive at this particular approach. Perhaps because of the competing impulses in this area—that is, the desire to accommodate religious freedom, on the one hand, and the desire to ensure that the government can regulate conduct according to consistently applied standards, on the other—the Court's path has not been an even one.

In some of the older cases, the Court refused to require exemptions from generally applicable laws to accommodate religious practices or beliefs. In *Braunfeld v. Brown*, 366 U.S. 599, 603 (1961), for example, the Court considered a claim by Orthodox Jews that a law requiring all businesses to close on Sundays interfered with the free exercise of their religion. The appellants argued that because their religious beliefs required them to close their businesses on Saturdays, which was their Sabbath, the effect of the law was to require them to close their businesses two days every week. The law thus put them to a choice between giving up a basic tenet of their faith, on the one hand, or facing serious economic disadvantage and the potential loss of livelihood, on the other.

The Court rejected their claim. The Court declared that "the freedom to act, even when the action is in accord with one's religious convictions, is not totally free from legislative restrictions." The Court noted that the statute at issue "does not make unlawful any religious practices of appellants ***. To strike down, without the most critical scrutiny, legislation which imposes only an indirect burden on the exercise of religion, i.e., legislation which does not make unlawful the religious practice itself, would radically restrict the operating latitude of the legislature." The Court noted that the State had "power to provide a weekly respite from all labor and, at the same time, to set one day of the week apart from the others as a day of rest, repose, recreation and tranquility." It then stated: "[I]f the State regulates conduct by enacting a general law within its power, the purpose and effect of which is to advance the State's secular goals, the statute is valid despite its indirect burden on religious observance unless the State may accomplish its purpose by means which do not impose such a burden." Because a system of exemptions from the one uniform day of rest might give economic advantages to a different set of businesses, and might require the State to assess the sincerity of the religious beliefs of applicants for an exemption, the Court concluded that the State was not required to adopt such a system. Justices Brennan, Stewart, and Douglas dissented.

Only two years after the decision in *Braunfeld*, however, the Court decided the case that follows. As you will see, the Court's approach in that case was different from the approach in *Braunfeld*. In addition, the outcome did not turn on whether the challenged regulation was neutral and generally applicable. In this respect, its approach was quite different from the Court's later approach in *Employment Division v. Smith*, which we will get to shortly.

————

Sherbert v. Verner

374 U.S. 398 (1963)

Mr. Justice BRENNAN delivered the opinion of the Court.

Appellant, a member of the Seventh-day Adventist Church was discharged by her South Carolina employer because she would not work on Saturday, the Sabbath Day of her faith. When she was unable to obtain other employment because from conscientious scruples she would not take Saturday work, she filed a claim for unemployment compensation benefits under the South Carolina Unemployment Compensation Act. That law provides that, to be eligible for benefits, a claimant must be "able to work and [is] available for work"; and, further, that a claimant is ineligible for benefits "[if] he has failed, without good cause [to] accept available suitable work when offered him by the employment office or the employer." The appellee Employment Security Commission, in administrative proceedings under the statute, found that appellant's restriction upon her availability for Saturday work brought her within the provision disqualifying for benefits insured workers who fail, without good cause, to accept "suitable work when offered [by] the employment office or the employer."

The door of the Free Exercise Clause stands tightly closed against any governmental regulation of religious beliefs as such. Government may neither compel affirmation of a repugnant belief, nor penalize or discriminate against individuals or groups because they hold religious views abhorrent to the authorities, nor employ the taxing power to inhibit the dissemination of particular religious views. On the other hand, the Court has rejected challenges under the Free Exercise Clause to governmental regulation of certain overt acts prompted by religious beliefs or principles, for "even when the action is in accord with one's religious convictions, [it] is not totally free from legislative restrictions." *Braunfeld v. Brown*, 366 U.S. 599, 603 (1961). The conduct or actions so regulated have invariably posed some substantial threat to public safety, peace or order.

Plainly enough, appellant's conscientious objection to Saturday work constitutes no conduct prompted by religious principles of a kind within the reach of state legislation. If, therefore, the decision of the South Carolina Supreme Court is to withstand appellant's constitutional challenge, it must be either because her disqualification as a beneficiary represents no infringement by the State of her constitutional rights of free exercise, or because any incidental burden on the free exercise of appellant's religion may be justified by a "compelling state interest in the regulation of a subject within the State's constitutional power to regulate." *NAACP v. Button*, 371 U.S. 415 (1963).

We turn first to the question whether the disqualification for benefits imposes any burden on the free exercise of appellant's religion. We think it is clear that it does. In a sense the consequences of such a disqualification to religious principles and practices may be only an indirect result of welfare legislation within the State's general competence to enact; it is true that no criminal sanctions directly compel appellant to work a six-day week. But this is only the beginning, not the end, of our inquiry. For "[i]f the purpose or effect of a law is to impede the observance of one or all religions or is to discriminate invidiously between religions, that law is constitutionally invalid even though the burden may be characterized as being only indirect." *Braunfield v. Braun*, 366 U.S., at 607. Here not only is it apparent that appellant's declared ineligibility for benefits derives solely from the practice of her religion, but the pressure upon her to forego that practice is unmistakable. The ruling forces her to choose between following the precepts of her religion and forfeiting benefits, on the one hand, and abandoning one of the precepts of her religion in order to accept work, on the other hand. Governmental imposition of such a choice puts the same kind of burden upon the free exercise of religion as would a fine imposed against appellant for her Saturday worship.

> **Take Note**
>
> The Court describes here the substantial burden imposed by the law. What is the burden? Is it relevant that the appellant is seeking employment benefits, which are generally available not as a matter of constitutional right but instead as a matter of legislative grace? That is, does it matter that what she seeks is a "privilege," not a right? We briefly considered the significance of that difference (to the extent that there is one) in Chapter 9, when we considered Procedural Due Process, and in Chapter 14, when we considered the "unconstitutional conditions" doctrine.

We must next consider whether some compelling state interest enforced in the eligibility provisions of the South Carolina statute justifies the substantial infringement of appellant's First Amendment right. It is basic that no showing merely of a rational relationship to some colorable state interest would suffice; in this highly sensitive constitutional area, "[o]nly the gravest abuses, endangering paramount interest, give occasion for permissible limitation," *Thomas v. Collins*, 323 U.S. 516, 530 (1945). No such abuse or danger has been advanced in the present case. The appellees suggest no more than a possibility that the filing of fraudulent claims by unscrupulous claimants feigning religious objections to Saturday work might not only dilute the unemployment compensation fund but also hinder the scheduling by employers of necessary Saturday work. But that possibility is not apposite here because no such objection appears to have been made before the South Carolina Supreme Court, and we are unwilling to assess the importance of an asserted state interest without the views of the state court. Nor, if the contention had been made below, would the record appear to sustain it; there is no proof whatever to warrant such fears of malingering or deceit as those which the respondents now advance. Even if consideration of such evidence is not foreclosed by the prohibition against judicial inquiry into the truth or falsity of religious beliefs—a question as to which we intimate no view since it is not before us—it is highly doubtful whether such evidence would be sufficient to warrant a substantial infringement of religious liberties. For even if the possibility of spurious claims did threaten to dilute the fund and disrupt the scheduling of work, it would plainly be incumbent upon the appellees to demonstrate that no alternative forms of regulation would combat such abuses without infringing First Amendment rights.

> **Practice Pointer**
>
> What was the state interest that South Carolina advanced here? Can you think of any other state interest that would have been more compelling?

In these respects, then, the state interest asserted in the present case is wholly dissimilar to the interests which were found to justify the less direct burden upon religious practices in *Braunfeld v. Brown.* [The statute at issue in that case was] saved by a countervailing factor which finds no equivalent in the instant case—a strong state interest in providing one uniform day of rest for all workers. That secular objective could be achieved, the Court found, only by declaring Sunday to be that day of rest. Requiring exemptions for Sabbatarians, while theoretically possible, appeared to present an administrative problem of such magnitude, or to afford the exempted class so great a competitive advantage, that such a requirement would have rendered the entire statutory scheme unworkable. In the present case no such justifications underlie the determination of the state court that appellant's religion makes her ineligible to receive benefits.

In holding as we do, plainly we are not fostering the "establishment" of the Seventh-day Adventist religion in South Carolina, for the extension of unemployment benefits to Sabbatarians in common with Sunday worshippers reflects nothing more than the governmental obligation of neutrality in the face of religious differences, and does not represent that involvement of religious with secular institutions which it is the object of the Establishment Clause to forestall. Nor does the recognition of the appellant's right to unemployment benefits under the state statute serve to abridge any other person's religious liberties. Nor do we, by our decision today, declare the existence of a constitutional right to unemployment benefits on the part of all persons whose religious convictions are the cause of their unemployment. This is not a case in which an employee's religious convictions serve to make him a nonproductive member of society. Finally, nothing we say today constrains the States to adopt any particular form or scheme of unemployment compensation. Our holding today is only that South Carolina may not constitutionally apply the eligibility provisions so as to constrain a worker to abandon his religious convictions respecting the day of rest. This holding but reaffirms a principle that we announced a decade and a half ago, namely that no State may "exclude individual Catholics, Lutherans, Mohammedans, Baptists, Jews, Methodists, Non-believers, Presbyterians, or the members of any other faith, because of their faith, or lack of it, from receiving the benefits of public welfare legislation." *Everson v. Board of Education*, 330 U.S. 1, 16 (1947).

Mr. Justice STEWART, concurring in the result.

Because the appellant refuses to accept available jobs which would require her to work on Saturdays, South Carolina has declined to pay unemployment compensation benefits to her. Her refusal to work on Saturdays is based on the tenets of her religious faith. The Court says that South Carolina cannot under these circumstances declare her to be not "available for work" within the meaning of its statute because to do so would violate her constitutional right to the free exercise of her religion.

Yet what this Court has said about the Establishment Clause must inevitably lead to a diametrically opposite result. If the appellant's refusal to work on Saturdays were based on indolence, or on a compulsive desire to watch the Saturday television programs, no one would say that South Carolina could not hold that she was not "available for work" within the meaning of its statute. That being so, the Establishment Clause as construed by this Court not only permits but affirmatively requires South Carolina equally to deny the appellant's claim for unemployment compensation when her refusal to work on Saturdays is based upon her religious creed. For, as said in *Everson v. Board of Education*, 330 U.S. 1, 11 (1943), the Establishment Clause bespeaks "a government [stripped] of all power [to] support, or otherwise to assist any or all religions," and no State "can pass laws which aid one religion." *Id.* at 30. ***

> **Take Note**
>
> Do you agree that, under *Everson's* principle of neutrality, the Establishment Clause requires South Carolina to decline to pay benefits under the circumstances here? Isn't it a neutral, generally applicable law? Or is Justice Stewart's point that a state cannot, consistently with that principle, grant an *exemption* only to adherents of a particular religious faith? If so, do you agree?

To require South Carolina to so administer its laws as to pay public money to the appellant under the circumstances of this case is thus clearly to require the State to violate the Establishment Clause as construed by this Court. This poses no problem for me, because I think the Court's mechanistic concept of the Establishment Clause is historically unsound and constitutionally wrong. I think the process of constitutional decision in the area of the relationships between government and religion demands considerably more than the invocation of broad-brushed rhetoric of the kind I have quoted. And I think that the guarantee of religious liberty embodied in the Free Exercise Clause affirmatively requires government to create an atmosphere of hospitality and accommodation to individual belief or disbelief. In short, I think our Constitution commands the positive protection by government of religious freedom—not only for a minority, however small—not only for the majority, however large—but for each of us.

Mr. Justice HARLAN, whom Mr. Justice WHITE joins, dissenting.

Since virtually all of the mills in the Spartanburg area were operating on a six-day week, the appellant was "unavailable for work," and thus ineligible for benefits, when personal considerations prevented her from accepting employment on a full-time basis in the industry and locality in which she had worked. *** [I]n no proper sense can it be said that the State discriminated against the appellant on the basis of her religious beliefs or that she was denied benefits *because* she was a Seventh-day Adventist. She was denied benefits just as any other claimant would be denied benefits who was not "available for work" for personal reasons.

What the Court is holding is that if the State chooses to condition unemployment compensation on the applicant's availability for work, it is constitutionally compelled to carve out an exception—and to provide benefits—for those whose unavailability is due to their religious convictions. Such a holding has particular significance in two respects.

First, despite the Court's protestations to the contrary, the decision necessarily overrules *Braunfeld* ***. [J]ust as in *Braunfeld*—where exceptions to the Sunday closing laws for Sabbatarians would have been inconsistent with the purpose to achieve a uniform day of rest and would have required case-by-case inquiry into religious beliefs—so here, an exception to the rules of eligibility based on religious convictions would necessitate judicial examination of those convictions and would be at odds with the limited purpose of the statute to smooth out the economy during periods of industrial instability.

Second, [under the Court's holding the] State [must] single out for financial assistance those whose behavior is religiously motivated, even though it denies such assistance to others whose identical behavior (in this case, inability to work on Saturdays) is not religiously motivated. It has been suggested that such singling out of religious conduct for special treatment may violate the constitutional limitations on state action. *** My own view [is] that at least under the circumstances of this case it would be a permissible accommodation of religion for the State, if it chose to do so, to create an exception to its eligibility requirements for persons like the appellant. The constitutional obligation of "neutrality" is not so narrow a channel that the slightest deviation from an absolutely straight course leads to condemnation. *** For very much the same reasons, however, I cannot subscribe to the conclusion that the State is constitutionally compelled to carve out an exception to its general rule of eligibility in the present case. Those situations in which the Constitution may require special treatment on account of religion are, in my view, few and far between, and this view is amply supported by the course of constitutional litigation in this area.

Points for Discussion

a. Strict Scrutiny?

In requiring the state to articulate a "compelling interest" before applying a neutral law to burden an individual's religious freedom, is the Court effectively applying strict scrutiny to such applications of state regulation? Does it make sense to apply such searching scrutiny to laws that not only are neutral and generally applicable, but also do not appear to have been applied with any invidious purpose? In *Sherbert*, for example, there was no contention that South Carolina had intentionally singled out the appellant for adverse treatment because of her religious beliefs; to the contrary, the claim was that South Carolina's presumably neutral application of a neutral law happened to burden appellant because of her particular beliefs. Is this the type of government action that, in other contexts, triggers strict scrutiny? Is it consistent with the Court's approach in *Washington v. Davis*, 426 U.S. 229 (1976), which (we saw in Chapter 11) held that neutral laws that disproportionately affect persons of a particular race are not subject to strict scrutiny under the Equal Protection Clause? Is it consistent with the Court's approach in *United States v. O'Brien*, 391 U.S. 367 (1968), which (we saw in Chapter 14) held that content-neutral, generally applicable regulations of conduct that incidentally burden expression are not subject to strict scrutiny under the First Amendment?

How much of the outcome in *Sherbert* turned on the importance of the public benefit at stake? Can we expect other neutral, generally applicable laws to survive this form of scrutiny when they do not provide something as desirable as unemployment compensation? Notice that, upon finding a "substantial burden" on appellant's religious freedom, the Court insisted upon a compelling interest. Under other neutral, generally applicable laws, is there reason to think that the burden on religious freedom will be less substantial than the burden at issue in *Sherbert*?

b. Compelling State Interest

What would be an example of a compelling state interest that could justify a substantial burden on religious freedom? This question is difficult to answer. Not surprisingly, the Supreme Court in most cases has not been clear on the subject. In *Goldman v. Weinberger*, 475 U.S. 503 (1986), for example, the Supreme Court held that the Air Force's interest in uniformity of appearance and other factors justified a regulation prohibiting an officer from wearing a yarmulke while on duty. But the Court did not specifically describe the Air Force's interest as "compelling." Is the Air Force's interest in uniformity more "compelling" than a state's interest in ensuring that only those who have sought work and could not find it are eligible to receive benefits from a limited pot of state funds?

In the following case, which also pre-dated the Court's decision in *Employment Division v. Smith*, the Court did not apply the *Smith* standard for determining when a law may permissibly burden a religious practice. After you have read *Smith*, consider whether *Yoder* is still good law. If nothing else, note that the case established the principle that the Free Exercise Clause protects only practices that are rooted in religious belief.

———————

Wisconsin v. Yoder

406 U.S. 205 (1972)

Mr. Chief Justice BURGER delivered the opinion of the Court.

Respondents Jonas Yoder and Wallace Miller are members of the Old Order Amish religion, and respondent Adin Yutzy is a member of the Conservative Amish Mennonite Church. They and their families are residents of Green County, Wisconsin. Wisconsin's compulsory school-attendance law required them to cause their children to attend public or private school until reaching age 16 but the respondents declined to send their children, ages 14 and 15, to public school after they complete the eighth grade. The children were not enrolled in any private school, or within any recognized exception to the compulsory-attendance law, and they are conceded to be subject to the Wisconsin statute.

On complaint of the school district administrator for the public schools, respondents were charged, tried, and convicted of violating the compulsory-attendance law in Green County Court and were fined the sum of $5 each. Respondents defended on the ground that the application of the compulsory-attendance law violated their rights under the First and Fourteenth Amendments. The trial testimony showed that respondents believed, in accordance with the tenets of Old Order Amish communities generally, that their children's attendance at high school, public or private, was contrary to the Amish religion and way of life. They believed that by sending their children to high school, they would not only expose themselves to the danger of the censure of the church community, but, as found by the county court, also endanger their own salvation and that of their children. The State stipulated that respondents' religious beliefs were sincere.

There is no doubt as to the power of a State, having a high responsibility for education of its citizens, to impose reasonable regulations for the control and duration of basic education. *See, e.g.,* *Pierce v. Society of Sisters*, 268 U.S. 510, 534 (1925). Providing public schools ranks at the very apex of the function of a State. Yet even this paramount responsibility was, in *Pierce*, made to yield to the right of parents to provide an equivalent education in a privately operated system. There the Court held that Oregon's statute compelling attendance in a public school from age eight to age 16 unreasonably interfered with the interest of parents in directing the rearing of their off-

> **Make the Connection**
>
> We considered the Court's decision in *Pierce*, and the right of parents to control the upbringing of their children, in Chapter 8.

spring, including their education in church-operated schools. As that case suggests, the values of parental direction of the religious upbringing and education of their children in their early and formative years have a high place in our society. Thus, a State's interest in universal education, however highly we rank it, is not totally free from a balancing process when it impinges on fundamental rights and interests, such as those specifically protected by the Free Exercise Clause of the First Amendment, and the traditional interest of parents with respect to the religious upbringing of their children so long as they, in the words of *Pierce*, "prepare [them] for additional obligations." 268 U.S. at 535.

It follows that in order for Wisconsin to compel school attendance beyond the eighth grade against a claim that such attendance interferes with the practice of a legitimate religious belief, it must appear either that the State does not deny the free exercise of religious belief by its requirement, or that there is a state interest of sufficient magnitude to override the interest claiming protection under the Free Exercise Clause. Long before there was general acknowledgment of the need for universal formal education, the Religion Clauses had specifically and firmly fixed the right to free exercise of religious beliefs, and buttressing this fundamental right was an equally firm, even if less explicit, prohibition against the establishment of any religion by government. The values underlying these two provisions relating to religion have been zealously protected, sometimes even at the expense of other interests of admittedly high social importance. The invalidation of financial aid to parochial schools by government grants for a salary subsidy for teachers is but one example of the extent to which courts have gone in this regard, notwithstanding that such aid programs were legislatively determined to be in the public interest and the service of sound educational policy by States and by Congress. *Lemon v. Kurtzman*, 403 U.S. 602 (1971).

We come then to the quality of the claims of the respondents concerning the alleged encroachment of Wisconsin's compulsory school-attendance statute on their rights and the rights of their children to the free exercise of the religious beliefs they and their forbears have adhered to for almost three centuries. In evaluating those claims we must be careful to determine whether the Amish religious faith and their mode of life are, as they claim, inseparable and interdependent. A way of life, however virtuous and admirable, may not be interposed as a barrier to reasonable state regulation of education if it is based on purely secular considerations; to have the protection of the Religion Clauses, the claims must be rooted in religious belief. Although a determination of what is a "religious" belief or practice entitled to constitutional protection may present a most delicate question, the very concept of ordered liberty precludes allowing every person to make his own standards on matters of conduct in which society as a whole has important interests. Thus, if the Amish asserted their claims because of their

> **Take Note**
>
> In this passage, the Court explains that, to be protected by the Free Exercise Clause, a practice must be rooted in a legitimate "religious belief." The Clause accordingly does not protect acts undertaken solely for secular reasons. The state in this case conceded that the respondents were motivated by "sincere" religious beliefs. What would the Court's inquiry have been like if the state had not made that concession?

subjective evaluation and rejection of the contemporary secular values accepted by the majority, much as Thoreau rejected the social values of his time and isolated himself at Walden Pond, their claims would not rest on a religious basis. Thoreau's choice was philosophical and personal rather than religious, and such belief does not rise to the demands of the Religion Clauses.

Giving no weight to such secular considerations, however, we see that the record in this case abundantly supports the claim that the traditional way of life of the Amish is not merely a matter of personal preference, but one of deep religious conviction, shared by an organized group, and intimately related to daily living. That the Old Order Amish daily life and religious practice stem from their faith is shown by the fact that it is in response to their literal interpretation of the Biblical injunction from the Epistle of Paul to the Romans, "be not conformed to this world." This command is fundamental to the Amish faith. Moreover, for the Old Order Amish, religion is not simply a matter of theocratic belief. As the expert witnesses explained, the Old Order Amish religion pervades and determines virtually their entire way of life, regulating it with the detail of the Talmudic diet through the strictly enforced rules of the church community.

> **Take Note**
>
> The trial in this case included testimony from experts who described Amish religious beliefs. What if the state had offered experts to rebut that testimony? Could the judge find one set of experts not credible? Misinformed?

The impact of the compulsory-attendance law on respondents' practice of the Amish religion is not only severe, but inescapable, for the Wisconsin law affirmatively compels them, under threat of criminal sanction, to perform acts undeniably at odds with fundamental tenets of their religious beliefs. Nor is the impact of the compulsory-attendance law confined to grave interference with important Amish religious tenets from a subjective point of view. It carries with it precisely the kind of objective danger to the free exercise of religion that the First Amendment was designed to prevent. As the record shows, compulsory school attendance to age 16 for Amish children carries with it a very real threat of undermining the Amish community and religious practice as they exist today; they must either abandon belief and be assimilated into society at large, or be forced to migrate to some other and more tolerant region.

In sum, the unchallenged testimony of acknowledged experts in education and religious history, almost 300 years of consistent practice, and strong evidence of a sustained faith pervading and regulating respondents' entire mode of life support the claim that enforcement of the State's requirement of compulsory formal education after the eighth grade would gravely endanger if not destroy the free exercise of respondents' religious beliefs.

The State advances two primary arguments in support of its system of compulsory education. It notes, as Thomas Jefferson pointed out early in our history, that some degree of education is necessary to prepare citizens to participate effectively and intelligently in our open political system if we are to preserve freedom and independence. Further, education prepares individuals to be self-reliant and self-sufficient participants in society. We accept these propositions.

However, the evidence adduced by the Amish in this case is persuasively to the effect that an additional one or two years of formal high school for Amish children in place of their long-established program of informal vocational education would do little to serve those interests. Respondents' experts testified at trial, without challenge, that the value of all education must be assessed in terms of its capacity to prepare the child for life. It is one thing to say that compulsory education for a year or two beyond the eighth grade may be necessary when its goal is the preparation of the child for life in modern society as the majority live, but it is quite another if the goal of education be viewed as the preparation of the child for life in the separated agrarian community that is the keystone of the Amish faith.

> **Take Note**
>
> In this passage, the Court applies a form of "means-ends analysis" for determining whether the state can apply its law to the respondents. The Court concludes that the means chosen by the state (i.e., compulsory education until age 16) is not necessary to achieve the state's ends (i.e., preparing individuals to participate in society). Under the Court's approach, how weighty must the state's interest be? How closely tailored to achieving that interest must the challenged regulation be?

The State attacks respondents' position as one fostering "ignorance" from which the child must be protected by the State. No one can question the State's duty to protect children from ignorance but this argument does not square with the facts disclosed in the record. Whatever their idiosyncrasies as seen by the majority, this record strongly shows that the Amish community has been a highly successful social unit within our society, even if apart from the conventional "mainstream." Its members are productive and very law-abiding members of society; they reject public welfare in any of its usual modern forms. The Congress itself recognized their self-sufficiency by authorizing exemption of such groups as the Amish from the obligation to pay social security taxes.

There is nothing in this record to suggest that the Amish qualities of reliability, self-reliance, and dedication to work would fail to find ready markets in today's society. Absent some contrary evidence supporting the State's position, we are unwilling to assume that persons possessing such valuable vocational skills and habits are doomed to become burdens on society should they determine to leave the Amish faith, nor is there any basis in the record to warrant a finding that an additional one or two years of formal school education beyond the eighth grade would serve to eliminate any such problem that might exist.

For the reasons stated we hold, with the Supreme Court of Wisconsin, that the First and Fourteenth Amendments prevent the State from compelling respondents to cause their children to attend formal high school to age 16. Our disposition of this case, however, in no way alters our recognition of the obvious fact that courts are not school boards or legislatures, and are ill-equipped to determine the "necessity" of discrete aspects of a State's program of compulsory education. This should suggest that courts must move with great circumspection in performing the sensitive and delicate task of weighing a State's legitimate social concern when faced with religious claims for exemption from generally applicable education requirements. It cannot be overemphasized that we are not dealing with a way of life and mode of education by a group claiming to have recently discovered some "progressive" or more enlightened process for rearing children for modern life.

Mr. Justice DOUGLAS, dissenting in part.

I agree with the Court that the religious scruples of the Amish are opposed to the education of their children beyond the grade schools, yet I disagree with the Court's conclusion that the matter is within the dispensation of parents alone. The Court's analysis assumes that the only interests at stake in the case are those of the Amish parents on the one hand, and those of the State on the other. The difficulty with this approach is that, despite the Court's claim, the parents are seeking to vindicate not only their own free exercise claims, but also those of their high-school-age children.

On this important and vital matter of education, I think the children should be entitled to be heard. While the parents, absent dissent, normally speak for the entire family, the education of the child is a matter on which the child will often have decided views. He may want to be a pianist or an astronaut or an oceanographer. To do so he will have to break from the Amish tradition.

It is the future of the student, not the future of the parents, that is imperiled by today's decision. If a parent keeps his child out of school beyond the grade school, then the child will be forever barred from entry into the new and amazing world of diversity that we have today. The child may decide that that is the preferred course, or he may rebel. It is the student's judgment, not his parents', that is essential if we are to give full meaning to what we have said about the Bill of Rights and of the right of students to be masters of their own destiny. *** [But the] views of the two children in question were not canvassed by the Wisconsin courts. The matter should be explicitly reserved so that new hearings can be held on remand of the case.

————————

Points for Discussion

a. Neutral and Generally Applicable Laws?

Was the law at issue in *Yoder* neutral—that is, did it have a purpose neither to advance nor inhibit religious practice? Was it a law of general applicability—that is, did it apply evenly to the religious and the non-religious alike? If so, then why did the Court invalidate it? Must courts grant exemptions from such laws for every person who sincerely asserts that his religious beliefs preclude compliance, assuming he can substantiate the genuineness of his religious convictions? Or is the form of scrutiny that the Court applied in *Yoder*—something very much like strict scrutiny, although the court did not explicitly call it that—flexible enough to ensure that truly important laws are enforced uniformly?

Imagine, for example, a person who adheres to a sect of Christianity that teaches that the only acceptable "tax" in God's eyes is a tithe to the Church, and that any other form of tax—including federal income taxes—violates the Biblical injunction against "false idols." Does the Court's approach in *Yoder* require the government to exempt him from the obligation to pay income taxes? If not, why? Because the government has a more compelling interest in raising revenues than it does in ensuring an educated polity? Or because there is no other way to advance its interest? Or is it simply impossible to draw a principled distinction?

b. What is a Religious Belief?

If the Establishment Clause protects only practices rooted in religious beliefs, courts presumably must distinguish religious beliefs from other kinds of beliefs. The Supreme Court has never devised a clear definition. How should religion be defined? Should it be a function of the adherent's sincerity? The number of adherents to the religion? The extent to which the beliefs seem within the plausible range of acceptable views? Isn't the very inquiry in tension with the idea of free exercise of religion?

Consider the view of then-Dean (and now Judge) Guido Calabresi:

> There may be some beliefs which are considered *so* outlandish that they do not count as religions at all, even for purposes of the [religion clauses]. In fact that is a subterfuge—for no principled distinction can be made between cults and religions. It may, nonetheless, be a useful—if dangerous—lie ***. By denying that some cults are religions at all, we may be able to give full protection in the face of majoritarian pressures to any number of other religions which are *not* "acceptable," but which could not be termed non-religious under any reasonable definition of religion.

Guido Calabresi, Ideals, Beliefs, Attitudes, and the Law 60-61 (1985). Do you agree that there is no "principled" way to distinguish among claims of religious beliefs? If so, is Judge Calabresi's approach defensible?

———————————

In the following case, the Court appeared to depart from *Sherbert* and *Yoder* to establish a new standard for claims under the Free Exercise Clause. Consider carefully what the Court says about its precedents, and whether the standard it articulates—new or not—is sensible.

———————————

Employment Div., Dept. of Human Resources of Oregon v. Smith

494 U.S. 872 (1990)

Justice SCALIA delivered the opinion of the Court.

Oregon law prohibits the knowing or intentional possession of a "controlled substance" unless the substance has been prescribed by a medical practitioner. The law defines "controlled substance" as a drug classified in Schedules I through V of the Federal Controlled Substances Act, as modified by the State Board of Pharmacy. Persons who violate this provision by possessing a controlled substance listed on Schedule I are "guilty of a Class B felony." As compiled by the State Board of Pharmacy under its statutory authority, Schedule I contains the drug peyote, a hallucinogen derived from the plant *Lophophora williamsii Lemaire*.

Respondents Alfred Smith and Galen Black (hereinafter respondents) were fired from their jobs with a private drug rehabilitation organization because they ingested peyote for sacramental purposes at a ceremony of the Native American Church, of which both are members. When respondents applied to petitioner Employment Division (hereinafter petitioner) for unemployment compensation, they were determined to be ineligible for benefits because they had been discharged for work-related "misconduct." ***

The free exercise of religion means, first and foremost, the right to believe and profess whatever religious doctrine one desires. Thus, the First Amendment obviously excludes all "governmental regulation of religious *beliefs* as such." *Sherbert v. Verner,* 374 U.S. 398, 402 (1963). The government may not compel affirmation of religious belief, see *Torcaso v. Watkins,* 367 U.S. 488 (1961), punish the expression of religious doctrines it believes to be false, *United States v. Ballard,* 322 U.S. 78, 86-88 (1944), impose special disabilities on the basis of religious views or religious status, see *McDaniel v. Paty,* 435 U.S. 618 (1978), or lend its power to one or the other side in controversies over religious authority or dogma, see *Presbyterian Church in U.S. v. Mary Elizabeth Blue Hull Memorial Presbyterian Church,* 393 U.S. 440, 445-452 (1969).

But the "exercise of religion" often involves not only belief and profession but the performance of (or abstention from) physical acts: assembling with others for a worship service, participating in sacramental use of bread and wine, proselytizing, abstaining from certain foods or certain modes of transportation. It would be true, we think (though no case of ours has involved the point), that a State would be "prohibiting the free exercise [of religion]" if it sought to ban such acts or abstentions only when they are engaged in for religious reasons, or only because of the religious belief that they display. It would doubtless be unconstitutional, for example, to ban the casting of "statues that are to be used for worship purposes," or to prohibit bowing down before a golden calf.

Make the Connection

The case that follows—*Church of the Lukumi Babalu Aye, Inc. v. City of Hialeah*—involved (in the Court's view) just such a statute.

Respondents in the present case, however, seek to carry the meaning of "prohibiting the free exercise [of religion]" one large step further. They contend that their religious motivation for using peyote places them beyond the reach of a criminal law that is not specifically directed at their religious practice, and that is concededly constitutional as applied to those who use the drug for other reasons. They assert, in other words, that "prohibiting the free exercise [of religion]" includes requiring any individual to observe a generally applicable law that requires (or forbids) the performance of an act that his religious belief forbids (or requires). As a textual matter, we do not think the words must be given that meaning. It is no more necessary to regard the collection of a general tax, for example, as "prohibiting the free exercise [of religion]" by those citizens who believe support of organized government to be sinful, than it is to regard the same tax as "abridging the freedom [of] the press" of those publishing companies that must pay the tax as a condition of staying in business. It is a permissible reading of the text, in the one case as in the other, to say that if prohibiting the exercise of religion (or burdening the activity of printing) is not the object of the tax but merely the incidental effect of a generally applicable and otherwise valid provision, the First Amendment has not been offended.

Our decisions reveal that the latter reading is the correct one. We have never held that an individual's religious beliefs excuse him from compliance with an otherwise valid law prohibiting conduct that the State is free to regulate. On the contrary, the record of more than a century of our free exercise jurisprudence contradicts that proposition. As described succinctly by Justice Frankfurter in *Minersville School Dist. Bd. of Ed. v. Gobitis,* 310 U.S. 586, 594-595 (1940): "Conscientious scruples have not, in the course of the long struggle for religious toleration, relieved the individual from obedience to a general law not aimed at the promotion or restriction of religious beliefs. The mere possession of religious convictions which contradict the relevant concerns of a political society does not relieve the citizen from the discharge of political responsibilities." We first had occasion to assert that principle in *Reynolds v. United States,* 98 U.S. 145 (1878), where we rejected the claim that criminal laws against polygamy could not be constitutionally applied to those whose religion commanded the practice. "Laws," we said, "are made for the government of actions, and while they cannot interfere with mere religious belief and opinions, they may with practices. [Can] a man excuse his practices to the contrary because of his religious belief? To permit this would be to make the professed doctrines of religious belief superior to the law of the land, and in effect to permit every citizen to become a law unto himself." *Id. at 166-167.*

> **FYI**
>
> In *Gobitis*, the Court rejected a free exercise challenge to a requirement that school children recite the pledge of allegiance. The Court overruled *Gobitis*, however, in *West Virginia State Board of Education v. Barnette,* 319 U.S. 624 (1943). In light of that fact, should the Court rely on *Gobitis* here?

Our most recent decision involving a neutral, generally applicable regulatory law that compelled activity forbidden by an individual's religion was *United States v. Lee,* 455 U.S. 252, 258-261 (1982). There, an Amish employer, on behalf of himself and his employees, sought exemption from collection and payment of Social Security taxes on the ground that the Amish faith prohibited participation in governmental support programs. We rejected the claim that an exemption was constitutionally required. There would be no way, we observed, to distinguish the Amish believer's objection to Social Security taxes from the religious objections that others might have to the collection or use of other taxes. "If, for example, a religious adherent believes war is a sin, and if a certain percentage of the federal budget can be identified as devoted to war-related activities, such individuals would have a similarly valid claim to be exempt from paying that percentage of the income tax. The tax system could not function if denominations were allowed to challenge the tax system because tax payments were spent in a manner that violates their religious belief." Id. at 260.

The only decisions in which we have held that the First Amendment bars application of a neutral, generally applicable law to religiously motivated action have involved not the Free Exercise Clause alone, but the Free Exercise Clause in conjunction with other constitutional protections, such as freedom of speech and of the press, see *Cantwell v. Connecticut,* 310 U.S. 296, 304-307 (1940) (invalidating a licensing system for religious and charitable solicitations under which the administrator had discretion to deny a license to any cause he deemed nonreligious); *Murdock v. Pennsylvania,* 319 U.S. 105 (1943) (invalidating a flat tax on solicitation as applied to the dissemination of religious ideas); or the right of parents, acknowledged in *Pierce v. Society of Sisters,* 268 U.S. 510 (1925), to direct the education of their children, see *Wisconsin v. Yoder,* 406 U.S. 205 (1972) (invalidating compulsory school-attendance laws as applied to Amish parents who refused on religious grounds to send their children to school). ***

The present case does not present such a hybrid situation, but a free exercise claim unconnected with any communicative activity or parental right. Respondents urge us to hold, quite simply, that when otherwise prohibitable conduct is accompanied by religious convictions, not only the convictions but the conduct itself must be free from governmental regula-

> **Take Note**
>
> The Court here distinguishes _Yoder_ on the ground that it involved the constitutional right of parents to direct the education of their children. Having read _Yoder_, do you agree that this fact was central to the decision?

tion. We have never held that, and decline to do so now. There being no contention that Oregon's drug law represents an attempt to regulate religious beliefs, the communication of religious beliefs, or the raising of one's children in those beliefs, the rule to which we have adhered ever since _Reynolds_ plainly controls. "Our cases do not at their farthest reach support the proposition that a stance of conscientious opposition relieves an objector from any colliding duty fixed by a democratic government." *Gillette v. United States,* 401 U.S. 437, 461 (1971).

Respondents argue that even though exemption from generally applicable criminal laws need not automatically be extended to religiously motivated actors, at least the claim for a religious exemption must be evaluated under the balancing test set forth in *Sherbert v. Verner,* 374 U.S. 398 (1963). Under the _Sherbert_ test, governmental actions that substantially burden a religious practice must be justified by a compelling governmental interest. Applying that test we have, on three occasions, invalidated state unemployment compensa-

> **Take Note**
>
> In this passage, the Court states that the *Sherbert* test, which requires a compelling state interest for laws that burden religious practices, has been applied only in cases involving claims for unemployment compensation. Isn't *Smith* just such a case? The Court seems to suggest that the neutral, generally applicable law at issue here is the criminal prohibition on the possession of a controlled substance. But isn't the challenge here to the state's refusal to provide unemployment compensation? Is the Court effectively overruling *Sherbert* without explicitly saying so?

tion rules that conditioned the availability of benefits upon an applicant's willingness to work under conditions forbidden by his religion. See *Sherbert; Thomas v. Review Bd. of Indiana Employment Security Div.,* 450 U.S. 707 (1981); *Hobbie v. Unemployment Appeals Comm'n of Florida,* 480 U.S. 136 (1987). We have never invalidated any governmental action on the basis of the *Sherbert* test except the denial of unemployment compensation. Although we have sometimes purported to apply the *Sherbert* test in contexts other than that, we have always found the test satisfied, see *United States v. Lee,* 455 U.S. 252 (1982); *Gillette v. United States,* 401 U.S. 437 (1971). In recent years we have abstained from applying the *Sherbert* test (outside the unemployment compensation field) at all. In *Bowen v. Roy,* 476 U.S. 693 (1986), we declined to apply *Sherbert* analysis to a federal statutory scheme that required benefit applicants and recipients to provide their Social Security numbers. The plaintiffs in that case asserted that it would violate their religious beliefs to obtain and provide a Social Security number for their daughter. We held the statute's application to the plaintiffs valid regardless of whether it was necessary to effectuate a compelling interest. In *Lyng v. Northwest Indian Cemetery Protective Assn.,* 485 U.S. 439 (1988), we declined to apply *Sherbert* analysis to the Government's logging and road construction activities on lands used for religious purposes by several Native American Tribes, even though it was undisputed that the activities "could have devastating effects on traditional Indian religious practices," 485 U.S., at 451. In *Goldman v. Weinberger,* 475 U.S. 503 (1986), we rejected application of the *Sherbert* test to military dress regulations that forbade the wearing of yarmulkes. ***

Even if we were inclined to breathe into *Sherbert* some life beyond the unemployment compensation field, we would not apply it to require exemptions from a generally applicable criminal law. The *Sherbert* test, it must be recalled, was developed in a context that lent itself to individualized governmental assessment of the reasons for the relevant conduct. [A] distinctive feature of unemployment compensation programs is that their eligibility criteria invite consideration of the particular circumstances behind an applicant's unemployment ***. [O]ur decisions in the unemployment cases stand for the proposition that where the State has in place a system of individual exemptions, it may not refuse to extend that system to cases of "religious hardship" without compelling reason. *Bowen v. Roy,* 476 U.S., at 708.

Whether or not the decisions are that limited, they at least have nothing to do with an across-the-board criminal prohibition on a particular form of conduct. Although, as noted earlier, we have sometimes used the *Sherbert* test to analyze free exercise challenges to such laws, we have never applied the test to invalidate one. We conclude today that the sounder approach, and the approach in accord with the vast majority of our precedents, is to hold the test inapplicable to such challenges. The government's ability to enforce generally applicable prohibitions of socially harmful conduct, like its ability to carry out other aspects of public policy, "cannot depend on measuring the effects of a governmental action on a religious objector's spiritual development." Lyng, 485 U.S., at 451. To make an individual's obligation to obey such a law contingent upon the law's coincidence with his religious beliefs, except where the State's interest is "compelling"—permitting him, by virtue of his beliefs, "to become a law unto himself," Reynolds v. United States, 98 U.S., at 167—contradicts both constitutional tradition and common sense.

The "compelling government interest" requirement seems benign, because it is familiar from other fields. But using it as the standard that must be met before the government may accord different treatment on the basis of race or before the government may regulate the content of speech is not remotely comparable to using it for the purpose asserted here. What it produces in those other fields—equality of treatment and an unrestricted flow of contending speech—are constitutional norms; what it would produce here—a private right to ignore generally applicable laws—is a constitutional anomaly.[3]

Nor is it possible to limit the impact of respondents' proposal by requiring a "compelling state interest" only when the conduct prohibited is "central" to the individual's religion. It is no more appropriate for judges to determine the "centrality" of religious beliefs before applying a "compelling interest" test in the free exercise field, than it would be for them to determine the "importance" of ideas before applying the "compelling interest" test in the free speech field. What principle of law or logic can be brought to bear to contradict a believer's assertion that a particular act is "central" to his personal faith? *** Repeatedly and in many different contexts, we have warned that courts must not presume to determine the place of a particular belief in a religion or the plausibility of a religious claim. See, *e.g.*, *United States v. Ballard*, 322 U.S. 78, 85-87 (1944).

If the "compelling interest" test is to be applied at all, then, it must be applied across the board, to all actions thought to be religiously commanded. Moreover, if "compelling interest" really means what it says (and watering it down here would subvert its rigor in the other fields where it is applied), many laws will not meet the test. Any society adopting such a system would be courting anarchy, but that danger increases in direct proportion to the society's diversity of religious beliefs, and its determination to coerce or suppress none of them. Precisely because "we are a cosmopolitan nation made up of people of

---

[3] Just as we subject to the most exacting scrutiny laws that make classifications based on race, so too we strictly scrutinize governmental classifications based on religion, see *McDaniel v. Paty*, 435 U.S. 618 (1978). But we have held that race-neutral laws that have the effect of disproportionately disadvantaging a particular racial group do not thereby become subject to compelling-interest analysis under the Equal Protection Clause, see *Washington v. Davis*, 426 U.S. 229 (1976); and we have held that generally applicable laws unconcerned with regulating speech that have the effect of interfering with speech do not thereby become subject to compelling-interest analysis under the First Amendment, see *Citizen Publishing Co. v. United States*, 394 U.S. 131, 139 (1969) (antitrust laws). Our conclusion that generally applicable, religion-neutral laws that have the effect of burdening a particular religious practice need not be justified by a compelling governmental interest is the only approach compatible with these precedents.

almost every conceivable religious preference," and precisely because we value and protect that religious divergence, we cannot afford the luxury of deeming *presumptively invalid*, as applied to the religious objector, every regulation of conduct that does not protect an interest of the highest order. The rule respondents favor would open the prospect of constitutionally required religious exemptions from civic obligations of almost every conceivable kind—ranging from compulsory military service, *Gillette v. United States*, 401 U.S. 437 (1971), to the payment of taxes; to health and safety regulation such as manslaughter and child neglect laws, compulsory vaccination laws, drug laws, and traffic laws; to social welfare legislation such as minimum wage laws, child labor laws, animal cruelty laws, environmental protection laws, and laws providing for equality of opportunity for the races, see, *e.g.*, *Bob Jones University v. United States*, 461 U.S. 574, 603-604 (1983). The First Amendment's protection of religious liberty does not require this.

Values that are protected against government interference through enshrinement in the Bill of Rights are not thereby banished from the political process. Just as a society that believes in the negative protection accorded to the press by the First Amendment is likely to enact laws that affirmatively foster the dissemination of the printed word, so also a society that believes in the negative protection accorded to religious belief can be expected to be solicitous of that value in its legislation as well. It is therefore not surprising that a number of States have made an exception to their drug laws for sacramental peyote use. But to say that a nondiscriminatory religious-practice exemption is permitted, or even that it is desirable, is not to say that it is constitutionally required, and that the appropriate occasions for its creation can be discerned by the courts. It may fairly be said that leaving accommodation to the political process will place at a relative disadvantage those religious practices that are not widely engaged in; but that unavoidable consequence of democratic government must be preferred to a system in which each conscience is a law unto itself or in which judges weigh the social importance of all laws against the centrality of all religious beliefs.

Because respondents' ingestion of peyote was prohibited under Oregon law, and because that prohibition is constitutional, Oregon may, consistent with the Free Exercise Clause, deny respondents unemployment compensation when their dismissal results from use of the drug.

Justice O'CONNOR, with whom Justice BRENNAN, Justice MARSHALL, and Justice BLACKMUN join as to Parts I and II, concurring in the judgment.

Although I agree with the result the Court reaches in this case, I cannot join its opinion. In my view, today's holding dramatically departs from well-settled First Amendment jurisprudence, appears unnecessary to resolve the question presented, and is incompatible with our Nation's fundamental commitment to individual religious liberty.

The First Amendment [does] not distinguish between laws that are generally applicable and laws that target particular religious practices. Indeed, few States would be so naive as to enact a law directly prohibiting or burdening a religious practice as such. Our free exercise cases have all concerned generally applicable laws that had the effect of significantly burdening a religious practice. If the First Amendment is to have any vitality, it ought not be construed to cover only the extreme and hypothetical situation in which a State directly targets a religious practice.

To say that a person's right to free exercise has been burdened, of course, does not mean that he has an absolute right to engage in the conduct. Under our established First Amendment jurisprudence, we have recognized that the freedom to act, unlike the freedom to believe, cannot be absolute. Instead, we have respected both the First Amendment's express textual mandate and the governmental interest in regulation of conduct by requiring the government to justify any substantial burden on religiously motivated conduct by a compelling state interest and by means narrowly tailored to achieve that interest.

The Court endeavors to escape from our decisions in *Cantwell* and *Yoder* by labeling them "hybrid" decisions, but there is no denying that both cases expressly relied on the Free Exercise Clause, see *Cantwell*, 310 U.S., at 303-307; *Yoder*, 406 U.S., at 219-229, and that we have consistently regarded those cases as part of the mainstream of our free exercise jurisprudence. Moreover, in each of the other cases cited by the Court to support its categorical rule, we rejected the particular constitutional claims before us only after carefully weighing the competing interests. That we rejected the free exercise claims in those cases hardly calls into question the applicability of First Amendment doctrine in the first place. Indeed, it is surely unusual to judge the vitality of a constitutional doctrine by looking to the win-loss record of the plaintiffs who happen to come before us.

FYI

In *Cantwell*, the Court reversed a conviction under a statute that required a person to obtain a license before soliciting money for religious causes. The Court relied on the First Amendment's protections for the freedom of speech and the free exercise of religion.

In my view, [the] essence of a free exercise claim is relief from a burden imposed by government on religious practices or beliefs, whether the burden is imposed directly through laws that prohibit or compel specific religious practices, or indirectly through laws that, in effect, make abandonment of one's own religion or conformity to the religious beliefs of others the price of an equal place in the civil community. A State that makes criminal an individual's religiously motivated conduct burdens that individual's free exercise of religion in the severest manner possible ***. I would have thought it beyond argument that such laws implicate free exercise concerns. Indeed, we have never distinguished between cases in which a State conditions receipt of a benefit on conduct prohibited by religious beliefs and cases in which a State affirmatively prohibits such conduct.

Once it has been shown that a government regulation or criminal prohibition burdens the free exercise of religion, we have consistently asked the government to demonstrate that unbending application of its regulation to the religious objector "is essential to accomplish an overriding governmental interest," *Lee*, 455 U.S., at 257-258, or represents "the least restrictive means of achieving some compelling state interest." *Thomas*, 450 U.S., at

718. To me, the sounder approach—the approach more consistent with our role as judges to decide each case on its individual merits—is to apply this test in each case to determine whether the burden on the specific plaintiffs before us is constitutionally significant and whether the particular criminal interest asserted by the State before us is compelling. Even if, as an empirical matter, a government's criminal laws might usually serve a compelling interest in health, safety, or public order, the First Amendment at least requires a case-by-case determination of the question, sensitive to the facts of each particular claim.

The Court today gives no convincing reason to depart from settled First Amendment jurisprudence. There is nothing talismanic about neutral laws of general applicability or general criminal prohibitions, for laws neutral toward religion can coerce a person to violate his religious conscience or intrude upon his religious duties just as effectively as laws aimed at religion. *** As the language of the [Free Exercise] Clause itself makes clear, an individual's free exercise of religion is a preferred constitutional activity. A law that makes criminal such an activity therefore triggers constitutional concern—and heightened judicial scrutiny—even if it does not target the particular religious conduct at issue. Our free speech cases similarly recognize that neutral regulations that affect free speech values are subject to a balancing, rather than categorical, approach. See, *e.g.,* United States v. O'Brien, 391 U.S. 367, 377 (1968). The Court's parade of horribles not only fails as a reason for discarding the compelling interest test, it instead demonstrates just the opposite: that courts have been quite capable of applying our free exercise jurisprudence to strike sensible balances between religious liberty and competing state interests.

[T]he Court today suggests that the disfavoring of minority religions is an "unavoidable consequence" under our system of government and that accommodation of such religions must be left to the political process. In my view, however, the First Amendment was enacted precisely to protect the rights of those whose religious practices are not shared by the majority and may be viewed with hostility. The history of our free exercise doctrine amply demonstrates the harsh impact majoritarian rule has had on unpopular or emerging religious groups such as the Jehovah's Witnesses and the Amish. Indeed, "[t]he very purpose of a Bill of Rights was to withdraw certain subjects from the vicissitudes of political controversy, to place them beyond the reach of majorities and officials and to establish them as legal principles to be applied by the courts." *West Virginia State Bd. of Educ. v. Barnette,* 319 U.S., at 638. *** The compelling interest test reflects the First Amendment's mandate of preserving religious liberty to the fullest extent possible in a pluralistic society. For the Court to deem this command a "luxury" is to denigrate "[t]he very purpose of a Bill of Rights."

The Court's holding today not only misreads settled First Amendment precedent; it appears to be unnecessary to this case. I would reach the same result applying our established free exercise jurisprudence. I believe that granting a selective exemption in this case would seriously impair Oregon's compelling interest in prohibiting possession of peyote by its citizens. Under such circumstances, the Free Exercise Clause does not require the State to accommodate respondents' religiously motivated conduct. *** Accordingly, I concur in the judgment of the Court.

Justice BLACKMUN, with whom Justice BRENNAN and Justice MARSHALL join, dissenting.

I agree with Justice O'CONNOR's analysis of the applicable free exercise doctrine ***. As she points out, "the critical question in this case is whether exempting respondents from the State's general criminal prohibition will unduly interfere with fulfillment of the governmental interest." I do disagree, however, with her specific answer to that question.

In weighing the clear interest of respondents Smith and Black (hereinafter respondents) in the free exercise of their religion against Oregon's asserted interest in enforcing its drug laws, it is important to articulate in precise terms the state interest involved. It is not the State's broad interest in fighting the critical "war on drugs," [but] the State's narrow interest in refusing to make an exception for the religious, ceremonial use of peyote. *** Oregon has never sought to prosecute respondents, and does not claim that it has made significant enforcement efforts against other religious users of peyote. The State's asserted interest thus amounts only to the symbolic preservation of an unenforced prohibition.

The State proclaims an interest in protecting the health and safety of its citizens from the dangers of unlawful drugs. It offers, however, no evidence that the religious use of peyote has ever harmed anyone. *** The fact that peyote is classified as a Schedule I controlled substance does not, by itself, show that any and all uses of peyote, in any circumstance, are inherently harmful and dangerous. The Federal Government, which created the classifications of unlawful drugs from which Oregon's drug laws are derived, apparently does not find peyote so dangerous as to preclude an exemption for religious use. [21 CFR § 1307.31 (1989).]

The carefully circumscribed ritual context in which respondents used peyote is far removed from the irresponsible and unrestricted recreational use of unlawful drugs. *** Not only does the church's doctrine forbid nonreligious use of peyote; it also generally advocates self-reliance, familial responsibility, and abstinence from alcohol. *** Far from promoting the lawless and irresponsible use of drugs, Native American Church members' spiritual code exemplifies values that Oregon's drug laws are presumably intended to foster.

Finally, the State argues that granting an exception for religious peyote use would erode its interest in the uniform, fair, and certain enforcement of its drug laws. The State fears that, if it grants an exemption for religious peyote use, a flood of other claims to religious exemptions will follow. It would then be placed in a dilemma, it says, between allowing a patchwork of exemptions that would hinder its law enforcement efforts, and risking a violation of the Establishment Clause by arbitrarily limiting its religious exemptions. *** The State's apprehension of a flood of other religious claims is purely speculative. Almost half the States, and the Federal Government, have maintained an exemption for religious peyote use for many years, and apparently have not found themselves overwhelmed by claims to other religious exemptions. *** The unusual circumstances that make the religious use of peyote compatible with the State's interests in health and safety and in preventing drug trafficking would not apply to other religious claims. Some religions, for example, might not restrict drug use to a limited ceremonial context, as does the Native

American Church. *** That the State might grant an exemption for religious peyote use, but deny other religious claims arising in different circumstances, would not violate the Establishment Clause. Though the State must treat all religions equally, and not favor one over another, this obligation is fulfilled by the uniform application of the "compelling interest" test to all free exercise claims, not by reaching uniform *results* as to all claims.

Finally, although I agree with Justice O'CONNOR that courts should refrain from delving into questions whether, as a matter of religious doctrine, a particular practice is "central" to the religion, I do not think this means that the courts must turn a blind eye to the severe impact of a State's restrictions on the adherents of a minority religion. Respondents believe, and their sincerity has *never* been at issue, that the peyote plant embodies their deity, and eating it is an act of worship and communion. Without peyote, they could not enact the essential ritual of their religion.

For these reasons, I conclude that Oregon's interest in enforcing its drug laws against religious use of peyote is not sufficiently compelling to outweigh respondents' right to the free exercise of their religion. Since the State could not constitutionally enforce its criminal prohibition against respondents, the interests underlying the State's drug laws cannot justify its denial of unemployment benefits.

Points for Discussion

a. The Theory of <u>Smith</u>

What is the theoretical basis of the Court's decision in <u>Smith</u> that the Free Exercise Clause does not require exemptions from neutral laws of general applicability? Is it the practical intuition that government cannot operate effectively when its laws cannot apply to those who object to their content? Is it the institutional concern that judges are ill suited to weigh the state's interest in its regulations against individuals' religious imperatives? Is it the commitment to democratic majoritarianism, which necessarily means that law will impose more burdens on religious minorities than on those who adhere to the majority faith?

Consider the view that Justice Stevens advanced in his concurring opinion in *Goldman v. Weinberger*, 475 U.S. 503 (1986), which the Court cited in <u>Smith</u> and which held that the Free Exercise Clause did not require the Air Force to exempt an observant Jew who wished to wear a yarmulke from a regulation prohibiting the wearing of headgear:

> Captain Goldman presents an especially attractive case for an exception from the uniform regulations that are applicable to all other Air Force personnel. His devotion to his faith is readily apparent. The yarmulke is a familiar and accepted sight. In addition to its religious significance for the wearer, the yarmulke may evoke the deepest respect and admiration—the symbol of a distinguished tradition and an eloquent rebuke to the ugliness of anti-Semitism. Captain Goldman's military duties are performed in a setting in which a modest departure from the uniform regulation creates almost no danger of impairment of the Air Force's military mission.

> [However, the] very strength of Captain Goldman's claim creates the danger that a similar claim on behalf of a Sikh or a Rastafarian might readily be dismissed as "so extreme, so unusual, or so faddish an image that public confidence in his ability to perform his duties will be destroyed." If exceptions from dress code regulations are to be granted on the basis of a multifactored test such as that proposed by Justice BRENNAN, inevitably the decisionmaker's evaluation of the character and the sincerity of the requester's faith—as well as the probable reaction of the majority to the favored treatment of a member of that faith—will play a critical part in the decision. For the difference between a turban or a dreadlock on the one hand, and a yarmulke on the other, is not merely a difference in "appearance"—it is also the difference between a Sikh or a Rastafarian, on the one hand, and an Orthodox Jew on the other. The Air Force has no business drawing distinctions between such persons when it is enforcing commands of universal application.

Is the real force of _Smith_'s rule the insight that the alternative—the compelling interest approach of _Sherbert_—is much worse, because it will require courts to become embroiled in disputes over which religions should "count"?

b. _Smith_ and Precedent

To what extent did _Smith_ change the law as articulated in _Yoder_ and _Sherbert_? To what extent does _Smith_ merely conform the articulated legal rules to the actual results of Free Exercise Clause precedents, including _Reynolds_ and _Goldman_?

c. Constitutional Interpretation

We have seen that Justice Scalia, who wrote the opinion for the Court in _Smith_, is an avowed originalist. Was his approach to constitutional interpretation in _Smith_ originalist? Did he focus on historical understandings of the meaning of the Free Exercise Clause? (Recall that the closest he came to an analysis of the meaning of the text was to suggest that the one the Court adopted was "a permissible reading.") If not, why is the Free Exercise Clause different from other constitutional provisions?

What rule would an originalist approach have yielded? Scholars have disagreed on the answer to this question. Professor Michael McConnell has argued that the approach of the Court in _Sherbert_ was "more consistent with the original understanding" than the approach of the Court in _Smith_. Michael W. McConnell, *Free Exercise Revisionism and the* Smith *Decision*, 57 U. Chi. L. Rev. 1109 (1990). Professor Philip Hamburger, however, has disputed that conclusion. See Philip A. Hamburger, *A Constitutional Right of Religious Exemption: An Historical Perspective*, 60 Geo. Wash. L. Rev. 915 (1992).

d. Religious Freedom Restoration Act

In 1993, Congress passed the Religious Freedom Restoration Act, 42 U.S.C. § 2000bb, in an effort to overrule _Smith_. The initial section of this act declares:

> The purposes of this chapter are—
>
> (1) to restore the compelling interest test as set forth in _Sherbert v. Verner, 374 U.S. 398 (1963)_ and _Wisconsin v. Yoder, 406 U.S. 205 (1972)_ and to guarantee its application in all cases where free exercise of religion is substantially burdened; and

(2) to provide a claim or defense to persons whose religious exercise is substantially burdened by government.

Id.. § 2000bb(b).

The portion of the act that applied to state (as opposed to federal) action was short-lived. In *City of Boerne v. Flores,* 521 U.S. 507 (1997), the Supreme Court held that Congress lacked the power to pass this act, at least as it applied to state laws. Although the Court has not squarely addressed the constitutionality of RFRA as applied to federal law, the Court has applied it to grant exemptions under federal law. See *Gonzales v. O Centro Espirita Beneficente Uniao do Vegetal,* 546 U.S. 418 (2006).

> **Make the Connection**
>
> We considered *City of Boerne*, and Congress's power to enforce the Fourteenth Amendment, in Chapter 13.

While the Supreme Court in <u>Smith</u> held that the government does not need a compelling state interest to justify the burden that a neutral law of general applicability imposes on religious practice, the Court did not specify what test should apply to a law that is not of general applicability or that is targeted at religious practices. In the following case, the Court concluded that the compelling interest test remains in effect for such laws.

Church of the Lukumi Babalu Aye, Inc. v. City of Hialeah

508 U.S. 520 (1993)

Justice KENNEDY delivered the opinion of the Court, except as to Part II-A-2.[*]

I

Petitioner Church of the Lukumi Babalu Aye, Inc. (Church), is a not-for-profit corporation organized under Florida law in 1973. The Church and its congregants practice the Santeria religion. The president of the Church is petitioner Ernesto Pichardo, who is also the Church's priest and holds the religious title of *Italero,* the second highest in the Santeria faith. In April 1987, the Church leased land in the City of Hialeah, Florida, and announced plans to establish a house of worship as well as a school, cultural center, and museum. Pichardo indicated that the Church's goal was to bring the practice of the Santeria faith, including its ritual of animal sacrifice, into the open. The Church began the process of obtaining utility service and receiving the necessary licensing, inspection, and zoning approvals. Although the Church's efforts at obtaining the necessary licenses and permits were far from smooth, it appears that it received all needed approvals by early August 1987.

---

[*] THE CHIEF JUSTICE, Justice SCALIA, and Justice THOMAS join all but Part II-A-2 of this opinion. Justice WHITE joins all but Part II-A of this opinion. Justice SOUTER joins only Parts I, III, and IV of this opinion.

The prospect of a Santeria church in their midst was distressing to many members of the Hialeah community, and the announcement of the plans to open a Santeria church in Hialeah prompted the city council to hold an emergency public session on June 9, 1987. *** In September 1987, the city council adopted three substantive ordinances addressing the issue of religious animal sacrifice. Ordinance 87-52 defined "sacrifice" as "to unnecessarily kill, torment, torture, or mutilate an animal in a public or private ritual or ceremony not for the primary purpose of food consumption," and prohibited owning or possessing an animal "intending to use such animal for food purposes." It restricted application of this prohibition, however, to any individual or group that "kills, slaughters or sacrifices animals for any type of ritual, regardless of whether or not the flesh or blood of the animal is to be consumed." The ordinance contained an exemption for slaughtering by "licensed establishment[s]" of animals "specifically raised for food purposes." Declaring, moreover, that the city council "has determined that the sacrificing of animals within the city limits is contrary to the public health, safety, welfare and morals of the community," the city council adopted Ordinance 87-71. That ordinance defined sacrifice as had Ordinance 87-52, and then provided that "[i]t shall be unlawful for any person, persons, corporations or associations to sacrifice any animal within the corporate limits of the City of Hialeah, Florida." The final Ordinance, 87-72, defined "slaughter" as "the killing of animals for food" and prohibited slaughter outside of areas zoned for slaughterhouse use. The ordinance provided an exemption, however, for the slaughter or processing for sale of "small numbers of hogs and/or cattle per week in accordance with an exemption provided by state law." All ordinances and resolutions passed the city council by unanimous vote. Violations of each of the four ordinances were punishable by fines not exceeding $500 or imprisonment not exceeding 60 days, or both.

II

The city does not argue that Santeria is not a "religion" within the meaning of the First Amendment. Nor could it. Although the practice of animal sacrifice may seem abhorrent to some, "religious beliefs need not be acceptable, logical, consistent, or comprehensible to others in order to merit First Amendment protection." *Thomas v. Review Bd. of Indiana Employment Security Div.,* 450 U.S. 707, 714 (1981). Given the historical association between animal sacrifice and religious worship, petitioners' assertion that animal sacrifice is an integral part of their religion "cannot be deemed bizarre or incredible." *Frazee v. Illinois Dept. of Employment Security,* 489 U.S. 829, 834, n. 2 (1989). Neither the city nor the courts below, moreover, have questioned the sincerity of petitioners' professed desire to conduct animal sacrifices for religious reasons. We must consider petitioners' First Amendment claim.

In addressing the constitutional protection for free exercise of religion, our cases establish the general proposition that a law that is neutral and of general applicability need not be justified by a compelling governmental interest even if the law has the incidental effect of burdening a particular religious practice. *Employment Div., Dept. of Human Resources of Ore. v. Smith,* 494 U.S. 872 (1990). Neutrality and general applicability are interrelated, and, as becomes apparent in this case, failure to satisfy one requirement is a likely indication that the other has not been satisfied. A law failing to satisfy these requirements must be justified by a compelling governmental interest and must be narrowly tailored to advance that interest. These ordinances fail to satisfy the *Smith* requirements. We begin by discussing neutrality.

A

At a minimum, the protections of the Free Exercise Clause pertain if the law at issue discriminates against some or all religious beliefs or regulates or prohibits conduct because it is undertaken for religious reasons. See, *e.g.*, *Braunfeld v. Brown*, 366 U.S. 599, 607 (1961) (plurality opinion). Indeed, it was "historical instances of religious persecution and intolerance that gave concern to those who drafted the Free Exercise Clause." *Bowen v. Roy*, 476 U.S. 693, 703 (1986) (opinion of Burger, C.J.).

1

Although a law targeting religious beliefs as such is never permissible, if the object of a law is to infringe upon or restrict practices because of their religious motivation, the law is not neutral, and it is invalid unless it is justified by a compelling interest and is narrowly tailored to advance that interest. There are, of course, many ways of demonstrating that the object or purpose of a law is the suppression of religion or religious conduct. To determine the object of a law, we must begin with its text, for the minimum requirement of neutrality is that a law not discriminate on its face. A law lacks facial neutrality if it refers to a religious practice without a secular meaning discernable from the language or context. Petitioners contend that three of the ordinances fail this test of facial neutrality because they use the words "sacrifice" and "ritual," words with strong religious connotations. We agree that these words are consistent with the claim of facial discrimination, but the argument is not conclusive. The words "sacrifice" and "ritual" have a religious origin, but current use admits also of secular meanings. See Webster's Third New International Dictionary 1961, 1996 (1971). See also 12 Encyclopedia of Religion, at 556 ("[T]he word *sacrifice* ultimately became very much a secular term in common usage"). The ordinances, furthermore, define "sacrifice" in secular terms, without referring to religious practices.

We reject the contention advanced by the city that our inquiry must end with the text of the laws at issue. *** Official action that targets religious conduct for distinctive treatment cannot be shielded by mere compliance with the requirement of facial neutrality. The Free Exercise Clause protects against governmental hostility which is masked, as well as overt.

The record in this case compels the conclusion that suppression of the central element of the Santeria worship service was the object of the ordinances. *** Apart from the text, the effect of a law in its real operation is strong evidence of its object. *** The subject at hand does implicate, of course, multiple concerns unrelated to religious animosity, for example, the suffering or mistreatment visited upon the sacrificed animals and health hazards from improper disposal. But the ordinances when considered together disclose an object remote from these legitimate concerns.

It is a necessary conclusion that almost the only conduct subject to Ordinances 87-40, 87-52, and 87-71 is the religious exercise of Santeria church members. The texts show that they were drafted in tandem to achieve this result. We begin with Ordinance 87-71. *** The definition [of "sacrifice"] excludes almost all killings of animals except for religious sacrifice, and the primary purpose requirement narrows the proscribed category even further, in particular by exempting kosher slaughter. We need not discuss whether this differential treatment of two religions is itself an independent constitutional violation. It suffices to recite this feature of the law as support for our conclusion that Santeria alone was the exclusive legislative concern. The net result [is] that few if any killings of animals are prohibited other than Santeria sacrifice, which is proscribed because it occurs during a ritual or ceremony and its primary purpose is to make an offering to the *orishas,* not food consumption. Indeed, careful drafting ensured that, although Santeria sacrifice is prohibited, killings that are no more necessary or humane in almost all other circumstances are unpunished.

Operating in similar fashion is Ordinance 87-52, which prohibits the "possess[ion], sacrifice, or slaughter" of an animal with the "inten[t] to use such animal for food purposes." This prohibition, extending to the keeping of an animal as well as the killing itself, applies if the animal is killed in "any type of ritual" and there is an intent to use the animal for food, whether or not it is in fact consumed for food. The ordinance exempts, however, "any licensed [food] establishment" with regard to "any animals which are specifically raised for food purposes," if the activity is permitted by zoning and other laws. This exception, too, seems intended to cover kosher slaughter. Again, the burden of the ordinance, in practical terms, falls on Santeria adherents but almost no others ***.

Ordinance 87-40 incorporates the Florida animal cruelty statute, Fla. Stat. § 828.12 (1987). Its prohibition is broad on its face, punishing "[w]hoever . . . unnecessarily . . . kills any animal." The city claims that this ordinance is the epitome of a neutral prohibition. The problem, however, is the interpretation given to the ordinance by respondent and the Florida attorney general. Killings for religious reasons are deemed unnecessary, whereas most other killings fall outside the prohibition. The city, on what seems to be a *per se* basis, deems hunting, slaughter of animals for food, eradication of insects and pests, and euthanasia as necessary. *** Respondent's application of the ordinance's test of necessity devalues religious reasons for killing by judging them to be of lesser import than nonreligious reasons. Thus, religious practice is being singled out for discriminatory treatment.

2

That the ordinances were enacted "'because of,' not merely 'in spite of,'" their suppression of Santeria religious practice, *Personnel Administrator of Mass. v. Feeney,* 442 U.S. 256, 279, n. 24 (1979), is revealed by the events preceding their enactment. Although respondent claimed at oral argument that it had experienced significant problems resulting from the sacrifice of animals within the city before the announced opening of the Church, the city council made no attempt to address the supposed problem before its meeting in June 1987, just weeks after the Church announced plans to open. The minutes and taped excerpts of the June 9 session, both of which are in

> **Take Note**
>
> This section did not receive the support of a majority of the Court.

the record, evidence significant hostility exhibited by residents, members of the city council, and other city officials toward the Santeria religion and its practice of animal sacrifice. The public crowd that attended the June 9 meetings interrupted statements by council members critical of Santeria with cheers and the brief comments of Pichardo with taunts. When Councilman Martinez, a supporter of the ordinances, stated that in prerevolution Cuba "people were put in jail for practicing this religion," the audience applauded. *** Other statements by members of the city council were in a similar vein. For example, *** Councilman Cardoso said that Santeria devotees at the Church "are in violation of everything this country stands for." Councilman Mejides [stated,] "The Bible says we are allowed to sacrifice an animal for consumption [but] for any other purposes, I don't believe that the Bible allows that." The president of the city council, Councilman Echevarria, asked: "What can we do to prevent the Church from opening?"

Various Hialeah city officials made comparable comments. The chaplain of the Hialeah Police Department told the city council that Santeria was a sin, "foolishness," "an abomination to the Lord," and the worship of "demons." He advised the city council: "We need to be helping people and sharing with them the truth that is found in Jesus Christ." He concluded: "I would exhort you ... not to permit this Church to exist." The city attorney commented that Resolution 87-66 indicated: "This community will not tolerate religious practices which are abhorrent to its citizens...." *** This history discloses the object of the ordinances to target animal sacrifice by Santeria worshippers because of its religious motivation.

3

In sum, the neutrality inquiry leads to one conclusion: The ordinances had as their object the suppression of religion. The pattern we have recited discloses animosity to Santeria adherents and their religious practices; the ordinances by their own terms target this religious exercise; the texts of the ordinances were gerrymandered with care to proscribe religious killings of animals but to exclude almost all secular killings; and the ordinances suppress much more religious conduct than is necessary in order to achieve the legitimate ends asserted in their defense. These ordinances are not neutral, and the court below committed clear error in failing to reach this conclusion.

B

We turn next to a second requirement of the Free Exercise Clause, the rule that laws burdening religious practice must be of general applicability. *Smith*, 494 U.S., at 879-881. All laws are selective to some extent, but categories of selection are of paramount concern when a law has the incidental effect of burdening religious practice. The Free Exercise Clause "protect[s] religious observers against unequal treatment," *Hobbie v. Unemployment Appeals Comm'n of Fla.*, 480 U.S. 136, 148 (1987) (STEVENS, J., concurring in judgment), and inequality results when a legislature decides that the governmental interests it seeks to advance are worthy of being pursued only against conduct with a religious motivation.

Respondent claims that Ordinances 87-40, 87-52, and 87-71 advance two interests: protecting the public health and preventing cruelty to animals. The ordinances are underinclusive for those ends. They fail to prohibit nonreligious conduct that endangers these interests in a similar or greater degree than Santeria sacrifice does. The underinclusion is substantial, not inconsequential. Despite the city's proffered interest in preventing cruelty to animals, the ordinances are drafted with care to forbid few killings but those occasioned by religious sacrifice. Many types of animal deaths or kills for nonreligious reasons are either not prohibited or approved by express provision. ***

The ordinances are also underinclusive with regard to the city's interest in public health, which is threatened by the disposal of animal carcasses in open public places and the consumption of uninspected meat. Neither interest is pursued by respondent with regard to conduct that is not motivated by religious conviction. The city does not [prohibit] hunters from bringing their kill to their houses, nor does it regulate disposal after their activity, [and] restaurants are outside the scope of the ordinances.

Ordinance 87-72, which prohibits the slaughter of animals outside of areas zoned for slaughterhouses, is underinclusive on its face. The ordinance includes an exemption for "any person, group, or organization" that "slaughters or processes for sale, small numbers of hogs and/or cattle per week in accordance with an exemption provided by state law." See Fla. Stat. § 828.24(3) (1991). Respondent has not explained why commercial operations that slaughter "small numbers" of hogs and cattle do not implicate its professed desire to prevent cruelty to animals and preserve the public health. Although the city has classified Santeria sacrifice as slaughter, subjecting it to this ordinance, it does not regulate other killings for food in like manner.

We conclude, in sum, that each of Hialeah's ordinances pursues the city's governmental interests only against conduct motivated by religious belief. The ordinances "ha[ve] every appearance of a prohibition that society is prepared to impose upon [Santeria worshippers] but not upon itself." *Florida Star v. B.J.F.,* 491 U.S. 524, 542 (1989) (SCALIA, J., concurring in part and concurring in judgment). This precise evil is what the requirement of general applicability is designed to prevent.

III

A law burdening religious practice that is not neutral or not of general application must undergo the most rigorous of scrutiny. To satisfy the commands of the First Amendment, a law restrictive of religious practice must advance "interests of the highest order" and must be narrowly tailored in pursuit of those interests. *McDaniel v. Paty,* 435 U.S. 618, 628 (1978), quoting *Wisconsin v. Yoder,* 406 U.S. 205, 215 (1972). *** A law that targets religious conduct for distinctive treatment or advances legitimate governmental interests only against conduct with a religious motivation will survive strict scrutiny only in rare cases. It follows from what we have already said that these ordinances cannot withstand this scrutiny.

[E]ven were the governmental interests compelling, the ordinances are not drawn in narrow terms to accomplish those interests. As we have discussed, all four ordinances are overbroad or underinclusive in substantial respects. The proffered objectives are not pursued with respect to analogous non-religious conduct, and those interests could be achieved by narrower ordinances that burdened religion to a far lesser degree. The absence of narrow tailoring suffices to establish the invalidity of the ordinances.

Justice SCALIA, with whom THE CHIEF JUSTICE joins, concurring in part and concurring in the judgment.

I join the judgment of the Court and all of its opinion except section 2 of Part II-A. I do not join that section because it departs from the opinion's general focus on the object of the *laws* at issue to consider the subjective motivation of the *lawmakers, i.e.,* whether the Hialeah City Council actually *intended* to disfavor the religion of Santeria. As I have noted elsewhere, it is virtually impossible to determine the singular "motive" of a collective legislative body, see, *e.g., Edwards v. Aguillard,* 482 U.S. 578, 636-639 (1987) (dissenting opinion), and this Court has a long tradition of refraining from such inquiries, see, *e.g., Fletcher v. Peck,* 6 Cranch (10 U.S.) 87, 130-131 (1810) (Marshall, C.J.); *United States v. O'Brien,* 391 U.S. 367, 383-384 (1968).

Justice BLACKMUN, with whom Justice O'CONNOR joins, concurring in the judgment.

The Court holds today that the city of Hialeah violated the First and Fourteenth Amendments when it passed a set of restrictive ordinances explicitly directed at petitioners' religious practice. With this holding I agree. I write separately to emphasize that the First Amendment's protection of religion extends beyond those rare occasions on which the government explicitly targets religion (or a particular religion) for disfavored treatment, as is done in this case. *** I continue to believe that Smith was wrongly decided, because it ignored the value of religious freedom as an affirmative individual liberty and treated the Free Exercise Clause as no more than an antidiscrimination principle.

[Justice SOUTER's opinion concurring in part and concurring in the judgment has been omitted.]

Points for Discussion

a. Triggering the Compelling Interest Test

The Court in *Church of the Lukumi Babalu Aye* announced a familiar test for laws that burden religious practice and that are not neutral or not of general application: such laws must advance a compelling interest and be narrowly tailored in pursuit of those interests. How exactly does the Court determine whether a law is neutral or of general applicability? Is there a difference between "neutrality" and "general applicability"? Can you think of a statute that is neutral but not generally applicable? Or a law that is generally applicable but not neutral?

b. Assessing Purpose

Justice Scalia declined to join the section of the Court's opinion finding a discriminatory purpose behind the challenged ordinances. Suppose that shortly after the Court's decision, the City enacted a new ordinance providing criminal penalties for the "killing of an animal by any person, group, or establishment who does not intend to eat the animal or sell the animal as food," and exempting from the prohibition "the killing of animals in the course of recreational hunting or fishing." Suppose further that at the session at which the City Council enacted the ordinance, every member of the Council declared that they were voting for it "to get around the Court's ruling."

Under Justice Scalia's approach, would this ordinance be constitutional? Is there a way to find that it impermissibly "targets" religious practice without referring to evidence of purpose? If it would be constitutional under Justice Scalia's approach, what does this suggest about his approach?

c. Another View

Professor Lino Graglia, a confirmed skeptic of judicial review, viewed this case in a different light. He began his article, *Church of the Lukumi Babalu Aye: Of Animal Sacrifice and Religious Persecution*, 85 Geo. L.J. 1 (1996), as follows:

> In recent years, residents of South Florida found themselves faced with a new and unsettling problem. The remains of animals, often accompanied by what appeared to be religious paraphernalia, were frequently encountered in public places. Carcasses were found in or along rivers and canals, at intersections, under trees, on lawns and doorsteps; a goat cut in two was found at a major Miami Beach intersection. *** Surely it was not to be expected that such spectacles would be tolerated in a modern American city, and the people of Hialeah quickly enacted ordinances specifically prohibiting them. It is a self-assigned function of intellectuals, however, to expand the boundaries of the expected and the tolerable ***. Thus, in *Church of the Lukumi Babalu Aye v. City of Hialeah*, the Justices of the Supreme Court, intellectuals all, could find no explanation for Hialeah's attempt to ban animal sacrifice other than religious prejudice.

What exactly is the basis for Professor Graglia's criticism: that the Court was wrong to conclude that the laws at issue were not neutral, that the city had a compelling interest in the laws, or that any legal rule that would produce the result in this case must be flawed?

—————

Hypothetical

As a matter of religious practice, some Muslim women cover their heads with scarves when in public places. Suppose that the Transportation Safety Administration issues a regulation requiring all passengers wearing headscarves to remove them when going through airport security lines. Is this regulation consistent with the Free Exercise Clause? Would you need any other information to conduct that inquiry? What if the regulation did not require the removal of other forms of headwear, such as yarmulkes or turbans? What if it required the removal of those, as well, but not the removal of baseball caps?

—————

As we have seen, the Establishment Clause and the Free Exercise Clause both protect religious freedom, but they do so in different ways. In the first part of the Chapter, we saw that the Establishment Clause protects religious freedom by ensuring that adherents of the majority religion cannot "force [or] influence a person to go to or to remain away from church against his will or force him to profess a belief or disbelief in any religion." *Everson v. Board of Education of Ewing Township,* 330 U.S. 1 (1947). The Free Exercise Clause appears to accomplish this goal even more directly.

Do the requirements imposed by the two Clauses ever conflict with each other? Sometimes, the government will defend against an Establishment Clause challenge by contending that it permissibly sought to accommodate religious practice. In *Board of Education of Kiryas Joel Village School District v. Grumet,* 512 U.S. 687 (1994), for example, the Court considered the constitutionality of a state decision to create a school district that embraced only adherents of one sect of Judaism, so that disabled students in the community would not have to attend public schools with children from outside of their religious community. The state contended that it had sought to accommodate the unique circumstances of one particular religious group, but the Court held that the policy violated the Establishment Clause.

Other times, the government will defend against a Free Exercise claim by arguing that it was seeking to avoid violating the Establishment Clause. Under what circumstances can the government rely on such an interest to defeat a Free Exercise claim? Consider the case that follows.

Locke v. Davey

540 U.S. 712 (2004)

Chief Justice REHNQUIST delivered the opinion of the Court.

The State of Washington established the Promise Scholarship Program to assist academically gifted students with postsecondary education expenses. In accordance with the State Constitution, students may not use the scholarship at an institution where they are pursuing a degree in devotional theology. We hold that such an exclusion from an otherwise inclusive aid program does not violate the Free Exercise Clause of the First Amendment.

Respondent, Joshua Davey, was awarded a Promise Scholarship, and chose to attend [a] private, Christian college affiliated with the Assemblies of God denomination ***. [H]e decided to pursue a double major in pastoral ministries and business management/administration. [After he learned that he could not use his scholarship to pursue a devotional theology degree, he filed suit challenging the state's refusal to permit him to use the scholarship for such studies.]

[T]he Establishment Clause and the Free Exercise Clause [are] frequently in tension.

Yet we have long said that "there is room for play in the joints" between them. *Walz v. Tax Comm'n of City of New York,* 397 U.S. 664, 669 (1970). In other words, there are some state actions permitted by the Establishment Clause but not required by the Free Exercise Clause.

Under our Establishment Clause precedent, the link between government funds and religious training is broken by the independent and private choice of recipients. See *Zelman v. Simmons-Harris,* 536 U.S. 639, 652 (2002). As such, there is no doubt that the State could, consistent with the Federal Constitution, permit Promise Scholars to pursue a degree in devotional theology ***. The question before us, however, is whether Washington, pursuant to its own constitution, which has been authoritatively interpreted as prohibiting even indirectly funding religious instruction that will prepare students for the ministry, can deny them such funding without violating the Free Exercise Clause.

> **Make the Connection**
>
> We considered the significance of the "independent and private choice of recipients" of government funds to decide how to spend those funds earlier in this Chapter, in *Zelman v. Simmons-Harris*.

Davey urges us to answer that question in the negative. He contends that under the rule we enunciated in *Church of Lukumi Babalu Aye, Inc. v. Hialeah,* 508 U.S. 520 (1993), the program is presumptively unconstitutional because it is not facially neutral with respect to religion. We reject his claim of presumptive unconstitutionality, however; to do otherwise would extend the *Lukumi* line of cases well beyond not only their facts but their reasoning. In *Lukumi,* the city of Hialeah *** sought to suppress ritualistic animal sacrifices of the Santeria religion. In the present case, the State's disfavor of religion (if it can be called that) is of a far milder kind. It imposes neither criminal nor civil sanctions on any type of religious service or rite. It does not deny to ministers the right to participate in the political affairs of the community. And it does not require students to choose between their religious beliefs and receiving a government benefit. The State has merely chosen not to fund a distinct category of instruction.

Justice SCALIA argues, however, that generally available benefits are part of the "baseline against which burdens on religion are measured." Because the Promise Scholarship Program funds training for all secular professions, Justice SCALIA contends the State must also fund training for religious professions. But training for religious professions and training for secular professions are not fungible. Training someone to lead a congregation is an essentially religious endeavor. Indeed, majoring in devotional theology is akin to a religious calling as well as an academic pursuit. And the subject of religion is one in which both the United States and state constitutions embody distinct views—in favor of free exercise, but opposed to establishment—that find no counterpart with respect to other callings or professions. That a State would deal differently with religious education for the ministry than with education for other callings is a product of these views, not evidence of hostility toward religion.

We can think of few areas in which a State's antiestablishment interests come more into play. Since the founding of our country, there have been popular uprisings against procuring taxpayer funds to support church leaders, which was one of the hallmarks of an "established" religion. *** Most states that sought to avoid an establishment of religion around the time of the founding placed in their constitutions formal prohibitions against using tax funds to support the ministry. The plain text of these constitutional provisions prohibited *any* tax dollars from supporting the clergy. *** That early state constitutions saw no problem in explicitly excluding *only* the ministry from receiving state dollars reinforces our conclusion that religious instruction is of a different ilk.

Far from evincing the hostility toward religion which was manifest in *Lukumi*, we believe that the entirety of the Promise Scholarship Program goes a long way toward including religion in its benefits. The program permits students to attend pervasively religious schools, so long as they are accredited. *** And under the Promise Scholarship Program's current guidelines, students are still eligible to take devotional theology courses. *** In short, we find neither in the history or text of [the] Washington Constitution, nor in the operation of the Promise Scholarship Program, anything that suggests animus toward religion. Given the historic and substantial state interest at issue, we therefore cannot conclude that the denial of funding for vocational religious instruction alone is inherently constitutionally suspect.

Without a presumption of unconstitutionality, Davey's claim must fail. The State's interest in not funding the pursuit of devotional degrees is substantial and the exclusion of such funding places a relatively minor burden on Promise Scholars. If any room exists between the two Religion Clauses, it must be here. We need not venture further into this difficult area in order to uphold the Promise Scholarship Program as currently operated by the State of Washington.

Justice SCALIA, with whom Justice THOMAS joins, dissenting.

In *Lukumi*, the [Court] held that "[a] law burdening religious practice that is not neutral ... must undergo the most rigorous of scrutiny," and that "the minimum requirement of neutrality is that a law not discriminate on its face." [*Lukumi* is] irreconcilable with today's decision, which sustains a public benefits program that facially discriminates against religion.

When the State makes a public benefit generally available, that benefit becomes part of the baseline against which burdens on religion are measured; and when the State withholds that benefit from some individuals solely on the basis of religion, it violates the Free Exercise Clause no less than if it had imposed a special tax. That is precisely what the State of Washington has done here. It has created a generally available public benefit, whose receipt is conditioned only on academic performance, income, and attendance at an accredited school. It has then carved out a solitary course of study for exclusion: theology. No field of study but religion is singled out for disfavor in this fashion.

The Court's reference to historical "popular uprisings against procuring taxpayer funds to support church leaders" is therefore quite misplaced. That history involved not the inclusion of religious ministers in public benefits programs like the one at issue here, but laws that singled them out for financial aid. *** One can concede the Framers' hostility to funding the clergy *specifically*, but that says nothing about whether the clergy had to be excluded from benefits the State made available to all.

The Court does not dispute that the Free Exercise Clause places some constraints on public benefits programs, but finds none here, based on a principle of "play in the joints." I use the term "principle" loosely, for that is not so much a legal principle as a refusal to apply *any* principle when faced with competing constitutional directives. *** Even if "play in the joints" were a valid legal principle, surely it would apply only when it was a close call whether complying with one of the Religion Clauses would violate the other. But that is not the case here. It is not just that "the State could, consistent with the Federal Constitution, permit Promise Scholars to pursue a degree in devotional theology." The establishment question *would not even be close* ***. Perhaps some formally neutral public benefits programs are so gerrymandered and devoid of plausible secular purpose that they might raise specters of state aid to religion, but an evenhanded Promise Scholarship Program is not among them.

[T]he interest to which the Court defers is not fear of a conceivable Establishment Clause violation, budget constraints, avoidance of endorsement, or substantive neutrality—none of these. It is a pure philosophical preference: the State's opinion that it would violate taxpayers' freedom of conscience *not* to discriminate against candidates for the ministry. This sort of protection of "freedom of conscience" has no logical limit and can justify the singling out of religion for exclusion from public programs in virtually any context. The Court never says whether it deems this interest compelling (the opinion is devoid of any mention of standard of review) but, self-evidently, it is not.

The Court makes no serious attempt to defend the program's neutrality, and instead identifies two features thought to render its discrimination less offensive. The first is the lightness of Davey's burden. The Court offers no authority for approving facial discrimination against religion simply because its material consequences are not severe. *** The Court has not required proof of "substantial" concrete harm with other forms of discrimination, see, *e.g., Brown v. Board of Education*, 347 U.S. 483, 493-495 (1954); cf. *Craig v. Boren*, 429 U.S. 190 (1976), and it should not do so here.

The other reason the Court thinks this particular facial discrimination less offensive is that the scholarship program was not motivated by animus toward religion. The Court does not explain why the legislature's motive matters, and I fail to see why it should. *** It is sufficient that the citizen's rights have been infringed.

Let there be no doubt: This case is about discrimination against a religious minority. Most citizens of this country identify themselves as professing some religious belief, but the State's policy poses no obstacle to practitioners of only a tepid, civic version of faith. Those the statutory exclusion actually affects—those whose belief in their religion is so strong that they dedicate their study and their lives to its ministry—are a far narrower set. One need not delve too far into modern popular culture to perceive a trendy disdain for deep religious conviction. In an era when the Court is so quick to come to the aid of other disfavored groups, see, *e.g., Romer v. Evans*, 517 U.S. 620, 635 (1996), its indifference in this case, which involves a form of discrimination to which the Constitution actually speaks, is exceptional.

Today's holding is limited to training the clergy, but its logic is readily extendible, and there are plenty of directions to go. What next? Will we deny priests and nuns their prescription-drug benefits on the ground that taxpayers' freedom of conscience forbids medicating the clergy at public expense? *** When the public's freedom of conscience is invoked to justify denial of equal treatment, benevolent motives shade into indifference and ultimately into repression. Having accepted the justification in this case, the Court is less well equipped to fend it off in the future. I respectfully dissent.

[Justice THOMAS's dissenting opinion is omitted.]

Points for Discussion

a. Free Exercise Clause

The Court reasoned that the challenged policy did not violate the Free Exercise Clause because it did not impose "criminal [or] civil sanctions," did not "deny to ministers the right to participate in the political affairs of the community," and did not "require students to choose between their religious beliefs and receiving a government benefit." Is this the test that we have seen for whether a challenged policy violates the Free Exercise Clause? Was the challenged policy similar to the law at issue in *Lukumi*? Is there a difference between singling out one particular religion for disfavored treatment (as in *Lukumi*) and treating all religious education regardless of denomination as a disfavored subject of instruction?

b. Establishment Clause

The Court concluded that it would not violate the Establishment Clause for the state to provide funding, on a neutral basis, to students who wish to pursue studies in devotional theology. Can you make an argument that the Court should conclude that such funding violates the Establishment Clause? Should it matter that the funds would be used for actual religious indoctrination? Given the Court's conclusion that it would not violate the Establishment Clause to fund such education, how could the state's interest in avoiding an Establishment Clause violation justify the exclusion at issue?

C. Government Involvement in Religious Disputes

The Free Exercise Clause clearly allows ecclesiastical bodies and leaders to establish religious doctrines without government interference. The Catholic Church, for example, is free to decide whether women should be ordained as priests. Rabbis may determine what is kosher and what is not. Muslim Imams may decide the exact days on which Ramadan begins and ends. Part of religious freedom, simply put, is the right to determine the tenets and practices of a particular faith.

In addition, we saw in the first section of this Chapter how the Establishment Clause prohibits excessive governmental entanglement with religion. In *Lemon v. Kurtzman*, 403 U.S. 602 (1971), for example, the Supreme Court invalidated state laws providing salary aid and other forms of assistance to parochial schools because of concerns that administration of the programs would unduly entangle the government in religious matters.

Together, these mandates of the Free Exercise and Establishment Clauses impose limits on the ability of the government to adjudicate disputes between and within religious organizations. Recognizing this, the Supreme Court has created a doctrine of judicial abstention that applies to certain ecclesiastic disputes. Although courts may decide some lawsuits between religious organizations (or between factions within the same religious organizations), the Court has held that the religion clauses prevent them from deciding issues of religious doctrine. If the ownership of property, the scope of the rights of clergy, or any other legal question turns on the tenets of faith, then the courts must leave the matter for religious bodies to decide.

————————

Presbyterian Church in U.S. v. Mary Elizabeth Blue Hull Memorial Presbyterian Church

393 U.S. 440 (1969)

Mr. Justice BRENNAN delivered the opinion of the Court.

Petitioner, Presbyterian Church in the United States, is an association of local Presbyterian churches governed by a hierarchical structure of tribunals which consists of, in ascending order, (1) the Church Session, composed of the elders of the local church; (2) the Presbytery, composed of several churches in a geographical area; (3) the Synod, generally composed of all Presbyteries within a State; and (4) the General Assembly, the highest governing body.

A dispute arose between petitioner, the general church, and two local churches in Savannah, Georgia—the respondents, Hull Memorial Presbyterian Church and Eastern Heights Presbyterian Church—over control of the properties used until then by the local churches. In 1966, the membership of the local churches, in the belief that certain actions and pronouncements of the general church were violations of that organization's constitution and departures from the doctrine and practice in force at the time of affiliation,[1] voted to withdraw from the general church and to reconstitute the local churches as an autonomous Presbyterian organization. The ministers of the two churches renounced the general church's jurisdiction and authority over them, as did all but two of the ruling elders. In response, the general church, through the Presbytery of Savannah, established an Administrative Commission to seek a conciliation. The dissident local churchmen remained steadfast; consequently, the Commission acknowledged the withdrawal of the local leadership and proceeded to take over the local churches' property on behalf of the general church until new local leadership could be appointed.

The local churchmen made no effort to appeal the Commission's action to higher church tribunals—the Synod of Georgia or the General Assembly. Instead, the churches filed separate suits in the Superior Court of Chatham County to enjoin the general church from trespassing on the disputed property, title to which was in the local churches. The cases were consolidated for trial. The general church moved to dismiss the actions and cross-claimed for injunctive relief in its own behalf on the ground that civil courts were without power to determine whether the general church had departed from its tenets of faith and practice. The motion to dismiss was denied, and the case was submitted to the jury on the theory that Georgia law implies a trust of local church property for the benefit of the general church on the sole condition that the general church adhere to its tenets of faith and practice existing at the time of affiliation by the local churches. Thus, the jury was instructed to determine whether the actions of the general church "amount to a fundamental or substantial abandonment of the original tenets and doctrines of the (general church), so that the new tenets and doctrines are utterly variant from the purposes for which the (general church) was founded." The jury returned a verdict for the local churches, and the trial judge thereupon declared that the implied trust had terminated and enjoined the general church from interfering with the use of the property in question. ***

It is of course true that the State has a legitimate interest in resolving property disputes, and that a civil court is a proper forum for that resolution. Special problems arise, however, when these disputes implicate controversies over church doctrine and practice. The approach of this Court in such cases was originally developed in *Watson v. Jones*, 80 U.S. (13 Wall.) 679 (1872), a pre-*Erie R. Co. v. Tompkins* diversity decision decided before the application of the First Amendment to the States but nonetheless informed by First Amendment considerations. There, as here, civil courts were asked to resolve a property dispute between a national Presbyterian organization and local churches of that organization. There, as here, the disputes arose out of a controversy over church doctrine. There, as here, the Court was asked to decree the termination of an implied trust because of departures from doctrine by the national organization. The *Watson* Court refused pointing

---

[1] The opinion of the Supreme Court of Georgia summarizes the claimed violations and departures from petitioner's original tenets of faith and practice as including the following: "ordaining of women as ministers and ruling elders, making pronouncements and recommendations concerning civil, economic, social and political matters, giving support to the removal of Bible reading and prayers by children in the public schools, adopting certain Sunday School literature and teaching neo-orthodoxy alien to the Confession of Faith and Catechisms, as originally adopted by the general church, and causing all members to remain in the National Council of Churches of Christ and willingly accepting its leadership which advocated named practices, such as the subverting of parental authority, civil disobedience and intermeddling in civil affairs." *** 224 Ga. 61, 62-63, 159 S.E.2d 690, 692 (1968).

out that it was wholly inconsistent with the American concept of the relationship between church and state to permit civil courts to determine ecclesiastical questions. In language which has a clear constitutional ring, the Court said

> In this country the full and free right to entertain any religious belief, to practice any religious principle, and to teach any religious doctrine which does not violate the laws of morality and property, and which does not infringe personal rights, is conceded to all. The law knows no heresy, and is committed to the support of no dogma, the establishment of no sect. *** All who unite themselves to such a body [the general church] do so with an implied consent to [its] government, and are bound to submit to it. But it would be a vain consent and would lead to the total subversion of such religious bodies, if any one aggrieved by one of their decisions could appeal to the secular courts and have them (sic) reversed. It is of the essence of these religious unions, and of their right to establish tribunals for the decision of questions arising among themselves, that those decisions should be binding in all cases of ecclesiastical cognizance, subject only to such appeals as the organism itself provides for.

The logic of this language leaves the civil courts no role in determining ecclesiastical questions in the process of resolving property disputes.

In *Kedroff v. St. Nicholas Cathedral of Russian Orthodox Church in North America*, 344 U.S. 94 (1952), the Court converted the principle of <u>Watson</u> [into] a constitutional rule. <u>Kedroff</u> grew out of a dispute between the Moscow-based general Russian Orthodox Church and the Russian Orthodox churches located in North America over an appointment to St. Nicholas Cathedral in New York City. The North American churches declared their independence from the general church, and the New York Legislature enacted a statute recognizing their administrative autonomy. The New York courts sustained the constitutionality of the statute and held that the North American churches' elected hierarch had the right to use the cathedral. This Court reversed, finding that the Moscow church had not acknowledged the schism, and holding the statute unconstitutional. The Court said:

> The opinion [in <u>Watson v. Jones</u>] radiates [a] spirit of freedom for religious organizations, an independence from secular control or manipulation—in short, power to decide for themselves, free from state interference, matters of church government as well as those of faith and doctrine. Freedom to select the clergy, where no improper methods of choice are proven, we think, must now be said to have federal constitutional protection as a part of the free exercise of religion against state interference.

Thus, the First Amendment severely circumscribes the role that civil courts may play in resolving church property disputes. It is obvious, however, that not every civil court decision as to property claimed by a religious organization jeopardizes values protected by the First Amendment. Civil courts do not inhibit free exercise of religion merely by opening their doors to disputes involving church property. And there are neutral principles of law, developed for use in all property disputes, which can be applied without "establishing" churches to which property is awarded. But First Amendment values are plainly jeopardized when church property litigation is made to turn on the resolution by civil courts of controversies over religious doctrine and practice. If civil courts undertake to resolve such controversies in order to adjudicate the property dispute, the hazards are ever present of inhibiting the free development of religious doctrine and of implicating secular interests in matters of purely ecclesiastical concern. *** Hence, States, religious organizations, and individuals must structure relationships involving church property so as not to require the civil courts to resolve ecclesiastical questions.

The Georgia courts have violated the command of the First Amendment. The departure-from-doctrine element of the implied trust theory which they applied requires the civil judiciary to determine whether actions of the general church constitute such a "substantial departure" from the tenets of faith and practice existing at the time of the local churches' affiliation that the trust in favor of the general church must be declared to have terminated. *** If the court should decide that a substantial departure has occurred, it must then go on to determine whether the issue on which the general church has departed holds a place of such importance in the traditional theology as to require that the trust be terminated. A civil court can make this determination only after assessing the relative significance to the religion of the tenets from which departure was found. Thus, the departure-from-doctrine element of the Georgia implied trust theory requires the civil court to determine matters at the very core of a religion—the interpretation of particular church doctrines and the importance of those doctrines to the religion. Plainly, the First Amendment forbids civil courts from playing such a role. [Reversed.]

Mr. Justice HARLAN, concurring.

I am in entire agreement with the Court's rejection of the "departure-from-doctrine" approach taken by the Georgia courts, as that approach necessarily requires the civilian courts to weigh the significance and the meaning of disputed religious doctrine. I do not, however, read the Court's opinion to go further to hold that the Fourteenth Amendment forbids civilian courts from enforcing a deed or will which expressly and clearly lays down conditions limiting a religious organization's use of the property which is granted. If, for example, the donor expressly gives his church some money on the condition that the church never ordain a woman as a minister or elder or never amend certain specified articles of the Confession of Faith, he is entitled to his money back if the condition is not fulfilled. In such a case, the church should not be permitted to keep the property simply because church authorities have determined that the doctrinal innovation is justified by the faith's basic principles.

> **Food for Thought**
>
> How does the hypothetical example that Justice Harlan offers here differ from the facts of the actual case? Is it clear that resolution of the donor's claim would not embroil the court in theological questions?

Points for Discussion

a. Involvement in Religious Disputes

Georgia law, which governed the dispute between the parties, made the question of property law (i.e., which party owned the land on which the churches were located) turn on the extent to which the general church had adhered to the tenets of its faith. It is not difficult to see why this standard risked embroiling the courts in a theological dispute. But what if that general church had produced a contract that it had entered into with the local church stating that, in the event of a dispute, it would have authority to control the property of the local churches by appointing leaders for those churches? Would application of ordinary contract principles to the dispute also violate the religion clauses? If not, why not? Exactly what types of judicial involvement in religious disputes do the religion clauses prohibit?

b. Is Abstention Mandatory?

The Court concluded that the resolution of this dispute—at least according to Georgia's "departure-from-doctrine" approach—would violate the religion clauses. Could the parties have forced the Court to resolve it by waiving their rights under this Clause? For example, suppose that a dispute arises within a church over a matter that involves some question of religious doctrine. After failed attempts to resolve the matter, the opposing sides decide that the most civil way to resolve the matter is to present it to a judge. Assuming an actual case or controversy, can the plaintiff and defendant ask a court to resolve the matter, thus waiving any Free Exercise claim? Judge Richard Posner, in dicta, expressed doubt:

> Judges have an interest independent of party preference for not being asked to decide an issue that they cannot resolve intelligently. Americans would, moreover, be deeply offended at the thought of their secular courts taking on the additional role of religious courts, as if the United States were a theocracy.

Tomic v. Catholic Diocese of Peoria, 442 F.3d 1036, 1042 (7th Cir. 2006).

c. Applying the Test

Imagine that a novice studying to become a Jesuit priest claims that he was sexually harassed by his superiors at seminary. The Jesuits do not offer a religious justification for the harassment the novice alleges; indeed, they condemn sexual harassment as inconsistent with their values and beliefs. But they dispute whether the harassment occurred. May a court decide this question? See *Bollard v. California Province of the Society of Jesus*, 196 F.3d 940 (9th Cir. 1999) (holding that the claim was not barred by the Free Exercise Clause). See also Ira C. Lupu & Robert Tuttle, *Sexual Misconduct and Ecclesiastical Immunity*, 2004 B.Y.U. L. Rev. 1789, 1896 (2004) (arguing that religious institutions should not have a general immunity from laws imposing liability for misconduct).

Executive Summary of This Chapter

Constitutional Provisions Addressing Freedom of Religion

The original Constitution addresses freedom of religion in Article VI, clause 3, which says "no religious Test shall ever be required as a Qualification to any Office or public Trust under the United States." The First Amendment augments the protection for the freedom of religion by saying: "Congress shall make no law respecting an establishment of religion, or prohibiting the free exercise thereof ***." The two clauses in this phrase have become known, respectively, as the **Establishment Clause** and the **Free Exercise Clause**. Although the text of these clauses refers to Congress, the Supreme Court has held that the Due Process clause of the Fourteenth Amendment makes both of these clauses applicable to the states, as well. *Cantwell v. Connecticut,* 310 U.S. 296, 303 (1940).

The Establishment Clause: Aid to Religious Institutions

The Establishment Clause not only prevents the federal and state governments from establishing an official religion, but also restricts certain kinds of interactions between the government and religious groups. One important question is whether or when government aid to religious institutions violates the Establishment Clause. The Court has declared that, as a general principle, "[n]o tax in any amount, large or small, can be levied to support any religious activities or institutions ***." This rule effectuates the principle of the **separation of church and state**. Because this principle, taken to its logical extreme, might forbid the government from providing a range of services to religious organizations, the Court has also held that the government may provide aid under certain circumstances to religious organizations if the government is "neutral in its relations with groups of religious believers and non-believers." *Everson v. Board of Education of Ewing Township*, 330 U.S. 1 (1947). This is generally known as the **neutrality principle**.

For many years, the Supreme Court sought to determine whether government actions complied with these principles by applying the *Lemon* **test**. In applying this test, courts consider (1) whether the challenged law has a secular purpose; (2) whether the principal or primary effect of the law is neither to advance nor inhibit religion; and (3) whether the law excessively entangles the government and religion. *Lemon v. Kurtzman,* 403 U.S. 602 (1971). The Supreme Court has not formally renounced the *Lemon* test, but it does not apply the test now as regularly as it did in the past.

The cases in this chapter provide various examples of the application of these principles. The government does not violate the Establishment Clause when it reimburses parents for costs incurred in transporting their children to parochial schools if the government also pays the costs of transporting children to public or other non-religious schools. *Everson v. Board of Education of Ewing Township*, 330 U.S. 1 (1947). The government does violate the Establishment Clause when it supplements teacher salaries at parochial schools or reimburses the schools for the cost of the salaries. *Lemon v. Kurtzman,* 403 U.S. 602 (1971). The government does not violate the Establishment Clause when it provides parents with vouchers to help cover the cost of educating their children if the vouchers can be redeemed at religious and non-religious schools alike. *Zelman v. Simmons-Harris,* 536 U.S. 639 (2002).

The Establishment Clause: Religion within Government

Another important issue is the extent to which the Establishment Clause restricts religious activities and symbols within the government. The Establishment Clause bars **prayer in public schools** if the prayer is an official or approved part of school activities. Indeed, prayer is banned in schools whether the students say the prayer or merely hear the prayer, whether the prayer is denominational or non-denominational, whether the prayer is silent or spoken, and whether student participation in the prayer is voluntary or involuntary. *Engel v. Vitale,* 370 U.S. 421 (1962); *Wallace v. Jaffree,* 472 U.S. 38 (1985); *Lee v. Weisman,* 505 U.S. 577 (1992).

The Supreme Court has held that the Establishment Clause does not always bar activities like prayer in public institutions other than public schools, however, if they are **deeply embedded in the history and tradition** of the country. *Marsh v. Chambers,* 463 U.S. 783 (1983). In addition, the Establishment Clause does not prevent the display of **religious symbols on government property** if the symbols have a secular purpose and do not amount to an endorsement of a particular religion or religion in general. *Lynch v. Donnelly,* 465 U.S. 668 (1984).

Free Exercise Clause: Burdens on Religious Practices

The Free Exercise Clause protects an individual freedom to engage in religious practices. The government may enforce a law that burdens a particular religious practice only if (1) the law is **both neutral and of general applicability**; or (2) the government has a **compelling interest for imposing the burden and the law is narrowly tailored** to advance that interest. A law is not neutral if the object of the law is to infringe upon or restrict practices because of their religious motivation. A law lacks general applicability if it is underinclusive, applying to religious practices but not to similar non-religious practices. *Employment Division, Dept. of Human Resources of Oregon v. Smith,* 494 U.S. 872 (1990); *Church of the Lukumi Babalu Aye, Inc. v. City of Hialeah,* 508 U.S. 520 (1993).

Government Involvement in Religious Disputes

Although courts may decide some disputes between or within religious organizations, the Supreme Court has held that the Religion Clauses prevent them from deciding **issues of religious doctrine**. If the ownership of property or the rights of clergy or any other legal question turns on the tenets of faith, the courts must leave the matter for a religious body to decide. *Presbyterian Church in U.S. v. Mary Elizabeth Blue Hull Memorial Presbyterian Church,* 393 U.S. 440 (1969).

POINT-COUNTERPOINT

Has the Court properly answered the question, "Whom should the First Amendment protect"?

POINT: PETER J. SMITH

The First Amendment is properly read to protect *dissenters*—those who choose not to accept the prevailing orthodoxy in matters of politics, religion, conscience, or opinion. This is not to say that the Amendment provides no protection to those who express popular views or adhere to the majority religion; but as a general matter, those people need no protection from majoritarian efforts to define what is orthodox. Although the Court has often construed the First Amendment to advance this end, there are substantial areas of doctrine that are in tension with this view of the Amendment.

For example, although the Court has often properly interpreted the Free Speech Clause to extend protection to persons who express unpopular political or cultural views, see, e.g., *Texas v. Johnson,* 491 U.S. 397 (1989) (burning the flag as a form of protest); *Cohen v. California,* 403 U.S. 15 (1971) (protesting the Vietnam War with colorful language), the Court has also concluded that entire categories of expression are not entitled to any protection at all, solely because of the content of the expression. The Court's cases on obscenity, for example, effectively permit the censorship of expression—including books and films—of which the majority disapproves. That approach presumably would have permitted local majorities to ban D. H. Lawrence's *Lady Chatterley's Lover* and Vladimir Nabokov's *Lolita* at the time that they were first published—and perhaps would tolerate it today, in some parts of the United States. This cannot be reconciled with the view that the First Amendment protects the expression of unpopular ideas. Nor can the categorical approach to the Free Speech Clause itself, which permits the Court—as opposed to individuals exercising their judgment and consciences—to decide which ideas have value and which do not.

The Religion Clauses also protect dissenters—those, that is, who adhere to minority religions, or to no religion at all. The Free Exercise Clause directly protects adherents of minority religions in their beliefs and worship, and the Establishment Clause, properly understood, protects all dissenters by ensuring that they are not marginalized by official endorsements of, or support for, a particular religion or for religion in general. But the Court's interpretation of the Religion Clauses, like its interpretation of the Free Speech Clause, has also not always advanced the First Amendment's central goal. For example, the non-preferentialist view of the Establishment Clause, towards which the Court has increasingly drifted, see, e.g., *Zelman v. Simmons-Harris,* 536 U.S. 639, 677-680 (2002) (upholding the use of vouchers at parochial schools); cf. *Lynch v. Donnelly,* 465 U.S. 668 (1984) (upholding an official public display of a Christian crèche), inevitably will marginalize adherents of certain minority religions. This is because once some religion is permitted in the public square, or some religious institutions are permitted to receive government subsidies, it will be impossible to permit true equal treatment for all religions. Even holiday displays that include Christian, Jewish, and Muslim symbols generally exclude Buddhists, Sikhs, Hindus, Shintoists, Animists, and adherents of countless other faiths. And the non-preferentialist view *by design* fails to protect those who choose not to adhere to *any* religion, because the *whole point* of the non-preferentialist view is to permit government to prefer religion to non-religion, as long as it does not prefer one religion to another. In practice, this approach provides government sanction to displays of the majority religion, but provides little or no protection to religious (or non-religious) dissenters.

We would do well to recall Justice Jackson's eloquent statement more than a half-century ago in *West Virginia State Board of Education v. Barnette*, 319 U.S. 624 (1943): "If there is any fixed star in our constitutional constellation, it is that no official, high or petty, can prescribe what shall be orthodox in politics, nationalism, religion, or other matters of opinion or force citizens to confess by word or act their faith therein. If there are any circumstances which permit an exception, they do not now occur to us."

————

COUNTERPOINT: GREGORY E. MAGGS

In *Loving v. Virginia*, 388 U.S. 1 (1967), which we considered in Chapter 11, the Supreme Court emphasized an important general point about the Constitution: constitutional rights are individual rights, not group rights. Accordingly, Virginia could not justify its law prohibiting intermarriage by arguing that the law applied to every *race* equally. Instead, Virginia had to show that its law treated each *person* equally. The state could not make this showing. Although Virginia would have allowed a white person to be married to Mr. Loving, the state did not allow the woman who wanted to be married to him to do so because of her race.

Although <u>Loving v. Virginia</u> was an Equal Protection case, this fundamental principle applies—or should apply—to all of the rights secured by the First Amendment. The First Amendment protects individual rights of free speech, of free exercise of religion, and so forth. Accordingly, a person's inclusion or membership in a particular group should not affect his or her rights. The First Amendment does not differentiate between those holding majority opinions and dissenters, between the religiously orthodox and the unorthodox, between the rich and the poor, or between anything comparable.

The Supreme Court, unfortunately, does not have a consistent record of applying this principle. A good example where the Court followed the principle is *Davis v. Federal Election Commission*, 128 S. Ct. 2759 (2008). In that case, the Supreme Court struck down the "millionaire's amendment," a statutory provision aimed at equalizing political candidates' campaign speech. The Court held that the government cannot burden the right of an individual candidate to spend however much of his own money he desires, even if this means that the wealthy as a group may have an advantage over the less affluent.

The Court, however, was not so faithful to the principle in *Buckley v. Valeo*, 424 U.S. 1 (1976). As discussed in the note following *NAACP v. Alabama ex rel. Patterson*, 357

U.S. 449 (1958), in Chapter 16, part of that case concerned a reporting requirement for donors to political campaigns. Although the court generally rejected the plaintiffs' claim that requiring donors to disclose their identities would substantially burden their freedom of association, it announced an exception for "minor parties" who can show "a reasonable probability that the compelled disclosure of a party's contributors' names will subject them to threats, harassment, or reprisals from either Government officials or private parties." *Buckley*, 424 U.S. at 74. This exception should not be limited to members of minor parties but should extend to any individual who can show a substantial burden on his or her freedom of association.

True, as a practical matter, legislatures are more likely to pass laws violating the First Amendment rights of minority groups—whether defined by political thought, religion, or some other characteristic—than of majority groups. Majority groups, in a democracy, usually can use their political power to prevent their own mistreatment. But this generalization does not change the fundamental nature of constitutional rights.

PART X: PROTECTION OF ECONOMIC LIBERTY

In Chapter 8, we considered the Court's efforts, in the late-nineteenth and early-twentieth centuries, to interpret the Due Process Clauses of the Fifth and Fourteenth Amendments to protect the "freedom of contract." As we saw, those efforts ultimately failed to produce enduring protections for economic rights.

But the original Constitution and the Bill of Rights also included at least two other explicit and direct protections for economic liberty. Article I, § 10, cl. 1 provides that "No State shall [pass] any *** Law impairing the Obligation of Contracts," and the Fifth Amendment provides that "private property shall [not] be taken for public use, without just compensation." In this Part, we consider these two provisions, known respectively as the "Contract Clause" and the "Takings Clause." As you read these materials, pay close attention to the tension between the government's interest in regulating private conduct and the economic interests of the persons regulated.

CHAPTER 18

Protection of Economic Liberty

A. Impairment of Contracts by State Laws

The conventional view is that the Contract Clause was designed to prevent states from enacting laws to help debtors at the expense of creditors. See Laurence H. Tribe, American Constitutional Law 613 (2d ed. 1988). Such a prohibition was thought not only to protect individuals from majoritarian efforts at redistribution, but also to maintain an incentive for the provision of credit by removing one source of risk that creditors would not be repaid.

The Contract Clause was a frequent source of litigation during the years of the Marshall Court. In perhaps the most important case, *Ogden v. Saunders*, 25 U.S. (12 Wheat.) 213 (1827), the Court held that although the Contract Clause imposes limits on the power of the state to interfere with *existing* contracts, it does not limit the power of states to regulate the terms of *future* contracts. The Court reasoned that state laws that existed at the time a contract was entered effectively constituted terms of the contract, and thus could not be said to "impair" an obligation arising under a contract but in conflict with those existing laws. Chief Justice Marshall dissented—the only time in his 34-year tenure that he dissented in a case involving a constitutional question—asserting that contractual obligations were essentially a matter of natural law, and that states accordingly could not interfere with them.

> **Food for Thought**
>
> If *Ogden* had come out the other way, could states reform the common law of contracts by, for example, enacting the Uniform Commercial Code?

In the nineteenth century, the Court decided, in a series of cases, that a state could interfere even with *existing* contracts if it had a valid government interest in doing so. See, e.g., *Stone v. Mississippi*, 101 U.S. 814 (1880). Although this approach tended to weaken substantially the importance of the Contract Clause as a limit on state authority, the ultimate effect was obscured by another doctrinal development. As we saw in Chapter 8, in the late-nineteenth and early-twentieth century the Court interpreted the Due Process Clauses to impose severe limits on the ability of the states (and, for that matter, the federal government) to interfere with private contractual relationships. Accordingly, during this period, the reach of the Contract Clause was not a particularly pressing question.

In the 1930s, however, the Court began to retreat from its aggressive protection of economic liberty through the Due Process Clauses. That made the question of the Contract

Clause's protections ripe once again. The Court offered its most important interpretation of the Clause in the case that follows.

————————

Home Building & Loan Ass'n v. Blaisdell

290 U.S. 398 (1934)

Mr. Chief Justice HUGHES delivered the opinion of the Court.

[In 1933, during the Great Depression, Minnesota enacted the Mortgage Moratorium Law, which authorized parties facing foreclosure to obtain from a court an extension of the time during which the mortgagee could not foreclose and an extension of the period of redemption after foreclosure. Extensions could be granted only until May 1, 1935, after which the statute would no longer be in effect. Extensions were conditioned upon the mortgagor's making continued payments, determined by the reasonable income or rental value of the property, to help to defray the cost of taxes, insurance, and the like. The Blaisdells obtained an order extending the contractual redemption period from May 2, 1932, to May 1, 1935, on the condition that they pay $40 per month to appellant, the mortgagee, during the extended period. Appellant challenged the constitutionality of the Act under the Contract Clause.]

Emergency does not create power. Emergency does not increase granted power or remove or diminish the restrictions imposed upon power granted or reserved. [But while] emergency does not create power, emergency may furnish the occasion for the exercise of power. *** [W]here constitutional grants and limitations of power are set forth in general clauses, which afford a broad outline, the process of construction is essential to fill in the details. That is true of the contract clause. [T]he reasons which led to the adoption of that clause, and of the other prohibitions of section 10 of article 1, are not left in doubt ***. The widespread distress following the revolutionary period and the plight of debtors had called forth in the States an ignoble array of legislative schemes for the defeat of creditors and the invasion of contractual obligations. Legislative interferences had been so numerous and extreme that the confidence essential to prosperous trade had been undermined and the utter destruction of credit was threatened. "The sober people of America" were convinced that some "thorough reform" was needed which would "inspire a general prudence and industry, and give a regular course to the business of society." The Federalist, No. 44.

> **Food for Thought**
>
> As the Court explains, the conventional view is that the Framers included the Contract Clause to prevent states from passing measures to provide relief to debtors at the expense of creditors. Why might this kind of relief be a concern? How does relief to debtors threaten to destroy debt? Isn't providing relief to debtors the whole point of the statute challenged in this case? If so, doesn't that mean that it must be unconstitutional?

But full recognition of the occasion and general purpose of the clause does not suffice to fix its precise scope. *** [The state] continues to possess authority to safeguard the vital interests of its people. *** Not only are existing laws read into contracts in order to fix obligations as between the parties, but the reservation of essential attributes of sovereign power is also read into contracts as a postulate of the legal order. The policy of protecting contracts against impairment presupposes the maintenance of a government by virtue of which contractual relations are worth while—a government which retains adequate authority to secure the peace and good order of society. This principle of harmonizing the constitutional prohibition with the necessary residuum of state power has had progressive recognition in the decisions of this Court.

Undoubtedly, [t]he reserved power cannot be construed so as to destroy the limitation, nor is the limitation to be construed to destroy the reserved power in its essential aspects. They must be construed in harmony with each other. This principle precludes a construction which would permit the state to adopt as its policy the repudiation of debts or the destruction of contracts or the denial of means to enforce them. But it does not follow that conditions may not arise in which a temporary restraint of enforcement may be consistent with the spirit and purpose of the constitutional provision and thus be found to be within the range of the reserved power of the state to protect the vital interests of the community.

[I]f state power exists to give temporary relief from the enforcement of contracts in the presence of disasters due to physical causes such as fire, flood, or earthquake, that power cannot be said to be nonexistent when the urgent public need demanding such relief is produced by other and economic causes. It is no answer to say that this public need was not apprehended a century ago, or to insist that what the provision of the Constitution meant to the vision of that day it must mean to the vision of our time. If by the statement that what the Constitution meant at the time of its adoption it means today, it is intended to say that the great clauses of the Constitution must be confined to the interpretation which the framers, with the conditions and outlook of their time, would have placed upon them, the statement carries its own refutation. It was to guard against such a narrow conception that Chief Justice Marshall uttered the memorable warning: "We must never forget, that it is a constitution we are expounding." *McCulloch v. Maryland*, 4 Wheat. 316, 407 (1819). *** The vast body of law which has been developed was unknown to the fathers, but it is believed to have preserved the essential content and the spirit of the Constitution. With a growing recognition of public needs and the relation of individual right to public security, the court has sought to prevent the perversion of the clause through its use as an instrument to throttle the capacity of the states to protect their fundamental interests.

Take Note

Is Chief Justice Hughes suggesting here that the original meaning of the Constitution is not (or need not be) the meaning of the Constitution today? If so, you will find no more explicit statement of this idea in any Supreme Court opinion. Or does Hughes mean that when the Court applies the original meaning of the provisions of the Constitution to modern circumstances, results that the Framers did not anticipate might follow? If Hughes means the latter, did he apply the Clause properly in this case?

Applying the criteria established by our decisions, we conclude: An emergency existed in Minnesota which furnished a proper occasion for the exercise of the reserved power of the state to protect the vital interests of the community. The declarations of the existence of this emergency by the Legislature and by the Supreme Court of Minnesota cannot be regarded as a subterfuge or as lacking in adequate basis. *** The legislation was addressed to a legitimate end; that is, the legislation was not for the mere advantage of particular individuals but for the protection of a basic interest of society. *** The conditions upon which the period of redemption is extended do not appear to be unreasonable. [T]he integrity of the mortgage indebtedness is not impaired; interest continues to run; the validity of the sale and the right of a mortgagee-purchaser to title or to obtain a deficiency judgment, if the mortgagor fails to redeem within the extended period, are maintained; and the conditions of redemption, if redemption there be, stand as they were under the prior law. *** The mortgagee-purchaser during the time that he cannot obtain possession [is] not left without compensation for the withholding of possession. *** The relief afforded by the statute has regard to the interest of mortgagees as well as to the interest of mortgagors. The legislation seeks to prevent the impending ruin of both by a considerate measure of relief. The legislation is temporary in operation [and] is limited to the exigency which called it forth.

We are of the opinion that the Minnesota statute as here applied does not violate the contract clause of the Federal Constitution. Whether the legislation is wise or unwise as a matter of policy is a question with which we are not concerned.

Mr. Justice SUTHERLAND, [joined by Mr. Justice VAN DEVANTER, Mr. Justice McREYN-OLDS, and Mr. Justice BUTLER,] dissenting.

If the contract impairment clause, when framed and adopted, meant that the terms of a contract for the payment of money could not be altered [by] a state statute enacted for the relief of hardly pressed debtors to the end and with the effect of postponing payment or enforcement during and because of an economic or financial emergency, it is but to state the obvious to say that it means the same now. *** The provisions of the Federal Constitution, undoubtedly, are pliable in the sense that in appropriate cases they have the capacity of bringing within their grasp every new condition which falls within their meaning. But, their meaning is changeless; it is only their application which is extensible. Constitutional grants of power and restrictions upon the exercise of power are not flexible as the doctrines of the common law are flexible.

The whole aim of construction, as applied to a provision of the Constitution, is to discover the meaning, to ascertain and give effect to the intent of its framers and the people who adopted it. *** A candid consideration of the history and circumstances which led up to and accompanied the framing and adoption of this clause will demonstrate conclusively that it was framed and adopted with the specific and studied purpose of preventing legislation designed to relieve debtors especially in time of financial distress.

[T]he question is not whether an emergency furnishes the occasion for the exercise of that state power, but whether an emergency furnishes an occasion for the relaxation of the restrictions upon the power imposed by the contract impairment clause; and the difficulty is that the contract impairment clause forbids state action under any circumstances, if it have the effect of impairing the obligation of contracts. That clause restricts every state power in the particular specified, no matter what may be the occasion. *** The Minnesota statute either impairs the obligation of contracts or it does not. *** If it does, the emergency no more furnishes a proper occasion for its exercise than if the emergency were nonexistent.

A statute which materially delays enforcement of the mortgagee's contractual right of ownership and possession does not modify the remedy merely; it destroys, for the period of delay, all remedy so far as the enforcement of that right is concerned. The phrase "obligation of a contract" in the constitutional sense imports a legal duty to perform the specified obligation of that contract, not to substitute and perform, against the will of one of the parties, a different, albeit equally valuable, obligation. And a state, under the contract impairment clause, has no more power to accomplish such a substitution than has one of the parties to the contract against the will of the other.

Points for Discussion

a. Emergencies and the Contract Clause

Did the Court uphold the regulation because the state was faced with an "emergency"? If so, would the Court have permitted this form of regulation if there had been no exigent circumstances? How did the Court decide if there was an emergency? In making such a determination, should it have deferred to the legislature that enacted the challenged regulation?

b. What's Left?

If the state can interfere with contractual obligations—here, by effectively redefining the parties' respective rights under a pre-existing contract—to advance some legitimate state interest, then what limit does the Contract Clause impose? Does the Clause have any continuing vitality after the decision in *Blaisdell*? Consider the case that follows.

Allied Structural Steel Company v. Spannaus

438 U.S. 234 (1978)

Mr. Justice STEWART delivered the opinion of the Court.

[Appellant, an Illinois corporation with an office in Minnesota, maintained a pension plan that entitled employees who were at least 65 years old at retirement to receive benefits as long as the company was still in business and the plan was still in effect. In 1974, Minnesota enacted the Private Pension Benefits Protection Act, which required certain employers in Minnesota to pay a "pension funding charge" if they (1) terminated a pension plan or closed a Minnesota office and (2) at the time of termination or closure, existing pension funds were not sufficient to pay pensions to employees who had worked at least 10 years. When appellant closed its Minnesota office, at least nine of the newly discharged employees did not have vested pension rights under the company's plan but qualified for pension benefits under the Act because they had been employed by the company for more than 10 years. The State assessed appellant a pension funding charge of approximately $185,000, and appellant challenged the constitutionality of the Act under the Contract Clause.]

There can be no question of the impact of the Minnesota Private Pension Benefits Protection Act upon the company's contractual relationships with its employees. The Act substantially altered those relationships by superimposing pension obligations upon the company conspicuously beyond those that it had voluntarily agreed to undertake. But it does not inexorably follow that the Act, as applied to the company, violates the Contract Clause of the Constitution.

The language of the Contract Clause appears unambiguously absolute, [but] it is to be accepted as a commonplace that the Contract Clause does not operate to obliterate the police power of the States. *** If the Contract Clause is to retain any meaning at all, however, it must be understood to impose *some* limits upon the power of a State to abridge existing contractual relationships, even in the exercise of its otherwise legitimate police power. [The Court in *Blaisdell*] implied that if the Minnesota moratorium legislation had not [been a reasonable response to an emergency,] it would have been invalid under the Contract Clause. *** The most recent Contract Clause case in this Court was *United States Trust Co. v. New Jersey*, 431 U.S. 1 (1977). *** Evaluating with particular scrutiny a modification of a contract to which the State itself was a party, the Court in that case held that legislative alteration of the rights and remedies of Port Authority bondholders violated the Contract Clause because the legislation was neither necessary nor reasonable.

In applying these principles to the present case, the first inquiry must be whether the state law has, in fact, operated as a substantial impairment of a contractual relationship.[1] The severity of the impairment measures the height of the hurdle the state legislation must clear. Minimal alteration of contractual obligations may end the inquiry at its first stage. Severe impairment, on the other hand, will push the inquiry to a careful examination of the nature and purpose of the state legislation.

The severity of an impairment of contractual obligations can be measured by the factors that reflect the high value the Framers placed on the protection of private contracts. Contracts enable individuals to order their personal and business affairs according to their particular needs and interests. Once arranged, those rights and obligations are binding under the law, and the parties are entitled to rely on them. *** The company [had] no reason to anticipate that its employees' pension rights could become vested except in accordance with the terms of the plan. It relied heavily, and reasonably, on this legitimate

---

[1] The novel construction of the Contract Clause expressed in the dissenting opinion is wholly contrary to the decisions of this Court. The narrow view that the Clause forbids only state laws that diminish the duties of a contractual obligor and not laws that increase them [has] been expressly repudiated. *Detroit United R. Co. v. Michigan*, 242 U.S. 238 (1916). The even narrower view that the Clause is limited in its application to state laws relieving debtors of obligations to their creditors is, as the dissent recognizes, completely at odds with this Court's decisions. See *Dartmouth College v. Woodward*, 17 U.S. (4 Wheat.) 518 (1819).

contractual expectation in calculating its annual contributions to the pension fund. The effect of Minnesota's Private Pension Benefits Protection Act on this contractual obligation was severe. [A]lthough the company's past contributions were adequate when made, they were not adequate when computed under the 10-year statutory vesting requirement. The Act thus forced a current recalculation of the past 10 years' contributions based on the new, unanticipated 10-year vesting requirement. Not only did the state law thus retroactively modify the compensation that the company had agreed to pay its employees from 1963 to 1974, but also it did so by changing the company's obligations in an area where the element of reliance was vital—the funding of a pension plan.

[T]here is no showing in the record before us that this severe disruption of contractual expectations was necessary to meet an important general social problem. [And] because the Act applies only to private employers who have at least 100 employees, at least one of whom works in Minnesota, and who have established voluntary private pension plans, [it] can hardly be characterized, like the law at issue in the *Blaisdell* case, as one enacted to protect a broad societal interest rather than a narrow class. [Finally, the] legislation [was] not enacted to deal with a situation remotely approaching the broad and desperate emergency economic conditions of the early 1930's—conditions of which the Court in *Blaisdell* took judicial notice.

Food for Thought

The "narrow class" to whom the challenged Act applies includes most employees who work at large employers in Minnesota. Do you agree with the Court's view that a statute designed to ensure the retirement security of workers in that class does not serve a "broad societal interest"? Or that retirement insecurity does not properly constitute an "emergency" that justifies state regulation? What was the Minnesota legislature's view of these questions?

This Minnesota law simply does not possess the attributes of those state laws that in the past have survived challenge under the Contract Clause of the Constitution. The law was not even purportedly enacted to deal with a broad, generalized economic or social problem. It did not operate in an area already subject to state regulation at the time the company's contractual obligations were originally undertaken, but invaded an area never before subject to regulation by the State. It did not effect simply a temporary alteration of the contractual relationships of those within its coverage, but worked a severe, permanent, and immediate change in those relationships—irrevocably and retroactively. And its narrow aim was leveled, not at every Minnesota employer, not even at every Minnesota employer who left the State, but only at those who had in the past been sufficiently enlightened as voluntarily to agree to establish pension plans for their employees. *** [I]f the Contract Clause means anything at all, it means that Minnesota could not constitutionally do what it tried to do to the company in this case.

Mr. Justice BRENNAN, with whom Mr. Justice WHITE and Mr. Justice MARSHALL join, dissenting.

Minnesota [adopted] the Act to remedy [what was viewed as a serious] social problem: the frustration of expectation interests that can occur when an employer closes a single plant and terminates the employees who work there. *** The Minnesota Act addresses this problem by selecting a period [after] which this generally unforeseen contingency may not be the basis for depriving employees of their accumulated pension fund credits. [T]he Act will impose only minor economic burdens on employers whose pension plans have been adequately funded. *** Indeed, without the Act, the closing of the plant would create a windfall for the employer, because, due to the resulting surplus in the fund, his future contributions would be reduced.

The Act does not relieve either the employer or his employees of any existing contract obligation. Rather, the Act simply creates an additional, supplemental duty of the employer, no different in kind from myriad duties created by a wide variety of legislative measures which defeat settled expectations but which have nonetheless been sustained by this Court. For this reason, the Minnesota Act, in my view, does not implicate the Contract Clause in any way. The basic fallacy of today's decision is its mistaken view that the Contract Clause protects all contract-based expectations, including that of an employer that his obligations to his employees will not be legislatively enlarged beyond those explicitly provided in his pension plan.

[T]he Framers never contemplated that the Clause would limit the legislative power of States to enact laws creating duties that might burden some individuals in order to benefit others *** [T]he sole evil at which the Contract Clause was directed was the theretofore rampant state legislative interference with the ability of creditors to obtain the payment or security provided for by contract. The Framers regarded the Contract Clause as simply an adjunct to the currency provisions of Art. I, § 10, which operated primarily to bar legislation depriving creditors of the payment of the full value of their loans. The Clause was thus intended by the Framers to be applicable only to laws which altered the obligations of contracts by effectively relieving one party of the obligation to perform a contract duty. *** This evil is identified with admirable precision: "Law[s] *impairing* the Obligation of Contracts." It is nothing less than an abuse of the English language to interpret, as does the Court, the term "impairing" as including laws which create new duties. While such laws may be conceptualized as "enlarging" the obligation of a contract when they add to the burdens that had previously been imposed by a private agreement, such laws cannot be prohibited by the Clause because they do not dilute or nullify a duty a person had previously obligated himself to perform.

Under the Court's opinion, any law that may be characterized as "superimposing" new obligations on those provided for by contract is to be regarded as creating "sudden, substantial, and unanticipated burdens" and then to be subjected to the most exacting scrutiny. The validity of such a law will turn upon whether judges see it as a law that deals with a generalized social problem, whether it is temporary (as few will be) or permanent, whether it operates in an area previously subject to regulation, and, finally, whether its duties apply to a broad class of persons. The necessary consequence of the extreme malleability of these rather vague criteria is to vest judges with broad subjective discretion to protect property interests that happen to appeal to them.

————————

Points for Discussion

a. Scope of State Power

In concluding that the statute upset the contract-based expectations of the company, the Court emphasized that the challenged state law regulated in an "area never before subject to regulation by the State." But isn't this argument circular? If the Court had concluded that Minnesota had authority to regulate in this fashion, then wouldn't any company's expectations (after the decision) incorporate the possibility of state regulation? If the Court's point is that state regulation simply cannot *retroactively* change the terms of a contract, then why would it matter that the state regulation is in response to some form of emergency?

b. Outlier or More Recent Trend?

Is *Allied Structural Steel* an outlier, or does it represent the Court's willingness to apply the Contract Clause more aggressively? It turns out that *Allied Structural Steel* is the only case since *Blaisdell* in which the Court invoked the Contract Clause to invalidate a state law that interfered with private contracts. In cases involving contracts between private parties since *Allied Structural Steel*, the Court has upheld the challenged state regulation, often expressly distinguishing the case. In *United States Trust Co. v. New Jersey*, 431 U.S. 1 (1977), however, the Court struck down a state law that effectively changed the terms of a contract to which the state itself was a party. There are reasons, however, to be particularly skeptical of such action. (Can you articulate what they are?)

B. Takings of Private Property

"**Eminent domain**"—the power of government to force a transfer of property—traces back at least as far as ancient Rome. The Constitution does not expressly authorize the federal government to exercise the power of eminent domain. Article I, § 8, which lists Congress's enumerated powers, does not include such a provision, but the Necessary and Proper Clause, along with Congress's other affirmative powers, presumably permits the exercise of the power of eminent domain. And the Fifth Amendment has long been viewed as a "tacit recognition of [the] pre-existing power" of eminent domain. *United States v. Carmack*, 329 U.S. 230, 241-242 (1946). The Fifth Amendment, after listing the grand jury requirement, the double jeopardy rule, and the entitlement to due process, states: "nor shall private property be taken for public use, without just com-

> **Make the Connection**
>
> Recall that in *Barron v. Baltimore*, which we considered in Chapter 7, the Court held that the Takings Clause does not apply to the states. After the ratification of the Fourteenth Amendment, however, the Court held that the Takings Clause was "incorporated" and thus applied to limit state, as well as federal, action. See *Chicago, Burlington & Quincy Railroad v. Chicago*, 166 U.S. 226 (1897).

pensation." This is known as the "**Takings Clause**."

FYI

The Court has consistently held that, when the government takes property, "just compensation" is determined by assessing the loss to the owner, measured by the market value at the time of the taking. See, e.g., *Kirby Forest Industries, Inc. v. United States*, 467 U.S. 1 (1984).

The Clause itself suggests several questions that must be resolved in any case arising under the Clause. First, in order to apply the Clause, the Court must have some way to determine what constitutes a taking. Second, the Clause, although inartfully drafted, seems to limit the government's power of eminent domain to instances in which the taking is for a "public use." Accordingly, courts are sometimes called upon to determine whether a taking satisfies this requirement. Third, when the government has taken property for a public use, the Takings Clause requires the government to pay "just compensation." In the materials that follow, we will focus on the first two questions.

---

1. Introduction

United States v. Causby

328 U.S. 256 (1946)

Mr. Justice DOUGLAS delivered the opinion of the Court.

[Respondents raised chickens on their land, which was less than one-half mile from an airport used by United States military aircraft. The planes passed over the property day and night at very low altitudes. The noise frightened the chickens, some of which died when they responded by flying into walls. Respondents eventually concluded that they could not use their property as a commercial chicken farm. The United States Court of Claims concluded that the United States had taken an easement over the property, and that the value of the property destroyed and the easement taken was $2,000.]

If, by reason of the frequency and altitude of the flights, respondents could not use this land for any purpose, their loss would be complete. It would be as complete as if the United States had entered upon the surface of the land and taken exclusive possession of it. [In] those circumstances there would be a taking. *** The fact that the planes never touched the surface would be [irrelevant]. The owner's right to possess and exploit the land—that is to say, his beneficial ownership of it—would be destroyed. It would not be a case of incidental damages arising from a legalized nuisance. *** There is no material difference between the supposed case and the present one, except that here enjoyment and use of the land are not completely destroyed. But that does not seem to us to be controlling. The path of glide for airplanes might reduce a valuable factory site to grazing land, an orchard to a vegetable patch, a residential section to a wheat field. Some value would remain. But the use of the airspace immediately above the land would limit the utility of the land and cause a diminution in its value.

[T]he airspace is a public highway. Yet it is obvious that if the landowner is to have full enjoyment of the land, he must have exclusive control of the immediate reaches of the enveloping atmosphere. Otherwise buildings could not be erected, trees could not be planted, and even fences could not be run. *** The landowner owns at least as much of the space above the ground as he can occupy or use in connection with the land. The fact that he does not occupy it in a physical sense—by the erection of buildings and the like—is not material. [T]he flight of airplanes, which skim the surface but do not touch it, is as much an appropriation of the use of the land as a more conventional entry upon it. We would not doubt that if the United States erected an elevated railway over respondents' land at the precise altitude where its planes now fly, there would be a partial taking, even though none of the supports of the structure rested on the land. The reason is that there would be an intrusion so immediate and direct as to subtract from the owner's full enjoyment of the property and to limit his exploitation of it. *** While the owner does not in any physical manner occupy that stratum of airspace or make use of it in the conventional sense, he does use it in somewhat the same sense that space left between buildings for the purpose of light and air is used. The superadjacent airspace at this low altitude is so close to the land that continuous invasions of it affect the use of the surface of the land itself. We think that the landowner, as an incident to his ownership, has a claim to it and that invasions of it are in the same category as invasions of the surface.

Flights over private land are not a taking, unless they are so low and so frequent as to be a direct and immediate interference with the enjoyment and use of the land. [T]he Court of Claims plainly establish that there was a diminution in value of the property and that the frequent, low-level flights were the direct and immediate cause. Since on this record it is not clear whether the easement taken is a permanent or a temporary one, it would be premature for us to consider whether the amount of the award made by the Court of Claims was proper. The judgment is reversed and the cause is remanded to the Court of Claims so that it may make the necessary findings in conformity with this opinion.

> **Food for Thought**
>
> If the government had built an airport ten miles away from respondents' property—far enough away that the chickens were not frightened by the sound, but close enough that a person on the property could clearly hear the sound of the jets overhead—isn't it likely that the value of the property would have gone down? Would that have constituted a taking, as well? If not, what is the difference?

Mr. Justice BLACK, [with whom Mr. Justice BURTON joins,] dissenting.

The Court's opinion seems to indicate that the mere flying of planes through the column of air directly above respondents' land does not constitute a "taking." Consequently, it appears to be noise and glare, to the extent and under the circumstances shown here, which make the government a seizer of private property. But [the] concept of taking property as used in the Constitution has heretofore never been given so sweeping a meaning. The Court's opinion presents no case where a man who makes noise or shines light onto his neighbor's property has been ejected from that property for wrongfully taking possession of it. Nor would anyone take seriously a claim that noisy automobiles passing on a highway are taking wrongful possession of the homes located thereon, or that a city elevated train which greatly interferes with the sleep of those who live next to it wrongfully takes their property. ***

Nor do I reach a different conclusion because of the fact that the particular circumstance which under the Court's opinion makes the tort here absolutely actionable, is the passing of planes through a column of air at an elevation of eighty-three feet directly over respondents' property. It is inconceivable to me that the Constitution guarantees that the airspace of this Nation needed for air navigation, is owned by the particular persons who happen to own the land beneath to the same degree as they own the surface below. No rigid Constitutional rule, in my judgment, commands that the air must be considered as marked off into separate compartments by imaginary metes and bounds in order to synchronize air ownership with land ownership. I think that the Constitution entrusts Congress with full power to control all navigable airspace *** under the assumption that the Commerce Clause of the Constitution gave Congress the same plenary power to control navigable airspace as its plenary power over navigable waters. Today's opinion is, I fear, an opening wedge for an unwarranted judicial interference with the power of Congress to develop solutions for new and vital and national problems. In my opinion this case should be reversed on the ground that there has been no "taking" in the Constitutional sense.

> **Food for Thought**
>
> Does the fact that Congress has "plenary" power over the navigable airspace really answer the question in this case whether there was a taking in the first place? Isn't the Takings Clause a limitation on Congress's affirmative powers?

Points for Discussion

a. Types of Takings

The Court has identified two distinct types of takings. First, when the government actually takes title to property, or authorizes a "physical occupation" of it, the Court will find a "physical" or "possessory" taking, triggering the requirement of just compensation. Second, the Court has sometimes recognized "regulatory takings." As the Court has explained, when the government "merely regulates the *use* of property, compensation is required only if considerations such as the purpose of the regulation or the extent to which it deprives the owner of the economic use of the property suggest that the regulation has unfairly singled out the property owner to bear a burden that should be borne by the public as a whole." *Yee v. City of Escondido*, *infra* (emphasis added).

Which type of taking was at issue in *Causby*? Did the Court conclude that the government effectively physically occupied the respondents' land? Or that the government's interference with the respondents' use of their land was sufficiently great to amount to a regulatory taking?

b. Definition of "Property"

In dissent, Justice Black suggested that because a common-law claim for ejectment would have failed, there could not have been any taking for constitutional purposes. Justice Black, in other words, appeared to define the respondents' property rights by reference to existing—and presumably state—law. How did the Court determine the scope of the respondents' property interests? Does the Takings Clause require the Court to define property rights? Or does it leave that definition to other sources of positive law—such as state common or statutory law?

c. Applying *Causby*

If the Environmental Protection Agency promulgated a regulation restricting the amount of methane—which is produced in large quantities by chickens on chicken farms—that can permissibly be emitted into the air, would owners of chicken farms be able to recover for a taking? In what way would such a takings claim be different from the claim in *Causby*?

d. Nuisance, Sovereign Immunity, and Takings

State tort law in most states provides a cause of action for "nuisance," which consists of the intentional and unreasonable "invasion of another's interest in the private use and enjoyment of land." Restatement (Second) of the Law of Torts § 822 (1965). Courts in other cases have imposed liability for this tort on airports that have caused unreasonable noise for their neighbors. *See, e.g., Krueger v. Mitchell*, 332 N.W.2d 733, 742 (Wis. 1983).

Wouldn't it have been easier and less controversial for the Causbys to have sued the government under this traditional tort theory rather than to try to convince the Court that the government had invaded its property by flying planes overhead? The answer is that, even if the government appears to have caused a nuisance, the Causbys could not have prevailed under this tort theory. The federal government has not waived its sovereign immunity for the tort of nuisance. In contrast, the federal government does not assert sovereign immunity from takings claims. As a result, the Causbys, like many other plaintiffs with grievances against the government, were careful to couch their claim in terms of a taking. In light of the Fifth Amendment, *could* the federal government assert sovereign immunity to defeat a takings claim?

---

2. Physical Takings

It is clear that the government effects a taking when it actually confiscates property, by taking title and possession. But the Court has made clear that the government also "takes" property within the meaning of the Takings Clause when it physically occupies property that is otherwise held privately. In *Loretto v. Teleprompter Manhattan CATV Corp.*, 458 U.S. 419 (1982), for example, the Court concluded that a city ordinance that required owners of apartment buildings to make space available for cable television providers to run wires constituted a compensable taking. The Court explained that the government takes property whenever a "physical intrusion reaches the extreme form of a permanent physical occupation," regardless of how small the amount of space occupied.

How far does the concept of the "physical intrusion" extend? Consider the following case.

Yee v. City of Escondido

503 U.S. 519 (1992)

Justice O'CONNOR delivered the opinion of the Court.

[Most mobile home owners rent the land on which their homes sit. The California Mobilehome Residency Law limits the bases upon which a mobile home park owner may terminate a mobile home owner's tenancy, and provides that while a rental agreement is in effect, the park owner generally may not require the removal of a mobile home when it is sold or disapprove of the purchaser, provided that the purchaser has the ability to pay the rent. In 1988, the voters of Escondido approved a rent control ordinance that set rents at their 1986 levels and prohibited rent increases without the approval of the City Council. Under the ordinance, park owners could apply for rent increases at any time, and the Council had to approve any increases it determined to be "just, fair and reasonable." Petitioners, John and Irene Yee, owners of a mobile home park in the city of Escondido, filed suit seeking damages and a declaration that, under those circumstances, the rent control ordinance was unconstitutional.]

Petitioners do not claim that the ordinary rent control statutes regulating housing throughout the country violate the Takings Clause. Cf. *Pennell v. City of San Jose*, 485 U.S. 1 (1988). Instead, their argument is predicated on the unusual economic relationship between park owners and mobile home owners. Park owners may no longer set rents or decide who their tenants will be. As a result, according to petitioners, any reduction in the rent for a mobile home pad causes a corresponding increase in the value of a mobile home, because the mobile home owner now owns, in addition to a mobile home, the right to occupy a pad at a rent below the value that would be set by the free market. *** And because the Mobilehome Residency Law permits the mobile home owner to sell the mobile home in place, the mobile home owner can

Food for Thought

Why did California enact the statute at issue here? Why does it apply only to mobile home owners who are renting property, as opposed to all tenants?

receive a premium from the purchaser corresponding to this increase in value. *** As a result, petitioners conclude, the rent control ordinance has transferred a discrete interest in land—the right to occupy the land indefinitely at a submarket rent—from the park owner to the mobile home owner. Petitioners contend that what has been transferred from park owner to mobile home owner is no less than a right of physical occupation of the park owner's land.

This argument, while perhaps within the scope of our regulatory taking cases, cannot be squared easily with our cases on physical takings. The government effects a physical taking only where it *requires* the landowner to submit to the physical occupation of his land. "This element of required acquiescence is at the heart of the concept of occupation." *FCC v. Florida Power Corp.*, 480 U.S. 245, 252 (1987). Thus whether the government floods a landowner's property, *Pumpelly v. Green Bay Co.*, 13 Wall. 166 (1872), or does no more than require the landowner to suffer the installation of a cable, *Loretto v. Teleprompter Manhattan CATV Corp.*, 458 U.S. 419 (1982), the Takings Clause requires compensation if the government authorizes a compelled physical invasion of property.

But the Escondido rent control ordinance, even when considered in conjunction with the California Mobilehome Residency Law, authorizes no such thing. Petitioners voluntarily rented their land to mobile home owners. At least on the face of the regulatory scheme, neither the city nor the State compels petitioners, once they have rented their property to tenants, to continue doing so. To the contrary, the Mobilehome Residency Law provides that a park owner who wishes to change the use of his land may evict his tenants, albeit with 6 or 12 months notice. Put bluntly, no government has required any physical invasion of petitioners' property. Petitioners' tenants were invited by petitioners, not forced upon them by the government. While the "right to exclude" is doubtless, as petitioners assert, "one of the most essential sticks in the bundle of rights that are commonly characterized as property," we do not find that right to have been taken from petitioners on the mere face of the Escondido ordinance. *** A different case would be presented were the statute, on its face or as applied, to compel a landowner over objection to rent his property or to refrain in perpetuity from terminating a tenancy.

On their face, the state and local laws at issue here merely regulate petitioners' *use* of their land by regulating the relationship between landlord and tenant. "This Court has consistently affirmed that States have broad power to regulate housing conditions in general and the landlord-tenant relationship in particular without paying compensation for all economic injuries that such regulation entails." *Loretto*, 458 U.S. at 440. When a landowner decides to rent his land to tenants, the government may place ceilings on the rents the landowner can charge, see, *e.g., Pennell*, 485 U.S. at 12, n. 6, or require the landowner to accept tenants he does not like, see, *e.g., Heart of Atlanta Motel, Inc. v. United States*, 379 U.S. 241, 261 (1964), without automatically having to pay compensation. *** In the words of Justice Holmes, "while property may be regulated to a certain extent, if regulation goes too far it will be recognized as a taking." *Pennsylvania Coal Co. v. Mahon*, 260 U.S. 393, 415 (1922).

Petitioners emphasize that the ordinance transfers wealth from park owners to incumbent mobile home owners. Other forms of land use regulation, however, can also be said to transfer wealth from the one who is regulated to another. Ordinary rent control often transfers wealth from landlords to tenants by reducing the landlords' income and the tenants' monthly payments ***. Traditional zoning regulations can transfer wealth from those whose activities are prohibited to their neighbors. *** The mobile home owner's ability to sell the mobile home at a premium may make this wealth transfer more *visible* than in the ordinary case, [but] the existence of the transfer in itself does not convert regulation into physical invasion.

[Petitioners also contend] that the ordinance amounts to compelled physical occupation because it deprives petitioners of the ability to choose their incoming tenants. Again, this effect may be relevant to a regulatory taking argument, [but] it does not convert regulation into the unwanted physical occupation of land. Because they voluntarily open their property to occupation by others, petitioners cannot assert a *per se* right to compensation based on their inability to exclude particular individuals.

In this Court, petitioners attempt to challenge the ordinance [as] a regulatory taking. [This claim was] not fairly included in the question on which we granted certiorari.

———————

Points for Discussion

a. Physical Occupation

In <u>Loretto</u>, the Court found a taking when the government required landlords to accept the installation of cable wires on their property. In <u>Yee</u>, the Court found that there was not a taking when the government required landlords to accept tenants on their property. Why did the cases come out differently? Does it matter that the tenants in <u>Yee</u> would not occupy the land "permanently"? Should it matter?

b. Rent Control

The Court declined to consider the petitioners' claim that the ordinance constituted a regulatory, as opposed to a physical, taking because it was not properly presented. Would that claim have been stronger? Several years before it decided <u>Yee</u>, the Court in *Pennell v. City of San Jose*, 485 U.S. 1 (1988), upheld a rent control ordinance that automatically permitted landlords to raise rents by up to 8 percent each year and provided for hearings to determine the validity of increases of more than that amount. In such hearings, the examiner was required to take into account seven factors, including whether the rent increase would produce "hardship" for the tenant. The Court stated that it was "premature" to decide whether the ordinance effected a transfer of the landlord's property to the tenant, because a hearing examiner had apparently never relied upon that factor. Justices Scalia and O'Connor, however, would have held that the tenant-hardship provision effected a taking of the landlord's property. Should rent control ordinances give rise to a government obligation to pay just compensation? If so, would it be as a physical taking or a regulatory taking?

———————

3. Regulatory Takings

A physical taking occurs, as we have seen, when the government actually confiscates or invades property. But the government can also impair a property owner's interests by regulating the property and thus reducing its value. Does regulation therefore constitute a taking for which the government must pay compensation? Justice Oliver Wendell Holmes famously addressed this question in *Pennsylvania Coal Co. v. Mahon*, 260 U.S. 393, 413 (1922), by saying: "The general rule at least is that while property may be regulated to a certain extent, if regulation goes too far it will be recognized as a taking."

The Supreme Court has repeated this principle in many cases, but has never defined the words "too far" in precise terms. Still, it is clear that most regulations of property do not go too far. Stop signs and speed limits restrict how you can drive your car, but the government does not have to pay you compensation for these restrictions. Similarly, local ordinances may restrict the hours at which you may operate your noisy lawn mower, but your city does not have to pay you for this imposition. State laws, moreover, may restrict your ability to sell home-made beer, but this is not a taking, either. Rather, only extreme laws that essentially deprive the property owner of the entire value of property or nearly all of the normal uses of property constitute regulatory takings. In reading the cases that follow, consider what arguments might justify this approach.

Penn Central Transportation Co. v. City of New York

438 U.S. 104 (1978)

Mr. Justice BRENNAN delivered the opinion of the Court.

[The New York City Landmarks Preservation Law authorizes the Landmarks Preservation Commission to designate as a landmark property that has "a special character or special historical or aesthetic interest or value as part of the development, heritage or cultural characteristics of the city, state or nation." Such a designation permits the property owner to alter the exterior architectural features of the landmark or to construct any exterior improvement on the landmark site only with the advance approval of the Commission. In 1967, the Commission designated Grand Central Terminal as a landmark. Shortly thereafter, Penn Central, which owned the Terminal, and UGP Properties, with whom it had entered into a lease agreement, applied to the Commission for permission to construct a new office building above the Terminal. The application included two proposed construction plans: the first provided for the office to be built above the existing façade of the terminal; and the second involved tearing down a portion of the Terminal. The Commission rejected the first proposal, stating that it would impair the dramatic view of the Terminal from the South, and rejected the second proposal on the ground that "[t]o protect a Landmark, one does not tear it down." Penn Central filed suit claiming that the denial of their application effected a taking of their property for which they had not received just compensation.]

"Government hardly could go on if to some extent values incident to property could not be diminished without paying for every such change in the general law," *Pennsylvania Coal Co. v. Mahon*, 260 U.S. 393, 413 (1922), and this Court has accordingly recognized, in a wide variety of contexts, that government may execute laws or programs that adversely affect recognized economic values. Exercises of the taxing power are one obvious example. A second are the decisions in which this Court has dismissed "taking" challenges on the ground that, while the challenged government action caused economic harm, it did not interfere with interests that were sufficiently bound up with the reasonable expectations of the claimant to constitute "property" for Fifth Amendment purposes.

More importantly for the present case, in instances in which a state tribunal reasonably concluded that "the health, safety, morals, or general welfare" would be promoted by prohibiting particular contemplated uses of land, this Court has upheld land-use regulations that destroyed or adversely affected recognized real property interests. See *Nectow v. Cambridge*, 277 U.S. 183, 188 (1928). Zoning laws are, of course, the classic example, which have been viewed as permissible governmental action even when prohibiting the most beneficial use of the property.

Zoning laws generally do not affect existing uses of real property, but "taking" challenges have also been held to be without merit in a wide variety of situations when the challenged governmental actions prohibited a beneficial use to which individual parcels had previously been devoted and thus caused substantial individualized harm. *** *Goldblatt v. Hempstead*, 369 U.S. 590 (1962), is a recent example. There, a 1958 city safety ordinance banned any excavations below the water table and effectively prohibited the claimant from continuing a sand and gravel mining business that had been operated on the particular parcel since 1927. The Court upheld the ordinance against a "taking" challenge, although the ordinance prohibited the present and presumably most beneficial use of the property and [severely] affected a particular owner. The Court assumed that the ordinance did not prevent the owner's reasonable use of the property since the owner made no showing of an adverse effect on the value of the land. *** It is, of course, implicit in *Goldblatt* that a use restriction on real property may constitute a "taking" if not reasonably necessary to the effectuation of a substantial public purpose, or perhaps if it has an unduly harsh impact upon the owner's use of the property.

> **Take Note**
>
> Didn't the regulation in *Mahon* permit a "reasonable use" of the property and serve a substantial public purpose, as the Court held the regulation in *Goldblatt* did? Is there some way to distinguish the cases? Which is the regulation in *Penn Central* more like?

Pennsylvania Coal Co. v. Mahon is the leading case for the proposition that a state statute that substantially furthers important public policies may so frustrate distinct investment-backed expectations as to amount to a "taking." There the claimant had sold the surface rights to particular parcels of property, but expressly reserved the right to remove the coal thereunder. A Pennsylvania statute, enacted after the transactions, forbade any mining of coal that caused the subsidence of any house, unless the house was the property of the owner of the underlying coal and was more than 150 feet from the improved property of another. Because the statute made it commercially impracticable to mine the coal, *id.,* at 414 and thus had nearly the same effect as the complete destruction of rights claimant had reserved from the owners of the surface land, the Court held that the statute was invalid as effecting a "taking" without just compensation.

[Appellants observe] that the airspace above the Terminal is a valuable property interest, citing *United States v. Causby*. They urge that the Landmarks Law has deprived them of any gainful use of their "air rights" above the Terminal and that, irrespective of the value of the remainder of their parcel, the city has "taken" their right to this superadjacent airspace, thus entitling them to "just compensation" measured by the fair market value of these air rights. [But the] submission that appellants may establish a "taking" simply by showing that they have been denied the ability to exploit a property interest that they heretofore had believed was available for development is quite simply untenable. *** "Taking" jurisprudence does not divide a single parcel into discrete segments and attempt to determine whether rights in a particular segment have been entirely abrogated. In deciding whether a particular governmental action has effected a taking, this Court focuses rather both on the character of the action and on the nature and extent of the interference with rights in the parcel as a whole—here, the city tax block designated as the "landmark site."

[T]he New York City law does not interfere in any way with the present uses of the Terminal. Its designation as a landmark not only permits but contemplates that appellants may continue to use the property precisely as it has been used for the past 65 years: as a railroad terminal containing office space and concessions. So the law does not interfere with what must be regarded as Penn Central's primary expectation concerning the use of the parcel. More importantly, on this record, we must regard the New York City law as permitting Penn Central not only to profit from the Terminal but also to obtain a "reasonable return" on its investment.

> **Make the Connection**
>
> Is the Court's conclusion here consistent with the Court's decision in *Causby*, which seemed to recognize a taking because of a regulation's effect on the airspace over an individual's property? Is there a way to distinguish *Causby*?

On this record, we conclude that the application of New York City's Landmarks Law has not effected a "taking" of appellants' property. The restrictions imposed are substantially related to the promotion of the general welfare and not only permit reasonable beneficial use of the landmark site but also afford appellants opportunities further to enhance not only the Terminal site proper but also other properties.

Mr. Justice REHNQUIST, with whom THE CHIEF JUSTICE and Mr. Justice STEVENS join, dissenting.

Only in the most superficial sense of the word can this case be said to involve "zoning." Typical zoning restrictions may, it is true, so limit the prospective uses of a piece of property as to diminish the value of that property in the abstract because it may not be used for the forbidden purposes. But any such abstract decrease in value will more than likely be at least partially offset by an increase in value which flows from similar restrictions as to use on neighboring properties. All property owners in a designated area are placed under the same restrictions, not only for the benefit of the municipality as a whole but also for the common benefit of one another. In the words of Mr. Justice Holmes, speaking for the Court in [*Mahon*,] there is "an average reciprocity of advantage." Where a relatively few individual buildings, all separated from one another, are singled out and treated differently from surrounding buildings, no such reciprocity exists.

[T]he Court has frequently emphasized that the term "property" as used in the Taking Clause includes the entire "group of rights inhering in the citizen's [ownership]." *United States v. General Motors Corp.*, 323 U.S. 373 (1945). *** While neighboring landowners are free to use their land and "air rights" in any way consistent with the broad boundaries of New York zoning, Penn Central, absent the permission of appellees, must forever maintain its property in its present state. The property has been thus subjected to a nonconsensual servitude not borne by any neighboring or similar properties. *** Appellees have thus destroyed—in a literal sense, "taken"—substantial property rights of Penn Central.

Unlike [permissible] land-use regulations, appellees' actions do not merely *prohibit* Penn Central from using its property in a narrow set of noxious ways. Instead, appellees have placed an *affirmative* duty on Penn Central to maintain the Terminal in its present state and in "good repair." Appellants are not free to use their property as they see fit within broad outer boundaries but must strictly adhere to their past use except where appellees conclude that alternative uses would not detract from the landmark. While Penn Central may continue to use the Terminal as it is presently designed, appellees otherwise "exercise complete dominion and control over the surface of the land." [*Causby*.]

> **Take Note**
>
> In what way does the Takings Clause prevent the government from imposing on the few the costs of actions that benefit the many? Should that principle apply in this case to require compensation to Penn Central?

Appellees have imposed a substantial cost on less than one-tenth of one percent of the buildings in New York City for the general benefit of all its people. It is exactly this imposition of general costs on a few individuals at which the "taking" protection is directed. *** Appellees in response would argue that a taking only occurs where a property owner is denied *all* reasonable value of his property. The Court has frequently held that, even where a destruction of property rights would not *otherwise* constitute a taking, the inability of the owner to make a reasonable return on his property requires compensation under the Fifth Amendment. But the converse is not true. A taking does not become a noncompensable exercise of police power simply because the government in its grace allows the owner to make some "reasonable" use of his property.

Andrus v. Allard

444 U.S. 51 (1979)

Mr. Justice BRENNAN delivered the opinion of the Court.

[The Eagle Protection Act and the Migratory Bird Treaty Act are conservation statutes designed to prevent the destruction of certain species of birds. The Acts prohibit commercial transactions in parts of birds that are protected under the statutes, and regulations promulgated by the Secretary of the Interior apply the prohibition to birds killed before the statutes were in force. Appellees were engaged in the trade of Indian artifacts, a number of which are partly composed of feathers of birds protected by the statute, and some of them were prosecuted for selling artifacts in violation of the statute and regulations. They brought suit alleging that the regulations violated the Fifth Amendment.]

We [disagree] with the District Court's holding that, as construed to authorize the prohibition of commercial transactions in pre-existing avian artifacts, the Eagle Protection and Migratory Bird Treaty Acts violate appellees' Fifth Amendment property rights because the prohibition wholly deprives them of the opportunity to earn a profit from those relics. *** Suffice it to say that government regulation—by definition—involves the adjustment of rights for the public good. Often this adjustment curtails some potential for the use or economic exploitation of private property. To require compensation in all such circumstances would effectively compel the government to regulate by *purchase*.

The regulations challenged here do not compel the surrender of the artifacts, and there is no physical invasion or restraint upon them. Rather, a significant restriction has been imposed on one means of disposing of the artifacts. But the denial of one traditional property right does not always amount to a taking. At least where an owner possesses a full "bundle" of property rights, the destruction of one "strand" of the bundle is not a taking, because the aggregate must be viewed in its entirety. In this case, it is crucial that appellees retain the rights to possess and transport their property, and to donate or devise the protected birds.

It is, to be sure, undeniable that the regulations here prevent the most profitable use of appellees' property. Again, however, that is not dispositive. When we review regulation, a reduction in the value of property is not necessarily equated with a taking. In the instant case, it is not clear that appellees will be unable to derive economic benefit from the artifacts; for example, they might exhibit the artifacts for an admissions charge. At any rate, loss of future profits—unaccompanied by any physical property restriction—provides a slender reed upon which to rest a takings claim. *** For example, the Court has sustained regulations prohibiting the sale of alcoholic beverages despite the fact that individuals were left with previously acquired stocks. *Everard's Breweries v. Day*, 265 U.S. 545 (1924)

> **Take Note**
>
> The Court states that the loss of future profits is not sufficient to constitute a taking. If the government prohibited transactions involving stock certificates, would the loss of future profits be sufficient to constitute a taking? Why is this case (and cases involving Prohibition) different?

It is true that appellees must bear the costs of these regulations. But, within limits, that is a burden borne to secure "the advantage of living and doing business in a civilized community." *Pennsylvania Coal Co. v. Mahon,* 260 U.S. 393, 422 (1922) (Brandeis, J., dissenting). We hold that the simple prohibition of the sale of lawfully acquired property in this case does not effect a taking in violation of the Fifth Amendment.

Points for Discussion

a. Finding a Regulatory Taking

What is the test for determining whether government regulation of private property has effected a taking? Is it simply a multi-factored test that considers all of the circumstances? The Court in <u>Penn Central</u> suggested that a claim of a regulatory taking in most cases will fail if the regulation advances some valid government interest. But don't most exercises of the power of eminent domain—including classic physical takings—presumably advance some legitimate government interest? (Indeed, doesn't the Public Use Clause require at least that much?) Why should the context of regulatory takings be any different?

b. History and Regulatory Takings

Before the Court's decision in *Pennsylvania Coal Co. v. Mahon,* 260 U.S. 393 (1922), to which the Court refers in <u>Penn Central</u>, the Court had typically found a compensable taking only when the government had confiscated property or physically occupied it. Since <u>Mahon</u>, however, the Court has recognized the possibility that government regulation of private property could amount to a taking if, in the words of Justice Holmes in <u>Mahon</u>, the regulation goes "too far." Does the fact that the Court did not recognize the possibility of a regulatory taking until 1922 suggest that the interpretation of the Takings Clause to embrace regulatory takings is inconsistent with the original meaning? Or does it simply reflect the fact that the government did not seek to regulate private property aggressively until more than 100 years after the founding?

c. The Consequences of Requiring Compensation

What are the possible consequences of requiring the government to pay a property owner for a particular regulation? One, of course, is that the property owner will receive compensation for a loss of the property's value. But another, perhaps more likely, consequence is that the government will not impose the regulation in the first place, because paying compensation would be too expensive. Is it any wonder that some libertarian thinkers have urged a more generous view on what constitutes a regulatory taking for which compensation must be paid? *See, e.g.,* Richard Epstein, Takings 57 (1985) (advancing the central thesis that the "protection afforded by the [takings] clause to each part of an endowment of private property is equal to the protection it affords the whole—no more and no less").

Lucas v. South Carolina Coastal Council

505 U.S. 1003 (1992)

Justice SCALIA delivered the opinion of the Court.

[In 1986, Lucas purchased two lots on the Isle of Palms in South Carolina with the intention of building single-family homes on each, as had the owners of the immediately adjacent lots. In 1988, before Lucas began construction, the South Carolina legislature enacted the Beachfront Management Act, which prevented construction on land within a certain distance of the coastline, in order to stem beach erosion. Lucas's property fell within this restricted area. He brought suit claiming that the regulation effected a taking without just compensation.]

[In *Pennsylvania Coal Co. v. Mahon,* 260 U.S. 393 (1922), Justice Holmes offered the] oft-cited maxim that, "while property may be regulated to a certain extent, if regulation goes too far it will be recognized as a taking." [But] our decision in <u>Mahon</u> offered little insight into when, and under what circumstances, a given regulation would be seen as going "too far" for purposes of the Fifth Amendment. In 70-odd years of succeeding "regulatory takings" jurisprudence, we have generally eschewed any "set formula" for determining how far is too far, preferring to "engage in essentially ad hoc, factual inquiries." *Penn Central Transportation Co. v. New York City,* 438 U.S. 104, 124 (1978) We have, however, described at least two discrete categories of regulatory action as compensable without case-specific inquiry into the public interest advanced in support of the restraint. The first encompasses regulations that compel the property owner to suffer a physical "invasion" of his property. In general (at least with regard to permanent invasions), no matter how minute the intrusion, and no matter how weighty the public purpose behind it, we have required compensation. [See, e.g. *United States v. Causby,* 328 U.S. 256 (1946) (physical invasions of airspace).] The second situation in which we have found categorical treatment appropriate is where regulation denies all economically beneficial or productive use of land.

[T]otal deprivation of beneficial use is, from the landowner's point of view, the equivalent of a physical appropriation. [And] regulations that leave the owner of land without economically beneficial or productive options for its use—typically, as here, by requiring land to be left substantially in its natural state—carry with them a heightened risk that private property is being pressed into some form of public service under the guise of mitigating serious public harm. [These reasons support] our frequently expressed belief that when the owner of real property has been called upon to sacrifice *all* economically beneficial uses in the name of the common good, that is, to leave his property economically idle, he has suffered a taking.

> ### Food for Thought
>
> In what way is the regulation here different from the regulation challenged in <u>Andrus</u>? Couldn't Lucas sit on the beach and watch the sunset, or charge people to use his beachfront property—say for picnics or parties—just as the appellees in <u>Andrus</u> could charge people to see their artifacts?

It is correct that many of our prior opinions have suggested that "harmful or noxious uses" of property may be proscribed by government regulation without the requirement of compensation. For a number of reasons, however, we think the South Carolina Supreme Court was too quick to conclude that that principle decides the present case. *** "Harmful or noxious use" analysis was [simply] the progenitor of our more contemporary statements that "land-use regulation does not effect a taking if it 'substantially advances legitimate state interests.'" *Nollan v. California Coastal Comm'n,* 483 U.S. 825, 834 (1987) The transition from our early focus on control of "noxious" uses to our contemporary understanding of the broad realm within which government may regulate without compensation was an easy one, since the distinction between "harm-preventing" and "benefit-conferring" regulation is often in the eye of the beholder. It is quite possible, for example, to describe in *either* fashion the ecological, economic, and esthetic concerns that inspired the South Carolina Legislature in the present case. One could say that imposing a servitude on Lucas's land is necessary in order to prevent his use of it from "harming" South Carolina's ecological resources; or, instead, in order to achieve the "benefits" of an ecological preserve. *** Whether Lucas's construction of single-family residences on his parcels should be described as bringing "harm" to South Carolina's adjacent ecological resources thus depends principally upon whether the describer believes that the State's use interest in nurturing those resources is so important that *any* competing adjacent use must yield.

When it is understood that "prevention of harmful use" was merely our early formulation of the police power justification necessary to sustain (without compensation) *any* regulatory diminution in value; and that the distinction between regulation that "prevents harmful use" and that which "confers benefits" is difficult, if not impossible, to discern on an objective, value-free basis; it becomes self-evident that noxious-use logic cannot serve as a touchstone to distinguish regulatory "takings"—which require compensation—from regulatory deprivations that do not require compensation. *A fortiori* the legislature's recitation of a noxious-use justification cannot be the basis for departing from our categorical rule that total regulatory takings must be compensated. If it were, departure would virtually always be allowed, [essentially nullifying] _Mahon_'s affirmation of limits to the noncompensable exercise of the police power.

Where the State seeks to sustain regulation that deprives land of all economically beneficial use, we think it may resist compensation only if the logically antecedent inquiry into the nature of the owner's estate shows that the proscribed use interests were not part of his title to begin with. This accords, we think, with our "takings" jurisprudence, which has traditionally been guided by the understandings of our citizens regarding the content of, and the State's power over, the "bundle of rights" that they acquire when they obtain title to property. It seems to us that the property owner necessarily expects the uses of his property to be restricted, from time to time, by various measures newly enacted by the State in legitimate exercise of its police powers ***. In the case of land, [however, we] think the notion pressed by the Council that title is somehow held subject to the "implied limitation" that the State may subsequently eliminate all economically valuable use is inconsistent with the historical compact recorded in the Takings Clause that has become part of our constitutional culture.

[C]onfiscatory regulations, *i.e.,* regulations that prohibit all economically beneficial use of land, [cannot] be newly legislated or decreed (without compensation), but must inhere in the title itself, in the restrictions that background principles of the State's law of property and nuisance already place upon land ownership. A law or decree with such an effect must, in other words, do no more than duplicate the result that could have been achieved in the courts—by adjacent landowners (or other uniquely affected persons) under the State's law of private nuisance, or by the State under its complementary power to abate nuisances that affect the public generally, or otherwise.

[As] it would be required to do if it sought to restrain Lucas in a common-law action for public nuisance, South Carolina must identify background principles of nuisance and property law that prohibit the uses he now intends in the circumstances in which the property is presently found. Only on this showing can the State fairly claim that, in proscribing all such beneficial uses, the Beachfront Management Act is taking nothing.

Justice KENNEDY, concurring in the judgment.

I agree with the Court that nuisance prevention accords with the most common expectations of property owners who face regulation, but I do not believe this can be the sole source of state authority to impose severe restrictions. Coastal property may present such unique concerns for a fragile land system that the State can go further in regulating its development and use than the common law of nuisance might otherwise permit.

Justice BLACKMUN, dissenting.

The Court creates its new takings jurisprudence based on the trial court's finding that the property had lost all economic value. This finding is almost certainly erroneous. Petitioner still can enjoy other attributes of ownership, such as the right to exclude others, "one of the most essential sticks in the bundle of rights that are commonly characterized as property." *Kaiser Aetna v. United States,* 444 U.S. 164, 176 (1979) Petitioner can picnic, swim, camp in a tent, or live on the property in a movable trailer. Petitioner also retains the right to alienate the land, which would have value for neighbors and for those prepared to enjoy proximity to the ocean without a house.

If one fact about the Court's takings jurisprudence can be stated without contradiction, it is that "the particular circumstances of each case" determine whether a specific restriction will be rendered invalid by the government's failure to pay compensation. This is so because although we have articulated certain factors to be considered, including the economic impact on the property owner, the ultimate conclusion "necessarily requires a weighing of private and public interests." [Our cases show that] the State has full power to prohibit an owner's use of property if it is harmful to the public.

Justice STEVENS, dissenting.

The Court's holding today effectively freezes the State's common law, denying the legislature much of its traditional power to revise the law governing the rights and uses of property. Until today, I had thought that we had long abandoned this approach to constitutional law. *** Arresting the development of the common law is not only a departure from our prior decisions; it is also profoundly unwise. The human condition is one of constant learning and evolution—both moral and practical. Legislatures implement that new learning; in doing so they must often revise the definition of property and the rights of property owners. *** Of course, some legislative redefinitions of property will effect a taking and must be compensated—but it certainly cannot be the case that every movement away from common law does so.

In addition to lacking support in past decisions, the Court's new rule is wholly arbitrary. A landowner whose property is diminished in value 95% recovers nothing, while an owner whose property is diminished 100% recovers the land's full value. *** [E]ven assuming that petitioner's property was rendered valueless, the risk inherent in investments of the sort made by petitioner, the generality of the Act, and the compelling purpose motivating the South Carolina Legislature persuade me that the Act did not effect a taking of petitioner's property.

———————

Points for Discussion

a. Rules v. Standards

Although the general test for finding a regulatory taking is a multi-factored standard, Justice Scalia sought in his opinion in _Lucas_ to offer a categorical rule to address one potentially common set of circumstances. There is a long-standing debate over the relative virtues of rules and standards. *See, e.g.,* Kathleen M. Sullivan, *The Justices of Rules and Standards,* 106 Harv. L. Rev. 22 (1992); Antonin Scalia, *The Rule of Law as a Law of Rules,* 56 U. Chi. L. Rev. 1175 (1989). Whatever the merits of rules in other contexts, is there any reason to think that they are particularly important in the context of regulatory takings?

b. Background Principles of Property Law

Justice Stevens criticized the majority for "freez[ing]" state common law. After the Court's decision in _Lucas_, can a state modify its law of nuisance (or, for that matter, its laws defining property rights) to achieve the same result that the state sought in _Lucas_? After all, if a state decides to define more expansively the circumstances that constitute a nuisance, then arguably it would have broader power to regulate to abate those nuisances without incurring the obligation to pay just compensation. At bottom, the question is whether the Takings Clause provides a constitutional definition of property (or at least empowers judges to create one), or instead relies on positive state-law definitions of property.

Justice Scalia stated that to avoid the obligation to pay compensation after depriving private land of all economically beneficial use, the state must identify "background principles" of nuisance and property law that prohibit the uses in question. By "background," did he mean principles embodied in the Constitution, or that at least existed at the time of the framing of the Constitution? Or did he mean principles that are a function of state law, but that already existed at the time of the state's action (or the purchase of the property)? If the latter, _Lucas_ effectively means that the state may not limit property rights retroactively, but may do so prospectively. But at common law, of course, principles of property law evolved over time, and were often applied retrospectively to the litigants in the cases that produced new rules. In any event, if states can—even if only prospectively—reduce the value of private property by redefining the law of nuisance or other property laws, is the Takings Clause really a strong protection for private ownership of property? Can a state alter property laws prospectively without affecting the current owner of existing property?

c. What Happened Next

The parties settled this case, with the state paying Lucas $850,000 for the property, plus additional sums in damages and costs. The state did not keep the property in an undeveloped state. Instead, it resold the property to a developer. What does this subsequent history suggest about the justice of the Supreme Court's decision?

----

4. Public Use

Most takings claims seek the payment of compensation as a remedy for the taking. But sometimes property owners would rather keep their property than be paid compensation for their loss of some or all of their rights in the property. One possible avenue for such property owners is to contend that the government lacks authority to take the property, because the taking is not for a "public use." The following case considers the meaning of that term.

Kelo v. City of New London

545 U.S. 469 (2005)

Justice STEVENS delivered the opinion of the Court.

[After years of economic decline in New London, Connecticut, state and local officials charged the New London Development Corporation (NLDC), a private nonprofit entity, with developing and implementing an economic revitalization project in the City's Fort Trumbull area. After the state authorized some initial funding for the project, the pharmaceutical company Pfizer, Inc. announced that it would build a $300 million research facility near Fort Trumbull. NLDC proposed a development plan to build residences, parkland, shops, a museum, and office space next to the proposed research facility. The city council approved the plan and gave NLDC authority to acquire property by purchase or through eminent domain. NLDC was able successfully to negotiate the purchase of most of the real estate in the 90-acre development area, but after negotiations with petitioners failed, NLDC initiated condemnation proceedings. NLDC did not contend that petitioners' property was blighted, but rather sought to condemn it because it was in the development area. Petitioners brought suit claiming that the city's proposed disposition of the property did not qualify as a "public use" within the meaning of the Fifth Amendment.]

Two polar propositions are perfectly clear. On the one hand, it has long been accepted that the sovereign may not take the property of *A* for the sole purpose of transferring it to another private party *B,* even though *A* is paid just compensation. On the other hand, it is equally clear that a State may transfer property from one private party to another if future "use by the public" is the purpose of the taking; the condemnation of land for a railroad with common-carrier duties is a familiar example. Neither of these propositions, however, determines the disposition of this case.

[T]he City's development plan was not adopted "to benefit a particular class of identifiable individuals." On the other hand, this is not a case in which the City is planning to open the condemned land—at least not in its entirety—to use by the general public. [But] this "Court long ago rejected any literal requirement that condemned property be put into use for the general public." Indeed, while many state courts in the mid-19th century endorsed "use by the public" as the proper definition of public use, that narrow view steadily eroded over time. Not only was the "use by the public" test difficult to administer (*e.g.,* what proportion of the public need have access to the property? at what price?), but it proved to be impractical given the diverse and always evolving needs of society. Accordingly, when this Court began applying the Fifth Amendment to the States at the close of the 19th century, it embraced the broader and more natural interpretation of public use as "public purpose." See, *e.g., Fallbrook Irrigation Dist. v. Bradley,* 164 U.S. 112 (1896).

> **Take Note**
>
> The Court states that the "public use" requirement of the Fifth Amendment is satisfied if the taking serves a "public purpose." Is this a legitimate interpretation of the provision? Wouldn't taking land from a wealthy person who owns significant acreage and giving it to a poor person who owns no land arguably serve a "public purpose," albeit one whose desirability would be hotly debated? Yet the Court also says that the state cannot take property from A simply to give it to B. Does the "public purpose" standard have any real content? Conversely, is taking land from A to give it to B really materially different from taking it from A to give it to a private railroad?

Without exception, our cases have defined ["public purpose"] broadly, reflecting our long-standing policy of deference to legislative judgments in this field. In *Berman v. Parker,* 348 U.S. 26 (1954), this Court upheld a redevelopment plan targeting a blighted area of Washington, D.C. The owner of a department store located in the area challenged the condemnation, pointing out that his store was not itself blighted and arguing that the creation of a "better balanced, more attractive community" was not a valid public use. Writing for a unanimous Court, Justice Douglas refused to evaluate this claim in isolation, deferring instead to the legislative and agency judgment that the area "must be planned as a whole" for the plan to be successful.

In *Hawaii Housing Authority v. Midkiff,* 467 U.S. 229 (1984), the Court considered a Hawaii statute whereby fee title was taken from lessors and transferred to lessees (for just compensation) in order to reduce the concentration of land ownership. *** [W]e concluded that the State's purpose of eliminating the "social and economic evils of a land oligopoly" qualified as a valid public use. 467 U.S., at 241-242. Our opinion also rejected the contention that the mere fact that the State immediately transferred the properties to private individuals upon condemnation somehow diminished the public character of the taking. *Id.*, at 244.

Take Note

Is the Court taking a non-originalist approach in considering society's evolving needs? Or is it simply applying the original meaning of the Takings Clause to changed circumstances?

Viewed as a whole, our jurisprudence has recognized that the needs of society have varied between different parts of the Nation, just as they have evolved over time in response to changed circumstances. *** For more than a century, our public use jurisprudence has wisely eschewed rigid formulas and intrusive scrutiny in favor of affording legislatures broad latitude in determining what public needs justify the use of the takings power.

Those who govern [New London] were not confronted with the need to remove blight in the Fort Trumbull area, but their determination that the area was sufficiently distressed to justify a program of economic rejuvenation is entitled to our deference. The City has carefully formulated an economic development plan that it believes will provide appreciable benefits to the community, including—but by no means limited to—new jobs and increased tax revenue. As with other exercises in urban planning and development, the City is endeavoring to coordinate a variety of commercial, residential, and recreational uses of land, with the hope that they will form a whole greater than the sum of its parts. *** Given the comprehensive character of the plan, the thorough deliberation that preceded its adoption, and the limited scope of our review, it is appropriate for us, as it was in *Berman*, to resolve the challenges of the individual owners, not on a piecemeal basis, but rather in light of the entire plan. Because that plan unquestionably serves a public purpose, the takings challenged here satisfy the public use requirement of the Fifth Amendment.

To avoid this result, petitioners urge us to adopt a new bright-line rule that economic development does not qualify as a public use. [But promoting] economic development is a traditional and long-accepted function of government. There is, moreover, no principled way of distinguishing economic development from the other public purposes that we have recognized.

It is further argued that without a bright-line rule nothing would stop a city from transferring citizen *A*'s property to citizen *B* for the sole reason that citizen *B* will put the property to a more productive use and thus pay more taxes. Such a one-to-one transfer of property, executed outside the confines of an integrated development plan, is not presented in this case. While such an unusual exercise of government power would certainly raise a suspicion that a private purpose was afoot, the hypothetical

Food for Thought

Once the Court has decided that a taking is for a public use as long as it serves a public purpose, and that legislative judgments are entitled to deference, doesn't it necessarily follow that the hypothetical cases suggested by petitioners would be a permissible exercise of the state's power of eminent domain? If so, what does that suggest about the Court's approach?

cases posited by petitioners can be confronted if and when they arise. They do not warrant the crafting of an artificial restriction on the concept of public use.

In affirming the City's authority to take petitioners' properties, we do not minimize the hardship that condemnations may entail, notwithstanding the payment of just compensation. We emphasize that nothing in our opinion precludes any State from placing further restrictions on its exercise of the takings power. Indeed, many States already impose "public use" requirements that are stricter than the federal baseline. *** As the submissions of the parties and their *amici* make clear, the necessity and wisdom of using eminent domain to promote economic development are certainly matters of legitimate public debate. This Court's authority, however, extends only to determining whether the City's proposed condemnations are for a "public use" within the meaning of the Fifth Amendment to the Federal Constitution. Because over a century of our case law interpreting that provision dictates an affirmative answer to that question, we may not grant petitioners the relief that they seek.

Justice KENNEDY, concurring.

A court applying rational-basis review under the Public Use Clause should strike down a taking that, by a clear showing, is intended to favor a particular private party, with only incidental or pretextual public benefits. *** A court confronted with a plausible accusation of impermissible favoritism to private parties should treat the objection as a serious one and review the record to see if it has merit, though with the presumption that the government's actions were reasonable and intended to serve a public purpose. Here, the trial court [concluded that] benefiting Pfizer was not "the primary motivation or effect of this development plan [and that respondents were not] motivated by a desire to aid [other] particular private entities." *** [W]hile there may be categories of cases in which the transfers are so suspicious, or the procedures employed so prone to abuse, or the purported benefits are so trivial or implausible, that courts should presume an impermissible private purpose, no such circumstances are present in this case.

Justice O'CONNOR, with whom THE CHIEF JUSTICE, Justice SCALIA, and Justice THOMAS join, dissenting.

In [*Berman* and *Midkiff*], the extraordinary, precondemnation use of the targeted property inflicted affirmative harm on society—in *Berman* through blight resulting from extreme poverty and in *Midkiff* through oligopoly resulting from extreme wealth. *** Thus a public purpose was realized when the harmful use was eliminated. Because each taking *directly* achieved a public benefit, it did not matter that the property was turned over to private use. Here, in contrast, New London does not claim that Susette Kelo's and Wilhelmina Dery's well-maintained homes are the source of any social harm.

> **Take Note**
>
> Justice O'Connor wrote the Court's opinion in *Midkiff*, finding a public use. Is her distinction here convincing? Is the social harm of inequitable distribution of wealth meaningfully different from the social harm of community economic distress?

In moving away from our decisions sanctioning the condemnation of harmful property use, the Court today significantly expands the meaning of public use. It holds that the sovereign may take private property currently put to ordinary private use, and give it over for new, ordinary private use, so long as the new use is predicted to generate some secondary benefit for the public—such as increased tax revenue, more jobs, maybe even esthetic pleasure. But nearly any lawful use of real private property can be said to generate some incidental benefit to the public. Thus, if predicted (or even guaranteed) positive side effects are enough to render transfer from one private party to another constitutional, then the words "for public use" do not realistically exclude *any* takings, and thus do not exert any constraint on the eminent domain power.

The Court [suggests] two limitations on what can be taken after today's decision. First, it maintains a role for courts in ferreting out takings whose sole purpose is to bestow a benefit on the private transferee—without detailing how courts are to conduct that complicated inquiry. *** The trouble with economic development takings is that private benefit and incidental public benefit are, by definition, merged and mutually reinforcing. [Moreover, if] it is true that incidental public benefits from new private use are enough to ensure the "public purpose" in a taking, why should it matter, as far as the Fifth Amendment is concerned, what inspired the taking in the first place?

A second proposed limitation is implicit in the Court's opinion. The logic of today's decision is that eminent domain may only be used to upgrade—not downgrade—property. [T]his constraint has no realistic import. For who among us can say she already makes the most productive or attractive possible use of her property? The specter of condemnation hangs over all property. Nothing is to prevent the State from replacing any Motel 6 with a Ritz-Carlton, any home with a shopping mall, or any farm with a factory.

Any property may now be taken for the benefit of another private party, but the fallout from this decision will not be random. The beneficiaries are likely to be those citizens with disproportionate influence and power in the political process, including large corporations and development firms. As for the victims, the government now has license to transfer property from those with fewer resources to those with more. The Founders cannot have intended this perverse result.

> ### Food for Thought
>
> Is the parade of horribles that Justice O'Connor envisions likely to come to pass? Isn't the Just Compensation Clause—which requires the government to pay for the property that it takes—specifically designed to avoid such uses of the power of eminent domain, by internalizing the costs of the taking?

Justice THOMAS, dissenting.

Today's decision is simply the latest in a string of our cases construing the Public Use Clause to be a virtual nullity, without the slightest nod to its original meaning. In my view, the Public Use Clause, originally understood, is a meaningful limit on the government's eminent domain power.

If the Public Use Clause served no function other than to state that the government may take property through its eminent domain power—for public or private uses—then it would be surplusage. *** The most natural reading of the Clause is that it allows the government to take property only if the government owns, or the public has a legal right to use, the property, as opposed to taking it for any public purpose or necessity whatsoever. At the time of the founding, dictionaries primarily defined the noun "use" as "[t]he act of employing any thing to any purpose." 2 S. Johnson, A Dictionary of the English Language 2194 (4th ed. 1773). When the government takes property and gives it to a private individual, and the public has no right to use the property, it strains language to say that the public is "employing" the property, regardless of the incidental benefits that might accrue to the public from the private use. *** The Constitution's text, in short, suggests that the Takings Clause authorizes the taking of property only if the public has a right to employ it, not if the public realizes any conceivable benefit from the taking.

> ### Food for Thought
>
> Justice Thomas focuses on the text of the Takings Clause. But is his reading the only one possible? Can you see how the clause could be read literally to suggest that there is *no* limit on the government's ability to take property for *private* uses—and no requirement that the government pay just compensation when it does so? How helpful is a close textual analysis of the Takings Clause?

The public purpose interpretation of the Public Use Clause also unnecessarily duplicates a similar inquiry required by the Necessary and Proper Clause. The Takings Clause is a prohibition, not a grant of power: The Constitution does not expressly grant the Federal Government the power to take property for any public purpose whatsoever. Instead, the Government may take property only when necessary and proper to the exercise of an expressly enumerated power. [A] taking is permissible under the Necessary and Proper Clause only if it serves a valid public purpose. Interpreting the Public Use Clause likewise to limit the government to take property only for sufficiently public purposes [renders the Public Use Clause] surplusage.

Our current Public Use Clause jurisprudence [has] rejected this natural reading of the Clause. *** When faced with a clash of constitutional principle and a line of unreasoned cases wholly divorced from the text, history, and structure of our founding document, we should not hesitate to resolve the tension in favor of the Constitution's original meaning.

———

Points for Discussion

a. Defining Public Use

It is virtually always possible to find some "public" purpose to the government's seizure of private property. Accordingly, the dissenting Justices criticized the Court for effectively reading the Public Use Clause out of the Fifth Amendment. But are the tests for public use proposed in the dissents any more manageable? Consider the following hypothetical exercises of the eminent domain power: (1) The government seizes private property to build a public park. (2) The government seizes private property to build a park open to members of the public willing to pay $50 per year as a usage fee. (3) The government seizes private property to build a park open to members of the public willing to pay $1,000 per year as a usage fee. (4) The government seizes private property to build a golf course open to members of the public willing to pay $1,000 per year in membership fees and $50 per round of golf. Presumably all of the Justices would agree that the first example satisfies the public use requirement. But as the price of access to the park goes up, the extent to which the benefit of the taking is shared goes down. At what point, under the dissent's approach, would the limitation on meaningful access violate the "public use" requirement?

b. Deference to State and Local Government

The Court concluded that deference is warranted to the judgment of state and local officials about what constitutes a public use. Does it make sense to defer to the government when what is at issue is the Constitution's protection for individual property rights? Would the Court defer to a police officer's view about whether the search of a private home was "reasonable" within the meaning of the Fourth Amendment? About whether a particular form of punishment is "cruel and unusual" within the meaning of the Eighth Amendment? If not, why is the Public Use Clause different?

c. The Takings Clause and Original Meaning

Justice Thomas sought the original meaning of the Takings Clause by consulting the understanding of the constitutional text in the late eighteenth century. But the Takings Clause applies to state action only by virtue of incorporation by the Fourteenth Amendment. Shouldn't Justice Thomas have sought the meaning of the public use requirement in 1868, when the Fourteenth Amendment was ratified? Is it possible for the clause to have one meaning with respect to action by the federal government and a different meaning with respect to action by state and local governments?

d. Subsequent History

In the wake of *Kelo*, several states considered and adopted restrictions on their own power of eminent domain. Does this development tend to demonstrate that the Court was wrong, or does it instead vindicate it?

Executive Summary of This Chapter

The **Contract Clause** imposes some limits on the authority of the states to interfere with contractual relationships. It does not prevent states from regulating the terms of future contracts, *Ogden v. Saunders* (1827), but under some circumstances it prohibits the states from abridging the terms of existing contracts. Whether a state law that affects the terms of existing contracts violates the Contract Clause turns on the weight of the governmental interest advanced by the regulation, *Stone v. Mississippi* (1880), the exigency of the circumstances that produced the need for the regulation, *Home Building & Loan Ass'n v. Blaisdell* (1934), and the extent of the interference with the contract, *Allied Structural Steel*

Company v. Spannaus (1978).

The **Takings Clause** of the Fifth Amendment limits the power of the government to take private property. Although the Clause originally applied only to the federal government, *Barron v. Baltimore* (1833), the Court has since held that it applies to the states by virtue of incorporation by the Due Process Clause of the Fourteenth Amendment, *Chicago, Burlington & Quincy Railroad v. Chicago* (1897). When analyzing a claim under the Takings Clause, the Court must address three principal questions: First, has there been a compensable taking? Second, if so, was the taking for a "public use"? Third, if so, has the government paid the person deprived of property "just compensation"?

The Court has recognized two types of takings. The government effects a **physical taking** (or **possessory taking**) when it actually confiscates property, by taking title and possession, or authorizes a compelled physical invasion of property that is otherwise held privately. *Loretto v. Teleprompter Manhattan CATV Corp.* (1982). Short of actual confiscation, the government effects a physical taking only where it *requires* the landowner to submit to the physical occupation of his land. *Yee v. City of Escondido* (1992).

Government regulation that reduces the value of private property can, under certain narrow circumstances, also amount to a taking. This type of taking is known as a **regulatory taking**. Regulatory takings occur only when government regulation goes "too far." *Pennsylvania Coal Co. v. Mahon* (1922). In determining whether a given regulation effects a regulatory taking, the Court considers the government's interest in the regulation and the extent to which the regulation interferes with the investment-backed expectations of the person alleging the deprivation. *Penn Central Transportation Co. v. City of New York* (1978); *Andrus v. Allard* (1979). Regulations that deprive an owner of land of all economically beneficial use effect a compensable taking unless background principles of nuisance and property law prohibit the uses to which the property owner seeks to put the land. *Lucas v. South Carolina Coastal Council* (1992).

The government may take private property only for a **public use**. Under this requirement, the government may not take the property of one private party for the sole purpose of transferring it to another private party, even if it pays just compensation to the person deprived of the property. But the "public use" requirement of the Fifth Amendment is satisfied as long as the taking serves a "public purpose." In determining whether a taking serves a public purpose, the Court defers to the governmental judgment supporting the taking. *Kelo v. City of New London* (2005). Applying this standard, the Court has found the public use requirement satisfied when the government has taken property to redevelop blighted areas, *Berman v. Parker* (1954); to reduce the concentration of land ownership, *Hawaii Housing Authority v. Midkiff* (1984); and to promote economic development in a depressed area, *Kelo v. City of New London* (2005).

If there has been a compensable taking, the government is obligated to pay **just compensation** for the deprivation. Just compensation is determined by assessing the loss to the owner, measured by the market value at the time of the taking. *Kirby Forest Industries, Inc. v. United States* (1984).

PART XI: CONSTITUTIONAL LIMITATIONS ON NON-GOVERNMENTAL CONDUCT

Throughout this book, we have seen many examples of how state and federal governmental units and governmental officials have taken actions that have violated the Constitution. Congress, for instance, has infringed the Constitution by enacting laws that contravene the freedom of speech. See, e.g., *Buckley v. Valeo,* 424 U.S. 1 (1976). The President has sometimes violated the Constitution by taking actions for which he lacks authority. See *Youngstown Sheet & Tube Co. v. Sawyer,* 343 U.S 579 (1952). And the states have enacted laws that violate the Equal Protection Clause, see, e.g., *Loving v. Virginia,* 388 U.S. 1 (1967), and other provisions.

But one question that we have addressed only circumspectly—in Chapter 13, on Congress's power to enforce the Reconstruction Amendments—is this: Do acts by private individuals or corporations ever violate the Constitution? The general answer to this question, subject to important exceptions, is no. The **state action doctrine** says that while the Constitution imposes limits on the action of the state and federal governments and governmental officials—action that is called "state action" for simplicity—the Constitution generally does not limit the actions of private parties.

The state action doctrine has a textual explanation. Most provisions in the Constitution by their terms address the government rather than private individuals. For example, suppose that parents require their minor children to attend a particular church. Are the parents violating the First Amendment's protection of the free exercise of religion? Simply reading the First Amendment reveals the answer. The First Amendment says that "*Congress shall make *no law* respecting an establishment of religion, or prohibiting the free exercise thereof ***.*" The Amendment does not purport to address non-governmental action that has some effect on religious practice. The parents' action therefore does not violate the constitutional protection of the free exercise of religion.

There are, however, some very important exceptions to this doctrine. First, as we saw in Chapter 13, the Thirteenth Amendment, which prohibits slavery and involuntary servitude, does not confine its prohibition to governmental action. Instead, it provides that neither "shall *exist* within the United States, or any place subject to their jurisdiction" (emphasis added). Indeed, slavery, although supported and enabled in many ways by state and federal legal institutions, was principally a problem of private action, and it is unsurprising that the constitutional prohibition on the institution does not limit itself to governmental conduct. And in the *Civil Rights Cases,* 109 U.S. 3 (1883), discussed below, the Supreme Court interpreted the Thirteenth Amendment to apply to both state and private conduct.

Second, as we will see in this Chapter, even when provisions of the Constitution that by their terms limit only governmental action are at issue, the state action doctrine is subject to exceptions or special cases. In particular, the **traditional public function exception** says that if private individuals are performing actions that have traditionally been performed exclusively by the government, their actions may be deemed to be state action. The **judicial enforcement exception** provides that, at least in some instances, a court's decision to uphold a private action may violate the Constitution. Finally, under the **joint participation exception**, sometimes when a private party and a state actor jointly participate in an activity, they are both engaged in state action.

Points for Discussion

a. Structural and Institutional Considerations

As a matter of policy, why would the drafters of the Constitution have chosen to address—with the one significant exception discussed above—only state action and not the action of private citizens? The Supreme Court has explained that the state action requirement "preserves an area of individual freedom by limiting the reach of federal law and federal judicial power." *Lugar v. Edmonson Oil Co.*, 457 U.S. 922, 936 (1982). Can you think of an illustration of this idea? Can you think of any alternative explanation for why the drafters focused only on the conduct of the state and federal governments?

b. New Proposals

The ill-fated experiment with "Prohibition"—the constitutional ban on the manufacture, sale, or transportation of "intoxicating liquors"—for many years served as a cautionary tale for those who hoped to amend the Constitution to apply to private conduct. Nevertheless, in the last few decades there have been several proposals to amend the Constitution to prohibit certain forms of private action, though all have failed in Congress.

For example, a proposed amendment to prohibit "physical desecration of the flag" passed the House of Representatives in 2005 by the requisite two-thirds vote but fell one vote short in the Senate the following year. And a proposed amendment to define marriage as "the union of a man and a woman" failed to obtain the two-thirds majority in both houses of Congress. Why do you think that these amendments failed? Is it solely because of the strong feelings about the particular conduct regulated? Or did they fail in part because of a strong belief that the Constitution generally is not an appropriate vehicle for the regulation of private conduct?

> **Make the Connection**
>
> The proposed "flag burning" amendment was a response to the Supreme Court's decision in *Texas v. Johnson*, which we considered in Chapter 14.

CHAPTER 19

The State Action Doctrine

A. The General Requirement of State Action

The decision in <u>*The Civil Rights Cases*</u>, which we consider below, concerned a collection of lawsuits arising under the Civil Rights Act of 1875. This sweeping legislation, enacted 89 years before the Civil Rights Act of 1964, would have banned most private racial discrimination in the United States. But the Supreme Court held that the legislation was unconstitutional, concluding that Congress lacked the power to address racial discrimination by private parties under either § 5 of the Fourteenth Amendment or § 2 of the Thirteenth Amendment.

Make the Connection

We considered Congress's power to enforce the Reconstruction Amendments in Chapter 13.

The civil rights legislation and the decision are very important in the history of racial inequality in the United States. Most law students are familiar with how the Supreme Court led the drive to end discrimination in the mid-twentieth century in landmark decisions such as *Shelley v. Kraemer*, 334 U.S. 1 (1948), and *Brown v. Board of Education*, 347 U.S. 483 (1954). Some readers may be surprised to learn that Congress had sought to outlaw private racial discrimination in a sweeping law enacted decades earlier, but that the Supreme Court had invalidated the legislation.

The decision in the <u>*Civil Rights Cases*</u> is also significant because of the clarity with which it addressed the state action doctrine. A significant part of the Court's analysis under the Fourteenth Amendment concerned the fact that the challenged statute addressed private discrimination as opposed to discrimination by the government. Read the case carefully to discern the Court's logic.

The Civil Rights Cases

109 U.S. 3 (1883)

BRADLEY, J.

These cases are all founded on the first and second sections of the act of congress known as the "Civil Rights Act," passed March 1, 1875, entitled "An act to protect all citizens in their civil and legal rights." Two of the cases, those against Stanley and Nichols, are indictments for denying to persons of color the accommodations and privileges of an inn or hotel; two of them, those against Ryan and Singleton, are [for] denying to individuals the privileges and accommodations of a theater ***. The case of Robinson and wife against the Memphis & Charleston Railroad Company [is] to recover the penalty of $500 given by the second section of the act; and the *gravamen* was the refusal by the conductor of the railroad company to allow the wife to ride in the ladies' car, for the reason, as stated in one of the counts, that she was a person of African descent. ***

It is obvious that the primary and important question in all the cases is the constitutionality of the law; for if the law is unconstitutional none of the prosecutions can stand. *** The sections of the law referred to provide as follows:

> Section 1. That all persons within the jurisdiction of the United States shall be entitled to the full and equal enjoyment of the accommodations, advantages, facilities, and privileges of inns, public conveyances on land or water, theaters, and other places of public amusement; subject only to the conditions and limitations established by law, and applicable alike to citizens of every race and color, regardless of any previous condition of servitude.

> Sec. 2. That any person who shall violate the foregoing section by denying to any citizen, except for reasons by law applicable to citizens of every race and color, and regardless of any previous condition of servitude, the full enjoyment of any of the accommodations, advantages, facilities, or privileges in said section enumerated, or by aiding or inciting such denial, shall, for every such offense, forfeit and pay the sum of $500 to the person aggrieved thereby, to be recovered in an action of debt, with full costs; and shall, also, for every such offense, be deemed guilty of a misdemeanor, and upon conviction thereof shall be fined not less than $500 nor more than $1,000, or shall be imprisoned not less than 30 days nor more than one year ***.

Make the Connection

In Chapter 3, we saw in *Heart of Atlanta Motel v. United States* that the Court concluded that Congress had the power to enact the Civil Rights Act of 1964 under the Commerce Clause. How is the Civil Rights Act of 1875 different from that law?

Has congress constitutional power to make such a law? ***

The first section of the fourteenth amendment—which is the one relied on—after declaring who shall be citizens of the United States, and of the several states, is prohibitory in its character, and prohibitory upon the states. *** It is state action of a particular character that is prohibited. Individual invasion of individual rights is not the subject-matter of the amendment. It has a deeper and broader scope. It nullifies and makes void all state legislation, and state action of every kind, which impairs the privileges and immunities of citizens of the United States, or which injures them in life, liberty, or property without due process of law, or which denies to any of them the equal protection of the laws. It not only does this, but, in order that the national will, thus declared, may not be a mere *brutum fulmen*, the last section of the amendment invests congress with power to enforce it by appropriate legislation. To enforce what? To enforce the prohibition. To adopt appropriate legislation for correcting the effects of such prohibited state law and state acts, and thus to render them effectually null, void, and innocuous. This is the legislative power conferred upon congress, and this is the whole of it. It does not invest congress with power to legislate upon subjects which are within the domain of state legislation; but to provide modes of relief against state legislation, or state action, of the kind referred to. It does not authorize congress to create a code of municipal law for the regulation of private rights; but to provide modes of redress against the operation of state laws, and the action of state officers, executive or judicial, when these are subversive of the fundamental rights specified in the amendment. Positive rights and privileges are undoubtedly secured by the fourteenth amendment; but they are secured by way of prohibition against state laws and state proceedings affecting those rights and privileges, and by power given to congress to legislate for the purpose of carrying such prohibition into effect; and such legislation must necessarily be predicated upon such supposed state laws or state proceedings, and be directed to the correction of their operation and effect. ***

> **Definition**
>
> *Brutum fulmen* is Latin for "inert thunder"; figuratively, the phrase means "an empty noise" or "empty threat" or something that is ineffectual. See Black's Law Dictionary.

> **Take Note**
>
> In these paragraphs, the Court concludes that the Fourteenth Amendment addresses only state action. Why does this conclusion matter in this case, which involves claims arising not under the Fourteenth Amendment but instead under a federal statute?

And so in the present case, until some state law has been passed, or some state action through its officers or agents has been taken, adverse to the rights of citizens sought to be protected by the fourteenth amendment, no legislation of the United States under said amendment, nor any proceeding under such legislation, can be called into activity, for the prohibitions of the amendment are against state laws and acts done under state authority. ***

In this connection it is proper to state that civil rights, such as are guaranteed by the constitution against state aggression, cannot be impaired by the wrongful acts of individuals, unsupported by state authority in the shape of laws, customs, or judicial or executive proceedings. The wrongful act of an individual, unsupported by any such authority, is simply a private wrong, or a crime of that individual; an invasion of the rights of the injured party, it is true, whether they affect his person, his property, or his reputation; but if not sanctioned in some way by the state, or not done under state authority, his rights remain in full force, and may presumably be vindicated by resort to the laws of the state for redress. An individual cannot deprive a man of his right to vote, to hold property, to buy and to sell, to sue in the courts, or to be a witness or a juror; he may, by force or fraud, interfere with the enjoyment of the right in a particular case; he may commit an assault against the person, or commit murder, or use ruffian violence at the polls, or slander the good name of a fellow-citizen; but unless protected in these wrongful acts by some shield of state law or state authority, he cannot destroy or injure the right; he will only render himself amenable to satisfaction or punishment; and amenable therefor to the laws of the state where the wrongful acts are committed. Hence, in all those cases where the constitution seeks to protect the rights of the citizen against discriminative and unjust laws of the state by prohibiting such laws, it is not individual offenses, but abrogation and denial of rights, which it denounces, and for which it clothes the congress with power to provide a remedy. This abrogation and denial of rights, for which the states alone were or could be responsible, was the great seminal and fundamental wrong which was intended to be remedied. And the remedy to be provided must necessarily be predicated upon that wrong. It must assume that in the cases provided for, the evil or wrong actually committed rests upon some state law or state authority for its excuse and perpetration.

Of course, these remarks do not apply to those cases in which congress is clothed with direct and plenary powers of legislation over the whole subject, accompanied with an express or implied denial of such power to the states, as in the regulation of commerce with foreign nations, among the several states, and with the Indian tribes, the coining of money, the establishment of post-offices and post-roads, the declaring of war, etc. In these cases congress has power to pass laws for regulating the subjects specified, in every detail, and the conduct and transactions of individuals respect thereof. But where a subject is not submitted to the general legislative power of congress, but is only submitted thereto for the purpose of rendering effective some prohibition against particular state legislation or state action in reference to that subject, the power given is limited by its object, and any legislation by congress in the matter must necessarily be corrective in its character, adapted to counteract and redress the operation of such prohibited state laws or proceedings of state officers.

[T]he power of congress to adopt direct and primary, as distinguished from corrective, legislation on the subject in hand, is sought, in the second place, from the thirteenth amendment, which abolishes slavery. *** This amendment, as well as the fourteenth, is undoubtedly self-executing without any ancillary legislation, so far as its terms are applicable to any existing state of circumstances. By its own unaided force it abolished slavery, and established universal freedom. Still, legislation may be necessary and proper to meet all the various cases and circumstances to be affected by it, and to prescribe proper modes of redress for its violation in letter or spirit. And such legislation may be primary and direct in its character; for the amendment is not a mere prohibition of state laws establishing or upholding slavery,

> **Take Note**
>
> The Court here begins to discuss the Thirteenth Amendment, which it recognizes addresses private as well as state action. Why then does the Thirteenth Amendment not give Congress the power to pass the law at issue in this case?

but an absolute declaration that slavery or involuntary servitude shall not exist in any part of the United States.

It is true that slavery cannot exist without law any more than property in lands and goods can exist without law, and therefore the thirteenth amendment may be regarded as nullifying all state laws which establish or uphold slavery. But it has a reflex character also, establishing and decreeing universal civil and political freedom throughout the United States; and it is assumed that the power vested in congress to enforce the article by appropriate legislation, clothes congress with power to pass all laws necessary and proper for abolishing all badges and incidents of slavery in the United Stated; and upon this assumption it is claimed that this is sufficient authority for declaring by law that all persons shall have equal accommodations and privileges in all inns, public conveyances, and places of public amusement; the argument being that the denial of such equal accommodations and privileges is in itself a subjection to a species of servitude within the meaning of the amendment. Conceding the major proposition to be true, that congress has a right to enact all necessary and proper laws for the obliteration and prevention of slavery, with all its badges and incidents, is the minor proposition also true, that the denial to any person of admission to the accommodations and privileges of an inn, a public conveyance, or a theater, does subject that person to any form of servitude, or tend to fasten upon him any badge of slavery? If it does not, then power to pass the law is not found in the thirteenth amendment.

> **Make the Connection**
>
> We discussed Congress's power to enforce the Thirteenth Amendment, and in particular the Court's decision in *Jones v. Alfred H. Mayer Co.*, 392 U.S. 409, 440 (1968), in Chapter 13. Recall that the Court in *Jones* relied on this language in the *Civil Rights Cases*, and then concluded that "Congress has the power under the Thirteenth Amendment rationally to determine what are the badges and the incidents of slavery, and the authority to translate that determination into effective legislation." As you read the rest of the Court's opinion, consider whether the Court in *Jones* otherwise shared the Court's view here of Congress's power to enforce the Thirteenth Amendment.

The long existence of African slavery in this country gave us very distinct notions of what it was, and what were its necessary incidents. Compulsory service of the slave for the benefit of the master, restraint of his movements except by the master's will, disability to hold property, to make contracts, to have a standing in court, to be a witness against a white person, and such like burdens and incapacities were the inseparable incidents of the institution. Severer punishments for crimes were imposed on the slave than on free persons guilty of the same offenses. *** The only question under the present head, therefore, is, whether the refusal to any persons of the accommodations of an inn, or a public conveyance, or a place of public amusement, by an individual, and without any sanction or support from any state law or regulation, does inflict upon such persons any manner of servitude, or form of slavery, as those terms are understood in this country? ***

After giving to these questions all the consideration which their importance demands, we are forced to the conclusion that such an act of refusal has nothing to do with slavery or involuntary servitude, and that if it is violative of any right of the party, his redress is to be sought under the laws of the state; or, if those laws are adverse to his rights and do not protect him, his remedy will be found in the corrective legislation which congress has adopted, or may adopt, for counteracting the effect of state laws, or state action, prohibited by the fourteenth amendment. It would be running the slavery argument into the ground to make it apply to every act of discrimination which a person may see fit to make as to the guests he will entertain, or as to the people he will take into his coach or cab or car, or admit to his concert or theater, or deal with in the matters of intercourse or business. Innkeepers and public carriers, by the laws of all the states, so far as we are aware, are bound, to the extent of their facilities, to furnish proper accommodation to all unobjectionable persons who in good faith apply for them. If the laws themselves make any unjust discrimination, amenable to the prohibitions of the fourteenth amendment, congress has full power to afford a remedy under that amendment and in accordance with it.

HARLAN, J., dissenting.

The thirteenth amendment, my brethren concede, did something more than to prohibit slavery as an *institution*, resting upon distinctions of race, and upheld by positive law. They admit that it established and decreed universal *civil freedom* throughout the United States. But did the freedom thus established involve nothing more than exemption from actual slavery? Was nothing more intended than to forbid one man from owning another as property? Was it the purpose of the nation simply to destroy the institution, and then remit the race, theretofore held in bondage, to the several states for such protection, in their civil rights, necessarily growing out of freedom, as those states, in their discretion, choose to provide? Were the states, against whose solemn protest the institution was destroyed, to be left perfectly free, so far as national interference was concerned, to make or allow discriminations against that race, as such, in the enjoyment of those fundamental rights that inhere in a state of freedom? ***

Congress has not, in these matters, entered the domain of state control and supervision. It does not assume to prescribe the general conditions and limitations under which inns, public conveyances, and places of public amusement shall be conducted or managed. It simply declares in effect that since the nation has established universal freedom in this country for all time, there shall be no discrimination, based merely upon race or color, in respect of the legal rights in the accommodations and advantages of public conveyances, inns, and places of public amusement.

I am of the opinion that such discrimination practiced by corporations and individuals in the exercise of their public or quasi-public functions is a badge of servitude, the imposition of which congress may prevent under its power [by] appropriate legislation, to enforce the thirteenth amendment; and consequently, without reference to its enlarged power under the fourteenth amendment, the act of March 1, 1875, is not, in my judgment, repugnant to the constitution.

It remains now to consider these cases with reference to the power congress has possessed since the adoption of the fourteenth amendment. The assumption that this amendment consists wholly of prohibitions upon state laws and state proceedings in hostility to its provisions, is unauthorized by its language. The first clause of the first section—"all persons born or naturalized in the United States, and subject to the jurisdiction thereof, are citizens of the United States, and of the state wherein they reside"—is of a distinctly affirmative character. In its application to the colored race, previously liberated, it created and granted, as well citizenship of the United States, as citizenship of the state in which they respectively resided. It introduced all of that race, whose ancestors had been imported and sold as slaves, at once, into the political community known as the "People of the United States." They became, instantly, citizens of the United States, and of their respective states. Further, they were brought, by this supreme act of the nation, within the direct operation of that provision of the constitution which declares that "the citizens of each state shall be entitled to all privileges and immunities of citizens in the several states."

But what was secured to colored citizens of the United States—as between them and their respective states—by the grant to them of state citizenship? With what rights, privileges, or immunities did this grant from the nation invest them? There is one, if there be no others—exemption from race discrimination in respect of any civil right belonging to citizens of the white race in the same state. That, surely, is their constitutional privilege when within the jurisdiction of other states. And such must be their constitutional right, in their own state, unless the recent amendments be "splendid baubles," thrown out to delude those who deserved fair and generous treatment at the hands of the nation. Citizenship in this country necessarily imports equality of civil rights among citizens of every race in the same state. It is fundamental in American citizenship that, in respect of such rights, there shall be no discrimination by the state, or its officers, or by individuals, or corporations exercising public functions or authority, against any citizen because of his race or previous condition of servitude. ***

Points for Discussion

a. The Fourteenth Amendment

The "syllogism" is a form of reasoning that consists of a major premise, a minor premise, and a conclusion. A classic example of a syllogism is as follows: All men are mortal; Socrates is a man; therefore, Socrates is mortal. In the *Civil Rights Cases*, the syllogism for the Fourteenth Amendment issue appears to be this: Section 5 of the Fourteenth Amendment gives Congress only the power to address violations of § 1 of the Fourteenth Amendment; private discrimination does not violate § 1 of the Fourteenth Amendment; therefore, § 5 does not give Congress the power to address private discrimination.

How does the Court explain its minor premise (i.e. that private discrimination does not violate § 1)? Why does the dissent disagree with the majority on this point? Note that the Supreme Court used the same reasoning in *United States v. Morrison*, 529 U.S. 598 (2000), which we considered (in relevant part) in Chapter 13. In *Morrison*, the Court concluded that Congress could not use its power under § 5 of the Fourteenth Amendment to prohibit gender-motivated violence by private actors because § 1 of the Amendment does not apply to purely private conduct. If the Court's minor premise in the <u>Civil Rights Cases</u> was wrong, does that mean that the Court was wrong in <u>Morrison</u>, as well?

b. The Thirteenth Amendment

According to the Court, what justifies the conclusion that only state action can violate the Fourteenth Amendment even though (in its view) certain types of private action can violate the Thirteenth Amendment? What is the disagreement between the majority and dissent with respect to the Thirteenth Amendment?

c. The State Action Doctrine and Federalism

If the Constitution does not limit the actions of private individuals, then any restrictions on their actions must come from legislation or the common law. If Congress lacks the power to regulate certain forms of private conduct, then any limitations on that conduct must come from state law (if at all). Does it make sense to leave to the states the sole authority to determine the legality of private discrimination? Even if it makes sense today, did it make sense in 1883, when the Court decided the <u>Civil Rights Cases</u>? What does the Court's reasoning suggest more generally about the ability of the United States to address social problems? What has history shown?

d. Missed Opportunity to End Racial Discrimination?

How different would the United States have been if the Supreme Court had upheld the Civil Rights Act of 1875? Immediately after the Supreme Court decided the <u>Civil Rights Cases</u>, did Congress miss an opportunity to use the Commerce Clause as an alternative source of power for enacting the law? In a portion of the opinion omitted here, the Court suggested that Congress might have power to end discrimination in the territories and the District of Columbia, which are subject to plenary regulation by Congress. Should Congress at least have responded to the Court's decision by enacting such a statute?

———————————

B. The Public Function Exception

As explained above, the state action doctrine rests on the conclusion that the Constitution generally addresses the conduct of the government but not private parties. This principle raises several important questions: What happens when private parties assume the functions traditionally undertaken by the state? Can the government evade the Constitution's requirements by outsourcing governmental functions to private parties? For example, suppose that a town's police department hires a private detective to look for clues. Can the private detective search any building without a warrant and then successfully argue that the search did not violate the Fourth Amendment because a private detective is not a state actor?

The Supreme Court has addressed these questions by creating what has become known as the **public function exception** to the state action doctrine. Under the public function exception, private parties may be deemed to be state actors when they engage in activities "traditionally exclusively reserved to the State." *Jackson v. Metropolitan Edison Co.*, 419 U.S. 345, 352 (1974). In reading the cases that follow, attempt to discern which public functions are "traditionally exclusively" reserved to the state.

Marsh v. State of Alabama

326 U.S. 501 (1946)

Mr. Justice BLACK delivered the opinion of the Court.

In this case we are asked to decide whether a State, consistently with the First and Fourteenth Amendments, can impose criminal punishment on a person who undertakes to distribute religious literature on the premises of a company-owned town contrary to the wishes of the town's management. The town, a suburb of Mobile, Alabama, known as Chickasaw, is owned by the Gulf Shipbuilding Corporation. Except for that it has all the characteristics of any other American town. The property consists of residential buildings, streets, a system of sewers, a sewage disposal plant and a "business block" on which business places are situated. A deputy of the Mobile County Sheriff, paid by the company, serves as the town's policeman. Merchants and service establishments have rented the stores and business places on the business block and the United States uses one of the places as a post office from which six carriers deliver mail to the people of Chickasaw and the adjacent area. The town and the surrounding neighborhood, which cannot be distinguished from the Gulf property by anyone not familiar with the property lines, are thickly settled, and according to all indications the residents use the business block as their regular shopping center. To do so, they now, as they have for many years, make use of a company-owned paved street and sidewalk located alongside the store fronts in order to enter and leave the stores and the post office. Intersecting company-owned roads at each end of the business block lead into a four-lane public highway which runs parallel to the business block at a distance of thirty feet. There is nothing to stop highway traffic from coming onto the business block and upon arrival a traveler may make free use of the facilities available there. In short the town and its shopping district are accessible to and freely used by the public in general and there is nothing to distinguish them from any other town and shopping center except the fact that the title to the property belongs to a private corporation.

Appellant, a Jehovah's Witness, came onto the sidewalk we have just described, stood near the post-office and undertook to distribute religious literature. In the stores the corporation had posted a notice which read as follows: "This Is Private Property, and Without Written Permission, No Street, or House Vendor, Agent or Solicitation of Any Kind Will Be Permitted." Appellant was warned that she could not distribute the literature without a permit and told that no permit would be issued to her. She protested that the company rule could not be constitutionally applied so as to prohibit her from distributing religious writings. When she was asked to leave the sidewalk and Chickasaw she declined. The deputy sheriff arrested her and she was charged in the state court with violating Title 14, Section 426 of the 1940 Alabama Code which makes it a crime to enter or remain on the premises of another after having been warned not to do so. Appellant contended that to construe the state statute as applicable to her activities would abridge her right to freedom of press and religion contrary to the First and Fourteenth Amendments to the Constitution. This contention was rejected and she was convicted. ***

Had the title to Chickasaw belonged not to a private but to a municipal corporation and had appellant been arrested for violating a municipal ordinance rather than a ruling by those appointed by the corporation to manage a company-town it would have been clear that appellant's conviction must be reversed. Under our decision in *Lovell v. Griffin*, 303 U.S. 444 (1938), and others which have followed that case, neither a state nor a municipality can completely bar the distribution of literature containing religious or political ideas on its streets, sidewalks and public places or make the right to distribute dependent on a flat license tax or permit to be issued by an official who could deny it at will. *** From these decisions it is clear that had the people of Chickasaw owned all the homes, and all the stores, and all the streets, and all the sidewalks,

> **Make the Connection**
>
> Why does the First Amendment prohibit an ordinary municipality from barring the distribution of literature on a public sidewalk? Recall the materials that we discussed in Chapter 14.

all those owners together could not have set up a municipal government with sufficient power to pass an ordinance completely barring the distribution of religious literature. Our question then narrows down to this: Can those people who live in or come to Chickasaw be denied freedom of press and religion simply because a single company has legal title to all the town? For it is the state's contention that the mere fact that all the property interests in the town are held by a single company is enough to give that company power, enforceable by a state statute, to abridge these freedoms.

We do not agree that the corporation's property interests settle the question. The State urges in effect that the corporation's right to control the inhabitants of Chickasaw is coextensive with the right of a homeowner to regulate the conduct of his guests. We can not accept that contention. Ownership does not always mean absolute dominion. The more an owner, for his advantage, opens up his property for use by the public in general, the more do his rights become circumscribed by the statutory and constitutional rights of those who use it. Thus, the owners of privately held bridges, ferries, turnpikes and railroads may not operate them as freely as a farmer does his farm. Since these facilities are built and operated primarily to benefit the public and since their operation is essentially a public function, it is subject to state regulation. And, though the issue is not directly analogous to the one before us we do want to point out by way of illustration that such regulation may not result in an operation of these facilities, even by privately owned companies, which unconstitutionally interferes with and discriminates against interstate commerce. ***

We do not think it makes any significant constitutional difference as to the relationship between the rights of the owner and those of the public that here the State, instead of permitting the corporation to operate a highway, permitted it to use its property as a town, operate a "business block" in the town and a street and sidewalk on that business block. Whether a corporation or a municipality owns or possesses the town the public in either case has an identical interest in the functioning of the community in such manner that the channels of communication remain free. As we have heretofore stated, the town of Chickasaw does not function differently from any other town. The "business block" serves as the community shopping center and is freely accessible and open to the people in the area and those passing through. The managers appointed by the corporation cannot curtail the liberty of press and religion of these people consistently with the purposes of the Constitutional guarantees, and a state statute, as the one here involved, which enforces such action by criminally punishing those who attempt to distribute religious literature clearly violates the First and Fourteenth Amendments to the Constitution.

Many people in the United States live in company-owned towns. These people, just as residents of municipalities, are free citizens of their State and country. Just as all other citizens they must make decisions which affect the welfare of community and nation. To act as good citizens they must be informed. In order to enable them to be properly informed their information must be uncensored. There is no more reason for depriving these people of the liberties guaranteed by the First and Fourteenth Amendments than there is for curtailing these freedoms with respect to any other citizen. *** Reversed and remanded.

Mr. Justice REED, [joined by the CHIEF JUSTICE and Mr. Justice BURTON,] dissenting.

Our Constitution guarantees to every man the right to express his views in an orderly fashion. An essential element of "orderly" is that the man shall also have a right to use the place he chooses for his exposition. The rights of the owner, which the Constitution protects as well as the right of free speech, are not outweighed by the interests of the trespasser, even though he trespasses in behalf of religion or free speech. We cannot say that Jehovah's Witnesses can claim the privilege of a license, which has never been granted, to hold their meetings in other private places, merely because the owner has admitted the public to them for other limited purposes. Even though we have reached the point where this Court is required to force private owners to open their property for the practice there of religious activities or propaganda distasteful to the owner, because of the public interest in freedom of speech and religion, there is no need for the application of such a doctrine here. Appellant, as we have said, was free to engage in such practices on the public highways, without becoming a trespasser on the company's property.

Points for Discussion

a. Competing First Amendment Rights?

The Court discusses some of the consequences that might flow if the Court were to conclude that this case did not involve state action. In particular, the opinion asserts that millions of Americans who live in company towns would not have the full protection that the Constitution provides in traditional, state-run municipalities. But what are the consequences of the Court's decision that there *is* state action? Must the Gulf Ship Building Company provide all of the rights that a state would? For example, must it hold elections for a local government?

What are the implications of the holding in <u>Marsh</u> for ordinary rights of free association? Suppose that all of the property in the town were owned not by a corporation but instead by one private individual. Does the Court's holding mean that this private individual would not be able to choose which messages, religious or otherwise, are distributed on his property? Do ordinary property owners face a similar limitation? If not, doesn't the Court's holding in <u>Marsh</u> abridge the free speech or associational rights of the property owner?

b. Public Function Exception or State Involvement?

Is the Court's conclusion in <u>Marsh</u> based on the fact that the company that owns the town is effectively acting in a "public" capacity? The Court reasoned that if individual owners of property joined together to establish a municipality, they could not evade the limits that the Constitution imposes on state action, and that the company here similarly was effectively acting in a public capacity. But the Court also stated that "a state statute, as the one here involved, which enforces [the exclusion of the appellant] by criminally punishing those who attempt to distribute religious literature clearly violates the First and Fourteenth Amendments to the Constitution." Does that mean that the state action requirement was satisfied by the judicial enforcement of the state ordinance that makes it a crime to enter or remain on the premises of another after having been warned not to do so? We will consider this theory of state action below, when we discuss <u>Shelley v. Kraemer</u>.

c. Company Towns

Company towns flourished in the United States at the start of the twentieth century. Businesses built them near factories and mines to house employees who otherwise could not afford housing or could not travel long distances to work because they lacked transportation. Company towns became less common with the advent of cars, and only a few traditional company towns still exist. Indeed, in modern times, a complete reversal has occurred; to promote employment and economic growth, some communities now provide sites for factories. See Marilyn Geewax, *"Company Towns" are Back, but not Like the Old Days*, Atlanta Const., Jan. 7, 1996, at G3.

————————

The Court held in <u>Marsh v. Alabama</u> that a company town serves a traditional public function. This conclusion certainly seems plausible because towns ordinarily are run by governments, not by businesses. But what about something smaller than a company town, such as a large shopping mall that serves only some, but not all, of the functions of a town? This question vexed the Supreme Court for many years, but was finally resolved in the case that follows.

————————

Hudgens v. National Labor Relations Board

424 U.S. 507 (1976)

Mr. Justice STEWART delivered the opinion of the Court.

A group of labor union members who engaged in peaceful primary picketing within the confines of a privately owned shopping center were threatened by an agent of the owner with arrest for criminal trespass if they did not depart. *** The petitioner, Scott Hudgens, is the owner of the North DeKalb Shopping Center, located in suburban Atlanta, Ga. The center consists of a single large building with an enclosed mall. Surrounding the building is a parking area which can accommodate 2,640 automobiles. The shopping center houses 60 retail stores leased to various businesses. One of the lessees is the Butler Shoe Co. Most of the stores, including Butler's, can be entered only from the interior mall.

In January 1971, warehouse employees of the Butler Shoe Co. went on strike to protest the company's failure to agree to demands made by their union in contract negotiations. The strikers decided to picket not only Butler's warehouse but its nine retail stores in the Atlanta area as well, including the store in the North DeKalb Shopping Center. On January 22, 1971, four of the striking warehouse employees entered the center's enclosed mall carrying placards which read: "Butler Shoe Warehouse on Strike, AFL-CIO, Local 315." The general manager of the shopping center informed the employees that they could not picket within the mall or on the parking lot and threatened them with arrest if they did not leave. The employees departed but returned a short time later and began picketing in an area of the mall immediately adjacent to the entrances of the Butler store. After the picketing had continued for approximately 30 minutes, the shopping center manager again informed the pickets that if they did not leave they would be arrested for trespassing. The pickets departed.

It is, of course, a commonplace that the constitutional guarantee of free speech is a guarantee only against abridgment by government, federal or state. Thus, while statutory or common law may in some situations extend protection or provide redress against a private corporation or person who seeks to abridge the free expression of others, no such protection or redress is provided by the Constitution itself.

This elementary proposition is little more than a truism. But even truisms are not always unexceptionably true, and an exception to this one was recognized almost 30 years ago in *Marsh v. Alabama*, 326 U.S. 501 (1946). *** It was the *Marsh* case that in 1968 provided the foundation for the Court's decision in *Amalgamated Food Employees Union v. Logan Valley Plaza*, 391 U.S. 308 (1968). That case involved peaceful picketing within a large shopping center near Altoona, Pa. One of the tenants of the shopping center was a retail store that employed a wholly nonunion staff. Members of a local union picketed the store, carrying signs proclaiming that it was nonunion and that its employees were not receiving union wages or other union benefits. The picketing took place on the shopping center's property in the immediate vicinity of the store. A Pennsylvania court issued an injunction that required all picketing to be confined to public areas outside the shopping center, and the Supreme Court of Pennsylvania affirmed the issuance of this injunction.

This Court held that the doctrine of the *Marsh* case required reversal of that judgment.

The Court's opinion pointed out that the First and Fourteenth Amendments would clearly have protected the picketing if it had taken place on a public sidewalk: "[S]treets, sidewalks, parks, and other similar public places are so historically associated with the exercise of First Amendment rights that access to them for the purpose of exercising such rights cannot constitutionally be denied broadly and absolutely." The Court's opinion then reviewed the *Marsh* case in detail, emphasized the similarities between the business block in Chickasaw, Ala., and the Logan Valley shopping center and unambiguously concluded: "The shopping center here is clearly the functional equivalent of the business district of Chickasaw involved in *Marsh*." Upon the basis of that conclusion, the Court held that the First and Fourteenth Amendments required reversal of the judgment of the Pennsylvania Supreme Court.

Four years later the Court had occasion to reconsider the *Logan Valley* doctrine in *Lloyd Corp. v. Tanner*, 407 U.S. 551 (1972). That case involved a shopping center covering some 50 acres in downtown Portland, Ore. On a November day in 1968 five young people entered the mall of the shopping center and distributed handbills protesting the then ongoing American military operations in Vietnam. Security guards told them to leave, and they did so, "to avoid arrest." They subsequently brought suit in a Federal District Court, seeking declaratory and injunctive relief. The trial court ruled in their favor, holding that the distribution of handbills on the shopping center's property was protected by the First and Fourteenth Amendments. The Court of Appeals for the Ninth Circuit affirmed the judgment, expressly relying on this Court's *Marsh* and *Logan Valley* decisions. This Court reversed the judgment of the Court of Appeals.

The Court in its *Lloyd* opinion did not say that it was overruling the *Logan Valley* decision. Indeed a substantial portion of the Court's opinion in *Lloyd* was devoted to pointing out the differences between the two cases, noting particularly that, in contrast to the hand-billing in *Lloyd*, the picketing in *Logan Valley* had been specifically directed to a store in the shopping center and the pickets had had no other reasonable opportunity to reach their intended audience. But the fact is that the reasoning of the Court's opinion in *Lloyd* cannot be squared with the reasoning of the Court's opinion in *Logan Valley*.

It matters not that some Members of the Court may continue to believe that the *Logan Valley* case was rightly decided. Our institutional duty is to follow until changed the law as it now is, not as some Members of the Court might wish it to be. And in the performance of that duty we make clear now, if it was not clear before, that the rationale of *Logan Valley* did not survive the Court's decision in the *Lloyd* case.

If a large self-contained shopping center is the functional equivalent of a municipality, as *Logan Valley* held, then the First and Fourteenth Amendments would not permit control of speech within such a center to depend upon the speech's content. For while a municipality may constitutionally impose reasonable time, place, and manner regulations on the use of its streets and sidewalks for First Amendment purposes, and may even forbid altogether such use of some of its facilities, what a municipality may not do under the First and Fourteenth Amendments is to discriminate in the regulation of expression on the basis of the content of that expression. *** It conversely follows, therefore, that if the respondents in the *Lloyd* case did not have a First Amendment right to enter that shopping center to distribute handbills concerning Vietnam, then the pickets in the present case did not have a First Amendment right to enter this shopping center for the purpose of advertising their strike against the Butler Shoe Co.

We conclude, in short, that under the present state of the law the constitutional guarantee of free expression has no part to play in a case such as this. *** Vacated and remanded.

Mr. Justice MARSHALL, with whom Mr. Justice BRENNAN joins, dissenting.

The Court adopts the view that *Marsh* has no bearing on this case because the privately owned property in *Marsh* involved all the characteristics of a typical town. But there is nothing in *Marsh* to suggest that its general approach was limited to the particular facts of that case. The underlying concern in *Marsh* was that traditional public channels of communication remain free, regardless of the incidence of ownership. Given that concern, the crucial fact in *Marsh* was that the company owned the traditional forums essential for effective communication; it was immaterial that the company also owned a sewer system and that its property in other respects resembled a town.

In *Logan Valley* we recognized what the Court today refuses to recognize[:] that the owner of the modern shopping center complex, by dedicating his property to public use as a business district, to some extent displaces the "State" from control of historical First Amendment forums, and may acquire a virtual monopoly of places suitable for effective communication. The roadways, parking lots, and walkways of the modern shopping center may be as essential for effective speech as the streets and sidewalks in the municipal or company-owned town. I simply cannot reconcile the Court's denial of any role for the First Amendment in the shopping center with *Marsh*'s recognition of a full rule for the First Amendment on the streets and sidewalks of the company-owned town.

Points for Discussion

a. Distinguishing a Company Town from a Shopping Center

The Court in *Marsh* made clear that the owner of a company town serves a traditional public function, whereas the Court in *Hudgens* concluded that the owner of a large shopping mall does not. Accordingly, the former is a state actor limited by the First Amendment, while the latter is not. What factors differentiate the two? What factors should be most important? Does the Court's willingness in *Hudgens* to overrule *Logan Valley* suggest that *Marsh* is vulnerable to the same fate?

b. Universities and Company Towns

Private university campuses are sometimes similar to company towns. They have residence halls where students sleep, cafeterias where they eat, stores where they can shop, buildings where they study and work, sidewalks, stadiums, open gathering places, and so forth. If a private university limits speech on campus, does it violate the First Amendment under the public function exception to the state action doctrine? In other words, is a private university more like a company town or a shopping mall? What arguments might you make for each side? Can the issue be avoided by concluding that higher education is not traditionally an *exclusively* public function? See *Greenya v. George Washington University,* 512 F.2d 556, 561 n.10 (1975).

C. The Judicial Enforcement Exception

The **judicial enforcement exception** to the state action doctrine provides that some private action can effectively become public action when a court acts to uphold the private action. The exception begins with the unobjectionable premise that judicial decisions are a form of state action; after all, judges and courts are part of the government. The theory of the exception is that although private conduct alone does not violate the Constitution, a court's enforcement of that private conduct may constitute state action. Thus, in the famous case of *Shelley v. Kraemer,* 334 U.S. 1 (1948), the Supreme Court concluded that although private homeowners do not violate the Constitution by engaging in race discrimination against prospective neighbors, a state court violates the Equal Protection Clause by enforcing such private discrimination. In reading the case, think carefully about how far this logic should extend.

Shelley v. Kraemer

334 U.S. 1 (1948)

Mr. Chief Justice VINSON delivered the opinion of the Court.

On February 16, 1911, thirty out of a total of thirty-nine owners of property fronting both sides of Labadie Avenue between Taylor Avenue and Cora Avenue in the city of St. Louis signed an agreement, which was subsequently recorded, providing in part:

> [T]he said property is hereby restricted to the use and occupancy for the term of Fifty (50) years from this date, so that it shall be a condition all the time and [in] subsequent conveyances and shall attach to the land, as a condition precedent to the sale of the same, that hereafter no part of said property or any portion thereof shall be, for said term of Fifty-years, occupied by any person not of the Caucasian race ***.

On August 11, 1945, pursuant to a contract of sale, petitioners Shelley, who are Negroes, for valuable consideration received from one Fitzgerald a warranty deed to [a house subject to this restrictive covenant]. *** On October 9, 1945, respondents, as owners of other property subject to the terms of the restrictive covenant, brought suit in Circuit Court of the city of St. Louis praying that petitioners Shelley be restrained from taking possession of the property and that judgment be entered divesting title out of petitioners Shelley and revesting title in the immediate grantor or in such other person as the court should direct. *** The Supreme Court of Missouri sitting en banc *** held the agreement effective and concluded that enforcement of its provisions violated no rights guaranteed to petitioners by the Federal Constitution. At the time the court rendered its decision, petitioners were occupying the property in question. [A companion case involved the enforcement of a similar restrictive covenant.]

It is *** clear that restrictions on the right of occupancy of the sort sought to be created by the private agreements in these cases could not be squared with the requirements of the Fourteenth Amendment if imposed by state statute or local ordinance. We do not understand respondents to urge the contrary. In the case of *Buchanan v. Warley*, 245 U.S. 60 (1917), a unanimous Court declared unconstitutional the provisions of a city ordinance which denied to colored persons the right to occupy houses in blocks in which the greater number of houses were occupied by white persons, and imposed similar restrictions on white persons with respect to blocks in which the greater number of houses were occupied by colored persons. During the course of the opinion in that case, this Court stated: "The Fourteenth Amendment and these statutes enacted in furtherance of its purpose operate to qualify and entitle a colored man to acquire property without state legislation discriminating against him solely because of color."

> **FYI**
>
> *Buchanan v. Warley* was litigated by the NAACP and was one of the organization's earliest judicial victories in campaigning for equal rights. Although the decision did not end all discrimination in residential housing, it was still "a symbolic watershed, showing that civil rights progress could be made through the courts." Susan D. Carle, *Race, Class, and Legal Ethics in the Early NAACP (1910-1920)*, 20 Law & Hist. Rev. 97, 128 (2002).

But the present cases, unlike those just discussed, do not involve action by state legislatures or city councils. Here the particular patterns of discrimination and the areas in which the restrictions are to operate, are determined, in the first instance, by the terms of agreements among private individuals. Participation of the State consists in the enforcement of the restrictions so defined. The crucial issue with which we are here confronted is whether this distinction removes these cases from the operation of the prohibitory provisions of the Fourteenth Amendment.

Since the decision of this Court in the *Civil Rights Cases*, 109 U.S. 3 (1883) the principle has become firmly embedded in our constitutional law that the action inhibited by the first section of the Fourteenth Amendment is only such action as may fairly be said to be that of the States. That Amendment erects no shield against merely private conduct, however discriminatory or wrongful.

We conclude, therefore, that the restrictive agreements standing alone cannot be regarded as a violation of any rights guaranteed to petitioners by the Fourteenth Amendment. So long as the purposes of those agreements are effectuated by voluntary adherence to their terms, it would appear clear that there has been no action by the State and the provisions of the Amendment have not been violated.

But here there was more. These are cases in which the purposes of the agreements were secured only by judicial enforcement by state courts of the restrictive terms of the agreements. The respondents urge that judicial enforcement of private agreements does not amount to state action; or, in any event, the participation of the State is so attenuated in character as not to amount to state action within the meaning of the Fourteenth Amendment. Finally, it is suggested, even if the States in these cases may be deemed to have acted in the constitutional sense, their action did not deprive petitioners of rights guaranteed by the Fourteenth Amendment. We move to a consideration of these matters.

That the action of state courts and of judicial officers in their official capacities is to be regarded as action of the State within the meaning of the Fourteenth Amendment, is a proposition which has long been established by decisions of this Court. That principle was given expression in the earliest cases involving the construction of the terms of the Fourteenth Amendment. ***

One of the earliest applications of the prohibitions contained in the Fourteenth Amendment to action of state judicial officials occurred in cases in which Negroes had been excluded from jury service in criminal prosecutions by reason of their race or color. These cases demonstrate, also, the early recognition by this Court that state action in violation of the Amendment's provisions is equally repugnant to the constitutional commands whether directed by state statute or taken by a judicial official in the absence of statute. Thus, in *Strauder v. West Virginia*, 100 U.S. 303 (1880), this Court declared invalid a state statute restricting jury service to white persons as amounting to a denial of the equal protection of the laws to the colored defendant in that case. ***

> **Make the Connection**
>
> We considered the Court's decision in *Strauder*, and discrimination on the basis of race, in Chapter 11.

We have no doubt that there has been state action in these cases in the full and complete sense of the phrase. The undisputed facts disclose that petitioners were willing purchasers of properties upon which they desired to establish homes. The owners of the properties were willing sellers; and contracts of sale were accordingly consummated. It is clear that but for the active intervention of the state courts, supported by the full panoply of state power, petitioners would have been free to occupy the properties in question without restraint.

These are not cases, as has been suggested, in which the States have merely abstained from action, leaving private individuals free to impose such discriminations as they see fit. Rather, these are cases in which the States have made available to such individuals the full coercive power of government to deny to petitioners, on the grounds of race or color, the

Take Note

The Court explains here why this case involves state action even if private racial discrimination is not state action. Suppose that the case involved instead a claim for an injunction to enforce a contractual provision that prohibited the parties from publicly discussing the terms of a prior settlement. Would a court's grant of such an injunction to enforce a private agreement constitute state action in violation of the First Amendment? If not, why is this case different?

enjoyment of property rights in premises which petitioners are willing and financially able to acquire and which the grantors are willing to sell. The difference between judicial enforcement and nonenforcement of the restrictive covenants is the difference to petitioners between being denied rights of property available to other members of the community and being accorded full enjoyment of those rights on an equal footing.

[We do not] find merit in the suggestion that property owners who are parties to these agreements are denied equal protection of the laws if denied access to the courts to enforce the terms of restrictive covenants and to assert property rights which the state courts have held to be created by such agreements. The Constitution confers upon no individual the right to demand action by the State which results in the denial of equal protection of the laws to other individuals. And it would appear beyond question that the power of the State to create and enforce property interests must be exercised within the boundaries defined by the Fourteenth Amendment. Cf. *Marsh v. Alabama*, 326 U.S. 501 (1946).

[Reversed.]

Points for Discussion

a. How Far Does *Shelley*'s Reasoning Extend?

The Court concluded in *Shelley* that judicial enforcement of the racially restrictive covenants would involve state action because judges and courts are state actors. Many scholars have questioned this reasoning. Dean Erwin Chemerinsky, for example, writes:

> If any decision by a state court represents state action, then ultimately all private actions must comply with the Constitution. Anyone who believes that his or her rights have been violated can sue in state court. If the court dismisses the case because the state law does not forbid the violation, there is state action sustaining the infringement of the right ***. It is difficult to imagine anything that cannot be transformed into state action under this reasoning. *** The Court [never] has taken *Shelley* this far, but nor has it articulated any clear limiting principles.

Erwin Chemerinsky, *Constitutional Law: Principles and Policies* 528 (3d ed. 2006). See also Kimberly A. Yuracko, *Education Off the Grid: Constitutional Constraints on Homeschooling*, 96 Cal. L. Rev. 123, 151-178 (2008) (discussing three different views about how far *Shelley* should be interpreted to extend).

Consider this example: In *Hudgens v. National Labor Relations Board*, 424 U.S. 507

(1976), the Supreme Court held that a private shopping mall's decision to exclude picketers was not state action. The Court therefore upheld the action. Wasn't the Supreme Court's action in enforcing the shopping mall's decision to exclude the picketers itself a form of state action? Did the Court's action convert the shopping mall's otherwise private action into state action? If not, how does this example differ from the circumstances at issue in *Shelley*? Can you articulate a limiting principle for the rule announced in *Shelley*?

b. Current Federal Law and Discrimination in Housing

When the Court decided *Shelley*, racially restrictive covenants did not violate federal (or, for that matter, state) statutory law. It also was not clear at the time whether Congress had power (even assuming that it had the will) under the Commerce Clause to prohibit the use or enforcement of such restrictive covenants. Given the analytical problems that the decision raises, is it fair to conclude that the Court's resolution of the question in *Shelley* reflected more the Court's concern that there was no effective way to stop this invidious practice than it did the Court's view about the state action doctrine?

Congress eventually did act. Title VIII of the Civil Rights Act of 1968 now prohibits discrimination on the basis of race (or other status-based distinctions) in the sale, rental, or financing of housing. 42 U.S.C. § 3601 *et seq.* In light of the Court's reasoning in *Shelley*, did Congress have authority to enact this statute pursuant to its authority to enforce the Fourteenth Amendment? (Recall our consideration in Chapter 13 of Congress's enforcement powers.) If not, does the Commerce Clause as currently interpreted confer the requisite authority? (Recall our consideration in Chapter 3 of Congress's power under the Commerce Clause.)

————

D. The Joint Participation (or Entanglement) Exception

The Supreme Court also has recognized the **joint participation exception** (sometimes called the **entanglement exception**) to the state action doctrine. Under this doctrine, some private parties will be deemed to be state actors in certain circumstances when they are acting with the state or state officers. The Supreme Court has held that a private party may be held liable for a deprivation of a constitutional right if two elements are present:

> First, the deprivation must be caused by the exercise of some right or privilege created by the State or by a rule of conduct imposed by the state or by a person for whom the State is responsible. *** Second, the party charged with the deprivation must be a person who may fairly be said to be a state actor. This may be because he is a state official, because he has acted together with or has obtained significant aid from state officials, or because his conduct is otherwise chargeable to the State.

Lugar v. Edmondson Oil Co., 457 U.S. 922, 937 (1982).

The second of these two elements—that the private party "may fairly be said to be a state actor"—is, as its terms suggest, an indefinite standard. The only way to determine whether this element is satisfied is to consider all the facts and to compare them to the Court's precedents. Consider the cases that follow.

Burton v. Wilmington Parking Authority

365 U.S. 715 (1961)

Mr. Justice CLARK delivered the opinion of the Court.

In this action for declaratory and injunctive relief it is admitted that the Eagle Coffee Shoppe, Inc., a restaurant located within an off-street automobile parking building in Wilmington, Delaware, has refused to serve appellant food or drink solely because he is a Negro. The parking building is owned and operated by the Wilmington Parking Authority, an agency of the State of Delaware, and the restaurant is the Authority's lessee. Appellant claims that such refusal abridges his rights under the Equal Protection Clause of the Fourteenth Amendment to the United States Constitution. The Supreme Court of Delaware has held that Eagle was acting in "a purely private capacity" under its lease; that its action was not that of the Authority and was not, therefore, state action within the contemplation of the prohibitions contained in that Amendment. It also held that under 24 Del. Code § 1501,[1] Eagle was a restaurant *** and that as such it "is not required (under Delaware law) to serve any and all persons entering its place of business." ***

The Authority was created by the City of Wilmington pursuant to 22 Del. Code §§ 501-515. It is "a public body corporate and politic, exercising public powers of the State as an agency thereof." Its statutory purpose is to provide adequate parking facilities for the convenience of the public and thereby relieve the "parking crisis, which threatens the welfare of the community ***."

The first project undertaken by the Authority was the erection of a parking facility on Ninth Street in downtown Wilmington. *** Before it began actual construction of the facility, the Authority was advised by its retained experts that the anticipated revenue from the parking of cars and proceeds from sale of its bonds would not be sufficient to finance the construction costs of the facility. Moreover, the bonds were not expected to be marketable if payable solely out of parking revenues. To secure additional capital needed for its "debt-service" requirements, and thereby to make bond financing practicable, the Authority decided it was necessary to enter long-term leases with responsible tenants for commercial use of some of the space available in the projected "garage building." The public was invited to bid for these leases.

---

[1] The statute provides that: "No keeper of an inn, tavern, hotel, or restaurant, or other place of public entertainment or refreshment of travelers, guests, or customers shall be obliged, by law, to furnish entertainment or refreshment to persons whose reception or entertainment by him would be offensive to the major part of his customers, and would injure his business. As used in this section, 'customer' includes all who have occasion for entertainment or refreshment."

In April 1957 such a private lease, for 20 years and renewable for another 10 years, was made with Eagle Coffee Shoppe, Inc., for use as a "restaurant, dining room, banquet hall, cocktail lounge and bar and for no other use and purpose." The multi-level space of the building which was let to Eagle, although "within the exterior walls of the structure, has no marked public entrance leading from the parking portion of the facility into the restaurant proper [whose main entrance] is located on Ninth Street." In its lease the Authority covenanted to complete construction expeditiously, including completion of "the decorative finishing of the leased premises and utilities therefor, without cost to Lessee," including necessary utility connections, toilets, hung acoustical tile and plaster ceilings; vinyl asbestos, ceramic tile and concrete floors; connecting stairs and wrought iron railings; and wood-floored show windows. Eagle spent some $220,000 to make the space suitable for its operation and, to the extent such improvements were so attached to realty as to become part thereof, Eagle to the same extent enjoys the Authority's tax exemption.

Other portions of the structure were leased to other tenants, including a bookstore, a retail jeweler, and a food store. Upon completion of the building, the Authority located at appropriate places thereon official signs indicating the public character of the building, [and] they flew from mastheads on the roof both the state and national flags.

In August 1958 appellant parked his car in the building and walked around to enter the restaurant by its front door on Ninth Street. Having entered and sought service, he was refused it. Thereafter he filed this declaratory judgment action in the Court of Chancery. * * *

[T]he Delaware Supreme Court seems to have placed controlling emphasis on its conclusion, as to the accuracy of which there is doubt, that only some 15% of the total cost of the facility was "advanced" from public funds; that the cost of the entire facility was allocated three-fifths to the space for commercial leasing and two-fifths to parking space; that anticipated revenue from parking was only some 30.5% of the total income, the balance of which was expected to be earned by the leasing; that the Authority had no original intent to place a restaurant in the building, it being only a happenstance resulting from the bidding; that Eagle expended considerable moneys on furnishings; that the restaurant's main and marked public entrance is on Ninth Street without any public entrance direct from the parking area; and that "the only connection Eagle has with the public facility [is] the furnishing of the sum of $28,700 annually in the form of rent which is used by the Authority to defray a portion of the operating expense of an otherwise unprofitable enterprise." While these factual considerations are indeed validly accountable aspects of the enterprise upon which the State has embarked, we cannot say that they lead inescapably to the conclusion that state action is not present. Their persuasiveness is diminished when evaluated in the context of other factors which must be acknowledged.

The land and building were publicly owned. As an entity, the building was dedicated to "public uses" in performance of the Authority's "essential governmental functions." The costs of land acquisition, construction, and maintenance are defrayed entirely from donations by the City of Wilmington, from loans and revenue bonds and from the proceeds of rentals and parking services out of which the loans and bonds were payable. Assuming that the distinction would be significant, the commercially leased areas were not surplus state property, but constituted a physically and financially integral and, indeed, indispensable part of the State's plan to operate its project as a self-sustaining unit. Upkeep and maintenance of the building, including necessary repairs, were responsibilities of the Authority and were payable out of public funds. It cannot be doubted that the peculiar relationship of the restaurant to the parking facility in which it is located confers on each an incidental variety of mutual benefits. Guests of the restaurant are afforded a convenient place to park their automobiles, even if they cannot enter the restaurant directly from the parking area. Similarly, its convenience for diners may well provide additional demand for the Authority's parking facilities. Should any improvements effected in the leasehold by Eagle become part of the realty, there is no possibility of increased taxes being passed on to it since the fee is held by a tax-exempt government agency. Neither can it be ignored, especially in view of Eagle's affirmative allegation that for it to serve Negroes would injure its business, that profits earned by discrimination not only contribute to, but also are indispensable elements in, the financial success of a governmental agency.

Addition of all these activities, obligations and responsibilities of the Authority, the benefits mutually conferred, together with the obvious fact that the restaurant is operated as an integral part of a public building devoted to a public parking service, indicates that degree of state participation and involvement in discriminatory action which it was the design of the Fourteenth Amendment to condemn. It is irony amounting to grave injustice that in one part of a single building, erected and maintained with public funds by an agency of the State to serve a public purpose, all persons have equal rights, while in another portion, also serving the public, a Negro is a second-class citizen, offensive because of his race, without rights and unentitled to service, but at the same time fully enjoys equal access to nearby restaurants in wholly privately owned buildings. As the Chancellor pointed out, in its lease with Eagle the Authority could have affirmatively required Eagle to discharge the responsibilities under the Fourteenth Amendment imposed upon the private enterprise as a consequence of state participation. But no State may effectively abdicate its responsibilities by either ignoring them or by merely failing to discharge them whatever the motive may be. It is of no consolation to an individual denied the equal protection of the laws that it was done in good faith. *** By its inaction, the Authority, and through it the State, has not only made itself a party to the refusal of service, but has elected to place its power, property and prestige behind the admitted discrimination. The State has so far insinuated itself into a position of interdependence with Eagle that it must be recognized as a joint participant in the challenged activity, which, on that account, cannot be considered to have been so "purely private" as to fall without the scope of the Fourteenth Amendment.

Because readily applicable formulae may not be fashioned, the conclusions drawn from the facts and circumstances of this record are by no means declared as universal truths on the basis of which every state leasing agreement is to be tested. Owing to the very "largeness" of government, a multitude of relationships might

> **Take Note**
>
> The Court acknowledges here that no simple test exists for when the joint participation exception applies to convert otherwise private action into state action. Instead, the answer depends on all the facts and circumstances. Can you identify the facts that were dispositive here?

appear to some to fall within the Amendment's embrace, but that, it must be remembered, can be determined only in the framework of the peculiar facts or circumstances present. Therefore respondents' prophecy of nigh universal application of a constitutional precept so peculiarly dependent for its invocation upon appropriate facts fails to take into account "Differences in circumstances (which) beget appropriate differences in law," *Whitney v. State Tax Comm.*, 309 U.S. 530, 542 (1940). Specifically defining the limits of our inquiry, what we hold today is that when a State leases public property in the manner and for the purpose shown to have been the case here, the proscriptions of the Fourteenth Amendment must be complied with by the lessee as certainly as though they were binding covenants written into the agreement itself. [Reversed.]

Mr. Justice STEWART, concurring.

I agree that the judgment must be reversed, but I reach that conclusion by a route much more direct than the one traveled by the Court. In upholding Eagle's right to deny service to the appellant solely because of his race, the Supreme Court of Delaware relied upon a statute of that State which permits the proprietor of a restaurant to refuse to serve "persons whose reception or entertainment by him would be offensive to the major part of his customers." There is no suggestion in the record that the appellant as an individual was such a person. The highest court of Delaware has thus construed this legislative enactment as authorizing discriminatory classification based exclusively on color. Such a law seems to me clearly violative of the Fourteenth Amendment. I think, therefore, that the appeal was properly taken, and that the statute, as authoritatively construed by the Supreme Court of Delaware, is constitutionally invalid.

Mr. Justice HARLAN, whom Mr. Justice WHITTAKER joins, dissenting.

The Court's opinion, by a process of first undiscriminatingly throwing together various factual bits and pieces and then undermining the resulting structure by an equally vague disclaimer, seems to me to leave completely at sea just what it is in this record that satisfies the requirement of "state action."

————

Points for Discussion

a. The Standard for Application of the Joint Participation Exception

What exactly is the standard for application of the joint participation exception? Is it simply that otherwise private action is state action when the private actor can "fairly be said to be a state actor"? See *Lugar v. Edmondson Oil Co.*, 457 U.S. 922 (1982). What are the advantages and disadvantages of such an open-ended standard?

b. What Facts Are Significant?

Suppose that the Eagle Coffee Shop were not a tenant in the government-owned garage, but instead were simply a neighbor next door to the parking garage. Would the case have come out the same way? If not, exactly which facts were significant for the

Court's conclusion in *Burton*?

c. Alternative Grounds for Finding State Action

Justice Stewart did not rest his concurrence on the joint participation exception. Instead, he concluded that the statute that authorized the Eagle Coffee Shop to exclude Burton itself was unconstitutional, because it permitted "discriminatory classification based exclusively on color." Given the state action doctrine, is this a valid basis for granting relief to Mr. Burton? What if the statute had conferred a right on private store owners to refuse to serve persons "for any reason, or no reason"? Would such a statute also, in Justice Stewart's view, violate the Fourteenth Amendment?

Edmonson v. Leesville Concrete Co., Inc.

500 U.S. 614 (1991)

Justice KENNEDY delivered the opinion of the Court.

Thaddeus Donald Edmonson, a construction worker, was injured in a jobsite accident at Fort Polk, Louisiana, a federal enclave. Edmonson sued Leesville Concrete Company for negligence in [federal district court], claiming that a Leesville employee permitted one of the company's trucks to roll backward and pin him against some construction equipment. Edmonson invoked his Seventh Amendment right to a trial by jury.

During *voir dire,* Leesville used two of its three peremptory challenges authorized by statute to remove black persons from the prospective jury. Citing our decision in *Batson v. Kentucky,* 476 U.S. 79 (1986), Edmonson, who is himself black, requested that the District Court require Leesville to articulate a race-neutral explanation for striking the two jurors. The District Court denied the request on the ground that *Batson* does not apply in civil proceedings. ***

> **Definition**
>
> In a jury trial, each party can challenge any juror for cause (e.g., bias) and can challenge a limited number of jurors without giving any cause. Challenges made without giving cause are called "peremptory challenges." See Black's Law Dictionary (8th ed. 2004).

> **Make the Connection**
>
> In *Batson v. Kentucky*, the Supreme Court held that a prosecutor—who is clearly a state actor—may not use peremptory challenges in a racially discriminatory manner. We briefly considered this decision in Chapter 11, in conjunction with our discussion of *Strauder v. West Virginia*.

The Constitution structures the National Government, confines its actions, and, in regard to certain individual liberties and other specified matters, confines the actions of the States. With a few exceptions, such as the provisions of the Thirteenth Amendment, constitutional guarantees of individual liberty and equal protection do not apply to the actions of private entities.

This fundamental limitation on the scope of constitutional guarantees "preserves an area of individual freedom by limiting the reach of federal law" and "avoids imposing on the State, its agencies or officials, responsibility for conduct for which they cannot fairly be blamed." *Lugar v. Edmondson Oil Co.*, 457 U.S. 922, 936-937 (1982). One great object of the Constitution is to permit citizens to structure their private relations as they choose subject only to the constraints of statutory or decisional law.

To implement these principles, courts must consider from time to time where the governmental sphere ends and the private sphere begins. Although the conduct of private parties lies beyond the Constitution's scope in most instances, governmental authority may dominate an activity to such an extent that its participants must be deemed to act with the authority of the government and, as a result, be subject to constitutional constraints. This is the jurisprudence of state action, which explores the "essential dichotomy" between the private sphere and the public sphere, with all its attendant constitutional obligations.

We begin our discussion within the framework for state-action analysis set forth in *Lugar*. There we considered the state-action question in the context of a due process challenge to a State's procedure allowing private parties to obtain prejudgment attachments. We asked first whether the claimed constitutional deprivation resulted from the exercise of a right or privilege having its source in state authority, and second, whether the private party charged with the deprivation could be described in all fairness as a state actor.

There can be no question that the first part of the *Lugar* inquiry is satisfied here. By their very nature, peremptory challenges have no significance outside a court of law. Their sole purpose is to permit litigants to assist the government in the selection of an impartial trier of fact. While we have recognized the value of peremptory challenges in this regard, particularly in the criminal context, there is no constitutional obligation to allow them. Peremptory challenges are permitted only when the government, by statute or decisional law, deems it appropriate to allow parties to exclude a given number of persons who otherwise would satisfy the requirements for service on the petit jury.

Given that the statutory authorization for the challenges exercised in this case is clear, the remainder of our state-action analysis centers around the second part of the *Lugar* test, whether a private litigant in all fairness must be deemed a government actor in the use of peremptory challenges. Although we have recognized that this aspect of the analysis is often a factbound inquiry, [our] precedents establish that, in determining whether a particular action or course of conduct is governmental in character, it is relevant to examine the following: the extent to which the actor relies on governmental assistance and benefits, see *Burton v. Wilmington Parking Authority*, 365 U.S. 715 (1961); whether the actor is performing a traditional governmental function, see *Marsh v. Alabama*, 326 U.S. 501 (1946); and whether the injury caused is aggravated in a unique way by the incidents of governmental authority, see *Shelley v. Kraemer*, 334 U.S. 1 (1948). Based on our application of these three principles to the circumstances here, we hold that the exercise of peremptory challenges by the defendant in the District Court was pursuant to a course of state action.

*** It cannot be disputed that, without the overt, significant participation of the government, the peremptory challenge system, as well as the jury trial system of which it is a part, simply could not exist. As discussed above, peremptory challenges have no utility outside the jury system, a system which the government alone administers. *** The trial judge exercises substantial control over *voir dire* in the federal system. The judge determines the range of information that may be discovered about a prospective juror, and so affects the exercise of both challenges for cause and peremptory challenges. In some cases, judges may even conduct the entire *voir dire* by themselves, a common practice in the District Court where the instant case was tried. The judge oversees the exclusion of jurors for cause, in this way determining which jurors remain eligible for the exercise of peremptory strikes. In cases involving multiple parties, the trial judge decides how peremptory challenges shall be allocated among them. When a lawyer exercises a peremptory challenge, the judge advises the juror he or she has been excused.

As we have outlined here, a private party could not exercise its peremptory challenges absent the overt, significant assistance of the court. The government summons jurors, constrains their freedom of movement, and subjects them to public scrutiny and examination. *** By enforcing a discriminatory peremptory challenge, the court "has not only made itself a party to the [biased act], but has elected to place its power, property and prestige behind the [alleged] discrimination." *Burton v. Wilmington Parking Authority*, 365 U.S., at 725. *** [Reversed and remanded.]

Justice O'CONNOR, with whom THE CHIEF JUSTICE and Justice SCALIA join, dissenting.

The Court concludes that the action of a private attorney exercising a peremptory challenge is attributable to the government and therefore may compose a constitutional violation. This conclusion is based on little more than that the challenge occurs in the course of a trial. Not everything that happens in a courtroom is state action. A trial, particularly a civil trial is by design largely a stage on which private parties may act; it is a forum through which they can resolve their disputes in a peaceful and ordered manner. The government erects the platform; it does not thereby become responsible for all that occurs upon it. As much as we would like to eliminate completely from the courtroom the specter of racial discrimination, the Constitution does not sweep that broadly. Because I believe that a peremptory strike by a private litigant is fundamentally a matter of private choice and not state action, I dissent.

Justice SCALIA, dissenting.

The concrete benefits of the Court's newly discovered constitutional rule are problematic. It will not necessarily be a net help rather than hindrance to minority litigants in obtaining racially diverse juries. In criminal cases, *Batson v. Kentucky*, 476 U.S. 79 (1986), already prevents the *prosecution* from using race-based strikes. The effect of today's decision (which logically must apply to criminal prosecutions) will be to prevent the *defendant* from doing so—so that the minority defendant can no longer seek to prevent an all-white jury, or to seat as many jurors of his own race as possible. To be sure, it is ordinarily more difficult to *prove* race-based strikes of white jurors, but defense counsel can generally be relied upon to do what we say the Constitution requires. So in criminal cases, today's decision represents a net loss to the minority litigant. In civil cases that is probably not true—but it does not represent an unqualified gain either. *Both* sides have peremptory challenges, and they are sometimes used to *assure* rather than to *prevent* a racially diverse jury.

Points for Discussion

a. The Court's Approach

The Court identified three "principles" to help to guide the decision whether a particular course of action was "governmental in character." Which, if any, of these three principles did the Court rely upon in concluding that a private litigant's racially discriminatory exercise of peremptory challenges constitutes state action?

b. Justice O'Connor's Dissent

Did Justice O'Connor disagree with the open-ended standard applied by the Court or just the Court's application of that standard? If the latter, which facts were dispositive in her view?

c. Justice Scalia's Dissent

Justice Scalia's prediction came to pass. In a subsequent case, *Georgia v. McCollum*, 505 U.S. 42, 52 (1992), the Supreme Court extended *Edmonson* and held that a criminal defendant could not use peremptory challenges in a racially discriminatory manner. Can a criminal defendant, on trial by the state, "be fairly said to be a state actor?"

In the previous two cases, in which the Court concluded that private parties and the government were jointly participating in an activity, it was the private party that engaged in the action that allegedly violated someone's constitutional rights. The following case is a "mirror image" joint participation case. Again a private party and the government are ostensibly jointly participating in an activity, but in this case it is the government that takes the action that allegedly violates someone's constitutional rights. In such a case, can the private party be held responsible for the government's action?

National Collegiate Athletic Association v. Tarkanian

488 U.S. 179 (1988)

Justice STEVENS delivered the opinion of the Court.

When he became head basketball coach at the University of Nevada, Las Vegas (UNLV), in 1973, Jerry Tarkanian inherited a team with a mediocre 14-14 record. Four years later the team won 29 out of 32 games and placed third in the championship tournament sponsored by the National Collegiate Athletic Association (NCAA), to which UNLV belongs.

Yet in September 1977 UNLV informed Tarkanian that it was going to suspend him. No dissatisfaction with Tarkanian, once described as "the 'winningest' active basketball coach," motivated his suspension. Rather, the impetus was a report by the NCAA detailing 38 violations of NCAA rules by UNLV personnel, including 10 involving Tarkanian. The NCAA had placed the university's basketball team on probation for two years and ordered UNLV to show cause why the NCAA should not impose further penalties unless UNLV severed all ties during the probation between its intercollegiate athletic program and Tarkanian.

Facing demotion and a drastic cut in pay, Tarkanian brought suit in Nevada state court, alleging that he had been deprived of his Fourteenth Amendment due process rights in violation of 42 U.S.C. § 1983. Ultimately Tarkanian obtained injunctive relief and an award of attorney's fees against both UNLV and the NCAA. NCAA's liability may be upheld only if its participation in the events that led to Tarkanian's suspension constituted "state action" prohibited by the Fourteenth Amendment and was performed "under color of" state law within the meaning of § 1983. We granted certiorari to review the Nevada Supreme Court's holding that the NCAA engaged in state action when it conducted its investigation and recommended that Tarkanian be disciplined. We now reverse.

UNLV is a branch of the University of Nevada, a state-funded institution. The university is organized and operated pursuant to provisions of Nevada's State Constitution, statutes, and regulations. In performing their official functions, the executives of UNLV unquestionably act under color of state law.

The NCAA is an unincorporated association of approximately 960 members, including virtually all public and private universities and 4-year colleges conducting major athletic programs in the United States. Basic policies of the NCAA are determined by the members at annual conventions. Between conventions, the Association is governed by its Council, which appoints various committees to implement specific programs.

One of the NCAA's fundamental policies "is to maintain intercollegiate athletics as an integral part of the educational program and the athlete as an integral part of the student body, and by so doing, retain a clear line of demarcation between college athletics and professional sports." It has therefore adopted rules, which it calls "legislation," governing the conduct of the intercollegiate athletic programs of its members. This NCAA legislation applies to a variety of issues, such as academic standards for eligibility, admissions, financial aid, and the recruiting of student athletes. By joining the NCAA, each member agrees to abide by and to enforce such rules.

The NCAA's bylaws provide that its enforcement program shall be administered by a Committee on Infractions. The Committee supervises an investigative staff, makes factual determinations concerning alleged rule violations, and is expressly authorized to "impose appropriate penalties on a member found to be in violation, or recommend to the Council suspension or termination of membership." In particular, the Committee may order a member institution to show cause why that member should not suffer further penalties unless it imposes a prescribed discipline on an employee; it is not authorized, however, to sanction a member institution's employees directly. The bylaws also provide that representatives of member institutions "are expected to cooperate fully" with the administration of the enforcement program. ***

[From 1972 to 1976, the Committee on Infractions investigated allegations that Tarkanian and others at UNLV had violated NCAA requirements governing the recruitment of student athletes.] It requested UNLV to investigate and provide detailed information concerning each alleged incident. *** With the assistance of the Attorney General of Nevada and private counsel, UNLV conducted a thorough investigation of the charges. On October 27, 1976, it filed a comprehensive response containing voluminous exhibits and sworn affidavits. The response denied all of the allegations and specifically concluded that Tarkanian was completely innocent of wrongdoing. Thereafter, the Committee conducted four days of hearings at which counsel for UNLV and Tarkanian presented their views of the facts and challenged the credibility of the NCAA investigators and their informants. Ultimately the Committee decided that many of the charges could not be supported, but it did find 38 violations of NCAA rules, including 10 committed by Tarkanian. Most serious was the finding that Tarkanian had violated the University's obligation to provide full cooperation with the NCAA investigation. ***

The Committee proposed a series of sanctions against UNLV, including a 2-year period of probation during which its basketball team could not participate in postseason games or appear on television. The Committee also requested UNLV to show cause why additional penalties should not be imposed against UNLV if it failed to discipline Tarkanian by removing him completely from the University's intercollegiate athletic program during the probation period. UNLV appealed most of the Committee's findings and proposed sanctions to the NCAA Council. After hearing arguments from attorneys representing UNLV and Tarkanian, the Council on August 25, 1977, unanimously approved the Committee's investigation and hearing process and adopted all its recommendations.

Promptly after receiving the NCAA report, the president of UNLV directed the University's vice president to schedule a hearing to determine whether the Committee's recommended sanctions should be applied. Tarkanian and UNLV were represented at that hearing; the NCAA was not. Although the vice president expressed doubt concerning the sufficiency of the evidence supporting the Committee's findings, he concluded that "given the terms of our adherence to the NCAA we cannot substitute—biased as we must be—our own judgment on the credibility of witnesses for that of the infractions committee and the Council." With respect to the proposed sanctions, he advised the president that he had three options:

> "1. Reject the sanction requiring us to disassociate Coach Tarkanian from the athletic program and take the risk of still heavier sanctions, *e.g.,* possible extra years of probation.
>
> 2. Recognize the University's delegation to the NCAA of the power to act as ultimate arbiter of these matters, thus reassigning Mr. Tarkanian from his present position—though tenured and without adequate notice—even while believing that the NCAA was wrong.
>
> 3. Pull out of the NCAA completely on the grounds that you will not execute what you hold to be their unjust judgments."

Pursuant to the vice president's recommendation, the president accepted the second option and notified Tarkanian that he was to "be completely severed of any and all relations, formal or informal, with the University's Intercollegiate athletic program during the period of the University's NCAA probation."

The day before his suspension was to become effective, Tarkanian filed an action in Nevada state court for declaratory and injunctive relief ***. [After lengthy proceedings, the state courts concluded that the suspension violated the Due Process Clause of the Fourteenth Amendment. The courts enjoined UNLV from suspending Tarkanian and enjoined the NCAA from conducting "any further proceedings against the University," from enforcing its show-cause order, and from taking any other action against the University. The Nevada trial court also awarded Tarkanian attorney's fees of almost $196,000, of which the NCAA had to pay 90%. The NCAA challenged its liability on grounds that it was not a state actor.]

> **Food for Thought**
>
> The state court held that both UNLV and the NCAA had violated Tarkanian's rights. But only the NCAA sought review in the Supreme Court. Why didn't UNLV seek review of the judgment, as well?

In the typical case raising a state-action issue, a private party has taken the decisive step that caused the harm to the plaintiff, and the question is whether the State was sufficiently involved to treat that decisive conduct as state action. *** Thus, in the usual case we ask whether the State provided a mantle of authority that enhanced the power of the harm-causing individual actor.

This case uniquely mirrors the traditional state-action case. Here the final act challenged by Tarkanian—his suspension—was committed by UNLV. A state university without question is a state actor. When it decides to impose a serious disciplinary sanction upon one of its tenured employees, it must comply with the terms of the Due Process Clause of the Fourteenth Amendment ***. Thus when UNLV notified Tarkanian that he was being separated from all relations with the university's basketball program, it acted under color of state law within the meaning of 42 U.S.C. § 1983.

> **Make the Connection**
>
> We considered the doctrine of "procedural due process," and its application to state efforts to terminate employees, in Chapter 9.

The mirror image presented in this case requires us to step through an analytical looking glass to resolve the case. Clearly UNLV's conduct was influenced by the rules and recommendations of the NCAA, the private party. But it was UNLV, the state entity, that actually suspended Tarkanian. Thus the question is not whether UNLV participated to a critical extent in the NCAA's activities, but whether UNLV's actions in compliance with the NCAA rules and recommendations turned the NCAA's conduct into state action.

We examine first the relationship between UNLV and the NCAA regarding the NCAA's rulemaking. UNLV is among the NCAA's members and participated in promulgating the

Association's rules; it must be assumed, therefore, that Nevada had some impact on the NCAA's policy determinations. Yet the NCAA's several hundred other public and private member institutions each similarly affected those policies. Those institutions, the vast majority of which were located in States other than Nevada, did not act under color of Nevada law. It necessarily follows that the source of the legislation adopted by the NCAA is not Nevada but the collective membership, speaking through an organization that is independent of any particular State.

Tarkanian further asserts that the NCAA's investigation, enforcement proceedings, and consequent recommendations constituted state action because they resulted from a delegation of power by UNLV. UNLV, as an NCAA member, subscribed to the statement in the Association's bylaws that NCAA "enforcement procedures are an essential part of the intercollegiate athletic program of each member institution." It is, of course, true that a State may delegate authority to a private party and thereby make that party a state actor. Thus, we recently held that a private physician who had contracted with a state prison to attend to the inmates' medical needs was a state actor. *West v. Atkins*, 487 U.S. 42 (1988). But UNLV delegated no power to the NCAA to take specific action against any university employee. The commitment by UNLV to adhere to NCAA enforcement procedures was enforceable only by sanctions that the NCAA might impose on UNLV itself.

Indeed, the notion that UNLV's promise to cooperate in the NCAA enforcement proceedings was tantamount to a partnership agreement or the transfer of certain university powers to the NCAA is belied by the history of this case. It is quite obvious that UNLV used its best efforts to retain its winning coach—a goal diametrically opposed to the NCAA's interest in ascertaining the truth of its investigators' reports. During the several years that the NCAA investigated the alleged violations, the NCAA and UNLV acted much more like adversaries than like partners engaged in a dispassionate search for the truth. The NCAA cannot be regarded as an agent of UNLV for purposes of that proceeding. It is more correctly characterized as an agent of its remaining members which, as competitors of UNLV, had an interest in the effective and evenhanded enforcement of the NCAA's recruitment standards. Just as a state-compensated public defender acts in a private capacity when he or she represents a private client in a conflict against the State, *Polk County v. Dodson*, 454 U.S. 312, 320 (1981), the NCAA is properly viewed as a private actor at odds with the State when it represents the interests of its entire membership in an investigation of one public university.

Finally, Tarkanian argues that the power of the NCAA is so great that [UNLV] had no practical alternative to compliance with its demands. We are not at all sure this is true, but even if we assume that a private monopolist can impose its will on a state agency by a threatened refusal to deal with it, it does not follow that such a private party is therefore acting under color of state law.

In final analysis the question is whether "the conduct allegedly causing the deprivation of a federal right [can] be fairly attributable to the State." *Lugar v. Edmondson Oil Co.*, 457 U.S. 922, 937 (1982). It would be ironic indeed to conclude that the NCAA's imposition of sanctions against UNLV—sanctions that UNLV and its counsel, including the Attorney

General of Nevada, steadfastly opposed during protracted adversary proceedings—is fairly attributable to the State of Nevada. It would be more appropriate to conclude that UNLV has conducted its athletic program under color of the policies adopted by the NCAA, rather than that those policies were developed and enforced under color of Nevada law. [Reversed and remanded.]

Justice WHITE, with whom Justice BRENNAN, Justice MARSHALL, and Justice O'CONNOR join, dissenting.

*** Had UNLV refused to suspend Tarkanian, and the NCAA responded by imposing sanctions against UNLV, it would be hard indeed to find any state action that harmed Tarkanian. But that is not this case. Here, UNLV did suspend Tarkanian, and it did so because it embraced the NCAA rules governing conduct of its athletic program and adopted the results of the hearings conducted by the NCAA concerning Tarkanian, as it had agreed that it would. Under these facts, I would find that the NCAA acted jointly with UNLV and therefore is a state actor.

Points for Discussion

a. Opposing Goals

The Court concluded in *Tarkanian* that the NCAA was not a state actor, even though it jointly engaged in some activity with UNLV, because the NCAA and UNLV were diametrically opposed to each other in their goals. Suppose that the university's leadership had in fact been appalled by Coach Tarkanian's alleged misconduct and wanted to oust him from his position to remove a stain on the university's name, even if the consequence would be a less powerful basketball program. (Remember, anything is possible in a hypothetical question.) Would the case have come out differently?

b. Another Mirror Image Case

In *Dennis v. Sparks*, 449 U.S. 24 (1980), the Duval County Ranch Company bribed a Texas state judge to issue an injunction preventing Orville Dennis from producing oil on his property. When Dennis learned of the bribery, he sued the company, its owners, and the judge under 42 U.S.C. § 1983, claiming that through the bribery they had conspired to deprive him of his right to due process under the Fourteenth Amendment. The private parties argued that they could not have deprived Dennis of his right to due process because they were not state actors. But the Supreme Court concluded:

> [T]o act "under color of" state law for § 1983 purposes does not require that the defendant be an officer of the State. It is enough that he is a willful participant in joint action with the State or its agents. [H]ere the allegations were that an official act of the defendant judge was the product of a corrupt conspiracy involving bribery of the judge. Under these allegations, the private parties conspiring with the judge were acting under color of state law; and it is of no consequence in this respect that the judge himself is immune from damages liability.

Id. at 28. In what way was *Dennis* a "mirror image" joint participation case? Why was the result different from the result in *Tarkanian*?

———————

Executive Summary of This Chapter

The **state action doctrine** recognizes that the Constitution restrains the actions of federal, state, and local governments and government officials, but generally does not limit the actions of private individuals and corporations. *The Civil Rights Cases,* 109 U.S. 3 (1883).

The **public function exception** to the state action doctrine requires courts to apply constitutional limitations to private entities when they engage in functions traditionally exclusively reserved to the government. Under this doctrine, the Court has held that a company town must afford speakers the protection of the First Amendment, *Marsh v. State of Alabama,* 326 U.S. 501 (1946), but that a shopping center need not, *Hudgens v. NLRB,* 424 U.S. 507 (1976).

The **judicial enforcement exception** to the state action doctrine says that a court's enforcement of a private agreement may constitute state action. Accordingly, judicial enforcement of a restrictive covenant that requires a party to discriminate on the basis of race violates the Fourteenth Amendment. *Shelley v. Kraemer,* 334 U.S. 1 (1948). But the Supreme Court has not extended this rationale to its logical limits, perhaps because any private action could be upheld by a court and thus transformed into state action.

The **joint participation** exception (sometimes called the **entanglement exception**) to the state action doctrine provides that a private party may be held liable for a deprivation of a right if two elements are present: (1) the deprivation is caused by the exercise of some right or privilege created by the State or by a rule of conduct imposed by the state or by a person for whom the State is responsible; and (2) the party charged with the deprivation must be a person who may fairly be said to be a state actor. *Lugar v. Edmondson Oil Co.,* 457 U.S. 922, 937 (1982). Whether someone can "fairly be said to be a state actor" depends on all the facts and circumstances. Applying this test, the Court has concluded that a private litigant who exercised a peremptory challenge in a racially discriminatory fashion engaged in state action. *See id.* Similarly, a private restaurant that had a lease in a government-owned building was deemed to be a state actor when it discriminated against a customer. *Burton v. Wilmington Parking Authority,* 365 U.S. 715 (1961). But a private intercollegiate sports organization was deemed not to be a state actor, even though it jointly acted with a state university, because the two institutions had opposing goals. *National Collegiate Athletic Association v. Tarkanian,* 488 U.S. 179 (1988).

———————

The Constitution of the United States of America

We the People of the United States, in Order to form a more perfect Union, establish Justice, insure domestic Tranquility, provide for the common defence, promote the general Welfare, and secure the Blessings of Liberty to ourselves and our Posterity, do ordain and establish this Constitution for the United States of America.

ARTICLE I

SECTION 1. All legislative Powers herein granted shall be vested in a Congress of the United States, which shall consist of a Senate and House of Representatives.

SECTION 2. [1] The House of Representatives shall be composed of Members chosen every second Year by the People of the several States, and the Electors in each State shall have the Qualifications requisite for Electors of the most numerous Branch of the State Legislature.

[2] No Person shall be a Representative who shall not have attained to the Age of twenty five Years, and been seven Years a Citizen of the United States, and who shall not, when elected, be an Inhabitant of that State in which he shall be chosen.

[3] [Representatives and direct Taxes shall be apportioned among the several States which may be included within this Union, according to their respective Numbers, which shall be determined by adding to the whole Number of free Persons, including those bound to Service for a Term of Years, and excluding Indians not taxed, three fifths of all other Persons.] The actual Enumeration shall be made within three Years after the first Meeting of the Congress of the United States, and within every subsequent Term of ten Years, in such Manner as they shall by Law direct. The Number of Representatives shall not exceed one for every thirty Thousand, but each State shall have at Least one Representative; and until such enumeration shall be made, the State of New Hampshire shall be entitled to chuse three, Massachusetts eight, Rhode-Island and Providence Plantations one, Connecticut five, New-York six, New Jersey four, Pennsylvania eight, Delaware one, Maryland six, Virginia ten, North Carolina five, South Carolina five, and Georgia three.

Take Note

The bracketed text has been modified by Section 2 of the Fourteenth Amendment.

[4] When vacancies happen in the Representation from any State, the Executive Authority thereof shall issue Writs of Election to fill such Vacancies.

[5] The House of Representatives shall chuse their Speaker and other Officers; and shall have the sole Power of Impeachment.

SECTION 3. [1] The Senate of the United States shall be composed of two Senators from each State, [chosen by the Legislature thereof for six Years]; and each Senator shall have one Vote.

Take Note

The bracketed text in the first two clauses of Section 3 has been modified by the Seventeenth Amendment.

[2] Immediately after they shall be assembled in Consequence of the first Election, they shall be divided as equally as may be into three Classes. The Seats of the Senators of the first Class shall be vacated at the Expiration of the second Year, of the second Class at the Expiration of the fourth Year, and of the third Class at the Expiration of the sixth Year, so that one third may be chosen every second Year; [and if Vacancies happen by Resignation, or otherwise, during the Recess of the Legislature of any State, the Executive thereof may make temporary Appointments until the next Meeting of the Legislature, which shall then fill such Vacancies.]

[3] No Person shall be a Senator who shall not have attained to the Age of thirty Years, and been nine Years a Citizen of the United States, and who shall not, when elected, be an Inhabitant of that State for which he shall be chosen.

[4] The Vice President of the United States shall be President of the Senate, but shall have no Vote, unless they be equally divided.

[5] The Senate shall chuse their other Officers, and also a President pro tempore, in the Absence of the Vice President, or when he shall exercise the Office of President of the United States.

[6] The Senate shall have the sole Power to try all Impeachments. When sitting for that Purpose, they shall be on Oath or Affirmation. When the President of the United States is tried, the Chief Justice shall preside: And no Person shall be convicted without the Concurrence of two thirds of the Members present.

[7] Judgment in Cases of Impeachment shall not extend further than to removal from Office, and disqualification to hold and enjoy any Office of honor, Trust or Profit under the United States: but the Party convicted shall nevertheless be liable and subject to Indictment, Trial, Judgment and Punishment, according to Law.

SECTION 4. [1] The Times, Places and Manner of holding Elections for Senators and Representatives, shall be prescribed in each State by the Legislature thereof; but the Congress may at any time by Law make or alter such Regulations, except as to the Places of chusing Senators.

[2] The Congress shall assemble at least once in every Year, and such Meeting shall be [on the first Monday in December], unless they shall by Law appoint a different Day.

Take Note

The bracketed text has been modified by Section 2 of the Twentieth Amendment.

Section 5. [1] Each House shall be the Judge of the Elections, Returns and Qualifications of its own Members, and a Majority of each shall constitute a Quorum to do Business; but a smaller Number may adjourn from day to day, and may be authorized to compel the Attendance of absent Members, in such Manner, and under such Penalties as each House may provide.

[2] Each House may determine the Rules of its Proceedings, punish its Members for disorderly Behaviour, and, with the Concurrence of two thirds, expel a Member.

[3] Each House shall keep a Journal of its Proceedings, and from time to time publish the same, excepting such Parts as may in their Judgment require Secrecy; and the Yeas and Nays of the Members of either House on any question shall, at the Desire of one fifth of those Present, be entered on the Journal.

[4] Neither House, during the Session of Congress, shall, without the Consent of the other, adjourn for more than three days, nor to any other Place than that in which the two Houses shall be sitting.

Section 6. [1] The Senators and Representatives shall receive a Compensation for their Services, to be ascertained by Law, and paid out of the Treasury of the United States. They shall in all Cases, except Treason, Felony and Breach of the Peace, be privileged from Arrest during their Attendance at the Session of their respective Houses, and in going to and returning from the same; and for any Speech or Debate in either House, they shall not be questioned in any other Place.

[2] No Senator or Representative shall, during the Time for which he was elected, be appointed to any civil Office under the Authority of the United States, which shall have been created, or the Emoluments whereof shall have been encreased during such time; and no Person holding any Office under the United States, shall be a Member of either House during his Continuance in Office.

Section 7. [1] All Bills for raising Revenue shall originate in the House of Representatives; but the Senate may propose or concur with Amendments as on other Bills.

[2] Every Bill which shall have passed the House of Representatives and the Senate, shall, before it become a Law, be presented to the President of the United States: If he approve he shall sign it, but if not he shall return it, with his Objections to that House in which it shall have originated, who shall enter the Objections at large on their Journal, and proceed to reconsider it. If after such Reconsideration two thirds of that House shall agree to pass the Bill, it shall be sent, together with the Objections, to the other House, by which it shall likewise be reconsidered, and if approved by two thirds of that House, it shall become a Law. But in all such Cases the Votes of both Houses shall be determined by yeas and Nays, and the Names of the Persons voting for and against the Bill shall be entered on the Journal of each House respectively. If any Bill shall not be returned by the President within ten Days (Sundays excepted) after it shall have been presented to him, the Same shall be a Law, in like Manner as if he had signed it, unless the Congress by their Adjournment prevent its Return, in which Case it shall not be a Law.

[3] Every Order, Resolution, or Vote to which the Concurrence of the Senate and House of Representatives may be necessary (except on a question of Adjournment) shall be presented to the President of the United States; and before the Same shall take Effect, shall be approved by him, or being disapproved by him, shall be repassed by two thirds of the Senate and House of Representatives, according to the Rules and Limitations prescribed in the Case of a Bill.

SECTION 8. [1] The Congress shall have Power To lay and collect Taxes, Duties, Imposts and Excises, to pay the Debts and provide for the common Defence and general Welfare of the United States; but all Duties, Imposts and Excises shall be uniform throughout the United States;

[2] To borrow Money on the credit of the United States;

[3] To regulate Commerce with foreign Nations, and among the several States, and with the Indian Tribes;

[4] To establish an uniform Rule of Naturalization, and uniform Laws on the subject of Bankruptcies throughout the United States;

[5] To coin Money, regulate the Value thereof, and of foreign Coin, and fix the Standard of Weights and Measures;

[6] To provide for the Punishment of counterfeiting the Securities and current Coin of the United States;

[7] To establish Post Offices and post Roads;

[8] To promote the Progress of Science and useful Arts, by securing for limited Times to Authors and Inventors the exclusive Right to their respective Writings and Discoveries;

[9] To constitute Tribunals inferior to the supreme Court;

[10] To define and punish Piracies and Felonies committed on the high Seas, and Offences against the Law of Nations;

[11] To declare War, grant Letters of Marque and Reprisal, and make Rules concerning Captures on Land and Water;

[12] To raise and support Armies, but no Appropriation of Money to that Use shall be for a longer Term than two Years;

[13] To provide and maintain a Navy;

[14] To make Rules for the Government and Regulation of the land and naval Forces;

[15] To provide for calling forth the Militia to execute the Laws of the Union, suppress Insurrections and repel Invasions;

[16] To provide for organizing, arming, and disciplining, the Militia, and for governing such Part of them as may be employed in the Service of the United States, reserving to the States respectively, the Appointment of the Officers, and the Authority of training the

Militia according to the discipline prescribed by Congress;

[17] To exercise exclusive Legislation in all Cases whatsoever, over such District (not exceeding ten Miles square) as may, by Cession of particular States, and the Acceptance of Congress, become the Seat of the Government of the United States, and to exercise like Authority over all Places purchased by the Consent of the Legislature of the State in which the Same shall be, for the Erection of Forts, Magazines, Arsenals, dock-Yards, and other needful Buildings;—And

[18] To make all Laws which shall be necessary and proper for carrying into Execution the foregoing Powers, and all other Powers vested by this Constitution in the Government of the United States, or in any Department or Officer thereof.

Section 9. [1] The Migration or Importation of such Persons as any of the States now existing shall think proper to admit, shall not be prohibited by the Congress prior to the Year one thousand eight hundred and eight, but a Tax or duty may be imposed on such Importation, not exceeding ten dollars for each Person.

[2] The Privilege of the Writ of Habeas Corpus shall not be suspended, unless when in Cases of Rebellion or Invasion the public Safety may require it.

[3] No Bill of Attainder or ex post facto Law shall be passed.

Take Note

The bracketed text has been modified by the Sixteenth Amendment.

[4] No Capitation, or other direct, Tax shall be laid, [unless in Proportion to the Census or enumeration herein before directed to be taken.]

[5] No Tax or Duty shall be laid on Articles exported from any State.

[6] No Preference shall be given by any Regulation of Commerce or Revenue to the Ports of one State over those of another; nor shall Vessels bound to, or from, one State, be obliged to enter, clear, or pay Duties in another.

[7] No Money shall be drawn from the Treasury, but in Consequence of Appropriations made by Law; and a regular Statement and Account of the Receipts and Expenditures of all public Money shall be published from time to time.

[8] No Title of Nobility shall be granted by the United States: And no Person holding any Office of Profit or Trust under them, shall, without the Consent of the Congress, accept of any present, Emolument, Office, or Title, of any kind whatever, from any King, Prince, or foreign State.

Section 10. [1] No State shall enter into any Treaty, Alliance, or Confederation; grant Letters of Marque and Reprisal; coin Money; emit Bills of Credit; make any Thing but gold and silver Coin a Tender in Payment of Debts; pass any Bill of Attainder, ex post facto Law, or Law impairing the Obligation of Contracts, or grant any Title of Nobility.

[2] No State shall, without the Consent of the Congress, lay any Imposts or Duties on

Imports or Exports, except what may be absolutely necessary for executing [its] inspection Laws: and the net Produce of all Duties and Imposts, laid by any State on Imports or Exports, shall be for the Use of the Treasury of the United States; and all such Laws shall be subject to the Revision and Controul of the Congress.

[3] No State shall, without the Consent of Congress, lay any Duty of Tonnage, keep Troops, or Ships of War in time of Peace, enter into any Agreement or Compact with another State, or with a foreign Power, or engage in War, unless actually invaded, or in such imminent Danger as will not admit of delay.

ARTICLE II

SECTION 1. [1] The executive Power shall be vested in a President of the United States of America. He shall hold his Office during the Term of four Years, and, together with the Vice President, chosen for the same Term, be elected, as follows:

[2] Each State shall appoint, in such Manner as the Legislature thereof may direct, a Number of Electors, equal to the whole Number of Senators and Representatives to which the State may be entitled in the Congress: but no Senator or Representative, or Person holding an Office of Trust or Profit under the United States, shall be appointed an Elector.

[3] [The Electors shall meet in their respective States, and vote by Ballot for two Persons, of whom one at least shall not be an Inhabitant of the same State with themselves. And they shall make a List of all the Persons voted for, and of the Number of Votes for each; which List they shall sign and certify, and transmit sealed to the Seat of the Government of the United States, directed to the President of the Senate. The President of the Senate shall, in the Presence of the Senate and House of Representatives, open all the Certificates, and the Votes shall then be counted. The Person having the greatest Number of Votes shall be the President, if such Number be a Majority of the whole Number of Electors appointed; and if there be more than one who have such Majority, and have an equal Number of Votes, then the House of Representatives shall immediately chuse by Ballot one of them for President; and if no Person have a Majority, then from the five highest on the List the said House shall in like Manner chuse the President. But in chusing the President, the Votes shall be taken by States, the Representation from each State having one Vote; A quorum for this purpose shall consist of a Member or Members from two thirds of the States, and a Majority of all the States shall be necessary to a Choice. In every Case, after the Choice of the President, the Person having the greatest Number of Votes of the Electors shall be the Vice President. But if there should remain two or more who have equal Votes, the Senate shall chuse from them by Ballot the Vice President.]

Take Note

The bracketed text has been superseded by the Twelfth Amendment, part of which in turn was modified by Section 3 of the Twentieth Amendment.

[4] The Congress may determine the Time of chusing the Electors, and the Day on which they shall give their Votes; which Day shall be the same throughout the United States.

[5] No Person except a natural born Citizen, or a Citizen of the United States, at the time of the Adoption of this Constitution, shall be eligible to the Office of President; neither shall any Person be eligible to that Office who shall not have attained to the Age of thirty five Years, and been fourteen Years a Resident within the United States.

[6] [In Case of the Removal of the President from Office, or of his Death, Resignation, or Inability to discharge the Powers and Duties of the said Office, the Same shall devolve on the Vice President, and the Congress may by Law provide for the Case of Removal, Death, Resignation or Inability, both of the President and Vice President, declaring what Officer shall then act as President, and such Officer shall act accordingly, until the Disability be removed, or a President shall be elected.]

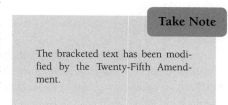

Take Note

The bracketed text has been modified by the Twenty-Fifth Amendment.

[7] The President shall, at stated Times, receive for his Services, a Compensation, which shall neither be increased nor diminished during the Period for which he shall have been elected, and he shall not receive within that Period any other Emolument from the United States, or any of them.

[8] Before he enter on the Execution of his Office, he shall take the following Oath or Affirmation:—"I do solemnly swear (or affirm) that I will faithfully execute the Office of President of the United States, and will to the best of my Ability, preserve, protect and defend the Constitution of the United States."

SECTION 2. [1] The President shall be Commander in Chief of the Army and Navy of the United States, and of the Militia of the several States, when called into the actual Service of the United States; he may require the Opinion, in writing, of the principal Officer in each of the executive Departments, upon any Subject relating to the Duties of their respective Offices, and he shall have Power to grant Reprieves and Pardons for Offences against the United States, except in Cases of Impeachment.

[2] He shall have Power, by and with the Advice and Consent of the Senate, to make Treaties, provided two thirds of the Senators present concur; and he shall nominate, and by and with the Advice and Consent of the Senate, shall appoint Ambassadors, other public Ministers and Consuls, Judges of the supreme Court, and all other Officers of the United States, whose Appointments are not herein otherwise provided for, and which shall be established by Law: but the Congress may by Law vest the Appointment of such inferior Officers, as they think proper, in the President alone, in the Courts of Law, or in the Heads of Departments.

[3] The President shall have Power to fill up all Vacancies that may happen during the Recess of the Senate, by granting Commissions which shall expire at the End of their next Session.

SECTION 3. He shall from time to time give to the Congress Information of the State of the Union, and recommend to their Consideration such Measures as he shall judge necessary and expedient; he may, on extraordinary Occasions, convene both Houses, or either of them, and in Case of Disagreement between them, with Respect to the Time of Adjournment, he may adjourn them to such Time as he shall think proper; he shall receive Ambassadors and other public Ministers; he shall take Care that the Laws be faithfully executed, and shall Commission all the Officers of the United States.

SECTION 4.   The President, Vice President and all civil Officers of the United States, shall be removed from Office on Impeachment for, and Conviction of, Treason, Bribery, or other high Crimes and Misdemeanors.

ARTICLE III

SECTION 1.   The judicial Power of the United States shall be vested in one supreme Court, and in such inferior Courts as the Congress may from time to time ordain and establish.   The Judges, both of the supreme and inferior Courts, shall hold their Offices during good Behaviour, and shall, at stated Times, receive for their Services a Compensation, which shall not be diminished during their Continuance in Office.

SECTION 2.   [1] The judicial Power shall extend to all Cases, in Law and Equity, arising under this Constitution, the Laws of the United States, and Treaties made, or which shall be made, under their Authority;—to all Cases affecting Ambassadors, other public Ministers and Consuls;—to all Cases of admiralty and maritime Jurisdiction;—to Controversies to which the United States shall be a Party;—to Controversies between two or more States;[—between a State and Citizens of another State;]—between Citizens of different States;—between Citizens of the same State claiming Lands under Grants of different States, [and between a State, or the Citizens thereof, and foreign States, Citizens or Subjects.]

Take Note

The bracketed text has been modified by the Eleventh Amendment.

[2] In all Cases affecting Ambassadors, other public Ministers and Consuls, and those in which a State shall be Party, the supreme Court shall have original Jurisdiction.   In all the other Cases before mentioned, the supreme Court shall have appellate Jurisdiction, both as to Law and Fact, with such Exceptions, and under such Regulations as the Congress shall make.

[3] The Trial of all Crimes, except in Cases of Impeachment, shall be by Jury; and such Trial shall be held in the State where the said Crimes shall have been committed; but when not committed within any State, the Trial shall be at such Place or Places as the Congress may by Law have directed.

SECTION 3.   [1] Treason against the United States, shall consist only in levying War against them, or in adhering to their Enemies, giving them Aid and Comfort.   No Person shall be convicted of Treason unless on the Testimony of two Witnesses to the same overt Act, or on Confession in open Court.

[2] The Congress shall have Power to declare the Punishment of Treason, but no Attainder of Treason shall work Corruption of Blood, or Forfeiture except during the Life of the Person attainted.

ARTICLE IV

SECTION 1. Full Faith and Credit shall be given in each State to the public Acts, Records, and judicial Proceedings of every other State. And the Congress may by general Laws prescribe the Manner in which such Acts, Records and Proceedings shall be proved, and the Effect thereof.

SECTION 2. [1] The Citizens of each State shall be entitled to all Privileges and Immunities of Citizens in the several States.

[2] A Person charged in any State with Treason, Felony, or other Crime, who shall flee from Justice, and be found in another State, shall on Demand of the executive Authority of the State from which he fled, be delivered up, to be removed to the State having Jurisdiction of the Crime.

[3] [No Person held to Service or Labour in one State, under the Laws thereof, escaping into another, shall, in Consequence of any Law or Regulation therein, be discharged from such Service or Labour, but shall be delivered up on Claim of the Party to whom such Service or Labour may be due.]

> **Take Note**
>
> The bracketed text has been superseded by the Thirteenth Amendment.

SECTION 3. [1] New States may be admitted by the Congress into this Union; but no new State shall be formed or erected within the Jurisdiction of any other State; nor any State be formed by the Junction of two or more States, or Parts of States, without the Consent of the Legislatures of the States concerned as well as of the Congress.

[2] The Congress shall have Power to dispose of and make all needful Rules and Regulations respecting the Territory or other Property belonging to the United States; and nothing in this Constitution shall be so construed as to Prejudice any Claims of the United States, or of any particular State.

SECTION 4. The United States shall guarantee to every State in this Union a Republican Form of Government, and shall protect each of them against Invasion; and on Application of the Legislature, or of the Executive (when the Legislature cannot be convened), against domestic Violence.

ARTICLE V

The Congress, whenever two thirds of both Houses shall deem it necessary, shall propose Amendments to this Constitution, or, on the Application of the Legislatures of two thirds of the several States, shall call a Convention for proposing Amendments, which, in either Case, shall be valid to all Intents and Purposes, as Part of this Constitution, when ratified by the Legislatures of three fourths of the several States, or by Conventions in three fourths thereof, as the one or the other Mode of Ratification may be proposed by the Congress; Provided that no Amendment which may be made prior to the Year One thousand eight hundred and eight shall in any Manner affect the first and fourth Clauses in the Ninth

Section of the first Article; and that no State, without its Consent, shall be deprived of its equal Suffrage in the Senate.

ARTICLE VI

[1] All Debts contracted and Engagements entered into, before the Adoption of this Constitution, shall be as valid against the United States under this Constitution, as under the Confederation.

[2] This Constitution, and the Laws of the United States which shall be made in Pursuance thereof; and all Treaties made, or which shall be made, under the Authority of the United States, shall be the supreme Law of the Land; and the Judges in every State shall be bound thereby, any Thing in the Constitution or Laws of any State to the Contrary notwithstanding.

[3] The Senators and Representatives before mentioned, and the Members of the several State Legislatures, and all executive and judicial Officers, both of the United States and of the several States, shall be bound by Oath or Affirmation, to support this Constitution; but no religious Test shall ever be required as a Qualification to any Office or public Trust under the United States.

ARTICLE VII

The Ratification of the Conventions of nine States, shall be sufficient for the Establishment of this Constitution between the States so ratifying the Same.

ARTICLES IN ADDITION TO, AND AMENDMENT OF THE CONSTITUTION OF THE UNITED STATES OF AMERICA, PROPOSED BY CONGRESS, AND RATIFIED BY THE LEGISLATURES OF THE SEVERAL STATES, PURSUANT TO THE FIFTH ARTICLE OF THE ORIGINAL CONSTITUTION:

AMENDMENT I [1791]

Congress shall make no law respecting an establishment of religion, or prohibiting the free exercise thereof; or abridging the freedom of speech, or of the press; or the right of the people peaceably to assemble, and to petition the Government for a redress of grievances.

AMENDMENT II [1791]

A well regulated Militia, being necessary to the security of a free State, the right of the people to keep and bear Arms, shall not be infringed.

AMENDMENT III [1791]

No Soldier shall, in time of peace be quartered in any house, without the consent of the Owner, nor in time of war, but in a manner to be prescribed by law.

Food for Thought

The Amendments are listed at the end of the text of the original document. Would it matter, for purposes of interpreting the Constitution, if instead the text of the Amendments were integrated with the language of the original document, in the relevant provisions? For example, would it matter if the text of the Eleventh Amendment were incorporated into Section 2 of Article 3, rather than simply included here at the end?

AMENDMENT IV [1791]

The right of the people to be secure in their persons, houses, papers, and effects, against unreasonable searches and seizures, shall not be violated, and no Warrants shall issue, but upon probable cause, supported by Oath or affirmation, and particularly describing the place to be searched, and the persons or things to be seized.

AMENDMENT V [1791]

No person shall be held to answer for a capital, or otherwise infamous crime, unless on a presentment or indictment of a Grand Jury, except in cases arising in the land or naval forces, or in the Militia, when in actual service in time of War or public danger; nor shall any person be subject for the same offence to be twice put in jeopardy of life or limb; nor shall be compelled in any criminal case to be a witness against himself, nor be deprived of life, liberty, or property, without due process of law; nor shall private property be taken for public use, without just compensation.

AMENDMENT VI [1791]

In all criminal prosecutions, the accused shall enjoy the right to a speedy and public trial, by an impartial jury of the State and district wherein the crime shall have been committed, which district shall have been previously ascertained by law, and to be informed of the nature and cause of the accusation; to be confronted with the witnesses against him; to have compulsory process for obtaining witnesses in his favor, and to have the Assistance of Counsel for his defence.

AMENDMENT VII [1791]

In Suits at common law, where the value in controversy shall exceed twenty dollars, the right of trial by jury shall be preserved, and no fact tried by a jury, shall be otherwise re-examined in any Court of the United States, than according to the rules of the common law.

AMENDMENT VIII [1791]

Excessive bail shall not be required, nor excessive fines imposed, nor cruel and unusual punishments inflicted.

AMENDMENT IX [1791]

The enumeration in the Constitution, of certain rights, shall not be construed to deny or disparage others retained by the people.

AMENDMENT X [1791]

The powers not delegated to the United States by the Constitution, nor prohibited by it to the States, are reserved to the States respectively, or to the people.

AMENDMENT XI [1798]

The Judicial power of the United States shall not be construed to extend to any suit in law or equity, commenced or prosecuted against one of the United States by Citizens of another State, or by Citizens or Subjects of any Foreign State.

AMENDMENT XII [1804]

The Electors shall meet in their respective states and vote by ballot for President and Vice-President, one of whom, at least, shall not be an inhabitant of the same state with themselves; they shall name in their ballots the person voted for as President, and in distinct ballots the person voted for as Vice-President, and they shall make distinct lists of all persons voted for as President, and of all persons voted for as Vice-President, and of the number of votes for each, which lists they shall sign and certify, and transmit sealed to the seat of the government of the United States, directed to the President of the Senate;—the President of the Senate shall, in the presence of the Senate and House of Representatives, open all the certificates and the votes shall then be counted;—The person having the greatest number of votes for President, shall be the President, if such number be a majority of the whole number of Electors appointed; and if no person have such majority, then from the persons having the highest numbers not exceeding three on the list of those voted for as President, the House of Representatives shall choose immediately, by ballot, the President. But in choosing the President, the votes shall be taken by states, the representation from each state having one vote; a quorum for this purpose shall consist of a member or members from two-thirds of the states, and a majority of all the states shall be necessary to a choice. [And if the House of Representatives shall not choose a President whenever the right of choice shall devolve upon them, before the fourth day of March next following, then the Vice-President shall act as President, as in case of the death or other constitutional disability of the President.] The person having the greatest number of votes as Vice-President, shall be the Vice-President, if such number be a majority of the whole number of Electors appointed, and if no person have a majority, then from the two highest numbers on the list, the Senate shall choose the Vice-President; a quorum for the purpose shall consist of two-thirds of the whole number of Senators, and a majority of the whole number shall be necessary to a choice. But no person constitutionally ineligible to the office of President shall be eligible to that of Vice-President of the United States.

> **Take Note**
>
> The bracketed text has been superseded by the Twentieth Amendment.

AMENDMENT XIII [1865]

SECTION 1. Neither slavery nor involuntary servitude, except as a punishment for crime whereof the party shall have been duly convicted, shall exist within the United States, or any place subject to their jurisdiction.

SECTION 2. Congress shall have power to enforce this article by appropriate legislation.

AMENDMENT XIV [1868]

SECTION 1. All persons born or naturalized in the United States, and subject to the jurisdiction thereof, are citizens of the United States and of the State wherein they reside. No State shall make or enforce any law which shall abridge the privileges or immunities of citizens of the United States; nor shall any State deprive any person of life, liberty, or property, without due process of law; nor deny to any person within its jurisdiction the equal protection of the laws.

SECTION 2. Representatives shall be apportioned among the several States according to their respective numbers, counting the whole number of persons in each State, excluding Indians not taxed. [But when the right to vote at any election for the choice of electors for President and Vice-President of the United States, Representatives in Congress, the Executive and Judicial officers of a State, or the members of the Legislature thereof, is denied to any of the male inhabitants of such State, being twenty-one years of age, and citizens of the United States, or in any way abridged, except for participation in rebellion, or other crime, the basis of representation therein shall be reduced in the proportion which the number of such male citizens shall bear to the whole number of male citizens twenty-one years of age in such State.]

Take Note

The bracketed text has been modified by the Twenty-Sixth Amendment.

SECTION 3. No person shall be a Senator or Representative in Congress, or elector of President and Vice-President, or hold any office, civil or military, under the United States, or under any State, who, having previously taken an oath, as a member of Congress, or as an officer of the United States, or as a member of any State legislature, or as an executive or judicial officer of any State, to support the Constitution of the United States, shall have engaged in insurrection or rebellion against the same, or given aid or comfort to the enemies thereof. But Congress may by a vote of two-thirds of each House, remove such disability.

SECTION 4. The validity of the public debt of the United States, authorized by law, including debts incurred for payment of pensions and bounties for services in suppressing insurrection or rebellion, shall not be questioned. But neither the United States nor any State shall assume or pay any debt or obligation incurred in aid of insurrection or rebellion against the United States, or any claim for the loss or emancipation of any slave; but all such debts, obligations and claims shall be held illegal and void.

SECTION 5. The Congress shall have the power to enforce, by appropriate legislation, the provisions of this article.

AMENDMENT XV [1870]

SECTION 1. The right of citizens of the United States to vote shall not be denied or abridged by the United States or by any State on account of race, color, or previous condition of servitude.

SECTION 2. The Congress shall have the power to enforce this article by appropriate legislation.

AMENDMENT XVI [1913]

The Congress shall have power to lay and collect taxes on incomes, from whatever source derived, without apportionment among the several States, and without regard to any census or enumeration.

AMENDMENT XVII [1913]

[1] The Senate of the United States shall be composed of two Senators from each State, elected by the people thereof, for six years; and each Senator shall have one vote. The electors in each State shall have the qualifications requisite for electors of the most numerous branch of the State legislatures.

[2] When vacancies happen in the representation of any State in the Senate, the executive authority of such State shall issue writs of election to fill such vacancies: Provided, That the legislature of any State may empower the executive thereof to make temporary appointments until the people fill the vacancies by election as the legislature may direct.

[3] This amendment shall not be so construed as to affect the election or term of any Senator chosen before it becomes valid as part of the Constitution.

AMENDMENT XVIII [1919]

SECTION 1. After one year from the ratification of this article the manufacture, sale, or transportation of intoxicating liquors within, the importation thereof into, or the exportation thereof from the United States and all territory subject to the jurisdiction thereof for beverage purposes is hereby prohibited.

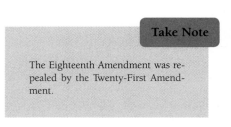

Take Note

The Eighteenth Amendment was repealed by the Twenty-First Amendment.

SECTION 2. The Congress and the several States shall have concurrent power to enforce this article by appropriate legislation.

SECTION 3. This article shall be inoperative unless it shall have been ratified as an amendment to the Constitution by the legislatures of the several States, as provided in the Constitution, within seven years from the date of the submission hereof to the States by the Congress.

AMENDMENT XIX [1920]

[1] The right of citizens of the United States to vote shall not be denied or abridged by the United States or by any State on account of sex.

[2] Congress shall have power to enforce this article by appropriate legislation.

Amendment XX [1933]

Section 1. The terms of the President and the Vice President shall end at noon on the 20th day of January, and the terms of Senators and Representatives at noon on the 3d day of January, of the years in which such terms would have ended if this article had not been ratified; and the terms of their successors shall then begin.

Section 2. The Congress shall assemble at least once in every year, and such meeting shall begin at noon on the 3d day of January, unless they shall by law appoint a different day.

Section 3. If, at the time fixed for the beginning of the term of the President, the President elect shall have died, the Vice President elect shall become President. If a President shall not have been chosen before the time fixed for the beginning of his term, or if the President elect shall have failed to qualify, then the Vice President elect shall act as President until a President shall have qualified; and the Congress may by law provide for the case wherein neither a President elect nor a Vice President shall have qualified, declaring who shall then act as President, or the manner in which one who is to act shall be selected, and such person shall act accordingly until a President or Vice President shall have qualified.

Section 4. The Congress may by law provide for the case of the death of any of the persons from whom the House of Representatives may choose a President whenever the right of choice shall have devolved upon them, and for the case of the death of any of the persons from whom the Senate may choose a Vice President whenever the right of choice shall have devolved upon them.

Section 5. Sections 1 and 2 shall take effect on the 15th day of October following the ratification of this article.

Section 6. This article shall be inoperative unless it shall have been ratified as an amendment to the Constitution by the legislatures of three-fourths of the several States within seven years from the date of its submission.

Amendment XXI [1933]

Section 1. The eighteenth article of amendment to the Constitution of the United States is hereby repealed.

Section 2. The transportation or importation into any State, Territory, or Possession of the United States for delivery or use therein of intoxicating liquors, in violation of the laws thereof, is hereby prohibited.

Section 3. This article shall be inoperative unless it shall have been ratified as an amendment to the Constitution by conventions in the several States, as provided in the Constitution, within seven years from the date of the submission hereof to the States by the Congress.

Amendment XXII [1951]

Section 1. No person shall be elected to the office of the President more than twice, and no person who has held the office of President, or acted as President, for more than two years of a term to which some other person was elected President shall be elected to the office of President more than once. But this Article shall not apply to any person holding the office of President when this Article was proposed by Congress, and shall not prevent any person who may be holding the office of President, or acting as President, during the term within which this Article becomes operative from holding the office of President or acting as President during the remainder of such term.

Section 2. This article shall be inoperative unless it shall have been ratified as an amendment to the Constitution by the legislatures of three-fourths of the several States within seven years from the date of its submission to the States by the Congress.

Amendment XXIII [1961]

Section 1. The District constituting the seat of Government of the United States shall appoint in such manner as Congress may direct:

A number of electors of President and Vice President equal to the whole number of Senators and Representatives in Congress to which the District would be entitled if it were a State, but in no event more than the least populous State; they shall be in addition to those appointed by the States, but they shall be considered, for the purposes of the election of President and Vice President, to be electors appointed by a State; and they shall meet in the District and perform such duties as provided by the twelfth article of amendment.

Section 2. The Congress shall have power to enforce this article by appropriate legislation.

Amendment XXIV [1964]

Section 1. The right of citizens of the United States to vote in any primary or other election for President or Vice President, for electors for President or Vice President, or for Senator or Representative in Congress, shall not be denied or abridged by the United States or any State by reason of failure to pay poll tax or other tax.

Section 2. The Congress shall have power to enforce this article by appropriate legislation.

Amendment XXV [1967]

Section 1. In case of the removal of the President from office or of his death or resignation, the Vice President shall become President.

Section 2. Whenever there is a vacancy in the office of the Vice President, the President shall nominate a Vice President who shall take office upon confirmation by a majority vote of both Houses of Congress.

Section 3. Whenever the President transmits to the President pro tempore of the

Senate and the Speaker of the House of Representatives his written declaration that he is unable to discharge the powers and duties of his office, and until he transmits to them a written declaration to the contrary, such powers and duties shall be discharged by the Vice President as Acting President.

SECTION 4. [1] Whenever the Vice President and a majority of either the principal officers of the executive departments or of such other body as Congress may by law provide, transmit to the President pro tempore of the Senate and the Speaker of the House of Representatives their written declaration that the President is unable to discharge the powers and duties of his office, the Vice President shall immediately assume the powers and duties of the office as Acting President.

[2] Thereafter, when the President transmits to the President pro tempore of the Senate and the Speaker of the House of Representatives his written declaration that no inability exists, he shall resume the powers and duties of his office unless the Vice President and a majority of either the principal officers of the executive department or of such other body as Congress may by law provide, transmit within four days to the President pro tempore of the Senate and the Speaker of the House of Representatives their written declaration that the President is unable to discharge the powers and duties of his office. Thereupon Congress shall decide the issue, assembling within forty-eight hours for that purpose if not in session. If the Congress, within twenty-one days after receipt of the latter written declaration, or, if Congress is not in session, within twenty-one days after Congress is required to assemble, determines by two-thirds vote of both Houses that the President is unable to discharge the powers and duties of his office, the Vice President shall continue to discharge the same as Acting President; otherwise, the President shall resume the powers and duties of his office.

AMENDMENT XXVI [1971]

SECTION 1. The right of citizens of the United States, who are eighteen years of age or older, to vote shall not be denied or abridged by the United States or by any State on account of age.

SECTION 2. The Congress shall have power to enforce this article by appropriate legislation.

AMENDMENT XXVII [1992]

No law, varying the compensation for the services of the Senators and Representatives, shall take effect, until an election of representatives shall have intervened.

FYI

The Twenty-Seventh Amendment was proposed on September 25, 1789, along with the Amendments that became the Bill of Rights. The amendment was ratified quickly by six states, but not by the rest of the states. The amendment had no "sunset provision," however, and over time it was ratified by other states until, in 1992, Michigan became the 38th state to ratify it, satisfying the three-fourths requirement.

Index

References are to pages

Reminder: In addition to this index, the full text of this book is
electronically searchable on-line.

ABORTION: 65, 100, 106, 472, 504, 537-74, 588, 612, 747, 749, 819, 874, 914-18

ADVISORY OPINIONS: 79-82, 103

AFFIRMATIVE ACTION: 89, 634, 639, 653, 681-82, 687-88, 693-722, 727, 739, 777, 803

AMENDMENT PROCESS: 12, 20, 242-43, 650-51, 844

APPOINTMENT: 26, 403, 422, 440-50, 455, 463

APPORTIONMENT: 68-71, 103, 654, 723-27, 777, 780, 792-804

ARTICLES OF CONFEDERATION: 4-6, 15, 43, 106-07, 129, 215, 218, 221, 224, 254, 268, 311, 316, 347, 424

BICAMERALISM AND PRESENTMENT: 395, 408, 412, 414-21, 463

BILL OF RIGHTS: 3, 10, 12, 15-16, 19, 23, 25-26, 154, 213, 245, 467-69, 472, 474-75, 483, 485-514, 538-39, 541, 544, 547, 550, 554, 616, 627, 629, 631, 637, 659, 779, 804, 829, 853, 859-60, 930, 952, 995, 997, 1015, 1038, 1044-46, 1057, 1085, 1088, 1090, 1093, 1126-27, 1131-34, 1154, 1170, 1174, 1198, 1205, 1207, 1235

BILLS OF ATTAINDER: 54, 106, 245, 395, 410, 458-64, 467, 478, 616

CASE OR CONTROVERSY: 45, 78-82, 87, 95-96, 103

CHILD LABOR
    And Commerce Clause: 142-44
    And Taxing Power: 187-89

CHILD PORNOGRAPHY: 902, 943-47, 968, 971, 1009, 1010, 1012

CIVIL RIGHTS ACT OF 1964: 157, 160-61, 163, 176, 674, 680, 693, 827, 831, 1273-74

CIVIL RIGHTS ACT OF 1875: 686, 847, 1273-74, 1280

COMMANDER-IN-CHIEF CLAUSE: 335, 355 367, 391, 896

COMMERCIAL SPEECH: 909, 921, 970, 973-82, 1012

CONSTITUTIONAL CONVENTION: 4-5, 9, 22, 43, 54, 59, 107, 215, 234, 325, 406-07, 424, 455, 467, 471, 616, 654, 794, 829, 835, 859, 1153

CONTENT-BASED RESTRICTIONS: 863 et seq.

CONTINENTAL CONGRESS: 3-4, 347, 619, 1153

CONTRACEPTION: 537 -74, 585

CONTRACT CLAUSE: 469-70, 514, 1237-45, 1269

DEFAMATION: 921, 927-37, 965, 1008, 1030-31

DISABILITY: 653, 740-41, 764-71, 778, 850

DISCRIMINATION
    Against interstate commerce: 267 et seq.
    Age: 761 et seq.
    Alienage: 755 et seq.
    Disability: 740-42, 764 et seq.
    Gender: 727 et seq.
    Parents' marital status: 759 et seq.
    Race: 654 et seq.
    Sexual orientation: 771 et seq., 1078-82

DORMANT COMMERCE CLAUSE DOCTRINE: 129, 134, 216, 245, 253-308, 313, 323, 469, 474, 552

DUE PROCESS
    Incorporation: 485-505, 637
    Procedural due process: 513, 537, 543, 598, 605, 619-29, 805, 850, 1189, 1303
    Substantive due process: 170, 477, 492, 497, 499, 501, 504-05, 508, 513-617, 619, 634, 638, 655, 779, 818, 850, 1051, 1082

ECONOMIC ACTIVITY
    And Commerce Clause: 163-66, 171-85, 238, 243
    And Contract Clause: 123-70
    And Due Process Clause: 514-30

Education
And Commerce Clause: 163-71
Fundamental right: 807-15

Eighth Amendment: 19, 66-67, 472, 493, 503, 508, 594, 1088, 1269

Eleventh Amendment: 65, 228-29, 231, 236-37

Eminent Domain: 1245-70

Equal Protection Clause: 19-20, 36, 68-69, 71, 103, 163, 290, 306-08, 313, 323, 475, 480-81, 484, 524, 533-36, 540, 554, 563, 567, 575-76, 585-88, 590-91, 598, 602, 633-822, 827, 829, 838-41, 1271, 1288, 1293

Establishment Clause
Incorporation: 507-09, 1089-91
Meaning: 1085 et seq.

Executive Power
Appointment: 327, 421-50
Domestic Affairs: 327 et seq.
Foreign Affairs: 339 et seq.
Immunity: 377 et seq.
In times of war: 354 et seq.
Privilege: 371 et seq.
Removal: 421-50

Familial Rights: 577-580, 604

First Amendment: 13-14, 23, 186, 204, 213, 242, 290, 472, 474, 492, 503-04, 508, 513-14, 538, 547, 615, 755, 781, 800, 808-09, 811, 842-44, 857-1233, 1271, 1282-1283, 1286-88, 1291, 1306

First Congress: 9-10, 111, 261, 417, 424, 453, 455, 568, 616, 1100, 1132-33, 1141, 1143, 1153-54, 1157, 1174

Fifteenth Amendment: 241, 474, 658, 681, 722, 782, 821, 827, et seq.

Foreign Affairs: 107, 335, 339-54, 367, 380, 389, 895-901

Foreign Law: 66-67, 226, 591-92

FOURTEENTH AMENDMENT: 13-14, 19-20, 36, 61, 63, 65, 69-71, 157, 161-63, 170, 175, 233, 238, 245, 272, 274, 306, 309-11, 320, 469, 474 et seq., 619 et seq., 653 et seq., 799 et seq., 827 et seq.

FREEDOM OF ASSOCIATION: 615, 773, 857, 905, 909, 984, 1051-83, 1233

FREEDOM OF SPEECH: 14, 77, 468, 495, 507, 538, 617, 649, 755, 857, 859 et seq.

FREEDOM OF THE PRESS: 467-68, 649, 857, 869, 896, 964, 1015 et seq.

FREEDOM OF RELIGION: 649, 857, 1052, 1085 et seq.

GENDER DISCRIMINATION: 524, 567, 728, 733-55, 815, 847

GENERAL WELFARE CLAUSE: 195-96, 219, 1082

HOMOSEXUALITY
      And substantive due process: 582 et seq.
      Discrimination: 771 et seq., 1071-77

IMPLIED POWERS: 109-28, 330, 347

INCORPORATION: 485-509, 514, 637-38, 659, 860, 1010, 1015, 1021, 1049, 1085, 1089-90, 1144, 1179, 1269-70

INTERMEDIATE SCRUTINY
      Gender Discrimination: 37, 730 et seq.
      Parents' Marital Status: 759 et seq.

INTERSTATE COMMERCE
      Congress's power: 129 et seq.
      Meaning of: 283 et seq.

JUDICIAL POWER: 12, 43-108, 228-31, 290, 325, 353, 385, 412, 428-29, 432, 444, 447, 557, 666, 1272

JUDICIAL REVIEW: 13, 17, 45 et seq.

JUDICIAL SUPREMACY: 64-67, 102, 845

JURISDICTION
      Congressional control: 98 et seq.
      Appellate: 46-60
      Original: 49-50, 53-54, 57, 59, 78, 101-02, 106

JUST COMPENSATION: 472, 1245 et seq.

JUSTICIABILITY: 67 et seq., 372, 800-02

LEGISLATIVE POWER: 11, 109 et seq.

LEGISLATIVE VETO: 404, 410-13

LIBEL: 859, 895, 897, 902, 927-35, 937, 939, 946, 965, 968, 1011

LINE ITEM VETO: 414-19, 421

MARRIAGE
    And race: 574 et seq., 678 et seq.
    Fundamental right: 535-536, 538-539, 574 et seq.

MILITARY: 4, 12, 14, 24-31, 34, 98-99, 101, 202, 205, 241, 330-31, 335-37, 353, 356-58, 360 – 65, 369-71, 375-76, 387, 389, 391-93, 407, 638, 661-68, 702, 734, 736-37, 752-55, 826, 884-85, 888, 895, 921, 950, 954, 1078-83, 1141, 1159, 1203, 1205, 1209, 1246, 1286

MOOTNESS: 81-82, 103

NATURAL LAW: 233-35, 469-72, 474, 484, 490-91, 505, 523, 616-17, 728, 1237

NECESSARY AND PROPER CLAUSE: 109, 120-28, 138, 181, 190, 196, 201-02, 205, 232, 238, 242, 279, 313, 403, 424, 634, 821, 838, 841, 853, 1089, 1245, 1268

NEUTRALITY PRINCIPLE: 1091 et seq.

NEW DEAL: 145, 148-49, 154, 176, 196, 224, 398, 436, 448, 905

NINTH AMENDMENT: 23, 538-40, 543-45, 547, 615, 1045, 1047-48

NON-DELEGATION DOCTRINE: 145, 398, 403, 463

NON-ORIGINALISM: 16, 18, 36

NON-PREFERENTIALISM: 1088, 1135, 1146, 1157, 1167

NOTICE: 619 et seq.

OBSCENITY: 588, 902, 921, 932, 937-48, 956, 959, 965, 966, 968, 970, 973, 1008, 1010, 1012, 1231

ORIGINALISM: 16-22, 36, 39-41, 194, 686-87, 1088

OVERBREADTH: 902-913, 942

POLITICAL QUESTION DOCTRINE: 45, 48, 67-78, 98, 103, 105, 315, 353, 389, 727

POLL TAX: 722, 781-85, 817, 820

PRAYER
    In schools: 1123 et seq.
    Legislative: 1100 et seq., 1120 et seq., 1153 et seq.

PREEMPTION: 245-53, 255, 257, 258, 290, 322, 757

PRIOR RESTRAINTS: 863, 894-902, 1011, 1019, 1040

PRIVACY: 376, 538-42, 544-47, 550, 552, 563, 574, 784, 881, 937, 961, 1045, 1117, 1145

PRIVILEGES AND IMMUNITIES CLAUSE: 12, 245, 308-13, 324, 478, 499, 631

PRIVILEGES OR IMMUNITIES CLAUSE: 475-85, 494, 498-500, 504- 05, 508, 615, 728, 758, 822, 853

PROCEDURAL DUE PROCESS: 513, 537, 543, 598, 605, 619-29, 805, 850, 1189, 1303

PROTECTIONISM: 268-69, 282-83, 289, 299

PUNITIVE DAMAGES: 174, 232, 247-52, 932, 936, 1020, 1038

RACIAL DISCRIMINATION: 85, 158-60, 162, 514, 576-77, 634, 637, 649, 654 et seq.

RATIONAL-BASIS TEST: 157, 169, 526, 529, 564, 634, 642, 647, 733, 768

RECONSTRUCTION AMENDMENTS: 12, 206, 474, 476, 479, 483, 650, 674, 783, 821-55, 1271, 1273

RELIGION, SEE FREEDOM OF RELIGION

REMOVAL POWER: 423-24, 435, 437-38, 444, 453

REVOLUTION: 2, 4, 109, 424, 619, 861, 1015, 1085, 1125

RIGHT TO DIE: 598-611

RIPENESS: 81-82, 103, 353

SECOND AMENDMENT: 22-37, 39-41, 223-24, 493-97, 500-02, 504, 646

SEGREGATION
    Racial: 20, 61, 63-64, 87, 160, 163, 551, 557, 636-38, 650-51, 662, 682-89, 692 et
        seq., 712-13, 715, 719-20, 904, 950, 1065
    Gender: 733-39

SEPARATION OF POWERS: 35, 69, 76, 86-88, 94, 96, 167, 325-463, 465, 541, 552, 591, 764,
    822, 846, 898-99, 1000

SEXUAL ORIENTATION: 585, 634, 653, 771-78, 1066-83

SLAVERY: 7, 12-13, 64-65, 241, 243, 471, 474, 476, 483, 500, 514, 581, 631, 637, 649-50,
    654-58, 681, 821, 823-27, 851, 853, 855, 1185, 1271, 1276-78

SPENDING POWER: 186, 192-200, 216, 239, 241, 913, 1119

STANDING: 82 et seq., 1119-20

STATE ACTION: 69, 157, 198-99, 206, 266, 273, 304, 472, 475, 486-87, 493-94, 504, 513-
    14, 522, 547, 573, 594, 606, 658, 676-77, 770, 780, 797, 809-10, 817, 819, 824-25,
    828-31, 833, 836-37, 840, 847-51, 853, 905, 938, 1001, 1063, 1090, 1130, 1139,
    1179, 1192, 1220, 1241, 1269, 1271-72, 1306

STATE SOVEREIGN IMMUNITY: 228-40

STERILIZATION: 533-37, 612, 779

STRICT SCRUTINY: 27, 32, 37, 535, 540, 563, 576, 634-35, 639, 647, 667-68, 671, 673,
    676-77, 692-93, 696, 700-02, 704, 713, 716-17, 719, 721-22, 724, 726, 730, 733,
    737-38, 755-56, 758-59, 761, 767, 776-78, 796, 800, 810, 815, 819, 863-64, 866,
    868-69, 873-75, 877-78, 888, 948, 969, 877, 981, 1010, 1012, 1193, 1198, 1216

SUBSTANTIVE DUE PROCESS: 170, 477, 492, 497, 499, 501, 504-05, 508, 513-15, 519, 530,
    537, 549-50, 552, 554, 575, 580-81, 589, 594, 598, 601, 605-29, 634, 638, 655,
    779, 818, 850, 1051, 1082

SUPREME COURT: 43 et seq.

SUSPECT CLASSES: 14, 760-61, 763-65, 772, 775, 778, 807-08, 811-14, 816, 819

SYMBOLIC CONDUCT: 921, 948-56

TAKINGS CLAUSE: 474, 514, 1235, 1245-70

TAXATION
    Congress's Taxing Power: 186 et seq.
    State: 109-18, 303-05

TENTH AMENDMENT: 107, 125, 143-44, 153, 187-88, 190, 194, 202-05, 208, 211, 213-15, 218, 233-35, 316, 318, 504, 544-45, 575, 822, 835, 853-55

TERM LIMITS: 313 et seq.

THIRTEENTH AMENDMENT: 13, 474, 476, 650, 656, 658, 821-28, 831, 851, 855, 1271, 1273, 1276, 1277, 1278, 1280, 1297

TIME, PLACE OR MANNER REGULATIONS: 863-64, 866, 878-83, 888, 950, 959, 981, 985, 1286

TREATIES: 11, 57, 59, 66, 78-79, 201, 204-05, 239, 245-46, 316, 327, 344, 348-50, 353-54, 409, 499, 591, 649, 975

TWENTY-FIRST AMENDMENT: 154, 197-99, 1271

TWENTY-FOURTH AMENDMENT: 781

UNCONSTITUTIONAL CONDITIONS: 625, 757, 863, 913-20, 1011, 1035, 1189

UNDUE BURDEN TEST: 573

UNENUMERATED RIGHTS: 501, 504, 520, 530, 608, 615-17, 811, 1045

UNIFORM NATIONAL STANDARD TEST: 258-64

VAGUENESS: 902-13, 942, 959, 1038

VOTING
    And discrimination: 832-35
    Apportionment: 792-96
    Redistricting: 722 et seq., 798-804
    Right to vote: 780 et seq.

WAR ON TERROR: 101, 360, 362, 391-92

WELFARE: 804-07

✝